Current Law

STATUTES
ANNOTATED
1993

VOLUME ONE

AUSTRALIA
The Law Book Company
Brisbane : Sydney : Melbourne : Perth

CANADA
Carswell
Ottawa : Toronto : Calgary : Montreal : Vancouver

Agents:
Steimatzky's Agency Ltd., Tel Aviv;
N. M. Tripathi (Private) Ltd., Bombay;
Eastern Law House (Private) Ltd., Calcutta;
M.P.P. House, Bangalore;
Universal Book Traders, Delhi;
Aditya Books, Delhi;
MacMillan Shuppan KK, Tokyo;
Pakistan Law House, Karachi

Current Law

STATUTES ANNOTATED

1993

VOLUME ONE

SWEET & MAXWELL EDITORIAL TEAM
SARAH ANDREWS
MELANIE BHAGAT
ALASTAIR BRUNKER
CAROLINE EADIE
PHILIPPA JOHNSON
SOPHIE LOWE
CERI PICKERING
ALICE WILEY

W. GREEN EDITORIAL TEAM
ELANOR BOWER
CHARLOTTE HALL
PETER NICHOLSON

LONDON

SWEET & MAXWELL

EDINBURGH

W. GREEN

1994

Published by
SWEET & MAXWELL LIMITED
of South Quay Plaza, 183 Marsh Wall, London,
and W. GREEN LIMITED
of Alva Street, Edinburgh,
Typeset by MFK Typesetting Ltd., Hitchin, Herts.
and printed in Great Britain
by The Bath Press,
Bath, Avon.

ISBN This Volume only : 0 421 51860 X
As a set   : 0 421 51850 2

CONTENTS

CHRONOLOGICAL TABLE

VOLUME ONE

Annotators' names are in italic

VOLUME ONE

c. 1. Gas (Exempt Supplies) Act 1993
   2. British Coal and British Rail (Transfer Proposals) Act 1993
   3. Social Security Act 1993
   4. Consolidated Fund Act 1993
   5. Damages (Scotland) Act 1993
       Ann Paton, Q.C., M.A., LL.B.
   6. Bankruptcy (Scotland) Act 1993
       Professor William McBryde, Vice Principal, University of Dundee
   7. Consolidated Fund (No. 2) Act 1993
   8. Judicial Pensions and Retirement Act 1993
       John Mesher, Barrister, Professor Associate, Department of Law, University of Sheffield
   9. Prisoners and Criminal Proceedings (Scotland) Act 1993
       Dr. D.J.J. McManus, LL.B., Ph.D., University of Dundee
   10. Charities Act 1993
       Jean Warburton, LL.B., Solicitor, Senior Lecturer, University of Liverpool
   11. Clean Air Act 1993
       Professor Neil Hawke, Professor of Law, De Montfort University
   12. Radioactive Substances Act 1993
       Gillian Irvine, Solicitor, Simmons & Simmons
   13. Carrying of Knives etc. (Scotland) Act 1993
       Robert Shiels, Solicitor
   14. Disability (Grants) Act 1993
   15. Protection of Animals (Scotland) Act 1993
   16. Foreign Compensation (Amendment) Act 1993
   17. Non-Domestic Rating Act 1993
   18. Reinsurance (Acts of Terrorism) Act 1993

INDEX OF SHORT TITLES

STATUTES 1993

(References are to chapter numbers of 1993)

GAS (EXEMPT SUPPLIES) ACT 1993

(1993 c. 1)

An Act to amend section 5 of the Gas Act 1986; and for connected purposes.

[19th January 1993]

PARLIAMENTARY DEBATES
Hansard, H.L. Vol. 538, col. 1232; Vol. 540, col. 677; Vol. 541, col. 178; H.C. Vol. 216, col. 1237.

INTRODUCTION
This Act inserts and substitutes various new provisions in the Gas Act 1986.

Section 5 (prohibition on unauthorised supply) is replaced with a new s.5, which makes provisions for various exceptions and exemptions from the scope of the provision, in the interest of safety. A new s.6A is added and s.36 is amended in accordance with the alterations to s.5 in order that exemptions under s.5 are regulated and registered.

Prohibition on unauthorised supply: exception and exemptions

1. For section 5 of the Gas Act 1986 there shall be substituted the following section—

"Prohibition on unauthorised supply

5.—(1) Subject to subsections (2) and (3) and sections 6 and 6A below, a person who supplies gas through pipes to any premises shall be guilty of an offence unless he is authorised to do so under section 7 or 8 below.

(2) Subsection (1) above is not contravened by a person supplying, for use in a building or part of a building in which he has an interest, gas supplied to the building by a person authorised to supply it by or under section 6, 6A, 7 or 8 below.

(3) Subsection (1) above is not contravened by a person supplying to any premises gas which consists wholly or mainly of propane or butane if—

    (a) the contract for the supply contains provisions empowering a person authorised by the supplier to enter the premises where in his opinion it is necessary to do so for the purpose of averting danger to life or property; and

    (b) those provisions are in terms approved for the purposes of this subsection by the Secretary of State.

(4) A person guilty of an offence under this section shall be liable—

    (a) on summary conviction to a fine not exceeding the statutory maximum;

    (b) on conviction on indictment, to a fine.

(5) No proceedings shall be instituted in England and Wales in respect of an offence under this section except by or on behalf of the Secretary of State or the Director."

Exemptions from prohibition on unauthorised supply

2. After section 6 of the Gas Act 1986 there shall be inserted the following section—

"Exemptions from section 5

6A.—(1) The Secretary of State may, after consultation with the Director, by order grant exemption from section 5(1) above, but subject to compliance with such conditions (if any) as may be specified in the order.

(2) An exemption may be granted either—
(a) to persons of a particular class; or
(b) to a particular person;

and an exemption granted to persons of a particular class shall be published in such manner as the Secretary of State considers appropriate for bringing it to the attention of persons of that class.

(3) An exemption, unless previously revoked in accordance with any term contained in the exemption, shall continue in force for such period as may be specified in or determined by or under the exemption."

Keeping of register

3. In section 36 of the Gas Act 1986 (keeping of register), for subsections (1) and (2) there shall be substituted the following subsections—

"(1) The Director shall keep a register of notifications and directions under section 6 above, exemptions granted under section 6A above to particular persons, authorisations under section 7 or 8 above and final and provisional orders at such premises and in such form as he may determine.

(2) Subject to any direction given under subsection (3) below, the Director shall cause to be entered in the register the provisions of—
(a) every notification or direction under section 6 above;
(b) every exemption granted under section 6A above to a particular person and every revocation of such exemption;
(c) every revocation made otherwise than by order of an exemption granted under that section to persons of a particular class;
(d) every authorisation under section 7 or 8 above and every modification or revocation of, and every direction or consent given or determination made under, such an authorisation; and
(e) every final or provisional order, every revocation of such an order and every notice under section 28(6) above."

Short title, commencement and extent

4.—(1) This Act may be cited as the Gas (Exempt Supplies) Act 1993.

(2) This Act shall come into force on such day as the Secretary of State may by order made by statutory instrument appoint; and different days may be so appointed for different provisions or for different purposes.

(3) This Act does not extend to Northern Ireland.

INDEX

References in roman type are to sections of this Act: references in italic are to sections of the Gas Act 1986

BRITISH COAL AND BRITISH RAIL (TRANSFER PROPOSALS) ACT 1993*

(1993 c. 2)

An Act to confer powers on the British Coal Corporation and the British Railways Board to act in relation to proposals for the transfer of any of their functions, property, rights or liabilities to any other body or person; and for connected purposes. [19th January 1993]

PARLIAMENTARY DEBATES

Hansard, H.C. Vol. 208, col. 22; Vol. 210, col. 599; H.L. Vol. 539, col. 9; Vol. 540, cols. 1173, 1208, 1256; Vol. 541, cols. 498, 723, 749.

The Bill was discussed in Standing Committee A between June 4 and 18, 1992.

INTRODUCTION AND GENERAL NOTE

This Act has been described as an important first legislative step to bringing the benefits of the private sector and privatisation to the state-owned coal and rail industries (*Hansard*, H.C. Vol. 208, col. 22).

The Act is similar to the paving legislation for previous privatisations (see, for example, s.1 of the Public Utility Transfers and Water Charges Act 1988).

Both British Coal and British Rail are creatures of statute and can take only those actions which they are permitted to take under the legislation which affects them. The need for this Act is to put beyond doubt the ability of British Coal and British Rail to advise on their own demise, which may otherwise be considered to be against their interests and possibly *ultra vires*. The Act also ensures that British Coal and British Rail have sufficient powers to incur the very substantial expenditure required to prepare for privatisation.

The Act consists of only two sections, which are succinctly summarised by the Earl of Caithness in his speech moving the bill for its second Lords reading:

"Clause 1 of the Bill confers on British Coal and British Rail powers to act in relation to proposals for the transfer of their commercial activities to the private sector or proposals for the establishment of new arrangements for their other activities. In particular it empowers them to consider and take advice on proposals for privatisation, advise the Government on such proposals and draw up plans for implementing such proposals. They will be able to employ external advisers to assist them in all these tasks.

Clause 2 simply gives the short title of the Bill, sets out the financial provisions and extends the Bill to Northern Ireland. The financial provisions deal with the source of any loans and clarify the destination of any repayments should either British Coal or British Rail require additional funding to meet costs incurred in preparation for privatisation" (*Hansard*, H.L. Vol. 539, col. 9).

The Act does not give either British Coal or British Rail powers to implement any scheme for privatisation. That will be a matter for subsequent (and what is described as the main privatisation) legislation of these two industries.

COMMENCEMENT

The Act came into force on January 19, 1993.

Power to act in relation to proposals for transfer of functions, property etc.

1.—(1) Where the Secretary of State is at any time proposing that any functions, property, rights or liabilities of a relevant corporation, that is to say, the British Coal Corporation or the British Railways Board, or of any subsidiary of a relevant corporation, should be transferred to any other body or person ("the transferee"), the functions of the relevant corporation shall include the power to do anything which in their opinion is appropriate for the purpose of—

(a) facilitating the implementation of the proposal; or

(b) facilitating the implementation of, or securing a modification of, any related proposals of the Secretary of State.

(2) Any reference in this section to the transfer of any functions of a relevant corporation includes a reference to the conferring of functions on

---

*Annotations by Ian MacPherson, Partner at Nabarro Nathanson.

any body or person in connection with, or in consequence of, the transfer to that, or any other, body or person of any functions, property, rights or liabilities of the relevant corporation or of any of its subsidiaries; and, accordingly, where the proposal is for the conferring of functions on a body or person, any reference in this section to "the transferee" is a reference to that body or person.

(3) The proposals which are to be regarded for the purposes of this section as related to a proposal of the Secretary of State for the transfer of any functions, property, rights or liabilities of a relevant corporation or a subsidiary of a relevant corporation ("the transferor") shall include any proposal relating to, or to any matter connected with,—

    (a) any relevant property, rights or liabilities which would be affected by the transfer, or any such property, rights or liabilities after their proposed transfer;

    (b) the exercise, whether before or after the transfer, of any function which it is proposed to transfer to the transferee;

    (c) the establishment or formation, flotation, control, finances or employees of the transferee or (where the transferee is a body corporate) of any body corporate which is, or in pursuance of any proposal of the Secretary of State may become, a member of the same group as the transferee;

and in this subsection "relevant property, rights or liabilities" means property, rights or liabilities of the transferor or of any other member of the same group as the transferor.

(4) Any power of a relevant corporation to do anything under this section in relation to a proposal for the transfer of any functions, property, rights or liabilities, or in relation to any related proposals, shall include power to do that thing whether or not with a view to promoting the interests of the relevant corporation.

(5) The powers conferred by this section in relation to any proposal shall be exercisable whether or not Parliament has given any approval on which the implementation of the proposal depends and are without prejudice to any power conferred otherwise than by virtue of this section.

(6) For the purposes of this section a body corporate is a member of the same group as another body corporate if it is a holding company or subsidiary of that other body corporate or if it is another subsidiary of that other body corporate's holding company.

(7) In this section—

    (a) any reference to a subsidiary or holding company is a reference to a subsidiary or holding company (as the case may be) within the meaning of section 736 of the Companies Act 1985;

    (b) any reference to a body, or to a body corporate, includes a reference to a body or body corporate (as the case may be) which has not been established or formed but which may be established or formed in pursuance of any proposal of the Secretary of State;

    (c) any reference to functions, property, rights or liabilities is a reference to functions, property, rights or liabilities whether exercisable, situate or subsisting in the United Kingdom or elsewhere.

GENERAL NOTE

This section gives both British Coal and British Rail power to act in relation to proposals of the Secretary of State for the transfer of functions, property, rights or liabilities to another body or person. Neither British Coal nor British Rail has the power to implement any such proposal merely to "facilitate" the implementation.

Subs. (1)

As with previous paving legislation, the starting point is a proposal by the Secretary of State made at any time. This Act differs from the Public Utility Transfers and Water Charges Act

1988 in that the Secretary of State may propose the transfer of any functions, property, rights or liabilities, whereas under the 1988 Act the proposal related only to property or functions (although rights and liabilities were classed as related proposals).

British Coal and British Rail shall have the power to do anything which in their opinion is appropriate for the purpose of (a) facilitating the implementation of the Secretary of State's proposal or (b) facilitating the implementation of or securing a modification of any related proposals of the Secretary of State. It is difficult to appreciate the reason for the distinction between the powers granted dependent upon whether it is a basic proposal or a related one. The former makes no reference to "securing a modification", whereas the latter does. As the powers given to British Coal and British Rail are widely drawn, *i.e.* to take appropriate steps at their discretion, it is unlikely that such steps would be open to challenge except in extreme cases.

Subs. (2)

This subsection removes any doubt that the transfer of functions includes a reference to the conferring of functions. It remains to be seen how the main privatisations of British Coal and British Rail will be proposed, but this subsection embraces the potential for the granting or bestowing of (perhaps new) functions or arrangements but which are to be treated as transfers, thus enabling British Coal and British Rail to consider and advise on the same.

Subs. (3)

This subsection defines the meaning of related proposals referred to in subs. (1).

Subs. (4)

This subsection empowers British Coal and British Rail to do anything under s.1 notwithstanding that it might be held to be against their interests.

Subs. (5)

This subsection makes it clear that it is not a requirement for Parliament to have approved the Secretary of State's proposal for the powers of s.1 to be exercisable. Also, the powers of the section are without prejudice to any other powers; accordingly British Coal and British Rail would still be permitted to act and rely on enabling powers they have under other legislation.

Subss. (6) and (7)

The term "subsidiary" and "holding company" have the same meaning as in the Companies Act 1985.

References to a body corporate include those which do not presently exist but may be formed in pursuance of a proposal.

The functions, property, rights and liabilities may be in the U.K. or elsewhere in the world.

Short title, financial provision and extent

2.—(1) This Act may be cited as the British Coal and British Rail (Transfer Proposals) Act 1993.

(2) Any increase attributable to the provisions of this Act in the sums payable under any other enactment out of—

(a) money provided by Parliament, or

(b) the National Loans Fund,

shall be paid out of money so provided or, as the case may be, out of that Fund.

(3) Any sums received in consequence of this Act by the Secretary of State under any other enactment shall be paid—

(a) to the extent that they represent interest on, or payments in or towards repayment of, sums issued out of the National Loans Fund, into that Fund; and

(b) subject to paragraph (a) above, into the Consolidated Fund;

but this subsection is without prejudice to the power conferred on the Secretary of State by section 2(5) of the Coal Industry Act 1980 (which permits certain sums received by him to be applied under section 2(1) of that Act as money provided by Parliament).

(4) This Act extends to Northern Ireland.

GENERAL NOTE

This section gives the short title of the Act, sets out financial provisions and extends the Act to Northern Ireland.

INDEX

References are to section numbers

SOCIAL SECURITY ACT 1993*

(1993 c. 3)

An Act to amend sections 3 and 85 of the Social Security Act 1986, to provide for the making of certain payments into the National Insurance Fund, and for connected purposes.   **[29th January 1993]**

PARLIAMENTARY DEBATES

Hansard, H.C. Vol. 215, cols. 46, 595; H.L. Vol. 541, cols. 818, 1367.

INTRODUCTION AND GENERAL NOTE

The Social Security Act 1993 contains two major provisions. Section 1(1) deals with the relationship between approved personal pensions and the state earnings-related pension scheme (SERPS) from April 1993. Section 2 deals with the Treasury grant to the National Insurance Fund.

Personal pensions

The purpose of s.1(1) was succinctly described by Lord Henley, the Parliamentary Under-Secretary of State for Social Security, in the second reading of the Act in the House of Lords (*Hansard*, H.L. Vol. 541, col. 819 (January 19, 1993)).

"[It] provides for a 1 per cent. addition to the contribution rebate for those aged 30 and over. It does so by amending the provisions in the Social Security Act 1986 which set out the amount of the minimum contributions paid to an earner's personal pension scheme. It will apply to those who are 30 or over at the beginning of the tax year commencing this coming April and to those who are over 30 at the beginning of any future tax year. As indicated in the Explanatory and Financial Memorandum to the Bill, the annual cost is estimated to be about £165 million from 1994/95. This cost will fall on the National Insurance Fund from 1994–95 because, in order to reduce the burden on employers, minimum contributions are paid by DSS direct to personal pension providers after the end of the tax year. We estimate that about 2 million personal pension holders will benefit.

The 1 per cent. additional rebate is a temporary measure which is intended to ensure that the majority of personal pension holders continue to find it worthwhile to maintain their pensions in the short term.

For the longer term we will be considering proposals for replacing the present flat rate rebate structure and the 1 per cent. additional rebate by an age related system which is intended to be in place from April 1996. We will be looking at the rebate structure not only for personal pensions but also for money purchase and salary related occupational schemes."

When a salary-related or money-purchase pension scheme is contracted out of SERPS, the social security contributions paid by the member of the scheme and the employer are reduced and in return the member's eventual SERPS pension will be reduced by the amount of the guaranteed minimum pension (GMP) paid by the scheme. For the period from April 1988 to April 1993 the reduction (rebate) in social security contributions was 3.8 per cent. for the employer and 2 per cent. for the employee. For the period from April 1993 to April 1998 the amounts are 3 per cent. and 1.8 per cent. The method where an employee wishes to replace a SERPS pension by a personal pension is slightly different. The full social security contributions are paid, but at the end of the tax year the DSS pays the amount of the rebate, plus the tax relief on the employee's portion, to the nominated personal pension scheme. These are the "minimum contributions". The eventual SERPS pension is then reduced by the notional GMP that would have been calculated from the minimum contributions in a salary-related scheme.

From April 1988 to April 1993, an additional rebate of 2 per cent. has been applied to schemes which first contracted out after January 1, 1986 (Social Security Act 1986, s.7) and to personal pension schemes (Social Security Act 1986, s.3(1)(b)). This is the "incentive payment" to encourage contracting out of SERPS and the establishment of personal pension schemes. Those provisions cease to have effect in April 1993. The 1993 Act provides only for the 1 per cent. incentive payment from April 1993 onwards to be paid for personal pensions. The Government's argument is that for contracted-out salary-related schemes the ordinary rebate of 4.8 per cent. recommended by the Government Actuary is the appropriate compensation for providing the GMP. It acknowledges that there are many similarities between money-purchase

---

*Annotations by John Mesher, Reader in Law and Simmons & Simmons Research Fellow in Pensions Law, University of Sheffield.

schemes and personal pensions. However, for a contracted-out money-purchase scheme the contributions are paid into the scheme every month. The minimum contribution to a personal pension scheme is not paid by the DSS until the end of the tax year. The Government estimates this disadvantage at half a per cent. In addition, it is argued that the level of administrative charges for personal pensions, being individual contracts, is higher and that because there is no obligation on the employer to put any contribution in, the individual member needs an extra incentive in order to continue using a personal pension to replace SERPS (see Lord Henley, *Hansard*, H.L. Vol. 541, col. 1370 (January 28, 1993)). The 1 per cent. incentive is limited to those of 30 or over because it is thought that the financial balance for members under that age (whose contributions will have a longer period to build up investment growth) is already sufficiently against SERPS.

The Government is committed to introducing an age-related rebate system in April 1996 for contracted-out salary-related and money-purchase schemes as well as for personal pensions.

The National Insurance Fund

The purpose of s.2 was also clearly summarised by Lord Henley (*Hansard*, H.L. Vol. 541, col. 820 (January 19, 1993)).

"The National Insurance Fund was originally set up with income from employers, employees and the state, but the former Treasury supplement which the Government abolished in 1989 was outdated and inflexible. The fund had to take a supplement whether it needed it or not, even when it was in surplus. The grant proposed by the Bill is more suited to today's needs. It is flexible; it is not automatic; it will be called upon only when needed.

Clause 2 contains the detailed provisions for the Treasury grant. The House will note that slightly different arrangements are proposed for 1993–94 than for later years, but they are based upon the well-established principle in managing the National Insurance Fund that we should plan its finances for the year ahead with the aim of maintaining a prudential minimum balance of some two months of benefit expenditure. The Government Actuary has advised that such a figure will represent an entirely adequate safety margin if events turn out differently from forecast.

In the current year, the balance has fallen below the two month level and we expect to carry forward the equivalent of just over a month's benefit expenditure at April 1993. This is not a cause for concern. The balance is fulfilling the very purpose for which it was designed. But it does mean that in order to plan for a two month balance at April 1994 we need to recover that lost ground. That is why the maximum amount of grant proposed for 1993–94 is higher than for subsequent years.

The House will note that the maximum grant available for 1993–94 will be 20 per cent. of estimated expenditure on benefits—nearly £8 billion. In later years the maximum will be 17 per cent."

The Government Actuary estimated that in 1993–94 a grant of 19.6 per cent. would be required in order to maintain the balance of two months' expenditure. This was on the assumptions set out in the Chancellor of the Exchequer's 1992 Autumn Statement, of unemployment averaging 2.8 million and average earnings increasing by 5 per cent. in 1993–94. The opposition expressed concern that in fact the receipts and liabilities of the Fund in 1993–94 might turn out to be lower and higher respectively, throwing doubt on the sufficiency of the 20 per cent. maximum. The Government's response was that an adverse experience compared to the estimate could be accommodated within the balance of two months' expenditure. If not, social security contributions might have to be increased. The opposition also made much of the costs of the rebates and incentive payments to personal pensions, which the National Audit Office found to have amounted to £9.3 billion from 1988 to 1993. The savings to SERPS were calculated to be £3.4 billion, but only on the basis that personal pension holders ceased to be outside SERPS in April 1993.

Other provisions

Section 1(3) corrects an oversight. There was previously no provision for meeting the expenses of administering the payment of minimum contributions to personal pension schemes out of the National Insurance Fund. The DSS's expenses (otherwise payable out of the Consolidated Fund) were in fact reimbursed out of the Fund, as was expressly provided for contracted-out schemes. Section 5(3) provides that s.1(3) shall be deemed always to have had effect, so that the accounting adjustment has been retrospectively validated.

Pension schemes: payments by Secretary of State under Part I of Social Security Act 1986

1.—(1) In section 3 of the Social Security Act 1986 (amount of minimum

contributions to personal pension schemes) in subsection (1) (calculation of contributions)—
   (a) at the end of paragraph (a) after "and" there shall be inserted—
      "(aa) where—
                     (i) the tax year in which the tax week falls ends before such date as may be prescribed, and
                     (ii) the earner was over the age of 30 on the 6th April with which the tax year began,
                 1 per cent. of any such earnings", and
   (b) paragraph (b) (which does not have effect in relation to tax weeks ending after 5th April 1993) shall be omitted.
   (2) In subsection (5) of that section (provision that may be made by regulations) after paragraph (c) there shall be inserted—
      "(cc) for the manner in which an earner's age is to be verified for the purposes of subsection (1)(aa) above".
   (3) In section 85 of that Act (financial provision) after subsection (8) there shall be inserted—
      "(8A) There shall be paid out of the National Insurance Fund into the Consolidated Fund, at such times and in such manner as the Treasury may direct, such sums as the Secretary of State may estimate (in accordance with any directions given by the Treasury) to be the amount of the administrative expenses incurred by him in exercising his functions relating to—
      (a) minimum contributions paid by him under Part I of this Act; and
      (b) payments by him under section 7 above."

Payments into National Insurance Fund out of money provided by Parliament

   2.—(1) During the tax year 1993–94 there shall be paid into the National Insurance Fund out of money provided by Parliament such amounts as the Secretary of State may from time to time determine, not exceeding in aggregate 20 per cent. of estimated benefit expenditure for the financial year ending with 31st March 1994.
   (2) If, before the beginning of the tax year 1994–95 or any subsequent tax year, the Secretary of State with the consent of the Treasury by order provides that this subsection is to have effect with respect to that tax year, there shall during that tax year be paid into the National Insurance Fund out of money provided by Parliament such amounts as the Secretary of State may from time to time determine, not exceeding in aggregate the prescribed percentage of estimated benefit expenditure for the financial year ending with 31st March in that tax year.
   (3) In subsection (2) above "the prescribed percentage" means such percentage, not exceeding 17 per cent., as may be specified in the order under that subsection.
   (4) In this section "estimated benefit expenditure", in relation to a financial year, means the amount estimated by the Government Actuary or the Deputy Government Actuary, before the beginning of that financial year, to be that of the aggregate of the amounts that may be expected to be paid out of the National Insurance Fund in that financial year—
   (a) under paragraphs (a), (b), (c) and (d) of section 163(1) of the Social Security Administration Act 1992, and
   (b) under sections 106(2), 122(1) and 123(1) of the Employment Protection (Consolidation) Act 1978.
   (5) The Secretary of State may exercise his power to make a determination under subsection (1) above or an order or determination under subsection (2) above only if he thinks it expedient to do so with a view to

adjusting the level at which the National Insurance Fund stands for the time being and having regard to estimated benefit expenditure for the financial year ending with 31st March in the tax year to which the determination or order is to relate.

(6) The Secretary of State shall consult the Treasury before making any determination under subsection (1) or (2) above.

(7) Amounts payable under this section shall be paid at such times and in such manner as the Treasury may direct.

(8) An order under subsection (2) above shall be made by statutory instrument; and a statutory instrument containing such an order shall not be made unless a draft of the instrument has been laid before Parliament and approved by a resolution of each House of Parliament.

(9) In section 1 of the Social Security Contributions and Benefits Act 1992 (outline of contributory system) at the end of subsection (1) there shall be added "and amounts payable under section 2 of the Social Security Act 1993".

Corresponding provision for Northern Ireland

3. An Order in Council under paragraph 1(1)(b) of Schedule 1 to the Northern Ireland Act 1974 (legislation for Northern Ireland in the interim period) which states that it is made only for purposes corresponding to those of this Act—

(a) shall not be subject to paragraph 1(4) and (5) of that Schedule (affirmative resolution of both Houses of Parliament); but

(b) shall be subject to annulment in pursuance of a resolution of either House of Parliament.

Interpretation and repeals

4.—(1) In this Act "tax year" means the 12 months beginning with 6th April in any year; and "the tax year 1993–94" and "the tax year 1994–95" mean respectively the tax year beginning with 6th April 1993 and the tax year beginning with 6th April 1994.

(2) The enactments specified in the Schedule to this Act are hereby repealed to the extent specified in the third column of that Schedule.

Short title, commencement and extent

5.—(1) This Act may be cited as the Social Security Act 1993.

(2) The following provisions of this Act shall not have effect with respect to any tax year before the tax year 1993–94—

section 1(1) and (2), and
section 4(2) and the Schedule.

(3) Section 1(3) of this Act shall be deemed always to have had effect.

(4) Section 3 of this Act and this section extend to Northern Ireland, but otherwise this Act does not extend there.

Section 4(2)   SCHEDULE

REPEALS

Chapter	Short title	Extent of repeal
1986 c.50.	The Social Security Act 1986.	In section 3, in subsection (1) the words "Subject to subsection (2) below" and paragraph (b), subsection (2) and, in subsection (5)(d), the words from "and as if" to the end.

INDEX

References are to section and Schedule numbers

CONSOLIDATED FUND ACT 1993

(1993 c. 4)

An Act to apply certain sums out of the Consolidated Fund to the service of the year ending on 31st March 1993. [18th February 1993]

PARLIAMENTARY DEBATES
Hansard, H.C. Vol. 219, col. 72; H.L. Vol. 542, col. 1249.

INTRODUCTION
This Act makes provision for the allocation of £1,893,716,000 for the Consolidated Fund for the service of the year ending March 31, 1993.

Issue out of the Consolidated Fund for the year ending 31st March 1993

1. The Treasury may issue out of the Consolidated Fund of the United Kingdom and apply towards making good the supply granted to Her Majesty for the service of the year ending on 31st March 1993 the sum of £1,893,716,000.

Short title

2. This Act may be cited as the Consolidated Fund Act 1993.

INDEX

References are to section numbers

DAMAGES (SCOTLAND) ACT 1993*

(1993 c. 5)

An Act to clarify and amend the law of Scotland concerning the right of certain relatives of a deceased person, and the right of executors, to claim damages in respect of the death of the deceased from personal injuries; to make provision regarding solatium where personal injuries result in loss of expectation of life; and for connected purposes.

[18th February 1993]

PARLIAMENTARY DEBATES

Hansard, H.L. Vol. 539, col. 1192; Vol. 540, cols. 266, 1067; H.C. Vol. 217, cols. 112, 1372. The Bill was discussed in 2nd Scottish Standing Committee on January 27, 1993.

INTRODUCTION AND GENERAL NOTE

Where a person suffers injury or disease through the fault or negligence of another, and dies either instantaneously or after a period of time, certain rights arise on the death: (a) *relatives' rights*: the deceased's relatives may be entitled to claim damages in respect of loss of society, loss of support, loss of services, and funeral expenses, if the death resulted from the negligence and not from extraneous causes; (b) *executor's rights*: the deceased's executor is entitled to recover damages in respect of any patrimonial loss such as loss of wages, loss of pension, expenses and outlays, suffered by the deceased during the period prior to death: see generally the Damages (Scotland) Act 1976; Walker, *Delict* (2nd ed.), Chap. 22; McEwan and Paton, *Damages in Scotland* (2nd ed.), Chap. 13.

The 1976 Act made it impossible for the executor to recover any *non-patrimonial* loss (solatium for pain and suffering) to which the deceased had become entitled prior to his death. While claims for *patrimonial* loss transmitted to the executor on death, claims for solatium were extinguished on death, and could not pass to the executor whether or not an action had already been raised by the deceased: s.2 of the Damages (Scotland) Act 1976; *Allison* v. *British Rail Engineering*, 1978 S.L.T. (Notes) 34; *Hansard*, H.L. Vol. 539, col. 1199. In this respect, the 1976 Act altered the previous law, under which transmission of claims for solatium had been possible to some extent, as an executor had been able to continue an action seeking damages for solatium which had been raised by the deceased prior to death, although he had not been able to initiate such an action: *Stewart* v. *London, Midland & Scottish Railway Co.*, 1943 S.C. (H.L.) 19; *Smith* v. *Stewart & Co.*, 1960 S.C. 329, 334.

The effect of s.2 upon claims for solatium caused disquiet, particularly in relation to victims of mesothelioma, asbestosis, pneumoconiosis, and other insidious industrial diseases. A significant number of victims were unable to survive sufficiently long to recover the damages for solatium due to them. There was a perception that defenders and their agents might be tempted to permit or encourage delays, so that the pursuer died either before an action had been raised, or before settlement or completion of an action. If the claim for solatium was extinguished, any damages payable to the executory estate were often significantly reduced.

With this in mind, the Secretary of State for Scotland made a reference to the Scottish Law Commission: "To consider the case for amending the law of damages in Scotland having regard to the possibility that there may be an incentive inherent in the present law for a defender to postpone making settlement or reaching proof until after the death of the pursuer in order to minimise the amount of any compensation to be paid." In November 1990 the Scottish Law Commission published a Discussion Paper ("The Effect of Death on Damages", Discussion Paper No. 89) which attracted widespread interest and response. In March 1992 the Scottish Law Commission published their *Report on The Effect of Death on Damages*, Scot. Law Com. No. 134 (hereinafter referred to as "the Report"). They commented at para. 1.13, "On the basis of our survey . . . we can only say that there may be at least an inducement to delay inherent in the present law. No evidence was submitted to us that the state of the law is being exploited. But that is not conclusive. The very possibility of exploitation may be sufficient reason for reform. And the case may be all the stronger if, as is said, delay is otherwise endemic in the processes in which personal injury claims are pursued"; and, at para. 1.18, "Our point is that delay of one sort or another probably cannot be wholly eliminated. There are too many potential causes of delay, and therefore an ever-present possibility of exploitation."

---

* Annotations by Ann Paton, Q.C., M.A., LL.B.

In their Report at para. 4.1, the Scottish Law Commission stated that it was not their purpose to carry out a comprehensive review of the 1976 Act. Their aim was limited to correcting a perceived defect in the law, and recommending other changes only where they seemed necessary as part of a coherent solution to the problem posed in their remit. The Report contained a draft Bill which formed the basis of the Damages (Scotland) Act 1993. The Bill was introduced by Lord Macaulay of Bragar, received cross-party support, and made swift progress through Parliament. The Damages (Scotland) Act 1993 received the Royal Assent on February 18, 1993.

The 1993 Act makes the following changes, all in the form of amendments to the Damages (Scotland) Act 1976;

(a) Section 1(1): loss of society is replaced (s.1(4) of the 1976 Act)

"Loss of society", as defined in ss.1(4) and 10 of the 1976 Act, is replaced by a broader, more flexible concept incorporating several elements, namely distress and anxiety suffered by the relative of the injured person prior to the death; grief and sorrow on the death; and the loss of such non-patrimonial benefit as the relative might have been expected to derive from the deceased's society and guidance if the deceased had not died.

(b) Section 1(2) and (3): provisional damages and loss of support (s.1(5A) of the 1976 Act)

A new subsection is inserted in the 1976 Act, specifically providing that an award of provisional damages to the deceased during his life will not bar a claim for damages by a relative; but in quantifying loss of support there is to be taken into account any part of the provisional award relating to future patrimonial loss intended to cover the period after the date of death.

(c) Section 2: transmissibility of relative's right (s.1A of the 1976 Act)

A new section is inserted in the 1976 Act providing that where a relative entitled to damages in respect of a death himself dies, his claim for both patrimonial and non-patrimonial loss transmits to his executor, restricted to the period prior to the relative's own death. This alters the previous law, under which only claims for patrimonial loss transmitted.

(d) Section 3: transmissibility of claim for solatium (s.2 of the 1976 Act)

Section 2 is replaced by a new section which provides that all rights to damages in respect of personal injuries vested in a person before his death pass to his executor on his death, including a right to damages by way of solatium, but restricted to the period prior to death. There are special provisions for defamation.

(e) Section 5: diminished life expectancy (s.9A of the 1976 Act)

A new section is inserted in the 1976 Act providing that solatium may reflect a reduction in life expectancy only where the injured person is, was at any time, or is likely to become, aware of that reduction.

COMMENCEMENT

In terms of s.8(3), the 1993 Act came into force two months after the day on which it was passed. The Act received the Royal Assent on February 18, 1993, and came into force on April 18, 1993. However, some of the provisions are retrospective and take effect in relation to deaths occurring on or after July 16, 1992: see s.6 *infra*.

Rights of relatives of a deceased person

1.—(1) In section 1(4) of the Damages (Scotland) Act 1976 (in this Act referred to as "the 1976 Act") for the words from "the loss" to the end there shall be substituted the words "all or any of the following—

(a) distress and anxiety endured by the relative in contemplation of the suffering of the deceased before his death;

(b) grief and sorrow of the relative caused by the deceased's death;

(c) the loss of such non-patrimonial benefit as the relative might have been expected to derive from the deceased's society and guidance if the deceased had not died,

and the court in making an award under this subsection shall not be required to ascribe specifically any part of the award to any of paragraphs (a), (b) and (c) above.".

(2) At the beginning of subsection (5) of that section there shall be added the words "Subject to subsection (5A) below,".

(3) After subsection (5) of that section there shall be inserted the following subsection—

"(5A) Where a deceased has been awarded a provisional award of damages under section 12(2) of the Administration of Justice Act 1982, the making of that award does not prevent liability from arising under this section but in assessing for the purposes of this section the amount of any loss of support suffered by a relative of the deceased the court shall take into account such part of the provisional award relating to future patrimonial loss as was intended to compensate the deceased for a period beyond the date on which he died.".

DEFINITIONS

"loss of support": s.1 of the Damages (Scotland) Act 1976.

GENERAL NOTE

Subs. (1)

A "loss of society award" was defined in s.1(4) of the Damages (Scotland) Act 1976 as "such sum of damages, if any, as the court thinks just by way of compensation for the loss of such non-patrimonial benefit as the relative might have been expected to derive from the deceased's society and guidance if he had not died". Loss of society replaced the previous award of solatium for grief and suffering on the death of a relative: see Walker, *Delict* (2nd ed.), p. 720.

In their Report at para. 2.7, the Scottish Law Commission doubted whether, on a strict reading of s.1(4), the definition of loss of society properly included grief caused by the death, or distress in contemplating the suffering of the deceased before death, although in practice the courts appeared to recognise such elements. At paras. 2.21 and 2.31 the Commission further commented that the expectation that the statutory definition of loss of society would encourage more generous awards had not been borne out in practice; and also that the decisions in *Dingwall* v. *Walter Alexander & Sons (Midland)*, 1981 S.L.T. 313 and *Donald* v. *Strathclyde Passenger Transport Executive*, 1986 S.L.T. 625 made the law on the content of a loss of society award difficult to determine.

The Commission recommended the tripartite formula now contained in subparas. (a)–(c), pointing out that the reformulation "is not intended to change the basis of the loss of society award, as it is now interpreted by the courts, but merely to clarify it and secure it legislatively" (para. 4.45). The award is no longer called a "loss of society award": ss.1(1) and 7(1) of the 1993 Act.

The court is not required specifically to allocate damages to one or other of the elements, but may do so if it thinks fit.

Subss. (2) and (3)

A new subs. (5A) is inserted in s.1 of the 1976 Act, making it clear that where an injured person has received provisional damages, and then dies, the award of provisional damages does not bar claims by relatives, but should be taken into account when quantifying loss of support.

As was said in the course of Parliamentary debate (*Hansard*, Vol. 540, col. 267) the need for this amendment is best illustrated by an example: a shipyard worker is diagnosed as having scars on his lungs and being unfit for work; he is warned of a risk of mesothelioma developing at an unspecified future date. He seeks and is awarded provisional damages, including an award in respect of future loss of earnings. Some years later, he develops mesothelioma, and dies before he has an opportunity to return to court. Two questions arise: (i) do the provisions of s.1(2) of the 1976 Act prevent a claim being made by the relatives; (ii) is there a possibility of overlap between the loss of earnings included in the provisional award, and the loss of support claims by the relatives?

The new subs. (5A) clarifies the position by providing that an award of provisional damages does not prevent claims by relatives, but that in assessing loss of support, the court is to take into account "such part of the provisional award relating to future patrimonial loss as was intended to compensate the deceased for a period beyond the date on which he died".

Transmissibility to executor of rights of deceased relative

2. After section 1 of the 1976 Act there shall be inserted the following section—

"Transmissibility to executor of rights of deceased relative

1A. Any right to damages under any provision of section 1 of this Act which is vested in the relative concerned immediately before his death shall be transmitted to the relative's executor; but, in determining the amount of damages payable to an executor by virtue of this section, the court shall have regard only to the period ending immediately before the relative's death.".

GENERAL NOTE

By the insertion of a new s.1A in the 1976 Act (as extended by s.6(1) and (2) of the 1993 Act), a relative's rights to damages in respect of either loss of society (deaths pre-1993 Act) or solatium (deaths pre-1976 Act) or any of the elements detailed in the amended s.1(4) of the 1976 Act (deaths post-1993 Act) become transmissible to his executor. Accordingly, if the relative himself dies, his executor may raise an action or be sisted as pursuer in an existing action to recover these damages. (While a relative's right to claim damages for solatium on a death was replaced by the right to claim damages for loss of society by the Damages (Scotland) Act 1976, the 1993 Act, in ss.2 and 6(2), allows for the remote possibility of rights to solatium which may have arisen before the commencement of the 1976 Act and which have not become time-barred under the Prescription and Limitation (Scotland) Act 1973).

Section 1A alters the law as it stood under the unamended 1976 Act, in terms of which a relative's non-patrimonial loss did not transmit to his executor. As the Scottish Law Commission pointed out at para. 4.41 *et seq.*, it is difficult in the context of transmissibility logically to distinguish between the non-patrimonial award of solatium (made transmissible to the executor by s.3 of the 1993 Act) and the non-patrimonial award arising on the death of a relative.

Transmissibility to executor of deceased's right to solatium for his injuries

3. For section 2 of the 1976 Act there shall be substituted the following section—

> **"Rights transmitted to executor in respect of deceased person's injuries**
>
> 2.—(1) Subject to the following provisions of this section, there shall be transmitted to the executor of a deceased person the like rights to damages in respect of personal injuries (including a right to damages by way of solatium) sustained by the deceased as were vested in him immediately before his death.
>
> (2) There shall not be transmitted to the executor under this section a right to damages by way of compensation for patrimonial loss attributable to any period after the deceased's death.
>
> (3) In determining the amount of damages by way of solatium payable to an executor by virtue of this section, the court shall have regard only to the period ending immediately before the deceased's death.
>
> (4) In so far as a right to damages vested in the deceased comprised a right to damages (other than for patrimonial loss) in respect of injury resulting from defamation or any other verbal injury or other injury to reputation sustained by the deceased, that right shall be transmitted to the deceased's executor only if an action to enforce that right had been brought by the deceased before his death and had not been concluded by then within the meaning of section 2A(2) of this Act.".

DEFINITIONS

"concluded": s.2A(2) of the Damages (Scotland) Act 1976, as inserted by s.4 of the Damages (Scotland) Act 1993.

"personal injuries": s.10(1) of the Damages (Scotland) Act 1976, as amended by the Schedule to the Damages (Scotland) Act 1993.

GENERAL NOTE

Section 2 of the 1976 Act is replaced by a section which provides, *inter alia*, that solatium is transmissible to an executor on the death of the injured person.

New s.2(1)

A claim for damages for solatium is no longer extinguished on the death of the victim, but passes to the executor, who may either initiate an action in order to recover the damages, or sist himself as pursuer in an existing action: s.2A(1) of the 1976 Act (see *infra*). Thus claims for damages for solatium transmit to the executor in the same way as claims for damages for patrimonial loss.

New s.2(2) and (3)

In relation to both solatium and patrimonial loss, the executor is entitled to claim damages only in respect of the period prior to death. The shorter the period between injury and death, the smaller the claims for solatium and patrimonial loss are likely to be.

New s.2(4)

Claims in respect of defamation, verbal injury, or injury to reputation do not transmit to the executor unless an action has already been raised by the deceased and has not been concluded. The Scottish Law Commission in their Report at para. 4.30 *et seq.* considered that such claims were special in that (1) they were very personal to the claimant, who might have good reason for electing not to sue; and (2) on one view, it was not clear under the present law how such claims were affected by the death of the claimant.

Concluded. This is in effect defined in s.2A(2) of the 1976 Act (as inserted by s.4 of the 1993 Act): " . . . an action shall not be taken to be concluded while any appeal is competent or before any appeal taken has been disposed of."

Enforcement by executor of rights transmitted to him

4. After section 2 of the 1976 Act there shall be inserted the following section—

"Enforcement by executor of rights transmitted to him

2A.—(1) For the purpose of enforcing any right transmitted to an executor under section 1A or 2 of this Act the executor shall be entitled—

(a) to bring an action; or

(b) if an action for that purpose had been brought by the deceased but had not been concluded before his death, to be sisted as pursuer in that action.

(2) For the purpose of subsection (1) above, an action shall not be taken to be concluded while any appeal is competent or before any appeal taken has been disposed of."

GENERAL NOTE

This is a technical provision which in part re-enacts the old s.2(1) and (2) of the 1976 Act. The new s.2A provides for the enforcement of any right transmitted to an executor in terms of s.1A and s.2 of the 1976 Act as amended. The executor may bring an action, or may be sisted as a pursuer in an action already raised by the deceased and not yet concluded.

Section 2A(2) provides a definition of an action which has not been "concluded".

Solatium for loss of expectation of life

5. After section 9 of the 1976 Act there shall be inserted the following section—

"Solatium for loss of expectation of life

9A.—(1) In assessing, in an action for damages in respect of personal injuries, the amount of damages by way of solatium, the court shall, if—

(a) the injured person's expectation of life has been reduced by the injuries; and

(b) the injured person is, was at any time or is likely to become, aware of that reduction,

have regard to the extent that, in consequence of that awareness, he has suffered or is likely to suffer.

(2) Subject to subsection (1) above, no damages by way of solatium shall be recoverable in respect of loss of expectation of life.

(3) The court in making an award of damages by way of solatium shall not be required to ascribe specifically any part of the award to loss of expectation of life.".

DEFINITIONS
"personal injuries": s.10(1) of the Damages (Scotland) Act 1976, as amended by the Schedule to the Damages (Scotland) Act 1993.

GENERAL NOTE

A new s.9A is inserted in the 1976 Act, providing for entitlement to damages in respect of the pain and suffering attributable to the victim's awareness that his life expectancy has been reduced. The Scottish Law Commission commented that awards of solatium to date may on occasion have included an element reflecting loss of life expectancy, but in their view *awareness* of that loss was an essential prerequisite of the award. Section 9 thus supersedes decisions such as *Dalgleish* v. *Glasgow Corporation*, 1976 S.C. 32, in so far as these decisions provided authority for the proposition that damages for loss of life expectancy may be awarded to unconscious, unaware victims.

The court is not required to treat any damages for loss of expectation of life as a separate award, but may do so if it thinks fit.

Section 9A is inserted after s.9 of the 1976 Act, which deals with the computation of patrimonial loss where the victim's expectation of life is diminished.

Transitional and retrospective provisions

6.—(1) Section 1A of the 1976 Act (as substituted by section 2 of this Act) shall have effect as if it expressly provided that the reference to a right to damages under section 1 of the 1976 Act included a reference to a right under that section as it existed at the time when the right vested, and section 2A shall have effect accordingly.

(2) Section 1A of the 1976 Act shall also have effect as if it provided that the reference to a right to damages under section 1 of the 1976 Act included a reference to a right to damages by way of solatium in respect of the death of a person under the law in force before 13th May 1976, and section 2A shall have effect accordingly.

(3) Section 9A of the 1976 Act shall not affect any proceedings commenced before this Act comes into operation.

(4) Subject to the following provisions of this section, this Act shall have effect only in relation to deaths occurring on or after its commencement.

(5) Notwithstanding section 3 of the 1976 Act, section 1A of that Act shall have effect, subject to subsection (8) below, in the case of the death on or after 16 July 1992 of the relative concerned.

(6) Notwithstanding section 2 of the 1976 Act as it existed prior to the commencement of this Act, that section as substituted by section 3 of this Act shall have effect, subject to subsections (7) and (8) below, in the case of the death on or after 16 July 1992 of a person in whom was vested immediately before his death a right to damages in respect of personal injuries.

(7) Subsection (6) above shall not apply in the case of a death before the commencement of this Act in so far as it would enable an executor to recover damages (other than for patrimonial loss) in respect of injury resulting from defamation or any other verbal injury or other injury to reputation sustained by the deceased.

(8) Neither subsection (5) nor (6) above shall apply where the rights to damages which transmitted to the deceased's executor under section 1 or 2 of the 1976 Act prior to the commencement of this Act have been subject to—

(a) a full and final settlement; or
(b) determination by a court in a final judgment within the meaning of section 19A(3) of the Prescription and Limitation (Scotland) Act 1973,

before the commencement of this Act.

(9) In calculating whether a claim made by an executor by virtue of subsection (5) or (6) above is unenforceable by virtue of the provisions of Part II of the Prescription and Limitation (Scotland) Act 1973, the period

starting with the date of death and ending with the commencement of this Act shall not be taken into account.

DEFINITIONS

"personal injuries": s.10(1) of the Damages (Scotland) Act 1976, as amended by the Schedule to the Damages (Scotland) Act 1993.

GENERAL NOTE

Transitional and retrospective provisions

General rule

The general rule, subject to special retrospective provisions (see *infra*), is that the 1993 Act only has effect in relation to deaths occurring on or after its commencement on April 18, 1993: s.6(4); but see subss. (1), (2), (5), (6), (7) and (8).

Retrospective commencement of some provisions

As a result of the desire to bring the benefits of the 1993 Act to victims and relatives as quickly as possible (*Hansard*, H.L. Vol. 539, col. 1196), the Act makes retrospective provision for the transmissibility of non-patrimonial claims on the death of a relative (s.1A of the 1976 Act, as amended), and for the transmissibility of solatium on the death of a victim (s.2 of the 1976 Act, as amended). The date July 16, 1992 was selected, being the date on which the Damages (Scotland) Bill was introduced in Parliament.

Claims in respect of injury resulting from defamation or any other verbal injury or other injury to reputation are specifically excluded from the retrospective provisions: subs. (7).

Transmission of non-patrimonial claims on death of relative: subss. (1), (2) and (5). If a death occurred before April 18, 1993, a relative of the deceased may have acquired, *inter alia*, a claim for loss of society (or for solatium, if the death occurred before May 13, 1976). If a death occurs on or after April 18, 1993, a relative of the deceased may acquire, *inter alia*, a claim in respect of one or more of the elements detailed in the amended s.1(4) of the 1976 Act.

In either case, if that relative, in whom that claim has vested, himself died on or after July 16, 1992, subss. (1), (2) and (5) provide that the claim transmits to his executor. Subsection (2) makes specific provision for rights which may have vested before the commencement of the 1976 Act (May 13, 1976) and which have not become time-barred under the Prescription and Limitation (Scotland) Act 1973, although the Scottish Law Commission described such a situation as being "likely to be only a very remote possibility".

Transmission of solatium on death of victim: subs. (6). The new s.2 of the 1976 Act, as amended, providing for the transmissibility to the executor of the victim's rights to damages (including a right to damages by way of solatium), is to have effect in the case of any death occurring on or after July 16, 1992. Thus where a person dies on or after July 16, 1992, with vested rights to claim damages in respect of personal injuries, those rights (including the right to damages by way of solatium) transmit to the executor.

Retrospective commencement not to affect claims settled or subject to final judgment

Subsection (8) excludes from the effect of the 1993 Act cases where death claims have, prior to the commencement of the 1993 Act, been subject to either (a) a full and final settlement; or (b) determination by a court in a final judgment. "Final judgment" is defined in s.19A(3) of the Prescription and Limitation (Scotland) Act 1973 as "an interlocutor of a court of first instance which, by itself, or taken along with previous interlocutors, disposes of the subject matter of a cause notwithstanding that judgment may not have been pronounced on every question raised or that the expenses found due may not have been modified, taxed or decerned for; but the expression does not include an interlocutor dismissing a cause by reason only of a provision mentioned in subsection (1) . . . " (*i.e.* the three-year limitation provisions in personal injuries claims).

Loss of expectation of life

The new s.9A, providing for damages by way of solatium where a victim is aware of loss of life expectancy, is not to affect any proceedings commenced prior to April 18, 1993. The commencement of an action has been defined as the date of citation: *Miller* v. *N.C.B.*, 1960 S.C. 376 *per* Lord President at p. 383; (*cf.* authorities cited in Walker, *The Law of Prescription* (4th ed.) at p. 97).

Limitation

For limitation purposes, the period starting with the date of death and ending with April 18,

1993 (date of commencement of the 1993 Act), is not to be taken into account. Thus in the case of any death occurring between July 16, 1992 and April 18, 1993, the triennium begins running on April 19, 1993. In the case of any death occurring on or after April 19, 1993, the triennium begins running on the date of death.

Interpretation, minor and consequential amendments and repeals

7.—(1) In any enactment passed or made before this Act, unless the context otherwise requires, any reference to a loss of society award shall be construed as a reference to an award under section 1(4) of the 1976 Act as amended by section 1 of this Act.

(2) The enactments mentioned in the Schedule to this Act shall have effect subject to the minor and consequential amendments respectively specified in that Schedule.

(3) The following provisions of the 1976 Act are hereby repealed—
Section 3;
In section 10(1) the definition of "loss of society award";
Section 11;
Section 12(3) and (4);
Schedule 2.

Short title, application to Crown, commencement and extent

8.—(1) This Act may be cited as the Damages (Scotland) Act 1993.
(2) This Act binds the Crown.
(3) This Act shall come into force at the end of the period of 2 months beginning with the day on which it is passed.
(4) This Act extends to Scotland only.

Section 7   SCHEDULE

CONSEQUENTIAL AMENDMENTS

The Damages (Scotland) Act 1976 (c.13)

1. In section 4 for the words from "nor is" to "said section 1" there shall be substituted the words "or by a deceased relative's executor under section 1A of this Act; nor is a claim by a relative of a deceased person or by a deceased relative's executor for damages under the said section 1 or (as the case may be) the said section 1A".

2. At the end of section 6(3)(b) there shall be added the words "or, if the relative has died, by the relative's executor".

3. In section 10(1) at the end of the definition of "personal injuries" there shall be added the words "and injury resulting from defamation or any other verbal injury or other injury to reputation".

The Administration of Justice Act 1982 (c.53)

4. In section 13(1) at the end of the definition of "personal injuries" there shall be added the words "and injury resulting from defamation or any other verbal injury or other injury to reputation".

The International Transport Conventions Act 1983 (c.14)

5. In Schedule 1, in paragraph 1(2) for the words from "as defined in" to the end there shall be substituted the words "or for an award under section 1(4) of the Damages (Scotland) Act 1976 as amended by section 1 of the Damages (Scotland) Act 1993.".

The Criminal Justice Act 1988 (c.33)

6. In section 111(4)(c) for the words from "for loss" to the end there shall be substituted the words "may be made to any person who is a member of the deceased's immediate family (within the meaning of section 10(2) of the Damages (Scotland) Act 1976), being the kind of award described in section 1(4) of that Act; and".

INDEX

References are to section and Schedule numbers

BANKRUPTCY (SCOTLAND) ACT 1993*

(1993 c. 6)

An Act to amend the Bankruptcy (Scotland) Act 1985; and for connected purposes.　　　　　　　　　　　　　　**[18th February 1993]**

PARLIAMENTARY DEBATES
　Hansard, H.C. Vol. 209, cols. 898, 988; Vol. 212, col. 791; Vol. 215, col. 75; Vol. 219, col. 73; H.L. Vol. 540, col. 10; Vol. 541, cols. 37, 71, 775, 1120.
　The Bill was discussed in Scottish Grand Committee on June 4 and 8, 1992 and in 1st Scottish Standing Committee between June 30 and October 20, 1992.

GENERAL NOTE
　This Act amends, and in some respects considerably alters, the system of bankruptcy law which was introduced into Scotland by the Bankruptcy (Scotland) Act 1985 (the "1985 Act"). The 1985 Act gave effect, with some modifications, to the proposals in a Report by the Scottish Law Commission on *Bankruptcy and Related Aspects of Insolvency and Liquidation* ("S.L.C.") which was published in February 1982 (Scot. Law Com. No. 68). The working of the 1985 Act produced some unexpected features which gave rise to a demand for further reform.
　The effect which was not foreseen by the Scottish Law Commission was the attraction of its scheme for "small assets" cases. The term "small assets" is not used in the 1985 Act, but is a popular (although inaccurate) phrase for the procedure in Sched. 2 to the 1985 Act which applies when a debtor's assets are unlikely to pay a dividend. If the appropriate procedure is followed the interim trustee reports to the statutory meeting of creditors that the debtor's assets are unlikely to be sufficient to pay a dividend and, following a report to the sheriff, the interim trustee is appointed permanent trustee (s.23(4), 1985 Act). Schedule 2 then applies with the consequence that public funds are available to meet the outlays and remuneration of both interim and permanent trustees (Sched. 2, para. 9).
　The Scottish Law Commission did not expect the availability of public funds to produce a large increase in the number of sequestrations. The Commission estimated that expenditure other than internal to the office of the Accountant of Court (who was to be the Accountant in Bankruptcy) "is likely to fall within the range of £6,000 to £7,500" per annum (S.L.C., para. 4.45). The total increase in expenditure for the Accountant's office was estimated at £30,000 to £40,000 per annum (S.L.C., para. 4.43). The basis of these figures was annual numbers of sequestrations of 120 or 150 a year with small assets cases being about 10 per cent. In the event these estimates turned out to be grossly incorrect.
　Before the 1985 Act came into operation there were under 300 sequestrations a year. After the Act the increase in numbers was dramatic. Using figures from the Accountant in Bankruptcy's Annual Reports the figures for financial years were:

1986/87	*1987/88*	*1988/89*	*1989/90*	*1990/91*	*1991/92*
560	951	1612	2618	5451	8584

*Annotations by Professor William W. McBryde, Vice Principal, University of Dundee.

For various reasons it is not possible to provide precise figures on the number of cases which are "small assets" cases but they represent over 80 per cent. of the totals. Most of these were cases where the debtor arranged his or her own sequestration by signing a trust deed and relying on the power of the trustee to petition for the debtor's sequestration; the so-called "trust deed route". In 1986, 75 per cent. of all awards of sequestration were granted on the petition of a qualified creditor. By 1991–92 these petitions constituted only 13 per cent. of the total. In contrast the number of trustee petitions increased from 31 in 1986–87 to 7,471 in 1991–92.

The level of Government expenditure in 1991/92 amounted to some £19.7 million divided between the administrative costs of the Accountant in Bankruptcy (£1.2m) and gross payments to or on behalf of trustees (£18.5m). The Government estimated that if the volume of sequestrations continued to grow at the same rate as over the previous six years and if the scheme of the 1985 Act was unaltered the total cost would increase to £50m by 1993/94, and to over £80m by 1994/95 (*Explanatory and Financial Memorandum* to the Bill). These estimates were disputed in some quarters because of assumptions about the continued growth in numbers and costs but nevertheless the estimates provided part of the motivation for the present Act.

The discrepancy between what the Scottish Law Commission predicted and what actually happened is considerable, including the expense to the taxpayer in millions of pounds since April 1, 1986 (the date of commencement of most of the 1985 Act). Social and economic factors may have been responsible for some part of the increase in sequestrations. The boom was also assisted by (1) the availability of public funds to pay for trustees' fees and outlays; and (2) the device of the "trust deed route" by which a debtor signed a trust deed and the trustee immediately petitioned for sequestration. A debtor could, therefore, arrange his or her sequestration without the consent of a creditor and in this process be assisted by a trustee who was guaranteed payment from public funds. It is not surprising that, in an appropriate case, this was a procedure with some attraction to a debtor who was being pressed for payment but wished an end to diligence and a discharge of all debts; it certainly was a procedure with benefits to insolvency practitioners some of whom marketed their services. As the hypothesis is that in "small assets" cases there will not be a dividend to creditors the procedures had little appeal to creditors who could view substantial sums of taxpayers' money being used to prevent enforcement of their claims for debt.

The Government's aims have been (1) to control the public expenditure involved and to have a service which is cost effective and good value for money; and (2) to strike the correct balance between the interests of debtors and creditors (see *Hansard*, H.L. Vol. 540, col. 12).

The Act deals with the difficulties in the following ways:

(1) The Accountant in Bankruptcy may become the interim or permanent trustee and will so act in many "small assets" cases (see new s.2(2) of the 1985 Act as substituted by s.2; new s.25A of the 1985 Act as inserted by s.7). This is a major change in the philosophy which has applied in Scottish sequestrations because for the first time the day to day administration of sequestrations will be the responsibility of a Government appointed officer. The Scottish Law Commission resisted the introduction of an Official Receiver into Scotland, ironically on the grounds of expense (S.L.C., para. 2.32). Where there are sufficient assets to pay a dividend the private sector will probably carry out the work as in the past.

(2) A system of summary administration is introduced where the liabilities and assets of the debtor do not exceed certain figures (s.6 inserting s.23A and Schedule 2A into the 1985 Act).

(3) The right of a trustee under a trust deed to petition for sequestration is limited to defined circumstances (s.3 inserting new s.5(2) in the 1985 Act) and the court must be satisfied that the trustee's averments are true (s.4(4) inserting new s.12(3) in the 1985 Act).

(4) A debtor may petition for sequestration without the concurrence of a qualified creditor *but* only if certain conditions are satisfied including that the debtor is apparently insolvent or a trustee under a trust deed has been unable to make the trust deed protected because of objections from creditors (s.3 inserting s.5(2B) in the 1985 Act). Informal sampling suggests that only a small percentage of debtors at present sequestrated under the "trust deed route" have been made apparently insolvent by creditors. The result, at least in the short term, may be a considerable reduction in the number of sequestrations.

(5) The procedure for making a trust deed protected is amended with the intention of increasing the popularity of trust deeds (Sched. 1, para. 32 inserting new para. 5 in Sched. 5 of the 1985 Act). There were very few protected trust deeds under the 1985 Act in part because of the difficulty of obtaining the consent of the required number and value of creditors within the specified time limit.

(6) Various amendments to the 1985 Act are designed to make procedures simpler and cheaper, *e.g.* the removal of any need for a notice in the *London Gazette* (Sched. 1, para. 4, inserting a new s.15(6) in the 1985 Act); the ability of the Accountant in Bankruptcy as interim trustee to dispense with a statutory meeting of creditors if appropriate procedure is followed (s.5, inserting a new s.21A in the 1985 Act).

(7) The opportunity is taken to remove some doubts or difficulties which arose from the 1985 Act.

(8) Transitional arrangements may be made to control the remuneration of permanent trustees (s.9).

The Government has promised that on enactment the Statutory Publications Office will produce a revised edition of the 1985 Act incorporating the amendments made to it (*Official Report*, First Scottish Standing Committee, July 14, 1992, col. 391).

One of the most interesting developments after the Act is in force may be attempts to revive the "trust deed route" to sequestration. This possibility is not entirely removed by the Act, although it is a matter for speculation how far practitioners and debtors may use some variants of the devices which are hinted at in these annotations. The overall effect of the Act, however, is that while public funds remain available for sequestrations, because the Accountant in Bankruptcy may now act as interim and permanent trustee, there are obstacles in the way of a debtor arranging his or her own sequestration. Some of the drafting, despite protests to the contrary, seems designed to prevent many of those who used the remedy of sequestration from continuing to do so. Whether or not this is the correct policy is debatable. As it is put in a classic American text:

"The purpose of bankruptcy law, properly used rather than abused, is to serve as a financial hospital for people sick with debt. If hospital admissions rise dramatically, there are at least two explanations for the increase. It may be that doctors have started admitting patients who are not seriously ill and who could be treated as outpatients. Or the crowded hospital wards may simply reflect a breakdown of health in the community. If the hospital population suddenly rose, no sensible person would close the hospital doors and announce that the problem had been solved. Instead, medical researchers would examine the patients to find out if they were really sick and, if so, why." (T.A. Sullivan, E. Warren, J.L. Westbrook, *As We Forgive Our Debtors*, O.U.P., 1989, p. 6).

Private practitioners will examine the extent to which they can provide a service, and make a profit, through (1) trust deeds; (2) as interim and permanent trustees with or without a certificate of summary administration; and (3) as agents or nominees of the Accountant in Bankruptcy in small assets cases. The Government intended,

"to introduce the provisions of the Bill so that the Accountant in Bankruptcy would be appointed the trustee in most small assets cases. The Accountant would then retain a proportion of cases in-house, but allocate the remainder to insolvency practitioners on the same basis as under the 1985 Act. Those cases would be allocated on a fixed-price basis. That would allow all concerned—the Accountant in Bankruptcy and the insolvency practitioners … the opportunity to gain experience under the new régime. That should permit a fairer comparison to be made between public sector and private sector provision when full market testing is undertaken" (*Hansard*, H.C. Vol. 219, col. 74).

COMMENCEMENT

In terms of s.12(3), on the passing of the Act there comes into force section 8 (which allows for regulations to prescribe the fees and outlays payable to the Accountant in Bankruptcy), section 9 (which provides for transitional arrangements on the remuneration of permanent trustees), a provision about the finality of a sheriff's decision (Sched. 1, para. 22(5)), and retrospective provisions about the effect of a debtor's discharge on securities (Sched. 1, paras. 23, 31(4) and (5)). The remainder of the Act may come into force on appointed days.

In broad terms there may, for a time, be four main legislative provisions which govern sequestrations in Scotland:

(1) the Bankruptcy (Scotland) Act 1913 which applies in the case of petitions presented before April 1, 1986;
(2) the Bankruptcy (Scotland) Act 1985 which, as it has been amended in minor ways from time to time, will apply to sequestration petitions presented on or after April 1, 1986 until the day this present Act was passed;
(3) The 1985 Act as amended by amongst other provisions those of the present Act which are brought into force on the Royal Assent; and
(4) When section 2 of this Act (and presumably most of the remainder of the Act) is brought into force, the 1985 Act as amended by, in particular, the substantive provisions of this Act.

The critical date in each case is the date of presentation of the petition (see, *e.g.* ss.9(1) and 12(6)) which means the time when the petition is received by the clerk of court (s.73(6) of the 1985 Act as inserted by Sched. 1, para. 29(7) of this Act).

APPLICATION

The Act extends to Scotland only except in so far as it amends an enactment which applies to England, Wales or Northern Ireland (s.12(8)). There is in fact very little which applies to non-Scottish legislation. There are minor and consequential amendments to the Insolvency Act 1986 (s.11(1) and (2)) and to the Criminal Justice Act 1988 (Sched. 2).

DEFINITIONS
The Act provides that expressions used in the Act shall have the same meaning as those expressions used in the 1985 Act. The Act does change some of the definitions in the 1985 Act (*e.g.* the definition of "trust deed"). The Bill when first introduced proposed to change the meaning of "the date of sequestration", which would have had widespread consequences. After representations from professional bodies the proposed change was modified and later in substance abandoned. The new definition is similar to the old with an addition to clarify the effect of more than one warrant to cite (s.4(5) substituting for s.12(4) of the 1985 Act).

For most purposes the important definitions are contained in the 1985 Act as amended and it is these definitions which are referred to in the annotations to the sections of the Act.

Accountant in Bankruptcy

1.—(1) In the Bankruptcy (Scotland) Act 1985 (in this Act referred to as "the 1985 Act"), for section 1 (functions of the Accountant in Bankruptcy) there shall be substituted the following sections—

"Accountant in Bankruptcy

1.—(1) The Accountant in Bankruptcy shall be appointed by the Secretary of State on such terms and conditions as the Secretary of State may, with the approval of the Treasury, determine.

(2) The Accountant in Bankruptcy shall have such staff appointed by the Secretary of State on such terms and conditions as the Secretary of State may, with the approval of the Treasury, determine.

(3) The Secretary of State may appoint a member of the staff to be Depute Accountant in Bankruptcy to exercise all of the functions of the Accountant in Bankruptcy at any time when the Accountant in Bankruptcy is unable to do so.

(4) The Secretary of State may pay to the Accountant in Bankruptcy and his staff such remuneration and allowances as the Secretary of State may, with the approval of the Treasury, determine.

(5) The Secretary of State may, with the approval of the Treasury, make such arrangements as he considers appropriate for the provision of superannuation, pensions or gratuities for the Accountant in Bankruptcy and his staff.

Supervisory functions of the Accountant in Bankruptcy

1A.—(1) The Accountant in Bankruptcy shall have the following general functions in the administration of sequestration and personal insolvency—

(a) the supervision of the performance by—
　　(i) interim trustees (not being the Accountant in Bankruptcy);
　　(ii) permanent trustees; and
　　(iii) commissioners,
of the functions conferred on them by this Act or any other enactment (including an enactment contained in subordinate legislation) or any rule of law and the investigation of any complaints made against them;

(b) the maintenance of a register (in this Act referred to as the "register of insolvencies"), in such form as may be prescribed by the Court of Session by act of sederunt, which shall contain particulars of—
　　(i) estates which have been sequestrated; and
　　(ii) trust deeds which have been sent to him for registration under paragraph 5(1)(e) of Schedule 5 to this Act;

(c) the preparation of an annual report which shall be presented

6–4

to the Secretary of State and the Court of Session and shall contain—
> (i) statistical information relating to the state of all sequestrations of which particulars have been registered in the register of insolvencies during the year to which the report relates;
> (ii) particulars of trust deeds registered as protected trust deeds in that year; and
> (iii) particulars of the performance of the Accountant in Bankruptcy's functions under this Act; and

(d) such other functions as may from time to time be conferred on him by the Secretary of State.

(2) If it appears to the Accountant in Bankruptcy that a person mentioned in paragraph (a) of subsection (1) above has failed without reasonable excuse to perform a duty imposed on him by any provision of this Act or by any other enactment (including an enactment contained in subordinate legislation) or by any rule of law, he shall report the matter to the court which, after hearing that person on the matter, may remove him from office or censure him or make such other order as the circumstances of the case may require.

(3) Where the Accountant in Bankruptcy has reasonable grounds to suspect that an offence has been committed—

(a) by a person mentioned in paragraph (a) of subsection (1) above in the performance of his functions under this Act or any other enactment (including an enactment contained in subordinate legislation) or any rule of law; or

(b) in relation to a sequestration, by the debtor in respect of his assets, his dealings with them or his conduct in relation to his business or financial affairs; or

(c) in relation to a sequestration, by a person other than the debtor in that person's dealings with the debtor, the interim trustee or the permanent trustee in respect of the debtor's assets, business or financial affairs,

he shall report the matter to the Lord Advocate.

(4) The Accountant in Bankruptcy shall—

(a) make the register of insolvencies, at all reasonable times, available for inspection; and

(b) provide any person, on request, with a certified copy of any entry in the register.

Performance of certain functions of the Accountant in Bankruptcy

1B.—(1) The functions of the Accountant in Bankruptcy, other than functions conferred by section 1A of this Act, may be carried out on his behalf by any member of his staff authorised by him to do so.

(2) Without prejudice to subsection (1) above, the Accountant in Bankruptcy may appoint on such terms and conditions as he considers appropriate such persons as he considers fit to perform on his behalf any of his functions in respect of the sequestration of the estate of any debtor.

(3) A person appointed under subsection (2) above shall comply with such general or specific directions as the Accountant in Bankruptcy may from time to time give to such person as to the performance of his functions in relation to any sequestration.

(4) The Accountant in Bankruptcy may pay to a person appointed under subsection (2) above such fee as he may consider appropriate.

Directions

1C.—(1) The Secretary of State may, after consultation with the Lord President of the Court of Session, give to the Accountant in Bankruptcy general directions as to the performance of his functions under this Act.

(2) Directions under this section may be given in respect of all cases or any class or description of cases, but may not be given in respect of any particular case.

(3) The Accountant in Bankruptcy shall comply with any directions given to him under this section."

(2) When a person is first appointed to be the Accountant in Bankruptcy under section 1 of the 1985 Act as inserted by subsection (1) above, the Accountant of Court shall cease to be the Accountant in Bankruptcy.

(3) On such appointment—

(a) the Accountant of Court shall deliver to the Accountant in Bankruptcy all registers, records, documents and other material in his possession relating to the functions of the Accountant in Bankruptcy before the commencement of this section; and

(b) there shall be transferred to and vest in the Accountant in Bankruptcy all property, rights, liabilities, functions and responsibilities of the Accountant of Court which, immediately before the commencement of this section, were vested in the Accountant of Court in connection with his functions in the administration of sequestrations and personal insolvency under the Bankruptcy (Scotland) Act 1913 or, in his capacity as Accountant in Bankruptcy, under the 1985 Act.

DEFINITIONS

"Accountant in Bankruptcy": s.73(1) and s.1 of the 1985 Act as amended.

"business": s.73(1) of the 1985 Act.

"commissioner": ss.30(1) and 73(1) of the 1985 Act.

"court": s.73(1) of the 1985 Act.

"debtor": s.73(1) of the 1985 Act.

"interim trustee": ss.2 and 73(1) of the 1985 Act.

"permanent trustee": ss.3 and 73(1) of the 1985 Act.

"protected trust deed": s.73(1) of the 1985 Act.

"register of insolvencies": s.73(1) of the 1985 Act as amended by Sched. 1, para. 29(3) to this Act.

"trust deed": s.73(1) of the 1985 Act as amended by Sched. 1, para. 29(6) to this Act and new s.5(4A) of the 1985 Act as inserted by s.3(4).

GENERAL NOTE

This section makes changes in the nature of the office of Accountant in Bankruptcy. The office will be separate from that of Accountant of Court and the appointment will be made by the Secretary of State who to an extent can control the activities of the Accountant and his staff. Part of the reason is that the Accountant in Bankruptcy is considered to be exercising an executive function with a responsibility for effective use of public funds (*Hansard*, Official Report, First Scottish Standing Committee, July 2, 1992, cols. 68, 71). The Accountant's functions will be very similar to those under the 1985 Act except that it will no longer be necessary to maintain a list of interim trustees.

The office of Accountant in Bankruptcy was created by the Bankruptcy (Scotland) Act 1856 (s.156) and was united with the office of Accountant of Court by the Judicial Factors (Scotland) Act 1889, s.1. The Scottish Law Commission considered, but rejected, the proposal that there should be a separate Accountant in Bankruptcy (S.L.C., para. 4.2). This separation will now take place.

When the Bill was introduced the proposal was that the Accountant in Bankruptcy would become interim trustee in all cases. By this and other means there would have been control on the cost of the sequestration process and a reduction in the amount of public funds spent on the sequestration process. After representations the Bill was amended so that private sector insolvency practitioners could be nominated as interim trustees, although it was envisaged that nomination would be accepted only when there were sufficient assets to meet the trustee's fees and outlays or where the petitioner agreed to underwrite the trustee's costs. In the other cases, which in the past have been in the large majority, the Accountant in Bankruptcy would act as trustee with the cost of this operation being the contribution of the public purse to the sequestration process. This replaced the previous provision in para. 9 of Sched. 2 to the 1985 Act under which public funds were paid to private sector insolvency practitioners.

For one office to carry out sequestrations throughout Scotland is a daunting task. It is envisaged that as well as an expansion of the staff of the Accountant (who may carry out routine administration on behalf of the Accountant), the Accountant may appoint agents to act on his (or her) behalf (new s.1B(2)). These may be insolvency practitioners who will be paid by the Accountant (new s.1B(4)). The Accountant, however, can appoint anyone he considers fit to perform his functions and so work might be delegated to, for example, solicitors with experience of investigation of debt problems or with particular expertise in legal issues which are arising. The Accountant may also nominate a person to be permanent trustee in certain cases (s.7 inserting s.25A in the 1985 Act). The Accountant may be expected to introduce competition into the process of selection of his or her agents for the purpose of ensuring value for money and quality of service (*Hansard*, H.C. Vol. 209, cols. 908–9).

Subs. (1)

This substitutes a new s.1 in the 1985 Act. The functions of the Accountant in Bankruptcy may be classified as (1) the supervision of the performance of those involved in the sequestration process; (2) the maintenance of a register and the preparation of an annual report; and (3)· the reporting of alleged offences to the Lord Advocate. The Accountant may be given general directions by the Secretary of State.

One function which the Accountant does not have is to give advice to individual debtors, despite repeated attempts in Parliament to suggest that this was necessary (*Hansard*, H.C. Vol. 209, col. 945; *Official Report*, First Scottish Standing Committee, July 2, 1992, col. 86; July 7, 1992, col. 129). The Accountant will prepare a general guide for debtors and may answer queries but a duty to provide advice to individuals (including advice on the need for sequestration) was seen as a potential conflict with a duty to control public expenditure.

Supervision

The duties of supervision are similar to those already existing but are extended beyond the performance of duties under the 1985 Act to cover functions conferred by any enactment or rule of law. In the event of misconduct by a trustee the sanctions available to the Accountant include (1) a request that the offender initiate action (*e.g.* resign from office as trustee); (2) a report to the individual's professional body for disciplinary action to be considered; (3) a report to the body which granted a permit to act as an insolvency practitioner (which may, or may not, be the same as the individual's professional organisation); (4) a report to the Lord Advocate if an offence may have been committed (new s.1A(3)); (5) a report to the court (new s.1A(2)); (6) an application for removal of an interim trustee from office (new s.13(2) as inserted by Sched. 1, para. 2); and (7) an application for removal of a permanent trustee from office (s.29(1) of the 1985 Act). The Accountant can ask a trustee for information, whether or not the trustee is in office (new s.2(4) inserted by s.2; s.3(1)(*g*) of the 1985 Act).

The Accountant does not have a function in supervising the performance of trustees under trust deeds although he may audit accounts and fix remuneration (Sched. 5, para. 1 of the 1985 Act).

The Accountant's own actions, as trustee or otherwise, were said to be subject to judicial review (*Official Report*, First Scottish Standing Committee, July 7, 1992, cols. 113 and 121) and also to an action based on negligence (*Official Report*, First Scottish Standing Committee, July 7, 1992, cols. 206–10). There is also a general provision, which may apply to the Accountant acting as permanent trustee, whereby the debtor, a creditor, or any person having an interest may challenge actions of a permanent trustee by application to the sheriff (new s.3(7) added by Sched. 1, para. 1).

Records

The Accountant must maintain a register of insolvencies as previously. The register has particulars of sequestrated estates and of protected trust deeds. The register is open to public inspection. It does not contain information on all trust deeds including those which the trustee tried but failed to have protected. There is, therefore, no record of every trust deed and no easily available information on the extent of use of trust deeds.

The duty to maintain a list of interim trustees and the need for the list disappear. This list was introduced by s.1(1)(*b*) of the 1985 Act. The intention was to provide a list from which interim trustees could be appointed by the court (s.13(1) of the 1985 Act now replaced by a new s.13—see Sched. 1, para. 2). In practice the interim trustee was nominated in the petition and the nominee was usually appointed. After s.2 of this Act is in force, the interim trustee will be either the person nominated in the petition or the Accountant. The list of interim trustees will, however, remain in existence for the purpose of s.28(5) of the 1985 Act (replacement of permanent trustee) in respect of petitions presented prior to the commencement of s.2 of this Act.

Offences
  The duty to report offences to the Lord Advocate is similar to the previous provision. The Accountant "shall" report when he has the required "reasonable grounds to suspect". The duty is wider than under the 1985 Act which was limited to offences under that Act. Now the duty extends to offences under any enactment or at common law.

Directions to the Accountant
  There is a new provision in s.1C that the Secretary of State may give general directions after consultation with the Lord President. This enables the Secretary of State to exercise a measure of control. The Accountant retains an independence in respect of individual cases.

Appointment and functions of interim trustee

2. For section 2 of the 1985 Act (interim trustee) there shall be substituted the following section—

"Appointment and functions of interim trustee

2.—(1) Where the court awards sequestration of the debtor's estate and the petition for the sequestration—
  (a) nominates a person to be interim trustee;
  (b) states that the person satisfies the conditions mentioned in subsection (3) below; and
  (c) has annexed to it a copy of the undertaking mentioned in subsection (3)(c) below,
the court may, if it appears to the court that the person satisfies those conditions and if no interim trustee has been appointed in pursuance of subsection (5) below, appoint that person to be interim trustee in the sequestration.

(2) Where the court awards sequestration of the debtor's estate and—
  (a) it does not appoint a person to be interim trustee in pursuance of subsection (1) above; and
  (b) no interim trustee has been appointed in pursuance of subsection (5) below,
the court shall appoint the Accountant in Bankruptcy to be interim trustee in the sequestration.

(3) The conditions referred to in subsection (1) above are that the person—
  (a) resides within the jurisdiction of the Court of Session;
  (b) is qualified to act as an insolvency practitioner; and
  (c) has given an undertaking, in writing, that he will act—
        (i) as interim trustee; and
        (ii) where no permanent trustee is elected, as permanent trustee,
in the sequestration.

(4) The interim trustee's general functions shall be—
  (a) to safeguard the debtor's estate pending the appointment of a permanent trustee under this Act;
  (b) to ascertain the reasons for the debtor's insolvency and the circumstances surrounding it;
  (c) to ascertain the state of the debtor's liabilities and assets;
  (d) to administer the sequestration process pending the appointment of a permanent trustee; and
  (e) whether or not he is still acting in the sequestration, to supply the Accountant in Bankruptcy with such information

as the Accountant in Bankruptcy considers necessary to enable him to discharge his functions under this Act.

(5) Where a petition for sequestration is presented by a creditor or a trustee acting under a trust deed, the court may appoint an interim trustee before sequestration is awarded—

(a) if the debtor consents; or

(b) if the trustee acting under the trust deed or any creditor shows cause.

(6) For the purpose of the appointment of an interim trustee under subsection (5) above—

(a) where a person is nominated as mentioned in subsection (1)(a) above and the provisions of that subsection apply, the court may appoint that person; and

(b) where such a person is not appointed, the court shall appoint the Accountant in Bankruptcy.

(7) Where the petition for sequestration was presented by a creditor or the trustee acting under a trust deed, the interim trustee shall, as soon as practicable, notify the debtor of his appointment."

DEFINITIONS

"Accountant in Bankruptcy": s.73(1) and s.1 of the 1985 Act as amended.

"court": s.73(1) of the 1985 Act.

"debtor": s.73(1) of the 1985 Act.

"interim trustee": ss.2 and 73(1) of the 1985 Act.

"permanent trustee": ss.3 and 73(1) of the 1985 Act.

"qualified to act as an insolvency practitioner": s.73(1) of the 1985 Act and ss.388 and 389 of the Insolvency Act 1986.

"trust deed": s.73(1) of the 1985 Act as amended by Sched. 1, para. 29(6) to this Act and new s.5(4A) of the 1985 Act as inserted by s.3(4).

GENERAL NOTE

As originally drafted this section provided for the appointment of the Accountant in Bankruptcy as interim trustee in every case unless a certificate of summary administration was granted, when the Accountant or his nominee would have become permanent trustee. This would have made the Accountant trustee even in cases where the assets were sufficient to pay trustees' fees and outlays and a dividend to creditors. The result was protests from those representing trustees (see, *e.g Hansard*, H.C. Vol. 209, cols. 909–910). As now enacted, the section allows the petitioner to nominate an interim trustee and in specified circumstances the nominee may be appointed. Otherwise the Accountant will be appointed interim trustee.

The intention of the 1985 Act was to have an interim trustee followed by a permanent trustee in every case. An interim trustee was to be appointed at the time of award of sequestration (or as soon as may be thereafter) (s.13(1) of the 1985 Act). In cases of a petition by a creditor or a trustee under a trust deed an interim trustee could be appointed at an earlier stage—usually with the first order on cause shown, *e.g.* where there was a need to have management and preservation of the debtor's business by a trustee prior to the award (s.13(1) of the 1985 Act).

The present Act modifies the existing pattern by making provision for the Accountant in Bankruptcy to become interim trustee in all cases where a nominated person is not appointed. An insolvency practitioner who is nominated as interim trustee must give a written undertaking to act as interim and permanent trustee.

New s.2(1)

This applies to any petition for sequestration. A nominated trustee must provide a written undertaking to act as interim and, if so appointed, as permanent trustee (new s.2(3)(*c*)). In most cases an insolvency practitioner will not consent so to act unless there is an assurance of payment of fees and outlays, *e.g.* because the debtor's assets are sufficient for this purpose, or because a third party has agreed to pay or to indemnify the trustee. This was in effect the position in all cases prior to the 1985 Act. Similarly a permanent trustee who is *elected* must give an undertaking in writing to act (new s.24(2)(*e*) inserted by Sched. 1, para. 12(3)).

In "small assets" cases it may be difficult to find a private practitioner prepared to act as trustee. A petition and award of sequestration will be possible, however, because the Accountant in Bankruptcy (or his nominee) will act as a trustee (new s.2(2) and new s.25A as inserted by s.7). To that extent public funds remain available to assist the sequestration process. A difficulty for a debtor who wishes to petition are the requirements for a debtor's petition (new s.5(2B) of the 1985 Act; see notes to s.3). Nor is a creditor likely to petition if it is known that there will be insufficient assets to pay any dividend.

The court is given a discretion on whether or not to appoint the person nominated in the petition as interim trustee. If the court decides to reject the nominee, the interim trustee will be the Accountant in Bankruptcy. The court in its discretion should give effect to the rule that no one should act as interim trustee if he would be disqualified from acting as permanent trustee (s.24(2) of the 1985 Act), for example if the nominated trustee was a creditor, a person associated with a creditor, or other person opposed to the general interests of creditors (new s.13(6) of the 1985 Act as inserted by Sched. 1, para. 2).

In the limited circumstances of a petition by a creditor or a trustee under a trust deed, an interim trustee might have been appointed before the award of sequestration (new s.2(5)). In that event there is no need, in the normal case, to have another appointment at the time of award of sequestration.

The petition must state the requirements of (a) to (b) *and* the court must be satisfied that the conditions are met, before the appointment of a nominated person as interim trustee.

The interim trustee has a duty to notify his or her appointment to the debtor as soon as practicable (new s.2(7)).

New s.2(2)

If the court has appointed an insolvency practitioner as interim trustee prior to the award of sequestration it is not contemplated that the trustee will be replaced by the Accountant in Bankruptcy.

In contrast to the new s.2(1), the court "shall" appoint the Accountant interim trustee when the necessary conditions are satisfied.

New s.2(3)

This repeats what used to be the qualification for inclusion in the list of interim trustees (old s.2(2) of the 1985 Act). Similar qualifications, amongst others, apply to the person who may be elected permanent trustee (s.24(2) of the 1985 Act). In any event no one should act as interim trustee if he or she would be disqualified from being the permanent trustee (new s.13(6) as inserted by Sched. 1, para. 2).

The provision for a written undertaking is new and replaces and extends a statutory requirement which used to require a person who was appointed interim trustee to act (old s.13(2) of the 1985 Act). The purpose is to prevent resignation if the trustee discovers that there are insufficient assets to pay his or her fees and outlays. The grounds for resignation are limited (new s.13(3) of the 1985 Act as substituted by Sched. 1, para. 2).

New s.2(4)

There is no change in the general functions of an interim trustee. To an extent the statutory duties of an interim trustee may now be wider than those of a permanent trustee when a certificate of summary administration is granted. In summary administration a permanent trustee would consider the financial benefit to the estate and the interests of creditors before ascertaining the reasons for the debtor's insolvency, the circumstances surrounding it and the state of the debtor's assets and liabilities (new Sched. 2A, para. 1, inserted by s.6(2)). No such limitation expressly applies to an interim trustee.

New s.2(5)

The early appointment of someone to administer an insolvent estate is a feature of Scottish insolvency practice which will also be found in liquidations and administration orders. The appointment of an interim trustee before the award of sequestration is limited to cases of a petition by a creditor or a trustee acting under a trust deed.

In a debtor's petition sequestration may be awarded "forthwith" in the normal case (new s.12(1) inserted by s.4(2)). This removes the need to have a pre-sequestration appointment of an interim trustee, but only in those cases where there is no delay. If there were a delay in the award of sequestration in a debtor's petition serious difficulties could arise, in the absence of an interim trustee, if the debtor was carrying on a business. At common law a debtor who has decided to petition for sequestration may be committing a criminal offence if transactions involving credit are entered into. Also goods delivered might have to be returned (see McBryde on *Bankruptcy* (W. Green) (1989), pp. 223–4). In certain circumstances the cessation of some trading activities, while the petition for sequestration is being considered, might not be in the best interests of the creditors or, to name two examples, of the animals on the debtor's farm or the guests in the debtor's hotel. The debtor could sign a trust deed, although this appears a cumbersome, short lived and, for the time involved, expensive, expedient.

In a creditor or trustee's petition the court has a discretion on whether or not to appoint an interim trustee prior to award. The appointment is, in some ways, a drastic step because, under present practice, it may be made before the debtor is aware of the petition. Not everyone relishes the sudden appearance of an insolvency practitioner on the door step with powers, which include an ability to carry on the debtor's business (now conferred without special application to the court—s.18(2) of the 1985 Act as amended by Sched. 1, para. 6) and a power to close down a business. Nor is the debtor even given any right to have service of the petition on him or her or to apply for recall of the interim trustee's appointment (except in the limited circumstances mentioned in the new s.13(2) which would lead to the appointment of another interim trustee). The debtor must wait until the normal procedures under s.12(2) of the 1985 Act have been carried out by the petitioner before the opportunity of opposition to the petition arises. It may be wise for a trading debtor to lodge a caveat in the appropriate Sheriff Court and the Court of Session if the presentation of a petition is feared (see McBryde, *Bankruptcy* (W. Green), pp. 49–50).

The interim trustee has a duty to notify his appointment to the debtor as soon as practicable (new s.2(7)).

New s.2(6)
For the early appointment of an interim trustee there is applied the provisions on nomination in the petition and, in default of the appointment of the nominee, the appointment of the Accountant. Because the provisions of subs. (1)(a) apply it is not possible for a person to agree to be interim trustee with the intention of resigning if he or she discovers that there are insufficient assets to pay trustees' fees and outlays. Any nominated interim trustee must give the written undertaking required by new s.2(3)(*c*) and will be subject to the revised rules which limit resignation (new s.13(3) as substituted by Sched. 1, para. 2).

In a pre-sequestration award appointment it is very likely that the Accountant, if appointed, would delegate work to an insolvency practitioner, at any rate if there was a potential need to carry on a business.

New s.2(7)
The duty is to notify the debtor of the appointment. Where the appointment is made pre-sequestration, under new s.2(5), there is not any duty to give the debtor a copy of the petition. Until service of the petition the debtor could be unaware of the averments being made by the petitioner.

Petitions for sequestration

3.—(1) Section 5 of the 1985 Act (procedure for the sequestration of the estate of a living debtor) shall be amended as follows.

(2) For subsection (2) (persons who may petition) there shall be substituted the following subsections—

"(2) The sequestration of the estate of a living debtor shall be on the petition of—
  (a) the debtor, if either subsection (2A) or (2B) below applies to him;
  (b) a qualified creditor or qualified creditors, if the debtor is apparently insolvent; or
  (c) the trustee acting under a trust deed if, and only if, one or more of the conditions in subsection (2C) below is satisfied.

(2A) This subsection applies to the debtor if a qualified creditor or qualified creditors concur in the petition.

(2B) This subsection applies to the debtor where—
  (a) the total amount of his debts (including interest) at the date of presentation of the petition is not less than £1,500;
  (b) an award of sequestration has not been made against him in the period of 5 years ending on the day before the date of presentation of the petition; and
  (c) the debtor either—
    (i) is apparently insolvent; or
    (ii) has granted a trust deed and the trustee has complied with the requirements of sub-sub-paragraphs (a) to (c) of paragraph 5(1) of Schedule 5 to this Act but has received

notification as mentioned in sub-sub-paragraph (d) of that paragraph,

and for the purposes of this paragraph a debtor shall not be apparently insolvent by reason only that he has granted a trust deed or that he has given notice to his creditors as mentioned in paragraph (b) of section 7(1) of this Act.

(2C) The conditions mentioned in subsection (2)(c) above are—

(a) that the debtor has failed to comply—

(i) with any obligation imposed on him under the trust deed with which he could reasonably have complied; or

(ii) with any instruction or requirement reasonably given to or made of him by the trustee for the purposes of the trust deed; or

(b) that the trustee avers in his petition that it would be in the best interests of the creditors that an award of sequestration be made."

(3) In subsection (4) delete "£750" where it appears and substitute "£1,500".

(4) After subsection (4) there shall be inserted the following subsection—

"(4A) In this Act, "trust deed" means a voluntary trust deed granted by or on behalf of the debtor whereby his estate (other than such of his estate as would not, under section 33(1) of this Act, vest in the permanent trustee if his estate were sequestrated) is conveyed to the trustee for the benefit of his creditors generally."

(5) In subsection (6) (copy of petition to be sent to the Accountant in Bankruptcy) for the words from "send" to "section" there shall be substituted the words ", on the day the petition for sequestration is presented under this section, send a copy of the petition".

(6) After subsection (6) there shall be inserted the following subsection—

"(6A) Where the petitioner is the debtor—

(a) he shall lodge with the petition a statement of assets and liabilities; and

(b) he shall, on the day the petition is presented, send to the Accountant in Bankruptcy such statement of assets and liabilities as was lodged in court in pursuance of paragraph (a) above."

(7) After subsection (8) there shall be inserted the following subsections—

"(9) If the debtor—

(a) fails to send to the Accountant in Bankruptcy in accordance with subsection (6A)(b) above such statement of assets and liabilities; or

(b) fails to disclose any material fact in such statement of assets and liabilities; or

(c) makes a material misstatement in such statement of assets and liabilities,

he shall be guilty of an offence and liable on summary conviction to a fine not exceeding level 5 on the standard scale or to imprisonment for a term not exceeding 3 months or to both such fine and imprisonment.

(10) In any proceedings for an offence under subsection (9) above, it shall be a defence for the accused to show that he had a reasonable excuse for—

(a) failing to send to the Accountant in Bankruptcy in accordance with subsection (6A)(b) above such statement of assets and liabilities; or

(b) failing to disclose a material fact; or

(c) making a material misstatement."

DEFINITIONS
"Accountant in Bankruptcy": s.73(1) and s.1 of the 1985 Act, as amended.

"apparently insolvent": ss.7 and 73(1) of the 1985 Act.
"court": s.73(1) of the 1985 Act.
"debtor": s.73(1) of the 1985 Act.
"qualified creditor": s.73(1) and s.5(4) of the 1985 Act as amended by subs. (3) above.
"standard scale": s.73(1) of the 1985 Act.
"statement of assets and liabilities": s.73(1) of the 1985 Act as amended by Sched. 1, para. 29.
"trust deed": s.73(1) of the 1985 Act, and as amended by Sched. 1, para. 29(6); and new s.5(4A) of the 1985 Act as inserted by subs. (4) above.

GENERAL NOTE

This is the section which most severely limits the ability of debtors to arrange their own sequestrations. It remains open to a debtor to petition with the concurrence of a qualified creditor. The "trust deed route" is more difficult than under the 1985 Act because the trustee under a trust deed should petition for sequestration only if the conditions in the new s.5(2C) exist and the court must be satisfied that the trustee's averments are true (see s.4(4) inserting new s.12(3) in the 1985 Act). Otherwise the debtor cannot petition for his or her own sequestration unless the conditions of the new s.5(2B) are complied with and these include that the debtor is apparently insolvent or a trustee under a trust deed has tried but failed to make the trust deed protected. Many of the present instances of debtors arranging sequestrations through the trust deed route will not result in sequestrations under these new rules because the debtor will not be apparently insolvent or the grounds for conversion of a trust deed to a sequestration will not exist. The result may be no formal insolvency procedures there being insufficient assets for a trustee to be persuaded to act under a trust deed.

It is to this section that most of the creative thought of practitioners and advice agencies will be directed because (1) the trust deed route has become part of the insolvency culture; and (2) some of those who advise debtors, including insolvency practitioners, would wish to preserve for debtors, in appropriate cases, the ability to arrange sequestration as a possible solution to pressing debt problems. This is not to deny that voluntary arrangements and trust deeds have some advantages.

It is impossible to predict what will happen (just as the availability of the trust deed route was not obvious to everyone, including the Scottish Law Commission, at the time of the passing of the 1985 Act). Ingenious minds may, however, consider the following factors:

(1) The debtor may petition for sequestration if the trustee under a trust deed has tried and failed to make the trust deed protected. A trustee might be persuaded to act, for a while, under a trust deed (*e.g.* on payment of fees and outlays from the debtor's assets and/or a third party). The debtor could sign a trust deed which has terms to which a majority in number or a third in value of the creditors are almost bound to object. To take an extreme example—a clause to the effect that by their express or implied accession the creditors agree to discharge all debts due by the debtor on the expiry of three months from the date of the trust deed. The clause could be varied to include an offer by the debtor to each creditor, *e.g.* a payment of 10p if asked. If a creditor does not object the creditor will be treated as acceding to the deed because of the terms of Sched. 5, new para. 5(2) of the 1985 Act (inserted by Sched. 1, para. 32(2)). The almost inevitable objections allow the debtor to petition for sequestration.

(2) It may not be too difficult for the debtor to fail to comply with a trust deed the terms of which are within the debtor's control, *e.g.* an obligation similar to the new s.19 to provide a statement of assets and liabilities within a specified time. Nor is it difficult for a debtor to fail to comply with reasonable instructions, *e.g.* a failure to attend meetings with the trustee. Some redrafting of standard styles might be necessary to make it easy for a debtor to be in breach of obligations. Nor should anything be done which might prejudice an eventual discharge of the debtor. But disorganisation, confusion, and inattention to detail might be said to be normal for some debtors and appropriate emphasis on these failings might allow the trustee under the trust deed to seek sequestration with its potential for administration of the estate at the public expense by the Accountant in Bankruptcy.

(3) If the trustee under a trust deed discovers that there are insufficient funds to pay him or her for further administration, and the trustee wishes to resign, what would happen if, in these circumstances, the trustee petitioned for sequestration (without, of course, a nominee as new trustee) and averred that sequestration was in the best interests of the creditors? Would it help if the trust deed gave the trustee express power to resign or to petition in the event described? There may be a difficulty for a sole trustee who cannot resign in terms of the Trusts (Scotland) Act 1921, s.3 unless a new trustee is assumed or the court appoints a new trustee or a judicial factor (*cf. Kennedy Petr.*, 1983 S.L.T. (Sh. Ct.) 10). But it is arguable that that provision is limited to those trustees who derive the power to resign from the 1921 Act and not to those who have a power to resign conferred by the trust deed. An express power to resign (which was necessary for resignation at common law) may overcome difficulty in the application of

statutory powers (*Maxwell's Trs.* v. *Maxwell* (1874) 2 R. 71; *Scott* v. *Muir's Trs.* (1894) 22 R. 78).

(4) The spectre of the fictitious debt haunts some of the discussion of "arranged sequestrations". The argument is that a debtor can arrange to owe money to a relative or friend. The amount need not be as high as £1,500 because any debt can be used to create apparent insolvency (provided that the s.7(1)(*d*) notice procedure is not used when the debt must be not less than £750). In total the debtor's debts must be not less than £1,500 but the debt which creates apparent insolvency can be for a smaller sum. Signature to an appropriate document is easy; control of gratuitous debts is difficult. It may be that court action and diligence, or summary diligence, could follow on an appropriate document. The apparent insolvency which results enables the debtor to petition for sequestration. The Accountant in Bankruptcy may then act as trustee. The difficulty is that the process from creation of a debt to apparent insolvency involves a certain amount of knowledge and possibly also professional help.

(5) A variation on (4) arises if the fictitious or arranged debt is not less than £1,500 and that creditor is willing to petition for sequestration. Apparent insolvency can be created by the debtor giving notice to his creditors. Alternatively the creditor can concur in the debtor's petition.

(6) Diligence by a creditor might be welcomed by a debtor (and not be helpful to creditors). If apparent insolvency is established the debtor can petition for sequestration (without the consent of any creditor). Also diligence could be a good reason for a petition by a trustee under a trust deed. No responsible person would suggest that a debtor should collude in the existence of diligence. That is not to say that this would never happen.

Questions might arise as to the legal and moral implications of a trustee for creditors providing assistance to a debtor. Part of the answer is provided in *Archer Car Sales (Airdrie) Ltd.* v. *Gregory's Tr.*, 1993 S.L.T. 223 at p. 225 *per* Temporary Judge J.M.S. Horsburgh, Q.C.:

> "I reject the argument that *per se* the second respondent's status as trustee for the creditors was tainted by his having previously advised the debtor. In many cases investigations by trustees for creditors into debtors' finances take place after the execution of trust deeds, but with small assets cases I consider it is both convenient and reasonable that such investigations may take place before the deeds are signed. I also consider it reasonable that in such cases debtors may have received advice on their financial circumstances from persons appointed their trustees under trust deeds subsequently entered. There is nothing in the Act which strikes at the appointment of a debtor's adviser as trustee for his creditors.
>
> Once the trust deed is signed, the trustee must take up a position independent of the debtor, and he has a responsibility for investigating the debtor's financial affairs. I consider that responsibility may be properly discharged by taking into account investigations made prior to the signing of the trust deed."

New s.5(2)

The same category as under the 1985 Act can petition for the sequestration of the estate of the living debtor, although the definition of qualified creditor is altered by a change to s.5(4) so that the creditor, or creditors, must have a debt of not less than £1,500. A debtor petitioner also needs debts of the same amount, although in this case it is specifically provided that interest may be included.

It is one of the oddities that a trustee under a trust deed can petition only in the case of the estate of a living debtor (or a deceased debtor). It is commonly thought that a trust deed in respect of a partnership, or other entity mentioned in s.6 of the 1985 Act, cannot be converted into a sequestration. Vain attempts were made to change the law but the Government would not contemplate what was seen as a complicated amendment at a late stage in the Bill (*Hansard*, H.L. Vol. 541, cols. 784–785, 1120–1122). There may also be another reason for a reluctance to legislate. A trust deed in respect of a partnership should be signed by all the partners. If the deed contains a mandate to the trustee to petition for sequestration, it is an open question as to whether or not the trustee could petition for sequestration. A mandate in a trust deed was recognised by the 1913 Act (s.20 of the Bankruptcy (Scotland) Act 1913; Goudy, *Bankruptcy*, p. 127). The Scottish Law Commission believed that the matter was best left to rules of court (S.L.C., para. 7.3). The issue might be solved by rules of court; but even so it is possible that a carefully drafted trust deed could have the desired effect.

New s.5(2A) and (2B)

The main change is to the circumstances in which a debtor may petition, discussed in the General Note above. There is some concern that sequestration can be used by a debtor as a method for avoiding liability for debts. While in many cases debtors are unlucky, confused, careless, naive or otherwise subject to human misfortune or failing, there are a number of rogues. There could be a deliberate or reckless course of action which involves incurring large debts followed by sequestration. Repeated over a lifetime it might be possible to abuse the system of sequestration. The 1985 Act has not been in force long enough for there to be useful statistics on the number of "repeaters". Nevertheless, the ability of a debtor to petition for sequestration is removed if there has been a prior award in the previous five years. This is similar to a provision in English law (Insolvency Act 1986, s.273(1)).

The requirement that a debtor petitioner would have to be apparently insolvent (unless the trust deed rules apply) is a fundamental change. To petition for sequestration a debtor did not need to be notour bankrupt under the Bankruptcy (Scotland) Act 1856, s.13, or the Bankruptcy (Scotland) Act 1913, s.11, or apparently insolvent under the 1985 Act, s.5(2). On the other hand, in all these cases the debtor needed the concurrence of a qualified creditor or creditors, which no longer applies.

It is not enough that the debtor is unable to pay his or her debts (*cf.* Insolvency Act 1986, s.272(1)). There must be apparent insolvency which in practice is commonly established by the expiry of the days of charge without payment. This and other methods of creating apparent insolvency are detailed in s.7 of the 1985 Act. The amount of the debt is irrelevant except in the case of a s.7(1)(*d*) notice (where the minimum amount remains £750). There is some worry that harassment of debtors might result because the use of diligence to enforce debts may allow the debtor to sequestrate. The disreputable creditor may have extra reason for the avoidance of legal methods of recovery. Arrestments remain a useful diligence because they do not create apparent insolvency.

To prevent the debtor arranging his or her own apparent insolvency the grant of a trust deed or a circular to creditors do not constitute apparent insolvency for the purposes of a debtor's petition.

New s.5(3)

The change in the amount of qualifying debt to £1,500 is mentioned in the note to subs. (2) above. This was the result of an opposition amendment, accepted by the Government (*Official Report*, First Scottish Standing Committee, July 9, 1992, cols. 269–271). A change was not made to the £750 required for a s.7(1)(*d*) notice, but this amount may be altered by regulation.

New s.5(4)

The definition of trust deed may have more significance than at first appears. A trust deed is a voluntary arrangement and it can be drafted in any terms which are likely to appeal to creditors and the debtor. For example, Sir Walter Scott's trust deed allowed the author to keep his official salaries, his liferent of Abbotsford and its furnishings, antiques, library and pictures. In return he contracted to pay in his entire revenue from literary sources (E. Quayle, *The Ruin of Sir Walter Scott* (London 1968), pp. 212–215).

In so far as there remains a "trust deed route" to sequestration it is necessary to define trust deed otherwise a very limited amount of assets could be put in trust (*e.g.* all one's future income from literary sources!) and it is not intended that in these circumstances the trustee could petition for sequestration or obtain the benefits of a protected trust deed under the new Sched. 5, para. 5 (see Sched. 1, para. 32(2)).

It is one of the criticisms of common styles of trust deeds that they convey all the assets, present and future, of the debtor (see McBryde on *Bankruptcy* (W. Green), p. 244). It is difficult to believe that a properly advised debtor would ever sign such a deed and yet that advice must be commonly given. It is preferable to limit the assets to those which would transfer to a permanent trustee in a sequestration (see Steven L. Henderson, *The Bankruptcy (Scotland) Act 1985—A Practical Guide* (Tolley) (1987), p. 226). In this way a debtor retains a right to his or her clothes, furnishings and income, to the extent that these items are excluded from a sequestration. The new definition of trust deed recognises this point, although it refers to s.33(1) of the 1985 Act only (which exempts property excluded from poinding and trust property) and omits reference to s.32(1) (which vests income in the debtor). The meaning of the word "estate" is uncertain but it is used in the context of heritable estate and moveable property in s.31, of acquirenda in s.32(6), of dealings by the debtor in s.32(8), and of the exclusion of the landlord's hypothec in s.33(2). There are also several references in various sections to "property" and "assets" which make it difficult to decide the precise meaning of each term. Income is possibly not "estate" and need not be conveyed to the trustee to enable the trust deed to come within the statutory definition. This is far from certain because the definition of "whole estate of the debtor" in s.31(8) includes income. (Section 2 of the 1913 Act did have a definition of "property" and "estate" which showed that both terms had a similar and very wide meaning).

It would be logical to allow a trust deed to become protected whatever it does with the debtor's income. A contribution order from a sheriff under s.32(2) cannot be sought under a trust deed, and so any suitable provision in respect of income must be in the deed and carefully drafted deeds will vary according to the circumstances.

New s.5(5)

In s.5(6) of the 1985 Act it was provided that the petitioner should send a copy of any petition presented to the Accountant in Bankruptcy. This provision had two defects: (1) there was no time limit for compliance; and (2) there was no sanction for non-compliance. Now it is stated that the copy of the petition must be sent on the day the petition for sequestration is presented. This provision must be complied with or the court cannot award sequestration (s.4(2) inserting new s.12(1) in the 1985 Act; and s.4(4) inserting new s.12(3)).

Unless the court is satisfied that the petitioner has complied with subs. (6) the court cannot award sequestration (new s.12(1) inserted by s.4(2)). It is inevitable that there will be breaches of the new s.5(6). There is only one day on which compliance with the subsection is possible. The subsection must be followed in every petition. An application to the sheriff under s.63 of the 1985 Act may cure a defect in procedure.

New s.5(6A)

Where the debtor is a petitioner the debtor must lodge a statement of assets and liabilities. The debtor has to send the list to the Accountant on the day the petition is presented which poses the same problems as the requirement to send a copy petition to the Accountant (see note to subs. (5)). Unless the court is satisfied that the debtor has complied with subs. (6A) the court cannot award sequestration (new s.12(1) inserted by s.4(2)). How the court will satisfy itself that the debtor has sent the statement to the Accountant "on the day the petition is presented" remains to be seen. The Accountant will use the statement (the accuracy of which cannot be guaranteed) to decide whether or not to apply for a certificate of summary administration within the remarkably short period of seven days as specified in the terms of new s.12(1A) inserted by s.4(3).

If the interim trustee is not the Accountant in Bankruptcy the debtor must send the statement of assets and liabilities to the interim trustee within seven days of the appointment of the interim trustee (new s.19(1) inserted by Sched. 1, para. 7). A similar requirement applies even when the petition is by a creditor or a trustee under a trust deed (new s.19(2) inserted by Sched. 1, para. 7). The statement is produced at the statutory meeting (new s.23(3), inserted by Sched. 1, para. 11(2)).

The definition of "statement of affairs" in s.73(1) of the 1985 Act as amended includes a list of the debtor's income and expenditure as well as assets and liabilities and other prescribed information. This is an interesting departure from the traditional approach which has tended to view insolvency and sequestration in terms of assets and liabilities only. Some lenders have been concerned that a debtor may be able to pay debts over a period by the use of income, but income has largely been disregarded in an assessment of an insolvent's state. The concentration on the value of assets and liabilities may be more appropriate for the trading debtor (and for a period until 1856 there were restrictions in Scotland on the sequestration of non-trading debtors, as in other legal systems—S.L.C., para. 5.2, n.3). For a debtor in employment with assets of little value, however, there might be the prospect of repayment of debts from income.

Attempts failed to amend the Bill so that income was taken into account at the time of a decision on the award of sequestration. Sequestration is a summary process and difficult decisions on what may be disputed facts were not thought to be appropriate. Nor did the Government accept changes to the procedure for seeking a contribution order under s.32(2) of the 1985 Act to allow creditor participation. In practice there appear to have been relatively few applications by permanent trustees to the sheriff seeking a contribution from the debtor's income. Recent figures suggest that 35 per cent. of debtors are in employment but that only five per cent. are contributing from that income (*Hansard*, H.L. Vol. 541, col. 798). The whole issue of income of debtors was one of the great controversies during the passing of the Bill and the problems were discussed several times (*Official Report*, First Scottish Standing Committee, July 9, 1992, cols. 340–354; *Hansard*, H.C. Vol. 212, cols. 791–801; H.L. Vol. 541, cols. 50–51, 69–73, 782).

The concerns expressed by lenders have been addressed by compelling the debtor to state income and expenditure in the statement of assets and liabilities, and the provision of this statement to the Accountant in Bankruptcy, the interim trustee, and its production at the statutory meeting where it may be inspected by creditors. This information may lead to more requests that the debtor in employment makes a contribution from income. When there is a certificate of summary administration the permanent trustee has to ask the debtor to give a written account of his or her state of affairs every six months (new Sched. 2A, para. 2, inserted by s.6(2)). This should cover changes in the debtor's income. A similar procedure would be prudent in all cases.

New s.5(9) and (10)

Level 5 is £5,000 since the coming into force of the Criminal Justice Act 1991, s.17(1) on October 1, 1992.

Award of sequestration

4.—(1) Section 12 of the 1985 Act (when sequestration is awarded) shall be amended as follows.

(2) For subsection (1) there shall be substituted the following subsection—

"(1) Where a petition for the sequestration of his estate is presented by the debtor, unless cause is shown why sequestration cannot competently be awarded, the court shall award sequestration forthwith if it is satisfied—
  (a) that the petition has been presented in accordance with the provisions of this Act;
  (b) that either subsection (2A) or (2B) of section 5 of this Act applies to the debtor; and
  (c) that the provisions of subsections (6) and (6A) of that section have been complied with."

(3) After subsection (1) there shall be inserted the following subsection—

"(1A) Where a petition is presented as mentioned in subsection (1) above, the Accountant in Bankruptcy may, not later than 7 days after the date on which sequestration is awarded, apply to the court for the grant of a certificate for the summary administration of the sequestration of the debtor's estate."

(4) For subsection (3) there shall be substituted the following subsections—

"(3) Where, on a petition for sequestration presented by a creditor or a trustee acting under a trust deed, the court is satisfied—
  (a) that, if the debtor has not appeared, proper citation has been made of the debtor;
  (b) that the petition has been presented in accordance with the provisions of this Act;
  (c) that the provisions of subsection (6) of section 5 of this Act have been complied with;
  (d) that, in the case of a petition by a creditor, the requirements of this Act relating to apparent insolvency have been fulfilled; and
  (e) that, in the case of a petition by a trustee, the averments in his petition as to any of the conditions in subsection (2C) of the said section 5 are true,

it shall, subject to subsection (3A) below, award sequestration forthwith.

(3A) Sequestration shall not be awarded in pursuance of subsection (3) above if—
  (a) cause is shown why sequestration cannot competently be awarded; or
  (b) the debtor forthwith pays or satisfies, or produces written evidence of the payment or satisfaction of, or gives or shows that there is sufficient security for the payment of—
    (i) the debt in respect of which he became apparently insolvent; and
    (ii) any other debt due by him to the petitioner and any creditor concurring in the petition."

(5) For subsection (4) there shall be substituted the following subsection—

"(4) In this Act "the date of sequestration" means—
  (a) where the petition for sequestration is presented by the debtor, the date on which sequestration is awarded;
  (b) where the petition for sequestration is presented by a creditor or a trustee acting under a trust deed—
    (i) the date on which the court grants warrant under subsection (2) above to cite the debtor; or

(ii) where more than one such warrant is granted, the date on which the first such warrant is granted."

DEFINITIONS

"Accountant in Bankruptcy": s.73(1), and s.1 of the 1985 Act as amended.
"apparently insolvent": ss.7 and 73(1) of the 1985 Act.
"court": s.73(1) of the 1985 Act.
"debtor": s.73(1) of the 1985 Act.
"security": s.73(1) of the 1985 Act.
"trust deed": s.73(1) of the 1985 Act and as amended by Sched. 1, para. 29(6); and new s.5(4A) of the 1985 Act as inserted by s.3(4).

GENERAL NOTE

The time when a petition for sequestration is presented is defined by s.73(6), 1985 Act inserted by Sched. 1, para. 29(7).

This section alters the procedure prior to and at the time of award of the sequestration for the purposes of (1) ensuring compliance with the provisions of the 1985 Act; and (2) to enable the introduction of the procedure which may lead to a certificate of summary administration.

If the court is satisfied on various matters it "shall" award sequestration "forthwith" (new s.12(1) and (3)). The award is not discretionary; nor should there be any delay in the normal case because of the consequences, particularly for creditors who are not parties to the process (McBryde, *Bankruptcy* (W. Green), pp. 54–55).

The policy that sequestration is a summary process is deeply ingrained in Scottish procedure. It has been argued that this is a defect because the court cannot consider whether sequestration is a more appropriate remedy than, say, a trust deed or an arrangement for payment of debts out of income (*e.g. Hansard*, H.C. Vol. 209, col. 918; *Official Report*, First Scottish Standing Committee, July 9, 1992, cols. 273–276, 354). English law has a procedure for voluntary arrangement under which the debtor may make a proposal to creditors, and execution or other legal process, including a bankruptcy petition, may not proceed (Insolvency Act 1986, Part VIII). The Government view was that a debt arrangement scheme, administered by the court, would be complex and expensive (*Hansard*, H.L. Vol. 541, cols. 52–55).

Summary administration is a new procedure introduced by the Act. It has the following features:

(1) When there is summary administration the duties of a permanent trustee (not an interim trustee) are modified. In particular the permanent trustee complies with duties under ss.3 and 39 of the 1985 Act only to the extent that it would be, in the view of the trustee, of financial benefit to the estate of the debtor and in the interests of creditors (new Sched. 2A of the 1985 Act inserted by s.6(2)). This, for example, is intended to avoid the argument that a permanent trustee has a statutory duty to trace assets, or investigate the causes of the insolvency, even in circumstances where it is unlikely that there will be any dividend to creditors.

(2) The court "shall" grant a certificate of summary administration where the aggregate amount of the debtor's unsecured liabilities does not exceed £20,000 and the aggregate amount of the debtor's assets (excluding heritage) does not exceed £2,000 (s.23A(1) and (2) of the 1985 Act inserted by s.6(1)). The intention is to apply summary administration particularly to many of those "small assets" cases in which, at present, the debtor arranges his or her sequestration using the "trust deed route".

(3) The application for a certificate of summary administration may be made at four stages: (a) by the Accountant in Bankruptcy not later than seven days after the award of sequestration (s.12(1A) of the 1985 Act inserted by s.4(3) above); (b) where the Accountant in Bankruptcy as interim trustee does not call a statutory meeting (s.21B(2) of the 1985 Act inserted by s.5); (c) when a statutory meeting is called but no creditor attends or no permanent trustee is appointed (s.24(3B) and (4A) of the 1985 Act inserted by Sched. 1, paras. 12(4) and (6)); and (d) when the statutory meeting of creditors elects a permanent trustee and, in his report of the meeting to the sheriff, the interim trustee applies for a certificate (new s.25(2A) of the 1985 Act inserted by Sched. 1, para. 13(2)).

(4) With one exception the permanent trustee will be the Accountant in Bankruptcy or his nominee (s.25A(1) of the 1985 Act inserted by s.7) and Sched. 2 to the Act applies in addition to Sched. 2A. The exception is when a trustee has been elected by the creditors at the statutory meeting but in his report to the sheriff the interim trustee seeks a certificate (new s.25(2A) of the 1985 Act inserted by Sched. 1, para. 13(2)). The permanent trustee who was elected would act under the rules of summary administration in Sched. 2A but, as an elected trustee, Sched. 2 to the 1985 Act would not apply.

(5) By and large the rules try to have a decision on an application for certificate of summary administration before a permanent trustee is in office. There are, however, rules in the new

s.23A(9) which limit the circumstances in which a certificate may be granted. A certificate may not be granted when the application is made by the Accountant and the court has appointed an interim trustee who is not the Accountant or after the election of a permanent trustee before the election is confirmed by the sheriff or "where no such person has been elected, unless the court at the same time appoints the interim trustee as permanent trustee". The drafting of these provisions raises some questions, but the effect is to prevent the Accountant using an application for a certificate to enable the Accountant to oust a private practitioner from the office of permanent trustee.

New s.12(1)

This is drafted to ensure that the court satisfies itself that the debtor's petition complies with the provisions mentioned. Rules of court may specify some of the details (*e.g.* the form of certificate on the posting of the copy petition to the Accountant). If everything is in order the court "shall" award sequestration "forthwith". Sequestration is intended to be a summary remedy but delay was a feature in some cases under the 1985 Act.

New s.12(1A)

It seems that the Accountant can make the application only where the Accountant is interim trustee. If a nominated person is appointed interim trustee an application by the Accountant is prohibited by new s.23A(9) inserted by s.6(1). The logic behind the very short period of seven days is difficult to understand. First the Accountant may not know the date on which sequestration is awarded (which could be different from the day the petition is presented when the debtor sends a copy petition to the Accountant and a statement of assets and liabilities) and the Accountant may for a time be unaware of his appointment. Secondly, there is bound to be a delay in transmission of information to the Accountant by post, even if the debtor timeously complies with the Act. Thirdly, little allowance is made for holidays and seasonal delays. Fourthly, the only real time limit should be to make the application before a permanent trustee is in office. It may save money to abbreviate the period of office of the Accountant as interim trustee, but it may be more important to have a mature consideration of facts. The Accountant could make an application under s.63 if there is a failure to comply with the time limit. Also the time could be varied by regulation under new s.72A (inserted by Sched. 1, para. 28).

New s.12(3)

The court must also be satisfied of certain conditions in the case of a petition by a creditor or a trustee under a trust deed. Subject to the new s.12(3A) the court "shall" award sequestration "forthwith".

There are three main grounds on which sequestration might not be awarded: (a) failure to comply with the conditions listed in the new s.12(3); (b) cause being shown why sequestration cannot be competently awarded (*e.g.* the court has no jurisdiction); and (c) payment, satisfaction, or sufficient security by the debtor in respect of the debt which produced apparent insolvency, and the petitioners' and concurring creditors' debts.

The phrase "cause is shown why sequestration cannot competently be awarded" applies also to a petition by the debtor. The generality of this phrase has allowed a court to refuse to award sequestration on a petition by a creditor before the expiry of the period of a three week demand served by that creditor, although the creditor founded on the different ground of expiry of the days of charge which constituted apparent insolvency. The creditor was personally barred from seeking sequestration having faced the debtor with "directly contradictory ultimata" (*Unity Trust Bank plc.* v. *Ahmed*, 1993 S.C.L.R. 53).

The last ground of "sufficient security", in the new s.12(3A)(*b*), repeats the provisions of s.12(3)(*b*) of the 1985 Act. What is "sufficient" may not be capable of immediate ascertainment. Similarly it may be necessary to make further enquiry to determine the amount of "any other debt due by him to the petitioner". Therefore, although sequestration is a summary process and answers are not normally lodged nor dilatory proceedings allowed (*Scottish Milk Marketing Board* v. *Wood*, 1936 S.C. 604; *Sales Lease Ltd.* v. *Minty*, 1993 S.C.L.R. 130) circumstances may arise in which the court can neither award sequestration nor refuse to award sequestration without further enquiry (*Royal Bank of Scotland plc.* v. *Forbes*, 1988 S.L.T. 73). There is a conflict of judicial opinion on whether a pre-existing security is sufficient security for payment of a debt (*Drybrough & Co. Ltd.* v. *Brown*, 1989 S.C.L.R. 279; *Bank of Scotland* v. *Mackay*, 1991 S.L.T. 163; *per contra Royal Bank of Scotland plc.* v. *Forbes sup. cit.*; *National Westminster Bank plc.* v. *W.J. Elrick & Co.*, 1991 S.L.T. 709). Even if it is sufficient security the court will not enter into a prolonged investigation of the value of assets and sequestration may be awarded with the possibility of recall if sufficient security exists (*National Westminster Bank plc.* v. *W.J. Elrick & Co., sup. cit.* at p. 713, *per* Lord Kirkwood).

To prevent an award of sequestration it may not be possible to challenge the obligation on which the creditor's debt is based. If the apparent insolvency has been constituted, the procedures are in order, and no question of payment or security for the debt arises, sequestration must be awarded; at a later stage there could be a recall of the award but that is after the interests of creditors have been protected (*Wright* v. *Tennent Caledonian Breweries Ltd.*, 1991 S.L.T. 823 at p. 827 per L.P. Hope; see also *Mackay* v. *Bank of Scotland*, 1992 S.L.T. 158; a challenge prior to sequestration is another issue—*James Finlay Corp. Ltd.* v. *McCormack*, 1986 S.L.T. 106). Sequestration may not be prevented by allegations that the decree proceeded on a forged document (*Sales Lease Ltd.* v. *Minty*, 1993 S.C.L.R. 130) or that there is a discrepancy between the charge and the petitioner's oath (*Lord Advocate* v. *Mackenzie*, 1993 S.C.L.R. 153).

If the debtor wishes to challenge the validity of diligence it may be necessary to do so in an action of suspension or reduction (*cf. Dickson* v. *United Dominions Trust Ltd. (No. 2)*, 1983 S.L.T. 502; *Dickson* v. *United Dominions Trust Ltd.*, 1988 S.L.T. 19; *Scottish & Newcastle Breweries* v. *Mann*, 1989 S.C.L.R. 118); it may be incompetent to challenge *ex facie* regular diligence in the course of sequestration proceedings (*Inland Revenue* v. *Gibb*, 1963 S.L.T. (Notes) 66).

New s.12(4)

Various changes to the meaning of "the date of sequestration" were proposed by the Government as the Bill progressed through Parliament. This date is of critical effect in the application of the sequestration process (see McBryde on *Bankruptcy*, pp. 48–9 where 16 events are listed). In particular alteration of the date would affect the time of vesting in a permanent trustee under s.31 of the 1985 Act, the ability of the debtor to deal with property (s.32(8)) and the effect of diligence (s.37(1)). There are merits in the present rules which should not be altered except after full consideration.

The final version of new s.12(4) preserves the existing meaning with a clarification in the case where there is more than one warrant to cite. The decision in *Campbell* v. *Sheriff*, 1991 S.L.T. (Sh. Ct.) 37 lead to uncertainty and variation in practice when the court granted a warrant to re-serve (see D.C. Coull, "Developments in Personal Insolvency Law", 1991 S.L.T. (News) 219, at p. 220; Note by the Accountant in Bankruptcy, "Date of Sequestration—Re-Service Cases", August 1991). There were good reasons why the first warrant should be the date of sequestration as the Sheriff Principal observed in *MacDonald's Tr.* v. *MacDonald*, 1992 S.L.T. (Sh. Ct.) 25. *Campbell* has been said to be wrongly decided (*Arthur* v. *H.M. Advocate*, 1993 G.W.D. 3–145). The controversy is removed by the terms of the new subsection.

Calling of statutory meeting

5. After section 21 of the 1985 Act there shall be inserted the following sections—

> **"Calling of statutory meeting where interim trustee is Accountant in Bankruptcy**
> 21A.—(1) Subject to subsections (5) and (6) below, where the interim trustee is the Accountant in Bankruptcy, the statutory meeting may be held at such time and place as the interim trustee may determine.
> (2) Not later than 60 days after the date of the sequestration, or such longer period as the sheriff may on cause shown allow, the interim trustee shall give notice to every creditor known to him of whether he intends to call the statutory meeting.
> (3) A notice given under subsection (2) above shall—
>> (a) be accompanied by a copy of the interim trustee's statement of the debtor's affairs; and
>> (b) where the interim trustee is notifying his intention not to hold the statutory meeting, inform creditors—
>>> (i) of the effect of subsections (4) and (5) below; and
>>> (ii) whether he intends to apply for the grant of a certificate for the summary administration of the sequestration of the debtor's estate.

(4) Within 7 days of the giving of notice under subsection (2) above, any creditor may request the interim trustee to call the statutory meeting.

(5) Where a request or requests under subsection (4) above are made by not less than one quarter in value of the debtor's creditors, the interim trustee shall call the statutory meeting not later than 28 days, or such other period as the sheriff may on cause shown allow, after the giving of notice under subsection (2) above.

(6) Where the interim trustee gives notice under subsection (2) above that he intends to call the statutory meeting, such meeting shall be called not later than 28 days after the giving of such notice.

(7) Not less than 7 days before the date fixed for the statutory meeting, the interim trustee shall notify every creditor known to him of the date, time and place of the meeting, and shall in such notice invite the submission of such claims as have not already been submitted and inform them of his duties under section 23(3) of this Act.

(8) The creditors may continue the statutory meeting to a date not later than 7 days after the end of the period mentioned in subsection (6) above or such longer period as the sheriff may on cause shown allow.

(9) This section applies in any case where the Accountant in Bankruptcy is the interim trustee.

Procedure where no statutory meeting called

21B.—(1) Where the interim trustee does not call the statutory meeting and the period mentioned in section 21A(4) of this Act has expired, he shall—

   (a) forthwith make a report to the sheriff on the circumstances of the sequestration; and

   (b) provide to the sheriff a copy of the interim trustee's statement of the debtor's affairs.

(2) In the case of a sequestration which falls within subsection (1) above—

   (a) section 25A of this Act shall apply; and

   (b) the interim trustee may apply to the sheriff for the grant of a certificate for the summary administration of the sequestration of the debtor's estate."

DEFINITIONS

"Accountant in Bankruptcy": s.73(1) and s.1 of the 1985 Act as amended.
"debtor": s.73(1) of the 1985 Act.
"interim trustee": ss.2 and 73(1) of the 1985 Act.
"statutory meeting": s.73(1) and new s.20A of the 1985 Act.
"the creditors": s.73(4) of the 1985 Act.

GENERAL NOTE

Under s.21(1) of the 1985 Act the interim trustee must call a meeting of creditors (referred to as the "statutory meeting") to be held within 28 days of the date of award of sequestration, unless the sheriff extends the period. This was a mandatory requirement applying to all sequestrations. In some cases the meeting achieved little either because the creditors did not attend or because even if the creditors did attend there were insufficient assets for any prospect of payment to them of a dividend. A Government Minister said that in 80 per cent. to 90 per cent. of cases no creditor attends (*Official Report*, First Scottish Standing Committee, July 14, 1992, col. 387). The result was the appointment of the interim trustee as a permanent trustee and the application of the "small assets" procedure in Sched. 2. There was not any election of a permanent trustee by the creditors (the difference between the *appointment* and the *election* of a permanent trustee is critical to the understanding of the 1985 Act—see McBryde on *Bankruptcy* (W. Green), pp. 88–9). The comments made by the creditors at the meeting, or the questions asked, did not assist the process of sequestration. The meeting did, however, add to the cost of the sequestration. One method of reduction in the expense of sequestrations is to remove the need for the statutory meeting, particularly in cases where the meeting would be unlikely to have an election of a permanent trustee by creditors or achieve any other useful purpose.

The Accountant will be interim trustee in the circumstances mentioned in the notes to s.2. Where the Accountant in Bankruptcy is the interim trustee this new section allows him (or her) to intimate to creditors that he does not intend to hold a statutory meeting. The creditors are given certain information and the chance to request a meeting. They need not meet for the purpose of making this request. If the Accountant receives requests within a short time limit from a quarter in value of the creditors he must call the meeting.

If no statutory meeting is called the sequestration will proceed with the Accountant in Bankruptcy, or his nominee, as permanent trustee (with Sched. 2 applying—see new s.25A) and there may, or may not, be a summary administration.

If the Accountant is *not* the interim trustee the statutory meeting must be held within the 28 days or such longer period as the sheriff on cause shown may allow (s.21(1) of the 1985 Act as amended by Sched. 1, para. 10). The period of 28 days will be altered to 60 days by regulation because experience with the number of requests to extend the period shows that 28 days may be too short (*Official Report*, First Scottish Standing Committee, July 14, 1992, col. 398; *Hansard*, H.L. Vol. 541, col. 797).

New s.21A(1)

An interim trustee, other than the Accountant, has to call the meeting to be held in such place as, in the opinion of the person calling the meeting, is the most convenient for the majority of the creditors (Sched. 6, para. 10 of the 1985 Act). The Government carried out consultation about whether interim trustees, other than the Accountant, might be allowed to dispense with the statutory meeting. This was thought, however, to be a significant reduction in creditors' rights, particularly when in most cases where an insolvency practitioner was trustee there would be sufficient assets for the creditors to have an interest (*Hansard*, H.C. Vol. 212, col. 828).

An interim trustee, other than the Accountant, has a 28 day period under this Act in which to *hold* the meeting unless steps are taken to obtain an extension of this period from the sheriff (and the 28 day period will be extended to 60 days by regulation). Under this subsection the Accountant is given a discretion on both time and place. The Accountant must, however, give notice to creditors within the 60 day period mentioned in subs. (2).

New s.21A(2)

The requirement is to give notice to "every creditor known to him". The trustee may learn of the existence of creditors from a variety of sources including responses to the *Edinburgh Gazette* notice which must be published by the interim trustee as soon as an award of sequestration has been granted (new s.15(6) of the 1985 Act, substituted by Sched. 1, para. 4) and any newspaper advertisements which may be inserted. When the debtor is the petitioner the debtor has a duty to lodge with the petition a copy of his statement of assets and liabilities (s.5(6A) of the 1985 Act, inserted by s.3(6)). When the petitioner is a creditor or a trustee under a trust deed the debtor has a duty to deliver a statement of assets and liabilities to the interim trustee within seven days of notification of the interim trustee's appointment (new s.19(1) of the 1985 Act substituted by Sched. 1, para. 7(1)). In both cases the statement must be accompanied by such other information as may be prescribed.

The interim trustee must give a notice in all cases. If there is to be a statutory meeting, there must be a notice calling the meeting and the time limits in subss. (6) and (7) apply. It seems that the interim trustee may have to give two notices: (1) a notice of intention to call a meeting; and (2) a notice calling the meeting. In practice attempts may be made to avoid a double circulation to creditors, if it is possible for one circulation to fulfil the purposes of both subs. (2) and subs. (7).

New s.21A(4)

A creditor has a very short time limit within which to request a statutory meeting. Argument is bound to arise about the meaning of "seven days of the giving of notice" and what constitutes a "request" by a creditor. This drafting is to be contrasted with the precision in the new procedure for a protected trust deed under which there is a reference to a trustee who "has not received notification in writing" from a majority of creditors within a time limit (see new Sched. 5, para. 5(1)(*d*) of the 1985 Act, inserted by Sched. 1, para. 32(2)). It is possible that the Accountant may avoid problems with the technicalities of creditors' requests and call a meeting under s.21A(1) whenever it appears desirable to do so and despite a previous indication of a contrary intent under s.21A(2).

New s.21A(5) and (6)

Part of the reason for short time limits for creditors' requests is, that if the appropriate majority make a request for a meeting, the 28 days within which the interim trustee must *call* the meeting starts to run from the giving of notice under subs. (2) (unless the sheriff decides otherwise). Similarly if the trustee wishes to hold a meeting he must *call* it within the same 28 days. It is probably the intention that the meeting should be *held* within the 28 days because of the terms of subs. (8), but the meaning is not entirely clear.

New s.21A(8)

In terms of s.73(4) of the 1985 Act the reference to "the creditors" in the context of them doing something means a reference to the majority in value of such creditors as vote at a meeting of creditors.

New s.21B

The effect of this section is that the Accountant in Bankruptcy, or his nominee, becomes permanent trustee.

Summary administration

6.—(1) After section 23 of the 1985 Act, there shall be inserted the following section—

> **"Summary administration**
> 23A.—(1) Where an application is made to the court under this Act for the grant of a certificate for the summary administration of the sequestration of the debtor's estate, the court shall, subject to subsection (9) below, grant such a certificate where it appears to the court that—
>> (a) the aggregate amount of the debtor's liabilities does not exceed £20,000; and
>> (b) the aggregate amount of the debtor's assets does not exceed £2,000.
> (2) In calculating—
>> (a) the aggregate amount of the debtor's liabilities under paragraph (a) of subsection (1) above, no account shall be taken of any debt to the extent that a creditor holds a security for that debt; and
>> (b) the aggregate amount of the debtor's assets under paragraph (b) of that subsection, no account shall be taken of—
>>> (i) any heritable property of his; or
>>> (ii) any property of his which, under section 33(1) of this Act, does not vest in the permanent trustee.
> (3) For the purposes of an application under subsection (1) above made by—
>> (a) the Accountant in Bankruptcy; or
>> (b) an interim trustee who is not the Accountant in Bankruptcy,
> a certificate by the Accountant in Bankruptcy or, as the case may be, the interim trustee as to the aggregate amounts of the debtor's liabilities and assets shall be sufficient evidence of such aggregate amounts.
> (4) Where a certificate for the summary administration of the sequestration of the debtor's estate is granted—
>> (a) in any case where the application for the certificate was made by the Accountant in Bankruptcy, section 25A of this Act; and
>> (b) in every case, Schedule 2A to this Act (which modifies the duties of the permanent trustee),
> shall apply to the sequestration.
> (5) The debtor, a creditor, the permanent trustee or the Accountant in Bankruptcy may, at any time, apply to the sheriff to withdraw the certificate for the summary administration of the sequestration of the debtor's estate.

(6) Where an application is made under subsection (5) above by a person who is not the permanent trustee, the applicant shall send a copy of the application to the permanent trustee who shall prepare and present to the sheriff a report on all of the circumstances of the sequestration.

(7) If it appears to the sheriff, on considering an application under subsection (5) above and any report under subsection (6) above, that it is no longer appropriate for the sequestration to be subject to summary administration, he shall withdraw the certificate and the sequestration of the estate shall proceed as if the certificate had not been granted.

(8) The sheriff clerk shall send to the permanent trustee and, where he is not the permanent trustee, the Accountant in Bankruptcy a copy of the sheriff's decision on any application under subsection (5) above.

(9) The court shall not grant an application as mentioned in subsection (1) above—

(a) in any case where the application is made by the Accountant in Bankruptcy and the court has appointed as interim trustee a person who is not the Accountant in Bankruptcy; or

(b) in any other case—

(i) where a person has been elected as permanent trustee, before the sheriff has confirmed the election of that person as permanent trustee; or

(ii) where no such person has been elected, unless the court at the same time appoints the interim trustee as permanent trustee."

(2) After Schedule 2 to the 1985 Act there shall be inserted the following Schedule—

"SCHEDULE 2A

MODIFICATION OF DUTIES OF PERMANENT TRUSTEE IN SUMMARY ADMINISTRATION

1. The permanent trustee shall comply with the requirements of sections 3 and 39 of this Act only in so far as, in his view, it would be of financial benefit to the estate of the debtor and in the interests of creditors to do so.

2. The permanent trustee shall, until the debtor is discharged under this Act, at the end of—

(a) the period of 6 months beginning with the date of sequestration; and

(b) each subsequent period of 6 months,

require the debtor to give an account in writing of his current state of affairs.

3.—(1) Where the Accountant in Bankruptcy is not the permanent trustee, the permanent trustee shall comply with any general or specific directions given to him by the Accountant in Bankruptcy.

(2) Directions given under this paragraph may be given in respect of any particular case, all cases or any class or description of case.

4.—(1) The permanent trustee shall, as soon as a certificate for the summary administration of the sequestration of the debtor's estate has been granted, publish in the Edinburgh Gazette a notice stating that such a certificate has been granted and that he has been appointed permanent trustee and, where no notice under section 15(6) of this Act has been published in respect of the sequestration—

(a) stating that sequestration of the debtor's estate has been awarded; and

(b) inviting the submission of claims to him.

(2) A notice under sub-paragraph (1) above shall also contain such additional information as may be prescribed.

5. Except in the case of an application for the grant of a certificate for the summary administration of the sequestration of the debtor's estate under section 25(2A) of this Act, Schedule 2 to this Act shall have effect in respect of a sequestration to which this Schedule applies."

DEFINITIONS

"Accountant in Bankruptcy": s.73(1) and s.1 of the 1985 Act as amended.

"court": s.73(1) of the 1985 Act.

"creditors": s.73(4) of the 1985 Act.

"date of sequestration": s.73(1) of the 1985 Act and new s.12(4) as inserted by s.4(5).

"debtor": s.73(1) of the 1985 Act.

"interim trustee": ss.2 and 73(1) of the 1985 Act.

"permanent trustee": ss.3 and 73(1) of the 1985 Act.

"prescribed": s.73(1) of the 1985 Act.

"security": s.73(1) of the 1985 Act.

GENERAL NOTE

The General Note to s.4 explains the reasons for, and part of the procedure applicable to, the grant of a certificate of summary administration. The procedure in this section is largely self explanatory. Subsections (3) and (9) were added during the course of the passage of the Bill and they reflect concerns which were raised.

The main effect of the grant of a certificate is to limit the work which a permanent trustee must carry out. The certificate enables a trustee to explain to a persistent creditor why the trustee does not wish to investigate or to litigate or otherwise to pursue a particular action. But both with and without a certificate the trustee has discretion and the significance of the presence or absence of a certificate might be exaggerated. The circumstances in which it would be worthwhile to seek withdrawal of an existing certificate must be limited and in practice largely confined to a creditor who is critical of the trustee.

New s.23A(1) and (2)

The amounts of £20,000 and £2,000 could be altered by regulation (new s.72A, inserted by Sched. 1, para. 28). To the extent that the various calculations have to be made on the basis of the information provided by a debtor in a statement of assets and liabilities, much is being asked of the comprehension of debtors, no matter how clearly expressed the prescribed forms may be, and of the accuracy of the information provided.

Liabilities

In the calculation of liabilities no account is taken of a debt "to the extent that a creditor holds a security for that debt". This obviously applies to standard securities and other charges. But the definition of "security" is very broad: "any security, heritable or moveable, or any right of lien, retention or preference" (s.73(1) of the 1985 Act). This raises questions, the full impact of which cannot be analysed here, on the extent to which diligence may be a security. Diligence can give a preference. Effective diligence may give a creditor a security for payment. Bell, for example, described an arrestment on the dependence as an "arrestment for security" and an "arrestment in security" (Prin., para. 2275; Comm. 5th *ed.* i, 7; 7th *ed.* i, 7) and he referred to a creditor being secured by an inhibition (Prin., para. 2306; Comm. 5th *ed.* ii. 144; 7th *ed.* ii. 136). Gretton has taken a different view (G.L. Gretton, *The Law of Inhibition and Adjudication* (W. Green, 1987), pp. 81–2), but, it is submitted that a wide view of the word "security" may be appropriate: (1) because that can be justified by reference to old authority (which cannot all be discussed here but see *Woodside* v. *Esplin* (1847) 9 D. 1486; *Hay* v. *Durham* (1850) 12 D. 676; *Gibson* v. *Greig* (1853) 16 D. 233; *Mitchell* v. *Motherwell* (1888) 16 R. 122 and other cases cited in Goudy, *Bankruptcy* (T. & T. Clark, 4th ed. 1914), p. 187); and (2) the wide definition in s.73(1) of the 1985 Act, which is similar to the definition in the Bankruptcy (Scotland) Act 1856 (s.4) and the Bankruptcy (Scotland) Act 1913 (s.2).

The definition of "security" in s.73(1) of the 1985 Act is not limited like the definition of "secured creditor" to a security over any part of the debtor's estate. It appears relevant to consider a security in the form of a claim against a cautioner or a security over heritage which belongs to someone other than the debtor.

Arguments are bound to arise about the creditor who has a security of dubious worth. The phrase "to the extent that a creditor holds a security for that debt" suggests that the value of any security has to be calculated and deducted in a determination of the amount of the debtor's liabilities. A creditor with a third postponed standard security, for example, may not in reality have a security for all, or part, of his debt.

Assets

The exclusion of heritable property from a calculation of the debtor's assets is significant. Some 20 per cent. of all sequestrations involve heritable property, usually the debtor's house (*Hansard*, H.L. Vol. 541, col. 66). A debtor with a house, subject to a security, but with a reasonable amount of free proceeds available after a sale, has an asset out of which it may be possible to pay for the cost of sequestration and produce a dividend for creditors.

The reasons for the exclusion of heritage from the assets figure include (1) to the extent that much heritage is fully or nearly fully secured the exclusion does not prejudice creditors; and (2) the difficulty which inclusion would produce in identifying "small assets" cases, given the wide divergence on value of heritage and of outstanding loan, which do not directly affect the complexity of insolvency administration or the wisdom of a summary procedure.

The exclusion of property which does not vest in the permanent trustee removes from the calculation certain property exempted from poinding and trust property.

New s.23A(3)

An application for a certificate may be made at an early stage in the sequestration process. In the case of a debtor's petition the Accountant in Bankruptcy may apply to the court not later than seven days after the date on which sequestration is awarded (new s.12(1A) of the 1985 Act, inserted by s.4(3)). The Accountant is likely to have to base the calculation of the debtor's assets and liabilities required by subs. (2) above on the debtor's statement of assets and liabilities. Debtors' statements will be of varying accuracy. The debtor may be suffering from the trauma of insolvency as well as ignorant of all the relevant figures and of the complexities arising from the assets and liabilities which should be excluded from the calculation. To prevent the necessity for the court to have a detailed examination of the figures in every case it is provided that the Accountant's (or the interim trustee's) certificate shall be sufficient, but not conclusive, evidence.

New s.23A(4)

If someone other than the Accountant in Bankruptcy is interim trustee, the Accountant cannot apply for a certificate (new s.23A(9)). When the Accountant applies for and is granted a certificate the Accountant, or his nominee, will become permanent trustee and Sched. 2 (as well as Sched. 2A) will apply. This is the effect of the reference to s.25A.

New s.23A(9)

This limits the circumstances in which a certificate of summary administration may be granted. In cases where there are assets sufficient to pay for a trustee and to pay a dividend to creditors it is probable that the debtor's petition will nominate an interim trustee who will be prepared to act. It is not intended that the Accountant should be able to take over the sequestration (by becoming permanent trustee under new s.25A(1)) through the route of applying for a certificate of summary administration.

A similar philosophy explains subs. (9)(b). If the creditors have elected a permanent trustee, this may produce one instance in which a permanent trustee other than the Accountant or his nominee operates under summary administration (see the notes to s.4). The Accountant cannot interrupt this process by application for a certificate immediately prior to the trustee's confirmation in office. If the meeting of creditors does not elect a trustee (*e.g.* because no creditor attends) the interim trustee, if a private sector trustee, would report the meeting to the sheriff and become permanent trustee. He might apply for a certificate of summary administration (s.24(3B), (4) and (4A) of the 1985 Act inserted by Sched. 1, paras. 12(4)–(6)). Again the Accountant could not halt the normal process by an application for a certificate.

New Sched. 2A

The reality was that in many of the "small assets" cases under the 1985 Act a full process of discovery of the reasons for the debtor's insolvency and the tracing of assets was mostly a waste of time, money and effort. For Sched. 2 cases the Accountant issued guidance on the extent to which public funds might pay for investigation work (Circular 1, December, 1988 quoted in McBryde, *Bankruptcy*, p. 190).

The statutory duties on trustees may have arisen in part because one of the underlying philosophies in the Scottish Law Commission Report was the need to detect offences which might have been committed by debtors (S.L.C., paras. 2.31, 2.44, 4.8). Most debtors are not criminals and, in any event, prosecution for minor insolvency offences does not appear to be common (these views are impressions from talking to insolvency practitioners—research into this point, which the Scottish Law Commission failed to do, would be valuable, and will hopefully be undertaken in the future).

The modified duties in a summary administration are intended to dispense with unnecessary work. Section 3 of the 1985 Act lists the general functions of a permanent trustee and s.39 is concerned with the management and realisation of estate. The reference to the whole of s.39 is somewhat curious because much of that section is concerned with the involvement of the Accountant or commissioners or creditors in the realisation of estate. It would be somewhat remarkable if the trustee could dispense with procedures which involve these categories of persons, although in most cases the permanent trustee will be the Accountant. Section 39(2) which relates, *inter alia,* to carrying on the debtor's business and legal proceedings, confers powers which are already subject to the permanent trustee's views on what "would be beneficial for the administration of the estate . . ." but in summary administration the phrase is "*financial* benefit to the estate . . .".

There is, therefore, a twofold standard: (1) of financial benefit to the estate; and (2) in the interests of creditors. It might be of financial benefit to trace an asset, *e.g.* to challenge a cheque which might be a fraudulent preference, but of no interest to creditors who would not receive any dividend even if the challenge was successful. The Accountant, as permanent trustee, should not act merely for the purpose of increasing the recovery of money for the benefit of his office and the public purse. The interests of creditors are a relevant factor.

Permanent trustees, other than the Accountant, are subject to directions from the Accountant (para. 3(1)). It may be that even the Accountant is subject to directions from the creditors or the court because of the terms of s.39(1) of the 1985 Act; doubt arises because of the reference to s.39, a point discussed above.

The requirement for the permanent trustee to make contact with the debtor every six months is good practice. The Accountant asks all trustees to follow this practice.

The adherence to the value (and expense) of an Edinburgh Gazette notice is remarkable in a procedure designed to cut cost.

Appointment of permanent trustee

7. After section 25 of the 1985 Act there shall be inserted the following section—

"Appointment of permanent trustee in certain cases

25A.—(1) Where this section applies as mentioned in section 21B(2), 23A(4) or 24(3A) of this Act, the court shall appoint as permanent trustee—

(a) the Accountant in Bankruptcy; or

(b) such person as may be nominated by the Accountant in Bankruptcy (being a person who is not ineligible for election as permanent trustee under section 24(2) of this Act) if that person consents to the nomination.

(2) Where this section applies as mentioned in section 28(5) of this Act, if either of the persons mentioned in paragraphs (a) and (b) of subsection (1) above applies to the sheriff for appointment as permanent trustee, the sheriff shall so appoint such person.

(3) Where a person is appointed to be permanent trustee under this section, the provisions of this Act shall apply to the sequestration subject to such modifications, and with such further provisions, as are set out in Schedule 2 to this Act."

DEFINITIONS

"Accountant in Bankruptcy": s.73(1) and s.1 of the 1985 Act as amended.

"court": s.73(1) of the 1985 Act.

"permanent trustee": ss.3 and 73(1) of the 1985 Act.

GENERAL NOTE

This section provides for the court to appoint the Accountant in Bankruptcy, or his nominee, as permanent trustee in the following cases: (1) following a report from the Accountant in Bankruptcy who as interim trustee has not called a statutory meeting (s.21B(2)); (2) where an application for a certificate of summary administration is granted on an application made by the Accountant in Bankruptcy (s.23A(4)); (3) where the Accountant in Bankruptcy is interim trustee and no creditor attends the statutory meeting or no permanent trustee is elected (s.24(3A)); and (4) where a permanent trustee has died or resigned and in the subsequent procedure no new permanent trustee is elected (new s.28(5)).

The Accountant will not normally become permanent trustee in cases where there are assets above the limits for summary administration and a private practitioner has been appointed interim trustee. In that case even if no permanent trustee was elected at the statutory meeting, the interim trustee would be appointed permanent trustee by the sheriff, as was the position before this Act (see s.24(4) of the 1985 Act, as amended), and the trustee would be obliged to act.

The person nominated by the Accountant must be eligible to be permanent trustee. Amongst other constraints this prevents the nomination of someone who is not a qualified insolvency practitioner. By nomination the Accountant will be able to arrange for work to be carried out throughout Scotland using insolvency practitioners of his choosing. The person nominated will have the responsibilities of a permanent trustee. As an alternative the Accountant can delegate some or all of the work of permanent trustees under the terms of the new s.1B to persons who need not be insolvency practitioners (see notes to s.1), and the Accountant would remain the trustee.

When the Accountant in Bankruptcy, or his nominee, becomes permanent trustee the procedure in the sequestration is modified as specified in Sched. 2. If, as will commonly be the case, there is a certificate of summary administration, Sched. 2A will also apply.

Fees for the Accountant in Bankruptcy

8. After section 69 of the 1985 Act there shall be inserted the following section—

> **"Fees for the Accountant in Bankruptcy**
> 69A. The Secretary of State may prescribe—
> (a) the fees and outlays to be payable to the Accountant in Bankruptcy in respect of the exercise of any of his functions under this Act;
> (b) the time and manner in which such fees and outlays are to be paid; and
> (c) the circumstances, if any, in which the Accountant in Bankruptcy may allow exemption from payment or the remission or modification of payment of any fees or outlays payable or paid to him."

DEFINITIONS
"Accountant in Bankruptcy": s.73(1) and s.1 of the 1985 Act as amended.

GENERAL NOTE
This replaces s.1(6) of the 1985 Act with a more extensive provision. The Accountant will charge or incur fees and outlays in the supervision of sequestrations, the auditing of accounts and the determination of trustees' fees. He will also charge for work when he is interim or permanent trustee.

Remuneration of permanent trustee

9.—(1) This section applies in the case of any sequestration in respect of which the petition is presented during the period beginning with the day on which this Act is passed and ending with the commencement of section 2 of this Act, being a sequestration to which Schedule 2 to the 1985 Act applies and in respect of which the permanent trustee is entitled to payment of his outlays and remuneration by virtue of paragraph 9 of that Schedule.

(2) In the case of any sequestration to which this section applies, section 53 of the 1985 Act shall apply for the purposes of the determination of the remuneration and outlays of the permanent trustee subject to the provisions of regulations made under this section.

(3) Regulations under this section may prescribe—
(a) the work in respect of which remuneration and outlays may be claimed, including work undertaken while the permanent trustee was acting as interim trustee;

(b) an amount which shall be paid in respect of remuneration and outlays in respect of any sequestration to which this section applies; and

(c) a scale of fees relating to the nature and extent of work undertaken to apply for the purposes of determining the remuneration and outlays in respect of any such sequestration.

(4) Such regulations may enable the Accountant in Bankruptcy, having taken into account the matters mentioned in paragraphs (a) and (b) of section 53(4) of the 1985 Act, to determine whether, in relation to any sequestration to which this section applies, the remuneration and outlays shall be—

(a) the amount mentioned in subsection (3)(b) above; or

(b) determined by reference to the scale mentioned in subsection (3)(c) above.

(5) Section 72 of the 1985 Act shall apply to regulations made under this section as it applies to regulations made under that Act.

(6) A determination by the Accountant in Bankruptcy in pursuance of regulations made under this section may be appealed to the sheriff in accordance with subsection (6) of the said section 53.

DEFINITIONS
"Accountant in Bankruptcy": s.73(1) and s.1 of the 1985 Act as amended.
"interim trustee": s.73(1) and new s.2 of the 1985 Act.
"permanent trustee": s.73(1) and s.3 of the 1985 Act.

GENERAL NOTE
The time when a petition is presented is defined in new s.73(6) inserted by Sched. 1, para. 29.

This is an interim measure to provide for control on the level of payments from public funds in "small assets" cases. The section came into force on the passing of the Act (s.12(3)). The section applies to petitions presented on and after that day, but not to sequestrations where the petition was prior to the date of Royal Assent. The section ceases to apply to new cases after s.2 of this Act comes into force, at which time, presumably, all, or almost all, of this Act will be in force and appropriate regulations will have been made. It is understood that because of the time scale in the introduction of the new procedures under the Act the powers to make regulations under this section will never be used.

Finance

10.—(1) There shall be paid into the Consolidated Fund any fees received by the Accountant in Bankruptcy in pursuance of regulations made under section 69A of the 1985 Act.

(2) There shall be paid out of money provided by Parliament—

(a) any fees paid in pursuance of section 1B(4) of the 1985 Act as inserted by section 1(1) of this Act;

(b) any administrative expenses incurred by the Secretary of State under this Act; and

(c) any increase attributable to this Act in the sums so payable under any other Act.

DEFINITIONS
"Accountant in Bankruptcy": s.73(1) and s.1 of the 1985 Act as amended.

GENERAL NOTE
The Accountant in Bankruptcy will receive fees, *e.g.* for work as interim or permanent trustee. He will have to pay fees, *e.g* to those to whom he has delegated work under the new s.1B(4) of the 1985 Act. This section makes normal provisions for the origin and destination of the monies.

Amendments and repeals

11.—(1) In section 388 of the Insolvency Act 1986 (meaning of "act as insolvency practitioner"), for subsection (5) there shall be substituted the following subsection—

"(5) Nothing in this section applies to anything done by—

(a) the official receiver; or

(b) the Accountant in Bankruptcy (within the meaning of the Bankruptcy (Scotland) Act 1985)."

(2) In section 389 of that Act (acting without qualification an offence), in subsection (2) at the end there shall be inserted the words "or the Accountant in Bankruptcy (within the meaning of the Bankruptcy (Scotland) Act 1985)."

(3) The 1985 Act shall have effect subject to the amendments in Schedule 1 to this Act.

(4) The enactments mentioned in Schedule 2 to this Act are repealed to the extent mentioned in the third column.

DEFINITIONS
"Accountant in Bankruptcy": s.73(1) and s.1 of the 1985 Act as amended.

GENERAL NOTE
The effect of the amendments to the Insolvency Act are to allow the Accountant in Bankruptcy to act as interim or permanent trustee without being a qualified insolvency practitioner.

Short title, interpretation, commencement and extent

12.—(1) This Act may be cited as the Bankruptcy (Scotland) Act 1993.

(2) Expressions used in this Act and in the 1985 Act shall have the same meaning in this Act as they do in that Act.

(3).The following provisions shall come into force on the day on which this Act is passed, namely—

section 8;

section 9;

this section; and

paragraphs 22(5), 23 and 31(4) and (5) of Schedule 1 and, so far as relating to those paragraphs, section 11.

(4) Subject to subsection (3) above, this Act shall come into force on such day as the Secretary of State may by order made by statutory instrument appoint; and different days may be so appointed for different purposes and for different provisions.

(5) An order under subsection (4) above may contain such transitional provisions and savings as appear to the Secretary of State necessary or expedient in connection with the provisions brought into force (whether wholly or partly) by the order.

(6) Notwithstanding anything in an order made under subsection (4) above, nothing in any provision commenced by such an order shall have effect as regards any sequestration in respect of which the petition is presented before such commencement.

(7) Subject to subsection (8) below, this Act extends to Scotland only.

(8) The amendment by this Act of an enactment which extends to England and Wales or Northern Ireland extends also to England and Wales or, as the case may be, Northern Ireland.

GENERAL NOTE

Subs. (3) to (6)
Some provisions in the Act are retrospective, namely, those which protect the rights of secured creditors on discharge of the debtor (Sched. 1, paras. 23(3) and (4), and paras. 31(4) and (5)). The sections coming into force on the passing of the Act are listed in subs. (3). Sections 8 and 9 are largely concerned with the fees and outlays payable to the Accountant in Bankruptcy and to permanent trustees. Otherwise the Act will come into force by order.

SCHEDULES

       SCHEDULE 1

MISCELLANEOUS AMENDMENTS OF THE 1985 ACT

GENERAL NOTE

There are two main provisions in this Schedule: (1) a series of amendments to the 1985 Act which arise from the Accountant in Bankruptcy's new rôle as interim or permanent trustee; and (2) reform of certain parts of the 1985 Act which gave rise to difficulty or obscurity.

Duties of permanent trustee

1. In section 3 (duties of the permanent trustee) at the end there shall be added the following subsections—

"(5) Paragraph (g) of subsection (1) above and subsection (3) above shall not apply in any case where the permanent trustee is the Accountant in Bankruptcy.

(6) A permanent trustee may apply to the sheriff for directions in relation to any particular matter arising in the sequestration.

(7) Where the debtor, a creditor or any other person having an interest is dissatisfied with any act, omission or decision of the permanent trustee, he may apply to the sheriff and, on such an application being made, the sheriff may confirm, annul or modify any act or decision of the permanent trustee or may give him directions or make such order as he thinks fit."

DEFINITIONS

"Accountant in Bankruptcy": s.73(1) and s.1 of the 1985 Act, as amended.
"debtor": s.73(1) of the 1985 Act.
"permanent trustee": ss.3 and 73(1) of the 1985 Act.

GENERAL NOTE

Section 3(1)(*g*) provides that a permanent trustee must give information to the Accountant in Bankruptcy. This is superfluous when the Accountant is a permanent trustee.

The ability of the permanent trustee to apply to the sheriff for directions is new. It is intended to provide a way of obtaining a court decision in a way which may be easier and cheaper than the alternatives (*e.g* of a Special Case in the Court of Session, an action of declarator or an action against a creditor or other person). On the other hand when a similar power was given by statute to trustees under a trust deed the Court of Session was not inclined to favour a petition with an *ex parte* application, a relatively informal procedure and the request for a decision on complex issues, particularly when another form of action was more appropriate (*Andrew's Trs.* v. *Maddeford*, 1935 S.C. 857; *Peel's Trs.* v. *Drummond*, 1936 S.C. 786; *Henderson's Trs.* v. *Henderson*, 1938 S.C. 461; *Grant's Tr.* v. *Hunter*, 1938 S.C. 501).

The procedure to be followed, including the extent to which creditors and others are given notice, may be specified by rules of court. A similar right to apply to the sheriff is given to a debtor, a creditor or any other person with an interest to challenge any act, omission or decision of a permanent trustee. These provisions do not apply to interim trustees because it is thought inappropriate to have the delay which the court applications would involve during the period of administration by an interim trustee which should be for a short period and for limited purposes. The overall effect is to emphasise the role of the sheriff in sequestrations. It might, for example, be difficult to convince the Accountant that the expense of a Court of Session application was necessary if the alternative of these sheriff court applications would have fulfilled the same purpose.

Resignation and removal of interim trustee

2. For section 13 (appointment and resignation of interim trustee) there shall be substituted the following section.

"Resignation, removal etc. of interim trustee

13.—(1) Where, under section 1A(2) of this Act, the court removes from office an interim trustee, the court shall, on the application of the Accountant in Bankruptcy, appoint a new interim trustee.

(2) Without prejudice to section 1A(2) of this Act or to subsection (1) above, where the court is satisfied that an interim trustee—

(a) is unable to act (whether by, under or by virtue of a provision of this Act or from any other cause whatsoever); or

(b) has so conducted himself that he should no longer continue to act in the sequestration,

the court, on the application of the debtor, a creditor or the Accountant in Bankruptcy, shall remove from office the interim trustee and appoint a new interim trustee.

(3) An interim trustee (not being the Accountant in Bankruptcy) may apply to the court for authority to resign office; and if the court is satisfied that the grounds mentioned in paragraph (a) or (b) of subsection (2) above apply in relation to the interim trustee, it shall grant the application.

(4) Where, following an application under subsection (3) above, the interim trustee resigns office, the court shall appoint a new interim trustee.

(5) Where the interim trustee has died, the court, on the application of the debtor, a creditor or the Accountant in Bankruptcy, shall appoint a new interim trustee.

(6) No one (other than the Accountant in Bankruptcy) shall act as interim trustee in a sequestration if he would, by virtue of section 24(2) of this Act, be disqualified from acting as permanent trustee in that sequestration; but where an interim trustee is, by virtue of this subsection, prohibited from so acting, he shall forthwith make an application under subsection (3) above.

(7) Subsections (1) and (2) of section 2 of this Act shall apply as regards the appointment of an interim trustee under this section as if for any reference to—

(a) the court awarding sequestration of the debtor's estate, there was substituted a reference to the court appointing a new interim trustee; and

(b) the petition for sequestration there was substituted a reference to the application under this section for the appointment of a new interim trustee."

DEFINITIONS

"Accountant in Bankruptcy": s.73(1) and s.1 of the 1985 Act, as amended.
"court": s.73(1) of the 1985 Act.
"debtor": s.73(1) of the 1985 Act.
"interim trustee": s.73(1) and new s.2 of the 1985 Act.

GENERAL NOTE

The old s.13 dealt with the appointment, resignation and removal of an interim trustee. The appointment provisions are in the new s.2. This replacement of s.13 covers aspects of resignation, removal and death. The philosophy of the 1985 Act that there shall always be an interim trustee is maintained. Provision is made for a court appointment of a new trustee on the application of various parties. Just as the original petition for sequestration might, or might not, have nominated an interim trustee, with various consequences (see notes to s.2), so also an application for a new interim trustee might nominate an individual with similar consequences.

The Accountant in Bankruptcy cannot resign. Also a nominated interim trustee has to lodge a written undertaking to act (new s.2(3) of the 1985 Act). Therefore, the circumstances in which an interim trustee might be allowed to resign are limited.

Inhibition on debtor's heritable estate

3. In section 14 (recording of award of sequestration) in subsection (4) for the word "shall" where it first occurs there shall be substituted the word "may".

GENERAL NOTE

Section 14(4) provides for the renewal of the inhibition over the debtor's estate by the recording of a further memorandum by the permanent trustee before the expiry of three years from the date of sequestration. This requirement was mandatory although it was not always followed, particularly if the debtor had no heritable estate, or no estate with a reasonable prospect of a realisable equity after meeting the demands of secured creditors. To avoid unnecessary expense it is now provided that the permanent trustee "may" record the memorandum. The trustee will be expected to renew the inhibition in cases where it is necessary to preserve rights for the benefit of the creditors who have claims in the sequestration.

Interim trustee's Gazette notice

4. In section 15 (further provisions relating to the award of sequestration) for subsection (6) there shall be substituted the following subsection—

"(6) The interim trustee shall, as soon as an award of sequestration has been granted, publish in the Edinburgh Gazette a notice—
(a) stating that sequestration of the debtor's estate has been awarded;
(b) inviting the submission of claims to him; and
(c) giving such other information as may be prescribed."

DEFINITIONS
"debtor": s.73(1) of the 1985 Act.
"interim trustee": s.73(1) and new s.2 of the 1985 Act.
"prescribed": s.73(1) of the 1985 Act.

GENERAL NOTE
Section 15(6) of the 1985 Act provided for intimation of the award of sequestration by notices in the *London* and *Edinburgh Gazettes*. The *London Gazette* notice appears to have served very little purpose in practice and, therefore, there was an unnecessary expense. The reworded s.15(6) restricts the notice to the *Edinburgh Gazette* and also allows for prescribed information to be added in addition to the request for submission of claims.

Petitions for recall of sequestration

5.—(1) Section 16 (petitions for recall of sequestration) shall be amended as follows.
(2) In subsection (4)(a) after the word "of" there shall be inserted the words "the award of".

GENERAL NOTE
This alters the time limit for presentation of certain petitions for the recall of sequestration. The present time limit is 10 weeks from the "date of sequestration". The actual award of sequestration in a creditor's petition will be at a later date, which may vary, *e.g.* if there is difficulty effecting service on the debtor or negotiations over payment by the debtor or arguments about the competence of the petition. It is also more logical to have a time limit for recall of an award of sequestration to run from the date of the award.

Preservation of debtor's estate

6. In section 18(2) (powers to enable preservation of the debtor's estate)—
(a) for the words "2(1)(a)" there shall be substituted the words "2(4)(a)"; and
(b) at the end there shall be added—
    "(h) carry on any business of the debtor or borrow money in so far as it is necessary for the interim trustee to do so to safeguard the debtor's estate."

DEFINITIONS
"business": s.73(1) of the 1985 Act.
"debtor": s.73(1) of the 1985 Act.
"interim trustee": s.73(1) and new s.2 of the 1985 Act.

GENERAL NOTE
Apart from one consequential change in a cross reference this provision removes the necessity for an interim trustee to obtain special authority from the court to carry on the business of the debtor or borrow money. It was one of the oddities of s.18 of the 1985 Act that the interim trustee had power, without the sanction of the court, to close down the debtor's business, but no power, except with court sanction, to preserve the business by carrying it on. This distinction between closing down and carrying on a business was based on spurious grounds (see McBryde, *Bankruptcy*, pp. 72–3) and, in any event, the need for a court application was sometimes inconvenient.
Even although court sanction is now unnecessary the ability to apply for this sanction has been retained because s.18(3) has not been amended. This might be useful if there were doubt as to whether the interim trustee's actions were "necessary . . to safeguard the debtor's estate". That question may arise if there were a prospect of the interim trustee incurring expense and running the business at a loss. Court sanction might not remove the personal liability of the trustee but could be some comfort if there are charges by creditors of imprudent or negligent trading by the trustee.

Statement of assets and liabilities

7.—(1) For section 19 (requirement on debtor to deliver list of assets and liabilities) there shall be substituted the following section—

"Statement of assets and liabilities etc.

19.—(1) Where the petitioner for sequestration is the debtor he shall, not later than 7 days after the appointment of the interim trustee (where he is not the Accountant in Bankruptcy), send to the interim trustee such statement of assets and liabilities as was lodged in court in pursuance of section 5(6A)(a) of this Act.

(2) Where the petitioner for sequestration is a creditor or a trustee acting under a trust deed, the debtor shall, not later than 7 days after having been notified by the interim trustee as mentioned in section 2(7) of this Act, send to the interim trustee a statement of assets and liabilities.

(3) If the debtor—

(a) fails to send to the interim trustee in accordance with subsection (1) or (2) above such statement of assets and liabilities; or

(b) fails to disclose any material fact in such statement of assets and liabilities; or

(c) makes a material misstatement in such statement of assets and liabilities,

he shall be guilty of an offence and liable on summary conviction to a fine not exceeding level 5 on the standard scale or to imprisonment for a term not exceeding 3 months or to both such fine and imprisonment.

(4) In any proceedings for an offence under subsection (3) above, it shall be a defence for the accused to show that he had a reasonable excuse for—

(a) failing to send to the interim trustee in accordance with subsection (1) or (2) above such statement of assets and liabilities; or

(b) failing to disclose a material fact; or

(c) making a material misstatement."

DEFINITIONS

"Accountant in Bankruptcy": s.73(1) and s.1 of the 1985 Act as amended.
"court": s.73(1) of the 1985 Act.
"debtor": s.73(1) of the 1985 Act.
"interim trustee": s.73(1) and new s.2 of the 1985 Act.
"standard scale": s.73(1) of the 1985 Act.
"statement of assets and liabilities": s.73(1) of the 1985 Act as amended by Sched. 1, para. 29.
"trust deed": s.73(1) of the 1985 Act as amended by Sched. 1, para. 29(6) to this Act and new s.5(4A) of the 1985 Act, as inserted by s.3(4).

GENERAL NOTE

Under the new s.6A (inserted by s.3(6)) where the petitioner is the debtor he must lodge with the petition a statement of assets and liabilities and send a copy to the Accountant. The new s.19(1) provides for a statement to be sent to the interim trustee (where he or she is not the Accountant). A similar obligation arises when a creditor or a trustee under a trust deed petitions.

Statement of debtor's affairs

8.—(1) Section 20 (duty to prepare statement of debtor's affairs) shall be amended as follows.

(2) For subsection (1) there shall be substituted the following subsection—

"(1) When the interim trustee has received the statement of assets and liabilities, he shall, as soon as practicable, prepare a statement of the debtor's affairs so far as within the knowledge of the interim trustee and shall indicate in the statement of the debtor's affairs whether, in his opinion, the debtor's assets are unlikely to be sufficient to pay any dividend whatsoever in respect of the debts mentioned in paragraphs (e) to (h) of section 51(1) of this Act."

(3) In paragraph (a) of subsection (2) for the words "a copy of the debtor's list" there shall be substituted the words "the statement".

(4) After subsection (5) there shall be inserted the following subsection—

"(5A) Subsections (2) and (3) above do not apply in any case where the Accountant in Bankruptcy is the interim trustee."

DEFINITIONS

"Accountant in Bankruptcy": s.73(1) and s.1 of the 1985 Act as amended.
"debtor": s.73(1) of the 1985 Act.
"interim trustee": s.73(1) and new s.2 of the 1985 Act.
"statement of assets and liabilities": s.73(1) of the 1985 Act as amended by Sched. 1, para. 29.

GENERAL NOTE

The existing requirement was for the interim trustee to prepare a preliminary statement of the debtor's affairs "on receipt" of the debtor's list or, as it is now called, statement of assets and liabilities. The time has been changed to "as soon as practicable" which allows the trustee some opportunity to check information and to make inquiries. The statement is no longer "preliminary" because in practice it may be the only statement produced by the debtor. A copy of the statement and other documents have to be sent to the Accountant in Bankruptcy and this is obviously inappropriate when the interim trustee is the Accountant.

Calling of statutory meeting

9. Before section 21 there shall be inserted the following section—

"Statutory meeting
20A. A meeting of creditors called by the interim trustee under section 21 or 21A of this Act shall, in this Act, be referred to as "the statutory meeting"."
10.—(1) Section 21 (calling of statutory meeting) shall be amended as follows.
(2) In subsection (1) for the words from the beginning to "statutory meeting")" there shall be substituted the words "Where the interim trustee is not the Accountant in Bankruptcy he shall call the statutory meeting".
(3) After subsection (1) there shall be inserted the following subsection—
"(1A) The statutory meeting shall be held at such time and place as the interim trustee determines."
(4) After subsection (3) there shall be inserted the following subsection—
"(4) This section does not apply in any case where the Accountant in Bankruptcy is the interim trustee."

DEFINITIONS
"Accountant in Bankruptcy": s.73(1) and s.1 of the 1985 Act as amended.
"interim trustee": s.73(1) and new s.2 of the 1985 Act.
"statutory meeting": s.73(1) of the 1985 Act and new s.20A of the 1985 Act.

GENERAL NOTE
When the Accountant in Bankruptcy is interim trustee the new s.21A applies to the calling of the statutory meeting. Otherwise s.21, as amended above, applies. Whoever is interim trustee the statutory meeting may be held at such time and place as the interim trustee determines (subject to the time limit which governs the date of the meeting). In practice the result may be that the meeting is held in the trustee's office, if that is convenient for the majority of creditors (see Sched. 6, para. 10 to the 1985 Act).

Proceedings at statutory meeting

11.—(1) Section 23 (proceedings at statutory meeting before the election of permanent trustee) shall be amended as follows.
(2) In subsection (3)—
(a) for paragraph (a) there shall be substituted the following paragraph—
"(a) shall make available for inspection—
(i) the statement of assets and liabilities; and
(ii) his statement of the debtor's affairs prepared under section 20(1) of this Act;"; and
(b) for paragraph (d) there shall be substituted the following paragraph—
"(d) shall determine whether it is necessary to revise his statement of the debtor's affairs and, if he determines that it is necessary to revise the statement, he shall do so either at, or as soon as possible after, the statutory meeting."
(3) For subsection (5) there shall be substituted the following subsection—
"(5) Where the interim trustee has revised his statement of the debtor's affairs, he shall, as soon as possible after the statutory meeting, send a copy of the revised statement to every creditor known to him."

DEFINITIONS
"debtor": s.73(1) of the 1985 Act.
"interim trustee": s.73(1) and new s.2 of the 1985 Act.
"permanent trustee": ss.3 and 73(1) of the 1985 Act.
"statement of assets and liabilities": s.73(1) of the 1985 Act as amended by Sched. 1, para. 29.
"statutory meeting": new s.20A of the 1985 Act inserted by para. 9 above.

GENERAL NOTE

The interim trustee must now make available for inspection the debtor's statement of assets and liabilities (which will include details of the debtor's income and expenditure for reasons mentioned in the notes to new s.5(6A) inserted by s.3(6)). The trustee no longer has to prepare a final statement of the debtor's affairs. He (or she) may, but only if he determines it necessary, revise his earlier statement prepared under new s.20(1) (inserted by para. 8(2) above). Only when the statement is revised is it necessary to send a copy to every creditor. This removes the expense which used to arise when a final statement was always prepared and sent to every creditor and the Accountant. It also follows that it is inappropriate for the new procedure to incorporate intimation as to whether or not the trustee intends to apply for a certificate of discharge.

Election of permanent trustee

12.—(1) Section 24 (election of permanent trustee) shall be amended as follows.

(2) For subsection (1) there shall be substituted the following subsection—

"(1) At the statutory meeting, the creditors shall, at the conclusion of the proceedings under section 23(3) of this Act, proceed to the election of the permanent trustee."

(3) In subsection (2) at the end there shall be inserted the following paragraphs—

"(e) a person who has not given an undertaking, in writing, to act as permanent trustee;

(f) the Accountant in Bankruptcy."

(4) After subsection (3) there shall be inserted the following subsections—

"(3A) In any case where the Accountant in Bankruptcy is the interim trustee, if—

(a) no creditor entitled to vote in the election of the permanent trustee attends the statutory meeting; or

(b) no permanent trustee is elected,

the Accountant in Bankruptcy shall forthwith report the proceedings at the statutory meeting to the sheriff and section 25A of this Act shall apply.

(3B) Where a report is made in pursuance of subsection (3A) above, the Accountant in Bankruptcy may apply to the sheriff for the grant of a certificate for the summary administration of the sequestration of the debtor's estate."

(5) In subsection (4) at the beginning there shall be inserted the following words—

"In any case where the Accountant in Bankruptcy is not the interim trustee,".

(6) After subsection (4) there shall be inserted the following subsection—

"(4A) Where a report is made in pursuance of subsection (4) above, the interim trustee may apply to the sheriff for the grant of a certificate for the summary administration of the sequestration of the debtor's estate."

DEFINITIONS

"Accountant in Bankruptcy": s.73(1) and s.1 of the 1985 Act as amended.
"debtor": s.73(1) of the 1985 Act.
"interim trustee": s.73(1) and new s.2 of the 1985 Act.
"permanent trustee": ss.3 and 73(1) of the 1985 Act.
"statutory meeting": new s.20A of the 1985 Act inserted by para. 9 above.
"the creditors": s.73(4) of the 1985 Act.

GENERAL NOTE

Para. 12(1)

This is a rewording of the existing provision, although it appears to obscure rather than clarify the situations in which the creditors proceed to election because of the deletion of the cross reference to s.23(4).

Para. 12(3)

A permanent trustee who is elected has to give a written undertaking to act. This is to prevent a trustee assuming office, finding that there are insufficient assets to pay his or her fees and outlays, and then resigning. It is similar to the requirement which applies to a nominated interim trustee (new s.2(3)(c)). The Accountant in Bankruptcy cannot be elected permanent trustee.

Paras. 12(4) to (6)

These are consequential amendments which cover the possibility that there may not be the election of a permanent trustee and either the Accountant in Bankruptcy or, as the case may be, a private practitioner as interim trustee reports to the sheriff, and is appointed permanent trustee. The interim trustee may apply for a certificate of summary administration (see notes to ss.4 and 6).

Procedure on election of permanent trustee

13.—(1) Section 25 (confirmation of permanent trustee) shall be amended as follows.
(2) After subsection (2) there shall be inserted the following subsection—
"(2A) Where a report is made in pursuance of subsection (1) above, the interim trustee may apply to the sheriff for the grant of a certificate for the summary administration of the sequestration of the debtor's estate."
(3) In paragraph (b) of subsection (6) at the end there shall be added the words "and giving such other information as may be prescribed."

DEFINITIONS
"debtor": s.73(1) of the 1985 Act.
"interim trustee": s.73(1) and new s.2 of the 1985 Act.
"prescribed": s.73(1) of the 1985 Act.

GENERAL NOTE
Paragraph 12(6) above inserted s.24(4A) so that an interim trustee could apply for a certificate of summary administration where no permanent trustee had been elected. Even if a permanent trustee is elected, the interim trustee (but not the permanent trustee) can apply for a certificate of summary administration.

Termination of interim trustee's functions

14.—(1) Section 26 (termination of functions of interim trustee) shall be amended as follows.
(2) In subsection (1) for the words from "a" to "liabilities" there shall be substituted the words "the statement of assets and liabilities, and a copy".
(3) In subsection (4) after the word "issue" there shall be inserted the words "; and the decision of the sheriff on such an appeal shall be final".
(4) After subsection (5) there shall be inserted the following subsection—
"(5A) This section does not apply in any case where the Accountant in Bankruptcy is the interim trustee."

DEFINITIONS
"Accountant in Bankruptcy": s.73(1) and s.1 of the 1985 Act as amended.
"interim trustee": s.73(1) and new s.2 of the 1985 Act.
"statement of assets and liabilities": s.73(1) of the 1985 Act as amended by Sched. 1, para. 29.

GENERAL NOTE
When an interim trustee does not become permanent trustee his or her accounts are audited by, and the amount of outlays and remuneration fixed by, the Accountant in Bankruptcy. The Accountant's determination may be appealed by various persons. The sheriff's decision is now made final.
Where the interim trustee is the Accountant s.26 does not apply. Instead the new s.26A applies.

Accountant in Bankruptcy to account for intromissions

15.—(1) After section 26 (termination of interim trustee's functions) there shall be inserted the following section.

"Accountant in Bankruptcy to account for intromissions
26A.—(1) This section applies in any case where the Accountant in Bankruptcy was the interim trustee and some other person becomes the permanent trustee.
(2) The Accountant in Bankruptcy shall, on confirmation of the permanent trustee in office, hand over to the permanent trustee everything in his possession which relates to the sequestration and which he obtained in his capacity as interim trustee (including the statement of assets and liabilities); and thereupon he shall cease to act as interim trustee.
(3) The Accountant in Bankruptcy shall, not later than 3 months after the confirmation in office of the permanent trustee, supply to the permanent trustee—

(a) his accounts of his intromissions (if any) as interim trustee with the debtor's estate;

(b) a determination of his fees and outlays calculated in accordance with regulations made under section 69A of this Act; and

(c) a copy of the notice mentioned in subsection 4(b) below.

(4) The Accountant in Bankruptcy shall send to the debtor and to all creditors known to him—

(a) a copy of the determination mentioned in subsection (3)(b) above; and

(b) a notice in writing stating—

(i) that the Accountant in Bankruptcy has commenced the procedure under this Act leading to discharge in respect of his actings as interim trustee;

(ii) that the accounts of his intromissions (if any) with the debtor's estate are available for inspection at such address as the Accountant in Bankruptcy may determine;

(iii) that an appeal may be made to the sheriff under subsection (5) below; and

(iv) the effect of subsection (7) below.

(5) The permanent trustee, the debtor and any creditor may appeal to the sheriff against—

(a) the determination of the Accountant in Bankruptcy mentioned in subsection (3)(b) above;

(b) the discharge of the Accountant in Bankruptcy in respect of his actings as interim trustee; or

(c) both such determination and discharge.

(6) An appeal under subsection (5) above shall be made not more than 14 days after the issue of the notice mentioned in subsection (4)(b) above; and the decision of the sheriff on such an appeal shall be final.

(7) Where—

(a) the requirements of this section have been complied with; and

(b) no appeal is made to the sheriff under subsection (5) above or such an appeal is made but is refused as regards the discharge of the Accountant in Bankruptcy,

the Accountant in Bankruptcy shall be discharged from all liability (other than any liability arising from fraud) to the creditors or to the debtor in respect of any act or omission of the Accountant in Bankruptcy in exercising the functions of interim trustee in the sequestration.

(8) The permanent trustee, on being confirmed in office, shall make such insertions in the sederunt book as are appropriate to provide a record of the sequestration process before his confirmation."

DEFINITIONS

"Accountant in Bankruptcy": s.73(1) and s.1 of the 1985 Act as amended.

"debtor": s.73(1) of the 1985 Act.

"interim trustee": s.73(1) and new s.2 of the 1985 Act.

"permanent trustee": ss.3 and 73(1) of the 1985 Act.

"sederunt book": ss.3 and 73(1) of the 1985 Act.

"statement of assets and liabilities": s.73(1) of the 1985 Act as amended by Sched. 1, para. 29(5).

GENERAL NOTE

This section, the terms of which are largely self explanatory, provides for the end of the Accountant in Bankruptcy's functions as interim trustee in cases where some other person becomes permanent trustee.

Discharge of interim trustee

16.—(1) Section 27 (discharge of interim trustee) shall be amended as follows.

(2) After subsection (4) there shall be inserted the following subsection—

"(4A) The decision of the sheriff in an appeal under subsection (4) above shall be final."

(3) After subsection (7) there shall be inserted the following subsection—

"(7A) This section does not apply in any case where the Accountant in Bankruptcy is the interim trustee."

DEFINITIONS
"Accountant in Bankruptcy": s.73(1) and s.1 of the 1985 Act, as amended.
"interim trustee": s.73(1) and new s.2 of the 1985 Act.

GENERAL NOTE

After certain procedure the Accountant may grant or refuse to grant a certificate of discharge to an interim trustee (other than himself). Various persons may appeal the Accountant's determination to the sheriff. The sheriff's decision is now final.

Replacement of permanent trustee

17.—(1) Section 28 (resignation and death of permanent trustee) shall be amended as follows.

(2) For subsection (1) there shall be substituted the following subsections—

"(1) The permanent trustee may apply to the sheriff for authority to resign office and, where the sheriff is satisfied that either of the grounds mentioned in paragraphs (a) and (b) of section 13(2) of this Act applies to the permanent trustee, he shall grant the application.

(1A) The sheriff may make the granting of an application under subsection (1) above subject to the election of a new permanent trustee and to such conditions as he thinks appropriate in all the circumstances of the case."

(3) In subsection (4), after the words "subsection (1)," there shall be inserted the word "(1A),".

(4) For subsection (5) there shall be substituted the following subsection—

"(5) Where no new permanent trustee is elected in pursuance of subsection (2) or (3) above, the provisions of section 25A of this Act shall apply."

(5) After subsection (7) there shall be inserted the following subsection—

"(8) The decision of the sheriff on an appeal under subsection (7) above shall be final."

DEFINITIONS
"permanent trustee": s.73(1) and s.3 of the 1985 Act.

GENERAL NOTE

The alterations to s.28 make it more difficult for a permanent trustee to resign. The trustee will have given a written undertaking to act. The intention is to prevent the trustee resigning merely because there are insufficient assets. No longer may a meeting of creditors accept the resignation. The trustee must apply to the sheriff who can grant the application only if either of the grounds in the new s.13(2) exist.

Removal of permanent trustee

18. In section 29 (removal of permanent trustee and provision for where the permanent trustee does not act) in each of subsections (1)(b), (5) and (6) where they occur, for the words "1(3)" there shall be substituted the words "1A(2)".

GENERAL NOTE
This is a consequential amendment of a cross reference.

Removal of commissioner from office

19. In section 30(4) (removal of commissioner from office) for the words "1(3)" there shall be substituted the words "1A(2)".

GENERAL NOTE
This is a consequential amendment of a cross reference.

Warrant for arrest of debtor etc.

20.—(1) Section 46 (measures to secure the attendance of the debtor and others at private and public examinations) shall be amended as follows.

(2) In subsection (1)—
  (a) in paragraph (a) at the end there shall be added the words "to apprehend";
  (b) in paragraph (b) for the words from "request" to the end of the paragraph there shall be substituted the words "grant a warrant for the arrest of"; and

    (c) after paragraph (b)—
        (i) the words "to apprehend" shall cease to have effect; and
        (ii) after the word "and" there shall be inserted the word "to".
  (3) In the proviso to subsection (1) for the words from "paragraph (a)" to "made" there shall be substituted the words "this subsection shall not be granted".

DEFINITIONS
    "debtor": s.73(1) of the 1985 Act.

GENERAL NOTE
    Section 46(1) of the 1985 Act allowed the Court of Session or the sheriff to request a court in another part of the U.K. to take appropriate steps to apprehend the debtor or other person required for private or public examination. The difficulty was uncertainty as to the procedure. The amendments give power to the Scottish courts to grant warrant for arrest. The effect would then be to apply the Insolvency Act 1986, s.426(7) and the Criminal Law Act 1977, s.38 which together would allow the enforcement of the warrant throughout the U.K.

Accounting period

    21.—In section 52 (estate to be distributed in respect of accounting periods), for subsections (1) and (2) there shall be substituted the following subsections—
    "(1) The permanent trustee shall make up accounts of his intromissions with the debtor's estate in respect of each accounting period.
    (2) In this Act "accounting period" shall be construed as follows—
      (a) the first accounting period shall be the period of 6 months beginning with the date of sequestration; and
      (b) any subsequent accounting period shall be the period of 6 months beginning with the end of the last accounting period; except that—
        (i) in a case where the Accountant in Bankruptcy is not the permanent trustee, the permanent trustee and the commissioners or, if there are no commissioners, the Accountant in Bankruptcy agree; or
        (ii) in a case where the Accountant in Bankruptcy is the permanent trustee, he determines,
      that the accounting period shall be such other period beginning with the end of the last accounting period as may be agreed or, as the case may be determined, it shall be that other period.
    (2A) An agreement or determination under subsection (2)(b)(i) or (ii) above—
      (a) may be made in respect of one or more than one accounting period;
      (b) may be made before the beginning of the accounting period in relation to which it has effect and, in any event, shall not have effect unless made before the day on which such accounting period would, but for the agreement or determination, have ended;
      (c) may provide for different accounting periods to be of different durations,
    and shall be recorded in the sederunt book by the permanent trustee."

DEFINITIONS
    "Accountant in Bankruptcy": s.73(1) and s.1 of the 1985 Act as amended.
    "accounting period": s.73(1) of the 1985 Act and new s.52(2) of the 1985 Act.
    "commissioner": ss.30(1) and 73(1) of the 1985 Act.
    "date of sequestration": s.73(1) of the 1985 Act and new s.12(4) of the 1985 Act.
    "debtor": s.73(1) of the 1985 Act.
    "permanent trustee": ss.3 and 73(1) of the 1985 Act.
    "sederunt book": ss.3 and 73(1) of the 1985 Act.

GENERAL NOTE
    The permanent trustee must make up his or her accounts for each accounting period. Under the 1985 Act the accounting periods were periods of 26 weeks commencing with the date of sequestration. The effect was to require accounts even for periods when there were few or no intromissions of much consequence. This added to the expense, particularly in "small assets" cases. Also the period of 26 weeks caused problems with some computer software. The main change is to have a first accounting period of six months. Thereafter the accounting periods can be varied if the appropriate procedure is followed.

Procedure after end of accounting periods

22.—(1) Section 53 (procedure after end of accounting periods) shall be amended as follows.

(2) For subsection (2) there shall be substituted the following subsections—

"(2) Subject to subsection (2A) below, all accounts in respect of legal services incurred by the permanent trustee shall, before payment thereof by him, be submitted for taxation to the auditor of the court before which the sequestration is pending.

(2A) Where—

(a) any such account has been agreed between the permanent trustee and the person entitled to payment in respect of that account (in this subsection referred to as "the payee");

(b) the permanent trustee is not an associate of the payee; and

(c) the commissioners have not determined that the account should be submitted for taxation,

the permanent trustee may pay such account without submitting it for taxation."

(3) In subsection (3)(a)—

(a) in sub-paragraph (i) before the word "audit" there shall be inserted the word "may"; and

(b) in sub-paragraph (ii) before the word "issue" there shall be inserted the word "shall".

(4) In subsection (5) for the words "the final" there shall be substituted the word "any".

(5) In subsection (6) at the end there shall be added the words "; and the decision of the sheriff on such an appeal shall be final."

DEFINITIONS

"accounting period": s.73(1) of the 1985 Act and new s.52(2) of the 1985 Act.

"associate": ss.73(1) and 74 of the 1985 Act.

"commissioner": ss.30(1) and 73(1) of the 1985 Act.

"court": s.73(1) of the 1985 Act.

"permanent trustee": ss.3 and 73(1) of the 1985 Act.

GENERAL NOTE

These amendments continue the policy of making the process of sequestration simpler and cheaper.

At present the permanent trustee cannot pay accounts for legal services without either taxation or the approval of the Accountant (s.53(2) of the 1985 Act). This requirement is relaxed, subject to safeguards, so that, in the normal case, payment can be made if the trustee and the payee agree the account.

Auditing of accounts at the end of every accounting period ceases to be mandatory, by alterations to s.53(3). Adjustments to the trustee's remuneration can be made when fixing remuneration in respect of any accounting period: under the 1985 Act (s.53(5)) an adjustment could be made only at the end of the final accounting period.

Extent of discharge under section 54

23.—(1) Section 55 (effect of discharge under section 54) shall be amended as follows.

(2) In subsection (1) for the words "subsection (2)" there shall be substituted the words "subsections (2) and (3)".

(3) After subsection (2) there shall be inserted the following subsection—

"(3) The discharge of the debtor under the said section 54 shall not affect any right of a secured creditor—

(a) for a debt in respect of which the debtor has been discharged to enforce his security for payment of the debt and any interest due and payable on the debt until the debt is paid in full; or

(b) for an obligation in respect of which the debtor has been discharged to enforce his security in respect of the obligation."

(4) Section 55 of the 1985 Act shall be deemed always to have had effect as amended by this paragraph.

DEFINITIONS

"debtor": s.73(1) of the 1985 Act.

"secured creditor": s.73(1) of the 1985 Act.

"security": s.73(1) of the 1985 Act.

GENERAL NOTE

The 1985 Act introduced a procedure under which there was, in the normal case, an "automatic" discharge of the debtor after three years. What the Act failed to take account of was the argument that discharge of a debt in principle discharges any associated security. When a property was fully secured, the secured creditor might be paid out of the debtor's income; the permanent trustee would not have an interest to sell until the value of the property had risen or the amount of the secured loan had decreased. If, however, the debtor obtained a discharge, it was possible that the permanent trustee could sell the property unencumbered by any security. The arguments which could produce this result were stated in "The Discharge of a Debtor and Securities", 1991 S.L.T. (News), 195–8.

Before there was a suitable opportunity to test the position in the courts an alteration to s.55 of the 1985 Act was proposed in the Bill and the change was to be retrospective. On the assumption that the change would be enacted there was not any point in litigation.

A secured creditor is now not prejudiced by the discharge of the debtor. This brings Scots law into line with English law (Insolvency Act 1986, s.281(2)). The change came into force on the day the Act was passed (s.12(3)).

The word "security" has a wide meaning which is discussed in the notes to s.6(1) inserting new s.23A(2) into the 1985 Act.

Discharge of permanent trustee

24.—(1) Section 57 (discharge of permanent trustee) shall be amended as follows.

(2) After subsection (4) there shall be inserted the following subsection—

"(4A) The decision of the sheriff on an appeal under subsection (4) above shall be final."

(3) After subsection (7) there shall be inserted the following subsection—

"(8) This section does not apply in any case where the Accountant in Bankruptcy is the permanent trustee."

DEFINITIONS

"Accountant in Bankruptcy": ss.1 and 73(1) of the 1985 Act.
"permanent trustee": ss.3 and 73(1) of the 1985 Act.

GENERAL NOTE

This paragraph clarifies that the decision of the sheriff is final when there is an appeal against the Accountant's determination on the grant or refusal of a certificate of discharge to a permanent trustee. Section 57 does not apply when the Accountant is a permanent trustee; the applicable provisions are in the new s.58A.

Unclaimed dividends

25. In section 58 (disposal of unclaimed dividends) in subsections (1) and (3) in both places where they occur, after the words "section 57(1)(a)" there shall be inserted the words "or 58A(3)".

GENERAL NOTE

The new s.58A(3) applies to the deposit of unclaimed dividends by the Accountant where he has acted as permanent trustee. This paragraph makes consequential amendments to s.58 on the right to unclaimed dividends and the eventual transfer of balances to the Secretary of State.

Discharge of Accountant in Bankruptcy

26. After section 58 of the 1985 Act there shall be inserted the following section—

"Discharge of Accountant in Bankruptcy

58A.—(1) This section applies where the Accountant in Bankruptcy has acted as the permanent trustee in any sequestration.

(2) After the Accountant in Bankruptcy has made a final division of the debtor's estate, he shall insert in the sederunt book—

(a) his final accounts of his intromissions (if any) with the debtor's estate;
(b) the scheme of division (if any); and
(c) a determination of his fees and outlays calculated in accordance with regulations made under section 69A of this Act.

(3) The Accountant in Bankruptcy shall deposit any unclaimed dividends and any unapplied balances in an appropriate bank or institution.

(4) The Accountant in Bankruptcy shall send to the debtor and to all creditors known to him—

(a) a copy of the determination mentioned in subsection (2)(c) above; and
(b) a notice in writing stating—
(i) that the Accountant in Bankruptcy has commenced the procedure under this Act leading to discharge in respect of his actings as permanent trustee;
(ii) that the sederunt book relating to the sequestration is available for inspection at such address as the Accountant in Bankruptcy may determine;
(iii) that an appeal may be made to the sheriff under subsection (5) below; and
(iv) the effect of subsection (7) below.
(5) The debtor and any creditor may appeal to the sheriff against—
(a) the determination of the Accountant in Bankruptcy mentioned in subsection (2)(c) above;
(b) the discharge of the Accountant in Bankruptcy in respect of his actings as permanent trustee; or
(c) both such determination and discharge.
(6) An appeal under subsection (5) above shall be made not more than 14 days after the issue of the notice mentioned in subsection (4)(b) above; and the decision of the sheriff on such an appeal shall be final.
(7) Where—
(a) the requirements of this section have been complied with; and
(b) no appeal to the sheriff is made under subsection (5) above or such an appeal is made but is refused as regards the discharge of the Accountant in Bankruptcy,
the Accountant in Bankruptcy shall be discharged from all liability (other than any liability arising from fraud) to the creditors or to the debtor in respect of any act or omission of the Accountant in Bankruptcy in exercising the functions of permanent trustee in the sequestration.
(8) Where the Accountant in Bankruptcy is discharged from all liability as mentioned in subsection (7) above, he shall make an entry in the sederunt book recording such discharge.
(9) Where the Accountant in Bankruptcy—
(a) has acted as both interim trustee and permanent trustee in a sequestration;
(b) has not been discharged under section 26A(7) of this Act,
references in this section to his acting as or exercising the functions of permanent trustee shall be construed as including references to his acting as or exercising the functions of interim trustee; and subsection (7) above shall have effect accordingly."

DEFINITIONS
"Accountant in Bankruptcy": ss.1 and 73(1) of the 1985 Act as amended.
"appropriate bank or institution": s.73(1) of the 1985 Act.
"debtor": s.73(1) of the 1985 Act.
"interim trustee": s.73(1) of the 1985 Act and new s.2 of the 1985 Act.
"permanent trustee": ss.3 and 73(1) of the 1985 Act.
"sederunt book": ss.3(1) and 73(1) of the 1985 Act.

GENERAL NOTE
This procedure for discharge of the Accountant in Bankruptcy follows, with appropriate variations, the procedure which would be adopted by other permanent trustees under ss.53(10) and 57.

Commencement of summary proceedings

27.—(1) Section 68 (summary proceedings) shall be amended as follows.
(2) In subsection (1)—
(a) at the beginning there shall be inserted the words "Subject to subsection (1A) below,"; and
(b) for the word "6" there shall be substituted the word "12".
(3) After subsection (1) there shall be inserted the following subsection—
"(1A) No such proceedings shall be commenced by virtue of this section more than three years after the commission of the offence."
(4) In subsection (2) for the words "subsection (1) above" there shall be substituted the words "this section".

This extends the period within which the Lord Advocate may commence summary proceedings from six to 12 months after the date on which the Advocate has sufficient evidence to justify proceedings. On the other hand there is now a time limit of three years from the commission of the offence.

Variation of references to time, money etc.

28. After section 72 (regulations) of the 1985 Act there shall be inserted the following section—

> **"Variation of references to time, money etc.**
> 72A. For any reference in this Act to—
> (a) a period of time;
> (b) an amount of money; or
> (c) a fraction,
> there shall be substituted a reference to such other period or, as the case may be, amount or fraction as may be prescribed."

DEFINITIONS
"prescribed": s.73(1) of the 1985 Act.

GENERAL NOTE
This new section allows for changes without the need for primary legislation. For example it would be possible to take account of the effect of inflation to alter the level of debt required for a s.7(1)(*d*) notice, or for a petition, or the amount of liabilities and assets required for a certificate of summary administration.

Interpretation

29.—(1) Section 73 (interpretation) shall be amended as follows.

(2) In subsection (1) the definition of "accounting period" for the words "52(1) and (6)" there shall be substituted the words "52(2)".

(3) In subsection (1) in the definition of "register of insolvencies" for the words "1(1)(c)" there shall be substituted the words "1A(1)(b)".

(4) In subsection (1) in the definition of "statutory meeting" for the words "section 21(1)" there shall be substituted the words "section 20A".

(5) In subsection (1) after the definition of "standard scale" there shall be inserted the following—

> ""statement of assets and liabilities" means a document (including a copy of a document) in such form as may be prescribed containing—
> (i) a list of the debtor's assets and liabilities;
> (ii) a list of his income and expenditure; and
> (iii) such other information as may be prescribed;".

(6) In subsection (1) for the definition of "trust deed" there shall be substituted the following—

> ""trust deed" has the meaning assigned by section 5(4A) of this Act;".

(7) At the end there shall be added the following subsection—

> "(6) Any reference in this Act, howsoever expressed, to the time when a petition for sequestration is presented shall be construed as a reference to the time when the petition is received by the clerk of the court."

Adaptation of procedure where permanent trustee not elected

30.—(1) Schedule 2 (which provides for the adaptation of procedure under the Act where a permanent trustee is not elected) shall be amended as follows.

(2) In paragraph 1 at the beginning there shall be inserted the words "Except where the permanent trustee is the Accountant in Bankruptcy,".

(3) For paragraph 2 there shall be substituted the following paragraphs—

> "2.—(1) In place of section 25, sub-paragraph (2) below shall have effect.
> (2) The sheriff clerk shall issue to the permanent trustee an act and warrant in such form as shall be prescribed by the Court of Session by act of sederunt.
> 2A. Sections 26 and 26A shall apply as if for any reference to the confirmation of the permanent trustee in office there was substituted a reference to the permanent trustee receiving the act and warrant issued in pursuance of paragraph 2(2) above."

(4) For paragraph 3 there shall be substituted the following paragraph—

"3.—(1) In place of subsections (1A) to (5) of section 28, sub-paragraph (2) below shall have effect.

(2) Where the permanent trustee resigns under subsection (1) of section 28 of this Act or dies—

(a) the Accountant in Bankruptcy; or

(b) such person as may be nominated by the Accountant in Bankruptcy (being a person who is not ineligible for election as permanent trustee under section 24(2) of this Act) if that person consents to the nomination,

may apply to the sheriff for appointment as permanent trustee; and, on such an application being made, the sheriff shall appoint the Accountant in Bankruptcy or, as the case may be, the person nominated by him to be the permanent trustee."

(5) For paragraph 4 there shall be substituted the following paragraph—

"4.—(1) Section 29 shall have effect as follows.

(2) Where the permanent trustee is the Accountant in Bankruptcy, subsections (1) to (6) shall not have effect.

(3) In any other case—

(a) subsection (5) shall not have effect but sub-paragraph (2) of paragraph 3 above shall apply where the permanent trustee has been removed from office under subsection (1)(b) of section 29 of this Act or following an appeal under subsection (4) of that section as that sub-paragraph applies where he resigns or dies; and

(b) subsection (6) shall have effect as if for the words from "(b)" to the end there were substituted the words—

"(b) appoint as permanent trustee—

(i) the Accountant in Bankruptcy; or

(ii) such person as may be nominated by the Accountant in Bankruptcy (being a person who is not ineligible for election as permanent trustee under section 24(2) of this Act) if that person consents to the nomination."

(4) In every case—

(a) subsection (7) shall not have effect; and

(b) subsection (8) shall have effect as if for the word "(5)" there were substituted the word "(6)"."

(6) In paragraph 5 for the words "4(a) or (b)" there shall be substituted the words "4(3)(a) or (b)".

(7) In paragraph 7—

(a) after the words "section 39" there shall be inserted the words ", subsection (1) shall not have effect where the permanent trustee is the Accountant in Bankruptcy and"; and

(b) for sub-paragraph (b) there shall be substituted the following sub-paragraph—

"(b) in subsection (2) the words "but if there are commissioners only with the consent of the commissioners, the creditors or the court" shall not have effect, and—

(i) if the permanent trustee is the Accountant in Bankruptcy, no consent shall be required for the actings mentioned in that subsection; and

(ii) in any other case, the consent of the Accountant in Bankruptcy shall be required for such actings."

(8) After paragraph 7 there shall be inserted the following paragraph—

"7A. In section 43 (money received by permanent trustee) for subsection (1) there shall be substituted the following subsection—

"(1) Subject to subsection (2) below, all money received by—

(a) the Accountant in Bankruptcy in respect of his actings as permanent trustee shall be deposited by him in the name of the debtor's estate or in the name of the Secretary of State in an appropriate bank or institution;

(b) the permanent trustee (where he is not the Accountant in Bankruptcy) in the exercise of his functions shall be deposited by him in the name of the debtor's estate in an appropriate bank or institution."."

(9) In paragraph 8—

(a) at the beginning there shall be inserted the words "Except where the permanent trustee is the Accountant in Bankruptcy,".

(10) For paragraph 9 there shall be substituted the following paragraph—

"9.—(1) Where the permanent trustee is the Accountant in Bankruptcy, section 53 shall have effect as follows.

(2) For subsections (1) to (7) there shall be substituted the following subsections—

"(1) At the end of each accounting period, the Accountant in Bankruptcy shall prepare accounts of his intromissions with the debtor's estate, and he shall make a determination of his fees and outlays calculated in accordance with regulations made under section 69A of this Act.

(2) Such accounts and determination shall be available for inspection by the debtor and the creditors not later than 6 weeks after the end of the accounting period to which they relate.

(3) In making a determination as mentioned in subsection (1) above, the Accountant in Bankruptcy may take into account any adjustment which he may wish to make in the amount of his remuneration fixed in respect of any earlier accounting period.

(4) Not later than 8 weeks after the end of an accounting period, the debtor or any creditor may appeal to the sheriff against the determination of the Accountant in Bankruptcy; and the decision of the sheriff on such an appeal shall be final.

(5) On the expiry of the period within which an appeal may be made under subsection (4) above, the Accountant in Bankruptcy shall pay to the creditors their dividends in accordance with the scheme of division."

(3) In subsection (10) for the words "the audited" there shall be substituted the word "his"."

DEFINITIONS

"Accountant in Bankruptcy": ss.1 and 73(1) of the 1985 Act as amended.
"accounting period": s.73(1) of the 1985 Act and new s.52(2) of the 1985 Act.
"act and warrant": s.73(1) of the 1985 Act.
"appropriate bank or institution": s.73(1) of the 1985 Act.
"commissioner": ss.30(1) and 73(1) of the 1985 Act.
"court": s.73(1) of the 1985 Act.
"debtor": s.73(1) of the 1985 Act.
"permanent trustee": ss.3 and 73(1) of the 1985 Act.
"prescribed": s.73(1) of the 1985 Act.
"the creditors": s.73(4) of the 1985 Act.

GENERAL NOTE

Most of the changes are a consequence of other alterations to the 1985 Act, including the possibility that the Accountant in Bankruptcy may be permanent trustee. There are two exceptions.

Paragraph 30(8) allows the Accountant in Bankruptcy to deposit funds in the name of the Secretary of State. This enables one account to be used, rather than many individual accounts in the name of debtors' estates.

Paragraph 30(10) amends para. 9 of Sched. 2 and removes the provision under which public funds would meet the cost of trustees' fees and outlays, in certain cases commonly referred to as "small assets" cases. This is perhaps the most significant change in the Act. So dramatic is the alteration that the new para. 9 is about a different topic.

Discharge on composition

31.—(1) Schedule 4 (discharge on composition) shall be amended as follows.

(2) In paragraph 2, after the words "permanent trustee" there shall be inserted the words ", where he is not the Accountant in Bankruptcy,".

(3) In paragraph 9—

(a) in sub-paragraph (1), after the words "permanent trustee" there shall be inserted the words ", where he is not the Accountant in Bankruptcy,";

(b) after sub-paragraph (1) there shall be inserted the following sub-paragraph—

"(1A) Where the offer of composition is approved and the permanent trustee is the Accountant in Bankruptcy, the permanent trustee shall prepare accounts of his intromissions with the debtor's estate and he shall make a determination of his fees and outlays calculated in accordance with regulations made under section 69A of this Act.";

(c) after sub-paragraph (2) there shall be inserted the following sub-paragraph—

"(3) Subsections (2), (3), (4), (5) and (10) of section 53 of this Act as adapted by paragraph 9(2) and (3) of Schedule 2 to this Act shall apply, subject to any necessary modifications, in respect of the accounts and determination prepared under sub-paragraph (1A) above as they apply in respect of the accounts and determination prepared under the said section 53 as so adapted."

(4) Paragraph 16 shall be renumbered sub-paragraph (1) of that paragraph and there shall be added at the end the following sub-paragraph—

"(2) The discharge of the debtor by virtue of an order under paragraph 11 above shall not affect any right of a secured creditor—

(a) for a debt in respect of which the debtor has been discharged to enforce his security for payment of the debt and any interest due and payable on the debt until the debt is paid in full; or

(b) for an obligation in respect of which the debtor has been discharged to enforce his security in respect of the obligation."

(5) Paragraph 16 of Schedule 4 to the 1985 Act shall be deemed always to have had effect as amended by this paragraph.

DEFINITIONS

"Accountant in Bankruptcy": ss.1 and 73(1) of the 1985 Act as amended.
"debtor": s.73(1) of the 1985 Act.
"permanent trustee": ss.3 and 73(1) of the 1985 Act.
"secured creditor": s.73(1) of the 1985 Act.
"security": s.73(1) of the 1985 Act.

GENERAL NOTE

There are two main effects of these alterations to Sched. 4: (1) to allow for the possibility that the Accountant in Bankruptcy may be permanent trustee; and (2) to preserve the rights of secured creditors on discharge of the debtor in accordance with the change introduced in other cases by the new s.55 (see notes to para. 23).

Voluntary trust deeds for creditors

32.—(1) Schedule 5 (which makes provisions as to voluntary trust deeds for creditors) shall be amended as follows.

(2) For paragraph 5 (which sets out the conditions for a trust deed becoming a protected trust deed) there shall be substituted the following paragraph—

"5.—(1) Paragraphs 6 and 7 of this Schedule shall apply in respect of a trust deed if—

(a) the trustee is a person who would not be disqualified under section 24(2) of this Act from acting as the permanent trustee if the debtor's estate were being sequestrated;

(b) after the trust deed has been delivered to him, the trustee publishes in the Edinburgh Gazette the notice specified in sub-paragraph (3) below;

(c) not later than one week after the date of publication of such notice, the trustee sends to every creditor known to him—

(i) a copy of the trust deed;

(ii) a copy of the notice; and

(iii) such other information as may be prescribed;

(d) within the period of 5 weeks beginning with the date of publication of such notice, the trustee has not received notification in writing from a majority in number or not less than one third in value of the creditors that they object to the trust deed and do not wish to accede to it; and

(e) immediately after the expiry of the said period of 5 weeks, the trustee sends to the Accountant in Bankruptcy for registration in the register of insolvencies a copy of the trust deed with a certificate endorsed thereon that it is a true copy and that he has not received notification as mentioned in sub-sub-paragraph (d) above.

(2) Any creditor who has been sent a copy of the notice referred to in sub-paragraph (1)(b) above and who has not notified the trustee as mentioned in sub-paragraph (1)(d) above that he objects to the trust deed shall be treated for all purposes as if he had acceded to the trust deed; and any reference in this Act to a creditor who has acceded to a trust deed shall include a reference to a creditor who is treated for all purposes as if he had so acceded.

(3) The notice mentioned in sub-paragraph (1)(b) above shall be in the prescribed form and shall contain such information as may be prescribed.

(4) The Secretary of State may by regulations amend sub-paragraphs (1) to (3) above by replacing them, varying them or adding to or deleting anything from them.

(5) Regulations made under sub-paragraph (4) above may contain such amendments of this Act as appear to the Secretary of State to be necessary in consequence of any amendment made by the regulations to the said sub-paragraphs (1) to (3)."

(3) In paragraph 6, for sub-paragraph (a) there shall be substituted the following sub-paragraph—

"(a) subject to paragraph 7 of this Schedule, a creditor who has—

(i) not been sent a copy of the notice as mentioned in paragraph 5(1)(c) above; or

(ii) notified the trustee of his objection to the trust deed as mentioned in paragraph 5(1)(d) above,

shall have no higher right to recover his debt than a creditor who has acceded to the trust deed;".

(4) In paragraph 7, in sub-paragraph (1)—

(a) for the words "who has not acceded to the trust deed" there shall be substituted the words "who has not been sent a copy of the notice as mentioned in paragraph 5(1)(c) above or who has notified the trustee of his objection to the trust deed as mentioned in paragraph 5(1)(d) above"; and

(b) in sub-sub-paragraph (a), for the words "paragraph 5(b)" there shall be substituted the words "paragraph 5(1)(b)".

(5) In paragraph 10, for the words "who has not acceded to the trust deed" in both places where they occur there shall be substituted the words "who has not been sent a copy of the notice as mentioned in paragraph 5(1)(c) above or who has notified the trustee of his objection to the trust deed as mentioned in paragraph 5(1)(d) above".

(6) In paragraph 11, for the words "who has not acceded to a protected trust deed" there shall be substituted the words "who has not been sent a copy of the notice as mentioned in paragraph 5(1)(c) above or who has notified the trustee of his objection to the trust deed as mentioned in paragraph 5(1)(d) above".

DEFINITIONS

"Accountant in Bankruptcy": ss.1 and 73(1) of the 1985 Act as amended.

"debtor": s.73(1) of the 1985 Act.

"prescribed": s.73(1) of the 1985 Act.

"protected trust deed": s.73(1) of the 1985 Act.

"register of insolvencies": s.73(1) of the 1985 Act and new s.1A(b) of the 1985 Act, as inserted by s.1(1).

"trust deed": s.73(1) of the 1985 Act as amended by Sched. 1, para. 29(6) of this Act and new s.5(4A) of the 1985 Act, inserted by s.3(4).

GENERAL NOTE

One of the major innovations of the 1985 Act was the introduction of the protected trust deed. The trust deed was protected to a large extent against the possibility of diligence by a non-acceding creditor and against the possibility of being superseded by sequestration on the petition of a non-acceding creditor. In fact protected trust deeds were unpopular with the number being registered not reaching double figures in recent years.

The reasons for the unpopularity of protected trust deeds include: (1) the emergence of the device of the "trust deed route" (see General Note to the Act) and the availability of sequestration at the public expense; and (2) the procedure for making a trust deed protected, which involved the accession of a majority in number and not less than two thirds in value of the creditors in a period of four weeks. The Act removes the obvious recourse to the "trust deed route" (see notes to s.3). The revision of Sched. 5 attempts to deal with the procedural obstacles.

The reality is that creditors may appear apathetic to a trust deed, or may not be sufficiently organised to give a decision on accession within a short time period, or, as a matter of policy, some creditors may neither accede to trust deeds nor oppose them. The solution adopted to solve these problems is to place the onus on a creditor to object to a trust deed. The trustee sends a copy of the trust deed and other information to each known creditor. The trust deed becomes protected unless within five weeks the trustee receives written notification from a majority in number *or* not less than one third in value of the creditors that they object to the trust deed and do not wish to accede to it.

Para. 32(2)

This sets out the new para. 5 which states how a trust deed becomes protected. Paragraphs 6 and 7, as amended, narrate the consequences of a deed being protected.

Before delivery of the trust deed, the deed might be revocable by the debtor (McBryde, *Bankruptcy*, p. 242). After delivery, but not within any specified time, the trustee may set in motion the procedure which might lead to the deed becoming protected. The first step is an *Edinburgh Gazette* notice. Periods run from the date of publication of that notice: (1) a one week period to send specified information to known creditors; (2) a five week period for creditors to object; (3) *immediately* after the five week period, the transmission of a certified copy of the trust deed and a certificate of non-notification to the Accountant in Bankruptcy; and (4) a six week period for certain creditors to present a petition for sequestration (new para. 7(1)).

As with most procedures there are traps for the unwary. The period of one week from publication of the *Gazette* notice is short and the documentation to be sent out may need careful checking particularly when there are numerous creditors. The effect of a failure to send part of what is required to one creditor is obscure. The trustee is not required by the Act to certify that he or she has made the correct distribution within the specified time. On the other hand a creditor who is affected by the protected status of the trust deed may wish evidence that the procedure has been in order.

A creditor who wishes to object must (a) make the objection in writing; (b) state two things—an objection to the trust deed and a wish not to accede; and (c) make sure that the objection is actually received by the trustee within the five week period. No reason for objection need be stated and any reason given could be illogical.

A trustee might receive a variety of statements from creditors; some, with the benefit of legal advice, may draft an objection which clearly follows the terms of the Act—others may clearly protest about the deed in lay person's terms—and there will be those who write letters with grumbles about the debtor or secured lenders or government policy or the like. To avoid difficult decisions on whether, for example, discontent with life, and the debtor in particular, equates to objection to the deed and non-accession, it may be easier for the trustee to offer a form for completion by creditors. On the other hand some might view this as encouragement of a response, when silence would result in a protected deed.

A procedure which relies entirely on documents being sent and received is fraught with the problems of non-receipt. The cynic may say that it would have been so much easier to make trust deeds protected if there had to be a meeting of creditors at which the requisite number of creditors would have had to object. The Act does mention the creditor who has not been sent a notice in the amendments to paras. 6, 7, 10 and 11.

The trustee must send the notice to "every creditor known to him". A creditor of whose existence the trustee is unaware would be affected by the protected status of the deed as would a creditor who objected. The uncertain case is of the creditor known to the trustee who, by mistake, is not sent a notice. On an analogy with cases involving the calling of meetings of corporations and clubs, it may be that failure to send notice to one individual can invalidate the proceedings (*Smyth* v. *Darley* (1849) 2 H.L.C. 789; *Portuguese Consolidated Copper Mines Ltd.* [1889] 42 Ch.D. 160; *Young* v. *Ladies Imperial Club Ltd.* [1920] 2 K.B. 523; *Musselwhite* v. *C.H. Musselwhite & Son Ltd.* [1962] Ch. 964; *John* v. *Rees* [1970] Ch. 345 at p. 402 *per* Megarry J.).

The trust deed will become protected unless the trustee receives the required objection from a majority in number and not less than one third in value of the creditors. The phrase "value of the creditors" means "in relation to any matter, the value of their claims as accepted for the purposes of that matter" (s.73(3) of the 1985 Act).

The phrase "the creditors" is defined in s.73(4) of the 1985 Act but by reference to votes at a meeting. For the purposes of para. 5 it appears that any creditor, even a secured creditor or a creditor with a postponed ranking, is a creditor.

Paras. 32 (3) to (6)

Creditors who have not been sent a notice or who have objected have limited rights. These are (1) presentation of a petition for sequestration of the debtor's estate within six weeks of the *Gazette* notice, or at any time on the grounds of unduly prejudicial distribution of the estate; and (2) receipt of a recorded delivery notice about the trustee's discharge with a right to apply to the court on limited grounds to escape the effect of the discharge (paras. 10 to 12 as amended).

Section 11   SCHEDULE 2

REPEALS

Chapter	Short title	Extent of repeal
52 & 53 Vict. c. 39.	The Judicial Factors (Scotland) Act 1889.	In section 2, the words "Without prejudice to section 1(2) of the Bankruptcy (Scotland) Act 1985 (Accountant of Court to be Accountant in Bankruptcy),".
1985 c. 66.	The Bankruptcy (Scotland) Act 1985.	In section 18, in subsection (3), paragraph (a). In section 20, in subsection (2)(b), the word "preliminary". In section 23, subsection (4). In section 25, in subsection (6)(b), the words "in the prescribed form". In section 28, in subsection (2), the words "paragraph (b) of".

Repeals—*cont.*

Chapter	Short title	Extent of repeal
		In section 46, in subsection (1), after paragraph (b) the words "to apprehend".
		In section 52, subsection (6).
		In section 53, in subsection 3(a), the word "shall".
		In section 73, in subsection (1), the definition of "list of interim trustees".
1987 c. 41.	The Criminal Justice (Scotland) Act 1987.	In section 37, in subsection (3), the words "(which provides that nothing in the section is to apply to anything done by the official receiver)".
1988 c. 33.	The Criminal Justice Act 1988.	In section 87, in subsection (3), the words "(which provides that nothing in the section is to apply to anything done by the official receiver)".

INDEX

References in roman type are to sections of this Act: those in italic are to sections of the Bankruptcy (Scotland) Act 1985

CONSOLIDATED FUND (No. 2) ACT 1993

(1993 C. 7)

An Act to apply certain sums out of the Consolidated Fund to the service of the years ending on 31st March 1992 and 1993.   [29th March 1993]

PARLIAMENTARY DEBATES
All discussions were informal with no substantial debates noted in *Hansard*.

INTRODUCTION
This is the second Consolidated Fund Act this year and provides for the provision of £131,142,154.72 from the Treasury for the year ending March 31, 1992 and £2,654,112,000 for the year ending March 31, 1993 to make good the supply granted to the Queen for the service of the appropriate year.

Issue out of the Consolidated Fund for the year ending 31st March 1992

1. The Treasury may issue out of the Consolidated Fund of the United Kingdom and apply towards making good the supply granted to Her Majesty for the service of the year ending on 31st March 1992 the sum of £131,142,154.72.

Issue out of the Consolidated Fund for the year ending 31st March 1993

2. The Treasury may issue out the Consolidated Fund of the United Kingdom and apply towards making good the supply granted to Her Majesty for the service of the year ending on 31st March 1993 the sum of £2,654,112,000.

Short title

3. This Act may be cited as the Consolidated Fund (No. 2) Act 1993.

INDEX

References are to section number

CONSOLIDATED FUND,
  issue out of, 2

SHORT TITLE, 1

JUDICIAL PENSIONS AND RETIREMENT ACT 1993*

(1993 c. 8)

ARRANGEMENT OF SECTIONS

PART I

NEW ARRANGEMENTS FOR JUDICIAL PENSIONS

Application of Part I

---

* Annotations by John Mesher, Barrister, Professor Associate, Department of Law, University of Sheffield.

27. Completion of proceedings after retirement.

An Act to make further provision with respect to the pensions and other benefits payable in respect of service in certain judicial, and related, offices and in certain senior public investigative offices; to amend the law relating to the date on which the holders of certain judicial, and related, offices are required to vacate those offices; and for purposes connected therewith.   **[29th March 1993]**

PARLIAMENTARY DEBATES
    Hansard, H.L. Vol. 538, cols. 118, 137, 664, 723; Vol. 539, cols. 1020, 1039, 1097, 1216; Vol. 540, cols. 330, 370; Vol. 543, col. 1612; H.C. Vol. 215, col. 425; Vol. 219, col. 78.
    The Bill was discussed in Standing Committee D between January 19 and 21, 1993.

INTRODUCTION AND GENERAL NOTE
    The Act deals with two separate, but related matters. The first is to provide for a unified pension scheme for new appointees to judicial office. The second is to provide for a lower normal retirement age of 70 for new appointees to judicial office. The link between the two matters is that under the new judicial pension scheme an officer must have 20 years' service in order to receive a full pension on retirement, as opposed to the 15 years under the schemes currently applicable to judges of the High Court and above and to circuit judges and others of comparable status in England and Wales. If a newly appointed judicial officer has to retire at 70, a full pension cannot be earned if the appointment is made after the age of 50. By the same token, a person appointed at the age of 50 will have to continue in service until the age of 70, instead of being able to retire on a full pension at the age of 65. A sustained attack on the principles of the new judicial pension scheme was mounted in the House of Lords. Some concessions and improvements were made, but the basic structure remained unchanged.
    In February 1990, during the Committee stage of the then Courts and Legal Services Bill, the Lord Chancellor announced that he would carry out a radical examination of judicial pension

arrangements. Proposals were published in a consultation paper in December 1990. The Bill introduced in the House of Lords follows that consultation process. The broad principles adopted were described as follows:

"It is in the interest of us all in a free society that our judges should be men and women of the highest calibre, able and willing to carry out the heavy public duties which we expect of them. It is right, therefore, that the pension Parliament provides to our judges should be sufficiently substantial to attract, or at least not deter, those candidates best fitted to serve. At the same time, as a member of the Government, I am mindful that judicial pensions are paid from the public purse" (Lord Chancellor, *Hansard*, H.L. Vol. 538, col. 119).

The cost of the overall pensions package was estimated to be about the same under the old and the new schemes—around 28 per cent. of pay (*Hansard*, H.C. Vol. 219, col. 79).

The general scheme of the Act was succinctly set out by the Parliamentary Secretary to the Lord Chancellor's Department at the end of the Third Reading debate in the House of Commons.

"The occasion for the Bill was the change in the tax treatment of pension schemes introduced by the Finance Acts of 1987 and 1989. That legislation provided the means by which the Revenue applied common standards to all modern occupational pension schemes. Those standards were not applied to the judicial pension schemes[, h]owever, pending a thorough-going review of those schemes and consultation with the judiciary on the design of improved arrangements. The Bill is the product of that review and consultation. Its provisions apply the same standards to judicial pension arrangements as the Revenue applies to all public service and private sector occupational pension schemes. It brings judicial pension arrangements into line with modern tax law.

The Government have also taken this opportunity to make a number of other significant changes to the judicial pension arrangements. In place of a plethora of judicial pension schemes with different accrual periods, contribution rates and benefit levels, they have created a unified scheme embracing all salaried judicial officers in the United Kingdom. As well as being inherently fairer than the existing position, this will remove the barriers which the current arrangements place in the way of judges moving between the different levels of the judiciary on promotion. Following representations, the Bill was amended by the Government in several important respects in the other place further to improve the level of benefits it provides. The judicial pension arrangements provided by the Bill now constitute an attractive package which compares favourably with other public service and private sector occupational pension schemes.

The Bill also makes provision, following consultation, for setting a new general retirement age of 70 for all judicial officers first appointed after the Bill comes into force. That uniform arrangement will replace the present variety of retirement ages. The choice of the age of 70 instead of another age has not been without its critics. The right retirement age for the judiciary is clearly a matter of judgment. It is the Government's view, however, that 70 is the appropriate age; it takes account both of the need for experience and maturity of judgment and the fact that the burdens of office can be onerous.

I think that it is right at this stage of the Bill to say a quick word about commencement. If the Bill is given a Third Reading, completes its final stage in the other place and goes on to receive Royal Assent, there will still be a considerable amount of work to be done in the form of regulations—many of an actuarial nature—before it can be fully implemented. It is my noble and learned Friend the Lord Chancellor's present intention that both the pensions and retirement provisions of the Bill be commenced simultaneously. However, in view of the work I have just mentioned, it is unlikely that the Bill can be brought into force much before the end of 1993" (Mr J. M. Taylor, *Hansard*, H.C. Vol. 219, cols. 94–5). By the end of October 1993 no regulations had been published and the estimate was that the Act would not be brought into force until April 1994.

The new judicial pension scheme

Section 1 and Sched. 1 define which judicial officers are covered by the new arrangements.

Sections 2 and 3 define the entitlement to a pension on retirement and s.4 provides for the payment of a lump sum on retirement.

Sections 5 to 8 provide for pensions for the surviving spouse and for children on the death of a judicial officer.

Section 9 provides for judicial officers to make contributions towards such pensions.

Section 10 enables judicial officers to make additional voluntary contributions to the scheme.

Section 11 prohibits membership of more than one judicial pension scheme and s.12 allows the transfer of existing pension rights from judicial office into the new scheme.

Section 13 allows a judicial officer to be a member of a personal pension scheme instead of the judicial pension scheme.

Sections 14 and 15 deal with holders of particular offices and ss.16 to 18 deal with technical matters.

Section 19 provides for the payment of extra benefits to judicial officers whose earnings have exceeded the amount of the earnings cap under s.590C(1) of the Income and Corporation Taxes Act 1988.

Section 20 provides for appeals where a person is aggrieved by decisions under the scheme.

Section 21 deals with judicial officers paid by local authorities in England and Wales.

Section 22 provides for pensions payable under the Act to be increased in line with price inflation under the Pensions (Increase) Act 1971.

Section 23 and Sched. 2 provide for transfers in and out of the scheme.

Section 24 and Sched. 3 make a number of minor amendments.

Section 25 and Sched. 4 make provisions relating to the pensions of certain senior investigative officers.

Retirement dates

Section 26, together with Scheds. 6 and 7, introduces the new standard retirement age of 70 and s.27 allows the completion of current proceedings after the retirement date.

Miscellaneous

Sections 28 and 29 deal with supplementary matters. Section 30 is the interpretation section. Section 31 provides for commencement of the Act by Ministerial order and, together with Sched. 8, makes minor and consequential amendments.

PART I

NEW ARRANGEMENTS FOR JUDICIAL PENSIONS

Application of Part I

Persons to whom this Part applies

1.—(1) This Part applies—

(a) to any person who first holds qualifying judicial office on or after the appointed day;

(b) to any person—

(i) who, immediately before the appointed day, was holding any qualifying judicial office, service in which was, in his case, subject to a judicial pension scheme; and

(ii) who, on or after that day, ceases to hold that office and is appointed to some other qualifying judicial office, service in which would (apart from this Act) have been subject, in his case, to some other judicial pension scheme;

(c) to any person who was not holding qualifying judicial office immediately before the appointed day, by virtue of having retired from such office, but who, on or after that day, is again appointed to such office; and

(d) to any person who makes an election under subsection (2) below for this Part to apply to him;

but this subsection is subject to the following provisions of this Act.

(2) Any person—

(a) who holds qualifying judicial office on the appointed day, and

(b) who held such office at any time before that day,

shall be entitled, in such circumstances as may be prescribed and subject to subsection (5) below, to make an election for this Part to apply to him, if it would not otherwise do so.

(3) Any election under subsection (2) above must be made within such time and in such manner as may be prescribed and shall be irrevocable.

(4) The circumstances that may be prescribed under subsection (2) above, and the time that may be prescribed under subsection (3) above, include

circumstances or times which permit the making of an election notwithstanding that the person in question has retired from qualifying judicial office or has died; and, without prejudice to section 29(3) and (4) below, where any such circumstances or times are so prescribed—

    (a) the person in question shall be treated for such purposes as may be prescribed as if he had, at such times as may be prescribed, been a person to whom this Part applies; and

    (b) any right to make an election notwithstanding the person's death shall be exercisable by his personal representatives.

(5) Except as provided by section 13 below, this Part does not apply to a person at any time when an election under that section is in force in respect of him; nor shall he make an election under subsection (2) above at any such time.

(6) For the purposes of this Act, a person shall be regarded as holding, or serving in, qualifying judicial office at any time when he holds, on a salaried basis, any one or more of the offices specified in Schedule 1 to this Act; and any reference in this Act to a "qualifying judicial office" is a reference to any office so specified if it is held on a salaried basis.

(7) For the purposes of subsection (6) above, a person holds an office "on a salaried basis" if and so long as, and to the extent that—

    (a) his service in the office is remunerated by payment of a salary; and

    (b) that salary is not subject to terms which preclude rights to pensions and other benefits accruing by reference to it;

and the reference in that subsection to an office being held on a salaried basis shall be construed accordingly.

(8) The appropriate Minister may by order amend either Part of Schedule 1 to this Act by adding offices to those for the time being there specified.

(9) In this section, "prescribed" means prescribed in regulations made by the appropriate Minister.

(10) In this Part "the appointed day" means the day appointed under section 31 below for the coming into force of this Part other than subsection (8) above.

DEFINITIONS
    "the appropriate Minister": s.30(1).
    "judicial pension scheme": s.30(1).
    "qualifying judicial office": subs. (6).
    "serve": s.30(1).

GENERAL NOTE

Subs. (1)
    The general rule is that the new judicial pension scheme only applies to those who first hold qualifying judicial office (*i.e.* one of the offices specified in Sched. 1 which is held on a salaried basis (subs. (6))) on or after the day on which the Act is brought into force (para. (a)). Subsection (1)(b), (c) and (d) apply Part I of the Act to certain of those who held qualifying judicial office before that date. In those cases, s.12 requires any entitlements under the previous judicial pension scheme to be transferred to the new scheme.
    Under subs. (1)(b), any judicial officer who transfers from one qualifying judicial office to another office which would have been subject to a different judicial pension scheme comes under the new scheme. The prime example will be where a judge is promoted. There are a number of different schemes applying to different categories of judicial officer and the problems of moving from one to another were said to constitute a barrier to promotion. For instance, the Lord Chancellor (*Hansard*, H.L. Vol. 538, col. 119) mentioned the case of a circuit judge promoted to the High Court, who could then take a pension based on the High Court judge's salary, but only by reference to the service in the High Court. If he or she wished to aggregate the service in both offices, the pension would be based on the salary of a circuit judge at the date of retirement. Once the new scheme comes into operation, on such a promotion, membership of the new scheme will be required, with aggregation of past service under s.12. Whether the requirement to give up a 15-year accrual scheme for a 20-year accrual

scheme will deter judges from accepting promotion can only be assessed once the regulations under s.12 are made.

The terms of subs. (1)(b)(ii) are intended to ensure that it does not apply when a judicial officer takes on a second and concurrent office (*Hansard*, H.L. Vol. 539, col. 1020). It also does not apply where the transfer is between offices which both fell within the same existing judicial pension scheme.

Subsection (1)(c) deals with the unusual case of a person who had retired from qualifying judicial office and is appointed to a qualifying judicial office after the Act comes into force. Such persons come under the new scheme.

Subsection (1)(d) allows judicial officers who continue in a qualifying office on the day on which the Act comes into force to elect to join the new scheme. The conditions are set out in subss. (2)–(5). The critics of the new scheme suggested that no one with entitlements under the existing judicial pension schemes would wish to make such an election, but officers in the less generous schemes might well wish to transfer.

Subss. (2)–(5)

Subsection (2) defines those who are entitled to elect to join the new scheme, although otherwise they would fall outside subs. (1)(a). The election must by virtue of subs. (3) be made within the time prescribed in regulations. Draft regulations were circulated before the Report stage in the House of Lords, which would permit an election to be made at any time after the coming into force of the Act up to the end of three months, subsequently extended to six months, from the date of retirement, providing that a pension had not come into payment (*Hansard*, H.L. Vol. 539, cols. 1022 and 1024). Subsection (4) allows regulations to permit an election to be made by the personal representatives of a deceased judicial officer. In general, a person who has elected to join a personal pension scheme under s.13 cannot make an election under subs. (2). There is provision in s.13 for allowing such a person back into the judicial pension scheme.

Subss. (6)–(8)

Qualifying judicial offices are listed in Sched. 1. Offices may be added to the list by Ministerial order (subs. (8)). Only those who hold or serve in qualifying judicial office "on a salaried basis" fall within the new scheme. The phrase is defined in subs. (7). The intention is to differentiate salaried officers from those who are paid on the basis of a daily or weekly fee, but subs. (7)(b) allows the terms of a salaried appointment to exclude entitlement to pension benefits.

Pensions for judicial officers

The judicial officer's entitlement to a pension

2.—(1) Any person to whom this Part applies—
  (a) who retires from qualifying judicial office on or after the day on which he attains the age of 65, and
  (b) who has, at the time of that retirement, completed, in the aggregate, at least 5 years' service in qualifying judicial office,
shall be entitled during his life to a pension at the appropriate annual rate.
  (2) Any person to whom this Part applies—
  (a) who retires from qualifying judicial office on or after the day on which he attains the age of 60, but before attaining the age of 65, and
  (b) who has, at the time of that retirement, completed, in the aggregate, at least 5 years' service in qualifying judicial office,
shall be entitled during his life to a pension at the appropriate annual rate, actuarially reduced.
  (3) In any case where—
  (a) a person to whom this Part applies retires from qualifying judicial office before he has attained the age of 65 or before he has completed, in the aggregate, at least 5 years' service in such office, and
  (b) the appropriate Minister is satisfied by means of a medical certificate that, by reason of infirmity of mind or body, the person is incapable of discharging the duties of his qualifying judicial office and that the incapacity is likely to be permanent,
the person shall be entitled during his life to a pension at the appropriate annual rate (and subsection (2) above shall not have effect in relation to that

retirement, notwithstanding that the conditions in paragraphs (a) and (b) of that subsection may be satisfied in the particular case).

(4) Where a person to whom this Part applies is removed from a qualifying judicial office, his removal from that office shall be treated for the purposes of this Part as his retirement from qualifying judicial office; and if—

(a) he has not attained the age of 60 at the date of that retirement, and

(b) the appropriate Minister recommends that his accrued rights under this Part should be given immediate effect,

the person shall be entitled during his life to a pension at the appropriate annual rate, actuarially reduced.

(5) Where a person to whom a pension under this section has commenced to be paid resumes service in qualifying judicial office—

(a) the resumption of service shall not affect his entitlement to payment of the pension for any period before the resumption,

(b) he shall not be entitled to payment of the pension for any period during the resumed service, and

(c) at the end of the period of resumed service—

(i) his entitlement (and that of any other person) to a pension or other benefit under this Part, and

(ii) the rate or amount of any such pension or other benefit,

shall be determined (subject to section 4(4) below) as if no pension under this section had previously commenced to be paid to him.

(6) A pension under this section shall be payable at such intervals, not exceeding three months, as the Treasury may determine.

(7) For the purposes of this Part—

(a) in determining the length of a person's period of service in any qualifying judicial office, it is immaterial whether he works full-time or part-time, but if he holds two or more qualifying judicial offices concurrently, no day shall be counted more than once;

(b) in determining the length of a person's period of service in any qualifying judicial office, there shall be left out of account—

(i) any service in such office before the day on which this Part first applied to him (except to the extent to which it is given effect under or by virtue of section 12 below);

(ii) in the case of an office which becomes a qualifying judicial office by virtue of an order under section 1(8) above, any service in that office before the day on which it becomes such an office (except to the extent to which it is given effect under or by virtue of section 12 below);

(iii) any service in qualifying judicial office at a time when an election under section 13 below is in force in respect of him; and

(iv) any service in such office in respect of which he has taken a cash equivalent in accordance with paragraph 6 of Schedule 2 to this Act;

(c) in any case falling within subsection (3) above where, at the date of the retirement, the person has not attained the age of 65, the aggregate length of his period of service shall be increased by the addition of a period equal in length to one half of that which—

(i) begins immediately after the date of the retirement; and

(ii) ends with the day on which he would attain the age of 65;

(d) where any payment in respect of a pension under this section has become due, the pension shall be treated as commencing to be paid, notwithstanding that no payment has in fact been made in respect of it, and for this purpose a payment in respect of a pension shall be treated as becoming due on the first day of the period for which it is payable;

(e) "actuarially reduced", in relation to the rate of a pension, means reduced by such amount as may be prescribed in, or determined in accordance with, regulations made under this section by the appropriate Minister with the concurrence of the Treasury;

(f) where a person ceases to hold qualifying judicial office in consequence of infirmity of mind or body, the cessation (however brought about) shall be taken for the purposes of this Part to constitute retirement, not removal, from such office.

(8) In this Act "judicial pension" means a pension under this section.

DEFINITIONS
"appropriate annual rate": ss.3 and 30(1).
"the appropriate Minister": s.30(1).
"qualifying judicial office": ss.1(6) and 30(1).
"service": ss.1(6) and 30(1).

GENERAL NOTE
Section 2 sets out the circumstances in which a pension is payable to a judicial officer on retirement in various circumstances. Section 3 defines how the pension is calculated.

Subs. (1)
The primary circumstance for entitlement is retirement at or after the age of 65 with at least five years' qualifying service (for which see subs. (7)). If a judicial officer leaves either with less than five years' service or is below the age of 60 (see subs. (2)) it appears that the only entitlement is to transfer the cash equivalent of accrued rights to some arrangement specified in para. 6 of Sched. 2. The "appropriate rate" of pension under s.3 is half of pensionable pay for someone who has completed at least 20 years' service and one-fortieth of pensionable pay for each year of service for someone who has completed less than 20 years.

Subs. (2)
If the retirement is in the same circumstances as in subs. (1) except that the judicial officer is aged less than 65, but at least 60, the appropriate rate of pension is payable immediately, subject to an actuarial reduction (see subs. (7)(e)).

Subs. (3)
Subsection (3) applies to retirement under the age of 65 or with less than five years' service when the judicial officer is, by reason of infirmity of mind or body, incapable of discharging the duties of his office, and that incapacity is likely to be permanent. An immediate pension is then payable at the appropriate rate, but calculated, in the case of someone retiring below the age of 65, on the basis of the actual period of service plus half the period from the date of retirement until the age of 65. That provision did not appear in the original Bill, which would have restricted the rate of pension to that calculated on actual service to the date of retirement. There was particularly strong pressure in the House of Lords against that restricted rule, especially comparing it to the provisions for High Court judges under the existing judicial pension schemes and to examples from other jurisdictions. Following discussions about the scope for improvements in the new scheme and practice in existing public service schemes, the enhancement was made (*Hansard*, H.L. Vol. 540, col. 381).

If the judicial officer ceases to hold office in consequence of infirmity of mind or body, that cessation is to be treated as retirement, not removal from office (subs. (7)(f)). This avoids the problems exposed in *Young* v. *Associated Newspapers* (1971) 11 K.I.R. 413 and *Dorrell* v. *May & Baker* (unreported, May 11, 1990) and *Harris* v. *Lord Shuttleworth* [1992] O.P.L.R. 151 where rules were strictly in terms of "retirement".

Subs. (4)
Where a judicial officer is removed from office, as the Lord Chancellor is often under the officer's terms of service entitled to do for misbehaviour or incapacity, an immediate pension can be paid at the appropriate rate, actuarially reduced. But the entitlement only arises if the Lord Chancellor or the Secretary of State for Scotland makes a recommendation to that effect.

Subs. (5)
If a judicial officer has retired and begun to receive a pension under the new scheme, but then resumes service in a qualifying judicial office, the entitlement to pension ceases. On retirement from the resumed office the entitlement to pension will be determined afresh on the aggregate period of qualifying service. The effect of s.4(4) is that if the judicial officer received a lump sum

on the first retirement that amount must be set off against any entitlement to a lump sum on the second retirement.

The appropriate annual rate

3.—(1) In the case of a person who has, at the time of his retirement from qualifying judicial office, completed, in the aggregate, at least 20 years' service in such office, the "appropriate annual rate" for the purposes of this Act is an annual rate equal to one-half of his pensionable pay.

(2) In the case of a person not falling within subsection (1) above, the "appropriate annual rate" for the purposes of this Act is an amount equal to one-fortieth of his pensionable pay, multiplied by the aggregate length of his service in qualifying judicial office (expressed in years and fractions of a year).

(3) For the purposes of this Act—

(a) a person's "pensionable pay" is the greater of the following amounts, that is to say—

(i) the pension-capped salary payable to him in respect of his service in qualifying judicial office in the period of twelve months ending with the day on which, within the meaning of section 590C (1) of the Income and Corporation Taxes Act 1988 (earnings cap), his participation in the scheme constituted by this Part ceases; and

(ii) the greatest amount of pension-capped salary payable to him in respect of such service in any other period of twelve consecutive months falling within the period of three years ending with that day;

(b) a person's "pension-capped salary" for any period of twelve months is so much of his aggregate salary in respect of service in qualifying judicial office in that period as, within the meaning of section 590C(1) of the Income and Corporation Taxes Act 1988 (earnings cap), does not exceed the permitted maximum for the year of assessment in which his participation in the scheme constituted by this Part ceases;

(c) a person's salary in respect of service in any qualifying judicial office shall be taken to accrue due from day to day, at the rate for the time being in force, throughout the period for which he holds the office;

(d) if, in consequence of periods of ill-health, the rate at which a person's salary in respect of service in any qualifying judicial office is payable to him for any period falling within the three years mentioned in paragraph (a)(ii) above is less than it would have been apart from the periods of ill-health, he shall be treated as if that salary had been payable to him throughout that period at the rate at which it would have been payable, apart from the periods of ill-health;

(e) in determining a person's salary in respect of his service in qualifying judicial office, there shall be left out of account any part of the salary which is paid on terms which preclude rights to pensions and other benefits accruing by reference to it;

but paragraphs (a) and (b) above are subject to regulations under subsections (4) and (5) below.

(4) Regulations may make provision for any case where a person to whom this Part applies serves in qualifying judicial office neither—

(a) throughout the whole of the period of twelve months mentioned in subsection (3)(a)(i) above; nor

(b) throughout any other such period of twelve consecutive months as is mentioned in subsection (3)(a)(ii) above;

and any such regulations may, in particular, provide for such a person's pensionable pay and pension-capped salary to be determined for the purposes of this Act as if he had served in his qualifying judicial office (whether full-time or part-time) throughout the whole of the period of twelve months mentioned in paragraph (a) above and had been paid in respect of that service a salary of an amount determined by reference to the annual rate of salary payable in his case in respect of service in that office in that period.

(5) Regulations may also make provision for any case where the service in qualifying judicial office of a person to whom this Part applies is, or has at some time been, only part-time, within the meaning of the regulations; and any such regulations may, in particular, provide for the amount of salary by reference to which his pension-capped salary (and accordingly his pensionable pay) would fall to be determined, apart from this subsection, to be reduced, for the purpose of making any such determination, in accordance with the regulations.

(6) In this section, "regulations" means regulations made by the appropriate Minister with the concurrence of the Treasury.

DEFINITIONS
"qualifying judicial office": ss. 1(6) and 30(1).

GENERAL NOTE
Section 3 is perhaps the most contentious part of the Act, containing the fundamental provisions on the calculation of entitlement to pension.

Subss. (1) and (2)
The effect of subss. (1) and (2) is that the rate of pension to which a person within the new scheme is entitled under s.2 is one-fortieth of pensionable pay for each year of service up to a maximum of twenty years. The maximum pension is thus half of pensionable pay. There will also be entitlement to a lump sum under s.4. The combination of the two is considered to be the equivalent of a pension of two-thirds of final salary, the normal maximum allowed under the Income and Corporation Taxes Act 1988. Once a pension is payable it is to be increased annually in line with price inflation under the Pensions (Increase) Act 1971, s.22.

See subs. (3) for the meaning of "pensionable pay".

The standard 20-year accrual for a full pension replaces a variety of periods under different judicial pension schemes. The existing schemes for High Court judges and above, for circuit judges and for industrial tribunal chairmen provide a pension of half pay after 15 years' service. The existing schemes for district judges, for stipendiary magistrates and for Scottish sheriffs (the equivalent of English circuit judges) have 20-year accruals, while the schemes for some other judicial officers have longer periods. One argument for the change was to secure simplification and to remove impediments to promotions between offices in different schemes. But the fundamental reason was said to be to bring the scheme into line with the standards applied generally to occupational pension schemes in the public and private sectors, on the basis of general fairness. Under the Finance Act 1987, 20 years is the minimum accrual period in which a tax-approved scheme can provide maximum benefits so that the new scheme is the most tax-efficient that could be secured on the basis of the general law. The judicial pension scheme has the added advantage, not available under the general law to schemes with such accrual rates, that "retained benefits", benefits deriving from earlier employment or self-employment, do not have to be added to the benefits of the scheme in restricting those benefits to the Revenue limits.

The fundamental argument against a 20-year accrual period was that, since promotion for judges tends to be the exception rather than the rule, the need to serve out 20 years rather than 15 for a full pension might lead to judges "soldiering on" for that purpose when their enthusiasm and critical edge had waned. That might lead to a diminution in the quality of justice, and might even lead to an increase in the average age of the judiciary if judges served until very near the maximum age, rather than retiring soon after the minimum pension age was reached. Because most barristers would not have made provision for their pensions while in practice they would need to serve in judicial office long enough to earn the full pension. It was also argued that the combination of a lowering of the retiring age to 70 and the change to a 20-year pension scheme would mean that judges would have to be appointed between the ages of 40 and 45. Most candidates would at that age be too young for the necessary qualities of experience and sound judgment to have developed, while the legal profession would be deprived of some senior practitioners at the height of their powers.

A fierce argument along these lines, although with much elaboration and drawing of unfavourable comparisons with overseas systems, was pressed, particularly in the House of Lords, by present and retired judges. However, the Government was not persuaded. A theme which recurs in the debates on other elements of the scheme in which improvements were urged is the Lord Chancellor's insistence on the importance of members of the judicial pension scheme being able to keep the full value of their retained benefits plus the full benefits of the judicial pension scheme and the counter-argument that before the age of 50 or so successful barristers have such high expenditure on mortgages, school fees, etc. that they cannot be expected to make any provision for their pensions in retirement and so would not have any retained benefits. It is difficult to envisage much public sympathy for this last point, although the other arguments pressed by the opponents of the new scheme raised matters of high principle.

Subs. (3)
The annual pension payable in any particular circumstance is the appropriate fraction of "pensionable pay". Under para. (a) the basic meaning of "pensionable pay" is the judicial officer's salary in the last 12 months of service or the highest amount paid in any continuous period of 12 months within the last three years of service. In the existing judicial pension schemes, the pension is based on the annual rate of salary payable at the date of retirement. The change was argued by opponents to be to the disadvantage of those who could otherwise have retired just after a pay rise, which in the public sector often lagged behind the increases in the cost of living for which the pay rise was to compensate. However, the evidence was that under the existing scheme there was no bunching of the dates of retirement around dates of pay rises. The Government would not concede the common provision in public and private sector schemes to base a pension on the best 12 months salary (or an average over three years) in the last ten years of service, increased in line with price inflation to the date of the end of service.
Under para. (b) only "pension-capped salary" comes into the definition of "pensionable salary" in para. (a). That is salary up to the permitted maximum ("the cap") prescribed for the tax year during which service ends. The amount of the cap for the tax year 1993–94 was £75,000. Section 590C(5) and (6) of the Income and Corporation Taxes Act 1988 supplies a formula for increasing the cap in line with price inflation. There was no increase in 1993–94 over 1992–93. Although the main part of the judicial pension scheme is thus limited, s.19 allows for separate payments, calculated in the same way, for salary which is greater than the cap.
Under para. (d) a person is assumed to have received full salary if that salary has in fact been reduced during a period of ill-health. The standard conditions of service allow absence for sickness on full pay for six months, followed by half pay for another six months.

Subs. (4)
Where service ends after less than a year, regulations may provide for the actual pay to be scaled up to an annual figure.

Subs. (5)
Regulations may make provision for part-time service.

Derivative benefits

Lump sum on the judicial officer's retirement or death

4.—(1) Where a judicial pension commences to be paid to a person, there shall also be paid to him a lump sum of an amount equal to two and one-quarter times the annual rate of the pension.
(2) Where a judicial pension commences to be paid to a person, but he dies so soon thereafter that the aggregate of—
(a) the sums paid or payable to him on account of that pension, including any increases under the Pensions (Increase) Act 1971, and
(b) the lump sum paid or payable to him under subsection (1) above,
falls short of an amount equal to five times the annual rate in force in respect of that pension immediately before his death, including any increases under the Pensions (Increase) Act 1971, his personal representatives shall be granted a lump sum equal to the deficiency.
(3) Where a person to whom this Part applies dies while holding qualifying judicial office, a lump sum of an amount equal to twice the amount of his pensionable pay shall be payable—
(a) to the person (if any) nominated by him for the purposes of this subsection by notice in writing to the administrators of the scheme constituted by this Part; or
(b) in default of any such nomination, to his personal representatives;

and, in determining a person's pensionable pay for the purposes of this subsection, his death shall be treated as his retirement from qualifying judicial office.

(4) A person to whom a lump sum is paid under subsection (1) above but who resumes service in qualifying judicial office shall not be required to refund the lump sum; but if the whole or any part of it is not refunded, an amount equal to so much of it as has not been refunded shall be deducted from any lump sum which subsequently becomes payable to or in respect of him under subsection (1), (2) or (3) above.

DEFINITIONS
"judicial pension": s.30(1).
"pensionable pay": ss.3(3) and 30(1).
"qualifying judicial office": ss.1(6) and 30(1).

GENERAL NOTE

Subs. (1)
Where a judicial officer is entitled to a pension on retirement there is also entitlement to a lump sum of two and one-quarter times the annual rate of pension. Such a lump sum is not subject to income tax. In the existing judicial pension schemes, the lump sum is twice the annual pension, *i.e.* a maximum of one year's salary at the rate payable at the end of service. There was pressure for the lump sum to be increased to three times the annual pension, as is common in other public service schemes. The reply was that the lower multiple was appropriate because retained benefits in the form of a tax-free lump sum could be enjoyed in a scheme with a rapid accrual of entitlement (Lord Chancellor, *Hansard*, H.L. Vol. 539, col. 1101).

See subs. (4) for the position where a person resumes qualifying judicial office after retiring and taking a lump sum. The lump sum is not repayable, but is set off against any further entitlement under this section.

Subs. (2)
Where a judicial officer dies after retirement, an additional lump sum is payable to the personal representatives if the pension paid plus the lump sum under subs. (1) amounts to less than five times the annual pension (taking into account increases for inflation under the Pensions (Increase) Act 1971). The additional lump sum makes up the difference. The provision constitutes a considerable improvement on the present situation.

Subs. (3)
Where a judicial officer dies in service, a lump sum of twice pensionable pay (see s.3(3)) is payable to the person nominated by the judicial officer or, if no nomination has been made, to the personal representatives. Once again, the justification for the lower amount than in some other schemes is the availability of retained benefits (Lord Chancellor, *Hansard*, H.L. Vol. 539, col. 1104).

Surviving spouse's pension

5.—(1) In any case where—

(a) a person ("the deceased") to whom this Part applies dies leaving a surviving spouse, and

(b) their marriage took place before the deceased retired from qualifying judicial office,

the surviving spouse shall be entitled to a pension for life (a "surviving spouse's pension") in respect of the deceased's service in such office, at an annual rate equal to one-half of the annual rate of the deceased's judicial pension.

(2) A pension under this section shall be payable at such intervals, not exceeding three months, as the Treasury may determine.

(3) If the surviving spouse re-marries, the Treasury may, on or at any time after the re-marriage, direct that the pension shall cease to be payable.

(4) Where a direction has been given under subsection (3) above, the Treasury may at any time direct that payment of the pension is to be resumed.

(5) Where the deceased dies while holding qualifying judicial office, his death shall be treated for the purposes of subsection (1)(b) above as his retirement from such office.

(6) For the purposes of this section, "the annual rate of the deceased's judicial pension" means—

(a) where a judicial pension under subsection (1) or (3) of section 2 above had commenced to be paid to the deceased, the appropriate annual rate of that pension;

(b) where a judicial pension under subsection (2) or (4) of that section had commenced to be paid to the deceased, the appropriate annual rate of that pension, as actuarially reduced under that section;

(c) where no judicial pension had commenced to be paid to the deceased, the rate that would have been the appropriate annual rate of his judicial pension under subsection (3) of that section—

(i) had he not died, but retired from qualifying judicial office on the date of death; and

(ii) had the appropriate Minister been satisfied in his case as mentioned in paragraph (b) of that subsection.

DEFINITIONS
    "judicial pension": s.30(1).
    "qualifying judicial office": ss.1(6) and 30(1).

GENERAL NOTE

Subs. (1)
    Where a judicial officer dies after retirement and was receiving a pension, any surviving spouse is normally entitled to a pension of half the rate of pension payable to the judicial officer (subs. (6)(a) and (b)), unless their marriage took place after the judicial officer's retirement. The justification of the exception is that because of the high levels of pay involved, provision for post-retirement marriage would be relatively expensive (*Hansard*, H.L. Vol. 539, col. 1224). Once in payment the pension is increased in line with price inflation under the Pensions (Increase) Act 1971.
    Where the judicial officer dies in service or before starting to receive a pension there is also a pension for the surviving spouse, but in this case the rate is half of what would have been paid to the judicial officer if he or she had taken ill-health retirement under s.2(3) (subs. (6)(c)). This is to compensate for the low entitlements accrued in the early years of service. Otherwise, if the judicial officer died early in the appointment, the surviving spouse's pension would be small.
    Although the lump sum on death in service may, under s.4(3)(a), go to anyone, the surviving spouse's pension is restricted to a legally married spouse.

Subss. (3) and (4)
    If the surviving spouse re-marries, the pension does not cease automatically, but the Treasury may direct that payment shall cease, subject to the possibility of resumption under subs. (4). A similar provision was introduced into the existing judicial pension schemes by s.80 of the Courts and Legal Services Act 1990, in place of an absolute prohibition on the payment of pensions to surviving spouses who re-marry. There is no guidance in the legislation as to how the Treasury might exercise its discretion.
    Any children's pension payable under s.6 does not cease on the surviving spouse's re-marriage.

Grant and payment of a children's pension

6.—(1) Upon the death of a person to whom this Part applies ("the deceased") a pension in respect of his service in qualifying judicial office shall be granted for the benefit of such persons as may from time to time be the eligible children of the deceased (a "children's pension").

(2) The persons who, for the purposes of this Part, are the "eligible children" of the deceased at any time are—

(a) any natural children of the deceased,

(b) any step-children of the deceased,

(c) any children adopted by the deceased before his retirement from qualifying judicial office, and

(d) any children adopted by the deceased after his retirement from qualifying judicial office and in respect of whom a direction is given under subsection (5) below,

who are for the time being in their period of childhood and full-time education.

(3) Only one children's pension shall be granted in respect of the service of any one person, but—

(a) the rate of the pension shall vary in accordance with section 8 below, according to the number of his eligible children for the time being;

(b) the pension shall be paid to such person or persons as the Treasury may from time to time direct, and different parts of the pension may be directed to be paid to different persons; and

(c) the person to whom all or any part of the pension is paid shall apply the sum paid to him, without distinction, for the benefit of all the persons who are for the time being eligible children of the deceased or, as the case may be, for the benefit of such of them as the Treasury may from time to time direct.

(4) A children's pension—

(a) shall be paid so long as and whenever there are eligible children of the deceased; and

(b) shall be payable at such intervals, not exceeding three months, as the Treasury may determine.

(5) The Treasury may direct that a person ("the child") who was adopted by the deceased is to be regarded as falling within paragraph (d) of subsection (2) above if they are satisfied—

(a) that the deceased had, before his retirement from qualifying judicial office, formed the intention of adopting the child; and

(b) that, immediately before that retirement, the child was wholly or mainly dependent on the deceased.

(6) Where the deceased died while holding qualifying judicial office, his death shall be treated for the purposes of subsection (2)(c) above as his retirement from such office.

(7) In this section, "step-children of the deceased" means—

(a) any natural children of any person to whom the deceased was at any time married who, at the time of the marriage, either had been born or were in gestation;

(b) any children adopted by such a person before the marriage to the deceased; and

(c) any children adopted by such a person after the marriage to the deceased in a case where the adoption proceedings were pending at the time of the marriage.

(8) For the purposes of this section the "natural children" of any person are any children of whom that person is the genetic father or mother.

<small>DEFINITIONS</small>
"qualifying judicial office": ss.1(6) and 30(1).

<small>GENERAL NOTE</small>

Subs. (1)
On the death of a judicial officer either in service or after retirement a pension is payable so long as there is at least one "eligible child" of the deceased. Sections 6 and 7 determine who counts as an eligible child. Section 8 deals with the rate of the pension.

Subs. (2)
Any natural or step-child can be an eligible child, as can any child adopted before the judicial officer's retirement. A child adopted after the judicial officer's retirement can only qualify if there is a direction under subs. (5).
Children are only eligible during childhood and full-time education, as defined by s.7.

Subs. (3)
Paragraph (a) allows the rate of the pension to vary according to how many eligible children there are and paras. (b) and (c) allow payments to be made either to the children or to someone else for their benefit.

Subs. (5)
The Treasury may, if satisfied that a deceased judicial officer had before his or her death formed the intention of adopting a child who was wholly or mainly dependent on the judicial officer, direct that the child counts for the purposes of subs. (2)(d).

Subss. (7) and (8)
Step-children and natural children are defined.

Children's pension: meaning of "period of childhood and full-time education"

7.—(1) For the purposes of section 6 above, a person is in his "period of childhood and full-time education" at any time if, and only if, at that time—
(a) he has not attained the age of 16;
(b) he is receiving full-time instruction at any university, college, school or other educational establishment; or
(c) he is undergoing training by any person ("the employer") for any trade, profession or vocation in such circumstances that—
   (i) he is required to devote the whole of his time to the training for a period of not less than two years; and
   (ii) while he is undergoing the training, the emoluments receivable by him, or payable by the employer in respect of him, do not exceed the maximum allowable remuneration, disregarding for this purpose any emoluments receivable or payable by way of return of any premium paid in respect of the training.

(2) A person shall not be regarded for the purposes of this section as coming within paragraph (b) or (c) of subsection (1) above at any time unless he has come within one or other of those paragraphs at all times since he attained the age of 16.

(3) Where there is a period during which a person comes within neither paragraph (b) nor paragraph (c) of subsection (1) above, then, if the Treasury think fit and are satisfied that the person's full-time education ought not to be regarded as completed, they may direct either—
(a) that that period shall be disregarded for the purposes of subsection (2) above; or
(b) that the person shall be regarded for the purposes of this section as having come within paragraph (b) or (c) of subsection (1) above throughout that period.

(4) For the purposes of this section—
"emoluments" means any salary, fees, wages, perquisites or profits or gains whatsoever, and includes the value of free board, lodging or clothing;
"the maximum allowable remuneration" at any time is an annual rate (£1,614 a year, at the passing of this Act) equal to that at which a pension of £250 a year—
   (a) first awarded under the principal civil service pension scheme on 1st June 1972, and
   (b) increased from time to time by the amount of increase that would be applied under the Pensions (Increase) Act 1971 to such a pension,
would (as so increased) be payable at that time.

(5) Where a premium has been paid in respect of the training of a person, all emoluments at any time receivable by him, or payable by the employer in respect of him, shall be taken for the purposes of subsection (1)(c)(ii) above to be receivable or payable by way of return of the premium, unless and to

the extent that the amount of those emoluments exceeds in the aggregate the amount of the premium.

GENERAL NOTE

A person is in their period of childhood and full-time education while under 16, while (regardless of age) receiving full-time education at some educational establishment or while undergoing training by an employer at very low pay. In general, if there is a gap in the satisfaction of one of those conditions the person can no longer meet the definition (subs. (2)). However, if the Treasury is satisfied that the person's full-time education ought not to be regarded as completed it has the discretion to direct that subs. (2) does not apply or that a period is to be treated as one of education or training (subs. (3)).

Rate of children's pension

8.—(1) Where the deceased leaves no surviving spouse, the annual rate of a children's pension shall be—
  (a) while the eligible children of the deceased are two or more in number, two-thirds of the annual rate of the deceased's judicial pension; and
  (b) while there is only one eligible child of the deceased, one-third of the annual rate of the deceased's judicial pension.

(2) Where the deceased leaves a surviving spouse, the annual rate of a children's pension during the life of the surviving spouse shall be—
  (a) while the eligible children of the deceased are two or more in number, one-half of the annual rate of the deceased's judicial pension; and
  (b) while there is only one eligible child of the deceased, one-quarter of the annual rate of the deceased's judicial pension;
and the annual rate of the children's pension after the death of the surviving spouse shall be the rate specified in paragraph (a) or, as the case may be, paragraph (b) of subsection (1) above.

(3) Where the deceased leaves a surviving spouse who remarries, the Treasury may, if they think fit, direct that subsection (1) above shall apply instead of subsection (2) above as respects any period when the surviving spouse has a spouse.

(4) "The annual rate of the deceased's judicial pension" has the same meaning for the purposes of this section as it has for the purposes of section 5 above.

DEFINITIONS

"children's pension": ss.6 and 30(1).
"the deceased": ss.6 and 30(1).
"judicial pension": s.30(1).

GENERAL NOTE

Subs. (1)

If the deceased judicial officer leaves no surviving spouse at the date of death, the total children's pension is one third of the rate of pension then payable to the deceased or, if he or she died in service, the pension that would have been paid on ill-health retirement, for each eligible child up to two in number.

Subs. (2)

If the deceased judicial officer leaves a surviving spouse, the rates are initially one-quarter for each eligible child up to two in number.
If the surviving spouse then dies, the rate is calculated as in subs. (1).

Subs. (3)

If the surviving spouse remarries, the Treasury may direct that the rate of the children's pension should be calculated under subs. (1) rather than subs. (2). Presumably, this will normally be done when the surviving spouse's pension ceases under s.5(3).

Contribution towards cost of surviving spouse's and children's pension

9.—(1) Such contributions as may be prescribed by regulations made for the purposes of this section shall be made towards the cost of the liability for any pension or pensions under sections 5 to 8 above in respect of a person's service in qualifying judicial office.

(2) No contribution shall be made by a person for any period of service during which an election under section 13 below is in force in respect of him.

(3) The prescribed contributions shall be in the form of deductions from the salary payable in respect of the service.

(4) In the case of persons to whom this Part applies by virtue of section 1(1)(b), (c) or (d) above, the prescribed contributions may (notwithstanding subsection (3) above) be in the form of either—
  (a) deductions from the salary payable in respect of the service, or
  (b) a reduction of any lump sum payable under section 4 above in respect of the service,
or partly in one of those forms and partly in the other.

(5) The power to make regulations under this section shall be exercisable by the appropriate Minister with the concurrence of the Treasury.

DEFINITIONS
  "service": s.30(1).

GENERAL NOTE
  Regulations may require judicial officers to pay contributions towards pensions for surviving spouses and children. The amount suggested was 3 per cent. (Lord Chancellor, *Hansard*, H.L. Vol. 539, col. 1236). Under the existing 15-year judicial pension schemes the rate is 4 per cent. for married judicial officers and the obligation to contribute ceases after 15 years' payments. It may, therefore, be expected that regulations under this section will not require contributions by deductions from salary for more than 20 years.

  For those appointed to qualifying judicial office for the first time after the Act comes into force, contributions can only be made by deduction from salary (subs. (2)). For the others to whom the Act applies, contribution can be made by a reduction of the tax-free lump sum.

  It appears to be consistent with the scheme of the Act that a judicial officer cannot decline to take part in the scheme and to pay contributions accordingly except where an election for a personal pension is made under s.13.

Additional voluntary contributions

Additional benefits from voluntary contributions

10.—(1) Regulations may make provision—
  (a) entitling any person to whom this Part applies to make voluntary contributions towards the cost of the provision of additional benefits, whether under the scheme constituted by this Part or otherwise; or
  (b) imposing conditions with respect to the exercise by any such person of any entitlement (whether or not under paragraph (a) above) which he may have to make any such voluntary contributions.

(2) Regulations may make provision for the purpose of imposing, in a case where a person to whom this Part applies makes voluntary contributions, upper limits with respect to—
  (a) the aggregate value of the aggregable benefits which may be paid to or in respect of any such person; and
  (b) the amount which any such person may pay by way of such contributions;
and, without prejudice to the generality of paragraph (b) above, any such regulations may, in particular, impose such an upper limit on the amount which a person may pay by way of voluntary contributions as will, so far as reasonably practicable, secure that the aggregate value referred to in paragraph (a) above will not exceed the limit prescribed under that paragraph.

(3) Regulations may—
  (a) prescribe the manner in which aggregable benefits are to be valued for the purpose of any such aggregation as is mentioned in subsection (2) above;

(b) confer on the administrators of the scheme constituted by this Part power to require a person to whom this Part applies who is making, or who wishes to make, voluntary contributions to provide such information as they may require concerning any retained benefits of his;

(c) permit the disclosure by those administrators of any information which they may obtain concerning any such retained benefits—

(i) to, or to any officers of, the Commissioners of Inland Revenue; or

(ii) to, or to any servants or agents of, any authorised provider who is, or may be, concerned in the investment of the voluntary contributions or the provision of the additional benefits in question.

(4) Regulations—

(a) may not prohibit the payment of voluntary contributions;

(b) may not impose any limit on the amount which a person may pay by way of voluntary contributions, other than either or both of the following, that is to say—

(i) such upper limit as may be imposed by virtue of subsection (2)(b) above; or

(ii) an upper limit corresponding to that for the time being fixed by or under section 594 of the Income and Corporation Taxes Act 1988 (exempt statutory schemes);

(c) must secure that any voluntary contributions paid by a person are used to provide additional benefits for or in respect of him; and

(d) must secure that the value of such additional benefits is reasonable, having regard to—

(i) the amount paid by way of voluntary contributions;

(ii) the value of the other benefits provided under the scheme constituted by this Part; and

(iii) the general value of benefits available to a person under any contract of life insurance entered into by him with an insurance company to which Part II of the Insurance Companies Act 1982 (regulation of insurance companies carrying on insurance business within the United Kingdom) applies;

but paragraphs (c) and (d) above have effect only in relation to a voluntary contributions scheme constituted by or under this Part.

(5) Regulations may, in particular—

(a) provide that the value of additional benefits offered on payment of voluntary contributions shall be determined in accordance with prescribed rules based on tables prepared for the purposes of the regulations by the Government Actuary;

(b) prescribe the manner in which it is to be determined in any case whether the amount of a person's contributions exceeds any such limit as is mentioned in subsection (4)(b) above;

(c) provide for any administrative expenses incurred by any person by virtue of this section to be defrayed out of sums received by way of voluntary contributions;

(d) provide for the manner in which voluntary contributions are to be made;

(e) make provision for, and in connection with, the valuation of a person's accrued rights—

(i) under any occupational or personal pension scheme, which are to be transferred into a voluntary contributions scheme, or

(ii) under any voluntary contributions scheme, which on termination of his membership of that scheme may fall to be transferred into another scheme;

(f) prescribe the additional benefits which are to be available under a voluntary contributions scheme and the rates and times at which those benefits are to be payable;

(g) make provision for and in connection with the making of elections between different benefits available under voluntary contributions schemes;

(h) provide for the terms on which a person may terminate his membership of a voluntary contributions scheme;

(j) provide for the terms on which surplus funds may be refunded to a person who has made payments by way of voluntary contributions to a voluntary contributions scheme;

(k) specify any authorised providers—

    (i) who are to invest any prescribed voluntary contributions, or

    (ii) who are to provide any prescribed additional benefits,

and, if two or more authorised providers are so specified, may make provision entitling any person who makes prescribed payments by way of voluntary contributions to elect between those authorised providers.

(6) Regulations may provide for such additional benefits arising under or by virtue of this section as may be prescribed—

(a) to be charged on, and paid out of, the Consolidated Fund; or

(b) to be paid out of money provided by Parliament.

(7) The power to make regulations under this section shall be exercisable by the appropriate Minister with the concurrence of the Treasury.

(8) In this section—

"aggregable benefits" means—

    (a) any pensions or other benefits under this Part, other than such additional benefits as are mentioned in subsection (1) above;

    (b) such additional benefits so mentioned as may be prescribed; and

    (c) such retained benefits as may be prescribed;

"authorised provider", in relation to the investment of any sums paid by way of voluntary contributions or the provision of any benefit, means a person who is authorised under Chapter III of Part I of the Financial Services Act 1986 to invest those sums or, as the case may be, to provide that benefit;

"employment" has the same meaning as it has in the Social Security Pensions Act 1975 (and accordingly includes employment as a self-employed earner, within the meaning of that Act);

"occupational pension scheme" has the meaning given by section 66(1) of the Social Security Pensions Act 1975 or, in relation to Northern Ireland, Article 2(2) of the Social Security Pensions (Northern Ireland) Order 1975;

"personal pension scheme" has the meaning given by section 84(1) of the Social Security Act 1986 or, in relation to Northern Ireland, Article 2(2) of the Social Security (Northern Ireland) Order 1986;

"prescribed" means specified in, or determined in accordance with, regulations;

"regulations" means regulations under this section;

"relevant benefits" has the meaning given by section 612(1) of the Income and Corporation Taxes Act 1988;

"retained benefits", in the case of any person, means any rights retained by him to relevant benefits under any occupational or personal pension scheme which has, or which may be expected to qualify for, tax-exemption or tax-approval, being rights which accrued during some previous employment;

"surplus funds", in relation to a person and any voluntary contributions scheme, means any funds which are, or have been, held for the purposes of that voluntary contributions scheme and which fall to be returned to him in consequence of any such limit as is mentioned in subsection (4)(b) above;

"tax-exemption" and "tax-approval" have the meaning given by section 84(1) of the Social Security Act 1986;

"voluntary contributions scheme" means any occupational pension scheme if and to the extent that it is a scheme under which such additional benefits as are mentioned in subsection (1) above are, or are to be, provided;

and, where a person's voluntary contributions are made by deduction from salary, any reference to payment of, or by way of, voluntary contributions shall be taken to include a reference to the making of voluntary contributions by deduction or, as the case may require, to any voluntary contributions so made.

(9) Without prejudice to section 29(6) below, regulations under this section may make different provision for different classes or descriptions of voluntary contributions scheme.

(10) Without prejudice to subsections (5)(c) and (d) and (6) above, there may be paid out of money provided by Parliament—

(a) any sums required for or in connection with the operation or administration of any prescribed voluntary contributions scheme; or

(b) any administrative expenses incurred under or by virtue of this section by a Minister of the Crown or government department.

(11) Any sums received under this section may be paid into the Consolidated Fund.

GENERAL NOTE

This section allows regulations to provide for judicial officers to make contributions to an additional voluntary contribution scheme, to a free-standing additional voluntary contribution scheme or to buy added years.

In introducing the amendments, the Lord Chancellor said:

"I am now in a position, with the Revenue's agreement, to allow judicial officers to make additional voluntary contributions to increase their own benefits provided that they do so within the limits which apply to all other tax-approved occupational pension schemes. That means that any retained benefits from other personal or occupational pension schemes of which a scheme member has been a member, will have to be declared and taken into account for the purposes of assessing the scope for each individual to make additional voluntary contributions. Such contributions will attract tax relief at the highest rate" (*Hansard*, H.L. Vol. 540, col. 419).

Relationship with other pension schemes

Provision against pensions under two or more judicial pension schemes

11.—(1) Where this Part applies, or would, apart from section 13 below, apply, to a person—

(a) no other judicial pension scheme, apart from—

(i) any scheme established by regulations under section 10 above which may fall to be regarded as a judicial pension scheme, and

(ii) the scheme constituted by section 19 below,

shall have effect in relation to him; and

(b) no pension or lump sum under any such scheme shall be paid to or in respect of him.

(2) Subsection (1) above is without prejudice to a person's accrued rights to benefit under any such scheme in respect of service before the relevant day; and, in the case of a person to whom this Part applies, any such rights which he may have shall accordingly be given effect in accordance with section 12 below.

(3) Subsections (1) and (2) above shall not—

(a) preclude the payment of a pension or other benefits under—

(i) the principal civil service pension scheme, or

(ii) the principal civil service pension scheme for the civil service of Northern Ireland,

in respect of service before the relevant day, or

(b) affect any rights to a pension or other benefits under either of those schemes in respect of such service,

unless at least some of that service was in qualifying judicial office.

(4) In this section, the "relevant day", in the case of any person, means the day on which this Part first applies, or would, apart from section 13(8)(a) below, first apply, to him.

DEFINITIONS

"judicial pension scheme": s.30(1).
"the principal civil service pension scheme": s.30(1).
"the principal civil service pension scheme for the civil service of Northern Ireland": s.30(1).
"qualifying judicial office": ss.1(6) and 30(1).

GENERAL NOTE

A person who comes within s.1(1) cannot be a member of any other judicial pension scheme than that constituted by the Act, leaving aside the additional voluntary contribution scheme under s.10 and the scheme for salary over the cap set out in s.19. Therefore, when a judicial officer who was a member of an existing judicial pension scheme comes under the new scheme by virtue of s.1(1)(b), (c) or (d), the accrued rights must be transferred in accordance with s.12.

Transfer of rights of persons holding qualifying judicial office before commencement

12.—(1) Where this Part begins to apply to a person by virtue of paragraph (b), (c) or (d) of section 1(1) above—

(a) any relevant rights of his shall be transferred to the scheme constituted by this Part; and

(b) entitlement to, and the rate or amount of, any judicial pension or derivative benefit payable under this Part to or in respect of him shall accordingly be determined by reference to—

(i) the rights so transferred; and

(ii) his service in qualifying judicial office on or after the relevant day.

(2) Regulations may make provision—

(a) for calculating, whether by actuarial assessment or otherwise, the amount or value of the rights transferred under subsection (1) above, and

(b) prescribing the manner in which those rights are to be given effect under this Part,

and, without prejudice to the generality of paragraph (b) above, regulations under that paragraph may provide for those rights to be so given effect by crediting the person in question with such service on or after the relevant day as may be prescribed.

(3) For the purposes of this section—

(a) a person's "relevant rights" are his accrued rights to benefit under any judicial pension scheme constituted otherwise than by or under this Act; but

(b) rights under—

(i) the principal civil service pension scheme, or

(ii) the principal civil service pension scheme for the civil service of Northern Ireland,

shall not be regarded as relevant rights for the purposes of this section unless at least some of the person's service which was subject to the scheme in question was service in qualifying judicial office and, in that event, all his rights under that scheme shall be regarded as relevant rights.

(4) In this section—

"prescribe" means prescribe in regulations;

"regulations" means regulations made by the appropriate Minister with the concurrence of the Treasury;

"the relevant day", in relation to any person, means the day on which this Part first applies to him.

DEFINITIONS
"the appropriate Minister": s.30(1).
"derivative benefit": s.30(1).
"judicial pension": s.30(1).
"qualifying judicial office": ss.1(6) and 30(1).

GENERAL NOTE
Where a person comes into the new judicial pension scheme by virtue of s.1(1)(b), (c) or (d), the accrued rights under the previous judicial pension scheme must be transferred into the new scheme. Regulations will provide for the valuation of those accrued rights and their treatment in the new scheme.

Election for personal pension instead of judicial pension

13.—(1) A person to whom this Part applies, or to whom it would apply apart from this section, may be a member of a personal pension scheme while holding qualifying judicial office if, and only if, he serves on the appropriate Minister a written notice of election, which shall—
    (a) identify the personal pension scheme in question; and
    (b) be expressed to take effect on a date not less than three months after service of the notice;
and, in accordance with section 1(5) above, where a person makes an election under this section, he shall not be regarded as a person to whom this Part applies at any time when the election is in force.
    (2) An election made by a person under this section—
    (a) shall be irrevocable, except as provided by the following provisions of this section; and
    (b) shall not affect any rights of his which accrued under this Part before the election comes into force;
and, in accordance with section 2(7)(b)(iii) above, any service of his in qualifying judicial office while the election is in force shall be left out of account in determining the length of his service in such office for the purposes of this Part.
    (3) Where an election under this section is in force and the person who made it continues to hold qualifying judicial office, he may make a written application to the appropriate Minister requesting that he should once again become a person to whom this Part applies.
    (4) If, on an application under subsection (3) above, the appropriate Minister is satisfied that the applicant is in good health, he may direct that this Part shall once again apply to the applicant with effect from a date (his "date of re-admission") not less than three months after service of the application.
    (5) A person's election under this section shall cease to be in force on his date of re-admission.
    (6) An applicant under subsection (3) above shall—
    (a) provide such evidence relating to his health, and
    (b) submit to any such medical examination,
as may be reasonably required by the appropriate Minister.
    (7) The appropriate Minister shall give written notice of his decision on an application under subsection (3) above to the applicant not later than three months after service of the application.
    (8) Where an election (whenever made) under any of the corresponding provisions is in force in respect of a person on the relevant day—

(a) the election shall have effect for the purposes of this Part, and shall continue in force, as if made under this section; and

(b) if and so long as the election remains in force, the person shall be precluded from making an election under section 1(2) above;

but if, on an application under subsection (3) above in relation to the election, the appropriate Minister directs that this Part shall apply to that person, the election shall, in accordance with subsection (5) above, cease to be in force for the purposes of this Part (as well as for those of the Act or instrument containing the corresponding provision), paragraphs (a) and (b) above shall cease to have effect in relation to it, and the application shall have effect as the applicant's election under section 1(2) above.

(9) In this section—

"the corresponding provisions" means—

(a) section 14A(3) of the 1981 Act;

(b) section 116A(3) of the County Courts Act (Northern Ireland) 1959;

(c) section 2A(3) of the Resident Magistrates' Pensions Act (Northern Ireland) 1960;

(d) section 2A(3) of the Lands Tribunal and Compensation Act (Northern Ireland) 1964;

(e) section 2A(1) of the Superannuation (Miscellaneous Provisions) Act (Northern Ireland) 1969;

(f) paragraph 7A(3) of Schedule 10 to the Social Security (Northern Ireland) Act 1975;

and, in the case of any other judicial pension scheme, any provision of that scheme which confers a right to elect for a pension under a personal pension scheme;

"personal pension scheme" means a scheme in respect of which there is in force a current appropriate scheme certificate issued by the Occupational Pensions Board in accordance with section 2 of the Social Security Act 1986 or, in the case of qualifying judicial office held in Northern Ireland, in accordance with Article 4 of the Social Security (Northern Ireland) Order 1986;

"the relevant day", in the case of any person, means the day on which this Part first applies, or would, apart from any election under this section or the corresponding provisions, first apply to him.

DEFINITIONS

"the appropriate Minister": s.30(1).

"qualifying judicial office": ss.1(6) and 30(1).

GENERAL NOTE

A judicial officer who would otherwise come under the new judicial pension scheme may elect to join a personal pension scheme instead. In that situation any service while such an election is in force does not count towards length of service for the purposes of the judicial scheme. Since under subs. (2)(b) the election is not to affect any accrued rights, it appears that a judicial officer may either leave any accrued rights (which it seems will be based on salary before the date on which participation in the scheme ceases (s.3(3)(a))) in the scheme or take a cash equivalent under Sched. 2.

In order to make the election, the personal pension scheme of which the judicial officer wishes to become a member must be identified. But it does not seem to be necessary that the judicial officer should actually become a member of the personal pension scheme or continue to pay contributions if once he has become a member. Of course, if no contributions are paid, no tax relief is given and no rights are earned.

The election is expressed to be irrevocable (subs. (2)(a)), but the appropriate Minister may re-admit a person if satisfied that the applicant is in good health (subss. (3) to (7)). There is then power to accept the cash equivalent of rights accrued under the personal pension scheme into the new judicial pension scheme (Sched. 2, Pt. II).

Supplemental provisions

Application of this Part to holders of the office of Lord Chancellor

14.—(1) Not more than one pension shall be paid under section 2 above and the Lord Chancellor's Pension Act 1832 to a person to whom this Part applies who has also held the office of Lord Chancellor.

(2) In determining the appropriate annual rate of a pension payable under section 2 above to such a person as is mentioned in subsection (1) above who either—

(a) was holding the office of Lord Chancellor immediately before the appointed day, or

(b) first held that office on or after that day,

the length of his service in qualifying judicial office shall be treated as increased by the aggregate length of his periods of service in the office of Lord Chancellor (excluding any day of service in that office which is also a day of service in qualifying judicial office).

(3) Where a pension under the Lord Chancellor's Pension Act 1832 is, or would, but for his death, have been, paid to such a person as is mentioned in subsection (1) above (so that no derivative benefits are payable to or in respect of him under this Act) Part II of the 1981 Act shall continue to have effect with respect to the derivative benefits, within the meaning of that Part, which are payable to or in respect of him by virtue of his service in the office of Lord Chancellor, and shall do so notwithstanding anything in section 11 or 12 above.

(4) Except as provided by subsection (3) above, no pension or other benefit shall be paid under that Part of that Act to or in respect of a person to whom this Part applies.

DEFINITIONS
"derivative benefit": s.30(1).
"qualifying judicial office": ss.1(6) and 30(1).

Circuit judges: the Recorder of London and the Common Serjeant

15. Subject to sections 1(8) above and 21 below and to any regulations under section 38 or 39A of the Superannuation Act 1965 (employment in more than one public office), nothing in this Part shall apply in relation to the pensions and other benefits payable to or in respect of a person in respect of his service as a Circuit judge by virtue of holding the office of Recorder of London or Common Serjeant; and accordingly—

(a) those matters shall continue to be provided for as mentioned in section 7 of the City of London (Courts) Act 1964 (remuneration, pensions and other benefits in respect of those offices to be defrayed by the Common Council); and

(b) service as a Circuit judge by virtue of holding either of those offices shall not be regarded as service in qualifying judicial office.

DEFINITIONS
"qualifying judicial office": ss.1(6) and 30(1).

Disregard of abatement of pension under s.65 of the Social Security Act 1973 etc.

16. In making any calculation for the purposes of sections 4 to 8 above, any abatement of a pension falling to be made under any order made under—

(a) section 65 of the Social Security Act 1973 (modification etc. of public service pension schemes), or

(b) Article 61 of the Social Security Pensions (Northern Ireland) Order 1975 (corresponding provision for Northern Ireland),

shall be left out of account.

Effect of certain nullity decrees

17. Where a marriage which is voidable, but not void from the beginning, is declared null by any court, the same results shall follow under this Part as would have followed if the marriage had not been voidable but had been dissolved at the date of the declaration of nullity.

Continuity of tax treatment

18.—(1) For the purposes of Chapter I of Part XIV of the Income and Corporation Taxes Act 1988 (retirement benefit schemes) the provisions of this Part shall be regarded as amendments, for such persons as are mentioned in section 1(1) above, of the statutory schemes constituted by or under the 1981 Act; and, accordingly, any scheme constituted by this Part—

(a) shall be taken to have been established before 14th March 1989; and

(b) is a relevant statutory scheme for the purposes of that Chapter.

(2) Expressions used in this section and in Chapter I of Part XIV of the Income and Corporation Taxes Act 1988 have the same meaning in this section as they have in that Chapter.

<small>DEFINITIONS</small>
"the 1981 Act": s.30(1).
"relevant statutory scheme": Income and Corporation Taxes Act 1988, s.611A.

PART II

MISCELLANEOUS, GENERAL AND SUPPLEMENTARY PROVISIONS

Additional benefits in respect of disregarded earnings

Benefits in respect of earnings in excess of pension-capped salary

19.—(1) This section applies in any case where—

(a) a pension or lump sum is payable under Part I above to or in respect of a person to whom that Part applies (the "judicial officer"); and

(b) the amount which constitutes the judicial officer's pensionable pay is less than it would have been, had pension-capped salary fallen to be determined under section 3(3)(b) above, in his case, without the limit imposed by reference to the permitted maximum there mentioned;

but nothing in this subsection applies in relation to any additional benefits provided under section 10 above.

(2) Where this section applies, payments by way of pension or lump sum shall be made to or in respect of the judicial officer amounting to the difference between—

(a) the rate or amount payable in respect of the pension or lump sum referred to in subsection (1) above; and

(b) the rate or amount that would have been payable in respect of that pension or lump sum, had pension-capped salary fallen to be determined under section 3(3)(b) above, in his case, without the limit imposed by reference to the permitted maximum there mentioned.

(3) No contributions shall be payable under or by virtue of section 9 above in respect of the cost of the liability to make payments under this section.

(4) For the purposes of Chapter I of Part XIV of the Income and Corporation Taxes Act 1988 (retirement benefit schemes) this section shall be taken to constitute a statutory scheme, within the meaning of that Chapter,—

(a) which is separate and distinct from any such scheme constituted by Part I above (or by any other enactment or instrument); and

(b) which is not capable of being a relevant statutory scheme, within the meaning of that Chapter.

(5) The appropriate Minister may by regulations make provision for implementing this section; and any such regulations may, in particular, make provision—

(a) for or with respect to the calculation of benefits under this section;
(b) for or with respect to the time at which and method by which payments under this section are to be made.

DEFINITIONS
"the appropriate Minister": s.30(1).
"pensionable pay": ss.3(3) and 30(1).
"pension-capped salary": ss.3(3) and 30(1).

GENERAL NOTE
Benefits under the main judicial pensions scheme are limited by the "cap" in s.3(3) on the salary to be taken into account. Section 19 provides for a separate non-contributory scheme to pay benefits to make up the difference as if there had been no cap.

General provisions connected with the new schemes

Appeals

20.—(1) If any person to whom this section applies is aggrieved by any decision taken by the administrators of a relevant pension scheme concerning—

(a) the interpretation of the rules of the scheme, or
(b) the exercise of any discretion under the scheme,

he shall have a right of appeal to the appropriate Minister against that decision.

(2) On deciding an appeal under this section, the appropriate Minister may give to the administrators such directions as he considers necessary or expedient for implementing his decision.

(3) The persons to whom this section applies are the following—

(a) any person to whom Part I above applies or has applied;
(b) the widow or widower, or any surviving dependant, of a person who served in qualifying judicial office but who has died; and
(c) where the decision relates to the question—

    (i) whether a person who claims to be such a person as is mentioned in paragraph (a) or (b) above is such a person, or

    (ii) whether a person who claims to be entitled to become a person to whom Part I above applies is so entitled,

the person so claiming.

(4) Regulations may make provision as to the manner in which, and time within which, appeals under this section are to be brought.

(5) The administrators shall be entitled to appear and be heard on any appeal under this section.

(6) In this section—

"regulations" means regulations made by the appropriate Minister;

"relevant pension scheme" means any scheme constituted under or by virtue of Part I or section 19 above for the payment of pensions or other benefits;

"rules", in relation to a relevant pension scheme, means the provisions of Part I and section 19 above and of any regulations or orders made under or by virtue of that Part or that section.

DEFINITIONS
"the administrators": s.30(1).
"the appropriate Minister": s.30(1).
"qualifying judicial office": ss.1(6) and 30(1).

GENERAL NOTE
There is to be an appeal to the appropriate Minister for any person aggrieved by an

interpretation of the rules of the new judicial pension scheme or the exercise of any discretion under the scheme.

Pensions payable to judicial officers etc. by local authorities in England and Wales

21.—(1) This section applies in any case where—

(a) an order under section 1(8) above amends Schedule 1 to this Act by the addition of any office ("the office") to those for the time being specified in that Schedule; and

(b) immediately before the coming into force of the order, a local authority was under a liability to defray, whether in whole or in part, pensions or other benefits payable in respect of service in the office.

(2) Where this section applies, the appropriate Minister may by order made with the consent of the Treasury—

(a) provide for the local authority to be discharged, to such extent as may be prescribed, from the liability to pay pensions or other benefits in respect of such service in the office as may be prescribed; and

(b) require the local authority instead to make prescribed payments to the Treasury.

(3) In framing the provisions of an order under subsection (2) above, regard shall be had to the desirability of securing so far as reasonably practicable—

(a) that the payments required to be made by the local authority are such as to reimburse the Treasury in respect of so much of—

    (i) any pension or lump sum payable under Part I above, or

    (ii) any sums payable by way of pension or lump sum under section 19 above,

to or in respect of any person to whom Part I above applies as may reasonably be regarded as attributable to his service in the office; and

(b) that the local authority is discharged, to a corresponding extent, from the liability to pay any pension or other benefit to or in respect of such a person in respect of his service in the office.

(4) In this section—

"local authority" means any county council, district council, London Borough Council or the Common Council of the City of London;

"prescribed" means specified in, or determined in accordance with, an order under subsection (2) above.

(5) Nothing in this section applies in relation to any pension or other benefits payable under or by virtue of section 10 above.

(6) This section is without prejudice to the generality of section 29 below.

DEFINITIONS
"the appropriate Minister": s.30(1).

Application of the Pensions (Increase) Act 1971

22.—(1) In the Pensions (Increase) Act 1971, in Schedule 2 (which specifies the pensions and other benefits which fall to be increased under or by virtue of that Act) after paragraph 4 (and beneath the heading relating to the administration of justice) there shall be inserted—

"4A. A pension payable under Part I or section 19 of the Judicial Pensions and Retirement Act 1993, other than a pension payable under or by virtue of section 10 of that Act."

(2) The pensions in relation to which the Pensions (Increase) Act 1971 extends to Northern Ireland shall include pensions payable under Part I or section 19 above, other than pensions payable under or by virtue of section 10 above; and, accordingly, in section 19(2)(a) of that Act, after the words "Pension Fund" there shall be inserted the words "or payable under Part I or

section 19 of the Judicial Pensions and Retirement Act 1993 (otherwise than under or by virtue of section 10 of that Act)".

(3) In subsection (2) above, "pensions" has the same meaning as it has in the Pensions (Increase) Act 1971.

GENERAL NOTE
  Pensions payable under the present Act, apart from those payable from an additional voluntary contribution scheme under s.10, are included in the requirement of the Pensions (Increase) Act 1971 to be increased in line with price inflation, once they come into payment.

Transfer of accrued benefits

23. Schedule 2 to this Act shall have effect with respect to the transfer of accrued rights into and out of the pension schemes constituted by Part I or section 19 above (other than any such transfer which falls to be made under section 12 above).

GENERAL NOTE
  See the notes to Sched. 2.

Corresponding minor amendments to other enactments

24. Schedule 3 to this Act (which makes certain minor amendments corresponding to provisions of this Act) shall have effect.

Pensions for senior public investigative officers

The Comptroller and Auditor General and the Parliamentary and Health Service Commissioners etc.

25. The amendments made by Schedule 4 to this Act shall have effect, as from the coming into force of this section, with respect to the pensions and other benefits payable to or in respect of a person (whenever appointed) who holds, or has held, any one or more of the following offices, that is to say—
  (a) Comptroller and Auditor General;
  (b) Parliamentary Commissioner for Administration;
  (c) Health Service Commissioner for England;
  (d) Health Service Commissioner for Scotland;
  (e) Health Service Commissioner for Wales;
  (f) Comptroller and Auditor General for Northern Ireland;
  (g) Northern Ireland Parliamentary Commissioner for Administration;
  (h) Northern Ireland Commissioner for Complaints.

Retirement date for certain judicial officers etc.

Retirement date for holders of certain judicial offices etc.

26.—(1) Subject to the following provisions of this section, a person holding any of the offices for the time being specified in Schedule 5 to this Act (a "relevant office") shall vacate that office on the day on which he attains the age of 70 or such lower age as may for the time being be specified for the purpose in the enactments and instruments relating to that office, whenever passed or made.

(2) Any reference in this section to a person's holding an office includes a reference to his being a member of, or otherwise included in, any panel or list of persons appointed, nominated, approved or otherwise selected to serve from time to time in that office (whether or not the panel or list is required by or under any enactment); and any reference in this section or Schedule 5 to this Act to any particular office or to an office of any class or description, or to a person's appointment to, or vacation of, an office, shall be construed accordingly.

(3) Subject to the transitional provision referred to in subsection (11) below, subsection (1) above applies whether the person was appointed to the office before or after the coming into force of this section; but nothing in this Act, or in any amendment made by it, shall be taken—
- (a) to preclude a person from vacating his office before the compulsory retirement date for that office in his case; or
- (b) to prevent a person's appointment to an office coming to an end before that date, in accordance with the terms on which he was appointed.

(4) Subsections (5) and (6) below apply in relation to any holder (whenever appointed) of a relevant office for which the compulsory retirement date in his case falls on or after the day on which he attains the age of 70, except—
- (a) Lord of Appeal in Ordinary;
- (b) judge of the Supreme Court of England and Wales;
- (c) Lord President of the Court of Session, Lord Justice Clerk or other judge of the Court of Session;
- (d) Lord Chief Justice of Northern Ireland or Lord Justice of Appeal, or judge of the High Court, in Northern Ireland.

(5) If, in a case where this subsection applies, the appropriate Minister considers it desirable in the public interest that the holder of a relevant office should continue in that office after his compulsory retirement date, he may authorise the person to continue in office, either generally or for such purpose as he may notify to the person, for a period not exceeding one year and not extending beyond the day on which the person attains the age of 75.

(6) If, on the expiration of the period for which a person is authorised to continue in office—
- (a) by virtue of subsection (5) above, or
- (b) by any previous exercise of the power conferred by this subsection,

the appropriate Minister considers it desirable in the public interest to retain the person in office for a further period, he may authorise him to continue in office, either generally or for such purpose as he may notify to the person, for a further period not exceeding one year and not extending beyond the day on which the person attains the age of 75.

(7) After the day on which a person attains the age of 75, he shall not hold any relevant office nor shall he—
- (a) be a member of the Judicial Committee of the Privy Council, unless he is the Lord Chancellor;
- (b) participate in the hearing and determination of any appeal, or any petition for leave to appeal, to the House of Lords, unless he is the Lord Chancellor;
- (c) act as a judge under or by virtue of section 9(1) of the Supreme Court Act 1981;
- (d) hold office as a deputy Circuit judge, within the meaning of section 24 of the Courts Act 1971;
- (e) sit and act as a judge under or by virtue of section 7 of the Judicature (Northern Ireland) Act 1978;
- (f) act as a deputy, or as a temporary additional officer, under subsection (1) of section 91 of the Supreme Court Act 1981 by virtue of subsection (3) of that section (persons who would otherwise be disqualified by age);
- (g) hold office as a deputy district judge in any district registry under subsection (1) of section 102 of that Act by virtue of subsection (3) of that section (persons who would otherwise be disqualified by age) or, in the case of a person who has previously held the office of district judge for a county court district, as a deputy district judge under section 8 of the County Courts Act 1984;
- (h) hold any office—

(i) to which appointments are made by or under any Act or statutory instrument;

(ii) for which there would, apart from this paragraph, be no compulsory retirement date; and

(iii) for appointment to which only persons who have held relevant office are eligible;

and this subsection applies whether or not the person was invited to act as a judge, or was appointed to the office in question, or to some other office by virtue of which he would (apart from this subsection) hold the office in question, before the appointed day.

(8) After the day on which a person attains the age of 70, he shall not be appointed or re-appointed as—

(a) one of the additional members, referred to in subsection (5) of section 9 of the Wireless Telegraphy Act 1949, of the appeal tribunal established under that section;

(b) the person, or one of the persons, constituting a tribunal for the purposes of section 150(3) of the Mines and Quarries Act 1954, or as an assessor assisting such a tribunal;

(c) an assessor assisting with an inquiry under section 52 of the Merchant Shipping Act 1970;

(d) chairman of a vaccine damage tribunal in Northern Ireland constituted under regulation 7 of the Vaccine Damage Payments Regulations 1979;

(e) chairman of a tribunal constituted under section 47 of the Building Societies Act 1986;

(f) chairman of a tribunal constituted under section 28 of the Banking Act 1987;

(g) an arbitrator, or (in Scotland) an arbiter, under paragraph 9(2) of Schedule 10 to the Electricity Act 1989;

(h) chairman of a tribunal constituted under Schedule 3 to the Education (Schools) Act 1992;

(j) chairman of a tribunal constituted under section 59 of the Friendly Societies Act 1992.

(9) The appropriate Minister may by order—

(a) amend Schedule 5 to this Act by adding offices to those for the time being specified in that Schedule; or

(b) amend subsection (8) above by adding offices to those for the time being specified in that subsection.

(10) As from the appointed day, the enactments and instruments mentioned in Schedule 6 to this Act shall have effect with the amendments specified in that Schedule; but those amendments are subject to section 27 below and Schedule 7 to this Act.

(11) Schedule 7 to this Act shall have effect for the purpose of making transitional provision in relation to persons holding relevant offices immediately before the appointed day; and—

(a) subsections (1) and (3) above are subject to the provisions of that Schedule; and

(b) any reference in this section to the compulsory retirement date for an office shall be construed in accordance with those provisions.

(12) In this section—

"the appointed day" means the day appointed under section 31 below for the coming into force of this section;

"the compulsory retirement date" for an office means the day on which a holder of that office is or, apart from any continuation power, would be required by any enactment or statutory instrument to vacate that office, being either—

(a) the day on which he attains a particular age; or

(b) a day falling to be determined by reference to his attaining a particular age;

"continuation power" means a power conferred by an enactment or statutory instrument on a Minister of the Crown to authorise the holder of an office to continue in that office until a later day than that on which, apart from any exercise of the power, he would be required by any enactment or statutory instrument to vacate that office;

and any reference to vacating an office includes a reference to retiring from it.

DEFINITIONS

"the appropriate Minister": s.30(1).

GENERAL NOTE

Subs. (1)

Subsection (1) imposes the obligation to retire on reaching the age of 70 on all holders of the judicial offices listed in Sched. 5. It applies whenever the judicial officer was appointed (subs. (3)), but subs. (11) and Sched. 7 allow those appointed before the Act comes into force to keep their existing agreed retirement ages. See subs. (4)–(6) for the circumstances in which specified persons may continue in office up to the age of 75.

The reduction from the existing retirement ages of 75 or 72, depending on the office and the date of appointment, was very generally welcomed. As the Lord Chancellor said in introducing the legislation (*Hansard*, H.L. Vol. 538, col. 122), "I have discussed these matters with some of my senior colleagues and we consider that a retirement age of 70 would be more appropriate to modern conditions. I therefore consulted earlier this year on a new and general retirement age of 70. I am pleased to say that the consultations indicated that there was general support for this". In the House of Commons, the Parliamentary Secretary to the Lord Chancellor's Department quoted what Lord Taylor L.C.J. had said in his Dimbleby lecture (Standing Committee D, col. 30, January 19, 1993):

"In my view being intellectually alert and having all one's faculties is not necessarily enough. Once a judge is into his 70s, he may fully understand the case and be capable of giving a reasoned judgment, but I believe he is less likely to be receptive to new ideas and even new laws. I therefore welcome the proposal presently before Parliament to reduce the judges' retirement age to 70. But, wisdom and judgment do require maturity and I would not reduce the age limit to 65".

There was pressure from the Law Society and the Bar Council, supported by the opposition, for the retirement age to be 65. However, a move directly to that position would exacerbate the main problem identified in the move to the age of 70. That was that the increase in the years of service necessary for a full pension would mean that unless judges were appointed at earlier ages they could not earn a full pension before retirement. The average ages of judges on appointment in 1992 was: High Court, 52.5; circuit judges, 49.1; district judges, 48; full-time chairmen of industrial tribunals, 52.5; stipendiary magistrates, 43.3 (Standing Committee D, col. 26, January 19, 1993).

Subsection (1) does not preclude legislation prescribing retirement ages for particular offices from specifying a lower age than 70. Under subs. (3)(b) the terms of appointment to an office may specify a lower age than 70, providing that that does not breach any other statutory provision. The Lord Chancellor might in practice be able to reduce the compulsory retirement age without further general legislation.

Subs. (2)

Some judges, for example, deputy High Court judges, do not have a continuing appointment, but are members of a panel from which appointments are made for particular periods or cases. They come under the same rule as in subs. (1).

Subs. (3)

Subsection (1) applies whenever the judge is appointed, but subject to the protection of subs. (11) and Sched. 7 for those in office at the date on which the Act comes into force. The provision that a judicial officer may retire before the compulsory retirement age seems scarcely necessary. The provision that a person's terms of appointment may prescribe an earlier age for compulsory retirement is of more importance, in possibly allowing a reduction in compulsory retirement age by administrative action.

Subss. (4)–(6)

Where the Lord Chancellor or the Secretary of State for Scotland considers that it is desirable in the public interest for a judicial officer to continue in office after the compulsory retirement date, he may continue that appointment for a year at a time, but not beyond the 75th birthday. A similar power has been used in the past where there is a shortage of judges of a particular kind or of a particular speciality. Originally, the proposal was that the power should be applicable to all the judicial officers listed in Sched. 5. However, the Lord Chancellor was persuaded by the arguments that there might be a public perception that a judge might be influenced by the fact that his continuance in office depended on the decision of a Minister, particularly if dealing with judicial review of government action (*Hansard*, H.L. Vol. 539, col. 1258). Therefore, subs. (4) excludes judges of the High Court or Court of Session and above from the possibility of continuance in office after the compulsory retirement age.

These provisions apply to all judicial officers, whenever appointed.

See subs. (7) for the possibility of retired judicial officers acting after retirement and s.27 for the completion of proceedings with which a judicial officer is dealing at the date of compulsory retirement.

Subs. (7)
Subsection (7) applies an overall maximum age limit for judicial activity of 75. This will mainly affect the possibility of retired judicial officers acting on an ad hoc basis after retirement.

Subs. (11)
The effect of Sched. 7 is that those who hold judicial office on the date on which the Act comes into force retain the same compulsory retirement date as they had immediately before that date, either under the terms of an original appointment or under a continuation power.

Completion of proceedings after retirement

27.—(1) Notwithstanding that a person has vacated or otherwise ceased to hold an office to which this section applies—
   (a) he may act as if he had not ceased to hold the office for the purpose of continuing to deal with, giving judgment in, or dealing with any ancillary matter relating to, any case begun before him before he ceased to hold that office; and
   (b) for that purpose, and for the purpose of any proceedings arising out of any such case or matter, he shall be treated as being or, as the case may be, as having been a holder of that office;
but nothing in this subsection shall authorise him to do anything if he ceased to hold the office by virtue of his removal from it.

(2) Where a person has vacated or otherwise ceased to hold a qualifying judicial office but the office in question is one to which this section applies, then, notwithstanding anything in subsection (1) above, any remuneration that may be paid in respect of service of his in that office by virtue of that subsection shall be remuneration by payment of fees (and not a salary) and accordingly that service shall not be regarded as service in qualifying judicial office.

(3) The offices to which this section applies are—
   (a) any relevant office, within the meaning of section 26 above;
   (b) any office falling within any of the paragraphs of subsection (7) of that section;
   (c) Queen's Coroner and Attorney and Master of the Crown Office and Registrar of Criminal Appeals;
   (d) Vice Judge Advocate General;
   (e) Assistant Judge Advocate General;
   (f) Deputy Judge Advocate;
   (g) Chairman of the Criminal Injuries Compensation Board.

(4) If and to the extent that any prohibition imposed by subsection (7) of section 26 above would not, apart from this subsection, be regarded as a prohibition on the holding of an office, it shall be treated for the purposes of this section as if it were such a prohibition, and references in this section to office, or to vacating or otherwise ceasing to hold office, shall be construed accordingly.

GENERAL NOTE

Section 27 allows a holder of one of the offices listed in subs. (3) to continue to act on a fee-paid basis after the date of retirement (other than a deemed retirement on removal from office) in order to continue to deal with a case begun before him or her before that date.

Miscellaneous and supplementary provisions

Payments charged on Consolidated Fund etc.

28.—(1) There shall be charged on, and paid out of, the Consolidated Fund—

(a) any pension or lump sum under Part I above payable to or in respect of a person who has held any of the qualifying judicial offices specified in Part I of Schedule 1 to this Act; and

(b) any payments by way of pension or lump sum authorised under section 19 above to be made to or in respect of such a person.

(2) Except as provided by subsection (1) above—

(a) any pension or lump sum payable under Part I above, and

(b) any payment authorised to be made under section 19 above,

shall be met out of money provided by Parliament.

(3) There shall be charged on, and paid out of, the Consolidated Fund any increase attributable to the provisions of this Act in the sums charged on, and payable out of, that Fund by or under any other enactment.

(4) There shall be paid out of money provided by Parliament any increase attributable to this Act in the sums payable out of money so provided under any other enactment.

(5) Any administrative expenses incurred under this Act by a Minister of the Crown or government department shall be defrayed out of money provided by Parliament.

(6) Any sums received by the Treasury under section 21 above shall be paid into the Consolidated Fund.

(7) Nothing in this section applies in relation to any pension or other benefits payable under or by virtue of section 10 above.

Regulations and orders

29.—(1) Any power conferred by this Act to make regulations or an order shall be exercisable by statutory instrument.

(2) A statutory instrument which contains (whether alone or with other provisions) regulations or an order under this Act, other than an order under section 31(2) below, shall be subject to annulment in pursuance of a resolution of either House of Parliament.

(3) Any power conferred by this Act to make regulations or an order includes power, exercisable in the same manner, to make such transitional, consequential, supplementary or incidental provision or savings as may appear to the authority making the regulations or order to be necessary or expedient for the purposes of, or in connection with, the regulations or order.

(4) The provision that may be made under or by virtue of subsection (3) above includes provision modifying the operation of this Act or any other enactment.

(5) The amendment by this Act of any provision contained in regulations or an order shall not be taken to have prejudiced any power to make further regulations or orders amending or revoking that provision.

(6) Regulations and orders under this Act may make different provision for different cases or classes of case.

Regulations under the Act may be made by the negative resolution procedure.

Interpretation

30.—(1) In this Act—

"the 1981 Act" means the Judicial Pensions Act 1981;

"actuarially reduced" has the meaning given by section 2(7)(e) above;

"the administrators", in relation to a pension scheme, means the persons entrusted with the administration of the scheme;

"appropriate annual rate", in relation to a judicial pension, shall be construed in accordance with section 3 above;

"the appropriate Minister" means—

(a) in relation to any judicial office whose jurisdiction is exercised exclusively in relation to Scotland, the Secretary of State; or

(b) subject to paragraph (a) above, the Lord Chancellor;

"children's pension" has the meaning given by section 6 above;

"commence to be paid", in relation to any judicial pension, shall be construed in accordance with section 2(7)(d) above;

"the deceased", in connection with any surviving spouse's or children's pension, shall be construed in accordance with section 5 or 6 above, as the case may be;

"derivative benefit" means a lump sum under section 4 above or a surviving spouse's or children's pension;

"eligible children", in relation to the deceased, shall be construed in accordance with section 6 above;

"judicial pension" means a pension under section 2 above;

"judicial pension scheme" means any public service pension scheme, as defined in—

(a) section 66(1) of the Social Security Pensions Act 1975, or

(b) Article 2(2) of the Social Security Pensions (Northern Ireland) Order 1975,

under which pensions and other benefits are payable in respect of service in one or more qualifying judicial offices (whether or not in respect of service in such offices alone);

"pensionable pay" has the meaning given by section 3(3) above;

"pension-capped salary" has the meaning given by section 3(3) above;

"the principal civil service pension scheme" means a scheme made under section 1 of the Superannuation Act 1972 which is the principal civil service pension scheme within the meaning of section 2 of that Act;

"the principal civil service pension scheme for the civil service of Northern Ireland" means a scheme made under Article 3 of the Superannuation (Northern Ireland) Order 1972 which is the principal civil service pension scheme within the meaning of Article 4 of that Order;

"qualifying judicial office" has the meaning given by section 1(6) above;

"serve" and "service", in relation to qualifying judicial office, shall be construed in accordance with section 1(6) above;

"stipendiary magistrate", in England and Wales, includes a metropolitan stipendiary magistrate;

"surviving spouse's pension" has the meaning given by section 5 above.

(2) In the case of a person who has retired from qualifying judicial office on more than one occasion, references in this Act to his retirement from such office are references to the last of those occasions.

(3) For the purposes of this Act, a person shall be regarded as vacating, or retiring from, an office at the end of the last day of his service in that office.

(4) Any reference in this Act to a pension or lump sum, or any salary or other money, being paid or payable to a person includes a reference to its being paid or payable for him.

(5) In determining for any purpose of this Act the accrued rights of a person under a judicial pension scheme which confers a power (but does not expressly impose a duty) to pay a pension or other benefit under the scheme, it shall be assumed that there is a duty to exercise the power (and to do so in such a way as will provide the greatest pension or other benefit authorised to be paid).

(6) Where a calculation falls to be performed under this Act, any resulting fraction of £1 shall be rounded up to the next whole £1.

Short title, supplementary provisions and extent

31.—(1) This Act may be cited as the Judicial Pensions and Retirement Act 1993.

(2) The provisions of this Act shall come into force on such day as the appropriate Minister may by order made by statutory instrument appoint; and different days may be appointed for different provisions or for different purposes of the same provision.

(3) The enactments and instruments mentioned in Schedule 8 to this Act shall have effect with the amendments there specified (being minor amendments and amendments consequential on the provisions of this Act).

(4) The enactments and instruments specified in Schedule 9 to this Act are repealed or revoked to the extent specified in the third column of that Schedule.

(5) Section 21 above extends to England and Wales only.

(6) The amendments, repeals and revocations in section 22 above and Schedules 3, 4, 6, 8 and 9 to this Act have the same extent as the enactment or instrument to which they relate.

(7) Subject to subsections (5) and (6) above, this Act extends to Northern Ireland.

SCHEDULES

Section 1   SCHEDULE 1

THE OFFICES WHICH MAY BE QUALIFYING JUDICIAL OFFICES

PART I

JUDGES

Lord of Appeal in Ordinary
Lord Chief Justice of England
Master of the Rolls
Lord President of the Court of Session
Lord Chief Justice of Northern Ireland
Lord Justice Clerk
Lord Justice of Appeal (in England and Wales or Northern Ireland)
President of the Family Division
Vice-Chancellor
High Court Judge (in England and Wales or Northern Ireland)
Judge of the Court of Session
Circuit judge
Sheriff Principal or sheriff in Scotland
County Court Judge in Northern Ireland
Stipendiary Magistrate in England and Wales
Resident Magistrate appointed under the Magistrates' Courts Act (Northern Ireland) 1964

PART II

OTHER APPOINTMENTS

Court officers

Master, Queen's Bench Division
Queen's Coroner and Attorney and Master of the Crown Office and Registrar of Criminal Appeals
Admiralty Registrar
Master, Chancery Division
Registrar in Bankruptcy of the High Court
Taxing Master of the Supreme Court
District Judge of the Principal Registry of the Family Division
Registrar of civil appeals
Master of the Court of Protection
District judge
Any of the offices from time to time specified in column 1 of Schedule 3 to the Judicature (Northern Ireland) Act 1978, other than—
    (a) Principal Secretary to the Lord Chief Justice;
    (b) Legal Secretary to the Lord Chief Justice; and
    (c) Official Solicitor

Members of tribunals

Chief or other Social Security Commissioner, excluding appointments in pursuance of section 52(2) of the Social Security Administration Act 1992
Chief or other Social Security Commissioner for Northern Ireland, excluding appointments in pursuance of section 50(2) of the Social Security Administration (Northern Ireland) Act 1992
Chief or other Child Support Commissioner, excluding appointments in pursuance of paragraph 4 of Schedule 4 to the Child Support Act 1991
Chief or other Child Support Commissioner for Northern Ireland, excluding appointments in pursuance of paragraph 4 of Schedule 4 to the Child Support Act 1991 as that paragraph has effect by virtue of paragraph 8 of that Schedule
President of social security appeal tribunals, medical appeal tribunals, disability appeal tribunals and child support appeal tribunals
President of social security appeal tribunals, medical appeal tribunals, disability appeal tribunals and child support appeal tribunals for Northern Ireland
Chairman of social security appeal tribunals, medical appeal tribunals and disability appeal tribunals
Chairman of social security appeal tribunals, medical appeal tribunals and disability appeal tribunals in Northern Ireland
Chairman of child support appeal tribunals
Chairman of child support appeal tribunals in Northern Ireland
President of the Industrial Tribunals (England and Wales)
President of the Industrial Tribunals (Scotland)
President or Vice-President of the Industrial Tribunals and the Fair Employment Tribunal, appointed under section 3 of the Fair Employment (Northern Ireland) Act 1989
Chairman of industrial tribunals appointed in pursuance of regulations under section 128 of the Employment Protection (Consolidation) Act 1978
Chairman of industrial tribunals or of the Fair Employment Tribunal appointed in pursuance of regulations under Article 30 of the Industrial Training (Northern Ireland) Order 1984 or appointed under section 3(1)(c) of the Fair Employment (Northern Ireland) Act 1989
President or other member of the Lands Tribunal, the Lands Tribunal for Scotland or the Lands Tribunal for Northern Ireland

Other offices whose holders are appointed by the Lord Chancellor

Judge Advocate General
Vice Judge Advocate General
Assistant Judge Advocate General
Deputy Judge Advocate
Judge Advocate of Her Majesty's Fleet
President or Vice-President of Value Added Tax Tribunals

Chairman of value added tax tribunals

Commissioner for the special purposes of the Income Tax Acts appointed under section 4 of the Taxes Management Act 1970

President or other member of the Immigration Appeal Tribunal

President of the pensions appeal tribunals established under the Pensions Appeal Tribunals Act 1943

President or chairman of the Transport Tribunal

Chief, or any other, immigration adjudicator under the Immigration Act 1971

Other offices

Chairman of the Criminal Injuries Compensation Board incorporated under section 108(1) of the Criminal Justice Act 1988

Chairman of the Foreign Compensation Commission

Chairman of the Scottish Land Court

President of the Industrial Court appointed in pursuance of Article 91 of the Industrial Relations (Northern Ireland) Order 1992

Section 23   SCHEDULE 2

TRANSFER OF ACCRUED BENEFITS

PART I

GENERAL

Interpretation

1. In this Schedule—

"authorised insurance company" means an insurance company authorised under section 3 or 4 of the Insurance Companies Act 1982 (or any similar previous enactment) to carry on ordinary long-term insurance business;

"contracted-out scheme" has the same meaning as it has for the purposes of Part III of the Social Security Pensions Act 1975 and, in relation to Northern Ireland, Part IV of the Social Security Pensions (Northern Ireland) Order 1975;

"disregarded service", in relation to any member of a scheme, means any period of service in qualifying judicial office during which an election under, or an election having effect as if made under, section 13 of this Act is in force in respect of the qualifying member;

"guaranteed minimum pension" has the same meaning as in the Social Security Pensions Act 1975 and, in relation to Northern Ireland, the Social Security Pensions (Northern Ireland) Order 1975;

"member", in relation to a scheme, means a person to whom Part I of this Act applies or has applied;

"normal pension age" means the earliest age at which, if his service in qualifying judicial office had continued until retirement at that age, a member of the scheme constituted by Part I of this Act might have been entitled to receive a pension under the scheme at the appropriate annual rate (otherwise than by reason of infirmity of mind or body);

"occupational pension scheme" has the meaning given by section 66(1) of the Social Security Pensions Act 1975 or, in relation to Northern Ireland, Article 2(2) of the Social Security Pensions (Northern Ireland) Order 1975;

"personal pension scheme" has the meaning given by section 84(1) of the Social Security Act 1986 or, in relation to Northern Ireland, Article 2(2) of the Social Security (Northern Ireland) Order 1986;

"prescribed" means prescribed by regulations;

"protected rights" has the same meaning as in the Social Security Pensions Act 1975 and, in relation to Northern Ireland, the Social Security Pensions (Northern Ireland) Order 1975;

"qualifying member" means a person to whom Part II of this Schedule applies;

"qualifying service" means the service by reference to which a qualifying member's entitlement to benefit under the scheme is calculated; and

"scheme" means the relevant occupational pension scheme constituted by Part I or section 19 of this Act.

Regulations

2. Regulations for the purposes of this Schedule may be made, with the concurrence of the Treasury, by the Lord Chancellor or, in relation to Scotland, the Secretary of State.

Other provisions about transfer values

3. Part II of Schedule 1A to the Social Security Pensions Act 1975 (transfer values) and Part II of Schedule 1A to the Social Security Pensions (Northern Ireland) Order 1975 (corresponding Northern Ireland provisions) shall not apply in relation to those schemes to which this Schedule applies.

PART II

TRANSFERS OUT

Qualifying members

4.—(1) Where the conditions mentioned in sub-paragraph (2) below are satisfied, this Part of this Schedule applies to any person—
 (a) to or in respect of whom benefits are payable under a scheme; and
 (b) whose qualifying service ends after this Schedule comes into force.
 (2) The conditions are that—
 (a) his qualifying service ends at least one year before he reaches normal pension age; and
 (b) on the date on which it ends—
   (i) he has accrued rights to benefit under the scheme; or
   (ii) he would have such rights if his service in qualifying judicial office had also ended on that date.

Qualifying member's right to a transfer payment

5.—(1) When his qualifying service ends, a qualifying member acquires a right to the cash equivalent at the relevant date of any benefits—
 (a) which have accrued to, or in respect of him, under the scheme; or
 (b) where service of his in qualifying judicial office is disregarded service, which would have so accrued if his service in qualifying judicial office had ended on the same date as that on which his qualifying service ended.
 (2) In this paragraph "the relevant date" means—
 (a) the date when the qualifying member's qualifying service ends, or
 (b) the date of any application which he has made under paragraph 6 below and which has not been withdrawn,
whichever is the later.

Method of taking cash benefit

6.—(1) A qualifying member who acquires a right to a cash equivalent under paragraph 5 above may only take it by exercising the option conferred by this paragraph.
 (2) The option is that of requiring the Treasury to use the cash equivalent in whichever of the following ways the qualifying member chooses—
 (a) for acquiring transfer credits allowed under the rules of another occupational pension scheme—
   (i) whose trustees or managers are able and willing to accept him; and
   (ii) which satisfies prescribed requirements;
 (b) for acquiring rights allowed under the rules of a personal pension scheme—
   (i) whose trustees or managers are able and willing to accept him; and
   (ii) which satisfies prescribed requirements;
 (c) for purchasing from one or more authorised insurance companies—
   (i) chosen by the qualifying member, and
   (ii) willing to accept payment on his account from the Treasury,
  one or more annuities which satisfy prescribed requirements;
 (d) for subscribing to other pension arrangements which satisfy prescribed requirements.
 (3) Without prejudice to the generality of the power to prescribe requirements under sub-paragraph (2) above, such requirements may provide that pension arrangements or a scheme or annuity must satisfy such requirements of the Commissioners of Inland Revenue as may be prescribed.
 (4) A qualifying member may exercise his option in different ways in relation to different portions of his cash equivalent.

(5) A qualifying member who exercises his option must do so in relation to the whole of his cash equivalent or, where sub-paragraph (6) below applies, in relation to the whole of the reduced cash equivalent.

(6) Where—

(a) the trustees or managers of—

    (i) an occupational pension scheme which is not a contracted-out scheme, or

    (ii) a personal pension scheme which is not an appropriate scheme under section 2 of the Social Security Act 1986, Article 4 of the Social Security (Northern Ireland) Order 1986 or under any prescribed provision, or

    (ii) a self-employed pension arrangement within the meaning of regulation 2D of the Occupational Pension Schemes (Transfer Values) Regulations 1985, regulation 2D of the Occupational Pension Schemes (Transfer Values) Regulations (Northern Ireland) 1985, regulation 2A of the Personal Pension Schemes (Transfer Values) Regulations 1987, regulation 2A of the Personal Pension Schemes (Transfer Values) Regulations (Northern Ireland) 1987 or any other prescribed provision,

are able or willing to accept a transfer payment only in respect of a qualifying member's rights other than his accrued rights to a guaranteed minimum pension or his protected rights; and

(b) the member has not required the Treasury to use the portion of his cash equivalent which represents a guaranteed minimum pension or protected rights in any of the ways specified in sub-paragraph (2) above,

paragraph 5 above, this paragraph and paragraph 7 below are to be read as conferring on the member an option only in respect of the reduced cash equivalent.

(7) In this paragraph "reduced cash equivalent" means a sum equal to the balance of the cash equivalent to which the qualifying member would be entitled if sub-paragraph (6) above did not apply, after deduction of an amount sufficient for the Treasury to meet its liability in respect of the member's guaranteed minimum pension or protected rights or those of his widow, or her widower.

Calculation of cash equivalents

7.—(1) Cash equivalents are to be calculated and verified in the prescribed manner.

(2) Regulations made under sub-paragraph (1) above may, in particular, provide—

(a) that in calculating cash equivalents account shall be taken—

    (i) of any surrender or forfeiture of the whole or part of a qualifying member's pension which occurs before the Treasury does what is needed to comply with the choice made by him in exercising his option;

    (ii) in a case where paragraph 6(6) above applies, of the need to deduct an appropriate amount to provide a guaranteed minimum pension or give effect to protected rights; and

(b) that in prescribed circumstances a qualifying member's cash equivalent shall be increased or reduced.

(3) Without prejudice to the generality of sub-paragraph (2) above, the circumstances that may be specified by virtue of paragraph (b) of that sub-paragraph include the length of time which elapses between the termination of a qualifying member's qualifying service and his exercise of the option conferred by paragraph 6 above.

Time within which option must be exercised

8.—(1) A qualifying member may only exercise his option on or before the last option date.

(2) The last option date is—

(a) the date which falls one year before the date on which the qualifying member reaches normal pension age, or

(b) the end of the period of six months beginning with the date on which his qualifying service ends,

whichever is the later.

(3) A qualifying member loses the right to any cash equivalent under this Schedule if—

(a) his pension becomes payable before he reaches normal pension age; or

(b) he fails to exercise his option on or before the last option date.

Option to be exercised in writing

9.—(1) A qualifying member may only exercise his option by making an application in writing to the Treasury.

(2) In any case where—

(a) a qualifying member has exercised his option, and

(b) the Treasury has done what is needed to comply with the choices made by him in exercising his option,

the Treasury shall be discharged from any obligation to provide benefits to which the cash equivalent related except, in any such cases as are mentioned in paragraph 6(6) above, to the extent that an obligation to provide guaranteed minimum pensions or give effect to protected rights continues to subsist.

(3) If the Treasury receives an application under this paragraph, it shall be its duty, subject to the following provisions of this paragraph, to do what is needed to comply with the choice made by the qualifying member in exercising his option—

(a) within twelve months of the date on which it receives his application, or

(b) by the date on which he attains normal pension age,

whichever is the earlier.

Cancellation of exercise of option

10.—(1) A qualifying member may cancel the exercise of his option by giving the Treasury notice in writing that he no longer wishes it to be exercised.

(2) No such notice shall have effect if it is given to the Treasury at a time when, in order to comply with the choice made by the qualifying member in exercising his option, the Treasury has entered into an agreement with a third party to use the whole or part of his cash equivalent in a way specified in paragraph 6(2)(a), (b), (c) or (d) above.

(3) A qualifying member who withdraws an application may make another.

PART III

TRANSFERS IN

Application to accept payment into scheme

11.—(1) Where a member of a scheme has asked the appropriate Minister to accept a payment representing the cash equivalent of his accrued rights in any other qualifying scheme, that Minister may—

(a) to the extent to which it does not exceed the prescribed limit, accept the payment or any part of it; or

(b) refuse to accept the payment or any part of it.

(2) A request under sub-paragraph (1) above must be made—

(a) in writing;

(b) before the person making it has reached normal pension age; and

(c) not less than one year before he becomes entitled to a pension on retirement from his qualifying service.

(3) In this paragraph—

"the prescribed limit" means the limit prescribed by regulations made by virtue of paragraph 13(a) below;

"qualifying scheme" means—

(a) an occupational pension scheme, a personal pension scheme, or an annuity purchased from an authorised insurance company, which satisfies prescribed requirements; or

(b) other prescribed pension arrangements.

Cancellation of request

12.—(1) A member may, by notice in writing given to the appropriate Minister, cancel a request made by him under paragraph 11 above, at any time before it has been accepted.

(2) A transferring member who withdraws an application may make another.

Regulations

13. Regulations may—

(a) prescribe limits on the amounts which the appropriate Minister may accept under paragraph 11(1) above;

(b) make provision as to the manner in which payments are to be accepted into a scheme under this Part of this Schedule;

(c) make provision as to the benefits which are to be provided to a member to reflect any such payment accepted with respect to him;

(d) prescribe formulae, based on tables of factors provided by the Government Actuary, to be used when performing any calculation relating to the acceptance of transfer payments or the provision of benefits.

GENERAL NOTE
Paragraph 3 takes the new judicial pension scheme out of the ordinary provisions relating to transfer values.

So far as Pt. II on transfers out of the scheme are concerned, it appears that it can only operate either where a judicial officer leaves service or makes an election relating to a personal pension scheme under s.13. In the first case, if the officer takes up some other employment or self-employment, the cash equivalent of accrued rights may be transferred into another occupational pension scheme or personal pension scheme or into an annuity. If the officer has no other employment or self-employment, then it seems that the only option apart from leaving the accrued rights in the judicial pension scheme is to use the cash equivalent to buy an annuity. In the second case, it would seem that the officer can transfer accrued rights into the personal pension scheme mentioned in the election or into an annuity. Much will depend on the terms of the regulations which are still to be made.

A cash equivalent cannot be taken unless the judicial officer's qualifying service ends at least one year before normal pension age, currently 65 (s.2(1)(a)).

Under Pt. II, cash equivalents from other schemes may be accepted into the judicial pension scheme. Because retained benefits from previous schemes do not have to be brought into account, this option will not be of interest to anyone who can serve the necessary years for a full pension under the judicial scheme.

Section 24   SCHEDULE 3

CORRESPONDING MINOR AMENDMENTS TO OTHER PENSIONS ENACTMENTS

PART I

AMENDMENTS OF THE 1981 ACT

Dependent children: maximum allowable remuneration

1.—(1) In section 21 of the 1981 Act (meaning of "period of childhood and full-time education") in subsection (1)(c)(ii), for the words from "do not exceed" to "a year" there shall be substituted the words "do not exceed the maximum allowable remuneration".

(2) After subsection (3) of that section (meaning of "emoluments") there shall be inserted—

"(3A) For the purposes of subsection (1)(c)(ii) above, the "maximum allowable remuneration" at any time is an annual rate (£1,614 a year, at the passing of the Judicial Pensions and Retirement Act 1993) equal to that at which a pension of £250 a year—

(a) first awarded under the principal civil service pension scheme on 1st June 1972, and

(b) increased from time to time by the amount of increase that would be applied under the Pensions (Increase) Act 1971 to such a pension,

would (as so increased) be payable at that time, rounding any resulting fraction of £1 up to the next whole £1."

(3) Subsections (5) and (6) of that section (orders increasing the earnings limit in subsection (1)(c)(ii)) shall cease to have effect.

Appeals

2.—(1) Section 15 of the 1981 Act (which provides that the decision of the Treasury on certain questions shall be final) shall cease to have effect.

(2) After section 32 of that Act there shall be inserted—

"Appeals

32A.—(1) If any person to whom this section applies is aggrieved by any decision taken by the administrators of a relevant pension scheme concerning—

(a) the interpretation of the rules of the scheme, or

(b) the exercise of any discretion under the scheme,

he shall have a right to appeal to the appropriate Minister against that decision.

(2) On deciding an appeal under this section, the appropriate Minister may give to the administrators such directions as he considers necessary or expedient for implementing his decision.

(3) The persons to whom this section applies are the following—

(a) any member of the scheme;

(b) the widow or widower, or any surviving dependant, of a deceased member of the scheme;

(c) where the decision relates to the question—

(i) whether a person who claims to be such a person as is mentioned in paragraph (a) or (b) above is such a person, or

(ii) whether a person who claims to be entitled to become a member of the scheme is so entitled,

the person so claiming.

(4) Regulations may make provision as to the manner in which, and time within which, appeals under this section are to be brought.

(5) The administrators shall be entitled to appear and be heard on any appeal under this section.

(6) In this section—

"the administrators", in relation to a pension scheme, means the persons entrusted with the administration of the scheme;

"the appropriate Minister" means—

(a) in relation to any judicial office whose jurisdiction is exercised exclusively in relation to Scotland, the Secretary of State; or

(b) subject to paragraph (a) above, the Lord Chancellor;

"member", in relation to a pension scheme, means a person whose service in an office is, was or is to be subject to the scheme;

"regulations" means regulations made by the appropriate Minister;

"relevant pension scheme" means any pension scheme constituted under or by virtue of this Act;

"rules", in relation to a relevant pension scheme, means the provisions of this Act, and of any regulations or orders made under this Act, so far as relating to that scheme."

Additional voluntary contributions

3.—(1) Section 33A of the 1981 Act (which confers power to make regulations entitling any member of a judicial pension scheme constituted by that Act or by the Sheriffs' Pensions (Scotland) Act 1961 to make voluntary contributions towards the provision of additional benefits under the scheme) shall be amended in accordance with the following provisions of this paragraph.

(2) In subsection (1), after the word "provision" there shall be inserted "(a)" and for the words "under the scheme" there shall be substituted the words "whether under the scheme or otherwise; or

(b) imposing conditions with respect to the exercise by any such person of any entitlement (whether or not under paragraph (a) above) which he may have to make any such voluntary contributions."

(3) After that subsection there shall be inserted—

"(1A) The regulations may make provision for the purpose of imposing, in a case where a member makes voluntary contributions, upper limits with respect to—

(a) the aggregate value of the agreeable benefits which may be paid to or in respect of any such member; and

(b) the amount which any such member may pay by way of such contributions;

and, without prejudice to the generality of paragraph (b) above, the regulations may, in particular, impose such an upper limit on the amount which a member may pay by way of voluntary contributions as will, so far as reasonably practicable, secure that the aggregate value referred to in paragraph (a) above will not exceed the limit prescribed under that paragraph.

(1B) The regulations may—

(a) prescribe the manner in which aggregable benefits are to be valued for the purpose of any such aggregation as is mentioned in subsection (1A) above;

(b) confer on the administrators of a judicial pension scheme power to require a member who is making, or who wishes to make, voluntary contributions to provide such information as they may require concerning any retained benefits of his;

(c) permit the disclosure by those administrators of any information which they may obtain concerning any such retained benefits—

(i) to, or to any officers of, the Commissioners of Inland Revenue; or

(ii) to, or to any servants or agents of, any authorised provider who is, or may be, concerned in the investment of the voluntary contributions or the provision of the additional benefits in question."

(4) In subsection (2), in paragraph (b) (no limit on voluntary contributions, other than an upper limit corresponding to that imposed by section 594 of the Income and Corporation Taxes Act 1988) after the words "other than" there shall be inserted the words "either or both of the following, that is to say—

(i) such upper limit as may be imposed by virtue of subsection (1A)(b) above; or
(ii)".

(5) At the end of that subsection there shall be added the words—
"but paragraphs (c) and (d) above have effect only in relation to a voluntary contributions scheme constituted by or under this Act or the Sheriffs' Pensions (Scotland) Act 1961."

(6) In subsection (3) (regulations about valuation of benefits etc.)—

(a) the word "and" immediately preceding paragraph (b) shall be omitted; and

(b) in that paragraph, for the words "limit imposed by virtue of" there shall be substituted the words "such limit as is mentioned in".

(7) At the end of that subsection there shall be added—
"(c) provide for any administrative expenses incurred by any person by virtue of this section to be defrayed out of sums received by way of voluntary contributions;

(d) provide for the manner in which voluntary contributions are to be made;

(e) make provision for, and in connection with, the valuation of a person's accrued rights—
(i) under any occupational or personal pension scheme, which are to be transferred into a voluntary contributions scheme, or
(ii) under any voluntary contributions scheme, which on termination of his membership of that scheme may fall to be transferred into another scheme;

(f) prescribe the additional benefits which are to be available under a voluntary contributions scheme and the rates and times at which those benefits are to be payable;

(g) make provision for and in connection with the making of elections between different benefits available under voluntary contributions schemes;

(h) provide for the terms on which a person may terminate his membership of a voluntary contributions scheme;

(j) provide for the terms on which surplus funds may be refunded to a person who has made payments by way of voluntary contributions to a voluntary contributions scheme;

(k) specify any authorised providers—
(i) who are to invest any prescribed voluntary contributions, or
(ii) who are to provide any prescribed additional benefits,
and, if two or more authorised providers are so specified, may make provision entitling any person who makes prescribed payments by way of voluntary contributions to elect between those authorised providers."

(8) Subsection (4) (limitation of voluntary contributions by reference to maximum entitlement of members) shall be omitted and before subsection (5) there shall be inserted—
"(4A) The regulations may provide for such additional benefits arising under or by virtue of this section as may be prescribed—
(a) to be charged on, and paid out of, the Consolidated Fund; or
(b) to be paid out of money provided by Parliament."

(9) After subsection (5) there shall be inserted—
"(5A) The regulations may make different provision for different classes or descriptions of voluntary contributions scheme."

(10) After subsection (8) there shall be added—
"(9) In this section—
"administrators", in relation to any scheme, means the persons entrusted with the administration of that scheme;
"aggregable benefits" means—
(a) any pensions or other benefits under a judicial pension scheme, other than such additional benefits as are mentioned in subsection (1) above;
(b) such additional benefits so mentioned as may be prescribed; and
(c) such retained benefits as may be prescribed;
"authorised provider", in relation to the investment of any sums paid by way of voluntary contributions or the provision of any benefit, means a person who is authorised under Chapter III of Part I of the Financial Services Act 1986 to invest those sums or, as the case may be, to provide that benefit;
"employment" has the same meaning as it has in the Social Security Pensions Act 1975 (and accordingly includes employment as a self-employed earner, within the meaning of that Act);
"judicial pension scheme" has the meaning given by section 14A(2) above;
"member" means member of a judicial pension scheme;
"occupational pension scheme" has the meaning given by section 66(1) of the Social Security Pensions Act 1975 or, in relation to Northern Ireland, Article 2(2) of the Social Security Pensions (Northern Ireland) Order 1975;

"personal pension scheme" has the meaning given by section 84(1) of the Social Security Act 1986 or, in relation to Northern Ireland, Article 2(2) of the Social Security (Northern Ireland) Order 1986;

"prescribed" means specified in, or determined in accordance with, the regulations;

"relevant benefits" has the meaning given by section 612(1) of the Income and Corporation Taxes Act 1988;

"retained benefits", in the case of any person, means any rights retained by him to relevant benefits under any occupational or personal pension scheme which has, or which may be expected to qualify for, tax-exemption or tax-approval, being rights which accrued during some previous employment;

"surplus funds", in relation to a person and any voluntary contributions scheme, means any funds which are, or have been, held for the purposes of that voluntary contributions scheme and which fall to be returned to him in consequence of any such limit as is mentioned in subsection (2)(b) above;

"tax-exemption" and "tax-approval" have the meaning given by section 84(1) of the Social Security Act 1986;

"voluntary contributions", in relation to any member of a judicial pension scheme, means voluntary contributions towards the provision of additional benefits, whether under that scheme or otherwise;

"voluntary contributions scheme" means any occupational pension scheme if and to the extent that it is a scheme under which such additional benefits as are mentioned in subsection (1) above are, or are to be, provided;

and, where a person's voluntary contributions are made by deduction from salary, any reference to payment of, or by way of, voluntary contributions shall be taken to include a reference to the making of voluntary contributions by deduction or, as the case may require, to any voluntary contributions so made.

(10) Without prejudice to subsections (3)(c) and (d) and (4A) above, there may be paid out of money provided by Parliament—

    (a) any sums required for or in connection with the operation or administration of any prescribed voluntary contributions scheme; or

    (b) any administrative expenses incurred under or by virtue of this section by a Minister of the Crown or government department.

(11) Any sums received under this section may be paid into the Consolidated Fund."

PART II

AMENDMENT OF THE SHERIFFS' PENSIONS (SCOTLAND) ACT 1961

Appeals

4. After section 9 of the Sheriffs' Pensions (Scotland) Act 1961 there shall be inserted—

"Appeals

9A.—(1) If any person to whom a pension is payable under this Act is aggrieved by any decision taken by the administrators of a pension scheme constituted by this Act concerning—

    (a) the interpretation of the provisions of the scheme, or

    (b) the exercise of any discretion under the scheme,

he shall have a right of appeal to the Secretary of State.

(2) On deciding an appeal under this section, the Secretary of State may give to the administrators such directions as he considers necessary or expedient for implementing his decision.

(3) The Secretary of State may by regulations make provision as to the manner in which, and time within which, appeals under this section are to be brought.

(4) The administrators shall be entitled to appear and be heard on any appeal under this section.

(5) In this section, "the administrators", in relation to a pension scheme, means the persons entrusted with the administration of the scheme."

PART III

AMENDMENTS OF NORTHERN IRELAND PROVISIONS

Interpretation

5. In this Part of this Schedule—

8–44

"the 1951 Act" means the Judicial Pensions Act (Northern Ireland) 1951;

"the 1959 Act" means the County Courts Act (Northern Ireland) 1959;

"the 1960 Act" means the Resident Magistrates' Pensions Act (Northern Ireland) 1960;

"the 1964 Order" means the Lands Tribunal (Salaries and Superannuation) Order (Northern Ireland) 1964;

"the 1969 Act" means the Superannuation (Miscellaneous Provisions) Act (Northern Ireland) 1969;

"the 1975 Act" means the Social Security (Northern Ireland) Act 1975.

Dependent children: maximum allowable remuneration

6.—(1) In subsection (1)(c)(ii) of each of the following enactments (which give the meaning of "period of childhood and full-time education"), that is to say—

(a) section 9 of the 1951 Act,

(b) section 125 of the 1959 Act,

(c) section 7 of the 1960 Act,

for the words from "do not exceed" to "a year" there shall be substituted the words "do not exceed the maximum allowable remuneration".

(2) In paragraph 1(c)(ii) of Article 9 of the 1964 Order (which gives the meaning of "period of childhood and full-time education"), for the words from "do not exceed" to "a year" there shall be substituted the words "do not exceed the maximum allowable remuneration".

(3) The subsection set out in sub-paragraph (4) below shall be inserted—

(a) numbered as subsection (2A), after subsection (2) of section 9 of the 1951 Act;

(b) numbered as subsection (2A), after subsection (2) of section 125 of the 1959 Act;

(c) numbered as subsection (4A), after subsection (4) of section 7 of the 1960 Act.

(4) The subsection inserted by sub-paragraph (3) above is as follows—

"( ) For the purposes of subsection (1)(c)(ii), the "maximum allowable remuneration" at any time is an annual rate (£1,614 a year, at the passing of the Judicial Pensions and Retirement Act 1993) equal to that at which a pension of £250 a year—

(a) first awarded under the principal civil service pension scheme (within the meaning of that Act) on 1st June 1972, and

(b) increased from time to time by the amount of increase that would be applied under the Pensions (Increase) Act 1971 to such a pension,

would (as so increased) be payable at that time, rounding any resulting fraction of £1 up to the next whole £1."

(5) A paragraph in the same terms as the subsection set out in sub-paragraph (4) above, but with the substitution of the word "paragraph" for the word "subsection", shall be inserted, numbered as paragraph (2A), after paragraph (2) of Article 9 of the 1964 Order.

(6) Paragraph 18 of Schedule 1 to the Superannuation (Amendment) Act (Northern Ireland) 1966 (orders increasing the earnings limit in subsection (1)(c)(ii) of each of the sections specified in sub-paragraph (1) above) shall cease to have effect.

Appeals

7.—(1) The following enactments (which correspond to section 15 of the 1981 Act) shall cease to have effect, that is to say—

(a) section 116(6) of the 1959 Act;

(b) section 14 of the 1960 Act;

(c) paragraph 6(4) of Schedule 10 to the 1975 Act.

(2) The section set out in sub-paragraph (3) below shall be inserted—

(a) numbered as section 132A, after section 132 of the 1959 Act;

(b) numbered as section 21A, after section 21 of the 1960 Act.

(3) The section inserted by sub-paragraph (2) above is as follows—

"Appeals

.—(1) If any person to whom this section applies is aggrieved by any decision taken by the administrators of a relevant pension scheme concerning—

(a) the interpretation of the rules of the scheme, or

(b) the exercise of any discretion under the scheme,

he shall have a right of appeal to the Lord Chancellor against that decision.

(2) On deciding an appeal under this section, the Lord Chancellor may give to the administrators such directions as he considers necessary or expedient for implementing his decision.

(3) The persons to whom this section applies are the following—
(a) any member of the scheme;
(b) the widow or widower, or any surviving dependant, of a deceased member of the scheme;
(c) where the decision relates to the question—
(i) whether a person who claims to be such a person as is mentioned in paragraph (a) or (b) is such a person, or
(ii) whether a person who claims to be entitled to become a member of the scheme is so entitled,
the person so claiming.

(4) The Lord Chancellor may by regulations make provision as to the manner in which, and time within which, appeals under this section are to be brought.

(5) Regulations made under this section shall be subject to annulment in like manner as a statutory instrument and section 5 of the Statutory Instruments Act 1946 shall apply accordingly.

(6) The administrators shall be entitled to appear and be heard on any appeal under this section.

(7) In this section—
"the administrators", in relation to a pension scheme, means the persons entrusted with the administration of the scheme;
"member", in relation to a pension scheme, means a person whose service in an office is, was or is to be subject to the scheme;
"relevant pension scheme" means any pension scheme constituted under or by virtue of this Act;
"rules", in relation to a relevant pension scheme, means the provisions of this Act, and of any regulations or orders made under this Act, so far as relating to that scheme."

(4) A paragraph in the same terms as the section set out in sub-paragraph (3) above, but with the substitution of the words "this paragraph" for the words "this section", wherever occurring, shall be inserted, numbered as paragraph 7B, after paragraph 7A of Schedule 10 to the 1975 Act.

Additional voluntary contributions

8.—(1) The following enactments (which correspond to section 33A of the 1981 Act), that is to say—
(a) section 11A of the 1951 Act,
(b) section 127A of the 1959 Act, and
(c) section 9A of the 1960 Act,
shall be amended in accordance with the following provisions of this paragraph.

(2) In subsection (1), after the word "provision" there shall be inserted "(a)" and for the words "under the scheme" there shall be substituted the words "whether under the scheme or otherwise; or
(b) imposing conditions with respect to the exercise by any such person of any entitlement (whether or not under paragraph (a)) which he may have to make any such voluntary contributions."

(3) After that subsection there shall be inserted—
"(1A) The regulations may make provision for the purpose of imposing, in a case where a member makes voluntary contributions, upper limits with respect to—
(a) the aggregate value of the aggregable benefits which may be paid to or in respect of any such member; and
(b) the amount which any such member may pay by way of such contributions;
and, without prejudice to the generality of paragraph (b), the regulations may, in particular, impose such an upper limit on the amount which a member may pay by way of voluntary contributions as will, so far as reasonably practicable, secure that the aggregate value referred to in paragraph (a) will not exceed the limit prescribed under that paragraph.

(1B) The regulations may—
(a) prescribe the manner in which aggregable benefits are to be valued for the purpose of any such aggregation as is mentioned in subsection (1A);
(b) confer on the administration of a judicial pension scheme power to require a member who is making, or who wishes to make, voluntary contributions to provide such information as they may require concerning any retained benefits of his;
(c) permit the disclosure by those administrators of any information which they may obtain concerning any such retained benefits—

(i) to, or to any officers of, the Commissioners of Inland Revenue; or

(ii) to, or to any servants or agents of, any authorised provider who is, or may be, concerned in the investment of the voluntary contributions or the provisions of the additional benefits in question."

(4) In subsection (2), in paragraph (b) (no limit on voluntary contributions, other than an upper limit corresponding to that imposed by section 594 of the Income and Corporation Taxes Act 1988) after the words "other than" there shall be inserted the words "either or both of the following, that is to say—

(i) such upper limit as may be imposed by virtue of subsection (1A)(b); or

(ii)".

(5) At the end of that subsection there shall be added the words—

"but paragraphs (c) and (d) have effect only in relation to a voluntary contributions scheme constituted by or under this Act."

(6) In subsection (3) (regulations about valuation of benefits etc.)—

(a) the word "and" immediately preceding paragraph (b) shall be omitted; and

(b) in that paragraph, for the words "limit imposed by virtue of" there shall be substituted the words "such limit as is mentioned in".

(7) At the end of that subsection there shall be added—

"(c) provide for any administrative expenses incurred by any person by virtue of this section to be defrayed out of sums received by way of voluntary contributions;

(d) provide for the manner in which voluntary contributions are to be made;

(e) make provision for, and in connection with, the valuation of a person's accrued rights—

(i) under any occupational or personal scheme, which are to be transferred into a voluntary contributions scheme, or

(ii) under any voluntary contributions scheme, which on termination of his membership of that scheme may fall to be transferred into another scheme;

(f) prescribe the additional benefits which are to be available under a voluntary contributions scheme and the rates and times at which those benefits are to be payable;

(g) make provision for and in connection with the making of elections between different benefits available under voluntary contributions schemes;

(h) provide for the terms on which a person may terminate his membership of a voluntary contributions scheme;

(j) provide for the terms on which surplus funds may be refunded to a person who has made payments by way of voluntary contributions to a voluntary contributions scheme;

(k) specify any authorised providers—

(i) who are to invest any prescribed voluntary contributions, or

(ii) who are to provide any prescribed additional benefits,

and, if two or more authorised providers are so specified, may make provision entitling any person who makes prescribed payments by way of voluntary contributions to elect between those authorised providers."

(8) Subsection (4) (limitation of voluntary contributions by reference to maximum entitlement of members) shall be omitted and before subsection (5) there shall be inserted—

"(4A) The regulations may provide for such additional benefits arising under or by virtue of this section as may be prescribed—

(a) to be charged on, and paid out of, the Consolidated Fund of the United Kingdom; or

(b) to be paid out of money provided by the Parliament of the United Kingdom."

(9) After subsection (6) there shall be added—

"(7) In this section—

"administrators", in relation to any scheme, means the persons entrusted with the administration of that scheme;

"aggregable benefits" means—

(a) any pensions or other benefits under a judicial pension scheme, other than such additional benefits as are mentioned in subsection (1);

(b) such additional benefits so mentioned as may be prescribed; and

(c) such retained benefits as may be prescribed;

"authorised provider", in relation to the investment of any sums paid by way of voluntary contributions or the provision of any benefit, means a person who is authorised under Chapter III of Part I of the Financial Services Act 1986 to invest those sums or, as the case may be, to provide that benefit;

"employment" has the same meaning as it has in the Social Security Pensions (Northern Ireland) Order 1975 (and accordingly includes employment as a self-employed earner, within the meaning of that Order);

"judicial pension scheme" means a scheme constituted by this Act;

"member" means member of a judicial pension scheme;

"occupational pension scheme" has the meaning given by Article 2(2) of the Social Security Pensions (Northern Ireland) Order 1975;

"personal pension scheme" has the meaning given by Article 2(2) of the Social Security (Northern Ireland) Order 1986;

"prescribed" means specified in, or determined in accordance with, the regulations;

"relevant benefits" has the meaning given by section 612(1) of the Income and Corporation Taxes Act 1988;

"retained benefits", in the case of any person, means any rights retained by him to relevant benefits under any occupational or personal pension scheme which has, or which may be expected to qualify for, tax-exemption or tax-approval, being rights which accrued during some previous employment;

"surplus funds", in relation to a person and any voluntary contributions scheme, means any funds which are, or have been, held for the purposes of that voluntary contributions scheme and which fall to be returned to him in consequence of any such limit as is mentioned in subsection (2)(b);

"tax-exemption" and "tax-approval" have the meaning given by Article 2(2) of the Social Security (Northern Ireland) Order 1986;

"voluntary contributions", in relation to any member of a judicial pension scheme, means voluntary contributions towards the provision of additional benefits, whether under that scheme or otherwise;

"voluntary contributions scheme" means any occupational pension scheme if and to the extent that it is a scheme under which such additional benefits as are mentioned in subsection (1) are, or are to be, provided;

and, where a person's voluntary contributions are made by deduction from salary, any reference to payment of, or by way of, voluntary contributions shall be taken to include a reference to the making of voluntary contributions by deduction or, as the case may require, to any voluntary contributions so made.

(8) Without prejudice to subsections (3)(c) and (d) and (4A), there may be paid out of money provided by the Parliament of the United Kingdom—

(a) any sums required for or in connection with the operation or administration of any prescribed voluntary contributions scheme; or

(b) any administrative expenses incurred under or by virtue of this section by a Minister of the Crown or government department.

(9) Any sums received under this section may be paid into the Consolidated Fund of the United Kingdom."

GENERAL NOTE

The main object of these amendments to the provisions governing existing judicial pension schemes is to allow a more flexible scheme for additional voluntary contributions, plus freestanding additional contribution schemes and the purchase of added years. They also incorporate the equivalent of the appeal process set out in s.20.

Section 25   SCHEDULE 4

PENSIONS FOR SENIOR PUBLIC INVESTIGATIVE OFFICERS

PART I

THE COMPTROLLER AND AUDITOR GENERAL

1. For section 13 of the Superannuation Act 1972 (pension provision for the Comptroller and Auditor General) there shall be substituted—

"The Comptroller and Auditor General

13.—(1) A person who first holds office on or after the appointed day as the Comptroller and Auditor General (in this section referred to as "the Comptroller") shall be entitled, if he was a member of a judicial pension scheme immediately before he first holds that office, to elect between—

(a) the scheme of pensions and other benefits under that judicial pension scheme (his "former scheme");

(b) (if different from his former scheme) the scheme of pensions and other benefits constituted by Part I of the 1993 Act ("the 1993 scheme"); and

(c) the scheme of pensions and other benefits applicable under section 1 of this Act to the civil service of the State ("the civil service scheme");

and, if he is not entitled to make an election under this subsection or if he is so entitled but fails to make such an election, he shall be treated as if he had been so entitled and had elected for the civil service scheme.

(2) If a person who held the office of Comptroller before the appointed day has made an election under the former enactments for the old judicial scheme, he shall be entitled to make an election under this subsection between—

(a) the old judicial scheme; and

(b) the 1993 scheme;

and, if he fails to make an election under this subsection, he shall be taken to have elected for the old judicial scheme.

(3) If a person who held the office of Comptroller before the appointed day—

(a) has made an election under the former enactments for the civil service scheme, or

(b) has failed to make an election under those enactments (so that he is taken to have elected for the civil service scheme),

he shall be treated as if he had been entitled to make an election under this section and had elected for the civil service scheme.

(4) Where a person elects under this section for his former scheme, that scheme shall, subject to regulations under this section, apply as if his service as Comptroller were service which was subject, in his case, to that scheme.

(5) A person who elects under subsection (1)(b) or (2)(b) above for the 1993 scheme, shall be entitled, when he ceases to hold office as Comptroller, to a pension under Part I of the 1993 Act at the appropriate annual rate (within the meaning of that Act) if he has held that office for at least 5 years and either—

(a) he has attained the age of 65; or

(b) he is disabled by permanent infirmity for the performance of the duties of the office;

and, subject to the following provisions of, and regulations under, this section, the provisions of Part I of that Act (other than sections 1(1) to (4) and 2) and of sections 19, 20 and 23 of, and Schedule 2 to, that Act (which provide for benefits in respect of earnings in excess of pension-capped salary, appeals and transfer of accrued rights) shall apply in relation to him and his service in the office of Comptroller as they apply in relation to a person to whom Part I of that Act applies.

(6) Subject to regulations under this section, in the application of provisions of the 1993 Act by virtue of subsection (5) above, a person who elects for the 1993 scheme shall be treated—

(a) as if the office of Comptroller were a qualifying judicial office (within the meaning of that Act) by virtue of inclusion among the offices specified in Part I of Schedule 1 to that Act;

(b) as if his election under this section were an election such as is mentioned in paragraph (d) of section 1(1) of that Act (so that, in particular, section 12 of that Act, which provides for the transfer of accrued rights into the scheme, applies);

(c) as if his pension by virtue of this section were a pension under section 2 of that Act (and, accordingly, a judicial pension, within the meaning of that Act); and

(d) for the purpose of determining, in the event of his death, the rate of any surviving spouse's or children's pension payable under section 5 to 8 of that Act in respect of his service as Comptroller, as if references in those sections to the annual rate of the deceased's judicial pension were references—

(i) where a pension had commenced to be paid to him by virtue of subsection (5) above, to the appropriate annual rate of that pension; or

(ii) where no such pension had commenced to be paid to him, to the rate that would have been the appropriate annual rate of the pension payable to him by virtue of subsection (5)(b) above, had he not died, but been disabled by permanent infirmity for the performance of the duties of his office on and after the date of death;

and, in the application of that Act to the Comptroller (whether by virtue of subsection (1)(a) or (b) or (2)(b) above) the references to the appropriate Minister in sections 13 (election for personal pension), 19 (benefits in respect of earnings in excess of pension-capped salary) and 20 (appeals) of, and Schedule 2 (transfer of accrued rights) to, that Act shall be taken as references to the Treasury and the power conferred by paragraph 2 of that Schedule to make regulations shall be exercisable by the Treasury.

(7) Where a person elects under this section for the civil service scheme, the principal civil service pension scheme within the meaning of section 2 of this Act and for the time being in force shall, subject to regulations under this section, apply as if his service as Comptroller were service in employment in the civil service of the State.

(8) Where a person elects under this section for the old judicial scheme, that scheme and the former enactments shall, subject to regulations under this section, continue to have effect in relation to him and his service in the office of Comptroller.

(9) Any power to make an election under this section shall be exercisable within such time and in such manner as may be prescribed in regulations under this section.

(10) The Treasury may make regulations for purposes supplementary to the other provisions of this section.

(11) Any such regulations may, without prejudice to section 38 or 39A of the Superannuation Act 1965 (employment in more than one public office), make special provision with respect to the pensions and other benefits payable to or in respect of a person to whom—

(a) his former scheme,
(b) the 1993 scheme,
(c) the civil service scheme, or
(d) the old judicial scheme,

applies, or has applied, in respect of any service other than service as Comptroller.

(12) The provision that may be made by virtue of subsection (11) above includes provision—

(a) for aggregating—

(i) other service falling within his former scheme, the 1993 scheme or the old judicial scheme with service as Comptroller, or

(ii) service as Comptroller with such other service,

for the purpose of determining qualification for, or entitlement to, or the amount of, benefit under the scheme in question;

(b) for increasing the amount of the benefit payable under any of the schemes mentioned in paragraph (a)(i) above, in the case of a person to whom that scheme applied in respect of an office held by him before appointment as Comptroller, up to the amount that would have been payable under that scheme if he had retired from that office on the ground of permanent infirmity immediately before his appointment.

(13) Any statutory instrument made by virtue of this section shall be subject to annulment in pursuance of a resolution of the House of Commons.

(14) Any pension or other benefit granted by virtue of this section shall be charged on, and issued out of, the Consolidated Fund.

(15) In this section—

"the 1981 Act" means the Judicial Pensions Act 1981;

"the 1993 Act" means the Judicial Pensions and Retirement Act 1993;

"the appointed day" means the day on which Part I of Schedule 4 to the 1993 Act comes into force;

"the former enactments" means section 13 of this Act, as it had effect from time to time before the appointed day;

"judicial pension scheme" means any public service pension scheme, as defined in—

(a) section 66(1) of the Social Security Pensions Act 1975, or

(b) Article 2(2) of the Social Security Pensions (Northern Ireland) Order 1975,

under which pensions and other benefits are payable in respect of service in one or more qualifying judicial offices, within the meaning of the 1993 Act, but does not include the civil service scheme;

"the old judicial scheme" means the statutory scheme of pensions and other benefits applicable under or by virtue of the 1981 Act to the judicial offices listed in section 1 of that Act."

PART II

THE PARLIAMENTARY COMMISSIONER FOR ADMINISTRATION

2. For Schedule 1 to the Parliamentary Commissioner Act 1967 (pension provision for the Parliamentary Commissioner for Administration) there shall be substituted—

"Section 2   SCHEDULE 1

PENSIONS AND OTHER BENEFITS

Persons taking office after the appointed day

1. A person who first holds office as the Commissioner on or after the appointed day

shall be entitled, if he was a member of a judicial pension scheme immediately before he first holds that office, to elect between—

(a) the scheme of pensions and other benefits under that judicial pension scheme (his "former scheme");

(b) (if different from his former scheme) the scheme of pensions and other benefits constituted by Part I of the 1993 Act ("the 1993 scheme"); and

(c) the scheme of pensions and other benefits applicable under section 1 of the Superannuation Act 1972 to the civil service of the State ("the civil service scheme");

and, if he is not entitled to make an election under this paragraph, or if he is so entitled but fails to make such an election, he shall be treated as if he had been so entitled and had elected for the civil service scheme.

Transitional provision for persons appointed before the appointed day

2.—(1) If a person who held the office of Commissioner before the appointed day has made an election under the former enactments for the old judicial scheme, he shall be entitled to make an election under this sub-paragraph between—

(a) the old judicial scheme; and

(b) the 1993 scheme;

and, if he fails to make an election under this sub-paragraph, he shall be taken to have elected for the old judicial scheme.

(2) If a person who held the office of Commissioner before the appointed day—

(a) has made an election under the former enactments for the civil service scheme, or

(b) has failed to make an election under those enactments (so that he is taken to have elected for the civil service scheme),

he shall be treated as if he had been entitled to make an election under this Schedule and had elected for the civil service scheme.

Effect of election to continue in former scheme

3. Where a person elects under this Schedule for his former scheme, that scheme shall, subject to regulations under this Schedule, apply as if his service as Commissioner were service which was subject, in his case, to that scheme.

Effect of election for the 1993 scheme

4.—(1) A person who elects under paragraph 1(b) or 2(1)(b) above for the 1993 scheme, shall be entitled, when he ceases to hold office as Commissioner, to a pension under Part I of the 1993 Act at the appropriate annual rate (within the meaning of that Act) if he has held that office for at least 5 years and either—

(a) he has attained the age of 65; or

(b) he is disabled by permanent infirmity for the performance of the duties of the office;

and, subject to the following provisions of, and regulations under, this Schedule, the provisions of Part I of that Act (other than sections 1(1) to (4) and 2) and of sections 19, 20 and 23 of, and Schedule 2 to, that Act (which provide for benefits in respect of earnings in excess of pension-capped salary, appeals and transfer of accrued rights) shall apply in relation to him and his service in the office of Commissioner as they apply in relation to a person to whom Part I of that Act applies.

(2) Subject to regulations under this Schedule, in the application of provisions of the 1993 Act by virtue of sub-paragraph (1) above, a person who elects for the 1993 scheme shall be treated—

(a) as if the office of Commissioner were a qualifying judicial office (within the meaning of that Act) by virtue of inclusion among the offices specified in Part I of Schedule 1 to that Act;

(b) as if his election under this Schedule were an election such as is mentioned in paragraph (d) of section 1(1) of that Act (so that, in particular, section 12 of that Act, which provides for the transfer of accrued rights into the scheme, applies);

(c) as if his pension by virtue of this Schedule were a pension under section 2 of that Act (and, accordingly, a judicial pension, within the meaning of that Act); and

(d) for the purpose of determining, in the event of his death, the rate of any surviving spouse's or children's pension payable under sections 5 to 8 of that Act in respect of his service as Commissioner, as if references in those sections to the annual rate of the deceased's judicial pension were references—

(i) where a pension had commenced to be paid to him by virtue of sub-paragraph (1) above, to the appropriate annual rate of that pension; or

(ii) where no such pension had commenced to be paid to him, to the rate that would have been the appropriate annual rate of the pension payable to him by virtue of sub-paragraph (1)(b) above, had he not died, but been disabled by permanent infirmity for the performance of the duties of his office on and after the date of death;

and, in the application of that Act to the Commissioner (whether by virtue of paragraph 1(a) or (b) or 2(1)(b) above) the references to the appropriate Minister in sections 13 (election for personal pension), 19 (benefits in respect of earnings in excess of pension-capped salary) and 20 (appeals) of, and Schedule 2 (transfer of accrued rights) to, that Act shall be taken as references to the Treasury and the power conferred by paragraph 2 of that Schedule to make regulations shall be exercisable by the Treasury.

Effect of election for, or to continue in, the civil service scheme

5. Where a person elects under this Schedule for the civil service scheme, the principal civil service pension scheme within the meaning of section 2 of the Superannuation Act 1972 and for the time being in force shall, subject to regulations under this Schedule, apply as if his service as Commissioner were service in employment in the civil service of the State.

Effect of election to continue in the old judicial scheme

6. Where a person elects under this Schedule for the old judicial scheme, that scheme and the former enactments shall, subject to regulations under this Schedule, continue to have effect in relation to him and his service in the office of Commissioner.

Time for, and manner of, election

7. Any power to make an election under this Schedule shall be exercisable within such time and in such manner as may be prescribed in regulations under this Schedule.

Regulations

8.—(1) The Treasury may make regulations for purposes supplementary to the other provisions of this Schedule.

(2) Any such regulations may, without prejudice to section 38 or 39A of the Superannuation Act 1965 (employment in more than one public office), make special provision with respect to the pensions and other benefits payable to or in respect of a person to whom—

(a) his former scheme,
(b) the 1993 scheme,
(c) the civil service scheme, or
(d) the old judicial scheme,

applies, or has applied, in respect of any service other than service as Commissioner.

(3) The provision that may be made by virtue of sub-paragraph (2) above includes provision—

(a) for aggregating—
(i) other service falling within his former scheme, the 1993 scheme or the old judicial scheme with service as Commissioner, or
(ii) service as Commissioner with such other service,
for the purpose of determining qualification for, or entitlement to, or the amount of, benefit under the scheme in question;
(b) for increasing the amount of the benefit payable under any of the schemes mentioned in paragraph (a)(i) above, in the case of a person to whom that scheme applied in respect of an office held by him before appointment as Commissioner, up to the amount that would have been payable under that scheme if he had retired from that office on the ground of permanent infirmity immediately before his appointment.

(4) Any statutory instrument made by virtue of this Schedule shall be subject to annulment in pursuance of a resolution of the House of Commons.

Pensions and benefits to be charged on the Consolidated Fund

9. Any pension or other benefit granted by virtue of this Schedule shall be charged on, and issued out of, the Consolidated Fund.

Interpretation

10. In this Schedule—

"the 1981 Act" means the Judicial Pensions Act 1981;

"the 1993 Act" means the Judicial Pensions and Retirement Act 1993;

"the appointed day" means the day on which Part II of Schedule 4 to the 1993 Act comes into force;

"the former enactments" means Schedule 1 to this Act, as it had effect from time to time before the appointed day;

"judicial pension scheme" means any public service pension scheme, as defined in—

    (a) section 66(1) of the Social Security Pensions Act 1975, or

    (b) Article 2(2) of the Social Security Pensions (Northern Ireland) Order 1975,

under which pensions and other benefits are payable in respect of service in one or more qualifying judicial offices, within the meaning of the 1993 Act, but does not include the civil service scheme;

"the old judicial scheme" means the statutory scheme of pensions and other benefits applicable under or by virtue of the 1981 Act to the judicial offices listed in section 1 of that Act."

PART III

THE HEALTH SERVICE COMMISSIONERS

The Health Service Commissioners for England and for Wales

3.—(1) Section 107 of the National Health Service Act 1977 (which makes provision with respect to the salaries and pensions of the Health Service Commissioners for England and for Wales) shall be amended in accordance with the following provisions of this paragraph.

(2) In subsection (2) (which applies Schedule 1 to the Parliamentary Commissioner Act 1967 in relation to persons who have held office as a Health Service Commissioner) for the words "who have held office", in both places where they occur, there shall be substituted the words "who hold, or have held, office".

(3) In subsection (6) (persons not to make simultaneously different elections in pursuance of paragraph 1 of that Schedule in respect of different offices)—

    (a) in paragraph (a), after the words "paragraph 1" there shall be inserted the words "or 2"; and

    (b) in paragraph (b), for the words "that paragraph" there shall be substituted the words "either of those paragraphs".

(4) In subsection (7) (which, among other things, provides for different regulations to be made under paragraph 4 of that Schedule in relation to different offices) for the words "paragraph 4" there shall be substituted the words "paragraph 8".

(5) The amendments made by sub-paragraphs (2) to (4) above have effect only in relation to Schedule 1 to the Parliamentary Commissioner Act 1967, as substituted by Part II above; and accordingly in any case where—

    (a) a person makes an election under paragraph 2(1)(a) of that Schedule for the old judicial scheme there mentioned, and

    (b) the former enactments mentioned in paragraph 6 of that Schedule continue to apply by virtue of that paragraph,

the amendments made by sub-paragraphs (3) and (4) above shall be disregarded in the continuing application of section 107 of the National Health Service Act 1977 in relation to those former enactments as they continue to have effect in relation to that person and that scheme.

The Health Service Commissioner for Scotland

4.—(1) Section 91 of the National Health Service (Scotland) Act 1978 (which makes provision with respect to the salary and pension of the Health Service Commission for Scotland) shall be amended in accordance with the following provisions of this paragraph.

(2) In subsection (2) (which applies Schedule 1 to the Parliamentary Commissioner Act 1967 in relation to persons who have held office as the Health Service Commissioner) for the words "who have held office", in both places where they occur, there shall be substituted the words "who hold, or have held, office".

(3) In subsection (6) (persons not to make simultaneously different elections in pursuance of paragraph 1 of that Schedule in respect of different offices)—

    (a) in paragraph (a), after the words "paragraph 1" there shall be inserted the words "or 2"; and

(b) in paragraph (b), for the words "that paragraph" there shall be substituted the words "either of those paragraphs".

(4) In subsection (7) (which, among other things, provides for different regulations to be made under paragraph 4 of that Schedule in relation to different offices) for the words "paragraph 4" there shall be substituted the words "paragraph 8".

(5) The amendments made by sub-paragraphs (2) to (4) above have effect only in relation to Schedule 1 to the Parliamentary Commissioner Act 1967, as substituted by Part II above; and accordingly in any case where—

(a) a person makes an election under paragraph 2(1)(a) of that Schedule for the old judicial scheme there mentioned, and

(b) the former enactments mentioned in paragraph 6 of that Schedule continue to apply by virtue of that paragraph,

the amendments made by sub-paragraphs (3) and (4) above shall be disregarded in the continuing application of section 91 of the National Health Service (Scotland) Act 1978 in relation to those former enactments as they continue to have effect in relation to that person and that scheme.

PART IV

THE COMPTROLLER AND AUDITOR GENERAL FOR NORTHERN IRELAND

5.—(1) The Audit (Northern Ireland) Order 1987 shall be amended in accordance with the following provisions of this paragraph.

(2) In Article 2(2) (interpretation), in the definition of "the appointed day" after the word "means" there shall be inserted the words "(except in Article 4A)".

(3) In paragraph (4) of Article 4 (pension of the Comptroller and Auditor General), after the words "Northern Ireland" (where they occur for the second time) there shall be inserted the words "unless he elects under Article 4A for it to be treated otherwise".

(4) After that Article there shall be inserted the following Article—

"*Pension of Comptroller and Auditor General: supplementary*

4A.—(1) This Article applies to a person—

(a) who first holds office on or after the appointed day as the Comptroller and Auditor General; and

(b) who, immediately before he first holds that office, is a member of a judicial pension scheme.

(2) A person to whom this Article applies shall be entitled to elect between—

(a) the scheme of pensions and other benefits under the judicial pension scheme mentioned in paragraph (1)(b) (his "former scheme");

(b) (if different from his former scheme) the scheme of pensions and other benefits constituted by Part I of the 1993 Act ("the 1993 scheme"); and

(c) the scheme of pensions and other benefits applicable under the Superannuation (Northern Ireland) Order 1972 to the civil service of Northern Ireland ("the civil service scheme");

and, if he fails to make an election under this paragraph, he shall be treated as if he had elected for the civil service scheme.

(3) Where a person elects under this Article for his former scheme, that scheme shall, subject to regulations under this Article, apply as if his service as Comptroller and Auditor General were service which was subject, in his case, to that scheme.

(4) A person who elects under paragraph (2)(b) for the 1993 scheme, shall be entitled, when he ceases to hold office as Comptroller and Auditor General, to a pension under Part I of the 1993 Act at the appropriate annual rate (within the meaning of that Act) if he has held that office for at least five years and either—

(a) he has attained the age of 65; or

(b) he is disabled by permanent infirmity for the performance of the duties of the office;

and, subject to the following provisions of, and regulations under, this Article, the provisions of Part I of that Act (other than sections 1(1) to (4) and 2) and of sections 19, 20 and 23 of, and Schedule 2 to, that Act (which provide for benefits in respect of earnings in excess of pension-capped salary, appeals and transfer of accrued rights) shall apply in relation to him and his service in the office of Comptroller and Auditor General as they apply in relation to a person to whom Part I of that Act applies.

(5) Subject to regulations under this Article, in the application of provisions of the 1993 Act by virtue of paragraph (4), a person who elects for the 1993 scheme shall be treated—

(a) as if the office of the Comptroller and Auditor General were a qualifying judicial office (within the meaning of that Act) by virtue of inclusion among the offices specified in Part I of Schedule 1 to that Act;

(b) as if his election under this Article were an election such as is mentioned in paragraph (d) of section 1(1) of that Act (so that, in particular, section 12 of that Act, which provides for the transfer of accrued rights into the scheme, applies);

(c) as if his pension by virtue of this Article were a pension under section 2 of that Act (and, accordingly, a judicial pension, within the meaning of that Act); and

(d) for the purpose of determining, in the event of his death, the rate of any surviving spouse's or children's pension payable under sections 5 to 8 of that Act in respect of his service as Comptroller and Auditor General, as if references in those sections to the annual rate of the deceased's judicial pension were references—

(i) where a pension had commenced to be paid to him by virtue of paragraph (4), to the appropriate annual rate of that pension; or

(ii) where no such pension had commenced to be paid to him, to the rate that would have been the appropriate annual rate of the pension payable to him by virtue of paragraph (4)(b), had he not died, but been disabled by permanent infirmity for the performance of the duties of his office on and after the date of death;

and, in the application of that Act to the Comptroller and Auditor General (whether by virtue of paragraph (2)(a) or (b)) the references to the appropriate Minister in sections 13 (election for personal pension), 19 (benefits in respect of earnings in excess of pension-capped salary) and 20 (appeals) of, and Schedule 2 (transfer of accrued rights) to, that Act shall be taken as references to the Treasury and the power conferred by paragraph 2 of that Schedule to make regulations shall be exercisable by the Treasury.

(6) Where a person elects under this Article for the civil service scheme, Article 4(4) shall apply in relation to his service as Comptroller and Auditor General.

(7) Any power to make an election under this Article shall be exercisable within such time and in such manner as may be prescribed in regulations under this Article. ·

(8) The Treasury may make regulations for purposes supplementary to the other provisions of this Article.

(9) Any such regulations may, without prejudice to section 38 of the Superannuation Act (Northern Ireland) 1967 or section 39A of the Superannuation Act 1965 (employment in more than one public office), make special provision with respect to the pensions and other benefits payable to or in respect of a person to whom—

(a) his former scheme,

(b) the 1993 scheme, or

(c) the civil service scheme,

applies, or has applied, in respect of any service other than service as Comptroller and Auditor General.

(10) The provision that may be made by virtue of paragraph (9) includes provision—

(a) for aggregating—

(i) other service falling within his former scheme or the 1993 scheme with service as Comptroller and Auditor General, or

(ii) service as Comptroller and Auditor General with such other service,

for the purpose of determining qualification for, or entitlement to, or the amount of, benefit under the scheme in question;

(b) for increasing the amount of the benefit payable under either of the schemes mentioned in sub-paragraph (a)(i), in the case of a person to whom that scheme applied in respect of an office held by him before appointment as Comptroller and Auditor General, up to the amount that would have been payable under that scheme if he had retired from that office on the ground of permanent infirmity immediately before his appointment.

(11) Regulations made under this Article shall be subject to annulment in like manner as a statutory instrument and section 5 of the Statutory Instruments Act 1946 shall apply accordingly.

(12) Any pension or other benefit granted by virtue of this Article (except a pension or other benefit under the civil service scheme) shall be charged on, and issued out of, the Consolidated Fund of the United Kingdom.

(13) In this Article—

"the 1993 Act" means the Judicial Pensions and Retirement Act 1993;

"the appointed day" means the day on which Part IV of Schedule 4 to the 1993 Act comes into force;

"judicial pension scheme" means any public service pension scheme, as defined in—

(a) section 66(1) of the Social Security Pensions Act 1975, or

(b) Article 2(2) of the Social Security Pensions (Northern Ireland) Order 1975, under which pensions and other benefits are payable in respect of service in one or more qualifying judicial offices, within the meaning of the 1993 Act, but does not include the civil service scheme."

PART V

THE NORTHERN IRELAND PARLIAMENTARY COMMISSIONER FOR ADMINISTRATION AND THE NORTHERN IRELAND COMMISSIONER FOR COMPLAINTS

6.—(1) The Parliamentary Commissioner Act (Northern Ireland) 1969 shall be amended in accordance with the following provisions of this paragraph.

(2) In subsection (3) of section 2 (power to determine the pension and other benefits payable to person who has held office as Commissioner) at the beginning there shall be inserted the words "Subject to subsections (4A) and (4B),".

(3) After subsection (4) of that section there shall be inserted the following subsections—

"(4A) Subsection (3) shall not apply in relation to pension and other benefits payable to or in respect of a person who first holds the office of Commissioner on or after the day appointed for the coming into force of Part V of Schedule 4 to the Judicial Pensions and Retirement Act 1993.

(4B) The provisions of Schedule 1A shall have effect with respect to the pensions and other benefits to be paid to or in respect of persons who have held office as Commissioner."

(4) In subsection (5) of that section, at the end there shall be added the words "or by virtue of Schedule 1A".

(5) In subsection (6) of that section, at the beginning there shall be inserted the words "Except insofar as Schedule 1A otherwise provides".

(6) Immediately before Schedule 1 there shall be inserted the following Schedule—

"Section 2   SCHEDULE 1A

PENSIONS AND OTHER BENEFITS

Persons taking office after the appointed day

1. A person who first holds office as the Commissioner on or after the appointed day shall be entitled, if he was a member of a judicial pension scheme immediately before he first holds that office, to elect between—

    (a) the scheme of pensions and other benefits under that judicial pension scheme (his "former scheme");

    (b) (if different from his former scheme) the scheme of pensions and other benefits constituted by Part I of the 1993 Act ("the 1993 scheme"); and

    (c) the scheme of pensions and other benefits applicable under Article 3 of the Superannuation (Northern Ireland) Order 1972 to the civil service of Northern Ireland ("the civil service scheme");

and, if he is not entitled to make an election under this paragraph, or if he is so entitled but fails to make such an election, he shall be treated as if he had been so entitled and had elected for the civil service scheme.

Transitional provision for persons appointed before the appointed day

2. If a person who held the office of Commissioner before the appointed day has made an election under the former enactment for the old judicial scheme, he shall be entitled to make an election under this sub-paragraph between—

    (a) the old judicial scheme; and

    (b) the 1993 scheme;

and, if he fails to make an election under this sub-paragraph, he shall be taken to have elected for the old judicial scheme.

Effect of election to continue in former scheme

3. Where a person elects under this Schedule for his former scheme, that scheme shall, subject to regulations under this Schedule, apply as if his service as Commissioner were service which was subject, in his case, to that scheme.

Effect of election for the 1993 scheme

4.—(1) A person who elects under paragraph 1(b) or 2(b) for the 1993 scheme, shall be entitled, when he ceases to hold office as Commissioner, to a pension under Part I of the 1993 Act at the appropriate annual rate (within the meaning of that Act) if he has held that office for at least 5 years and either—

(a) he has attained the age of 65; or

(b) he is disabled by permanent infirmity for the performance of the duties of the office;

and, subject to the following provisions of, and regulations under, this Schedule, the provisions of Part I of that Act (other than sections 1(1) to (4) and 2) and of sections 19, 20 and 23 of, and Schedule 2 to, that Act (which provide for benefits in respect of earnings in excess of pension-capped salary, appeals and transfer of accrued rights) shall apply in relation to him and his service in the office of Commissioner as they apply in relation to a person to whom Part I of that Act applies.

(2) Subject to regulations under this Schedule, in the application of provisions of the 1993 Act by virtue of sub-paragraph (1), a person who elects for the 1993 scheme shall be treated—

(a) as if the office of Commissioner were a qualifying judicial office (within the meaning of that Act) by virtue of inclusion among the offices specified in Part I of Schedule 1 to that Act;

(b) as if his election under this Schedule were an election such as is mentioned in paragraph (d) of section 1(1) of that Act (so that, in particular, section 12 of that Act, which provides for the transfer of accrued rights into the scheme, applies);

(c) as if his pension by virtue of this Schedule were a pension under section 2 of that Act (and, accordingly, a judicial pension, within the meaning of that Act); and

(d) for the purpose of determining, in the event of his death, the rate of any surviving spouse's or children's pension payable under sections 5 to 8 of that Act in respect of his service as Commissioner, as if references in those sections to the annual rate of the deceased's judicial pension were references—

(i) where a pension had commenced to be paid to him by virtue of sub-paragraph (1), to the appropriate annual rate of that pension; or

(ii) where no such pension had commenced to be paid to him, to the rate that would have been the appropriate annual rate of the pension payable to him by virtue of sub-paragraph (1)(b), had he not died, but been disabled by permanent infirmity for the performance of the duties of his office on and after the date of death;

and, in the application of that Act to the Commissioner (whether by virtue of paragraph 1(a) or (b) or 2(b)) the references to the appropriate Minister in sections 13 (election for personal pension), 19 (benefits in respect of earnings in excess of pension-capped salary) and 20 (appeals) of, and Schedule 2 (transfer of accrued rights) to, that Act shall be taken as references to the Treasury and the power conferred by paragraph 2 of that Schedule to make regulations shall be exercisable by the Treasury.

Effect of election for, or to continue in, the civil service scheme

5. Where a person elects under this Schedule for the civil service scheme, the principal civil service pension scheme within the meaning of Article 4 of the Superannuation (Northern Ireland) Order 1972 and for the time being in force shall apply as if his service as Commissioner were service in employment in the civil service of Northern Ireland.

Effect of election to continue in the old judicial scheme

6. Where a person elects under this Schedule for the old judicial scheme, that scheme and the former enactment shall continue to have effect in relation to him and his service in the office of Commissioner.

Time for, and manner of, election

7. Any power to make an election under this Schedule shall be exercisable within such time and in such manner as may be prescribed in regulations under this Schedule.

Regulations

8.—(1) The Treasury may make regulations for purposes supplementary to the other provisions of this Schedule.

(2) Any such regulations may, without prejudice to section 38 of the Superannuation Act (Northern Ireland) 1967 or section 39A of the Superannuation Act 1965 (employment in

more than one public office), make special provision with respect to the pensions and other benefits payable to or in respect of a person to whom—

    (a) his former scheme,

    (b) the 1993 scheme,

    (c) the civil service scheme, or

    (d) the old judicial scheme,

applies, or has applied, in respect of any service other than service as Commissioner.

    (3) The provision that may be made by virtue of sub-paragraph (2) includes provision—

        (a) for aggregating—

            (i) other service falling within his former scheme, the 1993 scheme or the old judicial scheme with service as Commissioner, or

            (ii) service as Commissioner with such other service,

        for the purpose of determining qualification for, or entitlement to, or the amount of, benefit under the scheme in question;

        (b) for increasing the amount of the benefit payable under any of the schemes mentioned in paragraph (a)(i), in the case of a person to whom that scheme applied in respect of an office held by him before appointment as Commissioner, up to the amount that would have been payable under that scheme if he had retired from that office on the ground of permanent infirmity immediately before his appointment.

    (4) Regulations made under this Schedule shall be subject to annulment in like manner as a statutory instrument and section 5 of the Statutory Instruments Act 1946 shall apply accordingly.

Pensions and benefits to be charged on the Consolidated Fund

    9. Any pension or other benefit granted by virtue of this Schedule (except a pension or other benefit under the civil service scheme or the old judicial scheme) shall be charged on, and issued out of, the Consolidated Fund of the United Kingdom.

Interpretation

    10. In this Schedule—

"the 1993 Act" means the Judicial Pensions and Retirement Act 1993;

"the appointed day" means the day on which Part V of Schedule 4 to the 1993 Act comes into force;

"the former enactment" means the Parliamentary Commissioner and Commissioner for Complaints (Pension) Order (Northern Ireland) 1973 as it had effect from time to time before the appointed day;

"judicial pension scheme" means any public service pension scheme, as defined in—

        (a) section 66(1) of the Social Security Pensions Act 1975, or

        (b) Article 2(2) of the Social Security Pensions (Northern Ireland) Order 1975,

    under which pensions and other benefits are payable in respect of service in one or more qualifying judicial offices, within the meaning of the 1993 Act, but does not include the civil service scheme;

"the old judicial scheme" means the scheme of pensions and other benefits set out in Part II of the Parliamentary Commissioner and Commissioner for Complaints (Pension) Order (Northern Ireland) 1973."

    7.—(1) The Commissioner for Complaints Act (Northern Ireland) 1969 shall be amended in accordance with the following provisions of this paragraph.

    (2) In subsection (2) of section 2 (remuneration), at the end there shall be added the words "or payable by virtue of Schedule 1A".

    (3) In subsection (3) of that section, at the beginning there shall be inserted "Except insofar as Schedule 1A otherwise provides".

    (4) After that subsection there shall be added—

        "(4) The provisions of Schedule 1A shall have effect with respect to the pensions and other benefits to be paid to or in respect of persons who have held office as Commissioner."

    (5) After subsection (1) of section 13 (power to make provision by order) there shall be inserted the following subsection—

        "(1A) Paragraph (c) of subsection (1) shall not apply in relation to pension and other benefits payable to or in respect of a person who first holds the office of Commissioner on or after the day appointed for the coming into force of Part V of Schedule 4 to the Judicial Pensions and Retirement Act 1993."

    (6) Immediately before Schedule 1 there shall be inserted as Schedule 1A the Schedule set out in paragraph 6(6) above.

SCHEDULE 5

RETIREMENT PROVISIONS: THE RELEVANT OFFICES

Lord of Appeal in Ordinary
Judge of the Supreme Court of England and Wales, other than the Lord Chancellor
Deputy judge of the High Court
Lord President of the Court of Session
Lord Justice Clerk
Judge of the Court of Session
Temporary Judge of the Court of Session
Lord Chief Justice of Northern Ireland
Lord Justice of Appeal in Northern Ireland
Judge of the High Court of Justice in Northern Ireland
Circuit judge
Sheriff principal or sheriff in Scotland
Temporary sheriff principal or temporary sheriff in Scotland
County Court judge in Northern Ireland
Deputy County Court judge in Northern Ireland
Master, Queen's Bench Division
Deputy or temporary Master, Queen's Bench Division, appointed under subsection (1) of section 91 of the Supreme Court Act 1981 otherwise than by virtue of subsection (3) of that section
Admiralty Registrar
Deputy or temporary Admiralty Registrar appointed under subsection (1) of section 91 of the Supreme Court Act 1981 otherwise than by virtue of subsection (3) of that section
Master, Chancery Division
Deputy or temporary Master, Chancery Division, appointed under subsection (1) of section 91 of the Supreme Court Act 1981 otherwise than by virtue of subsection (3) of that section
Registrar in Bankruptcy of the High Court
Deputy or temporary Registrar in Bankruptcy of the High Court appointed under sub-section (1) of section 91 of the Supreme Court Act 1981 otherwise than by virtue of subsection (3) of that section
Taxing Master of the Supreme Court
Deputy or temporary Taxing Master of the Supreme Court appointed under subsection (1) of section 91 of the Supreme Court Act 1981 otherwise than by virtue of subsection (3) of that section
District judge of the principal registry of the Family Division
Deputy or temporary district judge of the principal registry of the Family Division appointed under subsection (1) of section 91 of the Supreme Court Act 1981 otherwise than by virtue of subsection (3) of that section
Registrar of Civil Appeals
Deputy or temporary Registrar of Civil Appeals appointed under subsection (1) of section 91 of the Supreme Court Act 1981 otherwise than by virtue of subsection (3) of that section
Master of the Court of Protection
Deputy or temporary Master of the Court of Protection appointed under subsection (1) of section 91 of the Supreme Court Act 1981 otherwise than by virtue of subsection (3) of that section
District judge (whether appointed under section 100 of the Supreme Court Act 1981 or section 6 of the County Courts Act 1984)
Deputy district judge appointed under section 102 of the Supreme Court Act 1981, except in a case where the person in question has previously held office as a district judge for a district registry
Deputy district judge appointed under section 8 of the County Courts Act 1984, except in a case where the person in question has previously held office as a district judge for a county court district
Recorder
Assistant Recorder
Any appointment under section 70 or 75(1) of the Judicature (Northern Ireland) Act 1978 to an office from time to time specified in column 1 of Schedule 3 to that Act (statutory office) or any appointment under section 74 of that Act to act in any such office
Stipendiary magistrate in England and Wales
Resident Magistrate appointed under the Magistrates' Courts Act (Northern Ireland) 1964

Deputy Resident Magistrate appointed under the Magistrates' Courts Act (Northern Ireland) 1964

Chief or other Social Security Commissioner (including appointments in pursuance of section 52(2) of the Social Security Administration Act 1992)

Chief or other Child Support Commissioner (including appointments in pursuance of paragraph 4 of Schedule 4 to the Child Support Act 1991)

Chief or other Social Security Commissioner for Northern Ireland (including appointments in pursuance of section 50(2) of the Social Security Administration (Northern Ireland) Act 1992)

Chief or other Child Support Commissioner for Northern Ireland (including appointments in pursuance of paragraph 4 of Schedule 4 to the Child Support Act 1991 as that paragraph has effect by virtue of paragraph 8 of that Schedule)

President of social security appeal tribunals, medical appeal tribunals, disability appeal tribunals and child support appeal tribunals

President of social security appeal tribunals, medical appeal tribunals, disability appeal tribunals and child support appeal tribunals in Northern Ireland

Chairman of social security appeal tribunals, medical appeal tribunals and disability appeal tribunals

Chairman of child support appeal tribunals

Chairman of social security appeal tribunals, medical appeal tribunals and disability appeal tribunals in Northern Ireland

Chairman of child support appeal tribunals in Northern Ireland

Chairman of vaccine damage tribunals

Chairman of the Foreign Compensation Commission

Commons Commissioner

President of the Industrial Tribunals (England and Wales)

President of the Industrial Tribunals (Scotland)

President or Vice-President of Industrial Tribunals and of the Fair Employment Tribunal (Northern Ireland)

Chairman of industrial tribunals, appointed in pursuance of regulations under section 128 of the Employment Protection (Consolidation) Act 1978

Chairman of industrial tribunals in Northern Ireland, appointed in pursuance of regulations under Article 30 of the Industrial Training (Northern Ireland) Order 1984

Chairman of the Fair Employment Tribunal, appointed under section 3(1)(c) of the Fair Employment (Northern Ireland) Act 1989

President of the Industrial Court appointed in pursuance of Article 91 of the Industrial Relations (Northern Ireland) Order 1992

Member of the Employment Appeal Tribunal appointed under section 135(2)(c) of the Employment Protection (Consolidation) Act 1978

President or other member of the Lands Tribunal, the Lands Tribunal for Scotland or the Lands Tribunal for Northern Ireland

Judge Advocate General

Judge Advocate of Her Majesty's Fleet

President of Value Added Tax Tribunals

Chairman of value added tax tribunals

Commissioner for the special purposes of the Income Tax Acts appointed under section 4 of the Taxes Management Act 1970

Deputy Special Commissioner appointed under section 4A of the Taxes Management Act 1970

President or other member of the Immigration Appeal Tribunal

Immigration adjudicator

President or other member of Pensions Appeal Tribunals

Chairman or other member of a Mental Health Review Tribunal constituted under the Mental Health Act 1983

Member of the Financial Services Tribunal appointed by the Lord Chancellor

Chairman of a tribunal constituted for the purposes of sections 14 and 15 of the Misuse of Drugs Act 1971

Chairman of an advisory body constituted for the purposes of section 14 of the Misuse of Drugs Act 1971

Appointed member of the Restrictive Practices Court, within the meaning of section 3 of the Restrictive Practices Court Act 1976

Chairman or other member of the tribunal constituted by section 706 of the Income and Corporation Taxes Act 1988

Arbitrator appointed under paragraph 1(5) of Schedule 11 to the Agricultural Holdings Act 1986

Chairman, deputy-chairman or other member of an Agricultural Land Tribunal (other than an assessor added to the Tribunal under paragraph 16(2) of Schedule 9 to the Agriculture Act 1947)

President of the Aircraft and Shipbuilding Industries Arbitration Tribunal

Chairman of a tribunal established by section 29 of the Betting, Gaming and Lotteries Act 1963

Chairman or deputy chairman of the Copyright Tribunal

Chairman or deputy chairman of the Data Protection Tribunal

Chairman of an Independent Schools Tribunal

President of a tribunal constituted under Schedule 3 to the Industry Act 1975

Chairman of the tribunal constituted under Schedule 9 to the National Health Service Act 1977

Chairman of the Plant Varieties and Seeds Tribunal

Chairman of a Registered Homes Tribunal constituted under the Registered Homes Act 1984

Chairman or other member of Rent Assessment Committees appointed by the Lord Chancellor under Schedule 10 to the Rent Act 1977

President or chairman of the Transport Tribunal

President of the tribunal established under section 9 of the Wireless Telegraphy Act 1949

Wreck commissioner appointed under section 82 of the Merchant Shipping Act 1970

Chairman of a Reinstatement Committee constituted under the Reserve Forces (Safeguard of Employment) Act 1985

Section 26   SCHEDULE 6

RETIREMENT DATES FOR CERTAIN JUDICIAL OFFICES

The Judicial Committee of the Privy Council

1.—(1) At the end of section 3 of the Appellate Jurisdiction Act 1887 (Judicial Committee of the Privy Council to include such members of the Privy Council as are holding or have held high judicial office) there shall be added the words "but no person shall be a member of that Committee by virtue of this section at any time after the day on which he attains the age of seventy-five years unless he is for the time being the Lord Chancellor of Great Britain."

(2) At the end of section 1 of the Judicial Committee Act 1881 (person holding, or who has held, the office of Lord Justice of Appeal, if a member of the Privy Council, to be a member of the Judicial Committee) there shall be added the words "but no person shall be a member of that Committee by virtue of this section at any time after the day on which he attains the age of seventy-five years."

Lords of Appeal

2. In section 5 of the Appellate Jurisdiction Act 1876, after paragraph (3) (peers who hold, or have held, high judicial office to be Lords of Appeal) there shall be added the words—

"but this section is subject to sections 26(7)(b) and 27 of the Judicial Pensions and Retirement Act 1993 (prohibition on participating in the hearing and determination of appeals after attaining the age of seventy-five years, except for the purpose of completing proceedings already begun)."

Lords of Appeal in Ordinary and senior judges in Scotland and Northern Ireland

3. In subsection (1) of section 2 of the Judicial Pensions Act 1959 (which provides that any Lord of Appeal in Ordinary, Lord Justice General, Lord Justice Clerk, Senator of the College of Justice in Scotland, Lord Chief Justice of Northern Ireland, Lord Justice of Appeal in Northern Ireland or Judge of the High Court of Justice in Northern Ireland is to vacate his office on the day on which he attains the age of 75) for the words "seventy-five" there shall be substituted the word "seventy".

Judges of the Supreme Court

4. In subsection (2) of section 11 of the Supreme Court Act 1981 (which provides that any judge of the Supreme Court, other than the Lord Chancellor, is to vacate his office no later than the day on which he attains the age of 75) for the words "seventy-five" there shall be substituted the word "seventy".

Acting and deputy judges

5.—(1) In section 9 of the Supreme Court Act 1981, after subsection (1) (persons who may act as judges) there shall be inserted—

"(1A) A person shall not act as a judge by virtue of subsection (1) after the day on which he attains the age of 75."

(2) After subsection (4) of that section (appointment of deputy High Court judges) there shall be inserted—

"(4A) No appointment of a person as a deputy judge of the High Court shall be such as to extend beyond the day on which he attains the age of 70, but this subsection is subject to section 26(4) to (6) of the Judicial Pensions and Retirement Act 1993 (Lord Chancellor's power to authorise continuance in office up to the age of 75)."

(3) In subsection (6)(b) of that section (which refers to subsection (7) of that section, relating to the completion of proceedings after retirement), for the words "subject to subsection (7)" there shall be substituted the words "subject to section 27 of the Judicial Pensions and Retirement Act 1993".

Temporary Judges of the Court of Session

6.—(1) In paragraph 5 of Schedule 4 to the Law Reform (Miscellaneous Provisions) (Scotland) Act 1990 (appointment of temporary judges of the Court of Session) for the words "75 years" there shall be substituted the words "70 years".

(2) The said paragraph 5 as amended by sub-paragraph (1) above shall be numbered sub-paragraph (1) and there shall be added the following sub-paragraph—

"(2) Sub-paragraph (1) above is subject to section 26(4) to (6) of the Judicial Pensions and Retirement Act 1993 (power to authorise continuance in office up to the age of 75)."

Acting judges of the High Court or Court of Appeal in Northern Ireland

7. In section 7 of the Judicature (Northern Ireland) Act 1978, in subsection (1) (which provides that certain judges and former judges may, at the request of the Lord Chancellor, sit as judges of the High Court or Court of Appeal in Northern Ireland)—

(a) the words "at any time" shall be omitted; and

(b) at the end, there shall be added the words "at any time on or before the day on which he attains the age of seventy-five."

Circuit judges

8.—(1) Section 17 of the Courts Act 1971 (retirement of Circuit judges) shall be amended in accordance with the following provisions of this paragraph.

(2) For subsection (1) (which requires a Circuit judge to vacate his office at the end of the completed year of service in which he attains the age of 72, subject to the possibility of extended appointment) there shall be substituted—

"(1) Subject to subsection (4) below and to subsections (4) to (6) of section 26 of the Judicial Pensions and Retirement Act 1993 (power to authorise continuance in office up to the age of 75), a Circuit judge shall vacate his office on the day on which he attains the age of 70."

(3) Subsection (2) (which contains power to continue a Circuit judge's appointment up to the age of 75 and which is superseded by section 26(4) to (6) of this Act) shall cease to have effect.

(4) Subsection (3) (day on which certain persons are to be regarded as completing a year of service) shall cease to have effect.

Recorders, deputy Circuit judges and assistant Recorders

9.—(1) In section 21 of the Courts Act 1971, in subsection (5) (Recorder not to hold office after the end of the completed year of service in which he attains the age of 72) for the words from "the end of" onwards there shall be substituted the words "the day on which he attains the age of seventy, but this subsection is subject to section 26(4) to (6) of the Judicial Pensions and Retirement Act 1993 (Lord Chancellor's power to authorise continuance in office up to the age of 75)."

(2) In section 24 of that Act (deputy Circuit judges and assistant Recorders), after subsection (1) there shall be inserted—

"(1A) No appointment of a person under subsection (1) above shall be such as to extend—

(a) in the case of appointment as a deputy Circuit judge, beyond the day on which he attains the age of seventy-five; or

(b) in the case of appointment as an assistant Recorder, beyond the day on which he attains the age of seventy;

but paragraph (b) above is subject to section 26(4) to (6) of the Judicial Pensions and Retirement Act 1993 (Lord Chancellor's power to authorise continuance in office up to the age of 75)."

Sheriffs

10. In the Sheriff Courts (Scotland) Act 1971, after section 5 (qualification for offices of sheriff principal and sheriff) there shall be inserted—

"Retiring age for sheriff principal and sheriff
5A.—(1) A sheriff principal or sheriff shall vacate his office on the day on which he attains the age of 70.
(2) Subsection (1) above is subject to section 26(4) to (6) of the Judicial Pensions and Retirement Act 1993 (power to authorise continuance in office up to the age of 75)."

Temporary sheriffs

11. In section 11 of the Sheriff Courts (Scotland) Act 1971 (power to appoint temporary sheriffs principal and temporary sheriffs), after subsection (4) there shall be inserted the following subsections—

"(4A) No appointment under this section of a person to be a temporary sheriff principal or temporary sheriff shall extend beyond the day on which the person reaches the age of 70.
(4B) Subsection (4A) above is subject to section 26(4) to (6) of the Judicial Pensions and Retirement Act 1993 (power to authorise continuance in office up to the age of 75)."

County Court Judge in Northern Ireland

12. In section 105 of the County Courts Act (Northern Ireland) 1959, for subsection (4) (which requires every judge to vacate his office at the end of the completed year of service in which he attains the age of 72, but subject to a proviso for judges who would not have completed 15 years' service) there shall be substituted—

"(4) Every judge shall vacate his office on the day on which he attains the age of seventy years; but this subsection is subject to section 26(4) to (6) of the Judicial Pensions and Retirement Act 1993 (Lord Chancellor's power to authorise continuance in office up to the age of 75)."

Deputy judge of a county court in Northern Ireland

13. In section 107 of the County Courts Act (Northern Ireland) 1959, for subsection (4) (which provides that, except in the case of a former judge, a deputy judge shall not hold office after the end of the completed year of service in which he attains the age of 72) there shall be substituted—

"(4) Neither the initial term for which a deputy judge is appointed nor any extension of that term under subsection (3) shall be such as to continue his appointment as a deputy judge after the day on which he attains the age of seventy; but this subsection is subject to section 26(4) to (6) of the Judicial Pensions and Retirement Act 1993 (Lord Chancellor's power to authorise continuance in office up to the age of 75)."

Officers of the Supreme Court

14.—(1) Section 92 of the Supreme Court Act 1981 (tenure of office of certain officers of the Supreme Court) shall be amended in accordance with the following provisions of this paragraph.
(2) In subsection (1) (certain Masters, Registrars and other officers of the Supreme Court to vacate office at the end of the completed year of service in which they attain the age of 72)—
(a) after the words "Subject to the following provisions of this section" there shall be inserted the words "and to subsections (4) to (6) of section 26 of the Judicial Pensions and Retirement Act 1993 (Lord Chancellor's power to authorise continuance in office up to the age of 75)"; and
(b) for the words from "at the end" onwards there shall be substituted the words "on the day on which he attains the age of seventy years."
(3) In subsection (2B) (offices to which subsection (2A) applies) the words "and the office of Queen's Coroner and Attorney and Master of the Crown Office and Registrar of Criminal Appeals" shall be omitted.
(4) Subsection (2C) (which makes provision for determining the day on which persons who successively hold offices falling within column 1 of Part I or II of Schedule 2 to that Act are to be regarded as completing a year of service, and which is of no further utility) shall cease to have effect.
(5) After that subsection there shall be inserted—

"(2D) Subject to the following provisions of this section, a person who holds an office to which this subsection applies shall vacate it on the day on which he attains the age of sixty-two years.

(2E) Subsection (2D) applies to the office of Queen's Coroner and Attorney and Master of the Crown Office and Registrar of Criminal Appeals."

(6) Subsection (3) (which contains power to continue a person's appointment to an office to which subsection (1) applies up to the age of 75 and which is superseded by section 26(4) to (6) of this Act) shall cease to have effect.

(7) In subsection (4) (offices to which subsection (1) or (2A) applies to be held during good behaviour) for the words "or (2A)" there shall be substituted the words ", (2A) or (2D)".

Deputy and temporary officers of the Supreme Court

15. In section 91 of the Supreme Court Act 1981, in subsection (3) (which permits certain appointments as a deputy or temporary officer to be made, notwithstanding that the person would be disqualified by age from holding the office in question) after paragraph (c) there shall be added—

"but no appointment by virtue of this subsection shall be such as to extend beyond the day on which the person in question attains the age of seventy-five years."

Deputy district judges of district registries of the High Court

16. In section 102 of the Supreme Court Act 1981, at the end of subsection (3) (which permits certain appointments as a deputy district judge of a district registry of the High Court to be made, notwithstanding that the person would be disqualified by age from holding the office in question) there shall be added the words "; but no appointment by virtue of this subsection shall be such as to extend beyond the day on which the person in question attains the age of seventy-five years."

District judges and deputy district judges of county courts

17.—(1) In section 8 of the County Courts Act 1984 (deputy district judges) after subsection (1) there shall be inserted—

"(1A) Any appointment of a person as a deputy district judge—

(a) if he has previously held office as a district judge, shall not be such as to extend beyond the day on which he attains the age of 75 years; and

(b) in any other case, shall not be such as to extend beyond the day on which he attains the age of 70 years, but subject to section 26(4) to (6) of the Judicial Pensions and Retirement Act 1993 (power to authorise continuance in office up to the age of 75)."

(2) Section 11 of that Act (tenure of office of district judge etc) shall be amended in accordance with the following provisions of this paragraph.

(3) For subsections (1) and (2) (which provide for a person to whom subsection (1) applies to vacate his office at the end of the completed year of service in which he attains the age of 72) there shall be substituted—

"(1) This subsection applies to the office of district judge.

(2) Subject to the following provisions of this section and to subsections (4) to (6) of section 26 of the Judicial Pensions and Retirement Act 1993 (Lord Chancellor's power to authorise continuance in office up to the age of 75), a person who holds an office to which subsection (1) applies shall vacate his office on the day on which he attains the age of 70 years."

(4) Subsection (3) (which confers power to continue district judges etc. in office up to the age of 75 and which is superseded by section 26(4) to (6) of this Act) shall cease to have effect.

Statutory officers in Northern Ireland

18. In section 71 of the Judicature (Northern Ireland) Act 1978, for subsection (3) (which provides that a statutory officer, within the meaning of that Act, is to retire at the end of the completed year of service in which he attains the age of 72, but subject to the substitution of a lower age, under subsection (4)) there shall be substituted—

"(3) Subject to subsection (4) below and to subsections (4) to (6) of section 26 of the Judicial Pensions and Retirement Act 1993 (Lord Chancellor's power to authorise continuance in office beyond the age of 70, up to the age of 75), a statutory officer shall retire on the day on which he attains the age of 70 years."

Stipendiary magistrates in England and Wales

19.—(1) Section 14 of the Justices of the Peace Act 1979 (retirement of stipendiary magistrates) shall be amended in accordance with the following provisions of this paragraph.

(2) At the beginning of that section there shall be inserted—

"(1A) A stipendiary magistrate appointed after the coming into force of section 26 of the Judicial Pensions and Retirement Act 1993 shall vacate his office on the day on which he attains the age of 70."

(3) In subsection (1) (persons appointed on or after 25th October 1968)—

(a) after the words "25th October 1968" there shall be inserted the words "and before the coming into force of section 26 of the Judicial Pensions and Retirement Act 1993"; and

(b) the proviso (which provides that the Lord Chancellor may authorise a person to continue in office up to the age of 72 and which is superseded by section 26(4) to (6) of this Act) shall cease to have effect.

(4) Subsection (2) (which relates to appointments before 25th October 1968 and which is spent) shall be omitted.

(5) At the end of that section there shall be added—

"(3) Subsections (1A) and (1) above are subject to section 26(4) to (6) of the Judicial Pensions and Retirement Act 1993 (Lord Chancellor's power to authorise continuance in office up to the age of 75)."

Resident Magistrates in Northern Ireland

20. For section 1 of the Resident Magistrates' Pensions Act (Northern Ireland) 1960 (Resident Magistrate to vacate office at the end of the completed year of service in which he attains the age of 70, but with power to continue in office up to the age of 72) there shall be substituted—

"Retiring age of resident magistrates

1. Every resident magistrate (whether appointed before or after the passing of this Act) shall vacate his office on the day on which he attains the age of seventy; but this section is subject to section 26(4) to (6) of the Judicial Pensions and Retirement Act 1993 (Lord Chancellor's power to authorise continuance in office up to the age of 75)."

Social security: Commissioners, and the President and chairmen of appeal tribunals

21.—(1) Paragraph 1 of Schedule 2 to the Social Security Administration Act 1992 (tenure of office as Commissioner, President or full-time chairman) shall be amended in accordance with the following provisions of this paragraph.

(2) In sub-paragraph (2) (which requires such a person to vacate office at the end of the completed year of service in which he attains the age of 72) for the words from "at the end of" onwards there shall be substituted the words "on the day on which they attain the age of 70, but subject to section 26(4) to (6) of the Judicial Pensions and Retirement Act 1993 (power to authorise continuance in office up to the age of 75)."

(3) Sub-paragraph (3) (which contains power to continue such a person's appointment up to the age of 75 which is superseded by section 26(4) to (6) of this Act) shall cease to have effect.

(4) In sub-paragraph (5) (consultation with Lord Advocate before exercising powers under sub-paragraph (3) or (4)) the words "(3) or" shall be omitted.

(5) In sub-paragraph (6) (sub-paragraph (2) or (3) not to apply in relation to deputy Commissioners) the words "or (3)" shall be omitted.

(6) In sub-paragraph (7) (which provides that nothing in sub-paragraph (2) or (4) applies to a Commissioner appointed before 23rd May 1980) the words "(2) or" (which are of no further practical utility) shall be omitted.

Social security: Commissioners, and the President and chairmen of appeal tribunals in Northern Ireland

22.—(1) Paragraph 1 of Schedule 2 to the Social Security Administration (Northern Ireland) Act 1992 (tenure of office as Commissioner, President or full-time chairman) shall be amended in accordance with the following provisions of this paragraph.

(2) In sub-paragraph (2) (which requires such a person to vacate office at the end of the completed year of service in which he attains the age of 72) for the words from "at the end of" onwards there shall be substituted the words "on the day on which they attain the age of 70, but subject to section 26(4) to (6) of the Judicial Pensions and Retirement Act 1993 (power to authorise continuance in office up to the age of 75)."

(3) Sub-paragraph (3) (which contains power to continue such a person's appointment up to the age of 75 and which is superseded by section 26(4) to (6) of this Act) shall cease to have effect.

(4) In sub-paragraph (6) (sub-paragraph (2) or (3) not to apply in relation to deputy Commissioners) the words "or (3)" shall be omitted.

Child support: Commissioners and chairmen of appeal tribunals

23.—(1) In Schedule 3 to the Child Support Act 1991 (child support appeal tribunals), in paragraph 4—

(a) in sub-paragraph (3) (chairman of child support appeal tribunals to retire at the end of the completed year of service in which he reaches the age of 72) for the words from "at the end" to the end of that sub-paragraph there shall be substituted the words "on the date on which he reaches the age of 70; but this sub-paragraph is subject to section 26(4) to (6) of the Judicial Pensions and Retirement Act 1993 (power to authorise continuance in office up to the age of 75)"; and

(b) sub-paragraph (4) (which contains power to continue a chairman's appointment up to the age of 75 and which is superseded by section 26(4) to (6) of this Act) shall cease to have effect.

(2) In Schedule 4 to that Act (Child Support Commissioners), in paragraph 1—

(a) in sub-paragraph (1) (Child Support Commissioner to retire at the end of the completed year of service in which he reaches the age of 72) for the words from "at the end" to the end of that sub-paragraph there shall be substituted the words "on the date on which he reaches the age of 70; but this sub-paragraph is subject to section 26(4) to (6) of the Judicial Pensions and Retirement Act 1993 (power to authorise continuance in office up to the age of 75)"; and

(b) sub-paragraph (2) (which contains power to continue a Commissioner's appointment up to the age of 75 and which is superseded by section 26(4) to (6) of this Act) shall cease to have effect.

(3) In paragraph 4 of that Schedule (deputy Child Support Commissioners) at the beginning of paragraph (b) of sub-paragraph (2) there shall be inserted the words "Subject to sub-paragraph (2A)", and after that sub-paragraph there shall be inserted—

"(2A) No appointment of a person to be a deputy Child Support Commissioner shall be such as to extend beyond the date on which he reaches the age of 70; but this sub-paragraph is subject to section 26(4) to (6) of the Judicial Pensions and Retirement Act 1993 (power to authorise continuance in office up to the age of 75)."

(4) In paragraph 7 of that Schedule (Lord Chancellor to consult the Lord Advocate before exercising certain powers under the Schedule) for the words "paragraph 1(2) or (3)" there shall be substituted the words "paragraph 1(3)".

Chairmen of child support appeal tribunals in Northern Ireland

24. In Schedule 3 to the Child Support (Northern Ireland) Order 1991 (child support appeal tribunals), in paragraph 4—

(a) in sub-paragraph (3) (chairman of child support appeal tribunals to retire at the end of the completed year of service in which he reaches the age of 72) for the words from "at the end" to the end of that sub-paragraph there shall be substituted the words "on the date on which he reaches the age of 70; but this sub-paragraph is subject to section 26(4) to (6) of the Judicial Pensions and Retirement Act 1993 (power to authorise continuance in office up to the age of 75)"; and

(b) sub-paragraph (4) (which contains power to continue such a chairman's appointment up to the age of 75 and which is superseded by section 26(4) to (6) of this Act) shall cease to have effect.

Chairman of the Foreign Compensation Commission

25. In section 1 of the Foreign Compensation Act 1950 (constitution of the Foreign Compensation Commission), at the beginning of subsection (3) there shall be inserted the words "Subject, in the case of the chairman, to subsection (3A) of this section," and after that subsection there shall be inserted—

"(3A) The chairman of the Commission shall vacate his office on the day on which he attains the age of seventy years; but this subsection is subject to section 26(4) to (6) of the Judicial Pensions and Retirement Act 1993 (power to authorise continuance in office up to the age of seventy-five years)."

Commons Commissioners

26. In section 17 of the Commons Registration Act 1965 (which includes provision for the appointment of Commons Commissioners) after subsection (1) there shall be inserted—

"(1A) A Commons Commissioner shall vacate his office on the day on which he attains the age of seventy years; but this subsection is subject to section 26(4) to (6) of the Judicial Pensions and Retirement Act 1993 (power of Lord Chancellor to authorise continuance in office up to the age of seventy-five years)."

President and chairmen of industrial tribunals

27.—(1) The Industrial Tribunals (England and Wales) Regulations 1965 shall be amended in accordance with sub-paragraphs (2) and (3) below.

(2) For regulation 3(2) (which requires the President of Industrial Tribunals (England and Wales) to vacate office at the end of the completed year of service in which he attains the age of 72) there shall be substituted—

"(2) The President shall vacate his office on the day on which he attains the age of seventy years, but subject to section 26(4) to (6) of the Judicial Pensions and Retirement Act 1993 (Lord Chancellor's power to authorise continuance in office up to the age of 75)."

(3) In regulation 5, at the beginning of paragraph (5) (terms of membership of panels) there shall be inserted the words "Subject to paragraph (6)" and after that paragraph there shall be inserted—

"(6) A member of a panel of chairmen appointed under paragraph (2) shall vacate his office on the day on which he attains the age of seventy years, but subject to section 26(4) to (6) of the Judicial Pensions and Retirement Act 1993 (Lord Chancellor's power to authorise continuance in office up to the age of 75)."

(4) The Industrial Tribunals (Scotland) Regulations 1965 shall be amended in accordance with sub-paragraphs (5) and (6) below.

(5) For regulation 3(2) (which requires the President of Industrial Tribunals (Scotland) to vacate office at the end of the completed year of service in which he attains the age of 72) there shall be substituted—

"(2) The President shall vacate office on the day on which he attains the age of seventy years, but subject to section 26(4) to (6) of the Judicial Pensions and Retirement Act 1993 (power to authorise continuance in office up to the age of 75)."

(6) In regulation 5, at the beginning of paragraph (5) (terms of membership of panels) there shall be inserted the words "Subject to paragraph (6)" and after that paragraph there shall be inserted—

"(6) A member of a panel of chairmen appointed under paragraph (2) shall vacate his office on the day on which he attains the age of seventy years, but subject to section 26(4) to (6) of the Judicial Pensions and Retirement Act 1993 (powers to authorise continuance in office up to the age of 75)."

President, Vice-President and chairmen of industrial tribunals and of the Fair Employment Tribunal

28.—(1) In subsection (3) of section 3 of the Fair Employment (Northern Ireland) Act 1989 (which requires the President and Vice President of the Industrial Tribunals and the Fair Employment Tribunal each to vacate his office at the end of the completed year of service in which he attains the age of 72), for the words from "at the end of" onwards there shall be substituted the words "on the day on which he attains the age of 70, but subject to subsection (4) below and subsections (4) to (6) of section 26 of the Judicial Pensions and Retirement Act 1993 (power to authorise continuance in office up to the age of 75)".

(2) In regulation 3 of the Industrial Tribunals Regulations (Northern Ireland) 1965 (membership of tribunals), at the beginning of paragraph (5) there shall be inserted the words "Subject to paragraph (6)" and after that paragraph there shall be inserted—

"(6) A member of a panel of chairmen appointed under paragraph (2) shall vacate his office on the day on which he attains the age of seventy years, but subject to section 26(4) to (6) of the Judicial Pensions and Retirement Act 1993 (Lord Chancellor's power to authorise continuance in office up to the age of 75)."

President of the Industrial Court in Northern Ireland

29. In Article 91 of the Industrial Relations (Northern Ireland) Order 1992, at the beginning of paragraph (3) (terms of appointment of president and other members of the Industrial Court) there shall be inserted the words "Subject, in the case of the president, to paragraph (3A)," and after that paragraph there shall be inserted—

"(3A) The president shall vacate his office on the day on which he attains the age of 70; but this paragraph is subject to section 26(4) to (6) of the Judicial Pensions and Retirement Act 1993."

Members of the Employment Appeal Tribunal

30. In Schedule 11 to the Employment Protection (Consolidation) Act 1978 (which includes provision concerning the tenure of office of those members of the Employment Appeal Tribunal who are appointed under section 135(2)(c) of that Act), in paragraph 2 (which

provides that such a member may by notice resign his membership), after the word "member" there shall be inserted "(a)", and at the end of that paragraph there shall be inserted "; and

(b) shall vacate his office on the day on which he attains the age of 70;

but paragraph (b) is subject to section 26(4) to (6) of the Judicial Pensions and Retirement Act 1993 (power to authorise continuance in office up to the age of 75)."

The Lands Tribunal and the Lands Tribunal for Scotland

31. In section 2 of the Lands Tribunal Act 1949, after subsection (5) (terms of appointment to membership of the Tribunal) there shall be inserted—

"(5A) No person shall be appointed a member of the Tribunal for a term which extends beyond the day on which he attains the age of seventy, except in accordance with section 26(4) to (6) of the Judicial Pensions and Retirement Act 1993 (power to authorise continuance in office up to the age of 75)."

The Lands Tribunal for Northern Ireland

32. In section 2 of the Lands Tribunal and Compensation Act (Northern Ireland) 1964, for paragraph (b) of subsection (2) (which requires a member to vacate his office at the end of the completed year of service in the course of which he attains the age of 72) there shall be substituted—

"(b) shall vacate his office on the day on which he attains the age of seventy years, but subject to section 26(4) to (6) of the Judicial Pensions and Retirement Act 1993 (Lord Chancellor's power to authorise continuance in office up to the age of 75); and".

Judge Advocate of Her Majesty's Fleet

33. In section 28 of the Courts-Martial (Appeals) Act 1951, in subsection (3) (Judge Advocate of the Fleet to vacate office at the end of the completed year of service in which he attains the age of 70, with a proviso for continuance in office up to the age of 72)—

(a) for the words from "at the end" to "seventy years" there shall be substituted the words "on the day on which he attains the age of seventy years, but subject to section 26(4) to (6) of the Judicial Pensions and Retirement Act 1993 (power to authorise continuance in office up to the age of 75)"; and

(b) the proviso (which is superseded by section 26(4) to (6) of this Act) shall cease to have effect.

Judge Advocate General and related offices

34. In subsection (2) of section 32 of that Act (which makes similar provision for the Judge Advocate General and also provides for certain other judicial officers to vacate office at the end of the completed year of service in which they attain the age of 65, but with a proviso for continuance in office up to the age of 70)—

(a) after the words "The Judge Advocate General shall" there shall be inserted the words ", subject to section 26(4) to (6) of the Judicial Pensions and Retirement Act 1993 (power to authorise continuance in office up to the age of 75),";

(b) for the words "at the end of the completed year of service in the course of which", in both places where they occur, there shall be substituted the words "on the day on which"; and

(c) the proviso (which in relation to the Judge Advocate General is superseded by section 26(4) to (6) of this Act) shall cease to have effect.

Value added tax tribunals

35.—(1) In Schedule 8 to the Value Added Tax Act 1983, in paragraph 3, for sub-paragraphs (1) and (1A) (President of Value Added Tax Tribunals to vacate office at the end of the completed year of service in which he attains the age of 72, but with power to continue his appointment up to the age of 75) there shall be substituted—

"(1) The President—

(a) may resign his office at any time; and

(b) shall vacate his office on the day on which he attains the age of 70;

but paragraph (b) above is subject to section 26(4) to (6) of the Judicial Pensions and Retirement Act 1993 (power to authorise continuance in office up to the age of 75)."

(2) In paragraph 7 of that Schedule, for sub-paragraphs (3C) and (3D) (which make similar provision in relation to a chairman of value added tax tribunals) there shall be substituted—

"(3C) A chairman of value added tax tribunals—

(a) may resign his office at any time; and

(b) shall vacate his office on the day on which he attains the age of 70;

but paragraph (b) above is subject to section 26(4) to (6) of the Judicial Pensions and Retirement Act 1993 (power to authorise continuance in office up to the age of 75)."

Special, and deputy Special, Commissioners for Income Tax

36.—(1) In section 4 of the Taxes Management Act 1970 (Special Commissioners) after subsection (3) there shall be inserted—

"(3A) A Special Commissioner—
(a) may resign his office at any time; and
(b) shall vacate his office on the day on which he attains the age of seventy years;
but paragraph (b) above is subject to section 26(4) to (6) of the Judicial Pensions and Retirement Act 1993 (power to authorise continuance in office up to the age of 75)."

(2) In section 4A of that Act, at the end of subsection (2) (which provides that a person shall not be qualified for appointment as a deputy Special Commissioner unless he is qualified for appointment as a Special Commissioner) there shall be added the words "(and, accordingly, no appointment of a person as a deputy Special Commissioner shall be such as to extend beyond the day on which he attains the age of seventy years, but subject to section 26(4) to (6) of the Judicial Pensions and Retirement Act 1993)".

President or other member of the Immigration Appeal Tribunal

37. In Part II of Schedule 5 to the Immigration Act 1971 (the Immigration Appeal Tribunal) in paragraph 8 (terms of appointment) at the beginning of sub-paragraph (1) there shall be inserted the words "Subject to the following provisions of this paragraph" and at the end of that paragraph there shall be added—

"(3) A member of the Tribunal shall vacate his office on the day on which he attains the age of seventy, but subject to section 26(4) to (6) of the Judicial Pensions and Retirement Act 1993 (power to authorise continuance in office up to the age of 75)."

Immigration adjudicators

38. In Part I of Schedule 5 to the Immigration Act 1971 (immigration adjudicators) in paragraph 2 (terms of appointment) at the beginning of sub-paragraph (1) there shall be inserted the words "Subject to the following provisions of this paragraph" and at the end of that paragraph there shall be added—

"(3) An adjudicator shall vacate his office on the day on which he attains the age of seventy, but subject to section 26(4) to (6) of the Judicial Pensions and Retirement Act 1993 (power to authorise continuance in office up to the age of 75)."

Pensions Appeal Tribunals

39. In the Schedule to the Pensions Appeal Tribunals Act 1943, for paragraph 2 (appointment, remuneration and removal of members) there shall be substituted—

"2.—(1) The members of the Tribunals shall be appointed by the Lord Chancellor.
(2) There shall be paid to them such remuneration as the Treasury may determine.
(3) The Lord Chancellor may, if he thinks fit, remove any member of such a Tribunal.
(4) Subject to sub-paragraph (3) above and to subsections (4) to (6) of section 26 of the Judicial Pensions and Retirement Act 1993 (power to authorise continuance in office up to the age of 75), a member of such a Tribunal shall vacate his office on the day on which he attains the age of seventy years."

Mental Health Review Tribunals

40. In Schedule 2 to the Mental Health Act 1983 (which makes provision with respect to Mental Health Review Tribunals), at the beginning of paragraph 2 there shall be inserted the words "Subject to paragraph 2A below," and after that paragraph there shall be inserted—

"2A. A member of a Mental Health Review Tribunal shall vacate office on the day on which he attains the age of 70 years; but this paragraph is subject to section 26(4) to (6) of the Judicial Pensions and Retirement Act 1993 (power to authorise continuance in office up to the age of 75 years)."

The Financial Services Tribunal

41. In Schedule 6 to the Financial Services Act 1986, in paragraph 1 (which includes provision concerning the term of office of persons appointed to the panel from which persons are nominated to serve on the Financial Services Tribunal) at the beginning of sub-paragraph (1) there shall be inserted the words "Subject to the following provisions of this paragraph," and after sub-paragraph (2) there shall be added—

"(3) A member of the panel appointed by the Lord Chancellor shall vacate his office on the day on which he attains the age of seventy years; but this sub-paragraph is subject to section 26(4) to (6) of the Judicial Pensions and Retirement Act 1993 (power to authorise continuance in office up to the age of seventy-five years)."

Tribunals and advisory bodies under the Misuse of Drugs Act 1971

42.—(1) Schedule 3 to the Misuse of Drugs Act 1971 (which includes provision in relation to tribunals and advisory bodies established for the purposes of sections 14 and 15 of that Act) shall be amended in accordance with this paragraph.

(2) In paragraph 1 (membership of tribunals) after sub-paragraph (2) there shall be inserted—

"(2A) The chairman of a tribunal shall vacate his office on the day on which he attains the age of seventy years; but this sub-paragraph is subject to section 26(4) to (6) of the Judicial Pensions and Retirement Act 1993 (power to authorise continuance in office up to the age of seventy-five years)."

(3) In paragraph 13 (membership of advisory bodies) after sub-paragraph (1) there shall be inserted—

"(1A) The chairman of an advisory body shall vacate his office on the day on which he attains the age of seventy years; but this sub-paragraph is subject to section 26(4) to (6) of the Judicial Pensions and Retirement Act 1993 (power to authorise continuance in office up to the age of seventy-five years)."

Restrictive Practices Court

43.—(1) In section 3 of the Restrictive Practices Court Act 1976 (appointed members of the Restrictive Practices Court), in subsection (2)—

(a) at the beginning, there shall be inserted the words "Subject to subsection (2A) below,"; and

(b) the words "(not less than three years)" shall cease to have effect.

(2) After that subsection there shall be inserted—

"(2A) No appointment of a person to be an appointed member shall be such as to extend beyond the day on which he attains the age of seventy years; but this subsection is subject to section 26(4) to (6) of the Judicial Pensions and Retirement Act 1993 (power to authorise continuance in office up to the age of seventy-five years);".

Tribunals constituted under section 706 of the Income and Corporation Taxes Act 1988

44. Section 706 of the Income and Corporation Taxes Act 1988 (appointment of a tribunal to hear appeals in connection with the cancellation of tax advantages from certain transactions in securities) shall be numbered as subsection (1) of that section, and at the end of that section there shall be added—

"(2) A person appointed as chairman or other member of the tribunal shall vacate his office on the day on which he attains the age of 70; but this subsection is subject to section 26(4) to (6) of the Judicial Pensions and Retirement Act 1993 (power to authorise continuance in office up to the age of 75)."

Arbitrator appointed under the Agricultural Holdings Act 1986

45. In Schedule 11 to the Agricultural Holdings Act 1986 (which makes provision in relation to the determination by arbitration of matters arising under that Act), after sub-paragraph (5) of paragraph 1 there shall be added—

"(6) A member of the panel constituted for the purposes of this Schedule shall vacate his office on the day on which he attains the age of seventy years; but this sub-paragraph is subject to section 26(4) to (6) of the Judicial Pensions and Retirement Act 1993 (power to authorise continuance in office up to the age of seventy-five years)."

Agricultural Land Tribunals

46.—(1) Schedule 9 to the Agriculture Act 1947 (constitution etc of Agricultural Land Tribunals) shall be amended in accordance with this paragraph.

(2) In paragraph 13 (which relates to the chairmen of such Tribunals), in sub-paragraph (2)—

(a) at the beginning there shall be inserted the words "Subject to sub-paragraph (2A) of this paragraph,"; and

(b) for the words "three years" there shall be substituted "such period as may be specified in the terms of his appointment".

(3) After that sub-paragraph there shall be inserted—

"(2A) No appointment of a person to be the chairman shall be such as to extend beyond the day on which he attains the age of seventy years; but this sub-paragraph is subject to section 26(4) to (6) of the Judicial Pensions and Retirement Act 1993 (power to authorise continuance in office up to the age of seventy-five years)."

(4) Paragraph 14 (which provides for there to be a panel of deputy-chairmen for each such Tribunal) shall be numbered as sub-paragraph (1) of that paragraph, and at the end of that paragraph there shall be added—

"(2) A member of the panel of deputy-chairmen shall vacate his office on the day on which he attains the age of seventy years; but this sub-paragraph is subject to section 26(4) to (6) of the Judicial Pensions and Retirement Act 1993 (power to authorise continuance in office up to the age of seventy-five years)."

(5) In paragraph 15 (which provides for there to be panels of persons representing farmers' and landowners' interests), after sub-paragraph (1) there shall be inserted—

"(1A) A member of either of the panels drawn up under sub-paragraph (1) of this paragraph shall vacate his office on the day on which he attains the age of seventy years; but this sub-paragraph is subject to section 26(4) to (6) of the Judicial Pensions and Retirement Act 1993 (power to authorise continuance in office up to the age of seventy-five years)."

The Aircraft and Shipbuilding Industries Arbitration Tribunal

47. In section 42 of the Aircraft and Shipbuilding Industries Act 1977, at the beginning of subsection (5) (which makes provision in relation to the terms of appointment of the members of the Aircraft and Shipbuilding Industries Arbitration Tribunal) there shall be inserted the words "Subject to subsection (5A) below," and after that subsection there shall be inserted—

"(5A) No appointment of a person to be the president of the arbitration tribunal shall be such as to extend beyond the day on which he attains the age of 70; but this subsection is subject to section 26(4) to (6) of the Judicial Pensions and Retirement Act 1993 (power to authorise continuance in office up to the age of 75)."

Chairman of a tribunal established by section 29 of the Betting, Gaming and Lotteries Act 1963

48. In section 29 of the Betting, Gaming and Lotteries Act 1963 (appointment of a tribunal to hear appeals concerning bookmakers' levy) at the end of subsection (2) there shall be added the words ", but subject, in the case of the chairman, to subsection (2A) of this section", and after that subsection there shall be inserted—

"(2A) The chairman of any such tribunal shall vacate his office on the day on which he attains the age of seventy years; but this subsection is subject to section 26(4) to (6) of the Judicial Pensions and Retirement Act 1993 (power to authorise continuance in office up to the age of seventy-five years)."

The Copyright Tribunal

49. In section 146 of the Copyright, Designs and Patents Act 1988 (membership of the Copyright Tribunal) after subsection (3) there shall be inserted—

"(3A) A person who is the chairman or a deputy chairman of the Tribunal shall vacate his office on the day on which he attains the age of 70 years; but this subsection is subject to section 26(4) to (6) of the Judicial Pensions and Retirement Act 1993 (power to authorise continuance in office up to the age of 75 years)."

The Data Protection Tribunal

50. In Schedule 2 to the Data Protection Act 1984, in paragraph 8 (tenure of office of members of the Data Protection Tribunal), at the beginning of sub-paragraph (1) there shall be inserted the words "Subject to the following provisions of this paragraph," and at the end of that paragraph there shall be added—

"(3) A person who is the chairman or a deputy chairman of the Tribunal shall vacate his office on the day on which he attains the age of seventy years; but this sub-paragraph is subject to section 26(4) to (6) of the Judicial Pensions and Retirement Act 1993 (power to authorise continuance in office up to the age of seventy-five years)."

Independent Schools Tribunals

51. In Schedule 6 to the Education Act 1944 (constitution etc. of Independent Schools Tribunals) at the beginning of paragraph 3 there shall be inserted the words "Subject, in the case of a member of the legal panel, to paragraph 3A below," and after that paragraph there shall be inserted—

"3A. No appointment of a person to be a member of the legal panel shall be such as to extend beyond the day on which he attains the age of seventy years; but this paragraph is subject to section 26(4) to (6) of the Judicial Pensions and Retirement Act 1993 (power to authorise continuance in office up to the age of seventy-five years)."

President of a tribunal constituted under Schedule 3 to the Industry Act 1975

52.—(1) In Schedule 3 to the Industry Act 1975, paragraph 6 (terms of appointment of members of a tribunal established to arbitrate in a dispute arising under that Act) shall be numbered as sub-paragraph (1) of that paragraph.

(2) At the beginning of that sub-paragraph there shall be inserted the words "Subject, in the case of the president of a tribunal, to sub-paragraph (2) below", and after that sub-paragraph there shall be added—

"(2) No appointment of a person to be the president of a tribunal shall be such as to extend beyond the day on which he attains the age of 70 years; but this paragraph is subject to section 26(4) to (6) of the Judicial Pensions and Retirement Act 1993 (power to authorise continuance in office up to the age of 75 years)."

Tribunal constituted under Schedule 9 to the National Health Service Act 1977

53. In regulation 26 of the National Health Service (Service Committees and Tribunal) Regulations 1974 (tenure of office of chairman of Tribunal constituted under section 46 of the National Health Service Act 1977) at the beginning of paragraph (1) there shall be inserted the words "Subject to paragraph (1A)," and after that paragraph there shall be inserted—

"(1A) The chairman shall vacate his office on the day on which he attains the age of 70; but this paragraph is subject to section 26(4) to (6) of the Judicial Pensions and Retirement Act 1993 (power to authorise continuance in office up to the age of 75)."

Chairman of the Plant Varieties and Seeds Tribunal

54. In paragraph 1 of Schedule 4 to the Plant Varieties and Seeds Act 1964, at the beginning of sub-paragraph (2) (tenure of office of chairman of the Plant Varieties and Seeds Tribunal) there shall be inserted the words "Subject to sub-paragraph (2A) of this paragraph," and after that sub-paragraph there shall be inserted—

"(2A) No appointment of a person to be the chairman of the Tribunal shall be such as to extend beyond the day on which he attains the age of 70; but this sub-paragraph is subject to section 26(4) to (6) of the Judicial Pensions and Retirement Act 1993 (power to authorise continuance in office up to the age of 75)."

Chairman of a Registered Homes Tribunal

55. In section 40 of the Registered Homes Act 1984, at the beginning of subsection (6) (terms of appointment of persons to the panels of chairmen and other members of Registered Homes Tribunals), there shall be inserted the words "Subject, in the case of a person appointed to the legal panel, to subsection (7) below," and after that subsection there shall be added—

"(7) No appointment of a person to the legal panel shall be such as to extend beyond the day on which he attains the age of seventy years; but this subsection is subject to section 26(4) to (6) of the Judicial Pensions and Retirement Act 1993 (power to authorise continuance in office up to the age of seventy-five years)."

Rent Assessment Committees

56. In Schedule 10 to the Rent Act 1977, after paragraph 2 (appointment by Lord Chancellor or Secretary of State of persons to constitute the panels from which the members of rent assessment committees are selected) there shall be inserted—

"2A. No appointment of a person to any panel by the Lord Chancellor shall be such as to extend beyond the day on which the person attains the age of seventy years; but this sub-paragraph is subject to section 26(4) to (6) of the Judicial Pensions and Retirement Act 1993 (Lord Chancellor's power to authorise continuance in office up to the age of seventy-five years)."

The Transport Tribunal

57.—(1) Paragraph 3 of Schedule 4 to the Transport Act 1985 (tenure of office of judicial members) shall be amended in accordance with the following provisions of this paragraph.

(2) In sub-paragraph (1) (judicial member to hold office until the end of the completed year of service in which he attains the age of 72 and then retire)—

(a) after the words "Subject to the following provisions of this paragraph" there shall be inserted the words "and to subsections (4) to (6) of section 26 of the Judicial Pensions and Retirement Act 1993 (power to authorise continuance in office up to the age of seventy-five)"; and

(b) for the words "the end of the completed year of service in which he attains the age of seventy-two" there shall be substituted the words "the day on which he attains the age of seventy".

(3) Sub-paragraph (2) (which contains power to continue the member's appointment up to the age of 75 and which is superseded by section 26(4) to (6) of this Act) shall cease to have effect.

Tribunal established under section 9 of the Wireless Telegraphy Act 1949

58. In Schedule 2 to the Wireless Telegraphy Act 1949, in paragraph 1 (period for which members of the appeal tribunal established under section 9 of that Act are to hold office) after sub-paragraph (1) there shall be inserted—

"(1A) No appointment of a person to be the president of the appeal tribunal shall be such as to extend beyond the day on which he attains the age of seventy years; but this sub-paragraph is subject to section 26(4) to (6) of the Judicial Pensions and Retirement Act 1993 (power to authorise continuance in office up to the age of seventy-five years).

(1B) No person shall be appointed after the day on which he attains the age of seventy years to act as one of the additional members of the appeal tribunal under subsection (5) of section 9 of this Act."

Wreck commissioner

59. In section 82 of the Merchant Shipping Act 1970 (appointment of wreck commissioners) after subsection (1) there shall be inserted—

"(1A) A wreck commissioner shall vacate his office on the day on which he attains the age of seventy years; but this subsection is subject to section 26(4) to (6) of the Judicial Pensions and Retirement Act 1993 (power to authorise continuance in office up to the age of seventy-five years)."

Chairman of a Reinstatement Committee

60. In Schedule 2 to the Reserve Forces (Safeguard of Employment) Act 1985, paragraph 2 (composition of Reinstatement Committees) shall be numbered as sub-paragraph (1) of that paragraph and at the end of that paragraph there shall be added—

"(2) A member of the panel of persons referred to in sub-paragraph (1)(a) shall vacate his office on the day on which he attains the age of seventy years; but this sub-paragraph is subject to section 26(4) to (6) of the Judicial Pensions and Retirement Act 1993 (power to authorise continuance in office up to the age of seventy-five years)."

Tribunals constituted for the purposes of section 150(4) of the Mines and Quarries Act 1954

61. In Schedule 3 to the Mines and Quarries Act 1954, at the end of paragraph 1 (constitution of tribunals to inquire into whether a certificate of competency granted under that Act should be withdrawn or suspended) there shall be added the words "; but no person shall be appointed—

(a) as the person, or one of the persons, constituting such a tribunal, or

(b) as an assessor to assist any such tribunal,

after the day on which he attains the age of seventy years."

Courts of inquiry under section 52 of the Merchant Shipping Act 1970

62. In rule 5 of the Merchant Shipping (Section 52 Inquiries) Rules 1982 (appointment of courts of inquiry for the purposes of section 52 of the Merchant Shipping Act 1970) after paragraph (3) there shall be added—

"(4) A person shall not be appointed after the day on which he attains the age of 70 to assist with a section 52 inquiry as an assessor."

Chairman of a vaccine damage tribunal in Northern Ireland

63. In regulation 7 of the Vaccine Damage Payments Regulations 1979 (constitution etc. of vaccine damage tribunals), in paragraph (1B), at the end of sub-paragraph (a) (which provides for the chairman of a vaccine damage tribunal in Northern Ireland to be appointed by the Secretary of State) there shall be added the words "but no person shall be so appointed after the day on which he attains the age of 70".

Chairman of a tribunal constituted under section 47 of the Building Societies Act 1986

64. In section 47 of the Building Societies Act 1986 (tribunals to hear appeals against certain decisions of the Building Societies Commission) after subsection (3) there shall be inserted—

"(3A) A person shall not be appointed after the day on which he attains the age of 70 to be the chairman of a tribunal under this section."

Chairman of a tribunal constituted under section 28 of the Banking Act 1987

65. In section 28 of the Banking Act 1987 (tribunals to hear appeals against certain decisions of the Bank of England), after subsection (3) there shall be inserted—
"(3A) A person shall not be appointed after the day on which he attains the age of 70 to be the chairman of a tribunal under this section."

Arbitrators appointed under Schedule 10 to the Electricity Act 1989

66. In paragraph 9 of Schedule 10 to the Electricity Act 1989, after sub-paragraph (2) (appointment of arbitrator etc. to determine third parties' claims for compensation arising out of certain transfers of property etc.) there shall be added—
"(3) A person shall not be appointed after the day on which he attains the age of 70 to be an arbitrator or arbiter under sub-paragraph (2) above."

Chairman of a tribunal constituted under Schedule 3 to the Education (Schools) Act 1992

67. In Schedule 3 to the Education (Schools) Act 1992 (tribunals to hear appeals in relation to the registration of school inspectors), at the end of paragraph 1 there shall be added—
"(3) A person shall not be appointed after the day on which he attains the age of 70 to be the Chairman of a tribunal."

Chairman of a tribunal constituted under section 59 of the Friendly Societies Act 1992

68. In section 59 of the Friendly Societies Act 1992 (tribunal to hear appeals against certain decisions of the Friendly Societies Commission), after subsection (3) there shall be inserted—
"(3A) A person shall not be appointed after the day on which he attains the age of 70 to be the chairman of a tribunal under this section."

Section 26   SCHEDULE 7

RETIREMENT DATES: TRANSITIONAL PROVISIONS

Interpretation

1.—(1) In this Schedule—
"potential retirement date", in relation to any office, shall be construed in accordance with paragraph 5 below;
"re-appointment" to an office includes extension of a subsisting appointment to the office, otherwise than by the exercise of a continuation power.
(2) For the purposes of this Schedule, a person's office—
(a) is "salaried" if and so long as his service in the office is remunerated by payment of a salary; and
(b) is "fee-paid" if and so long as his service in the office is remunerated by the payment of fees;
and any reference in this Schedule to a person's being "salaried" or "fee-paid" shall be construed accordingly.
(3) Subsection (3) of section 26 of this Act applies for the purposes of this Schedule as it applies for the purposes of that section.
(4) Expressions used in this Schedule and in section 26 of this Act have the same meaning in this Schedule as they have in that section.
(5) This Schedule is without prejudice to subsections (4) to (6) of section 26 of this Act, but is subject to subsection (7) of that section and to section 27 of this Act.

Salaried offices

2.—(1) This paragraph applies to any person who for the time being holds, or who is seeking appointment or re-appointment to, a salaried relevant office (in this paragraph referred to as his "post-commencement office"), if—
(a) immediately before the appointed day, he was holding that or any other salaried relevant office (in this paragraph referred to as his "pre-commencement office");
(b) he has at all times on and after that day held some one or other salaried relevant office (whether the same office or not); and
(c) his potential retirement date by reference to his pre-commencement office falls later than

the date that would, apart from this paragraph, be the compulsory retirement date for the post-commencement office in his case.

(2) If and so long as this paragraph applies to a person—

(a) nothing in section 26 of, and no amendment made by Schedule 6 to, this Act shall—

   (i) require him to vacate his post-commencement office before his potential retirement date by reference to his pre-commencement office; or

   (ii) affect his eligibility for appointment or re-appointment to the post-commencement office; and

(b) that potential retirement date shall be taken for the purposes of section 26 of this Act (and, accordingly, of this Schedule) to be the compulsory retirement date for the post-commencement office in his case.

(3) If a person has two or more pre-commencement offices (so that he would, apart from this sub-paragraph, have two or more potential retirement dates) his potential retirement date for the purposes of this paragraph—

(a) shall be determined by reference only to that one of his pre-commencement offices to which he was first appointed, or

(b) shall be such later date, falling on or before the day on which he attains the age of 75, as may be agreed in writing by him and the appropriate Minister, determined by reference to that pre-commencement office;

and any reference in this Schedule to the person's potential retirement date by reference to his pre-commencement office shall be construed accordingly.

(4) If immediately before the appointed day—

(a) a person who holds a salaried relevant office ("office A") also holds another relevant office ("office B"), but

(b) in consequence of holding office A, he is either—

   (i) unremunerated in respect of his service in office B, or

   (ii) remunerated by payment of a supplement, in respect of that service, to the salary payable in respect of his service in office A,

then, in determining for the purposes of sub-paragraph (3) above the number of pre-commencement offices which that person has, and to which of them he was first appointed, he shall be taken to hold office B at that time as a salaried relevant office and to have been so holding it at all previous times when the conditions in paragraphs (a) and (b) above were fulfilled.

Fee-paid offices

3.—(1) This paragraph applies to any person who for the time being holds, or who is seeking re-appointment to, a fee-paid relevant office, if—

(a) immediately before the appointed day, he was holding that office as a fee-paid office;

(b) he has at all times on and after that day held that office as a fee-paid office; and

(c) his potential retirement date by reference to that office falls later than the date that would, apart from this paragraph, be the compulsory retirement date for that office in his case.

(2) If and so long as this paragraph applies to a person—

(a) nothing in section 26 of, and no amendment made by Schedule 6 to, this Act shall—

   (i) require him to vacate the office referred to in sub-paragraph (1) above before his potential retirement date by reference to that office; or

   (ii) affect his eligibility for re-appointment to that office as a fee-paid office; and

(b) that potential retirement date shall be taken for the purposes of section 26 of this Act (and, accordingly, of this Schedule) to be the compulsory retirement date for that office in his case.

Persons holding a relevant office by virtue of a continuation power

4. Where, immediately before the appointed day, a person was holding a relevant office by virtue of the exercise of a continuation power, nothing in section 26 of this Act or this Schedule, and no amendment made by Schedule 6 to this Act, shall affect the continuing validity of that exercise of that power in relation to that person.

Ascertainment of potential retirement date

5.—(1) For the purposes of this Schedule, a person's potential retirement date by reference to an office is—

(a) in a case where, immediately before the appointed day, he was holding that office otherwise than by virtue of the exercise of a continuation power, the day on which he would have been required by any enactment or statutory instrument to vacate that office, apart from this Act and apart from any continuation power;

(b) in a case where, immediately before the appointed day, he was holding that office by virtue of the exercise of a continuation power, the last day of the period for which he is authorised to continue in that office by virtue of that exercise of the continuation power; or

(c) in the case of an office to which any of the following sub-paragraphs applies (offices for which there was no compulsory retirement date before the appointed day, but whose standard terms of appointment, or whose arrangements with respect to retirement, are reflected in the provisions of the sub-paragraph in question), the day specified in the sub-paragraph as the appropriate day.

(2) This sub-paragraph applies to each of the following offices, as a salaried office—

(a) Social Security Commissioner appointed before 23rd May 1980;

(b) President or other member of the Lands Tribunal, or of the Lands Tribunal for Scotland, set up under the Lands Tribunal Act 1949;

(c) Commissioner for the special purposes of the Income Tax Acts, appointed under section 4 of the Taxes Management Act 1970;

(d) President or other member of the Immigration Appeal Tribunal;

(e) Chairman of the Foreign Compensation Commission;

(f) Chief or other Commons Commissioner;

(g) Chairman of industrial tribunals, appointed in pursuance of regulations under section 128 of the Employment Protection (Consolidation) Act 1978;

(h) Chairman of industrial tribunals or of the Fair Employment Tribunal, appointed in pursuance of regulations under Article 30 of the Industrial Training (Northern Ireland) Order 1984 or appointed under section 3(1)(c) of the Fair Employment (Northern Ireland) Act 1989;

(j) president of the Industrial Court appointed in pursuance of Article 91 of the Industrial Relations (Northern Ireland) Order 1992;

(k) President of Pensions Appeal Tribunals;

and the appropriate day in the case of an office to which this sub-paragraph applies is the last day of the completed year of service in that office in which the person attains the age of 72.

(3) In the case of the office of immigration adjudicator (whose usual terms of appointment, whether as a salaried or a fee-paid office, require the holder to vacate it on the day on which he attains the age of 70)—

(a) this sub-paragraph applies only in those cases where, immediately before the appointed day, the office is held on terms which require the person in question to vacate it on the day on which he attains the age of 72; and

(b) where this sub-paragraph applies, the appropriate day is the day on which that person attains that age;

and, accordingly, no person shall have a potential retirement date by reference to that office (whether held as a salaried or a fee-paid office) in any other case.

(4) This sub-paragraph applies to the office of deputy judge of the High Court, as a fee-paid office; and the appropriate day in the case of an office to which this sub-paragraph applies is the day on which the person attains the age of 75.

(5) This sub-paragraph applies to each of the following offices, as a fee-paid office—

(i) in the case of appointments under subsection (1) of section 91 of the Supreme Court Act 1981 otherwise than by virtue of subsection (3) of that section, each of the following offices—

(a) deputy or temporary Master, Queen's Bench Division;

(b) deputy or temporary Admiralty Registrar;

(c) deputy or temporary Master, Chancery Division;

(d) deputy or temporary Registrar in Bankruptcy of the High Court;

(e) deputy or temporary Taxing Master of the Supreme Court;

(f) deputy or temporary Registrar of Civil Appeals;

(g) deputy or temporary Master of the Courts of Protection;

(ii) assistant Recorder;

(iii) chairman of social security appeal tribunals, medical appeal tribunals and disability appeal tribunals in England and Wales;

(iv) chairman of child support appeal tribunals, in England and Wales;

(v) Chairman of the Foreign Compensation Commission;

(vi) Commons Commissioner;

(vii) chairman of industrial tribunals, appointed in pursuance of regulations under section 128 of the Employment Protection (Consolidation) Act 1978;

(viii) chairman of industrial tribunals or of the Fair Employment Tribunal, appointed in pursuance of regulations under Article 30 of the Industrial Training (Northern Ireland) Order 1984 or appointed under section 3(1)(c) of the Fair Employment (Northern Ireland) Act 1989;

(ix) president of the Industrial Court appointed in pursuance of Article 91 of the Industrial Relations (Northern Ireland) Order 1992;

(x) President or other member of the Lands Tribunal, or of the Lands Tribunal for Scotland, set up under the Lands Tribunal Act 1949;

(xi) Commissioner for the special purposes of the Income Tax Acts, appointed under section 4 of the Taxes Management Act 1970;

(xii) deputy Special Commissioner, appointed under section 4A of the Taxes Management Act 1970;

(xiii) President or other member of the Immigration Appeal Tribunal;

(xiv) President or other member of Pensions Appeal Tribunals;

(xv) Chairman or member of a Mental Health Review Tribunal constituted under the Mental Health Act 1983;

(xvi) member of the Financial Services Tribunal appointed by the Lord Chancellor;

(xvii) chairman of a tribunal constituted for the purposes of sections 14 and 15 of the Misuse of Drugs Act 1971;

(xviii) chairman of an advisory body constituted for the purposes of section 14 of the Misuse of Drugs Act 1971;

(xix) appointed member of the Restrictive Practices Court, within the meaning of section 3 of the Restrictive Practices Court Act 1976;

(xx) chairman or other member of the tribunal constituted by section 706 of the Income and Corporation Taxes Act 1988;

(xxi) arbitrator appointed under paragraph 1(5) of Schedule 11 to the Agricultural Holdings Act 1986;

(xxii) chairman or deputy-chairman of an Agricultural Land Tribunal;

(xxiii) President of the Aircraft and Shipbuilding Industries Arbitration Tribunal;

(xxiv) Chairman of a tribunal established by section 29 of the Betting, Gaming and Lotteries Act 1963;

(xxv) chairman or deputy chairman of the Copyright Tribunal;

(xxvi) chairman or deputy chairman of the Data Protection Tribunal;

(xxvii) chairman of an Independent Schools Tribunal;

(xxviii) president of a tribunal constituted under Schedule 3 to the Industry Act 1975;

(xxix) chairman of the tribunal constituted under Schedule 9 to the National Health Service Act 1977;

(xxx) Chairman of the Plant Varieties and Seeds Tribunal;

(xxxi) chairman of a Registered Homes Tribunal constituted under the Registered Homes Act 1984;

(xxxii) President of the tribunal established under section 9 of the Wireless Telegraphy Act 1949;

(xxxiii) wreck commissioner appointed under section 82 of the Merchant Shipping Act 1970;

(xxxiv) Chairman of a Reinstatement Committee constituted under the Reserve Forces (Safeguard of Employment) Act 1985;

and the appropriate day in the case of an office to which this sub-paragraph applies is the last day of the completed year of service in the office in which the person attains the age of 72.

(6) This sub-paragraph applies to each of the following offices, as a fee-paid office—

(a) deputy or temporary district judge of the principal registry of the Family Division appointed under subsection (1) of section 91 of the Supreme Court Act 1981 otherwise than by virtue of subsection (3) of that section;

(b) deputy district judge appointed under section 102 of the Supreme Court Act 1981, except in a case where the person in question has previously held office as a district judge for a district registry;

(c) deputy district judge appointed under section 8 of the County Courts Act 1984, except in a case where the person in question has previously held office as a district judge for a county court district;

(d) Deputy Resident Magistrate, appointed under the Magistrates' Courts Act (Northern Ireland) 1964;

(e) member of an Agricultural Land Tribunal, other than chairman, deputy chairman or an assessor added to the Tribunal under paragraph 16(2) of Schedule 9 to the Agriculture Act 1947;

(f) chairman or other member of Rent Assessment Committees appointed by the Lord Chancellor under Schedule 10 to the Rent Act 1977;

and the appropriate day in the case of an office to which this sub-paragraph applies is the last day of the completed year of service in that office in which the person attains the age of 70.

(7) This sub-paragraph applies to the office of member of the Employment Appeal Tribunal appointed under section 135(2)(c) of the Employment Protection (Consolidation) Act 1978, as a fee-paid office; and the appropriate day in the case of an office to which this sub-paragraph applies is the 31st March next following the day on which the person attains the age of 70.

SCHEDULE 8

MINOR AND CONSEQUENTIAL AMENDMENTS

The Courts-Martial (Appeals) Act 1951

1. Section 35 of the Courts-Martial (Appeals) Act 1951 (pension arrangements for Vice Judge Advocate General, Assistant Judge Advocates General and Deputy Judge Advocates) shall be numbered as subsection (1) of that section and at the end of that section there shall be added—

"(2) The foregoing subsection shall not have effect in relation to a person to whom Part I of the Judicial Pensions and Retirement Act 1993 applies, except to the extent provided by or under that Act."

The County Courts Act (Northern Ireland) 1959

2. At the end of section 116 of the County Courts Act (Northern Ireland) 1959 (pensions of county court judges in Northern Ireland) there shall be added—

"(7) This Part shall not have effect in relation to a person to whom Part I of the Judicial Pensions and Retirement Act 1993 applies, except to the extent provided by or under that Act."

The Resident Magistrates' Pensions Act (Northern Ireland) 1960

3. In section 2 of the Resident Magistrates' Pensions Act (Northern Ireland) 1960 (pensions of resident magistrates in Northern Ireland) after subsection (1) there shall be inserted—

"(1A) This Act shall not have effect in relation to a person to whom Part I of the Judicial Pensions and Retirement Act 1993 applies, except to the extent provided by or under that Act."

The Foreign Compensation Act 1962

4. In section 3 of the Foreign Compensation Act 1962, after subsection (1) (which makes provision for the pensions or other benefits payable to or in respect of members of the Foreign Compensation Commission) there shall be inserted—

"(1A) Subsection (1) above shall not have effect in relation to a chairman or former chairman of the Commission who is a person to whom Part I of the Judicial Pensions and Retirement Act 1993 applies, except to the extent provided by or under that Act."

The Lands Tribunal and Compensation Act (Northern Ireland) 1964

5. In section 2 of the Lands Tribunal and Compensation Act (Northern Ireland) 1964 (pensions of members of the Lands Tribunal for Northern Ireland) after subsection (5) there shall be inserted—

"(5A) Subsection (5), so far as relating to allowances and gratuities by way of super-annuation, shall not have effect in relation to persons to whom Part I of the Judicial Pensions and Retirement Act 1993 applies, except to the extent provided by or under that Act."

The Superannuation Act 1965

6. In section 39A of the Superannuation Act 1965 (superannuation benefits in respect of persons who have been employed in two or more judicial offices) in subsection (6), in the definition of "judicial office", after the word "means" there shall be inserted—

"(a) any qualifying judicial office, within the meaning of the Judicial Pensions and Retirement Act 1993, and
(b)".

The Superannuation (Miscellaneous Provisions) Act (Northern Ireland) 1969

7. In section 2 of the Superannuation (Miscellaneous Provisions) Act (Northern Ireland) 1969 (pensions for president of the industrial court, president and vice-president of the industrial tribunals and the Fair Employment Tribunal, etc. in Northern Ireland) after sub-section (1) there shall be inserted—

"(1A) Subsection (1) shall not apply in relation to a person to whom Part I of the Judicial Pensions and Retirement Act 1993 applies, except to the extent provided by or under that Act."

The Taxes Management Act 1970

8. In section 4 of the Taxes Management Act 1970, after subsection (6) (pensions, allowances and gratuities payable to or in respect of Special Commissioners) there shall be inserted—

"(6A) Subsection (6) above, so far as relating to pensions (including allowances and gratuities), shall not have effect in relation to a person to whom Part I of the Judicial Pensions and Retirement Act 1993 applies, except to the extent provided by or under that Act."

The Immigration Act 1971

9. In Schedule 5 to the Immigration Act 1971, paragraphs 3 and 9 (which, among other things, make provision for the pensions, allowances and gratuities etc. payable to or in respect of immigration adjudicators and members of the Immigration Appeal Tribunal) shall each be numbered as sub-paragraph (1) and at the end of each of those paragraphs there shall be added—

"(2) Sub-paragraph (1)(b) above shall not have effect in relation to a person to whom Part I of the Judicial Pensions and Retirement Act 1993 applies, except to the extent provided by or under that Act."

The Administration of Justice Act 1973

10.—(1) Section 10 of the Administration of Justice Act 1973 (which, as it has effect by virtue of subsection (8) thereof, provides for certain widows' and children's pensions in Northern Ireland to be increased) shall be amended as follows—

(a) in subsections (1), (2)(a) and (3), after the words "or widow's" in each place there shall be inserted the words "or widower's";

(b) in subsection (2)—

(i) in paragraph (b), after the word "widow", where it occurs for the first time, there shall be inserted the words "or widower", and

(ii) in sub-paragraph (i) of that paragraph, for the words from "was" to "and" there shall be substituted the words "left a spouse and he or";

(c) in subsection (4)—

(i) after the word "him" or "his" in each place there shall be inserted the words "or her", and

(ii) in sub-paragraph (c), after the word "widow's" there shall be inserted the word "widower's"; and

(d) in subsection (5), after the word "widow's" there shall be inserted the word "widower's".

(2) In Schedule 3 to the Administration of Justice Act 1973 (which sets out the enactments in relation to which section 10 of that Act has effect), in paragraph 3, for the reference to the Department of Health and Social Services for Northern Ireland there shall be substituted a reference to the Department of Economic Development.

The Social Security (Northern Ireland) Act 1975

11. In paragraph 6 of Schedule 10 to the Social Security (Northern Ireland) Act 1975 (pensions of social security commissioners in Northern Ireland) after sub-paragraph (1) there shall be inserted—

"(1A) Sub-paragraph (1) shall not have effect in relation to a person to whom Part I of the Judicial Pensions and Retirement Act 1993 applies, except to the extent provided by or under that Act."

The Social Security Pensions Act 1975

12. In section 59C of the Social Security Pensions Act 1975, after subsection (2) (rights of appeal to the Pensions Ombudsman on matters of fact or law) there shall be inserted—

"(2A) Subsection (2) above does not have effect in relation to any scheme constituted under or by virtue of—

(a) the Sheriffs' Pensions (Scotland) Act 1961;

(b) the Judicial Pensions Act 1981; or

(c) the Judicial Pensions and Retirement Act 1993."

The Social Security Pensions (Northern Ireland) Order 1975

13. In Article 69C of the Social Security Pensions (Northern Ireland) Order 1975, after paragraph (2) (rights of appeal to the Pensions Ombudsman on matters of fact or law) there shall be inserted—

"(2A) Paragraph (2) does not have effect in relation to any scheme constituted under or by virtue of—
(a) Part XIII of the County Courts Act (Northern Ireland) 1959;
(b) the Resident Magistrates' Pensions Act (Northern Ireland) 1960;
(c) Schedule 10 to the Social Security (Northern Ireland) Act 1975;
(d) the Judicial Pensions Act 1981; or
(e) the Judicial Pensions and Retirement Act 1993."

The Judicature (Northern Ireland) Act 1978

14. At the end of section 72 of the Judicature (Northern Ireland) Act 1978 (pension arrangements for statutory officers) there shall be added—
"(4) This section does not apply to a person to whom Part I of the Judicial Pensions and Retirement Act 1993 applies, except to the extent provided by or under that Act."

The Supreme Court Act 1981

15.—(1) In section 12 of the Supreme Court Act 1981, in subsection (7) (pensions to be payable to or in respect of the judges mentioned in subsection (1) in accordance with section 2 of the 1981 Act) after the words "section 2 of the Judicial Pensions Act 1981" there shall be inserted the words "or, in the case of a judge who is a person to whom Part I of the Judicial Pensions and Retirement Act 1993 applies, in accordance with that Act".

(2) In section 93 of that Act (certain officers to be treated as employed in the civil service of the State for the purposes of salary and pension), in subsection (2) (exception, in respect of pension, for persons holding offices specified in paragraph 1 of Schedule 1 to the 1981 Act) for the words from "an office" onwards there shall be substituted the words "qualifying judicial office, within the meaning of the Judicial Pensions and Retirement Act 1993."

(3) In section 102 of that Act (deputy district judges for district registries of the High Court), for subsection (5) (which includes a reference to section 91(5) of that Act, a provision which is repealed by this Act) there shall be substituted—
"(5) Subsection (6) of section 91 applies in relation to a deputy district judge appointed under this section as it applies in relation to a person appointed under that section."

The Value Added Tax Act 1983

16.—(1) In Schedule 8 to the Value Added Tax Act 1983, in paragraph 3, after sub-paragraph (4) (remuneration, pensions, allowances and gratuities payable to or in respect of the President of Value Added Tax Tribunals) there shall be inserted—
"(4A) Sub-paragraph (4) above, so far as relating to pensions, allowances and gratuities, shall not have effect in relation to a person to whom Part I of the Judicial Pensions and Retirement Act 1993 applies, except to the extent provided by or under that Act."

(2) In paragraph 7 of that Schedule, after sub-paragraph (4) (remuneration, pensions, allowances and gratuities payable to or in respect of chairmen of value added tax tribunals) there shall be inserted—
"(4A) Sub-paragraph (4) above, so far as relating to pensions, allowances and gratuities, shall not have effect in relation to a person to whom Part I of the Judicial Pensions and Retirement Act 1993 applies, except to the extent provided by or under that Act."

The County Courts Act 1984

17. In the County Courts Act 1984—
(a) section 7 (which relates to assistant district judges), and
(b) in section 9 (qualifications for appointment) the words "assistant district judge",
shall cease to have effect.

The Social Security Act 1986

18.—(1) In section 12 of the Social Security Act 1986 (member's right to make voluntary contributions) in subsection (10A) (which precludes the application of the section in relation to pensions under the 1981 Act etc.) after the word "under" there shall be inserted the words "the Judicial Pensions and Retirement Act 1993,".

(2) In section 17 of that Act (general power to modify statutory provisions) in subsection (3) (which specifies the Acts in relation to which the power to make consequential provision under subsection (2) is exercisable) after paragraph (h) there shall be inserted—
"(j) the Judicial Pensions and Retirement Act 1993."

The Social Security (Northern Ireland) Order 1986

19.—(1) In Article 14 of the Social Security (Northern Ireland) Order 1986 (member's right to make voluntary contributions) in paragraph (10A) (which precludes the application of the Article in relation to pensions under the 1981 Act) after the word "under" there shall be inserted the words "the Judicial Pensions and Retirement Act 1993 or".

(2) In Article 18 of that Order (general power to modify statutory provisions) in paragraph (3) (which specifies the provisions in relation to which the power to make consequential provision under paragraph (2) is exercisable) after paragraph (k) there shall be added—

"(l) the Judicial Pensions and Retirement Act 1993."

The Criminal Justice Act 1988

20. In Schedule 6 to the Criminal Justice Act 1988, in paragraph 3, after sub-paragraph (2) (pensions, allowances and gratuities payable to or in respect of members of the Criminal Injuries Compensation Board) there shall be added—

"(3) Sub-paragraph (2) above does not apply to a chairman or former chairman of the Board who is a person to whom Part I of the Judicial Pensions and Retirement Act 1993 applies, except to the extent provided by or under that Act."

The Child Support Act 1991

21.—(1) In paragraph 4 of Schedule 3 to the Child Support Act 1991, after sub-paragraph (7) (remuneration of, and pensions, allowances or gratuities for, full-time chairmen of child support appeal tribunals) there shall be added—

"(8) Sub-paragraph (7), so far as relating to pensions, allowances or gratuities, shall not have effect in relation to any person to whom Part I of the Judicial Pensions and Retirement Act 1993 applies, except to the extent provided by or under that Act."

(2) In Schedule 4 to that Act, at the end of paragraph 2 (remuneration and expenses of, and pensions, allowances or gratuities for, Child Support Commissioners) there shall be added—

"(3) Sub-paragraph (1), so far as relating to pensions, allowances or gratuities, shall not have effect in relation to any person to whom Part I of the Judicial Pensions and Retirement Act 1993 applies, except to the extent provided by or under that Act."

The Child Support (Northern Ireland) Order 1991

22. In paragraph 4 of Schedule 3 to the Child Support (Northern Ireland) Order 1991, after sub-paragraph (7) (remuneration of, and pensions, allowances or gratuities for, full-time chairmen of child support appeal tribunals for Northern Ireland) there shall be added—

"(8) Sub-paragraph (7), so far as relating to pensions, allowances or gratuities, shall not have effect in relation to any person to whom Part I of the Judicial Pensions and Retirement Act 1993 applies, except to the extent provided by or under that Act."

The Social Security Administration Act 1992

23. In Schedule 2 to the Social Security Administration Act 1992, paragraph 2 (remuneration, pensions, allowances and gratuities payable to or in respect of the President and full-time chairmen of social security appeal tribunals etc.) shall be numbered as sub-paragraph (1) and after that sub-paragraph there shall be added—

"(2) Sub-paragraph (1) above, so far as relating to pensions, allowances and gratuities, shall not have effect in relation to persons to whom Part I of the Judicial Pensions and Retirement Act 1993 applies, except to the extent provided by or under that Act."

The Social Security Administration (Northern Ireland) Act 1992

24. In Schedule 2 to the Social Security Administration (Northern Ireland) Act 1992, paragraph 3 (remuneration, pensions, allowances and gratuities payable to or in respect of the President and full-time chairmen of social security appeal tribunals etc.) shall be numbered as sub-paragraph (1) and after that sub-paragraph there shall be added—

"(2) Sub-paragraph (1) above, so far as relating to pensions, allowances and gratuities, shall not have effect in relation to persons to whom Part I of the Judicial Pensions and Retirement Act 1993 applies, except to the extent provided by or under that Act."

SCHEDULE 9

REPEALS AND REVOCATIONS

Chapter or number	Short title	Extent of repeal or revocation
14 & 15 Geo. 6. c.46.	The Courts-Martial (Appeals) Act 1951.	In section 28, the proviso to subsection (3). In section 32, the proviso to subsection (2).
1951 c.20 (N.I.).	The Judicial Pensions Act (Northern Ireland) 1951.	In section 11A, in subsection (3), the word "and" immediately preceding paragraph (b), and subsection (4).
1959 c.25 (N.I.).	The County Courts Act (Northern Ireland) 1959.	Section 116(6). In section 127A, in subsection (3), the word "and" immediately preceding paragraph (b), and subsection (4).
1960 c.2 (N.I.).	The Resident Magistrates' Pensions Act (Northern Ireland) 1960.	In section 9A, in subsection (3), the word "and" immediately preceding paragraph (b), and subsection (4). Section 14.
9 & 10 Eliz. 2. c.42.	The Sheriffs' Pensions (Scotland) Act 1961.	Section 6. Section 9. In section 10, in the definition of "sheriff", the words "except in subsection (2) of section six".
1966 c.27 (N.I.).	The Superannuation (Amendment) Act (Northern Ireland) 1966.	In Schedule 1, paragraph 18.
1969 c.7 (N.I.).	The Superannuation (Miscellaneous Provisions) Act (Northern Ireland) 1969.	Section 2(5).
1970 c.9.	The Taxes Management Act 1970.	Section 4A(5).
1971 c.23.	The Courts Act 1971.	Section 17(2) and (3). Section 24(4).
1975 c.15.	The Social Security (Northern Ireland) Act 1975.	In Schedule 10, paragraph 6(4).
1976 c.33.	The Restrictive Practices Court Act 1976.	In section 3(2), the words "(not less than three years)".
1978 c.23.	The Judicature (Northern Ireland) Act 1978.	In section 7(1), the words "at any time". Section 8(4).
1979 c.55.	The Justices of the Peace Act 1979.	In section 14, the proviso to subsection (1), and subsection (2).
1981 c.20.	The Judicial Pensions Act 1981.	Section 15. Section 21(5) and (6). In section 33A, in subsection (3), the word "and" immediately preceding paragraph (b), and subsection (4). In Schedule 1, in paragraph 1, the entry "Assistant district judge".
1981 c.54.	The Supreme Court Act 1981.	Section 9(7). Section 91(5). In section 92, in subsection (2B), the words from "and the office" onwards, and subsections (2C) and (3). Section 103.
1984 c.28.	The County Courts Act 1984.	Section 7. Section 8(2). In section 9, the words "assistant district judge". Section 11(3).
1985 c.67.	The Transport Act 1985.	In Schedule 4, paragraph 3(2).
1990 c.41.	The Courts and Legal Services Act 1990.	In Schedule 18, paragraph 42(b).

Chapter or number	Short title	Extent of repeal or revocation
1991 c.48.	The Child Support Act 1991.	In Schedule 3, paragraph 4(4) and, in paragraph 8, the word "(4)". In Schedule 4, paragraph 1(2).
S.I. 1991/2628 (N.I. 23).	The Child Support (Northern Ireland) Order 1991.	In Schedule 3, paragraph 4(4).
1992 c.5.	The Social Security Administration Act 1992.	In Schedule 2, in paragraph 1, sub-paragraph (3), in sub-paragraph (5) the words "(3) or", in sub-paragraph (6) the words "or (3)" and, in sub-paragraph (7), the words "(2) or".
1992 c.8.	The Social Security Administration (Northern Ireland) Act 1992.	In Schedule 2, in paragraph 1, sub-paragraph (3) and, in sub-paragraph (6), the words "or (3)".

INDEX

PRISONERS AND CRIMINAL PROCEEDINGS (SCOTLAND) ACT 1993*

(1993 c. 9)

ARRANGEMENT OF SECTIONS

PART I

DETENTION, TRANSFER AND RELEASE OF OFFENDERS

---

* Annotations by Dr. J. J. McManus, LL.B., Ph.D., University of Dundee.

PART III

GENERAL

An Act to amend the law of Scotland with respect to the detention, transfer and release of persons serving sentences of imprisonment etc. or committed or remanded in custody; to make further provision as regards evidence and procedure in criminal proceedings in Scotland; and for connected purposes.   [29th March 1993]

PARLIAMENTARY DEBATES
Hansard, H.L. Vol. 357, cols. 553, 687, 824; Vol. 358, cols. 384, 551, 875; H.C. Vol. 212, col. 237; Vol. 216, col. 449.
    The Bill was discussed in First Scottish Standing Committee between October 29 and November 11, 1992.

INTRODUCTION AND GENERAL NOTE
    This Act is in two distinct, and generally unrelated, parts. Part 1 deals mainly with early release from sentences of imprisonment and detention and brings together in one Act all the provisions relating to early release in Scotland. Part 2 amends aspects of the law relating to evidence and procedure in criminal cases.

Part 1

The Pre-existing System
    The pre-existing system, governed mainly by the Criminal Procedure (Scotland) Act 1975 and the Prisons (Scotland) Act 1989, will continue to cover all persons sentenced before the implementation date of the new Act, with the exception of children sentenced under ss.206 or 312 of the 1975 Act still in custody on implementation date, all others sentenced to periods of less than two years and still in custody on the date of implementation, persons sentenced to life imprisonment or equivalent for offences other than murder, and persons to whom s.3 (compassionate release) may apply.
    Provisions relating to remission date from the 1930s, and parole was introduced to Scotland in 1967. Initially introduced as a reward for good behaviour, which had to be positively earned under the "marks" system, remission, of one-third of the total sentence, had become an automatic deduction from sentence for all convicted prisoners and inmates with a determinate sentence, including fine defaulters. Only loss of some or all of that third as a result of disciplinary infractions committed within the establishment could delay release beyond the two-thirds date (Prisons (Scotland) Act 1989, s.39; Prisons (Scotland) Rules 1952 (S.I. 1952 No. 565), rr.37 and 42; Young Offenders (Scotland) Rules 1965 (S.I. 1965 No. 195), rr.42 and 44). The only exception to this were those sentenced under ss.206 and 312 of the Criminal Procedure

(Scotland) Act 1975 (*i.e.* children under the age of 16 sentenced under solemn or summary procedure to determinate sentences of detention, to be served in a place to be determined by the Secretary of State), who received no remission.

On release with remission, there was no further liability at all in relation to the sentence for those aged over 21 on sentence. Those who were under the age of 21 when sentenced were subject to recall to custody for a maximum period of three months for a breach of the post-release licence, which automatically applied to all young offenders who had been sentenced to a period of more than six months (s.12 of the Criminal Justice (Scotland) Act 1963, as amended). The six- or 12-month period of this liability ran from the date of release. Accordingly, the remission period was effectively discounted from the sentence totally.

The introduction of parole created the possibility of a determinate-sentence prisoner being released from custody even earlier in the sentence. A creation of the "Treatment Era" of penal philosophy, the idea underlying parole was that a person's response to custody might be such that it would be possible to allow the prisoner to serve part of the sentence in the community without risk to the public. The idea was first formally mooted in a Labour Party study-group paper, written by Lord Longford in 1964 ("Crime—A Challenge to us All"). A Government White Paper entitled "The Adult Offender" the following year outlined proposals which became law in the Criminal Justice Act 1967.

The minimum period required to be served in custody before consideration for parole was set by the 1967 Act (now contained in the Prisons (Scotland) Act 1989, s.22(1)(2)) at one-third of the total sentence or one year, whichever was the longer, in the case of all prisoners over 16 sentenced to determinate periods. For those sentenced under ss.206 and 312 of the Criminal Procedure (Scotland) Act 1975, there has been no minimum qualifying period.

The Parole Board for Scotland was established in 1968. Its function has been to advise the Secretary of State in the exercise of his power under the 1967 Act. A positive recommendation by the Board has been a necessary, but not sufficient, condition for the release of any prisoner on parole. The Secretary of State has retained the discretion to overturn a positive recommendation. In addition to the four types of people required by statute (Prisons (Scotland) Act 1989, Sched. 1) to be appointed to the Board (a psychiatrist, a holder or former holder of high judicial office, a person experienced in supervision or after-care of discharged prisoners and a person who has made a study of the causes of crime or the treatment of offenders), membership has usually included a former prison governor, a retired senior police officer, a sheriff and up to 10 others from a wide variety of backgrounds. The names and designations of members are given in the Board's annual reports, published by HMSO each year.

The power to appoint local review committees, contained now in s.18 of the 1989 Act, has been exercised, and every establishment which regularly holds parole-eligible prisoners has had a committee appointed. One member of the committee, not being the prison governor or his representative, has interviewed the prisoner to help with the making of the prisoner's representations. Thereafter, the whole committee has met to make a recommendation on each case to the Secretary of State. Cases not recommended for parole by the local review committee have been scrutinised by officials of the Scottish Office in one of two ways: adult male prisoners' cases have been "prediction scored", *i.e.* a set of criteria developed by researchers at Edinburgh University has been applied and, if this system indicated a low risk of reoffending, the case was remitted to the Parole Board. All cases involving females, and those of males under the age of 21, have been "sifted", that is, examined by two officials of the Scottish Office who, if they disagree with a negative recommendation of a local review committee, have been able to refer the case to the Board. Cases which have not passed one of these hurdles have generally not been referred to the Board, though a small number have been referred on a "for information only" basis, with an indication that the Secretary of State will not consider release.

From 1968 onwards, parole has also been the only method by which prisoners sentenced to indeterminate sentences (life imprisonment, detention for life, detention without limit of time or detention at Her Majesty's pleasure) can be released from custody. The system for these groups has operated slightly differently. After approximately four years of the sentence has been completed, the case is considered by the Preliminary Review Committee, a body with no statutory power and no set constitution. This committee has recommended a date for the first formal review of the case, at which a full parole dossier has been completed and put before the appropriate local review committee. The dossier has then gone, with the local review committee's recommendation, to the Scottish Office. If officials considered that a release programme was appropriate at that time, the case was passed to the Secretary of State who, if he also thought release appropriate, then had to consult the sentencing judge, if available, and the Lord Justice General. If everyone still agreed that release would be appropriate, the case would then be formally referred to the Parole Board for its decision. Again a positive recommendation from the Board has been essential before the release could take place. Cases not recommended by the local review committee and cases recommended by it, but not considered appropriate by the Scottish Office officials, the Secretary of State, or the judiciary, could be referred to the

Board on a "for information only" basis. The Board could not authorise release in these cases on its own.

All persons released on parole have been subject to licence. In the case of life-sentence prisoners, the licence has continued for life; for determinate-sentence prisoners, other than those sentenced under ss.205 and 312 of the Criminal Procedure (Scotland) Act 1975, the licence has expired at the two-thirds date of the sentence, even if remission had been forfeited while the person was in custody. Those who had been detained under ss.205 or 312 remained on licence until the expiry of the full original sentence.

The standard licence has required the parolee to be under the supervision of a social worker from a named local authority, to report to that social worker as required, not to change address or employment without reporting this to the social worker, to be of good behaviour and to keep the peace and not to travel outwith Great Britain without the prior permission of the supervisor. In addition, the Parole Board could add further conditions as it saw fit. Commonly, these might be not to contact particular individuals, to undertake alcohol or drugs counselling, or to reside in a certain place.

Breach of any licence condition could lead to variation or revocation of the licence. In the case of revocation, the person has been returned to custody and can be kept until the end of the original sentence (subject to remission and possible reconsideration for parole). Courts were also empowered to order revocation of licence upon conviction for a further offence (Prisons (Scotland) Act 1989, s.28(8)), but this was rarely done. The Secretary of State has been empowered to recall a parolee to custody without consulting the Parole Board when it appears to him expedient in the public interest so to do (1989 Act, s.28(2)), and the Board could recommend recall to the Secretary of State under s.28(1). Recalled persons were entitled to be told the reasons for their recall and could make representations, in writing, against their recall. Any such representations must be considered by the Board, as must all cases where the Secretary of State has issued the recall order without consulting the Board. If the Parole Board then decided that the person should be immediately re-released, the Secretary of State had no power to prevent the immediate release of the prisoner. There has been no set standard of proof against which allegations of breach of licence must be measured. The Board could take into consideration allegations which had not been sufficiently substantiated to result in a criminal conviction when the grounds for recall were failure to be of good behaviour and to keep the peace.

In its annual reports, the Board has detailed the number of cases considered, the numbers granted parole and the number of breaches of licence referred to it, along with its response to the alleged breaches, in each year. On average, there have been some 850 cases eligible for parole each year (though the number has increased significantly from 1986 onwards), of whom an average of 12 per cent. have not wished to be considered. Of those eligible, between 16 per cent. and 38 per cent. have been granted some parole (not necessarily the full period available under the statute), and the recall rate, expressed as percentage of those actually paroled, has never exceeded 10.2 per cent., and was only 0.4 per cent. in 1986.

The Case for Reform

Perhaps it was this remarkably high "success" rate which kept parole off the public and political agenda for most of its life, but the whole idea of remission had also never really attracted any public concern. Maybe, therefore, it was public ignorance of the systems for early release which ensured that they never attracted the attention of the media or the politicians. This, however, all changed in the 1980s.

Three factors can be highlighted as contributors to the growth of concern which led to this new Act: the demise of the "treatment model" of imprisonment and its replacement by notions of justice and prisoners' rights; the introduction of short-term parole on a virtually automatic basis in England and Wales; and the change in parole policy introduced in 1983 south of the border and in 1984 in Scotland.

The treatment model of imprisonment naturally wanted to accord the executive some power over release dates, in order that those who responded to the treatment could be released early and those who did not respond could be kept for further doses. In according the executive this power, there was a tendency to assume that it would always be exercised in favour of the prisoner and there was thus no need for legal protections. Although the parole systems in Great Britain (interestingly, Northern Ireland has never had a parole system) never gave the executive the same degree of power as the American system of discretionary sentencing (the "one-to 10-year" sentences available in the 1960s), they nonetheless gave the executive a significant input into determining the actual time to be spent in custody. Equally, the systems devised for decision-making were secretive, based on reports on the prisoner which the prisoner was not allowed to see; there was no right to a hearing in person; reasons for decisions were not given to prisoners; and there was no right of appeal.

The "rights" movement objected both to the principle of the executive's having any say in determining release dates and to the lack of due process or natural justice in the decision-making processes which were adopted. The best expression of the movement's objections are still two American books from 1971—The American Friends Service Committee, *Struggle for Justice*, and N. Kittrie, *The Right to be Different*. It is, however, difficult to imagine that a change in penal philosophy on its own would have produced the rethink about penal strategy of which this measure is a part. Thus, the other factors have a crucial importance.

The qualifying limits for consideration for parole had originally been set at one year or one-third of the sentence. Amendments to the 1967 Act, especially the Criminal Justice Act 1982, s.33(a), allowed the Secretary of State to reduce the qualifying period. This power was never used in Scotland, but the Home Secretary exercised it in England to reduce the minimum period to six months, thereby making parole available to those serving sentences of one year or more. In consequence of the numbers involved, parole became virtually automatic for short-sentence prisoners. Indeed, the main motivation for introducing the lower limit in England was to reduce the prison population. This was briefly achieved, but at a cost to the public and political image of the parole system.

The third crucial factor was the introduction, paradoxically at the same time as the announcement of the implementation of the lower threshold, of a much more restrictive policy in relation to the granting of parole to prisoners serving long sentences. Both announcements were made at the Conservative Party Conference in 1983 by the then newly appointed Home Secretary, Mr Leon Brittan. Both applied only to England and Wales, but the Secretary of State for Scotland decided in December 1984 that the restrictive policy in relation to long-term prisoners should apply also in Scotland. As was the case in England and Wales, the policy was to be retrospective and to take effect immediately.

Under this policy, the Secretary of State indicated that he would normally only consider granting parole for the last few months of sentences over five years imposed for offences of violence or for offences involving drugs. Equally, the Secretary of State indicated that he would not normally exercise his discretion to release life-sentence prisoners who had been sentenced for a murder involving the death of a police officer, murder by terrorists, sexual or sadistic murders of children, or murders committed by firearm in the commission of crime (*Hansard*, H.C. Vol. 70, col. 90). The legality of this new policy was challenged and established in the English case of *Findlay* v. *Secretary of State* [1984] 3 All E.R. 801, where the House of Lords held, unanimously, that the Secretary of State was entitled to adopt such a policy so long as each case was considered. This led to the Scottish formulation of the policy including the phrase "unless in exceptional circumstances", a phrase which has never been defined.

While perhaps politically popular, this policy has not been well received by many people involved in the prison system. The Parole Board for Scotland has frequently spoken out against it, voluntary organisations like SACRO have opposed it, and many prison governors and staff have joined with prisoners in expressing disquiet at it. Some indeed identify the policy as one of the major contributors to the series of riots and hostage-takings which occurred in Scottish prisons between 1986 and 1988. Its contribution, if any, to this is impossible to measure, but it is undoubtedly true that the policy was an important factor in highlighting the parole system and focusing concern about it, to such an extent that pressure for a formal review of the system was overwhelming.

Kincraig and Carlisle

The Government's response was to establish, in July 1987, a committee under the chairmanship of Lord Carlisle to review parole and related issues in England and Wales. A separate committee was duly established in December 1987, under the chairmanship of Lord Kincraig, to conduct a similar review for Scotland. The full terms of reference of the Scottish Committee were:

"To consider the present arrangements in Scotland for modifying the effects of custodial sentences and in particular:
  (a) the objectives of the parole system, and whether it should be retained in its present or in a modified form, including any changes which should be made to:
    (i) the current criteria for eligibility for parole;
    (ii) the current criteria for remission;
  (b) whether as an alternative or a supplement to the present arrangements any different scheme might be introduced for the release of prisoners, for stated purposes, before the completion of the sentence ordained by the court;
  (c) whether there should be any extension of the role of the judiciary in relation to the present parole or remission systems, or in relation to any alternative arrangements for the modification of the effects of custodial sentences;

(d) the role of the social work services in supervising convicted offenders released on licence;

(e) the current provisions for periods spent in custody on remand to be taken into account in the determination of sentences;

(f) whether or not powers should be conferred upon the courts to suspend sentences, or to ordain part-suspended sentences, in what circumstances and on what conditions;

(g) the conditions which should attach to parole, remission or any equivalent scheme;

(h) whether the conclusions reached in the context of determinate sentences have any relevance to current policy on life-sentence prisoners;

(i) the overall resource implications and cost-effectiveness of the existing systems and of any modifications or alternatives which may be suggested:

and to make recommendations."

The committee reported in February 1989 (*Parole and Related Issues in Scotland*, Cm. 598, 1989) and the Government made its response in July of the following year (*Parole and Related Issues in Scotland*, SHHD, 1990). The Committee rejected the arguments in favour of the total abolition of parole, but agreed with the general move towards giving the sentence of the court a real meaning—"real-time sentencing", in the American jargon. Accordingly, the basic strategy of the report was to ensure that no part of the sentence could be totally written off, but not to insist that all of it need necessarily be spent in prison. Remission, it was suggested, should be abolished and replaced by a system of "conditional release". Under conditional release, a person released from prison would be recalled automatically on conviction for a crime for which imprisonment was a possible penalty and would serve the balance of the original sentence outstanding on the date of the commission of the subsequent offence before, and in addition to, any sentence imposed for the subsequent offence. A necessary consequence of the abolition of remission was the disappearance of the power of prison governors to award forfeiture of remission as a disciplinary penalty for offences against prison discipline.

Given that conditional release would impose greater restrictions on prisoners after release than the remission system, the committee considered that it would be possible to extend the proportion of the sentence to which the release could apply. Accordingly, it recommended that prisoners sentenced to non-parole-eligible sentences should serve only one-half of the sentence in prison and should be conditionally released for the second half. It also recommended that there should be no compulsory social-work supervision for such prisoners on release, but that a statutory duty should be imposed on social-work departments to provide assistance to any former prisoner who sought it. Such a duty was created by the insertion of a new s.17(1)(c) into the Social Work (Scotland) Act 1968 by s.61(4)(a) of the Law Reform (Miscellaneous Provisions) (Scotland) Act 1990.

In relation to parole, the committee considered that it was proper for there to be some system for recognising the possibility of change in a prisoner, or in knowledge of a prisoner, during a sentence which rendered it unnecessary for the prisoner to be kept in custody for the full time decreed by the sentencing court. When the change was such that the prisoner was no longer perceived as a threat to the public, it might be appropriate to order that the balance of the sentence be served under supervision in the community, subject to the possibility of recall if the released person showed signs of being a risk to public safety. The committee did not consider that such changes could come about quickly, and accordingly felt that the existing threshold for consideration for parole was inappropriate. It recommended that the minimum sentence qualifying for parole should be five years, and that prisoners should serve a minimum of one-half of the total sentence before qualifying for parole consideration. All sentences under five years would thus qualify for the one-half conditional discharge, and those of five years or more for parole consideration at that stage. Since acceptance of this recommendation would greatly reduce the number of cases for parole consideration, there would be no need for the sifting process carried out by local review committees, which could, therefore, be abolished.

The committee suggested that parole should be the only mechanism by which prisoners sentenced to five years or more could be released early from prison, but that the Parole Board should be obliged to release all such prisoners at the two-thirds stage of the sentence, subject to whatever conditions were thought appropriate and to the possibility of recall for the balance of the sentence for breach of such conditions.

The committee recommended no major changes in the constitution of the Parole Board or in the relationship between the Board and the Secretary of State. It carefully avoided criticising the decision to introduce the restrictive policy in 1984, but made clear its opinion that it was not necessary to have such policies to protect the public and did criticise the application of the policy with retrospective effect. On procedural matters, the committee suggested that all parole dossiers should be open to the prisoners concerned; that reasons for decisions should be given for parole decisions in accordance with criteria to be clearly expressed in Statute; that prisoners should have the right to present their representations in person to a panel of three Parole Board members; that parole advisers should be available to help prisoners make their representations to the Board; that a judge's report should be added to all parole dossiers; that the contents of dossiers should be generally reviewed; and that breach-of-licence cases where the prisoner disputed the alleged facts should be resolved by a formal hearing by a panel of the Board. In addition, the committee suggested that supervision of ex-prisoners on parole should be considerably improved.

In relation to life sentence prisoners, the committee considered that the establishment of the House of Lords Select Committee effectively removed this topic from its remit, but it did suggest reviewing the procedures for considering their cases, putting a time limit on the supervision element of their licences and empowering the Parole Board to specify recall periods.

The Government's Response

In general, as will be seen from the Act itself, the Government accepted the main recommendations of the report. Only some of the recommendations required legislation. Many of the others, including review of the contents of parole dossiers, the giving of reasons for decisions, and making dossiers available to prisoners, are not covered in the legislation, but these are being addressed by the Parole Board and the Scottish Office, and pilot projects are already underway. The major differences between the report's recommendations and the Government's response as in the Act are:

—the selection of four years rather than five as the dividing line between long-term, and therefore parole-eligible, prisoners and short-term prisoners qualifying for automatic conditional release at half sentence;

—according courts discretion, rather than making it mandatory, to recall prisoners on conviction for another imprisonable offence during a period of conditional release;

—allowing prison governors the power to extend the period to be spent in prison as a response to disciplinary offences within the establishment;

—creating the possibility of compulsory social work supervision on release for short-term prisoners, though only on the order of a court at the time of passing sentence;

—instead of the proposal that a panel of three members of the Board should see candidates for parole, the Government proposed that prisoners should be entitled to see an individual from the Board;

—while the relationship between the Board and the Secretary of State should remain basically the same, the Secretary of State should have power to delegate his decision-making power totally to the Board in specific classes of case.

Conclusion

The proposals contained in this Act closely mirror those contained in the English Criminal Justice Act 1991, which were brought into effect in October 1992. They provide a legislative framework for early release which is more in conformity with current penological theory, but non-legislative developments will be equally important in producing a system which conforms with current notions of procedural justice. It is important that the new Act is brought into force as quickly as possible in order to remedy the perceived inequity between Scotland and the rest of Britain. It is equally important that the actual operation of the parole scheme is kept under review, not least since it seems likely that the European Court of Human Rights may soon be involved in adjudicating on the system for release of non-discretionary lifers and could also have an interest in the procedures for taking prisoners' representations before a parole decision and parolees' representations when recall is being considered.

Part 2

Part 2 of this Act is, in effect, a miscellaneous provisions measure, implementing a variety of recommendations from the Law Commission, Scottish Office research studies and the Kincraig Committee. The only general theme running through much of this part of the Act is the move to make courts more efficient, in terms of the admissibility of certain forms of evidence, the protection of child witnesses and the fuller use of judicial time.

Parliamentary Discussion

The only point of real contention during the Parliamentary stages of the Bill, which started life in the Lords, arose in relation to the provision, in Part 2 of the Act, for taking evidence from abroad through live video-link in cases under solemn procedure (s.32 of the Act). In the House of Lords, this clause was amended to exclude its application in cases covered by the War Crimes Act 1991. The Government saw this as an attempt by the Lords to resurrect principled objections to the War Crimes Act itself, and accordingly did not accept the proposed Lords' amendment. The Lords decided not to press their objections at the stage of consideration of Commons amendments (March 25, 1993). It was also in Part 2 that two new provisions appeared during the Parliamentary stages, one relating to corroboration in cases under the Wildlife and Countryside Act 1981 and the other introducing a Crown right of appeal against sentence. Neither of these proved controversial.

Part 1 of the Act provoked little controversy on the main matters of principle. An attempt was made by Opposition members in both houses to apply the provisions relating to the release of discretionary lifers to all lifers. This would have been consistent with the recommendations of the House of Lords Select Committee report on *Murder and Life Imprisonment* (H.L. Paper 78: July 1989). The Government resisted this on the basis that requiring all judges to set "tariff" periods on life sentences would devalue the unique denunciatory effect of the mandatory life sentence.

Opposition members of the committee in the Commons made a concerted move to introduce a provision limiting the number of years a Parole Board member could serve on the Board. They argued that long periods of service in this capacity would reduce the ability of members to remain in touch with public feeling and would produce a set body of establishment figures making the decisions. The Government responded by pointing out that only two existing members had served more than four years and that all appointments were reviewed at the end of each three-year period of appointment.

ABBREVIATIONS
    The 1975 Act: the Criminal Procedure (Scotland) Act 1975
    The 1984 Act: the Mental Health (Scotland) Act 1984
    The 1989 Act: the Prisons (Scotland) Act 1989

PART I

DETENTION, TRANSFER AND RELEASE OF OFFENDERS

Early release

Release of short-term, long-term and life prisoners

1.—(1) As soon as a short-term prisoner has served one-half of his sentence the Secretary of State shall, without prejudice to any supervised release order to which the prisoner is subject, release him unconditionally.

(2) As soon as a long-term prisoner has served two-thirds of his sentence, the Secretary of State shall release him on licence.

(3) After a long-term prisoner has served one-half of his sentence the Secretary of State may, if recommended to do so by the Parole Board under this section, release him on licence.

(4) If recommended to do so by the Parole Board under this section, the Secretary of State may, after consultation with—

    (a) the Lord Justice General, whom failing the Lord Justice Clerk; and
    (b) if available, the trial judge,

release on licence a life prisoner who is not a discretionary life prisoner.

(5) The Parole Board shall not make a recommendation under subsection (4) above unless the Secretary of State has referred the case to the Board for its advice.

(6) Notwithstanding the foregoing provisions of this section, the Secretary of State shall not release a person who is serving—

    (a) a sentence of imprisonment for a term and one or more sentences of imprisonment for life; or
    (b) more than one sentence of imprisonment for life,

unless and until the requirements of those provisions are satisfied in respect of each of those sentences.

(7) A person to whom subsection (6) above applies shall, when released on licence under this section, be released on a single licence under subsection (4) above.

(8) Schedule 1 to this Act, which makes special provision as respects the release of persons serving both a sentence of imprisonment imposed on conviction of an offence and a term of imprisonment or detention referred to in section 5(1)(a) or (b) of this Act, shall have effect.

DEFINITIONS
    "discretionary life prisoner": s.2(1)(a)(b).

"short-term prisoner" and "long-term prisoner": s.27.
"supervised release order": s.14.

GENERAL NOTE

Subs. (1)
The Kincraig Committee recommended that the new system to replace remission for short-term prisoners should be called "conditional release", though the only condition suggested was that the released person should not commit any offences during the second half of the original sentence. Subsection 1 makes it clear that there are to be no conditions unless imposed under s.14 of this Act. For the potential consequences of another offence during the release period, see s.16.

Subs. (2)
This replaces the existing remission of one-third of the sentence with release on licence for the same period for long-term prisoners who are not given parole. Grounds for revocation of licence are given in s.17 and are considerably wider than those available to the courts for ordering a short-term prisoner to continue serving the original sentence. Accordingly, this subsection ensures that long-term prisoners will be subject to restrictions on their liberty for the full time imposed by the sentencing court.

Subs. (3)
The existing system whereby qualification for parole comes at one-third of total sentence or one year, whichever is longer, is replaced by this provision limiting parole consideration to those sentenced to four years or more once they have served one-half of the total sentence.

Subss. (4)–(7)
These continue, without any change, the existing provisions (s.26 of the 1989 Act) in relation to persons sentenced to life imprisonment for murder.

Subs. (8)
This deals with concurrent and consecutive sentences where at least one of such sentences was imposed for contempt of court or in default of fines, both of these to be known as "non-offence sentences". All prisoners in this situation whose sentences have been ordered to run consecutively will be required to serve the relevant proportion of the non-offence sentence *after* the date on which they would have qualified for release under the relevant subsections (subss. (1)–(3) above). When the sentences are ordered to run wholly concurrently, only the offence sentence will be taken into account in calculating the release date, but long-term prisoners in this situation will not be eligible for parole consideration (Scheds. 1, para. 3(b)). Operation of this provision would require a non-offence sentence of four years or more. Partly concurrent sentences will be treated on the basis of which of them is due to expire first. No reduction under subs. (1) or (2) will be given to the sentence due to expire first, but a reduction will apply to the term due to expire last. In relation to an offence term which is due to expire last, s.1(3) will apply to it only if the relevant portion of the non-offence term has already been served. It would be a rare happening if this was not the case.

Duty to release discretionary life prisoners

2.—(1) In this Part of this Act "discretionary life prisoner", subject to subsection (9)(a) below and except where the context otherwise requires, means a life prisoner—
  (a) whose sentence was imposed for an offence the sentence for which is not fixed by law; and
  (b) in respect of whom the court which sentenced him for that offence made the order mentioned in subsection (2) below.

(2) The order referred to in subsection (1)(b) above is an order that subsections (4) and (6) below shall apply to the life prisoner as soon as he has served such part of his sentence ("the relevant part") as is specified in the order, being such part as the court considers appropriate taking into account—
  (a) the seriousness of the offence, or of the offence combined with other offences associated with it; and
  (b) any previous conviction of the life prisoner.

(3) Where a court which imposes life imprisonment for an offence such as is mentioned in subsection (1)(a) above decides not to make such order as is mentioned in subsection (2) above, it shall state its reasons for so deciding; and for the purposes of any appeal or review, any such order and any such decision shall each constitute part of a person's sentence within the meaning of the 1975 Act.

(4) Where this subsection applies, the Secretary of State shall, if directed to do so by the Parole Board, release a discretionary life prisoner on licence.

(5) The Parole Board shall not give a direction under subsection (4) above unless—

(a) the Secretary of State has referred the prisoner's case to the Board; and

(b) the Board is satisfied that it is no longer necessary for the protection
'   of the public that the prisoner should be confined.

(6) Where this subsection applies, a discretionary life prisoner may, subject to subsection (7) below, at any time require the Secretary of State to refer his case to the Parole Board.

(7) No requirement shall be made under subsection (6) above—

(a) where the prisoner is also serving a sentence of imprisonment for a term, before he has served one-half of that sentence; and

(b) where less than two years has elapsed since the disposal of any (or the most recent if more than one) previous reference of his case to the Board under subsection (5)(a) or (6) above or under section 17(3) of this Act.

(8) In determining for the purposes of subsection (4) or (6) above whether a discretionary life prisoner has served the relevant part of his sentence, no account shall be taken of any time during which he was unlawfully at large.

(9) Where a life prisoner is serving two or more sentences of imprisonment for life—

(a) he is a discretionary life prisoner only if the requirements of subsection (1) above are satisfied in respect of each of those sentences;

(b) notwithstanding the terms of any order under subsection (2) above, subsections (4) and (6) above shall not apply to him until he has served the relevant part of each of those sentences; and

(c) he shall, if released on licence under subsection (4) above, be so released on a single licence.

GENERAL NOTE

This is an entirely new section, introduced as a result of the European Court of Human Rights decision in the English case of *Thynne, Wilson and Gunnell* v. *U.K.*, Series A, No. 190–A; *The Independent*, November 2, 1990, E.C.H.R.). The Court held that "discretionary lifers", that is, those sentenced to life imprisonment for offences other than those for which the sentence is established by law, should have their release dates determined by a judicial process as of right once they have served the part of their sentence which would have been appropriate having regard to the nature of the offence on its own. While the English practice of sentencing judges in these cases stating a "tariff" period at the time of sentence may have contributed to this judgment, the judgment required that the system throughout the U.K. be reviewed. The law south of the border was changed in the Criminal Justice Act 1991; this provision closely follows that example. It is thought that there are some 30 prisoners in Scotland serving life sentences for offences other than murder, but the number has been increasing in recent times.

The main changes introduced by this section are, first, that sentencing courts will be required to address the question of whether or not to fix a tariff period ("the relevant part") in passing a discretionary life sentence, with any decision, including a decision not to specify any period of time, being subject to appeal, and, secondly, that the Secretary of State will have no discretion to refuse a Parole Board's recommendation for the release of such prisoners once he has referred their case to the Board and the Board is satisfied that the prisoner's further detention is not necessary in the interests of public protection. Additionally, such prisoners may require the Secretary of State to refer their cases to the Parole Board at any time after the expiry of the "relevant part" and at not less than two-yearly intervals thereafter.

Schedule 5, para. 6, of the Act requires the Secretary of State, in consultation with the Lord Justice General and the trial judge, if available, to review all existing discretionary life sentences and to consider whether, if s.2 had been in force at the time of sentence, an order would have been made under it and, if so, what order. This should be done as quickly as possible after this Act comes into force, and the provisions of this section will apply to any prisoners for whom a "relevant part" is set.

Though it is not spelled out in the Act, it is proposed that the Scottish Parole Board will follow the practice now adopted in England and Wales for dealing with such cases. There the parole board sits, at the establishment holding the prisoner, as a panel of three, made up of a High Court judge, a psychiatrist and a lay member, and gives the prisoner or his representative the right of audience at the hearing before reaching a decision. The only indication within the body of the Act that the same procedures may be followed in Scotland is the provision in Sched. 4, para. 4, adding a new s.21(1)(aa) to the Legal Aid (Scotland) Act 1986 permitting the award of legal aid for any case the referral of which is required under s.2(6) of this Act. It thus seems likely that a body of case-law will be established reasonably quickly, and it may be that this will be only the beginning of a more open and systematic treatment of all life sentences, and may even contribute to the development of more general Parole Board practices in relation to determinate sentence prisoners.

Power to release prisoners on compassionate grounds

3.—(1) The Secretary of State may at any time, if satisfied that there are compassionate grounds justifying the release of a person serving a sentence of imprisonment, release him on licence.

(2) Before so releasing any long-term prisoner or any life prisoner, the Secretary of State shall consult the Parole Board unless the circumstances are such as to render consultation impracticable.

(3) The release of a person under subsection (1) above shall not constitute release for the purpose of a supervised release order.

GENERAL NOTE

This section creates a totally new power and one which will be available for existing as well as future prisoners. Under pre-existing law (ss.11(2)(3) and 27 of the 1989 Act), the Secretary of State only had power to order the temporary release of prisoners for medical purposes. Such prisoners continued as prisoners, although, in the case of those released under s.27, the sentence ceased to run while the prisoner was released. If such a person were to die while on temporary release, it would still count as a death in custody and both humanitarian and practical considerations make this undesirable.

The only other methods of releasing a prisoner early were through the parole scheme and by exercise of the Royal Prerogative of Mercy. Both of these have limitations. The parole scheme can only come into operation when the prisoner has served the appropriate proportion of the sentence. If the only reason for granting parole to an eligible prisoner were a compassionate one, and that reason were no longer to apply at some time after release, this could be grounds for recall. It would, however, seem out of place with other recall decisions for the Parole Board to order recall on the basis, for example, that a parolee had had a remission from a life-threatening illness. On the other hand, the problem with the Royal Prerogative is that, once exercised, the beneficiary becomes totally free of all conditions and it would be very difficult to revoke the grant. Accordingly, it had become the practice for compassionate cases to be referred to the Parole Board for consideration of release.

The new power is designed to avoid these problems. While "compassionate" is not defined, it seems likely that medical grounds will be the commonest reason for exercising the power. It is not, however, a power which is likely to be exercised frequently. Subsection (2) gives the Parole Board some input into the decision-making process, but only on a consultative basis. There was some discussion during the Parliamentary stages of the Act about providing an appeals mechanism, but the Government resisted this idea. Undertakings were, however, given that reasons for any refusal would be given to prisoners. Release will be subject to licence.

Persons detained under Mental Health (Scotland) Act 1984

4.—(1) Notwithstanding that a transfer direction and a restriction direction (those expressions having the same meanings as in the Mental Health (Scotland) Act 1984) have been given in respect of a person serving a sentence of imprisonment, this Part of this Act shall apply to the person as if he continued to serve that sentence while detained in, and as if he had not been removed to, hospital.

(2) In section 71(7)(a) of the said Act of 1984 (categories of prisoner who may be transferred to hospital), the words "in criminal proceedings" shall cease to have effect.

(3) For sections 74 and 75 of the said Act of 1984 there shall be substituted the following section—

"Further provision as to transfer directions and restriction directions

74.—(1) This subsection applies where a transfer direction and a restriction direction have been given in respect of a person—

(a) serving a sentence of imprisonment; or

(b) who is detained (other than in respect of a criminal offence) under or by virtue of the Immigration Act 1971,

if the Secretary of State is satisfied, at a time when the person would but for those directions be, by virtue of the circumstance mentioned in paragraph (a) or (b) above, in prison or being detained other than in a hospital, as to the matters mentioned in subsection (2) below.

(2) The matters referred to in subsection (1) above are—

(a) that either—

(i) the person is not suffering from mental disorder of a nature or degree which makes it appropriate for him to be liable to be detained in a hospital for medical treatment; or

(ii) that it is not necessary for the health or safety of the person or for the protection of other persons that he should receive such treatment; and

(b) that it is not appropriate for the person to remain liable to be recalled to hospital for further treatment.

(3) Where subsection (1) above applies, the Secretary of State shall by warrant direct that the person be remitted to any prison or other institution or place in which he might have been detained had he not been removed to hospital and that he be dealt with there as if he had not been so removed.

(4) Where subsection (1) above does not apply only because the Secretary of State is not satisfied as to the matter mentioned in subsection (2)(b) above, he may either—

(a) by warrant give such direction as is mentioned in subsection (3) above; or

(b) decide that the person shall continue to be detained in hospital.

(5) If a direction is given under subsection (3) or (4)(a) above, then on the person's arrival in the prison or other institution or place to which remitted by virtue of that subsection the transfer direction and the restriction direction shall cease to have effect.

(6) This subsection applies where a transfer direction and a restriction direction have been given in respect of such person as is mentioned in subsection (1) above and he has thereafter been released under Part I of the Prisoners and Criminal Proceedings (Scotland) Act 1993.

(7) Where subsection (6) above applies—

(a) the transfer direction and the restriction direction shall forthwith cease to have effect; and

(b) the person shall thereupon be discharged from hospital unless a report is furnished in respect of him under subsection (9) below.

(8) A transfer direction or restriction direction given in respect of a person detained (other than in respect of a criminal offence) under or by virtue of the Immigration Act 1971 shall, if it does not first cease to have effect under subsection (5) above or under section 65(2) of this Act, cease to have effect when his liability to be so detained comes to an end.

(9) Not earlier than 28 days before a restriction direction given in respect of a person ceases to have effect other than by virtue of sub-section (8) above, the responsible medical officer shall obtain from another medical practitioner a report on the condition of the person in the prescribed form and thereafter shall assess the need for the detention of the person to be continued; and, if it appears to the responsible medical officer that it is necessary in the interests of the health or safety of the person or for the protection of others that the person should continue to be liable to be detained in hospital, the officer shall furnish to the managers of the hospital where the person is liable to be detained and to the Mental Welfare Commission a report to that effect in the prescribed form along with the report of the other medical practitioner.

(10) Where a report has been furnished under subsection (9) above the person shall, after the restriction direction ceases to have effect, be treated as if he had, on the date on which the restriction direction ceased to have effect, been admitted to the hospital in pursuance of an application for admission; but the provisions of sections 30(5) and (6) and 35 of this Act shall apply to the person and that report as they apply to a patient the authority for whose detention in hospital has been renewed in pursuance of subsection (4) of, and to a report under subsection (3) of, the said section 30.

(11) For the purposes of section 40(2) of the Prisons (Scotland) Act 1989 (discounting from sentence periods while unlawfully at large) a person who, having been transferred to hospital in pursuance of a transfer direction from a prison or young offenders institution, is at large in circumstances in which he is liable to be taken into custody under any provision of this Act, shall be treated as unlawfully at large and absent from the prison or young offenders institution.

(12) In this section "prescribed" means prescribed by regulations made by the Secretary of State.".

GENERAL NOTE

Prisoners sentenced to imprisonment but subsequently transferred to mental hospitals under the Mental Health Act 1984 have always caused some problems for the Parole Board. The legal situation, as confirmed in subs. (1), has been that they are entitled to be considered for parole in exactly the same way as other prisoners. Nonetheless, since their transfer to hospital has been based on the judgment that they are suffering from a mental illness and are a danger to themselves or to others, it is highly unlikely that they would be seen as good candidates for parole. Accordingly, the parole review process is likely to be a mere formality, but a formality which could have adverse effects on the treatment being undertaken in the hospital. The most appropriate action, therefore, would be for the transfer order to be rescinded when the person is well again and for the parole process to be undertaken while the person is in prison. This could cause two potential problems: first, the person could be disadvantaged in having the date of the parole review set back to allow up-to-date reports to be obtained from the prison; secondly, it may be the case that the person's mental illness was occasioned by imprisonment or that a return to prison would otherwise provoke a relapse and return directly to the community would ensure continued well-being. This problem is not resolved by continuing the existing law.

Subs. (1)

This also makes it clear that, on the expiry of a sentence of a transferred prisoner at the one-half or two-thirds stage, depending on the length of the sentence, the person must be released from hospital unless further detention can be authorised under the normal civil committal powers given by the 1984 Act. It remains possible, of course, for a transferred prisoner who recovers from a mental illness to be returned to prison at any stage before the end of the sentence.

Subs. (2)

This amends the existing law (s.71 of the 1984 Act) to ensure that all civil prisoners are treated in the same way. There was considerable debate in Committee stage and at Report stage of the Act in the House of Commons about the position of those detained under the Immigration Act 1971, despite ministerial assurances that no one in this position had ever been transferred to a mental hospital.

Subs. (3)

This replaces ss.74 and 75 of the 1984 Act with provisions which are identical save in the following regards:

s.74(1): paragraph (b) is a new addition;

s.74(2): paragraph (a) incorporates the old paras. (a) and (b);

s.74(3): was the old s.74(1)(i);

s.74(4): replaces s.74(2) without s.74(2)(b), which is now s.74(6);

s.74(5): was part of s.74(2);

s.74(6): replaces s.74(2)(b), which simply allowed the Secretary of State the same powers of release as were applicable in the institution in which the person would have been detained had he not been transferred to a mental hospital;

s.74(7): paragraph (a) was previously in s.74(2) and (b) in s.74(4);

s.74(8): replaces s.75 and makes it clear that Immigration Act detainees are to be treated in exactly the same way as other civil prisoners;

s.74(9): replaces the former s.74(5);

s.74(10): replaces the former s.74(6);

s.74(11): replaces the former s.74(9).

Fine defaulters and persons in contempt of court

5.—(1) Subject to section 1(8) of this Act and to subsections (2) and (3) below, this Part of this Act (except sections 1(3), 16 and 27(5)) applies to a person on whom imprisonment, or as the case may be detention in a young offenders institution, has been imposed—

(a) under section 407 of the 1975 Act (imprisonment for non-payment of fine: summary proceedings) or under that section as applied by section 194 of that Act (imprisonment for non-payment of fine: solemn proceedings) or, by virtue of the appropriate one of those sections, under section 415(2) or 207(2) of that Act (detention of young offenders); or

(b) for contempt of court,

as it applies to a person sentenced to imprisonment, or on whom detention has been imposed, on conviction of an offence; and references in this Part of this Act to prisoners (whether short-term or long-term), or to prison, imprisonment, detention or sentences of imprisonment shall be construed accordingly.

(2) Where section 1(1) or (2) of this Act applies to a person by virtue of subsection (1) above, that section shall be construed as requiring the Secretary of State to release the person unconditionally as soon as, in the case of—

(a) a short-term prisoner, he has served one-half of his term of imprisonment; or

(b) a long-term prisoner, he has served two-thirds of his term of imprisonment,

and if during the term in question the prisoner is both released under section 3 of this Act and subsequently recalled under section 17(1) thereof, the period during which he is thereby lawfully at large shall be taken, for the purposes of paragraph (a) or (b) above, to be a period of imprisonment served.

(3) Notwithstanding subsection (1) above, section 11 of this Act shall not apply to a person to whom this Part of this Act applies by virtue of that subsection but whose release on licence is under section 3 of this Act; and that licence shall (unless revoked) remain in force only until the date on which, by virtue of subsection (2) above, his release would have been required had he not been released earlier.

GENERAL NOTE

Persons imprisoned for non-payment of fines or for contempt of court are to be treated exactly the same as sentenced prisoners for the purposes of calculating release dates, except that they are not to be eligible for consideration for parole. Nor are they to be liable to be ordered to serve the outstanding balance of their sentence on commission of a further crime after release, or to be kept in custody beyond the one-half or two-thirds date if, after release under s.3 of the Act, they are recalled to custody.

Imprisonment for non-payment of fines has been a topic of some controversy in Scotland in recent times. Fine defaulters have constituted up to 50 *per cent.* of receptions under sentence into Scottish penal establishments, though this figure has fallen to nearer 40 *per cent.* in 1990/91 (Scottish Office Criminal Justice Series Statistical Bulletin CRJ/1991/5), and, as Lord James Douglas-Hamilton pointed out for the Government at Committee stage of the Bill in the Commons (First Scottish Standing Committee, November 3, 1992, col. 52), fine defaulters account for less than five *per cent.* of the average daily population in penal establishments. The explanation for this difference is, of course, that fine defaulters generally serve very short periods in custody, often securing their release by having the outstanding balance of the fine paid for them. Nonetheless, they cause a significant amount of clerical and other work for prison staff, as well as providing the first experience of custody for a large number of people. They are probably also the factor which causes Scotland to have one of the highest rates of incarceration per head of the population in the Western World.

The Government has not been unaware of the problem. An abortive attempt was made in what became the Law Reform (Miscellaneous Provisions) Act 1990 to introduce a day-fine system, and Opposition Members of Parliament made reference to this during the Parliamentary stages of this Act. In addition, an experiment with supervised attendance orders is currently running, under which, instead of a custodial sentence for non-payment of fines, courts may order a person to undertake a period of supervised community work. The Kincraig Committee recommended that fine defaulters should not receive any automatic abatement of sentence, on the basis that fines should only be imposed at a level which means that default is a chosen course of action by the defaulter, who should not thereafter be given any discount on the penalty. Clearly, this was not accepted by the Government, since this Act effectively retains the old remission system for fine defaulters.

For the situation in relation to concurrent and consecutive sentences for fine default and an offence, see the discussion *supra* at s.1(8).

Application to young offenders and to children detained without limit of time

6.—(1) This Part of this Act applies—

(a) to persons on whom detention in a young offenders institution (other than detention without limit of time or for life) has been imposed under section 207(2) or 415(2) of the 1975 Act as the Part applies to persons serving equivalent sentences of imprisonment; and

(b) to—

    (i) persons sentenced under section 205 of that Act to be detained without limit of time or for life;

    (ii) children sentenced to be detained without limit of time under section 206 of that Act; and

    (iii) persons on whom detention without limit of time or for life is imposed under section 207(2) of that Act,

as the Part applies to persons sentenced to imprisonment for life, and references in the Part (except in this section, sections 1(8) and 5(1) and paragraph 1(b) of Schedule 1) to prisoners (whether short-term, long-term or life) or to prison, imprisonment or sentences of imprisonment shall be construed accordingly.

(2) A child detained without limit of time under section 206 of the 1975 Act may, on the recommendation of the Parole Board made at any time, be released on licence by the Secretary of State.

(3) The Secretary of State may, after consultation with the Parole Board, by order provide that, in relation to all children detained without limit of time under section 206 of the 1975 Act or to such class of those children as may be specified in the order, this section shall have effect subject to the modification that, in subsection (2), for the word "may" there shall be substituted the word "shall".

General Note

This section applies all the provisions of the Act to young offenders (those between the ages of 16 and 21) sentenced to detention and to all those under the age of 21 sentenced to be detained without limit of time or for life. The exclusion, in subs. (1)(b), of the provisions relating to consecutive or concurrent non-offence sentences makes the situation slightly easier for those under 21, but it is not thought that there are many such cases in practice. The words "at any time" in subs. (2) also make it clear that these indeterminate cases are to be treated differently from adult lifers. Adult cases can, under s.1(4) and (5) of this Act, only be considered by the Parole Board when the Secretary of State has referred the case to the Board. Equally, subs. (3) gives the Secretary of State power to delegate his authority to release children detained without limit of time to the Parole Board, a power which, in relation to adults, s.20(3)(a) of this Act confines to determinate-sentence cases.

In all, therefore, this section seems to discriminate in favour of young people sentenced to life or detention without limit of time. The reasons for this may lie in the adverse publicity such cases received in the media towards the end of 1991. *The Scotsman* of December 19 ran a feature which suggested, following an article in an English newspaper, that Scottish children sentenced for murder spent considerably longer in custody than their English counterparts and longer, indeed, than adults in Scotland. Though the numbers involved in Scotland are very small, and the offences usually very bad, the article suggested that the mechanisms for their release ensured that none would gain freedom until some time had been spent in an adult penal establishment. This had already prompted the relevant minister to consider granting increased freedoms to such offenders, and may lie behind the new provisions in this section.

Children detained in solemn proceedings

7.—(1) Where a child is detained under section 206 of the 1975 Act (detention of children convicted on indictment) and the period specified in the sentence—

    (a) is less than four years, he shall be released on licence by the Secretary of State as soon as (following commencement of the sentence) half the period so specified has elapsed;

    (b) is of four or more years, he shall be so released as soon as (following such commencement) two thirds of the period so specified has elapsed.

(2) A child detained under section 206 of the 1975 Act or in pursuance of an order under subsection (3) below may, on the recommendation of the Parole Board made at any time, be released on licence by the Secretary of State.

(3) If, after release under subsection (1) or (2) above and before the date on which the entire period specified in the sentence elapses (following commencement of the sentence), a child commits an offence in respect of which it is competent to impose imprisonment on a person aged 21 years or more (other than an offence in respect of which imprisonment for life is mandatory) and, whether before or after that date, pleads guilty to or is found guilty of it a court may, instead of or in addition to making any other order in respect of that plea or finding—

    (a) in a case other than that mentioned in paragraph (b) below, order that he be returned to detention for the whole or any part of the period which—

        (i) begins with the date of the order for his return; and

        (ii) is equal in length to the period between the date on which the new offence was committed and the date on which that entire period so elapses; and

    (b) in a case where that court is inferior to the court which imposed the sentence, refer the case to the superior court in question; and a court to which a case is so referred may make such order with regard to it as is mentioned in paragraph (a) above.

(4) The period for which a child is ordered under subsection (3) above to be returned to detention—

    (a) shall be taken to be a sentence of detention for the purposes of this Act and of any appeal; and

    (b) shall, as the court making that order may direct, either be served before and be followed by, or be served concurrently with, any sentence imposed for the new offence (being in either case disregarded in determining the appropriate length of that sentence).

(5) Sections 11(1), 12, 17 and 20(2) of this Act apply to children detained under section 206 of the 1975 Act as they apply to long-term prisoners; and references in those sections of this Act to prisoners, or to prison, imprisonment or sentences of imprisonment shall be construed accordingly.

(6) The Secretary of State may, after consultation with the Parole Board, by order provide that, in relation to all children detained under section 206 of the 1975 Act or to such class of those children as may be specified in the order, this section shall have effect subject to the modification that, in subsection (2), for the word "may" there shall be substituted the word "shall".

(7) In the foregoing provisions of this section any reference to a child being detained does not include a reference to his being detained without limit of time.

GENERAL NOTE

Under the previous dispensation, children sentenced under s.206 of the 1975 Act did not qualify for remission, but could be released by the Secretary of State at any time during the sentence. On release, all who had been sentenced to six months or more were subject to compulsory social-work supervision and were liable to be recalled to custody, for a maximum further period of three months.

This section accords such children sentenced to determinate periods the same release rights as other sentenced persons, but maintains the additional discretion of the Secretary of State to release them at any time. Release of those sentenced to less than four years will be unconditional. Those sentenced to four years or more will have a licence. All will be liable to be ordered to serve the balance of the sentence outstanding at the date of commission of any new offence for which imprisonment would be a competent sentence for a person over the age of 21.

Subs. (6)

This accords the Secretary of State power to delegate his decision-making authority in regard to the release of such children to the Parole Board.

Schedule 6, para. 4 ensures that this section will operate in relation to existing and future s.206 detainees immediately the section is brought into force.

Children detained in summary proceedings

8. For subsection (6) of section 413 of the 1975 Act (review of case and release of child detained in summary proceedings) there shall be substituted the following subsections—

"(6) Where a child is detained in residential care in pursuance of an order under—

(a) subsection (1) above, he shall be released from such detention not later than the date by which half the period specified in the order has (following commencement of the detention) elapsed but, without prejudice to subsection (6A) below, until the entire such period has so elapsed may be required by the local authority to submit to supervision in accordance with such conditions as they consider appropriate;

(b) subsection (1) above or (6B) below, the local authority may at any time review his case and may, in consequence of such review and after having regard to the best interests of the child and the need to protect members of the public, release the child—

(i) for such period and on such conditions as the local authority consider appropriate; or

(ii) unconditionally.

(6A) Where a child released under paragraph (a) or (b)(ii) of subsection (6) above is subject to a supervision requirement within the meaning of the 1968 Act, the effect of that requirement shall commence, or as the case may be resume, upon such release.

(6B) If, while released under paragraph (a) or (b) of subsection (6) above (and before the date on which the entire period mentioned in the said paragraph (a) has, following commencement of the detention, elapsed), a child commits an offence to which this section applies and (whether before or after that date) pleads guilty to or is found guilty of it a court may, instead of or in addition to making any other order in respect of that plea or finding, order that he be returned to the residential care of the authority which released him and that his detention in their care shall continue for the whole or any part of the period which—
>
> (a) begins with the date of the order for his return; and
>
> (b) is equal in length to the period between the date on which the new offence was committed and the date on which that entire period elapses.

(6C) An order under subsection (6B) above for return to residential care—

> (a) shall be taken to be an order for detention in residential care for the purposes of this Act and of any appeal; and
>
> (b) shall, as the court making that order may direct, either be for a period of residential care before and to be followed by, or to be concurrent with, any period of residential care to be imposed in respect of the new offence (being in either case disregarded in determining the appropriate length of the period so imposed).".

GENERAL NOTE

Children ordered to be detained under summary proceedings (according to s.413 of the 1975 Act, such children are detained in residential care, rather than "in a place to be decided by the Secretary of State") are also to benefit from the half-release provision, but may be subject to compulsory supervision until the end of the sentence. They, too, may be released at any earlier stage of the sentence, and will be subject to be ordered to return to residential care by a court on conviction of a further imprisonable offence during the period of release. All decisions about their release and any conditions to be attached to it will be taken by local authorities, with neither the Secretary of State nor the Parole Board having any jurisdiction.

Schedule 6, para. 5 makes this section retroactive on implementation, but children released will be subject to supervision and such other conditions as the local authority may decide. In addition, any supervision order under the Social Work (Scotland) Act 1968 will be (re)activated on the child's release.

Persons liable to removal from the United Kingdom

9.—(1) In relation to a long-term prisoner who is liable to removal from the United Kingdom, section 1(3) of this Act shall have effect as if the words ", if recommended to do so by the Parole Board," were omitted.

(2) In relation to a person who is liable to removal from the United Kingdom, section 12 of this Act shall have effect as if subsection (2) were omitted.

(3) For the purposes of this section, a person is liable to removal from the United Kingdom if he—

> (a) is liable to deportation under section 3(5) of the Immigration Act 1971 and has been notified of a decision to make a deportation order against him;
>
> (b) is liable to deportation under section 3(6) of that Act;
>
> (c) has been notified of a decision to refuse him leave to enter the United Kingdom; or
>
> (d) is an illegal immigrant within the meaning of section 33(1) of that Act.

GENERAL NOTE

Granting parole, subject to conditions and a licence requiring supervision, was always difficult when the potential parolee was subject to deportation at the end of a sentence. Not only would supervision be difficult to monitor, but also it would be virtually impossible to secure the recall to custody of the person if breach of the licence were to occur. This new section ensures that such prisoners are not disadvantaged. By subs. (1), the Parole Board will not be involved and the question of parole will be one for the Secretary of State on his own, and he shall have discretion, under subs. (2), not to insist on a supervision requirement in the parole licence. This section is not to be retroactive.

Life prisoners transferred to Scotland

10.—(1) In a case where a transferred life prisoner transferred from England and Wales (whether before or after the commencement of this section) is, by virtue of an order under section 34 of the Criminal Justice Act 1991, a discretionary life prisoner for the purposes of Part II of that Act, this Part of this Act except sections 1(4) and 2(9) shall apply as if—
  (a) the prisoner were a discretionary life prisoner within the meaning of section 2 of this Act; and
  (b) the relevant part of his sentence within the meaning of that section were the relevant part specified in the order under the said section 34.

(2) In the case of any other transferred life prisoner, subsection (3) below applies where the Lord Justice General, whom failing the Lord Justice Clerk, certifies his opinion that, if the prisoner had been sentenced for his offence in Scotland after the commencement of section 2 of this Act, the court by which he was so sentenced would have ordered that that section should apply to him as soon as he had served a part of his sentence specified in the certificate.

(3) In a case to which this subsection applies, this Part of this Act except sections 1(4) and 2(9) shall apply as if—
  (a) the transferred life prisoner were a discretionary life prisoner within the meaning of section 2 of this Act; and
  (b) the relevant part of his sentence within the meaning of that section were the part specified in the certificate.

(4) In this section "transferred life prisoner" means a person—
  (a) on whom a court in a country or territory outside Scotland has imposed one or more sentences of imprisonment or detention for an indeterminate period; and
  (b) who has been transferred to Scotland, in pursuance of—
      (i) an order made by the Secretary of State under section 26 of the Criminal Justice Act 1961 or section 2 of the Colonial Prisoners Removal Act 1884; or
      (ii) a warrant issued by the Secretary of State under the Repatriation of Prisoners Act 1984,
    there to serve, or to serve the remainder of, his sentence or sentences.

(5) Where a transferred life prisoner has been transferred to Scotland to serve the whole or part of two or more sentences referred to in subsection (4)(a) above—
  (a) he shall be treated as a discretionary life prisoner (within the meaning of section 2 of this Act) for the purposes of subsection (3) above only if the requirements of subsection (2) above are satisfied in respect of each of those sentences; and
  (b) notwithstanding the terms of any order under section 34 of the said Act of 1991 or of any certificate under subsection (2) above, subsections (4) and (6) of section 2 of this Act shall not apply to him until he has served the relevant part of each of those sentences.

GENERAL NOTE
   This section ensures that life-sentence prisoners transferred from any other jurisdiction will be treated in the same way as those sentenced in Scotland to equivalent sentences.

Duration of licence

11.—(1) Where a long-term prisoner is released on licence under this Part of this Act, the licence shall (unless revoked) remain in force until the entire period specified in his sentence (reckoned from the commencement of the sentence) has elapsed.

(2) Where a life prisoner is so released, the licence shall (unless revoked) remain in force until his death.

(3) Without prejudice to any order under section 212A of the 1975 Act, where a short-term prisoner is released on licence—

(a) under section 3(1) of this Act, the licence shall (unless revoked) remain in force until the date on which, but for such release, he would have been released under section 1(1) of this Act;

(b) by virtue of section 16(7) of this Act, the licence shall, unless revoked, remain in force until the entire period specified in his sentence (reckoned from the commencement of the sentence) has elapsed or, if resulting in a later date, until the period for which he was ordered to be returned to prison under or by virtue of subsection (2)(a) of that section has elapsed.

GENERAL NOTE

All long-term prisoners and life-sentence prisoners will remain on licence until the expiry of the full sentence imposed by the court (as opposed to the two-thirds date for parolees under the former provisions and no conditions at all for those released on remission alone). Those short-term prisoners released on licence under s.3 of this Act (compassionate release) will remain on licence until the date on which they would otherwise have been released (that is, the one-half date, subject to the possibility of additional days having been added to the sentence under s.24, *infra*). Those returned to prison having been released early from a short-term sentence, but having committed another imprisonable offence and having been sentenced to another short-term sentence in addition to being ordered to serve all or part of the original sentence outstanding at the time of the new offence, will remain on licence until the expiry of the later of the whole of the new sentence or the period for which the court ordered the person to be returned under the original sentence. All other short-term prisoners are to be released without a licence.

Conditions in licence

12.—(1) A person released on licence under this Part of this Act shall comply with such conditions as may be specified in that licence by the Secretary of State.

(2) Without prejudice to the generality of subsection (1) above and to the power of the Secretary of State under subsection (3) below to vary or cancel any condition, a licence granted under this Part of this Act shall include a condition requiring that the person subject to it—

(a) shall be under the supervision of a relevant officer of such local authority, or of a probation officer appointed for or assigned to such petty sessions area, as may be specified in the licence; and

(b) shall comply with such requirements as that officer may specify for the purposes of the supervision.

(3) The Secretary of State may from time to time under subsection (1) above insert, vary or cancel a condition in a licence granted under this Part of this Act; but in the case of a long-term or life prisoner no licence condition shall be included on release or subsequently inserted, varied or cancelled except—

(a) in the case of the inclusion of a condition in the licence of a discretionary life prisoner, in accordance with the recommendations of the Parole Board; and

(b) in any other case, after consulting the Board.

(4) For the purposes of subsection (3) above, the Secretary of State shall be treated as having consulted the Parole Board about a proposal to include, insert, vary or cancel a condition in any case if he has consulted the Board about the implementation of proposals of that description generally or in that class of case.

GENERAL NOTE
This section effectively replaces ss.8(2)(b) and 22(7) of the 1989 Act. The significant change is in relation to the licence conditions of discretionary lifers, where the Secretary of State cannot act without the recommendation of the Parole Board (subs. (3)(a)).

Supervision of persons released on licence

13. The Secretary of State may make rules for regulating the supervision of any description of person released, under this Part of this Act, on licence.

GENERAL NOTE
Through the Social Work Services Group of the Scottish Office, much work has now been done to promulgate national standards for social-work supervision in all areas of criminal justice. This section gives authority to the Secretary of State to make the standards relating to the supervision of released persons legally enforceable.

Supervised release of short-term prisoners

14.—(1) After section 212 of the 1975 Act there shall be inserted the following section—

"Supervised release orders

212A.—(1) Where a person is convicted of an offence and is sentenced to imprisonment for a term of not less than twelve months but less than four years, the court on passing sentence may, if it considers that it is necessary to do so to protect the public from serious harm from the offender on his release, make such order as is mentioned in subsection (2) below.

(2) The order referred to in subsection (1) above (to be known as a "supervised release order") is that the person, during a relevant period—

(a) be under the supervision either of a relevant officer of a local authority or of a probation officer appointed for or assigned to a petty sessions area (such local authority or the justices for such area to be designated under section 14(4) or 15(1) of the Prisoners and Criminal Proceedings (Scotland) Act 1993); and

(b) comply with—
(i) such requirements as are specified in the order; and
(ii) such requirements as that officer may reasonably specify,
for the purpose of securing the good conduct of the person or preventing, or lessening the possibility of, his committing a further offence (whether or not an offence of the kind for which he was sentenced).

(3) A supervised release order—

(a) shall be as nearly as possible in such form as may be prescribed by Act of Adjournal;

(b) for the purposes of any appeal or review constitutes part of the sentence of the person in respect of whom the order is made; and

(c) shall have no effect during any period in which the person is subject to a licence under Part I of the said Act of 1993.

(4) Before making a supervised release order as respects a person the court shall explain to him, in as straightforward a way as is practicable, the effect of the order and the possible consequences for him of any breach of it.

(5) The clerk of the court by which a supervised release order is made in respect of a person shall—

(a) forthwith send a copy of the order to the person and to the Secretary of State; and

(b) within seven days after the date on which the order is made, send to the Secretary of State such documents and information relating to the case and to the person as are likely to be of assistance to a supervising officer.

(6) In this section—

"relevant officer" has the same meaning as in Part I of the Prisoners and Criminal Proceedings (Scotland) Act 1993;

"relevant period" means such period as may be specified in the supervised release order, being a period—

(a) not exceeding twelve months after the date of the person's release; and

(b) no part of which is later than the date by which the entire term of imprisonment specified in his sentence has elapsed; and

"supervising officer" means, where an authority has or justices have been designated as is mentioned in subsection (2)(a) above for the purposes of the order, any relevant officer or, as the case may be, probation officer who is for the time being supervising for those purposes the person released.".

(2) Notwithstanding section 26 of the Criminal Justice Act 1961 and section 212A(1) of the 1975 Act, where a short-term prisoner within the meaning of the Criminal Justice Act 1991, being a prisoner in respect of whom section 44 of that Act (release of sexual offenders) applies, is transferred to a prison in Scotland to serve his sentence or the remainder of his sentence, the sheriff court for the area in which that prison is situated shall, on the application of the Secretary of State supported by any relevant documents or information received by the Secretary of State on the transfer of the prisoner to Scotland, make under this subsection, but subject to section 212A(2) to (6) of the 1975 Act, a supervised release order in respect of the prisoner.

(3) For the purposes of a supervised release order under subsection (2) above the relevant period within the meaning of section 212A(2) of the 1975 Act shall be whichever is the shorter of—

(a) the period of twelve months from the date of the prisoner's release; and

(b) the period from that date until the date by which the entire term of imprisonment specified in his sentence has (following commencement of the imprisonment) elapsed.

(4) The Secretary of State shall, not later than thirty days before the date of release of a short-term prisoner who is subject to a supervised release order, designate—

(a) the local authority for the area where the prisoner proposes to reside after release;

(b) the local authority for the area where the place from which he is to be released is situated; or

(c) the justices for the petty sessions area where he proposes to reside after release,

as the appropriate authority or, as the case may be, justices for the purposes of the order.

(5) As soon as practicable after designating a local authority or justices under subsection (4) above the Secretary of State shall—

(a) inform the prisoner in writing of the designation; and

(b) send to the authority or, as the case may be, to the clerk to the justices a copy of the supervised release order and of the relevant documents and information received by the Secretary of State by virtue of section 212A(5)(b) of the 1975 Act.

GENERAL NOTE

This section creates a totally new disposal for criminal courts. When imposing a custodial sentence of between 12 months and less than four years, a court may order that the person be subject to a "supervised release order" for a maximum of 12 months or the unexpired period of the total original sentence, whichever is the lesser. In effect, this will be very much like a probation order, with the important difference that the offender's consent will not be required before the imposition of a supervised release order.

This was the Government's response to concerns expressed about the Kincraig recommendation that short-term prisoners should not be subject to any compulsory supervision on release. Kincraig had criticised the lack of targeting in post-release supervision and the seemingly arbitrary nature of recall decisions during the licence period. These two objections are met by the provision that the post-release supervision order must be made at the time of sentencing by the original court and only in cases which meet the criteria enunciated in the new s.212(A)(1) of the 1975 Act and by the provisions for dealing with breaches of the supervised release order in s.18, *infra*.

Some social workers will be concerned that this is the first instance of supervision being imposed directly by a court without the consent of the supervisee, and with the difficulty this may cause in forming positive relationships with the supervisee. Subsection (4) makes clear the duty of the court to explain the meaning of the order, but the fact remains that the supervisee's consent is not required.

By making provision for the Secretary of State to refer the case of any prisoner transferred to Scotland to serve a sentence imposed after the commission of a sexual offence to a sheriff in order that the sheriff may consider the imposition of a supervised release order on that prisoner, subs. (2) implies that it is this category of offenders for which the new order is specifically designed. Any order made in these circumstances will be subject to the same procedural and administrative requirements set out for orders made by Scottish courts at the time of sentence.

For procedure on breach of an order, see s.18, *infra*.

Variation of supervised release order etc.

15.—(1) A person released subject to a supervised release order, or his supervising officer, may request the Secretary of State that a local authority or the justices for a petty sessions area (in this section referred to as the "second" designee) be designated under this subsection as the appropriate authority or justices for the purposes of the order in place of that or those for the time being designated under section 14(4) of this Act or this subsection (the "first" designee) if the person resides or proposes to reside in the area of the second designee.

(2) The Secretary of State shall, if he designates the second designee in accordance with the request, determine the date from which the designation shall have effect.

(3) As soon as practicable after a designation is made under subsection (1) above—

  (a) the Secretary of State shall—

    (i) inform the person subject to the supervised release order, the first designee and the second designee that the designation has been made and of the date determined under subsection (2) above; and

    (ii) send a copy of the supervised release order to the second designee; and

  (b) the first designee shall send to the second designee the relevant documents and information received by the first designee by virtue of section 14(5)(b) of this Act (or by virtue of this paragraph).

(4) The court which made a supervised release order may, on an application under this subsection by a person subject to the order (whether or not he has been released before the application is made) or by his supervising officer (or, if the person is not yet released, but a local authority stands or justices stand designated as the appropriate authority or justices in respect of the order, by a relevant officer of that authority or, as the case may be, a probation officer appointed for or assigned to the petty sessions area)—

  (a) amend, vary or cancel any requirement specified in or by virtue of the order;

(b) insert in the order a requirement specified for the purpose mentioned in section 212A(2)(b) of the 1975 Act,
whether or not such amendment, variation, cancellation or insertion accords with what is sought by the applicant; but the period during which the person is to be under supervision shall not thereby be increased beyond any period which could have been specified in making the order.

(5) If an application under subsection (4) above is by the supervising officer (or other relevant officer or probation officer) alone, the court shall cite the person who is subject to the order to appear before the court and shall not proceed under that subsection until it has explained to the person, in as straightforward a way as is practicable, the effect of any proposed amendment, variation, cancellation or insertion.

(6) The clerk of the court by which an amendment, variation, cancellation or insertion is made under subsection (4) above shall forthwith send a copy of the resultant order to the person subject to it and to the supervising officer.

GENERAL NOTE
This section allows a supervised release order to be transferred from one local authority or justices for a petty sessions area to any other on the application of the supervisor or supervisee and the amendment, variation, cancellation or insertion of any appropriate condition in the order, but not the cancellation of the order itself. The supervisee retains the right to have any variations fully explained.

Commission of offence by released prisoner

16.—(1) This section applies to a short-term or long-term prisoner sentenced to a term of imprisonment (in this section referred to as "the original sentence") by a court in Scotland and released under this Part of this Act or Part II of the Criminal Justice Act 1991 if—
    (a) before the date on which he would (but for his release) have served his sentence in full, he commits an offence punishable with imprisonment (other than an offence in respect of which imprisonment for life is mandatory); and
    (b) whether before or after that date, he pleads guilty to or is found guilty of that offence (in this section referred to as "the new offence") in a court in Scotland or England and Wales.

(2) Where the court mentioned in subsection (1)(b) above is in Scotland it may, instead of or in addition to making any other order in respect of the plea or finding—
    (a) in a case other than that mentioned in paragraph (b) below, order the person to be returned to prison for the whole or any part of the period which—
        (i) begins with the date of the order for his return; and
        (ii) is equal in length to the period between the date on which the new offence was committed and the date mentioned in subsection (1)(a) above; and
    (b) in a case where that court is inferior to the court which imposed the sentence mentioned in the said subsection (1)(a), refer the case to the superior court in question; and a court to which a case is so referred may make such order with regard to it as is mentioned in paragraph (a) above.

(3) Where the court mentioned in subsection (1)(b) above is in England and Wales it may, instead of or in addition to making any other order in respect of the plea or finding, refer the case to the court which imposed the original sentence and shall, if it does so, send to that court such particulars of that case as may be relevant.

(4) The court to which a case is referred under subsection (3) above may make such an order as is mentioned in subsection (2)(a) above in respect of the person.

(5) The period for which a person to whom this section applies is ordered under subsection (2) or (4) above to be returned to prison—

(a) shall be taken to be a sentence of imprisonment for the purposes of this Act and of any appeal; and

(b) shall, as the court making that order may direct, either be served before and be followed by, or be served concurrently with, any sentence of imprisonment imposed for the new offence (being in either case disregarded in determining the appropriate length of that sentence).

(6) In exercising its powers under section 254(3) or 453C(1) of the 1975 Act, the court hearing an appeal against an order under subsection (2) or (4) above may, if it thinks fit and notwithstanding subsection (2)(a), substitute for the period specified in the order a period not exceeding the period between the date on which the person was released and the date mentioned in subsection (1)(a) above.

(7) Where an order under subsection (2) or (4) above is made in respect of a person released on licence and he is sentenced in respect of the new offence to a term of imprisonment of less than four years, section 1(1) of this Act shall apply in respect of that sentence as if for the word "unconditionally" there were substituted the words "on licence".

GENERAL NOTE

Commission of any offence punishable by imprisonment during the period between the release date and the end of the total sentence imposed by the original court renders a released person subject to an order returning him to custody for up to the balance of the sentence outstanding at the time of commission of the new offence. The new offence must have been committed in Great Britain, and the court dealing with the new offence, if it is in England or Wales, or, if in Scotland and inferior to the court which imposed the original sentence, has a discretion to refer the case to the original court for it to exercise this power if it so chooses.

This power is in addition to the court's sentencing powers in relation to the new offence, though any new sentence may be ordered to be served before, after or concurrently with the period of the original sentence. Any order to resume serving the original sentence is subject to the same appeal rights and the provisions of this Act in the same way as any other sentence of imprisonment. Accordingly, a person may again qualify for release at one-half or two-thirds of the period ordered to be served, and perhaps even for parole consideration in the unlikely event of that period being four years or more.

The Kincraig Committee had suggested that recall for further offences committed during the period of release should automatically be ordered for the balance of the sentence outstanding at the time of the new offence.

Revocation of licence

17.—(1) Where—

(a) a long-term or life prisoner has been released on licence under this Part of this Act, the Secretary of State may revoke that licence and recall him to prison—

(i) if recommended to do so by the Parole Board; or

(ii) if revocation and recall are, in the opinion of the Secretary of State, expedient in the public interest and it is not practicable to await such recommendation;

(b) a short-term prisoner has been so released, the Secretary of State may revoke his licence and recall him to prison if satisfied that his health or circumstances have so changed that were he in prison his release under section 3(1) of this Act would no longer be justified.

(2) A person recalled under subsection (1) above shall, on his return to prison, be informed of the reasons for his recall and that he has the right to make written representations to the Secretary of State in that regard.

(3) The Secretary of State shall refer to the Parole Board the case of—
(a) a person recalled under subsection (1)(a)(i) above who makes representations under subsection (2) above; or
(b) a person recalled under subsection (1)(a)(ii) above.
(4) Where on a reference under subsection (3) above the Parole Board directs a prisoner's immediate release on licence, the Secretary of State shall under this section give effect to that direction.
(5) On the revocation of the licence of any person under the foregoing provisions of this section, he shall be liable to be detained in pursuance of his sentence and, if at large, shall be deemed to be unlawfully at large.
(6) A licence under this Part of this Act, other than the licence of a life prisoner, shall be revoked by the Secretary of State if all conditions in it have been cancelled; and where a person's licence has been revoked under this subsection the person shall be treated in all respects as if released unconditionally.

GENERAL NOTE
    This section continues the existing powers of the Parole Board and the Secretary of State to deal with breach of licence (s.28(1)–(5)(7)(10) and (11) of the 1989 Act), and adds a power for the Secretary of State to revoke licences granted under s.3 of this Act (compassionate release). The parts of the pre-existing powers not re-enacted are those relating to the power of sheriff and High Court to revoke parole licences on conviction of an offence punishable on indictment by imprisonment (*ibid.* subs. (6)), a power which was very rarely used.
    Kincraig recommended (para. 6.21) that recalled prisoners who disputed the facts which had led to their recall should be entitled to appear at a hearing conducted by a panel of the Board authorised to hear both sides on matters of fact. The Act fails to address the dissatisfaction expressed about revocation of licences when the grounds are other than conviction of a further offence. It seems likely, therefore, that prisoners in these circumstances will continue to seek judicial reviews of decisions.

Breach of supervised release order

    18.—(1) Where the court which imposed a supervised release order on a person is informed, by statement on oath by an appropriate officer, that the person has failed to comply with a requirement specified in or by virtue of that order, the court may—
(a) issue a warrant for the arrest of the person; or
(b) issue a citation requiring the person to appear before the court at such time as may be specified in the citation.
(2) If it is proved to the satisfaction of the court before which a person is brought, or appears, in pursuance of a warrant or citation issued under subsection (1) above that there has been such failure as is mentioned in that subsection, the court may—
(a) order him to be returned to prison for the whole or any part of the period which—
(i) begins with the date of the order for his return; and
(ii) is equal in length to the period between the date of the first proven failure referred to in the statement mentioned in subsection (1) above and the date on which supervision under the supervised release order would have ceased; or
(b) do anything in respect of the supervised release order that might have been done under section 15(4) of this Act on an application under that subsection in relation to that order.
(3) For the purposes of subsection (2) above, evidence of one witness shall be sufficient evidence.
(4) As soon as the period for which a person is ordered under subsection (2) above to be returned to prison expires, the Secretary of State shall release him unconditionally.
(5) For the purposes of this Act, any such period as is mentioned in subsection (4) above is neither a sentence nor a part of a sentence.

(6) The following are "appropriate officers" for the purposes of sub-section (1) above—

(a) the person's supervising officer;
(b) the director of social work of a local authority which is designated under section 14(4) or 15(1) of this Act as the appropriate authority for the purposes of the order;
(c) any officer appointed by that director for the purposes of this section.

GENERAL NOTE

The procedure established in this section for dealing with breach of a supervised attendance order is very similar to that for breach of probation. Note, however, that the power of the court is limited to imprisonment for the period outstanding between the first proven failure to comply with the order and the end of the original order or to variation of the order subject to the maximum duration of one year (subs. (2)). Return to prison, for any period, results in termination of the order on release, even if that release is before the end of the original order (subs. (4)). No clear standard of proof is set down for establishing breaches (subs. (2)), but the evidence of one witness is to be sufficient (subs. (3)).

Appeals in respect of decisions relating to supervised release orders

19.—(1) Within two weeks after a determination by a court—

(a) on an application under section 15(4); or
(b) under section 18(2),

of this Act, or within such longer period as the High Court may allow, the person subject to the supervised release order may lodge a written note of appeal with the Clerk of Justiciary, who shall send a copy to the court which made the determination and to the Secretary of State.

(2) A note of appeal under subsection (1) above shall be as nearly as possible in such form as may be prescribed by Act of Adjournal and shall contain a full statement of all the grounds of appeal; and except by leave of the High Court on cause shown it shall not be competent for an appellant to found any aspect of his appeal on a ground not contained in the note of appeal.

GENERAL NOTE

This section applies the same time limit and formal conditions to appeals against variation of a supervised release order or the imposition of imprisonment for breach of such an order as are generally applicable in relation to appeals against sentence by a sentenced person.

The Parole Board for Scotland

20.—(1) There shall continue to be a body to be known as the Parole Board for Scotland, which shall discharge the functions conferred on it by, or by virtue of, this Part of this Act.

(2) It shall be the duty of the Board to advise the Secretary of State with respect to any matter referred to it by him which is connected with the early release or recall of prisoners.

(3) The Secretary of State may, after consultation with the Board, by order provide that, in relation to such class of case as may be specified in the order, this Act shall have effect subject to the modifications that—

(a) in subsection (3) of section 1, for the word "may" there shall be substituted the word "shall" so however that nothing in this paragraph shall affect the operation of that subsection as it has effect in relation to a long-term prisoner who is liable to removal from the United Kingdom (within the meaning of section 9 of this Act);
(b) in section 12—
    (i) in subsection (3)(a), after the words "licence of a" there shall be inserted the words "long-term or"; and
    (ii) subsection (4) shall be omitted; and
(c) in section 17(1)(a), for the word "may" there shall be substituted the word "shall".

(4) The Secretary of State may by rules make provision with respect to the proceedings of the Board, including provision—

(a) authorising cases to be dealt with in whole or in part by a prescribed number of members of the Board in accordance with such procedure as may be prescribed;

(b) requiring cases to be dealt with at prescribed times; and

(c) as to what matters may be taken into account by the Board (or by such number) in dealing with a case.

(5) The Secretary of State may give the Board directions as to the matters to be taken into account by it in discharging its functions under this Part of this Act; and in giving any such directions the Secretary of State shall in particular have regard to—

(a) the need to protect the public from serious harm from offenders; and

(b) the desirability of preventing the commission by offenders of further offences and of securing their rehabilitation.

(6) The supplementary provisions in Schedule 2 to this Act shall have effect with respect to the Board.

GENERAL NOTE

This section, with its associated Sched. 2, continues the main provisions of s.18 of and Sched. 1 to the 1989 Act in relation to the Parole Board, with two significant additions. The first is the power granted by subs. (3) to the Secretary of State enabling him to delegate to the Board full authority for release decisions in relation to classes of case to be specified in an order. In the pre-existing system, the Parole Board merely advised the Secretary of State, and, while he could not parole anyone without the Board's consent, the final decision was always the Secretary of State's. Kincraig recommended no change in this arrangement (paras. 3.22–3.24), arguing that the Secretary of State was responsible to Parliament for decisions and that this was preferable to, for example, the Canadian system, where the totally independent Parole Board takes full responsibility for its own decisions. The system adopted in this Act represents a half-way house between the Canadian model and the pre-existing Scottish one. The Secretary of State will be able to end his direct involvement in the selected categories of case, to be chosen in consultation with the Parole Board, and to give directions to the Board, under subs. (5), as to the matters the Board should take into account. He will, however, remain answerable to Parliament for the exercise of his powers under this Act, although the Board itself will undoubtedly come under more direct scrutiny.

The second area of major change is the provisions in subss. (4)(c) and (5) enabling the Secretary of State to specify by rules the matters to be taken into account by the Board in making its decisions and to give directions having had regard to the matters specified in subs. (5)(a) and (b). Parole criteria have never been set out in any authoritative document, though the Scottish Home and Health Department published a pamphlet entitled "Parole: Your Questions Answered" in 1986, giving parole-eligible prisoners some idea of the procedures followed and the matters considered in decision-making. The Kincraig Committee (para. 5.6) recommended that the criteria for parole should be established in statute. If the Secretary of State exercises the power given by this section, and it is thought likely that he will as soon as the Act is implemented, this recommendation will be met. One possible consequence of this, especially when coupled with the giving of reasons for decisions, is that the whole parole process will become much more open to review by the courts, and a major objection of those opposed to parole will have been overcome.

Subs. (4)(a)

This continues the provision of s.18(3) of the 1989 Act enabling the Secretary of State to authorise the Board to deal with cases with less than its full membership present. The practice in England and Wales has been for the Parole Board to sit in panels of three to make their recommendations, while the Scottish Board has always met as a single body. It is not envisaged that the Scottish Board will now sit in panels, except when dealing with the cases of discretionary lifers referred under s.2 of this Act.

Subsection (6) and Sched. 2 retain the present constitution of the Board, with a small amendment specifying that the judicial member (Sched. 2, para. 2(a)) must be a current post-holder. Local review committees are, however, not mentioned in this Act. Their function has been explained in the Introduction (*supra*), and will not be required under the new dispensation because the number of cases to be considered each year will be such that the Parole Board itself will be able to see them all. Accordingly, the committees will cease to exist when the new Act is fully operational.

Parole advisers

21.—(1) The Secretary of State may appoint under this section persons (to be known as "parole advisers") to give advice to prisoners, or former prisoners, who wish to make representations to the Secretary of State or to the Parole Board as regards any matter concerning their release on licence under this Part of this Act or their return to prison or detention by virtue of this Part of this Act.

(2) The Secretary of State shall pay to parole advisers such remuneration and allowances as he may with the consent of the Treasury determine.

General Note
    With the demise of the local review committees, the one existing method by which a prisoner may obtain assistance from someone outside the prison in making representations to the Parole Board would end. The Kincraig Committee (para. 5.15) considered it generally important that prisoners should be able to obtain assistance with this process and recommended that an independent panel of parole advisers should be appointed to each prison holding parole-eligible prisoners to help with the preparation of representations. This section makes this possible, and provides for payment to such advisers, a power which was not available in relation to local review committee members. No qualifications for such advisers are specified.

Miscellaneous

Place of confinement of prisoners

22. For section 10 of the 1989 Act (place of confinement of prisoners) there shall be substituted the following section—

"Place of confinement of prisoners

10.—(1) A prisoner may be lawfully confined in any prison.

(2) Prisoners shall be committed to such prisons as the Secretary of State may from time to time direct, and may be moved by the Secretary of State from any prison to any other prison.

(3) The foregoing provisions of this section are without prejudice to section 11 of this Act and section 241 of the 1975 Act (transfer of prisoner in connection with hearing of appeal).".

General Note
    Sections 22–26 are, with the exception of s.24, unrelated to the first part of the Act and arise from a perceived need to change some parts of the Prisons (Scotland) Act 1989, which was a consolidation measure.
    Section 22 amends s.10 of the 1989 Act, which required the Secretary of State to designate certain prisons for certain purposes. This considerably reduced the flexibility of the limited penal estate and has restricted the Scottish Prison Service's ability to respond to localised overcrowding and to implement the plans announced in *Custody and Care* and *Opportunity and Responsibility* to give prisoners more choice over the establishment in which they serve their sentence. This new section should thus enable more efficient use of prison buildings.

Transfer of young offenders to prison or remand centre

23. After section 20 of the 1989 Act there shall be inserted the following section—

"Transfer of young offenders to prison or remand centre

20A.—(1) Subject to section 21 of this Act, an offender sentenced to detention in a young offenders institution shall be detained in such an institution unless a direction under subsection (2) below is in force in relation to him.

(2) The Secretary of State may from time to time direct that an offender sentenced to detention in a young offenders institution shall be detained in a prison or remand centre instead of in a young offenders institution, but if the offender is under 18 years of age at the time of the direction, only for a temporary purpose.

(3) Where an offender is detained in a prison or remand centre by virtue of subsection (2) above, any rules under section 39 of this Act which apply in relation to persons detained in that place shall apply to that offender; but subject to the foregoing and to subsection (4) below, the provisions of the 1975 Act, the Prisoners and Criminal Proceedings (Scotland) Act 1993 and this Act relating to the treatment and supervision of persons sentenced to detention in a young offenders institution shall continue to apply to the offender.

(4) Where an offender referred to in subsection (3) above attains the age of 21 years, subsection (3) of section 21 of this Act shall apply to him as if he had been transferred to prison under that section.".

GENERAL NOTE

Section 20 of the 1989 Act authorises the temporary detention of a young offender in a place other than a young offender institution or remand centre only until arrangements can be made for transfer to an appropriate place. Section 206 of the 1975 Act prohibits the detention of young offenders in adult establishments. This new section introduces greater flexibility into the system, but subject to the checks maintained in subss. (3) and (4). The number of young offender establishments, and their geographical distribution, mean that it can be difficult within the existing law to provide, for example, accommodation near to a young offender's home to enable family to make visits, or separate accommodation for particular young offenders who may have difficulty in associating with other young offenders, within the existing law. The new provision will overcome these problems.

Additional days for disciplinary offences

24. The following subsection shall be added at the end of section 39 of the 1989 Act (rules for the management of prisons and other institutions)—

"(7) Rules made under this section may provide for the award of additional days, not exceeding in aggregate one-sixth of the prisoner's sentence—

    (a) to a short-term or long-term prisoner within the meaning of Part I of the Prisoners and Criminal Proceedings (Scotland) Act 1993; or

    (b) conditionally on his eventually becoming such a prisoner, to a person remanded in custody,

where he is guilty, under such rules, of a breach of discipline.".

GENERAL NOTE

The whole question of the power of governors of prisons and visiting committees to award forfeiture of remission under the old dispensation has been the subject of much debate, and several court challenges, in recent times. Rule 43 of the Prison (Scotland) Rules 1952 (S.I. 1952 No. 565 (S.18)) authorises governors to withdraw up to 14 days' remission upon finding a prisoner guilty of an offence against prison discipline, whereas visiting committees can order forfeiture of an unlimited amount of remission under r. 45. The only procedural requirement laid down in the Rules was that in r. 40(1), requiring that, before a report is adjudicated, the prisoner should be informed of the offence for which he has been reported and given an opportunity of hearing the facts alleged against him and of being heard in his own defence.

The first legal challenges were mounted against the English Boards of Visitors' adjudications, the powers of these boards being slightly less than those of the Scottish equivalent. Eventually the English courts held, in *R.* v. *Secretary of State for the Home Department*, ex p. *Tarrant*; *R.* v. *Board of Visitors of Albany Prison*, ex p. *Leyland*; *R.* v. *Board of Visitors of Wormwood Scrubs Prison*, ex p. *Tangney, Clark, Anderson* [1985] Q.B. 251, that boards of visitors should consider granting legal representation to prisoners appearing before them when the amount of remission at stake was high and the prisoner unlikely to be able to represent himself properly. The decision in this case was announced while a European Court of Human Rights judgment was being awaited on another English case (*Campbell and Fell* v. *U.K.* [1983] E.H.R.R. 207). That decision re-enforced the approach taken by the English court, which was that the matter at issue in adjudications was one of the freedom of the individual, and therefore the rules of natural justice should be applied. Although both cases originated in England, the fact that the European Court's judgment was binding on the U.K. meant that the Scottish position had to be reviewed. A decision was then made not to make any further use of visiting committees in their disciplinary rôle. Thus, although the Rules still provide for this function to be exercised, executive practice ensures that it is not. One can only surmise that this decision indicated at least a lack of total confidence in the committees' abilities to function in front of legally qualified people. It should be noted that this new section does not accord visiting committees any power to award additional days to a sentence.

Submitting governors' adjudications to legal scrutiny took a little longer. It was eventually held, in *R.* v. *Deputy Governor of Parkhurst Prison*, ex p. *Leech*; *R.* v. *Deputy Governor of Long Lartin Prison*, ex p. *Prevot* [1988] A.C. 533, that, since governors are exercising a statutory power affecting the rights or legitimate expectations of subjects, they must act in conformity with the rules of natural justice and their decisions are subject to judicial review. The only Scottish case to date is *Doran* v. *Secretary of State* 1990 G.W.D. 29–1431, where again the court held that judicial review was appropriate. There has not yet, however, been a detailed examination of the procedure adopted by governors in the exercise of their powers.

In its consideration of this issue, the Kincraig Committee (Report, Chapter 7) considered that it was inappropriate for governors to have the power to extend a person's stay in prison without any of the protections available in courts of law before a person can be sentenced to custody. In any case, with the proposed system of conditional release, which was calculated to ensure good behaviour after release of the prisoner, there was seen to be no place for any power to extend the part of the sentence spent in custody unless it were to be exercised by a court in response to a further criminal offence committed in custody.

The Government has not accepted this recommendation, feeling that it is important for the maintenance of discipline in prisons that governors have the power to award "additional days", as provided in this section. During the House of Lords Report stage on this part of the Act, assurances were given that procedures for governors' adjudications had been reviewed, and a new system would shortly be introduced. Unfortunately, the Minister could not provide details of the remit of the committee which had conducted the review, nor a copy of the report, since the committee reported verbally (*Hansard*, H.L. Vol. 538, cols. 556–558). It is to be hoped that details of the new procedures to be introduced will be made fully public at the earliest opportunity. No doubt they will, in due course, be subject to review in the courts, especially since this section makes clear, in the adoption of the terminology of "additional days", that the power is one effectively to sentence someone to a further period of imprisonment.

The section also creates a new power for Scottish governors, the power given by the new s.39(7)(b) to a governor to add additional days conditionally to a sentence of imprisonment which may be given to a remand prisoner. This power has been available south of the border for some time, but there have been few indications of any demand for such a power in Scotland.

Provision in prison rules for directions

25. The following subsections shall be added at the end of section 39 of the 1989 Act (rules for the management of prisons and other institutions) after the subsection added by section 24 of this Act—

"(8) Without prejudice to any power to make standing orders or to issue directions or any other kind of instruction, rules made under this section may authorise the Secretary of State to supplement the rules by making provision by directions for any purpose specified in the rules; and rules so made or directions made by virtue of this subsection may authorise the governor, or any other officer, of a prison, or some other person or class of persons specified in the rules or directions, to exercise a discretion in relation to the purpose so specified.

(9) Rules made under this section may permit directions made by virtue of subsection (8) above to derogate (but only to such extent, or in such manner, as may be specified in the rules) from provisions of rules so made and so specified.

(10) Any reference, however expressed, in any enactment other than this section to rules made under this section shall be construed as including a reference to directions made by virtue of subsection (8) above.

(11) Directions made by virtue of subsection (8) above shall be published by the Secretary of State in such manner as he considers appropriate.".

GENERAL NOTE

This new addition to s.39 of the 1989 Act is an attempt to clear up confusion about the status of Standing Orders issued by, or on behalf of, the Secretary of State in relation to penal establishments. It has become common practice for many of the details of prison life, including many important details like the regulation of correspondence and visits allowed to prisoners, to be decided by means of these standing orders. Their legal status was never very clear, especially in view of the requirement in s.42(1) of the 1989 Act that the Secretary of State should exercise any rule-making power under that Act by means of statutory instrument. In addition, standing orders, with the exception of those relating to correspondence, have been secret and not generally available to prisoners or their legal advisers.

This new section goes some way towards clarifying the position. New subs. (8) creates a new concept for prisons, that of "directions". The Secretary of State may use such directions, if authorised by the rules (which, under the 1989 Act, must be made by statutory instrument), to supplement the rules and also, if and as specifically permitted in the rules, to derogate from the rules (subs. (9)). Subsection (10) requires all directions to be published.

The net change may thus not be a great improvement. Not only is the possibility of standing orders, other, presumably non-statutory, directions and other kinds of instruction left open, but there is also the prospect of rules authorising directions which can countermand the rules, albeit in limited and publicly defined ways. The task of the person seeking to establish what the position is in regard to any specific matter relating to imprisonment may become more, rather than less, difficult.

Further amendment of Mental Health (Scotland) Act 1984

26. In section 73 of the Mental Health (Scotland) Act 1984, subsection (3) (which provides for the continued detention in hospital of persons moved there by virtue of a transfer order while awaiting trial etc. even where that order has ceased to have effect) shall cease to have effect.

GENERAL NOTE

This sensible amendment to the Mental Health (Scotland) Act 1984 leaves open the possibility that a person detained under s.73 can continue to be detained subject to the normal civil committal procedure after the expiry of a transfer order from a penal establishment.

Interpretation

Interpretation of Part I

27.—(1) In this Part of this Act, except where the context otherwise requires—

"court" does not include a court-martial;

"discretionary life prisoner" has the meaning given by section 2 of this Act;

"life prisoner" means a person serving a sentence of imprisonment for life;

"local authority" means a regional or islands council;

"long-term prisoner" means a person serving a sentence of imprisonment for a term of four years or more;

"Parole Board" means the Parole Board for Scotland;

"petty sessions area" has the same meaning as in the Justices of the Peace Act 1979;

"relevant officer", in relation to a local authority, means an officer of that authority employed by them in the discharge of their functions under section 27(1) of the Social Work (Scotland) Act 1968 (supervision and care of persons put on probation or released from prison etc.);

"short-term prisoner" means a person serving a sentence of imprisonment for a term of less than four years;

"supervised release order" has the meaning given by section 212A (as inserted by section 14 of this Act) of the 1975 Act but includes any order under subsection (2) of the said section 14; and

"supervising officer" has the meaning given by the said section 212A.

(2) The Secretary of State may by order provide—

(a) that the references to four years in the definitions of "long-term prisoner" and "short-term prisoner" in subsection (1) above shall be construed as references to such other period as may be specified in the order;

(b) that any reference in this Part of this Act to a particular proportion of a prisoner's sentence shall be construed as a reference to such other proportion of a prisoner's sentence as may be so specified.

(3) An order under subsection (2) above may make such transitional provisions as appear to the Secretary of State necessary or expedient in connection with any provision made by the order.

(4) For the purposes of this Part of this Act so far as relating to licences or persons released on licence, the age of any person at the time when sentence was passed on him shall be deemed to have been that which appears to the Secretary of State to have been his age at that time.

(5) For the purposes of any reference, however expressed, in this Part of this Act to the term of imprisonment or other detention to which a person has been sentenced or which, having been sentenced, he has served (in whole or in part), consecutive terms and terms which are wholly or partly concurrent shall be treated as a single term.

(6) If additional days are awarded in accordance with rules made under section 39(7) of the 1989 Act (and are not remitted in accordance with such rules), the period which the prisoner (or eventual prisoner) must serve before becoming entitled to or eligible for release shall be extended by those additional days.

(7) Where (but for this subsection) a prisoner would, under any provision of this Act or of the 1975 Act, fall to be released on or by a day which is a Saturday, Sunday or public holiday he shall instead be released on or by the last preceding day which is not a Saturday, Sunday or public holiday.

GENERAL NOTE

Subs. (2)

This allows the Secretary of State to vary, by order, the definition of both long-term and short-term prisoner and the proportion of the sentence which must be served before release can be granted. In relation to parole, this repeats the power given to the Secretary of State by s.22(2) of the 1989 Act, but without specifying a minimum time to be served. In relation to remission or conditional release, it repeats the power granted by s.24 of the 1989 Act.

Subs. (6)

This continues the present provision in relation to those being released other than on parole, but extends it to cover those being released on parole. Currently, any award of loss of remission is ignored, at least in the direct sense, in calculating release dates for parole purposes.

Subs. (7)

This extends the provision of s.16 of the 1989 Act by adding public holidays to Saturdays and Sundays as days to be discounted when release of any prisoner falls due on one. Accordingly, a prisoner due for release on a public holiday Monday will be released on the preceding Friday.

PART II

CRIMINAL PROCEEDINGS

Evidence

Prints, samples etc. in criminal investigations

28.—(1) This section applies where a person has been arrested and is in custody, or is detained under section 2(1) of the Criminal Justice (Scotland) Act 1980 (detention and questioning).

(2) A constable may take from the person fingerprints, palmprints and such other prints and impressions of an external part of the body as the

constable may, having regard to the circumstances of the suspected offence in respect of which the person has been arrested or detained, reasonably consider it appropriate to take.

(3) All record of any prints or impressions taken under subsection (2) above shall be destroyed immediately following a decision not to institute criminal proceedings against the person or on the conclusion of such proceedings otherwise than with a conviction or an order under section 383 (absolute discharge) or 384(1) (probation) of the 1975 Act.

(4) A constable may, with the authority of an officer of a rank no lower than inspector, take from the person—

 (a) from the hair of an external part of the body, by means of cutting or combing, a sample of hair or other material;

 (b) from a fingernail or toenail or from under any such nail, a sample of nail or other material;

 (c) from an external part of the body, by means of swabbing or rubbing, a sample of blood or other body fluid, of body tissue or of other material.

(5) A constable may use reasonable force in exercising any power conferred by subsection (2) or (4) above.

(6) Nothing in this section shall prejudice—

 (a) any power of search;

 (b) any power to take possession of evidence where there is imminent danger of its being lost or destroyed; or

 (c) any power to take prints, impressions or samples under the authority of a warrant.

GENERAL NOTE

This section implements the recommendations of the Scottish Law Commission with regard to the taking of prints and samples in criminal cases (Scottish Law Commission, *Report on Evidence: Blood Group Tests, DNA Tests and Related Matters*, Paper No. 120, 1989). The Commission felt that the existing law was, on the whole, satisfactory in requiring a warrant from a sheriff for conducting any invasive search, but that provisions governing the taking of prints, etc. from any external part of the body needed to be clarified and applied equally to cases where lawful arrest had taken place as well as those where the detention was under s.2 of the Criminal Justice (Scotland) Act 1980. It was also felt that new provisions were required for the taking of samples which required greater invasion than the taking of prints or impressions, but not as much as involved in entering the body of the detainee or arrestee.

Subs. (1)

This ensures that the section applies to all persons arrested or detained by the police.

Subs. (2)

This clarifies the previous provision by the addition of the words "external parts of the body". A warrant will still be required for the taking of any other print or impression. Thus, it is suggested that, for example, the taking of dental impressions will require a warrant from a sheriff.

Subs. (3)

This continues the previous provision in s.2(1)(c) of the Criminal Justice (Scotland) Act 1980.

Subs. (4)

This subsection details the intermediate category of samples which can be taken without warrant, but with the authorisation of a police officer of at least inspector rank. There is no limit on the location at which the sample may be taken and no requirement that the authorising police officer should be physically present. It is submitted, in line with the recommendation of the Law Commission (*ibid.* para. 2.33), that subs. (4)(c) would not authorise sampling of saliva from inside the mouth, the taking of hair by the roots or anything else which required any degree of invasion into the person's body.

Subss. (5) and (6)

These provisions continue the existing rights of the police when taking samples, prints or impressions.

Evidence from documents

29. Schedule 3 to this Act, which makes provision regarding the admissibility in criminal proceedings of copy documents and of evidence contained in business documents, shall have effect.

GENERAL NOTE
  This section and its accompanying schedule (Sched. 3) give effect to many of the recommendations of the Scottish Law Commission as contained in its Report No. 137 (*Evidence: Report on Documentary Evidence and Proof of Undisputed Facts in Criminal Proceedings*, October 1992), published after this section first appeared during the Parliamentary stages of the Bill and in reply to *Lord Advocate's Reference (No. 1 of 1992)* 1992 S.L.T. 1010. The main purpose of the section is to render authenticated copies of documents admissible in criminal proceedings and to allow statements made in business documents to be admissible in criminal proceedings on the same basis as oral evidence on the same matter, thereby obviating the need for witnesses to be called to speak to such evidence. It repeals the Criminal Evidence Act 1965. See further discussion under Sched. 3, *infra*.

Admissibility of audio and video records

30.—(1) Section 32 of the 1980 Act (evidence by letter of request or on commission) shall be amended as follows.
  (2) After subsection (3) there shall be inserted the following subsection—
    "(3A) Where any such record as is mentioned in paragraph (b) of subsection (2) above, or any part of such record, is not a document in writing, that record or part shall not be received in evidence under subsection (3) above unless it is accompanied by a transcript of its contents.".
  (3) After subsection (5) there shall be inserted the following subsection—
    "(5A) In subsections (2) and (3) above, "record" includes, in addition to a document in writing—
      (a) any disc, tape, soundtrack or other device in which sounds or other data (not being visual images) are recorded so as to be capable (with or without the aid of some other equipment) of being reproduced therefrom; and
      (b) any film (including microfilm), negative, tape, disc or other device in which one or more visual images are recorded so as to be capable (as aforesaid) of being reproduced therefrom.".

GENERAL NOTE
  This section amends the provisions on the taking of evidence on commission (Criminal Justice (Scotland) Act 1980, s.32) to allow sound, other recorded data and/or visual recordings of such evidence to be presented in criminal cases. A transcript must accompany any record other than a document in writing (new s.3A). The existing provision in s.32(6), continuing the common-law power of courts to adjourn to the place where a witness is, is not affected by this.

Transcript of customs interview sufficient evidence

31. In section 60(1) of the Criminal Justice (Scotland) Act 1987 (which provides that certain transcripts of interviews between police officers and accused persons shall be received in evidence and be sufficient evidence of the making of the transcript and of its accuracy), after the words "accused person" there shall be inserted the words ", or between a person commissioned, appointed or authorised under section 6(3) of the Customs and Excise Management Act 1979 and an accused person,".

Evidence from abroad through television links in solemn proceedings

32. After section 32 of the 1980 Act there shall be inserted the following section—

"Evidence from abroad through television links in solemn proceedings

32A.—(1) In any solemn proceedings in the High Court or the sheriff court a person other than the accused may give evidence through a live television link if—

(a) the witness is outside the United Kingdom;

(b) an application under subsection (2) below for the issue of a letter of request has been granted; and

(c) the court is satisfied as to the arrangements for the giving of evidence in that manner by that witness.

(2) The prosecutor or the defence in any proceedings referred to in subsection (1) above may apply to a judge of the court in which the trial is to take place (or, if that court is not yet known, to a judge of the High Court) for the issue of a letter of request to—

(a) a court or tribunal exercising jurisdiction in a country or territory outside the United Kingdom where a witness is ordinarily resident; or

(b) any authority which the judge is satisfied is recognised by the government of that country or territory as the appropriate authority for receiving requests for assistance in facilitating the giving of evidence through a live television link,

requesting assistance in facilitating the giving of evidence by that witness through a live television link.

(3) An application under subsection (2) above shall be granted only if the judge is satisfied that—

(a) the evidence which it is averred the witness is able to give is necessary for the proper adjudication of the trial; and

(b) the granting of the application—

(i) is in the interests of justice; and

(ii) in the case of an application by the prosecutor, is not unfair to the accused.

(4) The power of the High Court to make Acts of Adjournal under the 1975 Act shall include power to make such provision as it considers necessary or expedient for the purposes of this section.".

GENERAL NOTE

This section allows the use of live video-links for the taking of evidence from witnesses outside the United Kingdom in solemn criminal proceedings, subject to certain safeguards. It brings the law of Scotland into line with that south of the border (Criminal Justice Act 1988). The court must be satisfied as to the arrangements for obtaining the evidence (subs. (1)(c)), and the letter of request to an appropriate foreign authority must be issued by the court which is to hear the case, or by the High Court if the court is not yet identified, on the application of either the prosecution or the defence (subs. (2)). The court must also be satisfied that the evidence to be obtained in this way is necessary for the trial and that the application is in the interests of justice (subs. (3)). The High Court is given power to make Acts of Adjournal for the implementation of this section (subs. (4)).

Evidence of children on commission

33.—(1) Without prejudice to section 32 of the 1980 Act (evidence by letter of request or on commission where witness is outwith United Kingdom or is ill or infirm) and subject to section 35 of this Act, where a child has been cited to give evidence in a trial the court may appoint a commissioner to take the evidence of the child if—

(a) in solemn proceedings, at any time before the oath is administered to the jury;

(b) in summary proceedings, at any time before the first witness is sworn; or

(c) in exceptional circumstances in either solemn or summary proceedings, during the course of the trial, application is made to the court in that regard; but to be so appointed a person must be, and for a period of at least five years have been, a member of the Faculty of Advocates or a solicitor.

(2) Proceedings before a commissioner appointed under subsection (1) above shall be recorded by video recorder.

(3) An accused shall not, except by leave of the commissioner, be present in the room where such proceedings are taking place but shall be entitled by such means as seem suitable to the commissioner to watch and hear the proceedings.

GENERAL NOTE

Sections 33–35 of this Act amend the provisions in the Law Reform (Miscellaneous Provisions) (Scotland) Act 1990 to provide further protection to child witnesses from having to face the accused person in open court. This is in addition to the existing powers of judges to clear a court of all but interested parties when a child witness is giving evidence. The provisions are based on the recommendations of the Law Commission's report *Report on Evidence of Children and Other Potentially Vulnerable Witnesses* (No. 125, 1990).

Section 33 permits a court to appoint a commissioner, who must be a solicitor or advocate of at least five years' standing, to take evidence from a child, defined in s.59 of the 1990 Act as a person under the age of 16 years, and for this evidence to be presented in video-recorded form to the court. The provision applies only for criminal trials in the sheriff court (solemn or summary procedure) or High Court (s.35, and s.59 of the 1990 Act). There is no requirement that notice be given of an application for evidence to be taken in this way, but the commissioner must always ensure that an accused person is allowed the facility both to watch and hear the evidence, presumably in video-recorded format, when the commissioner has held it inappropriate for the accused to be present in the room where the evidence is being taken.

Concealment by screen of accused from child giving evidence

34. Subject to section 35 of this Act, where a child has been cited to give evidence in a trial, the court may, on application being made to it, authorise the use of a screen to conceal the accused from the sight of the child while the child is present to give evidence; but arrangements shall be made to ensure that the accused is able to watch and hear as the evidence is given by the child.

GENERAL NOTE

The Law Commission (*ibid.* para. 4.17 *et seq.*) recognised that, despite some objections to the practice, courts were increasingly using their common-law power to allow screening of child witnesses from accused persons. This provision makes clear the legal basis on which, and the conditions under which, a court on application may permit screening of a child witness.

Circumstances in which application under section 33 or 34 may be granted or on transfer be deemed granted, etc.

35. Subsections (2) and (3) of section 56 (restrictions on power of court to grant application for child's evidence to be given by means of live television link) and sections 57 (transfer of case where accommodation or equipment is lacking) and 58 (identification of accused by child whose evidence is given by such link) of the Law Reform (Miscellaneous Provisions) (Scotland) Act 1990 shall apply in respect of an application under section 33 or 34 of this Act as those provisions of that Act apply in respect of an application under subsection (1) of the said section 56; and in sections 33 and 34 of this Act "child", "court" and "trial" have the same meanings as in the said sections 56 to 58.

GENERAL NOTE

This section continues the protection of the accused from prejudice by the operation of the rules to protect child witnesses. In particular, before granting any application to take the evidence of a child on commission or from behind a screen, or the third-party evidence of a child's identification of a suspect at an identification parade or otherwise, the court must have regard to the possible effect on the child if the application is not granted and whether the child would be better able to give evidence if the application were granted (s.56(2) of the 1990 Act). In addition, the court may take into account where appropriate the age and maturity of the child, the nature of the alleged offence, the nature of the evidence which the child is likely to give and the relationship, if any, between the child and the accused (s.56(3) of the 1990 Act). All definitions remain as in the 1990 Act.

It is clear from the decision of the Lord Justice-Clerk in *H.M. Advocate* v. *Birkett*, 1992 S.C.C.R. 850, that applications to take evidence in any other than the conventional way require to show cause before they will succeed. Nothing in these new provisions reduces this need.

Evidence as to taking or destruction of eggs

36. After section 19 of the Wildlife and Countryside Act 1981 there shall be inserted the following section—

"Evidence in Scotland as to taking or destruction of eggs

19A. In any proceedings in Scotland for an offence under section 1(1)(c) of, or by virtue of section 3(1)(a)(iii) of, this Act, the accused may be convicted on the evidence of one witness.".

GENERAL NOTE

Introduced during the Parliamentary stages of the Bill, this section recognises the difficulty in gathering evidence in remote locations where birds' eggs may be subject to theft or destruction. It is one further erosion of the corroboration requirement in Scots law.

Evidence by certificate

37. Schedule 1 to the 1980 Act (certain certificates to be sufficient evidence in relation to statutory offences) shall have effect subject to the amendments specified in Schedule 4 to this Act.

GENERAL NOTE

This section amends and updates earlier provisions relating to certificated evidence in statutory offences. A full list of the provisions under which evidence by certificate may be acceptable is given in Sched. 4.

Procedure

Adjournment for inquiry etc. in summary proceedings at first calling

38.—(1) Immediately preceding section 334 of the 1975 Act there shall be inserted the following section—

"Adjournment for inquiry at first calling

333A. Without prejudice to section 338(1) of this Act, at the first calling of the case in a summary prosecution the court may, in order to allow time for inquiry into the case or for any other cause which it considers reasonable, adjourn the case under this section, for such period as it considers appropriate, without calling on the accused to plead to any charge against him but remanding him in custody or on bail or ordaining him to appear at the diet thus fixed; and the court may from time to time so adjourn the case, so however that—
  (a) where the accused is remanded in custody, the total period for which he is so remanded under this subsection shall not exceed twenty-one days and no one period of adjournment shall, except on special cause shown, exceed seven days; and
  (b) where he is remanded on bail or ordained to appear, no one period of adjournment shall exceed twenty eight days.".

(2) Section 328 of the 1975 Act (which admits of adjournment for inquiry in summary proceedings only where an accused has been apprehended) shall cease to have effect.

GENERAL NOTE

Section 328 of the 1975 Act allowed continuation without plea in summary cases only where the accused had been apprehended. This new section extends this power to all summary cases, subject to the protection that an accused remanded in custody can be detained for a maximum of seven days at any one court appearance and a maximum of 21 days in total before a plea is required, and the case of an accused bailed or ordained to appear can be adjourned without plea for a maximum of 28 days. These provisions may be particularly useful when the fitness to plead of the accused is at issue.

New circumstances on notice of which preliminary diet may be ordered

39.—(1) Section 76 of the 1975 Act (which specifies various circumstances on notice of which a preliminary diet shall or may be ordered) shall be amended as follows.

(2) In subsection (1)—

(a) after paragraph (b) there shall be inserted the following paragraph—

"(bb) that there are documents the truth of the contents of which ought in his view to be admitted, or that there is any other matter which in his view ought to be agreed, the court may make such order as is mentioned in paragraph (a) above;"; and

(b) in paragraph (c), for the words "or (b)" there shall be substituted the words ", (b) or (bb)".

(3) In subsection (7)(c), after the word "paragraph" there shall be inserted the words "(bb) or".

GENERAL NOTE

Intended as supplementary to s.29, *supra*, this section adds to the matters which can be established at a preliminary diet in solemn cases with a view to releasing potential witnesses from liability to being called at the trial diet.

Taking of other proceedings while jury out

40.—(1) After section 155 of the 1975 Act there shall be inserted the following section—

"Taking of other proceedings while jury out

155A. During the period in which, in any criminal trial, the jury are retired to consider their verdict, the judge may sit in any other proceedings; and the trial shall not fail by reason only of his so doing.".

(2) After section 360 of that Act there shall be inserted the following heading and section—

"Interruption of proceedings

Interruption of summary proceedings for verdict in earlier trial

360A.—(1) Where the sheriff is sitting in any summary proceedings during the period in which the jury in any criminal trial in which he has presided are retired to consider their verdict, it shall be lawful, if he considers it appropriate to do so, to interrupt those proceedings—

(a) in order to receive the verdict of the jury and dispose of the cause to which it relates;

(b) to give a direction to the jury on any matter on which they may wish one from him, or to hear a request from them regarding any matter, as for example that a production may be made available for examination by them,

and the interruption shall not affect the validity of the proceedings nor cause the instance to fall in respect of any person accused in the proceedings.

(2) Subsection (5) of section 156 of this Act shall apply in respect of the interruption of summary proceedings as it applies in respect of the interruption of a trial.".

GENERAL NOTE

The general principle remains, as enunciated in s.136 of the 1975 Act, that criminal trials should be continuous. Sections 156 and 157 of that Act allowed the interruption of another criminal trial for the taking of a verdict from, or the giving of further instructions to, a jury from a previous criminal trial, or to take guilty pleas from other cases, other than murder cases.

Subsection (1) of this new section creates a new s.155A of the 1975 Act and empowers judges to conduct any other business while a jury is out without interrupting the continuity of the trial on which that jury is deliberating.

Subsection (2) extends this provision to permit the interruption of summary proceedings to allow a sheriff to deal with a jury deliberating on an earlier trial without affecting the validity of the summary proceedings.

Date of commencement of sentence

41.—(1) Each of sections 218 and 431 of the 1975 Act (consideration of time spent in custody) shall be amended as follows.

(2) After the word "shall" there shall be inserted "(a)".

(3) At the end there shall be added the following words—
> "or spent in custody awaiting extradition to the United Kingdom;
> (b) specify the date of commencement of the sentence; and
> (c) if that person—
>> (i) has spent a period of time in custody on remand awaiting trial or sentence; or
>> (ii) is an extradited prisoner for the purposes of this section,
> and the date specified under paragraph (b) above is not earlier than the date on which sentence is passed, state its reasons for not specifying an earlier date.".

(4) The existing words, as so amended, shall be subsection (1).

(5) After that subsection there shall be inserted the following subsections—
> "(2) A prisoner is an extradited prisoner for the purposes of this section if—
>> (a) he was tried for the offence in respect of which his sentence of imprisonment was imposed—
>>> (i) after having been extradited to the United Kingdom; and
>>> (ii) without having first been restored to the state from which extradited or having had an opportunity of leaving the United Kingdom; and
>> (b) he was for any period kept in custody while awaiting such extradition.
>
> (3) In this section "extradited to the United Kingdom" means returned to the United Kingdom—
>> (a) in pursuance of extradition arrangements (as defined in section 3 of the Extradition Act 1989);
>> (b) under any law which corresponds to that Act and is a law of a designated Commonwealth country (as defined in section 5(1) of that Act);
>> (c) under that Act as extended to a colony or under any corresponding law of a colony; or
>> (d) in pursuance of a warrant of arrest endorsed in the Republic of Ireland under the law of that country corresponding to the Backing of Warrants (Republic of Ireland) Act 1965.".

GENERAL NOTE

The Kincraig Committee recommended, by a majority, that all custodial sentences should be dated from the initial remand in custody, unless there were special reasons for a court to decide to order otherwise, in which case such reasons should be recorded at the time of sentence (*op. cit.* para. 10.22). The existing provision, in s.218 (solemn procedure) and s.432 (summary procedure) of the 1975 Act, requires courts when imposing a custodial sentence to "have regard to" any time spent in custody before sentence. It is, however, possible for a court to "have regard to" a period in custody without taking it into account in deciding on the sentence to be imposed (*Doolan* v. *Lockhart* 1987, G.W.D. 12–434). Other conventions have grown up governing the decision whether or not to backdate a sentence. Thus cooperation with the police on arrest (*Aird* v. *HMA* (unreported, 1987)), early intimation of a guilty plea (*Grant* v. *HMA*, 1988, G.W.D. 34–1439) and remand for reports following a guilty plea (*Morrison* v. *Scott*, 1987 S.C.C.R. 376) are all situations which have been held to indicate that sentences should be backdated. The courts, however, retain a discretion in the matter, unlike courts in England and most other jurisdictions.

The Thomson Committee (*Criminal Procedure in Scotland (Second Report)*, Cm. 6218, 1975) and SACRO (*Bail and Custodial Remand*, 1987) both considered this issue. Thomson recommended that sentences should always be backdated to the date of the plea where an accused lodges a plea of guilty by letter under s.102 of the 1975 Act. SACRO suggested that all time in custody on remand should automatically be deducted from any sentence.

This new section represents a compromise. It may be read as implying that the norm should be for all time spent in custody before sentence to count towards the sentence, but the court clearly retains a discretion not to backdate the sentence, though reasons for not doing so must be given.

Subs. (3)
Considerable confusion and extra work are caused for the prison service in England and Wales by the requirement that prison officers work out how long a prisoner has been held in custody. The Scottish provision avoids this by requiring the court to specify the starting date for any custodial sentence. Presumably the existing practice of the prosecution bringing this to the attention of the court will continue.

Subs. (5)
The new subs. (2) to both s.218 and s.431 of the 1975 Act makes clear that time spent in custody awaiting extradition to the United Kingdom can only be considered when the sentence is imposed after the extradition and where the person has not been restored to the country from which he had been extradited or had the opportunity of leaving the United Kingdom for any other country. This ensures that, for example, a person who, having been sentenced in the United Kingdom, escapes to another country and is arrested there and held pending deportation, cannot have that period of detention discounted from the sentence passed in the United Kingdom. Equally, if the person could have avoided detention in the United Kingdom by returning to the country from which extradited, or by going to any other country, the subsequent sentence can ignore the period spent in detention.

Appeal by Lord Advocate against sentence in solemn proceedings etc.

42.—(1) After section 228 of the 1975 Act (which provides for appeal by a person convicted on indictment) there shall be inserted the following section—

"Appeal by Lord Advocate against sentence in solemn proceedings
228A. Where a person has been convicted on indictment, the Lord Advocate may appeal against the sentence passed on conviction—

    (a) if it appears to the Lord Advocate that the sentence is unduly lenient; or

    (b) on a point of law.".

(2) In section 442 of that Act (which provides for appeal in summary proceedings)—

    (a) in subsection (1), after paragraph (b) there shall be inserted the following paragraph—

        "(c) the prosecutor in such proceedings may, in any class of case specified by order by the Secretary of State under this paragraph, so appeal against the sentence passed on such conviction if it appears to the prosecutor that the sentence is unduly lenient."; and

    (b) after subsection (2) there shall be added the following subsection—

        "(3) The power of the Secretary of State to make an order under paragraph (c) of subsection (1) above shall be exercisable by statutory instrument; and any order so made shall be subject to annulment in pursuance of a resolution of either House of Parliament.".

GENERAL NOTE

This section introduces a new power for the prosecution to appeal against a sentence imposed by a court, in solemn cases on the grounds of law or undue leniency and in summary cases on the grounds of undue leniency in classes of case to be specified by statutory instrument. It implements a Government election manifesto promise and parallels English provisions to the same effect. Since implementation in summary cases will require statutory instrument (subs. (3)), more guidance will be forthcoming from Parliament. However, in solemn cases discretion the exercise of the new power is left to the Lord Advocate, who, traditionally, has taken little part in the sentencing process. This could, therefore, mark the start of a new era in sentencing in Scotland.

Prosecutor's consent to or application for setting aside of conviction

43. For section 453 of the 1975 Act there shall be substituted the following section—

> **"Prosecutor's consent to or application for setting aside of conviction**
> 453.—(1) Where—
>   (a) an appeal has been taken under section 442(1)(a)(i) or (iii) of this Act or by suspension or otherwise and the prosecutor is not prepared to maintain the judgment appealed against he may, by a relevant minute, consent to the conviction being set aside either in whole or in part; or
>   (b) no such appeal has been taken but the prosecutor is, at any time, not prepared to maintain the judgment on which a conviction is founded he may, by a relevant minute, apply for the conviction so to be set aside.
> (2) For the purposes of subsection (1) above, a "relevant minute" is a minute, signed by the prosecutor—
>   (a) setting forth the grounds on which he is of the opinion that the judgment cannot be maintained; and
>   (b) written on the complaint or lodged with the clerk of court.
> (3) A copy of any minute under subsection (1) above shall be sent by the prosecutor to the convicted person or his solicitor and the clerk of court shall—
>   (a) thereupon ascertain, and note on the record, whether that person or solicitor desires to be heard by the High Court before the appeal, or as the case may be application, is disposed of; and
>   (b) thereafter transmit the complaint and relative proceedings to the Clerk of Justiciary.
> (4) The Clerk of Justiciary, on receipt of a complaint and relative proceedings transmitted under subsection (3) above, shall lay them before any judge of the High Court either in court or in chambers who, after hearing parties if they desire to be heard, may—
>   (a) set aside the conviction either in whole or in part and—
>   (i) award such expenses to the convicted person, both in the High Court and in the inferior court, as the judge may think fit; and
>   (ii) where the conviction is set aside in part, pass another (but not more severe) sentence in substitution for the sentence imposed in respect of that conviction; or
>   (b) refuse to set aside the conviction, in which case the complaint and proceedings shall be returned to the clerk of the inferior court.
> (5) Where an appeal has been taken and the complaint and proceedings in respect of that appeal returned under subsection (4)(b) above,

the appellant shall be entitled to proceed with the appeal as if it had been marked on the date of their being received by the clerk of the inferior court on such return.

(6) Where an appeal has been taken and a copy minute in respect of that appeal sent under subsection (3) above, the preparation of the draft stated case shall be delayed pending the decision of the High Court.

(7) The period from an application being made under subsection (1)(b) above until its disposal under subsection (4) above (including the day of application and the day of disposal) shall, in relation to the conviction to which the application relates, be disregarded in any computation of time specified in any provision of this Part of this Act relating to appeals.".

GENERAL NOTE

This new section makes several changes to the existing provisions in s.453 of the 1975 Act. Subsection (1)(b), allowing the prosecutor to initiate action when not prepared to maintain the judgment on which a conviction is founded in a summary case even when the convicted person has not appealed, is a new addition. The new subs. (4)(a)(i) replaces the old subs. (3), which limited expenses awardable to a convicted person after a conviction is set aside to £5.25. The new subs. (7)(a) and (b) increases the time limits for prosecutors to consent by minute to an appeal from the original 10 days (old subs. (5)(a) and (b)), and adds a time limit when the appellant is seeking the exercise of the *nobile officium*. Subsection (8) is new, establishing that other time limits cease to run when the prosecutor initiates the action under the new subs. (1)(b).

PART III

GENERAL

Expenses

44. There shall be paid out of money provided by Parliament—
(a) any sums required by the Secretary of State for defraying the expenses of the Parole Board for Scotland;
(b) any expenses incurred by the Secretary of State under section 21(2) of this Act;
(c) any administrative expenses incurred by the Secretary of State under this Act; and
(d) any increase attributable to this Act in the sums payable out of money so provided under any other Act.

Rules and orders

45.—(1) The power of the Secretary of State to make rules and orders under this Act shall be exercisable by statutory instrument.

(2) Any rule made under section 13 or 20(4) of this Act shall be subject to annulment in pursuance of a resolution of either House of Parliament.

(3) An order shall not be made under section 6(3), 7(6), 20(3) or 27(2) of this Act unless a draft of the order has been laid before Parliament and approved by a resolution of each House of Parliament.

Interpretation

46. In this Act—
"the 1975 Act" means the Criminal Procedure (Scotland) Act 1975;
"the 1980 Act" means the Criminal Justice (Scotland) Act 1980; and
"the 1989 Act" means the Prisons (Scotland) Act 1989.

Minor and consequential amendments, transitional provisions, savings and repeals

47.—(1) The enactments mentioned in Schedule 5 to this Act shall have effect subject to the amendments there specified (being minor amendments and amendments consequential on the preceding provisions of this Act).

(2) The transitional provisions and savings contained in Schedule 6 to this Act shall have effect; but nothing in this subsection shall be taken as prejudicing the operation of sections 16 and 17 of the Interpretation Act 1978 (effect of repeals).

(3) The enactments mentioned in Part I of Schedule 7 to this Act (which include some that are spent or no longer of practical utility) are hereby repealed to the extent specified in the third column of that Part and the instruments mentioned in Part II of that Schedule are hereby revoked to the extent specified in the third column of that Part.

Short title, commencement and extent

48.—(1) This Act may be cited as the Prisoners and Criminal Proceedings (Scotland) Act 1993.

(2) Subject to subsection (4) below, this Act shall come into force on such day as the Secretary of State may by order made by statutory instrument appoint, and different days may be appointed for different provisions and for different purposes.

(3) An order under subsection (2) above may make such transitional provisions and savings as appear to the Secretary of State necessary or expedient in connection with any provision brought into force by the order.

(4) This section and, in so far as relating to paragraph 5 of Schedule 5 to this Act, section 47(1) of this Act shall come into force on the day on which this Act is passed.

(5) Subject to subsection (6) below, this Act extends to Scotland only.

(6) This section and the following provisions of this Act also extend to England and Wales—

> section 12(2);
> section 14(4);
> section 15;
> section 16(1) and (3);
> section 27;
> section 46; and
> in section 47, subsection (1) in so far as relating to paragraphs 1(38) and
> > 3 of Schedule 5, and subsection (3) in so far as relating to the entry
> > in Schedule 7 in respect of the Criminal Justice Act 1991.

(7) Nothing in subsection (5) above affects the extent of this Act in so far as it amends or repeals any provision of the Army Act 1955, the Air Force Act 1955 or the Naval Discipline Act 1957.

GENERAL NOTE

It is anticipated that most of this Act will be brought into force in October 1993. See further comments on Sched. 6.

SCHEDULES

Section 1(8)   SCHEDULE 1

CONSECUTIVE AND CONCURRENT TERMS OF IMPRISONMENT

General

1. This Schedule applies as respects the release of a person on whom there has been imposed—
   (a) a term of imprisonment on conviction of an offence ("his offence term"); and
   (b) a term of imprisonment or detention mentioned in section 5(1)(a) or (b) of this Act ("his non-offence term").

Consecutive terms of imprisonment

2. Where his offence term and his non-offence term are consecutive—

(a) his offence term shall be taken to precede his non-offence term;
(b) notwithstanding section 1(1) to (3) of this Act, he shall not be released when he has served the proportion of his offence term mentioned in whichever of those subsections is (or are) relevant to the term in question but when he falls to be released by virtue of the application of section 5 of this Act to his non-offence term; and
(c) his non-offence term shall be taken as beginning on the date on which he would have been released under section 1(1) to (3) but for sub-paragraph (b) above.

Wholly concurrent terms of imprisonment

3. Where his offence term and his non-offence term are wholly concurrent—
(a) only the offence term shall be taken into account for the purposes of the provisions of this Part of this Act relating to his release; but
(b) he shall not be released under section 1(3) of this Act.

Partly concurrent terms of imprisonment

4. Where his offence term and his non-offence term are partly concurrent—
(a) section 1(1) or (2), or as the case may be those provisions as modified by section 5(2), of this Act shall apply in relation to the term which is due to expire later and shall not apply to the term which is due to expire first; and
(b) if the term due to expire later is his offence term, section 1(3) of this Act shall apply in relation to it only if the person has served such proportion of his non-offence term as would, but for sub-paragraph (a) above, entitle him to release under section 1(1) or (2), as modified by section 5(2), of this Act.

GENERAL NOTE
See discussion under s.1(8), *supra*.

Section 20(6)   SCHEDULE 2

THE PAROLE BOARD

Membership

1. The Parole Board shall consist of a chairman and not less than four other members appointed by the Secretary of State.
2. The Parole Board shall include among its members—
(a) a Lord Commissioner of Justiciary;
(b) a registered medical practitioner who is a psychiatrist;
(c) a person appearing to the Secretary of State to have knowledge and experience of the supervision or aftercare of discharged prisoners; and
(d) a person appearing to the Secretary of State to have made a study of the causes of delinquency or the treatment of offenders.
3. A member of the Parole Board shall hold and vacate office under the terms of the instrument by which he is appointed, but may at any time resign his office; and a person who ceases to hold office as a member of the Parole Board shall be eligible for reappointment.

Remuneration and allowances

4. There shall be paid to the members of the Board such remuneration and allowances as the Secretary of State may with the consent of the Treasury determine.
5. The expenses of the Board under paragraph 4 above and any other expenses incurred by the Board in discharging the functions mentioned in section 20(1) of this Act shall be defrayed by the Secretary of State.

Reports

6. The Board shall as soon as practicable after the end of each year make to the Secretary of State a report on the performance of its functions during that year, and the Secretary of State shall lay a copy of the report before Parliament.

GENERAL NOTE
The only alteration to the previous constitution of the Parole Board is the requirement in para. 2(a) that a Lord Commissioner of Justiciary be appointed. The previous provision required the appointment of a person "who holds or has held judicial office" (1989 Act, Sched. 1, para. 1(a)). Parliament was keen to secure the services of an existing High Court judge, especially for involvement in release of life-sentence prisoners.

SCHEDULE 3

DOCUMENTARY EVIDENCE IN CRIMINAL PROCEEDINGS

Production of copy documents

1.—(1) For the purposes of any criminal proceedings a copy of, or of a material part of, a document, purporting to be authenticated in such manner and by such person as may be prescribed, shall unless the court otherwise directs, be—

(a) deemed a true copy; and

(b) treated for evidential purposes as if it were the document, or the material part, itself, whether or not the document is still in existence.

(2) For the purposes of this paragraph it is immaterial how many removes there are between a copy and the original.

(3) In this paragraph, "copy" includes a transcript or reproduction.

Statements in business documents

2.—(1) Except where it is a statement such as is mentioned in paragraph 3(b) and (c) below, a statement in a document shall be admissible in criminal proceedings as evidence of any fact or opinion of which direct oral evidence would be admissible, if the following conditions are satisfied—

(a) the document was created or received in the course of, or for the purposes of, a business or undertaking or in pursuance of the functions of the holder of a paid or unpaid office;

(b) the document is, or at any time was, kept by a business or undertaking or by or on behalf of the holder of such an office; and

(c) the statement was made on the basis of information supplied by a person (whether or not the maker of the statement) who had, or may reasonably be supposed to have had, personal knowledge of the matters dealt with in it.

(2) Sub-paragraph (1) above applies whether the information contained in the statement was supplied directly or indirectly unless, in the case of information supplied indirectly, it appears to the court that any person through whom it was so supplied did not both receive and supply it in the course of a business or undertaking or as or on behalf of the holder of a paid or unpaid office.

(3) Where in any proceedings a statement is admitted as evidence by virtue of this paragraph—

(a) any evidence which, if—

(i) the maker of the statement; or

(ii) where the statement was made on the basis of information supplied by another person, such supplier,

had been called as a witness, would have been admissible as relevant to the witness's credibility shall be so admissible in those proceedings;

(b) evidence may be given of any matter which, if the maker or as the case may be the supplier had been called as a witness, could have been put to him in cross-examination as relevant to his credibility but of which evidence could not have been adduced by the cross-examining party; and

(c) evidence tending to prove that the maker or as the case may be the supplier, whether before or after making the statement or supplying the information on the basis of which the statement was made, made (in whatever manner) some other representation which is inconsistent with the statement shall be admissible for the purpose of showing that he has contradicted himself.

(4) In sub-paragraph (3)(c) above, "representation" does not include a representation in a precognition.

3. A statement in a document shall be admissible in criminal proceedings as evidence of the fact that the statement was made if—

(a) the document satisfies the conditions mentioned in sub-paragraph (1)(a) and (b) of paragraph 2 above;

(b) the statement is made, whether directly or indirectly, by a person who in those proceedings is an accused; and

(c) the statement, being exculpatory only, exculpates the accused.

Documents kept by businesses etc.

4. Unless the court otherwise directs, a document may in any criminal proceedings be taken to be a document kept by a business or undertaking or by or on behalf of the holder of a paid or unpaid office if it is certified as such by a docquet in the prescribed form and purporting to be authenticated, in such manner as may be prescribed—

(a) by a person authorised to authenticate such a docquet on behalf of the business or undertaking by which; or

(b) by, or by a person authorised to authenticate such a docquet on behalf of, the office-holder by whom,

the document was kept.

Statements not contained in business documents

5.—(1) In any criminal proceedings, the evidence of an authorised person that a document which satisfies the conditions mentioned in paragraph 2(1)(a) and (b) above does not contain a relevant statement as to a particular matter (or that no document, within a category of documents satisfying those conditions, contains such a statement) shall be admissible evidence whether or not the whole or any part of that document (or of the documents within that category and satisfying those conditions) has been produced in the proceedings.

(2) For the purposes of sub-paragraph (1) above, a relevant statement is a statement which is of the kind mentioned in paragraph 2(1)(c) above and which, in the ordinary course of events, the document (or the document had there been one) might reasonably have been expected to contain.

(3) The evidence referred to in sub-paragraph (1) above may, unless the court otherwise directs, be given by means of a certificate by the authorised person in the prescribed form and purporting to be authenticated in such manner as may be prescribed.

(4) In this paragraph, "authorised person" means a person authorised to give evidence—

(a) on behalf of the business or undertaking by which; or

(b) as or on behalf of the office-holder by or on behalf of whom,

the document is or was kept.

Additional evidence where evidence from business documents challenged

6.—(1) This sub-paragraph applies where—

(a) evidence has been admitted by virtue of paragraph 2(3) above; or

(b) the court has made a direction under paragraph 1(1), 4 or 5(3) above.

(2) Where sub-paragraph (1) above applies in solemn criminal proceedings the judge may, without prejudice to sections 149 and 149A of the 1975 Act, on a motion of the prosecutor or defence at any time before the commencement of the speeches to the jury, permit him to lead additional evidence of such description as the judge may specify.

(3) Subsections (2) and (3) of section 149 of the 1975 Act shall apply in relation to sub-paragraph (2) above as they apply in relation to subsection (1) of that section.

(4) Where sub-paragraph (1) above applies in summary criminal proceedings the judge may, without prejudice to sections 350 and 350A of the 1975 Act, on a motion of the prosecutor or defence after the close of that party's evidence and before the prosecutor proceeds to address the judge on the evidence, permit that party to lead additional evidence of such description as the judge may specify.

(5) Subsections (2) and (3) of section 350 of the 1975 Act shall apply in relation to sub-paragraph (4) above as they apply in relation to subsection (1) of that section.

General

7.—(1) Nothing in this Schedule—

(a) shall prejudice the admissibility of a statement made by a person other than in the course of giving oral evidence in court which is admissible otherwise than by virtue of this Schedule;

(b) shall affect the operation of the Bankers' Books Evidence Act 1879;

(c) shall apply to—

(i) proceedings commenced; or

(ii) where the proceedings consist of an application to the sheriff by virtue of section 42(2)(c) of the Social Work (Scotland) Act 1968, an application made,

before this Schedule comes into force.

(2) For the purposes of sub-paragraph (1)(c)(i) above, solemn proceedings are commenced when the indictment is served.

(3) In section 6 of the Bankers' Books Evidence Act 1879 (case in which banker not compellable to produce book), after the word "1988" there shall be inserted the words "or Schedule 3 to the Prisoners and Criminal Proceedings (Scotland) Act 1993".

8. In this Schedule—

"business" includes trade, profession or other occupation;

"criminal proceedings" includes any hearing by the sheriff under section 42 of the Social Work (Scotland) Act 1968 of an application for a finding as to whether grounds for the referral of a child's case to a children's hearing are established, in so far as the application relates to the commission of an offence by the child;

"document" includes, in addition to a document in writing—

(a) any map, plan, graph or drawing;

(b) any photograph;

(c) any disc, tape, sound track or other device in which sounds or other data (not being visual images) are recorded so as to be capable (with or without the aid of some other equipment) of being reproduced therefrom; and

(d) any film, negative, tape, disc or other device in which one or more visual images are recorded so as to be capable (as aforesaid) of being reproduced therefrom;

"film" includes a microfilm;

"made" includes allegedly made;

"prescribed" means prescribed by Act of Adjournal;

"statement" includes any representation (however made or expressed) of fact or opinion, including an instruction, order or request, but, except in paragraph 7(1)(a), does not include a statement which falls within one or more of the following descriptions—

(a) a statement in a precognition;

(b) a statement made for the purposes of or in connection with—

(i) pending or contemplated criminal proceedings; or

(ii) a criminal investigation; or

(c) a statement made by an accused person in so far as it incriminates a co-accused; and

"undertaking" includes any public or statutory undertaking, any local authority and any government department.

GENERAL NOTE

This Schedule brings Scots law in relation to admissibility of copies of documents as evidence in criminal proceedings much more up to date than was previously the case. Paragraph 1 provides that an authenticated copy is to be treated in the same way as an original unless the court directs otherwise. Paragraph 2 creates a presumption that statements in a document are to be admissible as evidence of their truth if three conditions are fulfilled: the document was created or received in the course of a business; the document was or is kept by a business; the statement was made on the basis of information supplied by a person who had or may reasonably be supposed to have had personal knowledge of the matters dealt with in it.

Paragraph 8 defines widely all the terms used in this Schedule.

Section 37   SCHEDULE 4

CERTIFICATES AS TO PROOF OF CERTAIN ROUTINE MATTERS

1. Schedule 1 to the 1980 Act (which makes provision as regards the sufficiency of evidence by certificate in certain routine matters) shall be amended as follows.

2. For the entry relating to the Wireless Telegraphy Act 1949, there shall be substituted the following entries—

"The Wireless Telegraphy Act 1949 (c.54) Section 1 in so far as it relates to the installation or use of a television receiver (within the meaning of that Act); and section 1A in so far as it relates to an intended such use.	A person authorised to do so by the British Broadcasting Corporation.	In relation to an address specified in the certificate, whether on a date so specified any television licence (within the meaning of that Act) was, in records maintained on behalf of the Corporation in relation to such licences, recorded as being in force; and, if so, particulars so specified of such record of that licence.
The Firearms Act 1968 (c.27)	A person authorised to do so by the Secretary of State.	In relation to a person identified in the certificate, that on a date specified therein— (a) he held, or as the case may be did not hold, a firearm certificate or shotgun cer-

tificate (within the meaning of that Act);

(b) he possessed, or as the case may be did not possess, an authority (which, as regards a possessed authority, shall be described in the certificate) given under section 5 of that Act by the Secretary of State.".

3. After the entry relating to the Immigration Act 1971, there shall be inserted the following entry—

"The Control of Pollution Act 1974 (c.40) Section 31(1) (permitting poisonous, noxious or polluting matter to enter controlled waters, etc.), 32(1) (permitting trade effluent or sewage effluent to be discharged into such waters, etc.) or 49(1)(a) (causing accumulated deposit to be carried away in suspension in inland waters) or regulations under section 31(4) (prohibition on carrying on without consent certain activities likely to pollute waters in designated areas).	Two persons authorised to do so by a river purification authority (within the meaning of that Act).	That they have analysed a sample identified in the certificate (by label or otherwise) and that the sample is of a nature and composition specified in the certificate."

4. For the entry relating to the Supplementary Benefits Act 1976, there shall be substituted the following entry—

"The Licensing (Scotland) Act 1976 (c.66)	A person authorised to do so by the Secretary of State.	In relation to a person identified in the certificate, that on a date specified therein he held, or as the case may be did not hold, a licence granted under that Act.".

5. After the entry relating to the Customs and Excise Management Act 1979, there shall be inserted the following entry—

"The Bail etc. (Scotland) Act 1980 (c.4)	The Clerk of Justiciary or the clerk of court.	In relation to a person identified in the certificate— (a) that on a date specified therein an order granting bail was made by a court so specified; and (b) that on a date so specified that order, or a condition thereof so specified, was in force.".

6. After the entry relating to the Forgery and Counterfeiting Act 1981, there shall be inserted the following entry—

"The Civic Government (Scotland) Act 1982 (c.45)	A person authorised to do so by the Secretary of State.	In relation to a person identified in the certificate, that on a date specified therein he held, or as the case may be did not hold, a licence under a provision so specified of that Act.".

7. At the end there shall be added the following entry—

"The Social Security Administration Act 1992 (c.5)	A person authorised to do so by the Secretary of State.	In relation to a person identified in the certificate—

the assessment, award, or
nature of any benefit
applied for by him;
(b) the transmission or handing over of any payment to
him.".

Section 47(1)   SCHEDULE 5

MINOR AND CONSEQUENTIAL AMENDMENTS

Criminal Procedure (Scotland) Act 1975 (c. 21)

1.—(1) The Criminal Procedure (Scotland) Act 1975 shall be amended as follows.
(2) In section 20B (record of proceedings at judicial examination)—
(a) in subsection (1), for the words "a shorthand writer" there shall be substituted the words "means of shorthand notes or by mechanical means";
(b) after subsection (1), there shall be inserted the following subsections—
"(1A) A shorthand writer shall—
(a) sign the shorthand notes taken by him of the questions, answers and declarations mentioned in subsection (1) above and certify the notes as being complete and correct; and
(b) retain the notes.
(1B) A person recording the questions, answers and declarations mentioned in subsection (1) above by mechanical means shall—
(a) certify that the record is true and complete;
(b) specify in the certificate the proceedings to which the record relates; and
(c) retain the record.
(1C) The prosecutor shall require the person who made the record mentioned in subsection (1) above, or such other competent person as he may specify, to make a transcript of the record in legible form; and that person shall—
(a) comply with the requirement;
(b) certify the transcript as being a complete and correct transcript of the record purporting to have been made and certified, and in the case of shorthand notes signed, by the person who made the record; and
(c) send the transcript to the prosecutor."; and
(c) for subsection (2) there shall be substituted the following subsection—
"(2) A transcript certified under subsection (1C)(b) above shall, subject to subsection (4) below, be deemed for all purposes to be a complete and correct record of the questions, answers and declarations mentioned in subsection (1) above.".
(3) In section 76(1)(b) (notice of intention to submit plea in bar of trial or to make certain preliminary applications), after the word "trials" there shall be inserted the words "or to raise a preliminary objection under section 67 of this Act".
(4) In section 108(2) (certain preliminary objections competent only where notice given)—
(a) the word "and" at the end of paragraph (b) shall cease to have effect; and
(b) after paragraph (c) there shall be inserted the following—
"; and
(d) no preliminary objection under section 67 of this Act shall be raised,".
(5) After section 137 there shall be inserted the following section—

"Verdict by judge alone
137A.—(1) Where, at any time after the jury has been sworn to serve in any trial, the prosecutor intimates to the court that he does not intend to proceed in respect of an offence charged in the indictment, the judge shall acquit the accused of that offence and the trial shall proceed only in respect of any other offence charged in the indictment.
(2) Where, at any time after the jury has been sworn to serve in any trial, the accused intimates to the court that he is prepared to tender a plea of guilty as libelled, or such other plea as the Crown is prepared to accept, in respect of any offence charged in the indict-ment, the judge shall accept the plea tendered and shall convict the accused accordingly.
(3) Where an accused is convicted under subsection (2) above of an offence—
(a) the trial shall proceed only in respect of any other offence charged in the indict-ment; and
(b) without prejudice to any other power of the court to adjourn the case or to defer

sentence, the judge shall not sentence him or make any other order competent following a conviction until a verdict has been returned in respect of every offence mentioned in paragraph (a) above.".

(6) In each of sections 179(1) (power of court in solemn proceedings to adjourn case before sentence) and 380(1) (corresponding power in summary proceedings), in the proviso, for the words "three weeks" there shall be substituted the following paragraphs—

"(a) where the accused is remanded in custody, three weeks; or

(b) where he is remanded on bail or is ordained to appear, eight weeks but only on cause shown and otherwise four weeks".

(7) In each of sections 186 (breach of probation order imposed in solemn proceedings) and 387 (corresponding provision as regards summary proceedings), after subsection (2) there shall be inserted the following subsection—

"(2A) for the purposes of subsection (2) above, evidence of one witness shall be sufficient evidence.".

(8) In section 205A(1) (recommendation as to minimum period of detention for person convicted of murder), for the words "26 of the Prisons (Scotland) Act 1989" there shall be substituted the words "1(4) of the Prisoners and Criminal Proceedings (Scotland) Act 1993".

(9) In section 233(1) (note of appeal), the existing words from "within six weeks" to the end shall be paragraph (a) and after that paragraph there shall be added the word "; or" and the following paragraph—

"(b) as the case may be, within four weeks of the passing of the sentence in open court, the Lord Advocate may lodge such a note with the Clerk of Justiciary, who shall send a copy to the said judge and to the convicted person or that person's solicitor.".

(10) In section 234(1) (presentation of appeal in writing), after the word "appellant" there shall be inserted the words "other than the Lord Advocate".

(11) In section 236B(2) (extension of certain periods), for the words "233(1)" there shall be substituted the words "233(1)(a)".

(12) In section 236C (signing of documents), after the words "to appeal" there shall be inserted the words "or (except where the appellant is the Lord Advocate) any".

(13) In section 238 (admission of appellant to bail), for subsections (1) and (2) there shall be substituted the following subsections—

"(1) The High Court may, if it thinks fit, on the application of a convicted person, admit him to bail pending the determination of—

(a) his appeal; or

(b) any appeal by the Lord Advocate against the sentence passed on conviction.

(2) A person who is admitted to bail under subsection (1) above shall, unless the High Court otherwise directs, appear personally in court on the day or days fixed for the hearing of the appeal or of any application for leave to appeal; and in the event of his failing to do so the court may—

(a) if he is the appellant—

(i) decline to consider the appeal or application; and

(ii) dismiss it summarily; or

(b) whether or not he is the appellant—

(i) consider and determine the appeal or application; or

(ii) without prejudice to section 3 of the Bail etc. (Scotland) Act 1980 (breach of conditions), make such other order as the court thinks fit.".

(14) In section 239(1) (notice of date of hearing), for—

(a) the words "appellant or applicant", in both places where they occur, there shall be substituted the words "convicted person"; and

(b) the word "latter", there shall be substituted the words "appellant or applicant".

(15) In section 240 (presence of appellant at hearing), for the word "An", where it first occurs, there shall be substituted the words "A convicted".

(16) After section 242 there shall be inserted the following section—

"Special provision where appellant is Lord Advocate

242A. Where the Lord Advocate is the appellant, sections 241 and 242 of this Act shall apply in respect of the convicted person, if in custody, as they apply to an appellant or applicant in custody.".

(17) In section 243 (provision as to warders attending court), for the words "the last foregoing section" there shall be substituted the words "section 242 of this Act".

(18) In section 252 (powers of High Court), after the words "228(1)" there shall be inserted the words "or 228A".

(19) In section 258 (sentence in absence), after the word "appellant" there shall be inserted the words "(or, where the Lord Advocate is the appellant, the convicted person)".

(20) In section 261 (notice of determination of appeal), after the word "applicant" there shall be inserted the words "(or, where the Lord Advocate is the appellant, to the convicted person)".

(21) In section 264 (disqualification, forfeiture, etc.), in each of subsections (1) and (2)—

(a) for the word "two" there shall be substituted the word "four"; and

(b) after the words "228(1)(b)" there shall be inserted the words "or 228A".

(22) In section 265 (fines and caution), after subsection (4) there shall be inserted the following subsection—

"(4A) A convicted person who has been sentenced to the payment of a fine and has duly paid it shall, if an appeal against sentence by the Lord Advocate results in the sentence being quashed and no fine, or a lesser fine than that paid, being imposed, be entitled, subject to any order of the High Court, to the return of the sum paid or as the case may be to the return of the amount by which that sum exceeds the amount of the lesser fine.".

(23) In section 268 (reckoning of time spent in custody pending appeal)—

(a) in subsection (1)—

(i) for the words "an appellant" there shall be substituted the words "a convicted person";

(ii) after the word "appeal" there shall be inserted the words ", or as the case may be of any appeal by the Lord Advocate against the sentence passed on conviction,"; and

(iii) for the word "this", where it occurs qualifying the word "sentence", there shall be substituted the word "that";

(b) for subsection (2) there shall be substituted the following subsection—

"(2) The time (including any period consequent on the recall of bail) during which a convicted person is in custody pending the determination of his appeal, or as the case may be of any appeal by the Lord Advocate against the sentence passed on conviction, shall subject to any direction which the High Court may give to the contrary be reckoned as part of any term of imprisonment under that sentence."; and

(c) in subsection (3), after the word "appellant" there shall be inserted the words "(or, where the appellant is the Lord Advocate, of a convicted person)".

(24) In section 269 (extract convictions)—

(a) for the word "two" there shall be substituted the word "four"; and

(b) after the words "228(1)(b)" there shall be inserted the words "or 228A".

(25) In section 270 (custody of trial documents, etc.)—

(a) in subsection (2)—

(i) for the words from the beginning to "proceedings" there shall be substituted the words "Until any period allowed under or by virtue of this Part of this Act for lodging intimation of intention to appeal (or any longer period allowed by virtue thereof for lodging a note of appeal) has elapsed, all documents and other productions produced at the trial of a convicted person shall be kept";

(ii) after the words "228(1)(b)" there shall be inserted the words "or 228A"; and

(iii) the words "of two weeks or any extension thereof authorised by the High Court" shall cease to have effect;

(b) in subsection (3)—

(i) after the words "228(1)(b)" there shall be inserted the words "or 228A"; and

(ii) for the words "to his" there shall be substituted the words ", as the case may be, to the convicted person's"; and

(c) in subsection (4)—

(i) after the words "228(1)(b)" there shall be inserted the words "or 228A"; and

(ii) for the words "such period of two weeks or extension thereof as aforesaid" there shall be substituted the words "the period mentioned in subsection (2) above".

(26) In section 273(1) (register of appeals), after the words "228(1)(b)" there shall be inserted the words "or 228A".

(27) For sections 274 and 275 (shorthand notes of trial etc.) there shall be substituted the following sections—

"Record of trial

274.—(1) The proceedings at the trial of any person who, if convicted, is entitled to appeal under this Part of this Act shall be recorded by means of shorthand notes or by mechanical means.

(2) A shorthand writer shall—

(a) sign the shorthand notes taken by him of such proceedings and certify them as being complete and correct; and

(b) retain the notes.

(3) A person recording such proceedings by mechanical means shall—

(a) certify that the record is true and complete;

(b) specify in the certificate the proceedings (or, as the case may be, the part of the proceedings) to which the record relates; and

(c) retain the record.

(4) The cost of making a record under subsection (1) above shall be defrayed, in accordance with scales of payment fixed for the time being by the Treasury, out of money provided by Parliament.

(5) In subsection (1) above "proceedings at the trial" means the whole proceedings including (without prejudice to that generality)—

(a) discussions—

(i) on any objection to the relevancy of the indictment;

(ii) with respect to any challenge of jurors; and

(iii) on all questions arising in the course of the trial;

(b) the decision of the court on any matter referred to in paragraph (a) above;

(c) the evidence led at the trial;

(d) any statement made by or on behalf of the accused whether before or after the verdict;

(e) the summing up by the judge;

(f) the speeches of counsel or agent;

(g) the verdict of the jury; and

(h) the sentence by the judge.

Transcripts of record and documentary productions

275.—(1) The Clerk of Justiciary may direct that a transcript of a record made under section 274(1) of this Act, or any part thereof, be made and delivered to him for the use of any judge.

(2) Subject to subsection (3) below, the Clerk of Justiciary shall, if he is requested to do so by—

(a) the Secretary of State; or

(b) any other person on payment of such charges as may be fixed for the time being by the Treasury,

direct that such a transcript be made and sent to the person who requested it.

(3) The Secretary of State may, after consultation with the Lord Justice General, by order made by statutory instrument provide that in any class of proceedings specified in the order the Clerk of Justiciary shall only make a direction under subsection (2)(b) above if satisfied that the person requesting the transcript is of a class of person so specified and, if purposes for which the transcript may be used are so specified, intends to use it only for such a purpose; and different purposes may be so specified for different classes of proceedings or classes of person.

(4) Where subsection (3) above applies as respects a direction, the person to whom the transcript is sent shall, if purposes for which that transcript may be used are specified by virtue of that subsection, use it only for such a purpose.

(5) A statutory instrument containing an order under subsection (3) above shall be subject to annulment in pursuance of a resolution of either House of Parliament.

(6) A direction under subsection (1) or (2) above may require that the transcript be made by the person who made the record or by such competent person as may be specified in the direction; and that person shall comply with the direction.

(7) A transcript made in compliance with a direction under subsection (1) or (2) above—

(a) shall be in legible form; and

(b) shall be certified by the person making it as being a correct and complete transcript of the whole or, as the case may be, the part of the record purporting to have been made and certified, and in the case of shorthand notes signed, by the person who made the record.

(8) The cost of making a transcript in compliance with a direction under subsection (1) or (2)(a) above shall be defrayed, in accordance with scales of payment fixed for the time being by the Treasury, out of money provided by Parliament.

(9) The Clerk of Justiciary shall, on payment of such charges as may be fixed for the time being by the Treasury, provide a copy of any documentary production lodged in connection with an appeal under this Part of this Act to such of the following persons as may request it—

(a) the prosecutor;

(b) any person convicted in the proceedings;

(c) any other person named in, or immediately affected by, any order made in the proceedings; and

(d) any person authorised to act on behalf of any of the persons mentioned in paragraphs (a) to (c) above.".

(28) In section 276 (minute book entry regarding appointment of shorthand writer), for the words from "taken" to the end there shall be substituted the words "recorded by means of (*specify means*) and appointed (*name*), (*designation*), (*address*), to do so.".

(29) In section 277(2) (list of provisions non-compliance with which may be waived), in the first column, under the entry relating to section 242, there shall be inserted the entry "242A".

(30) In section 334(1) (procedure at first diet)—

(a) after the word "prosecution" there shall be inserted the words "(whether or not a diet fixed by virtue of section 333A of this Act)"; and

(b) after the words "he shall" there shall be inserted the words ", unless the court adjourns (or further adjourns) the case under the said section 333A,".

(31) In section 350(1) (additional evidence)—

(a) for the words "after the close of that party's evidence and" there shall be substituted the words "at any time"; and

(b) in paragraph (b), for the words "time the party's evidence was closed" there shall be substituted the words "commencement of the trial".

(32) In section 413 (detention of children in summary proceedings)—

(a) in subsection (1)—

(i) the words "for such period, not exceeding one year, as the sheriff may determine" shall cease to have effect; and

(ii) at the end there shall be added the words "and shall, when making any such order, specify therein a period not exceeding one year"; and

(b) in subsection (7), after the word "(1)" there shall be inserted the words "(or (6B))".

(33) In section 442(1)(b)(ii) (prosecutor's appeal against sentence on point of law), for the words "in such proceedings" there shall be substituted the words "on such conviction".

(34) In section 442B (method of appeal against sentence alone)—

(a) after the words "Where a" there shall be inserted the word "convicted";

(b) after the word "Act", where it first occurs, there shall be inserted the words ", or the prosecutor desires so to appeal by virtue of section 442(1)(c) thereof,"; and

(c) for the proviso there shall be substituted the words "; but nothing in this section shall prejudice any right to proceed by bill of suspension, or as the case may be advocation, against an alleged fundamental irregularity relating to the imposition of the sentence.".

(35) In section 452A (disposal of stated case appeal)—

(a) in subsection (1), after the word "subject" there shall be inserted the words "to subsection (2) below and"; and

(b) for subsection (2) there shall be substituted the following subsection—

"(2) The High Court shall, in an appeal—

(a) against both conviction and sentence, subject to section 453D(1) of this Act, dispose of the appeal against sentence; or

(b) by the prosecutor, against sentence, dispose of the appeal,

by exercise of the power mentioned in section 453C(1) of this Act.".

(36) In section 453B (appeals against sentence only)—

(a) in each of subsections (1), (7) and (8), after the words "442(1)(a)(ii)" there shall be inserted the words ", or by virtue of section 442(1)(c),";

(b) for subsection (2) there shall be substituted the following subsection—

"(2) The note of appeal shall, where the appeal is—

(a) under section 442(1)(a)(ii) be lodged, within one week of the passing of the sentence, with the clerk of the court from which the appeal is to be taken; or

(b) by virtue of section 442(1)(c) be so lodged within four weeks of such passing.";

(c) in subsection (6), for the word "(2)" there shall be substituted the words "(2)(a)"; and

(d) in subsection (8), at the end, there shall be added the words "except that, for the purposes of such application to any appeal by virtue of section 442(1)(c), references in subsections (1) to (3) of section 446 to the appellant shall be construed as references to the convicted person and subsections (4) and (5) of section 446 shall be disregarded".

(37) In section 453C(3) (powers of High Court at time of disposal of appeal)—

(a) after the words "442(1)(a)(ii)" there shall be inserted the words ", or by virtue of section 442(1)(c),"; and

(b) for the word "appellant", in each place where it occurs, there shall be substituted the words "convicted person".

(38) In section 463(1) (application to England and Wales), in paragraph (a) for the words "and 189" there shall be substituted the words "189 and 212A(2) and (6)".

Mental Health (Scotland) Act 1984 (c. 36)

2.—(1) Section 65 of the Mental Health (Scotland) Act 1984 (appeal to sheriff by patient in respect of whom restriction direction has been given) shall be amended as follows.

(2) In subsection (1)(b), for the words "in the event of the patient's not being released on licence or discharged under supervision under subsection (2)(b)(ii) of this section he" there shall be substituted the words "the patient".

(3) For subsection (2) there shall be substituted the following subsection—

"(2) If the sheriff notifies the Secretary of State—

(a) that the patient would be entitled to be absolutely discharged, the Secretary of State shall by warrant direct that the patient be remitted to any prison or other institution or place in which he might have been detained had he not been removed to hospital and that he shall be dealt with there as if he had not been so removed;

(b) that the patient would be entitled to be conditionally discharged, the Secretary of State may—

(i) by warrant give such direction as is mentioned in paragraph (a) above; or

(ii) decide that the patient should continue to be detained in a hospital,

and (if a direction is given under this subsection) on the person's arrival in the prison or other institution or place to which remitted by virtue of this subsection, the restriction direction, together with the transfer direction given in respect of the person, shall cease to have effect.".

Repatriation of Prisoners Act 1984 (c. 47)

3.—(1) The Repatriation of Prisoners Act 1984 shall be amended as follows.

(2) In section 2 (transfer of prisoners out of United Kingdom), in subsection (4)(b), for sub-paragraph (ii) there shall be substituted the following sub-paragraph—

"(ii) released on licence under section 1(2), (3) or (4), 2(4) or 7(1) or (2) of the Prisoners and Criminal Proceedings (Scotland) Act 1993;".

(3) In section 3 (transfer of prisoners into United Kingdom), after subsection (8) there shall be inserted the following subsection—

"(9) The provisions contained by virtue of subsection (1)(c) above in a warrant under this Act shall, in the case of a person who is a transferred life prisoner for the purposes of section 48 of the Criminal Justice Act 1991 or section 10 of the Prisoners and Criminal Proceedings (Scotland) Act 1993 (life prisoners transferred to England and Wales or, as the case may be, Scotland) include provision specifying the part of his sentence which is treated by virtue of section 48 or section 10 as the relevant part of his sentence.".

(4) In the Schedule (operation of certain enactments in relation to prisoners transferred into United Kingdom), in paragraph 2, for sub-paragraph (1) there shall be substituted the following sub-paragraphs—

"(1) In determining for the purposes of any of the enactments relating to release on licence whether the prisoner has at any time served a particular proportion or part of his sentence specified in that provision, the prisoner's sentence shall, subject to sub-paragraph (2) below, be deemed to begin with the day on which the relevant provisions take effect.

(1A) In sub-paragraph (1) above "the enactments relating to release on licence" means—

(a) sections 33(1)(b) and (2), 34(3) and (5), 35(1) and 37(1) and (2) of the Criminal Justice Act 1991; and

(b) sections 1(2) and (3), 2(2) and (7) and 7(1) of the Prisoners and Criminal Proceedings (Scotland) Act 1993.";

and the amendment made to sub-paragraph (2) of that paragraph by paragraph 35(3)(b) of Schedule 11 to the Criminal Justice Act 1991 shall extend also to Scotland.

(5) For paragraph 3 of the Schedule there shall be substituted the following paragraph—

"3. Where the relevant provisions include provision equivalent to a sentence in relation to which section 35(2) of the Criminal Justice Act 1991 or, as the case may be, section 1(4) of the Prisoners and Criminal Proceedings (Scotland) Act 1993 (power to release life prisoners who are not discretionary life prisoners) applies, section 35(2) or, as the case may be, section 1(4) shall have effect as if the reference to consulting the trial judge were omitted.".

Legal Aid (Scotland) Act 1986 (c. 47)

4. In section 21(1) of the Legal Aid (Scotland) Act 1986 (definition of "criminal legal aid"), after paragraph (a) (but before the word "and" which immediately follows that paragraph) there shall be inserted the following paragraph—

"(aa) any case the referral of which is required, under section 2(6) of the Prisoners and Criminal Proceedings (Scotland) Act 1993, by a discretionary life prisoner;".

Road Traffic Offenders Act 1988 (c. 53)

5. In section 12(4) of the Road Traffic Offenders Act 1988, as proposed to be inserted by paragraph 85 of Schedule 4 to the Road Traffic Act 1991 (proof of identity of driver in summary proceedings for certain road traffic offences), for the words "Road Traffic Act 1988" in the first place where they occur there shall be substituted the words "this Act".

Prisons (Scotland) Act 1989 (c. 45)

6.—(1) The Prisons (Scotland) Act 1989 shall be amended as follows.

(2) In section 12 (photographing and measuring of prisoners)—
  (a) for the words "The Secretary of State may make regulations as to" there shall be substituted the words "Rules under section 39 of this Act may provide for"; and
  (b) the words "such regulations" shall cease to have effect.

(3) In section 14(1) (legalised police cells), after the word "under" there shall be inserted the words "section 39 of".

(4) In section 19 (provisions of 1989 Act applying to remand centres and young offenders institutions)—
  (a) in subsection (3), for the words "the rules" there shall be substituted the words "rules under section 39 of this Act"; and
  (b) in subsection (4), in sub-paragraph (iii) of the proviso—
          (i) for the words "paragraphs (i) and (ii)" there shall be substituted the words "paragraph (i)"; and
          (ii) for the words "of the Secretary of State" there shall be substituted the words "under section 39 of this Act".

(5) In section 21 (transfer to prison of persons over 21 etc.)—
  (a) in subsection (1), after the word "section" there shall be inserted the words "but without prejudice to section 20A(2) of this Act"; and
  (b) in subsection (3), after the words "1975 Act" there shall be inserted the words "the Prisoners and Criminal Proceedings (Scotland) Act 1993".

(6) In section 39(1) (rules for the management of prisons and other institutions)—
  (a) the word "and", where it occurs for the third time, shall cease to have effect; and
  (b) at the end there shall be added the words "and for any other matter as respects which it is provided in this Act that rules may be made under this section".

(7) In section 40(2) (no account to be taken, in calculating period of liability to detention, of period when unlawfully at large)—
  (a) after the word "institution", where it first occurs, there shall be inserted the words "or committed to a prison or remand centre";
  (b) after the word "sentence" there shall be inserted the words "or committal";
  (c) for the words "or young offenders institution" there shall be substituted the words ", young offenders institution or remand centre"; and
  (d) after the words "so detained," there shall be inserted the words "or the date on or by which a term or period of imprisonment or detention elapses or has been served,".

(8) In section 42(2) (procedure in relation to statutory instruments containing regulations or rules), for the words from "regulations" to the end there shall be substituted the words "an order made under section 37(1) or rules made under section 39 of this Act shall be subject to annulment in pursuance of a resolution of either House of Parliament".

(9) In section 43 (interpretation)—
  (a) in subsection (1), the definition of "sentence of imprisonment" shall cease to have effect; and
  (b) in subsection (2), the words "(other than in section 25)" shall cease to have effect.

GENERAL NOTE

Paragraph 1: Amendments to the Criminal Procedure (Scotland) Act 1975

Para. 1(2). This allows mechanical recording of proceedings at judicial examinations instead of shorthand records being taken, but subject to the same protections as apply in the case of shorthand records.

Para. 1(3). This is a tidying amendment to allow objections raised under s.67 of the 1975 Act (offences committed in a special capacity, where currently the special status is held to have been admitted if not challenged by a preliminary objection before a plea is entered) to be raised in a preliminary application.

Para. 1(4). This extends the prohibition, except by leave of the court on cause shown, of the raising of objections to the special status issue without notice having been given. It is, accordingly, the correlative restriction to the newly given ability (para. 1(3), *supra*) to raise this issue in a preliminary hearing.

Para. 1(5). This abolishes the need for the matters covered to be referred to juries for the return of purely formal verdicts.

Para. 1(6). While continuing the restriction on remands in custody before sentence to a maximum of three weeks, this provision extends non-custodial remands to a maximum of eight weeks, on cause shown, and four weeks in other cases. It is understood that difficulties in obtaining drivers' records from the DVLC have given rise to the need for this extension, and that it should not be used routinely for the obtaining of reports.

Para. 1(7). No standard of proof has ever been established for breaches of probation. This provision formally enables courts to find a breach proven on the evidence of one witness, thereby clearly asserting that the offence of breach of probation is different from normal offences in Scots law.

Para. 1(9)–(26). These provide for the effect of the introduction of the prosecution right of appeal under s.42 of the Act on the various time limits in solemn cases.

Para. 1(27). The provisions of para. 1(2) of this Schedule allowing recording by means of methods other than shorthand writing of proceedings at judicial examinations are extended to all trials. The new s.275 of the 1975 Act places a duty on the Clerk of Justiciary to provide transcripts to any person who the Secretary of State may, by order, determine to be appropriate, subject to that person's paying the appropriate fee and using the transcript only for approved purposes. It must be presumed that this will extend the availability of verbatim transcripts of court proceedings.

Para. 1(28). This allows for specification of recording means other than shorthand and requires the same personal authorisation as existing provisions.

Para. 1(30). This amendment is necessitated by s.38 of this Act, which introduces the possibility of a summary case's being continued without plea when the accused has not been apprehended.

Para. 1(31). Sub-paragraph (a) gives the court greater flexibility to take additional evidence at any time in the proceedings, before the prosecutor proceeds to address the judge on the evidence. Sub-paragraph (b) similarly extends the discretion of the court which was only previously exercisable in relation to evidence which was not available or known to be available, or seen to be material, at the time of the party's evidence being closed.

Para. 1(33)–(37). These provide for the introduction of the prosecutor's right of appeal in summary cases.

Paragraph 2: Amendments to the Mental Health (Scotland) Act 1984

Para. 2(3). The Secretary of State is compelled by the new s.65(2) of the 1984 Act to give effect to an absolute discharge granted by a sheriff and to return the person to whatever form of custody is otherwise appropriate. When the sheriff holds that a conditional discharge is appropriate, the Secretary of State is given discretion either to return the person to another form of custody or to continue the detention in a hospital. In either case the restriction order and the transfer order shall cease to have effect upon the person's transfer to the new location.

Paragraph 3: Amendments to the Repatriation of Prisoners Act 1984.
    These amendments are required in order to accommodate the new release procedures under the present Act.

Paragraph 4: Amendments to the Legal Aid (Scotland) Act 1986
    By providing for legal aid to be available to discretionary life-sentence prisoners seeking release after the expiry of the tariff period of their sentence under s.2 of the present Act, it is

made clear that these proceedings are legal ones and that the Parole Board, in dealing with the applications, is constituted as a court, as required by the European Convention (*Thynne, Wilson and Gunnell* v. *U.K.*, *The Independent*, November 2, 1990, E.C.H.R.).

Paragraph 6: Amendments to the Prisons (Scotland) Act 1989

Para. 6(2). This clarifies the position that the Secretary of State must exercise his powers by means of statutory instrument.

Para. 6(3). This is a tidying amendment.

Para. 6(4). This is a tidying amendment.

Para. 6(8). This is a further attempt to clarify the procedure for the making of rules by the Secretary of State under the 1989 Act. It continues the distinction between some which require simply to be laid before Parliament and some which are subject to annulment.

Para. 6(9). "Sentence of imprisonment" previously excluded committals in default of payment of any sum of money and failure to do or abstain from doing anything required to be done or left undone.

Section 47(2)   SCHEDULE 6

TRANSITIONAL PROVISIONS AND SAVINGS

1. In this Schedule—
   "existing provisions" means such provisions as relate to the detention or release of persons and are amended or repealed by this Act, as they had effect immediately before such amendment or repeal;
   "new provisions" means sections 1 to 21 and 27 of this Act (together with the provisions of the 1975 Act and of the Mental Health (Scotland) Act 1984 which so relate and are so amended);
   "existing child detainee" means any child ("child" having the meaning assigned to that expression by section 30 of the Social Work (Scotland) Act 1968) who, at the relevant date, is detained under section 206 of the 1975 Act other than without limit of time or is detained in residential care by virtue of section 413 of the 1975 Act;
   "existing licensee" means any person who, before the relevant date, has been released on licence under the 1989 Act;
   "existing life prisoner" means any person who, at the relevant date, is serving—
        (a) a sentence of imprisonment for life;
        (b) a sentence of detention without limit of time or for life under section 205 of the 1975 Act;
        (c) a sentence of detention without limit of time under section 206 of that Act; or
        (d) a period of detention without limit of time or for life under section 207(2) of that Act;
   "existing prisoner" means any person who, at the relevant date, is serving—
        (a) a sentence of imprisonment; or
        (b) a sentence of detention in a young offenders institution; and
   "relevant date" means the date of commencement of the new provisions.
2.—(1) Subject to sub-paragraph (2) and paragraph 7 below, the new provisions shall apply only to persons who are sentenced (or on whom detention is imposed) on or after the relevant date; and notwithstanding any repeal or amendment effected by or by virtue of this Act, but subject to that sub-paragraph and to the following paragraphs of this Schedule, the existing provisions shall continue to apply to persons sentenced (or on whom detention has been imposed) before that date.
   (2) Section 3 of this Act shall apply irrespective of the date on which a person is sentenced (or on which detention is imposed on him).
3. An existing prisoner whose sentence is for a term of less than two years and who, by the relevant date, has served—

(a) one-half or more of that sentence, shall be released unconditionally by the Secretary of State on that date;

(b) less than one-half of that sentence, shall be so released as soon as he has served one-half of that sentence.

4.—(1) An existing child detainee whose sentence under section 206 of the 1975 Act is for a period—

(a) of less than four years and who, by the relevant date, has served—

(i) one-half or more of that sentence, shall be released on licence by the Secretary of State on that date;

(ii) less than one-half of that sentence, shall be so released as soon as he has served one-half of that sentence;

(b) of four years or more and who, by the relevant date, has served—

(i) two-thirds or more of that sentence, shall be released on licence by the Secretary of State on that date;

(ii) less than two-thirds of that sentence, shall be so released as soon as he has served two-thirds of that sentence.

(2) An existing child detainee detained under section 206 of the 1975 Act may, on the recommendation of the Parole Board made at any time, be released on licence by the Secretary of State.

5.—(1) An existing child detainee who, by the relevant date, has completed—

(a) one-half or more of a period of detention in residential care for which he has been committed, shall be released from such care on that date;

(b) less than one-half of that period, shall be so released as soon as he has completed one-half of that period,

but until the entire such period has elapsed may be required by the appropriate local authority to submit to supervision in accordance with such conditions as they consider appropriate.

(2) Where a child released under sub-paragraph (1) above is subject to a supervision requirement within the meaning of the Social Work (Scotland) Act 1968, the effect of that requirement shall commence, or as the case may be resume, upon such release.

6.—(1) This paragraph applies where, in the case of an existing life prisoner, the Lord Justice General, whom failing the Lord Justice Clerk, after consultation with the trial judge, if available, certifies his opinion that, if section 2 of this Act had been in force at the time when the prisoner was sentenced, the court by which he was sentenced would have ordered that that section should apply to him as soon as he had served a part of his sentence specified in the certificate.

(2) In a case to which this paragraph applies, sections 1 to 27 of this Act except sections 1(4) and 2(9) shall apply as if—

(a) the existing life prisoner were a discretionary life prisoner within the meaning of section 2 of this Act; and

(b) the relevant part of his sentence within the meaning of that section were the part specified in the certificate.

(3) Where a person is serving two or more sentences of imprisonment for life or detention without limit of time or for life—

(a) he shall be treated as a discretionary life prisoner within the meaning of section 2 of this Act only if the requirements of sub-paragraph (1) above are satisfied in respect of each of those sentences; and

(b) notwithstanding the terms of any certificate under that sub-paragraph, subsections (4) and (6) of section 2 shall not apply to him until he has served the relevant part of each of those sentences.

7. Where a transferred life prisoner is a discretionary life prisoner for the purposes of Part II of the Criminal Justice Act 1991 by virtue of section 48 of or paragraph 9 of Schedule 12 to that Act, paragraph 6 above shall apply as if the certificate under the said section 48 or paragraph 9 were a certificate under sub-paragraph (1) of the said paragraph 6.

8. Unless revoked, a licence under—

(a) paragraph 4(1)(a)(i) or (b)(i) above shall remain in force until at least twelve months have elapsed after the date of release and until the entire period of sentence has elapsed;

(b) paragraph 4(1)(a)(ii) or (b)(ii) above shall remain in force until a date determined by the Parole Board, being a date not later than the date by which the entire period of sentence has elapsed.

9. Section 12 of this Act shall apply in respect of a licence granted under this Schedule.

GENERAL NOTE

Paragraph 2
The general principle is that the new system for early release and all other provisions of this

Act are not to be retrospective. However, sub-para. (2) will enable the provisions about compassionate release to be applied to all prisoners.

Paragraph 3
Release at half sentence is to be immediately available on the implementation of the Act for those sentenced to less than two years. Those sentenced to two years or more will continue to be dealt with in accordance with the pre-existing provisions. Accordingly, there will still be a need for local review committees until all those sentenced to determinate sentences of two years or more have reached the two-thirds date of their sentence.

Paragraph 4
The introduction of the new release arrangements is to be applied retrospectively to all child detainees under s.206 of the 1975 Act, and the provision allowing their consideration for release on parole at any stage of their sentence is continued.

Paragraph 5
Child detainees under s.413 of the 1975 Act are also to benefit from retrospective introduction of the new release provisions, though subject to social-work supervision during the part of the sentence spent in the community.

Paragraph 6
This allows the Lord Justice General, or the Lord Justice Clerk, to review, in consultation with the original trial judge, if available, the cases of all life-sentence prisoners, and to certify in the cases of those who appear to them to be discretionary life-sentence prisoners a "relevant part" in terms of s.2 of the Act. Accordingly, all discretionary life-sentence prisoners should have their cases reviewed, and a decision made whether or not a "relevant part" should be set. The same restrictions apply to this process as would have applied had the provision been in force at the time the discretionary life prisoner was sentenced, including the right of the prisoner to appeal against any such order or the failure to make an order (s.2(3)).

Paragraph 7
This extends the operation of para. 6, *supra*, to include prisoners transferred to Scotland from other parts of Great Britain.

Paragraph 8
This ensures that child detainees will receive at least one year's supervision under licence if released immediately on this Act's coming into force, even if their total sentence would have expired before that time. It also allows the Parole Board to determine the length of licence of those children who have not yet reached the one-half or two-thirds date of their sentence at the date of implementation, but who are subsequently released at that stage. In these cases, the licence cannot continue beyond the expiry of the total original sentence.

Paragraph 9
All licences issued under this Schedule are subject to the same conditions as licences to be granted under the main provisions of this Act.

Section 47(3)   SCHEDULE 7

REPEALS AND REVOCATIONS

PART I

REPEALS

Chapter	Short title	Extent of repeal
1 Edw. 8 & 1 Geo. 6 c.37.	The Children and Young Persons (Scotland) Act 1937.	In section 57(3), the words "or section 25 of the Prisons (Scotland) Act 1989".
3 & 4 Eliz 2 c.18.	The Army Act 1955.	Section 71AA(6B). In Schedule 5A, paragraph 10(6B).

Chapter	Short title	Extent of repeal
3 & 4 Eliz. 2 c.19.	The Air Force Act 1955.	Section 71AA(6B). In Schedule 5A, paragraph 10(6B).
5 & 6 Eliz. 2 c.53.	The Naval Discipline Act 1957.	Section 43AA(6B). In Schedule 4A, paragraph 10(6B).
1963 c.39.	The Criminal Justice (Scotland) Act 1963.	In paragraph 13 of Schedule 1, the words "(and, if that person is released from such a prison under the said section 214(7) or 423(7), section 30(3) of the Prisons (Scotland) Act 1989)".
1965 c.20.	The Criminal Evidence Act 1965.	The whole Act.
1969 c.48.	The Post Office Act 1969.	Section 93(4).
1975 c.21.	The Criminal Procedure (Scotland) Act 1975.	In section 108(2), the word "and" at the end of paragraph (b). Section 207(11). Section 212. Section 214. In section 270(2), the words "of two weeks or any extension thereof authorised by the High Court". Section 289D(1A)(e). Section 328. In section 413(1) the words "for such period, not exceeding one year, as the sheriff may determine". Section 415(11). Section 421. Section 423.
1980 c.55.	The Law Reform (Miscellaneous Provisions) (Scotland) Act 1980.	In part I of Schedule 1, in Group B, paragraph (v).
1980 c.62.	The Criminal Justice (Scotland) Act 1980.	In section 2, in subsection (5), paragraph (c) and the proviso to that paragraph; and in subsection (6) the words "or (c)". In Schedule 3, paragraph 12.
1981 c.49.	The Contempt of Court Act 1981.	Section 15(6).
1984 c.36.	The Mental Health (Scotland) Act 1984.	In section 71, subsection (2)(b); and in subsection (7)(a), the words "in criminal proceedings". Section 73(3).
1987 c.41.	The Criminal Justice (Scotland) Act 1987.	Section 62(1). In Schedule 1, paragraph 19.
1989 c.45.	The Prisons (Scotland) Act 1989.	In section 12, the words "such regulations". Section 16(1). Section 18. In section 19(4), in paragraph (b), the word "24,"; and in the proviso, sub-paragraph (ii). In section 21(3), the proviso. Sections 22 to 32. In section 39, in subsection (1) the word "and" where it occurs for the third time; and subsection (4). In section 42, in subsection (1) the words "22(2), 30(6) or (7), 32(5) or"; and subsections (3) and (4). In section 43, in subsection (1), the definitions of "local review committee",

Chapter	Short title	Extent of repeal
1991 c.53.	The Criminal Justice Act 1991.	"Parole Board" and "sentence of imprisonment"; in subsection (2), the words "(other than in section 25)"; and in subsection (5), the words "(other than in section 30)". Schedule 1. In Schedule 2, paragraphs 1, 3 to 5, 8, 13 to 15, 17 and 18. In Schedule 11, in paragraph 35, sub-paragraphs (2), (3)(a) and (4).

PART II

REVOCATIONS

Year and number	Title	Extent of revocation
S.I. 1952/565.	The Prison (Scotland) Rules 1952.	Rule 9.
S.I. 1976/1889.	The Prison (Scotland) Amendment Rules 1976.	The whole rules.

INDEX

References are to section and Schedule number

CHARITIES ACT 1993*

(1993 c. 10)

[A table showing the derivation of the provisions of this consolidation will be found at the end of this Act. The table has no official status.]

ARRANGEMENT OF SECTIONS

PART I

THE CHARITY COMMISSIONERS AND THE OFFICIAL CUSTODIAN FOR CHARITIES

---

* Annotations by Jean Warburton LL.B., Solicitor, Senior Lecturer in Law, University of Liverpool.

An Act to consolidate the Charitable Trustees Incorporation Act 1872 and, except for certain spent or transitional provisions, the Charities Act 1960 and Part I of the Charities Act 1992. [27th May 1993]

PARLIAMENTARY DEBATES
Hansard, H.L. Vol. 541, col. 816.

INTRODUCTION AND GENERAL NOTE

During the course of the debate on the Bill which became the Charities Act 1992, considerable concern was expressed about the difficulties of comprehension caused by the numerous amendments to earlier Acts. As a short term measure, ss.4 and 20 of the 1960 Act, as amended, were set out in full in Sched. 1 to the 1992 Act. The point was clearly taken, however, as this consolidation has appeared just over a year after the 1992 Act.

The Act consolidates the Charitable Trustees Incorporation Act 1872, the Charities Act 1960 and Part I of the Charities Act 1992. It is not, therefore, a consolidation of the whole of charity law. The Charitable Trusts Validation Act 1954 and the Recreational Charities Act 1958 remain separate as do the fundraising and public collections provisions of the 1992 Act.

The annotations to this Act indicate the source of each new section to assist reference to earlier commentaries.

ABBREVIATIONS
The 1872 Act	:	The Charitable Trusts Incorporation Act 1872
The 1960 Act	:	The Charities Act 1960
The 1985 Act	:	The Charities Act 1985
The 1992 Act	:	The Charities Act 1992
The 1992 Rules	:	Land Registration (Charities) Rules 1992 (S.I. 1992 No. 3005)
The White Paper	:	"Charities: A Framework For The Future" (1989) Cm 694
The Woodfield report	:	"Efficiency Scrutiny of the Supervision of Charities"

PART I

THE CHARITY COMMISSIONERS AND THE OFFICIAL CUSTODIAN FOR CHARITIES

The Charity Commissioners

1.—(1) There shall continue to be a body of Charity Commissioners for England and Wales, and they shall have such functions as are conferred on them by this Act in addition to any functions under any other enactment for the time being in force.

(2) The provisions of Schedule 1 to this Act shall have effect with respect to the constitution and proceedings of the Commissioners and other matters relating to the Commissioners and their officers and employees.

(3) The Commissioners shall (without prejudice to their specific powers and duties under other enactments) have the general function of promoting the effective use of charitable resources by encouraging the development of

better methods of administration, by giving charity trustees information or advice on any matter affecting the charity and by investigating and checking abuses.

(4) It shall be the general object of the Commissioners so to act in the case of any charity (unless it is a matter of altering its purposes) as best to promote and make effective the work of the charity in meeting the needs designated by its trusts; but the Commissioners shall not themselves have power to act in the administration of a charity.

(5) The Commissioners shall, as soon as possible after the end of every year, make to the Secretary of State a report on their operations during that year, and he shall lay a copy of the report before each House of Parliament.

DEFINITIONS
"charity": s.96(1).
"charity trustees": s.97(1).
"the Commissioners": s.97(1).
"trusts": s.97(1).

GENERAL NOTE
This section re-enacts s.1 of the 1960 Act and makes provision for the continuance of the Charity Commissioners for England and Wales as a public department. For the Commissioners' views as to their duties and the organisation of the Charity Commission into Charity support and Charity supervision, see [1991] Ch. Comm. Rep., para. 4 *et seq.*

Subs. (1)
Functions under any other enactment for the time being in force. For example, s.72 of the 1992 Act.

Subs. (3)
This subsection emphasises the general function of the Commissioners and its effect is to relieve the Commissioners, who are civil servants, see Sched. 1, para. 1(3), from the civil servants' normal obligation to obey the Secretary of State who appoints him and who is responsible to Parliament for him, unless there is a statutory power (as in this subsection) which gives him independence. As to the giving of advice, see s.29; as to the investigation and checking of abuse, see ss.8, 16(6) and 18(1)(2).

Subs. (4)
The trustees, and not the Commissioners, are wholly and solely responsible for the administration of a charity.

Subs. (5)
The annual report is made to the Secretary of State for Home Affairs who lays the report before Parliament. The Home Secretary, however, is not responsible for the decisions of the Commissioners in relation to particular charities because the discretion is theirs and not his. Insofar as the Commissioners are answerable for the exercise of their discretion, they are answerable to the courts, because an appeal lies from their decision to the courts and not to the Home Secretary, see ss.16(12) and 33 and *Mills* v. *Winchester Diocesan Board of Finance* [1989] Ch. 428.

The official custodian for charities

2.—(1) There shall continue to be an officer known as the official custodian for charities (in this Act referred to as "the official custodian") whose function it shall be to act as trustee for charities in the cases provided for by this Act; and the official custodian shall be by that name a corporation sole having perpetual succession and using an official seal which shall be officially and judicially noticed.

(2) Such officer of the Commissioners as they may from time to time designate shall be the official custodian.

(3) The official custodian shall perform his duties in accordance with such general or special directions as may be given him by the Commissioners, and his expenses (except those re-imbursed to him or recovered by him as trustee for any charity) shall be defrayed by the Commissioners.

(4) Anything which is required to or may be done by, to or before the official custodian may be done by, to or before any officer of the Commissioners generally or specially authorised by them to act for him during a vacancy in his office or otherwise.

(5) The official custodian shall not be liable as trustee for any charity in respect of any loss or of the mis-application of any property unless it is occasioned by or through the wilful neglect or default of the custodian or of any person acting for him; but the Consolidated Fund shall be liable to make good to a charity any sums for which the custodian may be liable by reason of any such neglect or default.

(6) The official custodian shall keep such books of account and such records in relation thereto as may be directed by the Treasury and shall prepare accounts in such form, in such manner and at such times as may be so directed.

(7) The accounts so prepared shall be examined and certified by the Comptroller and Auditor General, and the report to be made by the Commissioners to the Secretary of State for any year shall include a copy of the accounts so prepared for any period ending in or with the year and of the certificate and report of the Comptroller and Auditor General with respect to those accounts.

DEFINITIONS
    "charity": s.96(1).
    "the Commissioners": s.97(1).
    "the official custodian": s.97(1).

GENERAL NOTE
    This section re-enacts s.3 of the 1960 Act, with minor amendments, and provides for the continuation of the office of official custodian. The Commissioners have power to order any property of a charity to be vested in the official custodian under s.18(1), and the court or the Commissioners may order land to be vested in the official custodian under s.21(1). The official custodian's functions were drastically reduced by s.29 of the 1992 Act (which remains in force) which required the official custodian to divest herself of all property other than land and that held following an order under s.20 of the 1960 Act. As to the official custodian's strategy for divestment, see [1989] Ch. Comm. Rep., para. 107 *et seq.*

Subs. (1)
    This subsection gives the official custodian for charities corporate status. The definition of "charity trustees" in s.96 as persons having the general control and management of the administration of a charity, indicates that a trustee otherwise described in the Act, as in this subsection as "trustee for charities" is a trustee without such control and management. This is the position of the official custodian who merely holds the legal estate and of a corporation which acts as a custodian trustee under s.4 of the Public Trustee Act 1906 and, as such, has a similar function, but a custodian trustee is not a bare trustee (See *Brooke Bond & Co.'s Trust Deed, Re; Brooke v. Brooke Bond & Co.* [1963] Ch. 357).

Subs. (7)
    In practice, the annual accounts of the official custodian for charities together with the certificate and report of the Comptroller and Auditor General are set out as an appendix to the Commissioners' annual report.

PART II

REGISTRATION AND NAMES OF CHARITIES

Registration of charities

The register of charities

    3.—(1) The Commissioners shall continue to keep a register of charities, which shall be kept by them in such manner as they think fit.

(2) There shall be entered in the register every charity not excepted by subsection (5) below; and a charity so excepted (other than one excepted by

paragraph (a) of that subsection) may be entered in the register at the request of the charity, but (whether or not it was excepted at the time of registration) may at any time, and shall at the request of the charity, be removed from the register.

(3) The register shall contain—

(a) the name of every registered charity; and

(b) such other particulars of, and such other information relating to, every such charity as the Commissioners think fit.

(4) Any institution which no longer appears to the Commissioners to be a charity shall be removed from the register, with effect, where the removal is due to any change in its purposes or trusts, from the date of that change; and there shall also be removed from the register any charity which ceases to exist or does not operate.

(5) The following charities are not required to be registered—

(a) any charity comprised in Schedule 2 to this Act (in this Act referred to as an "exempt charity");

(b) any charity which is excepted by order or regulations;

(c) any charity which has neither—

(i) any permanent endowment, nor

(ii) the use or occupation of any land,

and whose income from all sources does not in aggregate amount to more than £1,000 a year;

and no charity is required to be registered in respect of any registered place of worship.

(6) With any application for a charity to be registered there shall be supplied to the Commissioners copies of its trusts (or, if they are not set out in any extant document, particulars of them), and such other documents or information as may be prescribed by regulations made by the Secretary of State or as the Commissioners may require for the purpose of the application.

(7) It shall be the duty—

(a) of the charity trustees of any charity which is not registered nor excepted from registration to apply for it to be registered, and to supply the documents and information required by subsection (6) above; and

(b) of the charity trustees (or last charity trustees) of any institution which is for the time being registered to notify the Commissioners if it ceases to exist, or if there is any change in its trusts or in the particulars of it entered in the register, and to supply to the Commissioners particulars of any such change and copies of any new trusts or alterations of the trusts.

(8) The register (including the entries cancelled when institutions are removed from the register) shall be open to public inspection at all reasonable times; and copies (or particulars) of the trusts of any registered charity as supplied to the Commissioners under this section shall, so long as it remains on the register, be kept by them and be open to public inspection at all reasonable times, except in so far as regulations made by the Secretary of State otherwise provide.

(9) Where any information contained in the register is not in documentary form, subsection (8) above shall be construed as requiring the information to be available for public inspection in legible form at all reasonable times.

(10) If the Commissioners so determine, subsection (8) above shall not apply to any particular information contained in the register and specified in their determination.

(11) Nothing in the foregoing subsections shall require any person to supply the Commissioners with copies of schemes for the administration of a charity made otherwise than by the court, or to notify the Commissioners of any change made with respect to a registered charity by such a scheme, or

require a person, if he refers the Commissioners to a document or copy already in the possession of the Commissioners, to supply a further copy of the document; but where by virtue of this subsection a copy of any document need not be supplied to the Commissioners, a copy of it, if it relates to a registered charity, shall be open to inspection under subsection (8) above as if supplied to the Commissioners under this section.

(12) If the Secretary of State thinks it expedient to do so—

(a) in consequence of changes in the value of money, or

(b) with a view to extending the scope of the exception provided for by subsection (5)(c) above,

he may by order amend subsection (5)(c) by substituting a different sum for the sum for the time being specified there.

(13) The reference in subsection (5)(b) above to a charity which is excepted by order or regulations is to a charity which—

(a) is for the time being permanently or temporarily excepted by order of the Commissioners; or

(b) is of a description permanently or temporarily excepted by regulations made by the Secretary of State,

and which complies with any conditions of the exception.

(14) In this section "registered place of worship" means any land or building falling within section 9 of the Places of Worship Registration Act 1855 (that is to say, the land and buildings which if the Charities Act 1960 had not been passed, would by virtue of that section as amended by subsequent enactments be partially exempted from the operation of the Charitable Trusts Act 1853), and for the purposes of this subsection "building" includes part of a building.

DEFINITIONS
"charity": s.96(1).
"charity trustees": s.97(1).
"the Commissioners": s.97(1).
"the court": s.97(1).
"exempt charity": s.96(1).
"institution": s.97(1).
"permanent endowment": s.97(1).
"the register": s.97(1).
"registered place of worship": subs. (14).
"trusts": s.97(1).

GENERAL NOTE
This section re-enacts s.4 of the 1960 Act as amended by s.4 of the 1992 Act and provides for the continuation of the register of charities. The register had become out of date and unreliable by the 1980s and major steps were taken to computerise the register and to update the information held; see [1990] Ch. Comm. Rep. para. 25 *et seq.* The 1992 Act also widened the categories of charities required to be registered. An annual return by charities keeps the register up to date (see s.48). The register provides potential donors, potential beneficiaries, voluntary bodies, social workers and other interested members of the public with access to basic information on the existence of registered charities and their purposes. The register also allows charities and local authorities to see what the other is doing, see ss.76–78. The requirement of registration has the effect of placing upon the Commissioners the primary responsibility for determining charitable status at law, subject to appeal to the Chancery Division of the High Court.

Subs. (1)
The register contains details of the name, objects and correspondent of each charity together with financial information.
In such manner. This allows the register to be kept on computer rather than by manual system.

Subs. (2)
As to objection to and appeal against registration, on the ground that the institution is not a charity, see s.4(2) and (3).

An excepted charity may apply for voluntary registration but not an exempt charity. If an excepted charity is entered on the register it becomes subject to the accounting and annual report obligations, see s.46(3) and (4).

Subs. (3)

This subsection permits the Commissioners to mark the register that the trustees of a particular charity have not complied with one or more of their statutory duties, for example, if they have not made an annual return as required by s.48 (see *Hansard*, H.L. Vol. 532, col. 884).

Subs. (4)

There are various ways in which an institution can lose its charitable status. Thus, a charitable company may change its objects, so that they are no longer charitable; or there may be a revocable trust which is revoked; or an institution may be found not to be charitable because a decision of the court shows that a particular purpose, until then supposed to be charitable, is in fact not so. Where the trusts are altered, the removal of the institution dates back to the date of the change.

As to the limited power of a charitable company to alter the trusts attaching to property which it holds, see s.64(1).

As to the duty of trustees to supply information, see subs. (7).

Subs. (5)

An "exempt charity" is exempt from the jurisdiction of the Commissioners. As to exempt charities, see Sched. 2.

A charity excepted by order or regulations from the requirements of registration is not thereby necessarily excepted from the other requirements of the Act, for example, those in s.36. A class of charities may be excepted because, for example, no great advantage is to be derived from registration (small church funds of a purely local application come within this category), or because it comprises charities having a national organisation, for example, the Boy Scouts.The following regulations, see subs. (13), except certain categories of charity from the requirement of registration:

(1) The Charities (Exception of Voluntary Schools from Registration) Regulations 1960 (S.I. 1960 No. 2366);

(2) The Charities (Exception of Certain Charities for Boy Scouts and Girl Guides from Registration) Regulations 1961 (S.I. 1961 No. 1044);

(3) The Charities (Exception from Registration and Accounts) Regulations 1963 and 1964 (S.I. 1963 No. 2074, S.I. 1964 No. 1825) (certain religious charities);

(4) The Charities (Exception from Registration and Accounts) Regulations 1965 (S.I. 1965 No. 1056) (certain armed forces charities);

(5) The Charities (Exception of Universities from Registration) Regulations 1966 (S.I. 1966 No. 965).

The 1992 Act brought within the obligation to register charities having no permanent endowment but an income of more than £1,000 a year.

The income limit under subs. (5)(c) may be amended by order under subs. (12).

Registered place of worship. Places of worship are excepted because the Registrar General under the Places of Worship Registration Act 1855, s.3 already has to register all places of worship certified to him under s.2 of that Act and s.7 thereof requires a list of certified places of worship to be printed and open to public inspection.

Subs. (6)

Under this subsection it is the duty of charity trustees to furnish particulars of unwritten trusts, whether declared originally by parol or attached by user, as well as to lodge trust instruments; as to this duty see subs. (7). The Commissioners consider that this subsection empowers them to call for information concerning an institution's activities or intended activities, copies of accounts and other documents issued on behalf of the institution or its promoters, see [1980] Ch. Comm. Rep., para. 89. An institution applying for registration is asked by the Commissioners to complete a questionnaire, RE 96, to supply such information.

Subs. (7)

This subsection makes it clear that trustees have a positive duty to apply for registration. The fact that the trustees have previously had correspondence with the Commissioners about a charity does not obviate the need to apply for registration nor does the fact that a charity is already registered for some other limited purpose under some other statutory provision, for example, with the Registrar of Companies.

Changes in trusts should in any event be notified to the Commissioners by charity trustees in the annual return, see s.48.

Subs. (8)

A copy of the register or extracts from it may be obtained under s.84.

Subs. (11)

This subsection obviates the need to furnish copies of schemes copies of which will be in the Commissioners' possession. Similarly with other documents, a person who knows that a particular document or copy is already in the possession of the Commissioners need not supply them with a further copy.

Effect of, and claims and objections to, registration

4.—(1) An institution shall for all purposes other than rectification of the register be conclusively presumed to be or to have been a charity at any time when it is or was on the register of charities.

(2) Any person who is or may be affected by the registration of an institution as a charity may, on the ground that it is not a charity, object to its being entered by the Commissioners in the register, or apply to them for it to be removed from the register; and provision may be made by regulations made by the Secretary of State as to the manner in which any such objection or application is to be made, prosecuted or dealt with.

(3) An appeal against any decision of the Commissioners to enter or not to enter an institution in the register of charities, or to remove or not to remove an institution from the register, may be brought in the High Court by the Attorney-General, or by the persons who are or claim to be the charity trustees of the institution, or by any person whose objection or application under subsection (2) above is disallowed by the decision.

(4) If there is an appeal to the High Court against any decision of the Commissioners to enter an institution in the register, or not to remove an institution from the register, then until the Commissioners are satisfied whether the decision of the Commissioners is or is not to stand, the entry in the register shall be maintained, but shall be in suspense and marked to indicate that it is in suspense; and for the purposes of subsection (1) above an institution shall be deemed not to be on the register during any period when the entry relating to it is in suspense under this subsection.

(5) Any question affecting the registration or removal from the register of an institution may, notwithstanding that it has been determined by a decision on appeal under subsection (3) above, be considered afresh by the Commissioners and shall not be concluded by that decision, if it appears to the Commissioners that there has been a change of circumstances or that the decision is inconsistent with a later judicial decision, whether given on such an appeal or not.

DEFINITIONS

"charity": s.96(1).
"charity trustees": s.97(1).
"the Commissioners": s.97(1).
"institution": s.97(1).
"the register": s.97(1).

GENERAL NOTE

This section re-enacts s.5 of the 1960 Act which deals with the effect of registration under s.3, objections to registration and applications for removal from the register.

Subs. (1)

Since a registered charity is conclusively presumed to be a charity as long as it remains registered, it must during that time be recognised by all, including the Commissioners of Inland Revenue and rating authorities, as a charity and entitled to the privileges thereof; see *Wynn* v. *Skegness Urban District Council* [1967] 1 W.L.R. 52; *Finch* v. *Poplar Borough Council* (1967) 66 L.G.R. 324, 327.

A testamentary gift for purposes which, at a date subsequent to the donor's death, are registered as charitable is valid (*Murawski's Will Trusts, Re; Lloyds Bank* v. *Royal Society for the Prevention of Cruelty to Animals* [1971] 1 W.L.R. 707).

As to relief from income and corporation tax see the Income and Corporation Taxes Act 1988, ss.9(4) and 505.

As to relief from non-domestic rates see the Local Government Finance Act 1988, ss.43(6) and 45(6).

Subs. (2)

The purpose of this provision is to protect people, especially next of kin, whose financial interests may be affected by the question whether or not a trust ought to be classified as a charity. Thus, if a testator leaves money to an institution on the basis that it is charitable, and his next of kin think that there is strong reason for claiming that it is no longer entitled to be regarded as a charity, and to be registered as such, they may make representations to the Commissioners to that effect. No time limit is placed on the making of representations, *i.e.* it makes no difference how long the institution has been on the register. The Inland Revenue Commissioners and rating authorities are affected by the registration of an institution as a charity and may make representations under this subsection.

Subs. (3)

Any proceedings under this provision should be started in the Chancery Division. There is no time limit for an appeal against a decision of the Commissioners under this subsection. The usual time limits apply to any further appeal to the High Court or the Court of Appeal. An appeal is not within the meaning of the term "charity proceedings" in s.33. Accordingly, the restrictions on taking charity proceedings do not apply.

For appeals under this subsection see *Incorporated Council of Law Reporting for England and Wales* v. *Att.-Gen.* [1972] Ch. 73; *I.R.C.* v. *McMullen* [1981] A.C. 1; *McGovern* v. *Att.-Gen.* [1982] Ch. 321.

Subs. (4)

As long as there is an appeal pending, other proceedings, for example, in relation to a claim for income tax, would presumably be stayed. The Commissioners are to take account of the fact that an appeal may be brought from the judge and a further appeal from the Court of Appeal to the House of Lords; so long as there is a likelihood of further appeal, the entry is to be in suspense. See (1985) 129 Sol. J. 880 (Fryer).

Subs. (5)

This subsection prevents the operation of the *res judicata* rule and enables the question of the status of an institution to be reopened if it was previously treated as charitable but no longer enjoys charitable status, and vice versa, see *National Anti-Vivisection Society* v. *I.R.C.* [1948] A.C. 31.

Status of registered charity (other than small charity) to appear on official publications etc.

5.—(1) This section applies to a registered charity if its gross income in its last financial year exceeded £5,000.

(2) Where this section applies to a registered charity, the fact that it is a registered charity shall be stated in English in legible characters—

(a) in all notices, advertisements and other documents issued by or on behalf of the charity and soliciting money or other property for the benefit of the charity;

(b) in all bills of exchange, promissory notes, endorsements, cheques and orders for money or goods purporting to be signed on behalf of the charity; and

(c) in all bills rendered by it and in all its invoices, receipts and letters of credit.

(3) Subsection (2)(a) above has effect whether the solicitation is express or implied, and whether the money or other property is to be given for any consideration or not.

(4) If, in the case of a registered charity to which this section applies, any person issues or authorises the issue of any document falling within paragraph (a) or (c) of subsection (2) above in which the fact that the charity is a registered charity is not stated as required by that subsection, he shall be guilty of an offence and liable on summary conviction to a fine not exceeding level 3 on the standard scale.

(5) If, in the case of any such registered charity, any person signs any document falling within paragraph (b) of subsection (2) above in which the fact that the charity is a registered charity is not stated as required by that subsection, he shall be guilty of an offence and liable on summary conviction to a fine not exceeding level 3 on the standard scale.

(6) The Secretary of State may by order amend subsection (1) above by substituting a different sum for the sum for the time being specified there.

DEFINITIONS
    "charity": s.96(1).
    "charity trustees": s.97(1).
    "documents": s.97(2).
    "financial year": s.97(1).
    "gross income": s.97(1).

GENERAL NOTE
    This section re-enacts s.3 of the 1992 Act. The purpose of the section is to require registered charities to include a statement that they are so registered on specified documents with a view to indicating that the charity is subject to the supervisory régime of the Commissioners. Serious concern, voiced at the time of the passing of the 1992 Act, about imposing undue burdens on the trustees of small charities led to the provision being restricted to charities with a gross income of more than £5,000 in the previous financial year.

Subs. (1)
    The £5,000 limit may be varied by order, see subs. (6).

Subs. (2)
    Charitable companies are required to state that they are so registered on documents by s.68.
    Legible characters. There is no requirement for printing. It is open to the trustees of a charity with few relevant transactions, for example, to write on a cheque that it is a charity, provided the writing is legible.
    To be signed on behalf of the charity. A charity which keeps its funds in a building society account and makes payment by means of a cheque issued by the building society is not required to place its name on that cheque as it is a cheque issued on behalf of the building society, see *Hansard*, H.L. Vol. 535, col. 379.

Subss. (4) and (5)
    Criminal liability is restricted to the charity trustee, employee, officer or promoter who is actually responsible for issuing or signing the relevant document. The relevant provisions for charitable companies are to be found in s.68(3) and s.349(3)(4) of the Companies Act 1985. The standard levels of maximum fine on summary conviction are to be found in s.37(2) of the Criminal Justice Act 1982 and the present third level is £1,000. No prosecution may be brought without the consent of the Director of Public Prosecutions, see s.94.

Charity names

Power of Commissioners to require charity's name to be changed

6.—(1) Where this subsection applies to a charity, the Commissioners may give a direction requiring the name of the charity to be changed, within such period as is specified in the direction, to such other name as the charity trustees may determine with the approval of the Commissioners.

(2) Subsection (1) above applies to a charity if—
  (a) it is a registered charity and its name ("the registered name")—
      (i) is the same as, or
      (ii) is in the opinion of the Commissioners too like,
    the name, at the time when the registered name was entered in the register in respect of the charity, of any other charity (whether registered or not);
  (b) the name of the charity is in the opinion of the Commissioners likely to mislead the public as to the true nature—
      (i) of the purposes of the charity as set out in its trusts, or

      (ii) of the activities which the charity carries on under its trusts in pursuit of those purposes;

(c) the name of the charity includes any word or expression for the time being specified in regulations made by the Secretary of State and the inclusion in its name of that word or expression is in the opinion of the Commissioners likely to mislead the public in any respect as to the status of the charity;

(d) the name of the charity is in the opinion of the Commissioners likely to give the impression that the charity is connected in some way with Her Majesty's Government or any local authority, or with any other body of persons or any individual, when it is not so connected; or

(e) the name of the charity is in the opinion of the Commissioners offensive;

and in this subsection any reference to the name of a charity is, in relation to a registered charity, a reference to the name by which it is registered.

(3) Any direction given by virtue of subsection (2)(a) above must be given within twelve months of the time when the registered name was entered in the register in respect of the charity.

(4) Any direction given under this section with respect to a charity shall be given to the charity trustees; and on receiving any such direction the charity trustees shall give effect to it notwithstanding anything in the trusts of the charity.

(5) Where the name of any charity is changed under this section, then (without prejudice to section 3(7)(b) above) it shall be the duty of the charity trustees forthwith to notify the Commissioners of the charity's new name and of the date on which the change occurred.

(6) A change of name by a charity under this section does not affect any rights or obligations of the charity; and any legal proceedings that might have been continued or commenced by or against it in its former name may be continued or commenced by or against it in its new name.

(7) Section 26(3) of the Companies Act 1985 (minor variations in names to be disregarded) shall apply for the purposes of this section as if the reference to section 26(1)(c) of that Act were a reference to subsection (2)(a) above.

(8) Any reference in this section to the charity trustees of a charity shall, in relation to a charity which is a company, be read as a reference to the directors of the company.

(9) Nothing in this section applies to an exempt charity.

DEFINITIONS
    "charity": s.96(1).
    "charity trustees": s.97(1).
    "the Commissioners": s.97(1).
    "company": s.97(1).
    "exempt charity": s.96(1).
    "the register": s.97(1).

GENERAL NOTE
    This section re-enacts s.4 of the 1992 Act and deals with the concerns echoed in the White Paper, para. 10.17 that confusion generated by similarly named charities was being exploited by fundraisers. The section gives the Commissioners very similar powers to those of the Registrar of Companies in ss.26–29 of the Companies Act 1985, to order a change of name in specified circumstances where confusion is likely to occur. Unlike the Registrar of Companies, the Commissioners have power to order a change of name only *after* registration.

Subs. (2)
    The same. Subsection (7) applies the guidance in s.26(3) of the Companies Act 1985 which states, for example, that the definite article can be ignored when deciding whether a name is the same.

Too like. The same wording is to be found in s.28(2) of the Companies Act 1985. Guidance notes issued by the Registrar of Companies indicate, for example, that a charity whose name is phonetically identical to another charity will be "too like".

Para. (c)
The proscribed words are specified in the Charities (Misleading Names) Regulations 1992 (S.I. 1992 No. 1901).

Subs. (8)
Charitable companies can be required to change their name by both the Commissioners and the Registrar of Companies.

Effect of direction under s.6 where charity is a company

7.—(1) Where any direction is given under section 6 above with respect to a charity which is a company, the direction shall be taken to require the name of the charity to be changed by resolution of the directors of the company.

(2) Section 380 of the Companies Act 1985 (registration etc. of resolutions and agreements) shall apply to any resolution passed by the directors in compliance with any such direction.

(3) Where the name of such a charity is changed in compliance with any such direction, the registrar of companies—

(a) shall, subject to section 26 of the Companies Act 1985 (prohibition on registration of certain names), enter the new name on the register of companies in place of the former name, and

(b) shall issue a certificate of incorporation altered to meet the circumstances of the case;

and the change of name has effect from the date on which the altered certificate is issued.

DEFINITIONS
"charity": s.96(1).
"company": s.97(1).

GENERAL NOTE
This section re-enacts s.5 of the 1992 Act. Charitable companies are subject to the jurisdiction of the Commissioners and the Registrar of Companies. Thus, a change of name must be registered with the Registrar of Companies.

Subs. (3)
The corresponding provision is s.28(6) of the Companies Act 1985.

PART III

COMMISSIONERS' INFORMATION POWERS

General power to institute inquiries

8.—(1) The Commissioners may from time to time institute inquiries with regard to charities or a particular charity or class of charities, either generally or for particular purposes, but no such inquiry shall extend to any exempt charity.

(2) The Commissioners may either conduct such an inquiry themselves or appoint a person to conduct it and make a report to them.

(3) For the purposes of any such inquiry the Commissioners, or a person appointed by them to conduct it, may direct any person (subject to the provisions of this section)—

(a) to furnish accounts and statements in writing with respect to any matter in question at the inquiry, being a matter on which he has or can reasonably obtain information, or to return answers in writing to any questions or inquiries addressed to him on any such matter, and to verify any such accounts, statements or answers by statutory declaration;

(b) to furnish copies of documents in his custody or under his control which relate to any matter in question at the inquiry, and to verify any such copies by statutory declaration;

(c) to attend at a specified time and place and give evidence or produce any such documents.

(4) For the purposes of any such inquiry evidence may be taken on oath, and the person conducting the inquiry may for that purpose administer oaths, or may instead of administering an oath require the person examined to make and subscribe a declaration of the truth of the matters about which he is examined.

(5) The Commissioners may pay to any person the necessary expenses of his attendance to give evidence or produce documents for the purpose of an inquiry under this section, and a person shall not be required in obedience to a direction under paragraph (c) of subsection (3) above to go more than ten miles from his place of residence unless those expenses are paid or tendered to him.

(6) Where an inquiry has been held under this section, the Commissioners may either—

(a) cause the report of the person conducting the inquiry, or such other statement of the results of the inquiry as they think fit, to be printed and published, or

(b) publish any such report or statement in some other way which is calculated in their opinion to bring it to the attention of persons who may wish to make representations to them about the action to be taken.

(7) The council of a county or district, the Common Council of the City of London and the council of a London borough may contribute to the expenses of the Commissioners in connection with inquiries under this section into local charities in the council's area.

DEFINITIONS
"charity": s.96(1).
"the Commissioners": s.97(1).
"exempt charity": s.96(1).
"local charity": s.96(1).

GENERAL NOTE
This section re-enacts s.6 of the 1960 Act as amended by s.6 of the 1992 Act and sets out the powers of the Commissioners to conduct inquiries. An inquiry under this section is a necessary pre-condition for the Commissioners exercising their powers under s.18.

Subs. (1)
The powers of inquiry of the Commissioners are very wide and the fact that a charity is not registered under s.3 does not mean that it cannot be the subject of an inquiry. Anyone may ask for an inquiry and it may be in public or in private. Inquiries may take many forms from an exchange of letters with the trustees to an inquiry on oath (see subs. (4)).

The Commissioners may institute an inquiry to ascertain whether the property of a charity is being applied for the purposes of its trusts; this will often involve a question of law on which the person conducting the inquiry must necessarily form and express a conclusion, see *Rule* v. *Charity Commissioners for England and Wales* [1979] Ch. Comm. Rep., para. 24 *et seq.*

Subs. (2)
The person conducting the inquiry need not be a member of the Commission. An inquiry may be conducted jointly by a person appointed and a member of the Commission staff, see [1990] Ch. Comm. Rep., para. 62. The report of the person conducting the inquiry may or may not be published, see subs. (6).

On an appeal to the High Court pursuant to ss.16(12) or 18(8) against an order for the removal of a trustee made by the Commissioners following an inquiry and report made under this section, it is open to the appellant to challenge findings of fact contained in the report, but a report to the extent that it is not challenged is to be treated as evidence, see *Jones* v. *Att.-Gen.*

[1974] Ch. 148. The report is only evidence of its contents in proceedings brought by the Commissioners or the Attorney General, see s.34.

Subs. (3)

The repeal of s.6(6) of the 1960 Act by s.6(4) of the 1992 Act means that it is no longer an answer to a request for information or documents from the Commissioners to claim to be holding property adversely to a charity. As to the general duty to produce accounts, see s.42.

Document. Information recorded otherwise than in legible form, for example, on a computer disk, must be produced in legible form, see s.97(2).

Subs. (6)

The publication of the report following an inquiry under this section is a matter in the discretion of the Commissioners. The amendment made by s.6 of the 1992 Act means that the Commissioners may publish a report even if they do not propose to take any action. Details of reports following inquiries under this section are contained in the Commissioners' annual report, see, for example, [1991] Ch. Comm. Rep., para. 111 *et seq.*

Power to call for documents and search records

9.—(1) The Commissioners may by order—

(a) require any person to furnish them with any information in his possession which relates to any charity and is relevant to the discharge of their functions or of the functions of the official custodian;

(b) require any person who has in his custody or under his control any document which relates to any charity and is relevant to the discharge of their functions or of the functions of the official custodian—

(i) to furnish them with a copy of or extract from the document, or

(ii) (unless the document forms part of the records or other documents of a court or of a public or local authority) to transmit the document itself to them for their inspection.

(2) Any officer of the Commissioners, if so authorised by them, shall be entitled without payment to inspect and take copies of or extracts from the records or other documents of any court, or of any public registry or office of records, for any purpose connected with the discharge of the functions of the Commissioners or of the official custodian.

(3) The Commissioners shall be entitled without payment to keep any copy or extract furnished to them under subsection (1) above; and where a document transmitted to them under that subsection for their inspection relates only to one or more charities and is not held by any person entitled as trustee or otherwise to the custody of it, the Commissioners may keep it or may deliver it to the charity trustees or to any other person who may be so entitled.

(4) No person properly having the custody of documents relating only to an exempt charity shall be required under subsection (1) above to transmit to the Commissioners any of those documents, or to furnish any copy of or extract from any of them.

(5) The rights conferred by subsection (2) above shall, in relation to information recorded otherwise than in legible form, include the right to require the information to be made available in legible form for inspection or for a copy or extract to be made of or from it.

DEFINITIONS

"charity": s.96(1).
"charity trustees": s.97(1).
"the Commissioners": s.97(1).
"exempt charity": s.96(1).
"the official custodian": s.97(1).

GENERAL NOTE

This section re-enacts s.7 of the 1960 Act as amended by s.7 of the 1992 Act. Following the

1992 Act, the Commissioners have power to call for any information, whether or not it is in documentary form.

Subs. (1)
Document. Information recorded otherwise than in legible form, for example on computer disk, must be produced in legible form, see s.97(2).

Any breach of an order under this section is enforceable by the Commissioners through the contempt procedure under s.88.

The repeal of s.7(4) of the 1960 Act by s.7(3) of the 1992 Act means that it is no longer an answer to a request for documents from the Commissioners to claim to be holding property adversely to a charity.

Subs. (2)
The Commissioners are entitled to legible copy of any information, however recorded, see subs. (5).

Subs. (3)
As to the preservation of charity documents, see also s.30(2).

Disclosure of information to and by Commissioners

10.—(1) Subject to subsection (2) below and to any express restriction imposed by or under any other enactment, a body or person to whom this section applies may disclose to the Charity Commissioners any information received by that body or person under or for the purposes of any enactment, where the disclosure is made by the body or person for the purpose of enabling or assisting the Commissioners to discharge any of their functions.

(2) Subsection (1) above shall not have effect in relation to the Commissioners of Customs and Excise or the Commissioners of Inland Revenue; but either of those bodies of Commissioners ("the relevant body") may disclose to the Charity Commissioners the following information—

(a) the name and address of any institution which has for any purpose been treated by the relevant body as established for charitable purposes;

(b) information as to the purposes of an institution and the trusts under which it is established or regulated, where the disclosure is made by the relevant body in order to give or obtain assistance in determining whether the institution ought for any purpose to be treated as established for charitable purposes; and

(c) information with respect to an institution which has for any purpose been treated as so established but which appears to the relevant body—

(i) to be, or to have been, carrying on activities which are not charitable, or

(ii) to be, or to have been, applying any of its funds for purposes which are not charitable.

(3) In subsection (2) above, any reference to an institution shall, in relation to the Commissioners of Inland Revenue, be construed as a reference to an institution in England and Wales.

(4) Subject to subsection (5) below, the Charity Commissioners may disclose to a body or person to whom this section applies any information received by them under or for the purposes of any enactment, where the disclosure is made by the Commissioners—

(a) for any purpose connected with the discharge of their functions, and

(b) for the purpose of enabling or assisting that body or person to discharge any of its or his functions.

(5) Where any information disclosed to the Charity Commissioners under subsection (1) or (2) above is so disclosed subject to any express restriction on the disclosure of the information by the Commissioners, the Commissioners' power of disclosure under subsection (4) above shall, in relation to the information, be exercisable by them subject to any such restriction.

(6) This section applies to the following bodies and persons—

(a) any government department (including a Northern Ireland department);

(b) any local authority;

(c) any constable; and

(d) any other body or person discharging functions of a public nature (including a body or person discharging regulatory functions in relation to any description of activities).

(7) In subsection (6)(d) above the reference to any such body or person as is there mentioned shall, in relation to a disclosure by the Charity Commissioners under subsection (4) above, be construed as including a reference to any such body or person in a country or territory outside the United Kingdom.

(8) Nothing in this section shall be construed as affecting any power of disclosure exercisable apart from this section.

(9) In this section "enactment" includes an enactment comprised in subordinate legislation (within the meaning of the Interpretation Act 1978).

DEFINITIONS

"charitable purposes": s.97(1).
"the Commissioners": s.97(1).
"enactment": subs. (9).
"institution": s.97(1).

GENERAL NOTE

This section re-enacts s.52 of the 1992 Act. The Finance Act 1986 inserted s.9(3) into the 1960 Act which permitted the Inland Revenue to pass information to the Commissioners where a charity appeared to be carrying on non-charitable activities or to be applying its income for non-charitable purposes. That section was very useful in providing information to recover funds for charity, see [1987] Ch. Comm. Rep., para. 28. Following the recommendation in para. 5.26 of the White Paper, provision was made in the 1992 Act for similar arrangements between the Commissioners and other Government departments and statutory bodies to assist in their functions.

Subs. (4)

Bodies which may look to the Commissioners for information include the Department of Trade and Industry and the Serious Fraud Office.

Subs. (6)

Any other body or person discharging functions of a public nature. This phrase is very wide and can extend to a private body. Some guidance as to the application of the paragraph can be obtained from the cases on judicial review, see, for example, *R. v. Panel on Take-overs and Mergers, ex p. Datafin (Norton Opax intervening)* [1987] 1 Q.B. 815; *R. v. Advertising Standards Authority, ex p. The Insurance Service* [1990] 9 T.L.R. 169; *R. v. Disciplinary Committee of the Jockey Club, ex p. Aga Khan* [1993] 2 All E.R. 853.

Supply of false or misleading information to Commissioners, etc.

11.—(1) Any person who knowingly or recklessly provides the Commissioners with information which is false or misleading in a material particular shall be guilty of an offence if the information—

(a) is provided in purported compliance with a requirement imposed by or under this Act; or

(b) is provided otherwise than as mentioned in paragraph (a) above but in circumstances in which the person providing the information intends, or could reasonably be expected to know, that it would be used by the Commissioners for the purpose of discharging their functions under this Act.

(2) Any person who wilfully alters, suppresses, conceals or destroys any document which he is or is liable to be required, by or under this Act, to produce to the Commissioners shall be guilty of an offence.

(3) Any person guilty of an offence under this section shall be liable—

(a) on summary conviction, to a fine not exceeding the statutory maximum;

(b) on conviction on indictment, to imprisonment for a term not exceeding two years or to a fine, or both.

(4) In this section references to the Commissioners include references to any person conducting an inquiry under section 8 above.

DEFINITIONS
"the Commissioners": subs. (4); s.97(1).
"documents": s.97(2).

GENERAL NOTE
This section re-enacts s.54 of the 1992 Act and strengthens the monitoring and supervisory powers of the Commissioners by the addition of a criminal offence of supplying false or misleading information. Fears that Draconian penalties could be imposed on charity trustees may be eased by the requirement that no prosecution may be brought without the consent of the Director of Public Prosecutions, see the note to s.94.

A person who fails to supply information in the form of the annual report or annual return may be guilty of a criminal offence under s.49.

Any person who fails to comply with a direction of the Commissioners to supply information may be in contempt of court, ss.87 and 88.

Subs. (1)
Knowingly or recklessly. Knowingly usually requires proof of knowlege on the part of the offender of all the material circumstances of the offence, *i.e.* that the information was false or misleading; see, for example, *R.* v. *Hallam* [1957] 1 Q.B. 569. The requirement of recklessness will probably be satisfied if the offender, either before giving the information, fails to give any thought to the possibility of there being any risk that it may be false or misleading, or, having recognised that there was such a risk, nevertheless goes on to give it, see *R.* v. *Lawrence* [1982] A.C. 510.

It was said in the course of the debate on the 1992 Act that it was not the intention that the inadvertent provision of false information should constitute an offence, see *Hansard*, H.L. P.B.C. col. 206.

Subs. (2)
Wilfully. The adverb has been held to apply to someone who is reckless as well as someone who does a deliberate act, see *R.* v. *Sheppard* [1981] A.C. 394; *R.* v. *Gittins* [1982] R.T.R. 363.

Subs. (3)
The statutory maximum fine is to be found in s.32 of the Magistrates' Courts Act 1980 and the present maximum is £5,000. No proceedings may be instituted except with the consent of the Director of Public Prosecutions, see s.94.

Data protection

12. An order under section 30 of the Data Protection Act 1984 (exemption from subject access provisions of data held for the purpose of discharging designated functions in connection with the regulation of financial services etc.) may designate for the purposes of that section, as if they were functions conferred by or under such an enactment as is there mentioned, any functions of the Commissioners appearing to the Secretary of State to be—

(a) connected with the protection of charities against misconduct or mismanagement (whether by trustees or other persons) in their administration; or

(b) connected with the protection of the property of charities from loss or misapplication or with the recovery of such property.

DEFINITIONS
"charity": s.96(1).
"the Commissioners": s.97(1).

GENERAL NOTE
This section re-enacts s.53 of the 1992 Act. Section 30 of the Data Protection Act 1984

exempts from the subject access provisions of the Act personal data which is held for the purposes of discharging designated statutory functions in any case in which application of those provisions to the data would be likely to prejudice the proper discharge of those functions. This section adds functions of the Commissioners to those which may be designated by the Secretary of State under s.30(2) of the 1984 Act. A possible function for designation may be the collection of information about a trustee who is suspected of misconduct or mismanagement with a view to making an order under s.18, particularly as an order may be made under s.18(1) without first giving notice to the trustee under s.18(12).

PART IV

APPLICATION OF PROPERTY CY-PRÈS AND ASSISTANCE AND SUPERVISION OF CHARITIES BY COURT AND COMMISSIONERS

Extended powers of court and variation of charters

Occasions for applying property cy-près

13.—(1) Subject to subsection (2) below, the circumstances in which the original purposes of a charitable gift can be altered to allow the property given or part of it to be applied cy-près shall be as follows—
  (a) where the original purposes, in whole or in part—
      (i) have been as far as may be fulfilled; or
      (ii) cannot be carried out, or not according to the directions given and to the spirit of the gift; or
  (b) where the original purposes provide a use for part only of the property available by virtue of the gift; or
  (c) where the property available by virtue of the gift and other property applicable for similar purposes can be more effectively used in conjunction, and to that end can suitably, regard being had to the spirit of the gift, be made applicable to common purposes; or
  (d) where the original purposes were laid down by reference to an area which then was but has since ceased to be a unit for some other purpose, or by reference to a class of persons or to an area which has for any reason since ceased to be suitable, regard being had to the spirit of the gift, or to be practical in administering the gift; or
  (e) where the original purposes, in whole or in part, have, since they were laid down,—
      (i) been adequately provided for by other means; or
      (ii) ceased, as being useless or harmful to the community or for other reasons, to be in law charitable; or
      (iii) ceased in any other way to provide a suitable and effective method of using the property available by virtue of the gift, regard being had to the spirit of the gift.
(2) Subsection (1) above shall not affect the conditions which must be satisfied in order that property given for charitable purposes may be applied cy-près except in so far as those conditions require a failure of the original purposes.
  (3) References in the foregoing subsections to the original purposes of a gift shall be construed, where the application of the property given has been altered or regulated by a scheme or otherwise, as referring to the purposes for which the property is for the time being applicable.
  (4) Without prejudice to the power to make schemes in circumstances falling within subsection (1) above, the court may by scheme made under the court's jurisdiction with respect to charities, in any case where the purposes for which the property is held are laid down by reference to any such area as is mentioned in the first column in Schedule 3 to this Act, provide for enlarging the area to any such area as is mentioned in the second column in the same entry in that Schedule.

(5) It is hereby declared that a trust for charitable purposes places a trustee under a duty, where the case permits and requires the property or some part of it to be applied cy-près, to secure its effective use for charity by taking steps to enable it to be so applied.

DEFINITIONS
"charity": s.96(1).
"charitable purposes": s.97(1).
"the court": s.97(1).

GENERAL NOTE
This section re-enacts s.13 of the 1960 Act and specifies the circumstances, short of absolute failure of trust, which are required to exist before the purposes of a charity can be altered and a scheme can be made directing a *cy-près* application, and it adds to the pre-1960 circumstances. It does not enable trusts to be altered to entirely different purposes, appearing to constitute a more urgent need, so long as it remains reasonably practicable to give effect to the original trusts. Nor does it attempt to regulate the finding of suitable new purposes once it has been decided that a scheme is necessary. Whilst the limitations on the extension of the *cy-près* doctrine must be appreciated, the Commissioners endeavour to apply the doctrine in any particular case as flexibly and sensibly as possible. For the Commissioners' guidelines, see [1989] Ch. Comm. Rep., para. 73 *et seq.* By virtue of s.16(1), the Commissioners have concurrent jurisdiction with the court to direct application *cy-près*.

Subs. (1)
In this subsection are set out the occasions when property may be applied *cy-près* and it effects a considerable relaxation of the pre-1960 position. It does not require a *cy-près* scheme where none was necessary before 1960, for example, to sell land, see *Oldham Metropolitan Borough Council* v. *Att.-Gen.* [1993] 2 All E.R. 432. Prior to the 1960 Act, the principle was that if the charity could be administered according to the directions of the founder, it must be so administered even though those original trusts had become largely outdated as a result of changing circumstances or otherwise.
The original purposes. These words are applicable to the trusts of the description as a whole and not generally in relation to its respective parts, see *Lepton's Charity, Re*; *Ambler* v. *Thomas* [1972] Ch. 276, 285. The original purposes mean the purposes as amended by subsequent schemes if relevant, see subs. (3).
The spirit of the gift. This refers to the basic intention underlying the gift, the intention being ascertainable from the terms of the relevant instrument read in the light of admissible evidence, *Lepton's Charity, Re*; *Ambler* v. *Thomas* [1972] Ch. 276, 285. It seems that the reference here is to the original gift and not to any variation which there may have been previously by scheme, and that is notwithstanding subs. (3).

Para. (a)(ii)
See *Dominium Student Hall Trust, Re* [1947] Ch. 183.

Para. (b)
See *Douglas, Re* [1905] 1 Ch. 279; *King, Re* [1923] 1 Ch. 243.

Para. (c)
A consolidation of charities was possible prior to 1960, see *Faraker, Re* [1912] 2 Ch. 488. There would appear to be an overlap with the general power to make schemes under s.16.

Para. (d)
For the Commissioners' views on the extension of the area of benefit, see [1984] Ch. Comm. Rep., para. 30 and for an example of the use of this paragraph see [1989] Ch. Comm Rep., para. 80.

Para. (e)(i)
Adequately provided for by other means. This is usually where the original benefits of the trust are now provided by the statutory services of public or local authorities; see, for example, [1975] Ch. Comm. Rep., para. 54 *et seq.*

Para. (e)(ii)
For purposes ceasing to be charitable, see *National Anti-Vivisection Society* v. *I.R.C.* [1948] A.C. 31, 74 and for removal from the register, see s.3(4).

Para. (e)(iii)

This sub-paragraph provides the widest relaxation of the pre-1960 *cy-près* circumstances. For examples as to the use of this sub-paragraph, see [1985] Ch. Comm. Rep., para. 35 *et seq.* and [1986] Ch. Comm. Rep., App. B.

A stipulation as to distribution of capital is an administrative provision and not an original purpose of the gift, and so cannot be removed under this subs., but the court is not fettered by the particular condition imposed by sub-para. (iii) and can, by the exercise of its inherent jurisdiction, remove such a stipulation, see *Laing (J.W.) Trust, Re* [1984] Ch. 143, 153–155.

Subs. (5)

This subsection is declaratory of the duty of a trustee expressed by Lord Simonds in *National Anti-Vivisection Society* v. *I.R.C.* [1948] A.C. 31, 74. The duty is expressly referred to in s.6 of the Disused Burial Grounds (Amendment) Act 1981.

Application cy-près of gifts of donors unknown or disclaiming

14.—(1) Property given for specific charitable purposes which fail shall be applicable cy-près as if given for charitable purposes generally, where it belongs—

(a) to a donor who after—

    (i) the prescribed advertisements and inquiries have been published and made, and

    (ii) the prescribed period beginning with the publication of those advertisements has expired,

cannot be identified or cannot be found; or

(b) to a donor who has executed a disclaimer in the prescribed form of his right to have the property returned.

(2) Where the prescribed advertisements and inquiries have been published and made by or on behalf of trustees with respect to any such property, the trustees shall not be liable to any person in respect of the property if no claim by him to be interested in it is received by them before the expiry of the period mentioned in subsection (1)(a)(ii) above.

(3) For the purposes of this section property shall be conclusively presumed (without any advertisement or inquiry) to belong to donors who cannot be identified, in so far as it consists—

(a) of the proceeds of cash collections made by means of collecting boxes or by other means not adapted for distinguishing one gift from another; or

(b) of the proceeds of any lottery, competition, entertainment, sale or similar money-raising activity, after allowing for property given to provide prizes or articles for sale or otherwise to enable the activity to be undertaken.

(4) The court may by order direct that property not falling within subsection (3) above shall for the purposes of this section be treated (without any advertisement or inquiry) as belonging to donors who cannot be identified where it appears to the court either—

(a) that it would be unreasonable, having regard to the amounts likely to be returned to the donors, to incur expense with a view to returning the property; or

(b) that it would be unreasonable, having regard to the nature, circumstances and amounts of the gifts, and to the lapse of time since the gifts were made, for the donors to expect the property to be returned.

(5) Where property is applied cy-près by virtue of this section, the donor shall be deemed to have parted with all his interest at the time when the gift was made; but where property is so applied as belonging to donors who cannot be identified or cannot be found, and is not so applied by virtue of subsection (3) or (4) above—

(a) the scheme shall specify the total amount of that property; and

(b) the donor of any part of that amount shall be entitled, if he makes a claim not later than six months after the date on which the scheme is made, to recover from the charity for which the property is applied a sum equal to that part, less any expenses properly incurred by the charity trustees after that date in connection with claims relating to his gift; and

(c) the scheme may include directions as to the provision to be made for meeting any such claim.

(6) Where—

(a) any sum is, in accordance with any such directions, set aside for meeting any such claims, but

(b) the aggregate amount of any such claims actually made exceeds the relevant amount,

then, if the Commissioners so direct, each of the donors in question shall be entitled only to such proportion of the relevant amount as the amount of his claim bears to the aggregate amount referred to in paragraph (b) above; and for this purpose "the relevant amount" means the amount of the sum so set aside after deduction of any expenses properly incurred by the charity trustees in connection with claims relating to the donors' gifts.

(7) For the purposes of this section, charitable purposes shall be deemed to "fail" where any difficulty in applying property to those purposes makes that property or the part not applicable cy-près available to be returned to the donors.

(8) In this section "prescribed" means prescribed by regulations made by the Commissioners; and such regulations may, as respects the advertisements which are to be published for the purposes of subsection (1)(a) above, make provision as to the form and content of such advertisements as well as the manner in which they are to be published.

(9) Any regulations made by the Commissioners under this section shall be published by the Commissioners in such manner as they think fit.

(10) In this section, except in so far as the context otherwise requires, references to a donor include persons claiming through or under the original donor, and references to property given include the property for the time being representing the property originally given or property derived from it.

(11) This section shall apply to property given for charitable purposes, notwithstanding that it was so given before the commencement of this Act.

DEFINITIONS
  "charitable purposes": s.97(1).
  "the Commissioners": s.97(1).
  "the court": s.97(1).
  "donor": subs. (10).
  "prescribed": subs. (8).
  "property": subs. (10).

GENERAL NOTE
  This section re-enacts s.14 of the 1960 Act as amended by s.15 of the 1992 Act and permits property contributed by unknown or disclaiming donors for charitable purposes which fail *ab initio* to be applied *cy-près* even though the donors have not shown a general charitable intention. It thus obviates the need to pay into court to await claims by donors, see *Ulverston and District New Hospital Building Trusts, Re*; *Birkett* v. *Barrow and Furness Hospital Management Committee* [1956] Ch. 622. The section is retrospective (subs. (11)).

Subs. (1)
  As to when a gift fails, see subs. (7).
  The form of the advertisements, etc., is to be prescribed by the Commissioners (subs. (8)). The requirement for specific procedures, rather than reasonable enquiries was substituted by s.15(1) of the 1992 Act.

Subs. (2)
  This specific protection for trustees means that the trustees do not need to rely on s.27 of the Trustee Act 1925.

Subs. (4)

Although the order is to be made by the court, the court may direct that a scheme for the application *cy-près* of the property in question be made by the Commissioners.

Subs. (5)

This subsection enables a donor, or his personal representatives, who has not been traced by means of inquiries under subs. (1)(a), but not subss. (3) or (4), to come forward within six months of the date of the scheme made applying *cy-près* the property given and to recover a sum equivalent to the amount so applied, less any expenses incurred by the trustees. If too many claims are made, an individual donor may receive only a proportion of his original gift, see subs. (6).

Liability to Capital Gains Tax may be affected by the deeming of the donor to have parted with all his interest at the time the gift was made.

Charities governed by charter, or by or under statute

15.—(1) Where a Royal charter establishing or regulating a body corporate is amendable by the grant and acceptance of a further charter, a scheme relating to the body corporate or to the administration of property held by the body (including a scheme for the cy-près application of any such property) may be made by the court under the court's jurisdiction with respect to charities notwithstanding that the scheme cannot take effect without the alteration of the charter, but shall be so framed that the scheme, or such part of it as cannot take effect without the alteration of the charter, does not purport to come into operation unless or until Her Majesty thinks fit to amend the charter in such manner as will permit the scheme or that part of it to have effect.

(2) Where under the court's jurisdiction with respect to charities or the corresponding jurisdiction of a court in Northern Ireland, or under powers conferred by this Act or by any Northern Ireland legislation relating to charities, a scheme is made with respect to a body corporate, and it appears to Her Majesty expedient, having regard to the scheme, to amend any Royal charter relating to that body, Her Majesty may, on the application of that body, amend the charter accordingly by Order in Council in any way in which the charter could be amended by the grant and acceptance of a further charter; and any such Order in Council may be revoked or varied in like manner as the charter it amends.

(3) The jurisdiction of the court with respect to charities shall not be excluded or restricted in the case of a charity of any description mentioned in Schedule 4 to this Act by the operation of the enactments or instruments there mentioned in relation to that description, and a scheme established for any such charity may modify or supersede in relation to it the provision made by any such enactment or instrument as if made by a scheme of the court, and may also make any such provision as is authorised by that Schedule.

DEFINITIONS

"charity": s.96(1).
"the court": s.97(1).

GENERAL NOTE

This section re-enacts s.15 of the 1960 Act as amended to deal with the abolition of the Parliament of Northern Ireland by the Northern Ireland Constitution Act 1973 and permits amendment of charities governed by Royal Charter and empowers the court to exercise jurisdiction over certain charities governed by or under statute.

Subs. (1)

By s.16(1) the Commissioners have jurisdiction concurrent with that of the court.

Subs. (3)

The charities listed in Sched. 4 are charities governed by various statutes, for example, the Endowed Schools Acts 1869 to 1948. See s.17 with regard to the alteration of trusts regulated by statute.

Powers of Commissioners to make schemes and act for protection of charities etc.

Concurrent jurisdiction with High Court for certain purposes

16.—(1) Subject to the provisions of this Act, the Commissioners may by order exercise the same jurisdiction and powers as are exercisable by the High Court in charity proceedings for the following purposes—
(a) establishing a scheme for the administration of a charity;
(b) appointing, discharging or removing a charity trustee or trustee for a charity, or removing an officer or employee;
(c) vesting or transferring property, or requiring or entitling any person to call for or make any transfer of property or any payment.

(2) Where the court directs a scheme for the administration of a charity to be established, the court may by order refer the matter to the Commissioners for them to prepare or settle a scheme in accordance with such directions (if any) as the court sees fit to give, and any such order may provide for the scheme to be put into effect by order of the Commissioners as if prepared under subsection (1) above and without any further order of the court.

(3) The Commissioners shall not have jurisdiction under this section to try or determine the title at law or in equity to any property as between a charity or trustee for a charity and a person holding or claiming the property or an interest in it adversely to the charity, or to try or determine any question as to the existence or extent of any charge or trust.

(4) Subject to the following subsections the Commissioners shall not exercise their jurisdiction under this section as respects any charity, except—
(a) on the application of the charity; or
(b) on an order of the court under subsection (2) above; or
(c) in the case of a charity other than an exempt charity, on the application of the Attorney General.

(5) In the case of a charity which is not an exempt charity and whose income from all sources does not in aggregate exceed £500 a year, the Commissioners may exercise their jurisdiction under this section on the application—
(a) of any one or more of the charity trustees; or
(b) of any person interested in the charity; or
(c) of any two or more inhabitants of the area of the charity if it is a local charity.

(6) Where in the case of a charity, other than an exempt charity, the Commissioners are satisfied that the charity trustees ought in the interests of the charity to apply for a scheme, but have unreasonably refused or neglected to do so and the Commissioners have given the charity trustees an opportunity to make representations to them, the Commissioners may proceed as if an application for a scheme had been made by the charity but the Commissioners shall not have power in a case where they act by virtue of this subsection to alter the purposes of a charity, unless 40 years have elapsed from the date of its foundation.

(7) Where—
(a) a charity cannot apply to the Commissioners for a scheme by reason of any vacancy among the charity trustees or the absence or incapacity of any of them, but
(b) such an application is made by such number of the charity trustees as the Commissioners consider appropriate in the circumstances of the case,

the Commissioners may nevertheless proceed as if the application were an application made by the charity.

(8) The Commissioners may on the application of any charity trustee or trustee for a charity exercise their jurisdiction under this section for the purpose of discharging him from his trusteeship.

(9) Before exercising any jurisdiction under this section otherwise than on an order of the court, the Commissioners shall give notice of their intention to do so to each of the charity trustees, except any that cannot be found or has no known address in the United Kingdom or who is party or privy to an application for the exercise of the jurisdiction; and any such notice may be given by post, and, if given by post, may be addressed to the recipient's last known address in the United Kingdom.

(10) The Commissioners shall not exercise their jurisdiction under this section in any case (not referred to them by order of the court) which, by reason of its contentious character, or of any special question of law or of fact which it may involve, or for other reasons, the Commissioners may consider more fit to be adjudicated on by the court.

(11) An appeal against any order of the Commissioners under this section may be brought in the High Court by the Attorney General.

(12) An appeal against any order of the Commissioners under this section may also, at any time within the three months beginning with the day following that on which the order is published, be brought in the High Court by the charity or any of the charity trustees, or by any person removed from any office or employment by the order (unless he is removed with the concurrence of the charity trustees or with the approval of the special visitor, if any, of the charity).

(13) No appeal shall be brought under subsection (12) above except with a certificate of the Commissioners that it is a proper case for an appeal or with the leave of one of the judges of the High Court attached to the Chancery Division.

(14) Where an order of the Commissioners under this section establishes a scheme for the administration of a charity, any person interested in the charity shall have the like right of appeal under subsection (12) above as a charity trustee, and so also, in the case of a charity which is a local charity in any area, shall any two or more inhabitants of the area and the council of any parish or (in Wales) any community comprising the area or any part of it.

(15) If the Secretary of State thinks it expedient to do so—

(a) in consequence of changes in the value of money, or
(b) with a view to increasing the number of charities in respect of which the Commissioners may exercise their jurisdiction under this section in accordance with subsection (5) above,

he may by order amend that subsection by substituting a different sum for the sum for the time being specified there.

DEFINITIONS
"charity": s.96(1).
"charity trustee": s.97(1).
"the Commissioners": s.97(1).
"the court": s.97(1).
"exempt charity": s.96(1).
"local charity": s.96(1).
"trusts": s.97(1).

GENERAL NOTE
This section re-enacts s.18 of the 1960 Act as amended by s.13 of the 1992 Act and gives the Charity Commissioners concurrent jurisdiction with the court for certain purposes.

Subs. (1)
A scheme. No alteration of the purposes of a charity can be made unless the *cy-près* doctrine is satisfied, see ss.13 and 14.
As to schemes affecting charities governed by Royal Charter or by statute, see ss.15 and 17.

A scheme may alter a previous scheme, see *Att.-Gen.* v. *St. John's Hospital, Bath* (1865) 1 Ch. App. 92, 106, including one made by the court, see *Weir Hospital, Re* [1910] 2 Ch. 124, 131.

A scheme may be used to alter administrative provisions of a charity, *Laing (J.W.) Trust, Re* [1984] Ch. 143.

Where the machinery for appointing trustees has broken down, the usual procedure of the Commissioners is to make a scheme setting up new provisions for appointment rather than simply appoint new trustees. A person who disobeys an order requiring transfer of property or payment to be called for or made is punishable for contempt of court under s.88(b).

As to publicity for proceedings, see s.20.

Subs. (2)

In practice the court usually directs the making of the scheme be referred to the Commissioners.

Subs. (4)

An application by a charity needs a majority of the trustees to concur. A trustee who is not in agreement can protect himself by applying to the Commissioners for advice under s.29.

As to the circumstances in which the Commissioners may exercise their powers without an application by the charity or an order of the court, see subss. (5)(6)(7) and (8).

The power for the Attorney General to apply for a scheme was added by s.13(1) of the 1992 Act.

Subs. (5)

As to income from all sources, see s.96(4). This subsection may be used by the Commissioners if the charity itself does not take advantage of the power under s.74 to transfer property or to modify its objects or use the power under s.75 to spend capital. The £500 income limit may be increased by the Secretary of State by order under subs. (15).

Subs. (6)

As to the duty on trustees to apply for a scheme, see s.13(5). The requirement of the Commissioners to apply to the Secretary of State was removed by s.13(4) of the 1992 Act.

This subsection only allows the Commissioners to make a scheme, it gives them no power, for example, to remove trustees without an application under subs. (4).

Subs. (9)

If the Commissioners wish to act in relation to a charity or its trustees without giving notice to the trustees they must act under s.18(1) and satisfy the conditions of the subsection.

Subs. (10)

This subsection does not deprive the Commissioners of jurisdiction over contentious cases but merely enables them to decline to exercise jurisdiction where they consider that the case might be better dealt with by the court, see *Burnham National Schools, Re* (1873) 17 Eq. 241 (a case on s.5 of the Charitable Trusts Act 1860). See also s.33(3).

Subs. (11)

The Attorney General has a right of appeal to the High Court in any case without leave and without limitation of time.

Subss. (12) and (13)

By s.18(9) there is no need to apply for leave to appeal against an order for the appointment of a receiver and manager or the removal of a trustee from office made under s.18, see *Jones* v. *Att.-Gen.* [1974] Ch. 148.

An application is not to be made to the court under subss. (12) and (13) for leave to appeal against an order of the Commissioners unless the applicant has requested the Commissioners to grant a certificate that it is a proper case for an appeal and the certificate has been refused, see R.S.C., Ord. 108, r.3 and *Childs* v. *Att.-Gen.* [1973] 1 W.L.R. 497. As to the procedure on an appeal under subs. (12), see generally R.S.C., Ord. 108. In the first instance only the Attorney General should be made the respondent to an appeal; if there is a difference of views between the Attorney General and the Commissioners they can be joined later, *Jones* v. *Charity Commissioners* (Practice note) [1972] 1 W.L.R. 784.

Further powers to make schemes or alter application of charitable property

17.—(1) Where it appears to the Commissioners that a scheme should be established for the administration of a charity, but also that it is necessary or desirable for the scheme to alter the provision made by an Act of Parliament establishing or regulating the charity or to make any other provision which goes or might go beyond the powers exercisable by them apart from this section, or that it is for any reason proper for the scheme to be subject to parliamentary review, then (subject to subsection (6) below) the Commissioners may settle a scheme accordingly with a view to its being given effect under this section.

(2) A scheme settled by the Commissioners under this section may be given effect by order of the Secretary of State, and a draft of the order shall be laid before Parliament.

(3) Without prejudice to the operation of section 6 of the Statutory Instruments Act 1946 in other cases, in the case of a scheme which goes beyond the powers exercisable apart from this section in altering a statutory provision contained in or having effect under any public general Act of Parliament, the order shall not be made unless the draft has been approved by resolution of each House of Parliament.

(4) Subject to subsection (5) below, any provision of a scheme brought into effect under this section may be modified or superseded by the court or the Commissioners as if it were a scheme brought into effect by order of the Commissioners under section 16 above.

(5) Where subsection (3) above applies to a scheme, the order giving effect to it may direct that the scheme shall not be modified or superseded by a scheme brought into effect otherwise than under this section, and may also direct that that subsection shall apply to any scheme modifying or superseding the scheme to which the order gives effect.

(6) The Commissioners shall not proceed under this section without the like application and the like notice to the charity trustees, as would be required if they were proceeding (without an order of the court) under section 16 above; but on any application for a scheme, or in a case where they act by virtue of subsection (6) or (7) of that section, the Commissioners may proceed under this section or that section as appears to them appropriate.

(7) Notwithstanding anything in the trusts of a charity, no expenditure incurred in preparing or promoting a Bill in Parliament shall without the consent of the court or the Commissioners be defrayed out of any moneys applicable for the purposes of a charity but this subsection shall not apply in the case of an exempt charity.

(8) Where the Commissioners are satisfied—

(a) that the whole of the income of a charity cannot in existing circumstances be effectively applied for the purposes of the charity; and

(b) that, if those circumstances continue, a scheme might be made for applying the surplus cy-près; and

(c) that it is for any reason not yet desirable to make such a scheme;

then the Commissioners may by order authorise the charity trustees at their discretion (but subject to any conditions imposed by the order) to apply any accrued or accruing income for any purposes for which it might be made applicable by such a scheme, and any application authorised by the order shall be deemed to be within the purposes of the charity.

(9) An order under subsection (8) above shall not extend to more than £300 out of income accrued before the date of the order, nor to income accruing more than three years after that date, nor to more than £100 out of the income accruing in any of those three years.

<small>DEFINITIONS</small>
    "charity": s.96(1).
    "the Commissioners": s.97(1).
    "the court": s.97(1).

"exempt charity": s.96(1).

This section re-enacts s.19 of the 1960 Act as amended by Sched. 3, para. 7 to the 1992 Act and makes provision for the Charity Commissioners to make schemes for, or alter the provisions of, charities regulated by statute.
As to publicity for schemes, see s.20.

Subs. (1)
It would appear that the power conferred by this subsection does not enable purposes to be altered in a manner which goes beyond the *cy-près* doctrine. A scheme made under this subsection is a form of legislation and there is a presumption that legislation does not permit confiscation without compensation; a non *cy-près* scheme would amount to confiscation from those entitled under the original trusts and any permissible *cy-près* variation thereof. For an example of a scheme under this subsection, see [1988] Ch. Comm. Rep., para. 66 (the Charities (University of Liverpool) Order 1988 (S.I. 1988 No. 1068)).

Subs. (3)
In other cases, for example where the provision altered is contained in a Private Act, a copy of the order must lie before each House of Parliament for 40 days and the order will thereafter be effective unless in the meantime either House shall have resolved that it should not be made (Statutory Instruments Act 1946, s.6(1)).

Subs. (4)
See s.16(1) and note the limitation in subs. (5).

Subs. (6)
The like application. See s.16(4)(a).
Like notice. See s.16(9).
It is for the Commissioners to decide whether there is jurisdiction to proceed under s.16 or whether resort should be had to the procedure of this section.

Power to act for protection of charities

18.—(1) Where, at any time after they have instituted an inquiry under section 8 above with respect to any charity, the Commissioners are satisfied—

(a) that there is or has been any misconduct or mismanagement in the administration of the charity; or

(b) that it is necessary or desirable to act for the purpose of protecting the property of the charity or securing a proper application for the purposes of the charity of that property or of property coming to the charity,

the Commissioners may of their own motion do one or more of the following things—

(i) by order suspend any trustee, charity trustee, officer, agent or employee of the charity from the exercise of his office or employment pending consideration being given to his removal (whether under this section or otherwise);

(ii) by order appoint such number of additional charity trustees as they consider necessary for the proper administration of the charity;

(iii) by order vest any property held by or in trust for the charity in the official custodian, or require the persons in whom any such property is vested to transfer it to him, or appoint any person to transfer any such property to him;

(iv) order any person who holds any property on behalf of the charity, or of any trustee for it, not to part with the property without the approval of the Commissioners;

(v) order any debtor of the charity not to make any payment in or towards the discharge of his liability to the charity without the approval of the Commissioners;

(vi) by order restrict (notwithstanding anything in the trusts of the charity) the transactions which may be entered into, or the nature or amount of the payments which may be made, in the administration of the charity without the approval of the Commissioners;

(vii) by order appoint (in accordance with section 19 below) a receiver and manager in respect of the property and affairs of the charity.

(2) Where, at any time after they have instituted an inquiry under section 8 above with respect to any charity, the Commissioners are satisfied—

(a) that there is or has been any misconduct or mismanagement in the administration of the charity; and

(b) that it is necessary or desirable to act for the purpose of protecting the property of the charity or securing a proper application for the purposes of the charity of that property or of property coming to the charity,

the Commissioners may of their own motion do either or both of the following things—

(i) by order remove any trustee, charity trustee, officer, agent or employee of the charity who has been responsible for or privy to the misconduct or mismanagement or has by his conduct contributed to it or facilitated it;

(ii) by order establish a scheme for the administration of the charity.

(3) The references in subsection (1) or (2) above to misconduct or mismanagement shall (notwithstanding anything in the trusts of the charity) extend to the employment for the remuneration or reward of persons acting in the affairs of the charity, or for other administrative purposes, of sums which are excessive in relation to the property which is or is likely to be applied or applicable for the purposes of the charity.

(4) The Commissioners may also remove a charity trustee by order made of their own motion—

(a) where, within the last five years, the trustee—

(i) having previously been adjudged bankrupt or had his estate sequestrated, has been discharged, or

(ii) having previously made a composition or arrangement with, or granted a trust deed for, his creditors, has been discharged in respect of it;

(b) where the trustee is a corporation in liquidation;

(c) where the trustee is incapable of acting by reason of mental disorder within the meaning of the Mental Health Act 1983;

(d) where the trustee has not acted, and will not declare his willingness or unwillingness to act;

(e) where the trustee is outside England and Wales or cannot be found or does not act, and his absence or failure to act impedes the proper administration of the charity.

(5) The Commissioners may by order made of their own motion appoint a person to be a charity trustee—

(a) in place of a charity trustee removed by them under this section or otherwise;

(b) where there are no charity trustees, or where by reason of vacancies in their number or the absence or incapacity of any of their number the charity cannot apply for the appointment;

(c) where there is a single charity trustee, not being a corporation aggregate, and the Commissioners are of opinion that it is necessary to increase the number for the proper administration of the charity;

(d) where the Commissioners are of opinion that it is necessary for the proper administration of the charity to have an additional charity trustee because one of the existing charity trustees who ought nevertheless to remain a charity trustee either cannot be found or does not act or is outside England and Wales.

(6) The powers of the Commissioners under this section to remove or appoint charity trustees of their own motion shall include power to make any such order with respect to the vesting in or transfer to the charity trustees of any property as the Commissioners could make on the removal or appointment of a charity trustee by them under section 16 above.

(7) Any order under this section for the removal or appointment of a charity trustee or trustee for a charity, or for the vesting or transfer of any property, shall be of the like effect as an order made under section 16 above.

(8) Subject to subsection (9) below, subsections (11) to (13) of section 16 above shall apply to orders under this section as they apply to orders under that section.

(9) The requirement to obtain any such certificate or leave as is mentioned in section 16(13) above shall not apply to—

(a) an appeal by a charity or any of the charity trustees of a charity against an order under subsection (1)(vii) above appointing a receiver and manager in respect of the charity's property and affairs, or

(b) an appeal by a person against an order under subsection (2)(i) or (4)(a) above removing him from his office or employment.

(10) Subsection (14) of section 16 above shall apply to an order under this section which establishes a scheme for the administration of a charity as it applies to such an order under that section.

(11) The power of the Commissioners to make an order under subsection (1)(i) above shall not be exercisable so as to suspend any person from the exercise of his office or employment for a period of more than 12 months; but (without prejudice to the generality of section 89(1) below), any such order made in the case of any person may make provision as respects the period of his suspension for matters arising out of it, and in particular for enabling any person to execute any instrument in his name or otherwise act for him and, in the case of a charity trustee, for adjusting any rules governing the proceedings of the charity trustees to take account of the reduction in the number capable of acting.

(12) Before exercising any jurisdiction under this section otherwise than by virtue of subsection (1) above, the Commissioners shall give notice of their intention to do so to each of the charity trustees, except any that cannot be found or has no known address in the United Kingdom; and any such notice may be given by post and, if given by post, may be addressed to the recipient's last known address in the United Kingdom.

(13) The Commissioners shall, at such intervals as they think fit, review any order made by them under paragraph (i), or any of paragraphs (iii) to (vii), of subsection (1) above; and, if on any such review it appears to them that it would be appropriate to discharge the order in whole or in part, they shall so discharge it (whether subject to any savings or other transitional provisions or not).

(14) If any person contravenes an order under subsection (1)(iv), (v) or (vi) above, he shall be guilty of an offence and liable on summary conviction to a fine not exceeding level 5 on the standard scale.

(15) Subsection (14) above shall not be taken to preclude the bringing of proceedings for breach of trust against any charity trustee or trustee for a charity in respect of a contravention of an order under subsection (1)(iv) or (vi) above (whether proceedings in respect of the contravention are brought against him under subsection (14) above or not).

(16) This section shall not apply to an exempt charity.

DEFINITIONS
   "charity": s.96(1).
   "charity trustees": s.97(1).
   "the Commissioners": s.97(1).
   "exempt charity": s.96(1).
   "the official custodian": s.97(1).

GENERAL NOTE

This section re-enacts s.20 of the 1960 Act as amended by s.8 of the 1992 Act and sets out the powers of the Commissioners to act for the protection of charities. Following the 1992 Act, the Commissioners are still required to hold a s.8 inquiry before acting to prevent abuse but only misconduct or mismanagement *or* the desirability to protect charity property has to be shown before the temporary and protective powers in subs. (1) can be exercised; both conditions have to be fulfilled before the remedial and permanent powers in subs. (2) can be exercised.

Subs. (1)

Para. (i)

The suspension may not be for more than 12 months, see subs. (11).

Para. (ii)

Cf. the more limited power to appoint additional trustees without a s.8 inquiry under subs. (5).

Para. (iii)

Any property, not merely land, may be vested in the official custodian, see the note to s.2. Charity trustees' powers in respect of land vested in the official custodian under this paragraph are restricted, see s.22(3).

Paras. (iv), (v) and (vi)

Breach of an order of the Commissioners under any of these paragraphs is a criminal offence, subs. (14).

Para. (vii)

For the circumstances in which the court has appointed a receiver, see *Att.-Gen.* v. *Schonfield* [1988] 1 W.L.R. 1182. See also s.9 for the supplementary provisions relating to an appointment. The Commissioners are not obliged to notify the charity trustees before making an order under this subsection, subs. (12).

Subs. (2)

The power to establish a scheme was added by s.8(2) of the 1992 Act. The Commissioners must give charity trustees notice before making an order under this subsection, subs. (12).

Subs. (3)

For controls on fundraising and remuneration therefor, see ss.58–64 of the 1992 Act.

Subs. (4)

Mental disorder. See the Mental Health Act 1983, s.1.

For trustees who are disqualified and thus do not need to be removed, see s.72.

The Commissioners must give charity trustees notice before making an order under this subsection, subs. (12).

Subs. (5)

For an example of the exercise of this power, see [1991] Ch. Comm. Rep., para. 129.

Subss. (6) and (7)

See s.16 and the notes thereto.

A person who disobeys an order requiring transfer of property is punishable for contempt of court, s.88.

Subs. (8)

Section 16(11)–(13) relates to appeals.

Subs. (9)

Although a charity trustee does not need leave to appeal against an order removing him from office, it is for him to show that the order was wrongly made. Where there has been an inquiry and a report, the report, to the extent that it is not challenged by the appellant, should be treated as evidence in the appeal, see *Jones* v. *Att.-Gen.* [1974] Ch. 148, 162.

Subs. (10)

Section 16(14) relates to appeals.

Subs. (14)

The offence relates to transfer of property and freezing orders. The standard levels of maximum fine on summary conviction are to be found in s.37(2) of the Criminal Justice Act 1982 and the present fifth level of fine is £5,000. The consent of the Director of Public Prosecutions is required before any proceedings may be brought under this subsection (s.94). See also the notes to subss. (6) and (7).

Supplementary provisions relating to receiver and manager appointed for a charity

19.—(1) The Commissioners may under section 18(1)(vii) above appoint to be receiver and manager in respect of the property and affairs of a charity such person (other than an officer or employee of theirs) as they think fit.

(2) Without prejudice to the generality of section 89(1) below, any order made by the Commissioners under section 18(1)(vii) above may make provision with respect to the functions to be discharged by the receiver and manager appointed by the order; and those functions shall be discharged by him under the supervision of the Commissioners.

(3) In connection with the discharge of those functions any such order may provide—

    (a) for the receiver and manager appointed by the order to have such powers and duties of the charity trustees of the charity concerned (whether arising under this Act or otherwise) as are specified in the order;

    (b) for any powers or duties exercisable or falling to be performed by the receiver and manager by virtue of paragraph (a) above to be exercisable or performed by him to the exclusion of those trustees.

(4) Where a person has been appointed receiver and manager by any such order—

    (a) section 29 below shall apply to him and to his functions as a person so appointed as it applies to a charity trustee of the charity concerned and to his duties as such; and

    (b) the Commissioners may apply to the High Court for directions in relation to any particular matter arising in connection with the discharge of those functions.

(5) The High Court may on an application under subsection (4)(b) above—

    (a) give such directions, or

    (b) make such orders declaring the rights of any persons (whether before the court or not),

as it thinks just; and the costs of any such application shall be paid by the charity concerned.

(6) Regulations made by the Secretary of State may make provision with respect to—

    (a) the appointment and removal of persons appointed in accordance with this section;

    (b) the remuneration of such persons out of the income of the charities concerned;

    (c) the making of reports to the Commissioners by such persons.

(7) Regulations under subsection (6) above may, in particular, authorise the Commissioners—

    (a) to require security for the due discharge of his functions to be given by a person so appointed;

    (b) to determine the amount of such a person's remuneration;

    (c) to disallow any amount of remuneration in such circumstances as are prescribed by the regulations.

DEFINITIONS
"charity": s.96(1).

"charity trustees": s.97(1).
"the Commissioners": s.97(1).

GENERAL NOTE

This section re-enacts s.20A of the 1960 Act inserted by s.9 of the 1992 Act and provides supplementary provisions relating to the appointment of a receiver and manager under s.18(1)(vii).

Subs. (2)

Section 89 gives the Commissioners power to include such incidental and supplementary provisions as they think expedient in any order they may make.

Subs. (4)

Section 29 empowers the Commissioners to give advice to charity trustees and protects charity trustees who act in accordance with such advice.

Publicity for proceedings under ss.16 to 18

20.—(1) The Commissioners shall not make any order under this Act to establish a scheme for the administration of a charity, or submit such a scheme to the court or the Secretary of State for an order giving it effect, unless not less than one month previously there has been given public notice of their proposals, inviting representations to be made to them within a time specified in the notice, being not less than one month from the date of such notice, and, in the case of a scheme relating to a local charity, other than an ecclesiastical charity, in a parish or (in Wales) a community, a draft of the scheme has been communicated to the parish or community council or, in the case of a parish not having a council, to the chairman of the parish meeting.

(2) The Commissioners shall not make any order under this Act to appoint, discharge or remove a charity trustee or trustee for a charity (other than the official custodian), unless not less than one month previously there has been given the like public notice as is required by subsection (1) above for an order establishing a scheme but this subsection shall not apply in the case of—

    (a) an order under section 18(1)(ii) above; or

    (b) an order discharging or removing a trustee if the Commissioners are of opinion that it is unnecessary and not in his interest to give publicity to the proposal to discharge or remove him.

(3) Before the Commissioners make an order under this Act to remove without his consent a charity trustee or trustee for a charity, or an officer, agent or employee of a charity, the Commissioners shall, unless he cannot be found or has no known address in the United Kingdom, give him not less than one month's notice of their proposal, inviting representations to be made to them within a time specified in the notice.

(4) Where notice is given of any proposals as required by subsections (1) to (3) above, the Commissioners shall take into consideration any representations made to them about the proposals within the time specified in the notice, and may (without further notice) proceed with the proposals either without modification or with such modifications as appear to them to be desirable.

(5) Where the Commissioners make an order which is subject to appeal under subsection (12) of section 16 above the order shall be published either by giving public notice of it or by giving notice of it to all persons entitled to appeal against it under that subsection, as the Commissioners think fit.

(6) Where the Commissioners make an order under this Act to establish a scheme for the administration of a charity, a copy of the order shall, for not less than one month after the order is published, be available for public inspection at all reasonable times at the Commissioners' office and also at some convenient place in the area of the charity, if it is a local charity.

(7) Any notice to be given under this section of any proposals or order shall give such particulars of the proposals or order, or such directions for obtaining information about them, as the Commissioners think sufficient and appropriate, and any public notice shall be given in such manner as they think sufficient and appropriate.

(8) Any notice to be given under this section, other than a public notice, may be given by post and, if given by post, may be addressed to the recipient's last known address in the United Kingdom.

DEFINITIONS
    "charity": s.96(1).
    "charity trustees": s.97(1).
    "the Commissioners": s.97(1).
    "the court": s.97(1).
    "ecclesiastical charity": s.96(1).
    "local charity": s.96(1).
    "the official custodian": s.97(1).

GENERAL NOTE
    This section re-enacts s.21 of the 1960 Act as amended to take account of local government re-organisation and makes provision for due publicity to be given to the exercise by the Commissioners of their powers under ss.16, 17 and 18. It is applied in relation to schemes made under s.4(1) of the Redundant Church and Other Religious Buildings Act 1969, by s.4(4) of that Act and to schemes amending the provisions regulating certain coal industry trusts by the Coal Industry Act 1987, s.5(8).

Subss. (1) and (2)
    The mode of publication is left to the discretion of the Commissioners (subs. (7)), whose normal practice is simply to ask for publication on a public notice board in the locality. In *Berkhamsted Grammar School, Re* [1908] 2 Ch. 25, 49 Warrington J. expressed the view that failure to send a draft of the scheme relating to a local charity to the parish council or parish meeting would not invalidate the scheme.
    Month. This is defined in the Interpretation Act 1978, s.5 and Sched. 1 as 'calendar month'. Where notice is given in months, the period of notice ends on the day of the month bearing the same number as that on which the notice is given, February being an exception, see *Dodds* v. *Walker* [1981] 1 W.L.R. 1027.
    As to the general power of the Commissioners to give or require some other person to give notice of the making or contents of orders, see s.89(2).

Subs. (4)
    The Commissioners should not take into consideration representations made to them after the specified time has expired, see *Errington* v. *Minister of Health* [1935] 1 K.B. 249.

Subs. (5)
    As to public notice, see the note to subss. (1) and (2); see also subs. (7).

Property vested in official custodian

Entrusting charity property to official custodian, and termination of trust

    21.—(1) The court may by order—
    (a) vest in the official custodian any land held by or in trust for a charity;
    (b) authorise or require the persons in whom any such land is vested to transfer it to him; or
    (c) appoint any person to transfer any such land to him;
but this subsection does not apply to any interest in land by way of mortgage or other security.

    (2) Where property is vested in the official custodian in trust for a charity, the court may make an order discharging him from the trusteeship as respects all or any of that property.

    (3) Where the official custodian is discharged from his trusteeship of any property, or the trusts on which he holds any property come to an end, the

court may make such vesting orders and give such directions as may seem to the court to be necessary or expedient in consequence.

(4) No person shall be liable for any loss occasioned by his acting in conformity with an order under this section or by his giving effect to anything done in pursuance of such an order, or be excused from so doing by reason of the order having been in any respect improperly obtained.

DEFINITIONS
    "charity": s.96(1).
    "the court": s.97(1).
    "the official custodian": s.97(1).
    "trusts": s.97(1).

GENERAL NOTE
    This section re-enacts s.16 of the 1960 Act as amended by Sched. 3, para. 4 to the 1992 Act to take account of the divestment of property, other than land, by the official custodian, see the note to s.2.
    For supplementary provisions, see s.22.

Subs. (1)
    An order either vesting the land in the official custodian or authorising or requiring persons to transfer it to her, is essential. A conveyance to her on its own is not sufficient.

Subs. (3)
    The Commissioners have power to discharge the official custodian as a "trustee for charity" under s.16(1)(b) and would appear to have concurrent jurisdiction with the court to make consequential vesting orders under s.16(1)(c).

Supplementary provisions as to property vested in official custodian

22.—(1) Subject to the provisions of this Act, where property is vested in the official custodian in trust for a charity, he shall not exercise any powers of management, but he shall as trustee of any property have all the same powers, duties and liabilities, and be entitled to the same rights and immunities, and be subject to the control and orders of the court, as a corporation appointed custodian trustee under section 4 of the Public Trustee Act 1906 except that he shall have no power to charge fees.

(2) Subject to subsection (3) below, where any land is vested in the official custodian in trust for a charity, the charity trustees shall have power in his name and on his behalf to execute and do all assurances and things which they could properly execute or do in their own name and on their own behalf if the land were vested in them.

(3) If any land is so vested in the official custodian by virtue of an order under section 18 above, the power conferred on the charity trustees by subsection (2) above shall not be exercisable by them in relation to any transaction affecting the land, unless the transaction is authorised by order of the court or of the Commissioners.

(4) Where any land is vested in the official custodian in trust for a charity, the charity trustees shall have the like power to make obligations entered into by them binding on the land as if it were vested in them; and any covenant, agreement or condition which is enforceable by or against the custodian by reason of the land being vested in him shall be enforceable by or against the charity trustees as if the land were vested in them.

(5) In relation to a corporate charity, subsections (2), (3) and (4) above shall apply with the substitution of references to the charity for references to the charity trustees.

(6) Subsections (2), (3) and (4) above shall not authorise any charity trustees or charity to impose any personal liability on the official custodian.

(7) Where the official custodian is entitled as trustee for a charity to the custody of securities or documents of title relating to the trust property, he

may permit them to be in the possession or under the control of the charity trustees without thereby incurring any liability.

DEFINITIONS
    "charity": s.96(1).
    "charity trustees": s.97(1).
    "the Commissioners": s.97(1).
    "the court": s.97(1).
    "the official custodian": s.97(1).

GENERAL NOTE
    This section re-enacts s.17 of the 1960 Act as amended by Sched. 3, para. 5 to the 1992 Act and contains supplementary provisions as to property vested in the official custodian, see s.21.

Subs. (1)
    This subsection makes clear that the function of the official custodian is that of a holding trustee, the powers of management being vested in the charity trustees; but it assimilates the position of the official custodian to that of a custodian trustee under the Public Trustee Act 1960, s.4, except that the official custodian may not charge fees, and a custodian trustee is not a bare trustee, see *Brooke Bond & Co.'s Trust Deed, Re*; *Brooke* v. *Brooke Bond & Co.* [1963] Ch. 357.

Subs. (2)
    As to when charity trustees may properly deal with land, see ss.36 to 39 and the notes thereto. Any land transaction entered into by the charity trustees must not involve the official custodian in personal liability (subs. (6)).

Subs. (3)
    This subsection ensures that land vested in the official custodian, following an order under s.18(1)(iii), is retained for the charity.

Subs. (4)
    Whilst this subsection permits the charity trustees to bind the charity property without the consent of the official custodian, they may not involve her in personal liability (subs. (6)).

Divestment in the case of land subject to Reverter of Sites Act 1987

    23.—(1) Where—
    (a) any land is vested in the official custodian in trust for a charity, and
    (b) it appears to the Commissioners that section 1 of the Reverter of Sites
        Act 1987 (right of reverter replaced by trust for sale) will, or is likely
        to, operate in relation to the land at a particular time or in particular
        circumstances,
the jurisdiction which, under section 16 above, is exercisable by the Commissioners for the purpose of discharging a trustee for a charity may, at any time before section 1 of that Act ("the 1987 Act") operates in relation to the land, be exercised by them of their own motion for the purpose of—
    (i) making an order discharging the official custodian from his trusteeship of the land, and
    (ii) making such vesting orders and giving such directions as appear to them to be necessary or expedient in consequence.
    (2) Where—
    (a) section 1 of the 1987 Act has operated in relation to any land which, immediately before the time when that section so operated, was vested in the official custodian in trust for a charity, and
    (b) the land remains vested in him but on the trust arising under that section,
the court or the Commissioners (of their own motion) may—
    (i) make an order discharging the official custodian from his trusteeship of the land, and
    (ii) (subject to the following provisions of this section) make such vesting

orders and give such directions as appear to it or them to be necessary or expedient in consequence.

(3) Where any order discharging the official custodian from his trusteeship of any land—

(a) is made by the court under section 21(2) above, or by the Commissioners under section 16 above, on the grounds that section 1 of the 1987 Act will, or is likely to, operate in relation to the land, or

(b) is made by the court or the Commissioners under subsection (2) above,

the persons in whom the land is to be vested on the discharge of the official custodian shall be the relevant charity trustees (as defined in subsection (4) below), unless the court or (as the case may be) the Commissioners is or are satisfied that it would be appropriate for it to be vested in some other persons.

(4) In subsection (3) above "the relevant charity trustees" means—

(a) in relation to an order made as mentioned in paragraph (a) of that subsection, the charity trustees of the charity in trust for which the land is vested in the official custodian immediately before the time when the order takes effect, or

(b) in relation to an order made under subsection (2) above, the charity trustees of the charity in trust for which the land was vested in the official custodian immediately before the time when section 1 of the 1987 Act operated in relation to the land.

(5) Where—

(a) section 1 of the 1987 Act has operated in relation to any such land as is mentioned in subsection (2)(a) above, and

(b) the land remains vested in the official custodian as mentioned in subsection (2)(b) above,

then (subject to subsection (6) below), all the powers, duties and liabilities that would, apart from this section, be those of the official custodian as trustee for sale of the land shall instead be those of the charity trustees of the charity concerned; and those trustees shall have power in his name and on his behalf to execute and do all assurances and things which they could properly execute or do in their own name and on their own behalf if the land were vested in them.

(6) Subsection (5) above shall not be taken to require or authorise those trustees to sell the land at a time when it remains vested in the official custodian.

(7) Where—

(a) the official custodian has been discharged from his trusteeship of any land by an order under subsection (2) above, and

(b) the land has, in accordance with subsection (3) above, been vested in the charity trustees concerned or (as the case may be) in any persons other than those trustees,

the land shall be held by those trustees, or (as the case may be) by those persons, as trustees for sale on the terms of the trust arising under section 1 of the 1987 Act.

(8) The official custodian shall not be liable to any person in respect of any loss or misapplication of any land vested in him in accordance with that section unless it is occasioned by or through any wilful neglect or default of his or of any person acting for him; but the Consolidated Fund shall be liable to make good to any person any sums for which the official custodian may be liable by reason of any such neglect or default.

(9) In this section any reference to section 1 of the 1987 Act operating in relation to any land is a reference to a trust for sale arising in relation to the land under that section.

DEFINITIONS
"charity": s.96(1).

"charity trustees": s.97(1).
"the Commissioners": s.97(1).
"the official custodian": s.97(1).
"the 1987 Act": subs. (1).

GENERAL NOTE

This section re-enacts s.31 of the 1992 Act. Section 1 of the Reverter of Sites Act 1987 abolished the right of reverter where land had been held for specific charitable purposes and substituted a trust for sale. On failure of the charitable purpose, the land remains vested in the persons in whom it was vested at that time but to be held on the trust for sale set out in the 1987 Act. It is clearly inconsistent with the very reduced functions of the official custodian that she should continue to hold land for purposes which are not charitable and on a trust which is not only active but which can also be problematic. Accordingly, the section makes provision for such property to be transferred from the official custodian to the persons who were trustees of the charity immediately before the specific charitable purpose ceased or who are the trustees when the vesting order is made if no reverter has occurred. For discussion of the 1987 Act, see D. Evans, "*Reverter of Sites Act 1987*" [1987] Conv. 408.

Establishment of common investment or deposit funds

Schemes to establish common investment funds

24.—(1) The court or the Commissioners may by order make and bring into effect schemes (in this section referred to as "common investment schemes") for the establishment of common investment funds under trusts which provide—

(a) for property transferred to the fund by or on behalf of a charity participating in the scheme to be invested under the control of trustees appointed to manage the fund; and

(b) for the participating charities to be entitled (subject to the provisions of the scheme) to the capital and income of the fund in shares determined by reference to the amount or value of the property transferred to it by or on behalf of each of them and to the value of the fund at the time of the transfers.

(2) The court or the Commissioners may make a common investment scheme on the application of any two or more charities.

(3) A common investment scheme may be made in terms admitting any charity to participate, or the scheme may restrict the right to participate in any manner.

(4) A common investment scheme may make provision for, and for all matters connected with, the establishment, investment, management and winding up of the common investment fund, and may in particular include provision—

(a) for remunerating persons appointed trustees to hold or manage the fund or any part of it, with or without provision authorising a person to receive the remuneration notwithstanding that he is also a charity trustee of or trustee for a participating charity;

(b) for restricting the size of the fund, and for regulating as to time, amount or otherwise the right to transfer property to or withdraw it from the fund, and for enabling sums to be advanced out of the fund by way of loan to a participating charity pending the withdrawal of property from the fund by the charity;

(c) for enabling income to be withheld from distribution with a view to avoiding fluctuations in the amounts distributed, and generally for regulating distributions of income;

(d) for enabling money to be borrowed temporarily for the purpose of meeting payments to be made out of the funds;

(e) for enabling questions arising under the scheme as to the right of a charity to participate, or as to the rights of participating charities, or as to any other matter, to be conclusively determined by the decision of the trustees managing the fund or in any other manner;

(f) for regulating the accounts and information to be supplied to participating charities.

(5) A common investment scheme, in addition to the provision for property to be transferred to the fund on the basis that the charity shall be entitled to a share in the capital and income of the fund, may include provision for enabling sums to be deposited by or on behalf of a charity on the basis that (subject to the provisions of the scheme) the charity shall be entitled to repayment of the sums deposited and to interest thereon at a rate determined by or under the scheme; and where a scheme makes any such provision it shall also provide for excluding from the amount of capital and income to be shared between charities participating otherwise than by way of deposit such amounts (not exceeding the amounts properly attributable to the making of deposits) as are from time to time reasonably required in respect of the liabilities of the fund for the repayment of deposits and for the interest on deposits, including amounts required by way of reserve.

(6) Except in so far as a common investment scheme provides to the contrary, the rights under it of a participating charity shall not be capable of being assigned or charged, nor shall any trustee or other person concerned in the management of the common investment fund be required or entitled to take account of any trust or other equity affecting a participating charity or its property or rights.

(7) The powers of investment of every charity shall include power to participate in common investment schemes unless the power is excluded by a provision specifically referring to common investment schemes in the trusts of the charity.

(8) A common investment fund shall be deemed for all purposes to be a charity; and if the scheme admits only exempt charities, the fund shall be an exempt charity for the purposes of this Act.

(9) Subsection (8) above shall apply not only to common investment funds established under the powers of this section, but also to any similar fund established for the exclusive benefit of charities by or under any enactment relating to any particular charities or class of charity.

DEFINITIONS
   "charity": s.96(1).
   "the Commissioners": s.97(1).
   "the court": s.97(1).
   "exempt charity": s.96(1).

GENERAL NOTE
   This section re-enacts s.22 of the 1960 Act as amended by Sched. 3, para. 9 to the 1992 Act to take account of divestment by the official custodian (see the note to s.2) and makes provision for the establishment of common investment funds by scheme. The Charity Commissioners are very concerned to encourage investment in common investment funds, particularly for small charities following divestment by the official custodian, see [1989] Ch. Comm. Rep., para. 111 *et seq.*

   The Charities Official Investment Fund was established by scheme in 1962. The C.O.I.F. Charities Fixed Interest and Deposit Fund was established by scheme in 1989, see [1989] Ch. Comm. Rep., para. 122.

   Sums of money contributed to common investment funds do not come within the definition of deposit in s.5(1) of the Banking Act 1987 so that such a fund is able to accept deposits for the purpose of common investment without having to become an authorised institution within the meaning of s.3(1) of that Act.

Subs. (1)
   Manage. A person appointed as manager is an exempt person for the purposes of the Financial Services Act 1986 s.3 (see s.45(1)(j) of that Act).

   The entitlement of the charity to the capital and income in the common investment fund is calculated not by reference to any par value of contributions made to the fund, but by reference to the relative value between contributions made by the charity and the total amount of the fund at the date of the contribution, the valuation being based not on par value but on the actual value whether the market value or assessed in some other way.

Subs. (2)
Any two or more charities. The application may be made by trustees of any two or more charitable trusts and it is immaterial that the trustees are in each case the same persons, *London University's Charitable Trusts, Re* [1964] Ch. 282.

Subs. (5)
A completely separate deposit fund cannot be created under this subsection, see [1989] Ch. Comm. Rep., para. 31. There is power to create a common deposit fund under s.25.

Subs. (7)
This subsection has the effect of extending, so far as charitable trusts are concerned, the range of trustee investments specified in s.1 of and Sched. 1 to the Trustee Investment Act 1961. See also ss.70 and 71 for the widening of investment powers.

Schemes to establish common deposit funds

25.—(1) The court or the Commissioners may by order make and bring into effect schemes (in this section referred to as "common deposit schemes") for the establishment of common deposit funds under trusts which provide—
   (a) for sums to be deposited by or on behalf of a charity participating in the scheme and invested under the control of trustees appointed to manage the fund; and
   (b) for any such charity to be entitled (subject to the provisions of the scheme) to repayment of any sums so deposited and to interest thereon at a rate determined under the scheme.

(2) Subject to subsection (3) below, the following provisions of section 24 above, namely—
   (a) subsections (2) to (4), and
   (b) subsections (6) to (9),
shall have effect in relation to common deposit schemes and common deposit funds as they have effect in relation to common investment schemes and common investment funds.

(3) In its application in accordance with subsection (2) above, subsection (4) of that section shall have effect with the substitution for paragraphs (b) and (c) of the following paragraphs—
   "(b) for regulating as to time, amount or otherwise the right to repayment of sums deposited in the fund;
   (c) for authorising a part of the income for any year to be credited to a reserve account maintained for the purpose of counteracting any losses accruing to the fund, and generally for regulating the manner in which the rate of interest on deposits is to be determined from time to time;".

DEFINITIONS
   "charity": s.96(1).
   "the Commissioners": s.97(1).

GENERAL NOTE
   This section re-enacts s.22A of the 1960 Act which was inserted by s.16 of the 1992 Act and provides for the setting up of common deposit funds unconnected to common investment funds, see the note to s.24(5). The provisions follow closely those relating to common investment funds in s.24.

Subs. (2)
   Common deposit funds are made subject to the same provisions as common investment funds; thus a scheme may only be made on the application of two or more charities although the trustees may be the same (*London University's Charitable Trusts, Re* [1964] Ch. 282). The scheme may be for any charity or may restrict the right to participate and should contain detailed provisions as to matters set out in s.24(4), including the remuneration of trustees and the right to borrow. By s.24(7) all charities now have power to participate in common deposit

funds. If all the participating charities are exempt, by s.24(8), the common deposit fund will be an exempt charity.

Additional powers of Commissioners

Power to authorise dealings with charity property etc.

26.—(1) Subject to the provisions of this section, where it appears to the Commissioners that any action proposed or contemplated in the administration of a charity is expedient in the interests of the charity, they may by order sanction that action, whether or not it would otherwise be within the powers exercisable by the charity trustees in the administration of the charity; and anything done under the authority of such an order shall be deemed to be properly done in the exercise of those powers.

(2) An order under this section may be made so as to authorise a particular transaction, compromise or the like, or a particular application of property, or so as to give a more general authority, and (without prejudice to the generality of subsection (1) above) may authorise a charity to use common premises, or employ a common staff, or otherwise combine for any purpose of administration, with any other charity.

(3) An order under this section may give directions as to the manner in which any expenditure is to be borne and as to other matters connected with or arising out of the action thereby authorised; and where anything is done in pursuance of an authority given by any such order, any directions given in connection therewith shall be binding on the charity trustees for the time being as if contained in the trusts of the charity; but any such directions may on the application of the charity be modified or superseded by a further order.

(4) Without prejudice to the generality of subsection (3) above, the directions which may be given by an order under this section shall in particular include directions for meeting any expenditure out of a specified fund, for charging any expenditure to capital or to income, for requiring expenditure charged to capital to be recouped out of income within a specified period, for restricting the costs to be incurred at the expense of the charity, or for the investment of moneys arising from any transaction.

(5) An order under this section may authorise any act notwithstanding that it is prohibited by any of the disabling Acts mentioned in subsection (6) below or that the trusts of the charity provide for the act to be done by or under the authority of the court; but no such order shall authorise the doing of any act expressly prohibited by Act of Parliament other than the disabling Acts or by the trusts of the charity or shall extend or alter the purposes of the charity.

(6) The Acts referred to in subsection (5) above as the disabling Acts are the Ecclesiastical Leases Act 1571, the Ecclesiastical Leases Act 1572, the Ecclesiastical Leases Act 1575 and the Ecclesiastical Leases Act 1836.

(7) An order under this section shall not confer any authority in relation to a building which has been consecrated and of which the use or disposal is regulated, and can be further regulated, by a scheme having effect under the Union of Benefices Measures 1923 to 1952, the Reorganisation Areas Measures 1944 and 1954, the Pastoral Measure 1968 or the Pastoral Measure 1983, the reference to a building being taken to include part of a building and any land which under such a scheme is to be used or disposed of with a building to which the scheme applies.

DEFINITIONS
"charity": s.96(1).
"charity trustees": s.97(1).
"the Commissioners": s.97(1).
"the court": s.97(1).
"trusts": s.97(1).

GENERAL NOTE

This section re-enacts s.23 of the 1960 Act and empowers the Charity Commissioners to authorise transactions beneficial to a charity thus obviating the need for the charity trustees to apply to the court under s.57 of the Trustee Act 1925. For a discussion of the use of the section, see [1977] Ch. Comm. Rep., para. 146 *et seq.*

Subs. (1)

For power to make orders which are not financially beneficial to a charity, see ss.27 and 28.

The practice of the Commissioners, adopted following the judgment of Buckley J. in *BIU Estates Limited* v. *The Chichester Diocesan Fund and Board of Finance (Incorporated)* (1963) 186 E.G. 261, is to make a formal order and not merely to issue a formally worded letter.

Subs. (4)

For the Commissioners' policy on replacement of capital, see [1963] Ch. Comm. Rep., paras. 20 to 23.

Subss. (5) and (6)

The disabling Acts limit the power to grant leases and other assurances of hereditaments being part of the possessions of, or appertaining to, any parsonage or other spiritual promotion.

The power of the Commissioners to make an order was unsuccessfully challenged *in Beaumont* v. *The National Trust for Places of Historic Interest and Natural Beauty* [1984] Ch. Comm. Rep., App. F.

Subs. (7)

Section 55(1) of the Pastoral Measure 1983, provides that the power of the court to make schemes under its jurisdiction with respect to charities, and the power of the Commissioners to make schemes under the Act, shall extend to the making of schemes with respect to consecrated chapels belonging to charities which are no longer needed for the purposes of the charity. Section 7(2) of the Redundant Churches and Other Religious Buildings Act 1969 provides that nothing in that Act shall be taken to prejudice any power of the court or the Commissioners to establish a scheme for the administration of a charity or the power of the Commissioners under s.26 of the Act to authorise dealings with trust property.

Power to authorise ex gratia payments etc.

27.—(1) Subject to subsection (3) below, the Commissioners may by order exercise the same power as is exercisable by the Attorney General to authorise the charity trustees of a charity—

(a) to make any application of property of the charity, or

(b) to waive to any extent, on behalf of the charity, its entitlement to receive any property,

in a case where the charity trustees—

(i) (apart from this section) have no power to do so, but

(ii) in all the circumstances regard themselves as being under a moral obligation to do so.

(2) The power conferred on the Commissioners by subsection (1) above shall be exercisable by them under the supervision of, and in accordance with such directions as may be given by, the Attorney General; and any such directions may in particular require the Commissioners, in such circumstances as are specified in the directions—

(a) to refrain from exercising that power; or

(b) to consult the Attorney General before exercising it.

(3) Where—

(a) an application is made to the Commissioners for them to exercise that power in a case where they are not precluded from doing so by any such directions, but

(b) they consider that it would nevertheless be desirable for the application to be entertained by the Attorney General rather than by them,

they shall refer the application to the Attorney General.

(4) It is hereby declared that where, in the case of any application made to them as mentioned in subsection (3)(a) above, the Commissioners determine the application by refusing to authorise charity trustees to take any

action falling within subsection (1)(a) or (b) above, that refusal shall not preclude the Attorney General, on an application subsequently made to him by the trustees, from authorising the trustees to take that action.

DEFINITIONS
   "charity": s.96(1).
   "charity trustees": s.97(1).
   "the Commissioners": s.97(1).

GENERAL NOTE
   This section re-enacts s.17 of the 1992 Act which removed the anomaly that the Attorney General, but not the Commissioners, had power to permit a charity to make *ex gratia* payments, for example, where a charity takes unknowingly at the expense of the testator's family.
   Prior to the 1992 Act, a charity never had the power to disclaim a legacy, as it would amount to an application of funds for non-charitable purposes. The only way a charity could refuse a legacy was by Act of Parliament as occurred in the Alcoholics Anonymous (Dispositions) Act 1986.

Subs. (1)
   Guidance as to the circumstances in which the power to make an *ex gratia* payment may be exercised can be obtained from *Snowdon, Re*; *Shackleton* v. *Eddy*; *Henderson, Re*; *Henderson* v. *Att.-Gen.* [1970] Ch. 700. In that case, Cross J. emphasised that payment should only be made where, if the charity were an individual, it would be morally wrong to refuse to make the payment.
   Guidance as the exercise of the power of waiver can be found in the *Alcoholics Anonymous* case [1986] Ch. Comm. Rep. App. D. There the Commissioners gave the necessary permission to expend funds to obtain an Act of Parliament where the charity placed considerable emphasis on self-reliance and to accept a legacy would have been contrary to the whole ethos of the charity.

Subs. (2)
   The continuing supervision by the Attorney General reflects his constitutional duty to represent the Crown in protecting charitable trusts.

Subs. (3)
   Following *Snowdon, Re* (above), if no individual charity is concerned the application should be made on behalf of the executors.

Power to give directions about dormant bank accounts of charities

   28.—(1) Where the Commissioners—
   (a) are informed by a relevant institution—
            (i) that it holds one or more accounts in the name of or on behalf of a particular charity ("the relevant charity"), and
            (ii) that the account, or (if it so holds two or more accounts) each of the accounts, is dormant, and
   (b) are unable, after making reasonable inquiries, to locate that charity or any of its trustees,
they may give a direction under subsection (2) below.
   (2) A direction under this subsection is a direction which—
   (a) requires the institution concerned to transfer the amount, or (as the case may be) the aggregate amount, standing to the credit of the relevant charity in the account or accounts in question to such other charity as is specified in the direction in accordance with subsection (3) below; or
   (b) requires the institution concerned to transfer to each of two or more other charities so specified in the direction such part of that amount or aggregate amount as is there specified in relation to that charity.
   (3) The Commissioners may specify in a direction under subsection (2) above such other charity or charities as they consider appropriate, having regard, in a case where the purposes of the relevant charity are known to them, to those purposes and to the purposes of the other charity or charities;

but the Commissioners shall not so specify any charity unless they have received from the charity trustees written confirmation that those trustees are willing to accept the amount proposed to be transferred to the charity.

(4) Any amount received by a charity by virtue of this section shall be received by the charity on terms that—

(a) it shall be held and applied by the charity for the purposes of the charity, but

(b) it shall, as property of the charity, nevertheless be subject to any restrictions on expenditure to which it was subject as property of the relevant charity.

(5) Where—

(a) the Commissioners have been informed as mentioned in subsection (1)(a) above by any relevant institution, and

(b) before any transfer is made by the institution in pursuance of a direction under subsection (2) above, the institution has, by reason of any circumstances, cause to believe that the account, or (as the case may be) any of the accounts, held by it in the name of or on behalf of the relevant charity is no longer dormant,

the institution shall forthwith notify those circumstances in writing to the Commissioners; and, if it appears to the Commissioners that the account or accounts in question is or are no longer dormant, they shall revoke any direction under subsection (2) above which has previously been given by them to the institution with respect to the relevant charity.

(6) The receipt of any charity trustees or trustee for a charity in respect of any amount received from a relevant institution by virtue of this section shall be a complete discharge of the institution in respect of that amount.

(7) No obligation as to secrecy or other restriction on disclosure (however imposed) shall preclude a relevant institution from disclosing any information to the Commissioners for the purpose of enabling them to discharge their functions under this section.

(8) For the purposes of this section—

(a) an account is dormant if no transaction, other than—

(i) a transaction consisting in a payment into the account, or

(ii) a transaction which the institution holding the account has itself caused to be effected,

has been effected in relation to the account within the period of five years immediately preceding the date when the Commissioners are informed as mentioned in paragraph (a) of subsection (1) above;

(b) a "relevant institution" means—

(i) the Bank of England;

(ii) an institution which is authorised by the Bank of England to operate a deposit-taking business under Part I of the Banking Act 1987;

(iii) a European deposit-taker as defined in regulation 82(3) of the Banking Coordination (Second Council Directive) Regulations 1992;

(iv) a building society which is authorised by the Building Societies Commission under section 9 of the Building Societies Act 1986 to raise money from its members; or

(v) such other institution mentioned in Schedule 2 to the Banking Act 1987 as the Secretary of State may prescribe by regulations; and

(c) references to the transfer of any amount to a charity are references to its transfer—

(i) to the charity trustees, or

(ii) to any trustee for the charity,

as the charity trustees may determine (and any reference to any amount received by a charity shall be construed accordingly).

(9) For the purpose of determining the matters in respect of which any of the powers conferred by section 8 or 9 above may be exercised it shall be assumed that the Commissioners have no functions under this section in relation to accounts to which this subsection applies (with the result that, for example, a relevant institution shall not, in connection with the functions of the Commissioners under this section, be required under section 8(3)(a) above to furnish any statements, or answer any questions or inquiries, with respect to any such accounts held by the institution).

This subsection applies to accounts which are dormant accounts by virtue of subsection (8)(a) above but would not be such accounts if sub-paragraph (i) of that provision were omitted.

(10) Subsection (1) above shall not apply to any account held in the name of or on behalf of an exempt charity.

DEFINITIONS
"charity": s.96(1).
"charity trustees": s.97(1).
"the Commissioners": s.97(1).
"dormant account": subs. (8)(a).
"relevant institution": subs. (8)(b).

GENERAL NOTE
This section re-enacts s.18 of the 1992 Act and gives the Commissioners power to bring back into circulation funds which have not been used for at least five years. The power originally appeared in s.12 of the Law Reform (Miscellaneous Provisions) (Scotland) Act 1990 to permit the Lord Advocate to deal with dormant accounts of Scottish charities. As the Commissioners commented in their 1990 report in relation to the Scottish provision, the success of the provision will depend upon the willingness of the banks and building societies to identify charity accounts and to inform the Commissioners.

It is intended to use the section in connection with the Commissioners' programme of local reviews of charities. A list of charities in a particular area will be supplied to local banks, which will then be able to provide information on dormant accounts, *Hansard*, H.L. Vol. 535, col. 399.

Subs. (1)
Reasonable inquiries. What is reasonable may vary from account to account and may cause difficulties in practice in determining whether a charity really cannot be located. The problems caused by a similar requirement in s.14 of the 1960 Act led to specific provisions being introduced, see s.14(1).

Subs. (3)
A charity would probably only be *considered appropriate* where it satisfied the usual *cy-près* condition for use of charity property on failure of the trust.

Subs. (4)
Paragraph (b) requires property which was part of the relevant charity's permanent endowment to remain subject to the same restrictions on expenditure.

Subs. (7)
The usual duties of confidentiality are waived solely for the purposes of this section. Banks and building societies are not within the general power to disclose information under s.10.

Subs. (8)
An account will be dormant if it is, for example, receiving interest payments direct into the account from an investment but no payments out are being made. If the Commissioners wish to deal with the investment generating the income, they will have to use their powers under s.16.

Subs. (9)
Banks themselves identify accounts as dormant in circumstances where no payments are being made, *i.e.* where sub-para. (i) of subs. (8)(a) does not apply, and can easily supply information about such accounts. Apparently, it would place too great a burden on banks and building societies to require them to give information about accounts within sub-para. (i), *Hansard*, H.L. Vol. 535, col. 400.

Power to advise charity trustees

29.—(1) The Commissioners may on the written application of any charity trustee give him their opinion or advice on any matter affecting the performance of his duties as such.

(2) A charity trustee or trustee for a charity acting in accordance with the opinion or advice of the Commissioners given under this section with respect to the charity shall be deemed, as regards his responsibility for so acting, to have acted in accordance with his trust, unless, when he does so, either—

    (a) he knows or has reasonable cause to suspect that the opinion or advice was given in ignorance of material facts; or

    (b) the decision of the court has been obtained on the matter or proceedings are pending to obtain one.

DEFINITIONS
    "charity trustees": s.97(1).
    "the Commissioners": s.97(1).
    "the court": s.97(1).
    "trust": s.97(1).

GENERAL NOTE
    This section re-enacts s.24 of the 1960 Act and empowers the Charity Commissioners to advise charity trustees.

Subs. (1)
    The Commissioners are empowered but not obliged to advise charity trustees. For the Commissioners' view of their powers under this section, see [1982] Ch. Comm. Rep., para. 24 *et seq.*
    When advising, the Commissioners must satisfy themselves that the action proposed by a trustee is within the powers of the trustee and a trustee must supply the Commissioners with sufficient evidence to allow them to make an informed decision, see [1991] Ch. Comm. Rep., para. 33 and *Marley* v. *Mutual Security Merchant Bank and Trust Co. Limited* [1991] 3 All E.R. 198, P.C.

Powers for preservation of charity documents

30.—(1) The Commissioners may provide books in which any deed, will or other document relating to a charity may be enrolled.

(2) The Commissioners may accept for safe keeping any document of or relating to a charity, and the charity trustees or other persons having the custody of documents of or relating to a charity (including a charity which has ceased to exist) may with the consent of the Commissioners deposit them with the Commissioners for safe keeping, except in the case of documents required by some other enactment to be kept elsewhere.

(3) Where a document is enrolled by the Commissioners or is for the time being deposited with them under this section, evidence of its contents may be given by means of a copy certified by any officer of the Commissioners generally or specially authorised by them to act for this purpose; and a document purporting to be such a copy shall be received in evidence without proof of the official position, authority or handwriting of the person certifying it or of the original document being enrolled or deposited as aforesaid.

(4) Regulations made by the Secretary of State may make provision for such documents deposited with the Commissioners under this section as may be prescribed by the regulations to be destroyed or otherwise disposed of after such period or in such circumstances as may be so prescribed.

(5) Subsections (3) and (4) above shall apply to any document transmitted to the Commissioners under section 9 above and kept by them under subsection (3) of that section, as if the document had been deposited with them for safe keeping under this section.

DEFINITIONS
    "charity": s.96(1).

"charity trustees": s.97(1).
"the Commissioners": s.97(1).

GENERAL NOTE
This section re-enacts s.25 of the 1960 Act and makes provision for the preservation of charity documents.
The Charity Commission is a department of public record. Public access is given to papers more than 30 years old, see [1981] Ch. Comm. Rep., para. 130.

Subs. (4)
No regulations have been made under this subsection at time of writing (June 1993).

Subs. (5)
Section 9(3) permits the Commissioners to retain documents provided to them after they have exercised their powers under s.9(1) to call for documents relating to any charity.

Power to order taxation of solicitor's bill

31.—(1) The Commissioners may order that a solicitor's bill of costs for business done for a charity, or for charity trustees or trustees for a charity, shall be taxed, together with the costs of the taxation, by a taxing officer in such division of the High Court as may be specified in the order, or by the taxing officer of any other court having jurisdiction to order the taxation of the bill.

(2) On any order under this section for the taxation of a solicitor's bill the taxation shall proceed, and the taxing officer shall have the same powers and duties, and the costs of the taxation shall be borne, as if the order had been made, on the application of the person chargeable with the bill, by the court in which the costs are taxed.

(3) No order under this section for the taxation of a solicitor's bill shall be made after payment of the bill unless the Commissioners are of opinion that it contains exorbitant charges; and no such order shall in any case be made where the solicitor's costs are not subject to taxation on an order of the High Court by reason either of an agreement as to his remuneration or the lapse of time since payment of the bill.

DEFINITIONS
"charity": s.96(1).
"charity trustees": s.97(1).
"the Commissioners": s.97(1).
"the court": s.97(1).

GENERAL NOTE
This section re-enacts s.26 of the 1960 Act and enables the Commissioners to obtain taxation of a solicitor's bill of costs if any item therein appears excessive.

Subs. (3)
The Solicitors Act 1974, s.70(4) provides that an order for taxation of costs shall not be made after the expiration of 12 months from the payment of the bill.

Legal proceedings relating to charities

Proceedings by Commissioners

32.—(1) Subject to subsection (2) below, the Commissioners may exercise the same powers with respect to—
  (a) the taking of legal proceedings with reference to charities or the property or affairs of charities, or
  (b) the compromise of claims with a view to avoiding or ending such proceedings,
as are exercisable by the Attorney General acting ex officio.

(2) Subsection (1) above does not apply to the power of the Attorney General under section 63(1) below to present a petition for the winding up of a charity.

(3) The practice and procedure to be followed in relation to any proceedings taken by the Commissioners under subsection (1) above shall be the same in all respects (and in particular as regards costs) as if they were proceedings taken by the Attorney General acting ex officio.

(4) No rule of law or practice shall be taken to require the Attorney General to be a party to any such proceedings.

(5) The powers exercisable by the Commissioners by virtue of this section shall be exercisable by them of their own motion, but shall be exercisable only with the agreement of the Attorney General on each occasion.

DEFINITIONS
   "charity": s.96(1).
   "the Commissioners": s.97(1).

GENERAL NOTE
   This section re-enacts s.26A of the 1960 Act which was inserted by s.28 of the 1992 Act and gives the Charity Commissioners the same powers as the Attorney General to take legal proceedings with reference to charities. The constitutional position of the Attorney General in relation to charities is preserved by the requirement that the Commissioners may only exercise their power to bring proceedings with the agreement of the Attorney General.

Subs. (1)
   Paragraph (b) gives specific power to the Commissioners to settle court actions; previously settlements were approved under s.23 of the 1960 Act.

Subs. (2)
   The Commissioners may petition to wind up a company under s.63(2).

Subs. (3)
   For the practice and procedure in charity proceedings brought by the Attorney General, see Tudor, *Charities*, 7th ed. p.329 *et seq.*

Subs. (4)
   This reverses the well-established rule that the Attorney General is a necessary party to charity proceedings, *Wellbeloved* v. *Jones* (1822) 1 S. & S. 43; *National Anti-Vivisection Society* v. *I.R.C.* [1948] A.C. 31.

Proceedings by other persons

33.—(1) Charity proceedings may be taken with reference to a charity either by the charity, or by any of the charity trustees, or by any person interested in the charity, or by any two or more inhabitants of the area of the charity if it is a local charity, but not by any other person.

(2) Subject to the following provisions of this section, no charity proceedings relating to a charity (other than an exempt charity) shall be entertained or proceeded with in any court unless the taking of the proceedings is authorised by order of the Commissioners.

(3) The Commissioners shall not, without special reasons, authorise the taking of charity proceedings where in their opinion the case can be dealt with by them under the powers of this Act other than those conferred by section 32 above.

(4) This section shall not require any order for the taking of proceedings in a pending cause or matter or for the bringing of any appeal.

(5) Where the foregoing provisions of this section require the taking of charity proceedings to be authorised by an order of the Commissioners, the proceedings may nevertheless be entertained or proceeded with if, after the order had been applied for and refused, leave to take the proceedings was obtained from one of the judges of the High Court attached to the Chancery Division.

(6) Nothing in the foregoing subsections shall apply to the taking of proceedings by the Attorney General, with or without a relator, or to the taking of proceedings by the Commissioners in accordance with section 32 above.

(7) Where it appears to the Commissioners, on an application for an order under this section or otherwise, that it is desirable for legal proceedings to be taken with reference to any charity (other than an exempt charity) or its property or affairs, and for the proceedings to be taken by the Attorney General, the Commissioners shall so inform the Attorney General, and send him such statements and particulars as they think necessary to explain the matter.

(8) In this section "charity proceedings" means proceedings in any court in England or Wales brought under the court's jurisdiction with respect to charities, or brought under the court's jurisdiction with respect to trusts in relation to the administration of a trust for charitable purposes.

DEFINITIONS
"charity": s.96(1).
"charity proceedings": subs. (8).
"charity trustees": s.97(1).
"the Commissioners": s.97(1).
"the court": s.97(1).
"exempt charity": s.96(1).
"local charity": s.96(1).
"trusts": s.97(1).

GENERAL NOTE
This section re-enacts s.28(1) to (8) of the 1960 Act as amended by Sched. 3, para. 10 to the 1992 Act and sets out the persons who may take charity proceedings and requires them to obtain the consent of the Charity Commissioners.

As to the form of proceedings, see R.S.C., Ord. 108.

Subs. (1)
Charity proceedings. See subs. (8). In all cases in which administration of the charity property is sought or which necessarily involves either whole or partial administration or execution of the trusts of the charity, an order of the Commissioners must be sought. On the other hand, an action brought solely to enforce a common law right, whether arising out of contract or common law obligation or common law duty, is not within the section, see *Rooke* v. *Dawson* [1895] 1 Ch. 485. Thus an action on a contract of service or to recover rents does not need the consent of the Commissioners. Nor is an order of the Commissioners necessary to enable charity trustees to pay a charitable fund into court under the Trustee Act 1925, see *Poplar and Blackwall Free Schools, Re* (1878) 8 Ch. D. 546.

Proceedings to determine a bone fide dispute as to whether or not a charitable trust exists are not "charity proceedings". It follows that only the Attorney General is entitled to maintain an action to establish the existence of a charitable trust; in such a case it is not open to a local authority or to local inhabitants to bring proceedings under subs. (1) and there is no question of an order under either subss. (2) or (5), see *Belling, Re* [1967] Ch. 425; *Hauxwell* v. *Barton-upon-Humber U.D.C.* [1974] Ch. 432.

Although proceedings with which they are concerned may not themselves be "charity proceedings", so as to require an order under this section, charity trustees will often require the protection of the court or the Commissioners before expending charitable funds in bringing or defending an action. In such a case they may seek an order under s.26 or advice under s.29. If the Commissioners decline to make an order under that section, the trustees may seek a *Beddoe* order (see *Beddoe, Re* [1893] 1 Ch. 547) from the court; but as a *Beddoe* summons is within the term "charity proceedings" it needs the authority of an order under subss. (2) or (5) of this section.

Any person interested in the charity. Generally speaking, a person who cannot in any circumstances be a beneficiary of a charity or take any interest under the trusts applicable to the property of the charity, for example, the executors of a donor, is not a person interested, *Bradshaw* v. *University College of Wales, Aberystwyth* [1988] 1 W.L.R. 190. Nor does the fact that a person has a contract with the trustees of a charity make him "a person interested", *Haslemere Estates* v. *Baker* [1982] 1 W.L.R. 1109, 1122. A person who makes a donation is "a person interested" and not a person enforcing contractual rights, *Brooks* v. *Richardson* [1986] 1

W.L.R. 385. A local authority may be "a person interested" in a charity operating in its area, *Hampton Fuel Allotment Society, Re* [1988] 3 W.L.R. 513, a case in which the Court of Appeal appeared to decide that there was no general rule to decide who was "a person interested".

Subs. (2)
If proceedings are commenced without the consent of the Commissioners, they will not be dismissed but ordered to be stood over in order to see whether such authority can be obtained, *Rooke* v. *Dawson* [1895] 1 Ch. 485.

Subs. (3)
For the powers of the Commissioners see s.16 and the limitation thereon in s.16(10).
Section 32 gives the Commissioners the same powers as the Attorney General to take proceedings with reference to charities.

Subs. (4)
A pending cause or matter. This means a cause or matter pending at the time of the · application, *Lister's Hospital, Re* (1855) 6 De G. M. & G. 184, 187.

Subs. (5)
An application to the court for leave to appeal must be made within 21 days after the refusal by the Commissioners of an order authorising the taking of proceedings, R.S.C., Ord. 108, r.3(2).

Subs. (7)
The Attorney General does not in practice commence proceedings against charity trustees except in a case referred to him by the Commissioners as one in which it is desirable for him to act, for example, after a s.8 inquiry.

Report of s.8 inquiry to be evidence in certain proceedings

34.—(1) A copy of the report of the person conducting an inquiry under section 8 above shall, if certified by the Commissioners to be a true copy, be admissible in any proceedings to which this section applies—
 (a) as evidence of any fact stated in the report; and
 (b) as evidence of the opinion of that person as to any matter referred to in it.
(2) This section applies to—
 (a) any legal proceedings instituted by the Commissioners under this Part of this Act; and
 (b) any legal proceedings instituted by the Attorney General in respect of a charity.
(3) A document purporting to be a certificate issued for the purposes of subsection (1) above shall be received in evidence and be deemed to be such a certificate, unless the contrary is proved.

DEFINITIONS
"the Commissioners": s.97(1).

GENERAL NOTE
This section re-enacts s.28A of the 1960 Act which was inserted by s.11 of the 1992 Act.
The report of a s.8 inquiry is central to any temporary and protective or remedial and permanent powers to be taken by the Commissioners under s.18. If proceedings were taken following such an inquiry, any statements of fact or opinion in the report would need to be proved in court, either by the author of the report giving evidence himself, or by serving a Civil Evidence Act notice, both of which can give rise to many practical difficulties. This section obviates the need for either procedure and makes a certified copy of the report evidence of the facts and opinions stated therein.

Subs. (1)
This subsection is in very similar form to that in s.441 of the Companies Act 1985 relating to a Department of Trade and Industry inspector's report on a company.

Subs. (2)
The section applies only when proceedings are instituted by the Commissioners or the

Attorney General. It would seem to follow that if, for example, the Commissioners proceeded to remove a trustee by *order* under s.18(2)(i) and the trustee then applied to the court for a declaration that he had been wrongfully removed, the contents of the s.8 inquiry report would have to be proved to the court in the usual way.

Meaning of "trust corporation"

Application of provisions to trust corporations appointed under s.16 or 18

35.—(1) In the definition of "trust corporation" contained in the following provisions—

(a) section 117(xxx) of the Settled Land Act 1925,
(b) section 68(18) of the Trustee Act 1925,
(c) section 205(xxviii) of the Law of Property Act 1925,
(d) section 55(xxvi) of the Administration of Estates Act 1925, and
(e) section 128 of the Supreme Court Act 1981,

the reference to a corporation appointed by the court in any particular case to be a trustee includes a reference to a corporation appointed by the Commissioners under this Act to be a trustee.

(2) This section shall be deemed always to have had effect; but the reference to section 128 of the Supreme Court Act 1981 shall, in relation to any time before 1st January 1982, be construed as a reference to section 175(1) of the Supreme Court of Judicature (Consolidation) Act 1925.

DEFINITIONS
  "the Commissioners": s.97(1).

GENERAL NOTE
  This section re-enacts s.21A of the 1960 Act which was inserted by s.14 of the 1992 Act and removes any doubt, prospectively and retrospectively, that a trust corporation appointed by the Commissioners has the same rights and duties as a trust corporation appointed by the court.

PART V

CHARITY LAND

Restrictions on dispositions

36.—(1) Subject to the following provisions of this section and section 40 below, no land held by or in trust for a charity shall be sold, leased or otherwise disposed of without an order of the court or of the Commissioners.

(2) Subsection (1) above shall not apply to a disposition of such land if—

(a) the disposition is made to a person who is not—
    (i) a connected person (as defined in Schedule 5 to this Act), or
    (ii) a trustee for, or nominee of, a connected person; and
(b) the requirements of subsection (3) or (5) below have been complied with in relation to it.

(3) Except where the proposed disposition is the granting of such a lease as is mentioned in subsection (5) below, the charity trustees must, before entering into an agreement for the sale, or (as the case may be) for a lease or other disposition, of the land—

(a) obtain and consider a written report on the proposed disposition from a qualified surveyor instructed by the trustees and acting exclusively for the charity;
(b) advertise the proposed disposition for such period and in such manner as the surveyor has advised in his report (unless he has there advised that it would not be in the best interests of the charity to advertise the proposed disposition); and
(c) decide that they are satisfied, having considered the surveyor's report, that the terms on which the disposition is proposed to be made are the best that can reasonably be obtained for the charity.

(4) For the purposes of subsection (3) above a person is a qualified surveyor if—

(a) he is a fellow or professional associate of the Royal Institution of Chartered Surveyors or of the Incorporated Society of Valuers and Auctioneers or satisfies such other requirement or requirements as may be prescribed by regulations made by the Secretary of State; and

(b) he is reasonably believed by the charity trustees to have ability in, and experience of, the valuation of land of the particular kind, and in the particular area, in question;

and any report prepared for the purposes of that subsection shall contain such information, and deal with such matters, as may be prescribed by regulations so made.

(5) Where the proposed disposition is the granting of a lease for a term ending not more than seven years after it is granted (other than one granted wholly or partly in consideration of a fine), the charity trustees must, before entering into an agreement for the lease—

(a) obtain and consider the advice on the proposed disposition of a person who is reasonably believed by the trustees to have the requisite ability and practical experience to provide them with competent advice on the proposed disposition; and

(b) decide that they are satisfied, having considered that person's advice, that the terms on which the disposition is proposed to be made are the best that can reasonably be obtained for the charity.

(6) Where—

(a) any land is held by or in trust for a charity, and

(b) the trusts on which it is so held stipulate that it is to be used for the purposes, or any particular purposes, of the charity,

then (subject to subsections (7) and (8) below and without prejudice to the operation of the preceding provisions of this section) the land shall not be sold, leased or otherwise disposed of unless the charity trustees have previously—

(i) given public notice of the proposed disposition, inviting representations to be made to them within a time specified in the notice, being not less than one month from the date of the notice; and

(ii) taken into consideration any representations made to them within that time about the proposed disposition.

(7) Subsection (6) above shall not apply to any such disposition of land as is there mentioned if—

(a) the disposition is to be effected with a view to acquiring by way of replacement other property which is to be held on the trusts referred to in paragraph (b) of that subsection; or

(b) the disposition is the granting of a lease for a term ending not more than two years after it is granted (other than one granted wholly or partly in consideration of a fine).

(8) The Commissioners may direct—

(a) that subsection (6) above shall not apply to dispositions of land held by or in trust for a charity or class of charities (whether generally or only in the case of a specified class or dispositions or land, or otherwise as may be provided in the direction), or

(b) that that subsection shall not apply to a particular disposition of land held by or in trust for a charity,

if, on an application made to them in writing by or on behalf of the charity or charities in question, the Commissioners are satisfied that it would be in the interests of the charity or charities for them to give the direction.

(9) The restrictions on disposition imposed by this section apply notwithstanding anything in the trusts of a charity; but nothing in this section applies—

(a) to any disposition for which general or special authority is expressly given (without the authority being made subject to the sanction of an order of the court) by any statutory provision contained in or having effect under an Act of Parliament or by any scheme legally established; or

(b) to any disposition of land held by or in trust for a charity which—
    (i) is made to another charity otherwise than for the best price that can reasonably be obtained, and
    (ii) is authorised to be so made by the trusts of the first-mentioned charity; or

(c) to the granting, by or on behalf of a charity and in accordance with its trusts, of a lease to any beneficiary under those trusts where the lease—
    (i) is granted otherwise than for the best rent that can reasonably be obtained; and
    (ii) is intended to enable the demised premises to be occupied for the purposes, or any particular purposes, of the charity.

(10) Nothing in this section applies—
(a) to any disposition of land held by or in trust for an exempt charity;
(b) to any disposition of land by way of mortgage or other security; or
(c) to any disposition of an advowson.

(11) In this section "land" means land in England or Wales.

<small>DEFINITIONS</small>
"charity": s.96(1).
"charity trustees": s.97(1).
"the Commissioners": s.97(1).
"exempt charity": s.96(1).
"land": subs. (11).

<small>GENERAL NOTE</small>
This section re-enacts s.32 of the 1992 Act which enacted the recommendation in the Woodfield report and the White Paper that the consent of the Commissioners should no longer be required by charity trustees to sell charity land, provided that statutory requirements are complied with. The statutory requirements are intended to protect charity property against mismanagement and abuse. A less strict régime applies to leases for seven years or less.

There is much to be said for the view that the requirements are merely a statutory statement of actions trustees should have been taking in any event to comply with their duties and obligations as trustees when dealing with charity land. The consent of the Commissioners is still required in those circumstances where a trustee would be in breach of his fiduciary duties, for example, by selling to himself or at less than market value.

Any provision in the trusts of a charity or an Act of Parliament or an order or scheme under the Education Act 1944 or 1973 which required the Commissioners to consent to any disposition of land of a charity ceased to have effect by s.36 of the 1992 Act.

Subs. (1)
The sale of any land held by a charity must comply with the section, not merely a sale of part of the permanent endowment or functional land.

Subs. (2)
A sale to any of the persons or bodies listed in Sched. 5, save a donor, would probably amount to a breach of the self-dealing rule by a charity trustee, see *Thompson's Settlement, Re* [1986] Ch. 99. A donor was included in the definition of *connected person* to prevent tax avoidance by the giving of property to a charity followed by a lease back to the donor at a low rent, *Hansard*, H.L. Vol. 535, col. 1251.

Subs. (3)
The trustees need not approve the terms of each sale in a full meeting of the trustees. It is sufficient for the trustees to set the policy for disposals and then to delegate decisions as to particular sales to a committee of their number who report back at regular intervals. The wording of para. (c) is sufficiently wide to cover sales by auction and sales by tender and allows trustees to set a reserve selling price, *Hansard*, H.L. Vol. 535, cols. 416 to 417.

Subs. (4)

The detailed requirements for the surveyor's report are set out in the Charities (Qualified Surveyors' Reports) Regulations 1992 (S.I. 1992 No. 2980). The report should include a description of the land, whether it is leased by or from the charity trustees, the easements or covenants to which the land is subject or the benefit of which it enjoys, whether or not any buildings in it are in good repair, whether alterations to any such buildings are desirable, advice as to the way the proposed disposition of the land is to be conducted, advice about VAT, the surveyor's opinion about the value of the land and, where appropriate, his suggested alternative ways of disposing of the land.

Subs. (5)

For the grant of a lease for seven years or less, advice does not have to be obtained from a qualified surveyor, nor does the proposed lease have to be advertised.

Subs. (6)

This subsection deals with charity land which is held *in specie*, such as almshouses. An almshouse resident, for example, only has a right to make representations to the trustees. Provided that the trustees can be shown to have considered the representations, to have complied with the rest of the section and are not otherwise in default, neither the beneficiaries nor the Commissioners can stop the sale; the sanction of the Commissioners is not required. Even this limited control is removed if the trustees intend to acquire replacement property or lease it for two years or less, see subs. (7).

Subs. (8)

This subsection allows the Commissioners to grant a charity exemption from subs. (6) for either all or some of its dispositions of land. The subsection was introduced to deal with problems of charities such as the National Trust which have a large number of straightforward land transactions, *Hansard*, H.L. Vol. 535, col. 191.

Subs. (9)

Paragraph (a) covers such statutory authority as ss.8–12 of the Housing Associations Act 1985 as amended by s.78(1) of and Sched. 6 to the 1992 Act for housing associations.

Paragraph (b) allows a charity to sell land at an undervalue to another charity to ensure that the land is retained for charitable purposes, provided that such a sale is authorised by the trust instrument.

Paragraph (c) allows a charity, such as a charity to provide housing for the poor, to grant a lease to a beneficiary at less than market rent.

Subs. (10)(b)

For the restrictions on mortgages, see s.38.

Supplementary provisions relating to dispositions

37.—(1) Any of the following instruments, namely—
  (a) any contract for the sale, or for a lease or other disposition, of land which is held by or in trust for a charity, and
  (b) any conveyance, transfer, lease or other instrument effecting a disposition of such land,
shall state—
  (i) that the land is held by or in trust for a charity,
  (ii) whether the charity is an exempt charity and whether the disposition is one falling within paragraph (a), (b) or (c) of subsection (9) of section 36 above, and
  (iii) if it is not an exempt charity and the disposition is not one falling within any of those paragraphs, that the land is land to which the restrictions on disposition imposed by that section apply.

(2) Where any land held by or in trust for a charity is sold, leased or otherwise disposed of by a disposition to which subsection (1) or (2) of section 36 above applies, the charity trustees shall certify in the instrument by which the disposition is effected—
  (a) (where subsection (1) of that section applies) that the disposition has been sanctioned by an order of the court or of the Commissioners (as the case may be), or

  (b) (where subsection (2) of that section applies) that the charity trustees have power under the trusts of the charity to effect the disposition, and that they have complied with the provisions of that section so far as applicable to it.

  (3) Where subsection (2) above has been complied with in relation to any disposition of land, then in favour of a person who (whether under the disposition or afterwards) acquires an interest in the land for money or money's worth, it shall be conclusively presumed that the facts were as stated in the certificate.

  (4) Where—
  (a) any land held by or in trust for a charity is sold, leased or otherwise disposed of by a disposition to which subsection (1) or (2) of section 36 above applies, but
  (b) subsection (2) above has not been complied with in relation to the disposition,

then in favour of a person who (whether under the disposition or afterwards) in good faith acquires an interest in the land for money or money's worth, the disposition shall be valid whether or not—
  (i) the disposition has been sanctioned by an order of the court or of the Commissioners, or
  (ii) the charity trustees have power under the trusts of the charity to effect the disposition and have complied with the provisions of that section so far as applicable to it.

  (5) Any of the following instruments, namely—
  (a) any contract for the sale, or for a lease or other disposition, of land which will, as a result of the disposition, be held by or in trust for a charity, and
  (b) any conveyance, transfer, lease or other instrument effecting a disposition of such land,

shall state—
  (i) that the land will, as a result of the disposition, be held by or in trust for a charity,
  (ii) whether the charity is an exempt charity, and
  (iii) if it is not an exempt charity, that the restrictions on disposition imposed by section 36 above will apply to the land (subject to subsection (9) of that section).

  (6) In section 29(1) of the Settled Land Act 1925 (charitable and public trusts)—
  (a) the requirement for a conveyance of land held on charitable, ecclesiastical or public trusts to state that it is held on such trusts shall not apply to any instrument to which subsection (1) above applies; and
  (b) the requirement imposed on a purchaser, in the circumstances mentioned in section 29(1) of that Act, to see that any consents or orders requisite for authorising a transaction have been obtained shall not apply in relation to any disposition in relation to which subsection (2) above has been complied with;

and expressions used in this subsection which are also used in that Act have the same meaning as in that Act.

  (7) Where—
  (a) the disposition to be effected by any such instrument as is mentioned in subsection (1)(b) or (5)(b) above will be a registered disposition, or
  (b) any such instrument will on taking effect be an instrument to which section 123(1) of the Land Registration Act 1925 (compulsory registration of title) applies,

the statement which, by virtue of subsection (1) or (5) above, is to be contained in the instrument shall be in such form as may be prescribed.

  (8) Where—
  (a) an application is duly made—

(i) for registration of a disposition of registered land, or
(ii) for registration of a person's title under a disposition of unregistered land, and
(b) the instrument by which the disposition is effected contains a statement complying with subsections (5) and (7) above, and
(c) the charity by or in trust for which the land is held as a result of the disposition is not an exempt charity,
the registrar shall enter in the register, in respect of the land, a restriction in such form as may be prescribed.
(9) Where—
(a) any such restriction is entered in the register in respect of any land, and
(b) the charity by or in trust for which the land is held becomes an exempt charity,
the charity trustees shall apply to the registrar for the restriction to be withdrawn; and on receiving any application duly made under this subsection the registrar shall withdraw the restriction.
(10) Where—
(a) any registered land is held by or in trust for an exempt charity and the charity ceases to be an exempt charity, or
(b) any registered land becomes, as a result of a declaration of trust by the registered proprietor, land held in trust for a charity (other than an exempt charity),
the charity trustees shall apply to the registrar for such a restriction as is mentioned in subsection (8) above to be entered in the register in respect of the land; and on receiving any application duly made under this subsection the registrar shall enter such a restriction in the register in respect of the land.
(11) In this section—
(a) references to a disposition of land do not include references to—
(i) a disposition of land by way of mortgage or other security,
(ii) any disposition of an advowson, or
(iii) any release of a rentcharge falling within section 40(1) below; and
(b) "land" means land in England or Wales;
and subsections (7) to (10) above shall be construed as one with the Land Registration Act 1925.

DEFINITIONS
"charity": s.96(1).
"charity trustees": s.97(1).
"the Commissioners": s.97(1).
"exempt charity": s.96(1).
"land": subs. (11).

GENERAL NOTE
This section re-enacts s.33 of the 1992 Act and contains provisions to ensure that the controls on the disposition of land in s.36 are complied with. The aim of the section is to alert those engaging in transactions to the fact that the trustees with whom they are dealing are subject to a special régime. In addition to alerting potential purchasers by requiring specific statements that the land is charity land in contracts and conveyances, the section also requires a restriction to be entered at the Land Registry in the case of registered land. A balance is struck in that the charity trustees' certificate is presumed to be correct in favour of a purchaser and a purchaser in good faith is protected in the event of non-compliance with the section.
The Land Registration (Charities) Rules 1992 (S.I. 1992 No. 3005) (the 1992 Rules) give detailed effect to this section by amending the Land Registration Rules 1925.

Subs. (1)
The requirement to include the necessary statement applies to *all* charities even if they do not have to comply with s.36. Thus, anyone dealing with a charitable housing association, for

example, will be alerted to the need to comply with the Housing Associations Act 1985. For the form of the statements, see the 1992 Rules (S.I. 1992 No. 3005), rr.5 and 9. Any contract for land in category (iii) must be conditional on the consent of the Commissioners being obtained or the conditions in s.36(2) being complied with: see *Richards (Michael) Properties* v. *Corporation of Wardens of St. Saviour's Parish, Southwark* [1975] 3 All E.R. 416; *Haslemere Estates* v. *Baker* [1982] 1 W.L.R. 1109.

Subs. (3)
A purchaser is protected even if it subsequently transpires that the facts stated in the certificate are incorrect.

Subs. (4)
This subsection protects a purchaser of property who is unaware that it is charity land and the subs. (2) has not been complied with.

Subs. (5)
For the form of the statements, see the 1992 Rules (S.I. 1992 No. 3005), rr.4 and 6.

Subs. (8)
Once a restriction has been entered on the register, no further transaction in relation to that title can take place unless the restriction is complied with, s.58 of the Land Registration Act 1925.
For the forms of the restriction see the Schedule to the 1992 Rules (S.I. 1992 No. 3005).

Subs. (10)
Rule 8 of the 1992 Rules makes it clear that the trustees are under an obligation to apply for a restriction as soon as the land becomes subject to charitable trusts.

Subs. (11)(a)(i)
For restrictions on mortgages, see s.38.

Restrictions on mortgaging

38.—(1) Subject to subsection (2) below, no mortgage of land held by or in trust for a charity shall be granted without an order of the court or of the Commissioners.
(2) Subsection (1) above shall not apply to a mortgage of any such land by way of security for the repayment of a loan where the charity trustees have, before executing the mortgage, obtained and considered proper advice, given to them in writing, on the matters mentioned in subsection (3) below.
(3) Those matters are—
(a) whether the proposed loan is necessary in order for the charity trustees to be able to pursue the particular course of action in connection with which the loan is sought by them;
(b) whether the terms of the proposed loan are reasonable having regard to the status of the charity as a prospective borrower; and
(c) the ability of the charity to repay on those terms the sum proposed to be borrowed.
(4) For the purposes of subsection (2) above proper advice is the advice of a person—
(a) who is reasonably believed by the charity trustees to be qualified by his ability in and practical experience of financial matters; and
(b) who has no financial interest in the making of the loan in question; and such advice may constitute proper advice for those purposes notwithstanding that the person giving it does so in the course of his employment as an officer or employee of the charity or of the charity trustees.
(5) This section applies notwithstanding anything in the trusts of a charity; but nothing in this section applies to any mortgage for which general or special authority is given as mentioned in section 36(9)(a) above.
(6) In this section—
"land" means land in England or Wales;

"mortgage" includes a charge.
(7) Nothing in this section applies to an exempt charity.

<small>DEFINITIONS</small>
"charity": s.96(1).
"charity trustees": s.97(1).
"the Commissioners": s.97(1).
"exempt charity": s.96(1).
"land": subs. (6).
"mortgage": subs. (6).

<small>GENERAL NOTE</small>
This section re-enacts s.34 of the 1992 Act. Following the recommendation that the Commissioners should no longer be required to consent to sales and leases of charity land (see the note to s.36), the White Paper, para. 7.14, recommended that trustees should be given power to borrow money on the security of a mortgage of charity land without the consent of the Commissioners, provided that proper advice was obtained on specific matters.

Subs. (3)
The Commissioners will be able to give formal or informal advice under s.29 as to whether a loan is necessary within para. (a).

Subs. (4)
Proper advice. Save for para. (b) the definition is very similar to that in s.6(4) of the Trustee Investment Act 1961. Thus, trustees may use the same person to advise on loans under this section as they do for advice on investments under the 1961 Act, including, where appropriate, one of the trust's officers or employees.

Supplementary provisions relating to mortgaging

39.—(1) Any mortgage of land held by or in trust for a charity shall state—
(a) that the land is held by or in trust for a charity,
(b) whether the charity is an exempt charity and whether the mortgage is one falling within subsection (5) of section 38 above, and
(c) if it is not an exempt charity and the mortgage is not one falling within that subsection, that the mortgage is one to which the restrictions imposed by that section apply;
and where the mortgage will be a registered disposition any such statement shall be in such form as may be prescribed.
(2) Where subsection (1) or (2) of section 38 above applies to any mortgage of land held by or in trust for a charity, the charity trustees shall certify in the mortgage—
(a) (where subsection (1) of that section applies) that the mortgage has been sanctioned by an order of the court or of the Commissioners (as the case may be), or
(b) (where subsection (2) of that section applies) that the charity trustees have power under the trusts of the charity to grant the mortgage, and that they have obtained and considered such advice as is mentioned in that subsection.
(3) Where subsection (2) above has been complied with in relation to any mortgage, then in favour of a person who (whether under the mortgage or afterwards) acquires an interest in the land in question for money or money's worth, it shall be conclusively presumed that the facts were as stated in the certificate.
(4) Where—
(a) subsection (1) or (2) of section 38 above applies to any mortgage of land held by or in trust for a charity, but
(b) subsection (2) above has not been complied with in relation to the mortgage,

then in favour of a person who (whether under the mortgage or afterwards) in good faith acquires an interest in the land for money or money's worth, the mortgage shall be valid whether or not—

    (i) the mortgage has been sanctioned by an order of the court or of the Commissioners, or

    (ii) the charity trustees have power under the trusts of the charity to grant the mortgage and have obtained and considered such advice as is mentioned in subsection (2) of that section.

(5) In section 29(1) of the Settled Land Act 1925 (charitable and public trusts)—

    (a) the requirement for a mortgage of land held on charitable, ecclesiastical or public trusts (as a "conveyance" of such land for the purposes of that Act) to state that it is held on such trusts shall not apply to any mortgage to which subsection (1) above applies; and

    (b) the requirement imposed on a mortgagee (as a "purchaser" for those purposes), in the circumstances mentioned in section 29(1) of that Act, to see that any consents or orders requisite for authorising a transaction have been obtained shall not apply in relation to any mortgage in relation to which subsection (2) above has been complied with;

and expressions used in this subsection which are also used in that Act have the same meaning as in that Act.

(6) In this section—

"mortgage" includes a charge, and "mortgagee" shall be construed accordingly;

"land" means land in England or Wales;

"prescribed" and "registered disposition" have the same meaning as in the Land Registration Act 1925.

DEFINITIONS
"charity": s.96(1).
"charity trustees": s.97(1).
"the Commissioners": s.97(1).
"exempt charity": s.96(1).
"land": subs. (6).
"mortgage": subs. (6).
"prescribed": subs. (6).
"registered disposition": subs. (6).

GENERAL NOTE
This section re-enacts s.35 of the 1992 Act and contains the same provisions in relation to mortgages as those in relation to sales and leases in s.37 (see the note to s.37).

Subs. (1)
For the form of the statements, see the Land Registration (Charities) Rules 1992 (S.I. 1992 No. 3005), r.9.

Release of charity rentcharges

40.—(1) Section 36(1) above shall not apply to the release by a charity of a rentcharge which it is entitled to receive if the release is given in consideration of the payment of an amount which is not less than ten times the annual amount of the rentcharge.

(2) Where a charity which is entitled to receive a rentcharge releases it in consideration of the payment of an amount not exceeding £500, any costs incurred by the charity in connection with proving its title to the rentcharge shall be recoverable by the charity from the person or persons in whose favour the rentcharge is being released.

(3) Neither section 36(1) nor subsection (2) above applies where a rentcharge which a charity is entitled to receive is redeemed under sections 8 to 10 of the Rentcharges Act 1977.

(4) The Secretary of State may by order amend subsection (2) above by substituting a different sum for the sum for the time being specified there.

DEFINITIONS
   "charity": s.96(1).

GENERAL NOTE
   This section re-enacts s.37(1) to (4) of the 1992 Act. Consistent with the intention of relieving the Commissioners from consent work (see the note to s.36) this section relieves them of the need to consent to the voluntary release of rentcharges by charities. This provision will be of decreasing importance in view of the fact that no new rentcharges have been capable of being created after August 22, 1977: s.2 of the Rentcharges Act 1977. The power of the Commissioners under s.27(2) to (8) of the 1960 Act to give notice to an estate owner to redeem a rentcharge was removed by s.37(5) of the 1992 Act.

Subs. (1)
   A release for less than ten years' purchase will have to comply with s.36 but the consent of the Commissioners will only be necessary if the trustees cannot satisfy the requirements of s.36(2).

Subs. (3)
   Sections 8–10 of the 1977 Act permit the owner of land affected by a rentcharge to apply for a redemption certificate from the Secretary of State and the price is settled according to a formula in s.10. Thus, the charity receives a fair price for the redemption of the rentcharge.

PART VI

CHARITY ACCOUNTS, REPORTS AND RETURNS

Duty to keep accounting records

41.—(1) The charity trustees of a charity shall ensure that accounting records are kept in respect of the charity which are sufficient to show and explain all the charity's transactions, and which are such as to—
   (a) disclose at any time, with reasonable accuracy, the financial position of the charity at that time, and
   (b) enable the trustees to ensure that, where any statements of accounts are prepared by them under section 42(1) below, those statements of accounts comply with the requirements of regulations under that provision.
   (2) The accounting records shall in particular contain—
   (a) entries showing from day to day all sums of money received and expended by the charity, and the matters in respect of which the receipt and expenditure takes place; and
   (b) a record of the assets and liabilities of the charity.
   (3) The charity trustees of a charity shall preserve any accounting records made for the purposes of this section in respect of the charity for at least six years from the end of the financial year of the charity in which they are made.
   (4) Where a charity ceases to exist within the period of six years mentioned in subsection (3) above as it applies to any accounting records, the obligation to preserve those records in accordance with that subsection shall continue to be discharged by the last charity trustees of the charity, unless the Commissioners consent in writing to the records being destroyed or otherwise disposed of.
   (5) Nothing in this section applies to a charity which is a company.

DEFINITIONS
   "charity": s.96(1).
   "charity trustees": s.97(1).
   "the Commissioners": s.97(1).
   "company": s.97(1).
   "financial year": s.97(1).

GENERAL NOTE

This section re-enacts s.19 of the 1992 Act and, consistent with the increased monitoring and supervisory rôle of the Commissioners, strengthens and particularises the requirements for charities to keep accounts and submit them regularly.

This section mirrors closely s.221 of the Companies Act 1985 which requires companies to keep accounting records.

Exempt charities are required to keep proper books of account by s.46.

Subs. (1)

The stated aim of this subsection is to require reasonable and proper accounts to be kept by a charity up to a reasonable date, not that accounts should be accurate to the previous day, *Hansard*, H.L. P.B.C., col. 86.

The previous obligation in s.32 of the 1960 Act simply to keep "proper books of account" is spelt out in far greater detail, requiring accurate records to be kept of all transactions which must comply with the regulations under s.42.

Subs. (2)

The requirements are far stricter than the former Charities (Statement of Account) Regulations 1960 (S.I. 1960 No. 2425), which merely asked for statements of the approximate amount of liabilities.

From day to day. This does not impose a requirement that books should be entered on a daily basis, merely that accounts should show on which day an amount was received, *Hansard*, H.L. P.B.C., col. 85.

Subs. (5)

Charitable companies are obliged to keep accounting records by s.221 of the Companies Act 1985. They do not have to produce a separate set of accounts to comply with ss.41–44.

Annual statements of accounts

42.—(1) The charity trustees of a charity shall (subject to subsection (3) below) prepare in respect of each financial year of the charity a statement of accounts complying with such requirements as to its form and contents as may be prescribed by regulations made by the Secretary of State.

(2) Without prejudice to the generality of subsection (1) above, regulations under that subsection may make provision—

(a) for any such statement to be prepared in accordance with such methods and principles as are specified or referred to in the regulations;

(b) as to any information to be provided by way of notes to the accounts;

and regulations under that subsection may also make provision for determining the financial years of a charity for the purposes of this Act and any regulations made under it.

(3) Where a charity's gross income in any financial year does not exceed £25,000, the charity trustees may, in respect of that year, elect to prepare the following, namely—

(a) a receipts and payments account, and

(b) a statement of assets and liabilities,

instead of a statement of accounts under subsection (1) above.

(4) The charity trustees of a charity shall preserve—

(a) any statement of accounts prepared by them under subsection (1) above, or

(b) any account and statement prepared by them under subsection (3) above,

for at least six years from the end of the financial year to which any such statement relates or (as the case may be) to which any such account and statement relate.

(5) Subsection (4) of section 41 above shall apply in relation to the preservation of any such statement or account and statement as it applies in

relation to the preservation of any accounting records (the references to subsection (3) of that section being read as references to subsection (4) above).

(6) The Secretary of State may by order amend subsection (3) above by substituting a different sum for the sum for the time being specified there.

(7) Nothing in this section applies to a charity which is a company.

DEFINITIONS
  "charity": s.96(1).
  "charity trustees": s.97(1).
  "company": s.97(1).
  "financial year": s.97(1).
  "gross income": s.97(1).

GENERAL NOTE
This section re-enacts s.20 of the 1992 Act and strikes a balance between the need for the Commissioners to have up-to-date financial information about charities (see the note to s.41), and the desire not to overburden the trustees of small charities. Thus, charities with an income below £25,000 are required to submit only a receipts and payments account and a statement of assets and liabilities rather than a full statement of accounts.

Subs. (1)
The Commissioners intend to produce a number of different model forms of account for charities.

Subs. (2)
The Accounting Standards Committee have now prepared the proposed amendments to the Statement of Recommended Practice 2 (SORP 2) for charity accounts and it is likely that the regulations will closely follow the amended SORP 2. The White Paper, paras. 4.18–4.19 indicated that the types of information which will be required will include a breakdown of administrative payments, differentiating between expenditure on property, office expenses, salaries and other remuneration, details of the gross and net receipts of fundraising efforts and details of grants made, including the names of institutional beneficiaries.

Subs. (3)
Although a charity will have ten months from the end of the financial year in which to submit its accounts to the Commissioners (see s.45(3)(a)), a charity whose income is approaching £25,000 may consider it advisable to work on the basis that it will have to produce a full statement of accounts under subs. (1) rather than the limited accounts under this subsection.

Subs. (5)
If a charity ceases to exist, the obligation to preserve accounts rests with the last charity trustees.

Subs. (7)
The form and content of the accounts for a charitable company are prescribed by s.228 of and Sched. 4 to the Companies Act 1985. Once regulations have been made under subs. (1), a separate accounting régime for charitable companies may be issued under the powers in s.257 of the 1985 Act to ensure that charitable companies are subject to the same accounting provision as unincorporated charities, *Hansard*, H.L. Vol. 535, col. 405.

Annual audit or examination of charity accounts

43.—(1) Subsection (2) below applies to a financial year of a charity ("the relevant year") if the charity's gross income or total expenditure in any of the following, namely—
  (a) the relevant year,
  (b) the financial year of the charity immediately preceding the relevant year (if any), and
  (c) the financial year of the charity immediately preceding the year specified in paragraph (b) above (if any),
exceeds £100,000.

(2) If this subsection applies to a financial year of a charity, the accounts of the charity for that year shall be audited by a person who—

(a) is, in accordance with section 25 of the Companies Act 1989 (eligibility for appointment), eligible for appointment as a company auditor, or

(b) is a member of a body for the time being specified in regulations under section 44 below and is under the rules of that body eligible for appointment as auditor of the charity.

(3) If subsection (2) above does not apply to a financial year of a charity, then (subject to subsection (4) below) the accounts of the charity for that year shall, at the election of the charity trustees, either—

(a) be examined by an independent examiner, that is to say an independent person who is reasonably believed by the trustees to have the requisite ability and practical experience to carry out a competent examination of the accounts, or

(b) be audited by such a person as is mentioned in subsection (2) above.

(4) Where it appears to the Commissioners—

(a) that subsection (2), or (as the case may be) subsection (3) above, has not been complied with in relation to a financial year of a charity within ten months from the end of that year, or

(b) that, although subsection (2) above does not apply to a financial year of a charity, it would nevertheless be desirable for the accounts of the charity for that year to be audited by such a person as is mentioned in that subsection,

the Commissioners may by order require the accounts of the charity for that year to be audited by such a person as is mentioned in that subsection.

(5) If the Commissioners make an order under subsection (4) above with respect to a charity, then unless—

(a) the order is made by virtue of paragraph (b) of that subsection, and

(b) the charity trustees themselves appoint an auditor in accordance with the order,

the auditor shall be a person appointed by the Commissioners.

(6) The expenses of any audit carried out by an auditor appointed by the Commissioners under subsection (5) above, including the auditor's remuneration, shall be recoverable by the Commissioners—

(a) from the charity trustees of the charity concerned, who shall be personally liable, jointly and severally, for those expenses; or

(b) to the extent that it appears to the Commissioners not to be practical to seek recovery of those expenses in accordance with paragraph (a) above, from the funds of the charity.

(7) The Commissioners may—

(a) give guidance to charity trustees in connection with the selection of a person for appointment as an independent examiner;

(b) give such directions as they think appropriate with respect to the carrying out of an examination in pursuance of subsection (3)(a) above;

and any such guidance or directions may either be of general application or apply to a particular charity only.

(8) The Secretary of State may by order amend subsection (1) above by substituting a different sum for the sum for the time being specified there.

(9) Nothing in this section applies to a charity which is a company.

DEFINITIONS
"charity": s.96(1).
"charity trustees": s.97(1).
"the Commissioners": s.97(1).
"company": s.97(1).
"financial year": s.97(1).
"gross income": s.97(1).
"independent examiner": s.97(1).

GENERAL NOTE
This section re-enacts s.21 of the 1992 Act which introduced the requirement for charities to have their accounts audited or independently examined. An obligation for all charities to audit their accounts would clearly be unduly burdensome and the section, therefore, requires those charities with income and expenditure of less than £100,000 a year to have their accounts independently examined rather than audited. A charity whose income or expenditure exceeds £100,000 in any financial year will have only ten months to have its accounts audited, even if the income level is exceeded by a last minute legacy.

Subs. (1)
The full audit requirement applies if the gross income or expenditure exceeds £100,000 in the last three financial years.
Total expenditure. In determining whether the £100,000 limit has been breached account must be taken of capital as well as income expenditure.

Subs. (2)
The persons who under s.25 of the Companies Act 1985 are eligible to audit company accounts are very limited. Paragraph (b) makes it possible, for example, for members of the Chartered Institute of Public Finance and Accountancy to act as charity auditors.

Subs. (3)
The requirement for an independent examiner is intended to be flexible so that the calibre of the examiner and the depth of the examination can be matched to the size and complexity of the charity. The type of person it is envisaged will be an independent examiner is a bank or building society manager, a local authority treasurer or a retired accountant, *Hansard*, H.L. Vol. 535, col. 408. Guidance will be issued by the Commissioners under subs. (7).

Subs. (4)
The Commissioners formerly had power to order the audit of a charity's accounts under s.8(3) of the 1960 Act. It is envisaged that the power under this subsection will be used in similar circumstances, *i.e.*, where abuse is suspected.

Subs. (5)
A charity with income and expenditure of less than £100,000 is given the opportunity to appoint its own auditor rather than have one imposed by the Commissioners.

Subs. (6)
The White Paper, para. 4.26 considered that the Commissioners should be empowered, but not obliged, to charge the charity for a compulsory audit and that trustees should be liable personally only if the need for the audit arose from a breach of trust. The phrase "shall be recoverable", however, would appear to give no discretion to the Commissioners and to make the trustees primarily liable for the cost of any audit ordered under subs. (4).

Subs. (9)
Charitable companies are required to have their accounts audited by s.236 of the Companies Act 1985. The Commissioners have power to investigate a charitable company's accounts under s.69.

Supplementary provisions relating to audits etc.

44.—(1) The Secretary of State may by regulations make provision—
(a) specifying one or more bodies for the purposes of section 43(2)(b) above;
(b) with respect to the duties of an auditor carrying out an audit under section 43 above, including provision with respect to the making by him of a report on—
    (i) the statement of accounts prepared for the financial year in question under section 42(1) above, or
    (ii) the account and statement so prepared under section 42(3) above,
    as the case may be;
(c) with respect to the making by an independent examiner of a report in respect of an examination carried out by him under section 43 above;

(d) conferring on such an auditor or on an independent examiner a right of access with respect to books, documents and other records (however kept) which relate to the charity concerned;

(e) entitling such an auditor or an independent examiner to require, in the case of a charity, information and explanations from past or present charity trustees or trustees for the charity, or from past or present officers or employees of the charity;

(f) enabling the Commissioners, in circumstances specified in the regulations, to dispense with the requirements of section 43(2) or (3) above in the case of a particular charity or in the case of any particular financial year of a charity.

(2) If any person fails to afford an auditor or an independent examiner any facility to which he is entitled by virtue of subsection (1)(d) or (e) above, the Commissioners may by order give—

(a) to that person, or

(b) to the charity trustees for the time being of the charity concerned,

such directions as the Commissioners think appropriate for securing that the default is made good.

(3) Section 727 of the Companies Act 1985 (power of court to grant relief in certain cases) shall have effect in relation to an auditor or independent examiner appointed by a charity in pursuance of section 43 above as it has effect in relation to a person employed as auditor by a company within the meaning of that Act.

DEFINITIONS

"charity": s.96(1).
"charity trustees": s.97(1).
"the Commissioners": s.97(1).
"independent examiner": s.97(1).

GENERAL NOTE

This section re-enacts s.22 of the 1992 Act and permits the Secretary of State to make regulations in relation to audit, to make audit an effective tool for monitoring and supervision by the Commissioners.

Subs. (1)

In relation to para. (f), the White Paper, para. 4.27, envisaged that such a dispensing power would be exercised in cases where adequate audit arrangements already existed, for example, where there were corporate trustees such as the trust companies of the major banks or where one of the trustees was a local authority.

Subs. (2)

A person who fails to obey an order of the Commissioners may be dealt with as being in contempt of court under s.88.

Subs. (3)

The power of the court to grant relief under s.727 of the Companies Act 1985 is from liability for negligence, default, breach of duty or breach of trust where the auditor or examiner has acted honestly and reasonably and ought fairly to be excused, *i.e.* on the same grounds as relief for trustees under s.61 of the Trustee Act 1925.

Annual reports

45.—(1) The charity trustees of a charity shall prepare in respect of each financial year of the charity an annual report containing—

(a) such a report by the trustees on the activities of the charity during that year, and

(b) such other information relating to the charity or to its trustees or officers,

as may be prescribed by regulations made by the Secretary of State.

(2) Without prejudice to the generality of subsection (1) above, regulations under that subsection may make provision—

(a) for any such report as is mentioned in paragraph (a) of that subsection to be prepared in accordance with such principles as are specified or referred to in the regulations;

(b) enabling the Commissioners to dispense with any requirement prescribed by virtue of subsection (1)(b) above in the case of a particular charity or a particular class of charities, or in the case of a particular financial year of a charity or of any class of charities.

(3) The annual report required to be prepared under this section in respect of any financial year of a charity shall be transmitted to the Commissioners by the charity trustees—

(a) within ten months from the end of that year, or

(b) within such longer period as the Commissioners may for any special reason allow in the case of that report.

(4) Subject to subsection (5) below, any such annual report shall have attached to it the statement of accounts prepared for the financial year in question under section 42(1) above or (as the case may be) the account and statement so prepared under section 42(3) above, together with—

(a) where the accounts of the charity for that year have been audited under section 43 above, a copy of the report made by the auditor on that statement of accounts or (as the case may be) on that account and statement;

(b) where the accounts of the charity for that year have been examined under section 43 above, a copy of the report made by the independent examiner in respect of the examination carried out by him under that section.

(5) Subsection (4) above does not apply to a charity which is a company, and any annual report transmitted by the charity trustees of such a charity under subsection (3) above shall instead have attached to it a copy of the charity's annual accounts prepared for the financial year in question under Part VII of the Companies Act 1985, together with a copy of the auditors' report on those accounts.

(6) Any annual report transmitted to the Commissioners under subsection (3) above, together with the documents attached to it, shall be kept by the Commissioners for such period as they think fit.

DEFINITIONS

"charity": s.96(1).
"charity trustees": s.97(1).
"the Commissioners": s.97(1).
"company": s.97(1).
"financial year": s.97(1).

GENERAL NOTE

This section re-enacts s.23 of the 1992 Act and the aim of the section is to make public the manner in which trustees have pursued the charity's objectives in the previous financial year, *Hansard*, H.L. P.B.C., col. 120.

An exempt charity is not required to produce an annual report and an excepted charity is only required to produce a report if it is registered or required to do so by the Commissioners, s.46.

Subs. (1)

The Accounting Standards Committee in the Statement of Recommended Practice for charity accounts and the White Paper, para. 4.21 considered that the trustees' report should deal with four matters: (a) the means employed to promote the charity's objects, noting any significant changes since the last report; (b) a review of the charity's activities and achievements during the financial year; (c) a review of the transactions and financial position of the charity; (d) an explanation of salient features of the financial report.

It is likely that the regulations will require the names of all the trustees, but not their addresses, to be included in the information to be supplied under para. (b), *Hansard*, H.L. Vol. 535, cols. 353, 374.

Subs. (2)
The dispensing power in para. (b) is likely to be used where the relevant information about a charity is available elsewhere in another form.

Subs. (3)
Failure to send the report to the Commissioners is made a criminal offence by s.49.

Subs. (4)
A charity with an income of £25,000 or less and expenditure below £100,000 will be required to attach simplified accounts which have been independently examined.

A charity with an income between £25,000 and £100,000 and expenditure below £100,000 will be required to attach a full statement of accounts which has been independently examined.

A charity with an income above £100,000 will be required to attach a full statement of accounts which has been audited.

Subs. (5)
Charitable companies are relieved from the obligation of preparing two different sets of accounts for the Companies Registry and the Commissioners.

Special provision as respects accounts and annual reports of exempt and other excepted charities

46.—(1) Nothing in sections 41 to 45 above applies to any exempt charity; but the charity trustees of an exempt charity shall keep proper books of account with respect to the affairs of the charity, and if not required by or under the authority of any other Act to prepare periodical statements of account shall prepare consecutive statements of account consisting on each occasion of an income and expenditure account relating to a period of not more than fifteen months and a balance sheet relating to the end of that period.

(2) The books of accounts and statements of account relating to an exempt charity shall be preserved for a period of six years at least unless the charity ceases to exist and the Commissioners consent in writing to their being destroyed or otherwise disposed of.

(3) Nothing in sections 43 to 45 above applies to any charity which—
(a) falls within section 3(5)(c) above, and
(b) is not registered.

(4) Except in accordance with subsection (7) below, nothing in section 45 above applies to any charity (other than an exempt charity or a charity which falls within section 3(5)(c) above) which—
(a) is excepted by section 3(5) above, and
(b) is not registered.

(5) If requested to do so by the Commissioners, the charity trustees of any such charity as is mentioned in subsection (4) above shall prepare an annual report in respect of such financial year of the charity as is specified in the Commissioners' request.

(6) Any report prepared under subsection (5) above shall contain—
(a) such a report by the charity trustees on the activities of the charity during the year in question, and
(b) such other information relating to the charity or to its trustees or officers,
as may be prescribed by regulations made under section 45(1) above in relation to annual reports prepared under that provision.

(7) Subsections (3) to (6) of section 45 above shall apply to any report required to be prepared under subsection (5) above as if it were an annual report required to be prepared under subsection (1) of that section.

(8) Any reference in this section to a charity which falls within section 3(5)(c) above includes a reference to a charity which falls within that provision but is also excepted from registration by section 3(5)(b) above.

DEFINITIONS
    "charity": s.96(1).
    "charity trustees": s.97(1).
    "the Commissioners": s.97(1).
    "exempt charity": s.96(1).
    "financial year": s.97(1).

GENERAL NOTE
    This section re-enacts s.32(1)(2) of the 1960 Act as amended by Sched. 3, para. 13 to the 1992 Act and s.24 of the 1992 Act. Without this section, the Commissioners would be handicapped in their monitoring and supervisory functions by an inability to obtain financial information about excepted charities.

Subs. (1)
    Exempt charities are listed in Sched. 2 and are those charities which are considered to be subject to an adequate outside system of supervision. The account obligations for exempt charities are those imposed formerly by s.32 of the 1960 Act.

Subs. (3)
    If a charity with an income of less than £1,000 chooses to register, it becomes subject to the obligations in ss.43 to 45.

Subs. (4)
    A charity excepted by order is liable to produce an annual report if it chooses to register.

Subs. (5)
    A request for an annual report is likely to be made where there is suspicion of abuse.

Subs. (6)
    In particular, trustees can be required to attach accounts to the report.

Public inspection of annual reports etc.

47.—(1) Any annual report or other document kept by the Commissioners in pursuance of section 45(6) above shall be open to public inspection at all reasonable times—
    (a) during the period for which it is so kept; or
    (b) if the Commissioners so determine, during such lesser period as they may specify.
    (2) Where any person—
    (a) requests the charity trustees of a charity in writing to provide him with a copy of the charity's most recent accounts, and
    (b) pays them such reasonable fee (if any) as they may require in respect of the costs of complying with the request,
those trustees shall comply with the request within the period of two months beginning with the date on which it is made.
    (3) In subsection (2) above the reference to a charity's most recent accounts is—
    (a) in the case of a charity other than one falling within any of paragraphs (b) to (d) below, a reference to the statement of accounts or account and statement prepared in pursuance of section 42(1) or (3) above in respect of the last financial year of the charity the accounts for which have been audited or examined under section 43 above;
    (b) in the case of such a charity as is mentioned in section 46(3) above, a reference to the statement of accounts or account and statement prepared in pursuance of section 42(1) or (3) above in respect of the last financial year of the charity in respect of which a statement of accounts or account and statement has or have been so prepared;
    (c) in the case of a charity which is a company, a reference to the annual accounts of the company most recently audited under Part VII of the Companies Act 1985; and

(d) in the case of an exempt charity, a reference to the accounts of the charity most recently audited in pursuance of any statutory or other requirement or, if its accounts are not required to be audited, the accounts most recently prepared in respect of the charity.

DEFINITIONS
"charity": s.96(1).
"charity trustees": s.97(1).
"the Commissioners": s.97(1).
"exempt charity": s.96(1).
"financial year": s.97(1).

GENERAL NOTE
This section re-enacts s.25 of the 1992 Act and gives the public two routes to obtain the accounts of a charity: by inspecting documents at the Charity Commission or by requesting the trustees to provide a copy.

Subs. (1)
The period of time for which annual reports and accounts are available is uncertain as s.45(6) allows the Commissioners to keep the documents for such period as they think fit.

Subs. (2)
Reasonable fee. Presumably, any charge which does not exceed that imposed by the Commissioners under the Charity Commissioners (Copies and Extracts) Regulations 1992 (S.I. 1992 No. 2986) will be regarded as reasonable.
Section 49 makes it a criminal offence to fail to provide a copy of a charity's accounts on request.

Annual returns by registered charities

48.—(1) Every registered charity shall prepare in respect of each of its financial years an annual return in such form, and containing such information, as may be prescribed by regulations made by the Commissioners.

(2) Any such return shall be transmitted to the Commissioners by the date by which the charity trustees are, by virtue of section 45(3) above, required to transmit to them the annual report required to be prepared in respect of the financial year in question.

(3) The Commissioners may dispense with the requirements of subsection (1) above in the case of a particular charity or a particular class of charities, or in the case of a particular financial year of a charity or of any class of charities.

DEFINITIONS
"charity": s.96(1).
"charity trustees": s.97(1).
"the Commissioners": s.97(1).
"financial year": s.97(1).

GENERAL NOTE
This section re-enacts s.26 of the 1992 Act. The purpose of the annual return is to ensure that the information held by the Commissioners on the register about each charity is up to date and accurate. The return will also give the Commissioners information for the purpose of monitoring charities for signs of maladministration and fraud, *Hansard*, H.L. P.B.C., cols. 136–137.

Subs. (1)
The type of information likely to be required in the return will include the names and addresses of the trustees, the number of the bank account, any changes in the charity's trust, and formal legal and administrative details.

Subs. (2)
The annual report, and hence the annual return, must be submitted within ten months of the end of the financial year in question. Section 49 makes it a criminal offence to fail to make the annual return.

Subs. (3)
The dispensing power is only likely to be used where the information in the annual return is readily available from another source.

Offences

49. Any person who, without reasonable excuse, is persistently in default in relation to any requirement imposed—
  (a) by section 45(3) above (taken with section 45(4) or (5), as the case may require), or
  (b) by section 47(2) or 48(2) above,
shall be guilty of an offence and liable on summary conviction to a fine not exceeding level 4 on the standard scale.

GENERAL NOTE
This section re-enacts s.27 of the 1992 Act. The specific offences are (1) failing to submit the annual report to the Commissioners; (2) failing to provide members of the public with copies of accounts and (3) failing to provide the Commissioners with the annual return. All the offences require the individual to be without reasonable excuse and to be persistently in default. It is envisaged that several reminders will have been sent by the Commissioners, and ignored, before any offence has been committed. One potential problem is that the correspondent of the charity may not tell the trustees about the reminders.
The standard levels of maximum fines on summary conviction are to be found in s.37(2) of the Criminal Justice Act 1982 and the present fourth level is £2,500. The consent of the Director of Public Prosecutions is required before any proceedings can be brought under this section, s.94(2)(d).

PART VII

INCORPORATION OF CHARITY TRUSTEES

Incorporation of trustees of a charity

50.—(1) Where—
  (a) the trustees of a charity, in accordance with section 52 below, apply to the Commissioners for a certificate of incorporation of the trustees as a body corporate, and
  (b) the Commissioners consider that the incorporation of the trustees would be in the interests of the charity,
the Commissioners may grant such a certificate, subject to such conditions or directions as they think fit to insert in it.
(2) The Commissioners shall not, however, grant such a certificate in a case where the charity appears to them to be required to be registered under section 3 above but is not so registered.
(3) On the grant of such a certificate—
  (a) the trustees of the charity shall become a body corporate by such name as is specified in the certificate; and
  (b) (without prejudice to the operation of section 54 below) any relevant rights or liabilities of those trustees shall become rights or liabilities of that body.
(4) After their incorporation the trustees—
  (a) may sue and be sued in their corporate name; and
  (b) shall have the same powers, and be subject to the same restrictions and limitations, as respects the holding, acquisition and disposal of property for or in connection with the purposes of the charity as they had or were subject to while unincorporated;
and any relevant legal proceedings that might have been continued or commenced by or against the trustees may be continued or commenced by or against them in their corporate name.
(5) A body incorporated under this section need not have a common seal.
(6) In this section—

"relevant rights or liabilities" means rights or liabilities in connection with any property vesting in the body in question under section 51 below; and

"relevant legal proceedings" means legal proceedings in connection with any such property.

DEFINITIONS
"charity": s.96(1).
"the Commissioners": s.97(1).
"relevant legal proceedings": subs. (6).
"relevant rights and liabilities": subs. (6).
"the trustees": s.62.

GENERAL NOTE
Charity trustees face the problem of the need to transfer the assets of the trust on any change of trustees. This problem was for a long time solved by the use of the official custodian, a route which is no longer available, see s.29 of the 1992 Act. This and the succeeding 12 sections provide an alternative solution to the use of a commercial custodian trustee, by providing a method for the trustee body to seek incorporation.

This section re-enacts s.1 of the 1872 Act as substituted by s.48 of and Sched. 4 to the 1992 Act and provides a simple procedure for incorporation by certificate from the Commissioners. Thereafter, the trustees of the charity may sue and be sued in their corporate name and hold property.

Subs. (1)
The terms of the certificate may be amended by the Commissioners under s.56. Breach of any condition or direction of the certificate by the trustees may be dealt with as a contempt of court, ss.58 and 88.

Subs. (3)
Section 54 provides that the liability of the trustees of the charity shall not be limited by incorporation.

Subs. (4)
The property of the charity is vested in the body corporate by s.51.

Estate to vest in body corporate

51. The certificate of incorporation shall vest in the body corporate all real and personal estate, of whatever nature or tenure, belonging to or held by any person or persons in trust for the charity, and thereupon any person or persons in whose name or names any stocks, funds or securities are standing in trust for the charity, shall transfer them into the name of the body corporate, except that the foregoing provisions shall not apply to property vested in the official custodian.

DEFINITIONS
"charity": s.96(1).
"the official custodian": s.97(1).

GENERAL NOTE
This section re-enacts s.2 of the 1872 Act as amended by s.48 of and Sched. 4 to the 1992 Act and vests the property of the charity in the corporate body after incorporation of trustees under s.50. The official custodian continues to hold land: s.29(3)(a) of the 1992 Act.

Applications for incorporation

52.—(1) Every application to the Commissioners for a certificate of incorporation under this Part of this Act shall—
    (a) be in writing and signed by the trustees of the charity concerned; and
    (b) be accompanied by such documents or information as the Commissioners may require for the purpose of the application.
  (2) The Commissioners may require—

(a) any statement contained in any such application, or
(b) any document or information supplied under subsection (1)(b) above,
to be verified in such manner as they may specify.

DEFINITIONS
 "the Commissioners": s.97(1).
 "the trustees": s.62.

GENERAL NOTE
 This section re-enacts s.3 of the 1872 Act as substituted by s.48 of and Sched. 4 to the 1992 Act and provides the method for application by trustees for incorporation.

Nomination of trustees, and filling up vacancies

53.—(1) Before a certificate of incorporation is granted under this Part of this Act, trustees of the charity must have been effectually appointed to the satisfaction of the Commissioners.

(2) Where a certificate of incorporation is granted vacancies in the number of the trustees of the charity shall from time to time be filled up so far as required by the constitution or settlement of the charity, or by any conditions or directions in the certificate, by such legal means as would have been available for the appointment of new trustees of the charity if no certificate of incorporation had been granted, or otherwise as required by such conditions or directions.

DEFINITIONS
 "charity": s.96(1).
 "the Commissioners": s.97(1).
 "the trustees": s.62.

GENERAL NOTE
 This section re-enacts s.4 of the 1872 Act as amended by s.48 of and Sched. 4 to the 1992 Act.

Liability of trustees and others, notwithstanding incorporation

54. After a certificate of incorporation has been granted under this Part of this Act all trustees of the charity, notwithstanding their incorporation, shall be chargeable for such property as shall come into their hands, and shall be answerable and accountable for their own acts, receipts, neglects, and defaults, and for the due administration of the charity and its property, in the same manner and to the same extent as if no such incorporation had been effected.

DEFINITIONS
 "charity": s.96(1).
 "the trustees": s.62.

GENERAL NOTE
 This section re-enacts s.5 of the 1872 Act as amended by s.48 of and Sched. 4 to the 1992 Act and retains the trustees' personal unlimited liability after incorporation of the trustee body.

Certificate to be evidence of compliance with requirements for incorporation

55. A certificate of incorporation granted under this Part of this Act shall be conclusive evidence that all the preliminary requirements for incorporation under this Part of this Act have been complied with, and the date of incorporation mentioned in the certificate shall be deemed to be the date at which incorporation has taken place.

GENERAL NOTE
 This section re-enacts s.6 of the 1872 Act as amended by s.48 of and Sched. 4 to the 1992 Act.

Power of Commissioners to amend certificate of incorporation

56.—(1) The Commissioners may amend a certificate of incorporation either on the application of the incorporated body to which it relates or of their own motion.

(2) Before making any such amendment of their own motion, the Commissioners shall by notice in writing—

(a) inform the trustees of the relevant charity of their proposals, and

(b) invite those trustees to make representations to them within a time specified in the notice, being not less than one month from the date of the notice.

(3) The Commissioners shall take into consideration any representations made by those trustees within the time so specified, and may then (without further notice) proceed with their proposals either without modification or with such modifications as appear to them to be desirable.

(4) The Commissioners may amend a certificate of incorporation either—

(a) by making an order specifying the amendment; or

(b) by issuing a new certificate of incorporation taking account of the amendment.

DEFINITIONS
"the Commissioners": s.97(1).
"incorporated body": s.62.
"the relevant charity": s.62.
"the trustees": s.62.

GENERAL NOTE
This section re-enacts s.6A of the 1872 Act which was inserted by s.48 of and Sched. 4 to the 1992 Act. Section 50(1) allows the Commissioners to grant a certificate of incorporation subject to conditions or directions and this section makes provision for amendment. The incorporated body may apply to the Commissioners for amendment of the certificate, for example, to change the number of trustees.

Records of applications and certificates

57.—(1) The Commissioners shall keep a record of all applications for, and certificates of, incorporation under this Part of this Act and shall preserve all documents sent to them under this Part of this Act.

(2) Any person may inspect such documents, under the direction of the Commissioners, and any person may require a copy or extract of any such document to be certified by a certificate signed by the secretary of the Commissioners.

DEFINITIONS
"the Commissioners": s.97(1).
"document": s.97(2).

GENERAL NOTE
This section re-enacts s.7 of the 1872 Act as amended by s.48 of and Sched. 4 to the 1992 Act.

Enforcement of orders and directions

58. All conditions and directions inserted in any certificate of incorporation shall be binding upon and performed or observed by the trustees as trusts of the charity, and section 88 below shall apply to any trustee who fails to perform or observe any such condition or direction as it applies to a person guilty of disobedience to any such order of the Commissioners as is mentioned in that section.

DEFINITIONS
"charity": s.96(1).
"the Commissioners": s.97(1).
"the trustees": s.62.

GENERAL NOTE

This section re-enacts s.8 of the 1872 Act as amended by s.48 of and Sched. 4 to the 1992 Act. By s.88, failure to perform a direction or order of the Commissioners may be dealt with as a contempt of court.

Gifts to charity before incorporation to have same effect afterwards

59. After the incorporation of the trustees of any charity under this Part of this Act every donation, gift and disposition of property, real or personal, lawfully made before the incorporation but not having actually taken effect, or thereafter lawfully made, by deed, will or otherwise to or in favour of the charity, or the trustees of the charity, or otherwise for the purposes of the charity, shall take effect as if made to or in favour of the incorporated body or otherwise for the like purposes.

DEFINITIONS

"charity": s.96(1).
"incorporated body": s.62.
"the trustees": s.62.

GENERAL NOTE

This section re-enacts s.10 of the 1872 Act and makes gifts to the charity take effect as gifts to the incorporated body of trustees.

Execution of documents by incorporated body

60.—(1) This section has effect as respects the execution of documents by an incorporated body.

(2) If an incorporated body has a common seal, a document may be executed by the body by the affixing of its common seal.

(3) Whether or not it has a common seal, a document may be executed by an incorporated body either—

(a) by being signed by a majority of the trustees of the relevant charity and expressed (in whatever form of words) to be executed by the body; or

(b) by being executed in pursuance of an authority given under subsection (4) below.

(4) For the purposes of subsection (3)(b) above the trustees of the relevant charity in the case of an incorporated body may, subject to the trusts of the charity, confer on any two or more of their number—

(a) a general authority, or

(b) an authority limited in such manner as the trustees think fit,

to execute in the name and on behalf of the body documents for giving effect to transactions to which the body is a party.

(5) An authority under subsection (4) above—

(a) shall suffice for any document if it is given in writing or by resolution of a meeting of the trustees of the relevant charity, notwithstanding the want of any formality that would be required in giving an authority apart from that subsection;

(b) may be given so as to make the powers conferred exercisable by any of the trustees, or may be restricted to named persons or in any other way;

(c) subject to any such restriction, and until it is revoked, shall, notwithstanding any change in the trustees of the relevant charity, have effect as a continuing authority given by the trustees from time to time of the charity and exercisable by such trustees.

(6) In any authority under subsection (4) above to execute a document in the name and on behalf of an incorporated body there shall, unless the contrary intention appears, be implied authority also to execute it for the

body in the name and on behalf of the official custodian or of any other person, in any case in which the trustees could do so.

(7) A document duly executed by an incorporated body which makes it clear on its face that it is intended by the person or persons making it to be a deed has effect, upon delivery, as a deed; and it shall be presumed, unless a contrary intention is proved, to be delivered upon its being so executed.

(8) In favour of a purchaser a document shall be deemed to have been duly executed by such a body if it purports to be signed—

(a) by a majority of the trustees of the relevant charity, or

(b) by such of the trustees of the relevant charity as are authorised by the trustees of that charity to execute it in the name and on behalf of the body,

and, where the document makes it clear on its face that it is intended by the person or persons making it to be a deed, it shall be deemed to have been delivered upon its being executed.

For this purpose "purchaser" means a purchaser in good faith for valuable consideration and includes a lessee, mortgagee or other person who for valuable consideration acquires an interest in property.

DEFINITIONS
"incorporated body": s.62.
"purchaser": subs. (8).
"the relevant charity": s.62.
"the trustees": s.62.

GENERAL NOTE
This section re-enacts s.12 of the 1872 Act as amended by s.48 of and Sched. 4 to the 1992 Act and permits the execution of documents by affixing a common seal or by a majority of trustees, or by a limited number of trustees under authority.

Subs. (2)
It is not necessary for an incorporated body to have a common seal, s.50(5).

Subs. (5)
For the avoidance of doubt, the resolution of the trustees should be recorded in writing.

Subs. (8)
Any document which is executed by a number of trustees should set out clearly the basis on which they sign and refer to the relevant resolution.

Power of Commissioners to dissolve incorporated body

61.—(1) Where the Commissioners are satisfied—

(a) that an incorporated body has no assets or does not operate, or

(b) that the relevant charity in the case of an incorporated body has ceased to exist, or

(c) that the institution previously constituting, or treated by them as constituting, any such charity has ceased to be, or (as the case may be) was not at the time of the body's incorporation, a charity, or

(d) that the purposes of the relevant charity in the case of an incorporated body have been achieved so far as is possible or are in practice incapable of being achieved,

they may of their own motion make an order dissolving the body as from such date as is specified in the order.

(2) Where the Commissioners are satisfied, on the application of the trustees of the relevant charity in the case of an incorporated body, that it would be in the interests of the charity for that body to be dissolved, the Commissioners may make an order dissolving the body as from such date as is specified in the order.

(3) Subject to subsection (4) below, an order made under this section with respect to an incorporated body shall have the effect of vesting in the

trustees of the relevant charity, in trust for that charity, all property for the time being vested—
  (a) in the body, or
  (b) in any other person (apart from the official custodian),
in trust for that charity.
  (4) If the Commissioners so direct in the order—
  (a) all or any specified part of that property shall, instead of vesting in the trustees of the relevant charity, vest—
        (i) in a specified person as trustee for, or nominee of, that charity, or
        (ii) in such persons (other than the trustees of the relevant charity) as may be specified;
  (b) any specified investments, or any specified class or description of investments, held by any person in trust for the relevant charity, shall be transferred—
        (i) to the trustees of that charity, or
        (ii) to any such person or persons as is or are mentioned in paragraph (a)(i) or (ii) above;
and for this purpose "specified" means specified by the Commissioners in the order.
  (5) Where an order to which this subsection applies is made with respect to an incorporated body—
  (a) any rights or liabilities of the body shall become rights or liabilities of the trustees of the relevant charity; and
  (b) any legal proceedings that might have been continued or commenced by or against the body may be continued or commenced by or against those trustees.
  (6) Subsection (5) above applies to any order under this section by virtue of which—
  (a) any property vested as mentioned in subsection (3) above is vested—
        (i) in the trustees of the relevant charity, or
        (ii) in any person as trustee for, or nominee of, that charity; or
  (b) any investments held by any person in trust for the relevant charity are required to be transferred—
        (i) to the trustees of that charity, or
        (ii) to any person as trustee for, or nominee of, that charity.
  (7) Any order made by the Commissioners under this section may be varied or revoked by a further order so made.

DEFINITIONS
  "the Commissioners": s.97(1).
  "incorporated body": s.62.
  "the relevant charity": s.62.
  "the trustees": s.62.

GENERAL NOTE
  This section re-enacts s.12A of the 1872 Act which was inserted by s.48 of and Sched. 4 to the 1992 Act and permits the Commissioners to dissolve an incorporated body of trustees returning the property to the trustees or some other persons as trustee for the charity.

Subs. (1)
  There is only a power to dissolve where the charity has ceased to operate, not where there is mismanagement or maladministration, *cf.* the power in relation to charitable companies under s.63. In any other circumstances, an application from the trustees is necessary under subs. (2).

Subs. (3)
  A dissolution order of the Commissioners automatically vests the property of the incorporated body in the trustees unless the Commissioners make an order under subs. (4).

Interpretation of Part VII

62. In this Part of this Act—
"incorporated body" means a body incorporated under section 50 above;
"the relevant charity", in relation to an incorporated body, means the charity the trustees of which have been incorporated as that body;
"the trustees", in relation to a charity, means the charity trustees.

GENERAL NOTE
This section re-enacts s.14 of the 1872 Act as substituted by s.48 of and Sched. 4 to the 1992 Act and supplies the definitions for Pt. VII of the Act.

PART VIII

CHARITABLE COMPANIES

Winding up

63.—(1) Where a charity may be wound up by the High Court under the Insolvency Act 1986, a petition for it to be wound up under that Act by any court in England or Wales having jurisdiction may be presented by the Attorney General, as well as by any person authorised by that Act.

(2) Where a charity may be so wound up by the High Court, such a petition may also be presented by the Commissioners if, at any time after they have instituted an inquiry under section 8 above with respect to the charity, they are satisfied as mentioned in section 18(1)(a) or (b) above.

(3) Where a charitable company is dissolved, the Commissioners may make an application under section 651 of the Companies Act 1985 (power of court to declare dissolution of company void) for an order to be made under that section with respect to the company; and for this purpose subsection (1) of that section shall have effect in relation to a charitable company as if the reference to the liquidator of the company included a reference to the Commissioners.

(4) Where a charitable company's name has been struck off the register of companies under section 652 of the Companies Act 1985 (power of registrar to strike defunct company off register), the Commissioners may make an application under section 653(2) of that Act (objection to striking off by person aggrieved) for an order restoring the company's name to that register; and for this purpose section 653(2) shall have effect in relation to a charitable company as if the reference to any such person aggrieved as is there mentioned included a reference to the Commissioners.

(5) The powers exercisable by the Commissioners by virtue of this section shall be exercisable by them of their own motion, but shall be exercisable only with the agreement of the Attorney General on each occasion.

(6) In this section "charitable company" means a company which is a charity.

DEFINITIONS
"charity": s.96(1).
"charitable company": subs. (6).
"the Commissioners": s.97(1).

GENERAL NOTE
This section re-enacts s.30 of the 1960 Act as amended by s.111(1) of the Companies Act 1989 and s.10 of the 1992 Act and sets out the circumstances in which the Attorney General and the Commissioners may apply to the court for a charitable company to be wound up.

Subs. (2)
The Commissioners need to be satisfied that there has been misconduct or mismanagement in the administration of the charity *or* that it is necessary or desirable to act for the purpose of protecting the property of the charity.
If a s.8 inquiry has not taken place, the Attorney General can still petition under subs. (1).

Subs. (3)
   Any application under s.651 of the Companies Act 1985 must be brought within two years of the date of dissolution. This allows such proceedings to be taken as might have been taken if the charitable company had not been dissolved, for example, to recover assets of the charity.

Subs. (4)
   By s.653(2) of the Companies Act 1985, any application must be made within 20 years of the publication of the s.652 notice in the Gazette.

Alteration of objects clause

   64.—(1) Where a charity is a company or other body corporate having power to alter the instruments establishing or regulating it as a body corporate, no exercise of that power which has the effect of the body ceasing to be a charity shall be valid so as to affect the application of—
   (a) any property acquired under any disposition or agreement previously made otherwise than for full consideration in money or money's worth, or any property representing property so acquired,
   (b) any property representing income which has accrued before the alteration is made, or
   (c) the income from any such property as aforesaid.
   (2) Where a charity is a company, any alteration by it—
   (a) of the objects clause in its memorandum of association, or
   (b) of any other provision in its memorandum of association, or any provision in its articles of association, which is a provision directing or restricting the manner in which property of the company may be used or applied,
is ineffective without the prior written consent of the Commissioners.
   (3) Where a company has made any such alteration in accordance with subsection (2) above and—
   (a) in connection with the alteration is required by virtue of—
         (i) section 6(1) of the Companies Act 1985 (delivery of documents following alteration of objects), or
         (ii) that provision as applied by section 17(3) of that Act (alteration of condition in memorandum which could have been contained in articles),
      to deliver to the registrar of companies a printed copy of its memorandum, as altered, or
   (b) is required by virtue of section 380(1) of that Act (registration etc. of resolutions and agreements) to forward to the registrar a printed or other copy of the special resolution effecting the alteration,
the copy so delivered or forwarded by the company shall be accompanied by a copy of the Commissioner's consent.
   (4) Section 6(3) of that Act (offences) shall apply to any default by a company in complying with subsection (3) above as it applies to any such default as is mentioned in that provision.

DEFINITIONS
   "charity": s.96(1).
   "the Commissioners": s.97(1).
   "company": s.97(1).

GENERAL NOTE
   This section re-enacts s.30A of the 1960 Act as amended by s.111(1) of the Companies Act 1989 and s.40 of the 1992 Act and ensures that the Commissioners can control the purpose for which property is held by charitable companies.

Subs. (1)
   Only property acquired after the change of objects can be used for non-charitable purposes.

Subs. (2)

The prior written consent. The Commissioners have previously indicated that they will intervene if they think that, by a fundamental change in the objects of a charitable company, the real intentions of the public who contributed are likely to be defeated, [1971] Ch. Comm. Rep., paras. 26–29.

A provision restricting payment of fees to directors would come within para. (b).

Subs. (3)

Special resolution. Charitable companies have power to alter their objects in the memorandum of association by special resolution under s.4 of the Companies Act 1985, as amended by s.110(2) of the Companies Act 1989.

Invalidity of certain transactions

65.—(1) Sections 35 and 35A of the Companies Act 1985 (capacity of company not limited by its memorandum; power of directors to bind company) do not apply to the acts of a company which is a charity except in favour of a person who—

(a) gives full consideration in money or money's worth in relation to the act in question, and

(b) does not know that the act is not permitted by the company's memorandum or, as the case may be, is beyond the powers of the directors,

or who does not know at the time the act is done that the company is a charity.

(2) However, where such a company purports to transfer or grant an interest in property, the fact that the act was not permitted by the company's memorandum or, as the case may be, that the directors in connection with the act exceeded any limitation on their powers under the company's constitution, does not affect the title of a person who subsequently acquires the property or any interest in it for full consideration without actual notice of any such circumstances affecting the validity of the company's act.

(3) In any proceedings arising out of subsection (1) above the burden of proving—

(a) that a person knew that an act was not permitted by the company's memorandum or was beyond the powers of the directors, or

(b) that a person knew that the company was a charity,

lies on the person making that allegation.

(4) Where a company is a charity, the ratification of an act under section 35(3) of the Companies Act 1985, or the ratification of a transaction to which section 322A of that Act applies (invalidity of certain transactions to which directors or their associates are parties), is ineffective without the prior written consent of the Commissioners.

DEFINITIONS

"charity": s.96(1).
"the Commissioners": s.97(1).
"company": s.97(1).

GENERAL NOTE

This section re-enacts s.30B of the 1960 Act which was inserted in that Act by s.111(1) of the Companies Act 1989 and limits the effect of ss.35 and 35A of the Companies Act 1985 which abolished the *ultra vires* doctrine and removed restrictions on the powers of directors in favour of third parties dealing with companies. The effect of this section is that commercial transactions beyond the capacity of a charitable company or the power of its directors are binding as are transactions with a person who does not know that he is dealing with a charity; other *ultra vires* transactions remain void.

Subs. (1)

The burden of proof is on the person making the allegation either that a person knew the act was not permitted or that he knew that the company was a charity, subs. (3).

As to knowledge of the charitable status of a company, see s.68.

Subs. (2)

The effect of this subsection is to protect a bone fide purchaser for full consideration of charity property.

Subs. (4)

Section 35(3) of the Companies Act 1985 permits ratification of *ultra vires* transactions. Section 322A of the Companies Act 1989 covers transactions where a director or a person connected with him is a party.

Requirement of consent of Commissioners to certain acts

66.—(1) Where a company is a charity—

(a) any approval given by the company for the purposes of any of the provisions of the Companies Act 1985 specified in subsection (2) below, and

(b) any affirmation by it for the purposes of section 322(2)(c) of that Act (affirmation of voidable arrangements under which assets are acquired by or from a director or person connected with him),

is ineffective without the prior written consent of the Commissioners.

(2) The provisions of the Companies Act 1985 referred to in subsection (1)(a) above are—

(a) section 312 (payment to director in respect of loss of office or retirement);

(b) section 313(1) (payment to director in respect of loss of office or retirement made in connection with transfer of undertaking or property of company);

(c) section 319(3) (incorporation in director's service contract of term whereby his employment will or may continue for a period of more than five years);

(d) section 320(1) (arrangement whereby assets are acquired by or from director or person connected with him);

(e) section 337(3)(a) (provision of funds to meet certain expenses incurred by director).

DEFINITIONS

"charity": s.96(1).
"the Commissioners": s.97(1).
"company": s.97(1).

GENERAL NOTE

This section re-enacts s.30BA of the 1960 Act which was inserted by s.41 of the 1992 Act and prevents charitable companies from carrying out certain transactions in relation to directors, which would be permissible under the Companies Acts, without the consent of the Commissioners, thus strengthening the control of the Charity Commissioners over charitable companies.

Subs. (1)

The prior written consent. In view of the extreme reluctance of the Commissioners and the courts to allow charity trustees to receive remuneration for their services, it is unlikely that the Commissioners will consent to directors of charitable companies receiving benefits in any of the cases set out in subs. (2) except in very exceptional circumstances, see [1988] Ch. Comm. Rep., para. 38; *Smallpiece* v. *Att.-Gen.* [1990] Ch. Comm. Rep., p.36.

Name to appear on correspondence etc.

67. Section 30(7) of the Companies Act 1985 (exemption from requirements relating to publication of name etc.) shall not, in its application to any company which is a charity, have the effect of exempting the company from the requirements of section 349(1) of that Act (company's name to appear in its correspondence etc.).

DEFINITIONS

"charity": s.96(1).

"company": s.97(1).

GENERAL NOTE
This section re-enacts s.30BB of the 1960 Act which was inserted by s.42 of the 1992 Act. Consistent with the desire to make public when an institution is subject to the supervision of the Commissioners (see the note to s.5) this section ensures that the name of a charitable company appears on all its correspondence, notices and bills.

Status to appear on correspondence etc.

68.—(1) Where a company is a charity and its name does not include the word "charity" or the word "charitable", the fact that the company is a charity shall be stated in English in legible characters—

(a) in all business letters of the company,
(b) in all its notices and other official publications,
(c) in all bills of exchange, promissory notes, endorsements, cheques and orders for money or goods purporting to be signed on behalf of the company,
(d) in all conveyances purporting to be executed by the company, and
(e) in all bills rendered by it and in all its invoices, receipts, and letters of credit.

(2) In subsection (1)(d) above "conveyance" means any instrument creating, transferring, varying or extinguishing an interest in land.

(3) Subsections (2) to (4) of section 349 of the Companies Act 1985 (offences in connection with failure to include required particulars in business letters etc.) shall apply in relation to a contravention of subsection (1) above, taking the reference in subsection (3)(b) of that section to a bill of parcels as a reference to any such bill as is mentioned in subsection (1)(e) above.

DEFINITIONS
"charity": s.96(1).
"company": s.97(1).

GENERAL NOTE
This section re-enacts s.30C of the 1960 Act which was inserted by s.111(1) of the Companies Act 1989 and amended by Sched. 3, para. 11 of the 1992 Act. The fact that a transaction which is *ultra vires* or beyond the powers of the directors will bind a charitable company if the other person did not know that he was dealing with a charity (see s.65(1)) provides one reason, at least, to publicise the charitable status of a company. Failure to comply with the section is a criminal offence, see subs. (3).

Subs. (1)
Legible characters. There is no requirement for printing. It is open to the directors of a charitable company with few relevant transactions, for example, to write on a cheque that it is a charity, providing that the writing is legible.

Investigation of accounts

69.—(1) In the case of a charity which is a company the Commissioners may by order require that the condition and accounts of the charity for such period as they think fit shall be investigated and audited by an auditor appointed by them, being a person eligible for appointment as a company auditor under section 25 of the Companies Act 1989.

(2) An auditor acting under subsection (1) above—

(a) shall have a right of access to all books, accounts and documents relating to the charity which are in the possession or control of the charity trustees or to which the charity trustees have access;
(b) shall be entitled to require from any charity trustee, past or present, and from any past or present officer or employee of the charity such information and explanation as he thinks necessary for the performance of his duties;

(c) shall at the conclusion or during the progress of the audit make such reports to the Commissioners about the audit or about the accounts or affairs of the charity as he thinks the case requires, and shall send a copy of any such report to the charity trustees.

(3) The expenses of any audit under subsection (1) above, including the remuneration of the auditor, shall be paid by the Commissioners.

(4) If any person fails to afford an auditor any facility to which he is entitled under subsection (2) above the Commissioners may by order give to that person or to the charity trustees for the time being such directions as the Commissioners think appropriate for securing that the default is made good.

DEFINITIONS
"charity": s.96(1).
"charity trustee": s.97(1).
"the Commissioners": s.97(1).
"company": s.97(1).

GENERAL NOTE
This section re-enacts s.8 of the 1960 Act as amended by the Companies Act 1989 (Eligibility for Appointment as Company Auditor) (Consequential Amendments) Regulations 1991 (S.I. 1991 No. 1997) and Sched. 3, para. 2 to the 1992 Act and retains the power of the Charity Commissioners to investigate the accounts of charitable companies.

Subs. (1)
Under s.25 of the Companies Act 1989 the persons eligible as auditors are current members of the recognised supervisory bodies who are eligible for appointment as auditors under the rules of that body.

Subs. (2)
Documents. Information recorded otherwise than in legible form, for example, on computer disk, must be produced in legible form, see s.97(2).

Subs. (3)
Cf. s.43(6) which lays the cost of audit ordered by the Commissioners of a non-company charity on the charity trustees.

Subs. (4)
A person guilty of disobedience to an order of the Commissioners requiring a default to be made good is liable to be committed for contempt, s.88.

PART IX

MISCELLANEOUS

Powers of investment

Relaxation of restrictions on wider-range investments

70.—(1) The Secretary of State may by order made with the consent of the Treasury—

(a) direct that, in the case of a trust fund consisting of property held by or in trust for a charity, any division of the fund in pursuance of section 2(1) of the Trustee Investments Act 1961 (trust funds to be divided so that wider-range and narrower-range investments are equal in value) shall be made so that the value of the wider-range part at the time of the division bears to the then value of the narrower-range part such proportion as is specified in the order;

(b) provide that, in its application in relation to such a trust fund, that Act shall have effect subject to such modifications so specified as the Secretary of State considers appropriate in consequence of, or in connection with, any such direction.

(2) Where, before the coming into force of an order under this section, a trust fund consisting of property held by or in trust for a charity has already been divided in pursuance of section 2(1) of that Act, the fund may, notwithstanding anything in that provision, be again divided (once only) in pursuance of that provision during the continuance in force of the order.

(3) No order shall be made under this section unless a draft of the order has been laid before and approved by a resolution of each House of Parliament.

(4) Expressions used in this section which are also used in the Trustee Investments Act 1961 have the same meaning as in that Act.

(5) In the application of this section to Scotland, "charity" means a recognised body within the meaning of section 1(7) of the Law Reform (Miscellaneous Provisions) (Scotland) Act 1990.

DEFINITIONS
"charity": subs. (5); s.96(1).

GENERAL NOTE
This section re-enacts s.38 of the 1992 Act. The investment powers laid down in the Trustee Investment Act 1961 have for long been considered to be unsatisfactory; the Law Reform Committee advised amendment in 1982 in their report: *"Powers and Duties of Trustees"*. Larger charities have been able to obtain schemes to widen their powers of investment but this section, together with s.71, is capable of giving all charities less restrictive powers ahead of any general reform of the law relating to the investment powers of trustees.

Subs. (1)
Paragraph (a) opens the way for charities to invest more than 50 per cent. of their funds in equities rather than gilts and para. (b) allows further easing of the rules in relation to investment by charities.

Subs. (2)
This subsection permits existing charities to take advantage of any relaxation of the rules regarding the proportion of funds which may be invested in equities.

Extension of powers of investment

71.—(1) The Secretary of State may by regulations made with the consent of the Treasury make, with respect to property held by or in trust for a charity, provision authorising a trustee to invest such property in any manner specified in the regulations, being a manner of investment not for the time being included in any Part of Schedule 1 to the Trustee Investments Act 1961.

(2) Regulations under this section may make such provision—

(a) regulating the investment of property in any manner authorised by virtue of subsection (1) above, and

(b) with respect to the variation and retention of investments so made,

as the Secretary of State considers appropriate.

(3) Such regulations may, in particular, make provision—

(a) imposing restrictions with respect to the proportion of the property held by or in trust for a charity which may be invested in any manner authorised by virtue of subsection (1) above, being either restrictions applying to investment in any such manner generally or restrictions applying to investment in any particular such manner;

(b) imposing the like requirements with respect to the obtaining and consideration of advice as are imposed by any of the provisions of section 6 of the Trustee Investments Act 1961 (duty of trustees in choosing investments).

(4) Any power of investment conferred by any regulations under this section—

(a) shall be in addition to, and not in derogation from, any power conferred otherwise than by such regulations; and

(b) shall not be limited by the trusts of a charity (in so far as they are not contained in any Act or instrument made under an enactment) unless it is excluded by those trusts in express terms;

but any such power shall only be exercisable by a trustee in so far as a contrary intention is not expressed in any Act or in any instrument made under an enactment and relating to the powers of the trustee.

(5) No regulations shall be made under this section unless a draft of the regulations has been laid before and approved by a resolution of each House of Parliament.

(6) In this section "property"—

(a) in England and Wales, means real or personal property of any description, including money and things in action, but does not include an interest in expectancy; and

(b) in Scotland, means property of any description (whether heritable or moveable, corporeal or incorporeal) which is presently enjoyable, but does not include a future interest, whether vested or contingent;

and any reference to property held by or in trust for a charity is a reference to property so held, whether it is for the time being in a state of investment or not.

(7) In the application of this section to Scotland, "charity" means a recognised body within the meaning of section 1(7) of the Law Reform (Miscellaneous Provisions) (Scotland) Act 1990.

DEFINITIONS
"charity": subs. (7); s.96(1).
"property": subs. (6).

GENERAL NOTE
See the note to s.70. This section empowers the Secretary of State to make regulations extending charity trustees' powers of investment.

Subs. (1)
The power to extend investments is a special power for the purposes of s.3 of the Trustee Investment Act 1961. Once regulations have been made, charities will be able to convert funds held in narrower, and wider, range investments into special property and invest in accordance with the regulations.

Subs. (3)
In sanctioning schemes extending investment powers, the courts have insisted that there are provisions for ensuring a core of 'safe' investments for every charity and for ensuring that proper advice is available and taken, see *Trustees of the British Museum* v. *Att. Gen.* [1984] 1 W.L.R. 418; *Steel* v. *Wellcome Custodian Trustees* [1988] 1 W.L.R. 167.

Disqualification for acting as charity trustee

Persons disqualified for being trustees of a charity

72.—(1) Subject to the following provisions of this section, a person shall be disqualified for being a charity trustee or trustee for a charity if—

(a) he has been convicted of any offence involving dishonesty or deception;

(b) he has been adjudged bankrupt or sequestration of his estate has been awarded and (in either case) he has not been discharged;

(c) he has made a composition or arrangement with, or granted a trust deed for, his creditors and has not been discharged in respect of it;

(d) he has been removed from the office of charity trustee or trustee for a charity by an order made—

(i) by the Commissioners under section 18(2)(i) above, or

(ii) by the Commissioners under section 20(1A)(i) of the Charities Act 1960 (power to act for protection of charities) or under section 20(1)(i) of that Act (as in force before the commencement of section 8 of the Charities Act 1992), or

(iii) by the High Court,

on the grounds of any misconduct or mismanagement in the administration of the charity for which he was responsible or to which he was privy, or which he by his conduct contributed to or facilitated;

(e) he has been removed, under section 7 of the Law Reform (Miscellaneous Provisions) (Scotland) Act 1990 (powers of Court of Session to deal with management of charities), from being concerned in the management or control of any body;

(f) he is subject to a disqualification order under the Company Directors Disqualification Act 1986 or to an order made under section 429(2)(b) of the Insolvency Act 1986 (failure to pay under county court administration order).

(2) In subsection (1) above—

(a) paragraph (a) applies whether the conviction occurred before or after the commencement of that subsection, but does not apply in relation to any conviction which is a spent conviction for the purposes of the Rehabilitation of Offenders Act 1974;

(b) paragraph (b) applies whether the adjudication of bankruptcy or the sequestration occurred before or after the commencement of that subsection;

(c) paragraph (c) applies whether the composition or arrangement was made, or the trust deed was granted, before or after the commencement of that subsection; and

(d) paragraphs (d) to (f) apply in relation to orders made and removals effected before or after the commencement of that subsection.

(3) Where (apart from this subsection) a person is disqualified under subsection (1)(b) above for being a charity trustee or trustee for any charity which is a company, he shall not be so disqualified if leave has been granted under section 11 of the Company Directors Disqualification Act 1986 (undischarged bankrupts) for him to act as director of the charity; and similarly a person shall not be disqualified under subsection (1)(f) above for being a charity trustee or trustee for such a charity if—

(a) in the case of a person subject to a disqualification order, leave under the order has been granted for him to act as director of the charity, or

(b) in the case of a person subject to an order under section 429(2)(b) of the Insolvency Act 1986, leave has been granted by the court which made the order for him to so act.

(4) The Commissioners may, on the application of any person disqualified under subsection (1) above, waive his disqualification either generally or in relation to a particular charity or a particular class of charities; but no such waiver may be granted in relation to any charity which is a company if—

(a) the person concerned is for the time being prohibited, by virtue of—

(i) a disqualification order under the Company Directors Disqualification Act 1986, or

(ii) section 11(1) or 12(2) of that Act (undischarged bankrupts; failure to pay under county court administration order),

from acting as director of the charity; and

(b) leave has not been granted for him to act as director of any other company.

(5) Any waiver under subsection (4) above shall be notified in writing to the person concerned.

(6) For the purposes of this section the Commissioners shall keep, in such manner as they think fit, a register of all persons who have been removed from office as mentioned in subsection (1)(d) above either—

(a) by an order of the Commissioners made before or after the commencement of subsection (1) above, or

(b) by an order of the High Court made after the commencement of section 45(1) of the Charities Act 1992;

and, where any person is so removed from office by an order of the High Court, the court shall notify the Commissioners of his removal.

(7) The entries in the register kept under subsection (6) above shall be available for public inspection in legible form at all reasonable times.

DEFINITIONS
"charity": s.96(1).
"charity trustees": s.97(1).
"the Commissioners": s.97(1).
"company": s.97(1).

GENERAL NOTE
This section re-enacts s.45 of the 1992 Act and embodies the recommendation in para. 5.4 of the White Paper that certain persons should be disqualified from trusteeship in order to strengthen the preventive powers of the Commissioners. The power is backed by a public register in subs. (6) and by a statutory offence of acting as a charity trustee whilst disqualified in s.73. The width of the section is tempered by the power of the Commissioners to grant a waiver under subs. (4) to individuals within the section.

Subs. (1)
Any offence involving dishonesty or deception. The White Paper, para. 5.4, considered that disqualifying offences should be confined to indictable offences involving theft, fraud, forgery or financial misapplication. Rather than list specific offences, however, the subsection uses a wide general phrase which is not limited to conviction on indictment. Clearly, conviction of an offence which by its very definition includes dishonesty or deception will bar a person from trusteeship. Relevant offences can be found, *inter alia*, in the Theft Acts 1968 and 1978, the Companies Act 1985, the Insolvency Act 1986 and the Financial Services Act 1986. It is less clear whether conviction of an offence, the statutory definition of which does not include dishonesty or deception, but the particularisation of the circumstances of the commission of which may involve dishonesty or deception, and did in the specific instance, is sufficient to satisfy para. (a). Although it is open to question, it is unlikely that a person who has been convicted of an offence which does not involve dishonesty or deception can be brought within para. (a) on the grounds that he actually had a dishonest intent at the time of commission of the offence. It is also open to question whether a person who was guilty of a strict liability offence involving deception but who was not dishonest would be liable to be disqualified from trusteeship.
For disqualification under para. (d) see the note to s.18. Section 7 of the Law Reform (Miscellaneous Provisions) (Scotland) Act 1990, para. (e), is in very similar terms to s.18.

Subs. (2)
This subsection bars from trusteeship any person who already comes within any of the paras. of subs. (1) at the commencement of the subsection. Such a person who is a trustee can apply for leave to continue as a trustee under subs. (4).

Subs. (3)
Leave is granted by the court under s.11 of the Company Directors Disqualification Act 1986 only after notice has been served on the official receiver, who is bound to attend to oppose the application if he is of the opinion that it is contrary to the public interest that the application be granted.

Subs. (4)
This subsection recognises that in the case of certain charities, for example, those for ex-offenders, it may be appropriate for convicted persons to be appointed as trustees.

Person acting as charity trustee while disqualified

73.—(1) Subject to subsection (2) below, any person who acts as a charity trustee or trustee for a charity while he is disqualified for being such a trustee by virtue of section 72 above shall be guilty of an offence and liable—

(a) on summary conviction, to imprisonment for a term not exceeding six months or to a fine not exceeding the statutory maximum, or both;

   (b) on conviction on indictment, to imprisonment for a term not exceed-
        ing two years or to a fine, or both.
  (2) Subsection (1) above shall not apply where—
   (a) the charity concerned is a company; and
   (b) the disqualified person is disqualified by virtue only of paragraph (b)
        or (f) of section 72(1) above.
  (3) Any acts done as charity trustee or trustee for a charity by a person
disqualified for being such a trustee by virtue of section 72 above shall not be
invalid by reason only of that disqualification.
  (4) Where the Commissioners are satisfied—
   (a) that any person has acted as charity trustee or trustee for a charity
        (other than an exempt charity) while disqualified for being such a
        trustee by virtue of section 72 above, and
   (b) that, while so acting, he has received from the charity any sums by
        way of remuneration or expenses, or any benefit in kind, in connec-
        tion with his acting as charity trustee or trustee for the charity,
they may by order direct him to repay to the charity the whole or part of any
such sums, or (as the case may be) to pay to the charity the whole or part of
the monetary value (as determined by them) of any such benefit.
  (5) Subsection (4) above does not apply to any sums received by way of
remuneration or expenses in respect of any time when the person concerned
was not disqualified for being a charity trustee or trustee for the charity.

DEFINITIONS
   "charity": s.96(1).
   "charity trustees": s.97(1).
   "the Commissioners": s.97(1).
   "company": s.97(1).

GENERAL NOTE
   This section re-enacts s.46 of the 1992 Act and strengthens the preventive power in s.72 by
making it a criminal offence to act as a trustee whilst disqualified. The provision in subs. (3) to
protect the interests of the charity and those doing business with it from the effects of
disqualification of a trustee, and that in subs. (4) to allow recovery of remuneration follow the
recommendations in para. 5.5 of the White Paper.

Subs. (1)
   The statutory maximum fine is to be found in s.32 of the Magistrates' Courts Act 1980 and the
present maximum is £5,000.

Subs. (2)
   It is a criminal offence for an undischarged bankrupt to act as a director of a company by s.11
of the Company Directors Disqualification Act 1976. Section 13 of the 1976 Act makes it an
offence for any person to act in contravention of an order disqualifying him from being a
company director.

Subs. (4)
   In the case of an exempt charity, the trustees themselves could take action to recover any
sums from a disqualified trustee or approach the Attorney General to act on their behalf.

Small charities

Power to transfer all property, modify objects etc.

  74.—(1) This section applies to a charity if—
   (a) its gross income in its last financial year did not exceed £5,000, and
   (b) it does not hold any land on trusts which stipulate that the land is to be
        used for the purposes, or any particular purposes, of the charity,
and it is neither an exempt charity nor a charitable company.
  (2) Subject to the following provisions of this section, the charity trustees
of a charity to which this section applies may resolve for the purposes of this
section—

(a) that all the property of the charity should be transferred to such other charity as is specified in the resolution, being either a registered charity or a charity which is not required to be registered;

(b) that all the property of the charity should be divided, in such manner as is specified in the resolution, between such two or more other charities as are so specified, being in each case either a registered charity or a charity which is not required to be registered;

(c) that the trusts of the charity should be modified by replacing all or any of the purposes of the charity with such other purposes, being in law charitable, as are specified in the resolution;

(d) that any provision of the trusts of the charity—
    (i) relating to any of the powers exercisable by the charity trustees in the administration of the charity, or
    (ii) regulating the procedure to be followed in any respect in connection with its administration,
should be modified in such manner as is specified in the resolution.

(3) Any resolution passed under subsection (2) above must be passed by a majority of not less than two-thirds of such charity trustees as vote on the resolution.

(4) The charity trustees of a charity to which this section applies ("the transferor charity") shall not have power to pass a resolution under subsection (2)(a) or (b) above unless they are satisfied—

(a) that the existing purposes of the transferor charity have ceased to be conducive to a suitable and effective application of the charity's resources; and

(b) that the purposes of the charity or charities specified in the resolution are as similar in character to the purposes of the transferor charity as is reasonably practicable;

and before passing the resolution they must have received from the charity trustees of the charity, or (as the case may be) of each of the charities, specified in the resolution written confirmation that those trustees are willing to accept a transfer of property under this section.

(5) The charity trustees of any such charity shall not have power to pass a resolution under subsection (2)(c) above unless they are satisfied—

(a) that the existing purposes of the charity (or, as the case may be, such of them as it is proposed to replace) have ceased to be conducive to a suitable and effective application of the charity's resources; and

(b) that the purposes specified in the resolution are as similar in character to those existing purposes as is practical in the circumstances.

(6) Where charity trustees have passed a resolution under subsection (2) above, they shall—

(a) give public notice of the resolution in such manner as they think reasonable in the circumstances; and

(b) send a copy of the resolution to the Commissioners, together with a statement of their reasons for passing it.

(7) The Commissioners may, when considering the resolution, require the charity trustees to provide additional information or explanation—

(a) as to the circumstances in and by reference to which they have determined to act under this section, or

(b) relating to their compliance with this section in connection with the resolution;

and the Commissioners shall take into account any representations made to them by persons appearing to them to be interested in the charity where those representations are made within the period of six weeks beginning with the date when the Commissioners receive a copy of the resolution by virtue of subsection (6)(b) above.

(8) Where the Commissioners have so received a copy of a resolution from any charity trustees and it appears to them that the trustees have complied

with this section in connection with the resolution, the Commissioners shall, within the period of three months beginning with the date when they receive the copy of the resolution, notify the trustees in writing either—

    (a) that the Commissioners concur with the resolution; or

    (b) that they do not concur with it.

    (9) Where the Commissioners so notify their concurrence with the resolution, then—

    (a) if the resolution was passed under subsection (2)(a) or (b) above, the charity trustees shall arrange for all the property of the transferor charity to be transferred in accordance with the resolution and on terms that any property so transferred—

        (i) shall be held and applied by the charity to which it is transferred ("the transferee charity") for the purposes of that charity, but

        (ii) shall, as property of the transferee charity, nevertheless be subject to any restrictions on expenditure to which it is subject as property of the transferor charity,

    and those trustees shall arrange for it to be so transferred by such date as may be specified in the notification; and

    (b) if the resolution was passed under subsection (2)(c) or (d) above, the trusts of the charity shall be deemed, as from such date as may be specified in the notification, to have been modified in accordance with the terms of the resolution.

    (10) For the purpose of enabling any property to be transferred to a charity under this section, the Commissioners shall have power, at the request of the charity trustees of that charity, to make orders vesting any property of the transferor charity—

    (a) in the charity trustees of the first-mentioned charity or in any trustee for that charity, or

    (b) in any other person nominated by those charity trustees to hold the property in trust for that charity.

    (11) The Secretary of State may by order amend subsection (1) above by substituting a different sum for the sum for the time being specified there.

    (12) In this section—

    (a) "charitable company" means a charity which is a company or other body corporate; and

    (b) references to the transfer of property to a charity are references to its transfer—

        (i) to the charity trustees, or

        (ii) to any trustee for the charity, or

        (iii) to a person nominated by the charity trustees to hold it in trust for the charity,

    as the charity trustees may determine.

DEFINITIONS

    "charitable company": subs. (12).
    "charity": s.96(1).
    "charity trustees": s.97(1).
    "the Commissioners": s.97(1).
    "exempt charity": s.96(1).
    "financial year": s.97(1).
    "gross income": s.97(1).

GENERAL NOTE

    This section re-enacts s.43 of the 1992 Act. The Charities Act 1985 was passed to improve the effectiveness of small charities by setting up new and simplified mechanisms to allow the alteration of objects of certain local charities for the poor, to facilitate the amalgamation of registered charities with an income of £200 or less and to permit the trustees of very small permanently endowed charities to spend capital as income. The response to the Act was modest and the Woodfield report considered that response would be better if the provisions of the 1985

Act were widened. Rather than amend the 1985 Act, ss.43 and 44 of the 1992 Act restated its aims in much wider terms and removed the requirement for the trustees to be unanimous. The opportunity was also taken to standardise the conditions which apply to transfer of property, modification of objects and the spending of capital.

The power to transfer property to another charity and the power to modify objects now extends to all charities with an income of £5,000 a year or less, regardless of the original objects and age of the charity.

Subs. (1)

The previous restriction of a local charity at least 50 years old was removed by s.43(1) of the 1992 Act for change of objects and the income limit for transfer of property was raised from £200 to £5,000. A charitable company has power to amend its objects by s.4 of the Companies Act 1985 after obtaining the written consent of the Commissioners under s.64.

Subs. (2)

In addition to being given the power to transfer property or alter objects, which was in the 1985 Act, small charities now also have the power to alter their administrative provisions. Any resolution to transfer property must meet the conditions in subs. (4) and a resolution to modify objects must meet the conditions in subs. (5). It is envisaged that the power in para. (d) will be used to deal with deficiencies in the trust instrument in relation to, *inter alia*, appointment of trustees, the conduct of meetings and investment powers, the White Paper, para. 6.11.

Not required to be registered. A charity with income of less than £1,000 a year does not need to register, see s.3(5). Thus, two small charities can merge, for example, without the need for registration.

Subs. (3)

Resolution. No form is laid down for the resolution but guidance can be obtained from the forms in Scheds. 1 and 2 to the 1985 Act.

Subs. (4)

The condition in para. (a) did not appear in s.3 of the 1985 Act and would appear capable of fettering the transfer of property from small charities unless a liberal view is taken by the Commissioners as to when a suitable and effective application of charity resources has ceased. A liberal interpretation is presumably intended as para. (b) omits any reference to the intentions of the founder and the spirit of the gift, *cf.* s.3(2)(b) of the 1985 Act.

Subs. (5)

Both para. (a) and (b) are easier to satisfy than their predecessors in s.2(2) of the 1985 Act and would appear to be slightly easier than the usual *cy-près* conditions, *cf.* s.13(1)(e).

Subs. (6)

There is no longer any requirement to send copies of the resolution to the local authority.

Subs. (7)

The founder of the charity is no longer required to approve any alteration of objects or transfer but can make representations to the Commissioners.

Subs. (9)

Paragraph (a)(ii) requires property which was part of the original charity's permanent endowment to remain subject to the same restrictions on expenditure.

Power to spend capital

75.—(1) This section applies to a charity if—

(a) it has a permanent endowment which does not consist of or comprise any land, and

(b) its gross income in its last financial year did not exceed £1,000,

and it is neither an exempt charity nor a charitable company.

(2) Where the charity trustees of a charity to which this section applies are of the opinion that the property of the charity is too small, in relation to its purposes, for any useful purpose to be achieved by the expenditure of income alone, they may resolve for the purposes of this section that the charity ought to be freed from the restrictions with respect to expenditure of capital to which its permanent endowment is subject.

(3) Any resolution passed under subsection (2) above must be passed by a majority of not less than two-thirds of such charity trustees as vote on the resolution.

(4) Before passing such a resolution the charity trustees must consider whether any reasonable possibility exists of effecting a transfer or division of all the charity's property under section 74 above (disregarding any such transfer or division as would, in their opinion, impose on the charity an unacceptable burden of costs).

(5) Where charity trustees have passed a resolution under subsection (2) above, they shall—

    (a) give public notice of the resolution in such manner as they think reasonable in the circumstances; and

    (b) send a copy of the resolution to the Commissioners, together with a statement of their reasons for passing it.

(6) The Commissioners may, when considering the resolution, require the charity trustees to provide additional information or explanation—

    (a) as to the circumstances in and by reference to which they have determined to act under this section, or

    (b) relating to their compliance with this section in connection with the resolution;

and the Commissioners shall take into account any representations made to them by persons appearing to them to be interested in the charity where those representations are made within the period of six weeks beginning with the date when the Commissioners receive a copy of the resolution by virtue of subsection (5)(b) above.

(7) Where the Commissioners have so received a copy of a resolution from any charity trustees and it appears to them that the trustees have complied with this section in connection with the resolution, the Commissioners shall, within the period of three months beginning with the date when they receive the copy of the resolution, notify the trustees in writing either—

    (a) that the Commissioners concur with the resolution; or

    (b) that they do not concur with it.

(8) Where the Commissioners so notify their concurrence with the resolution, the charity trustees shall have, as from such date as may be specified in the notification, power by virtue of this section to expend any property of the charity without regard to any such restrictions as are mentioned in subsection (2) above.

(9) The Secretary of State may by order amend subsection (1) above by substituting a different sum for the sum for the time being specified there.

(10) In this section "charitable company" means a charity which is a company or other body corporate.

DEFINITIONS

"charitable company": subs. (10).
"charity": s.96(1).
"charity trustees": s.97(1).
"the Commissioners": s.97(1).
"exempt charity": s.96(1).
"financial year": s.97(1).
"gross income": s.97(1).
"permanent endowment": s.97(1).

GENERAL NOTE

This section re-enacts s.44 of the 1992 Act which replaced s.4 of the Charities Act 1985 and widened the circumstances in which small charities can resolve to spend their capital, see the note to s.74. There are safeguards in that the resolution has to be advertised and the Commissioners have to concur in the resolution to spend capital.

Subs. (2)

Any useful purpose. It was indicated during debate on the 1992 Act (*Hansard*, H.L. P.B.C., col. 182) that this phrase meant "is the money able to relieve any need?", which may no longer be the case where capital is invested in ways which give a low yield and the income has been eroded by inflation. The section contains no power to amend the trusts and "any useful purpose" must be considered within the purposes of the trust.

Subs. (3)
 Resolution. Guidance as to the form of the resolution can be obtained from Sched. 3 to the 1985 Act.

Subs. (4)
 Before a transfer can be made, the conditions in s.74(2)(4) have to be satisfied.

Local charities

Local authority's index of local charities

76.—(1) The council of a county or of a district or London borough and the Common Council of the City of London may maintain an index of local charities or of any class of local charities in the council's area, and may publish information contained in the index, or summaries or extracts taken from it.

(2) A council proposing to establish or maintaining under this section an index of local charities or of any class of local charities shall, on request, be supplied by the Commissioners free of charge with copies of such entries in the register of charities as are relevant to the index or with particulars of any changes in the entries of which copies have been supplied before; and the Commissioners may arrange that they will without further request supply a council with particulars of any such changes.

(3) An index maintained under this section shall be open to public inspection at all reasonable times.

(4) A council may employ any voluntary organisation as their agent for the purposes of this section, on such terms and within such limits (if any) or in such cases as they may agree; and for this purpose "voluntary organisation" means any body of which the activities are carried on otherwise than for profit, not being a public or local authority.

(5) A joint board discharging any of a council's functions shall have the same powers under this section as the council as respects local charities in the council's area which are established for purposes similar or complementary to any services provided by the board.

DEFINITIONS
 "the Commissioners": s.97(1).
 "local charity": s.97(1).
 "the register": s.97(1).

GENERAL NOTE
 This section re-enacts s.10 of the 1960 Act as amended to take account of local government reorganisation and empowers county, district and London Borough councils to maintain indices of local charities.

Subs. (1)
 A local authority may itself be a charity trustee, for example for the purposes of a public park. In that capacity it must, of course, apply for registration under s.3.

Subs. (2)
 The central register constitutes the main source of information for local indices but additional information may be obtained from local charities.

Subs. (5)
 As to joint boards, see the Local Government Act 1972, s.263.

Reviews of local charities by local authority

77.—(1) The council of a county or of a district or London borough and the Common Council of the City of London may, subject to the following provisions of this section, initiate, and carry out in co-operation with the charity trustees, a review of the working of any group of local charities with the same or similar purposes in the council's area, and may make to the Commissioners such report on the review and such recommendations arising from it as the council after consultation with the trustees think fit.

(2) A council having power to initiate reviews under this section may co-operate with other persons in any review by them of the working of local charities in the council's area (with or without other charities), or may join with other persons in initiating and carrying out such a review.

(3) No review initiated by a council under this section shall extend to any charity without the consent of the charity trustees, nor to any ecclesiastical charity.

(4) No review initiated under this section by the council of a district shall extend to the working in any county of a local charity established for purposes similar or complementary to any services provided by county councils unless the review so extends with the consent of the council of that county.

(5) Subsections (4) and (5) of section 76 above shall apply for the purposes of this section as they apply for the purposes of that section.

DEFINITIONS
"charity": s.96(1).
"charity trustees": s.97(1).
"ecclesiastical charity": s.96(1).
"local charity": s.96(1).

GENERAL NOTE
This section re-enacts s.11 of the 1960 Act as amended to take account of local government reorganisation and empowers local authorities to review the workings of local charities. Such a review should indicate the scope of existing charitable activities and suggest how they may best be co-ordinated with statutory activities in the same area. The initiation and progress of local reviews and the establishment of schemes consequent on such reviews was an annual topic in the Commissioners' reports between 1963 and 1980. Local reviews which were initiated encountered resistance, see [1968] Ch. Comm. Rep., paras. 55–60. The White Paper at para. 6.2 recommended that the Commissioners as well as local authorities should have power to appoint voluntary organisations to carry out reviews but no provision was made for this in the 1992 Act.

Subs. (1)
Any group of local charities. A single charity cannot be reviewed. Although a review cannot be carried out without the co-operation of the charity trustees (see subs. (3)) and they must be consulted before a report is made to the Commissioners, the trustees have no power to prevent the local authority submitting a report of which they disapprove. As to the co-operation by charity trustees, see s.78(2)(a).

Subs. (2)
The White Paper, para. 6.2 took the view that local reviews would be more effective if undertaken by locally based voluntary bodies, for example Councils for Voluntary Service, rather than such bodies co-operating with the local authority.

Subs. (4)
Were it not for this provision, a county council could find that a review had already been initiated in its area by another local authority before it undertook a review.

Subs. (5)
Section 76(4) allows a local authority to employ a voluntary organisation as agent (see the note to subs. (2)) and s.76(5) gives a joint board the same powers as a council.

Co-operation between charities, and between charities and local authorities

78.—(1) Any local council and any joint board discharging any functions of such a council—

(a) may make, with any charity established for purposes similar or complementary to services provided by the council or board, arrangements for co-ordinating the activities of the council or board and those of the charity in the interests of persons who may benefit from those services or from the charity; and

(b) shall be at liberty to disclose to any such charity in the interests of those persons any information obtained in connection with the services provided by the council or board, whether or not arrangements have been made with the charity under this subsection.

In this subsection "local council" means the council of a county, or of a district, London borough, parish or (in Wales) community, and includes also the Common Council of the City of London and the Council of the Isles of Scilly.

(2) Charity trustees shall, notwithstanding anything in the trusts of the charity, have power by virtue of this subsection to do all or any of the following things, where it appears to them likely to promote or make more effective the work of the charity, and may defray the expense of so doing out of any income or money applicable as income of the charity, that is to say—

(a) they may co-operate in any review undertaken under section 77 above or otherwise of the working of charities or any class of charities;

(b) they may make arrangements with an authority acting under subsection (1) above or with another charity for co-ordinating their activities and those of the authority or of the other charity;

(c) they may publish information of other charities with a view to bringing them to the notice of those for whose benefit they are intended.

DEFINITIONS
"charity": s.96(1).
"charity trustees": s.97(1).
"local council": subs. (1).
"trusts": s.97(1).

GENERAL NOTE
This section re-enacts s.12 of the 1960 Act as amended to take account of local government reorganisation and allows consultation and co-operation between local authorities and charity trustees and between charities. For an example of co-operation between the trustees of an almshouse charity and a local authority in providing residential accommodation for poor persons, see [1972] Ch. Comm. Rep., para. 49.

Subs. (1)
As to joint boards, see Local Government Act 1972, s.263.
The powers conferred by this section belong to **all** councils, *cf.* ss.76 and 77 which apply only to councils of counties, districts and London boroughs.
For the powers of a local authority to make available information about services in their area provided by itself or others including charities, see the Local Government Act 1972, s.142(2).

Subs. (2)
As to disclosure of information, see also s.10.
A scheme may impose on charities trustees a duty, not merely a discretion, to enter into arrangements for the co-ordination of activities, see [1964] Ch. Comm. Rep., p.15.

Parochial charities

79.—(1) Where trustees hold any property for the purposes of a public recreation ground, or of allotments (whether under inclosure Acts or otherwise), for the benefit of inhabitants of a parish having a parish council, or for other charitable purposes connected with such a parish, except for an ecclesiastical charity, they may with the approval of the Commissioners and with the consent of the parish council transfer the property to the parish council or to persons appointed by the parish council; and the council or their appointees shall hold the property on the same trusts and subject to the same conditions as the trustees did.

This subsection shall apply to property held for any public purposes as it applies to property held for charitable purposes.

(2) Where the charity trustees of a parochial charity in a parish, not being an ecclesiastical charity nor a charity founded within the preceding 40 years, do not include persons elected by the local government electors, ratepayers or inhabitants of the parish or appointed by the parish council or parish meeting, the parish council or parish meeting may appoint additional charity trustees, to such number as the Commissioners may allow; and if there is a sole charity trustee not elected or appointed as aforesaid of any such charity, the number of the charity trustees may, with the approval of the Commissioners, be increased to three of whom one may be nominated by the person holding the office of the sole trustee and one by the parish council or parish meeting.

(3) Where, under the trusts of a charity other than an ecclesiastical charity, the inhabitants of a rural parish (whether in vestry or not) or a select vestry were formerly (in 1894) entitled to appoint charity trustees for, or trustees or beneficiaries of, the charity, then—

(a) in a parish having a parish council, the appointment shall be made by the parish council or, in the case of beneficiaries, by persons appointed by the parish council; and

(b) in a parish not having a parish council, the appointment shall be made by the parish meeting.

(4) Where overseers as such or, except in the case of an ecclesiastical charity, churchwardens as such were formerly (in 1894) charity trustees of or trustees for a parochial charity in a rural parish, either alone or jointly with other persons, then instead of the former overseer or churchwarden trustees there shall be trustees (to a number not greater than that of the former overseer or churchwarden trustees) appointed by the parish council or, if there is no parish council, by the parish meeting.

(5) Where, outside Greater London (other than the outer London boroughs), overseers of a parish as such were formerly (in 1927) charity trustees of or trustees for any charity, either alone or jointly with other persons, then instead of the former overseer trustees there shall be trustees (to a number not greater than that of the former overseer trustees) appointed by the parish council or, if there is no parish council, by the parish meeting.

(6) In the case of an urban parish existing immediately before the passing of the Local Government Act 1972 which after 1st April 1974 is not comprised in a parish, the power of appointment under subsection (5) above shall be exercisable by the district council.

(7) In the application of the foregoing provisions of this section to Wales—

(a) for references in subsections (1) and (2) to a parish or a parish council there shall be substituted respectively references to a community or a community council;

(b) for references in subsections (3)(a) and (b) to a parish, a parish council or a parish meeting there shall be substituted respectively references to a community, a community council or the district council;

(c) for references in subsections (4) and (5) to a parish council or a parish meeting there shall be substituted respectively references to a community council or the district council.

(8) Any appointment of a charity trustee or trustee for a charity which is made by virtue of this section shall be for a term of four years, and a retiring trustee shall be eligible for re-appointment but—

(a) on an appointment under subsection (2) above, where no previous appointments have been made by virtue of that subsection or of the corresponding provision of the Local Government Act 1894 or the Charities Act 1960, and more than one trustee is appointed, half of those appointed (or as nearly as may be) shall be appointed for a term of two years; and

(b) an appointment made to fill a casual vacancy shall be for the remainder of the term of the previous appointment.

(9) This section shall not affect the trusteeship, control or management of any voluntary school within the meaning of the Education Act 1944 or of any grant-maintained school.

(10) The provisions of this section shall not extend to the Isles of Scilly, and shall have effect subject to any order (including any future order) made under any enactment relating to local government with respect to local government areas or the powers of local authorities.

(11) In this section the expression "formerly (in 1894)" relates to the period immediately before the passing of the Local Government Act 1894, and the expression "formerly (in 1927)" to the period immediately before 1st April 1927; and the word "former" shall be construed accordingly.

DEFINITIONS
"charity": s.96(1).
"charitable purposes": s.97(1).
"charity trustees": s.97(1).
"the Commissioners": s.97(1).
"ecclesiastical charity": s.96(1).
"formerly (in 1894)": subs. (11).
"formerly (in 1927)": subs. (11).
"parochial charity": s.96(1).
"trusts": s.97(1).

GENERAL NOTE
This section re-enacts s.37 of the 1960 Act as amended to take account of local government re-organisation. That section was itself in large part a re-enactment of various provisions contained in s.14 of the Local Government Act 1894. The 1894 Act established parish councils and parish meetings in rural parishes and provided for the trusteeship of parochial charities. Section 11(1) of the Local Government Act 1972 provides for the grouping of parishes in England and s.29(1) of that Act provides for the grouping of communities in Wales. A grouping order must make provision for the application to the parishes or communities included in the group of all or any of the provisions of this section: see ss.11(3)(c) and 29(3)(c) of that Act.

Subs. (1)
Public recreation grounds, see *Hadden, Re* [1932] 1 Ch. 133.
Allotments. Charitable allotments can be broadly grouped into four categories as follows: (1) Allotment gardens for the benefit of the poor; (2) Allotment gardens on land belonging to charities held, not specifically for use as such, but for the purpose of producing income for the charity to relieve poverty in other ways; (3) Fuel allotments usually "allotted" under the Inclosure Acts and awards which require either that the land itself should be used to provide fuel for the benefit of poor persons, or that the land should be let and the income used for such purpose; (4) "Allotments" for purposes other than those mentioned in the first three categories, for example, to provide stone, chalk or marl for repairing public and private roads and buildings, for pasture, or for recreation or exercise, [1969] Ch. Comm. Rep., p.18.
The section will only apply where the relevant property is held upon charitable trust and not where, for example, a local authority hold land subject to covenants to use it as "a recreation ground and for no other purpose", see *Liverpool City Council* v. *Att. Gen.*, *The Times*, May 1, 1992.

Subss. (2)(3)(4) and (5)
For the term for which trustees are appointed, see subs. (8).

Subs. (9)
Voluntary school. See the Education Act 1944, s.9(2).
Grant maintained school. See the Education Reform Act 1988, s.52.

Subs. (10)
  This subsection anticipates any future local government re-organisation.

Scottish charities

Supervision by Commissioners of certain Scottish charities

80.—(1) The following provisions of this Act, namely—
(a) sections 8 and 9,
(b) section 18 (except subsection (2)(ii)), and
(c) section 19,
shall have effect in relation to any recognised body which is managed or controlled wholly or mainly in or from England or Wales as they have effect in relation to a charity.

(2) Where—
(a) a recognised body is managed or controlled wholly or mainly in or from Scotland, but
(b) any person in England and Wales holds any property on behalf of the body or of any person concerned in its management or control,
then, if the Commissioners are satisfied as to the matters mentioned in subsection (3) below, they may make an order requiring the person holding the property not to part with it without their approval.

(3) The matters referred to in subsection (2) above are—
(a) that there has been any misconduct or mismanagement in the administration of the body; and
(b) that it is necessary or desirable to make an order under that subsection for the purpose of protecting the property of the body or securing a proper application of such property for the purposes of the body;
and the reference in that subsection to the Commissioners being satisfied as to those matters is a reference to their being so satisfied on the basis of such information as may be supplied to them by the Lord Advocate.

(4) Where—
(a) any person in England and Wales holds any property on behalf of a recognised body or of any person concerned in the management or control of such a body, and
(b) the Commissioners are satisfied (whether on the basis of such information as may be supplied to them by the Lord Advocate or otherwise)—
    (i) that there has been any misconduct or mismanagement in the administration of the body, and
    (ii) that it is necessary or desirable to make an order under this subsection for the purpose of protecting the property of the body or securing a proper application of such property for the purposes of the body,
the Commissioners may by order vest the property in such recognised body or charity as is specified in the order in accordance with subsection (5) below, or require any persons in whom the property is vested to transfer it to any such body or charity, or appoint any person to transfer the property to any such body or charity.

(5) The Commissioners may specify in an order under subsection (4) above such other recognised body or such charity as they consider appropriate, being a body or charity whose purposes are, in the opinion of the Commissioners, as similar in character to those of the body referred to in paragraph (a) of that subsection as is reasonably practicable; but the Commissioners shall not so specify any body or charity unless they have received—
(a) from the persons concerned in the management or control of the body, or

(b) from the charity trustees of the charity,
as the case may be, written confirmation that they are willing to accept the
property.

(6) In this section "recognised body" has the same meaning as in Part I of
the Law Reform (Miscellaneous Provisions) (Scotland) Act 1990 (Scottish
charities).

DEFINITIONS
"charity": s.96(1).
"charity trustees": s.97(1).
"the Commissioners": s.97(1).
"recognised body": subs. (6) and s.1(7) of the Law Reform (Miscellaneous Provisions)
(Scotland) Act 1990.

GENERAL NOTE
This section re-enacts s.12 of the 1992 Act. There is no body in Scotland equivalent to the
Charity Commissioners and there is no register of charities. By Pt. 1 of the Law Reform
(Miscellaneous Provisions) (Scotland) Act 1990 a body accepted by the Inland Revenue
Commissioners as entitled to tax relief under s.505 of the Income and Corporation Taxes Act
1988 as applying its income for charitable purposes only and established under Scottish law or
managed or controlled mainly in or from Scotland ("a recognised body") was made subject to
the supervision of the Lord Advocate and the Court of Session. The supervisory powers also
extend to registered and non-registered charities which operate in Scotland. Sections 6 and 7 of
the 1990 Act are in very similar form to ss.8, 9 and 18 with the supervisory powers being largely
exercised by the Court of Session after inquiry by the Lord Advocate. Without further
provision, however, there would be certain bodies and property which would not be subject to
the supervision of either the Lord Advocate and the Court of Session or the Charity Commissioners, in particular, recognised bodies controlled from England or Wales and property of
recognised bodies held in England or Wales.

Subs. (3)
An inquiry in Scotland is conducted by the Lord Advocate, s.6 of the 1990 Act.

Subs. (4)
There is no equivalent to the official custodian in Scotland. Thus, the order equivalent to that
under s.18(1)(iii) in relation to a Scottish charity has to be a transfer of the property to another
charity.

Subs. (5)
The effect of the subsection is to require the transfer under subs. (4) to be *cy-près* the original
charity.

Administrative provisions about charities

Manner of giving notice of charity meetings, etc.

81.—(1) All notices which are required or authorised by the trusts of a
charity to be given to a charity trustee, member or subscriber may be sent by
post, and, if sent by post, may be addressed to any address given as his in the
list of charity trustees, members or subscribers for the time being in use at
the office or principal office of the charity.

(2) Where any such notice required to be given as aforesaid is given by
post, it shall be deemed to have been given by the time at which the letter
containing it would be delivered in the ordinary course of post.

(3) No notice required to be given as aforesaid of any meeting or election
need be given to any charity trustee, member or subscriber, if in the list
above mentioned he has no address in the United Kingdom.

DEFINITIONS
"charity": s.96(1).
"charity trustees": s.97(1).
"trusts": s.97(1).

GENERAL NOTE
This section re-enacts s.33 of the 1960 Act and makes provision for the giving of notices to charity trustees.

Manner of executing instruments

82.—(1) Charity trustees may, subject to the trusts of the charity, confer on any of their body (not being less than two in number) a general authority, or an authority limited in such manner as the trustees think fit, to execute in the names and on behalf of the trustees assurances or other deeds or instruments for giving effect to transactions to which the trustees are a party; and any deed or instrument executed in pursuance of an authority so given shall be of the same effect as if executed by the whole body.

(2) An authority under subsection (1) above—

(a) shall suffice for any deed or instrument if it is given in writing or by resolution of a meeting of the trustees, notwithstanding the want of any formality that would be required in giving an authority apart from that subsection;

(b) may be given so as to make the powers conferred exercisable by any of the trustees, or may be restricted to named persons or in any other way;

(c) subject to any such restriction, and until it is revoked, shall, notwithstanding any change in the charity trustees, have effect as a continuing authority given by the charity trustees from time to time of the charity and exercisable by such trustees.

(3) In any authority under this section to execute a deed or instrument in the names and on behalf of charity trustees there shall, unless the contrary intention appears, be implied authority also to execute it for them in the name and on behalf of the official custodian or of any other person, in any case in which the charity trustees could do so.

(4) Where a deed or instrument purports to be executed in pursuance of this section, then in favour of a person who (then or afterwards) in good faith acquires for money or money's worth an interest in or charge on property or the benefit of any covenant or agreement expressed to be entered into by the charity trustees, it shall be conclusively presumed to have been duly executed by virtue of this section.

(5) The powers conferred by this section shall be in addition to and not in derogation of any other powers.

DEFINITIONS
"charity": s.96(1).
"charity trustees": s.97(1).
"official custodian": s.97(1).
"trusts": s.97(1).

GENERAL NOTE
This section re-enacts s.34 of the 1960 Act as amended by Sched. 3, para. 14 to the 1992 Act and makes provision for charity trustees to delegate to not less than two of their number authority to execute deeds and other instruments.

Subs. (1)
The power to delegate may be limited by the terms of the trust.
Instruments. This includes, for example, cheques.

Subs. (3)
As to charity trustees executing and doing assurances and things in the name and on behalf of the official custodian, see s.22(2). As to the power of the charity trustees to bind land or interests in land vested in the official custodian, see s.22(4).

Transfer and evidence of title to property vested in trustees

83.—(1) Where, under the trusts of a charity, trustees of property held for the purposes of the charity may be appointed or discharged by resolution of a meeting of the charity trustees, members or other persons, a memorandum declaring a trustee to have been so appointed or discharged shall be sufficient evidence of that fact if the memorandum is signed either at the meeting by the person presiding or in some other manner directed by the meeting and is attested by two persons present at the meeting.

(2) A memorandum evidencing the appointment or discharge of a trustee under subsection (1) above, if executed as a deed, shall have the like operation under section 40 of the Trustee Act 1925 (which relates to vesting declarations as respects trust property in deeds appointing or discharging trustees) as if the appointment or discharge were effected by the deed.

(3) For the purposes of this section, where a document purports to have been signed and attested as mentioned in subsection (1) above, then on proof (whether by evidence or as a matter of presumption) of the signature the document shall be presumed to have been so signed and attested, unless the contrary is shown.

(4) This section shall apply to a memorandum made at any time, except that subsection (2) shall apply only to those made after the commencement of the Charities Act 1960.

(5) This section shall apply in relation to any institution to which the Literary and Scientific Institutions Act 1854 applies as it applies in relation to a charity.

DEFINITIONS
"charity": s.96(1).
"charity trustees": s.97(1).
"institution": s.97(1).
"trusts": s.97(1).

GENERAL NOTE
This section re-enacts s.35 of the 1960 Act and makes provision for the transfer of property on a change of trustees.

Subs. (1)
This subsection covers not only the situation where trustees may be appointed by a resolution of a meeting of the charity trustees or charity members but also where a trustee may be appointed by a resolution of another body, for example, the committee of a local sports club may have power to appoint a trustee of a charity for a recreation ground.

Subs. (2)
By s.40 of the Trustee Act 1925 the legal estate in the trust property (other than property within s.40(4)) will automatically vest in the newly appointed trustees and cease to be vested in any trustees who are discharged, provided that the memorandum is executed as a deed.

PART X

SUPPLEMENTARY

Supply by Commissioners of copies of documents open to public inspection

84. The Commissioners shall, at the request of any person, furnish him with copies of, or extracts from, any document in their possession which is for the time being open to inspection under Parts II to VI of this Act.

DEFINITIONS
"the Commissioners": s.97(1).

GENERAL NOTE
This section is derived from s.9(2) of the 1960 Act and s.25(2) of and Sched. 3, para. 3 to the 1992 Act. The documents covered include the register and annual reports of charities which include their accounts, s.47.

The Charity Commissioners may charge fees for the supply of copy documents, see s.85(1)(b) and the Charity Commissioners' Fees (Copies and Extracts) Regulations 1992 (S.I. 1992 No. 2986).

Fees and other amounts payable to Commissioners

85.—(1) The Secretary of State may by regulations require the payment to the Commissioners of such fees as may be prescribed by the regulations in respect of—
(a) the discharge by the Commissioners of such functions under the enactments relating to charities as may be so prescribed;
(b) the inspection of the register of charities or of other material kept by them under those enactments, or the furnishing of copies of or extracts from documents so kept.
(2) Regulations under this section may—
(a) confer, or provide for the conferring of, exemptions from liability to pay a prescribed fee;
(b) provide for the remission or refunding of a prescribed fee (in whole or in part) in circumstances prescribed by the regulations.
(3) Any regulations under this section which require the payment of a fee in respect of any matter for which no fee was previously payable shall not be made unless a draft of the regulations has been laid before and approved by a resolution of each House of Parliament.
(4) The Commissioners may impose charges of such amounts as they consider reasonable in respect of the supply of any publications produced by them.
(5) Any fees and other payments received by the Commissioners by virtue of this section shall be paid into the Consolidated Fund.

DEFINITIONS
"the Commissioners": s.97(1).
"documents": s.97(2).
"the register": s.97(1).

GENERAL NOTE
This section re-enacts s.51 of the 1992 Act. The provision proved to be one of the most controversial of the 1992 Act as it goes against the long-accepted understanding that the Commissioners do not charge for their services, *Hansard*, H.L. Vol. 535, col. 1180. The Woodfield report and the White Paper, however, saw no reason why the Commissioners should not charge and, indeed, considered that it would have positive advantages in making trustees consider whether advice should be obtained from professional advisers and in bringing a degree of consumer pressure to bear on the Commissioners.

Subs. (1)
It is envisaged that, initially, charges will be set for registration, consent orders for the disposition of land and for access to the computerised register by other than individuals. The fee for registration may be about £50 and that for consent orders on a sliding scale relating to the amount of the proceeds of sale. It is not envisaged that fees will be charged for filing annual reports and accounts, or for advice given by the Commissioners' to charities, see *Hansard*, H.L. Vol. 535, col. 1181.
As to charges for the supply of copies of documents and extracts from the register see the Charity Commissioners' Fees (Copies and Extracts) Regulations 1992 (S.I. 1992 No. 2986).

Subs. (2)
It is envisaged that regulations will relieve small charities from payment of fees so as not to deter them from using the services of the Commissioners, see the White Paper, paras. 9 and 10.

Subs. (3)
The regulations are required to be laid before both Houses of Parliament to ensure that charges are set at a reasonable level, *Hansard*, H.L. Vol. 535, col. 1180.

Subs. (4)
It is not the intention that a charge should be made for all leaflets as the provision of a free leaflet may be the most effective means of giving advice, see the White Paper, para. 9.21.

Regulations and orders

86.—(1) Any regulations or order of the Secretary of State under this Act—
  (a) shall be made by statutory instrument; and
  (b) (subject to subsection (2) below) shall be subject to annulment in pursuance of a resolution of either House of Parliament.
  (2) Subsection (1)(b) above does not apply—
  (a) to an order under section 17(2), 70 or 99(2);
  (b) to any regulations under section 71; or
  (c) to any regulations to which section 85(3) applies.
  (3) Any regulations of the Secretary of State or the Commissioners and any order of the Secretary of State under this Act may make—
  (a) different provision for different cases; and
  (b) such supplemental, incidental, consequential or transitional provision or savings as the Secretary of State or, as the case may be, the Commissioners consider appropriate.
  (4) Before making any regulations under section 42, 44 or 45 above the Secretary of State shall consult such persons or bodies of persons as he considers appropriate.

DEFINITIONS
"the Commissioners": s.97(1).

GENERAL NOTE
This section provides a usual method of making orders and regulations and draws together a number of provisions relating to specific orders and regulations under the 1960 and the 1992 Acts.

Subs. (2)
Section 17(2) refers to schemes settled by the Commissioners, ss.70 and 71, to changes in powers of investment, s.99(2), to commencement orders and s.85(3) to the payment of fees to the Commissioners.

Subs. (4)
Section 42 refers to annual statements of account, s.44 to audit of accounts and s.45 to annual reports.

Enforcement of requirements by order of Commissioners

87.—(1) If a person fails to comply with any requirement imposed by or under this Act then (subject to subsection (2) below) the Commissioners may by order give him such directions as they consider appropriate for securing that the default is made good.
  (2) Subsection (1) above does not apply to any such requirement if—
  (a) a person who fails to comply with, or is persistently in default in relation to, the requirement is liable to any criminal penalty; or
  (b) the requirement is imposed—
        (i) by an order of the Commissioners to which section 88 below applies, or
        (ii) by a direction of the Commissioners to which that section applies by virtue of section 90(2) below.

DEFINITIONS
"the Commissioners": s.97(1).

GENERAL NOTE
This section is derived from s.56(1)(2) and (6) of the 1992 Act and re-inforces the monitoring

and supervisory rôle of the Commissioners by giving them power to make orders to enforce compliance with the requirements of the Act. Failure to comply with such an order is capable of being a contempt of court, s.88(c).

Subs. (2)
  For those requirements giving rise to a criminal penalty, see the note to s.94(2).
  For those requirements imposed by an order of the Commissioners to which s.88 applies, see the note to s.88.
  Section 90(2) applies s.88 to a direction which has been varied by the Commissioners.

Enforcement of orders of Commissioners

88. A person guilty of disobedience—
  (a) to an order of the Commissioners under section 9(1), 44(2), 61, 73 or 80 above; or
  (b) to an order of the Commissioners under section 16 or 18 above requiring a transfer of property or payment to be called for or made; or
  (c) to an order of the Commissioners requiring a default under this Act to be made good;
may on the application of the Commissioners to the High Court be dealt with as for disobedience to an order of the High Court.

DEFINITIONS
  "the Commissioners": s.97(1).

GENERAL NOTE
  This section is derived from s.41 of the 1960 Act and s.56(3)(6) of the 1992 Act and provides that failure to comply with an order of the Commissioners is capable of being a contempt of court.

Para. (a)
  Section 9(1) refers to an order for the production of documents and information to the Commissioners, s.44(2) to an order to provide facilities for an auditor, s.61 to an order of the Commissioners on the dissolution of an incorporated body of trustees, s.73 to an order for repayment directed to a disqualified trustee and s.80 to orders in respect of certain Scottish charities.

Para. (b)
  See s.16(1)(c) and s.18(1)(iii).

Para. (c)
  See the note to s.87.

Other provisions as to orders of Commissioners

89.—(1) Any order made by the Commissioners under this Act may include such incidental or supplementary provisions as the Commissioners think expedient for carrying into effect the objects of the order, and where the Commissioners exercise any jurisdiction to make such an order on an application or reference to them, they may insert any such provisions in the order notwithstanding that the application or reference does not propose their insertion.

(2) Where the Commissioners make an order under this Act, then (without prejudice to the requirements of this Act where the order is subject to appeal) they may themselves give such public notice as they think fit of the making or contents of the order, or may require it to be given by any person on whose application the order is made or by any charity affected by the order.

(3) The Commissioners at any time within twelve months after they have made an order under any provision of this Act other than section 61 if they are satisfied that the order was made by mistake or on misrepresentation or

otherwise than in conformity with this Act, may with or without any application or reference to them discharge the order in whole or in part, and subject or not to any savings or other transitional provisions.

(4) Except for the purposes of subsection (3) above or of an appeal under this Act, an order made by the Commissioners under this Act shall be deemed to have been duly and formally made and not be called in question on the ground only of irregularity or informality, but (subject to any further order) have effect according to its tenor.

DEFINITIONS
"charity": s.96(1).
"the Commissioners": s.97(1).

GENERAL NOTE
This section is derived from s.40 of the 1960 Act and s.56(4)(5) and (6) of the 1992 Act and gives the Commissioners powers in relation to orders made by them.

Subs. (2)
For the duty of the Commissioners to give public notice of their intention to make orders, see s.20.

Subs. (3)
Where an application for an order has been made to the Commissioners, it cannot be withdrawn before the order is made, *Poor Lands Charity Bethnal Green, Re* [1891] 3 Ch. 400. Section 61 deals with the dissolution of an incorporated body of trustees.

Directions of the Commissioners

90.—(1) Any direction given by the Commissioners under any provision contained in this Act—
  (a) may be varied or revoked by a further direction given under that provision; and
  (b) shall be given in writing.
(2) Sections 88 and 89(1), (2) and (4) above shall apply to any such directions as they apply to an order of the Commissioners.
(3) In subsection (1) above the reference to the Commissioners includes, in relation to a direction under subsection (3) of section 8 above, a reference to any person conducting an inquiry under that section.
(4) Nothing in this section shall be read as applying to any directions contained in an order made by the Commissioners under section 87(1) above.

DEFINITIONS
"the Commissioners": s.97(1).

GENERAL NOTE
This section re-enacts s.57 of the 1992 Act and reinforces the supervisory and monitoring powers of the Commissioners by allowing them to vary directions in writing, failure to comply with which will be capable of being a contempt of court by the application of s.88.

Service of orders and directions

91.—(1) This section applies to any order or direction made or given by the Commissioners under this Act.
(2) An order or direction to which this section applies may be served on a person (other than a body corporate)—
  (a) by delivering it to that person;
  (b) by leaving it at his last known address in the United Kingdom; or
  (c) by sending it by post to him at that address.
(3) An order or direction to which this section applies may be served on a body corporate by delivering it or sending it by post—

(a) to the registered or principal office of the body in the United Kingdom, or

(b) if it has no such office in the United Kingdom, to any place in the United Kingdom where it carries on business or conducts its activities (as the case may be).

(4) Any such order or direction may also be served on a person (including a body corporate) by sending it by post to that person at an address notified by that person to the Commissioners for the purposes of this subsection.

(5) In this section any reference to the Commissioners includes, in relation to a direction given under subsection (3) of section 8 above, a reference to any person conducting an inquiry under that section.

DEFINITIONS
"the Commissioners": subs. (5) and s.97(1).

GENERAL NOTE
This section re-enacts s.76 of the 1992 Act and sets out the rules for service of documents under this Act.

Appeals from Commissioners

92.—(1) Provision shall be made by rules of court for regulating appeals to the High Court under this Act against orders or decisions of the Commissioners.

(2) On such an appeal the Attorney General shall be entitled to appear and be heard, and such other persons as the rules allow or as the court may direct.

DEFINITIONS
"the Commissioners": s.97(1).
"the court": s.97(1).

GENERAL NOTE
This section re-enacts s.42 of the 1960 Act and makes provision for appeals from orders and decisions of the Commissioners.

Subs. (1)
Rules of the court. See R.S.C., Ord. 108 and see also s.16(12)(13) and the notes thereto.

Miscellaneous provisions as to evidence

93.—(1) Where, in any proceedings to recover or compel payment of any rentcharge or other periodical payment claimed by or on behalf of a charity out of land or of the rents, profits or other income of land, otherwise than as rent incident to a reversion, it is shown that the rentcharge or other periodical payment has at any time been paid for twelve consecutive years to or for the benefit of the charity, that shall be prima facie evidence of the perpetual liability to it of the land or income, and no proof of its origin shall be necessary.

(2) In any proceedings, the following documents, that is to say,—

(a) the printed copies of the reports of the Commissioners for enquiring concerning charities, 1818 to 1837, who were appointed under the Act 58 Geo. 3. c. 91 and subsequent Acts; and

(b) the printed copies of the reports which were made for various counties and county boroughs to the Charity Commissioners by their assistant commissioners and presented to the House of Commons as returns to orders of various dates beginning with 8th December 1890, and ending with 9th September 1909,

shall be admissible as evidence of the documents and facts stated in them.

(3) Evidence of any order, certificate or other document issued by the Commissioners may be given by means of a copy retained by them, or taken

from a copy so retained, and certified to be a true copy by any officer of the Commissioners generally or specially authorised by them to act for this purpose; and a document purporting to be such a copy shall be received in evidence without proof of the official position, authority or handwriting of the person certifying it.

DEFINITIONS
"charity": s.96(1).
"the Commissioners": s.97(1).

GENERAL NOTE
This section re-enacts s.36 of the 1960 Act and includes several miscellaneous provisions as to evidence.

Restriction on institution of proceedings for certain offences

94.—(1) No proceedings for an offence under this Act to which this section applies shall be instituted except by or with the consent of the Director of Public Prosecutions.

(2) This section applies to any offence under—
(a) section 5;
(b) section 11;
(c) section 18(14);
(d) section 49; or
(e) section 73(1).

GENERAL NOTE
This section re-enacts s.55 of the 1992 Act. The need for the consent of the Director of Public Prosecutions to prosecutions was included because those who administer charities are unpaid volunteers. It was felt that some check was required to ensure that criminal proceedings are taken only where the transgression is a serious one, *Hansard*, H.L. Vol. 535, col. 1191. By s.1 of the Prosecution of Offences Act 1985, any Crown prosecutor who is in charge of a particular case may take any step or give any consent on behalf of the Director of Public Prosecutions.

Subs. (2)
The relevant offences are: Para. (a): failure to include a statement on specified documents that the institution is a charity; Para. (b): supplying false or misleading information to the Commissioners; Para. (c): failure to obey a stop order of the Commissioners in relation to property; Para. (d): failure to submit an annual report or return or to provide a member of the public with a copy of the charity's accounts; Para. (e): acting as a trustee whilst disqualified.

Offences by bodies corporate

95. Where any offence under this Act is committed by a body corporate and is proved to have been committed with the consent or connivance of, or to be attributable to any neglect on the part of, any director, manager, secretary or other similar officer of the body corporate, or any person who was purporting to act in any such capacity, he as well as the body corporate shall be guilty of that offence and shall be liable to be proceeded against and punished accordingly.

In relation to a body corporate whose affairs are managed by its members, "director" means a member of the body corporate.

GENERAL NOTE
This section re-enacts s.75 of the 1992 Act and ensures that where a company has committed an offence under this Act the officer whose conduct led to the offence will also be liable. A similar clause is to be found in s.12(7) of the Safety of Sports Grounds Act 1975 and s.36(8) of the Fire Safety and Safety of Places of Sport Act 1987.
Similar officer. This phrase would not include a junior clerk, *Hansard*, H.L. Vol. 535, col. 1246.

Construction of references to a "charity" or to particular classes of charity

96.—(1) In this Act, except in so far as the context otherwise requires—

"charity" means any institution, corporate or not, which is established for charitable purposes and is subject to the control of the High Court in the exercise of the court's jurisdiction with respect to charities;

"ecclesiastical charity" has the same meaning as in the Local Government Act 1894;

"exempt charity" means (subject to section 24(8) above) a charity comprised in Schedule 2 to this Act;

"local charity" means, in relation to any area, a charity established for purposes which are by their nature or by the trusts of the charity directed wholly or mainly to the benefit of that area or of part of it;

"parochial charity" means, in relation to any parish or (in Wales) community, a charity the benefits of which are, or the separate distribution of the benefits of which is, confined to inhabitants of the parish or community, or of a single ancient ecclesiastical parish which included that parish or community or part of it, or of an area consisting of that parish or community with not more than four neighbouring parishes or communities.

(2) The expression "charity" is not in this Act applicable—

(a) to any ecclesiastical corporation (that is to say, any corporation in the Church of England, whether sole or aggregate, which is established for spiritual purposes) in respect of the corporate property of the corporation, except to a corporation aggregate having some purposes which are not ecclesiastical in respect of its corporate property held for those purposes; or

(b) to any Diocesan Board of Finance within the meaning of the Endowments and Glebe Measure 1976 for any diocese in respect of the diocesan glebe land of that diocese within the meaning of that Measure; or

(c) to any trust of property for purposes for which the property has been consecrated.

(3) A charity shall be deemed for the purposes of this Act to have a permanent endowment unless all property held for the purposes of the charity may be expended for those purposes without distinction between capital and income, and in this Act "permanent endowment" means, in relation to any charity, property held subject to a restriction on its being expended for the purposes of the charity.

(4) References in this Act to a charity whose income from all sources does not in aggregate amount to more than a specified amount shall be construed—

(a) by reference to the gross revenues of the charity, or

(b) if the Commissioners so determine, by reference to the amount which they estimate to be the likely amount of those revenues,

but without (in either case) bringing into account anything for the yearly value of land occupied by the charity apart from the pecuniary income (if any) received from that land; and any question as to the application of any such reference to a charity shall be determined by the Commissioners, whose decision shall be final.

(5) The Commissioners may direct that for all or any of the purposes of this Act an institution established for any special purposes of or in connection with a charity (being charitable purposes) shall be treated as forming part of that charity or as forming a distinct charity.

DEFINITIONS
  "the Commissioners": s.97(1).
  "institution": s.97(1).
  "permanent endowment": s.97(1).

GENERAL NOTE
  This section re-enacts s.45 of the 1960 Act as amended by s.179(1)(4) of the Local Govern-

ment Act 1972, s.1(2) of and Sched. 3, para. 18 to the 1992 Act and s.44 of the Endowments and Glebe Measure 1976 (No. 4) and contains the definitions of 'charity' and particular classes of charity. The same definitions are applied in the Redundant Churches and other Religious Buildings Act 1969, see s.4(13) of the Act.

Subs. (1)
Court's jurisdiction. The court's jurisdiction extends to charities founded outside the jurisdiction but taking effect within it, *Duncan, Re* (1867) 2 Ch. App. 356, 360, 362, and to charities founded within the jurisdiction but taking effect outside it, *Ironmongers Company* v. *Att.-Gen.* (1844) 10 Cl. & F. 908. The fact that a Minister of the Crown is given certain powers of control over a charity does not place it outside the court's jurisdiction, *Construction Industry Training Board* v. *Att.-Gen.* [1973] Ch. 73, 91.
Is established. When considering whether an institution is established for charitable purposes, it is the foundation date which matters, *Incorporated Council of Law Reporting for England and Wales* v. *Att. Gen.* [1972] Ch. 73, 91.
Ecclesiastical charity. The Local Government Act 1894, s.75, provides that the expression shall include a charity the endowment whereof is held for some or one or more of the following purposes: (a) for any spiritual purpose which is a legal purpose; (b) for the benefit of any spiritual person or ecclesiastical officer as such; (c) for use, if a building, as a church, chapel, mission room, or Sunday School, or otherwise by any particular church or denomination; (d) for the maintenance, repair or improvement of any such building as aforesaid, or for the maintenance of divine service therein; (e) otherwise for the benefit of any particular church or denomination, or for any members thereof as such. Provided that where any endowment of a charity, other than a building held for any of the purposes aforesaid, is held in part only for some of those purposes aforesaid, the charity, so far as that endowment is concerned, shall be an ecclesiastical charity within the meaning of this Act: and the Charity Commissioners shall, on application by any person interested, make such provision for the apportionment and management of that endowment as seems to them to be necessary or expedient for giving effect to this Act. A charity providing temporal benefits for members of a church may come within para. (e), *Perry Almshouses, Re Ross' Charity, Re* [1899] 1 Ch. 21.

Subs. (2)
The corporate property of ecclesiastical corporations established for spiritual purposes is not by its nature subject to any trusts, and the ordinary courts have, therefore, no more jurisdiction over it than they have over the goods of private individuals; see *Att.-Gen.* v. *St. John's Hospital, Bedford* (1864) 2 De G. J. & S. 621, 635 (a case of a civil corporation in respect of which the same principle applies). Such property is dealt with under ecclesiastical law in the ecclesiastical courts. Where, however, a corporation aggregate, for example Christ Church, Oxford, has some purposes which are not ecclesiastical, in respect of its corporate property held for those purposes the court has jurisdiction.
Glebe land is held for the ecclesiastical purposes of an ecclesiastical corporation and is therefore outside the Act; it is immaterial whether or not it is let.
It is provided by s.8(2) of the Sharing of Church Buildings Act 1969 that a sharing agreement with respect to any church building which under the agreement is owned by the Church of England shall not affect the application to the building of s.96(2) of the Act. A parochial church council or diocesan board of finance is not established for spiritual purposes: such corporations are therefore within the Act, save in so far as diocesan boards of finance are taken out by para. (b). On the other hand, charities of both the Church of England and other denominations, wholly or mainly concerned with the advancement of religion are to a large extent excepted from the provisions of registration, see s.3(5).
Ecclesiastical corporations, although excluded from the Act, retain charitable status and consequent tax privileges.

Subs. (5)
This subsection allows the Commissioners to direct that separate accounts and annual returns are prepared in respect of an institution established for any special purposes of or in connection with a charity.

General interpretation

97.—(1) In this Act, except in so far as the context otherwise requires—
"charitable purposes" means purposes which are exclusively charitable according to the law of England and Wales;

"charity trustees" means the persons having the general control and management of the administration of a charity;

"the Commissioners" means the Charity Commissioners for England and Wales;

"company" means a company formed and registered under the Companies Act 1985 or to which the provisions of that Act apply as they apply to such a company;

"the court" means the High Court and, within the limits of its jurisdiction, any other court in England and Wales having a jurisdiction in respect of charities concurrent (within any limit of area or amount) with that of the High Court, and includes any judge or officer of the court exercising the jurisdiction of the court;

"financial year"—

(a) in relation to a charity which is a company, shall be construed in accordance with section 223 of the Companies Act 1985; and

(b) in relation to any other charity, shall be construed in accordance with regulations made by virtue of section 42(2) above;

but this definition is subject to the transitional provisions in section 99(4) below and Part II of Schedule 8 to this Act;

"gross income", in relation to charity, means its gross recorded income from all sources including special trusts;

"independent examiner", in relation to a charity, means such a person as is mentioned in section 43(3)(a) above;

"institution" includes any trust or undertaking;

"the official custodian" means the official custodian for charities;

"permanent endowment" shall be construed in accordance with section 96(3) above;

"the register" means the register of charities kept under section 3 above and "registered" shall be construed accordingly;

"special trust" means property which is held and administered by or on behalf of a charity for any special purposes of the charity, and is so held and administered on separate trusts relating only to that property but a special trust shall not, by itself, constitute a charity for the purposes of Part VI of this Act;

"trusts" in relation to a charity, means the provisions establishing it as a charity and regulating its purposes and administration, whether those provisions take effect by way of trust or not, and in relation to other institutions has a corresponding meaning.

(2) In this Act, except in so far as the context otherwise requires, "document" includes information recorded in any form, and, in relation to information recorded otherwise than in legible form—

(a) any reference to its production shall be construed as a reference to the furnishing of a copy of it in legible form; and

(b) any reference to the furnishing of a copy of, or extract from, it shall accordingly be construed as a reference to the furnishing of a copy of, or extract from, it in legible form.

(3) No vesting or transfer of any property in pursuance of any provision of Part IV or IX of this Act shall operate as a breach of a covenant or condition against alienation or give rise to a forfeiture.

DEFINITIONS
"charity": s.96(1).

GENERAL NOTE
This section derives from ss.16(5) and 46 of the 1960 Act, s.111(2) of the Companies Act 1989 and s.1(1)–(4) of the 1992 Act.

Subs. (2)
Information recorded in any form. For example, on microfiche or on computer disk.

Consequential amendments and repeals

98.—(1) The enactments mentioned in Schedule 6 to this Act shall be amended as provided in that Schedule.

(2) The enactments mentioned in Schedule 7 to this Act are hereby repealed to the extent specified in the third column of the Schedule.

Commencement and transitional provisions

99.—(1) Subject to subsection (2) below this Act shall come into force on 1st August 1993.

(2) Part VI, section 69 and paragraph 21(3) of Schedule 6 shall not come into force until such day as the Secretary of State may by order appoint; and different days may be appointed for different provisions or different purposes.

(3) Until the coming into force of all the provisions mentioned in subsection (2) above the provisions mentioned in Part I of Schedule 8 to this Act shall continue in force notwithstanding their repeal.

(4) Part II of Schedule 8 to this Act shall have effect until the coming into force of the first regulations made by virtue of section 42(2) above for determining the financial year of a charity for the purposes of the provisions mentioned in that Part.

Short title and extent

100.—(1) This Act may be cited as the Charities Act 1993.

(2) Subject to subsections (3) to (6) below, this Act extends only to England and Wales.

(3) Section 10 above and this section extend to the whole of the United Kingdom.

(4) Section 15(2) extends also to Northern Ireland.

(5) Sections 70 and 71 and so much of section 86 as relates to those sections extend also to Scotland.

(6) The amendments in Schedule 6 and the repeals in Schedule 7 have the same extent as the enactments to which they refer and section 98 above extends accordingly.

SCHEDULES

Section 1   SCHEDULE 1

CONSTITUTION ETC. OF CHARITY COMMISSIONERS

1.—(1) There shall be a Chief Charity Commissioner and two other commissioners.

(2) Two at least of the commissioners shall be persons who have a seven year general qualification within the meaning of section 71 of the Courts and Legal Services Act 1990.

(3) The chief commissioner and the other commissioners shall be appointed by the Secretary of State, and shall be deemed for all purposes to be employed in the civil service of the Crown.

(4) There may be paid to each of the commissioners such salary and allowances as the Secretary of State may with the approval of the Treasury determine.

(5) If at any time it appears to the Secretary of State that there should be more than three commissioners, he may with the approval of the Treasury appoint not more than two additional commissioners.

2.—(1) The chief commissioner may, with the approval of the Treasury as to number and conditions of service, appoint such assistant commissioners and other officers and such employees as he thinks necessary for the proper discharge of the functions of the Commissioners and of the official custodian.

(2) There may be paid to officers and employees so appointed such salaries or remuneration as the Treasury may determine.

3.—(1) The Commissioners may use an official seal for the authentication of documents, and their seal shall be officially and judicially noticed.

(2) The Documentary Evidence Act 1868, as amended by the Documentary Evidence Act 1882, shall have effect as if in the Schedule to the Act of 1868 the Commissioners were included in the first column and any commissioner or assistant commissioner and any officer authorised to act on behalf of the Commissioners were mentioned in the second column.

(3) The Commissioners shall have power to regulate their own procedure and, subject to any such regulations and to any directions of the chief commissioner, any one commissioner or any assistant commissioner may act for and in the name of the Commissioners.

(4) Where the Commissioners act as a board, then—

(a) if not more than four commissioners hold office for the time being, the quorum shall be two commissioners (of whom at least one must be a person having a qualification such as is mentioned in paragraph 1(2) above); and

(b) if five commissioners so hold office, the quorum shall be three commissioners (of whom at least one must be a person having such a qualification);

and in the case of an equality of votes the chief commissioner or in his absence the commissioner presiding shall have a second or casting vote.

(5) The Commissioners shall have power to act notwithstanding any vacancy in their number.

(6) It is hereby declared that the power of a commissioner or assistant commissioner to act for and in the name of the Commissioners in accordance with sub-paragraph (3) above may, in particular, be exercised in relation to functions of the Commissioners under sections 8, 18, 19 and 63 of this Act, including functions under sections 8, 18 and 19 as applied by section 80(1).

4. Legal proceedings may be instituted by or against the Commissioners by the name of the Charity Commissioners for England and Wales, and shall not abate or be affected by any change in the persons who are the commissioners.

DEFINITIONS
"the Commissioners": s.97(1).

GENERAL NOTE
This schedule re-enacts Sched. 1 to the 1960 Act as amended and provides for the constitution of the Charity Commissioners for England and Wales and certain related matters.

Para. (1)
The third Commissioner need not be a lawyer and the non-lawyer may be the Chief Commissioner.

Whilst appointed by the Secretary of State, the Commissioners are independent of him, see the note to s.1(3).

The power under subpara. (5) has been used to appoint two part-time Commissioners who are not lawyers.

Para. (3)
Section 2 of the Documentary Evidence Act 1868 provides that prima facie evidence of any order or regulation issued before or after the passing of the Act by or under the authority of any such Department of the Government or officer as is mentioned in the first column of the Schedule thereto may be given in all legal proceedings by the production of a copy or extract purporting to be certified and made by the person or the persons specified in the second column of that Schedule in connection with such Department or officer. No proof is required of the handwriting or official position of such person.

The effect of subpara. (4) is to give all the Commissioners equal standing except in connection with the functions given to the Chief Commissioner by paras. 2(1) and 3(3) and for the casting vote which the subpara. gives the Commissioner presiding at a meeting of the Board.

Para. (4)
This provision is necessary because the Commissioners are not incorporated and, therefore, without a provision to this effect any proceedings by or against them would have to be in the names of the persons who were actually the Commissioners for the time being.

Sections 3 and 96   SCHEDULE 2

EXEMPT CHARITIES

The following institutions, so far as they are charities, are exempt charities within the meaning of this Act, that is to say—

(a) any institution which, if the Charities Act 1960 had not been passed, would be exempted from the powers and jurisdiction, under the Charitable Trusts Acts 1853 to 1939, of the

Commissioners or Minister of Education (apart from any power of the Commissioners or Minister to apply those Acts in whole or in part to charities otherwise exempt) by the terms of any enactment not contained in those Acts other than section 9 of the Places of Worship Registration Act 1855;
- (b) the universities of Oxford, Cambridge, London, Durham and Newcastle, the colleges and halls in the universities of Oxford, Cambridge, Durham and Newcastle, Queen Mary and Westfield College in the University of London and the colleges of Winchester and Eton;
- (c) any university, university college, or institution connected with a university or university college, which Her Majesty declares by Order in Council to be an exempt charity for the purposes of this Act;
- (d) a grant-maintained school;
- (e) the National Curriculum Council;
- (f) the Curriculum Council for Wales;
- (g) the School Examinations and Assessment Council;
- (h) a higher education corporation;
- (i) a successor company to a higher education corporation (within the meaning of section 129(5) of the Education Reform Act 1988) at a time when an institution conducted by the company is for the time being designated under that section;
- (j) a further education corporation;
- (k) the Board of Trustees of the Victoria and Albert Museum;
- (l) the Board of Trustees of the Science Museum;
- (m) the Board of Trustees of the Armouries;
- (n) the Board of Trustees of the Royal Botanic Gardens, Kew;
- (o) the Board of Trustees of the National Museums and Galleries on Merseyside;
- (p) the trustees of the British Museum and the trustees of the Natural History Museum;
- (q) the Board of Trustees of the National Gallery;
- (r) the Board of Trustees of the Tate Gallery;
- (s) the Board of Trustees of the National Portrait Gallery;
- (t) the Board of Trustees of the Wallace Collection;
- (u) the Trustees of the Imperial War Museum;
- (v) the Trustees of the National Maritime Museum;
- (w) any institution which is administered by or on behalf of an institution included above and is established for the general purposes of, or for any special purpose of or in connection with, the last-mentioned institution;
- (x) the Church Commissioners and any institution which is administered by them;
- (y) any registered society within the meaning of the Industrial and Provident Societies Act 1965 and any registered society or branch within the meaning of the Friendly Societies Act 1974;
- (z) the Board of Governors of the Museum of London;
- (za) the British Library Board.

DEFINITIONS
  "charity": s.96(1).
  "the Commissioners": s.97(1).
  "exempt charity": s.96(1).
  "institution": s.97(1).

GENERAL NOTE
  This Schedule re-enacts Sched. 2 to the 1960 Act as amended. The general law of charity declared in the Act applies to exempt charities and, hence, they are subject to the jurisdiction of the court at the relation of the Attorney General but they are exempt from all the supervisory and restrictive powers of the Commissioners in the Act. On the other hand, the enabling powers of the Commissioners, for example, their power under s.26 to authorise dealings with charity property, are available to them on request. The basis of exemption is the fact that Parliament has been satisfied that there exist satisfactory arrangements for carrying out the objects of their trusts and safeguarding their property and that in the circumstances it would be superfluous to submit them to the control of the Commissioners or their constitution is such that supervision is unnecessary. Usually Parliament has provided for their supervision by some other means.
  So far as they are charities. These words take account of the fact that the Universities of Oxford and Cambridge, in so far as they are civil corporations, are the owners of corporate property which is not by its nature subject to any trust, so that the court has no more jurisdiction over it than it has over the goods of private individuals; *cf.*, ecclesiastical corporations which are removed entirely from the purview of the Act, see s.96(2).

Para. (a)
The institutions referred to are the Universities of: Birmingham (Birmingham University Act 1900, s.14); Liverpool (Liverpool University Act 1903, s.14); Manchester (Victoria University of Manchester Act 1904, s.11); Leeds (University of Leeds Act 1904, s.12); Sheffield (University of Sheffield Act 1905, s.11); Bristol (University of Bristol Act 1909, s.12); Reading (University of Reading Act 1926, s.10); Nottingham (University of Nottingham Act 1949, s.9); Southampton (University of Southampton Act 1953, s.10); the Representative Body of the Welsh Church and its property (Welsh Church Act 1914, s.13, Welsh Church (Temporalities) Act 1919, s.7(1)), and property within the Church Funds Investment Measure 1958.

Para. (c)
The Universities which have been exempted under this paragraph are those which undertook to submit their accounts to the University Funding Council (now the Higher Education Funding Council). The relevant orders are The Exempt Charities Orders: 1962 (No. 1343); 1965 (No. 1715); 1966 (No. 1460); 1967 (No. 821); 1969 (No. 1496); 1978 (No. 453); 1982 (No. 1661); 1983 (No. 1516); 1984 (No. 1976); 1987 (No. 1823); and 1987 (No. 2394).

Paras. (h) and (j)
The relevant bodies are mainly the former polytechnics, the majority of which are now universities.

Para. (j)
The relevant bodies under this paragraph are the former sixth form and tertiary colleges.

Section 13 SCHEDULE 3

ENLARGEMENT OF AREAS OF LOCAL CHARITIES

Existing area	*Permissible enlargement*
1. Greater London.	Any area comprising Greater London.
2. Any area in Greater London and not in, or partly in, the City of London.	(i) Any area in Greater London and not in, or partly in, the City of London; (ii) the area of Greater London exclusive of the City of London; (iii) any area comprising the area of Greater London, exclusive of the City of London; (iv) any area partly in Greater London and partly in any adjacent parish or parishes (civil or ecclesiastical), and not partly in the City of London.
3. A district.	Any area comprising the district.
4. Any area in a district.	(i) Any area in the district; (ii) the district; (iii) any area comprising the district; (iv) any area partly in the district and partly in any adjacent district.
5. A parish (civil or ecclesiastical), or two or more parishes, or an area in a parish, or partly in each of two or more parishes.	Any area not extending beyond the parish or parishes comprising or adjacent to the area in column 1.
6. In Wales, a community, or two or more communities, or an area in a community, or partly in each of two or more communities.	Any area not extending beyond the community or communities comprising or adjacent to the area in column 1.

Section 15 SCHEDULE 4

COURT'S JURISDICTION OVER CERTAIN CHARITIES GOVERNED BY OR UNDER STATUTE

1. The court may by virtue of section 15(3) of this Act exercise its jurisdiction with respect to charities—

(a) in relation to charities established or regulated by any provision of the Seamen's Fund Winding-up Act 1851 which is repealed by the Charities Act 1960;

(b) in relation to charities established or regulated by schemes under the Endowed Schools Act 1869 to 1948, or section 75 of the Elementary Education Act 1870 or by schemes given effect under section 2 of the Education Act 1973;

(c) in relation to allotments regulated by sections 3 to 9 of the Poor Allotments Management Act 1873;

(d) in relation to fuel allotments, that is to say, land which, by any enactment relating to inclosure or any instrument having effect under such an enactment, is vested in trustees upon trust that the land or the rents and profits of the land shall be used for the purpose of providing poor persons with fuel;

(e) in relation to charities established or regulated by any provision of the Municipal Corporations Act 1883 which is repealed by the Charities Act 1960 or by any scheme having effect under any such provision;

(f) in relation to charities regulated by schemes under the London Government Act 1899;

(g) in relation to charities established or regulated by orders or regulations under section 2 of the Regimental Charitable Funds Act 1935;

(h) in relation to charities regulated by section 79 of this Act, or by any such order as is mentioned in that section.

2. Notwithstanding anything in section 19 of the Commons Act 1876 a scheme for the administration of a fuel allotment (within the meaning of the foregoing paragraph) may provide—

(a) for the sale or letting of the allotment or any part thereof, for the discharge of the land sold or let from any restrictions as to the use thereof imposed by or under any enactment relating to inclosure and for the application of the sums payable to the trustees of the allotment in respect of the sale or lease; or

(b) for the exchange of the allotment or any part thereof for other land, for the discharge as aforesaid of the land given in exchange by the said trustees, and for the application of any money payable to the said trustees for equality of exchange; or

(c) for the use of the allotment or any part thereof for any purposes specified in the scheme.

Section 36(2)   SCHEDULE 5

MEANING OF "CONNECTED PERSON" FOR PURPOSES OF SECTION 36(2)

1. In section 36(2) of this Act "connected person", in relation to a charity, means—

(a) a charity trustee or trustee for the charity;

(b) a person who is the donor of any land to the charity (whether the gift was made on or after the establishment of the charity);

(c) a child, parent, grandchild, grandparent, brother or sister of any such trustee or donor;

(d) an officer, agent or employee of the charity;

(e) the spouse of any person falling within any of sub-paragraphs (a) to (d) above;

(f) an institution which is controlled—

      (i) by any person falling within any of sub-paragraphs (a) to (e) above, or

      (ii) by two or more such persons taken together; or

(g) a body corporate in which—

      (i) any connected person falling within any of sub-paragraphs (a) to (f) above has a substantial interest, or

      (ii) two or more such persons, taken together, have a substantial interest.

2.—(1) In paragraph 1(c) above "child" includes a stepchild and an illegitimate child.

(2) For the purposes of paragraph 1(e) above a person living with another as that person's husband or wife shall be treated as that person's spouse.

3. For the purposes of paragraph 1(f) above a person controls an institution if he is able to secure that the affairs of the institution are conducted in accordance with his wishes.

4.—(1) For the purposes of paragraph 1(g) above any such connected person as is there mentioned has a substantial interest in a body corporate if the person or institution in question—

(a) is interested in shares comprised in the equity share capital of that body of a nominal value of more than one-fifth of that share capital, or

(b) is entitled to exercise, or control the exercise of, more than one-fifth of the voting power at any general meeting of that body.

(2) The rules set out in Part I of Schedule 13 to the Companies Act 1985 (rules for interpretation of certain provisions of that Act) shall apply for the purposes of sub-paragraph

(1) above as they apply for the purposes of section 346(4) of that Act ("connected persons" etc.).

(3) In this paragraph "equity share capital" and "share" have the same meaning as in that Act.

Section 98(1) SCHEDULE 6

CONSEQUENTIAL AMENDMENTS

The Places of Worship Registration Act 1855 (c. 81)

1.—(1) Section 9 of the Places of Worship Registration Act 1855 shall be amended as follows.

(2) For "subsection (4) of section four of the Charities Act 1960" there shall be substituted "subsection (5) of section 3 of the Charities Act 1993".

(3) At the end there shall be added—

"(2) Section 89 of the said Act of 1993 (provisions as to orders under that Act) shall apply to any order under paragraph (b) above as it applies to orders under that Act."

The Open Spaces Act 1906 (c. 25)

2. At the end of section 4 of the Open Spaces Act 1906 there shall be added—

"(4) Section 89 of the Charities Act 1993 (provisions as to orders under that Act) shall apply to any order of the Charity Commissioners under this section as it applies to orders made by them under that Act."

The New Parishes Measure 1943 (No. 1)

3.—(1) The New Parishes Measure 1943 shall be amended as follows.

(2) In subsection (1)(b) of section 14 for "the Charities Act 1960" there shall be substituted "the Charities Act 1993".

(3) At the end of that section there shall be added—

"(4) Section 89 of the Charities Act 1993 (provisions as to orders under that Act) shall apply to any order under section (1)(b) above as it applies to orders under that Act."

(4) In section 31 for "the Charities Act 1960" there shall be substituted "the Charities Act 1993".

The Clergy Pensions Measure 1961 (No. 3)

4. In section 33 of the Clergy Pensions Measure 1961 for "section 32 of the Charities Act 1992" and "the Charities Act 1960" there shall be substituted respectively "section 36 of the Charities Act 1993" and "that Act".

The Finance Act 1963 (c. 25)

5. In section 65(2) of the Finance Act 1963 at the end of paragraph (a) there shall be added "or to any common investment scheme under section 24 or any common deposit scheme under section 25 of the Charities Act 1993;".

The Cathedrals Measure 1963 (No. 2)

6.—(1) The Cathedrals Measure 1963 shall be amended as follows.

(2) In section 20(2)(iii) for "section 32 of the Charities Act 1992" there shall be substituted "section 36 of the Charities Act 1993".

(3) In section 51 for "the Charities Act 1960" there shall be substituted "the Charities Act 1993".

The Incumbents and Churchwardens (Trusts) Measure 1964 (No. 2)

7. In section 1 of the Incumbents and Churchwardens (Trusts) Measure 1964 for "subsection (3) of section forty-five of the Charities Act 1960" there shall be substituted "section 96(3) of the Charities Act 1993".

The Leasehold Reform Act 1967 (c. 88)

8. In section 23(4) of the Leasehold Reform Act 1967 for "section 32 of the Charities Act 1992" there shall be substituted "section 36 of the Charities Act 1993".

The Greater London Council (General Powers) Act 1968 (c. xxxix)

9. In section 43 of the Greater London Council (General Powers) Act 1968, in the definition of "night café", for "section 4 of the Charities Act 1960" and "subsection (4) thereof" there shall be substituted respectively "section 3 of the Charities Act 1993" and "subsection (5) thereof".

The Redundant Churches and other Religious Buildings Act 1969 (c. 22)

10.—(1) The Redundant Churches and other Religious Buildings Act 1969 shall be amended as follows.

(2) In subsection (6) of section 4 for "section 18 of the Charities Act 1960" there shall be substituted "section 16 of the Charities Act 1993".

(3) In subsection (7) of that section for "subsection (4) of section 18 of that Act" there shall be substituted "subsection (4) of section 16 of that Act".

(4) In subsection (8) of that section for "section 18 of the Charities Act 1960" and (where next occurring) "section 18" there shall be substituted respectively "section 16 of the Charities Act 1993" and "section 16" and for "section 21" there shall be substituted "section 20".

(5) In subsection (13) of that section for "sections 45 and 46 of the Charities Act 1960" there shall be substituted "sections 96 and 97 of the Charities Act 1993".

(6) In section 7(2) for "the Charities Act 1960" and "section 23" there shall be substituted respectively "the Charities Act 1993" and "section 26".

The Sharing of Church Buildings Act 1969 (c. 38)

11.—(1) The Sharing of Church Buildings Act 1969 shall be amended as follows.

(2) In section 2(4) for "the Charities Act 1960" there shall be substituted "the Charities Act 1993".

(3) In subsection (1) of section 8 for "the Charities Act 1960" there shall be substituted "the Charities Act 1993".

(4) In subsection (2) of that section for "section 45(2) of the Charities Act 1960" there shall be substituted "section 96(2) of the Charities Act 1993".

(5) In subsection (3) of that section for "Section 32 of the Charities Act 1992" there shall be substituted "Section 36 of the Charities Act 1993".

The Local Government Act 1972 (c. 70)

12.—(1) The Local Government Act 1972 shall be amended as follows.

(2) In sections 11(3)(c) and 29(3)(c) for "section 37 of the Charities Act 1960" there shall be substituted "section 79 of the Charities Act 1993".

(3) In sections 123(6) and 127(4) for "the Charities Act 1960" there shall be substituted "the Charities Act 1993".

(4) In section 131(3) for "section 32 of the Charities Act 1992" and "section 32(9)(a) of that Act" there shall be substituted respectively "section 36 of the Charities Act 1993" and "section 36(9)(a) of that Act".

The Fire Precautions (Loans) Act 1973 (c. 11)

13. In section 1(7) of the Fire Precautions (Loans) Act 1973 for "Section 34 of the Charities Act 1992" there shall be substituted "Section 38 of the Charities Act 1993".

The Theatres Trust Act 1976 (c. 27)

14. In section 2(2)(d) of the Theatres Trust Act 1976 for "sections 32 and 34 of the Charities Act 1992" there shall be substituted "sections 36 and 38 of the Charities Act 1993".

The Interpretation Act 1978 (c. 30)

15. In Schedule 1 to the Interpretation Act 1978, in the definition of "Charity Commissioners" for "section 1 of the Charities Act 1960" there shall be substituted "section 1 of the Charities Act 1993".

The Reserve Forces Act 1980 (c. 9)

16.—(1) Section 147 of the Reserve Forces Act 1980 shall be amended as follows.

(2) In subsection (4) for "section 28 of the Charities Act 1960" there shall be substituted "section 33 of the Charities Act 1993".

(3) In subsection (5) for "section 28(5) of that Act of 1960" there shall be substituted "section 33(5) of that Act of 1993".

(4) In subsection (7) for "section 18 of the Charities Act 1960" there shall be substituted "section 16 of the Charities Act 1993".

(5) In subsection (10)(b) for "the Charities Act 1960" there shall be substituted "the Charities Act 1993".

The Disused Burial Grounds (Amendment) Act 1981 (c. 18)

17. In section 6 of the Disused Burial Grounds (Amendment) Act 1981 for "section 13(5) of the Charities Act 1960" there shall be substituted "section 13(5) of the Charities Act 1993".

The Pastoral Measure 1983 (No. 1)

18.—(1) The Pastoral Measure 1983 shall be amended as follows.

(2) In section 55(1) for "the Charities Act 1960" and "section 45(2)(b)" there shall be substituted "the Charities Act 1993" and "section 96(2)(c)".

(3) In section 63(3) for "the Charities Act 1960" there shall be substituted "the Charities Act 1993".

(4) In section 87(1) for "section 45 of the Charities Act 1960" there shall be substituted "section 96 of the Charities Act 1993".

(5) In paragraphs 11(6) and 16(1)(e) of Schedule 3 for "section 18 of the Charities Act 1960" there shall be substituted "section 16 of the Charities Act 1993".

The Rates Act 1984 (c. 33)

19. In section 3(9) of the Rates Act 1984 for "section 4 of the Charities Act 1960" there shall be substituted "section 3 of the Charities Act 1993".

The Companies Act 1985 (c. 6)

20.—(1) The Companies Act 1985 shall be amended as follows.

(2) In sections 35(4) and 35A(6) for "section 30B(1) of the Charities Act 1960" there shall be substituted "section 65(1) of the Charities Act 1993".

(3) In section 209(1)(c) and paragraph 11(b) of Schedule 13 after "the Charities Act 1960" there shall be inserted "or section 24 or 25 of the Charities Act 1993".

The Housing Associations Act 1985 (c. 69)

21.—(1) The Housing Associations Act 1985 shall be amended as follows.

(2) In section 10(1) for "sections 32 and 34 of the Charities Act 1992" there shall be substituted "sections 36 and 38 of the Charities Act 1993".

(3) In section 26(2) for the words from "section 8" onwards there shall be substituted "sections 41 to 45 of the Charities Act 1993 (charity accounts)".

(4) In section 35(2)(c) for "section 32 of the Charities Act 1992" there shall be substituted "section 36 of the Charities Act 1993".

(5) In section 38—
(a) in paragraph (a) for "the Charities Act 1960" there shall be substituted "the Charities Act 1993";
(b) in paragraph (b) for "section 4 of that Act" there shall be substituted "section 3 of that Act".

The Financial Services Act 1986 (c. 60)

22. In section 45(1)(j) of the Financial Services Act 1986 after "the Charities Act 1960" there shall be inserted ", section 24 or 25 of the Charities Act 1993".

The Coal Industry Act 1987 (c. 3)

23.—(1) In section 5 of the Coal Industry Act 1987 for subsection (8) there shall be substituted—

"(8) Sections 16(3), (9), (11) to (14), 17(1) to (5) and (7) and 20 of the Charities Act 1993 shall apply in relation to the powers of the Charity Commissioners and the making of schemes under this section as they apply in relation to their powers and the making of schemes under that Act and sections 89, 91 and 92 of that Act shall apply to orders and decisions under this section as they apply to orders and decisions under that Act."

(2) In subsection (8A) of that section for "section 29" (in both places) there shall be substituted "section 17".

The Reverter of Sites Act 1987 (c. 15)

24. In section 4(4) of the Reverter of Sites Act 1987 for "sections 40, 40A and 42 of the Charities Act 1960" there shall be substituted "sections 89, 91 and 92 of the Charities Act 1993".

The Income and Corporation Taxes Act 1988 (c. 1)

25. In Schedule 20 to the Income and Corporation Taxes Act 1988—
(a) in paragraph 3 after "the Charities Act 1960" there shall be inserted ", section 24 of the Charities Act 1993";
(b) in paragraph 3A after "the Charities Act 1960" there shall be inserted "or section 25 of the Charities Act 1993".

The Courts and Legal Services Act 1990 (c. 41)

26. In Schedule 11 to the Courts and Legal Services Act 1990, in the reference to a Charity Commissioner, for "under the First Schedule to the Charities Act 1960" there shall be substituted "as provided in Schedule 1 to the Charities Act 1993".

The London Local Authorities Act 1990 (c. vii)

27. In section 4 of the London Local Authorities Act 1990, in the definition of "night café", for "section 4 of the Charities Act 1960" and "subsection (4) thereof" there shall be substituted respectively "section 3 of the Charities Act 1993" and "subsection (5) thereof".

The London Local Authorities Act 1991 (c. xiii)

28. In section 4 of the London Local Authorities Act 1991, in the definition of "establishment for special treatment", for "section 4 of the Charities Act 1960" and "subsection (4) of that section" there shall be substituted respectively "section 3 of the Charities Act 1993" and "subsection (5) of that section".

The Charities Act 1992 (c. 41)

29.—(1) The Charities Act 1992 shall be amended as follows.

(2) In section 29(2)(b) after "Act" there shall be inserted "or section 18 of the Charities Act 1993".

(3) In section 30(1)(b) after "Act" there shall be inserted "or section 22(1) of the Charities Act 1993".

(4) In section 30(3)(a) after "Act" there shall be inserted "or section 18 of the Charities Act 1993".

(5) In section 58(1), in the definition of "charity" for "the Charities Act 1960" there shall be substituted "the Charities Act 1993" and in the definition of "company" for the words after "section" there shall be substituted "97 of the Charities Act 1993".

(6) In section 63(2) for "section 4 of the Charities Act 1960" there shall be substituted "section 3 of the Charities Act 1993".

(7) In section 72 for subsection (5) there shall be substituted—

"(5) Section 89(1), (2) and (4) of the Charities Act 1993 (provisions as to orders made by the Commissioners) shall apply to an order made by them under this section as it applies to an order made by them under that Act.

(6) In this section "charity" and "charitable purposes" have the same meaning as in that Act."

(8) In section 74 after subsection (3) there shall be inserted—

"(3A) Any person who knowingly or recklessly provides the Commissioners with information which is false or misleading in a material particular shall be guilty of an offence if the information is provided in circumstances in which he intends, or could reasonably be expected to know, that it would be used by them for the purpose of discharging their functions under section 72.

(3B) A person guilty of an offence under subsection (3A) shall be liable—
    (a) on summary conviction, to a fine not exceeding the statutory maximum;
    (b) on conviction or indictment, to imprisonment for a term not exceeding two years or to a fine, or both."

Other amendments

30. In the following provisions for "the Charities Act 1960" there shall be substituted "the Charities Act 1993"—

The National Health Service Reorganisation Act 1973 section 30(5).
The Consumer Credit Act 1974 section 189(1).
The Rent (Agriculture) Act 1976 section 5(3)(f).
The Rent Act 1977 section 15(2)(b).
The National Health Service Act 1977 section 96(2).
The Dioceses Measure 1978 section 19(4).
The Ancient Monuments and Archaeological Areas Act 1979 section 49(3).
The Greater London Council (General Powers) Act 1984 section 10(2)(n).
The Local Government Act 1985 section 90(4).
The Housing Act 1985 sections 525 and 622.
The Landlord and Tenant Act 1987 section 60(1).
The Education Reform Act 1988 sections 128(5) and 192(11).
The Copyright, Designs and Patents Act 1988 Schedule 6 paragraph 7.
The Housing Act 1988 Schedule 2 Part I Ground 6.
The University of Wales College of Cardiff Act 1988 section 9.
The Imperial College Act 1988 section 10.
The Local Government and Housing Act 1989 section 138(1).

Section 98(2)   SCHEDULE 7

REPEALS

Chapter	Short title	Extent of repeal
35 & 36 Vic. c. 24.	The Charitable Trustees Incorporation Act 1872.	The whole Act so far as unrepealed.
10 & 11 Geo. 5 c. 16.	The Imperial War Museum Act 1920.	Section 5.
24 & 25 Geo. 5 c. 43.	The National Maritime Museum Act 1934.	Section 7.
8 & 9 Eliz. 2 c. 58.	The Charities Act 1960.	The whole Act so far as unrepealed except— section 28(9) section 35(6) section 38(3) to (5) section 39(2) sections 48 and 49 Schedule 6.
1963 c. 33.	The London Government Act 1963.	Section 81(9)(b) and (c).
1963 c. xi.	The Universities of Durham and Newcastle-upon-Tyne Act 1963.	Section 10.
1965 c. 17.	The Museum of London Act 1965.	Section 11.
1972 c. 54.	The British Library Act 1972.	Section 4(2).
1972 c. 70.	The Local Government Act 1972.	Section 210(9).
1973 c. 16.	The Education Act 1973.	In section 2(7) the words from "but" onwards. In Schedule 1, paragraph 1(1) and (3).
1976 No. 4.	The Endowments and Glebe Measure 1976.	Section 44.
1983 c. 47.	The National Heritage Act 1983.	In Schedule 5, paragraph 4.

Chapter	Short title	Extent of repeal
1985 c. 9.	The Companies Consolidation (Consequential Provisions) Act 1985.	In Schedule 2 the entry relating to the Charities Act 1960.
1985 c. 20.	The Charities Act 1985.	Section 1.
1986 c. 60.	The Financial Services Act 1986.	In Schedule 16, paragraph 1.
1988 c. 40.	The Education Reform Act 1988.	In Schedule 12, paragraphs 9, 10, 63 and 64.
1989 c. 40.	The Companies Act 1989.	Section 111.
1989 c. xiii.	The Queen Mary and Westfield College Act 1989.	Section 10.
1990 c. 41.	The Courts and Legal Services Act 1990.	In Schedule 10, paragraph 14.
1992 c. 13.	The Further and Higher Education Act 1992.	In Schedule 8, paragraph 69.
1992 c. 41.	The Charities Act 1992.	The whole of Part I except— section 1(1) and (4) sections 29 and 30 section 36 sections 49 and 50 Section 75(b). Section 76(1)(a). In section 77, subsections (2)(a), (b) and (c) and in subsection (4) the figures 20, 22 and 23. Section 79(4) and (5). Schedules 1 to 4. In Schedule 6, paragraph 13(2). In Schedule 7, the entries relating to section 8 of the Charities Act 1960 and (so far as not in force at the date specified in section 99(1) of this Act) the Charities Act 1985.
1992 c. 44.	The Museums and Galleries Act 1992.	In Schedule 8, paragraphs 4 and 10. In Schedule 9, the entry relating to the Charities Act 1960.

Section 99(3), (4)   SCHEDULE 8

TRANSITIONAL PROVISIONS

PART I

PROVISIONS APPLYING PENDING COMING INTO FORCE OF PART VI ETC.

1. In the Charities Act 1960—
   section 8
   section 32
   Part V so far as relevant to those sections.
2. In the Charities Act 1985
   section 1
   sections 6 and 7 so far as relevant to section 1.

PART II

PROVISIONS APPLYING PENDING COMING INTO FORCE OF "FINANCIAL YEAR" REGULATIONS

Section 5

In section 5(1) of this Act "financial year"—
(a) in relation to a charity which is a company, shall be construed in accordance with section 223 of the Companies Act 1985;

(b) in relation to any other charity, means any period in respect of which an income and expenditure account is required to be prepared whether under section 32 of the Charities Act 1960 or by or under the authority of any other Act, whether that period is a year or not.

Sections 74 and 75

In sections 74(1)(a) and 75(1)(b) of this Act "financial year" means any period in respect of which an income and expenditure account is required to be prepared whether under section 32 of the Charities Act 1960 or by or under the authority of any other Act, whether that period is a year or not.

TABLE OF DERIVATIONS

Note:

1. The following abbreviations are used in this Table—

1872 = The Charitable Trustees Incorporation Act 1872 (c. 24)
1960 = The Charities Act 1960 (c. 58)
1992 = The Charities Act 1992 (c. 41)

Provision	Derivation
1	1960 s.1; 1992 Sch. 3, para. 1.
2	1960 s.3.
3	1960 ss.4, 43(1), 45(6); 1992 s.2, Sch. 1.
4	1960 ss.5, 43(1).
5	1992 s.3.
6	1992 s.4.
7	1992 s.5.
8	1960 s.6; 1992 s.6.
9	1960 s.7; 1992 s.7.
10	1992 s.52.
11	1992 s.54.
12	1992 s.53.
13	1960 s.13.
14	1960 s.14; 1992 s.15.
15	1960 s.15; Northern Ireland (Temporary Provisions) Act 1972 (c. 22) s.1(3); Northern Ireland Constitution Act 1973 (c. 36) Sch. 5, para. 1; Northern Ireland Act 1974 (c. 28) Sch. 1, para. 1(7).
16	1960 s.18; Local Government Act 1972 (c. 70) s.179(1)(4); 1992 s.13, Sch. 3, para. 6.
17	1960 s.19; 1992 Sch. 3, para. 7.
18	1960 s.20; 1992 s.8, Sch. 1.
19	1960 ss.20A, 43(1); 1992 s.9.
20	1960 s.21; Local Government Act 1972 (c. 70) s.179(1)(4); 1992 Sch. 3, para. 8.
21	1960 s.16; 1992 Sch. 3, para. 4.
22	1960 s.17; 1992 Sch. 3, para. 5.
23	1992 s.31.
24	1960 s.22.
25	1960 s.22A; 1992 s.16.
26	1960 s.23.
27	1960 s.23A; 1992 s.17.
28	1992 s.18; Banking Coordination (Second Council Directive) Regulations 1992 (S.I. 1992/3218) Sch. 10, para. 33.
29	1960 s.24.
30	1960 ss.25, 43(1).
31	1960 s.26.
32	1960 s.26A; 1992 s.28.
33	1960 s.28(1) to (8); 1992 Sch. 3, para. 10.
34	1960 s.28A; 1992 s.11.
35	1960 s.21A; 1992 s.14.
36	1992 s.32.
37	1992 s.33.
38	1992 s.34.

Provision	Derivation
39	1992 s.35.
40	1992 s.37(1) to (4).
41	1992 s.19.
42	1992 s.20.
43	1992 s.21.
44	1992 s.22.
45	1992 s.23.
46	1960 s.32(1)(2); 1992 s.24, Sch. 3, para. 13.
47	1992 s.25.
48	1992 s.26.
49	1992 s.27.
50	1872 s.1; 1992 Sch. 4, para. 1.
51	1872 s.2; 1992 Sch. 4, para. 2.
52	1872 s.3; 1992 Sch. 4, para. 3.
53	1872 s.4; 1992 Sch. 4, para. 4.
54	1872 s.5; 1992 Sch. 4, para. 5.
55	1872 s.6.
56	1872 s.6A; 1992 Sch. 4, para. 6.
57	1872 s.7; 1992 Sch. 4, para. 7.
58	1872 s.8; 1992 Sch. 4, para. 8.
59	1872 s.10.
60	1872 s.12; 1992 Sch. 4, para. 9 (part).
61	1872 s.12A; 1992 Sch. 4, para. 9 (part).
62	1872 s.14; 1992 Sch. 4, para. 10.
63	1960 s.30; Companies Act 1989 (c. 40) s.111(1); 1992 s.10.
64	1960 s.30A; Companies Act 1989 (c. 40) s.111(1); 1992 s.40.
65	1960 s.30B; Companies Act 1989 (c. 40) s.111(1).
66	1960 s.30BA; 1992 s.41.
67	1960 s.30BB; 1992 s.42.
68	1960 s.30C; Companies Act 1989 (c. 40) s.111(1); 1992 Sch. 3, para. 11.
69	1960 s.8; 1992 Sch. 3, para. 2; Companies Act 1989 (Eligibility for Appointment as Company Auditor) (Consequential Amendments) Regulations 1991 (S.I. 1991/1997).
70	1992 s.38.
71	1992 s.39.
72	1992 s.45.
73	1992 s.46.
74	1992 s.43.
75	1992 s.44.
76	1960 s.10; London Government Act 1963 (c. 33) s.81(9)(b); Local Government Act 1972 (c. 70) s.210(9)(a).
77	1960 s.11; London Government Act 1963 (c. 33) s.81(9)(b); Local Government Act 1972 (c. 70) s.210(9)(b).
78	1960 s.12; Local Government Act 1972 (c. 70) ss.179(1)(4), 210(9)(c).
79	1960 s.37; London Government Act 1963 (c. 33) s.4(4); Local Government Act 1972 (c. 70) ss.179(1)(4), 210(9)(e); Education Reform Act 1988 (c. 40) Sch. 12, para. 9.
80	1992 s.12.
81	1960 s.33.
82	1960 s.34; 1992 Sch. 3, para. 14.
83	1960 s.35.
84	1960 s.9; 1992 s.25(2), Sch. 3, para. 3.
85	1992 s.51.
86	1960 ss.4(8B), 18(14), 43(2A)(3); Education Act 1973 (c. 16) Sch. 1 para. 1(1); 1992 ss.2(7), 13(6), 77, Sch. 3, para. 17.
87	1992 s.56(1)(2)(6).
88	1960 s.41; 1992 s.56(3)(6), Sch. 3, para. 16.
89	1960 s.40; 1992 s.56(4)(5)(6).
90	1992 s.57.
91	1960 s.40A; 1992 s.76, Sch. 3, para. 15.
92	1960 s.42.

Provision	Derivation
93	1960 s.36.
94	1992 s.55.
95	1992 s.75.
96	1960 s.45(1) to (5); Local Government Act 1972 (c. 70) s.179(1)(4); 1992 s.1(2), Sch. 3, para. 18; Endowments and Glebe Measure 1976 (No. 4) s.44.
97	1960 ss.16(5) (part), 46; Companies Act 1989 (c. 40) s.111(2); 1992 s.1(1) to (4).
98	
99	
100	1960 s.49(2)(c); 1992 s.79(3)(4)(5).
Sch. 1	1960 Sch. 1; Courts and Legal Services Act 1990 (c. 41) Sch. 10, para. 14; 1992 s.12(1), Sch. 3, paras. 20, 21.
Sch. 2	
para. (a)	1960 Sch. 2, para. (a).
para. (b)	1960 Sch. 2, para. (b); Universities of Durham and Newcastle-upon-Tyne Act 1963 (c. xi) s.18; Queen Mary and Westfield College Act 1989 (c. xiii) s.10.
para. (c)	1960 Sch. 2, para. (c).
paras. (d) to (i)	Education Reform Act 1988 (c. 40) Sch. 12, paras. 10, 63, 64.
para. (j)	Further and Higher Education Act 1992 (c. 13) Sch. 8, para. 69.
paras. (k) to (n)	1960 Sch. 2, paras. (ca) to (cd); National Heritage Act 1983 (c. 47) Sch. 5, para. 4.
para. (o)	Local Government Reorganisation (Miscellaneous Provisions) Order 1990. (S.I. 1990/1765) art. 3(1)(b).
para. (p)	1960 Sch. 2, para. (d); Museums and Galleries Act 1992 (c. 44) Sch. 8, para. 4.
paras. (q) to (t)	1960 Sch. 2, paras. (ce) to (ch); Museums and Galleries Act 1992 (c. 44) Sch. 8, para. 10.
para. (u)	Imperial War Museum Act 1920 (c. 16) s.5.
para. (v)	National Maritime Museum Act 1934 (c. 43) s.7.
para. (w)	1960 Sch. 2, para. (e); Education Reform Act 1988 (c. 40) Sch. 12, paras. 10, 63, 64; Further and Higher Education Act 1992 (c. 13) Sch. 8, para. 69.
paras. (x)(y)	1960 Sch. 2, paras. (f)(g).
para. (z)	1960 Sch. 2, para. (h); Museum of London Act 1965 (c. 17) s.11.
para. (za)	1960 Sch. 2, para. (i); British Library Act 1972 (c. 54) s.4(2).
Sch. 3	1960 Sch. 3; London Government Act 1963 (c. 33) s.81(9)(c); Local Government Act 1972 (c. 70) ss.179(1)(4), 210(9)(f).
Sch. 4	1960 Sch. 4; Education Act 1973 (c. 16) s.2(7).
Sch. 5	1992 Sch. 2.
Sch. 6	1960 s.40(5) (as to paras. 1(3), 2, 3(3)) and 1992 ss.54(1)(b)(3), 56(4)(5) (as to para. 29(7)(8)).
Sch. 7	
Sch. 8	

TABLE OF DESTINATIONS

1872 CHARITABLE TRUSTEES INCORPORATION ACT 1872
c.24

1872	1993
s.1	s.50
2	51
3	52
4	53
5	54
6	55
6A	56
7	57
8	58
10	59
12	60
12A	61
14	62

IMPERIAL WAR MUSEUM ACT 1920
c.16

1920	1993
s.5	Sched. 2, para. (u)

NATIONAL MARITIME MUSEUM ACT 1934
c.43

1934	1993
s.7	Sched. 2, para. (v)

CHARITIES ACT 1960
c.58

1960	1993	1960	1993	1960	1993
s.1	s.1	s.23	s.26	s.40A	s.91
4	3	23A	27	41	88
(8B)	86	24	29	42	92
5	4	25	30	43(1)	3, 4, 19, 30
6	8	26	31	(2A)	86
7	9	26A	32	(3)	86
8	69	28(1)–(8)	33	45(1)–(5)	96
9	84	28A	34	(6)	3
10	75	30	63	46	97
11	77	30A	64	49(2)(c)	100
12	78	30B	65	Sched. 1	3; Sched. 1
13	13	30BA	66	Sched. 2,	
14	14	30BB	67	para. (a)	Sched. 2, para. (a)
15	15	30C	68	(b)	(b)
16	21	32(1)	46	(c)	(c)
5 (part)	97	(2)	46	(ca)–(cd)	(k)–(n)
17	22	33	81	(ce)–(ch)	(q)–(t)
18	16	34	82	(d)	(p)
(14)	86	35	83	(e)	(w)
19	17	36	93	(f)–(g)	(x)–(y)
20	18	37	79	(h)	(z)
20A	18	40	89	(i)	(2a)
21	20	(5) (as to		Sched. 3	Sched. 3
21A	35	paras.		4	4
22	24	1(3), 2,			
22A	25	3(3))	Sched. 6		

10–125

TABLE OF DESTINATIONS

LONDON GOVERNMENT ACT 1963
c.33

1963	1993
s.4(4)	s.9
81(9)(b)	76, 77
(c)	Sched. 3

UNIVERSITIES OF DURHAM AND NEWCASTLE-UPON-TYNE ACT 1963
c.XI

1963	1993
s.18	Sched. 2, para. (b)

MUSEUM OF LONDON ACT 1965
c.17

1965	1993
s.11	Sched. 2, para. (2)

NORTHERN IRELAND (TEMPORARY PROVISIONS) ACT 1972
c.22

1972	1993
s.1(3)	s.15

BRITISH LIBRARY ACT 1972
c.54

1972	1993
s.4(2)	Sched. 2, para. (2a)

LOCAL GOVERNMENT ACT 1972
c.70

1972	1993
s.179(1)	ss.16, 20, 78, 79, 96; Sched. 3
(4)	16, 20, 78, 79, 96; Sched. 3
210(9)(a)	76
(b)	77
(c)	78
(e)	79
(f)	Sched. 3

EDUCATION ACT 1973
c.16

1973	1993
s.2(7)	Sched. 4
Sched. 1, para 1(1)	s.86

NORTHERN IRELAND CONSTITUTION ACT 1973
c.36

1973	1993
Sched. 5, para. 1	s.15

10–126

TABLE OF DESTINATIONS

NORTHERN IRELAND ACT 1974
c.28

1974	1993
Sched. 1,	
para. 1(7) ...	s.15

ENDOWMENTS AND GLEBE MEASURE 1976 (No. 4)
c.17

1976	1993
s.44	s.96

NATIONAL HERITAGE ACT 1983
c.47

1983	1993
Sched. 5,	
para. 4	Sched. 2,
	paras. (k)–
	(n)

EDUCATION REFORM ACT 1988
c.40

1988	1993
Sched. 12,	
para. 9	s.79
10	Sched. 2,
	paras.
	(d)–(i), (w)
63	Sched. 2,
	paras.
	(d)–(i), (w)
64	Sched. 2,
	paras.
	(d)–(i), (w)

COMPANIES ACT 1989
c.40

1989	1993
s.111(1).	ss.63, 64, 65,
	68
(2).	97

QUEEN MARY AND WESTFIELD COLLEGE ACT 1989
c.XIII

1989	1993
s.10	Sched. 2,
	para. (b)

COMPANIES ACT 1989 (ELIGIBILITY FOR APPOINTMENT AS COMPANY AUDITOR) (CONSEQUENTIAL AMENDMENTS) REGULATIONS 1991
(S.I. 1991 No. 1997)

S.I. 1989 No. 1997	1993
....	s.69

COURTS AND LEGAL SERVICES ACT 1990
c.41

1990	1993
Sched. 10	
para. 14	Sched. 1

TABLE OF DESTINATIONS

LOCAL GOVERNMENT REORGANISATION (MISCELLANEOUS PROVISIONS) ORDER 1990
(S.I. 1990 No. 1765)

S.I. 1990 No. 1765	1993
art. 3(1)(b)....	Sched. 2, para. (o)

FURTHER AND HIGHER EDUCATION ACT 1992
c.13

1992	1993
Sched. 8, para. 69.....	Sched. 2, para. (j)–(w)

CHARITIES ACT 1992
c.41

1992	1993	1992	1993	1992	1993
s.1(1)........	s.97	s.31..........	s.23	s.79(4)........	s.100
(2)........	96, 97	32..........	36	(5).......	100
(3)–(4)....	97	33..........	37	Sched. 1......	18
2............	3	34..........	38	Sched. 2.....	Sched. 5
(7)........	86	35..........	39	Sched. 3,	
3...........	5	37(1)–(4)....	40	para. 1......	1
4...........	6	38..........	70	2.....	69
5...........	7	39..........	71	3.....	84
6...........	8	40..........	64	4.....	21
7...........	9	41..........	66	5.....	22
8...........	18	42..........	67	6.....	16
9...........	19	43..........	74	7.....	17
10..........	63	44..........	75	8.....	20
11..........	34	45..........	72	10....	33
12..........	80	46..........	73	11.....	68
(1).......	Sched. 1	51..........	85	13.....	46
13..........	16	52..........	10	14....	82
(6).......	86	53..........	12	15....	91
14..........	35	54..........	11	16....	88
15..........	14	(1)(b)(3)..	Sched. 6	17....	86
16..........	25	55..........	94	18.....	96
17..........	27	56(1).......	87	20.....	Sched. 1
18..........	28	(2).......	87	21.....	Sched. 1
19..........	41	(3).......	88	Sched. 4,	
20..........	42	(4).......	89, Sched. 6	para. 1......	50
21..........	43	(5).......	88	2.....	51
22..........	44	(as to		3.....	52
23..........	45	para.		4.....	53
24..........	46	29(7)(8)).	Sched. 6	5.....	54
25..........	47	(6).......	87, 88, 89	6....	56
(2).......	84	57..........	90	7.....	57
26..........	48	75..........	95	8.....	58
27..........	49	76..........	91	9 (in	
28..........	32	77..........	86	part).	60, 61
		79(3)........	100	10.....	62

MUSEUMS AND GALLERIES ACT 1992
c.44

1992	1993
Sched. 8, para. 4......	Sched. 2, para. (p)

BANKING COORDINATION (SECOND COUNCIL DIRECTIVE) REGULATIONS 1992
(S.I. 1992 No. 3218)

S.I. 1992 No. 3218	1993
Sched. 10, para. 33.....	s.28

INDEX

References are to sections and Schedule numbers

ACCOUNTS,
annual statements, 42
audit, 43–44
duty to keep records, 41
exempt and excepted charities, 46
investigation of charitable companies, 69
production at inquiries, 8(3)
public inspection, 47
ADVICE TO TRUSTEES, 29
ADVOWSONS, 36(10)(c), 37(11)(a)(ii)
ANNUAL REPORT, 45
exempt and excepted charities, 46
offence, 49
public inspection, 47
ANNUAL RETURN, 48
APPEALS,
against appointment of receiver and manager, 18(9)(a)
notices of orders subject to, 20(5)
regulations as to, 92
against removal of trustee or officer, 18(9)(b)
against schemes, 16(11)–(14)

CHARITABLE COMPANIES,
alteration of objects clause, 64
capacity, 65
change of name, 7
correspondence and official publications,
charitable status, 68
name, 67
invalidity of certain acts, 65
investigation of accounts, 69
payments to directors requiring consent, 66
property transactions, 65(2)
ratification under Companies Act 1985, 64(4)
winding up, 63
CHARITIES, INTERPRETATION, 96
CHARITY COMMISSIONERS,
advising trustees, 29
annual report, 1(5)
appeals from, 92
constitution and proceedings, 1(2), Sched. 1
continuation of body, 1(1)
dealings with property, authorising, 26
directions, 90, 91
dormant bank accounts, directions as to, 28
ex gratia payments, authorising, 27
fees payable to, 85
function, 1(3)
information powers, *see* INFORMATION POWERS

CHARITY COMMISSIONERS—*cont.*
legal proceedings,
authorising trustees and others, 33
by Commissioners, 32
object, 1(4)
orders, *see* ORDERS OF COMMISSIONERS
powers to protect charities, 18
CHARITY LAND,
advowson, 36(10)(c), 37(11)(a)(ii)
dispositions,
instruments, statements and certificates required, 37
restrictions applying, 36(1)
held for particular purpose, 36(6)
restrictions not applying,
advertised, 36(3)(b), 36(6)(i)
advowson, 36(10)(c)
best terms, 36(3)(c)
directions by Commissioners, 36(8)
disposition to another charity, 36(9)(b)
by exempt charity, 36(10)
lease at low rent to beneficiary for purpose of charity, 36(9)(c)
lease for not more than seven years, 36(3)–(5)
lease for two years, 36(7)(b)
mortgage, 36(10)(b)
to person not connected or trustee, 36(2)
replacement land acquired, 36(7)(a)
under statutory authority, 36(9)(a)
surveyor's report, 36(3)(a), 36(4)
mortgages,
not dispositions, 36(10)(b), 37(11)(a)(i)
requirements in instrument, 39
restrictions applying, 38(1)
restrictions not applying,
proper advice taken, 38(2)–(3)
statutory authority, 38(5)
permanent endowment not consisting of, 75(1)
rentcharge,
evidence of payment, 93
release of, 37(11)(a)(iii), 40
situation of, 36(11), 37(11)(b), 38(6)
see also VESTING OF PROPERTY
COMMENCEMENT, 99
COMMON DEPOSIT FUNDS, 25
COMMON INVESTMENT FUNDS, 24
CONNECTED PERSONS, 36(2)(a), Sched. 5
CONSEQUENTIAL AMENDMENTS, 98(1), Sched. 6
COURT'S JURISDICTION,
charities governed by statute, 15, Sched. 4
directions as to receiver's functions, 19(4)(b), 19(5)

CLEAN AIR ACT 1993*

(1993 c. 11)

[A table showing the derivation of the provisions of this consolidation will be found at the end of this Act. The table has no official status.]

---

* Annotations by Professor Neil Hawke, Professor of Law, De Montfort University, Leicester.

An Act to consolidate the Clean Air Acts 1956 and 1968 and certain related enactments, with amendments to give effect to recommendations of the Law Commission and the Scottish Law Commission.   [27th May 1993]

PARLIAMENTARY DEBATES
Hansard, H.L. Vol. 534, col. 343; Vol. 540, col. 921.
As a consolidating measure the majority of readings were formal with no debate.

INTRODUCTION AND GENERAL NOTE
This Act consolidates the Clean Air Acts 1956–1968; Part IV of the Control of Pollution Act 1974; and related legislation, as listed in the Table of Derivations, to be found at the end of the text of the Act. Significant provisions on air pollution are to be found in Parts I and III of the Environmental Protection Act 1990, as noted below. The new Clean Air Act contains various minor technical amendments giving effect to recommendations in a joint report of the Law Commission and the Scottish Law Commission (Report on the Consolidation of Certain Enactments relating to Clean Air: (1992) Law Comm. No. 209; Scot. Law Comm. No. 138).

The consolidation is a very useful development although the existence of other statutory provisions affecting clean air, particularly in the Environmental Protection Act 1990, emphasises a rather limited legislative agenda for the Clean Air Act 1993. But for the transfer of the statutory provisions on statutory nuisances from the Clean Air Acts the new consolidation would have been a rather more comprehensive exercise. Reference to Department of the Environment Circulars will remain a very useful guide to the disparate elements now consolidated:

28/69 : Clean Air Act 1968: Height of Chimneys
54/69 : Clean Air Act 1968
72/69 : Clean Air Act 1968
 7/76 : Control of Pollution Act 1974 Part IV
 2/77 : Regulations under the Control of Pollution Act Part IV
25/81 : Clean Air Acts 1956 and 1968: Chimney Heights
11/81 : Domestic Smoke Control and EC Directive on Sulphur Dioxide
 9/93 : Exchequer grant-aid in smoke control areas

References to various functions and responsibilities of the Secretary of State for the Environment under the Act are explained in note 2 to the Table of Derivations, set out at the end of the Act. Note 3 relates to fines in respect of summary offences. Throughout the Act, references to the "standard scale" in s.37 of the Criminal Justice Act 1982 are subject to the amendment of that scale by virtue of s.17 of the Criminal Justice Act 1991.

ARRANGEMENT OF THE ACT

Part I—Dark Smoke
Part I brings together, in ss.1 and 2 the offences relating to the emission of dark smoke from chimneys and from industrial or trade premises, formerly divided between the two Clean Air Acts of 1956 and 1968.

Part II—Smoke, Grit, Dust and Fumes
Part II is concerned primarily with furnaces and emissions to the atmosphere, bringing together a variety of provisions, again from the Acts of 1956 and 1968.

Part III—Smoke Control Areas
Part III relates to the designation (formerly under the Acts of 1956 and 1968) of smoke control areas, a critical area of control, particularly for the purpose of compliance with limit values and other requirements found in E.C. Directives.

Part IV—Control of certain forms of Air Pollution
Drawn from Pt. IV of the Control of Pollution Act 1974, these provisions are concerned principally with the regulation making power by which, *inter alia*, the lead content of motor fuel and the sulphur content of oil for engines and furnaces can be regulated, again for the purpose of compliance with a range of E.C. Directives.

Part V—Information about Air Pollution
Drawn from Pt. IV of the Control of Pollution Act 1974, this set of provisions contain a variety of essentially discretionary powers for the collection of information about atmospheric pollution, the particular value of which may be in relation to the Secretary of State's power to require local authorities to measure and record information and to transmit that information to the Department of the Environment, no doubt for the purpose (again) of ensuring compliance with E.C. requirements.

Part VI—Special Cases
Apart from a variety of miscellaneous provisions, there is a continuing reminder of the division between controls in Pts. I to III of the Clean Air Act and Pt. I of the Environmental Protection Act 1990, referred to below.

Part VII—Miscellaneous and General
This final part of the Act deals with, *inter alia*, the power to extend some provisions dealing with grit, dust and smoke, to fumes and gases, administration and enforcement and a variety of general matters.

The Environmental Protection Act 1990

Parts I and III
Part I of the Act of 1990, dealing with multi-media integrated pollution control and local authority air pollution control are expressly separated from Pts. I–III of the Clean Air Act by s.41 of the Act of 1993. This separation is achieved by reference to the categories of "processes" through which Pt. I controls operate. Accordingly, local authority enforcement of Pts. I–III of the Act of 1993 is severely, if not completely limited.

By virtue of the decision to site statutory nuisance provisions based on air pollution occurrences in the Act of 1990, the Act of 1993, unlike the former Clean Air Acts, is no longer the natural home for such controls. For this purpose, reference should be made to s.79(1)(b), (c) and (d), together with the statutory machinery for dealing with statutory nuisances in s.80, etc., and the statutory definitions provided for the following: "dust", "fumes", "gas" and "smoke" (s.79(7)).

ABBREVIATIONS
The Act : The Clean Air Act 1993

PART I

DARK SMOKE

Prohibition of dark smoke from chimneys

1.—(1) Dark smoke shall not be emitted from a chimney of any building, and if, on any day, dark smoke is so emitted, the occupier of the building shall be guilty of an offence.

(2) Dark smoke shall not be emitted from a chimney (not being a chimney of a building) which serves the furnace of any fixed boiler or industrial plant, and if, on any day, dark smoke is so emitted, the person having possession of the boiler or plant shall be guilty of an offence.

(3) This section does not apply to emissions of smoke from any chimney, in such classes of case and subject to such limitations as may be prescribed in regulations made by the Secretary of State, lasting for not longer than such periods as may be so prescribed.

(4) In any proceedings for an offence under this section, it shall be a defence to prove—

    (a) that the alleged emission was solely due to the lighting up of a furnace which was cold and that all practicable steps had been taken to prevent or minimise the emission of dark smoke;

    (b) that the alleged emission was solely due to some failure of a furnace, or of apparatus used in connection with a furnace, and that—

        (i) the failure could not reasonably have been foreseen, or, if foreseen, could not reasonably have been provided against; and

        (ii) the alleged emission could not reasonably have been prevented by action taken after the failure occurred; or

    (c) that the alleged emission was solely due to the use of unsuitable fuel and that—

        (i) suitable fuel was unobtainable and the least unsuitable fuel which was available was used; and

        (ii) all practicable steps had been taken to prevent or minimise the emission of dark smoke as the result of the use of that fuel;

or that the alleged emission was due to the combination of two or more of the causes specified in paragraphs (a) to (c) and that the other conditions specified in those paragraphs are satisfied in relation to those causes respectively.

(5) A person guilty of an offence under this section shall be liable on summary conviction—

    (a) in the case of a contravention of subsection (1) as respects a chimney of a private dwelling, to a fine not exceeding level 3 on the standard scale; and

    (b) in any other case, to a fine not exceeding level 5 on the standard scale.

(6) This section has effect subject to section 51 (duty to notify offences to occupier or other person liable).

DEFINITIONS

    "chimney": s.64(1).
    "dark smoke": s.3(1).
    "day": s.64(1).
    "fixed boiler or industrial plant": s.64(1).
    "practicable": s.64(1).
    "smoke": s.64(1).
    "standard scale": s.37 of the Criminal Justice Act 1982.

GENERAL NOTE

    This section prohibits dark smoke being emitted from the chimneys of buildings. The prohibition extends to "any" buildings and applies to "dark smoke" which must be as dark, or darker, than shade 2 on the Ringelmann Chart. As to the Ringelmann Chart, see the Report of the Committee on Air Pollution, Cmnd. 9322 (H.M.S.O.). Although the definition of "chimney" for the purpose of the section is wide, its width is not comparable with any provision which might have referred to emissions from any chimney situation on "premises". Note in this respect the following s.2 referring to the emission of dark smoke from "any industrial or trade premises". Accordingly, although s.1 would not apply to the burning of trade waste in a scrap yard, for example, an emission of dark smoke from such premises would be caught by s.2.

Subs. (1)

Building. The case law surrounding this term and its interpretation is to be treated with caution since it arises from a variety of other measures such as the Town and Country Planning legislation. Helpful indicators of what should, it is submitted, be a wide definition of "building" for present purposes are to be found in a planning case, *Cheshire County Council* v. *Woodward* [1962] 2 A.C. 126, where (at p.135), Lord Parker C.J., observed that: ". . . when the Act defines a building as including 'any structure or erection and any part of a building so defined', the Act is referring to any structure or erection which can be said to form part of the realty, and to change the physical character of the land". Again, in another planning case, *Buckinghamshire County Council* v. *Callingham* [1952] 2 A.C. 515, Morris L.J., (at p.528) observed that "small or model buildings may only be small structures or small erections, but they are, nevertheless, within the definition of the word 'buildings' ".

Occupier. Where different parts of a building are occupied by different persons, the reference to an "occupier" is a reference to the occupier or other person in control of the part of the building in which the relevant fireplace is situated: s.64(2). The occupier is "the appropriate person" to notify for the purpose of section 51, imposing a duty on the authorised officer of the local authority to notify an offence which is being, or has been committed under s.1.

On any day. A fresh offence is committed every day, *i.e.*, during a period of 24 hours, during which dark smoke is emitted.

Dark smoke. Although defined by s.3 as comprising smoke as dark, or darker, than shade 2 on the Ringelmann Chart, in proceedings under the present section the court may be satisfied that smoke is or is not dark smoke notwithstanding that there has been no actual comparison of the smoke with a chart of the Ringelmann type: s.3(2).

Guilty of an offence. Although each case will no doubt be regarded in its own statutory context it seems likely that the offence under the present section is one where *mens rea* is not a constituent element. Certainly a reversal of the onus of proof will aid proof of the offence and there is considerable judicial support for the proposition that, in the absence of strict liability and a reversal of the onus of proof, the offence may be incapable of "proof": *Alphacell* v. *Woodward* [1972] A.C. 824, H.L.

Subs. (2)

The effect of this subsection is to include plant such as stationary incinerators which may be independent of any building. A mobile incinerator would not be included unless there is some element of fixity on the subject land. Otherwise, use of the word "installed" in the definition of any "fixed boiler or industrial plant" seems to suggest something less than fixity may bring an item of plant within the subsection. Nevertheless, "installation" connotes a need for something more than mere parking or stationing of plant on land.

Boiler. This term is left undefined by the Act but see the Boiler Explosions Act 1892 (now repealed) defining a boiler as: ". . . any closed vessel used for generating steam, or for heating water, or for heating any other liquids, or into which steam is admitted for heating, steaming, boiling or any other similar purposes": s.3.

Possession. Unlike the offence in the previous subsection, the present offence assumes mere possession of a boiler or plant. A person has possession of whatever is to his knowledge physically in his custody or under his physical control: *R.* v. *Maio* [1989] V.R. 281. An object delivered to or placed on land without any request for delivery or knowledge of placement cannot amount to possession of that object: *R.* v. *Cavendish* [1961] 1 W.L.R. 1083; *R.* v. *Peaston* (1978) 69 Cr.App.R. 203.

Subs. (3)

The Secretary of State is able to prescribe, through regulations, exemption from the section of emissions of smoke from "any chimney" lasting for periods no longer than those prescribed. Under the predecessor provisions of subs. (2) of s.1 of the Clean Air Act 1956, the Secretary of State made the Dark Smoke (Permitted Periods) Regulations 1958 (S.I. 1958 No. 498) and the Dark Smoke (Permitted Periods) (Vessels) Regulations 1958 (S.I. 1958 No. 878). As to the making of regulations, and orders, see s.63, *post.*

Subs. (4)

The burden of establishing any of the defences lies with the person charged. The defence in para. (a) applies only to an emission of dark smoke taking place when a furnace is being lit up; presumably there would be no defence where dark smoke is emitted through the making up of a dying fire. No doubt it is possible to light a furnace from cold without emitting dark smoke but note the inclusion of the word "practicable" and its interpretation which includes the important variable relating to "financial implications": s.64(1). There is no obligation on a defendant in any proceedings to give notice to the prosecution of an intention to rely on any of the defences. These circumstances would suggest the importance of local authority inspection of the subject installation, and fuel, at the time of the offence for the purpose of ascertaining the true facts. Powers of entry are provided by s.56 but not in relation to a private dwelling: s.56(2). As to exemptions for the purposes of investigations or research relevant to the problem of air pollution, see s.45.

Unsuitable fuel; suitable fuel. These terms remain undefined by the Act but note the "relative" reference in s.4(2) to the burning of fuel: ". . . of a type for which the furnace was designed". The provisions of this section apply to railway locomotive engines and "vessels in waters" by virtue (respectively) of ss.43 and 44.

Prohibition of dark smoke from industrial or trade premises

2.—(1) Dark smoke shall not be emitted from any industrial or trade premises and if, on any day, dark smoke is so emitted the occupier of the premises and any person who causes or permits the emission shall be guilty of an offence.

(2) This section does not apply—

(a) to the emission of dark smoke from any chimney to which section 1 above applies; or

(b) to the emission of dark smoke caused by the burning of any matter prescribed in regulations made by the Secretary of State, subject to compliance with such conditions (if any) as may be so prescribed.

(3) In proceedings for an offence under this section, there shall be taken to have been an emission of dark smoke from industrial or trade premises in any case where—

(a) material is burned on those premises; and

(b) the circumstances are such that the burning would be likely to give rise to the emission of dark smoke,

unless the occupier or any person who caused or permitted the burning shows that no dark smoke was emitted.

(4) In proceedings for an offence under this section, it shall be a defence to prove—

(a) that the alleged emission was inadvertent; and

(b) that all practicable steps had been taken to prevent or minimise the emission of dark smoke.

(5) A person guilty of an offence under this section shall be liable on summary conviction to a fine not exceeding level 5 on the standard scale.

(6) In this section "industrial or trade premises" means—

(a) premises used for any industrial or trade purposes; or

(b) premises not so used on which matter is burnt in connection with any industrial or trade process.

(7) This section has effect subject to section 51 (duty to notify offences to occupier or other person liable).

DEFINITIONS

"chimney": s.64(1).

"dark smoke": s.3(1).

"day": s.64(1).

"emission": s.64(3).

"industrial or trade premises": subs. (6).

"occupier": s.64(2).

"practicable": s.64(1).

"standard scale": s.37 of the Criminal Justice Act 1982.

GENERAL NOTE

This section extends beyond s.1 by making it an offence to emit dark smoke from any industrial or trade premises otherwise than from a chimney. The scope of the section is marked out particularly by the potential width of the reference to "premises" (as opposed to the "chimney of any building" in s.1) and the conduct of the occupier and anyone who "causes or permits" the emission of dark smoke. The overlap with s.1 is recognised: the present section does not apply to the emission of dark smoke from any chimney within s.1. As to the application of s.3 to this provision see the note on "dark smoke" under s.1(1).

Subs. (1)

Premises. These were held to include a demolition site for the purpose of the present section in *Sheffield City Council* v. *A.D.H. Demolition* (1984) 82 L.G.R. 177. It was also held that the act of demolition is a "trade process" so that demolition contractors who burn debris on a site, thereby causing the emission of dark smoke, are in breach of the section.

On any day. A fresh offence is committed every day, *i.e.*, during a period of 24 hours during which dark smoke is emitted.

Causes or permits. In *Alphacell* v. *Woodward* [1972] A.C. 824, it was stated that a defendant who "causes" pollution must be involved in an "active operation" (Lord Wilberforce); or in "positive activities" (Lord Pearson); or a "positive act" (Lord Cross); or an "active operation of plant" (Lord Salmon); or his "acts" must be referable to an "operation of the works" (Viscount Dilhorne). It would appear that a mere passive "looking on" is insufficient for present purposes: *Wychavon District Council* v. *National Rivers Authority* (1992) 136 S.J. (LB) 260. *Cf. Window* v. *The Phosphate Co-operative Co. of Australia Ltd.* [1983] 2 V.R. 287. The inclusion of the word "permits" is stricter than the commonly found reference to "knowingly permits". This latter term indicates a failure by the defendant to prevent a polluting emission when there is evidence that it was known to him. Absence of any immediate requirement to establish the defendant's knowledge is an aid to proof, although presumably, the defendant will have to be shown to have sufficient control over premises as a pre-requisite, see, for example, *Price* v. *Cromack* [1975] 1 W.L.R. 988, a case illustrating the interrelationship between offences of "causing" and "knowingly permitting" in water pollution legislation.

Guilty of an offence. See the equivalent note to s.1.

Subs. (2)

Prescribed in regulations. Under the powers given by the now repealed s.1(3) of the Clean Air Act 1968 the Clean Air (Emission of Dark Smoke) (Exemption) Regulations 1969 (S.I. 1969 No. 1263) prescribe six categories of exempt material, as described by Circular 72/69 (Welsh Office 71/69).

Subs. (3)

The provisions of this subsection aid considerably the process of proof and enforcement since the onus is on the occupier or some other person alleged to have caused or permitted the emission to prove that no dark smoke was emitted where material is burned on premises in circumstances where such burning is "likely" to give rise to an emission of dark smoke.

Subs. (4)

It is a defence to proceedings under this section to prove both inadvertence and that all practicable steps had been taken to prevent or minimise the emission. Accordingly, proof (to the satisfaction of the court) that the variables that make up "practicable steps" are the only basis for reliance on inadvertence. There are close similarities with the definitions of "practicable" and "means" to be found in s.72 of the Control of Pollution Act 1974, for example: there is no obligation on a defendant in any proceedings to give notice to the prosecution of an intention to rely on the defence. These circumstances would suggest the importance of local authority inspection of the subject premises at the time of the offence or as soon as possible afterwards for the purpose of ascertaining the true facts. Powers of entry are provided by s.56 but not in relation to a private dwelling: s.56(2). As to exemptions for the purposes of investigations or research relevant to the problem of air pollution, see s.45.

Subs. (6)

"*Industrial or trade premises*". These premises are widely defined. The critical consideration is the purpose for which the premises are used: *Thames Water Authority* v. *Blue and White Launderettes* [1980] 1 W.L.R. 700, C.A. Even if premises are not used for industrial or trade purposes it will be sufficient if "matter is burnt in connection with any industrial or trade process".

As to a local authority's power of exemption in relation to the investigation of and research into, air pollution, see s.45.

Meaning of "dark smoke"

3.—(1) In this Act "dark smoke" means smoke which, if compared in the appropriate manner with a chart of the type known on 5th July 1956 (the date of the passing of the Clean Air Act 1956) as the Ringelmann Chart, would appear to be as dark as or darker than shade 2 on the chart.

(2) For the avoidance of doubt it is hereby declared that in proceedings—

(a) for an offence under section 1 or 2 (prohibition of emissions of dark smoke); or

(b) brought by virtue of section 17 (smoke nuisances in Scotland),

the court may be satisfied that smoke is or is not dark smoke as defined in subsection (1) notwithstanding that there has been no actual comparison of the smoke with a chart of the type mentioned in that subsection.

(3) Without prejudice to the generality of subsections (1) and (2), if the Secretary of State by regulations prescribes any method of ascertaining whether smoke is dark smoke as defined in subsection (1), proof in any such proceedings as are mentioned in subsection (2)—

(a) that that method was properly applied, and

(b) that the smoke was thereby ascertained to be or not to be dark smoke as so defined,

shall be accepted as sufficient.

DEFINITIONS
  "dark smoke": subs. (1).
  "smoke": s.64(1).

GENERAL NOTE
  The section sets out the essential meaning and definition of "dark smoke" for the purpose of the Act: ss.1 and 2 in particular. However, for the avoidance of doubt it is declared by subs. (2) that in any proceedings for an offence under these sections or, in Scotland, s.17, the court may be "satisfied" that smoke is or is not "dark smoke" notwithstanding an absence of actual comparison using the Ringelmann Chart. Difficulty in obtaining truly objective evidence may therefore justify reliance on some other evidence such as video or other photographic evidence. The Secretary of State is empowered by the section to prescribe "any method" for ascertaining whether smoke is dark smoke in relation to proceedings where there is no reliance on the Ringelmann Chart comparison.

Subs. (3)
  See the notes to ss.1 and 2, above.

PART II

SMOKE, GRIT, DUST AND FUMES

Installation of furnaces

Requirement that new furnaces shall be so far as practicable smokeless

4.—(1) No furnace shall be installed in a building or in any fixed boiler or industrial plant unless notice of the proposal to install it has been given to the local authority.

(2) No furnace shall be installed in a building or in any fixed boiler or industrial plant unless the furnace is so far as practicable capable of being operated continuously without emitting smoke when burning fuel of a type for which the furnace was designed.

(3) Any furnace installed in accordance with plans and specifications submitted to, and approved for the purposes of this section by, the local authority shall be treated as complying with the provisions of subsection (2).

(4) Any person who installs a furnace in contravention of subsection (1) or (2) or on whose instructions a furnace is so installed shall be guilty of an offence and liable on summary conviction—

(a) in the case of a contravention of subsection (1), to a fine not exceeding level 3 on the standard scale; and

(b) in the case of a contravention of subsection (2), to a fine not exceeding level 5 on that scale.

(5) This section does not apply to the installation of domestic furnaces.

(6) This section applies in relation to—

(a) the attachment to a building of a boiler or industrial plant which already contains a furnace; or

(b) the fixing to or installation on any land of any such boiler or plant,

as it applies in relation to the installation of a furnace in any fixed boiler or industrial plant.

DEFINITIONS
   "domestic furnace": s.64(1).
   "fixed boiler or industrial plant": s.64(1).
   "local authority": s.64(1).
   "practicable": s.64(1).
   "smoke": s.64(1).
   "standard scale": s.37 of the Criminal Justice Act 1982.

GENERAL NOTE
   All furnaces except domestic furnaces must be, so far as practicable, smokeless, *i.e.*, capable of being operated continuously without emitting smoke when burning fuel of a type for which the furnace was designed.
   Before any such furnace is installed, notice of the proposal to install must be given to the local authority. It would appear that even if a furnace is taken from one location to another or even altered in position, compliance with the section is required, including requirements for notification. Local authority decisions are not subject to appeal. Despite local authority approval for a furnace under this section there is no defence, by virtue of that approval, to proceedings under s.1 of this Act.
   The word "furnace" is undefined by the Act and case law gives only modest guidance. In a rating case, *British Steel Corporation* v. *Pittock (Valuation Officer)* 16 RRC 374; [1970] RA 423 (Lands Tribunal), it was held that the furnace in question was the whole agglomeration of bricks, steel and the parts and, as such, was a "structure". In similar proceedings in *Gudgion (Valuation Officer)* v. *Croydon Borough Council* 16 RRC 305; [1970] RA 341, cremators were held to be furnaces for rating purposes. Counsel for the respondents in this case resorted to the Oxford Shorter English Dictionary definition of "furnace": "An apparatus consisting essentially of a chamber to contain combustibles for the purpose of subjecting minerals, metals, etc., to the continuous action of intense heat". By contrast, but on this occasion for the purpose of determining the availability of allowances under the Income Tax Act 1952, it was held in *Bourne (Inspector of Taxes)* v. *Norwich Crematorium* [1967] 1 W.L.R. 691 that a furnace chamber and chimney tower at a crematorium did not amount to "an industrial building or structure" for the purpose of the Act.
   It seems that a "furnace" can include an "incinerator" for present purposes unless expressly excepted: see, for example, the note to s.5 and the reference there to reg. 6 of the Clean Air (Emission of Grit and Dust from Furnaces) Regulations 1971 (S.I. 1971 No. 162). The provisions of this section may be extended (by regulation) to cover fumes or prescribed gases, or both: s.47.

Subs. (2)
   As to a local authority's power of exemption in relation to the investigation of and research into air pollution, see s.45.

Limits on rate of emission of grit and dust

Emission of grit and dust from furnaces

   5.—(1) This section applies to any furnace other than a domestic furnace.

   (2) The Secretary of State may by regulations prescribe limits on the rates of emission of grit and dust from the chimneys of furnaces to which this section applies.

(3) If on any day grit or dust is emitted from a chimney serving a furnace to which this section applies at a rate exceeding the relevant limit prescribed under subsection (2), the occupier of any building in which the furnace is situated shall be guilty of an offence.

(4) In proceedings for an offence under subsection (3) it shall be a defence to prove that the best practicable means had been used for minimising the alleged emission.

(5) If, in the case of a building containing a furnace to which this section applies and which is served by a chimney to which there is no limit applicable under subsection (2), the occupier fails to use any practicable means there may be for minimising the emission of grit or dust from the chimney, he shall be guilty of an offence.

(6) A person guilty of an offence under this section shall be liable on summary conviction to a fine not exceeding level 5 on the standard scale.

DEFINITIONS
   "chimney": s.64(1).
   "domestic furnace": s.64(1).
   "occupier": s.64(2).
   "practicable": s.64(1).
   "standard scale": s.37 of the Criminal Justice Act 1982.

GENERAL NOTE
   This section empowers the prescription of limits on the quantities of grit and dust which may be emitted from chimneys of premises other than in the case of domestic furnaces. Where such limits are prescribed, it is an offence to exceed the limit, subject to the defence that the best practicable means have been used to minimise the emission. Although the word "practicable" receives a definition in the Act, there is no definition of the term "best practicable means", although there are few differences between that expression (as defined in s.72 of the Control of Pollution Act 1974, for example) and the definition of "practicable" under this Act. Where there are no prescribed limits, the occupier commits an offence where there is failure to use any practicable means "there may be" for minimising the emission of grit or dust from the chimney. In what is an offence of strict liability it is the defendant who is obliged to establish "practicable means".
   Under the powers given by the now repealed s.2(1) of the Clean Air Act 1968 the Clean Air (Emission of Grit and Dust from Furnaces) Regulations 1971 (S.I. 1971 No. 162) prescribe specific limits to the quantities of grit and dust which may be emitted from the furnaces defined by Scheds. 1 and 2. The Regulations are described by Circular 2/71 (Welsh Office 2/71). By virtue of reg. 6 the regulations do not apply to incinerators, *i.e.*, ". . . any appliance used to burn refuse or waste matter, whether solid or liquid, and whether or not the resulting heat is used for any purpose".
   The provisions of the present section apply also to any outdoor furnace: s.13. For the purpose of enforcing the requirements of s.5 here there is substituted a reference to a person having possession of the boiler or plant, rather than the "occupier of any building".
   As to a local authority's power of exemption in respect of investigation of and research into air pollution, see s.45.
   The provisions of this section may be extended (by regulation) to cover fumes or prescribed gases or both: s.47.

Arrestment plant for furnaces

Arrestment plant for new non-domestic furnaces

   6.—(1) A furnace other than a domestic furnace shall not be used in a building—
   (a) to burn pulverised fuel; or
   (b) to burn, at a rate of 45.4 kilograms or more an hour, any other solid matter; or
   (c) to burn, at a rate equivalent to 366.4 kilowatts or more, any liquid or gaseous matter,

unless the furnace is provided with plant for arresting grit and dust which has been approved by the local authority or which has been installed in accordance with plans and specifications submitted to and approved by the local authority, and that plant is properly maintained and used.

(2) Subsection (1) has effect subject to any exemptions prescribed or granted under section 7.

(3) The Secretary of State may by regulations substitute for any rate mentioned in subsection (1)(b) or (c) such other rate as he thinks fit: but no regulations shall be made so as to reduce any rate unless a draft of the regulations has been laid before and approved by each House of Parliament.

(4) Regulations under subsection (3) reducing any rate shall not apply to a furnace which has been installed, the installation of which has been begun, or an agreement for the purchase or installation of which has been entered into, before the date on which the regulations come into force.

(5) If on any day a furnace is used in contravention of subsection (1), the occupier of the building shall be guilty of an offence and liable on summary conviction to a fine not exceeding level 5 on the standard scale.

DEFINITIONS
    "domestic furnace": s.64(1).
    "local authority": s.64(1).
    "occupier": s.64(2).
    "standard scale": s.37 of the Criminal Justice Act 1982.

GENERAL NOTE
    Sections 6 and 8 are complementary in requiring that certain categories of furnace are provided with plant for arresting grit and dust (as approved by the local authority) and that that plant is properly maintained and used. In the case of the present section dealing with arrestment plant for new, non-domestic furnaces the Secretary of State may provide for exemptions from the foregoing requirements: s.7. Under the present section the Secretary of State may, by regulations, substitute the burning capacity of any non-domestic furnace. To date no regulations have been made for this purpose.

    The provisions of the present section apply also to any outdoor furnace: s.13. For the purpose of enforcing the requirements of s.6 here there is substituted a reference to a person having possession of the boiler or plant, rather than the "occupier of any building".

    Where an application is made for approval to the local authority, that authority is obliged to give a written notification of the decision, accompanied by reasons, if it is not to grant approval: s.9(1). The person making the application or any person "interested" in the subject building included in the application may, if dissatisfied with the authority's decision, appeal to the Secretary of State within 28 days of its notification: s.9(2).

    As to certain transitional arrangements, see Sched. 2, para. 6(1).

    As to a local authority's power of exemption in relation to the investigation of and research into, air pollution, see s.45.

    The provisions of this section may be extended (by regulation) to cover fumes or prescribed gases or both: s.47.

Exemptions from section 6

7.—(1) The Secretary of State may by regulations provide that furnaces of any class prescribed in the regulations shall, while used for a purpose so prescribed, be exempted from the operation of section 6(1).

(2) If on the application of the occupier of a building a local authority are satisfied that the emission of grit and dust from any chimney serving a furnace in the building will not be prejudicial to health or a nuisance if the furnace is used for a particular purpose without compliance with section 6(1), they may exempt the furnace from the operation of that subsection while used for that purpose.

(3) If a local authority to whom an application is duly made for an exemption under subsection (2) fail to determine the application and to give a written notice of their decision to the applicant within—

    (a) eight weeks of receiving the application; or

(b) such longer period as may be agreed in writing between the applicant and the authority,

the furnace shall be treated as having been granted an exemption from the operation of section 6(1) while used for the purpose specified in the application.

(4) If a local authority decide not to grant an exemption under subsection (2), they shall give the applicant a written notification of their decision stating their reasons, and the applicant may within twenty-eight days of receiving the notification appeal against the decision to the Secretary of State.

(5) On an appeal under this section the Secretary of State—

(a) may confirm the decision appealed against; or

(b) may grant the exemption applied for or vary the purpose for which the furnace to which the application relates may be used without compliance with section 6(1);

and shall give the appellant a written notification of his decision, stating his reasons for it.

(6) If on any day a furnace which is exempt from the operation of section 6(1) is used for a purpose other than a prescribed purpose or, as the case may be, a purpose for which the furnace may be used by virtue of subsection (2), (3) or (5), the occupier of the building shall be guilty of an offence and liable on summary conviction to a fine not exceeding level 5 on the standard scale.

DEFINITIONS
    "chimney": s.64(1).
    "day": s.64(1).
    "local authority": s.64(1).

GENERAL NOTE
    Exemptions may be granted by a local authority (or, on appeal, the Secretary of State) or by virtue of regulations prescribing exemptions from the operation of s.6, above. For this purpose the Clean Air (Arrestment Plant) (Exemption) Regulations 1969 (S.I. 1969 No. 1262) were made under the now repealed s.4 of the Clean Air Act 1968. Schedule 1 to the regulations set out the classes of furnace subject to exemption and the purpose for which exemption is granted.
    The occupier of a building, subject to the requirements of s.6, may seek exemption on an application to the local authority. If the local authority is satisfied that the emission of grit and dust from any chimney serving a furnace in the building will not be prejudicial to health or a nuisance: ". . . if the furnace is used for a particular purpose without compliance with section 6(1) . . .", exemption may be granted for that purpose. As to the procedures applicable, including facility for an appeal to the Secretary of State see, subss. (3) to (5). There is no express definition of the expression "prejudicial to health or a nuisance", as to which, see Pt. III of the Environmental Protection Act 1990.
    As to criminal enforcement, see subs. (6) and note that a fresh offence is committed every day, *i.e.*, during a period of 24 hours. Otherwise the offence defined by the subsection relates to use of a furnace for a purpose other than a prescribed purpose or a purpose for which it may be used by virtue of subss. (2), (3) or (5) of s.6.
    The provisions of the present section apply also to any outdoor furnace: s.13. As to the precise terms of the application, see the note to s.6.
    The provisions of this section may be extended (by regulation) to cover fumes or prescribed gases or both: s.47.

Requirement to fit arrestment plant for burning solid fuel in other cases

8.—(1) A domestic furnace shall not be used in a building—

(a) to burn pulverised fuel; or

(b) to burn, at a rate of 1.02 tonnes an hour or more, solid fuel in any other form or solid waste,

unless the furnace is provided with plant for arresting grit and dust which has been approved by the local authority or which has been installed in accordance with plans and specifications submitted to and approved by the local authority, and that plant is properly maintained and used.

(2) If a furnace is used in a building in contravention of subsection (1), the occupier of the building shall be guilty of an offence and liable on summary conviction to a fine not exceeding level 5 on the standard scale.

<small>DEFINITIONS</small>
　　"domestic furnace": s.64(1).
　　"local authority": s.64(1).
　　"occupier": s.64(2).
　　"standard scale": s.37 of the Criminal Justice Act 1982.

<small>GENERAL NOTE</small>
　　The provisions of this section are broadly similar (except in respect of burning capacity) to s.6. As to the parallels between the two provisions, see the note to s.6 and the note to s.9 relating to appeals to the Secretary of State. As to the application of this section to outdoor furnaces, see the note to s.6, referring to s.13.
　　As to certain transitional arrangements, see Sched. 2, para. 6(2) and (3).
　　As to a local authority's power of exemption in relation to the investigation of or research into, air pollution, see s.45.

Appeal to Secretary of State against refusal of approval

9.—(1) Where a local authority determine an application for approval under section 6 or 8, they shall give the applicant a written notification of their decision and, in the case of a decision not to grant approval, shall state their reasons for not doing so.
　　(2) A person who—
　　(a) has made such an application to a local authority; or
　　(b) is interested in a building with respect to which such an application has been made,
may, if he is dissatisfied with the decision of the authority on the application, appeal within twenty-eight days after he is notified of the decision to the Secretary of State; and the Secretary of State may give any approval which the local authority might have given.
　　(3) An approval given by the Secretary of State under this section shall have the like effect as an approval of the local authority.

<small>DEFINITIONS</small>
　　"local authority": s.64(1).

<small>GENERAL NOTE</small>
　　As to the facility for appeals in respect of decisions of a local authority under ss.6 and 8, see the note to s.6, referring to s.9.

Measurement of grit, dust and fumes

Measurement of grit, dust and fumes by occupiers

10.—(1) If a furnace in a building is used—
　　(a) to burn pulverised fuel;
　　(b) to burn, at a rate of 45.4 kilograms or more an hour, any other solid matter; or
　　(c) to burn, at a rate equivalent to 366.4 kilowatts or more, any liquid or gaseous matter,
the local authority may, by notice in writing served on the occupier of the building, direct that the provisions of subsection (2) below shall apply to the furnace, and those provisions shall apply accordingly.
　　(2) In the case of a furnace to which this subsection for the time being applies, the occupier of the building shall comply with such requirements as may be prescribed as to—

(a) making and recording measurements from time to time of the grit, dust and fumes emitted from the furnace;

(b) making adaptations for that purpose to the chimney serving the furnace;

(c) providing and maintaining apparatus for making and recording the measurements; and

(d) informing the local authority of the results obtained from the measurements or otherwise making those results available to them;

and in this subsection "prescribed" means prescribed (whether generally or for any class of furnace) by regulations made by the Secretary of State.

(3) If the occupier of the building fails to comply with those requirements, he shall be guilty of an offence and liable on summary conviction—

(a) to a fine not exceeding level 5 on the standard scale; or

(b) to cumulative penalties on continuance in accordance with section 50.

(4) The occupier of a building who by virtue of subsection (2) is under a duty to make and record measurements of grit, dust and fumes emitted from a furnace in the building shall permit the local authority to be represented during the making and recording of those measurements.

(5) The Secretary of State may by regulations substitute for any rate mentioned in subsection (1)(b) or (c) such other rate as he thinks fit; but regulations shall not be made under this subsection so as to reduce any rate unless a draft of the regulations has been laid before and approved by each House of Parliament.

(6) Any direction given by a local authority under subsection (1) with respect to a furnace in a building may be revoked by the local authority by a subsequent notice in writing served on the occupier of the building, without prejudice, however, to their power to give another direction under that subsection.

DEFINITIONS

"chimney": s.64(1).
"fumes": s.64(1).
"local authority": s.64(1).
"occupier": s.64(2).
"prescribed": subs. (2).
"standard scale": s.37 of the Criminal Justice Act 1982.

GENERAL NOTE

In the case of a furnace the burning capacity of which brings it within s.6, above, a local authority may, by notifying the occupier of the building in writing, direct that certain prescribed requirements will apply to the subject furnace. Those requirements, now prescribed in detail by the Clean Air (Measurement of Grit and Dust from Furnaces) Regulations 1971 (S.I. 1971 No. 161), relate to: (a) making and recording measurements from time to time of the grit, dust and fumes emitted; (b) making adaptations for that purpose to the chimney serving the furnace; (c) providing and maintaining apparatus for making and recording measurements; and (d) informing the local authority of results obtained, or otherwise making the results available to them. An occupier subject to the duty to make and record measurements is also subject to a duty to permit the local authority to be represented during the making and recording of the measurements. As to an extension of the duty to comply with prescribed requirements in relation to other categories of furnace, see the note to s.11. Failure to comply with the requirements of the section is an offence, of strict liability.

As to the application of the present section to outdoor furnaces under s.13, see the relevant note to s.5.

As to a local authority's power of exemption in relation to investigation of and research into, air pollution, see s.45.

Measurement of grit, dust and fumes by local authorities

11.—(1) This section applies to any furnace to which section 10(2) (duty to comply with prescribed requirements) for the time being applies and which is used—
  (a) to burn, at a rate less than 1.02 tonnes an hour, solid matter other than pulverised fuel; or
  (b) to burn, at a rate of less than 8.21 Megawatts, any liquid or gaseous matter.

(2) The occupier of the building in which the furnace is situated may, by notice in writing given to the local authority, request that authority to make and record measurements of the grit, dust and fumes emitted from the furnace.

(3) While a notice is in force under subsection (2)—
  (a) the local authority shall from time to time make and record measurements of the grit, dust and fumes emitted from the furnace; and
  (b) the occupier shall not be under a duty to comply with any requirements of regulations under subsection (2) of section 10 in relation to the furnace, except those imposed by virtue of paragraph (b) of that subsection;
and any such notice given by the occupier of a building may be withdrawn by a subsequent notice in writing given to the local authority by him or any subsequent occupier of that building.

(4) A direction under section 10(1) applying section 10(2) to a furnace which is used as mentioned in subsection (1)(a) or (b) of this section shall contain a statement of the effect of subsections (1) to (3) of this section.

DEFINITIONS
  "fumes": s.64(1).
  "local authority": s.64(1).
  "occupier": s.64(2).

GENERAL NOTE
  In the case of other furnaces beyond the terms of s.10, an occupier may require the local authority to undertake the making and recording of measurements of grit, dust and fumes emitted from the furnace. The occupier's notice may be withdrawn subsequently by the same or a subsequent occupier. While a notice is in force, the local authority is subject to a duty to make and record measurements "from time to time". Furthermore, the occupier will not be under a duty to comply with any requirements of the Clean Air (Measurement of Grit and Dust from Furnaces) Regulations 1971 (S.I. 1971 No. 161), except those relating to the making of adaptations to the chimney serving the furnace. Where a local authority serves a direction under s.10(1), it is obliged to notify the terms of the present section and, more particularly, the effect of s.11(1) to (3). As to the application of the present provisions to outdoor furnaces under s.13, see the note on that section appended to s.5.
  As to more general powers of information collection by a local authority, see Pt. V of the Act.
  The provisions of this section may be extended (by regulation) to cover prescribed gases: s.47.

Information about furnaces and fuel consumed

12.—(1) For the purpose of enabling the local authority properly to perform their functions under and in connection with sections 5 to 11, the local authority may, by notice in writing served on the occupier of any building, require the occupier to furnish to them, within fourteen days or such longer time as may be limited by the notice, such information as to the furnaces in the building and the fuel or waste burned in those furnaces as they may reasonably require for that purpose.

(2) Any person who, having been duly served with a notice under subsection (1)—
  (a) fails to comply with the requirements of the notice within the time limited; or

(b) furnishes any information in reply to the notice which he knows to be false in a material particular,

shall be guilty of an offence and liable on summary conviction to a fine not exceeding level 5 on the standard scale.

DEFINITIONS
"local authority": s.64(1).
"occupier": s.64(2).
"standard scale": s.37 of the Criminal Justice Act 1982.

GENERAL NOTE

This section, relating as it does to acquisition of information by a local authority, might well have been included in Pt. V of the Act concerning information about air pollution. The requirement of the section is to enable any local authority properly to perform the functions prescribed by ss.5 to 11, including functions under s.13 relating to outdoor furnaces, as to which, see the note to s.5, above. The obligation to furnish information requested is on the "occupier of any building", or (for the purpose of s.13), the "person having possession of the boiler or plant". As to the form and service of notices, see ss.283 and 285 of the Public Health Act 1936, as applied to the present Act by s.62. The two offences provided for in subs. (2) appear, respectively, to provide for strict liability (failure to comply with the requirements of the notice within the time limited) and a requirement for *mens rea* (furnishing any information in reply to the notice known by the defendant to be false in a material particular).

Outdoor furnaces

Grit and dust from outdoor furnaces, etc.

13.—(1) Sections 5 to 12 shall apply in relation to the furnace of any fixed boiler or industrial plant as they apply in relation to a furnace in a building.

(2) References in those sections to the occupier of the building shall, in relation to a furnace falling within subsection (1), be read as references to the person having possession of the boiler or plant.

(3) The reference in section 6(4) (and the reference in paragraph 6(1) and (3) of Schedule 5) to the installation and to the purchase of a furnace shall, in relation to a furnace which is already contained in any fixed boiler or industrial plant, be read as a reference to attaching the boiler or plant to the building or fixing it to or installing it on any land and to purchasing it respectively.

DEFINITIONS
"fixed boiler or industrial plant": s.64(1).
"occupier": s.64(2).

GENERAL NOTE

The section deals with the application of ss.5 to 12 to outdoor furnaces. As to the operation of the respective sections in relation to outdoor furnaces, see the notes to the above sections.

Height of chimneys

Height of chimneys for furnaces

14.—(1) This section applies to any furnace served by a chimney.

(2) An occupier of a building shall not knowingly cause or permit a furnace to be used in the building—

(a) to burn pulverised fuel;
(b) to burn, at a rate of 45.4 kilograms or more an hour, any other solid matter; or
(c) to burn, at a rate equivalent to 366.4 kilowatts or more, any liquid or gaseous matter,

unless the height of the chimney serving the furnace has been approved for the purposes of this section and any conditions subject to which the approval was granted are complied with.

(3) If on any day the occupier of a building contravenes subsection (2), he shall be guilty of an offence.

(4) A person having possession of any fixed boiler or industrial plant, other than an exempted boiler or plant, shall not knowingly cause or permit a furnace of that boiler or plant to be used as mentioned in subsection (2), unless the height of the chimney serving the furnace has been approved for the purposes of this section and any conditions subject to which the approval was granted are complied with.

(5) If on any day a person having possession of any boiler or plant contravenes subsection (3), he shall be guilty of an offence.

(6) A person guilty of an offence under this section shall be liable on summary conviction to a fine not exceeding level 5 on the standard scale.

(7) In this section "exempted boiler or plant" means a boiler or plant which is used or to be used wholly for any purpose prescribed in regulations made by the Secretary of State; and the height of a chimney is approved for the purposes of this section if approval is granted by the local authority or the Secretary of State under section 15.

DEFINITIONS
"chimney": s.64(1).
"day": s.64(1).
"exempted boiler or plant": subs. (7).
"fixed boiler or industrial plant": s.64(1).
"occupier": s.64(2).
"standard scale": s.37 of the Criminal Justice Act 1982.

GENERAL NOTE
Furnaces the burning capacity of which is the same as furnaces covered by s.6 and which are served by a chimney are subject to local authority approval by virtue of ss.14 and 15 in relation to the height of any such chimney. Controls in respect of other chimneys not serving a furnace are dealt with under s.16.

Subs. (2)
The requirement is that the occupier of a building shall not "knowingly cause or permit" a furnace to be used in a building to burn to the capacity described unless the chimney has been approved and any conditions complied with. As to the words "knowingly cause or permit", see the note to s.2 dealing with the words "causes or permits" used in that section. The addition of the word "knowingly" to the word "cause" imports the requirement of proof of a *mens rea* requirement.

Subs. (3)
On any day. A fresh offence (under subs. (2)) is committed every day, *i.e.*, during a period of 24 hours.

Subs. (4)
Possession. See the note to s.1(2), above. As to exempted boilers or plant, see the Clean Air (Height of Chimneys) (Exemption) Regulations 1969 (S.I. 1969 No. 411), explained in Circular 28/69 (Welsh Office 23/69). The requirement under this subsection is that a person in possession of a fixed boiler or industrial plant (other than one which is exempted) shall not "knowingly cause or permit" a furnace of that boiler or plant to be used in the manner described in subs. (2) unless (again) the height of the chimney has been approved by the local authority and any conditions complied with.

Subs. (5)
On any day. A fresh offence under subs. (4) is committed every day, *i.e.*, during a period of 24 hours. Note the error in the subsection, erroneously referring to subs. (3).
As to certain transitional arrangements, see Sched. 2, para. 7.

Applications for approval of height of chimneys of furnaces

15.—(1) This section applies to the granting of approval of the height of a chimney for the purposes of section 14.

(2) Approval shall not be granted by a local authority unless they are satisfied that the height of the chimney will be sufficient to prevent, so far as practicable, the smoke, grit, dust, gases or fumes emitted from the chimney from becoming prejudicial to health or a nuisance having regard to—

(a) the purpose of the chimney;
(b) the position and descriptions of buildings near it;
(c) the levels of the neighbouring ground; and
(d) any other matters requiring consideration in the circumstances.

(3) Approval may be granted without qualification or subject to conditions as to the rate or quality, or the rate and quality, of emissions from the chimney.

(4) If a local authority to whom an application is duly made for approval fail to determine the application and to give a written notification of their decision to the applicant within four weeks of receiving the application or such longer period as may be agreed in writing between the applicant and the authority, the approval applied for shall be treated as having been granted without qualification.

(5) If a local authority decide not to approve the height of a chimney, or to attach conditions to their approval, they shall give the applicant a written notification of their decision which—

(a) states their reasons for that decision; and
(b) in the case of a decision not to approve the height of the chimney, specifies—

> (i) the lowest height (if any) which they are prepared to approve without qualification; or
> (ii) the lowest height which they are prepared to approve if approval is granted subject to any specified conditions,

or (if they think fit) both.

(6) The applicant may within twenty-eight days of receiving a notification under subsection (5) appeal against the local authority's decision to the Secretary of State.

(7) On an appeal under this section the Secretary of State may confirm the decision appealed against or he may—

(a) approve the height of the chimney without qualification or subject to conditions as to the rate or quality, or the rate and quality, of emissions from the chimney; or
(b) cancel any conditions imposed by the local authority or substitute for any conditions so imposed any other conditions which the authority had power to impose.

(8) The Secretary of State shall give the appellant a written notification of his decision on an appeal under this section which—

(a) states his reasons for the decision; and
(b) in the case of a decision not to approve the height of the chimney, specifies—

> (i) the lowest height (if any) which he is prepared to approve without qualification; or
> (ii) the lowest height which he is prepared to approve if approval is granted subject to any specified conditions,

or (if he thinks fit) both.

(9) References in this section to "the applicant" shall, in a case where the original applicant notifies the local authority that his interest in the application has been transferred to another person, be read as references to that other person.

DEFINITIONS
 "chimney": s.64(1).
 "fumes": s.64(1).
 "local authority": s.64(1).

"practicable": s.64(4).
"smoke": s.64(1).
"the applicant": subs. (9).

GENERAL NOTE
This section sets out the procedural and substantive requirements in relation to local authority approval of chimney heights for furnaces. Before approval can be granted a local authority must be satisfied that the height of a chimney will be sufficient to prevent "so far as practicable" the smoke, grit, dust, gases or fumes emitted from becoming "prejudicial to health or a nuisance", having regard to the factors and variables set out in subs. (2). As to the likely scope and meaning of "prejudicial to health or a nuisance", see s.79 of the Environmental Protection Act 1990, dealing with statutory nuisances. Approval may be granted "without qualification" or subject to conditions as to the rate or quality, or the rate and quality, of emissions from the chimney. In this respect, the local authority may need to take account of limit and guide values in E.C. Directives on atmospheric pollution. As to particular concerns, see Directives 80/779 (sulphur dioxide); 82/884 (lead); and 85/203 (nitrogen dioxide) and *cf.* the Air Quality Standards Regulations 1989 (S.I. 1989 No. 317).

Height of other chimneys

16.—(1) This section applies where plans for the erection or extension of a building outside Greater London or in an outer London borough, other than a building used or to be used wholly for one or more of the following purposes, that is to say—
(a) as a residence or residences;
(b) as a shop or shops; or
(c) as an office or offices,
are in accordance with building regulations deposited with the local authority and the plans show that it is proposed to construct a chimney, other than one serving a furnace, for carrying smoke, grit, dust or gases from the building.
(2) The local authority shall reject the plans unless they are satisfied that the height of the chimney as shown on the plans will be sufficient to prevent, so far as practicable, the smoke, grit, dust or gases from becoming prejudicial to health or a nuisance having regard to—
(a) the purpose of the chimney;
(b) the position and descriptions of buildings near it;
(c) the levels of the neighbouring ground; and
(d) any other matters requiring consideration in the circumstances.
(3) If a local authority reject plans under the authority of this section—
(a) the notice given under section 16(6) of the Building Act 1984 shall specify that the plans have been so rejected; and
(b) any person interested in the building may appeal to the Secretary of State.
(4) On an appeal under subsection (3) the Secretary of State may confirm or cancel the rejection and, where he cancels the rejection, may, if he thinks it necessary, direct that the time for rejecting the plans otherwise than under the authority of this section shall be extended so as to run from the date on which his decision is notified to the local authority.
(5) In the application of this section to Scotland—
(a) any reference to plans deposited in accordance with building regulations shall be read as a reference to the plans, specifications and other information submitted with an application for a warrant under section 6 of the Building (Scotland) Act 1959;
(b) any reference to a local authority shall be read as a reference to a local authority within the meaning of that Act;
(c) any reference to the rejection of plans shall be read as a reference to the refusal of a warrant under section 6 of that Act;
and subsections (3) and (4) shall be omitted.

  "building": s.121(1) of the Building Act 1984.
  "building regulations": s.64(1).
  "chimney": s.64(1).
  "local authority": s.64(1).
  "practicable": s.64(1).
  "smoke": s.64(1).

GENERAL NOTE
  The provisions of this section relate to plans for the erection or extension of a building used or to be used for certain defined purposes indicated by subs. (1) where those plans are (in accordance with building regulations) deposited with the local authority and show that it is proposed to construct a chimney (other than one serving a furnace), for carrying smoke, grit, dust or gases but not "fumes", from the building. The basis for local authority decision-making is the same as it is in the case of powers exercisable under s.15(2). Rejection of plans by the local authority must be accompanied by a notice under s.16(6) of the Building Act 1984 and "any person interested in the building" (rather than the applicant alone under s.15) may appeal to the Secretary of State. As to the meaning of the term "building" for present purposes, see s.121 of the Building Act 1984. Guidance on the operation of the present section is given by Circular 25/81 (Welsh Office 12/81), containing a Memorandum on Chimney Heights.

Smoke nuisances in Scotland

Abatement of smoke nuisances in Scotland

17.—(1) Smoke other than—

(a) smoke emitted from a chimney of a private dwelling in a smoke control area;

(b) dark smoke emitted from a chimney of a building or from a chimney serving the furnace of any fixed boiler or industrial plant; or

(c) dark smoke emitted otherwise than as mentioned in paragraph (b) from industrial or trade premises within the meaning of section 2,

shall, if it is a nuisance to the inhabitants of the neighbourhood, be deemed for the purposes of the Public Health (Scotland) Act 1897 to be a nuisance liable to be dealt with summarily in manner provided by that Act.

(2) In any proceedings brought by virtue of this section in the case of smoke emitted from a chimney, it shall be a defence for the person against whom proceedings are taken for contravention of any interdict or decree granted under section 22 or 23 of the Public Health (Scotland) Act 1897 for the prevention, removal, remedy or discontinuance of a nuisance to prove that the best practicable means are being or have been employed to prevent the nuisance.

(3) This section extends to Scotland only.

DEFINITIONS
  "chimney": s.64(1).
  "dark smoke": s.3.
  "fixed boiler or industrial plant": s.64(1).
  "practicable": s.64(1).
  "smoke": s.64(1).

PART III

SMOKE CONTROL AREAS

Creation of smoke control areas

Declaration of smoke control area by local authority

18.—(1) A local authority may by order declare the whole or any part of the district of the authority to be a smoke control area; and any order made under this section is referred to in this Act as a "smoke control order".

(2) A smoke control order—

(a) may make different provision for different parts of the smoke control area;

(b) may limit the operation of section 20 (prohibition of emissions of smoke) to specified classes of building in the area; and

(c) may exempt specified buildings or classes of building or specified fireplaces or classes of fireplace in the area from the operation of that section, upon such conditions as may be specified in the order;

and the reference in paragraph (c) to specified buildings or classes of building include a reference to any specified, or to any specified classes of, fixed boiler or industrial plant.

(3) A smoke control order may be revoked or varied by a subsequent order.

(4) The provisions of Schedule 1 apply to the coming into operation of smoke control orders.

DEFINITIONS
"fireplace": s.64(1).
"fixed boiler or industrial plant": s.64(1).
"local authority": s.64(1).
"smoke control order": s.29.

GENERAL NOTE
A local authority has been empowered, in its own right, to declare the whole or part of its district to be a smoke control area since 1980. Formerly an order was subject to confirmation by the Secretary of State. That an order under this section is potentially very flexible is to be seen in the terms of subs. (2). The provisions of Sched. 1 provide for publicity in respect of orders prior to their being made by any local authority, as well as a facility for objection to the local authority. Any objection made but not withdrawn must be considered before the order is made: Sched. 1, para. 3. The power of the Secretary of State to require the creation of a smoke control area is contained in s.19. Default powers available to the Secretary of State under s.60 do not apply to local authority declaration of smoke control areas: s.60(7).
As to certain transitional arrangements, see Sched. 2, para. 8.
As to powers to permit two or more local authorities to combine for the purpose of declaring an area to be a smoke control area, see s.61(3).

Power of Secretary of State to require creation of smoke control areas

19.—(1) If, after consultation with a local authority, the Secretary of State is satisfied—

(a) that it is expedient to abate the pollution of the air by smoke in the district or part of the district of the authority; and

(b) that the authority have not exercised, or have not sufficiently exercised, their powers under section 18 (power to declare smoke control area) to abate the pollution,

he may direct the authority to prepare and submit to him for his approval, within such period not being less than six months from the direction as may be specified in the direction, proposals for making and bringing into operation one or more smoke control orders within such period or periods as the authority think fit.

(2) Any proposals submitted by a local authority in pursuance of a direction under subsection (1) may be varied by further proposals submitted by the authority within the period specified for the making of the original proposals or such longer period as the Secretary of State may allow.

(3) The Secretary of State may reject any proposals submitted to him under this section or may approve them in whole or in part, with or without modifications.

(4) Where a local authority to whom a direction under subsection (1) has been given—

(a) fail to submit proposals to the Secretary of State within the period specified in the direction; or

(b) submit proposals which are rejected in whole or in part, the Secretary of State may make an order declaring them to be in default and directing them for the purposes of removing the default to exercise their powers under section 18 in such manner and within such period as may be specified in the order.

(5) An order made under subsection (4) may be varied or revoked by a subsequent order so made.

(6) While proposals submitted by a local authority and approved by the Secretary of State under this section are in force, it shall be the duty of the authority to make such order or orders under section 18 as are necessary to carry out the proposals.

DEFINITIONS
"local authority": s.64(1).
"smoke": s.64(1).
"smoke control order": s.29.

GENERAL NOTE
The Secretary of State's power to require the creation of a smoke control area by a local authority may be exercised if he is satisfied that it is expedient to abate smoke pollution in the district or part of it, and that the authority has not exercised, or not "sufficiently exercised" their powers to declare a smoke control area to abate the pollution. Such powers are likely to be used for the purpose of ensuring compliance with limit values in the relevant E.C. Directives: see particularly Directive 80/779 (sulphur dioxide); 82/884 (lead); and 85/203 (nitrogen dioxide) and note the requirements of the Air Quality Standards Regulations 1989 (S.I. 1989 No. 317). In the circumstances above, the Secretary of State may direct an authority to prepare and submit to him for approval proposals for making and bringing into effect one or more smoke control orders. Failure to comply empowers the Secretary of State to declare the authority to be in default and to require removal of the default: subs. (4). For these purposes the default provisions of s.60 do not apply in so far as default comprises failure to submit proposals, a failure to comply with a requirement to remove a default or a failure to carry out the duty to implement proposals that have been approved: s.60(7).

Subs. (1)
Consultation. The requirement here is that the Secretary of State ". . . with a receptive mind, must, by such consultation, seek and welcome the aid and advice which those with local knowledge may be in a position to proffer . . ." in regard to a proposal tentatively evolved: *Rollo* v. *Minister of Town and Country Planning* [1948] 64 T.L.R. 25. Nevertheless, the existence of a policy in favour of a particular course of action, such as government policy to ensure compliance with limit values in E.C. Directives, does not necessarily mean that any consultation will not be undertaken without a receptive mind.

Satisfied . . . that it is expedient. These words appear to make the Secretary of State sole judge of what is "expedient": *Customs and Excise Commissioners* v. *Cure and Deeley* [1962] 1 Q.B. 340 ("appears to them to be necessary"). However, ". . . if the Minister does not act in good faith, or if he acts on extraneous considerations which ought not to influence him, or if he plainly misdirects himself in fact or in law, it may well be that a court would interfere; but if he honestly takes a view of the facts or of the law which could reasonably be entertained, then his decision is not to be set aside simply because thereafter someone thinks that his view was wrong" (*per* Lord Denning, M.R., in *Secretary of State for Employment* v. *ASLEF (No. 2)* [1972] 2 Q.B. 455).

Prohibition on emission of smoke in smoke control area

Prohibition on emission of smoke in smoke control area

20.—(1) If, on any day, smoke is emitted from a chimney of any building within a smoke control area, the occupier of the building shall be guilty of an offence.

(2) If, on any day, smoke is emitted from a chimney (not being a chimney of a building) which serves the furnace of any fixed boiler or industrial plant within a smoke control area, the person having possession of the boiler or plant shall be guilty of an offence.

(3) Subsections (1) and (2) have effect—
(a) subject to any exemptions for the time being in force under section 18, 21 or 22;
(b) subject to section 51 (duty to notify offences to occupier or other person liable).

(4) In proceedings for an offence under this section it shall be a defence to prove that the alleged emission was not caused by the use of any fuel other than an authorised fuel.

(5) A person guilty of an offence under this section shall be liable on summary conviction to a fine not exceeding level 3 on the standard scale.

(6) In this Part "authorised fuel" means a fuel declared by regulations of the Secretary of State to be an authorised fuel for the purposes of this Part.

DEFINITIONS
"authorised fuel": subs. (6).
"chimney": s.64(1).
"day": s.64(1).
"fixed boiler or industrial plant": s.64(1).
"occupier": s.64(2).
"smoke": s.64(1).
"standard scale": s.37 of the Criminal Justice Act 1982.

GENERAL NOTE
The present section creates two offences by virtue of subss. (1) and (2) although in each case a fresh offence is committed every day, *i.e.*, during a period of 24 hours. Both offences refer to "smoke" rather than "dark smoke". A smoke control order under s.18 may limit the operation of the present section to specified classes of building in the area. This power of limitation is in addition to exemptions available by virtue of ss.21 and 22. Section 21 empowers the Secretary of State, by order, to exempt any class of fireplace if satisfied that any such fireplace can be used for burning fuel, other than authorised fuels, without producing any smoke or a substantial quantity of smoke. Numerous Smoke Control Areas (Exempted Fireplaces) Orders have been made under the terms of s.11(4) of the Clean Air Act 1956, now repealed. The power of exemption under s.22, also available to the Secretary of State by order, permits suspension or relaxation of s.20 if it appears to be necessary or expedient to do so, in relation to the whole or any part of a smoke control area. Before making any such order under s.22, the Secretary of State is obliged to consult with the local authority unless satisfied that, on account of urgency, such consultation is impracticable. As soon as practicable after the making of an order the authority is obliged to take such steps as appear to them "suitable" for bringing the effect of the order to the notice of persons affected.

The present s.20 is also effective, subject to s.51 relating to the duty to notify offences to an occupier or other persons liable. In proceedings for either of the offences in s.20 it is a defence that the alleged smoke emission was not caused by any fuel other than authorised fuel. As to "authorised fuel", see the Smoke Control Areas (Authorised Fuels) Regulations 1991 (S.I. 1991 No. 1282) and the Smoke Control Areas (Authorised Fuels) (Amendment) Regulations 1992 (S.I. 1992 No. 72).

As to adaptations in or in connection with a dwelling to avoid contraventions of the present section, see ss.24 and 27, and the notes thereto.

As to a local authority's power of exemption in respect of investigations of and research into air pollution, see s.45.

Power by order to exempt certain fireplaces

21.—The Secretary of State may by order exempt any class of fireplace, upon such conditions as may be specified in the order, from the provisions of section 20 (prohibition of smoke emissions in smoke control area), if he is satisfied that such fireplaces can be used for burning fuel other than authorised fuels without producing any smoke or a substantial quantity of smoke.

DEFINITIONS
"authorised fuels": s.20(6).
"fireplace": s.64(1).
"smoke": s.64(1).

  See the note to s.20.

Exemptions relating to particular areas

   22.—(1) The Secretary of State may, if it appears to him to be necessary or
expedient so to do, by order suspend or relax the operation of section 20
(prohibition of smoke emissions in smoke control area) in relation to the
whole or any part of a smoke control area.
   (2) Before making an order under subsection (1) the Secretary of State
shall consult with the local authority unless he is satisfied that, on account of
urgency, such consultation is impracticable.
   (3) As soon as practicable after the making of such an order the local
authority shall take such steps as appear to them suitable for bringing the
effect of the order to the notice of persons affected.

DEFINITIONS
  "local authority": s.64(1).
  "smoke": s.64(1).

GENERAL NOTE
  See note to s.20.

Subs. (1)
  Appears . . . to be necessary or expedient. See note to s.19(1) on the phrase "*satisfied . . . that it
is expedient*".

Subs. (2)
  Consult. See the note to s.19(1) on "*consultation*".

Dealings with unauthorised fuel

Acquisition and sale of unauthorised fuel in a smoke control area

   23.—(1) Any person who—
   (a) acquires any solid fuel for use in a building in a smoke control area
       otherwise than in a building or fireplace exempted from the operation
       of section 20 (prohibition of smoke emissions in smoke control area);
   (b) acquires any solid fuel for use in any fixed boiler or industrial plant in
       a smoke control area, not being a boiler or plant so exempted; or
   (c) sells by retail any solid fuel for delivery by him or on his behalf to—
          (i) a building in a smoke control area; or
          (ii) premises in such an area in which there is any fixed boiler or
       industrial plant,
shall be guilty of an offence and liable on summary conviction to a fine not
exceeding level 3 on the standard scale.
   (2) In subsection (1), "solid fuel" means any solid fuel other than an
authorised fuel.
   (3) Subsection (1) shall, in its application to a smoke control area in which
the operation of section 20 is limited by a smoke control order to specified
classes of buildings, boilers or plant, have effect as if references to a building, boiler or plant were references to a building, boiler or plant of a class
specified in the order.
   (4) The power of the Secretary of State under section 22 (exemptions
relating to particular areas) to suspend or relax the operation of section 20 in
relation to the whole or any part of a smoke control area includes power to
suspend or relax the operation of subsection (1) in relation to the whole or
any part of such an area.
   (5) In proceedings for an offence under this section consisting of the sale
of fuel for delivery to a building or premises, it shall be a defence for the
person accused to prove that he believed and had reasonable grounds for
believing—

(a) that the building was exempted from the operation of section 20 or, in a case where the operation of that section is limited to specified classes of building, was not of a specified class; or

(b) that the fuel was acquired for use in a fireplace, boiler or plant so exempted or, in a case where the operation of that section is limited to specified classes of boilers or plant, in a boiler or plant not of a specified class.

DEFINITIONS

"fireplace": s.64(1).
"fixed boiler or industrial plant": s.64(1).
"smoke": s.64(1).
"smoke control order": s.29.
"solid fuel": subs. (2).
"standard scale": s.37 of the Criminal Justice Act 1982.

GENERAL NOTE

This section makes it an offence to obtain solid, smoke producing fuel for use in a smoke control area, or to sell such fuel by retail for delivery to premises in such an area. As to the various limitations and exemptions referred to, see the notes to ss.20 and 22.

Subs. (5)

Believed and had reasonable grounds for believing. As to possible interpretations of the words "reasonable grounds for belief", see *Nakkuda Ali* v. *M.F. de S. Jayaratne* [1951] A.C. 66 and (albeit in emergency, war-time circumstances) *Liversidge* v. *Anderson* [1942] A.C. 206. In *R.* v. *Banks* [1916] 2 K.B. 621, the court considered that the phrase "had reasonable cause to believe" means "had reasonable cause to believe, and did in fact believe". The test in the case of the present subsection requires the court to "match" the defendant's belief with objectively reasonable, constructive, grounds for belief.

As to a local authority's power of exemption in relation to investigation of or research into, air pollution, see s.45.

Adaptation of fireplaces

Power of local authority to require adaptation of fireplaces in private dwellings

24.—(1) The local authority may, by notice in writing served on the occupier or owner of a private dwelling which is, or when a smoke control order comes into operation will be, within a smoke control area, require the carrying out of adaptations in or in connection with the dwelling to avoid contraventions of section 20 (prohibition of smoke emissions in smoke control area).

(2) The provisions of Part XII of the Public Health Act 1936 with respect to appeals against, and the enforcement of, notices requiring the execution of works shall apply in relation to any notice under subsection (1).

(3) Any reference in those provisions to the expenses reasonably incurred in executing the works shall, in relation to a notice under subsection (1), be read as a reference to three-tenths of those expenses or such smaller fraction of those expenses as the local authority may in any particular case determine.

(4) In the application of this section to Scotland—

(a) subsections (2) and (3) shall be omitted;

(b) section 111 of the Housing (Scotland) Act 1987 (which provides for an appeal to the sheriff against certain notices, demands and orders under that Act) shall apply in relation to a notice under subsection (1) of this section as it applies in relation to a repair notice under that Act; and

(c) subject to any such right of appeal as is mentioned in paragraph (b), if any person on whom a notice under subsection (1) is served fails to execute the works required by the notice within the time limited by the notice, the local authority may themselves execute the works and may recover from that person three-tenths, or such smaller fraction as the local authority may in any particular case determine, of the expenses reasonably incurred by them in so doing.

DEFINITIONS
"expenses incurred in the execution of works": s.28(1).
"local authority": s.64(1).
"occupier": s.64(2).
"owner": s.64(1).
"smoke": s.64(1).
"smoke control order": s.29.

GENERAL NOTE
The average domestic coal burning grate may be unsuitable for the burning of "smokeless" fuels and considerable modifications and adaptations have to be undertaken in any smoke control area before smokeless fires become the norm. The present section empowers local authorities to make contributions towards the costs of necessary adaptations in private dwellings. Provisions of Pt. XII of the Public Health Act 1936 concerning appeals against, and enforcement of, notices requiring the execution of works are ss.283, 285, 290, 291, 293 and 294: subs. (2).

Subs. (1)
Adaptations in or in connection with a dwelling. This expression is defined by s.27 as referring to the execution of various works, in or outside the dwelling being works "reasonably necessary" to make what is in all the circumstances suitable provision for heating and cooking without contravention of s.20 and s.27.

Subs. (2)
Notice. The recipient of a notice must be told what is required of him, the time for doing it, and his right of appeal to the magistrates' court. An appeal may be taken on a number of grounds, *e.g.*, that (as owner) the notice should have been served on the occupier, or vice versa. Subject to the right of appeal, if the recipient defaults, the local authority may undertake the work and recover the expenses from him but without prejudice to proceedings to recover a fine. In any such proceedings for a fine the recipient of the notice may not raise an issue that should have been raised on appeal.

Expenditure incurred in relation to adaptations in private dwellings

25.—(1) Schedule 2 to this Act shall have effect with respect to certain expenditure incurred in adapting old private dwellings in smoke control areas.

(2) In this Part "old private dwelling" means any private dwelling other than one which either—

(a) was erected after 15th August 1964 (which was the date immediately preceding the time when the enactment replaced by this subsection came into force), or

(b) was produced by the conversion, after that date, of other premises, with or without the addition of premises erected after that date;

and for the purposes of this subsection a dwelling or premises shall not be treated as erected or converted after that date unless the erection or conversion was begun after it.

DEFINITIONS
"dwelling ... erected or converted": subs. (2).
"old private dwelling": s.29.
"premises": s.64(1).
"premises ... erected or converted": subs. (2).

GENERAL NOTE
Schedule 2 to the Act makes detailed provision for grants for expenditure in relation to adaptation of fireplaces as well as Exchequer contributions to certain expenditure. As to the withdrawal (subject to some limited exceptions) of Exchequer grant-aid, see Circular 9/93, indicating a need for reliance in future on Supplementary Credit Approvals.

Power of local authority to make grants towards adaptations to fireplaces in churches, chapels, buildings used by charities etc.

26.—(1) If, after the making of a smoke control order, the owner or occupier of any premises or part of any premises to which this section applies and which will be within a smoke control area as the result of the order incurs expenditure on adaptations in or in connection with the premises or part to avoid contraventions of section 20 (prohibition of smoke emissions in smoke control area), the local authority may, if they think fit, repay to him the whole or any part of that expenditure.

(2) This section applies to any premises or part of any premises which fall within one or more of the following paragraphs, that is to say—

    (a) any place of public religious worship, being, in the case of a place in England or Wales, a place which belongs to the Church of England or to the Church in Wales (within the meaning of the Welsh Church Act 1914) or which is for the time being certified as required by law as a place of religious worship;

    (b) any church hall, chapel hall or similar premises used in connection with any such place of public religious worship, and so used for the purposes of the organisation responsible for the conduct of public religious worship in that place;

    (c) any premises or part of any premises occupied for the purposes of an organisation (whether corporate or unincorporated) which is not established or conducted for profit and whose main objects are charitable or are otherwise concerned with the advancement of religion, education or social welfare.

DEFINITIONS

"adaptations in or in connection with the premises": s.27(1)(4).
"local authority": s.64(1).
"occupier": s.64(2).
"owner": s.64(1).
"premises": s.64(1).
"smoke": s.64(1).
"smoke control order": s.29.

GENERAL NOTE

While s.25 (and Sched. 2) make provision for repayment of expenditure in respect of the adaptation of private dwellings, the present section relates to churches, chapels and charitable organisations and their various buildings. As to the nature of works contemplated by the expression "adaptations in or in connection with . . ." the premises, see the note to s.24(1), adapted to refer to a "dwelling" for the purpose of that section.

Supplementary provisions

References to adaptations for avoiding contraventions of section 20

27.—(1) References in this Part to adaptations in or in connection with a dwelling to avoid contraventions of section 20 (prohibition of smoke emissions from smoke control area) shall be read as references to the execution of any of the following works (whether in or outside the dwelling), that is to say—

    (a) adapting or converting any fireplace; .

    (b) replacing any fireplace by another fireplace or by some other means of heating or cooking;

    (c) altering any chimney which serves any fireplace;

    (d) providing gas ignition, electric ignition or any other special means of ignition; or

    (e) carrying out any operation incidental to any of the operations mentioned in paragraphs (a) to (d);

being works which are reasonably necessary in order to make what is in all the circumstances suitable provision for heating and cooking without contraventions of section 20.

(2) For the purposes of this section the provision of any igniting apparatus or appliance (whether fixed or not) operating by means of gas, electricity or other special means shall be treated as the execution of works.

(3) Except for the purposes of section 24 (power of local authority to require certain adaptations), works which make such suitable provision as is mentioned in subsection (1) shall not be treated as not being adaptations to avoid contraventions of section 20 of this Act by reason that they go beyond what is reasonably necessary for that purpose, but any expenditure incurred in executing them in excess of the expenditure which would have been reasonably incurred in doing what was reasonably necessary shall be left out of account.

(4) References in this section to a dwelling include references to any premises or part of any premises to which section 26 (grants towards certain adaptations in churches and other buildings) applies.

DEFINITIONS
 "chimney": s.64(1).
 "dwelling": subs. (4).
 "fireplace": s.64(1).
 "heating": s.29.
 "smoke": s.64(1).

GENERAL NOTE
 The terms of this section are referred to elsewhere, in context. See the notes to ss.20, 24 and 26.

Subss. (1) and (3)
 Reasonably necessary. What is "reasonably necessary" is a matter of fact, for which supporting evidence will be required: *Coleen Properties* v. *Minister of Housing and Local Government* [1971] 1 W.L.R. 433, C.A.

Cases where expenditure is taken to be incurred on execution of works

28.—(1) References in this Part to expenses incurred in the execution of works include references to the cost of any fixed cooking or heating appliance installed by means of the execution of the works, notwithstanding that the appliance can be readily removed from the dwelling without injury to itself or the fabric of the dwelling.

(2) For the purposes of this Part a person who enters into either—

 (a) a conditional sale agreement for the sale to him, or

 (b) a hire-purchase agreement for the bailment or (in Scotland) hiring to him,

of a cooking or heating appliance shall be treated as having incurred on the date of the agreement expenditure of an amount equal to the price which would have been payable for the appliance if he had purchased it for cash on that date.

(3) References in this section to a dwelling include references to any premises or part of any premises to which section 26 (grants towards certain adaptations in churches and other buildings) applies.

DEFINITIONS
 "conditional sale agreement": s.29.
 "dwelling": subs. (3).
 "heating": s.29.
 "hire purchase agreement": s.29.
 "premises": s.64(1).

This section seeks, *inter alia*, to dispel any uncertainty for present purposes in relation to the installation of any "fixed cooking or heating appliance". Works of installation and the cost thereof is included in any reference to "expenses incurred in the execution of works", even though the appliance can be readily removed from the dwelling. As to references to expenses incurred in the execution of works, see the possible aid to interpretation provided by the present section in ss.24(3), 26(1) and 27(3).

Interpretation of Part III

29.—In this Part, except so far as the context otherwise requires—
  "authorised fuel" has the meaning given in section 20(6);
  "conditional sale agreement" means an agreement for the sale of goods under which—
> (a) the purchase price or part of it is payable by instalments; and
> (b) the property in the goods is to remain in the seller (notwithstanding that the buyer is to be in possession of the goods) until such conditions as to the payment of instalments or otherwise as may be specified in the agreement are fulfilled;

  "heating", in relation to a dwelling, includes the heating of water;
  "hire-purchase agreement" means an agreement, other than a conditional sale agreement, under which—
> (a) goods are bailed or (in Scotland) hired in return for periodical payments by the person to whom they are bailed or hired; and
> (b) the property in the goods will pass to that person if the terms of the agreement are complied with and one or more of the following occurs—
>> (i) the exercise of an option to purchase by that person;
>> (ii) the doing of any other specified act by any party to the agreement; and
>> (iii) the happening of any other specified event;

  "old private dwelling" has the meaning given in section 25; and
  "smoke control order" means an order made by a local authority under section 18.

PART IV

CONTROL OF CERTAIN FORMS OF AIR POLLUTION

Regulations about motor fuel

30.—(1) For the purpose of limiting or reducing air pollution, the Secretary of State may by regulations—
(a) impose requirements as to the composition and contents of any fuel of a kind used in motor vehicles; and
(b) where such requirements are in force, prevent or restrict the production, treatment, distribution, import, sale or use of any fuel which in any respect fails to comply with the requirements, and which is for use in the United Kingdom.

(2) It shall be the duty of the Secretary of State, before he makes any regulations under this section, to consult—
(a) such persons appearing to him to represent manufacturers and users of motor vehicles;
(b) such persons appearing to him to represent the producers and users of fuel for motor vehicles; and
(c) such persons appearing to him to be conversant with problems of air pollution,
as he considers appropriate.

(3) Regulations under this section—

(a) in imposing requirements as to the composition and contents of any fuel, may apply standards, specifications, descriptions or tests laid down in documents not forming part of the regulations; and

(b) where fuel is subject to such requirements, may, in order that persons to whom the fuel is supplied are afforded information as to its composition or contents, impose requirements for securing that the information is displayed at such places and in such manner as may be prescribed by the regulations.

(4) It shall be the duty of every local weights and measures authority to enforce the provisions of regulations under this section within its area; and subsections (2) and (3) of section 26 of the Trade Descriptions Act 1968 (reports and inquiries) shall apply as respects those authorities' functions under this subsection as they apply to their functions under that Act.

(5) The following provisions of the Trade Descriptions Act 1968 shall apply in relation to the enforcement of regulations under this section as they apply to the enforcement of that Act, that is to say—

section 27 (power to make test purchases);

section 28 (power to enter premises and inspect and seize goods and documents);

section 29 (obstruction of authorised officers);

section 30 (notice of test);

and section 33 of that Act shall apply to the exercise of powers under section 28 as applied by this subsection.

References to an offence under that Act in those provisions as applied by this subsection, except the reference in section 30(2) to an offence under section 28(5) or 29 of that Act, shall be construed as references to an offence under section 32 of this Act (provisions supplementary to this section) relating to regulations under this section.

(6) In relation to Scotland—

(a) nothing in subsection (4) authorises a local weights and measures authority to institute proceedings for an offence; and

(b) regulations under this section may provide that certificates issued by such persons as may be specified by the regulations in relation to such matters as may be so specified shall, subject to the provisions of the regulations, be received in evidence, and be sufficient evidence, of those matters in any proceedings for an offence under regulations made under this section;

and such regulations may apply any of the provisions of subsections (2) to (4) of section 31 of the Trade Descriptions Act 1968 (evidence by certificate).

(7) In Northern Ireland it shall be the duty of the Department of Economic Development to enforce the provisions of regulations under this section; and accordingly this section shall have effect in relation to Northern Ireland with the omission of subsection (4).

(8) It is hereby declared that in relation to Northern Ireland the references in subsection (5) to provisions of the Trade Descriptions Act 1968 are references to those provisions as modified by section 40(1)(b) and (c) of that Act.

(9) The Secretary of State shall for each financial year pay into the Consolidated Fund of Northern Ireland such sum as the Secretary of State and the Department of Economic Development for Northern Ireland may agree to be appropriate as representing the expenses incurred by that Department in enforcing the provisions of any regulations made under this section.

GENERAL NOTE

The regulation-making power conferred on the Secretary of State by this section is widely drawn, indicating that for the "... purpose of limiting or reducing air pollution ..." requirements may be imposed as to the composition and contents of "any" fuel of a kind used in motorvehicles. Furthermore, subs. (1) goes on to indicate that such requirements may "...

prevent or restrict the production, treatment, import, sale or use of any fuel which in any respect fails to comply . . ." As to the Secretary of State's discretion to consult, see the note to s.19(1) on the meaning of "consultation". Enforcement is the responsibility of every local weights and measures authority, adapting provisions of the Trade Descriptions Act 1968 as appropriate: subss. (4)–(6). As to the position in Northern Ireland, see subss. (7)–(9).

Apart from the facility for excluding liability on conviction on indictment or reducing the maximum fine on summary conviction, the offence of contravening or failing to comply with the regulations is triable either summarily or on indictment: s.32(2).

The Motor Fuel (Lead Content of Petrol) Regulations 1976 (S.I. 1976 No. 1866); the Motor Fuel (Sulphur Content of Gas Oil) Regulations 1976 (S.I. 1976 No. 1989); the Motor Fuel (Lead Content of Petrol) (Amendment) Regulations 1979 (S.I. 1979 No. 1); the Motor Fuel (Lead Content of Petrol) Regulations 1981 (S.I. 1981 No. 1523); the Motor Fuel (Lead Content of Petrol) (Amendment) Regulations 1985 (S.I. 1985 No. 1728); and the Motor Fuel (Lead Content of Petrol) (Amendment) Regulations 1989 (S.I. 1989 No. 547) have been made under the "predecessor" provision, s.75 of the Control of Pollution Act 1974. The present section and the regulations listed represent the vehicles for implementation of E.C. Directives 75/716 (as amended by Directive 87/219) on the Sulphur content of Gas Oil, 85/210 (as amended by 87/416) on the Lead content of Petrol, and 82/884 on limit values for lead in air.

In *Budden* v. *B.P. Oil and Shell Oil*; *Albery-Speyer* v. *B.P. Oil and Shell Oil* [1980] J.P.L. 586, the Court of Appeal struck out various claims arising from what was claimed to be the adverse impact on child health of exposure to vehicle emissions in the inner city. The fact that the petrol companies had complied with statutory regulations on the composition of petrol was decisive. However, Megaw L.J. went on to say that:

> ". . . this is not to say that the courts are bound to hold, where a limit has been prescribed in the interests of safety by statute or statutory regulations, that one who keeps within these limits cannot be guilty of negligence at common law".

The encouragement of local authorities to promote guide values as a result of E.C. legislation may suggest some circumstances in which there may well be an enforceable duty of care to observe and implement emission limits below formally legislated limits.

As to the operation of this section and this Part of the Act, see Circular 7/76 (Welsh Office 9/76).

Section 58 empowers a local authority to serve a notice on "any person" requiring him to furnish to that authority: ". . . any information so specified which the authority reasonably considers that it needs for the purposes of any function conferred on the authority by Part IV . . . of this Act . . .".

Regulations about sulphur content of oil fuel for furnaces or engines

31.—(1) For the purpose of limiting or reducing air pollution, the Secretary of State may by regulations impose limits on the sulphur content of oil fuel which is used in furnaces or engines.

(2) It shall be the duty of the Secretary of State, before he makes any regulations in pursuance of this section, to consult—

(a) such persons appearing to him to represent producers and users of oil fuel;

(b) such persons appearing to him to represent manufacturers and users of plant and equipment for which oil fuel is used; and

(c) such persons appearing to him to be conversant with problems of air pollution,

as he considers appropriate.

(3) Regulations under this section may—

(a) prescribe the kinds of oil fuel, and the kinds of furnaces and engines, to which the regulations are to apply;

(b) apply standards, specifications, descriptions or tests laid down in documents not forming part of the regulations; and

(c) without prejudice to the generality of section 63(1)(a), make different provision for different areas.

(4) It shall be the duty—

(a) of every local authority to enforce the provisions of regulations under this section within its area, except in relation to a furnace which is part of a process subject to Part I of the Environmental Protection Act 1990; and

(b) of the inspectors appointed under that Part to enforce those provisions in relation to such furnaces;

but nothing in this section shall be taken to authorise a local authority in Scotland to institute proceedings for any offence.

(5) In this section "oil fuel" means any liquid petroleum product produced in a refinery.

DEFINITIONS
"local authority": s.64(1).
"oil fuel": subs. (5).

GENERAL NOTE
The present section, together with s.30, also provides the Secretary of State with a regulation-making power again for the purpose of "limiting or reducing air pollution" but in this case what is regulated is the sulphur content of oil fuel which is used in furnaces or engines. Again, as with s.30, there is a widely drawn discretion in respect of consultation before regulations are made by the Secretary of State: as to the meaning of "consultation" in law, see the note to s.19(1). The duty to enforce the regulations lies with every local authority. The exception to the enforcement duty relates to any furnace which is part of a "process" subject to integrated pollution control or local authority air pollution control under Pt. I of the Environmental Protection Act 1990. Nevertheless there is a duty on inspectors appointed under Pt. I of that Act to enforce the regulations in relation to such furnaces. In the absence of any statutory definition of a "furnace", see the note to s.4. As to the application of the supplementary provisions of s.32 to the present section, see the note to s.30.

The Oil Fuel (Sulphur Content of Gas Oil) Regulations 1990 (S.I. 1990 No. 1096), have been made under the "predecessor" provision: s.76 of the Control of Pollution Act 1974. The present section and regulations represent the vehicle for implementation of E.C. Directive 75/716 (as amended by Directive 87/219).

As to the operation of this section and this Part of the Act, see Circular 7/76 (Welsh Office 9/76).

Section 58, empowering acquisition of information for the purposes of this Part of the Act, allows a local authority to serve a notice on "any person" requiring him to furnish that information.

Provisions supplementary to sections 30 and 31

32.—(1) Regulations under section 30 or 31 (regulation of content of motor fuel and fuel oil) may authorise the Secretary of State to confer exemptions from any provision of the regulations.

(2) A person who contravenes or fails to comply with any provision of regulations under section 30 or 31 shall be guilty of an offence and liable—

(a) on conviction on indictment, to a fine; and

(b) on summary conviction, to a fine not exceeding the statutory maximum;

but the regulations may in any case exclude liability to conviction on indictment or reduce the maximum fine on summary conviction.

(3) Regulations under section 30 or 31 shall, subject to any provision to the contrary in the regulations, apply to fuel used for, and to persons in, the public service of the Crown as they apply to fuel used for other purposes and to other persons.

(4) A local authority shall not be entitled by virtue of subsection (3) to exercise, in relation to fuel used for and persons in that service, any power conferred on the authority by virtue of sections 56 to 58 (rights of entry and inspection and other local authority powers).

DEFINITIONS
"local authority": s.64(1).
"statutory maximum": s.37 of the Criminal Justice Act 1982.

GENERAL NOTE
As to the operation of this section's supplementary provisions, see the note to ss.30 and 31. More generally, see Circular 7/76 (Welsh Office 9/76).

Subs. (3)

Public service of the Crown. In *Pfizer* v. *Ministry of Health* [1965] A.C. 512, the words in issue were "for the services of the Crown". The House of Lords decided that the treatment of National Health Service patients was a governmental function so that the use of drugs was "for the services of the Crown". Consequently, in the event of any dispute about application of regulations to fuel used for, and to persons in, the public service of the Crown, a significant, though not necessarily decisive, consideration may be the nature and status of any function being performed, *cf., Town Investments* v. *Secretary of State for the Environment* [1978] A.C. 359, H.L.

Cable burning

33.—(1) A person who burns insulation from a cable with a view to recovering metal from the cable shall be guilty of an offence unless the burning is part of a process subject to Part I of the Environmental Protection Act 1990.

(2) A person guilty of an offence under this section shall be liable on summary conviction to a fine not exceeding level 5 on the standard scale.

DEFINITIONS

"standard scale": s.37 of the Criminal Justice Act 1982.

GENERAL NOTE

Unless covered by an authorisation under Pt. I (for integrated pollution control or local authority air pollution control purposes), any person who burns insulation from a cable for the purpose of metal recovery is guilty of an offence. As a "process" (defined by the Environmental Protection (Prescribed Processes and Substances) Regulations 1991 (S.I. 1991 No. 472)), authorised under Pt. I, "cable burning" as a generic description may be referable to Sched. 1, Chap. 2 (Metal Production and Processing): "Any process for ... recovering by ... the use of heat ..." of any of a number of metals; para. 2.2, Non-ferrous metals Pt. A. Authorisations should be capable of ensuring that particularly toxic by-products of cable burning, such as PCBs (polychlorinated biphenols) are properly managed.

As to the operation of this and related provisions, see Circular 7/76 (Welsh Office 9/76). Enforcement is by a local authority (as defined by s.64(1)): s.55(1).

PART V

INFORMATION ABOUT AIR POLLUTION

Research and publicity

34.—(1) A local authority may—

(a) undertake, or contribute towards the cost of, investigation and research relevant to the problem of air pollution;

(b) arrange for the publication of information on that problem;

(c) arrange for the delivery of lectures and addresses, and the holding of discussions, on that problem;

(d) arrange for the display of pictures, cinematograph films or models, or the holding of exhibitions, relating to that problem; and

(e) prepare, or join in or contribute to the cost of the preparation of, pictures, films, models or exhibitions to be displayed or held as mentioned in paragraph (d).

(2) In acting under subsection (1)(b), a local authority shall ensure that the material published is presented in such a way that no information relating to a trade secret is disclosed, except with the consent in writing of a person authorised to disclose it.

(3) Breach of a duty imposed by subsection (2) shall be actionable.

(4) In any civil or criminal proceedings (whether or not arising under this Act) brought against a local authority, or any member or officer of a local authority, on the grounds that any information has been published, it shall be a defence to show that it was published in compliance with subsections (1) and (2).

DEFINITIONS
"local authority": s.64(1).

GENERAL NOTE
Subsection (1), paras. (a) and (b) are drawn from s.79(1) of the Control of Pollution Act 1974 while paras. (c)–(e) are drawn from s.25 of the Clean Air Act 1956, repeating in wider terms provisions found originally in the Public Health Act 1936. In so far as a local authority arranges (under subs. (1)(b)) for the publication of information on the problem of air pollution, that authority is obliged (under subs. (2)) to ensure that the material published is presented in such a way that no information relating to a trade secret is disclosed, except with the consent in writing of a person authorised to disclose it. Significantly, breach of this duty is actionable in tort: subs. (3). Where any civil or criminal proceedings are pursued against the local authority (or a member or officer of that authority), whether or not under the present Act, on the ground that any information has been published, it is a defence to show that the information was published in compliance with subss. (1) and (2): subs. (4). While such a defence is more naturally associated with the "public law" issue of statutory authority it may be doubtful whether such a defence is necessarily relevant to many other areas of criminal or civil liability that may arise.

The provisions of the present section (although discretionary) may be of crucial importance where, for example, the local authority would wish to publish information on, say, dust and grit emissions from foundry industries operating in its district. Publication of the subject information may be undertaken by virtue of the facilities in ss.12 and 34 of this Act but not before the dischargers' consent has been obtained in respect of any trade secret that may be involved: see Circular 2/77 (Welsh Office 6/77), para. 13 and the Control of Atmospheric Pollution (Research and Publicity) Regulations 1977 (S.I. 1977 No. 19).

As to other facilities enabling local authority collection of information, see ss.11 to 13.

Obtaining information

35.—(1) Without prejudice to the generality of section 34 (research, etc. by local authorities), local authorities may obtain information about the emission of pollutants and other substances into the air—

(a) by issuing notices under section 36 (information about emissions from premises);

(b) by measuring and recording the emissions, and for that purpose entering on any premises, whether by agreement or in exercise of the power conferred by section 56 (rights of entry and inspection); and

(c) by entering into arrangements with occupiers of premises under which they measure and record emissions on behalf of the local authority;

but references to premises in paragraphs (b) and (c) do not include private dwellings or caravans.

(2) A local authority shall not be entitled to exercise the power of entry mentioned in subsection (1)(b) for the purpose of measuring and recording such emissions on any premises unless—

(a) the authority has given to the occupier of the premises a notice in writing—

(i) specifying the kind of emissions in question and the steps it proposes to take on the premises for the purpose of measuring and recording emissions of that kind; and

(ii) stating that it proposes to exercise that power for that purpose unless the occupier requests the authority to serve on him a notice under section 36 (information about emissions from premises) with respect to the emissions; and

(b) the period of twenty-one days beginning with the day on which the notice was given has expired;

and the authority shall not be entitled to exercise that power if, during that period, the occupier gives a notice to the authority requesting it to serve on him a notice under section 36.

(3) Nothing in this section shall authorise a local authority to investigate emissions from any process subject to Part I of the Environmental Protection Act 1990 otherwise than—

(a) by issuing notices under section 36; or

(b) by exercising the powers conferred on the authority by section 34(1)(a) (investigation and research etc.) without entering the premises concerned.

(4) So long as a local authority exercises any of its powers under subsection (1), it shall from time to time consult the persons mentioned in subsection (5)—

(a) about the way in which the local authority exercises those powers (under this section and section 36); and

(b) about the extent to which, and the manner in which, any information collected under those powers should be made available to the public.

(5) The consultations required by subsection (4) shall be with—

(a) such persons carrying on any trade or business in the authority's area or such organisations appearing to the authority to be representative of those persons; and

(b) such persons appearing to the authority to be conversant with problems of air pollution or to have an interest in local amenity,

as appear to the authority to be appropriate.

(6) The consultations shall take place as the authority think necessary, but not less than twice in each financial year.

DEFINITIONS
"caravan": s.64(1).
"local authority": s.64(1).
"occupier": s.64(2).
"premises": s.64(1).
"private dwelling": s.64(4).

GENERAL NOTE

This section stipulates the various ways in which a local authority may obtain information about the emission of pollutants "and other substances" into the air. Operation of the section and its relationship with other provisions in Pt. V of the Act is explained in Circular 2/77 (Welsh Office 6/77). A local authority is obliged to maintain a register of information obtained by virtue of the Control of Atmospheric Pollution (Research and Publicity) Regulations 1977 (S.I. 1977 No. 19), reg. 6. Under subs. (1) there is one method of obtaining information (in para. (b)) that specifies an entry to premises for the purpose of measuring and recording emissions. Such entry may be by agreement or by virtue of the power conferred by s.56, relating to rights of entry and inspection. Other methods relate to the issue of a notice under s.36 or arrangements with occupiers of "premises" whereby they measure and record emissions on behalf of the authority. As to the exercise of the power of entry mentioned in subs. (1)(b) see subs. (2) but note that that power may not be exercised if, within stipulated time limits, the occupier gives notice to the local authority requesting service of a s.36 notice. If a local authority wishes to investigate emissions from any process subject to Pt. I of the Environmental Protection Act 1990 otherwise than by a s.36 notice or through investigatory powers under s.34(1)(a) the present section does not authorise any investigation without entry to the premises concerned: subs. (3). *Cf.*, s.36(3). Subsections (4)–(6) indicate various consultative requirements to be observed by any local authority wishing to exercise its powers under subs. (1). As to the legal obligations associated with consultation, see the note to s.19(1). *Cf.*, Circular 2/77, paras. 3 and 4.

Notices requiring information about air pollution

36.—(1) A local authority may by notice in writing require the occupier of any premises in its area to furnish, whether by periodical returns or by other means, such estimates or other information as may be specified or described in the notice concerning the emission of pollutants and other substances into the air from the premises.

(2) This section does not apply to premises in so far as they consist of a private dwelling or a caravan.

(3) If the notice relates to a process subject to Part I of the Environmental Protection Act 1990, the person on whom the notice is served shall not be obliged to supply any information which, as certified by an inspector

appointed under that Part, is not of a kind which is being supplied to the inspector for the purposes of that Part.

(4) The person on whom a notice is served under this section shall comply with the notice within six weeks of the date of service, or within such longer period as the local authority may by notice allow.

(5) A notice under this section shall not require returns at intervals of less than three months, and no one notice (whether or not requiring periodical returns) shall call for information covering a period of more than twelve months.

(6) Except so far as regulations made by the Secretary of State provide otherwise, this section applies to premises used for, and to persons in, the public service of the Crown as it applies to other premises and persons.

(7) A local authority shall not be entitled by virtue of subsection (6) to exercise, in relation to premises used for and persons in the public service of the Crown, any power conferred on the authority by virtue of sections 56 to 58 (rights of entry and other local authority powers).

(8) A person who—

(a) fails without reasonable excuse to comply with the requirements of a notice served on him in pursuance of this section; or

(b) in furnishing any estimate or other information in compliance with a notice under this section, makes any statement which he knows to be false in a material particular or recklessly makes any statement which is false in a material particular,

shall be guilty of an offence and liable on summary conviction to a fine not exceeding level 5 on the standard scale.

(9) Where a person is convicted of an offence under subsection (8) in respect of any premises and information of any kind, nothing in section 35(2) (limits on exercise of power of entry) shall prevent a local authority from exercising the power of entry there mentioned for the purpose of obtaining information of that kind in respect of the premises.

DEFINITIONS
  "caravan": s.64(1).
  "emission of substances": s.40.
  "local authority": s.64(1).
  "occupier": s.64(1).
  "premises": s.64(1).
  "private dwelling": s.64(4).
  "standard scale": s.37 of the Criminal Justice Act 1982.

GENERAL NOTE
  The detailed requirements associated with discretionary s.36 notices are to be found in the Control of Atmospheric Pollution (Research and Publicity) Regulations 1977 (S.I. 1977 No. 19), indicating that any such notice "... may relate to the emission of pollutants and other substances from any chimney, flue or other outlet used for the discharge, from any premises to the atmosphere, of any emission of ..." sulphur dioxide among other gases or particulate matter. As to the guidance available in relation to implementation and enforcement, see Circular 2/77 (Welsh Office 6/77). The Control of Atmospheric Pollution (Exempted Premises) Regulations 1977 (S.I. 1977 No. 18) indicate that s.36 notices shall not be available for use in relation to specified premises used for the public service of the Crown: subss. (6) and (7).
  Where a s.36 notice relates to a process subject to Pt. I of the Environmental Protection Act 1990 the person on whom the notice is served is not obliged to supply any information which, as certified by an inspector appointed under Pt. I, is not of a kind which is being supplied to the inspector for the purposes of that Part. As to limitations on local authority methods of obtaining information in relation to processes subject to Pt. I control under the Act of 1990, see s.35(3).
  As to the machinery for and regularity of, information collection, see subss. (4) and (5).
  As to offences, see subs. (8) and note that any conviction under this subsection gives the local authority freedom to operate outside the restrictions on the power of entry for the purpose of obtaining information in respect of the subject premises.

Subss. (6) and (7)
  Public service of the Crown. See the note to s.32(3).

Subs. (8)
  Reasonable excuse. It appears that this defence will operate where the evidence indicates that the defendant has no control over the circumstances surrounding the alleged offence: *Wellingborough Borough Council* v. *Gordon* [1991] J.P.L. 874, a case relating to statutory nuisance. Lack of finance, for example, will be insufficient as a reasonable excuse: *Saddleworth U. D. C.* v. *Aggregate and Sand* (1970) 114 S.J. 931.

Appeals against notices under section 36

37.—(1) A person served with a notice under section 36 (information about air pollution), or any other person having an interest in the premises to which the notice relates, may appeal to the Secretary of State—
  (a) on the ground that the giving to the authority or the disclosure to the public of all or part of the information required by the notice would—
        (i) prejudice to an unreasonable degree some private interest by disclosing information about a trade secret; or
        (ii) be contrary to the public interest; or
  (b) on the ground that the information required by the notice is not immediately available and cannot readily be collected or obtained by the recipient of the notice without incurring undue expenditure for the purpose.
  (2) If the Secretary of State allows the appeal he may direct the local authority to withdraw or modify the notice, or to take such steps as he may specify to ensure that prejudicial information is not disclosed to the public; and it shall be the duty of the authority to comply with the direction.
  (3) The Secretary of State may make regulations as to appeals under this section, including regulations about the time for bringing an appeal and the circumstances in which all or any part of the appellant's case is to be withheld from the respondent.
  (4) It shall be the duty of the Secretary of State, before he makes any regulations under subsection (3), to consult—
  (a) such persons appearing to him to represent local authorities;
  (b) such persons appearing to him to represent industrial interests; and
  (c) such persons appearing to him to be conversant with problems of air pollution,
as he considers appropriate.

DEFINITIONS
  "local authority": s.64(1).
  "premises": s.64(1).

GENERAL NOTE
  The facility for an appeal to the Secretary of State in respect of a s.36 notice is given to the person served as well as ". . . any other person having an interest in the premises . . .": the latter word being defined to include "land". Any such interest must undoubtedly comprehend a legal interest and include a person who has a mere licence in respect of the subject land, or part of it. The section defines two grounds of appeal in subs. (1): that disclosure of information to the public would prejudice to an unreasonable degree some private interest in connection with a trade secret, or would be contrary to the public interest; and that information required is not "immediately" available and cannot readily be collected or obtained by the recipient without incurring "undue expenditure" for the purpose.
  The person served with a notice under s.36 may find that an appeal is not determined within the time for compliance specified by the notice. In these circumstances the defendant may well be open to conviction for the offence under s.36(8)(a) unless the local authority extends the time for compliance.
  Appeals are governed by the Control of Atmospheric Pollution (Appeals) Regulations 1977 (S.I. 1977 No. 17). The Secretary of State has an obligation to consult before making regulations: subss. (3) and (4). As to the meaning in law of "consultation", see the note to s.19(1).

Operation of the appeal facility under the present regulations is described by Circular 2/77 (Welsh Office 6/77).

Information relating to any appeal relating to a s.36 notice must be entered on the public register provided for by the Control of Atmospheric Pollution (Research and Publicity) Regulations 1977 (S.I. 1977 No. 19), reg. 6(b).

Regulations about local authority functions under sections 34, 35 and 36

38.—(1) The Secretary of State shall by regulations prescribe the manner in which, and the methods by which, local authorities are to perform their functions under sections 34(1)(a) and (b), 35 and 36 (investigation and research etc. into, and the obtaining of information about, air pollution).

(2) It shall be the duty of the Secretary of State, before he makes regulations under this section, to consult—

(a) such persons appearing to him to represent local authorities;

(b) such persons appearing to him to represent industrial interests; and

(c) such persons appearing to him to be conversant with problems of air pollution,

as he considers appropriate.

(3) Regulations under this section may in particular—

(a) prescribe the kinds of emissions to which notices under section 36 (power to require information about air pollution) may relate;

(b) prescribe the kinds of information which may be required by those notices;

(c) prescribe the manner in which any such notice is to be given, and the evidence which is to be sufficient evidence of its having been given, and of its contents and authenticity;

(d) require each local authority to maintain in a prescribed form a register containing—

(i) information obtained by the authority by virtue of section 35(1) (powers of local authorities to obtain information), other than information as to which a direction under section 37(2) (appeals against notices under section 36) provides that the information is not to be disclosed to the public; and

(ii) such information (if any) as the Secretary of State may determine, or as may be determined by or under regulations, with respect to any appeal under section 37 against a notice served by the authority which the Secretary of State did not dismiss;

(e) specify the circumstances in which local authorities may enter into arrangements with owners or occupiers of premises under which they will record and measure emissions on behalf of the local authorities; and

(f) specify the kinds of apparatus which local authorities are to have power to provide and use for measuring and recording emissions, and for other purposes.

(4) Regulations made by virtue of subsection (3)(b) may in particular require returns of—

(a) the total volume of gases, whether pollutant or not, discharged from the premises in question over any period;

(b) the concentration of pollutant in the gases discharged;

(c) the total of the pollutant discharged over any period;

(d) the height or heights at which discharges take place;

(e) the hours during which discharges take place; or

(f) the concentration of pollutants at ground level.

(5) A register maintained by a local authority in pursuance of regulations made by virtue of subsection (3)(d) shall be open to public inspection at the principal office of the authority free of charge at all reasonable hours, and the authority shall afford members of the public reasonable facilities for

obtaining from the authority, on payment of reasonable charges, copies of entries in the register.

DEFINITIONS
"local authority": s.64(1).
"measurement": s.40.
"premises": s.64(1).

GENERAL NOTE
The Control of Atmospheric Pollution (Research and Publicity) Regulations 1977 (S.I. 1977 No. 19), were made under this section's predecessor, s.82 of the Control of Pollution Act 1974, as well as the powers under s.104(1) of that Act. As to the operation of the regulations in the context of broader statutory requirements found in Pt. V of the Act of 1993, see Circular 2/77 (Welsh Office 6/77). This Circular explains (in para. 5) the matters which are not covered by the regulations. Although the regulations refer to emissions of sulphur dioxide, as well as emissions of gas other than sulphur dioxide and emissions of particulate matter of all kinds, the essence of Pt. V of the Act is its discretionary nature. As such, the provisions stand apart from other provisions such as the Air Quality Standards Regulations 1989 (S.I. 1989 No. 317), seeking to ensure implementation, of limit values in particular, under various E.C. Directives: see, for example, the note to s.30, listing some of the more significant directives for present purposes. In the case of access to environmental information it should be noted that there may be some overlap between local authority information acquisition and public registration under the present Pt. V and information acquisition by the local authority, among others, for the purpose of the Environmental Protection Act 1990, Pt. I: see ss.35(3) and 36(3) of the Act of 1993. For the purpose of access, note also the provisions of the Environmental Information Regulations 1992 (S.I. 1992 No. 3240) which may raise two important questions, one of which has been anticipated previously. First, is subject information collected by and in the possession of some other "additional" agency? Second, when subject information is held on collection by a local authority with or without similar information being held by some other agency are the disclosure requirements of the Environmental Information Regulations more or less onerous than those found in the present statutory provisions? The more onerous requirements will be those that apply, by virtue of the 1992 Regulations, *cf.*, E.C. Directive 90/313. As to requirements for public registers, see S.I. 1977 No. 19, reg. 6, above.
There is a consultation requirement before the Secretary of State can make regulations under this section. As to the meaning of "consultation" in law, see the note to s.19(1).
As to the meaning of "emissions of substances into the atmosphere", see s.40. As to the meaning of "rate of emission of any substance", see s.64(3).

Provision by local authorities of information for Secretary of State

39.—(1) The Secretary of State may, for the purpose of obtaining information about air pollution, direct a local authority to make such arrangements as may be specified in the direction—

(a) for the provision, installation, operation and maintenance by the local authority of apparatus for measuring and recording air pollution; and

(b) for transmitting the information so obtained to the Secretary of State; but before giving the direction under this section the Secretary of State shall consult the local authority.

(2) Where apparatus is provided in pursuance of a direction under this section, the Secretary of State shall defray the whole of the capital expenditure incurred by the local authority in providing and installing the apparatus.

(3) It shall be the duty of the local authority to comply with any direction given under this section.

DEFINITIONS
"local authority": s.64(1).

GENERAL NOTE
The note to s.38 deals with the acquisition of various types of relevant environmental information. The present section allows the Secretary of State, by direction, to require that a local authority facilitates the measuring and recording of air pollution for transmission to the Secretary of State. However, prior to any such direction the Secretary of State is obliged to

consult with the local authority which is under a duty to comply with any direction, albeit in return for the capital costs involved. As to the meaning of "consultation" in law, see the note to s.19(1). The process of measurement for present purposes includes the taking of samples: s.40.

Interpretation of Part V

40. In this Part—
(a) references to the emission of substances into the atmosphere are to be construed as applying to substances in a gaseous or liquid or solid state, or any combination of those states; and
(b) any reference to measurement includes a reference to the taking of samples.

PART VI

SPECIAL CASES

Relation to Environmental Protection Act 1990

41.—(1) Parts I to III shall not apply to any process which is a prescribed process as from the date which is the determination date for that process.
(2) The "determination date" for a prescribed process is—
(a) in the case of a process for which an authorisation is granted, the date on which the enforcing authority grants it, whether in pursuance of the application or, on an appeal, of a direction to grant it, and
(b) in the case of a process for which an authorisation is refused, the date of the refusal or, on an appeal, of the affirmation of the refusal.
(3) In this section "authorisation", "enforcing authority" and "prescribed process" have the meaning given in section 1 of the Environmental Protection Act 1990 and the reference to an appeal is a reference to an appeal under section 15 of that Act.

DEFINITIONS
"appeal": subs. (3) and s.15 of the Environmental Protection Act 1990.
"authorisation": subs. (3) and s.1 of the Environmental Protection Act 1990.
"determination date": subs. (2).
"enforcing authority": subs. (3) and s.1 of the Environmental Protection Act 1990.
"prescribed process": subs. (3) and s.1 of the Environmental Protection Act 1990.

GENERAL NOTE
Parts I and III of the present Act are stated not to apply to any process which is a "prescribed process" as defined in detail by the Environmental Protection (Prescribed Processes and Substances) Regulations 1991 (S.I. 1991 No. 472), as amended by S.I. 1992 No. 614. The omission of any reference to Pt. II indicates the potential for duplication of controls in so far as the detailed requirements are not reflected in the foundations of both areas of regulation and control, albeit Pt. I of the Act of 1990 subdivides into integrated pollution control and local authority air pollution control. As to other areas that interface, see (in Pt. V), ss.35(3) and 36(3).

Colliery spoilbanks

42.—(1) This section applies to any mine or quarry from which coal or shale has been, is being or is to be got.
(2) The owner of a mine or quarry to which this section applies shall employ all practicable means—
(a) for preventing combustion of refuse deposited from the mine or quarry; and
(b) for preventing or minimising the emission of smoke and fumes from such refuse;
and, if he fails to do so, he shall be guilty of an offence.
(3) A person guilty of an offence under subsection (2) shall be liable on summary conviction—

(a) to a fine not exceeding level 5 on the standard scale; or

(b) to cumulative penalties on continuance in accordance with section 50.

(4) Neither the provisions of Part III of the Environmental Protection Act 1990 nor any provision of Parts I to III of this Act shall apply in relation to smoke, grit or dust from the combustion of refuse deposited from any mine or quarry to which this section applies.

(5) In the application of this section to Scotland, subsection (4) shall have effect as if for the reference to Part III of the Environmental Protection Act 1990 there were substituted a reference to section 16 of the Public Health (Scotland) Act 1897.

(6) In this section, "mine", "quarry" and "owner" have the same meaning as in the Mines and Quarries Act 1954.

DEFINITIONS

"fumes": s.64(1).
"mine": subs. (6) and s.180 of the Mines and Quarries Act 1954.
"owner": subs. (6) and s.180 of the Mines and Quarries Act 1954.
"practicable": s.64(1).
"quarry": subs. (6) and s.180 of the Mines and Quarries Act 1954.
"smoke": s.64(1).
"standard scale": s.37 of the Criminal Justice Act 1982.

GENERAL NOTE

This provision is based on enforcement through a simple (summary) sanction requiring only "practicable means" for the purpose of preventing combustion of refuse and preventing or minimising the emission of smoke and fumes from such refuse. Enforcement is by a local authority (as defined by s.64(1)): s.55(1). In so far as smoke, grit or dust from the combustion of waste "deposited" from a mine or quarry is generated, the statutory nuisance provisions of the Environmental Protection Act 1990 (Pt. III) together with Pts. I to III of the present Act will not apply and cannot be enforced in these circumstances.

Subss. (2) and (4)

Deposited. Although decided by reference to the provisions on unlawful deposition of controlled waste under Pt. I of the Control of Pollution Act 1974 it was held in *R.* v. *Metropolitan Stipendiary Magistrate*, ex p. *London Waste Regulatory Authority*; *Berkshire County Council* v. *Scott*, *The Times*, January 14, 1993 that a "deposit" is not restricted to a "final" deposit. The court was influenced by the fact that regulations provided exceptionally for lawful temporary deposits, as well as an objective of environmental protection. No doubt in the context of licensing of mine and quarry operations the term "deposit" may usefully be clarified through the terms of any necessary consent.

Subs. (4)

The provisions of this subsection may be extended (by regulation) to cover fumes or prescribed gases or both: s.47.

Railway engines

43.—(1) Section 1 (prohibition of emissions of dark smoke) shall apply in relation to railway locomotive engines as it applies in relation to buildings.

(2) In the application of section 1 to such engines, for the reference in subsection (1) of that section to the occupier of the building there shall be substituted a reference to the owner of the engine.

(3) The owner of any railway locomotive engine shall use any practicable means there may be for minimising the emission of smoke from the chimney on the engine and, if he fails to do so, he shall, if smoke is emitted from that chimney, be guilty of an offence.

(4) A person guilty of an offence under subsection (3) shall be liable on summary conviction—

(a) to a fine not exceeding level 5 on the standard scale; or

(b) to cumulative penalties on continuance in accordance with section 50.

(5) Except as provided in this section, nothing in Parts I to III applies to smoke, grit or dust from any railway locomotive engine.

DEFINITIONS
"chimney": s.64(1).
"dark smoke": s.3.
"occupier": s.64(2).
"practicable": s.64(1).
"smoke": s.64(1).
"standard scale": s.37 of the Criminal Justice Act 1982.

GENERAL NOTE

Again, as with s.42, regulation is based on a requirement for use of "practicable" means for minimising smoke emissions, enforced by a provision for summary conviction. The offence defined by subs. (3) is additional to those provided for in s.1. Otherwise nothing that is provided for in Pts. I to III of the Act in relation to smoke, grit or dust from any railway locomotive engine can be enforced. As to a local authority's power of exemption in respect of investigations of and research into air pollution, see s.45.

Subs. (5)

The provisions of this subsection may be extended (by regulation) to cover fumes or prescribed gases or both: s.47.

Vessels

44.—(1) Section 1 (prohibition of emissions of dark smoke) shall apply in relation to vessels in waters to which this section applies as it applies in relation to buildings.

(2) In the application of section 1 to a vessel—

(a) for the reference in subsection (1) of that section to the occupier of the building there shall be substituted a reference to the owner of, and to the master or other officer or person in charge of, the vessel;

(b) references to a furnace shall be read as including references to an engine of the vessel; and

(c) subsection (5) of that section shall be omitted;

and a person guilty of an offence under that section in relation to a vessel shall be liable on summary conviction to a fine not exceeding level 5 on the standard scale.

(3) For the purposes of this Act a vessel in any waters to which this section applies which are not within the district of any local authority shall be deemed to be within the district of the local authority whose district includes that point on land which is nearest to the spot where the vessel is.

(4) The waters to which this section applies are—

(a) all waters not navigable by sea-going ships; and

(b) all waters navigable by sea-going ships which are within the seaward limits of the territorial waters of the United Kingdom and are contained within any port, harbour, river, estuary, haven, dock, canal or other place so long as a person or body of persons is empowered by or under any Act to make charges in respect of vessels entering it or using facilities in it.

(5) In subsection (4) "charges" means any charges with the exception of light dues, local light dues and any other charges payable in respect of lighthouses, buoys or beacons and of charges in respect of pilotage.

(6) Except as provided in this section, nothing in Parts I to III applies to smoke, grit or dust from any vessel.

DEFINITIONS
"charges": subs. (4).
"dark smoke": s.3.
"local authority": s.64(1).
"occupier": s.64(1).
"standard scale": s.37 of the Criminal Justice Act 1982.

GENERAL NOTE
In contrast to the provision in s.43, the present section applying s.1 to vessels in "waters" (as defined by subs. (4)) provides for no additional offences beyond those defined by the first section of the Act. As to the penalties applicable, compare subs. (2) of the present section with s.1(5). With some exceptions, s.44 applies to vessels owned by the Crown: s.46(4). Except as indicated by this section, nothing else in Pts. I to III applies to smoke, dust or grit from a vessel: subs. (6). Furthermore, emissions of dark smoke for periods no longer than those specified by the Dark Smoke (Permitted Periods) (Vessels) Regulations 1958 (S.I. 1958 No. 878) do not count towards any liability arising by virtue of s.1 of the Act.

Subs. (6)
The provisions of this subsection may be extended (by regulation) to cover fumes or prescribed gases or both: s.47.

Exemption for purposes of investigations and research

45.—(1) If the local authority are satisfied, on the application of any person interested, that it is expedient to do so for the purpose of enabling investigations or research relevant to the problem of the pollution of the air to be carried out without rendering the applicant liable to proceedings brought under or by virtue of any of the provisions of this Act or the Environmental Protection Act 1990 mentioned below, the local authority may by notice in writing given to the applicant exempt, wholly or to a limited extent,—

(a) any chimney from the operation of sections 1 (dark smoke), 5 (grit and dust), 20 (smoke in smoke control area) and 43 (railway engines) of this Act and Part III of the Environmental Protection Act 1990 (statutory nuisances);

(b) any furnace, boiler or industrial plant from the operation of section 4(2) (new furnaces to be as far as practicable smokeless);

(c) any premises from the operation of section 2 (emissions of dark smoke);

(d) any furnace from the operation of sections 6 or 8 (arrestment plant) and 10 (measurement of grit, dust and fumes by occupier), and

(e) the acquisition or sale of any fuel specified in the notice from the operation of section 23 (acquisition and sale of unauthorised fuel in smoke control area),

in each case subject to such conditions, if any, and for such period as may be specified in the notice.

(2) Any person who has applied to the local authority for an exemption under this section may, if he is dissatisfied with the decision of the authority on the application, appeal to the Secretary of State; and the Secretary of State may, if he thinks fit, by notice in writing given to the applicant and the local authority, give any exemption which the authority might have given or vary the terms of any exemption which they have given.

DEFINITIONS
"chimney": s.64(1).
"dark smoke": s.3.
"fumes": s.64(1).
"local authority": s.64(1).
"occupier": s.64(1).
"practicable": s.64(1).
"smoke": s.64(1).

GENERAL NOTE
Applications under this section may be made by a very wide category of persons and the local authority has an equally wide discretion to grant an exemption if "... satisfied ... that it is expedient to do so ...". As to the need for a statutory discretion to be interpreted and applied consistently with the policy and objects of the Act, see, for example, *Padfield* v. *Minister of Agriculture, Fisheries and Food* [1968] A.C. 997, H.L. As to the range of provisions which may

attract exemption, see subs. (1)(a) to (e). Although an appeal is provided to the Secretary of State where an applicant is "dissatisfied" with the decision of the authority, no detailed statutory procedures or other requirements have been prescribed.

Crown premises, etc.

46.—(1) It shall be part of the functions of the local authority, in cases where it seems to them proper to do so, to report to the responsible Minister any cases of—

(a) emissions of dark smoke, or of grit or dust, from any premises which are under the control of any Government department and are occupied for the public service of the Crown or for any of the purposes of any Government department;

(b) emissions of smoke, whether dark smoke or not, from any such premises which are within a smoke control area;

(c) emissions of smoke, whether dark smoke or not, from any such premises which appear to them to constitute a nuisance to the inhabitants of the neighbourhood; or

(d) emissions of dark smoke from any vessel of Her Majesty's navy, or any Government ship in the service of the Secretary of State while employed for the purposes of Her Majesty's navy, which appear to them to constitute a nuisance to the inhabitants of the neighbourhood,

and on receiving any such report the responsible Minister shall inquire into the circumstances and, if his inquiry reveals that there is cause for complaint, shall employ all practicable means for preventing or minimising the emission of the smoke, grit or dust or for abating the nuisance and preventing a recurrence of it, as the case may be.

(2) Subsection (1) shall apply to premises occupied for the purposes of the Duchy of Lancaster or the Duchy of Cornwall as it applies to premises occupied for the public service of the Crown which are under the control of a Government department, with the substitution, in the case of the Duchy of Cornwall, for references to the responsible Minister of references to such person as the Duke of Cornwall or the possessor for the time being of the Duchy of Cornwall appoints.

(3) The fact that there subsists in any premises an interest belonging to Her Majesty in right of the Crown or of the Duchy of Lancaster, or to the Duchy of Cornwall, or belonging to a Government department or held in trust for Her Majesty for the purposes of a Government department, shall not affect the application of this Act to those premises so long as that interest is not the interest of the occupier of the premises, and this Act shall have effect accordingly in relation to the premises and that and all other interests in the premises.

(4) Section 44 (vessels) shall, with the omission of the reference in subsection (2) of that section to the owner, apply to vessels owned by the Crown, except that it shall not apply to vessels of Her Majesty's navy or to Government ships in the service of the Secretary of State while employed for the purposes of Her Majesty's navy.

(5) This Act (except Parts IV and V) shall have effect in relation to premises occupied for the service of a visiting force as if the premises were occupied for the public service of the Crown and were under the control of the Government department by arrangement with whom the premises are occupied.

(6) In this section—

"Government ship" has the same meaning as in section 80 of the Merchant Shipping Act 1906; and

"visiting force" means any such body, contingent or detachment of the forces of any country as is a visiting force for the purposes of any of the provisions of the Visiting Forces Act 1952.

DEFINITIONS
"dark smoke": s.3.
"Government ship": subs. (6).
"local authority": s.64(1).
"occupier": s.64(2).
"practicable": s.64(1).
"premises": s.64(1).
"smoke": s.64(1).
"visiting force": subs. (6).

GENERAL NOTE
A local authority is obliged to report to the responsible Minister any dark smoke, grit or dust outside a smoke control area, any smoke within a smoke control area, any smoke nuisance or any dark smoke from a vessel where the premises or vessel concerned are Crown property. Upon receipt of a report the responsible Minister is obliged to inquire into "all the circumstances". Thereafter, if the inquiry "... reveals that there is cause for complaint ..." all "practicable means for preventing or minimising the emission of smoke, grit or dust or for abating the nuisance and preventing a recurrence, as the case may be" must be employed. As such, this provision is not enforceable, at least to the extent that coercive remedies will not normally lie against the Crown: see s.21 of the Crown Proceedings Act 1947, for example.

Subs. (1)
The provisions of this subsection may be extended (by regulation) to cover fumes or prescribed gases or both: s.47.

Subss. (1)(2) and (5)
Public service of the Crown. See the note to s.32(3).

PART VII

MISCELLANEOUS AND GENERAL

Power to apply certain provisions to fumes and gases

Application to fumes and gases of certain provisions as to grit, dust and smoke

47.—(1) The Secretary of State may by regulations—
(a) apply all or any of the provisions of sections 5, 6, 7, 42(4), 43(5), 44(6) and 46(1) to fumes or prescribed gases or both as they apply to grit and dust;
(b) apply all or any of the provisions of section 4 to fumes or prescribed gases or both as they apply to smoke; and
(c) apply all or any of the provisions of section 11 to prescribed gases as they apply to grit and dust,
subject, in each case, to such exceptions and modifications as he thinks expedient.

(2) No regulations shall be made under this section unless a draft of the regulations has been laid before and approved by each House of Parliament.

(3) In the application of any provision of this Act to prescribed gases by virtue of regulations under this section, any reference to the rate of emission of any substance shall be construed as a reference to the percentage by volume or by mass of the gas which may be emitted during a period specified in the regulations.

(4) In this section—
"gas" includes vapour and moisture precipitated from vapour; and
"prescribed" means prescribed in regulations under this section.

DEFINITIONS
"fumes": s.64(1).
"gas": subs. (4).
"prescribed": s.64(1).
"smoke": s.64(1).

To date, the power to make regulations has not been exercised. Except in the case of s.11, the regulation-making power enables extension of selected provisions to include fumes or prescribed gases.

Power to give effect to international agreements

Power to give effect to international agreements

48. The Secretary of State may by regulations provide that any provisions of Parts IV and V, or of this Part (apart from this section) so far as relating to those Parts, shall have effect with such modifications as are prescribed in the regulations with a view to enabling the Government of the United Kingdom to give effect to any provision made by or under any international agreement to which the Government is for the time being a party.

Administration and enforcement

Unjustified disclosures of information

49.—(1) If a person discloses any information relating to any trade secret used in carrying on any particular undertaking which has been given to him or obtained by him by virtue of this Act, he shall, subject to subsection (2), be guilty of an offence and liable on summary conviction to a fine not exceeding level 5 on the standard scale.

(2) A person shall not be guilty of an offence under subsection (1) by reason of the disclosure of any information if the disclosure is made—

(a) in the performance of his duty;
(b) in pursuance of section 34(1)(b); or
(c) with the consent of a person having a right to disclose the information.

DEFINITIONS
"standard scale": s.37 of the Criminal Justice Act 1982.

GENERAL NOTE
In this section on the unjustified disclosure of information, there are various important prerequisites for a summary conviction: the existence of "any trade secret" used in "any particular undertaking" and given or obtained "by virtue of this Act". The offence is not, therefore, restricted to authorised officers of a responsible local authority. A variety of provisions in the Act are of significance for present purposes: note in particular, ss.12, 35, 36, 56, 57 and 58. By way of defence the defendant may plead that disclosure was in the performance of his duty: a potentially wide defence that could extend to include both substantive legal duties as well as more procedural matters of authority, for the purposes of delegation in particular: subs. (2)(a). Because the offence is seemingly one of strict liability, evidence of knowledge or belief is probably irrelevant, for example, where the defendant believed he had authority to release the information for independent scientific analysis. Other defences relate to consent and exercise by a local authority of its power (under s.34(1)(b)) to arrange for the publication of information on the problem of air pollution: subs. (2)(b)(c).

Subs. (1)
Obtained. The House of Lords, affirming a decision of the Court of Appeal in *Att.-Gen.'s Reference (No. 1 of 1988)* [1989] 2 W.L.R. 729 held that, for the purposes of the Company Securities (Insider Dealing) Act 1985, a person could be convicted *qua* "*tippee*" even if specific information about securities comes to him without any purpose or action on his part.

Cumulative penalties on continuance of certain offences

50.—(1) Where—

(a) a person is convicted of an offence which is subject to cumulative penalties on continuance in accordance with this section; and
(b) it is shown to the satisfaction of the court that the offence was substantially a repetition or continuation of an earlier offence by him after he had been convicted of the earlier offence,

the penalty provided by subsection (2) shall apply instead of the penalty otherwise specified for the offence.

(2) Where this subsection applies the person convicted shall be liable on summary conviction to a fine not exceeding—

    (a) level 5 on the standard scale; or

    (b) £50 for every day on which the earlier offence has been so repeated or continued by him within the three months next following his conviction of that offence,

whichever is the greater.

(3) Where an offence is subject to cumulative penalties in accordance with this section—

    (a) the court by which a person is convicted of the original offence may fix a reasonable period from the date of conviction for compliance by the defendant with any directions given by the court; and

    (b) where a court has fixed such a period, the daily penalty referred to in subsection (2) is not recoverable in respect of any day before the end of that period.

GENERAL NOTE

This section contains two important elements, relating to offences in the Act attracting cumulative penalties: see in particular ss.10(3), 42(3) and 43(4). Where there is a conviction in respect of an offence subject to cumulative penalties on continuance and the court is satisfied that the subject offence was substantially a repetition or continuation of an earlier offence after conviction for that offence, the special penalty prescribed by subs. (2) applies. The second important element is seen in the court's power to issue the defendant with directions to be complied with by a date fixed (representing a "reasonable period from the date of conviction") before which the daily penalty referred to in subs. (2) is not recoverable: subs. (3).

Duty to notify occupiers of offences

51.—(1) If, in the opinion of an authorised officer of the local authority—

    (a) an offence is being or has been committed under section 1, 2 or 20 (prohibition of certain emissions of smoke); or

    (b) in Scotland, a nuisance to which section 17 (smoke nuisances) applies exists or has existed,

he shall, unless he has reason to believe that notice of it has already been given by or on behalf of the local authority, as soon as may be notify the appropriate person, and, if his notification is not in writing, shall before the end of the four days next following the day on which he became aware of the offence, confirm the notification in writing.

(2) For the purposes of subsection (1), the appropriate person to notify is the occupier of the premises, the person having possession of the boiler or plant, the owner of the railway locomotive engine or the owner or master or other officer or person in charge of the vessel concerned, as the case may be.

(3) In any proceedings for an offence under section 1, 2 or 20 it shall be a defence to prove that the provisions of subsection (1) have not been complied with in the case of the offence; and if no such notification as is required by that subsection has been given before the end of the four days next following the day of the offence, that subsection shall be taken not to have been complied with unless the contrary is proved.

DEFINITIONS

    "authorised officer": s.64(1).

    "local authority": s.64(1).

    "occupier": s.64(2).

    "premises": s.64(1).

    "smoke": s.64(1).

GENERAL NOTE

This section, containing a duty to notify occupiers of offences, relates both to certain offences already committed as well as offences "being" committed, under ss.1, 2 or 20 as well as under s.17 relating to smoke nuisances in Scotland. Crucially the opinion concerning the offences is that of an "authorised officer" of the local authority exercising formally delegated powers by virtue of s.101 of the Local Government Act 1972. The duty to notify does not apply if the authorised officer has reason to believe the notice has been given already by or on behalf of the authority. Failure to comply with the duty is a defence in proceedings under ss.1, 2 or 20 unless it is established that notification was provided before the end of the four days next following the day of the offence. Normally the person to be served with the notice is the occupier of the premises.

Offences committed by bodies corporate

52.—(1) Where an offence under this Act which has been committed by a body corporate is proved to have been committed with the consent or connivance of, or to be attributable to any neglect on the part of, any director, manager, secretary or other similar officer of the body corporate or any person who was purporting to act in any such capacity, he as well as the body corporate shall be guilty of that offence and be liable to be proceeded against and punished accordingly.

(2) Where the affairs of a body corporate are managed by its members this section shall apply in relation to the acts and defaults of a member in connection with his functions of management as if he were a director of the body corporate.

GENERAL NOTE

This provision is representative of a growing number of similar provisions to be found in other areas of environmental legislation; s.157 of the Environmental Protection Act 1990, for example.

Subs. (1)

Consent. A director or other officer of the company who is aware of and agrees to a particular transaction would be taken to have consented to it for present purposes, or even to have connived in the decision or other transaction: *Huckerby* v. *Elliott* [1970] 1 All E.R. 189, *cf.*, *Bishopsgate Investment Management Trust* v. *Maxwell (No. 2)*, *The Times*, February 16, 1993.

Connivance. A passive standing by, sometimes referred to as "wilful blindness", would be sufficient evidence of connivance. Tacit agreement to the transaction amounts to connivance: *Huckerby* v. *Elliott*, *ibid.*

Neglect. A person subject to a duty to act but who, probably unreasonably, fails to act is probably in neglect of that duty. A director of a company owes a duty to that company, including a common law duty of care: *Smith and Fawcett, Re* [1942] Ch. 304; *City Equitable Fire*, *Re* [1925] Ch. 407. A negligent failure to comply with a s.36 notice, for example, might lead to the conviction of a director neglecting (without reasonable excuse) to respond to local authority requirements: s.36(8)(a). The expectations in the present context may be rather more onerous under the terms of the Company Directors Disqualification Act 1986 than they are at common law.

Director . . . or other similar officer. This form of words would, no doubt, cover a shadow director as a person used to acting on the instructions of another. Elsewhere the subsection recognises that irregularity of appointment will not affect operation of the section whether in relation to the appointment of directors or other officers.

Offence due to act or default of another

53.—(1) Where the commission by any person of an offence under this Act is due to the act or default of some other person, that other person shall be guilty of the offence.

(2) A person may be charged with and convicted of an offence by virtue of this section whether or not proceedings for the offence are taken against any other person.

GENERAL NOTE

This provision may assist on those occasions when, for example, an employee has operated independently and outside any system or procedure within the company: *Tesco Supermarkets* v. *Nattrass* [1972] A.C. 153, H.L. Many variables will determine whether the offence is attributable "to the act or default of some other person": for example, company delegation and other operational procedures, and the extent to which an employee (or indeed someone who may not be an employee) is closely supervised.

Power of county court to authorise works and order payments

54.—(1) If works are reasonably necessary in or in connection with a building in order to enable the building to be used for some purpose without contravention of any of the provisions of this Act (apart from Parts IV and V), the occupier of the building—

(a) may, if by reason of a restriction affecting his interest in the building he is unable to carry out the works without the consent of the owner of the building or some other person interested in the building and is unable to obtain that consent, apply to the county court for an order to enable the works to be carried out by him; and

(b) may, if he considers that the whole or any proportion of the cost of carrying out the works should be borne by the owner of the building or some other person interested in the building, apply to the county court for an order directing the owner or other person to indemnify him, either wholly or in part, in respect of that cost;

and on an application under paragraph (a) or (b) the court may make such order as may appear to the court to be just.

(2) In the application of this section to Scotland for any reference to the county court there shall be substituted a reference to the sheriff.

GENERAL NOTE

The jurisdiction of the County Court extends to compliance with requirements under Pts. I to III and VI. The jurisdiction of the court in proceedings (typically) between an occupier, on the one hand, and an owner or some other person interested in the building, on the other, is widely drawn; the court may make such order as appears to be "just".

General provisions as to enforcement

55.—(1) It shall be the duty of the local authority to enforce—

(a) the provisions of Parts I to III, section 33 and Part VI; and

(b) the provisions of this Part so far as relating to those provisions;

but nothing in this section shall be taken as extending to the enforcement of any building regulations.

(2) A local authority in England and Wales may institute proceedings for an offence under section 1 or 2 (prohibition of emissions of dark smoke) in the case of any smoke which affects any part of their district notwithstanding, in the case of an offence under section 1, that the smoke is emitted from a chimney outside their district and, in the case of an offence under section 2, that the smoke is emitted from premises outside their district.

(3) Nothing in this section shall be taken as authorising a local authority in Scotland to institute proceedings for an offence against this Act.

DEFINITIONS

"building regulations": s.64(1).
"chimney": s.64(1).
"dark smoke": s.3.
"local authority": s.64(1).
"premises": s.64(1).
"smoke": s.64(1).

GENERAL NOTE

Local authority enforcement duties extend to Pts. I to III, s.33 and Pt. IV but not to building regulations: in England and Wales, the Building Regulations 1991 (S.I. 1991 No. 2768). Subsection (2) empowers a local authority, under ss.1 and 2, to enforce the law where dark smoke emissions emanate from outside the district but are such that they affect that district. Section 60 contains default powers in favour of the Secretary of State but in respect of failure to perform "functions" indicating (presumably) that each Part of the Act referred to by s.55 contains such local authority "functions", *cf.*, s.56.

Rights of entry and inspection etc.

56.—(1) Any person authorised in that behalf by a local authority may at any reasonable time—

    (a) enter upon any land or vessel for the purpose of—

        (i) performing any function conferred on the authority or that person by virtue of this Act,

        (ii) determining whether, and if so in what manner, such a function should be performed, or

        (iii) determining whether any provision of this Act or of an instrument made under this Act is being complied with; and

    (b) carry out such inspections, measurements and tests on the land or vessel or of any articles on it and take away such samples of the land or articles as he considers appropriate for such a purpose.

(2) Subsection (1) above does not, except in relation to work under section 24(1) (adaptations to dwellings in smoke control area), apply in relation to a private dwelling.

(3) If it is shown to the satisfaction of a justice of the peace on sworn information in writing—

    (a) that admission to any land or vessel which a person is entitled to enter in pursuance of subsection (1) has been refused to that person or that refusal is apprehended or that the land or vessel is unoccupied or that the occupier is temporarily absent or that the case is one of emergency or that an application for admission would defeat the object of the entry; and

    (b) that there is reasonable ground for entry upon the land or vessel for the purpose for which entry is required,

then, subject to subsection (4), the justice may by warrant under his hand authorise that person to enter the land or vessel, if need be by force.

(4) A justice of the peace shall not issue a warrant in pursuance of subsection (3) in respect of any land or vessel unless he is satisfied—

    (a) that admission to the land or vessel in pursuance of subsection (1) was sought after not less than seven days notice of the intended entry had been served on the occupier; or

    (b) that admission to the land or vessel in pursuance of that subsection was sought in an emergency and was refused by or on behalf of the occupier; or

    (c) that the land or vessel is unoccupied; or

    (d) that an application for admission to the land or vessel would defeat the object of the entry.

(5) A warrant issued in pursuance of this section shall continue in force until the purpose for which the entry is required has been satisfied.

(6) In the application of this section to Scotland—

    (a) any reference to a justice of the peace shall be construed as including a reference to the sheriff; and

    (b) in subsection (3) for "on sworn information in writing" there is substituted "by evidence on oath".

DEFINITIONS
    "emergency": s.57(7).
    "local authority": s.64(1).
    "vessel": s.64(1).

GENERAL NOTE
    Entry to land may be demanded as of right under subs. (1) except in respect of a private dwelling although here entry may be demanded as of right for the purpose of s.24(1). Subsections (3)(4) and (5) apply stringent requirements to the issue, by a justice of the peace, of a warrant for entry to land or a vessel for the purposes of the Act. Supplementary provision in respect of rights of entry and inspection is to be found in the following s.57.

The right of entry is given to "any person authorised in that behalf by a local authority", suggesting a wide category extending across local authority members, officers and employees and perhaps even independent contractors: contrast s.287 of the Public Health Act 1936 referring to any "authorised officer". The terms of subs. (1) are drawn widely in referring (in para. (a)) to "any land or vessel". However, the broader investigatory powers are to be contrasted with the narrower references to, *inter alia*, "inspections, measurements and tests" carried out on "the land or vessel", indicating a possible restriction on more detailed investigatory activities on, for example, neighbouring land. For an earlier discussion of these issues, see *Senior* v. *Twelves* (1958) 56 L.G.R. 239, a case relating to s.287 of the Public Health Act 1936.

Provisions supplementary to section 56

57.—(1) A person authorised to enter upon any land or vessel in pursuance of section 56 shall, if so required, produce evidence of his authority before he enters upon the land or vessel.

(2) A person so authorised may take with him on to the land or vessel in question such other persons and such equipment as may be necessary.

(3) Admission to any land or vessel used for residential purposes and admission with heavy equipment to any other land or vessel shall not, except in an emergency or in a case where the land or vessel is unoccupied, be demanded as of right in pursuance of section 56(1) unless notice of the intended entry has been served on the occupier not less than seven days before the demand.

(4) A person who, in the exercise of powers conferred on him by virtue of section 56 or this section, enters upon any land or vessel which is unoccupied or of which the occupier is temporarily absent shall leave the land or vessel as effectually secured against unauthorised entry as he found it.

(5) It shall be the duty of a local authority to make full compensation to any person who has sustained damage by reason of—

    (a) the exercise by a person authorised by the authority of any of the powers conferred on the person so authorised by virtue of section 56 or this section; or

    (b) the failure of a person so authorised to perform the duty imposed on him by subsection (4),

except where the damage is attributable to the default of the person who sustained it; and any dispute as to a person's entitlement to compensation in pursuance of this subsection or as to the amount of the compensation shall be determined by arbitration.

(6) A person who wilfully obstructs another person acting in the exercise of any powers conferred on the other person by virtue of section 56 or this section shall be guilty of an offence and liable on summary conviction to a fine not exceeding level 3 on the standard scale.

(7) In section 56 and this section any reference to an emergency is a reference to a case where a person requiring entry to any land or vessel has reasonable cause to believe that circumstances exist which are likely to endanger life or health and that immediate entry to the land or vessel is necessary to verify the existence of those circumstances or to ascertain their cause or to effect a remedy.

DEFINITIONS
    "emergency": subs. (7).
    "local authority": s.64(1).
    "occupier": s.64(2).
    "standard scale": s.37 of the Criminal Justice Act 1982.
    "vessel": s.64(1).

GENERAL NOTE
This section contains a number of provisions supplementary to s.56, as noted therein.

Subs. (2)

Such other persons. It would appear that there is a right of entry for employees or contractors by virtue of these words as long as they are acting under the instructions of the person authorised for the purposes of s.56. However, actual entry must be effected by the person authorised. As to the varying nature of activities according to whether land entered or to be entered is the site of some non-compliance, see the note to s.56.

Subs. (5)

Full compensation. The word "full" is included, it seems, as a matter of emphasis. From the considerable litigation in relation to s.278 of the Public Health Act 1936 (the wording of which is very similar to that of the present provision) a number of principles emerge: (a) a claim is sustainable only where the dealings of the authority would have been actionable but for the existence of a statutory power: *Ricket* v. *Metropolitan Railway Co.* (1867) L.R. 2 H.L. 175; (b) many of the rules from the law of tort for the determination of compensation will apply equally for present purposes: the rules relating to remoteness, for example; (c) the *quantum* of compensation again follows the rules from the law of tort: *Cowper-Essex* v. *Acton Local Board* (1889) 14 App. Cas. 153; (d) compensation must arise from the lawful exercise of a power in the present Act, failing which the remedy is by action: *Imperial Gas, Light and Coke Co.* v. *Broadbent* (1859) 7 H.L. Cas. 800; (e) the negligent exercise of a statutory power precludes a claim under the present statutory provision: the remedy again is an action in tort: *Geddis* v. *Proprietors of Bann Reservoir* (1878) 3 App. Cas. 430; (f) a claim will not lie in respect of any damage not the subject of an exercise of the subject statutory power: *Horton* v. *Colwyn Bay and Colwyn District Council* [1908] 1 K.B. 327; (g) subject to occasional express exceptions, s.34(3), for example, compensation under subs. (5) is not claimable where damage is sustained through a breach of statutory duty.

Subs. (6)

Wilfully obstructs. In *Hinchcliffe* v. *Sheldon* [1955] 1 W.L.R. 1207 the court (for the purposes of s.2 of the Prevention of Crimes Amendment Act 1885) held that the proper approach is to consider whether (where the police are involved) the defendant has made it more difficult for them to carry out their duties, *cf.*, the many cases on the obstruction of a police officer in the execution of his duty, by virtue of s.51 of the Police Act 1964.

Power of local authorities to obtain information

58.—(1) A local authority may serve on any person a notice requiring him to furnish to the authority, within a period or at times specified in the notice and in a form so specified, any information so specified which the authority reasonably considers that it needs for the purposes of any function conferred on the authority by Part IV or V of this Act (or by this Part of this Act so far as relating to those Parts).

(2) The Secretary of State may by regulations provide for restricting the information which may be required in pursuance of subsection (1) and for determining the form in which the information is to be so required.

(3) Any person who—

(a) fails without reasonable excuse to comply with the requirements of a notice served on him in pursuance of this section; or

(b) in furnishing any information in compliance with such a notice, makes any statement which he knows to be false in a material particular or recklessly makes any statement which is false in a material particular,

shall be guilty of an offence and liable on summary conviction to a fine not exceeding level 5 on the standard scale.

DEFINITIONS

"local authority": s.64(1).

"standard scale": s.37 of the Criminal Justice Act 1982.

GENERAL NOTE

The power to seek information is limited to Pts. IV and V of the Act. A facility for obtaining information is provided by Pt. II and (presumably) the present section may be used by a local authority as part of its information gathering facilities for the purposes of enforcing Pts. I and III of the Act.

Subs. (1)

Reasonably considers that it needs. These words, arguably, confer a discretion on the local authority whose judgment on such a matter must normally be conclusive, on the authority of *Associated Provincial Picture Houses* v. *Wednesbury Corporation* [1948] 1 K.B. 223, but subject to a requirement for evidential support in relation to a matter of fact: *Coleen Properties* v. *Minister of Housing and Local Government* [1971] 1 W.L.R. 433, C.A.

Subs. (3)

Reasonable excuse. See the note to s.36(8).

Fails . . . to comply with the requirements of a notice. In *J.B. and M. Motor Haulage* v. *London Waste Regulation Authority, The Times,* November 28, 1990 it was held that justices could not convict a defendant for failure to furnish information without hearing evidence that would link that defendant to the offence of unlawful deposition of waste, contrary to s.3(3) of the Control of Pollution Act 1974.

Local inquiries

59.—(1) The Secretary of State may cause a local inquiry to be held in any case in which he considers it appropriate for such an inquiry to be held either in connection with a provision of this Act or with a view to preventing or dealing with air pollution at any place.

(2) Subsections (2) to (5) of section 250 of the Local Government Act 1972 (which contains supplementary provisions with respect to local inquiries held in pursuance of that section) shall, without prejudice to the generality of subsection (1) of that section, apply to inquiries in England and Wales in pursuance of subsection (1) as they apply to inquiries in pursuance of that section.

(3) Subsections (2) to (8) of section 210 of the Local Government (Scotland) Act 1973 (local inquiries) shall, without prejudice to the generality of subsection (1) of that section, apply to inquiries in Scotland in pursuance of subsection (1) as they apply to inquiries held in pursuance of that section.

GENERAL NOTE

The facility for the Secretary of State to hold a local inquiry is a common feature of several items of legislation, including the Town and Country Planning Act 1990. The purposes for which a local inquiry may be convened are widely defined by subs. (1). As such, a local inquiry here is referred to as a discretionary rather than a mandatory inquiry but nevertheless is subject to the Tribunals and Inquiries Act 1992 by virtue of S.I. 1975 No. 1379. The application of s.250(2) to (5) of the Local Government Act 1972 permits the adoption of a variety of powers in connection with the holding of a local inquiry under the present Act.

Default powers

60.—(1) If the Secretary of State is satisfied that any local authority (in this section referred to as the "defaulting authority") have failed to perform any functions which they ought to have performed, he may make an order—

(a) declaring the authority to be in default; and

(b) directing the authority to perform such of their functions as are specified in the order;

and he may specify the manner in which and the time or times within which those functions are to be performed by the authority.

(2) If the defaulting authority fails to comply with any direction contained in such an order, the Secretary of State may, instead of enforcing the order by mandamus, make an order transferring to himself such of the functions of the authority as he thinks fit.

(3) Where any functions of the defaulting authority are transferred in pursuance of subsection (2) above, the amount of any expenses which the Secretary of State certifies were incurred by him in performing those functions shall on demand be paid to him by the defaulting authority.

(4) Where any expenses are in pursuance of subsection (3) required to be paid by the defaulting authority in respect of any functions transferred in pursuance of this section—

(a) the expenses shall be defrayed by the authority in the like manner, and shall be debited to the like account, as if the functions had not been transferred and the expenses had been incurred by the authority in performing them; and

(b) the authority shall have the like powers for the purpose of raising any money required for the purpose of paragraph (a) as the authority would have had for the purpose of raising money required for defraying expenses incurred for the purposes of the functions in question.

(5) An order transferring any functions of the defaulting authority in pursuance of subsection (2) may provide for the transfer to the Secretary of State of such of the property, rights, liabilities and obligations of the authority as he considers appropriate; and where such an order is revoked the Secretary of State may, by the revoking order or a subsequent order, make such provision as he considers appropriate with respect to any property, rights, liabilities and obligations held by him for the purposes of the transferred functions.

(6) An order made under this section may be varied or revoked by a subsequent order so made.

(7) This section does not apply to a failure by a local authority—

(a) to discharge their functions under section 18 (declaration of smoke control areas);

(b) to submit proposals to the Secretary of State in pursuance of a direction under subsection (1) of section 19 (Secretary of State's power to require creation of smoke control area); or

(c) to perform a duty imposed on them by or by virtue of subsection (4) or (6) of that section.

(8) In this section "functions", in relation to an authority, means functions conferred on the authority by virtue of this Act.

DEFINITIONS
"functions": subs. (8).
"local authority": s.64(1).

GENERAL NOTE
The default powers available to the Secretary of State are based on widely defined margins. Failure to comply with a direction gives the Secretary of State two options, either to enforce the order by an application under R.S.C., Ord. 53 for an order of *mandamus* or by a transfer of the subject function to himself. The default powers are not available in relation to s.18 functions and are not available in relation to s.19(1), (4) and (6), in each case where there is failure by a local authority to submit proposals or perform a duty, as the case may be. Note the specific default provisions in s.19.

Subs. (1)
Satisfied. See *Secretary of State for Education and Science* v. *Tameside Metropolitan Borough Council* [1977] A.C. 1014, H.L. where it was held (in respect of default powers in the Education Act 1944 stipulating that the Secretary of State should be "... satisfied ... that any local authority ... have acted or are proposing to act unreasonably with respect to the exercise of any power conferred or the performance of any duty imposed by or under this Act") that a direction was *ultra vires* because there were no grounds for concluding that the authority had acted "unreasonably". Such a conclusion, it is submitted, may be justified more easily in relation to the less subjective wording of the present subsection.

Joint exercise of local authority functions

61.—(1) Sections 6, 7, 9 and 10 of the Public Health Act 1936 (provisions relating to joint boards) shall, so far as applicable, have effect in relation to this Act as if the provisions of this Act were provisions of that Act.

(2) Section 172 of the Public Health (Scotland) Act 1897 (constitution of port health authorities) shall have effect as if the provisions of this Act were provisions of that Act.

(3) Without prejudice to subsections (1) and (2), any two or more local authorities may combine for the purpose of declaring an area to be a smoke control area and in that event—

(a) the smoke control area may be the whole of the districts of those authorities or any part of those districts;

(b) the references in section 18, Schedule 1 and paragraph 1 of Schedule 2 to the local authority shall be read as references to the local authorities acting jointly;

(c) the reference in paragraph 1 of Schedule 1 to a place in the district of the local authority shall be construed as a reference to a place in each of the districts of the local authorities;

but, except as provided in this subsection, references in this Act to the local authority shall, in relation to a building or dwelling, or to a boiler or industrial plant, in the smoke control area, be read as references to that one of the local authorities within whose district the building, dwelling, boiler or plant is situated.

(4) For the avoidance of doubt it is hereby declared that where a port health authority or joint board has functions, rights or liabilities under this Act—

(a) any reference in this Act to a local authority or its district includes, in relation to those functions, rights or liabilities, a reference to the port health authority or board or its district;

(b) for the purposes of this Act, no part of the district of any such port health authority or board is to be treated, in relation to any matter falling within the competence of the authority or board, as forming part of the district of any other authority.

(5) Any premises which extend into the districts of two or more authorities shall be treated for the purposes of this Act as being wholly within such one of those districts—

(a) in England and Wales, as may from time to time be agreed by those authorities; or

(b) in Scotland, as may from time to time be so agreed or, in default of agreement, determined by the Secretary of State.

DEFINITIONS
"local authority": s.64(1).
"port health authority": s.64(1).
"premises": s.64(1).

GENERAL NOTE
A number of Acts have applied ss.6, 7, 9 and 10 of the Public Health Act 1936 in addition to the Clean Air Act 1993. The initiative for a joint board must come from one or more authorities. Generally, whatever functions are conferred by the order on the joint board cease to be the responsibility of the constituent authorities although some functions may be identified as being amenable to discharge concurrently by the board and constituent authorities. Nevertheless a board may delegate any function to a constituent authority. Joint action in respect of smoke control areas is provided for by subs. (3).

Application of certain provisions of Part XII of Public Health Act 1936 and corresponding Scottish legislation

62.—(1) In the application of this Act to England and Wales, the following provisions of Part XII of the Public Health Act 1936 shall have effect in relation to the provisions of this Act (apart from Parts IV and V) as if those provisions were provisions of that Act—

section 275 (power of local authority to execute works);
section 276 (power of local authority to sell materials);
section 278 (compensation to individuals for damage resulting from exercise of powers under Act);
section 283 (form of notices);

section 284 (authentication of documents);
section 285 (service of notices);
section 289 (power to require occupier to permit works to be executed by owner);
section 291 (expenses to be a charge on the premises);
section 293 (recovery of expenses);
section 294 (limitation of liability of certain owners);
section 299 (inclusion of several sums in one complaint, etc.);
section 305 (protection of members and officers of local authorities from personal liability).

(2) In the application of this Act to Scotland—

(a) the following enactments shall have effect in relation to the provisions of this Act (apart from Parts IV and V) as if those provisions were provisions of the Act in which that enactment is comprised—

(i) in the Public Health (Scotland) Act 1897, section 161 (joint owners) and section 164 (compensation); and

(ii) in the Housing (Scotland) Act 1987, section 131 and Schedule 9 (charging orders), section 319 (penalty for preventing execution of works), section 325 (furnishing information for service of documents), section 329 (default powers), section 330 (form of notices) and section 336 (limitation on liability of trustee);

(b) for the purposes of the application of section 329 of the Housing (Scotland) Act 1987 by virtue of paragraph (a) above, subsections (1) and (3) of section 196 of the Housing (Scotland) Act 1966 shall apply to section 329 as they originally applied to the provisions which it re-enacted;

(c) section 109 of the Housing (Scotland) Act 1987 (recovery by local authority of expenses) shall have effect as if the reference to section 108(3) of that Act included a reference to paragraph 1 of Schedule 2 to this Act; and

(d) section 319 of that Act (penalty for preventing execution of works) shall have effect as if subsection (1) of that section included a reference to this Act (apart from Parts IV and V) and as if sub-paragraphs (b) and (c) were omitted.

DEFINITIONS
"local authority": s.64(1).
"owner": s.64(1).
"premises": s.64(1).

GENERAL NOTE
Section 275 enables a local authority to act as contractor: (a) on behalf of an owner or occupier of premises called upon by the authority to execute works under the Act and (b) on behalf of a person carrying out certain other works not directly applicable for present purposes.

By agreement. As to the recovery of expenses, see ss.291 and 293, also having effect under the present Act.

Section 276 empowers a local authority to sell materials removed by them when carrying out work under the Act unless the owner claims them within three days of removal.

Section 278, dealing with compensation for damage resulting from an exercise of powers under the Act is analysed in the note to s.57(5).

Section 283 is a general provision indicating that formal notifications by a local authority must be in writing, a mandatory requirement: *Epping Forest District Council* v. *Essex Rendering* [1983] 1 W.L.R. 158.

Section 284 provides for the manner of authentication of notices and other documents reduced to writing in compliance with s.283. If a notice or other document is not so authenticated independent evidence would have to be adduced in any legal proceedings in which the document was material.

Section 285 provides for a number of alternative methods whereby a notice, demand, etc., required or authorised by the Act (or regulations under the Act) to be served on an individual, may be so served. If it can be proved that one of the methods has been adopted, the court will then hold that the document has in fact been duly served.

Section 289 empowers a magistrates' court, on a complaint by an owner of any premises, to require an occupier to execute works required for the purposes of Pts. I to III of the present Act. As to the jurisdiction and powers of the court for the purposes of s.289, see s.300 of the Public Health Act 1936.

Section 291 relates to expenses incurred by a local authority repayment of which is the responsibility of the owner of the subject premises. The expenses become a charge on the land and run with the land. The local authority has two remedies: to sue in the county court under s.293 (which also applies to the present Act) and to enforce a charge under the present section.

Section 293: see the note to s.291, above.

Section 294 allows for a limitation of the liability of certain owners in relation to a local authority's attempt to claim the recovery of its expenses.

Section 299 allows the inclusion in one complaint of more than one sum outstanding in relation to a local authority's claim in respect of expenses.

Section 305 stipulates that, provided that a member or officer of a local authority acts in good faith in carrying out any of the provisions of the present Act, any claim in respect of any such act lies against the local authority only.

General

Regulations and orders

63.—(1) Any power of the Secretary of State under this Act to make an order or regulations—

(a) includes power to make different provision in the order or regulations for different circumstances;

(b) includes power to make such incidental, supplemental and transitional provision as the Secretary of State considers appropriate; and

(c) is exercisable by statutory instrument except in the case of the powers conferred by sections 19(4) and 60 and paragraph 3 of Schedule 3.

(2) Any statutory instrument containing regulations made under this Act, except an instrument containing regulations a draft of which is required by section 6(3), 10(5) or 47(2) to be approved by a resolution of each House of Parliament, shall be subject to annulment in pursuance of a resolution of either House of Parliament.

(3) Any statutory instrument containing an order under section 21 or 22 shall be subject to annulment in pursuance of a resolution of either House of Parliament.

General provisions as to interpretation

64.—(1) In this Act, except so far as the context otherwise requires,—

"authorised officer" means any officer of a local authority authorised by them in writing, either generally or specially, to act in matters of any specified kind or in any specified matter;

"building regulations" means, as respects Scotland, any statutory enactments, byelaws, rules and regulations or other provisions under whatever authority made, relating to the construction, alteration or extension of buildings;

"caravan" means a caravan within the meaning of Part I of the Caravan Sites and Control of Development Act 1960, disregarding the amendment made by section 13(2) of the Caravan Sites Act 1968, which usually and for the time being is situated on a caravan site within the meaning of that Act;

"chimney" includes structures and openings of any kind from or through which smoke, grit, dust or fumes may be emitted, and, in particular, includes flues, and references to a chimney of a building include references to a chimney which serves the whole or a part of a building but is structurally separate from the building;

"dark smoke" has the meaning given by section 3(1);

"day" means a period of twenty-four hours beginning at midnight;

"domestic furnace" means any furnace which is—

(a) designed solely or mainly for domestic purposes, and

(b) used for heating a boiler with a maximum heating capacity of less than 16.12 kilowatts;

"fireplace" includes any furnace, grate or stove, whether open or closed;

"fixed boiler or industrial plant" means any boiler or industrial plant which is attached to a building or is for the time being fixed to or installed on any land;

"fumes" means any airborne solid matter smaller than dust;

"industrial plant" includes any still, melting pot or other plant used for any industrial or trade purposes, and also any incinerator used for or in connection with any such purposes;

"local authority" means—

> (a) in England and Wales, the council of a district or a London borough, the Common Council of the City of London, the Sub-Treasurer of the Inner Temple and the Under Treasurer of the Middle Temple; and
>
> (b) in Scotland, an islands or district council;

"owner", in relation to premises—

> (a) as respects England and Wales, means the person for the time being receiving the rackrent of the premises, whether on his own account or as agent or trustee for another person, or who would so receive the rackrent if the premises were let at a rackrent; and
>
> (b) as respects Scotland, means the person for the time being entitled to receive or who would, if the premises were let, be entitled to receive, the rents of the premises and includes a trustee, factor, tutor or curator and, in the case of public or municipal property, includes the persons to whom the management of the property is entrusted;

"port health authority" means, as respects Scotland, a port local authority constituted under Part X of the Public Health (Scotland) Act 1897 and includes a reference to a joint port health authority constituted under that Part;

"practicable" means reasonably practicable having regard, amongst other things, to local conditions and circumstances, to the financial implications and to the current state of technical knowledge, and "practicable means" includes the provision and maintenance of plant and its proper use;

"premises" includes land;

"smoke", includes soot, ash, grit and gritty particles emitted in smoke; and

"vessel" has the same meaning as in the Merchant Shipping Act 1894.

(2) Any reference in this Act to the occupier of a building shall, in relation to any building different parts of which are occupied by different persons, be read as a reference to the occupier or other person in control of the part of the building in which the relevant fireplace is situated.

(3) In this Act any reference to the rate of emission of any substance or any reference which is to be understood as such a reference shall, in relation to any regulations or conditions, be construed as a reference to the quantities of that substance which may be emitted during a period specified in the regulations or conditions.

(4) In this Act, except so far as the context otherwise requires, "private dwelling" means any building or part of a building used or intended to be used as such, and a building or part of a building is not to be taken for the purposes of this Act to be used or intended to be used otherwise than as a private dwelling by reason that a person who resides or is to reside in it is or is to be required or permitted to reside in it in consequence of his employment or of holding an office.

(5) In considering for the purposes of this Act whether any and, if so, what works are reasonably necessary in order to make suitable provision for heating and cooking in the case of a dwelling or are reasonably necessary in order to enable a building to be used for a purpose without contravention of any of the provisions of this Act, regard shall be had to any difficulty there may be in obtaining, or in obtaining otherwise than at a high price, any fuels which would have to be used but for the execution of the works.

(6) Any furnaces which are in the occupation of the same person and are served by a single chimney shall, for the purposes of sections 5 to 12, 14 and 15, be taken to be one furnace.

Application to Isles of Scilly

65. Parts IV and V, and this Part so far as relating to those Parts, shall have effect in their application to the Isles of Scilly with such modifications as the Secretary of State may by order specify.

Transitory provisions relating to Alkali, &c. Works Regulation Act 1906

66.—(1) Until the coming into force of the repeal by the Environmental Protection Act 1990 of the Alkali, &c. Works Regulation Act 1906—

(a) Part I of Schedule 3 shall have effect;

(b) this Act shall have effect subject to the modifications in Part II of that Schedule; and

(c) the Alkali, &c. Works Regulation Act 1906 shall continue to have effect as amended by Schedule 2 to the Clean Air Act 1956 notwithstanding the repeal by this Act of the last-mentioned Act.

(2) On the coming into force of the repeal by the Environmental Protection Act 1990 of the Alkali, &c. Works Regulation Act 1906, this section and Schedule 3 shall cease to have effect.

Consequential amendments, transitional provisions and repeals

67.—(1) The enactments specified in Schedule 4 shall have effect subject to the amendments set out in that Schedule, being amendments consequential on the preceding provisions of this Act.

(2) The transitional provisions and savings contained in Schedule 5 (which include provisions preserving the effect of transitional or saving provisions in enactments repealed by this Act) shall have effect.

(3) The enactments specified in Schedule 6 (which include spent enactments) are repealed to the extent specified in the third column of that Schedule.

Short title, commencement and extent

68.—(1) This Act may be cited as the Clean Air Act 1993.

(2) This Act shall come into force at the end of the period of three months beginning with the day on which it is passed.

(3) The following provisions of this Act (apart from this section) extend to Northern Ireland—

(a) section 30;

(b) section 32 so far as it relates to regulations under section 30; and

(c) section 67(3) and Schedule 6, so far as they relate to the repeal of sections 75 and 77 of the Control of Pollution Act 1974;

but otherwise this Act does not extend to Northern Ireland.

SCHEDULES

SCHEDULE 1

COMING INTO OPERATION OF SMOKE CONTROL ORDERS

1. Before making a smoke control order the local authority shall publish in the London Gazette and once at least in each of two successive weeks in some newspaper circulating in the area to which the order will relate a notice—
    (a) stating that the local authority propose to make the order, and its general effect;
    (b) specifying a place in the district of the local authority where a copy of the order and of any map or plan referred to in it may be inspected by any person free of charge at all reasonable times during a period of not less than six weeks from the date of the last publication of the notice; and
    (c) stating that within that period any person who will be affected by the order may by notice in writing to the local authority object to the making of the order.

2. Besides publishing such a notice, the local authority shall post, and keep posted throughout the period mentioned in paragraph 1(b), copies of the notice in such number of conspicuous places within the area to which the order will relate as appear to them necessary for the purpose of bringing the proposal to make the order to the notice of persons who will be affected.

3. If an objection is duly made to the local authority within the period mentioned in paragraph 1(b), and is not withdrawn, the local authority shall not make the order without first considering the objection.

4. Subject to paragraphs 5 and 6, an order shall come into operation on such date not less than six months after it is made as may be specified in it.

5. An order varying a previous order so as to exempt specified buildings or classes of building or specified fireplaces or classes of fireplace from the operation of section 20 (prohibition of smoke emissions in smoke control area) may come into operation on, or at any time after, the date on which it is made.

6. If, before the date on which the order is to come into operation, the local authority—
    (a) pass a resolution postponing its coming into operation; and
    (b) publish a notice stating the effect of the resolution in the London Gazette and once at least in each of two successive weeks in some newspaper circulating in the area to which the order will relate,
the order shall, unless its coming into operation is again postponed under this paragraph, come into operation on the date specified in the resolution.

7. In the application of this Schedule to Scotland, for any reference to the London Gazette there shall be substituted a reference to the Edinburgh Gazette.

SCHEDULE 2

SMOKE CONTROL ORDERS: EXPENDITURE ON OLD PRIVATE DWELLINGS

Grants for expenditure incurred in adaptation of fireplaces

1.—(1) This paragraph applies if, after the making of a smoke control order by a local authority, the owner or occupier of, or any person interested in, an old private dwelling which is or will be within a smoke control area as a result of the order incurs relevant expenditure.

(2) For the purposes of this paragraph "relevant expenditure" is expenditure on adaptations in or in connection with an old private dwelling to avoid contraventions of section 20 (prohibition of smoke emissions in smoke control area) which—
    (a) is incurred before the coming into operation of the order and with the approval of the local authority given for the purposes of this paragraph; or
    (b) is reasonably incurred in carrying out adaptations required by a notice given under section 24(1) (power of local authority to require certain adaptations).

(3) If the adaptations in question are carried out to the satisfaction of the local authority, the local authority—
    (a) shall repay to him seven-tenths of the relevant expenditure; and
    (b) may, if they think fit, also repay to him the whole or any part of the remainder of that expenditure.

(4) Where relevant expenditure is incurred by the occupier of a private dwelling who is not an owner of the dwelling and the adaptations in question consist of or include the provision of any cooking or heating appliance which can be readily removed from the dwelling without injury to itself or the fabric of the dwelling, the following provisions shall have effect as respects so much of the expenditure as represents the cost of the appliance, that is to say—
    (a) not more than seven-twentieths of that part of that expenditure shall be repaid until two years from the coming into operation of the order; and

(b) any further repayment of that part of that expenditure shall be made only if the appliance has not by then been removed from the dwelling and, if made, shall be made to the person who is the occupier of the dwelling at the end of the two years.

(5) The approval of a local authority to the incurring of expenditure may be given for the purposes of this paragraph, if the authority think fit in the circumstances of any particular case, after the expenditure has been incurred.

(6) This paragraph has effect subject to paragraph 4.

Exclusion of grants in case of unsuitable appliances

2. For the purposes of this Schedule, an appliance is unsuitable for installation in any area or (as the case may be) in any district or part of Great Britain if it tends, by reason of its consumption of fuel (of whatever kind) or its consumption of fuel at times when it is generally used, to impose undue strain on the fuel resources available for that area, district or part.

3.—(1) Sub-paragraph (2) applies if—
    (a) after a local authority have resolved to make a smoke control order declaring a smoke control area (not being an order varying a previous order so made); and
    (b) before notice of the making of the order is first published in accordance with Schedule 1,
the authority pass a resolution designating any class of heating appliance as being, in their opinion, unsuitable for installation in that area.

(2) No payment shall be made by the authority under paragraph 1 in respect of expenditure incurred in providing, or in executing works for the purpose of the installation of, any heating appliance of the class designated by the resolution in or in connection with a dwelling within the area to which the order relates.

(3) No payment shall be made under paragraph 1 by a local authority in respect of expenditure incurred in providing, or in executing works for the purpose of the installation of, any heating appliance which, when the expenditure was incurred, fell within any class of appliance for the time being designated for the purposes of this paragraph by the Secretary of State as being in his opinion—
    (a) unsuitable for installation in the district of that authority; or
    (b) generally unsuitable for installation in the part of Great Britain with which the Secretary of State is concerned,
unless the approval of the local authority in respect of that expenditure was given for the purposes of paragraph 1 at a time when the appliance in question did not fall within any class of appliance so designated.

(4) Retrospective approval of expenditure may only be given by a local authority by virtue of paragraph 1(5) in the case of expenditure incurred in providing, or in executing works for the purpose of the installation of, a heating appliance, if the appliance—
    (a) did not at the time when the expenditure was incurred; and
    (b) does not when the approval is given,
fall within a class of appliance for the time being designated by the Secretary of State for the purposes of this paragraph as regards the district of that authority or generally.

(5) In accordance with the preceding provisions of this Schedule, expenditure within sub-paragraph (3) or (4) shall be left out of account for the purposes of paragraph 1.

Exchequer contributions to certain expenditure

4.—(1) The Secretary of State may, out of money provided by Parliament, make a contribution towards the following expenses, of any local authority (if approved by him), that is to say—
    (a) any expenses of the local authority in making payments under paragraph 1;
    (b) any expenses incurred by them in making, in or in connection with old private dwellings owned by them or under their control, adaptations to avoid contraventions of section 20; and
    (c) any expenses incurred by them in carrying out adaptations required by notices under section 24 in or in connection with old private dwellings.

(2) A contribution under this paragraph in respect of any expenses shall be a single payment equal—
    (a) in the case of expenses mentioned in sub-paragraph (1)(a), to four-sevenths of the amount of the expenses;
    (b) in the case of expenses mentioned in sub-paragraph (1)(b), to two-fifths of the amount of the expenses; and
    (c) in the case of expenses mentioned in sub-paragraph (1)(c), to four-sevenths of the amount arrived at by deducting the recoverable amount from the amount of those expenses.

(3) In sub-paragraph (2)(c), "the recoverable amount" means, in relation to any expenses, the fraction of those expenses (whether three-tenths or some smaller fraction determined by the local authority, in the case of those expenses, under section 24(2) or (3)) which the local authority have power to recover from the occupier or owner by virtue of section 24(2) or (3).

Section 66(1)   SCHEDULE 3

PROVISIONS HAVING EFFECT UNTIL REPEAL OF ALKALI, &C. WORKS REGULATION ACT 1906

PART I

RELATION OF THIS ACT TO ALKALI, &C. WORKS REGULATION ACT 1906

1.—(1) In this Part of this Schedule—
"the Alkali Act" means the Alkali, &c. Works Regulation Act 1906; and
"work subject or potentially subject to the Alkali Act" means—
(a) so much of any work registered under section 9 of that Act as is directly concerned in the processes which necessitate its registration under that section; and
(b) so much of any work in the course of erection or alteration as will on completion of the erection or alteration be directly concerned in such processes.
(2) The Secretary of State may from time to time determine how much of any work mentioned in sub-paragraph (1) is or will be directly concerned as there mentioned and his determination shall, until revoked or varied by him, be conclusive.
2. Subject to paragraphs 3 and 4, Parts I to III of this Act shall not apply to any work subject or potentially subject to the Alkali Act.
3. If, on the application of the local authority, the Secretary of State is satisfied that in all the circumstances it is expedient to do so, he may by order exclude the application of paragraph 2 to the whole or any specified part of any work subject or potentially subject to the Alkali Act.
4. While, by virtue of an order under paragraph 3 above, paragraph 2 is excluded from applying to any work or to any specified part of any work—
(a) in any proceedings brought under section 1, 2 or 20 in respect of the emission of smoke from the work or (as the case may be) from the specified part of the work it shall be a defence to prove that the best practicable means had been employed to prevent or minimise the alleged emission;
(b) in any proceedings brought by virtue of section 17 (smoke nuisances in Scotland) in respect of smoke emitted from the work or (as the case may be) from the specified part of the work, the defence provided for by subsection (2) of that section shall be available whether the smoke was emitted from a chimney or not.
5. Any order made under paragraph 3 may be varied or revoked by a subsequent order of the Secretary of State.
6. Nothing in section 55 shall be taken as extending to the enforcement of any of the provisions of the Alkali Act.

PART II

MODIFICATIONS OF THIS ACT

7. In section 31(4)—
(a) in paragraph (a), after "1990" there is inserted "or a work subject to the Alkali Act"; and
(b) for paragraph (b) there is substituted—
"(b) of the inspectors appointed under Part I of the Environmental Protection Act 1990 or, as the case may be, under the Alkali Act, to enforce those provisions in relation to such furnaces;".
8. In section 33(1), after "1990" there is inserted "or the place at which he does so is a work registered in pursuance of section 9 of the Alkali, &c. Works Regulation Act 1906".
9. In section 35(3), after "1990" there is inserted "or any work subject to the Alkali Act".
10. In section 36, after subsection (3) there is inserted—
"(3A) If the notice relates to a work subject to the Alkali Act, the person on whom the notice is served shall not be obliged to supply any information which, as certified by an inspector appointed under that Act, is not of a kind which is being supplied to the inspector for the purposes of that Act."
11. At the end of section 40 there is inserted—
"and 'the Alkali Act' means the Alkali, &c. Works Regulation Act 1906 and 'a work subject to the Alkali Act' means a work registered under section 9 of the Alkali Act, excluding the whole or part of such a work while the work or part is the subject of an order made or treated as made under paragraph 3 of Schedule 3 to this Act."

SCHEDULE 4

CONSEQUENTIAL AMENDMENTS

The Health and Safety at Work etc. Act 1974 (c.37)

1. Section 80(1) of the Health and Safety at Work etc. Act 1974 shall apply to provisions in this Act which re-enact provisions previously contained in an Act passed before or in the same Session as that Act as it applies to provisions so contained.

The Control of Pollution Act 1974 (c.40)

2. In section 96(1) of the Control of Pollution Act 1974 after "pollution" there is inserted "other than air pollution".

The Public Health (Control of Disease) Act 1984 (c.22)

3. In section 7(4) of the Public Health (Control of Disease) Act 1984 for paragraph (e) there is substituted—
    "(e) the Clean Air Act 1993;".

The Environmental Protection Act 1990 (c.43)

4. In section 79(7) of the Environmental Protection Act 1990—
    (a) for "the Clean Air Act 1956 or the Clean Air Act 1968" there is substituted "the Clean Air Act 1993"; and
    (b) for "section 34(2) of the Clean Air Act 1956" there is substituted "section 3 of the Clean Air Act 1993".

The Atomic Weapons Establishment Act 1991 (c.46)

5. In the Schedule to the Atomic Weapons Establishment Act 1991 after paragraph 10A there is inserted—

"Clean Air Act 1993

10B.—(1) Subsection (1) of section 46 of the Clean Air Act 1992 (Crown premises) shall have effect, in relation to emissions from designated premises, as if—
    (a) references to premises under the control of a government department which are occupied for the public service of the Crown included a reference to designated premises; and
    (b) references to the responsible Minister were references to the Secretary of State.
    (2) For the purposes of section 36 of that Act (notices requiring information about air pollution), designated premises, and persons at such premises, shall be treated as premises used for, or persons in, the public service of the Crown.
    (3) For all other purposes of that Act any such premises shall be treated as Crown premises occupied by a government department."

The Radioactive Substances Act 1993 (c.12)

6. In Schedule 3 to the Radioactive Substances Act 1993—
    (a) for paragraph 2 there is substituted—
        "2. Section 16 of the Clean Air Act 1993."; and
    (b) for paragraph 12 there is substituted—
        "12. Sections 16 and 17 of the Clean Air Act 1993."

SCHEDULE 5

TRANSITIONAL PROVISIONS

PART I

GENERAL TRANSITIONAL PROVISIONS AND SAVINGS

Continuity of the law

1. The substitution of this Act for the enactments repealed by this Act does not affect the continuity of the law.

2. Any reference, whether express or implied, in this Act or any other enactment, instrument or document to a provision of this Act shall, so far as the context permits, be construed as including, in relation to the times, circumstances and purposes in relation to which the corresponding provision of the enactments repealed by this Act has effect, a reference to that corresponding provision.

3. Any document made, served or issued after the commencement of this Act which contains a reference to any of the enactments repealed by this Act shall be construed, except so far as a contrary intention appears, as referring or, as the case may require, including a reference to the corresponding provision of this Act.

4. Paragraphs 2 and 3 have effect without prejudice to the operation of sections 16 and 17 of the Interpretation Act 1978 (which relate to the effect of repeals).

General saving for old transitional provisions and savings

5.—(1) The repeal by this Act of a transitional provision or saving relating to the coming into force of a provision reproduced in this Act does not affect the operation of the transitional provision or saving, in so far as it is not specifically reproduced in this Act but remains capable of having effect in relation to the corresponding provision of this Act.

(2) The repeal by this Act of an enactment previously repealed subject to savings does not affect the continued operation of those savings.

(3) The repeal by this Act of a saving on the previous repeal of an enactment does not affect the operation of the saving in so far as it is not specifically reproduced in this Act but remains capable of having effect.

PART II

EXCLUSION AND MODIFICATION OF CERTAIN PROVISIONS OF THIS ACT

Requirements to fit arrestment plant: sections 6 & 8

6.—(1) Section 6(1) (arrestment plant for new non-domestic furnaces) does not apply to a furnace which was installed, the installation of which began or an agreement for the purchase or installation of which was entered into before 1st October 1969 (which was the day appointed for the coming into force of the enactments replaced by section 6).

(2) Subject to sub-paragraph (3), section 8(1) (arrestment plant for furnaces burning solid fuel in other cases) applies in relation to a furnace to which, by virtue of sub-paragraph (1), section 6 does not apply as it applies to a domestic furnace.

(3) Section 8(1) does not apply to a furnace which was installed, the installation of which began or an agreement for the purchase or installation of which was entered into—

    (a) in relation to a furnace in England and Wales, before 1st June 1958 (which was the day appointed as respects England and Wales for the coming into force of the enactments replaced by section 8); and

    (b) in relation to a furnace in Scotland, before 15th November 1958 (which was the day so appointed as respects Scotland).

Height of chimneys for furnaces: section 14

7.—(1) Subject to sub-paragraph (2) below, section 14 (height of chimneys for furnaces) does not apply to any furnace served by a chimney the construction of which was begun or the plans for which were passed before 1st April 1969 (which was the day appointed for the coming into force of the enactments replaced by section 14).

(2) Notwithstanding sub-paragraph (1), section 14 does apply to—

    (a) any furnace the combustion space of which has been increased on or after 1st April 1969; or

    (b) any furnace the installation of which was begun on or after that day and which replaces a furnace which had a smaller combustion space.

Smoke control orders

8.—(1) In relation to any smoke control order made by a local authority under section 18 of this Act which revokes or varies an order made under section 11 of the Clean Air Act 1956 before 13th November 1980 (which was the date of the passing of the Local Government, Planning and Land Act 1980, which amended section 11 of that Act to omit the requirement that an order made by a local authority should be confirmed by the Secretary of State) the provisions of this Act mentioned in the following provisions of this paragraph shall have effect subject to the modifications there mentioned.

(2) In section 18—

    (a) in subsection (1) after the word "order" where it first appears there shall be inserted the words "confirmed by the Secretary of State";

    (b) in subsection (3), after the word "order" where it first appears there shall be inserted the words "confirmed by the Secretary of State" and at the end there shall be inserted the words "so confirmed"; and

    (c) in subsection (4), after the words "to the" there shall be inserted the words "confirmation and".

(3) In section 26(1) and paragraph 1(1) of Schedule 2, for the word "making" there shall be substituted the word "confirmation".

9. The provisions of Part III of this Schedule (which are derived from Schedule 1 to the Clean Air Act 1956 as that Schedule had effect immediately before the date mentioned in paragraph 8(1) of this Schedule) shall apply in substitution for Schedule 1 to this Act in relation to any such order; and references in this Act, as it applies in relation to any such order, to Schedule 1 to this Act or to any specified provision of that Schedule shall be read as referring to Part III of this Schedule or the corresponding provision of that Part (as the case may be).

Colliery spoilbanks: section 42

10. Subsections (2) to (4) of section 42 (colliery spoilbanks) shall not apply to any deposit of refuse deposited from a mine or quarry before 5th July 1956 (the date of the passing of the Clean Air Act 1956) if at that date the deposit was no longer in use as such and was not under the control of the owner of the mine or quarry.

PART III

CONFIRMATION AND COMING INTO OPERATION OF CERTAIN SMOKE CONTROL ORDERS

11. In this Part of this Schedule "order" means a smoke control order.

12. After making an order, the local authority shall publish in the London Gazette and also once at least in each of two successive weeks in some newspaper circulating in the area to which the order relates a notice—

    (a) stating that the order has been made and its general effect;

    (b) specifying a place in the district of the local authority where a copy of the order and of any map or plan referred to in the order may be inspected by any person free of charge at all reasonable times during a period of not less than six weeks from the date of the last publication of the notice; and

    (c) stating that within that period any person who will be affected by the order may by notice in writing to the Secretary of State object to the confirmation of that order.

13. Besides publishing a notice as required by paragraph 12, the local authority who have made an order shall post, and keep posted throughout the period mentioned in that paragraph, copies of the notice in such number of conspicuous places within the area to which the order relates as appear to them necessary for the purpose of bringing the making of the order to the notice of persons affected.

14. If no objection is duly made to the Secretary of State within the period mentioned in paragraph 12(b), or if every objection so made is withdrawn, the Secretary of State may, if he thinks fit, confirm the order either with or without modifications.

15. In any case other than one within paragraph 14 the Secretary of State shall, before confirming the order, either—

    (a) cause a local inquiry to be held; or

    (b) afford to any person by whom an objection has been duly made in accordance with paragraph 12(c) and not withdrawn an opportunity of appearing before and being heard by a person appointed by him for the purpose;

and, after considering the objection and the report of the person who held the inquiry or the person so appointed, may confirm the order with or without modifications.

16. Section 250(2) to (5) of the Local Government Act 1972 (summoning of witnesses and production of documents before, and costs incurred at, local government inquiries held under that section) shall apply to an inquiry held under this Part of this Schedule by the Secretary of State as they apply to inquiries held under that section.

17. Subject to paragraphs 18 and 19, an order when confirmed shall come into operation on such date as may be specified in the order, not being earlier than six months from the date of the confirmation.

18. An order varying a previous order so as to exempt specified buildings or classes of building or specified fireplaces or classes of fireplace from the operation of section 18 may come into operation on, or at any time after, the date of its confirmation.

19.—(1) If, before the date on which an order is to come into operation, the local authority—
  (a) pass a resolution postponing its operation; and
  (b) publish a notice stating the effect of the resolution in the London Gazette and also once at least in each of two successive weeks in some newspaper circulating in the area to which the order relates;
the order shall, unless its coming into operation is again postponed under this paragraph, come into operation on the date specified in the resolution.

(2) A local authority shall not without the consent of the Secretary of State exercise their power under sub-paragraph (1) of postponing the coming into operation of an order for a period of more than twelve months or for periods amounting in all to more than twelve months.

20. In the application of this Part of this Schedule to Scotland, for any reference to the London Gazette there shall be substituted a reference to the Edinburgh Gazette.

Section 67(3)   SCHEDULE 6

REPEALS

Chapter	Short title	Extent of repeal
4 & 5 Eliz. 2. c.52.	The Clean Air Act 1956.	The whole Act.
1963 c.33.	The London Government Act 1963.	Section 40(4)(e). In Schedule 11, paragraphs 30 and 31.
1964 c.56.	The Housing Act 1964.	Section 95.
1968 c.62.	The Clean Air Act 1968.	The whole Act.
1970 c.38.	The Building (Scotland) Act 1970.	In Schedule 1, paragraph 5.
1972 c.70.	The Local Government Act 1972.	Section 180(3)(f).
1973 c.65.	The Local Government (Scotland) Act 1973.	In Schedule 15, paragraph 28. In Schedule 27, paragraph 128.
1974 c.39.	The Consumer Credit Act 1974.	In Schedule 4, paragraphs 15 and 16.
1974 c.40.	The Control of Pollution Act 1974.	Sections 75 to 84. Section 103. In section 109(3), the words "75, 77". In Schedule 2, paragraphs 19, 26 and 27. In Schedule 3, paragraph 16.
1980 c.65.	The Local Government, Planning and Land Act 1980.	Section 189. In Schedule 2, paragraphs 1 to 6 and 16.
1984 c.55.	The Building Act 1984.	In Schedule 5, paragraph 2. In Schedule 6, paragraph 5.
1987 c.26.	The Housing (Scotland) Act 1987.	In Schedule 23, paragraphs 6 and 14.
1989 c.17.	The Control of Smoke Pollution Act 1989.	The whole Act.
1990 c.43.	The Environmental Protection Act 1990.	Section 85. In Schedule 15, paragraphs 6, 7, 12 and 15(6) to (9).
1991 c.46.	The Atomic Weapons Establishment Act 1991.	In the Schedule, paragraphs 4 and 8(1).

TABLE OF DERIVATIONS

Notes:

1. The following abbreviations are used in this Table:—

1897	= The Public Health (Scotland) Act 1897 (c.38)
1936	= The Public Health Act 1936 (c.49)
1956	= The Clean Air Act 1956 (c.52)
1961	= The Public Health Act 1961 (c.64)
1963	= The London Government Act 1963 (c.33)

1964	=	The Housing Act 1964 (c.56)
1968	=	The Clean Air Act 1968 (c.62)
1970 c.38	=	The Building (Scotland) Act 1970 (c.38)
1972 c.70	=	The Local Government Act 1972 (c.70)
1973 c.65	=	The Local Government (Scotland) Act 1973 (c.65)
1974	=	The Control of Pollution Act 1974 (c.40)
1974 c.39	=	The Consumer Credit Act 1974 (c.39)
1975 c.21	=	The Criminal Procedure (Scotland) Act 1975 (c.21)
1980	=	The Local Government, Planning and Land Act 1980 (c.65)
1980 c.43	=	The Magistrates' Courts Act 1980 (c.43)
1984 c.55	=	The Building Act 1984 (c.55)
1987 c.26	=	The Housing (Scotland) Act 1987 (c.26)
1989	=	The Control of Smoke Pollution Act 1989 (c.17)
1989 c.29	=	The Electricity Act 1989 (c.29)
1990	=	The Environmental Protection Act 1990 (c.43)
S.I. 1974/2170	=	The Clean Air Enactments (Repeals and Modifications) Regulations 1974 (S.I. 1974/2170)
S.I. 1992/36	=	The Clean Air (Units of Measurement) Regulations 1992 (S.I. 1992/36)
R (followed by a number)	=	The recommendation set out in the paragraph of that number in the Appendix to the Report of the Law Commission and the Scottish Law Commission (Cm 2085).

2. Certain functions of the Minister of Housing and Local Government were transferred to the Secretary of State for Wales by the Secretary of State for Wales and Minister of Land and Natural Resources Order 1965 (S.I. 1965/319, Article 2(1), Schedule 1) and the remaining functions of that Minister were transferred to the Secretary of State by the Secretary of State for the Environment Order 1970 (S.I. 1970/1681, Article 2(1)). References to "the Minister" and "the appropriate Minister" in the Clean Air Acts 1956 and 1968 are therefore reproduced in the Bill as references to the Secretary of State.

3. Fines for summary offences under the enactments being consolidated (other than fines relating to continuing offences) were increased by the Criminal Justice Act 1982 (c.48) section 38(6), (8) and (9) and section 289F of the Criminal Procedure (Scotland) Act 1975 (c.21). In relation to summary offences all references in the enactments being consolidated to fines of specified amounts (other than those relating to continuing offences) were converted by section 46(1) of the Criminal Justice Act 1982 and section 289G(4) of the Criminal Procedure (Scotland) Act 1975 to references to fines at the corresponding level on the standard scale of fines for summary offences introduced by section 37 of the Criminal Justice Act 1982 and section 289G of the Criminal Procedure (Scotland) Act 1975. All references in the Bill to a fine of a specified level on the standard scale are derived from the operation of the enactments mentioned above.

Provision	*Derivation*
1(1)	1956 s.1(1)
(2)	1956 s.1(4)
(3)	1956 s.1(2)
(4)	1956 s.1(3)
(5)	1956 s.27(1); 1974 Sch. 2, para. 19(1)
(6)	1956 s.1(1)
2(1)	1968 s.1(1); 1989 s.2(1)
(2)	1968 s.1(2), (3)
(3)	1968 s.1(1A); 1989 s.2(2)
(4)	1968 s.1(4)
(5)	1968 s.1(1); 1974 Sch. 2, para. 26(a); 1968 s.1(5)
(6)	
(7)	1968 Sch. 1, para. 9
3	1956 s.34(2); 1968 Sch. 1, para. 11
4(1)	1956 s.3(3)
(2)	1956 s.3(1)

Provision	Derivation
4(3)	1956 s.3(2)
(4)	1956 ss.3(1), (3), 27(2), (4); Sch. 2, para. 19(2), (4); R1
(5), (6)	1956 s.3(4), (5)
5(1)	1968 s.2(5)
(2)	1968 s.2(1)
(3)	1968 s.2(2)
(4)	1968 s.2(3)
(5)	1968 s.2(4)
(6)	1968 s.2(2), (4); 1974 Sch. 2, para. 26(b), (c)
6(1), (2)	1968 s.3(1); S.I. 1992/36 reg. 3(3), (4)
(3)	1968 s.3(2)
(4)	1968 s.3(4)
(5)	1968 s.3(3); 1974 Sch. 2, para. 26(d)
7(1), (2)	1968 s.4(1), (2)
(3)–(5)	1968 s.4(4)–(6)
(6)	1968 s.4(7); 1974 Sch. 2, para. 26(e)
8(1)	1956 s.6(1); 1968 s.3(5): S.I. 1992/36 reg. 2(3)
(2)	1956 ss.6(1), 27(4); 1974 Sch. 2, para. 19(4); R1
9(1)	1968 s.3(6)
(2)	1956 s.6(4); 1968 s.3(5), (7)
(3)	1956 s.6(5); 1968 s.3(5)
10(1)	1956 s.7(1); 1968 s.5(1); S.I. 1992/36 reg. 2(4), (5)
(2)	1956 s.7(2), (3); 1968 Sch. 1, para. 2
(3)	1956 s.27(4)
(4)	1968 s.5(7)
(5)	1968 s.5(2)
(6)	1956 s.7(1) proviso
11	1968 s.5(3)–(6); S.I. 1992/36 reg. 3(5), (6)
12(1)	1956 s.8(1); 1968 Sch. 1, para. 3
(2)	1956 ss.8(2), 27(4); 1974 Sch. 2, para. 19(4)
13	1956 s.9; 1968 Sch. 1, para. 4; R2
14(1)	1968 s.6(10)
(2)	1968 s.6(1)
(3)	1968 s.6(1)
(4)	1968 s.6(2)
(5)	1968 s.6(2)
(6)	1968 s.6(1), (2); 1974 Sch. 2, para. 26(f)
(7)	1968 s.6(11)
15(1)	—
(2)–(4)	1968 s.6(4)–(6)
(5), (6)	1968 s.6(7)
(7), (8)	1968 s.6(8), (9)
(9)	1968 s.6(11)
16(1)	1956 s.10(1); 1961 Sch. 1, Pt. III; 1963 Sch. 11, Part I, para. 31; 1968 s.6(12)
(2)	1956 s.10(1)
(3)	1956 s.10(2), (3); 1984 c.55 Sch. 6, para. 5
(4)	1956 s.10(3)
(5)	1956 s.10(5); 1970 c.38 Sch. 1, Pt. II, para. 5; 1973 c.65 Sch. 15, para. 28

Provision	Derivation
17	1956 s.16(1), (3); 1968 Sch. 1, para. 5; 1989 s.1
18(1)	1956 s.11(1)
(2)	1956 ss.11(3), 11(10) proviso
(3), (4)	1956 s.11(5), (6)
19	1968 s.8(1) to (6)
20(1)	1956 s.11(2)
(2)	1956 s.11(10)
(3)(a)	1956 s.11(2)
(3)(b)	drafting
(4)	1956 s.11(2) proviso
(5)	1956 s.27(2); 1974 Sch. 2, para. 19(2)
(6)	1956 s.34(1)
21	1956 s.11(4)
22(1)	1956 s.11(7)
(2)	1956 s.11(7) proviso
(3)	1956 s.11(9)
23(1), (2)	1968 s.9(1), (2); 1974 Sch. 2, para. 27
(3)–(5)	1968 s.9(3)–(5)
24(1)–(3)	1956 s.12(2)
(4)	1956 s.12(3); 1987 c.26 Sch. 23, para. 6(1)
25(1)	drafting
(2)	1964 ss.95(1), 108(4)
26	1956 s.15(1), (2); 1980 Sch. 2, para. 2
27(1)	1956 s.14(1); 1964 s.95(9)
(2)	1964 s.95(9)
(3)	1956 s.14(1) proviso
(4)	1956 s.15(3)
28(1)	1956 s.14(2)
(2)	1956 s.14(2); 1974 c.39 Sch.4, Part I, para. 15
(3)	1956 s.15(3)
29	1956 s.34(1); 1974 c.39 Sch. 4, Part I, para. 16
30	1974 s.75; The Departments (Northern Ireland) Order 1982 (S.I. 1982/846 (N.I. 11))
31	1974 s.76; 1990 Sch. 15, para. 15(6)
32(1)	1974 ss.75(3)(b), 76(3)(c)
(2)–(4)	1974 s.77; 1975 c.21 s.289B(1); 1980 c.43 s.32(2)
33	1974 s.78; S.I. 1974/2170 reg. 10; 1990 Sch. 15, para. 15(7)
34(1)	1956 s.25; 1974 s.79(1)
(2)–(4)	1974 s.79(5)–(7)
35(1)–(3)	1974 ss.79(2)–(4), 84(1) (definition of "private dwelling"), 105(1) (definition of "notice"); 1990 Sch. 15, para. 15(8)
(4), (5)	1974 s.79(8)
(6)	1974 s.79(9)
36	1974 ss.80, 84(1) (definition of "private dwelling"), 105(1) (definitions of "notice" and "regulations"); 1990 Sch. 15, para. 15(9)
37	1974 s.81
38	1974 s.82
39	1974 s.83
40(a), (b)	1974 s.84(2), (3)
41	1956 s.16A; 1968 s.11A; 1990 Sch. 15, paras. 6, 12

Provision	Derivation
42(1), (2)	1956 s.18(1)
(3)	1956 ss.18(1), 27(4) proviso; 1974 Sch. 2, para. 19(4)
(4)	1956 s.18(2); 1968 Sch. 1, para. 1; 1990 Sch. 15, para. 7(1)
(5)	1956 s.18(5); 1990 Sch. 15, para. 7(2)
(6)	1956 s.18(4)
43(1), (2)	1956 s.19(1)
(3)	1956 s.19(2)
(4)	1956 s.27(4); 1974 Sch. 2, para. 19(3)
(5)	1956 s.19(3); 1968 Sch. 1, para. 1
44(1), (2)	1956 s.20(1); 27(1)
(3)	1956 s.20(2)
(4), (5)	1956 s.20(3)
(6)	1956 s.20(4); 1968 Sch. 1, para. 1
45(1)	1956 s.21(1); 1968 Sch. 1, para. 6; 1990 Sch. 15, para. 7(3)
(2)	1956 s.21(2)
46	1956 s.22; Defence (Transfer of Functions) (No. 1) Order 1964 (S.I. 1964/488) Sch. 1, Part I; 1968 Sch. 1, para. 1
47	1968 ss.7, 7A; 1990 s.85
48	1974 s.102(1)
49	1956 ss.26, 27(3); 1968 Sch. 1, para. 1; 1974 s.94, Sch. 2, para. 19(3); R3
50(1)	1956 s.27(4); 1974 Sch. 2, para. 19(4)
(2)	1956 s.27(4) proviso; 1974, Sch. 2, para. 19(4)
(3)	1936 s.297; 1956 s.31, Sch. 3, para. 2
51(1), (2)	1956 s.30(1); 1968 Sch. 1, para. 9; 1974 Sch. 3, para. 16(1)
(3)	1956 s.30(2); 1968, Sch. 1, para. 9; 1974, Sch. 3, para. 16(2)
52	1974 s.87(1); R4
53	1974 s.87(2); R4
54	1956 s.28; 1968 Sch. 1, para. 1
55(1)	1956 s.29(1); 1961 Sch. 1, Part III; 1968 Sch. 1, para. 1; R5
(2)	1956 s.29(2); 1968 Sch. 1, para. 8
(3)	1956 s.29(3); 1968 Sch. 1, para. 1
56	1897 s.18; 1936 s.287; 1956 s.31(1), Sch. 3, para. 1, Part III; 1974 s.91; R6
57	1897 s.18; 1936 ss.287(3), 288; 1956 s.31(1); 1974 s.92; R6
58	1974 s.93
59	1936 s.318; 1956 s.31(1); 1974 s.96; R7
60	1936 ss.322, 324, 325; 1956 s.31(1); 1968 s.8(7); 1974 s.97; R8
61	1956 s.31(1), (3), (4), (6); 1968 Sch. 1, para. 1; R9
62(1)	1956 s.31(1); 1968 Sch. 1, para. 1
(2)	1956 s.31(7), Sch. 3, Part III; 1968 Sch. 1, para. 1; 1987 c.26 Sch. 23, para. 6(2), (3)
63(1)	1956 s.33(1); 1968 s.12(1); R10
(2)	1956 s.33(1); 1968 s.12(2)
(3)	1956 s.33(1)
64(1)	1936 s.343(1); 1956 ss.31(1), 34(1); 1961 Sch. 1, Part III; 1968 s.13(1), Sch. 1, para. 10; 1972 c.70 s.180(1), (3)(f); 1973 c.65 Sch. 27, Part II, para. 128; 1974 s.84(1); S.I. 1992/36 regs. 2(2), 3(2); R11
(2)	1956 s.34(3)
(3)	1968 s.13(2)
(4)	1956 s.34(4); 1974 ss.30(1), 84(1), R12
(5)	1956 s.34(6)

Provision	Derivation
64(6)	1956 s.34(7); 1968 Sch. 1, para. 12
65	1974 s.107
66	1956 s.17
67	—
68(1), (2)	—
(3)	1956 s.36; 1968 s.15(6)
Sch. 1	1956 Sch. 1; 1980 Sch. 2, para. 5
Sch. 2	
para. 1(1)–(4)	1956 s.12(1); 1980 Sch. 2, para. 2
(5), (6)	1964 ss.95(4)(a), 108(4)
para. 2	1964 s.95(2)
para. 3(1), (2)	1964 s.95(2); 1968 s.10(5)
(3)	1964 s.95(3), (10)(b)
(4)	1964 s.95(4)(b)
(5)	1964 s.95(2), (3)
para. 4(1)	1956 s.13(1)
(2)	1956 s.13(2); 1964 s.95(7), (8)
(3)	1964 s.95(7)
Sch. 3, Part I	
para. 1	1968 s.11(6), (7)
paras. 2, 3	1968 s.11(1), (3)
para. 4	1968 s.11(3)
para. 5	1968 s.11(4)
para. 6	1956 s.29(1), proviso para. (a)
Part II	
para. 7	1974 s.76(4)(a)
para. 8	1974 s.78(1)
para. 9	1974 s.79(4)
para. 10	1974 s.80(3)
para. 11	1974 s.84(1)
Sch. 4	—
Sch. 5 Part I	—
paras. 1–5	
Part II para. 6(1)	1968 s.3(4); Clean Air Act 1968 (Commencement No. 2) Order 1969 (S.I. 1969/995); Clean Air Act 1968 (Commencement No. 2) (Scotland) Order 1969 (S.I. 1969/1006)
(2), (3)	1956 s.6(2); Clean Air Act 1956 (Appointed Day) Order 1958 (S.I. 1958/167); Clean Air Act 1956 (Appointed Day No. 2) (Scotland) Order 1958 (S.I. 1958/1931)
para. 7	1968 s.6(10); Clean Air Act 1968 (Commencement No. 1) Order 1968 (S.I. 1968/1922); Clean Air Act 1968 (Commencement No. 1) (Scotland) Order 1968 (S.I. 1968/1941)
paras. 8, 9	1980 Sch. 2, paras. 2(b) and 5(b)
para. 10	1956 s.18(3)
Part III	1956 Sch. 1 as originally enacted; 1968 s.10(1), (2), (4)
Sch. 6	—

TABLE OF DESTINATIONS

TABLE OF DESTINATIONS

CLEAN AIR ACT 1956 (APPOINTED DAY) ORDER 1958
(S.I. 1958 No. 167)

S.I. 1958 No.

167	1993
	Sched. 5,
	Pt. II,
	paras.
	6(2), (3)

CLEAN AIR ACT 1956 (APPOINTED DAY NO. 2) (SCOTLAND) ORDER 1958
(S.I. 1958 No. 1931)

S.I. 1958 No.

1931	1993
	Sched. 5,
	Pt. II,
	paras.
	6(2), (3)

PUBLIC HEALTH ACT 1961
c.64

1961	1993
Sched. 1,	
Pt. III	ss.16(1),
	55(1), 64(1)

LONDON GOVERNMENT ACT 1963
c.33

1963	1993
Sched. 11,	
Pt. I,	
para. 31	s.16(1)

HOUSING ACT 1964
c.56

1964	1993	1964	1993	1964	1993
s.95(1)	s.25(2)	s.95(4)(b)	Sched. 2,	s.95(10)(b)	Sched. 2,
(2)	Sched. 2,		para. 3(4)		para. 3(3)
	paras. 2,	(7)	Sched. 2,	107	65
	3(1), (2), (5)		paras.	108(4)	25(2),
(3)	Sched. 2,		4(2), (3)		Sched. 2,
	paras.	(8)	Sched. 2,		paras. 1(5),
	3(3), (5)		para. 4(2)	(6)	
(4)(a)	Sched. 2,	(9)	27(1), (2)		
	para. 1(5),				
	(6)				

DEFENCE (TRANSFER OF FUNCTIONS) (NO. 1) ORDER 1964
(S.I. 1964 No. 488)

S.I. 1964 No.

488	1993
Sched. 1,	
Pt. I	s.46

CLEAN AIR ACT 1968
c.62

CLEAN AIR ACT 1968 (COMMENCEMENT NO. 1) ORDER 1968
(S.I. 1968 NO. 1922)

CLEAN AIR ACT 1968 (COMMENCEMENT NO. 1) (SCOTLAND) ORDER 1968
(S.I. 1968 NO. 1941)

CLEAN AIR ACT 1968 (COMMENCEMENT NO. 2) ORDER 1969
(S.I. 1969 NO. 995)

TABLE OF DESTINATIONS

1974	1993
s.83 . . . . s.39	
84(1).	35(1)–(3),
	36, 64(1), (4)
	Sched. 3,
	Pt. II,
	para. 11
(2).	40(a)(b)
(3).	40(a)(b)
87(1).	52
(2).	53
91	56
92	57

1974	1993
s.93	s.58
94	49
96	59
97	60
102(1).	48
105(1).	35(1)–(3), 36
Sched. 2,	
para. 19(1) . .	1(5)
(2) . .	4(4), 20(5)
para. 19(3) . .	43(4), 49
(4) . .	4(4), 8(2),
	12(2), 42(3),
	50(1), (2)

1974	1993
Sched. 2—*cont.*	
para. 26(a) . .	s.2(5)
(b)(c) .	5(6)
(d) . .	6(5)
(e) . .	7(6)
(f) . . .	14(6)
27	23(1), (2)
Sched. 3,	
para. 16(1) . .	51(1), (2)
(2) . .	51(3)

CLEAN AIR ENACTMENTS (REPEALS AND MODIFICATIONS) REGULATIONS 1974
(S.I. 1974 No. 2170)

S.I. 1974 No. 2170	1993
reg. 10	s.33

CRIMINAL PROCEDURE (SCOTLAND) ACT 1975
c.21

1975	1993
s.289B(1)	s.32(2)–(4)

MAGISTRATES' COURTS ACT 1980
c.43

1980	1993
s.32(2).	s.32(2)–(4)
Sched. 2,	
para. 2	26, Sched. 2,
	para. 1(4)
(b) . . .	Sched. 5,
	Pt. II,
	paras. 8, 9
5	Sched. 1
(b) . . .	Sched. 5,
	Pt. II,
	paras. 8, 9

DEPARTMENTS (NORTHERN IRELAND) ORDER 1982
(S.I. 1982 No. 846 (N.I. 11))

S.I. 1982 No. 846	1993
	s.30

BUILDING ACT 1984
c.55

1984	1993
Sched. 6,	
para. 5	s.16(3)

TABLE OF DESTINATIONS

HOUSING (SCOTLAND) ACT 1987
c.26

1987	1993
Sched. 23,	
para. 6(1) . . .	s.24(4)
(2) . . .	62(2)
(3) . . .	62(2)

CONTROL OF SMOKE POLLUTION ACT 1989
c.17

1989	1993
s.1	s.17
2(1).	2(1)
(2).	2(3)

ENVIRONMENTAL PROTECTION ACT 1990
c.43

1990	1993
s.85	s.47
Sched. 15,	
para. 6	41
7(1) . . .	42(4)
(2) . . .	42(5)
(3) . . .	45(1)
12.	41
15(6) . .	31
(7) . .	33
(8) . .	35(1)–(3)
(9) . .	36

CLEAN AIR (UNITS OF MEASUREMENT) REGULATIONS 1992
(S.I. 1992 No. 36)

S.I. 1992 No.	
36	1993
reg. 2(2)	s.64(1)
(3)	8(1)
(4)	10(1)
(5)	10(1)
3(2)	64(1)
(3)	6(1), (2)
(4)	6(1), (2)
(5)	11
(6)	11

REPORT OF THE LAW COMMISSION AND THE SCOTTISH LAW COMMISSION
CM 2085

Cm. 2085	1993
R1	ss.4(4), 8(2)
R2	13
R3	49
R4	52, 53
R5	55(1)
R6	56, 57
R7	59
R8	60
R9	61
R10	63(1)
R11	64(1)
R12	64(4)

INDEX

References are to sections

RADIOACTIVE SUBSTANCES ACT 1993*

(1993 c. 12)

[A table showing the derivation of the provisions of this consolidation will be found at the end of this Act. The table has no official status.]

ARRANGEMENT OF SECTIONS

Preliminary

---

* Annotations by Gillian Irvine, Solicitor in Environmental Law Department of Simmons & Simmons.

An Act to consolidate certain enactments relating to radioactive substances with corrections and minor improvements made under the Consolidation of Enactments (Procedure) Act 1949. [27th May 1993]

PARLIAMENTARY DEBATES
Hansard, H.L. Vol. 543, col. 343; H.C. Vol. 223, col. 284.
As a consolidating measure the majority of readings were formal with no debate.

INTRODUCTION AND GENERAL NOTE

This Act is a consolidation of the Radioactive Substances Act 1960 which had been heavily amended in recent years and in particular by the Environmental Protection Act 1990. The Department of Environment felt that the previously existing structure of radioactive substances regulation would benefit from re-arrangement and also from the repeal of the now defunct provisions of the Radioactive Substances Act 1948.

The purpose of the consolidation was to restructure the provisions of the RSA 1960 in such a way as to better reflect and clarify Parliament's original intentions. As with all consolidations, no substantive amendments were introduced during the passage of the new 1993 Act through the Houses of Parliament and therefore no change to the law on radioactive substances has been made.

A Guide to the Administration of the Radioactive Substances Act 1960

This was published by the DoE, the Scottish Development Office, the Department of the Environment for Northern Ireland and the Welsh Office in 1982. Although somewhat confusingly the section numbers have been changed by the consolidation, the basic principles are still the same. Although some care must be taken in referring to this circular, as additional provisions in relation to enforcement and regulation have been introduced in recent years, a copy of the Guide is reproduced as Appendix 1.

The original motivation to introduce the Radioactive Substances Act 1960 came out of a report produced by an expert panel appointed by the Radioactive Substances Advisory Committee in 1956. That report, which concluded that the then existing laws on the regulation of radioactive substances would benefit from strengthening, was published in a White Paper "*The Control of Radioactive Waste*" Comm. 884. It is the recommendations and objectives set out in that report that are now contained in the legislation with additions made by the Environmental Protection Act 1990.

The 1993 Act regulates the keeping and using of radioactive materials as well as regulating the emotive matters of disposal and accumulation of radioactive waste.

Registration of Premises

Any person who keeps or uses radioactive material on premises used for the purpose of an undertaking must either be registered or subject to an exemption under the provisions of the Act (s.6).

Applications for registration are made to the chief inspector (Her Majesty's Inspectorate of Pollution in England and Wales, Her Majesty's Industrial Pollution Inspectorate in Scotland and the Alkali and Radiochemical Inspectorate in Northern Ireland). Application forms can be obtained from HMIP. Applications have to contain specified information and be accompanied by a fee (s.7). Copies of applications are sent to the local authority unless the circulation of an application has been restricted by the Secretary of State for reasons of national security (s.25).

The chief inspector may either refuse to grant a registration or grant one (which may be subject to conditions and limitations). When setting conditions or limitations the chief inspector must have regard only "to the amount and character of the radioactive waste likely to arise from the keeping or use of the radioactive material on the premises in question" (s.7(7)). Conditions and limitations may deal with the structure of premises, apparatus, equipment or appliances relating to the use of radioactive material. Additional conditions may require the production of information on the movement of radioactive material, or prohibit the sale of incorrectly labelled radioactive material.

Premises covered by available exemptions include those which are subject to a nuclear site licence (granted under the Nuclear Installations Act 1965) and premises on which clocks and watches which contain radioactive material are kept or used (although this exemption does not extend to premises on which clocks or watches are manufactured or repaired by processes involving the use of luminous material). Other exemptions are set out in statutory orders and include a wide range of low activity radioactive materials (see the General Note to s.7).

Registration of Mobile Radioactive Apparatus

In addition to the registration of premises, special provisions are made for mobile radioactive apparatus. Such equipment must be registered wherever it might be kept, used, lent or hired, unless such use is covered by an exemption (s.9).

The provisions on applications and the powers of the chief inspector for registering mobile radioactive apparatus are very similar to those for registering of premises, although the chief inspector may impose any limitations and conditions that he thinks fit (s.10). A registration of mobile radioactive apparatus is only valid in the country in which it was issued.

Exemptions from the necessity to register mobile radioactive apparatus are to be set out in statutory instruments; of which to date there have been none (s.11).

Cancellation of Variation of Registrations

The chief inspector may cancel or vary any registrations made in respect of premises or mobile radioactive apparatus at any time (s.12). Such cancellation or variation is subject to a right of appeal (s.26).

Authorisation of Disposal or Accumulation

It is useful to distinguish between "disposal" and "storage". Storage of radioactive waste is where the material is placed at a facility (either engineered or natural) with the intention of action being taken at a later time for its subsequent disposal. That later action may involve the retrieval of the substances, its in-site treatment or a declaration that no further action is needed and that the storage has, in the event, become disposal.

The disposal of radioactive waste is the dispersal of the waste into an environmental medium or placement in a facility with the intention of taking no further action apart from some possible monitoring for technical or reassurance purposes. In the U.K. it is only low-level waste such as that produced by hospitals, research facilities and industry, etc., *e.g.*, contaminated packaging, gloves, rags, glass, small tools, paper, filters and effluents which may be disposed of by way of incineration, landfill or discharge to sewers. Intermediate level waste and high level waste are generally accumulated in long-term storage facilities at Drigg, Cumbria.

The disposal (on land, into water or by discharge into the atmosphere) of any radioactive waste, on or from any premises is prohibited unless it is authorised by the chief inspector or is exempted under the Act (s.13). A similar prohibition applies to the disposal of any radioactive waste from mobile radioactive apparatus or the receipt of radioactive waste for the purpose of its disposal.

The exemptions cover premises with a nuclear site licence, the disposal of any radioactive waste arising from clocks and watches (on a similar basis as for registration) and others as set out in statutory instruments (see the General Note to s.15).

The accumulation of radioactive waste with a view to its subsequent disposal is also prohibited unless it is either authorised by the chief inspector or exempted (s.14). The exemption provisions are as for the disposal of radioactive waste (s.15).

Applications for both authorisation for disposal or accumulation are made to the chief inspector (s.16). However, where the disposal of radioactive waste is on or from a nuclear site, the power to authorise resides with the chief inspector and the appropriate Minister jointly. (For England, the appropriate Minister is the Minister of Agriculture, Fisheries and Food and for Wales and Scotland the responsibility is solely that of the Secretaries of State for Wales and Scotland respectively. In relation to Northern Ireland, the responsibility falls to the Department of the Environment for Northern Ireland and the Department of Agriculture (Northern Ireland) jointly).

As for registration, authorisation may be granted or refused. Where granted, the authorisation may be subject to such limitations or conditions as the chief inspector (or chief inspector and appropriate Minister) may think fit. Copies of applications will be sent to the local authority except where there are overriding issues of national security (s.25).

For the disposal of radioactive waste only, before an application is refused, limitations or conditions imposed or an authorisation varied or revoked, there is a right to a hearing (s.28). Additionally, local authorities and other appropriate persons may be given the opportunity of a hearing. (For discussion of this provision see the General Note to s.28).

The chief inspector may vary or revoke any authorisations for disposal or accumulation of radioactive waste in which case there is a right of appeal (s.17).

Central Control

The control of radioactive materials is a central and not a local government function. Local bodies are specifically prohibited from taking account of radioactivity when exercising their functions under public health and clean air legislation as enumerated in Sched. 3, or local enactments dealing with nuisances, pollution and waste discharges. However, the non-radioactive aspects of any substances must still be dealt with. For example, the discharge of waste effluent to a sewer must be properly authorised under the Water Industry Act 1991, regardless of whether or not it is radioactive. Where the chief inspector believes that the disposal of radioactive waste is likely to involve the need for any special precautions to be taken, he will consult with relevant authorities, including any local or water authorities, who would have to take special precautions, before the authority to dispose of waste is granted. Only where special precautions are necessary can the authority in question make a charge (s.18).

The Secretary of State can give directions to the chief inspector on the conduct of any applications or in relation to any registration or authorisation granted (ss.23 and 24).

Where the Secretary of State believes that inadequate provisions for the safe disposal or accumulation of radioactive waste are not available, he may arrange for such facilities to be provided. The Secretary of State may then make a charge for their use. The site at Drigg near Sellafield has been provided pursuant to this power. That site is owned and operated by British Nuclear Fuels Limited and is used for the disposal of solid waste which is considered unsuitable for special precaution tipping at a landfill site (s.29).

On a similar note, the Secretary of State has the power to dispose of radioactive waste where the premises on which it is are unoccupied or the occupier is absent or insolvent or for some other reason, and it is unlikely that the waste would be lawfully disposed of unless he intervened. The Secretary of State may recover his reasonably incurred costs from the occupier or owner of the premises (s.30).

Posting of Certificates

A copy of any certificate of registration or authorisation must be displayed at the appropriate premises (s.19). The chief inspector can require a registered or authorised person to retain and produce on request site and disposal documentation (s.20).

Enforcement and Prohibition Notices

The chief inspector can issue enforcement or prohibition notices in relation to any registration or authorisation.

The chief inspector may consider issuing an enforcement notice where there is either an actual or likely failure to comply with the conditions and limitations of an authorisation or registration.

Prohibition notices may be used where the continuation of an authorised or registered activity involves an imminent risk of pollution of the environment or of harm to human health. There is no pre-requisite to the service of such notice of non-compliance with any limitation or conditions. Prohibition notices are likely to be used in the event of an unauthorised or unusual happening.

When either a prohibition or enforcement notice has been served there is a right to a hearing (s.28).

Criminal Offences

The Act creates a number of criminal offences arising out of failure to obtain authorisations and registrations as well as other provisions of the Act (ss.32–37).

Rights of Entry

The Secretary of State appoints the chief inspector and inspectors to assist him. These inspectors are given extensive rights of entry to premises at any reasonable time for testing and inspecting, etc., for the purposes of enforcing a registration or authorisation (s.31).

Record Keeping

The chief inspector must keep copies of applications as well as documents issued by him or sent by him to local authorities. Additionally, he must keep a record of convictions under the Act (s.39). The chief inspector must send documentation to local authorities and those documents are to be made available to the public (s.39). (See DoE circulars 22/92 and 21/90 at Appendices 2 and 3).

The Crown

The Crown is generally bound by the Act (s.42). However, the Act does not apply to premises occupied for military or defence purposes, by Her Majesty in her personal capacity or by visiting forces. The Crown cannot be held criminally liable for an infringement of the Act, but the courts can make a declaration that an unlawful act or omission has been committed. Additionally, the Secretary of State may suspend the powers of entry available to chief inspectors in relation to Crown premises for reasons of national security.

Other Controls

Nuclear installations in the U.K. are regulated by the Nuclear Installations Act 1965. This Act provides for their licensing and inspection with a view to ensuring the maximum possible safety in their construction and operation. That Act also provides that where injury or damage results from the emission of ionising radiation from or in connection with a nuclear site, compensation is available.

The transportation by road of radioactive material is regulated by the Radioactive Material (Road Transport) Act 1991 and its attendant Regulations. That Act makes provision for the consignment and carriage of radioactive material in Great Britain and imposes strict requirements on the transportation of such material which are enforced by criminal sanctions, etc.

ABBREVIATIONS

the Act	:	The Radioactive Substances Act 1993
DoE	:	Department of the Environment
EPA 1990	:	Environmental Protection Act 1990
HMIP	:	Her Majesty's Inspectorate of Pollution
HMIPI	:	Her Majesty's Industrial Pollution Inspectorate
MAFF	:	Ministry of Agriculture, Fisheries and Food
MOD	:	Ministry of Defence
RSA 1960	:	Radioactive Substances Act 1960

Preliminary

Meaning of "radioactive material".

1.—(1) In this Act "radioactive material" means anything which, not being waste, is either a substance to which this subsection applies or an article made wholly or partly from, or incorporating, such a substance.

(2) Subsection (1) applies to any substance falling within either or both of the following descriptions, that is to say,—

    (a) a substance containing an element specified in the first column of Schedule 1, in such a proportion that the number of becquerels of that element contained in the substance, divided by the number of grams which the substance weighs, is a number greater than that specified in relation to that element in the appropriate column of that Schedule;

    (b) a substance possessing radioactivity which is wholly or partly attributable to a process of nuclear fission or other process of subjecting a substance to bombardment by neutrons or to ionising radiations, not being a process occurring in the course of nature, or in consequence of the disposal of radioactive waste, or by way of contamination in the course of the application of a process to some other substance.

(3) In subsection (2)(a) "the appropriate column"—

    (a) in relation to a solid substance, means the second column,

    (b) in relation to a liquid substance, means the third column, and

    (c) in relation to a substance which is a gas or vapour, means the fourth column.

(4) For the purposes of subsection (2)(b), a substance shall not be treated as radioactive material if the level of radioactivity is less than such level as may be prescribed for substances of that description.

(5) The Secretary of State may by order vary the provisions of Schedule 1, either by adding further entries to any column of that Schedule or by altering or deleting any entry for the time being contained in any column.

(6) In the application of this section to Northern Ireland, the reference in subsection (5) to the Secretary of State shall have effect as a reference to the Department of the Environment for Northern Ireland.

Definitions
    "article": s.47(1).
    "contamination": s.47(1).
    "prescribed": s.47(1).
    "substance": s.47(1).
    "waste": s.47(1).

General Note
    This definition of "radioactive material" is a reproduction of the definition within s.18 of the RSA 1960 except that the original reference to microcuries has been replaced with its metric equivalent, the becquerel. The Units of Measurement Regulations 1986 (S.I. 1986 No. 1082) were made pursuant to s.2(2) of the European Communities Act 1972 and set out the becquerel as the only unit of radiation authorised for any "specified circumstances" as defined in those Regulations. There are 37,000 becquerels to a microcurie and the amount set out in Sched. 1 represents an exact conversion.

Subs. (4)
    This subsection originated in the EPA 1990 and no substances have yet been prescribed as exempt from the definition of "radioactive material".

Subs. (5)
    The Secretary of State is empowered to change the parameters of what constitutes radioactive material, but to date no order has been made.

Meaning of "radioactive waste"

2. In this Act "radioactive waste" means waste which consists wholly or partly of—
  (a) a substance or article which, if it were not waste, would be radioactive material, or
  (b) a substance or article which has been contaminated in the course of the production, keeping or use of radioactive material, or by contact with or proximity to other waste falling within paragraph (a) or this paragraph.

DEFINITIONS
  "article": s.47(1).
  "contaminated": s.47(5).
  "radioactive material": s.1.
  "substance": s.47(1).
  "waste": s.47(1) and (4).

GENERAL NOTE
  The meaning of "waste" is considered in s.47(1) where it is given a wide interpretation and is to be judged largely by reference to the state of mind of the person discarding or wishing to dispose of the substance or material. In the case of *Berridge Incinerators* v. *Nottinghamshire County Council High Court*, 1987, unreported but cited at para. 2.7 of DoE Circular 13/88 on the *Collection and Disposal of Waste Regulations*, it was held by Deputy Judge P.J. Crawford, Q.C. that:
  "It is of course, a truism that one man's waste is another man's raw material. The fact that a price is paid by the collector of the material to its originator is, no doubt, relevant, but I do not regard it as crucial. If I have an old fireplace to dispose of to a passing rag and bone man, its character as waste is not affected by whether or not I can persuade the latter to pay me 50p for it. In my judgment, the correct approach is to regard the material from the point of view of the person who produces it. Is it something which is produced as a product, or even as a by-product of his business, or is it something to be disposed of as useless?"
  Circular 13/88 goes on to suggest, in the light of this decision, that disposal authorities may find it helpful to consider four questions from the point of view of the person producing the material when considering whether any particular material is waste: (a) Is it what would ordinarily be described as waste?; (b) Is the substance a scrap metal, effluent or other unwanted surplus?; (c) Is the substance or article required to be disposed of broken, worn out, contaminated or otherwise spoiled?; (d) Is the material being discarded or dealt with as if it were waste?
  The Circular suggests that an answer of "yes" to any of these questions indicates that the material is waste. This is consistent with the definition of "waste" given at s.47(1) and (4).
  Thus "radioactive waste" includes any scrap, surplus or spoiled "radioactive material" (as defined in s.1) and any other waste substance or article which has become radioactive or has acquired an increased concentration of radioactivity by any means.
  It should also be noted that radioactive waste is not a "controlled" waste for the purposes of Pt. II of the EPA 1990 (s.75 of that Act).

Meaning of "mobile radioactive apparatus"

3. In this Act "mobile radioactive apparatus" means any apparatus, equipment, appliance or other thing which is radioactive material and—
  (a) is constructed or adapted for being transported from place to place, or
  (b) is portable and designed or intended to be used for releasing radioactive material into the environment or introducing it into organisms.

DEFINITIONS
  "radioactive material": s.1.

GENERAL NOTE
  This definition was recast by the EPA 1990 to include plant which is mobile and designed for either releasing radioactive material into the environment or introducing it into organisms.

Constructed or Adapted

It is generally considered that this phrase "constructed or adapted" means originally constructed or subsequently altered so as to make suitable, see: *Hubbard* v. *Messenger* (1938) 1 K.B. 300 and *Davison* v. *Birmingham Industrial Co-operative Society* [1920] 90 LJKB 206.

Inspectors and chief inspector

Inspectors and chief inspector appointed by Secretary of State

4.—(1) The Secretary of State may appoint as inspectors, to assist him in the execution of this Act, such number of persons appearing to him to be qualified for the purpose as he may from time to time consider necessary or expedient.

(2) For the purposes of this Act the Secretary of State shall—

(a) appoint one of those inspectors to be chief inspector for England and Wales, and

(b) appoint one of them to be chief inspector for Scotland.

(3) A person may be appointed both as an inspector or as chief inspector under this section and as an inspector or as chief inspector under section 16 of the Environmental Protection Act 1990.

(4) The chief inspector may, to any extent, delegate his functions under this Act to any other inspector appointed under this section.

(5) The Secretary of State may make to or in respect of any person appointed by him under this section such payments, by way of remuneration, allowances or otherwise, as he may, with the approval of the Treasury, determine.

(6) In England and Wales, an inspector appointed under this section, if authorised to do so by the chief inspector, may, although not of counsel or a solicitor, prosecute before a magistrates' court proceedings for an offence under this Act.

(7) In the application of this section to Northern Ireland—

(a) references to the Secretary of State shall have effect as references to the Department of the Environment for Northern Ireland,

(b) the reference in subsection (5) to the Treasury shall have effect as a reference to the Department of Finance and Personnel in Northern Ireland,

(c) the reference in subsection (3) to section 16 of the Environmental Protection Act 1990 shall have effect as a reference to section 10 of the Alkali, &c. Works Regulation Act 1906,

(d) subsections (2) and (6) shall not apply;

and the Department of the Environment for Northern Ireland shall appoint one of the inspectors appointed by it under subsection (1) to be the chief inspector for Northern Ireland.

DEFINITIONS

"chief inspector": s.47(1).

GENERAL NOTE

This provision was introduced into the regulation of radioactive substances by the EPA 1990. It gives the Secretary of State power to appoint inspectors and a chief inspector to assist him in the execution of the Act.

Subs. (3)

Appointees may be inspectors both for the purposes of this Act and for the regulation of integrated pollution control under Part 1 of the EPA 1990. Both functions fall within the general remit of HMIP (or in Scotland HMIPI). Further information on the activities of HMIP in relation to radioactive substances can be found in the Fifth Annual Report for 1991/92. As to the activities and structure of HMIPI, reference may be made to the first report of HMIPI for 1987–88 (HMSO 1990). A further HMIPI report for April 1988–March 1992 is in the process of being prepared and should be available in Autumn 1993.

Subs. (6)

HMIP inspectors in England and Wales are given the power to conduct proceedings in a Magistrates' Court for offences under the Act.

Appointment of inspectors by Minister of Agriculture, Fisheries and Food

5.—(1) For the purposes of the execution of this Act in relation to any premises in England which are situated on a nuclear site, the Minister of Agriculture, Fisheries and Food may appoint as inspectors such number of persons appearing to him to be qualified for the purpose as he may from time to time consider necessary or expedient.

(2) The Minister of Agriculture, Fisheries and Food may make to or in respect of any person appointed by him under this section such payments, by way of remuneration, allowances or otherwise, as he may, with the approval of the Treasury, determine.

(3) This section shall have effect in relation to Northern Ireland as it has effect in relation to England, but with the substitution—

(a) for references to the Minister of Agriculture, Fisheries and Food of references to the Department of Agriculture for Northern Ireland, and

(b) for the reference to the Treasury of a reference to the Department of Finance and Personnel in Northern Ireland.

DEFINITIONS

"nuclear site": s.47(1).
"premises": s.47(1).

GENERAL NOTE

This provision enables the Minister of Agriculture, Fisheries and Food to appoint inspectors in relation to any premises on nuclear sites. Additionally MAFF is empowered to remunerate such persons appointed.

Registration relating to use of radioactive material and mobile radioactive apparatus

Prohibition of use of radioactive material without registration

6. No person shall, on any premises which are used for the purposes of an undertaking carried on by him, keep or use, or cause or permit to be kept or used, radioactive material of any description, knowing or having reasonable grounds for believing it to be radioactive material, unless either—

(a) he is registered under section 7 in respect of those premises and in respect of the keeping and use on those premises of radioactive material of that description, or

(b) he is exempted from registration under that section in respect of those premises and in respect of the keeping and use on those premises of radioactive material of that description, or

(c) the radioactive material in question consists of mobile radioactive apparatus in respect of which a person is registered under section 10 or is exempted from registration under that section.

DEFINITIONS

"mobile radioactive apparatus": s.3.
"premises": s.47(1).
"radioactive material": s.1.
"undertaking": s.47(1).

GENERAL NOTE

It is a criminal offence, pursuant to s.32, to keep or use radioactive material without registration. It is also an offence to cause or permit the keeping or using of radioactive material without the requisite registration. In all cases the offence must be committed with knowledge that or reasonable grounds for belief that the substance in question is radioactive material.

Permit and Cause

The different wording implies distinct offences and to "permit" an offence is generally considered to be a "looser and vaguer" term than to "cause", see *McCleod* v. *Buchanan* [1940] 2 All E.R. 179, 187, *per* Lord Wright and on the differences between "cause" and "permit", see *Shave* v. *Rosner* [1954] 2 Q.B. 113.

The term "cause" does not imply any intention or negligence and its meaning should be approached in an everyday commonsense way, see: *Alphacell* v. *Woodward* [1972] A.C. 824. However, in another water pollution case, *Wychavon District Council* v. *National Rivers Authority, The Independent* (1992) 136 S.J. (L.B.) 260 it was held that a person could only "cause" a discharge of sewage into controlled waters if he took some positive or deliberate act to bring it about. Failure to prevent a discharge was not enough to sustain a conviction. The facts of that case were such that had the appellants been charged with "knowingly permitting" they may well have been convicted. That case was further discussed and approved in *National Rivers Authority* v. *Welsh Development Agency* TLR, December 29, 1992.

However, to "cause" the keeping or use of radioactive material does imply some degree of positive participation or control on the defendant's part, see *McCleod* v. *Buchanan* [1940] 2 All E.R. 179. Somebody can only be said to have "caused" another person to have undertaken a particular course of action when he either knew or deliberately chose not to know what was being done (see *James & Son* v. *Smee*; *Green* v. *Burnett* [1955] 1 Q.B. 78).

To "permit" an act to occur imports the necessity for either express or implied permission for that act. Some knowledge of the facts constituting the offence is necessary to establish permitting, although turning a blind eye to events or allowing a course of action to occur during which the commission of an offence would be likely and not caring whether an offence occurs or not is sufficient (see *James & Son* v. *Smee, ibid.*).

Knowing or Having Reasonable Grounds for Believing

To make out an offence under this section the prosecution must prove that the defendant had the requisite knowledge (see *Gaumont British Distributors Limited* v. *Henry* [1939] 2 K.B. 711). As mentioned above, knowledge may be imputed to the person who turns a blind eye to the obvious (see *James & Son* v. *Smee, ibid.*). Additionally, where a person deliberately does not make enquiries, the results of which he does not wish to know, there is authority that this may constitute in law, actual knowledge of the facts in question (see *Knox* v. *Boyd* [1941] J.C. 82 and *Mallon* v. *Allon* [1964] 1 Q.B. 385, 394).

With regard to the terms "reasonable grounds for believing" case law implies that these words require not only that the person in question has reasonable grounds for believing but that he does also actually believe (see *R.* v. *Banks* [1916] 2 K.B. 621).

For a corporation to be found guilty of an offence under this provision the prosecution must prove that an individual for whom the corporation could be found responsible caused or permitted the commission of an offence with the requisite knowledge. A corporation is generally only liable for senior personnel who could be said to be exercising a "directing mind" over the company's affairs (see *Tesco Supermarkets* v. *Natrass* [1972] A.C. 153 and *R.* v. *Boal (Francis)* [1992] 1 Q.B. 591).

Person

Under s.5 of the Interpretation Act 1978, unless a contrary intention is apparent, the term "person" includes a body of persons incorporate or unincorporate.

Registration of users of radioactive material

7.—(1) Any application for registration under this section shall be made to the chief inspector and shall—

    (a) specify the particulars mentioned in subsection (2),

    (b) contain such other information as may be prescribed, and

    (c) be accompanied by the prescribed fee.

(2) The particulars referred to in subsection (1)(a) are—

    (a) the premises to which the application relates,

    (b) the undertaking for the purposes of which those premises are used,

    (c) the description or descriptions of radioactive material proposed to be kept or used on the premises, and the maximum quantity of radioactive material of each such description likely to be kept or used on the premises at any one time, and

    (d) the manner (if any) in which radioactive material is proposed to be used on the premises.

(3) On any application being made under this section, the chief inspector shall, subject to directions under section 25, send a copy of the application to each local authority in whose area the premises are situated.

(4) Subject to the following provisions of this section, where an application is made to the chief inspector for registration under this section in respect of any premises, the chief inspector may either—

(a) register the applicant in respect of those premises and in respect of the keeping and use on those premises of radioactive material of the description to which the application relates, or

(b) if the application relates to two or more descriptions of radioactive material, register the applicant in respect of those premises and in respect of the keeping and use on those premises of such one or more of those descriptions of radioactive material as may be specified in the registration, or

(c) refuse the application.

(5) An application for registration under this section which is duly made to the chief inspector may be treated by the applicant as having been refused if it is not determined within the prescribed period for determinations or within such longer period as may be agreed with the applicant.

(6) Any registration under this section in respect of any premises may (subject to subsection (7)) be effected subject to such limitations or conditions as the chief inspector thinks fit, and in particular (but without prejudice to the generality of this subsection) may be effected subject to conditions of any of the following descriptions—

(a) conditions imposing requirements (including, if the chief inspector thinks fit, requirements involving structural or other alterations) in respect of any part of the premises, or in respect of any apparatus, equipment or appliance used or to be used on any part of the premises for the purposes of any use of radioactive material from which radioactive waste is likely to arise,

(b) conditions requiring the person to whom the registration relates, at such times and in such manner as may be specified in the registration, to furnish the chief inspector with information as to the removal of radioactive material from those premises to any other premises, and

(c) conditions prohibiting radioactive material from being sold or otherwise supplied from those premises unless it (or the container in which it is supplied) bears a label or other mark—

(i) indicating that it is radioactive material, or

(ii) if the conditions so require, indicating the description of radioactive material to which it belongs,

and (in either case) complying with any relevant requirements specified in the conditions.

(7) In the exercise of any power conferred on him by subsection (4) or (6), the chief inspector, except in determining whether to impose any conditions falling within paragraph (b) or (c) of subsection (6), shall have regard exclusively to the amount and character of the radioactive waste likely to arise from the keeping or use of radioactive material on the premises in question.

(8) On registering a person under this section in respect of any premises, the chief inspector—

(a) shall furnish him with a certificate containing all material particulars of the registration, and

(b) subject to directions under section 25, shall send a copy of the certificate to each local authority in whose area the premises are situated.

DEFINITIONS
"chief inspector": s.4.
"local authority": s.47(1).

"prescribed": s.47(1).
"prescribed period for determination": s.47(1) and (2).
"radioactive material": s.1.
"radioactive waste": s.2.

GENERAL NOTE
This section sets out the provisions relating to the making of an application for a registration for the use or keeping of radioactive material.

Subs. (1)
To date (July 1993) no statutory instrument has been made prescribing further information to be furnished to the chief inspector on an application for registration.
As to the provisions relating to fees payable, see s.43.

Subss. (3) and (8)
Under s.25 the Secretary of State may, on the grounds of national security, restrict the copying of applications and certificates of registration to local authorities.

Subs. (4)
The provisions on appeals against a refusal to grant a registration, a deemed refusal to grant a registration or the imposition of conditions or limitations on a registration are set out in ss.26 and 27.

Subs. (5)
The prescribed period is four months beginning with the day on which the application was received.

Subs. (6)
The types of conditions that a chief inspector may impose upon a registration are set out at subs. (6). It should also be noted that under s.44(2) the Secretary of State is empowered to make regulations setting out general limitations or conditions applicable to registrations. Breach of limitations or conditions is a criminal offence under s.32. The new statutory controls imposed by Pt. I of the EPA 1990 on integrated pollution control and local authority air pollution control raise issues of duplication and overlap with other areas of control. One example is between Pt. I of the EPA 1990 and this Act. Section 28(2) of the EPA 1990 deals with this potential problem by providing that where activities within a prescribed process are regulated by both an authorisation under the EPA 1990 and by registration under this Act, then if different obligations are imposed as respects the same matter those obligations imposed by the EPA 1990 are not binding. Thus, any conditions imposed by this Act are superior to those imposed under the EPA 1990.

Subs. (8)
The certificate provided to the applicant must be posted at the registered premises pursuant to s.19.

Exemptions from registration under s.7

8.—(1) At any time while a nuclear site licence is in force in respect of a site, and at any time after the revocation or surrender of such a licence but before the period of responsibility of the licensee has come to an end, the licensee (subject to subsection (2)) is exempted from registration under section 7 in respect of any premises situated on that site and in respect of the keeping and use on those premises of radioactive material of every description.

(2) Where, in the case of any such premises as are mentioned in subsection (1), it appears to the chief inspector that, if the licensee had been required to apply for registration under section 7 in respect of those premises, the chief inspector would have imposed conditions such as are mentioned in paragraph (b) or (c) of subsection (6) of that section, the chief inspector may direct that the exemption conferred by subsection (1) of this section shall have effect subject to such conditions (being conditions which in the opinion of the chief inspector correspond to those which he would so have imposed) as may be specified in the direction.

(3) On giving a direction under subsection (2) in respect of any premises, the chief inspector shall furnish the licensee with a copy of the direction.

(4) Except as provided by subsection (5), in respect of all premises all persons are exempted from registration under section 7 in respect of the keeping and use on the premises of clocks and watches which are radioactive material.

(5) Subsection (4) does not exempt from registration under section 7 any premises on which clocks or watches are manufactured or repaired by processes involving the use of luminous material.

(6) The Secretary of State may by order grant further exemptions from registration under section 7, by reference to such classes of premises and undertakings, and such descriptions of radioactive material, as may be specified in the order.

(7) Any exemption granted by an order under subsection (6) may be granted subject to such limitations or conditions as may be specified in the order.

(8) In the application of this section to Northern Ireland, the reference in subsection (6) to the Secretary of State shall have effect as a reference to the Department of the Environment for Northern Ireland.

DEFINITIONS
"chief inspector": s.47(1).
"licensee": s.47(1).
"nuclear site licence": s.47(1).
"period of responsibility": s.47(1).
"premises": s.47(1).
"prescribed": s.47(1).
"radioactive material": s.1.
"undertaking": s.47(1).

GENERAL NOTE

Subs. (1)
Premises for which there is an operative nuclear site licence are exempted from the necessity for registration under s.7. Nuclear site licences are issued under the Nuclear Installations Act 1965.

Subs. (2)
If it appears to the chief inspector that s.7 type conditions are necessary at a nuclear site, he may impose such conditions by direction notwithstanding the exemption. Failure to comply with such limitations or conditions imposed is a criminal offence under s.32.

Subs. (6)
The following statutory instruments granting exemptions under this section are currently in force for England and Wales:
(1) The Radioactive Substances (Exhibitions) Exemption Order 1962 (S.I. 1962 No. 2645).
(2) The Radioactive Substances (Storage and Transit) Exemption Order 1962 (S.I. 1962 No. 2646).
(3) The Radioactive Substances (Phosphatic Substances, Rare Earths, etc.) Exemption Order 1962 (S.I. 1962 No. 2648).
(4) The Radioactive Substances (Lead) Exemption Order 1962 (S.I. 1962 No. 2649).
(5) The Radioactive Substances (Uranium and Thorium) Exemption Order 1962 (S.I. 1962 No. 2710).
(6) The Radioactive Substances (Prepared Uranium and Thorium Compounds) Exemption Order 1962 (S.I. 1962 No. 2711).
(7) The Radioactive Substances (Geological Specimens) Exemption Order 1962 (S.I. 1962 No. 2712).
(8) The Radioactive Substances (Schools, etc.) Exemption Order 1963 (S.I. 1963 No. 1832).
(9) The Radioactive Substances (Precipitated Phosphate) Exemption Order 1963 (S.I. 1963 No. 1836).
(10) The Radioactive Substances (Electronic Valves) Exemption Order 1967 (S.I. 1967 No. 1797).

(11) The Radioactive Substances (Smoke Detectors) Exemption Order 1980 (S.I. 1980 No. 953) as amended by S.I. 1991 No. 477.
(12) The Radioactive Substances (Gaseous Tritium Light Devices) Exemption Order 1985 (S.I. 1985 No. 1047).
(13) The Radioactive Substances (Luminous Articles) Exemption Order 1985 (S.I. 1985 No. 1048).
(14) The Radioactive Substances (Testing Instruments) Exemption Order 1985 (S.I. 1985 No. 1049).
(15) The Radioactive Substances (Substances of Low Activity) Exemption Order 1986 (S.I. 1986 No. 1002) as amended by S.I. 1992 No. 647.
(16) The Radioactive Substances (Hospitals) Exemption Order 1990 (S.I. 1990 No. 2512).
Similar orders have been issued in relation to exemptions for Scotland and Northern Ireland.

Prohibition of use of mobile radioactive apparatus without registration

9.—(1) No person shall, for the purpose of any activities to which this section applies—
    (a) keep, use, lend or let on hire mobile radioactive apparatus of any description, or
    (b) cause or permit mobile radioactive apparatus of any description to be kept, used, lent or let on hire,
unless he is registered under section 10 in respect of that apparatus or is exempted from registration under that section in respect of mobile radioactive apparatus of that description.
    (2) This section applies to activities involving the use of the apparatus concerned for—
    (a) testing, measuring or otherwise investigating any of the characteristics of substances or articles, or
    (b) releasing quantities of radioactive material into the environment or introducing such material into organisms.

DEFINITIONS
    "article": s.47(1).
    "chief inspector": s.47(1).
    "mobile radioactive apparatus": s.3.
    "substance": s.47(1).

GENERAL NOTE

Subs. (1)
    Breach of this provision is a criminal offence pursuant to s.32. For further discussion on the components of the crime, see the General Note to s.6.

Person
    As regards the meaning of "person" see further the General Note to s.6.
    For revocation and variation of registrations see s.12.
    For exemptions from registration see s.11.

Registration of mobile radioactive apparatus

10.—(1) Any application for registration under this section shall be made to the chief inspector and—
    (a) shall specify—
        (i) the apparatus to which the application relates, and
        (ii) the manner in which it is proposed to use the apparatus,
    (b) shall contain such other information as may be prescribed, and
    (c) shall be accompanied by the prescribed fee.
    (2) Where an application is made to the chief inspector for registration under this section in respect of any apparatus, the chief inspector may register the applicant in respect of that apparatus, either unconditionally or subject to such limitations or conditions as the chief inspector thinks fit, or may refuse the application.

(3) On any application being made the chief inspector shall, subject to directions under section 25, send a copy of the application to each local authority in whose area it appears to him the apparatus will be kept or will be used for releasing radioactive material into the environment.

(4) An application for registration under this section which is duly made to the chief inspector may be treated by the applicant as having been refused if it is not determined within the prescribed period for determinations or within such longer period as may be agreed with the applicant.

(5) On registering a person under this section in respect of any mobile radioactive apparatus, the chief inspector—

(a) shall furnish him with a certificate containing all material particulars of the registration, and

(b) shall, subject to directions under section 25, send a copy of the certificate to each local authority in whose area it appears to him the apparatus will be kept or will be used for releasing radioactive material into the environment.

DEFINITIONS

"chief inspector": s.47(1).
"mobile radioactive apparatus": s.3.
"prescribed": s.47(1).
"prescribed period for determinations": s.47(1) and (2).

GENERAL NOTE

This section sets out the provisions relating to applications for registration of mobile radioactive apparatus.

Subs. (1)

To date no statutory instrument has been made prescribing further information to be furnished to the chief inspector on an application for a registration.

As to the provision relating to fees payable, see s.43.

Application forms are available from HMIP.

Subs. (2)

The chief inspector has the power to impose conditions on a registration. Additionally, under s.44(2) the Secretary of State is empowered to make regulations setting out general limitations or conditions applicable to registrations. Breaches of limitations or conditions is a criminal offence pursuant to s.32.

The provisions on appeals against a refusal to grant a registration, a deemed refusal to grant a registration or the imposition of limitations or conditions to a registration are set out in ss.26 and 27.

Subss. (3) and (5)

Under s.25 the Secretary of State may, on the grounds of national security, direct that an application for registration or a certificate of registration should not be copied to the local authorities.

Subs. (4)

The prescribed period is four months beginning with the day on which the application was received.

Exemptions from registration under s.10

11.—(1) The Secretary of State may by order grant exemptions from registration under section 10, by reference to such classes of persons, and such descriptions of mobile radioactive apparatus, as may be specified in the order.

(2) Any exemption granted by an order under subsection (1) may be granted subject to such limitations or conditions as may be specified in the order.

(3) In the application of this section to Northern Ireland, the reference to the Secretary of State shall have effect as a reference to the Department of the Environment for Northern Ireland.

"mobile radioactive apparatus": s.3.

GENERAL NOTE

Subs. (1)
This provision sets out the exemption from the necessity to register mobile radioactive apparatus as required by s.9.

Person
See the General Note to s.6.

Subs. (2)
Non-compliance with a limitation or condition is a criminal offence under s.32.
The orders currently in force under this section are:
(1) The Radioactive Substances (Electronic Valves) Exemption Order 1967 (S.I. 1967 No. 1797).
(2) The Radioactive Substances (Testing Instruments) Exemption Order 1985 (S.I. 1985 No. 1049).
Similar orders have been issued in relation to exemptions for Scotland and Northern Ireland.

Cancellation and variation of registration

12.—(1) Where any person is for the time being registered under section 7 or 10, the chief inspector may at any time cancel the registration, or may vary it—
    (a) where the registration has effect without limitations or conditions, by attaching limitations or conditions to it, or
    (b) where the registration has effect subject to limitations or conditions, by revoking or varying any of those limitations or conditions or by attaching further limitations or conditions to the registration.
(2) On cancelling or varying a registration by virtue of this section, the chief inspector shall—
    (a) give notice of the cancellation or variation to the person to whom the registration relates, and
    (b) if a copy of the certificate was sent to a local authority in accordance with section 7(8) or 10(5), send a copy of the notice to that local authority.

DEFINITIONS
"chief inspector": s.47(1).
"local authority": s.47(1).

GENERAL NOTE
This provision empowers the chief inspector to cancel or vary any registration of premises for mobile apparatus made under s.7 or s.10 respectively. Where a registration has been varied or cancelled then the registered person may appeal to the Secretary of State pursuant to the provisions of ss.26 and 27.

Limitation or Condition
To breach a limitation or condition attached to a registration is a criminal offence pursuant to s.32.

Authorisation of disposal and accumulation of radioactive waste

Disposal of radioactive waste

13.—(1) Subject to section 15, no person shall, except in accordance with an authorisation granted in that behalf under this subsection, dispose of any radioactive waste on or from any premises which are used for the purposes of any undertaking carried on by him, or cause or permit any radioactive waste to be so disposed of, if (in any such case) he knows or has reasonable grounds for believing it to be radioactive waste.

(2) Where any person keeps any mobile radioactive apparatus for the purpose of its being used in activities to which section 9 applies, he shall not dispose of any radioactive waste arising from any such apparatus so kept by him, or cause or permit any such radioactive waste to be disposed of, except in accordance with an authorisation granted in that behalf under this subsection.

(3) Subject to subsection (4) and to section 15, where any person, in the course of the carrying on by him of an undertaking, receives any radioactive waste for the purpose of its being disposed of by him, he shall not, except in accordance with an authorisation granted in that behalf under this subsection, dispose of that waste, or cause or permit it to be disposed of, knowing or having reasonable grounds for believing it to be radioactive waste.

(4) The disposal of any radioactive waste does not require an authorisation under subsection (3) if it is waste which falls within the provisions of an authorisation granted under subsection (1) or (2), and it is disposed of in accordance with the authorisation so granted.

(5) In relation to any premises which—
(a) are situated on a nuclear site, but
(b) have ceased to be used for the purposes of an undertaking carried on by the licensee,
subsection (1) shall apply (subject to section 15) as if the premises were used for the purposes of an undertaking carried on by the licensee.

DEFINITIONS
"disposal": s.47(1).
"dispose of": s.47(1).
"mobile radioactive apparatus": s.3.
"nuclear site": s.47(1).
"period of responsibility": s.47(1).
"premises": s.47(1).
"radioactive waste": s.2.
"undertaking": s.47(1).

GENERAL NOTE

Subs. (1)
The disposal of radioactive waste is prohibited unless it is in accordance with an authorisation issued under this subsection, or exempted by s.15. The disposal of waste includes the removal of the waste from the premises as well as its deposit or destruction (s.47(1)). Pursuant to subs. (5) this subsection also applies to redundant nuclear sites.

Subs. (2)
The use of mobile radioactive apparatus to dispose of any radioactive waste arising from the use of such apparatus is prohibited unless authorised under this subsection or exempted pursuant to s.11.

Subs. (3)
The receipt of waste for disposal is prohibited unless authorised under this subsection or exempted under s.15. However, there is no need for an authority under this subsection where the disposal is already the subject of authorisation under subss. (1) or (2).
The provisions in relation to the application for an authorisation are set out at s.16.

Subs. (5)
The power of the Health and Safety Executive to attach conditions to nuclear site licences with regard to the discharge of substances on or from such a site is without prejudice to this subsection (Nuclear Installation Act 1965, s.4).
For the provisions on appeals in relation to applications for authorisations see ss.26 and 27.
For the right to a hearing before an application is refused or limitation or condition attached to it see s.28.
Contravention of this section is a criminal offence under s.32.
For discussion of the elements of the criminal offences, see the General Note to s.6.

Person
For the meaning of "person" see the General Note to s.6.

Accumulation of radioactive waste

14.—(1) Subject to the provisions of this section and section 15, no person shall, except in accordance with an authorisation granted in that behalf under this section, accumulate any radioactive waste (with a view to its subsequent disposal) on any premises which are used for the purposes of an undertaking carried on by him, or cause or permit any radioactive waste to be so accumulated, if (in any such case) he knows or has reasonable grounds for believing it to be radioactive waste.

(2) Where the disposal of any radioactive waste has been authorised under section 13, and in accordance with that authorisation the waste is required or permitted to be accumulated with a view to its subsequent disposal, no further authorisation under this section shall be required to enable the waste to be accumulated in accordance with the authorisation granted under section 13.

(3) Subsection (1) shall not apply to the accumulation of radioactive waste on any premises situated on a nuclear site.

(4) For the purposes of this section, where radioactive material is produced, kept or used on any premises, and any substance arising from the production, keeping or use of that material is accumulated in a part of the premises appropriated for the purpose, and is retained there for a period of not less than three months, that substance shall, unless the contrary is proved, be presumed—

(a) to be radioactive waste, and
(b) to be accumulated on the premises with a view to the subsequent disposal of the substance.

DEFINITIONS
    "disposal": s.47(1).
    "nuclear site": s.47(1).
    "premises": s.47(1).
    "radioactive material": s.1.
    "radioactive waste": s.2.
    "substance": s.47(1).
    "undertaking": s.47(1).
    "waste": s.47(1) and (4).

GENERAL NOTE

Subs. (1)
    The accumulation of radioactive waste with a view to its subsequent disposal is prohibited unless it is in accordance with an authority granted under this subsection.

Subs. (2)
    Where the accumulation of radioactive waste is in accordance with an authority granted under s.13 then no additional authority is required.

Subs. (3)
    The accumulation of radioactive waste on a nuclear site does not require authority under this subsection.

Subs. (4)
    For the purposes of this section the accumulation of radioactive material for at least three months is presumed to be both radioactive waste and accumulated with a view to its disposal and so must be authorised under subs. (1).
    For these purposes "months" means "calendar months", see s.5 of Interpretation Act 1978.
    The provisions for appeals in relation to applications for authorisations are contained in ss.26 and 27.
    It is a criminal offence pursuant to s.32 to fail to comply with the requirements of this section.

For a discussion on the elements and the criminal offences see the General Note to s.6.

Person
For the meaning of the word "person", see the General Note to s.6.

Further exemptions from ss.13 and 14

15.—(1) Sections 13(1) and (3) and 14(1) shall not apply to the disposal or accumulation of any radioactive waste arising from clocks or watches, but this subsection does not affect the operation of section 13(1) or section 14(1) in relation to the disposal or accumulation of radioactive waste arising from clocks or watches on or from premises which, by virtue of subsection (5) of section 8, are excluded from the operation of subsection (4) of that section.

(2) Without prejudice to subsection (1), the Secretary of State may by order exclude particular descriptions of radioactive waste from any of the provisions of section 13 or 14, either absolutely or subject to limitations or conditions; and accordingly such of those provisions as may be specified in an order under this subsection shall not apply to a disposal or accumulation of radioactive waste if it is radioactive waste of a description so specified, and (where the exclusion is subject to limitations or conditions) the limitations or conditions specified in the order are complied with.

(3) In the application of this section to Northern Ireland, the reference to the Secretary of State shall have effect as a reference to the Department of the Environment for Northern Ireland.

DEFINITIONS
"disposal": s.47(1).
"radioactive waste": s.2.

GENERAL NOTE
This section contains the exemptions from the necessity to hold an authorisation for disposing of or accumulating radioactive waste as required by ss.13 and 14.

Subs. (1)
The disposal or accumulation of radioactive waste from watches or clocks is exempted. However, there is no exemption for waste arising from clocks or watches on the premises at which they are manufactured or repaired by a process involving luminous material.

Subs. (2)
The Secretary of State may grant exemptions by way of statutory instrument. Those statutory instruments currently in force for England and Wales are:
(1) The Radioactive Substances (Storage in Transit) Exemption Order 1962 (S.I. 1962 No. 2646).
(2) The Radioactive Substances (Phosphatic Substances, Rare Earths, etc.) Exemption Order 1962 (S.I. 1962 No. 2648).
(3) The Radioactive Substances (Lead) Exemption Order 1962 (S.I. 1962 No. 2649).
(4) The Radioactive Substances (Uranium and Thorium) Exemption Order 1962 (S.I. 1962 No. 2710).
(5) The Radioactive Substances (Prepared Uranium and Thorium Compounds) Exemption Order 1962 (S.I. 1962 No. 2711).
(6) The Radioactive Substances (Geological Specimens) Exemption Order 1962 (S.I. 1962 No. 2712).
(7) The Radioactive Substances (Waste Closed Sources) Exemption Order 1963 (S.I. 1963 No. 1831).
(8) The Radioactive Substances (Schools, etc.) Exemption Order 1963 (S.I. 1963 No. 1832).
(9) The Radioactive Substances (Electronic Valves) Exemption Order 1967 (S.I. 1967 No. 1797).
(10) The Radioactive Substances (Smoke Detectors) Exemption Order 1980 (S.I. 1980 No. 953) as amended by S.I. 1991 No. 477.
(11) The Radioactive Substances (Gaseous Tritium Light Devices) Exemption Order 1985 (S.I. 1985 No. 1047).
(12) The Radioactive Substances (Luminous Articles) Exemption Order 1985 (S.I. 1985 No. 1048).

(13) The Radioactive Substances (Testing Instruments) Exemption Order 1985 (S.I. 1985 No. 1049).
(14) The Radioactive Substances (Substances of Low Activity) Exemption Order 1986 (S.I. 1986 No. 1002) as amended by S.I. 1992 No. 647.
(15) The Radioactive Substances (Hospitals) Exemption Order 1990 (S.I. 1990 No. 2512).
Similar orders have been issued in relation to exemptions for Scotland and Northern Ireland.

Grant of authorisations

16.—(1) In this section, unless a contrary intention appears, "authorisation" means an authorisation granted under section 13 or 14.

(2) Subject to subsection (3), the power to grant authorisations shall be exercisable by the chief inspector.

(3) In England, Wales and Northern Ireland, the power to grant authorisations under section 13(1) in respect of the disposal of radioactive waste on or from any premises situated on a nuclear site shall be exercisable by the chief inspector and the appropriate Minister; and the disposal of radioactive waste on or from any such premises in England, Wales or Northern Ireland shall not be treated as authorised under section 13(1) unless it is so authorised by both the chief inspector and that Minister.

(4) Any application for an authorisation shall be accompanied by the prescribed fee.

(5) Before granting an authorisation under section 13(1) in respect of the disposal of radioactive waste on or from premises situated on a nuclear site, the chief inspector and, where the premises are in England, Wales or Northern Ireland, the appropriate Minister shall each consult with such local authorities, relevant water bodies or other public or local authorities as appear to him to be proper to be consulted by him.

(6) On any application being made, the chief inspector shall, subject to directions under section 25, send a copy of the application to each local authority in whose area, in accordance with the authorisation applied for, radioactive waste is to be disposed of or accumulated.

(7) An application for an authorisation (other than an application to which subsection (3) applies) which is duly made to the chief inspector may be treated by the applicant as having been refused if it is not determined within the prescribed period for determinations or such longer period as may be agreed with the applicant.

(8) An authorisation may be granted—
(a) either in respect of radioactive waste generally or in respect of such one or more descriptions of radioactive waste as may be specified in the authorisation, and
(b) subject to such limitations or conditions as the chief inspector or, as the case may be, the chief inspector and the appropriate Minister think fit.

(9) Where any authorisation is granted, the chief inspector—
(a) shall furnish the person to whom the authorisation is granted with a certificate containing all material particulars of the authorisation, and
(b) shall, subject to directions under section 25, send a copy of the certificate—
    (i) to each local authority in whose area, in accordance with the authorisation, radioactive waste is to be disposed of or accumulated, and
    (ii) in the case of an authorisation to which subsection (5) applies, to any other public or local authority consulted in relation to the authorisation in accordance with that subsection.

(10) An authorisation shall have effect as from such date as may be specified in it; and in fixing that date, in the case of an authorisation where copies of the certificate are required to be sent as mentioned in subsection

(9)(b), the chief inspector or, as the case may be, the chief inspector and the appropriate Minister—

(a) shall have regard to the time at which those copies may be expected to be sent, and

(b) shall fix a date appearing to him or them to be such as will allow an interval of not less than twenty-eight days after that time before the authorisation has effect,

unless in his or their opinion it is necessary that the coming into operation of the authorisation should be immediate or should otherwise be expedited.

DEFINITIONS
"appropriate Minister": s.47(1).
"chief inspector": s.47(1).
"disposal": s.47(1).
"local authority": s.47(1).
"nuclear site": s.47(1).
"premises": s.47(1).
"prescribed period for determination": s.47(1) and (2).
"public or local authorities": s.47(1).
"radioactive waste": s.2.
"relevant water body": s.47(1).

GENERAL NOTE

Subss. (2) and (3)
The chief inspector has the power to grant authorisations for the disposal and accumulation of radioactive waste. However, in relation to an authorisation for the disposal of radioactive waste on or from a nuclear site situated in England and Wales and Northern Ireland, the authorisation must be granted jointly by both the chief inspector and the appropriate Minister.

For an authorisation to be granted the chief inspector (and where relevant, the Minister) must consult the statutory consultees which include local authorities, the National Rivers Authority, water undertakers, sewerage undertakers or local fisheries committees. (In Scotland, the River Purification Authority, a District Salmon Fishery Board and a Water Authority; and in Northern Ireland the Fisheries Conservation Board for Northern Ireland).

Subs. (4)
See s.43 for provisions on fees payable.

Subs. (6)
Unless the Secretary of State has directed that knowledge of the application should be restricted on the grounds of national security pursuant to s.25, the chief inspector must furnish relevant local authorities with copies of applications.

Subs. (7)
The prescribed period is four months beginning with the day on which the application was received.

Subs. (8)(b)
Limitations and conditions may be attached to an authorisation. Additionally, it is open to the Secretary of State to set out general limitations or conditions in regulations made pursuant to s.44. Breach of limitations and conditions is a criminal offence pursuant to s.32.

Subs. (9)(b)
Unless the Secretary of State has restricted knowledge of an authorisation on the grounds of national security pursuant to s.25, a copy of the certificate must be sent to the relevant local authorities and where an authorisation is for the disposal of radioactive waste on or from nuclear site premises, to the public and local authorities originally consulted.

Person
For a discussion of the meaning of the word "person" see the General Note to s.6.
For provisions on the right to appeal where an application is refused, deemed to be refused or has limitations or conditions attached to it see ss.25 and 26.
For the right to a hearing before an authorisation for the disposal of radioactive waste under s.13 is refused or condition or limitation imposed on such an authorisation see s.28.

Revocation and variation of authorisations

17.—(1) The chief inspector may at any time revoke an authorisation granted under section 13 or 14.

(2) The chief inspector may at any time vary an authorisation granted under section 13 or 14—

(a) where the authorisation has effect without limitations or conditions, by attaching limitations or conditions to it, or

(b) where the authorisation has effect subject to limitations or conditions, by revoking or varying any of those limitations or conditions or by attaching further limitations or conditions to the authorisation.

(3) Where any authorisation granted under section 13 or 14 is revoked or varied, the chief inspector—

(a) shall give notice of the revocation or variation to the person to whom the authorisation was granted, and

(b) if a copy of the certificate of authorisation was sent to a public or local authority in accordance with section 16(9)(b), shall send a copy of the notice to that authority.

(4) In relation to an authorisation granted by the chief inspector and the appropriate Minister, references in subsections (1) and (2) to the chief inspector shall have effect as references to the chief inspector and that Minister.

DEFINITIONS
"chief inspector": s.47(1).
"public or local authority": s.47(1).

GENERAL NOTE

Subs. (1)
This provision empowers the chief inspector to revoke or vary an authorisation for either the disposal or accumulation of radioactive waste. Where either a revocation or variation has been made then the authorised person may appeal to the Secretary of State pursuant to the provisions of s.26.

For the right to a hearing before an authorisation for the disposal of radioactive waste pursuant to s.13 or the imposition of conditions or limitations on such an authorisation, see s.28.

The breach of limitations or conditions attached to an authorisation is a criminal offence pursuant to s.32.

Functions of public and local authorities in relation to authorisations under s.13

18.—(1) If, in considering an application for an authorisation under section 13, it appears to the chief inspector (or, in a case where the power to grant the authorisation is exercisable by the chief inspector and the appropriate Minister, it appears to either the chief inspector or that Minister) that the disposal of radioactive waste to which the application relates is likely to involve the need for special precautions to be taken by a local authority, relevant water body or other public or local authority, the chief inspector or the appropriate Minister, as the case may be, shall consult with that public or local authority before granting the authorisation.

(2) Where a public or local authority take any special precautions in respect of radioactive waste disposed of in accordance with an authorisation granted under section 13, and those precautions are taken—

(a) in compliance with the conditions subject to which the authorisation was granted, or

(b) with the prior approval of the chief inspector (or, where the authorisation was granted by the chief inspector and the appropriate Minister, with the prior approval of either the chief inspector or that Minister) as being precautions which in the circumstances ought to be taken by that public or local authority, the public or local authority shall have power to make such charges, in respect of the taking of those precautions, as may be agreed between that authority and the person to whom the authorisation was granted, or as, in default of such agreement, may be determined by the chief inspector, and to recover the charges so agreed or determined from that person.

(3) Where an authorisation granted under section 13 requires or permits radioactive waste to be removed to a place provided by a local authority as a place for the deposit of refuse, it shall be the duty of that local authority to accept any radioactive waste removed to that place in accordance with the authorisation, and, if the authorisation contains any provision as to the manner in which the radioactive waste is to be dealt with after its removal to that place, to deal with it in the manner indicated in the authorisation.

DEFINITIONS
"chief inspector": s.47(1).
"disposal": s.47(1).
"disposed of": s.47(1).
"local authority": s.47(1).
"public or local authority": s.47(1).
"radioactive waste": s.2.
"relevant water body": s.47(1).

GENERAL NOTE

Subs. (1)
Under this provision where the disposal of radioactive waste is likely to need "special precautions to be taken" then the chief inspector (and where required by s.16, the Minister) must consult the relevant public or local authorities before granting an authorisation.

Subs. (2)
Where the public or local authority must take special precautions in disposing of radioactive waste then it has the power to make a charge for taking those precautions.

Subs. (3)
Where an authorisation to deal with radioactive waste either requires or permits that waste to be removed or disposed of at a local authority refuse site, the local authority is under a statutory duty to accept that waste and to deal with it in a manner required by the authorisation.

Further obligations relating to registration or authorisation

Duty to display documents

19. At all times while—
  (a) a person is registered in respect of any premises under section 7, or
  (b) an authorisation granted in respect of any premises under section 13(1) or 14 is for the time being in force,
the person to whom the registration relates, or to whom the authorisation was granted, as the case may be, shall cause copies of the certificate of registration or authorisation issued to him under this Act to be kept posted on the premises, in such characters and in such positions as to be conveniently read by persons having duties on those premises which are or may be affected by the matters set out in the certificate.

DEFINITIONS
"premises": s.47(1).

GENERAL NOTE
Certificates of registration of premises or authorisation for the disposal or accumulation of waste must be posted on the premises concerned.

Person
For the meaning of person, see the General Note to s.6.

Retention and production of site or disposal records

20.—(1) The chief inspector may, by notice served on any person to whom a registration under section 7 or 10 relates or an authorisation under section 13 or 14 has been granted, impose on him such requirements authorised by this section in relation to site or disposal records kept by that person as the chief inspector may specify in the notice.

(2) The requirements that may be imposed on a person under this section in relation to site or disposal records are—

(a) to retain copies of the records for a specified period after he ceases to carry on the activities regulated by his registration or authorisation, or

(b) to furnish the chief inspector with copies of the records in the event of his registration being cancelled or his authorisation being revoked or in the event of his ceasing to carry on the activities regulated by his registration or authorisation.

(3) In relation to authorisations under section 13 so far as the power to grant or revoke such authorisations is exercisable by the chief inspector and the appropriate Minister, references in subsections (1) and (2) of this section to the chief inspector shall be construed as references to the chief inspector and that Minister.

(4) In this section, in relation to a registration and the person registered or an authorisation and the person authorised—

"the activities regulated" by his registration or authorisation means—

    (a) in the case of registration under section 7, the keeping or use of radioactive material,

    (b) in the case of registration under section 10, the keeping, using, lending or hiring of the mobile radioactive apparatus,

    (c) in the case of an authorisation under section 13, the disposal of radioactive waste, and

    (d) in the case of an authorisation under section 14, the accumulation of radioactive waste,

"records" means records required to be kept by virtue of the conditions attached to the registration or authorisation relating to the activities regulated by the registration or authorisation, and "site records" means records relating to the condition of the premises on which those activities are carried on or, in the case of registration in respect of mobile radioactive apparatus, of any place where the apparatus is kept and "disposal records" means records relating to the disposal of radioactive waste on or from the premises on which the activities are carried on, and

"specified" means specified in a notice under this section.

<small>DEFINITIONS</small>
"chief inspector": s.47(1).

<small>GENERAL NOTE</small>
This provision sets out the obligation in relation to the retention and production of documentation.

Person
For the meaning of "person", see the General Note to s.6.

Enforcement notices and prohibition notices

Enforcement notices

21.—(1) Subject to the provisions of this section, if the chief inspector is of the opinion that a person to whom a registration under section 7 or 10 relates or to whom an authorisation was granted under section 13 or 14—

(a) is failing to comply with any limitation or condition subject to which the registration or authorisation has effect, or

(b) is likely to fail to comply with any such limitation or condition,

he may serve a notice under this section on that person.

(2) A notice under this section shall—

(a) state that the chief inspector is of that opinion,

(b) specify the matters constituting the failure to comply with the limitations or conditions in question or the matters making it likely that such a failure will occur, as the case may be, and

(c) specify the steps that must be taken to remedy those matters and the period within which those steps must be taken.

(3) In the case of an authorisation granted by the chief inspector and the appropriate Minister in accordance with section 16(3), the power to issue notices under this section shall be exercisable by the chief inspector or by that Minister as if references in subsections (1) and (2) to the chief inspector were references to the chief inspector or that Minister.

(4) Where a notice is served under this section the chief inspector or, where the notice is served by the appropriate Minister, that Minister shall—

(a) in the case of a registration, if a certificate relating to the registration was sent to a local authority under section 7(8) or 10(5), or

(b) in the case of an authorisation, if a copy of the authorisation was sent to a public or local authority under section 16(9)(b),

send a copy of the notice to that authority.

DEFINITIONS
    "appropriate Minister": s.47(1).
    "chief inspector": s.47(1).

GENERAL NOTE

Subs. (1)
An enforcement notice may be served in relation to either a registration or an authorisation not only where a condition or limitation is being contravened but also where such contravention appears likely to take place.

Subs. (2)
The requirement as to the matters to be contained in an enforcement notice are mandatory and it appears that any notice which on its face does not comply with these requirements will be a nullity and could then be ignored or challenged in proceedings, see *Miller-Mead* v. *Minister of Housing and Local Government* [1963] Q.B. 196, 226, *per* Upjohn L.J. In practice, it is unlikely that many notices will fail to comply with these requirements on their face; rather the question is likely to be whether a notice is bad for failure to specify the required matters with sufficient accuracy and precision. The most widely accepted test as to these matters in the case of planning enforcement notices is whether the notice tells the recipient "fairly what he has done wrong and what he must do to remedy" (*Miller-Mead* v. *Minister of Housing and Local Government* [1963] Q.B. 196, 232, Upjohn L.J.). There seems to be no reason why the same test should not be applied to notices served under s.21.

Provision as to appeals against enforcement notices are contained at ss.26 and 27. Under s.27, the Secretary of State may either quash or affirm the notice and in affirming may do so with modifications. Although it is not explicitly stated, this power may well allow the Secretary of State to correct defects in a notice, but it is questionable whether it would be possible to cure fundamental defects that make the notice a nullity. Reference to the considerable body of case law on defective enforcement notices under the Town and Country Planning Acts may provide some degree of assistance as to the likely attitude of the Courts on this question. In general the Courts have become increasingly reluctant to hold that notices cannot be served.

For provisions on the opportunity to have a hearing, see s.28.

Breach of enforcement notice is a criminal offence under s.32.

The power to issue enforcement notices was introduced by the EPA 1990 into the regulation of radioactive substances. The HMIP Fifth Annual Report for 1991–1992 (HMSO) reveals that the first of such enforcement notices was issued during that year to Lucas Aerospace for failing to notify the loss of radioactive sources, failure to implement security measures that had been previously requested by an inspector, and for having more radioactive sources than was permitted by the company's registration.

Another early enforcement notice was issued to a hospital in Chelmsford which was no longer incinerating its radioactive clinical waste but accumulating it instead. The notice obliged the hospital to recommence incineration.

Prohibition notices

22.—(1) Subject to the provisions of this section, if the chief inspector is of the opinion, as respects the keeping or use of radioactive material or of mobile radioactive apparatus, or the disposal or accumulation of radioactive waste, by a person in pursuance of a registration or authorisation under this Act, that the continuing to carry on that activity (or the continuing to do so in a particular manner) involves an imminent risk of pollution of the environment or of harm to human health, he may serve a notice under this section on that person.

(2) A notice under this section may be served whether or not the manner of carrying on the activity in question complies with any limitations or conditions to which the registration or authorisation in question is subject.

(3) A notice under this section shall—

(a) state the chief inspector's opinion,

(b) specify the matters giving rise to the risk involved in the activity, the steps that must be taken to remove the risk and the period within which those steps must be taken, and

(c) direct that the registration or authorisation shall, until the notice is withdrawn, wholly or to the extent specified in the notice cease to have effect.

(4) Where the registration or authorisation is not wholly suspended by the direction given under subsection (3), the direction may specify limitations or conditions to which the registration or authorisation is to be subject until the notice is withdrawn.

(5) In the case of an authorisation granted by the chief inspector and the appropriate Minister in accordance with section 16(3), the power to issue and withdraw notices under this section shall be exercisable by the chief inspector or by the appropriate Minister as if references in subsections (1) and (3) to the chief inspector were references to the chief inspector or that Minister.

(6) Where a notice is served under this section the chief inspector or, where the notice is served by the appropriate Minister, that Minister shall—

(a) in the case of a registration, if a certificate relating to the registration was sent to a local authority under section 7(8) or 10(5), or

(b) in the case of an authorisation, if a copy of the authorisation was sent to a public or local authority under section 16(9)(b),

send a copy of the notice to that authority.

(7) The chief inspector or, where the notice was served by the appropriate Minister, that Minister shall, by notice to the recipient, withdraw a notice under this section when he is satisfied that the risk specified in it has been removed; and on so doing he shall send a copy of the withdrawal notice to any public or local authority to whom a copy of the notice under this section was sent.

DEFINITIONS

"appropriate Minister": s.47(1).
"chief inspector": s.47(1).
"disposal": s.47(1).
"mobile radioactive apparatus": s.3.
"radioactive material": s.1.
"radioactive waste": s.2(1).

GENERAL NOTE
The chief inspector may serve a prohibition notice even where the activity in question is in full compliance with an authorisation or registration; the relevant issue is whether the activity involves imminent risk of pollution to the environment or harm to human health. The Act does not provide any definitions of pollution of the environment or harm to human health.

Subs. (2)
There are mandatory requirements as to what matters should be included within the notice and the comments made in relation to enforcement notices in the General Note to s.21 above should apply equally.

The provisions on the rights of appeal against a prohibition notice are set out at ss.26 and 27.

The provisions on the ability to seek a hearing in relation to a prohibition notice are set out at s.28.

Breach of a prohibition notice is a criminal offence under s.32.

The HMIP Annual Report 1991–1992 indicates that no prohibition notices were served in that period. Such notices are considered necessary for use in an emergency situation where there is a risk of serious pollution.

Powers of Secretary of State in relation to applications etc.

Power of Secretary of State to give directions to chief inspector

23.—(1) The Secretary of State may, if he thinks fit in relation to—
(a) an application for registration under section 7 or 10,
(b) an application for an authorisation under section 13 or 14, or
(c) any such registration or authorisation,
give directions to the chief inspector requiring him to take any of the steps mentioned in the following subsections in accordance with the directions.

(2) A direction under subsection (1) may require the chief inspector so to exercise his powers under this Act as—
(a) to refuse an application for registration or authorisation,
(b) to effect or grant a registration or authorisation, attaching such limitations or conditions (if any) as may be specified in the direction, or
(c) to vary a registration or authorisation, as may be so specified, or
(d) to cancel or revoke (or not to cancel or revoke) a registration or authorisation.

(3) The Secretary of State may give directions to the chief inspector, as respects any registration or authorisation, requiring him to serve a notice under section 21 or 22 in such terms as may be specified in the directions.

(4) The Secretary of State may give directions requiring the chief inspector to send such written particulars relating to, or to activities carried on in pursuance of, registrations effected or authorisations granted under any provision of this Act as may be specified in the directions to such local authorities as may be so specified.

(5) In the application of this section to Northern Ireland, references to the Secretary of State shall have effect as references to the Department of the Environment for Northern Ireland.

DEFINITIONS
"chief inspector": s.47(1).

GENERAL NOTE
This section sets out the powers of the Secretary of State to give directions on the conduct of all registrations and authorisations.

Power of Secretary of State to require certain applications to be determined by him

24.—(1) The Secretary of State may—
(a) give general directions to the chief inspector requiring him to refer applications under this Act for registrations or authorisations of any description specified in the directions to the Secretary of State for his determination, and

(b) give directions to the chief inspector in respect of any particular application requiring him to refer the application to the Secretary of State for his determination.

(2) Where an application is referred to the Secretary of State in pursuance of directions given under this section, the Secretary of State may cause a local inquiry to be held in relation to the application.

(3) The following provisions shall apply to inquiries in pursuance of subsection (2)—

(a) in England and Wales, subsections (2) to (5) of section 250 of the Local Government Act 1972 (supplementary provisions about local inquiries under that section) but with the omission, in subsection (4) of that section, of the words "such local authority or",

(b) in Scotland, subsections (2) to (8) of section 210 of the Local Government (Scotland) Act 1973 (power to direct inquiries), and

(c) in Northern Ireland, Schedule 8 to the Health and Personal Services (Northern Ireland) Order 1972 (provisions as to inquiries).

(4) After determining any application so referred, the Secretary of State may give the chief inspector directions under section 23 as to the steps to be taken by him in respect of the application.

(5) In the application of this section to Northern Ireland, references to the Secretary of State shall have effect as references to the Department of the Environment for Northern Ireland.

GENERAL NOTE

This section enables the Secretary of State to give either a general direction to the chief inspector that all applications of a particular type are referred to him or that an individual application be referred to him.

Power of Secretary of State to restrict knowledge of applications etc.

25.—(1) The Secretary of State may direct the chief inspector that in his opinion, on grounds of national security, it is necessary that knowledge of—

(a) any particular application for registration under section 7 or 10 or applications of any description specified in the directions, or

(b) any particular registration or registrations of any description so specified,

should be restricted.

(2) The Secretary of State or, in a case falling within section 16(3) in relation to premises in England, the Secretary of State and the Minister of Agriculture, Fisheries and Food, may direct the chief inspector that in his or their opinion, on grounds of national security, it is necessary that knowledge of—

(a) any particular application for authorisation under section 13 or 14 or applications of any description specified in the directions, or

(b) any particular authorisation under either of those sections or authorisations of any description so specified,

should be restricted.

(3) Where it appears to the chief inspector that an application, registration or authorisation is the subject of any directions under this section, the chief inspector shall not send a copy of the application or the certificate of registration or authorisation, as the case may be—

(a) to any local authority under any provision of section 7 or 10, or

(b) to any public or local authority under any provision of section 16.

(4) In the application of this section to Northern Ireland—

(a) references to the Secretary of State shall have effect as references to the Department of the Environment for Northern Ireland, and

(b) in subsection (2), the reference to England shall have effect as a reference to Northern Ireland and the reference to the Minister of Agriculture, Fisheries and Food shall have effect as a reference to the Department of Agriculture for Northern Ireland.

<small>DEFINITIONS</small>
"chief inspector": s.47(1).
"local authority": s.47(1).
"public or local authority": s.47(1).

<small>GENERAL NOTE</small>

Subs. (1)
The Secretary of State may prohibit on the grounds of national security the copying of applications or registrations to local authorities.

Subs. (2)
The same powers are afforded to the Secretary of State and the Minister of Agriculture, Fisheries and Food (acting jointly for nuclear sites) in relation to applications for authorisations and their circulation to public or local authorities.

Appeals

Registrations, authorisations and notices: appeals from decisions of chief inspector

26.—(1) Where the chief inspector—
(a) refuses an application for registration under section 7 or 10, or refuses an application for an authorisation under section 13 or 14,
(b) attaches any limitations or conditions to such a registration or to such an authorisation, or
(c) varies such a registration or such an authorisation, otherwise than by revoking a limitation or condition subject to which it has effect, or
(d) cancels such a registration or revokes such an authorisation,
the person directly concerned may, subject to subsection (3), appeal to the Secretary of State.

(2) A person on whom a notice under section 21 or 22 is served may, subject to subsections (3) and (4), appeal against the notice to the Secretary of State.

(3) No appeal shall lie—
(a) under subsection (1) in relation to authorisations which are subject to section 16(3);
(b) under subsection (1) or (2) in respect of any decision taken by the chief inspector in pursuance of a direction of the Secretary of State under section 23 or 24.

(4) No appeal shall lie under subsection (2) in respect of any notice served in England, Wales or Northern Ireland by the appropriate Minister in exercise of the power under section 21 or 22.

(5) In this section "the person directly concerned" means—
(a) in relation to a registration under section 7 or 10, the person applying for the registration or to whom the registration relates;
(b) in relation to an authorisation under section 13 or 14, the person applying for the authorisation or to whom it was granted;
and any reference to attaching limitations or conditions to a registration or authorisation is a reference to attaching limitations or conditions to it either in effecting or granting it or in exercising any power to vary it.

(6) In the application of this section to Northern Ireland, references to the Secretary of State shall have effect as references to the Department of the Environment for Northern Ireland.

DEFINITIONS
    "chief inspector": s.47(1).

GENERAL NOTE
    This section provides a right of appeal to the Secretary of State from most decisions taken by the chief inspector. However, there is no right of appeal (i) where the chief inspector has acted pursuant to a direction given by the Secretary of State under ss.23 or 24; or (ii) in respect of authorisations made or notices given relating to the disposal of radioactive waste on or from nuclear site premises.

Procedure on appeals under s.26

27.—(1) The Secretary of State may refer any matter involved in an appeal under section 26 to a person appointed by him for the purpose.

(2) An appeal under section 26 shall, if and to the extent required by regulations under subsection (7) of this section, be advertised in such manner as may be prescribed.

(3) If either party to the appeal so requests, an appeal shall be in the form of a hearing (which may, if the person hearing the appeal so decides, be held, or held to any extent, in private).

(4) On determining an appeal from a decision of the chief inspector under section 26 the Secretary of State—

(a) may affirm the decision,

(b) where that decision was the refusal of an application, may direct the chief inspector to grant the application,

(c) where that decision involved limitations or conditions attached to a registration or authorisation, may quash those limitations or conditions wholly or in part, or

(d) where that decision was a cancellation or revocation of a registration or authorisation, may quash the decision,

and where the Secretary of State does any of the things mentioned in paragraph (b), (c) or (d) he may give directions to the chief inspector as to the limitations and conditions to be attached to the registration or authorisation in question.

(5) On the determination of an appeal in respect of a notice under section 26(2), the Secretary of State may either cancel or affirm the notice and, if he affirms it, may do so either in its original form or with such modifications as he may think fit.

(6) The bringing of an appeal against a cancellation or revocation of a registration or authorisation shall, unless the Secretary of State otherwise directs, have the effect of suspending the operation of the cancellation or revocation pending the determination of the appeal; but otherwise the bringing of an appeal shall not, unless the Secretary of State so directs, affect the validity of the decision or notice in question during that period.

(7) The Secretary of State may by regulations make provision with respect to appeals under section 26 (including in particular provision as to the period within which appeals are to be brought).

(8) In the application of this section to Northern Ireland, references to the Secretary of State shall have effect as references to the Department of the Environment for Northern Ireland.

DEFINITIONS
    "chief inspector": s.47(1).

GENERAL NOTE
    This section governs the procedures for appeals made under s.26.

Subs. (1)
    The Secretary of State has the power to either determine the appeal himself or to transfer his jurisdiction to a person appointed by him.

Subs. (3)
The two modes of appeal contemplated are written representations or a hearing (which could be either public or private).

Subs. (4)
The Secretary of State is given a wide discretion as to the disposal of appeals including substitution of new conditions and modification of notices.

The Radioactive Substances (Appeals) Regulations 1990 (S.I. 1990 No. 2504) have been published under this section (as previously enacted) and set out the relevant procedures in more detail. In particular, notice of appeal should be given to the Secretary of State within two months of the date on which the decision or notice which is the subject of the appeal is sent to the appellant or the date on which application is deemed to have been refused for non-determination. Although a longer period may be allowed by the Secretary of State this would only occur in very compelling circumstances. HMIP have produced a guidance note to accompany these regulations which is available from HMIP on request. The note fleshes out the Regulations and is based on the well established system used for planning appeals.

A copy of the Appeals Regulations and the Guidance Note on Appeals are at Appendices 2 and 3.

Representations in relation to authorisations and notices where appropriate Minister is concerned

28.—(1) Before the chief inspector and the appropriate Minister—
(a) refuse an application for an authorisation under section 13, or
(b) attach any limitations or conditions to such an authorisation, or
(c) vary such an authorisation, otherwise than by revoking a limitation or condition subject to which it has effect, or
(d) revoke such an authorisation,
the person directly concerned shall, and such local authorities or other persons whom the Secretary of State and that Minister consider appropriate may, be afforded the opportunity of appearing before, and being heard by, a person appointed for the purpose by the Secretary of State and that Minister.

(2) In subsection (1)—
(a) "the person directly concerned", in relation to an authorisation under section 13, means the person applying for the authorisation or the person to whom the authorisation was granted, as the case may be, and
(b) any reference to attaching limitations or conditions to such an authorisation is a reference to attaching limitations or conditions to it either in granting the authorisation or in the exercise of any power to vary it.

(3) The appropriate Minister shall afford to any person—
(a) on whom he has served a notice under section 21 or 22, and
(b) who requests a hearing within the prescribed period,
an opportunity to appear before and be heard by a person appointed by him for the purpose.

(4) In the application of this section to Northern Ireland, references to the Secretary of State shall have effect as references to the Department of the Environment for Northern Ireland.

DEFINITIONS
"appropriate Minister": s.47(1).
"chief inspector": s.47(1).
"local authority": s.47(1).

GENERAL NOTE

Subs. (1)
Before any decision is made to: (i) refuse an application for an authorisation for the disposal of radioactive waste; (ii) attach any limitations or conditions to such authorisation; or (iii) vary or revoke such an authorisation, the person concerned has a right to a hearing.

Subs. (3)

There is also a right to a hearing where any enforcement or prohibition notice has been served pursuant to ss.21 and 22. This is not a right to be heard before a decision is made.

The wording of the RSA 1960 before it was amended by the EPA 1990 was very similar and was considered in *R.* v. *Secretary of State for the Environment*, ex p. *Dudley Metropolitan Borough Council* 90 J.P.L. 683, D.C.

The case concerned an application for judicial review by the local authority, of a decision by the Minister to grant an authorisation permitting the disposal of radioactive waste at Dudley in the West Midlands. The question before the Court was whether, in granting the authority to the company, the Secretary of State was under a duty to consider whether the local authority should be given the opportunity of a hearing under the old s.11(1)(c) of the RSA 1960. In this case, the applicant company did not, as it was entitled to do, seek a hearing. However, the Secretary of State did not consider whether or not the local authority should be given the opportunity of a hearing prior to granting the authorisation. The Court held that the Secretary of State was entitled to have a policy that unless the applicant requested one other relevant persons would not be given an opportunity for a hearing except in exceptional circumstances. Notwithstanding this, the Court went on to hold that the Secretary of State should have considered the question of whether a local authority that was opposed to an application should be given the right to a hearing, whether or not the applicant itself had asked for one. It was noted during the hearing that from the commencement of the RSA 1960 up until the date of this judgment, no hearing had been held under this provision.

Further powers of Secretary of State in relation to radioactive waste

Provision of facilities for disposal or accumulation of radioactive waste

29.—(1) If it appears to the Secretary of State that adequate facilities are not available for the safe disposal or accumulation of radioactive waste, the Secretary of State may provide such facilities, or may arrange for their provision by such persons as the Secretary of State may think fit.

(2) Where, in the exercise of the power conferred by this section, the Secretary of State proposes to provide, or to arrange for the provision of, a place for the disposal or accumulation of radioactive waste, the Secretary of State, before carrying out that proposal, shall consult with any local authority in whose area that place would be situated, and with such other public or local authorities (if any) as appear to him to be proper to be consulted by him.

(3) The Secretary of State may make reasonable charges for the use of any facilities provided by him, or in accordance with arrangements made by him, under this section, or, in the case of facilities provided otherwise than by the Secretary of State, may direct that reasonable charges for the use of the facilities may be made by the person providing them in accordance with any such arrangements.

(4) In the application of this section to Northern Ireland, references to the Secretary of State shall have effect as references to the Department of the Environment for Northern Ireland.

DEFINITIONS
"disposal": s.47(1).
"local authority": s.47(1).
"public or local authority": s.47(1).
"radioactive waste": s.2.

Power of Secretary of State to dispose of radioactive waste

30.—(1) If there is radioactive waste on any premises, and the Secretary of State is satisfied that—
(a) the waste ought to be disposed of, but
(b) by reason that the premises are unoccupied, or that the occupier is absent, or is insolvent, or for any other reason, it is unlikely that the waste will be lawfully disposed of unless the Secretary of State exercises his powers under this section,

the Secretary of State shall have power to dispose of that radioactive waste as the Secretary of State may think fit, and to recover from the occupier of the premises, or, if the premises are unoccupied, from the owner of the premises, any expenses reasonably incurred by the Secretary of State in disposing of it.

(2) In the application of subsection (1) to Northern Ireland, references to the Secretary of State shall have effect as references to the Department of the Environment for Northern Ireland.

(3) For the purposes of this section in its application to England and Wales and Northern Ireland, the definition of "owner" in section 343 of the Public Health Act 1936, and the provisions of section 294 of that Act (which limits the liability of owners who are only agents or trustees), shall apply—

(a) with the substitution in section 294 for references to a council of references to the Secretary of State or, in Northern Ireland, the Department of the Environment for Northern Ireland, and

(b) in relation to Northern Ireland, as if that Act extended to Northern Ireland.

(4) For the purposes of this section in its application to Scotland, the definition of "owner" in section 3 of the Public Health (Scotland) Act 1897 and the provisions of section 336 of the Housing (Scotland) Act 1987 shall apply, with the substitution in section 336 of references to the Secretary of State for references to a local authority.

DEFINITIONS
"disposed of": s.47(1).
"premises": s.47(1).
"radioactive waste": s.2.

GENERAL NOTE

Subs. (1)
The Secretary of State has the power to dispose of radioactive waste which ought to be disposed of, but is unlikely to be disposed of lawfully. When the Secretary of State has made use of his powers under this provision, he is entitled to recover any expenses reasonably incurred.

Subs. (3)
"Owner" is defined by reference to s.343 of the Public Health Act 1936. Under that Act "owner" is defined by reference to the person receiving or entitled to receive the rack rent of the premises. However, it should be noted that in Scotland, although the provisions by which the word "owner" is defined are very similar, they may be interpreted differently by the Scottish Courts.

Rights of entry

Rights of entry and inspection

31.—(1) Any person who is either an inspector appointed under section 4 or a person authorised in that behalf by the Secretary of State (in this section referred to as an "inspector") may, for the purposes of the execution of this Act,—

(a) enter, at any reasonable time or, in an emergency, at any time, upon any premises to which this subsection applies, with such equipment as the inspector may require,

(b) carry out such tests (including dismantling and subjecting to any process) and inspections and take such photographs on any such premises, and obtain and take away such samples from the premises, as the inspector may consider necessary or expedient,

(c) give directions that the whole or any part of such premises, or anything in them, be left undisturbed for so long as is reasonably necessary for the purpose of any tests or inspections, and

(d) require the occupier of any such premises, or any person with duties on or in connection with the premises, to provide the inspector with such facilities and assistance and such information relating to the use of the premises, or to permit him to inspect such documents relating thereto, as the inspector may require, and in the case of answers to his questions, to sign a declaration of the truth of the answers.

(2) Subsection (1) applies—

(a) to any premises in respect of which a person is for the time being registered under section 7,

(b) to any premises in respect of which a person is exempted from such registration by section 8(1), and

(c) to any premises in respect of which an authorisation granted under section 13(1) or 14 is for the time being in force.

(3) In relation to premises belonging to or used for the purposes of the United Kingdom Atomic Energy Authority, subsection (1) shall have effect subject to section 6(3) of the Atomic Energy Authority Act 1954 (which restricts entry to such premises where they have been declared to be prohibited places for the purposes of the Official Secrets Act 1911).

(4) Where an inspector has reasonable grounds for believing—

(a) that radioactive material has been or is being kept or used on any premises to which subsection (1) does not apply, or

(b) that radioactive waste has been or is being disposed of or accumulated on or from any such premises,

the inspector may exercise, in relation to those premises, any of the powers which are conferred by subsection (1) in relation to premises to which that subsection applies, but this subsection has effect subject to subsection (6) unless the premises fall within subsection (7).

(5) Any person authorised in that behalf by the Secretary of State may at any reasonable time enter upon any premises for the purpose of disposing of radioactive waste in the exercise of the powers conferred by section 30, but this subsection has effect subject to subsection (6) unless the premises fall within subsection (7).

(6) Subject to subsection (7), no power shall be exercisable by virtue of subsection (4) or (5) in respect of any premises except—

(a) with consent given by or on behalf of the occupier of the premises, or

(b) under the authority of a warrant granted under the provisions of Schedule 2, or

(c) where entry is required in a case of emergency.

(7) Subsection (6) does not apply in respect of—

(a) premises in respect of which—

(i) a person has been (but is no longer) registered under section 7, or

(ii) an authorisation has been (but is no longer) in force under section 13(1) or 14, or

(b) premises on which there are reasonable grounds for believing that mobile radioactive apparatus has been or is being kept or used.

(8) In England, subject to section 6(3) of the Atomic Energy Authority Act 1954, any person who is either an inspector appointed under section 5 of this Act or a person authorised in that behalf by the Minister of Agriculture, Fisheries and Food may, for the purposes of the execution of this Act in relation to any premises situated on a nuclear site, exercise in relation to any such premises (but not in relation to any other premises) any of the powers conferred by paragraphs (a) to (d) of subsection (1) of this section, as if references in those paragraphs to an inspector included a reference to a person appointed or authorised as mentioned in this subsection.

(9) An inspector appointed under section 4 or 5 shall not be liable in any civil or criminal proceedings for anything done in the purported exercise of his powers under this section if the court is satisfied that the act was done in good faith and that there were reasonable grounds for doing it.

(10) The provisions of Schedule 2 shall have effect for the purposes of this section.

(11) In this section any reference to a case of emergency is a reference to a case where a person requiring entry to any premises in pursuance of this section has reasonable cause to believe—

(a) that circumstances exist which are likely to endanger life or health, and

(b) that immediate entry to the premises is necessary to verify the existence of those circumstances or to ascertain their cause or to effect a remedy.

(12) In the application of this section to Northern Ireland—

(a) references to the Secretary of State shall have effect as references to the Department of the Environment for Northern Ireland, and

(b) subsection (8) shall apply as it applies in England, but as if the reference to the Minister of Agriculture, Fisheries and Food were a reference to the Department of Agriculture for Northern Ireland.

DEFINITIONS
"disposed of": s.47(1).
"mobile radioactive apparatus": s.3.
"premises": s.47(1).
"radioactive material": s.1.
"radioactive waste": s.2.

GENERAL NOTE
This section gives inspectors very wide powers of entry, testing, inspecting, sampling and requisitioning of information. Unlike other environmental statutes providing enforcing authorities with powers of investigation, etc., the Act does not exempt the necessity to produce any documentation on the grounds that it is covered by legal professional privilege.

Subs. (1)
Intentionally obstructing an inspector or other person in the exercise of his powers under this provision is a criminal offence pursuant to s.35.

Offences

Offences relating to registration or authorisation

32.—(1) Any person who—

(a) contravenes section 6, 9, 13(1), (2) or (3) or 14(1), or

(b) being a person registered under section 7 or 10, or being (wholly or partly) exempted from registration under either of those sections, does not comply with a limitation or condition subject to which he is so registered or exempted, or

(c) being a person to whom an authorisation under section 13 or 14 has been granted, does not comply with a limitation or condition subject to which that authorisation has effect, or

(d) being a person who is registered under section 7 or 10 or to whom an authorisation under section 13 or 14 has been granted, fails to comply with any requirement of a notice served on him under section 21 or 22,

shall be guilty of an offence.

(2) A person guilty of an offence under this section shall be liable—

(a) on summary conviction, to a fine not exceeding £20,000 or to imprisonment for a term not exceeding six months, or both;

(b) on conviction on indictment, to a fine or to imprisonment for a term not exceeding five years, or both.

GENERAL NOTE
This section creates some of the offences under the Act and prescribes the various penalties.

Subs. (1)
For discussion of the word "person" see the General Note to s.6.

For discussion of the elements of the criminal offences see the General Note to s.6.

Offences are given a maximum fine of £20,000 in a Magistrates' Court which is consistent with the maximum fines available under the Water Resources Act 1991 and the EPA 1990.

The HMIP Annual Report for 1991–1992 reveals that three prosecutions were taken and concluded in that year:

(a) AEA Technology were prosecuted for a failure of operating procedures in relation to telephone dials containing tritium. They were fined £3,000 plus costs of £1,395.

(b) BNFL Springfold were found guilty of breaching a condition of authorisation in relation to the disposal of low level radioactive waste. They were fined £7,500 plus costs of £6,140.

(c) Leicester Royal Infirmary were found guilty of unauthorised disposal of radioactive waste and fined £6,000 plus costs of £5,500.

Other recent prosecutions include:

(a) Plessey GEC Semiconductors Ltd., who pleaded guilty to holding a radioactive source without a certificate of registration and were fined £1,000 plus £2,261 costs in May 1993.

(b) Nicholls Institute Diagnostics, who pleaded guilty to accumulating radioactive waste without authorisation, holding radioactive material without a certificate of registration, and exceeding the limit for the holdings in their registration. They were fined £10,000 and ordered to pay costs of £2,726 in April 1993.

Offences relating to ss.19 and 20

33.—(1) Any person who contravenes section 19 shall be guilty of an offence and liable—

(a) on summary conviction, to a fine not exceeding the statutory maximum;

(b) on conviction on indictment, to a fine.

(2) Any person who without reasonable cause pulls down, injures or defaces any document posted in pursuance of section 19 shall be guilty of an offence and liable on summary conviction to a fine not exceeding level 2 on the standard scale.

(3) Any person who fails to comply with a requirement imposed on him under section 20 shall be guilty of an offence and liable—

(a) on summary conviction, to a fine not exceeding the statutory maximum or to imprisonment for a term not exceeding three months, or both;

(b) on conviction on indictment, to a fine or to imprisonment for a term not exceeding two years, or both.

GENERAL NOTE

This section creates the offence of breaching the provisions in s.19 relating to the posting of certificates of registration or authorisation and also an offence of defacing such displayed documents.

Subs. (3)

Failure to comply with the requirement to retain or produce documents or records issued pursuant to s.20 is an offence.

The maximum fine for this offence in the Magistrates' Court is the statutory maximum which is currently £5,000 (see s.17(1) of the Criminal Justice Act 1991 which amended the standard scale of fines set out in the Criminal Justice Act 1982).

Disclosure of trade secrets

34.—(1) If any person discloses any information relating to any relevant process or trade secret used in carrying on any particular undertaking which has been given to or obtained by him under this Act or in connection with the execution of this Act, he shall be guilty of an offence, unless the disclosure is made—

(a) with the consent of the person carrying on that undertaking, or

(b) in accordance with any general or special directions given by the Secretary of State, or

(c) in connection with the execution of this Act, or

(d) for the purposes of any legal proceedings arising out of this Act or of any report of any such proceedings.

(2) A person guilty of an offence under this section shall be liable—

(a) on summary conviction, to a fine not exceeding the statutory maximum or to imprisonment for a term not exceeding three months, or both;

(b) on conviction on indictment, to a fine or to imprisonment for a term not exceeding two years, or both.

(3) In this section "relevant process" means any process applied for the purposes of, or in connection with, the production or use of radioactive material.

(4) In the application of this section to Northern Ireland, the reference in subsection (1)(b) to the Secretary of State shall have effect as a reference to the Department of the Environment for Northern Ireland.

DEFINITIONS
"undertaking": s.47(1).

GENERAL NOTE
This section creates an offence of disclosing trade or process secrets without proper authority. For a note on "person" see the General Note to s.6.

The statutory maximum fine available on summary conviction is £5,000, see the General Note to s.33.

Obstruction

35.—(1) Any person who—

(a) intentionally obstructs an inspector or other person in the exercise of any powers conferred by section 31, or

(b) refuses or without reasonable excuse fails to provide facilities or assistance or any information or to permit any inspection reasonably required by an inspector or other person under that section,

shall be guilty of an offence.

(2) A person guilty of an offence under this section shall be liable—

(a) on summary conviction, to a fine not exceeding the statutory maximum;

(b) on conviction on indictment, to a fine.

GENERAL NOTE
This section creates the offence of obstructing an inspector acting in the course of his duties or failing to assist him.

An act of obstruction does not necessarily involve any actual physical violence as discussed in *Borrow* v. *Howland* [1896] 74 LT 787. The case of *Hinchcliffe* v. *Sheldon* [1955] 1 W.L.R. 1207 gives authority to the proposition to the fact that an act which makes it more difficult for the police to carry out their duty may amount to obstruction.

The statutory maximum fine, in relation to this section, is £5,000, see General Note to s.33 above.

Offences by bodies corporate

36.—(1) Where a body corporate is guilty of an offence under this Act, and that offence is proved to have been committed with the consent or connivance of, or to be attributable to any neglect on the part of, any director, manager, secretary or other similar officer of the body corporate, or any person who was purporting to act in any such capacity, he, as well as the body corporate, shall be guilty of that offence, and shall be liable to be proceeded against and punished accordingly.

(2) In this section "director", in relation to a body corporate established by or under any enactment for the purpose of carrying on under national ownership any industry or part of an industry or undertaking, being a body corporate whose affairs are managed by its members, means a member of that body corporate.

GENERAL NOTE

This provision is inserted in a great deal of statutes with the object of making directors and other senior officers of a company statutory principals in circumstances where they have a certain degree of personal responsibility and culpability.

Consent

"It would seem that where a director consents to the commission of an offence by his company, he is well aware of what is going on and agrees to it" (*Huckerby* v. *Elliott* [1970] 1 All E.R. 189, 194, Ashworth J.).

Connivance

This term implies acquiescence in the course of conduct reasonably likely to lead to the commission of the offence. "Where he [the director] connives at the offence committed by the company he is equally well aware of what is going on but his agreement is tacit, not actively encouraging what happens but letting it continue and saying nothing about it" (*Huckerby* v. *Elliott* (*ibid.*)). See also *Glanville Williams, Criminal Law: The General Part*, para. 284, describing connivance in the criminal law context as requiring "knowledge (including wilful blindness) plus negligent failure to prevent".

Neglect

This term implies "failure to perform a duty which the person knows or ought to know" (*Hughes, Re* [1943] 2 All E.R. 269). A director's duty is not absolute and some act or omission constituting neglect must be shown (*Huckerby* v. *Elliott* [1970] 1 All E.R. 189). As to the director's duties, see *City Equitable Fire Insurance Co., Re* [1925] Ch. 407. Duties may in certain circumstances be properly delegated: "a director may delegate, but each case is one of fact and of the circumstances of the case" (*Hirschler* v. *Birch* (1987) 151 J.P. 396, and see also *City Equitable Fire Insurance Co., Re* [1925] Ch. 407).

Director, manager, secretary or other similar officer

See *R.* v. *Boal (Francis)* [1992] 1 Q.B. 591, in which an employee manager of a bookshop was not held to be a "manager" for the purposes of the Fire Precautions Act 1971. See also *Armour* v. *Skeen* [1977] I.R.L.R. 310 in which the terms were held to include a senior officer of a Scottish Regional Council.

Or a person purporting to act in any such capacity

This term will cover directors or officers whose appointment is irregular or defective, see *Dean* v. *Hiesler* [1942] 2 All E.R. 340.

Offence due to another's fault

37. Where the commission by any person of an offence under this Act is due to the act or default of some other person, that other person may by virtue of this section be charged with and convicted of the offence whether or not proceedings for the offence are taken against the first-mentioned person.

GENERAL NOTE

This section allows a person whose acts or defaults result in the commission of an offence by another person, to be charged and convicted of the offence, whether or not proceedings are taken against the person who actually committed the offence. See *Olgeirsson* v. *Kitching* [1986] 1 W.L.R. 304 and *Meah* v. *Roberts; Lansley* v. *Roberts* [1978] 1 W.L.R. 1187 for discussion of this type of provision.

Restriction on prosecutions

38.—(1) Proceedings in respect of any offence under this Act shall not be instituted in England or Wales except—
  (a) by the Secretary of State,
  (b) by the chief inspector, or
  (c) by or with the consent of the Director of Public Prosecutions.
  (2) Proceedings in respect of any offence under this Act shall not be instituted in Northern Ireland except—
  (a) by the head of the Department of the Environment for Northern Ireland, or

(b) by or with the consent of the Attorney General for Northern Ireland.

(3) This section shall be deemed to have been enacted before the coming into operation of the Prosecution of Offences (Northern Ireland) Order 1972.

DEFINITIONS
  "chief inspector": s.47(1).

Public access to documents and records

Public access to documents and records

39.—(1) The chief inspector shall keep copies of—

(a) all applications made to him under any provision of this Act,
(b) all documents issued by him under any provision of this Act,
(c) all other documents sent by him to any local authority in pursuance of directions of the Secretary of State, and
(d) such records of convictions under section 32, 33, 34 or 35 as may be prescribed in regulations;

and he shall make copies of those documents available to the public except to the extent that that would involve the disclosure of information relating to any relevant process or trade secret or would involve the disclosure of applications or certificates as respects which the Secretary of State has directed that knowledge should be restricted on grounds of national security.

(2) Each local authority shall keep and make available to the public copies of all documents sent to the authority under any provision of this Act unless directed by the chief inspector or, as the case may be, the appropriate Minister and the chief inspector, that all or any part of any such document is not to be available for inspection.

(3) Directions under subsection (2) shall only be given for the purpose of preventing disclosure of relevant processes or trade secrets and may be given generally in respect of all, or any description of, documents or in respect of specific documents.

(4) The copies of documents required to be made available to the public by this section need not be kept in documentary form.

(5) The public shall have the right to inspect the copies of documents required to be made available under this section at all reasonable times and, on payment of a reasonable fee, to be provided with a copy of any such document.

(6) In this section "relevant process" has the same meaning as in section 34.

(7) In the application of this section to Northern Ireland, references to the Secretary of State shall have effect as references to the Department of the Environment for Northern Ireland.

DEFINITIONS
  "appropriate Minister": s.47(1).
  "chief inspector": s.47(1).
  "local authority": s.47(1).

GENERAL NOTE
  This provision was added to the laws on radioactive substances by the EPA 1990 and greatly extends the documents that should be sent to local authorities and in turn made available to the public. The *DoE Circular* 21/90 on *Local Authority Responsibilities for Public Access to Information under the Radioactive Substances Act 1960 as Amended by the Environmental Protection Act 1990* as supplemented by *DoE Circular* 22/92 explains the provisions on public access to information and gives guidance to local authorities on their obligations in respect of those provisions. Copies of these DoE Circulars are at Appendices 4 and 5.
  The local authorities are required to make available to the general public copies of all the documents sent to them by the chief inspector unless they have been directed otherwise by the

chief inspector that a particular document or part of a document must not be made available for inspection. Such direction would normally involve preventing. the disclosure of information relating to any relevant process or trade secret.

The public are entitled to both inspect and also take copies of documents held by the local authority. The local authority is entitled to make a reasonable charge for photocopying.

HMIP's regional offices should hold full sets of documentation relating to the local authorities within its region. HMIP is under the same obligation to allow inspection and photocopying as the local authorities.

Except for special rules relating to the rehabilitation of offenders under the Rehabilitation of Offenders Act 1974, local authorities should keep documents sent to them by the chief inspector for a minimum period of four years after the documents cease to have effect.

The Radioactive Substances (Records of Conviction) Regulations 1992 (S.I. 1992 No. 1685) sets out the prescribed information to be made available to the public. In relation to each conviction this is: the details of the offence; the name of the offender; the date of conviction; the penalty imposed; and the name of the court. However, spent convictions under the Rehabilitation of Offenders Act 1974 must be removed from the register.

Operation of other statutory provisions

Radioactivity to be disregarded for purposes of certain statutory provisions

40.—(1) For the purposes of the operation of any statutory provision to which this section applies, and for the purposes of the exercise or performance of any power or duty conferred or imposed by, or for the enforcement of, any such statutory provision, no account shall be taken of any radioactivity possessed by any substance or article or by any part of any premises.

(2) This section applies—

(a) to any statutory provision contained in, or for the time being having effect by virtue of, any of the enactments specified in Schedule 3, or any enactment for the time being in force whereby an enactment so specified is amended, extended or superseded, and

(b) to any statutory provision contained in, or for the time being having effect by virtue of, a local enactment whether passed or made before or after the passing of this Act (in whatever terms the provision is expressed) in so far as—

(i) the disposal or accumulation of waste or any description of waste, or of any substance which is a nuisance, or so as to be a nuisance, or of any substance which is, or so as to be, prejudicial to health, noxious, polluting or of any similar description, is prohibited or restricted by the statutory provision, or

(ii) a power or duty is conferred or imposed by the statutory provision on any local authority, relevant water body or other public or local authority, or on any officer of a public or local authority, to take any action (whether by way of legal proceedings or otherwise) for preventing, restricting or abating such disposals or accumulations as are mentioned in sub-paragraph (i).

(3) In this section—

"statutory provision"—

(a) in relation to Great Britain, means a provision, whether of a general or a special nature, contained in, or in any document made or issued under, any Act, whether of a general or a special nature, and

(b) in relation to Northern Ireland, has the meaning given by section 1(f) of the Interpretation Act (Northern Ireland) 1954,

"local enactment" means—

(a) a local or private Act (including a local or private Act of the Parliament of Northern Ireland or a local or private Measure of the Northern Ireland Assembly), or

(b) an order confirmed by Parliament (or by the Parliament of Northern Ireland or the Northern Ireland Assembly) or brought into operation in accordance with special parliamentary procedure,

and any reference to disposal, in relation to a statutory provision, is a reference to discharging or depositing a substance or allowing a substance to escape or to enter a stream or other place, as may be mentioned in that provision.

(4) The references to provisions of the Water Resources Act 1991 in Part I of Schedule 3 shall have effect subject to the power conferred by section 98 of that Act.

DEFINITIONS
"article": s.47(1).
"local authority": s.47(1).
"premises": s.47(1).
"public or local authority": s.47(1).
"relevant water body": s.47(1).
"substance": s.47(1).
"waste": s.47(1) and (4).

GENERAL NOTE
This provision provides that where any prescribed statutory powers or obligations are being exercised or performed no account is to be taken of any radioactivity of any substances, articles or premises dealt with by that statutory provision. The list of prescribed statutory provisions, other than local enactments, are set out at Sched. 3. The previous list at Sched. 1 to the RSA 1960 included at para. 8c the Control of Pollution (Special Waste) Regulations 1980. Reference to these regulations has been omitted from Sched. 3 to the Act. However, Sched. 5 provides that until s.30 of the Control of Pollution Act 1974 is repealed, Sched. 3 still includes those Special Waste regulations. Special waste under the EPA 1990 is excluded by s.78 of that Act which states that Pt. II of that Act does not apply to radioactive waste, although the Secretary of State may by regulation bring radioactive waste back into the ambit of that Act.

General

Service of documents

41.—(1) Any notice required or authorised by or under this Act to be served on or given to any person may be served or given by delivering it to him, or by leaving it at his proper address, or by sending it by post to him at that address.

(2) Any such notice may—

(a) in the case of a body corporate, be served on or given to the secretary or clerk of that body;

(b) in the case of a partnership, be served on or given to a partner or a person having the control or management of the partnership business.

(3) For the purposes of this section and of section 7 of the Interpretation Act 1978 (service of documents by post) in its application to this section, the proper address of any person on or to whom any such notice is to be served or given shall be his last known address, except that—

(a) in the case of a body corporate or their secretary or clerk, it shall be the address of the registered or principal office of that body;

(b) in the case of a partnership or person having the control or the management of the partnership business, it shall be the principal office of the partnership;

and for the purposes of this subsection the principal office of a company registered outside the United Kingdom or of a partnership carrying on business outside the United Kingdom shall be their principal office within the United Kingdom.

(4) If the person to be served with or given any such notice has specified an address in the United Kingdom other than his proper address within the

meaning of subsection (3) as the one at which he or someone on his behalf will accept notices of the same description as that notice, that address shall also be treated for the purposes of this section and section 7 of the Interpretation Act 1978 as his proper address.

(5) The preceding provisions of this section shall apply to the sending or giving of a document as they apply to the giving of a notice.

GENERAL NOTE

This is a new provision in the Act as set out in Proposal No. 4 of the Memorandum under Consolidation of Enactments (Procedure) Act 1949 and sets out the new standard conditions on service of documents under a statute.

Application of Act to Crown

42.—(1) Subject to the following provisions of this section, the provisions of this Act shall bind the Crown.

(2) Subsection (1) does not apply in relation to premises—

(a) occupied on behalf of the Crown for naval, military or air force purposes or for the purposes of the department of the Secretary of State having responsibility for defence, or

(b) occupied by or for the purposes of a visiting force.

(3) No contravention by the Crown of any provision of this Act shall make the Crown criminally liable; but the High Court or, in Scotland, the Court of Session may, on the application of any authority charged with enforcing that provision, declare unlawful any act or omission of the Crown which constitutes such a contravention.

(4) Notwithstanding anything in subsection (3), the provisions of this Act shall apply to persons in the public service of the Crown as they apply to other persons.

(5) If the Secretary of State certifies that it appears to him requisite or expedient in the interests of national security that the powers of entry conferred by section 31 should not be exercisable in relation to any Crown premises specified in the certificate, those powers shall not be exercisable in relation to those premises; and in this subsection "Crown premises" means premises held or used by or on behalf of the Crown.

(6) Where, in the case of any such premises as are mentioned in subsection (2)—

(a) arrangements are made whereby radioactive waste is not to be disposed of from those premises except with the approval of the chief inspector, and

(b) in pursuance of those arrangements the chief inspector proposes to approve, or approves, the removal of radioactive waste from those premises to a place provided by a local authority as a place for the deposit of refuse,

the provisions of section 18 shall apply as if the proposal to approve the removal of the waste were an application for an authorisation under section 13 to remove it, or (as the case may be) the approval were such an authorisation.

(7) Nothing in this section shall be taken as in any way affecting Her Majesty in her private capacity; and this subsection shall be construed as if section 38(3) of the Crown Proceedings Act 1947 (interpretation of references in that Act to Her Majesty in her private capacity) were contained in this Act.

(8) In this section "visiting force" means any such body, contingent or detachment of the forces of any country as is a visiting force for the purposes of any of the provisions of the Visiting Forces Act 1952.

(9) In the application of this section to Northern Ireland—

(a) references to the Crown shall include references to the Crown in right of Her Majesty's Government in Northern Ireland, and

(b) the reference in subsection (5) to the Secretary of State shall have effect as a reference to the Department of the Environment for Northern Ireland.

GENERAL NOTE

Subs. (1)
The general principle underlying this section is that the whole Act binds the Crown with the exception of three matters as set out in subss. (2), (3) and (4).

Subs. (2)
The Act is not binding on the Crown in relation to premises occupied on behalf of the Crown for military or defence purposes, or occupied by or for the purposes of visiting forces.

Subs. (3)
Contravention of the Act does not render the Crown criminally liable, but the enforcing authority may obtain a declaration of unlawfulness from the High Court or Court of Session.

Subs. (4)
The Secretary of State may issue a certificate excluding powers of entry to any Crown premises on the ground of national security.

Subs. (6)
This deals with the disposal of radioactive waste from military premises to which the controls of the Act do not apply. Administrative arrangements may be made that such waste is not to be disposed of except with the approval of the chief inspector. Where such arrangements are made, and approval is given or proposed for removal to a local authority refuse site, then the local authority must, by s.18(3)–(5), receive the waste. The local authority has statutory rights under these provisions to be consulted in advance as to any special precautions necessary and to recover charges in respect of those precautions.

The *DoE Circular* 22/92 on *Local Authority Responsibilities for Public Access to Information under the Radioactive Substances Act 1960 as Amended by the Environmental Protection Act 1990: Monitoring Data and Other Information*, helps to clarify the position on the MOD and visiting forces. A copy of this DoE Circular is at Appendix 5. Although MOD and visiting forces are exempt from the requirements of the Act, controls similar to those exercised over other radioactive material users are applied on an administrative basis. However, instead of registrations and authorisations, MOD and visiting forces receive "certificates of notification" recording the holding of radioactive material and "certificates of agreement" approving the disposal of radioactive wastes. These documents are to be sent to local authorities, except where there are overriding matters of national security. In this Circular the DoE clarify that the MOD and visiting forces have indicated a wish to comply with the spirit of public access to information provisions and copies of these documents as sent to local authorities are to be made available to the public as described in the General Note to s.39.

Fees and charges

43.—(1) The Secretary of State may, with the approval of the Treasury, make and from time to time revise, a scheme prescribing—
  (a) fees payable in respect of applications for registration under section 7 or 10 or an authorisation under section 13 or 14;
  (b) fees payable in respect of the variation of the registration under section 12 or, as the case may be, in respect of the variation of the authorisation under section 17;
  (c) charges payable by a person to whom such a registration relates or to whom such an authorisation has been granted in respect of the subsistence of that registration or authorisation;
and it shall be a condition of any such registration or authorisation that any applicable prescribed charge is paid in accordance with that scheme.
  (2) The power to make and revise a scheme under this section, so far as it relates to, or to applications for, authorisations under section 13 which may only be granted by the chief inspector and the Minister of Agriculture, Fisheries and Food shall not be exercisable without the consent of the Minister of Agriculture, Fisheries and Food.

(3) A scheme under this section may, in particular—

(a) provide for different fees or charges to be payable in different cases or circumstances, and

(b) provide for the times at which and the manner in which payments are to be made;

and a scheme may make such incidental, supplementary and transitional provision as appears to the Secretary of State to be appropriate and different schemes may be made and revised for different areas.

(4) The Secretary of State shall so frame a scheme under this section as to secure, so far as practicable, that the amounts payable under it are sufficient, taking one financial year with another, to cover—

(a) the expenditure of the chief inspector and the Minister of Agriculture, Fisheries and Food in exercising their functions under this Act in relation to registrations and authorisations,

(b) the expenditure of the Secretary of State in exercising in relation to Wales such of his functions under this Act in relation to registrations and authorisations as are exercised by the Minister of Agriculture, Fisheries and Food in relation to England.

(5) The Secretary of State shall, on making or revising a scheme under this section, lay a copy of the scheme or of the revisions before each House of Parliament.

(6) In the application of this section to Northern Ireland—

(a) references to the Secretary of State shall have effect as references to the Department of the Environment for Northern Ireland,

(b) references to the Minister of Agriculture, Fisheries and Food shall have effect as references to the Department of Agriculture for Northern Ireland,

(c) the reference to the Treasury shall have effect as a reference to the Department of Finance and Personnel in Northern Ireland,

(d) the reference to each House of Parliament shall have effect as a reference to the Northern Ireland Assembly, and

(e) subsection (4)(b) shall be omitted.

DEFINITIONS
"prescribed": s.47.
"chief inspector": s.47.

GENERAL NOTE
This section is a relatively new addition to the regulation of radioactive substances having been introduced by the EPA 1990 to provide a framework for making a scheme of charges payable in respect of applications for authorisations, registrations and variations as well as providing for the imposition of an annual subsistence charge for such authorisations and registrations.

Subss. (1) and (2)
The scheme must be approved by the Treasury and in some cases the consent of the Minister of Agriculture, Fisheries and Food must also be obtained.

Subs. (4)
The scheme must be designed to, so far as practicable, cover the expenditure of the Chief Inspector, the Minister of Agriculture, Fisheries and Food and the Secretary of State for Wales.

Although the scheme of charges was introduced as from April 1, 1991, the current scheme is set out in the Fees and Charges for Radioactive Substances Act Regulation 1993–1994. A copy of this scheme is at Appendix 6. Under this Regulation the fees are determined by reference to which one of four bands premises fall into.

Bands 1 and 2 cover British Nuclear Fuels plc. at Sellafield and other major nuclear power stations. These are charged on an individual time spent basis.

Band 3 includes those premises which dispose of or accumulate radioactive waste and are authorised under s.13 and s.14 (*e.g.*, hospitals or university laboratories). These are subject to an application/variation fee of £1,385 and an annual subsistence fee of £820. (In some cases there is a reduced annual subsistence fee of £80 per authorisation held). Additionally, as costs were not adequately covered in the first year of the charging scheme's operation, a supplementary charge of £210 for authorisations originally applied for in 1991–1992 is payable.

Band 4 premises are those which are registered under s.7 and s.10 for keeping or using radioactive material and use of mobile apparatus (*e.g.*, factories and holders of minor radioactive sources). These are charged at £500 per application, do not generally incur a subsistence fee, but where the application was made for the registration in 1991–1992 a supplementary charge of £80 is required to help recover HMIP's first year overrun on costs.

Regulations and orders: Great Britain

44.—(1) The Secretary of State may make regulations under this Act for any purpose for which regulations are authorised or required to be made under this Act.

(2) For the purpose of facilitating the exercise of any power under this Act to effect registrations, or grant authorisations, subject to limitations or conditions, the Secretary of State may make regulations setting out general limitations or conditions applicable to such classes of cases as may be specified in the regulations; and any limitations or conditions so specified shall, for the purposes of this Act, be deemed to be attached to any registration or authorisation falling within the class of cases to which those limitations or conditions are expressed to be applicable, subject to such exceptions or modifications (if any) as may be specified in any such registration or authorisation.

(3) Any power conferred by this Act to make regulations or orders shall be exercisable by statutory instrument.

(4) Any statutory instrument containing regulations or an order made under this Act, other than an order under Schedule 5, shall be subject to annulment in pursuance of a resolution of either House of Parliament.

(5) This section does not extend to Northern Ireland.

GENERAL NOTE

The limitations or conditions referred to in subs. (2) may be attached to registrations or authorisations granted pursuant to ss.7, 10, 13 and 14.

Breach of any such limitations or conditions is a criminal offence pursuant to s.32.

Regulations and orders: Northern Ireland

45.—(1) The Department of the Environment for Northern Ireland may make regulations under this Act for any purpose for which regulations are authorised or required to be made under this Act.

(2) For the purpose of facilitating the exercise of any power under this Act to effect registrations, or grant authorisations, subject to limitations or conditions, the Department of the Environment for Northern Ireland may make regulations setting out general limitations or conditions applicable to such classes of cases as may be specified in the regulations; and any limitations or conditions so specified shall, for the purposes of this Act, be deemed to be attached to any registration or authorisation falling within the class of cases to which those limitations or conditions are expressed to be applicable, subject to such exceptions or modifications (if any) as may be specified in any such registration or authorisation.

(3) Any power conferred by this Act to make regulations or orders shall be exercisable by statutory rule for the purposes of the Statutory Rules (Northern Ireland) Order 1979.

(4) Any regulations or orders made under this Act shall be subject to negative resolution within the meaning of section 41(6) of the Interpretation Act (Northern Ireland) 1954.

(5) This section extends to Northern Ireland only.

Effect of Act on other rights and duties

46. Subject to the provisions of section 40 of this Act, and of section 18 of the Interpretation Act 1978 (which relates to offences under two or more laws), nothing in this Act shall be construed as—

(a) conferring a right of action in any civil proceedings (other than proceedings for the recovery of a fine) in respect of any contravention of this Act, or

(b) affecting any restriction imposed by or under any other enactment, whether contained in a public general Act or in a local or private Act, or

(c) derogating from any right of action or other remedy (whether civil or criminal) in proceedings instituted otherwise than under this Act.

General interpretation provisions

47.—(1) In this Act, except in so far as the context otherwise requires—

"the appropriate Minister" means—

(a) in relation to England, the Minister of Agriculture, Fisheries and Food,

(b) in relation to Wales, the Secretary of State, and

(c) in relation to Northern Ireland, the Department of Agriculture for Northern Ireland,

"article" includes a part of an article,

"the chief inspector" means—

(a) in relation to England and Wales, the chief inspector for England and Wales appointed under section 4(2)(a),

(b) in relation to Scotland, the chief inspector for Scotland appointed under section 4(2)(b), and

(c) in relation to Northern Ireland, the chief inspector for Northern Ireland appointed under section 4(7),

"disposal", in relation to waste, includes its removal, deposit, destruction, discharge (whether into water or into the air or into a sewer or drain or otherwise) or burial (whether underground or otherwise) and "dispose of" shall be construed accordingly,

"local authority" (except where the reference is to a public or local authority) means—

(a) in England and Wales, the council of a county, district or London borough or the Common Council of the City of London or an authority established by the Waste Regulation and Disposal (Authorities) Order 1985,

(b) in Scotland, a regional, islands or district council, and

(c) in Northern Ireland, a district council,

"nuclear site" means—

(a) any site in respect of which a nuclear site licence is for the time being in force, or

(b) any site in respect of which, after the revocation or surrender of a nuclear site licence, the period of responsibility of the licensee has not yet come to an end,

"nuclear site licence", "licensee" and "period of responsibility" have the same meaning as in the Nuclear Installations Act 1965,

"premises" includes any land, whether covered by buildings or not, including any place underground and any land covered by water,

"prescribed" means prescribed by regulations under this Act or, in relation to fees or charges payable in accordance with a scheme under section 43, prescribed under that scheme,

"the prescribed period for determinations", in relation to any application under this Act, means, subject to subsection (2), the period of four months beginning with the day on which the application was received,

"public or local authority", in relation to England and Wales, includes a water undertaker or a sewerage undertaker,
"relevant water body" means—
(a) in England and Wales, the National Rivers Authority, a water undertaker, a sewerage undertaker or a local fisheries committee,
(b) in Scotland, a river purification authority within the meaning of the Rivers (Prevention of Pollution) (Scotland) Act 1951, a district salmon fishery board established under section 14 of the Salmon Act 1986 or a water authority within the meaning of the Water (Scotland) Act 1980, and
(c) in Northern Ireland, the Fisheries Conservation Board for Northern Ireland,
"substance" means any natural or artificial substance, whether in solid or liquid form or in the form of a gas or vapour,
"undertaking" includes any trade, business or profession and—
(a) in relation to a public or local authority, includes any of the powers or duties of that authority, and
(b) in relation to any other body of persons, whether corporate or unincorporate, includes any of the activities of that body, and
"waste" includes any substance which constitutes scrap material or an effluent or other unwanted surplus substance arising from the application of any process, and also includes any substance or article which requires to be disposed of as being broken, worn out, contaminated or otherwise spoilt.

(2) The Secretary of State may by order substitute for the period for the time being specified in subsection (1) as the prescribed period for determinations such other period as he considers appropriate.

(3) In determining, for the purposes of this Act, whether any radioactive material is kept or used on any premises, no account shall be taken of any radioactive material kept or used in or on any railway vehicle, road vehicle, vessel or aircraft if either—
(a) the vehicle, vessel or aircraft is on those premises in the course of a journey, or
(b) in the case of a vessel which is on those premises otherwise than in the course of a journey, the material is used in propelling the vessel or is kept in or on the vessel for use in propelling it.

(4) Any substance or article which, in the course of the carrying on of any undertaking, is discharged, discarded or otherwise dealt with as if it were waste shall, for the purposes of this Act, be presumed to be waste unless the contrary is proved.

(5) Any reference in this Act to the contamination of a substance or article is a reference to its being so affected by either or both of the following, that is to say,—
(a) absorption, admixture or adhesion of radioactive material or radioactive waste, and
(b) the emission of neutrons or ionising radiations,
as to become radioactive or to possess increased radioactivity.

(6) In the application of this section to Northern Ireland, the reference in subsection (2) to the Secretary of State shall have effect as a reference to the Department of the Environment for Northern Ireland.

GENERAL NOTE

Disposal
The DoE Guide to the administration of the Radioactive Substances Act (see Appendix 1) draws the distinction between "storage" and "disposal".

Storage is seen as the placement of radioactive substances in a facility with the intention of taking further action at a later time. That further action may include *in situ* treatment or a declaration that further action is no longer needed and that storage has become disposal.

Disposal is seen as the dispersal of radioactive waste into an environmental medium or its placement in a facility with no intention of further action, apart from precautionary monitoring.

Nuclear Site
Under the Nuclear Installations Act 1965, sites to be used for the operation of a nuclear reactor or other prescribed nuclear installations must be licensed by the Health and Safety Executive. Thus, licences under that Act are required for nuclear power stations (such as Sellafield, Dungeness or Bradwell), research reactors, private commercial reactors and processing plants (such as that proposed at Thorpe).

Premises
Under U.K. statutes generally, "premises" refers only to those situated in the U.K. However, under the Continental Shelf Act 1964 and in particular the Continental Shelf (Jurisdiction) Order 1980 (S.I. 1980 No. 184) for the purposes of this Act, any installation within the areas designated under the Continental Shelf Act as English, Scottish or Northern Irish are deemed to be situated within England, Scotland or Northern Ireland respectively.

For revocation and variation of registrations, see s.12.
For exemptions from registration, see s.8.

Waste
See further the General Note to s.2.

Index of defined expressions

48. The following Table shows provisions defining or otherwise explaining expressions for the purposes of this Act—

the appropriate Minister	section 47(1)
article	section 47(1)
the chief inspector	section 47(1)
contamination	section 47(5)
disposal	section 47(1)
licensee (in relation to a nuclear site licence)	section 47(1)
local authority	section 47(1)
mobile radioactive apparatus	section 3
nuclear site	section 47(1)
nuclear site licence	section 47(1)
period of responsibility (in relation to a nuclear site licence)	section 47(1)
premises	section 47(1)
prescribed	section 47(1)
the prescribed period for determinations	section 47(1) and (2)
public or local authority	section 47(1)
radioactive material	section 1
radioactive waste	section 2
relevant water body	section 47(1)
substance	section 47(1)
undertaking	section 47(1)
waste	section 47(1) and (4).

GENERAL NOTE
The addition of a list of terms defined in the Act is a welcome innovation which will assist in making statutes more user friendly.

Consequential amendments and transitional and transitory provisions

49.—(1) The enactments specified in Schedule 4 shall have effect subject to the amendments set out in that Schedule, being amendments consequential on the preceding provisions of this Act.

(2) The transitional and transitory provisions contained in Schedule 5 shall have effect.

Repeals

50. The enactments and instruments specified in Schedule 6 (which include spent enactments) are repealed or, as the case may be, revoked to the extent specified in the third column of that Schedule, but subject to any provision at the end of any Part of that Schedule.

Short title, commencement and extent

51.—(1) This Act may be cited as the Radioactive Substances Act 1993.
(2) This Act shall come into force at the end of the period of three months beginning with the day on which it is passed.
(3) This Act extends to Northern Ireland.

GENERAL NOTE
The Act came into force on August 27, 1993.

SCHEDULES

Section 1   SCHEDULE 1

SPECIFIED ELEMENTS

ELEMENT	BECQUERELS PER GRAM (BQ G^{-1})		
	Solid	Liquid	Gas or Vapour
1. Actinium	0.37	7.40×10^{-2}	2.59×10^{-6}
2. Lead	0.74	3.70×10^{-3}	1.11×10^{-4}
3. Polonium	0.37	2.59×10^{-2}	2.22×10^{-4}
4. Protoactinium	0.37	3.33×10^{-2}	1.11×10^{-6}
5. Radium	0.37	3.70×10^{-4}	3.70×10^{-5}
6. Radon	—	—	3.70×10^{-2}
7. Thorium	2.59	3.70×10^{-2}	2.22×10^{-5}
8. Uranium	11.1	0.74	7.40×10^{-5}

Section 31   SCHEDULE 2

EXERCISE OF RIGHTS OF ENTRY AND INSPECTION

1. A person entering upon any premises in the exercise of any power conferred by this Act shall, if so required, produce written evidence of his authority before entering.
2. Where it is shown to the satisfaction of a justice of the peace, on sworn information in writing, that admission to premises specified in the information is reasonably required by a person for the purpose of exercising a power conferred by this Act in respect of the premises, the justice, subject to paragraph 3, may by warrant under his hand authorise that person to enter upon the premises.
3. A justice of the peace shall not grant a warrant under paragraph 2 unless he is satisfied—
(a) that admission to the premises for the purpose of exercising the power in question was sought—
(i) in the case of premises to which section 31(1) applies, after not less than twenty-four hours' notice of the intended entry had been given to the occupier, or
(ii) in the case of any other premises, after not less than seven days' notice of the intended entry had been so given, or
(b) that admission to the premises for that purpose was sought in a case of emergency and was refused by or on behalf of the occupier, or
(c) that the premises are unoccupied, or
(d) that an application for admission would defeat the object of the entry.
4. Every warrant granted under this Schedule shall remain in force until the purpose for which the entry is required has been satisfied.
5. Any person who, in the exercise of a power conferred by this Act, enters any premises which are unoccupied, or of which the occupier is temporarily absent, shall leave the premises as effectually secured against unauthorised entry as he found them.

6. Before a person carries out any test on any premises, in the exercise of any power conferred by this Act, he shall consult with such persons having duties on the premises as may appear to him to be appropriate in order to secure that the carrying out of the test does not create any danger.

7. Any power of entry conferred by this Act shall, if exercised under the authority of a warrant granted under this Schedule or in a case of emergency, but not in any other case, include power to enter, if need be, by force.

8. Any power of entry, or of carrying out tests or inspections, or of obtaining or taking away samples, conferred on any person by this Act may be exercised by him either alone or together with any other persons.

9. In this Schedule any reference to a case of emergency shall be construed in accordance with section 31(11).

10. This Schedule shall have effect in relation to Scotland with the substitution for any reference to a justice of the peace of a reference to the sheriff.

Section 40   SCHEDULE 3

ENACTMENTS, OTHER THAN LOCAL ENACTMENTS, TO WHICH S.40 APPLIES

PART I

ENGLAND AND WALES

1. Sections 48, 81, 82, 141, 259 and 261 of the Public Health Act 1936.
2. Section 10 of the Clean Air Act 1956.
3. Section 5 of the Sea Fisheries Regulation Act 1966.
4. Section 4 of the Salmon and Freshwater Fisheries Act 1975.
5. Section 59 of the Building Act 1984.
6. The Planning (Hazardous Substances) Act 1990.
7. Part III of the Environmental Protection Act 1990.
8. Sections 72, 111 and 113(6) and Chapter III of Part IV of the Water Industry Act 1991 and paragraphs 2 to 4 of Schedule 8 to that Act so far as they re-enact provisions of sections 43 and 44 of the Control of Pollution Act 1974.
9. Sections 82, 84, 85, 86, 87(1), 88(2), 92, 93, 99, 161, 190, 202, 203 and 213 of and paragraph 6 of Schedule 25 to the Water Resources Act 1991.
10. Section 18 of the Water Act 1945 so far as it continues to have effect by virtue of Schedule 2 to the Water Consolidation (Consequential Provisions) Act 1991 or by virtue of provisions of the Control of Pollution Act 1974 not having been brought into force.

PART II

SCOTLAND

11. Sections 16, 17, 32, 41, 42 and 116 of the Public Health (Scotland) Act 1897.
12. Sections 10 and 16 of the Clean Air Act 1956.
13. The Sewerage (Scotland) Act 1968.
14. Sections 56A to 56N and 97B of the Town and Country Planning (Scotland) Act 1972.
15. Section 201 of the Local Government (Scotland) Act 1973.
16. Sections 30A, 30B, 30D, 31(1) to (5) and (7) to (10), 31A, 32, 34 to 42, 46, 53, 55 and 56(1) to (4) of the Control of Pollution Act 1974.
17. Sections 70, 71 and 75 of the Water (Scotland) Act 1980.

PART III

NORTHERN IRELAND

18. Sections 50, 51, 58, 107 and 129 of the Public Health (Ireland) Act 1878.
19. Section 26 of the Public Health Acts Amendment Act 1890.
20. Sections 35, 46, 49 and 51 of the Public Health Acts Amendment Act 1907.
21. Sections 26, 47 and 124 of the Fisheries Act (Northern Ireland) 1966.
22. Sections 5, 7 and 8 of the Water Act (Northern Ireland) 1972.
23. Article 34 of the Water and Sewerage Services (Northern Ireland) Order 1973.
24. The Clean Air (Northern Ireland) Order 1981.
25. The Pollution Control (Special Waste) Regulations (Northern Ireland) 1981.

SCHEDULE 4

CONSEQUENTIAL AMENDMENTS

The Continental Shelf Act 1964 (c. 29)

1. In section 7 of the Continental Shelf Act 1964, for "Radioactive Substances Act 1960" there is substituted "Radioactive Substances Act 1993".

The Nuclear Installations Act 1965 (c. 57)

2. In section 4(1)(d) of the Nuclear Installations Act 1965, for "sections 6 and 8 of the Radioactive Substances Act 1960" there is substituted "sections 13 and 16 of the Radioactive Substances Act 1993".

The Control of Pollution Act 1974 (c. 40)

3. In section 56(6) of the Control of Pollution Act 1974, for "Radioactive Substances Act 1960" (in both places) there is substituted "Radioactive Substances Act 1993".

The Pollution Control and Local Government (Northern Ireland) Order 1978 (S.I. 1978/1049 (N.I. 19))

4. In article 36(4) of the Pollution Control and Local Government (Northern Ireland) Order 1978—
   (a) for "Radioactive Substances Act 1960" there is substituted "Radioactive Substances Act 1993", and
   (b) in paragraph (b) for "1960" there is substituted "1993".

The Atomic Energy (Miscellaneous Provisions) Act 1981 (c. 48)

5. In section 4(1) of the Atomic Energy (Miscellaneous Provisions) Act 1981, in the definition of "radioactive substance", for "has the same meaning as in section 12 of the Radioactive Substances Act 1948" there is substituted "means any substance which consists of or contains any radioactive chemical element, whether natural or artificial".

The Environmental Protection Act 1990 (c. 43)

6. In section 28(2) of the Environmental Protection Act 1990, for "Radioactive Substances Act 1960" there is substituted "Radioactive Substances Act 1993".

7. In section 78 of that Act, for "Radioactive Substances Act 1960" (in both places) there is substituted "Radioactive Substances Act 1993".

8. In section 142(7) of that Act, for "the Radioactive Substances Act 1960" there is substituted "the Radioactive Substances Act 1993".

9. In section 156 of that Act, for "Radioactive Substances Act 1960" there is substituted "Radioactive Substances Act 1993".

The Atomic Weapons Establishment Act 1991 (c. 46)

10. After paragraph 10 of the Schedule to the Atomic Weapons Establishment Act 1991 there is inserted—

"*Radioactive Substances Act 1993*

10A.—(1) For the purposes of the Radioactive Substances Act 1993, so far as relating to authorisations required under section 13(1) of that Act for the disposal of radioactive waste, a relevant site in designated premises shall be treated as a site in respect of which a nuclear site licence is for the time being in force.

(2) For the purposes of sub-paragraph (1) above, "relevant site" means a site used by a contractor for the purposes of any activity which would, if section 1 of the Nuclear Installations Act 1965 applied to the site, require a nuclear site licence."

The Water Resources Act 1991 (c. 57)

11. In section 98 of the Water Resources Act 1991—
   (a) in subsection (1), for "Radioactive Substances Act 1960" there is substituted "Radioactive Substances Act 1993", and
   (b) in subsection (2)(b) for "1960" there is substituted "1993".

SCHEDULE 5

TRANSITIONAL AND TRANSITORY PROVISIONS

PART I

GENERAL TRANSITIONAL PROVISIONS AND SAVINGS

1. The substitution of this Act for the enactments repealed by this Act does not affect the continuity of the law.

2. Any reference, whether express or implied, in this Act or any other enactment, instrument or document to a provision of this Act shall, so far as the context permits, be construed as including, in relation to the times, circumstances and purposes in relation to which the corresponding provision of the enactments repealed by this Act has effect, a reference to that corresponding provision.

3. Any document made, served or issued after the commencement of this Act which contains a reference to any of the enactments repealed by this Act shall be construed, except so far as a contrary intention appears, as referring or, as the case may require, including a reference to the corresponding provision of this Act.

4. Paragraphs 2 and 3 have effect without prejudice to the operation of sections 16 and 17 of the Interpretation Act 1978 (which relate to the effect of repeals).

5. The power to amend or revoke the subordinate legislation reproduced in the definition of "local authority" in section 47(1) shall be exercisable in relation to the provision reproduced to the same extent as it was exercisable in relation to the subordinate legislation.

6. Subsection (1) of section 80 of the Health and Safety at Work etc. Act 1974 (general power to repeal or modify Acts or instruments) shall apply to provisions of this Act which re-enact provisions previously contained in the Radioactive Substances Act 1960 as it applies to provisions contained in Acts passed before the Health and Safety at Work etc. Act 1974.

7. In the application of paragraph 6 to Northern Ireland—
(a) the reference to subsection (1) of section 80 of the Health and Safety at Work etc. Act 1974 shall have effect as a reference to paragraph (1) of Article 54 of the Health and Safety at Work (Northern Ireland) Order 1978, and
(b) the reference to Acts passed before that Act shall have effect as a reference to statutory provisions passed or made before the making of that Order.

PART II

TRANSITORY MODIFICATIONS OF SCHEDULE 3

8.—(1) If—
(a) no date has been appointed before the commencement of this Act as the date on which paragraph 8 of Schedule 15 of the Environmental Protection Act 1990 (in this paragraph referred to as "the 1990 provision") is to come into force, or
(b) a date has been appointed which is later than that commencement,
paragraph 7 of Schedule 3 to this Act shall be omitted until the appointed day.
(2) In this paragraph "the appointed day" means—
(a) in the case mentioned in paragraph (a) of sub-paragraph (1) above, such day as may be appointed by the Secretary of State by order, and
(b) in the case mentioned in paragraph (b) of that sub-paragraph, the date appointed as the day on which the 1990 provision is to come into force.
9.—(1) If—
(a) no date has been appointed before the commencement of this Act as the date on which the repeal by Schedule 4 to the Control of Pollution Act 1974 of the provisions of the Radioactive Substances Act 1960 specified in sub-paragraph (2) below (in this paragraph referred to as "the 1974 repeal") is to come into force, or
(b) a date has been appointed which is later than that commencement,
Schedule 3 to this Act shall have effect until the appointed day with the modifications specified in sub-paragraph (3) below.
(2) The provisions of the Radioactive Substances Act 1960 referred to in sub-paragraph (1)(a) above are—
(a) in paragraph 3 of Schedule 1, the words "seventy-nine", and
(b) paragraph 8A of Schedule 1.
(3) The modifications of Schedule 3 to this Act referred to in sub-paragraph (1) above are as follows—
(a) in paragraph 1 after "48" there shall be inserted "79", and
(b) after paragraph 2 there shall be inserted—
"2A. Sections 2, 5 and 7 of the Rivers (Prevention of Pollution) Act 1961."

(4) In this paragraph "the appointed day" means—

(a) in the case mentioned in paragraph (a) of sub-paragraph (1) above, such day as may be appointed by the Secretary of State by order, and

(b) in the case mentioned in paragraph (b) of that sub-paragraph, the date appointed as the day on which the 1974 repeal is to come into force.

10.—(1) If—

(a) no date has been appointed before the commencement of this Act for the purposes of paragraph 17 of Schedule 4 to the Planning (Consequential Provisions) Act 1990, or

(b) a date has been appointed which is later than that commencement,

paragraph 6 of Schedule 3 to this Act shall be omitted until the appointed day.

(2) In this paragraph "the appointed day" means—

(a) in the case mentioned in paragraph (a) of sub-paragraph (1) above, such day as may be appointed by the Secretary of State by order, and

(b) in the case mentioned in paragraph (b) of that sub-paragraph, the date appointed for the purposes of paragraph 17 of Schedule 4 to the Planning (Consequential Provisions) Act 1990.

11. Until the commencement of the repeal by Part II of Schedule 16 to the Environmental Protection Act 1990 of subsection (5) of section 30 of the Control of Pollution Act 1974 (or, if the repeal of that subsection comes into force on different days, until the last of those days) Schedule 3 to this Act shall have effect—

(a) with the insertion after paragraph 4 of the following paragraph—

"4B. The Control of Pollution (Special Waste) Regulations 1980.", and

(b) with the insertion after paragraph 17 of the following paragraph—

"17A. The Control of Pollution (Special Waste) Regulations 1980."

12. Until the commencement of the repeal by Part II of Schedule 16 to the Environmental Protection Act 1990 of section 124 of the Civic Government (Scotland) Act 1982 (or, if the repeal of that section comes into force on different days, until the last of those days) Schedule 3 to this Act shall have effect with the insertion at the end of Part II of the following paragraph—

"17B. Section 124 of the Civic Government (Scotland) Act 1982."

Section 50　　　　　　　SCHEDULE 6

Repeals and revocations

Part I

Acts of the Parliament of the United Kingdom

Chapter	Short title	Extent of repeal
11 & 12 Geo. 6 c. 37.	The Radioactive Substances Act 1948.	The whole Act so far as unrepealed.
8 & 9 Eliz. 2 c. 34.	The Radioactive Substances Act 1960.	The whole Act.
1968 c. 47.	The Sewerage (Scotland) Act 1968.	In Schedule 1, paragraph 4.
1973 c. 65.	The Local Government (Scotland) Act 1973.	In Schedule 27, in Part II, paragraph 144.
1979 c. 2.	The Customs and Excise Management Act 1979.	In Schedule 4, in Part I of the Table following paragraph 12, the entry relating to the Radioactive Substances Act 1948.
1980 c. 45.	The Water (Scotland) Act 1980.	In Schedule 10, in Part II, the entry relating to the Radioactive Substances Act 1960.
1984 c. 55.	The Building Act 1984.	In Schedule 6, paragraph 7.
1986 c. 63.	The Housing and Planning Act 1986.	In Part II of Schedule 7, paragraph 1.
1989 c. 15.	The Water Act 1989.	In Schedule 25, paragraph 27.
1990 c. 11.	The Planning (Consequential Provisions) Act 1990.	In Schedule 2, paragraph 7. In Schedule 4, paragraph 17 and the entry relating to it in the Table in paragraph 1(1).
1990 c. 43.	The Environmental Protection Act 1990.	Sections 100 to 105. Schedule 5. In Schedule 15, paragraph 8.
1991 c. 46.	The Atomic Weapons Establishment Act 1991.	In the Schedule, paragraph 5.
1991 c. 60.	The Water Consolidation (Consequential Provisions) Act 1991.	In Schedule 1, paragraph 9.

Note: Except as provided in Part II of this Schedule, the repeal of the Radioactive Substances Act 1948 does not extend to Northern Ireland.

PART II

REPEALS IN RADIOACTIVE SUBSTANCES ACT 1948 EXTENDING TO NORTHERN IRELAND

Chapter	Short title	Extent of repeal
11 & 12 Geo. 6 c. 37.	The Radioactive Substances Act 1948.	Section 2. Section 5(1)(b). In section 7, in subsection (1), the words "except section two" and in subsection (2)(b), the words "(except section two)". Section 8(7). In section 9(1), the words "or orders". In section 10, the words "or order" in both places. In section 11, the words from the beginning to "under this Act and". In section 12, the definitions of "registered dental practitioner", "registered pharmacist" and "sale by way of wholesale dealing". Section 14(2)(f).

Note: These repeals extend to Northern Ireland only.

PART III

NORTHERN IRELAND LEGISLATION

Chapter or number	Short title	Extent of repeal
1966 c. 17 (N.I.).	The Fisheries Act (Northern Ireland) 1966.	In Schedule 7, the amendments of the Radioactive Substances Act 1960.
1972 c. 5 (N.I.).	The Water Act (Northern Ireland) 1972.	Section 31(1).
S.I. 1973/70 (N.I. 2).	The Water and Sewerage Services (Northern Ireland) Order 1973.	In Schedule 3, paragraph 1.
S.I. 1978/1049 (N.I. 19).	The Pollution Control and Local Government (Northern Ireland) Order 1978.	In Schedule 4, paragraph 5.

PART IV

SUBORDINATE LEGISLATION

Number	Title	Extent of revocation
S.I. 1974/1821.	The Radioactive Substances Act 1948 (Modification) Regulations 1974.	The whole instrument.
S.I. 1980/170.	The Control of Pollution (Special Waste) Regulations 1980	Regulation 3(2).

Number	Title	Extent of revocation
S.R. (N.I.) 1981/252.	The Pollution Control (Special Waste) Regulations (Northern Ireland) 1981.	Regulation 4(2).
S.I. 1985/1884.	The Waste Regulation and Disposal (Authorities) Order 1985.	In Schedule 2, paragraph 2.
S.I. 1991/2539.	The Control of Pollution (Radioactive Waste) (Scotland) Regulations 1991.	Regulation 4.

TABLE OF DERIVATIONS

Notes:

1. The following abbreviations are used in this Table:—

1960	= The Radioactive Substances Act 1960 (c. 34)
1968 c. 47	= The Sewerage (Scotland) Act 1968 (c. 47)
1973 c. 36	= The Northern Ireland Constitution Act 1973 (c. 36)
1973 c. 65	= The Local Government (Scotland) Act 1973 (c. 65)
1974 c. 40	= The Control of Pollution Act 1974 (c. 40)
1978 c. 30	= The Interpretation Act 1978 (c. 30)
1984 c. 55	= The Building Act 1984 (c. 55)
1986 c. 63	= The Housing and Planning Act 1986 (c. 63)
1989 c. 15	= The Water Act 1989 (c. 15)
1990	= The Environmental Protection Act 1990 (c. 43)
1990 c. 11	= The Planning (Consequential Provisions) Act 1990 (c. 11)
1991 c. 60	= The Water Consolidation (Consequential Provisions) Act 1991 (c. 60)
S.I. 1976/959	= The Control of Pollution (Radioactive Waste) Regulations 1976 (S.I. 1976/959)
S.I. 1980/1709	= The Control of Pollution (Special Waste) Regulations 1980 (S.I. 1980/1709)
S.I. 1985/1884	= The Waste Regulation and Disposal (Authorities) Order 1985 (S.I. 1985/1884)
S.I. 1989/1158	= The Control of Pollution (Radioactive Waste) Regulations 1989 (S.I. 1989/1158)
M (followed by a number)	= The proposal of that number in the Memorandum under the Consolidation of Enactments (Procedure) Act 1949 (16 Dec 1991, HC 148).

2. The Table does not show the effect of the Transfer of Functions (Wales) (No. 1) Order 1978 (S.I. 1978/272) or the Transfer of Functions (Radioactive Substances) (Wales) Order 1990 (S.I. 1990/2598).

Provision	Derivation
1	1960 ss.18(1)—(3A), 21(2)(a); 1990 s.100(3), Sch. 5 paras. 17, 20(a)(i).
2	1960 s.18(4).
3	1960 s.18(5): 1990 Sch. 5 para. 7(2).
4	1960 ss.11A, 12(7B), 20(a), 21(2)(a), (k), (l); 1990 s.100, Sch. 5 paras. 13(4), 18(a), 20(a).
5	1960 ss.8(1)(b), (c), 12(7)(a), 20(b), 21(2)(a); 1990 Sch. 5 paras. 18(a), 20(a)(i).
6	1960 s.1(1).
7	1960 s.1(2)—(6); 1990 s.100(2), Sch. 5 paras. 4(1), 6(1)(a), (b), 11(1).
8	1960 ss.2, 21(2)(a); 1990 s.100(2), (3), Sch. 5 para. 20(a)(i).
9	1960 s.3(1), (2); 1990 Sch. 5 para. 7(1).
10	1960 s.3(3)—(5); 1990 s.100(2), Sch. 5 paras. 6(2)(a), (b), 7(1), 11(2).
11	1960 ss.4, 21(2)(a); 1990 s.100(3), Sch. 5 para. 20(a)(i).

Provision	Derivation
12	1960 s.5; 1990 s.100(2), Sch. 5 para. 6(3).
13	1960 s.6(1)—(3), (6); 1990 Sch. 5 para. 7(3).
14	1960 s.7(1)—(3), (5).
15	1960 ss.6(4), (5), 7(4), 21(2)(a); 1990 s.100(3), Sch. 5 para. 20(a)(i).
16	1960 ss.8(1)—(5), (6), 20(b), 21(2)(a); 1990 s.100(2), Sch. 5 paras. 1, 4(2), 6(4), 11(3), 18(a), 20(a)(i); M2.
17	1960 s.8(7), (8); 1990 Sch. 5 para. 1(5); M2.
18	1960 s.9(3)—(5); 1990 s.100(2), Sch. 5 para. 2(1).
19	1960 s.11(3).
20	1960 s.8A; 1990 Sch. 5 para. 8.
21	1960 s.11B; 1990 s.102.
22	1960 s.11C; 1990 s.102.
23	1960 ss.12A, 21(2)(a); 1990 Sch. 5 paras. 12, 20(a)(i).
24	1960 ss.12B, 21(2)(a), (m); 1990 Sch. 5 paras. 12, 20(a).
25	1960 ss.1(7), 3(6), 8(5A), 21(2)(a); 1990 Sch. 5 paras. 6(1)(c), (2)(c), (4)(c), 20(a)(i).
26	1960 ss.11D(1)—(4), (12), 21(2)(a); 1990 Sch. 5 paras. 10, 20(a)(i); M3.
27	1960 ss.11D(5)—(11), 21(2)(a); 1990 Sch. 5 paras. 10, 20(a)(i).
28	1960 ss.11(1), (4), 11E, 20(f), 21(2)(a); 1990 Sch. 5 paras. 9(2), 10, 18(b), 20(a)(i).
29	1960 ss.10(1)—(3), 21(2)(a); 1990 s.100(3), Sch. 5 para. 20(a)(i).
30	1960 ss.10(4), (5), 20(e), 21(2)(a), (j); 1978 c. 30 s.17(2)(a); 1990 s.100(3), Sch. 5 para. 20(a)(i).
31	1960 s.12(1)—(6A), (7)(b), (7A), (8), (9), 20(b), 21(2)(a); 1990 s.100(3), Sch. 5 paras. 2(2), 13, 18(a), 20(a)(i).
32	1960 s.13(1), (2); 1990 Sch. 5 para. 14(2), (3).
33	1960 s.13(4A), (5), (6); 1990 Sch. 5 para. 14(5), (7), (8).
34	1960 ss.13(3), (4), 21(2)(a); 1990 s.100(3), Sch. 5 paras. 14(4), 20(a)(i).
35	1960 s.13(5); 1990 Sch. 5 para. 14(6), (7).
36	1960 s.13(8).
37	1960 s.13(9); 1990 Sch. 5 para. 14(10).
38	1960 ss.13(7), 21(3); 1973 c. 36 Sch. 5 para. 7(1); 1990 Sch. 5 para. 14(9).
39	1960 ss.13A, 21(2)(a); 1990 Sch. 5 paras. 15, 20(a)(i).
40	1960 ss.9(1), (2), (6), 21(2)(i); 1973 c. 36 Sch. 5 para. 1; 1991 c. 60 Sch. 1 para. 9(2).
41	1990 s.160; M4.
42	1960 ss.14, 21(2)(a), (o); 1990 s.104, Sch. 5 para. 20(a).
43	1960 ss.15A, 21(2)(a), (n); 1990 s.101, Sch. 5 para. 20(a).
44	1960 s.15; 1990 s.100(3).
45	1960 ss.15, 21(2)(a), (b), (c); 1990 s.100(3), Sch. 5 para. 20(a)(i).
46	1960 s.19(5).
47	1960 ss.19(1)—(4), 20(a), (c), 21(2)(a), (f), (g); Fisheries Act (Northern Ireland) 1966 (c. 17) Sch. 7; 1973 c. 65 Sch. 27 Part II para. 144; 1978 c. 30 s.17(2)(a); S.I. 1985/1884 Sch. 2 para. 2; Salmon Act 1986 (c. 62) s.14(2); 1989 c. 15 Sch. 25 para. 27(3); 1990 Sch. 5 paras. 3, 5 11(4), 18(a), 20(a).
48–50	—
51(1)—(2)	—
(3)	1960 s.21(2).
Sch. 1	1960 Sch. 3.
Sch. 2	1960 s.20(d), Sch. 2.
Sch. 3 Part I	1960 Sch. I Part I; S.I. 1976/959 reg. 4; 1978 c. 30 s.17(2)(a); 1984 c. 55 Sch. 6 para. 7; 1990 Sch. 15 para. 8; 1990 c. 11 Sch. 2 para. 6; 1991 c. 60 Sch. 1 para. 9(1).
Part II	1960 Sch. 1 Part II; 1968 c. 47 Sch. 1 para. 4; 1980 c. 45 Sch. 10 Part II; 1986 c. 63 Sch. 7 Part II para. 1; 1990 Sch. 5 para. 19(b); Control of Pollution (Radioactive Waste) (Scotland) Regulations 1991 (S.I. 1991/2539) reg. 4.
Part III	1960 Sch. 1 Part III; Fisheries Act (Northern Ireland) 1966 (c. 17) Sch. 7; Water Act (Northern Ireland) 1972 (c. 5) s.31(1); Water and Sewerage Services (Northern Ireland) Order 1973 (S.I. 1973/70 (N.I. 2)) Sch. 3 para. 1; Pollution Control (Special Waste) Regulations (Northern Ireland) 1981 (S.R. (N.I.) 1981/252).

Provision	Derivation
Sch. 4	—
Sch. 5 paras. 1–7	—
para. 8	1990 s.164(3), Sch. 15 para. 8.
para. 9	1974 c. 40 s.109(2), Sch. 4.
para. 10	1990 c. 11 Sch. 4 paras. 1, 17.
para. 11	S.I. 1980/1709 reg. 3(2); 1990 s.164(3).
para. 12	1990 s.164(3).
Sch. 6	—

TABLE OF DESTINATIONS

RADIOACTIVE SUBSTANCES ACT 1960
c.34

FISHERIES ACT (NORTHERN IRELAND) 1966
c.17

SEWERAGE (SCOTLAND) ACT 1968
c.47

TABLE OF DESTINATIONS

WATER ACT (NORTHERN IRELAND) 1972
c.5

1972	c.5
s.31(1)........	Sched. 3,
	Pt. III

NORTHERN IRELAND CONSTITUTION ACT 1973
c.36

1973	c.36
Sched. 5,	
para. 1	s.40
para. 7(1)...	38

LOCAL GOVERNMENT (SCOTLAND) ACT 1973
c.65

1973	c.65
Sched. 27,	
Pt. III,	
para. 144 ...	s.47

WATER AND SEWERAGE SERVICES (NORTHERN IRELAND) ORDER 1973
S.I. 1973 No. 70 (N.I. 2)

1973	S.I. 70 (N.I. 2)
Sched. 3,	
para. 1	Sched. 3,
	Pt. III

CONTROL OF POLLUTION ACT 1974
c.40

1974	c.40
s.109(2).......	Sched. 5,
	para. 9
Sched. 4	Sched. 5,
	para. 9

CONTROL OF POLLUTION (RADIOACTIVE WASTE) REGULATIONS 1976
S.I. 1976 No. 959

1976	S.I. 959
reg. 4.........	Sched. 3,
	Pt. I

INTERPRETATION ACT 1978
c.30

1978	c.30
s.17(2)(a)	ss.30, 47,
	Sched. 3,
	Pt. I

WATER (SCOTLAND) ACT 1980
c.45

1980	c.45
Sched. 10,	
Pt. II	Sched. 3,
	Pt. II

CONTROL OF POLLUTION (SPECIAL WASTE) REGULATIONS 1980
S.I. 1980 No. 1709

1980	S.I. 1709
reg. 3(2)	Sched. 5,
	para. 11

WATER CONSOLIDATION (CONSEQUENTIAL PROVISIONS) ACT 1991
c.60

CONTROL OF POLLUTION (RADIOACTIVE WASTE) (SCOTLAND) REGULATIONS 1991
S.I. 1991 No. 2539

APPENDICES

Appendix 1:	Radioactive Substances Act 1960: A Guide to the Administration of the Act.
Appendix 2:	Radioactive Substances (Appeals) Regulations 1990 (S.I. 1990 No. 2504).
Appendix 3:	Guidance Note on Appeals.
Appendix 4:	DoE Circular 21/90: Local Authority Responsibilities for Public Access to Information under the Radioactive Substances Act 1960 as amended by the Environmental Protection Act 1990.
Appendix 5:	DoE Circular 22/92: Local Authority Responsibilities for Public Access to Information under the Radioactive Substances Act 1960 as amended by the Environmental Protection Act 1990: Monitoring data and other information.
Appendix 6:	HMIP Report: Fees and Charges for Radioactive Substances Act Regulation 1993–94.

APPENDIX 1

RADIOACTIVE SUBSTANCES ACT 1960:
A GUIDE TO THE ADMINISTRATION OF THE ACT

PART I

NATURE OF CONTROLS
CONTROL OVER RADIOACTIVE MATERIALS AND WASTES

Registration of the keeping and use of radioactive materials on premises

1. Under s.1(1)(*a*) or 1(1)(*b*) of the Act no person may keep or use (or cause or permit to be kept or used) any radioactive material (for definitions of 'radioactive material' and 'radioactive waste' see paras. 14–16) on premises* which are used for the purposes of an undertaking† carried on by him unless he is registered or exempted either by the Act itself or by Exemption Orders made under the Act.

Registration of mobile radioactive apparatus

2. The control under s.1 involves the registration of premises where radioactive material is kept or used, but under s.3 there is a special registration procedure for mobile radioactive apparatus such as industrial radiography equipment which is used for testing or measuring and is moved from premises to premises.
3. Under s.3 no person may keep, use, lend or let on hire (or cause or permit to be kept, used, lent or let on hire) mobile radioactive apparatus, for the purpose of its being used in connection with the provision by him of certain specified 'services', unless he is registered.
4. The 'services' to which s.3 applies consist of using, lending or letting on hire mobile radioactive apparatus for testing, measuring or otherwise investigating any of the characteristics of substances or articles situated elsewhere than on premises occupied by the person providing the services (s.3(2)). The meaning of mobile radioactive apparatus is given in s.18(5) as 'any apparatus, equipment or appliance which is radioactive material and is constructed or adapted for being transported from place to place.'
5. Neither the person who is registered under s.3 nor the person to whose premises mobile radioactive apparatus is sent is required to register under s.1 (s.1(1)(*c*)).
6. However, where the person providing the services outlined in para. 4 above is registered under s.3, and also uses mobile radioactive apparatus on his own premises, he is required to register additionally under s.1 (s.1(1)(*a*)).
7. Section 3 certificates issued in England, Wales, Scotland and Northern Ireland are valid only in their respective countries.

Authorisation for disposal of radioactive waste

8. Under s.6(1) no person may dispose of any radioactive waste or cause or permit its disposal on or from any premises which are used for the purposes of an undertaking carried on by him except in accordance with an authorisation or unless he is excluded by an Exemption Order.
9. Under s.6(2) no person may dispose of any radioactive waste arising from a mobile radioactive apparatus kept by him except in accordance with an authorisation or unless he is excluded by an Exemption Order.
10. A person, who in the course of carrying on an undertaking receives radioactive waste for the purpose of disposing of it, may dispose of this waste only in accordance with an authorisation granted under s.6(3), unless the disposal is covered by an authorisation given under s.6(1) or 6(2), or unless excluded by an Exemption Order.
11. Disposal, in relation to radioactive waste, is defined in s.19(1) as including 'the removal, deposit, or destruction thereof, the discharge thereof, whether into water or into the air or into a sewer or drain or otherwise, or the burial thereof, whether underground or otherwise'. In practice a distinction is usually drawn between:

---

* The term 'premises' includes any land, whether covered by buildings or not, including any place underground and any land covered by water (s.19(1)). Where a vehicle, vessel or aircraft, in or on which there is radioactive material, is on premises in the course of a journey the registration requirements do not apply (s.19(2)(a)). Premises having a nuclear propelled ship (whether or not in the course of a journey) are also exempt from registration if the radioactive material in the vessel is there for the purpose of the nuclear propulsion unit (s.19(2)(b)).

† 'Undertaking' is defined in s.19 as including 'any trade, business or profession and, in relation to a public or local authority, includes any of the powers or duties of that authority, and, in relation to any other body or persons, whether corporate or unincorporate, includes any of the activities of that body'.

'storage' which is seen as emplacement in a facility, either engineered or natural, with the intention of taking further action at a later time, and in such a way and location that such action is expected to be feasible. The action may involve retrieval treatment in situ or a declaration that further action is no longer needed, and that storage has thus become disposal; and

'disposal' which is seen as dispersal of radioactive waste into an environmental medium or emplacement in a facility, either engineered or natural, with the intention of taking no further action apart from any monitoring which may be thought desirable either on technical grounds or to provide reassurance.

Authorisation for accumulation of radioactive waste

12. Under s.7(1) no person may accumulate or cause or permit to be accumulated with a view to subsequent disposal any radioactive waste on any premises which are used for the purposes of an undertaking carried on by him except in accordance with an authorisation.

13. Where substances arising from the production, keeping or use of radioactive material on premises are accumulated on the premises for more than three months, the substances are, by virtue of s.7(5), presumed to be radioactive waste and to be accumulated with a view to subsequent disposal unless the contrary is proved.

Definition of radioactive material and radioactive waste

14. The definitions of 'radioactive material' and 'radioactive waste' for the purposes of the Act are contained in s.18 and are set out in Appendix I to this [Appendix].

15. 'Radioactive material' includes the following substances and any articles made wholly or partly from or incorporating them:

　(*a*) A substance containing an element listed in the Third Schedule to the Act if the concentration of that element in that substance in microcuries per gramme of the substance is greater than the concentration specified in that schedule for the particular state of that substance (i.e. solid, liquid or gaseous);

　(b) Substances whose radioactivity is attributable either wholly or partly to a process of nuclear fission or other process whereby a substance is bombarded by neutrons or ionising radiations.

16. 'Radioactive waste' is defined in ss.18(4) and 19(1) and the meaning of 'contamination' is explained in s.19(4). Anything discharged, discarded or otherwise dealt with as though it were waste is presumed to be waste unless the contrary is proved (s.19(3)). The combined effect is that radioactive waste includes:

　(a) any scrap, surplus, or spoilt 'radioactive material';

　(b) any other waste substance or article (whether solid, liquid, gas or vapour) which has become radioactive or has acquired an increased concentration of radioactivity by any means.

Exemptions from registration and authorisation

17. The Act contains a wide definition of the term 'radioactive material'. However exemptions have been provided, in the Act itself or in orders made under it, in those cases where the amount of radioactive material is too small to justify registration. Exemptions have also been provided, subject to certain conditions, in cases where an equivalent control already exists under other powers.

Exemptions under the Act

18. The following exemptions are provided by the Act:

　(a) On premises of the United Kingdom Atomic Energy Authority (UKAEA) and on sites licensed under the Nuclear Installations Act 1965 (as amended), the keeping and use of radioactive materials are exempt from registration (ss.2(1) and 2(2)) and accumulation of such materials (with a view to subsequent disposal) are exempt from authorisation (s.7(3)). But wastes for disposal are not exempt from authorisation (s.6(1)). The UKAEA are also exempt from registration under s.3 for mobile radioactive apparatus (s.4(1)).

　(b) Except on premises where clocks or watches are manufactured or repaired by processes involving luminous material, the keeping and use of clocks and watches are exempt from registration (s.2(5)) and the accumulation and disposal of radioactive waste arising from them is exempt from authorisation (ss.6(4) and 7(4)).

　(c) The keeping and use of radioactive substances on the premises of National Health Service hospitals are excluded from registration except in Northern Ireland (s.14(1)), although similar control is exercised administratively. NHS hospitals are not however exempt from authorisations for disposal and accumulation. Other premises occupied by Crown establishments are excluded from the provisions of this Act, although in practice formal arrangements exist for similar controls to be exercised (ss.14(2) and 14(3)).

Exemptions by orders under the Act

19. A number of orders have been made under the Act providing for exemptions from registration and authorisation. Brief details of the existing Exemption Orders made under the Act are given in Appendix II to this [Appendix]. Many of the exemptions are subject to limitations and conditions not all of which are mentioned here; conditions requiring losses and breakages of sources to be reported are included in some orders. To find out the precise terms in which exemption is granted reference must be made to the orders, copies of which may be obtainable from Her Majesty's Stationery Office or through any bookseller. Separate Exemption Orders in similar terms have been made for England and Wales, Scotland, and Northern Ireland.

20. All existing Exemption Orders are currently being reviewed. Some orders are now obsolete and will therefore be revoked; others need to be modified. A new order will be made which will exempt users of substances of low activity and concentration from registration and from the need to obtain an authorisation for disposal. This Order will meet the recommendations of the Expert Group regarding the disposal of wastes with very low concentrations of radioactivity (mentioned below in para. 53); and will implement part of Art. 4 of the European Community Directive mentioned in para. 43. (This Article specifies types of radioactive substances in respect of which the general requirement about a system of reporting imposed on member states by Arts. 2 and 3 need not apply). Member states have to comply with the provisions of this Directive by December 3, 1982. Further orders may also be made. When the revision of exemption orders has been completed, probably in 1983, a supplement to this [Appendix] will be published to bring up to date the details contained in Appendix II. Until then, anyone who wishes to find out the most up-to-date information should contact the appropriate Department viz: the Department of the Environment, Welsh Office, Scottish Development Department or Department of the Environment for Northern Ireland. The addresses and telephone numbers of these Departments are given at Appendix III.

Exercise of control—controlling authorities

21. In England control under the Act is exercised by the Secretary of State for the Environment (the 'Secretary of State') and, in the case of disposals of radioactive waste on or from premises of the UKAEA and sites licensed under the Nuclear Installations Act 1965 (as amended), control is exercised jointly with the Minister of Agriculture, Fisheries and Food (the 'Minister'). In Wales control is exercised solely by the Secretary of State for Wales, and in Scotland control is exercised solely by the Secretary of State for Scotland. In Northern Ireland control is exercised solely by the Department of the Environment for Northern Ireland or in the case of disposals requiring joint control by that Department jointly with the Department of Agriculture (Northern Ireland).

Functions of local bodies

22. The control of radioactive wastes is a central government and not a local government responsibility. Under s.9(1) and (2) public and local authorities may not take account of radioactivity when exercising their powers under either the general public health legislation specified in the First Schedule to the 1960 Act or under any local enactments which empower them to control nuisances, pollution and the discharge of wastes. The non-radioactive properties of substances and wastes are still subject to these powers where they apply; for example, the requirements of legislation governing the discharge of an effluent into a public sewer or into a river would need to be satisfied in relation to the non-radioactive properties of the effluent. It should be noted that if radioactive waste authorised for disposal is also special waste as defined by Reg. 2 of the Control of Pollution (Special Waste) Regulations 1980, the requirements of those Regulations will also need to be met. In Northern Ireland the Pollution Control (Special Waste) Regulations (Northern Ireland) 1981 apply.

23. Local bodies may have an interest in the use of radioactive materials, and in the disposal and accumulation of radioactive waste in their areas. The Fire Service, for example, need to know the whereabouts of radioactive materials to enable them to take appropriate precautions in emergencies. Where it is proposed to issue an authorisation for a disposal which will require special precautions to be taken by a local or public authority, the Secretary of State (or Minister where appropriate) must consult that local or public authority before granting the authorisation (s.9(3)). Where it is proposed to issue an authorisation for disposal on or from the UKAEA's premises or sites licensed under the Nuclear Installations Act 1965 (as amended) the Secretary of State and Minister must consult such local and public authorities as seem appropriate before issuing the authorisation (s.8(2)). Even where the Act does not impose a requirement about consultation, the Secretary of State (and if appropriate the Minister) will, before giving an authorisation consult relevant local and public authorities where it seems justifiable to do so. The Secretary of State (and if appropriate the Minister) are required, unless national security considerations arise, to send copies of the certificates of registration and authorisation to the local authorities for the area (ss.1(6) and 8(5)(*b*)). Local authorities have been directed to make this information available to certain other public bodies, such as water undertakers, who have an interest in it.

Procedure for making applications—forms of application

24. Application forms for registration and authorisation may be obtained from and when completed should be submitted to the appropriate addressee set out in Appendix III. However, applications for authorisations for the UKAEA's premises or sites licensed under the Nuclear Installations Act 1965 (as amended) should be made by letter; and in England should be sent in parallel both to the Department of the Environment and to the Ministry of Agriculture, Fisheries and Food.

Completion of application forms

25. It may not always be possible for an applicant to state precisely the amount of radioactivity in the radioactive materials or radioactive wastes. If that is so the best possible estimates of the levels should be made, and it should be made clear that the figures are only estimates. Advice on methods of estimating levels of radioactivity may be obtained from the Radiochemical Inspectorate of the Department of the Environment (for England and Wales), HM Industrial Pollution Inspectorate in Scotland and the Alkali and Radiochemical Inspectorate of the Department of the Environment for Northern Ireland as appropriate. The addresses and telephone numbers are given in Appendix II.

Timing of applications

26. The time it will take to issue registration and authorisation certificates will vary according to the nature of the application. On certain types of application consultations with other authorities will be necessary and in all cases where limitations or conditions are proposed the person directly concerned must be given an opportunity to be heard by a person appointed by the Secretary of State (and if appropriate the Minister). An authorisation will normally take effect only after an interval of 28 days from the date of sending the copy to the local authority unless the Secretary of State (and if appropriate the Minister) are satisfied that there is an urgent reason why it should come into force before then. While simple registrations and authorisations may be obtained in a few weeks, it may take several months to deal with an application where consultations and a hearing are necessary. In order to ensure that registrations and authorisations may operate when they are required, it is essential for applications to be made well before that time.

Provisions governing registrations and authorisations—limitations and conditions

27. Registrations and authorisations may be granted subject to limitations and conditions. In deciding the terms of registration under section 1, the Secretary of State (and if appropriate the Minister) must, apart from two exceptions, have regard only to the amount and character of the radioactive waste likely to arise. The conditions attached to these registrations may, in particular, impose requirements (including requirements involving structural or other alterations) relating to the premises, apparatus, equipment or appliances involved in the use of the radioactive material. Two types of condition not determined by radioactive waste considerations may also be attached to these registrations:
  (i) conditions requiring information to be supplied to the Secretary of State about the movement of radioactive materials; and
  (ii) conditions prohibiting the sale or supply of these materials unless they are labelled or otherwise marked to indicate they are radioactive.

Opportunity for hearing objections

28. If an applicant or the person to whom the application relates objects to any limitations or conditions proposed to be attached to a registration or authorisation he must be given an opportunity to appear before, and be heard by, a person appointed by the relevant Secretary of State (and if appropriate the Minister) s.11(1) and (2). An applicant will therefore be advised of the form in which it is proposed to grant registration or authorisation. He will be invited to comment and if he objects, a hearing will be arranged. Similarly, before an application for registration or authorisation is refused, an opportunity to be heard will be given to the person directly concerned. The Secretary of State (and if appropriate the Minister) may give local authorities or other persons as he may consider appropriate an opportunity to be heard by a person appointed by him.

Certificates of registration and authorisation

29. Registration and authorisation certificates give details of the registration or authorisation and of any limitations or conditions attaching thereto.

Copies of certificates to be posted on premises

30. Persons who are registered under s.1 and to whom authorisations are granted under ss.6(1) or 7 must arrange for copies of the certificates to be posted on the premises concerned where they can be conveniently read by persons who work on the premises and whose duties might be affected (s.11(3)).

Cancellation and variation of registrations and authorisations

31. Under ss.5(1) and 8(7) the Secretary of State (and if appropriate the Minister) may at any time:
(a) cancel a registration or revoke an authorisation;
(b) revoke or vary any of the limitations or conditions subject to which a registration or authorisation has been granted; or
(c) attach limitations or conditions to a registration or authorisation.

32. Where it it proposed to vary an existing registration or authorisation (otherwise than by revoking a limitation or condition) the person directly concerned will be given an opportunity, if he objects to the variation, to appear before, and be heard by, a person appointed for the purpose by the Secretary of State (and if appropriate the Minister) (s.11(1) and (2)). There is no obligation on the Secretary of State (and the Minister) to give an opportunity for a hearing before cancelling an existing registration, or revoking an existing authorisation or a condition or limitation attached to a registration or authorisation. It may be necessary on grounds of public health to stop immediately a use of radioactive material or a discharge or accumulation of radioactive waste. A notification of any cancellation, revocation or variation will be sent to the person concerned and copied to the appropriate local authorities.

Rights of entry and inspection

33. In England and Wales the Radiochemical Inspectors appointed under the Act by the Secretary of State for the Environment have powers under s.12 to enter at any reasonable time with their equipment any premises in respect of which a registration or authorisation is in force, and to carry out such tests and inspections on the premises and obtain and take such samples of waste as they consider necessary or expedient. The occupier or other persons having duties on the premises may be required by the inspectors to provide them with information about the use of the premises and to permit the inspection of documents relating to the use. Radiochemical Inspectors, HM Alkali and Clean Air Inspectorate and Inspectors appointed under the Act by the Minister of Agriculture, Fisheries and Food (in England) and the Secretary of State for Wales (in Wales) have these powers in relation to premises of the UKAEA and to sites licensed under the Nuclear Installations Act 1965 (as amended). In Scotland these powers are exercised by HM Industrial Pollution Inspectorate and in Northern Ireland by the Alkali and Radiochemical Inspectorate.

34. Inspectors also have powers under s.12(4) and (5) to enter premises where they have reasonable grounds for believing that radioactive material or radioactive waste has been or is being handled without the necessary registration or authorisation, or to deal with wastes which might not otherwise be disposed of lawfully because, for instance, the premises are unoccupied or the occupier is absent. Except where entry is necessary to deal with an emergency, inspectors may not enter premises for these purposes without either consent given by or on behalf of the occupier, or under the authority of a warrant granted by a Justice of the Peace (in Scotland, the Sheriff).

Offences and penalties

35. Offences under s.13(1) include—
(a) keeping or using radioactive material (other than mobile radioactive apparatus in respect of which a person is registered or exempted under s.3) knowing or having reasonable grounds for believing it to be radioactive material, without being registered or exempted from registration under section 1;

(b) keeping, using, lending or letting on hire mobile radioactive apparatus for the purpose of providing services to which s.3 applies, without being registered or exempted from registration under s.3;

(c) failing to comply with any limitation or condition of registration or exemption from registration under s.1 or s.3;

(d) disposing of or accumulating radioactive waste, knowing or having reasonable grounds for believing it to be radioactive waste, otherwise than in accordance with an authorisation under s.6(1) or (3) or s.7(1) except where the disposal or accumulation requires no authorisation by virtue of the provisions of the Act or of any exemption order;

(e) disposing of radioactive waste arising from mobile radioactive apparatus kept for the purpose of providing services to which s.3 applies, otherwise than in accordance with an authorisation under s.6(2), except where the disposal requires no authorisation by virtue of the provisions of any exemption order;

(f) failing to comply with any limitation or condition of an authorisation under s.6 or s.7.

36. Under s.13(3) the unauthorised disclosure of information about processes connected with the production or use of radioactive materials or about trade secrets is treated as an offence.

37. Offences under s.13(5) include—

(a) failing to post copies of certificates of registration or authorisation on the premises to which they relate (see para. 30);

(b) obstructing an inspector in the exercise of his powers under the Act or failing without reasonable excuse to provide information or to permit an inspection reasonably required by an inspector.

38. Under s.13(6), it is an offence to pull down, injure or deface copies of certificates posted on premises in pursuance of s.11(3) (see para. 30), without reasonable cause.

39. Penalties for offences under the Act include fines up to £1000, imprisonment for terms of up to 3 months, or both on summary conviction. For conviction on indictment the Act prescribes no maximum for the fine, imprisonment for terms of up to 5 years, or both.

Proceedings in respect of offences

40. Proceedings in respect of offences may be instituted in England only by the Secretary of State for the Environment, in Wales by the Secretary of State for Wales or in both countries, by or with the consent of the Director of Public Prosecutions (s.13(7)). In Northern Ireland proceedings may be instituted only by the Department of the Environment for Northern Ireland or by or with the consent of the Attorney General for Northern Ireland (s.21(3)). Where a body corporate is guilty of an offence any director, manager, secretary or other similar officer of that body with whose consent or connivance, or through whose neglect, the offence is proved to have been committed is also guilty of that offence and is liable to be proceeded against and punished accordingly.

PART II

APPLICATION OF CONTROLS

Standards of control

41. An expert panel was set up in 1956 to advise on the Control of Radioactive Wastes and its report was appended to the White Paper of that name (Cmnd 884) published in November 1959. The Government accepted the report and the Radioactive Substances Act 1960 was based on its recommendations. In its acceptance of the report the Government stated that:

An important section of the panel's report is concerned with the standards by which the discharge of radioactive waste should be controlled. These standards are not immutable; they will be subject to review from time to time in the light of advice received from international and national advisory bodies. Neither will they provide a charter for the discharge of radioactive waste at will, provided that the discharges remain within specified upper limits; it is the essence of the prudent system of control that discharges should be kept not only within the upper limits of safety, but as far below them as can reasonably be achieved.

42. The International Commission on Radiological Protection (ICRP) is generally regarded as the appropriate body to provide guidance on radiological protection standards. The National Radiological Protection Board (NRPB), established as a national point of authoritative reference on radiological protection standards, has been directed by the Health Ministers to give advice on the acceptability of ICRP's recommendations for application in the United Kingdom.

43. The ICRP recommendations provide the basis for the European Community Directive, made under the Euratom Treaty, which lays down basic safety standards for the health protection of the general public and workers against the dangers of ionising radiation. The latest version of this Directive (80/836/Euratom) was adopted by the European Community on 15 July 1980.

44. In 1977 ICRP published a major review of its recommendations (ICRP 26) and it is the view of NRPB that the system of dose limitation recommended therein provides a satisfactory basis for controlling within the United Kingdom the exposure of persons to ionising radiations. The Expert Group which reviewed Cmnd. 884 recommended* that the radiological protection aspect of radioactive waste management practices should be based on the system of dose limitation in ICRP 26 as expanded in NRPB ASP2†. This and other relevant aspects of their recommendations and conclusions are accepted by the Government as an updating, where necessary, of the policies laid down in Cmnd. 884, and form the basis for the remainder of this [Appendix].

45. As was emphasised in 1959 standards and practices of radioactive waste management are not immutable, and these standards and practices will be subject to review from time to time.

Basic objectives

46. For the purposes of radiological protection, the basic objectives of radioactive waste management in the UK are:
  (a) that all practices giving rise to radioactive wastes must be justified, *i.e.* the need for the practice must be established in terms of its overall benefit;
  (b) radiation exposure of individuals and the collective dose to the population arising from radioactive wastes shall be reduced to levels which are as low as reasonably achievable, economic and social factors being taken into account;
  (c) the average effective dose equivalent from all sources, excluding natural background radiation and medical procedures, to representative members of a critical group of the general public shall not exceed 5 mSv (0·5 rem) in any one year.

47. The above objectives are an application to radioactive waste management of the system of dose limitation recommended in ICRP 26. NRPB notes, in its advice given in ASP2, that the use of a limit of 5 mSv in a year, combined with the technique of optimisation discussed in that document as the means of meeting objective (b), will in most cases result in an average dose rate equivalent to a critical group of less than 1 mSv per year of life-long whole body exposure from all sources of radiation. Hence the lifetime whole body dose equivalent of an individual will not normally exceed 70 mSv (7 rem). In some cases it may be necessary to pay particular attention to the lifetime dose equivalent likely to be accumulated by representative individuals in the critical group, taking account of all the age-related factors affecting their exposures.

48. Radioactive waste management includes the design and operation of plant insofar as it affects the generation of plant waste, and the handling, storage and conditioning of wastes, as well as waste disposal practices. In all these matters an important consideration is that the basic objectives shall be met.

Protection of other species

49. Consideration must be given not only to the radiological exposure of man but also to that of other living environmental resources. Whilst the underlying objective of minimisation of their exposure is common to that applied to the protection of man, it is generally considered adequate to restrict exposure at the 'population' rather than the 'individual' level when considering dose to organisms. The ICRP's opinion, as expressed in its recommendations, is that protection arrangements drawn up to ensure the health and safety of man will in general provide sufficient protection for other species.

Disposal routes

50. Where it can safely be done it is desirable to use conventional methods of waste disposal such as discharge to sewers or disposal on local authority refuse tips and this has been the practice since the first authorisations were issued. Among the factors taken into account are the nature and amount of radioactive waste and the facilities available locally. For example, the extent to which disposal can safely be made into the sewers will depend, among other things, on the volume of flow in sewers and where the sewage effluent is finally discharged. In the case of solid wastes the suitability of local authority refuse tips will depend on the nature of the tip and the amount of non-radioactive material available to cover the solid wastes. Each authorisation requires separate consideration; that is done on a case by case basis, taking into account the particular circumstances.

---

* A Review of CMND 884: 'The Control of Radioactive Wastes'. A Report by an Expert Group made to the Radioactive Waste Management Committee (1979). Obtainable from DoE price £1.35 plus postage.

† Recommendations of the International Commission on Radiological Protection (ICRP Publication 26): Advice to the Expert Group reviewing the White Paper Command 884 'The Control of Radioactive Wastes' ASP2 NRPB (HMSO).

51. Some low level radioactive wastes are not suitable for local disposal. Arrangements known as the National Disposal Service (NDS) have been made by the Department of the Environment under section 10 of the 1960 Act for dealing with these wastes. UKAEA and British Nuclear Fuels Limited (BNFL) accept wastes whose disposal via the service is permitted under an authorisation. The waste is generally either buried in trenches at the BNFL site at Drigg (para. 59), or suitably packaged by UKAEA and disposed of at sea in the Atlantic at a depth generally in excess of 4000 metres of water in accordance with internationally agreed conditions (paras. 61–64). Section 10(3) of the Act allows reasonable charges to be made for this service.

52. Where disposal routes are available they should be used to the full for disposal of current arisings and backlogs of the appropriate types of waste in order to prevent the unnecessary accumulation of waste requiring storage and surveillance at production sites. The disposal routes currently available are described below. In all cases it is desirable that the disposal arrangements adopted for a particular kind of waste should not be more elaborate than the characteristics of the waste actually require. The development of further disposal routes will be the responsibility of the Nuclear Industry Radioactive Waste Executive (NIREX) based at Harwell.

Disposal practices—solid wastes

Very low level wastes

53. Very low level solid waste, less than 0.4 Bq/g ($\sim 10^{-5}$ µCi/g) and organic solvent waste containing only carbon-14 or tritium at total concentration of less than 4 Bq/ml ($\sim 10^{-4}$ µCi/ml) can be exempted from consideration under the Act. A Low Activity Substances Exemption Order, which will cover both substances and wastes and will comply with the EC Directive, will be made.

Low level waste in domestic refuse

54. Small amounts of solid radioactive waste are authorised for disposal with ordinary refuse. The limits for such 'dustbin disposals' are:
  (a) 400 kBq (~ 10 µCi) in any 0.1 m^3 and;
  (b) 40 kBq (~ 1 µCi) per article.
However where the radioactive content is due solely to the presence of carbon-14 and/or tritium, those limits are relaxed to 4000 kBq (~ 100 µCi) in any 0.1 m^3 and not more than 400 kBq (~ 10 µCi) in any one item. A volume of 0.1 m^3 is taken to be the equivalent of one dustbin. Alpha emitters and strontium-90 are usually excluded from dustbin disposals. Dustbin disposals under these conditions present no hazard either to the refuse collectors or at the disposal site.

Incineration

55. This method of disposal is useful for wastes which are obnoxious or biologically toxic, and is sometimes advisable simply because the wastes concerned are combustible or inflammable. It often has the advantage of reducing the volume of solid waste ultimately requiring disposal, but on the other hand it suffers from the potential disadvantages that the radioactivity (from nuclides other than tritium and carbon-14) may be concentrated in the ash. Where the quantity and nature of the radionuclides and the throughput of ash production of the incinerator are known authorisations for disposal in this way are generally given on a case by case basis, taking all the local circumstances into account. However it is usual to permit disposals of up to 4 MBq (~ 100 µCi) a day of the commonly used tritium and carbon-14 without this detailed examination. Conditions concerning safe disposal of the ash are laid down, where necessary, in the authorisation for disposal of the waste to the incinerator, rather than in a separate authorisation.

Special precautions disposals

56. Within certain limits and provided that special precautions are observed, solid wastes which are too radioactive for dustbin disposal may be disposed of at suitable landfill sites. The appropriate precautions are specified in the authorisation for disposal. The ones usually employed are—
  (a) waste shall be conveyed to the disposal site in a sealed, plain, unlabelled plastic or multi-layer paper sack, in a closed metal bin;
  (b) at the disposal site the sack shall be removed from the bin and placed either at the foot of the tipping face or in a hole dug for it, and immediately covered with inactive refuse to a depth of not less than 1.5 m.

The usual limits are that no one sack shall contain more than 4 MBq ($\sim$100 µCi) of radionuclides of half life greater than one year and 40 MBq ($\sim$1 mCi) of others, except that where the radioactive content is due solely to the presence of carbon-14 and/or tritium the limit is 200 MBq ($\sim$5 mCi) per sack. There may be a further restriction of not more than 400 kBq ($\sim$10 µCi) of long lived activity in relation to any one article in the waste, where the activity is not due to carbon-14 or tritium.

57. Authorisations for special precautions disposals are only granted where the disposal will be at sites with the necessary characteristics and after consultation with the appropriate public and local bodies. The Act (section 9 (4)) allows the disposal authority to make a charge for special precautions disposals.

Demolition wastes and other high volume wastes which are of low specific activity or are lightly contaminated

58. Demolition wastes and other high volume wastes having a radioactive content of less than 4 Bq/g ($\sim$10^{-4} µCi/g) should be normally authorised for removal to a tip and burial at a depth of at least 1·5 m. Wastes of less than 0·4 Bq/g ($\sim$10^{-5} µCi/g) may be left on the site and, if significant economic savings can be made, this limit may be raised to 1 Bq/g ($\sim$3 × 10^{-5} µCi/g). Burial of wastes with higher specific activity on the site at which they arise should only be authorised in special circumstances.

Trench burial at a special site

59. The Drigg Site some 4 miles south of Sellafield is owned and operated by BNFL. It is currently the only site generally available in the UK for disposal of solid waste unsuitable for special precautions disposal. The wastes authorised to be disposed of at Drigg by BNFL are subject to the following restrictions:
  (a) that the waste is buried in the ground beneath at least 1·0 metre of top cover;
  (b) that no burial excavation penetrates through the boulder clay stratum;
  (c) that the dose rate at the surface of substantially unshielded waste containing radio-nuclides emitting beta particles or gamma radiation, does not exceed 7·5 mGy (0·75 rads) per hour;
  (d) that in all the matter (whether or not consisting wholly of the waste) buried on the site in any one day;
    (i) the alpha activity on the average does not exceed 740 MBq/m^3 (20 mCi/m^3); and
    (ii) the beta activity of beta emitting radionuclides which do not emit gamma radiation on the average does not exceed 2·2 GBq/m^3 (60 mCi/m^3).
60. The Government have accepted that additional sites for this type of waste burial should be identified.

Sea disposal of solid waste

61. The UK has regularly carried out disposal of packages of solid low level radioactive waste in the deep ocean since 1949. In recent years there has been an annual disposal at an internationally agreed site in the North Atlantic. This site is well away from shipping lanes, major fishing grounds and submarine cables.

62. The amount and type of waste disposed of at sea conforms to international agreements to which the UK is a signatory. The London Dumping Convention, which is implemented in the UK by the Dumping at Sea Act 1974, prohibits the sea disposal of waste defined as unsuitable by the International Atomic Energy Agency (IAEA) and requires the granting of a special licence by the competent national authority for the sea disposal of other radioactive waste. The IAEA currently recommends that only solid or solidified packaged waste* be disposed of at sea and defines as unsuitable any waste or other matters with a concentration exceeding:
  (a) 1 Ci/t (37 GBq/t) for alpha emitters but limited to 10^{-1} Ci/t (3·7 GBq/t) for radium-226 and supported polonium-210;
  (b) 10^2 Ci/t (3·7 TBq/t) for beta/gamma emitters with half lives of at least 0·5 years (excluding tritium) and beta/gamma emitters of unknown half lives; and
  (c) 10^6 Ci/t (37 P Bq/t) for tritium and beta/gamma emitters with half lives of less than 0·5 years.
    (NB the above activity concentrations must be averaged over a mass not exceeding 1000 t.).
In granting a licence, the competent national authority must take into account such matters as possible effects on marine life and the environment and the practical availability of land based methods of treatment or disposal. This licence is additional to authorisations under the

---

* Save for a relaxation for small quantities of liquids which must be absorbed onto a solid substrate.

Radioactive Substances Act 1960. The competent national authority for issuing licences for waste loaded in England is the Minister of Agriculture, Fisheries and Food and in Wales the Secretary of State for Wales; in Scotland it is the Secretary of State for Scotland; and in Northern Ireland, the Department of the Environment for Northern Ireland.

63. There is also a Multilateral Consultation and Surveillance Mechanism set up by the Organisation for Economic Co-operation and Development (OECD). This provides for the establishment and keeping under review of standards and recommended safety procedures, periodic assessments of the suitability of the disposal site, consultation with other member countries on each proposed disposal operation and surveillance of the disposal operation by an independent observer appointed by the Director-General of the Nuclear Energy Agency of the OECD.

64. The UK participates fully in relevant international studies including consideration by an expert group of a 'de minimis' level which would allow lightly contaminated wastes to be disposed of at sea without packaging and transport to the deep ocean.

Disposal practices—liquid wastes

65. Liquid wastes are disposed of either to surface waters or to the sea. Discharges from major nuclear establishments are evaluated individually and authorisations include quantitative limits with specific reference to individual nuclides where appropriate. Authorisations are kept under regular review in keeping with the spirit and principles of the ICRP recommendations. Currently when new or revised authorisations are issued, such opportunities are being used also to include a clause making specific reference to the ALARA principle (see para. 46(b)) in place of a previously mutually-accepted but unwritten understanding to this effect.

66. Disposal directly to the drains, without prior collection or storage in hold-up tanks, is the most convenient and radiologically safe method of disposal of relatively small amounts of low activity liquid radioactive waste. Authorisations are usually given in terms of activity per month with limits on individual radionuclides where this is necessary. Several GBq (a few Ci) a month, more for tritium, have been authorised for some establishments; others are able to operate with much smaller limits. Hospitals discharging the excreta of patients who have been given therapeutic or diagnostic doses of radioactive substances are amongst the premises having the largest authorisations, although such wastes are mainly of radionuclides with short half lives. The radioactive waste is diluted immediately with other waste waters and in most cases the average concentration in the effluent from the establishment is orders of magnitude below the permissible level for drinking water. There is no formal upper limit for the average concentration of radioactivity in liquid effluents. Each case is considered on its merits: taking account of the toxicity of the radionuclides discharged; the possibility that they may settle out in the sewerage system; their behaviour in the sewage treatment process and ultimately in the effluent, whether discharged to a soakaway, stream, river or the sea. The authorising departments continue to check their assessments by monitoring where appropriate.

Disposal practices—atmospheric discharges

67. New authorisations for emissions to atmosphere from major nuclear establishments are now being expressed in quantitative terms for the more radiologically significant emissions, as well as specifying that the best practicable means should be used to limit emissions. Existing authorisations will be amended on a programmed basis. Authorisations for emissions to atmosphere by other users of radioactive substances have usually included a specific limit on the activity which may be discharged in a given period. Such authorisations usually require discharges to be made directly from discharge points, in such a manner as to prevent re-entry into any part of the premises. Treatment techniques, such as filtration or absorption are rarely stipulated; if such techniques are employed, they must be relevant, and, from time to time after installation, their effectiveness must be demonstrated.

APPENDIX I

EXTRACT FROM SECTION 18 OF THE ACT GIVING THE DEFINITION OF
RADIOACTIVE MATERIAL AND RADIOACTIVE WASTE

18.—(1) In this Act 'radioactive material' means anything which, not being waste, is either a substance to which this subsection applies or an article made wholly or partly from, or incorporating, such a substance.

(2) The preceding subsection applies to any substances falling within either or both of the following descriptions, that is to say,—

(a) a substance containing an element specified in the first column of the Third Schedule to this Act, in such a proportion that the number of microcuries of that element contained in the substance, divided by the number of grammes which the substance weighs, is a number greater than that specified in relation to that element in the appropriate column of that Schedule;

(b) a substance possessing radioactivity which is wholly or partly attributable to a process of nuclear fission or other process of subjecting a substance to bombardment by neutrons or to ionising radiations, not being a process occurring in the course of nature, or in consequence of the disposal of radioactive waste, or by way of contamination in the course of the application of a process to some other substance.

(3) In paragraph (a) of the last preceding subsection 'the appropriate column'—

(a) in relation to a solid substance, means the second column;

(b) in relation to a liquid substance, means the third column; and

(c) in relation to a substance which is a gas or vapour means the fourth column.

(4) In this Act 'radioactive waste' means waste which consists wholly or partly of—

(a) a substance or article which, if it were not waste, would be radioactive material, or

(b) a substance or article which has been contaminated in the course of the production, keeping or use of radioactive material, or by contact with or proximity to other waste falling within the preceding paragraph or this paragraph.

THE THIRD SCHEDULE TO THE ACT

SPECIFIED ELEMENTS

Element	Microcuries per gramme		
	Solid	Liquid	Gas or Vapour
1. Actinium	1×10^{-5}	2×10^{-6}	7×10^{-11}
2. Lead	2×10^{-5}	1×10^{-7}	3×10^{-9}
3. Polonium	1×10^{-5}	7×10^{-7}	6×10^{-9}
4. Protoactinium	1×10^{-5}	9×10^{-7}	3×10^{-11}
5. Radium	1×10^{-5}	1×10^{-8}	1×10^{-9}
6. Radon	—		1×10^{-6}
7. Thorium	7×10^{-5}	1×10^{-6}	6×10^{-10}
8. Uranium	3×10^{-4}	2×10^{-5}	2×10^{-9}

APPENDIX II

EXEMPTION ORDERS

The Radioactive Substances (Civil Defence) Exemption Order

England and Wales S.I. 1962 No. 2641
Scotland S.I. 1962 No. 2767 (S.127)

The Order was introduced to conditionally exempt the local authority and industrial civil defence units which were in operation at that time from registration and authorisation. Civil defence work has undergone considerable reorganisation since 1962 and some of the exempted uses of radioactive material have been discontinued. It is proposed that the Order should be revoked.

The Radioactive Substances (Testing Instruments) Exemption Order

England and Wales S.I. 1962 No. 2643
Scotland S.I. 1962 No. 2764 (S. 124)
Northern Ireland SR & O 1962 No. 241

This Order applies to scientific and technical instruments which are used for measuring radioactivity and for investigating the properties of substances. These instruments incorporate or are accompanied by closed radioactive sources for the purpose of calibration. The Order gives conditional exemption from registration for the instruments and for mobile radioactive apparatus consisting of such instruments. The disposal of these sources by return to manufacturers is exempt from the need to have an authorisation. The possibility of extending the scope of this Order is currently under consideration.

The Radioactive Substances (Luminous Articles) Exemption Order

England and Wales S.I. 1962 No. 2644

Scotland S.I. 1962 No. 2761 (S. 121)
Northern Ireland SR & O 1962 No. 251

This Order applies to articles consisting of instruments, signs and indicators containing radioactive luminescent substances. The instruments are of two types. The first type contains luminous material which is substantially insoluble in water and is in the form of either glass, vitreous enamel or a similar substance. The second type of instrument incorporates tritium or krypton-85 gas in a sealed container. Both types of sign or instrument are conditionally exempted from registration and authorisation as are loose components of instruments and components of clocks or watches. The use of radioactive paint, glass or vitreous enamel in luminous instruments has largely been superseded by the use of gaseous tritium sources. These gaseous sources are to be dealt with in a separate Order and the provisions relating to the other types of signs, instruments and indicators will be modified.

The Radioactive Substances (Exhibitions) Exemption Order

England and Wales S.I. 1962 No. 2645
Scotland S.I. 1962 No. 2768 (S. 128)
Northern Ireland SR & O 1962 No. 250

The purpose of this Order is to exempt from registration the use of small quantities of radioactive materials at trade exhibitions. On any exhibition stand there must not be more than 1mCi of radionuclides in sealed and closed sources and not more than 3 open sources of specified radionuclides.

The Radioactive Substances (Storage in Transit) Exemption Order

England and Wales S.I. 1962 No. 2648
Scotland S.I. 1962 No. 2765 (S. 125)
Northern Ireland SR & O 1962 No. 246

This Order grants conditional exemption from registration for the temporary storage whilst in transit of a limited number of packages of radioactive material which would bear labels indicating their radioactive content. Not more than five such packages may be held at any one time and no package may be kept on the premises for longer than 2 weeks.

The Radioactive Substances (Phosphatic Substances, Rare Earths etc.) Exemption Order

England and Wales S.I. 1962 No. 2648
Scotland S.I. 1962 No. 2769 (S. 129)
Northern Ireland SR & O 1962 No. 249

The substances and articles to which this Order applies are radioactive material within the meaning of the Act because they contain one or more of the elements listed in the Third Schedule to the Act in concentrations higher than the appropriate limits included in that Schedule. Unconditional exemption from registration and authorisation is given for certain substances and articles which are derived from phosphatic ores or which contain the rare earth elements or titanium, yttrium, zirconium, niobium or hafnium. Exemption is also given for lighter flints.

The Radioactive Substances (Lead) Exemption Order

England and Wales S.I. 1962 No. 2649
Scotland S.I. 1962 No. 2762 (S. 122)
Northern Ireland SR & O 1962 No. 240

Unconditional exemption from the registration and authorisation requirements is given for substances and articles containing lead in common use.

The Radioactive Substances (Uranium and Thorium) Exemption Order

England and Wales S.I. 1962 No. 2710
Scotland S.I. 1962 No. 2766 (S. 126)
Northern Ireland SR & O 1962 No. 244

This Order exempts from registration and authorisation a number of common-place materials containing natural uranium and natural thorium which are radioactive within the meaning of the Act because their concentration of these elements exceed the appropriate limits included in the Third Schedule to the Act. These materials include thoriated tungsten used for electric lamp filaments, certain hard metal alloys, incandescent mantels, heat-resisting thoria ware made from thorium dioxide and uranium glass used for certain optical equipment.

The Radioactive Substances (Prepared Uranium and Thorium Compounds) Exemption Order

England and Wales S.I. 1962 No. 2711
Scotland S.I. 1962 No. 2766 (S. 126)
Northern Ireland SR & O 1962 No. 242

This Order applies to prepared compounds of either uranium or thorium from which each of the radioactive decay products has been substantially removed in the course of preparation. These compounds are commonly used in laboratories. Their use for demonstrating or investigating the characteristics of any material is exempt from registration provided that not more than 2 kilogrammes of uranium and thorium are held on the premises. Conditional exemption from authorisation is also given for these materials.

The Radioactive Substances (Geological Specimens) Exemption Order

England and Wales S.I. 1962 No. 2712
Scotland S.I. 1962 No. 2771 (S. 131)
Northern Ireland SR & O 1962 No. 248

This Order applies to specimens of natural rocks and natural minerals containing uranium or thorium or both. Exemption from registration is given for specimens kept for demonstration, investigation or sale provided that the amount of uranium and thorium in the specimens on the premises does not exceed 100 kilogrammes. Conditional exemption from authorisation is given for specimens which are substantially insoluble in water. Disposal may be by means of the local authority refuse disposal service or to a tip which is used for the deposit of substantial quantities of non-radioactive waste.

The Radioactive Substances (Waste Closed Sources) Exemption Order

England and Wales S.I. 1962 No. 1831
Scotland S.I. 1963 No. 1877 (S. 94)
Northern Ireland SR & O 1963 No. 222

This Order conditionally exempts waste closed sources from authorisation provided they are returned to a manufacturer who deals in the same kind of radioactive material, or to a person who is authorised under the 1960 Act to dispose of such sources. The Order also exempts waste closed sources from being authorised to remain in storage provided they are stored under certain conditions and not kept on premises for more than 12 weeks.

The Radioactive Substances (Schools etc.) Exemption Order

England and Wales S.I. 1963 No. 1832
Scotland S.I. 1963 No. 1878 (S. 95)
Northern Ireland SR & O 1963 No. 219

The Order applies to the following education establishments:
1. all schools, except those independent schools not recognised as efficient by the Department of Education and Science and the Welsh Office;
2. establishments of further education maintained or assisted by local education authorities;
3. independent establishments of further education either receiving grants from the DES or WO or which are recognised as efficient by the DES or WO;
4. colleges of education.

The Scottish Order exempts a somewhat similar range of premises.

The Order gives conditional exemption from registration for closed sources containing any radionuclides and also open sources which contain beta-gamma emitting radionuclides other than strontium-90. The total amount of active material which can be held on the premises is limited. Conditional exemption from authorisation is also given.

Because independent schools and independent colleges of further education are no longer recognised as 'efficient' for the purposes of the Education Act 1944 by the DES and WO, the Exemption Order will be revised to reflect the current position.

The Radioactive Substances (Hospitals Waste) Exemption Order (as amended)

England and Wales S.I. 1963 No. 1833 and S.I. 1974 No. 501

Scotland S.I. 1963 No. 1879 (S. 96) and S.I. 1974 No. 487 (S. 35)
Northern Ireland SR & O 1963 No. 217

This Order applies to national health service hospitals. Conditional exemption is given for the disposal from hospitals of wastes arising from the administration of very low doses of radioactive materials to patients. It therefore covers such things as waste from medical treatment, human excreta, articles which have contained radioactive substances used for medical treatment and residual ash arising from these wastes being burnt. The Order will be amended inter alia to take account of organisational changes in health service administration which come into effect on April 1, 1982.

The Radioactive Substances (Thorium X) Exemption Order (as amended)

England and Wales S.I. 1963 No. 1834 and S.I. 1974 No. 500
Scotland S.I. 1963 No. 1880 (S. 97) and S.I. 1974 No. 488 (S. 36)
Northern Ireland SR & O 1963 No. 221

This Order gives conditional exemption from registration for the keeping and use in certain hospitals, nursing homes and pharmacists' premises of prepared thorium-X for purposes of medical treatment. The manufacture of thorium-X ceased in the UK in 1975. The Order will therefore be revoked.

The Radioactive Substances (Attachments to Lightning Conductors) Exemption Order

England and Wales S.I. 1963 No. 1835
Scotland S.I. 1963 No. 1881 (S. 98)
Northern Ireland SR & O 1963 No. 216

This Order gives exemption from registration in respect of radioactive material in devices attached to lightning conductors. This exemption is subject to the condition that the occupier of the premises where the device is installed must notify the address and date of installation to the Secretary of State. There are also other conditions about safety notices, the manner in which the device is secured onto the lightning conductor and the notification of loss, damage or theft. The exemption applies only to installed devices.

The Radioactive Substances (Precipitated Phosphate) Exemption Order

England and Wales S.I. 1963 No. 1836
Scotland S.I. 1963 No. 1882 (S. 99)
Northern Ireland SR & O 1963 No. 218

The Order gives exemption from registration in respect of the keeping and use of substances which consist of or contain precipitated phosphate which is a by-product of the manufacture of sodium phosphate and contains among a number of metals a very small amount of uranium and its decay products.

The Radioactive Substances (Electronic Valves) Exemption Order

England and Wales S.I. 1967 No. 1797
Scotland S.I. 1967 No. 1803 (S. 166)
Northern Ireland SR & O 1967 No. 313

This Order gives exemption from registration and authorisation in respect of certain valves used in such things as telecommunications and radar equipment. Valves containing not more than specified low levels of radioactive material are exempted from registration and waste valves are exempted from authorisation if they are disposed of by means of the local authority refuse collection service. Manufacturers of these valves are not covered by these exemptions. It is proposed that the scope of this Order will be widened to cover other types of electronic tube.

The Radioactive Substances (Tokens for Vending Machines) Exemption Order

England and Wales S.I. 1968 No. 935
Scotland S.I. 1968 No. 954 (S. 100)
Northern Ireland SR & O 1968 No. 139

Unconditional exemption from registration and authorisation is given in respect of tokens incorporating small amounts of carbon-14 designed to facilitate self service at petrol stations and other automatic vending machines. These tokens were used experimentally at 4 places, but shortly after the Order was made the relevant Home Office and local authority regulations were changed and cash accepting machines were permitted at petrol stations. The Order will therefore be revoked.

The Radioactive Substances (Vouchers for Encashment Machines) Exemption Order

England and Wales S.I. 1968 No. 936
Scotland S.I. 1968 No. 953 (S. 99)
Northern Ireland SR & O 1968 No. 140

The Order applies to vouchers held by banks for use in automatic cash machines. Unconditional exemption from registration and authorisation is given for cash machine vouchers containing small amounts of carbon-14. The Order does not apply to the premises of the manufacturer of these vouchers or to that of their despatch agents.

The Radioactive Substances (Smoke Detectors) Exemption Order

England and Wales S.I. 1980 No. 953
Scotland S.I. 1980 No. 1599 (S. 126)
Northern Ireland SR & O 1980 No. 304

Conditional exemption from registration is given for loose smoke detectors which incorporate closed sources, containing not more than 40 kBq of americium-241 or for smoke detectors incorporating closed sources containing in the aggregate not more than 4 MBq of other radionuclides and their decay products and which are attached or affixed to premises. Not more than 100 of the 40 kBq smoke detectors may be kept on any premises without being registered unless they are attached or affixed to premises.

Exemption from registration is also given for the use of up to 10 americium-241 smoke detectors in mobile radioactive apparatus. The disposal of smoke detectors by return to manufacturers who deal in the same kind of radioactive material, or to persons who are authorised under the 1960 Act to dispose of such sources, is exempt from authorisation.

APPENDIX III

PROCEDURE FOR MAKING APPLICATIONS—
FORMS OF APPLICATION

Application forms are available from:

England	Department of the Environment, Room A502, Romney House, 43 Marsham Street, London SW1P 3PY Tel 01 212 6328
Wales	Welsh Office, Room 2002, New Crown Building, Cathays Park, Cardiff, South Glamorgan CF1 3NQ Tel 0222 824156
Scotland	Scottish Development Department, Room 510, Pentland House, 47 Robbs Loan, Edinburgh EH14 1TY Tel 031 443 8681 extension 381 or 227
Northern Ireland	Department of the Environment for Northern Ireland, Environmental Protection Branch, Stormont, Belfast BT4 3SS Tel 0232 63210

The appropriate forms are:

1. Application for registration under s.1 .... Form RSA1
2. Application for registration under s.3 (mobile radioactive apparatus) .... Form RSA2
3. Application for authorisation under s.6 for disposal of radioactive waste and/or for authorisation under s.7 for the accumulation of radioactive waste .... Form RSA3

In England applications for authorisations for UKAEA premises or licenced nuclear sites should be made by letter and sent both to the Department of the Environment and to:

Ministry of Agriculture, Fisheries and Food, Room 257, Great Westminster House, Horseferry Road, London SW1P 2AE
Tel 01 216 6111

APPENDIX IV
EXPLANATORY NOTE ON THE INTRODUCTION OF SI UNITS

The International System of Units (SI) is a set of units intended for use in all branches of science and the UK is committed to its adoption. The General Conference on Weights and Measures has adopted special names for SI units used in connection with radioactivity. The SI unit for the quantity of radioactivity is the becquerel (Bq). It is defined as a unit of activity equal to one nuclear disintegration per second. The becquerel has replaced the curie (Ci) which was based upon the activity of one gram of radium. Table I shows the relationship between the becquerel and the curie.

The SI unit for the quantity of absorbed radiation dose is the gray (Gy). It has replaced the rad. One gray is equal to 100 rads (see Table I). The quantity absorbed dose is multiplied by modifying factors characteristic of the type of radiation in order to generate a quantity dose equivalent which takes into account the different effectiveness of the various ionising radiations in causing harm to tissue. In the old system of units, the unit of dose equivalent was the rem. In the SI system the gray is related to the new unit of dose equivalent, the sievert (Sv), in exactly the same way. One sievert is equal to 100 rems (see Table I).

It should be noted that very much larger numbers are required to express activity in becquerels and the prefixes to be used with SI units, shown in Table II, allow for this.

Table III is a conversion table from curies to becquerels and Table IV from becquerels to curies.

UNITS OF RADIOACTIVITY
RELATIONSHIP BETWEEN SI UNITS AND NON SI-UNITS

TABLE I

Physical Quantity	SI Unit	Non-SI Unit	Relationship
Activity	becquerel (Bq)	curie (Ci)	1 Bq $= 2.7 \times 10^{-11}$ Ci $= 27$ pCi 1 Ci $= 3.7 \times 10^{10}$ Bq $= 37$ GBq
Absorbed Dose	gray (Gy)	rad (rad)	1 Gy $= 100$ rads 1 rad $= 0.01$ Gy $= 10$ mGy
Dose Equivalent	sievert (Sv)	rem (rem)	1 Sv $= 100$ rems 1 rem $= 0.01$ Sv $= 10$ mSv

PREFIXES FOR SI UNITS

TABLE II

Factor	Prefix	Symbol	Factor	Prefix	Symbol
10^{12}	tera	T	10^{-3}	milli	m
10^{9}	giga	G	10^{-6}	micro	μ
10^{6}	mega	M	10^{-9}	nano	n
10^{3}	kilo	k	10^{-12}	pico	p

CONVERSION FROM CURIES TO BECQUERELS

TABLE III

pCi nCi μCi mCi Ci	mBq Bq kBq MBq GBq	pCi nCi μCi mCi Ci	Bq kBq MBq GBq TBq
0·1	3·7	30	1·11
0·2	7·4	40	1·48
0·25	9·25	50	1·85
0·3	11·1	60	2·22
0·4	14·8	70	2·59
0·5	18·5	80	2·96
1	37	90	3·33
2	74	100	3·7
2·5	92·5	125	4·625
3	111	150	5·55
4	148	200	7·4
5	185	250	9·25
6	222	300	11·1
7	259	400	14·8
8	296	500	18·5
9	333	600	22·2
10	370	700	25·9
12	444	750	27·75
15	555	800	29·6
20	740	900	33·3
25	925	1000	37

Examples

2·5 nCi = 92·5 Bq	900 pCi = 33·3 Bq
0·2 μCi = 7·4 kBq	50 μCi = 1·85 MBq
5 mCi = 185 MBq	200 mCi = 7·4 GBq
20 Ci = 740 GBq	1000 Ci = 37 TBq

CONVERSION FROM BECQUERELS TO CURIES

TABLE IV

mBq Bq kBq MBq GBq	pCi nCi μCi mCi Ci	Bq kBq MBq GBq TBq	pCi nCi μCi mCi Ci
1	0·027	1	27
2	0·054	2	54
3	0·081	3	81
4	0·108	4	108
5	0·135	5	135
6	0·162	6	162
7	0·189	7	189
8	0·216	8	216
9	0·243	9	243
10	0·27	10	270
15	0·405	15	405
50	1·35	20	540
100	2·7	25	675
200	5·4	30	810
250	6·75	35	945
500	13·5	40	1080
750	20·25		
1000	27		

Examples

3 mBq	= 0·081 pCi		7 kBq	= 189 nCi
5 kBq	= 0·135 μCi		3 MBq	= 81 μCi
9 MBq	= 0·243 mCi		15 GBq	= 405 mCi
250 GBq	= 6·75 Ci		35 TBq	= 945 Ci

APPENDIX V
GLOSSARY OF TERMS

Radiation—The process of emitting energy as waves of particles. The energy thus radiated. Often used for 'Ionising radiation' (see below).

Ionisation—The process by which a neutral atom or molecule acquires an electric charge.

Ionising radiation—'Radiation' that produces 'Ionisation' in matter, *e.g.* alpha particles, beta particles, gamma rays, X rays and neutrons.

Absorbed dose—The quantity of energy imparted by ionising radiation to unit mass of matter, such as tissue.

Dose equivalent—The quantity obtained by multiplying the absorbed dose by a factor to allow for the different effectiveness of the various ionising radiations in causing harm to tissue. The factor for gamma rays, x-rays, and beta particles is 1, for neutrons 10, and for alpha particles 20.

Effective dose equivalent—The quantity obtained by multiplying the 'dose equivalents' to various tissues and organs by the risk weighting factor appropriate to each and summing the products.

Collective effective dose equivalent—The quantity obtained by multiplying the average 'effective dose equivalent' by the number of persons exposed to a given source of radiation.

Critical group—That group of members of the general public representative of those expected to receive the highest radiation dose as a result of the discharge of a particular radioisotope to the environment from a site.

Optimisation—The process which is used to assess whether the radiation exposure of individuals and the collective dose arising from radioactive wastes has been reduced to levels which are as low as reasonably achievable, economic and social factors being taken into account.

Lifetime dose equivalent—The integral or the summation of the instantaneous 'dose equivalent' rates over an individual's lifetime.

APPENDIX 2

ATOMIC ENERGY AND RADIOACTIVE SUBSTANCES

The Radioactive Substances (Appeals) Regulations 1990

(S.I. 1990 No. 2504)

Made - - - - - - - -	*10th December 1990*
Laid before Parliament - - - - -	*11th December 1990*
Coming into force - - - - - -	*1st January 1991*

The Secretary of State for the Environment as respects England, the Secretary of State for Wales as respects Wales and the Secretary of State for Scotland as respects Scotland, in exercise of their powers under sections 11D(6) and (11) of the Radioactive Substances Act 1960 (c. 34) and of all other powers enabling them in that behalf, hereby make the following Regulations:

Citation, commencement and interpretation

1.—(1) These Regulations may be cited as the Radioactive Substances (Appeals) Regulations 1990 and shall come into force on 1st January 1991.

(2) In these Regulations "the 1960 Act" means the Radioactive Substances Act 1960.

Notice of appeal

2.—(1) A person who wishes to appeal to the Secretary of State under section 11D of the 1960 Act shall give written notice of the appeal to the Secretary of State.

(2) The notice of appeal shall be accompanied by the following—

(a) a full statement of the appellant's case;

(b) a copy of any relevant application;

(c) a copy of any relevant certificate of registration or authorisation;

(d) a copy of any relevant correspondence between the appellant and the chief inspector;

(e) a copy of any decision or notice which is the subject-matter of the appeal;

(f) a statement indicating whether the appellant wishes the appeal to be in the form of a hearing or to be disposed of on the basis of written representations.

(3) Any request by the appellant that an appeal be withdrawn shall be made to the Secretary of State in writing.

Time limit for bringing appeal

3.—(1) Subject to paragraph (2) below, notice of appeal pursuant to regulation 2(1) above is to be given before the expiry of the period of two months beginning with the date on which—

(a) a copy of the decision or notice which is the subject-matter of the appeal is sent to the appellant; or

(b) the relevant application is treated as having been refused pursuant to section 1(3A), 3(4B) or 8(3B) (sections 1(3A), 3(4B) and 8(3B) were inserted by paragraph 11 of Schedule 5 to the Environmental Protection Act 1990) of the 1960 Act,

or before the expiry of such longer period as may be allowed by the Secretary of State.

(2) Where the appeal is against the decision of the chief inspector to cancel a registration or to revoke an authorisation, notice of appeal shall be given before the expiry of the period of 28 days beginning with the date on which notice of the decision is given to the appellant under section 5(2) or 8(8) (section 5(2) was amended by s.100(2) of the Environmental Protection Act 1990 and s.8(8) was amended by paragraph 1(5) of Sched. 5 to that Act) of the 1960 Act or before the expiry of such longer period as may be allowed by the Secretary of State.

Action upon receipt of notice of appeal

4.—(1) Upon receipt of a notice of appeal accompanied by the documents specified in regulation 2(2) above, the Secretary of State shall send to the chief inspector a copy of the notice of appeal, the statement of the appellant's case and the appellant's statement indicating whether he wishes the appeal to be in the form of a hearing or to be disposed of on the basis of written representations.

(2) Where the appeal is against a decision in respect of an application for an authorisation under section 6 of the 1960 Act on which the chief inspector consulted any local authority, local fisheries committee, river purification authority, statutory water undertakers or other public or local authority under section 9(3) of the 1960 Act (section 9(3) was amended as respects

England and Wales by para. 27(2)(b) of Sched. 25 to the Water Act 1989 (c. 15). It was further amended by s.100(2) of, and para. 2(1) of Sched. 5 to, the Environmental Protection Act 1990), the chief inspector shall notify the Secretary of State of the names of the authorities consulted.

(3) The Secretary of State shall send to any authority whose name is notified to him under paragraph (2) above a notice stating that an appeal has been lodged and that within a period of 21 days beginning with the date of service of that notice the authority may make representations to the Secretary of State with respect to the subject-matter of the appeal.

Written representations

5.—(1) Where the appellant informs the Secretary of State that he wishes the appeal to be disposed of on the basis of written representations, the chief inspector may submit written representations to the Secretary of State not later than 28 days after receiving a copy of the appellant's statements.

(2) The appellant may make further representations by way of reply to any representations from the chief inspector not later than 17 days after the date of submission of those representations by the chief inspector.

(3) Any representations made by the chief inspector or the appellant shall be dated and submitted to the Secretary of State on the date they bear.

(4) When the appellant or the chief inspector submits any representations to the Secretary of State under paragraph (3) above he shall at the same time send a copy to the other party.

(5) The Secretary of State shall send to the appellant and the chief inspector a copy of any representations made to him by the authorities mentioned in regulation 4(2) above and shall allow the appellant and the chief inspector a period of not less than 14 days in which to make representations thereon.

(6) The Secretary of State may in a particular case set later time limits than those mentioned in this regulation.

Hearings

6.—(1) The Secretary of State shall give the appellant and the chief inspector at least 28 days written notice of the date, time and place for the holding of any hearing unless they agree to a shorter period of notice.

(2) Subject to paragraph 3 below, in the case of a hearing which is to be held wholly or partly in public, the Secretary of State shall, at least 21 days before the date fixed for the hearing—
  (a) publish a copy of the notice mentioned in paragraph (1) above in at least one newspaper circulating in the locality in which the activity which is the subject-matter of the appeal is or would be carried on; and
  (b) in a case where the Secretary of State is informed under regulation 4(2) above that the chief inspector has consulted any authority, serve a copy of that notice on every authority which was consulted.

(3) The Secretary of State may vary the date fixed for the holding of any hearing and paragraphs (1) and (2) above shall apply to the variation of a date as they applied to the date originally fixed.

(4) The Secretary of State may also vary the time or place for the holding of a hearing but shall give such notice of any such variation as appears to him to be reasonable.

(5) After the conclusion of the hearing the person appointed to conduct the hearing shall make a report in writing to the Secretary of State which shall include his conclusions together with his recommendations or his reasons for not making any recommendations.

Notification of determination

7.—(1) The Secretary of State shall notify the appellant in writing of his determination of the appeal and of his reasons for it and, if a hearing is held, shall at the same time provide him with a copy of the report of the person who conducted the hearing.

(2) The Secretary of State shall at the same time send a copy of those documents to the chief inspector and to any authority to which he was required to give notice of the appeal under regulation 4(3) above.

Michael Heseltine
7th December 1990   Secretary of State for the Environment

David Hunt
10th December 1990   Secretary of State for Wales

Signed by authority of
the Secretary of State for Scotland

James Douglas-Hamilton
Parliamentary Under-Secretary of State,
Scottish Office

10th December 1990

APPENDIX 3

GUIDANCE NOTE ON APPEALS

APPEALS

1. This note explains the procedures to be followed when a person intends to appeal against a decision of the Chief Inspector under the Radioactive Substances Act 1960. The statutory framework for the appeals system is provided by the Radioactive Substances (Appeals) Regulations 1990, and the requirements of the regulations are included in this note. However, some of the procedures set out below are not covered by the regulations, and they take the form of a code of practice, based on the well-established systems used for planning appeals. Adherence to the code is important for the smooth running of the appeals system.

MAKING AN APPEAL

2. Regulation 2 requires an appeal to be made in writing to the Secretary of State and that the notice of appeal must be accompanied by the following information:
   (a) a full statement of the appellant's case (this must be given in all appeals);
   (b) a copy of any relevant application (for a registration or authorisation);
   (c) a copy of any relevant certificate of registration or authorisation;
   (d) a copy of any relevant correspondence between the appellant and the Chief Inspector;
   (e) a copy of any decision or notice which is the subject-matter of the appeal; and
   (f) a statement indicating whether the appellant wishes the appeal to be determined on the basis of written representations or a hearing (see paragraph 7 below).

3. If at any time the appellant wishes to withdraw an appeal, regulation 2(3) provides that he must do so in writing.

TIME LIMIT FOR BRINGING AN APPEAL

4. Regulation 3(1) states than an appeal must be made within two months of the relevant date. Although the Secretary of State has the power to allow a longer period he would only do so in the most compelling circumstances. The relevant date (except in the case of a cancellation or revocation notice) is either:
   (a) the date on which a copy of the decision or notice which is the subject-matter of the appeal was sent to the appellant; or
   (b) the date on which the appellant deemed, under the provisions of new section 1(3A), 3(4B) or 8(3B) of the Radioactive Substances Act 1960, that the application had been refused. These sections provide that an application may be deemed to have been refused once the time allowed to the Chief Inspector for determining an application (currently four months) has lapsed.

5. The date by which an appeal must be made against a notice of cancellation or revocation is provided for in regulation 3(2) which states that the notice of appeal must be given before the expiry of the period of 28 days beginning with the date on which the notice was sent to the appellant. The Secretary of State has the power to extend the 28 day period but would only do so in exceptional circumstances.

6. If the appeal is out of time and no extension is allowed, the Department of the Environment (or, in Wales, the Welsh Office), acting for the Secretary of State, will inform the appellant that the appeal will not be considered. If the appellant has not supplied the information required under regulation 2, the Department will notify the appellant that the appeal will not be considered until the additional information is provided. This additional information should be provided to the Department within the time period specified in paragraph 4 or 5 above.

ACTION ON RECEIPT OF AN APPEAL

7. Once an appeal is received and if the appellant has asked for the appeal to be determined by written representations, the Department will send a copy of the appeal to the Chief Inspector and ask him whether he is also content for the written procedure to apply (in view of new section 11D(7) of the Act both parties must agree to the written procedure). If he is, and if the Secretary of State has no objection (the Secretary of State is unlikely to object except in the most important cases where a hearing is more appropriate in the public interest), the appeal will then begin to be decided by the written procedure. If, however, the appellant *or* the Chief Inspector wish the appeal to be determined following a hearing then one will be arranged.

8. The Department will notify the appellant and the Chief Inspector of the method by which the appeal is to be determined.

9. Regulation 4(2) provides that the Secretary of State must, in the case of appeals against a decision in respect of an application for an authorisation under Section 6 of RSA 60, notify the relevant statutory consultees. Notification of the lodging of an appeal will also be given to those organisations consulted under administrative arrangements. The notice will state that an appeal has been lodged and that further representations may be made to the Secretary of State within 21 days. The time and place of a hearing (if any) and a notification of the decision will be sent to those who make further representations.

10. These procedures are designed to ensure that, whether an appeal is determined through the written representation procedure or following a hearing, background information is available at an early stage to the person appointed to consider the appeal.

WRITTEN REPRESENTATIONS

11. Appeals may be resolved through the written representations procedure. The procedure does have certain advantages; for example, by removing the need to attend the hearing it is less time consuming for the parties to the appeal. In addition, by removing any necessary time delay associated with making the administrative arrangements associated with a hearing (such as finding a location for the appeal to be heard) the overall time spent in considering the appeal will in all probability be substantially less than that involved in a hearing.

12. Under paragraph 2 above a full statement of case setting out the grounds of appeal will be provided by the appellant. Regulation 5 states that the Chief Inspector has up to 28 days from the date he receives notification of the appellant's wish for the appeal to be determined by written representations, to provide a reply to the Department. The Chief Inspector should send a copy of his response to the appellant at the same time as he submits it to the Department. The appellant will then be given 17 days to reply to the Chief Inspector's representations, and he should similarly copy his reply to the Chief Inspector when he submits it to the Department. The reply given by the appellant will normally end the written representations, unless the Department considers that the final response by the appellant has raised new considerations which should be put to the Chief Inspector.

13. Where third parties make representations under the provisions of paragraph 9 above, the appellant and Chief Inspector will have a period of not less than 14 days in which to respond to those representations. At the same time as sending their responses to the Department, the appellant and Chief Inspector should send a copy to each other.

14. The complete papers will then be passed to an appeals inspector so that he may make recommendations to the Secretary of State. The inspector may if he thinks fit require either the appellant or the Chief Inspector to furnish further particulars of any relevant facts or contentions. He may also notify the appellant and the Chief Inspector at any time that he wishes to visit the site.

HEARINGS

15. Regulation 6 states that where a hearing is to be held the Secretary of State shall serve on the appellant and the Chief Inspector (wherever possible after consultation with them) a notice specifying the date, time and place for the holding of a hearing. This notice must be given at least 28 days before the date of the hearing unless a shorter period is agreed. A copy of that notice shall be published, not less than 21 days before the hearing is to take place, in at least one newspaper circulating in the locality in which the activity which is the subject-matter of the appeal is or would be carried on. If the Secretary of State varies the date, time or place of the hearing he must publish and notify the revised details.

16. An important element of the hearing procedure is that the appeals inspector, who will be appointed by the Secretary of State to conduct the hearing, must be fully aware of the issues and arguments likely to be made at the hearing so that he can properly lead the discussion. It is therefore essential that at least 21 days before the hearing the appellant and the Chief Inspector provide a written statement to the Department containing full particulars of the case they will wish to make at the hearing. The statements will be passed to the appeals inspector to enable him to prepare for the hearing. At the same time as sending their statements to the Department, the appellant and Chief Inspector should send a copy to each other.

17. The procedure at a hearing will be left to the appeals inspector. Any interested party may participate, and the appeals inspector may hear the parties in whatever order he thinks most suitable for the clarification of the issues, although the appellant will be given the opportunity to make any final comments before the discussion is closed. He may, for instance, review the case based on the papers already provided and then outline what he considers to be the main issues and indicate those matters which require further explanation or clarification. This will not preclude the appellant or the Chief Inspector from referring to other aspects which they consider to be relevant. The approach that will be encouraged will be one of informality. For

example, hearings may often take the form of a round table discussion, rather than a formal presentation of evidence.

18. The Secretary of State may appoint an assessor to sit with the appeals inspector at a hearing to advise the inspector on such matters arising as the Secretary of State may specify. When an assessor is appointed the appellant and the Chief Inspector will be notified of the name of the assessor and of the matters on which he is appointed to advise.

19. Although there will be no formal procedure rules applying to the hearing, the rules of natural justice will apply. The inspector will thus be concerned to ensure that any interested parties who wish to give evidence have a fair opportunity to have their say, and before taking into account any matter (not being a matter of Government policy) which has not previously been raised by the parties, he will give them a full opportunity to comment on it. However, it will be open to him to refuse to hear evidence which is irrelevant or repetitious and is therefore wasting time. It is up to the parties to decide whether or not they wish to be professionally represented, although this should not normally be necessary in order to gain an effective hearing.

20. The exchange of written material prior to the hearing should normally obviate the need for this to be read out at the hearing. It is important that the parties should make every effort to avoid introducing at the hearing new material or documents not previously referred to, as this may necessitate adjournment of the hearing to a later date. If documents are made available at the hearing, the inspector will ask or allow questions on those points on which he, or others taking part in the hearing, require further information or clarification. Generally, the inspector will wish to ensure that participants have an adequate opportunity to ask questions, provided those questions are relevant and the discussion proceeds in an orderly manner. The appellant will be given the opportunity to make any final comments before the discussion is closed.

21. The appeals inspector may adjourn a hearing to such time, place and on such terms as he thinks fit, although the wishes of the main parties will be taken into account. An appeal may be heard even though the appellant (or the Chief Inspector) is not present.

22. It may appear to the appeals inspector that certain matters could be more satisfactorily resolved if he were to adjourn the hearing to the site, normally then to be concluded there. The appeals inspector would only do this when, having regard to all the circumstances, including weather conditions, he was also satisfied that:

(a) the discussion could proceed satisfactorily and that no one involved would be at a disadvantage;

(b) the main parties at the hearing had the opportunity to attend;

(c) no one participating in the hearing objected to the discussion being continued on the site.

23. The hearing shall take place in public unless the appellant or Chief Inspector apply for it to be held either wholly or partly in private. Any such application should be made to the appeals inspector as soon as it has been agreed that the appeal will be disposed of by a hearing, and should demonstrate that a public hearing would result in the disclosure of information relating to a relevant process or trade secret (within the meaning of section 13(3) of the Radioactive Substances Act 1960).

PROCEDURE AFTER WRITTEN REPRESENTATIONS OR A HEARING

24. The Secretary of State may take into account any new evidence or new matter of fact that comes to his attention after the conclusion of the hearing or the exchanges of written representations but before final determination of the appeal. If the new information is considered to be material to the decision, it will be referred to the parties for their comments. The hearing may be re-opened if this is considered necessary to properly investigate the new evidence. Where a hearing is re-opened, the same procedure as those for the original hearing will normally apply.

DECISIONS

25. At the conclusion of the hearing regulation 6(5) provides that the appeals inspector must make a written report to the Secretary of State containing his conclusions and recommendations (including, where appropriate, recommended conditions that should be attached to the registration or authorisation). Any assessor assisting the appeals inspector may also report in writing in respect of the matters on which he was appointed to advise. If he does so, that report will also be appended to the report of the appeals inspector. The appeals inspector will also notify the Secretary of State in writing of his recommendations following the written representation procedure.

26. The Secretary of State will then consider the report and issue a written decision. The appeals inspector's report (and any report made by an assessor) shall be appended to the Secretary of State's decision. The decision and the report will then be sent to the appellant and the Chief Inspector. A copy of the decision and any report will also be sent to any organisation

consulted under the provisions of paragraph 9 above, and a copy of the decision only will be provided to any other person who appeared at the hearing.

27. Where a decision of the Secretary of State on an appeal (considered at a hearing or by written representations) is quashed in proceedings before any court, the Secretary of State:

(a) shall send to those persons who appeared at a hearing, or those who made written representations, a written statement of the matters with respect to which further representations are invited for the further consideration of the appeal;

(b) shall afford to those persons the opportunity of making, within 21 days of the written statement, written representations to him in respect of those matters or of asking for the re-opening of the hearing (where one has been held); and

(c) may, if appropriate, cause the hearing to be re-opened (whether by the same or a different appeals inspector), and if he does so he shall follow the procedures set out in regulation 6 of the Radioactive Substances (Appeals) Regulations 1990.

APPENDIX 4

DoE Circular 21/90

4 December 1990

Local Authority responsibilities for public access to information under the Radioactive Substances Act 1960 as amended by the Environmental Protection Act 1990

Introduction

1. This circular explains the new provisions on public access to information introduced into the Radioactive Substances Act 1960 (RSA 60) by Part V of the Environmental Protection Act 1990, and gives guidance to local authorities on their new obligations under the Act. The new provisions reflect the Government's long standing commitment to openness in the matter of environmental information.

2. This circular does not cover the public access to information provisions in respect of Integrated Pollution Control or any other environmental matters dealt with by other parts of the Environmental Protection Act. Separate guidance will be issued to authorities on these subjects, as appropriate.

3. In reading this circular it should be noted that in Wales the functions of the Minister of Agriculture, Fisheries and Food are exercised by the Secretary of State for Wales.

Position before Environmental Protection Act 1990

4. This section sets out the position under RSA 60 before introduction of the Environmental Protection Act 1990. These provisions will remain unaffected by the new legislation.

Framework of controls

5. RSA 60 provides that no radioactive material shall be kept or used unless a registration is first granted by the Secretary of State under section 1 of the Act, or section 3 in respect of mobile radioactive apparatus. Similarly no radioactive waste shall either be accumulated or disposed of unless this is first authorised under section 6 or 7. These registrations and authorisations are issued subject to such conditions as are necessary in order to protect man and the environment.

6. RSA 60 already contains limited provisions for sending documents to local authorities but no requirement for these documents to be made available to the public. The Secretary of State and, where appropriate, the Minister of Agriculture, Fisheries and Food are required to send copies of the following documents to local authorities for their information:

(a) Certificates of registration issued under section 1 are sent to those local authorities in whose area the premises to which the certificate relates are situated;

(b) Certificates of authorisation issued under section 6 or 7 are sent to those local authorities in whose area, in accordance with the authorisation applied for, radioactive waste is to be disposed of or accumulated. Where an authorisation is granted by the Secretary of State and the Minister of Agriculture, Fisheries and Food under section 8(1) of RSA 60, a copy of the certificate is sent to any public or local authority consulted under section 8(2);

(c) Notices advising holders of section 1 certificates that their registration has been varied or cancelled are sent to those local authorities who were sent a copy of the original certificate; and

(d) Notices advising holders of section 6 or 7 certificates that their authorisation has been varied or revoked are sent to those local authorities and public bodies who were sent a copy of the original section 6 or 7 certificate.

Certificates of registration and authorisation are not copied to local authorities if the Secretary of State and/or the Minister of Agriculture, Fisheries and Food consider that knowledge of such certificates should be restricted, for reasons of national security.

Impact of Environmental Protection Act 1990

7. Part V of the Environmental Protection Act 1990 amends RSA 60 to provide that a much wider range of documents must be made available to local authorities. It further provides that the public is to have access to these documents, subject to the limitations of national security and confidentiality, which are described in paragraph 11 below.

8. In general local authorities are, with effect from the beginning of January 1991, to be sent copies of all documents issued by the Chief Inspector (who takes over from the Secretary of State responsibility for issuing registrations and authorisations etc.) and, where appropriate,

the Minister of Agriculture, Fisheries and Food, under any provision of RSA 60. Over and above those documents already required to be sent under RSA 60, the following additional documents are to be provided:

(a) New applications for registration:
- (i) Section 1 application forms are to be sent to each local authority in whose area the premises, to which the application relates, are situated;
- (ii) Section 3 application forms are to be sent to each local authority in whose area, it appears to the Chief Inspector, mobile apparatus will be kept or will be used for releasing radioactive material in to the environment; and
- (iii) Section 6 or 7 application forms are to be sent to each local authority in whose area, in accordance with the authorisation, radioactive waste is to be disposed of or accumulated;

Applications should be taken to include supporting material, for example maps and photos;
- (b) Certificates of registration issued under section 3 are to be sent to each local authority, in whose area it appears to the Chief Inspector, mobile apparatus will be kept or will be used for releasing radioactive material in to the environment;
- (c) Notices advising holders of certificates under section 3 that their registration has been varied or cancelled are to be sent to those local authorities who were provided with a copy of the original certificate of registration;
- (d) Enforcement and prohibition notices issued under sections 11B and 11C of RSA 60 are to be sent to those local authorities and public bodies who were provided with a copy of the relevant certificate of registration or authorisation;
- (e) Letters notifying those served with an enforcement notice that the conditions of the registration/authorisation, of which they were in breach, are now being complied with, are to be sent to those local authorities who were provided with a copy of the original enforcement notice;
- (f) Notices advising those served with a prohibition notice that the notice is now withdrawn are to be sent to those local authorities who were provided with a copy of the original prohibition notice;
- (g) Notices advising holders of section 1 and 3 certificates that their registration has been varied or cancelled following the determination of an appeal are to be sent to those local authorities who were provided with a copy of the original certificate of registration;
- (h) Notices advising holders of section 6 or 7 certificates that their authorisation has been varied or revoked following the determination of an appeal are to be sent to those local authorities who were provided with a copy of the original certificate of authorisation; and
- (i) Such records of convictions under section 13 of RSA 60 as prescribed in Regulations. Records of conviction are to be sent to those local authorities who were provided with a copy of the certificate connected with the infringement or who would have been sent a copy of the relevant certificate had the provisions of the Act been complied with. *It should be noted that these documents will not be provided until Parliament has approved the necessary Regulations.*

There is also a power for the Secretary of State to direct the Chief Inspector to send to local authorities such other documents as he specifies. It is intended that this power will be exercised in respect of the provision of monitoring data. The precise format in which this information is to be made available has not yet been determined, and further guidance will be issued once a decision has been reached.

Treatment of copy documents sent to local authorities before January 1991

9. As noted in paragraph 6 above, copies of a number of documents have been sent to authorities under the existing provisions of RSA 60. *Copies sent before the beginning of January 1991 should in no circumstances be made available to the public.* The Chief Inspector and, where appropriate, the Minister of Agriculture, Fisheries and Food are to examine all documents issued before 1991 to establish whether any information contained in them relates to any relevant process or trade secret within the meaning of section 13(3) of RSA 60. Once this examination is complete, fresh copies of these documents will be forwarded to authorities for the purpose of making them available to the public, accompanied by instructions, where appropriate, to withhold information found to be confidential. Given that there are in the region of 7,000 documents involved the exercise is likely to take some time, and authorities will probably receive their copies in batches, rather than as a single consignment. It is hoped that authorities should have received most of the copies due to them by December 1991.

Local authority responsibilities

10. Local authorities are required under the provisions of RSA 60 as amended to keep and

make available to the general public copies of all documents sent to them by the Chief Inspector (documents issued by the Minister of Agriculture, Fisheries and Food will be sent to local authorities via the Chief Inspector), except where the Chief Inspector, Secretary of State or Minister of Agriculture, Fisheries and Food has directed otherwise (see paragraph 11 below). The public are entitled to inspect and take copies of these documents. Each local authority is required to make the documents available for inspection at reasonable times free of charge and to provide photocopies of the documents on request at a reasonable charge. It is for each local authority to decide how to keep the documents they are sent by the Chief Inspector. These need not be kept in documentary form and may for example be stored on microfiche.

11. Where the Secretary of State or, as the case may be, the Secretary of State and the Minister of Agriculture, Fisheries and Food direct the Chief Inspector that knowledge of a document should be restricted on grounds of national security, the Chief Inspector will not send a copy of that document to the local authority. The Chief Inspector may also direct an authority that all or part of a document is not to be made available for inspection, if that would involve disclosure of information relating to any relevant process or trade secret (within the meaning of section 13(3) of RSA 60). Where an authority has been directed by the Chief Inspector not to disclose information from all or part of a document a statement must be held by the authority, and made available to the general public, indicating that the information exists but that it is confidential.

12. Her Majesty's Inspectorate of Pollution's regional offices will also hold a complete set of the documents sent by the Chief Inspector to local authorities in its region. The regional offices will be under an obligation to undertake a similar service to the general public as that provided by the local authorities in keeping and making available for inspection copies of the documents and providing, at a reasonable charge, copies of the documents to the public.

13. Local authorities shall, subject to paragraph 14 below, keep the documents sent to them for a minimum of four years after the document ceases to have effect. This period should be applied as follows to those documents listed under paragraph 8 above:

(a) Applications for registration or authorisation—four years after the certificate, to which the application refers, ceases to have effect. For unsuccessful applications—four years after the date of application;

(b) Certificates of registration or authorisation—four years after the certificate ceases to have effect;

(c) Notices advising holders of certificates that their registration or authorisation has been cancelled or varied—four years after the date of the notice;

(d) Enforcement notices—four years after the completion of the period specified in the notice;

(e) Prohibition notices—four years after the notice is withdrawn; and

(f) Withdrawal notices—four years after the date of the notice.

14. The Rehabilitation of Offenders Act 1974 shall apply to notices of records of convictions under section 13 of RSA 60.

Financial Effect of Proposals on Local Authorities

15. Since local authorities already receive copies of certificates of registration and authorisation, the receipt of further documents will not affect local authorities financially. However, the requirement to make these documents available to the public may involve some additional expenditure, but it is expected that this will be small. Local authorities already make other documents available to members of the public *e.g.* as part of the planning process, and there should be scope for using the same facilities for documents arising from RSA 60. Local authorities will of course be able to recoup any cost of photocopying through the provisions in RSA 60 which allow a charge to be made for this service.

Enquiries

16. Please address any enquiries on this circular to Mr. A.T. Barnes 071–276 8401 or if they relate to Welsh matters to Mr. R.L. Davies 0222–825393.

M.W. Jones, *Senior Principal in the Department of the Environment*
A.H.H. Jones, *Assistant Secretary in the Welsh Office*
P.M. Boyling, *Assistant Secretary in the Ministry of Agriculture, Fisheries and Food*

APPENDIX 5

DoE Circular 22/92

28 August 1992

Local authority responsibilities for public access to information under the Radioactive Substances Act 1960 as amended by the Environmental Protection Act 1990: monitoring data and other information

Introduction

1. This circular supplements Circular 21/90 (Department of the Environment), 56/90 (Welsh Office) and FMP 1102 (Ministry of Agriculture, Fisheries and Food), which explained the new provisions on public access to information introduced into the Radioactive Substances Act 1960 (RSA 60) by Part V of the Environmental Protection Act 1990, and gave guidance to local authorities on their new obligations in respect of these provisions. This circular provides further guidance and information on public access to monitoring data and other documents.

2. It should be noted that the Radioactive Substances Act 1960 is being consolidated, and it is hoped that the new Bill (known as the Radioactive Substances Bill) will become law later this year. All statutory references in this circular are based on the 1960 Act but the section numbers are likely to be different in the consolidated legislation.

3. In this circular, the definition of "local authority" is as set out in section 19(1) of RSA 60 and includes county councils, district councils and London boroughs.

Monitoring data—summary information

4. The Secretary of State has exercised his power under section 12A(4) of RSA 60 and has directed the Chief Inspector to send to *all* local authorities copies of annual reports of Her Majesty's Inspectorate of Pollution (HMIP) monitoring programmes of authorised discharges of radioactive wastes in England and Wales. The reports will include both summary data and an analysis of the main findings. Each local authority is required under section 13A(2) and (5) of RSA 60 to make these reports readily available for inspection by members of the public at reasonable times and to provide photocopies on request at a reasonable charge. As with other documents sent to local authorities under the public access to information provisions, the reports need not be held in documentary form.

5. In addition the Ministry of Agriculture, Fisheries and Food (MAFF) will be sending to those local authorities consulted on authorisations issued in respect of nuclear licensed sites—*i.e.* the authorities listed in Annex 1 to this circular—copies of the Ministry's annual Aquatic Environment Monitoring Report and Terrestrial Radioactivity Monitoring Programme Report. If your authority is not included on this list and wishes to receive copies please inform MAFF Marine Environmental Protection Division who will ensure that your authority is placed on the distribution list. The Division's address may be found at Annex 2.

6. The first HMIP and MAFF reports covered by these provisions are those for the year 1989. Reports for 1989 and 1990 have already been distributed to local authorities, and should now be made available to the public for inspection, if this has not already been done on an informal basis.

Monitoring data—detailed information

7. The more detailed monitoring data held by HMIP, from which the annual reports are prepared, will not be sent to local authorities. Instead, this data will be kept at HMIP regional offices and, unless it is confidential, will be made available to members of the public there on request. The reason for this approach is that the quantity of material is too large for it to be handled by all local authorities. Furthermore the information consists of raw data without any accompanying explanation or analysis, and is unlikely to be readily understood by the general public. Detailed environmental monitoring data retained by MAFF will be kept at the Ministry's Directorate of Fisheries Research (for aquatic monitoring data) and Food Safety Radiation Unit (for terrestrial monitoring data). The addresses of these two establishments are to be found at Annex 2. Unless it is confidential MAFF will where possible respond to reasonable requests from the public for information.

Monitoring data—information submitted by operators

8. Operators of the major sites authorised to dispose of radioactive waste are required as a condition of their authorisation to provide certain monitoring and discharge data to HMIP and,

where appropriate, MAFF. The Secretary of State has exercised his power under section 12A(4) of RSA 60 and directed the Chief Inspector to send copies of data provided to him to those local authorities consulted on the applications for authorisations containing a requirement to provide data (see Annex 1). MAFF will similarly supply copies of data which is provided exclusively to that Department. Local authorities should make copies of all such data available to the public, unless directed otherwise under section 13A(2) of RSA 60.

Ministry of Defence and Visiting Forces

9. The Ministry of Defence (MOD) and visiting forces are exempt from the requirements of RSA 60 but controls similar to those exercised over other users of radioactive material are applied on an administrative basis to MOD establishments and premises occupied by visiting forces. Instead of being issued with registrations and authorisations, MOD and visiting forces are sent documents known as "certificates of notification" which record the holding of radioactive material and "certificates of agreement" which approve the disposal of radioactive waste, each document specifying the conditions which are to be observed. It has long been our practice to send local authorities copies of such documents (known previously as "noting letters", "notification letters" or "letters of approval"), except in cases where national security considerations have been involved, and this policy is to continue.

10. MOD and visiting forces have indicated that they wish to comply with the spirit of the new public access to information provisions. Copies of certificates of notification, and certificates of agreement, and any variations or cancellations of these documents sent to local authorities should therefore be made available to the public in the same way as documents covered by the legislative provisions. To ensure local authorities hold a comprehensive set of MOD and visiting forces documents, fresh copies of those documents issued before the date of this circular will be sent to local authorities for the purpose of making them available to the public, provided there are no national security constraints. It is hoped that authorities will have received most of the copies due to them by June 1993.

Records of convictions

11. The Radioactive Substances (Records of Convictions) Regulations 1992 (S.I. 1992 No. 1685), provide that information relating to convictions for offences under section 13 of RSA 60 is to be made publicly available. HMIP is to keep copies of records of convictions which, in relation to each conviction, give details of the offence, the name of the offender, the date of the conviction, the penalty imposed and the name of the Court where the offender was convicted. Members of the public will be able to inspect the information at the appropriate HMIP regional office shown at Annex 2. Copies of records of convictions will be sent to those local authorities who were provided with a copy of the certificate connected with the infringement or who would have been sent a copy of the relevant certificate had the provisions of the Act been complied with, and local authorities are requested to make such copies available for public inspection.

12. Copies of records of convictions received by local authorities are subject to the provisions of the Rehabilitation of Offenders Act 1974, which requires that spent convictions relating to individuals (not corporations) must be removed from public scrutiny. Under section 9 of this Act, unauthorised disclosure of a spent conviction is a criminal offence and therefore local authorities should be very careful to remove relevant details from public inspection. HMIP has established internal procedures so as to notify local authorities in advance of the need to remove records of spent convictions relating to RSA 60 offences.

Financial Effect of Proposals on Local Authorities

13. The documents covered by this circular are to be supplied to local authorities without charge. The requirement to make these documents available to members of the public may involve some additional expenditure [but] it is expected that this will be small. Local authorities already make other documents issued under RSA 60 available to the public, and it should be possible to use the same facilities. Local authorities will of course be able to recoup any cost of photocopying through the provisions in RSA 60 which allow a charge to be made for this service.

Enquiries

14. Please address any enquiries on this circular to Mr A.T. Barnes 071–276 8401 (Department of the Environment), Mr. R.M. Bayliss 071–238 5878 (Ministry of Agriculture, Fisheries and Food), or Mr. R.L. Davies 0222 825393 (Welsh Office).

M.W. Jones, *Assistant Secretary in the Department of the Environment*

A.H.H. Jones, *Assistant Secretary in the Welsh Office*

G.F. Meekings, *Assistant Secretary in the Ministry of Agriculture, Fisheries and Food*

The Chief Executive
  County Councils ⎫
  District Councils ⎬ in England and Wales
  London Borough Councils
  Council of the Isles of Scilly

The Town Clerk, City of London

[DOE RW 2/12/54]
[WO WEP/57/95/3]
[MAFF FMP 1102]

ANNEX 1

Nuclear Licensed Site	*District Council*	*County Council*
Berkeley Power Station (Nuclear Electric)	Gloucester City Northavon Stroud Forest of Dean	Gloucestershire
Bradwell Power Station (Nuclear Electric)	Maldon Colchester Tendring	Essex
Dungeness Power Station (Nuclear Electric)	Shepway	Kent
Hartlepool Power Station (Nuclear Electric)	Hartlepool Borough	Cleveland
Heysham Power Station (Nuclear Electric)	Lancaster City Wyre	Lancashire Cumbria
Hinkley Point Power Station (Nuclear Electric)	Sedgemoor West Somerset Woodspring	Somerset Avon
Oldbury Power Station (Nuclear Electric)	Northavon Forest of Dean Bristol City	Avon Gloucestershire
Sizewell Power Station (Nuclear Electric)	Suffolk Coastal	Suffolk
Trawsfynydd Power Station (Nuclear Electric)	Meirionnydd Montgomeryshire	Gwynedd Powis
Wylfa Power Station (Nuclear Electric)	Ynys Môn (Isle of Anglesey Borough)	Gwynedd
Capenhurst Works (BNFL)	Chester City Ellesmere Port and Neston Borough	Cheshire
Drigg (BNFL) Sellafield (BNFL) Windscale (UKAEA)	Copeland Borough Carlisle City Eden South Lakeland Barrow-in-Furness Allerdale	Cumbria
Springfields (BNFL and UKAEA)	Preston Borough Fylde Borough South Ribble Borough West Lancashire Borough	Lancashire
Amersham International	Chiltern	Buckinghamshire

Harwell (UKAEA)	South Oxfordshire Oxford City Vale of White Horse Newbury	Oxfordshire Berkshire
Forrest Farm (Amersham International)	Cardiff City	South Glamorgan
TRIGA Reactor (ICI)	Stockton-on-Tees Borough	Cleveland
Rolls Royce	Derby City	Derbyshire
Manchester University Reactor	Warrington Borough	Cheshire

University of London Reactor	Windsor and
	  Maidenhead Royal
	  Borough
	Runnymede
	Surrey Heath
		Berkshire
		Surrey

Barrow Shipyard	Barrow-in-Furness Borough	Cumbria
Devonport Royal Dockyard	Plymouth City	Devon
Winfrith (UKAEA)	Weymouth and Portland Borough Purbeck West Dorset	Dorset Isle of Wight

ANNEX 2

HMIP REGIONAL OFFICES

1. East Division

Her Majesty's Inspectorate of Pollution, Howard House, 40–64 St John's Street, Bedford MK42 0DL.
Covers the counties of Bedfordshire, Berkshire, Buckinghamshire, Cambridgeshire, Essex, Greater London, Hampshire, Hertfordshire, Humberside (South), Isle of Wight, Kent, Leicestershire, Lincolnshire, Norfolk, Northamptonshire, Nottinghamshire, Oxfordshire, Suffolk, Surrey, East and West Sussex.

2. West Division

Her Majesty's Inspectorate of Pollution, Highwood Pavilions, Jupiter Road, Patchway, Bristol BS12 5SN.
Covers the counties of Avon, Cornwall, Derbyshire, Devon, Dorset, Gloucestershire, Hereford and Worcester, Merseyside, Shropshire, Somerset, Staffordshire, Warwickshire, West Midlands, Wiltshire and the whole of Wales.

3. North Division

Her Majesty's Inspectorate of Pollution, Stockdale House, 1st Floor, 8 Victoria Road, Headingley, Leeds LS6 1PF.
Covers the counties of Cheshire, Cleveland, Cumbria, Durham, Humberside (North), Lancashire, Greater Manchester, Northumberland, Tyne and Wear and North, South and West Yorkshire.

MAFF OFFICES

Fisheries Radiological Inspectorate, Directorate of Fisheries Research, Pakefield Road, Lowestoft, Suffolk NR33 0HT.
Food Safety Radiation Unit, Food Science Division, Ergon House, 17 Smith Square, London SW1P 3JR.
Marine Environmental Protection Division, Nobel House, 17 Smith Square, London SW1P 3JR.

APPENDIX 6

HMIP REPORT: FEES AND CHARGES FOR RADIOACTIVE SUBSTANCES ACT REGULATION 1993–94

INTRODUCTION AND EXPLANATORY NOTES

1. The Radioactive Substances Act 1960, as amended by the Environmental Protection Act 1990 provides for the Secretaries of State for the Environment and for Wales to introduce charges to recover the costs incurred by Her Majesty's Inspectorate of Pollution (HMIP) and by the Ministry of Agriculture, Fisheries and Food (MAFF) in regulating the holding of radioactive material and accumulation and disposal of radioactive waste under the Radioactive Substances Act 1960 ("the Act").

2. The revised Scheme of charges contained in pages 10–15 below has been made and will take effect from 1 April 1993. It will apply until superseded by revised rates, most likely in April 1994.

3. These notes outline and explain the system of charges. They do not form part of the Scheme.

RADIOACTIVE SUBSTANCES AUTHORISATIONS AND REGISTRATIONS FEES AND CHARGES SCHEME (ENGLAND AND WALES) REVISED 1993

4. The fees and charges under the Scheme are structured on the basis of the following four Bands:

Band 1:   British Nuclear Fuels Ltd reprocessing plant, Sellafield.

Band 2:   Other sites subject to licensing under section 1 of the Nuclear Installations Act 1965 (mainly nuclear power stations).

Band 3:   Authorisations under section 6 or section 7 of the Act to accumulate or dispose of radioactive waste.

Band 4:   Registrations under section 1 of the Act for the keeping and use of radioactive material, or under section 3 for the keeping and use of mobile radioactive apparatus, including use for tracer testing.

BAND 1 AND 2 OPERATORS' SITES

5. Charges will in these cases be calculated and billed to operators on the basis of actual time spent and costs incurred in relation to applications, authorisations and registrations relating to each individual site by HMIP and by MAFF, (Scheme, para. 14). HMIP has written to operators giving an indicative estimate of 1993–94 HMIP and MAFF costs for each site.

6. HMIP and MAFF will separately invoice operators for their respective charges. Invoices will be issued quarterly in arrears.

BAND 3 AUTHORISATIONS AND BAND 4 REGISTRATIONS

7. For Bands 3 and 4, charges are based on a system of flat-rate fees and charges as follows:
— an **application fee**, payable with each application for authorisation or registration, to cover the costs of consideration of applications;
— an annual **subsistence charge** for the holding of an authorisation or registration, to cover the cost of ongoing inspection and enforcement;
— a **variation fee** for variation of an authorisation or registration. This will apply whether the variation is made at the instigation of HMIP or requested by the holder. But the fee is not charged for a trivial variation, such as a change of holder's name or other administrative detail, which does not involve any material reconsideration of the authorisation or registration.
— a **supplementary charge**—see paras. 14–16 below.

8. The charges are as follows:

	Application or Variation Fee	Annual Subsistence Charge	Supplementary Charge (Scheme para 11)
Band 3: authorisation under sections 6 or 7 of the Act (Scheme, para 10(1)(d)):	**£1,385** per application	**£820** per authorisation held	**£210** per authorisation issued in response to a 1991–92 application

	Application or Variation Fee	Annual Subsistence Charge	Supplementary Charge (Scheme para 11)
authorisation under sections 6 or 7 of the Act in respect of a registration under section 1 of the Act where the registration is solely for the use of Technetium 99M, and the registered holding is less than 10 gigabecquerels (Scheme para 10(1)(e)):	£1,385 per application	£80 per authorisation held	£210 per authorisation issued in response to a 1991–92 application
authorisation under sections 6 or 7 of the Act in respect of registrations under section 1 or section 3 of the Act where the sum of the registered holdings does not exceed 20 megabecquerels. (Scheme para 10(1)(f)):	£1,385 per application	£80 per authorisation held	£210 per authorisation issued in response to a 1991–92 application
Band 4: registration under sections 1 or 3 of the Act:			
registration for one or more closed source(s), none of which exceeds 4 TBq (Scheme, para 10(1)(a)(i)); also registration for storage in transit (Scheme, para 10(1)(a)(v)):	£500 per application	Nil	£80 per registration, if issued in response to a 1991–92 application
registration for one or more closed source(s), any one of which exceeds 4 TBq (Scheme, para 10(1)(a)(ii)):	£500 per application	£80 per registration held	£80 "
registration for an open source, which is also the subject of an authorisation, or application for an authorisation (Scheme, para 10(1)(a)(iii)):	£500 per application	Nil	£80 "
registration for an open source which is not the subject of an authorisation, or application for an authorisation (Scheme, para 10(1)(a)(iv)):	£500 per application	£80 per registration held	£80 "
registration for one or more mobile source(s), other than a tracer test source (Scheme, para 10(1)(b)):	£500 per application	£80 per registration held	£80 "
registration for one or more tracer test source(s) (Scheme, para 10(1)(c)):	£500 per application	Nil	£80 "

9. Note in particular that:
  (i) MAFF is not involved in regulation of Band 3 and 4 authorisations and registrations.
  (ii) A single application may cover more than one registration, and a registration may cover more than one source. However open and closed sources require separate registrations. Subsistence is payable on each authorisation or registration held.

(iii) There is no subsistence charge (other than a supplementary charge in the case of a registration issued in response to an application submitted in 1991–92—see paras. 14–16 below) for the following:

　　— a registration for a source covered also by a section 6 or 7 authorisation or application, since there will not normally be any additional inspection or oversight beyond that carried out in relation to the authorisation, and covered by the subsistence charge for the authorisation;

　　— a tracer test registration, since tracer tests are generally short time-limited events, which do not normally require ongoing regulatory oversight;

　　— a registration for storage in transit, or for a closed source of less than 4 TBq, (other than mobile sources), since these relatively low-risk sources are not subject to frequent inspection;

(iv) For determining whether a registration covering more than one closed source is above or below the 4 TBq threshold, the activity content of the sources is **not** aggregated. The charging category is determined by **the individual source with the highest activity content**. For example, a registration covering two closed sources each of 3 TBq will nonetheless fall below the 4 TBq threshold.

Application Fee

10. The fee is payable for each application for authorisation or registration, and must accompany the application. HMIP may decline to start consideration of the application, and will not issue an authorisation or registration, if the application fee is outstanding.

Subsistence Charges

11. For existing authorisations, annual subsistence will be payable at the rates given above. HMIP will invoice operators during the course of 1993/94.

12. For new authorisations or registrations issued after 1 April 1993, the first subsistence charge will apply from the date at which the authorisation or registration comes into operation (normally 28 days after issue), at the rate of the relevant annual subsistence charge, adjusted *pro rata* to the remaining period to the following 31 March. HMIP will calculate the sum due and invoice the holder at the time of issuing the authorisation or registration. Subsequent subsistence charges will then be payable from each 1 April, at the rate in force at the time. HMIP will again invoice the holder when the charge is due.

13. To cover the costs associated with revocation of an authorisation or cancellation of a registration, there is no refund of the subsistence charge in the year that an authorisation is revoked or the registration cancelled. Exceptionally however where an operator has applied for revocation of an authorisation or cancellation of a registration in the previous financial year consideration will be given as to whether a subsistence charge is appropriate.

Supplementary Charge

14. Application fees for registrations and authorisations in 1991–92 were based on a lower estimate of the amount of regulatory time than was actually incurred in dealing with the applications. HMIP's costs for this activity in 1991–92 were therefore not fully covered by the income received. The Department is required by the legislation governing the charging Scheme to set fees and charges so as to balance regulatory costs and income, taking one financial year with another, and HMIP is therefore obliged to recoup an under-recovery in one year through its charges in later years.

15. The recoupment of the 1991–92 under-recovery is spread over four years, and is made through the subsistence charges **on those authorisations and registrations which have followed from applications submitted in 1991–92.** To continue recovery on this basis, there will be in 1993–94 a supplement of **£210** per authorisation resulting from an application received in 1991–92, and **£80** per registration (Scheme, para. 11).

16. Any supplementary charge due will be included in the subsistence charge invoice for the registration or authorisation.

Variation Fee

17. The variation fee will apply to a variation whether sought by the holder, or made at the instigation of HMIP. No fee will be charged, however, for a trivial variation such as a change of name or other major administrative detail which does not involve any material reconsideration of the authorisation or registration (Scheme, para. 12(2)).

18. Before issuing a variation or replacement certificate, HMIP will invoice the holder if a fee is payable and will not issue the variation until the fee is paid in full.

REVIEW OF AUTHORISATIONS AND REGISTRATIONS

19. To enable authorisations and registrations to be kept up-to-date the Act empowers HMIP (in the case of Band 1 and 2 operators, HMIP and MAFF), to review and vary them as necessary. The Environmental Protection Act 1990 provides that Integrated Pollution Control authorisations shall be reviewed at least every four years. Subject to staff resources, HMIP and where applicable MAFF will seek to review Radioactive Substances Act authorisations and registrations on a similar timescale. The review of existing authorisations and registrations will be programmed on the basis of priority, taking into account age of authorisation or registration, risk category and other factors.

20. Review may involve variation, or possibly in some cases re-application where it is necessary for HMIP or MAFF to carry out a comprehensive review of operating arrangements.

21. HMIP will advise operators when review is planned.

METHOD OF PAYMENT

22. For Band 3 and 4 applications, application fees should be sent together with the application to the RSA Application Unit at the relevant HMIP Field Operations Office. Addresses are given below. HMIP will invoice operators for subsistence charges and variation fees. The application form for authorisations and registrations asks applicants to indicate an invoicing address. Payment is due immediately on receipt of the invoice to the HMIP office which issued the invoice.

23. In the case of Band 1 and 2 sites, HMIP and MAFF will separately invoice operators for their respective charges. Payment is due immediately on receipt of the invoice, to the HMIP office which issued the invoice, or to MAFF, as indicated on the invoice.

24. Payments should be by cheque, made payable to Her Majesty's Inspectorate of Pollution, or the Ministry of Agriculture, Fisheries and Food as appropriate, and endorsed "Not Negotiable A/C Payee Only".

25. Any overpayment of a fee or charge will be repaid in full, but refunds of application fees will not be made after an authorisation or registration has been issued.

NON-PAYMENT OF FEES AND CHARGES

26. An authorisation or registration will not be issued if the relevant application fee is outstanding. It is a condition of authorisation or registration that all relevant charges are paid. In the event of failure to pay a subsistence charge, the authorisation or registration may be revoked or other enforcement action taken.

TAXATION

27. HMIP has received provisional guidance from Inland Revenue's Business Profits Division concerning the treatment for taxation purposes of fees and charges paid under the Scheme. The general rule is that revenue expenses are allowable for tax, capital expenses are not. In terms of the Scheme, the position appears to be:

Payment Type	Expense Type	Tax Position
Application Fee	Capital	Not Allowable
Subsistence Charge	Revenue	Allowable

including supplementary charge

Variation Fee	Depends on circumstances	

This guidance is provisional only. For a ruling, operators should contact their Tax Inspector.

INFORMATION ON HMIP COSTS

28. At the end of each financial year HMIP will publish accounts and information on fee and charge income, and regulatory expenditure.

QUESTIONS AND FURTHER INFORMATION

29. Please contact the local HMIP Operations Division Office if you have any questions or require further information about this Scheme—see below for addresses and telephone numbers.

30. Further copies of the Charging Scheme are also available from these offices.

OTHER POLLUTION CONTROL CHARGES

31. Cost-recovery charges also apply to Integrated Pollution Control, to local authority air pollution control, and to the National Rivers Authority (NRA) controls on water pollution. Details of these charges can be found in:

— "Pollution Control Charges for Integrated Pollution Control". Copies available from HMIP offices.
— Revised charges for local authority air pollution control for 1993–94 are available from DOE Air Quality Division, Room B350, Romney House, 43 Marsham Street, London SW1P 3PY.
— NRA leaflet "Charges for Discharges to Controlled Waters" as amended for 1993–94. Copies available from the NRA, Rivers House, Waterside Drive, Aztec West, Almondsbury, Bristol BS12 4UD.

HMIP ADDRESSES

RSA 60 applications, fees and charges are dealt with by the RSA Applications Units at HMIP Operations Divisions in Bedford, Bristol and Leeds. All correspondence and queries should be directed to these addresses:

HMIP Bedford Office

Responsible for:

RSA Applications Unit
HMIP Bedford Office
Howard House
40–64 St Johns Street
BEDFORD
MK42 0DL

Tel: 0234 272112
Fax: 0234 218355

South Humberside
Lincolnshire
Nottinghamshire
Essex
Berkshire
Hampshire
Surrey
West Sussex
East Sussex
Kent

Buckinghamshire
Oxfordshire
Hertfordshire
Northamptonshire
Cambridgeshire
Norfolk
Suffolk
Bedfordshire
Isle of Wight
Greater London

HMIP Bristol Office

Responsible for:

RSA Applications Unit
HMIP Bristol Office
Highwood Pavilions
Jupiter Road
Patchway
BRISTOL
BS12 5SN

Tel: 0272 319639
Fax: 0272 319650

Leicestershire
Derbyshire
Shropshire
Staffordshire
West Midlands
Hereford and
   Worcester
Warwickshire
Avon
Wiltshire

Gloucestershire
Somerset
Dorset
Devon
Cornwall
Wales

HMIP Leeds Office

Responsible for:

RSA Applications Unit
HMIP Leeds Office
Stockdale House
Headingley Business Park
8 Victoria Road
Headingley
LEEDS
LS6 1PF

Tel: 0532 786636
Fax: 0532 740464

Northumberland
Tyne and Wear
Durham
Cumbria
Cleveland
Yorkshire
Lancashire
Greater Manchester

Cheshire
North Humberside
Merseyside

DEPARTMENT OF THE ENVIRONMENT
HER MAJESTY'S INSPECTORATE OF POLLUTION

REVISED SCHEME OF FEES AND CHARGES UNDER THE RADIOACTIVE SUBSTANCES ACT 1960

The Secretary of State for the Environment as respects England and the Secretary of State for Wales as respects Wales, in exercise of their powers under Section 15A of the Radioactive Substances Act 1960 with the approval of the Treasury and the consent of the Minister of Agriculture, Fisheries and Food hereby make the following Scheme of fees and charges:

COMMENCEMENT AND CITATION

1. This Scheme may be referred to as the Radioactive Substances Authorisations and

Registrations Fees and Charges Scheme (England and Wales) Revised 1993. It shall come into operation on 1st April 1993.

INTERPRETATION

2. In this Scheme unless the contrary intention appears:
"the Act" means the Radioactive Substances Act 1960.
"the Chief Inspector" means the Chief Inspector of Her Majesty's Inspectorate of Pollution, appointed in relation to England and Wales under section 11A(2) of the Act.
"the Minister" means the Minister of Agriculture, Fisheries and Food.

APPLICATION

3. The Scheme applies to:
(a) an application for registration made under section 1 or section 3 of the Act on or after 1st April 1993, or in the case of a site subject to licensing under the Nuclear Installations Act 1965, under consideration at that date;
(b) an application for authorisation made under section 6 or section 7 of the Act on or after 1st April 1993, or in the case of a site subject to licensing under the Nuclear Installations Act 1965, under consideration at that date;
(c) the subsistence of a registration under section 1 or section 3 of the Act;
(d) the subsistence of an authorisation under section 6 or section 7 of the Act;
(e) the variation of a registration or authorisation on or after 1st April 1993.

APPLICATION FEE

4. Except in those cases described in paragraph 14 below, an application fee shall accompany the application to which it relates, and shall be as follows:

An application for registration made under section 1 or section 3 of the Act:	**£500** per application
An application for authorisation made under section 6 or section 7 of the Act:	**£1,385** per application

SUBSISTENCE CHARGE

5. Except in those cases described in paragraph 14 below, a charge shall be payable in respect of the subsistence of each registration or authorisation on demand to the Chief Inspector on or after 1st April 1993.
6. In the case of a registration or authorisation in operation at 1st April 1993, (except in those cases described in paragraph 8 below) the charge shall be the annual subsistence charge as provided by paragraph 10 of this Scheme.
7. In the case of a registration or authorisation granted on or after 1st April 1993, (except in those cases described in paragraph 9 below), the charge shall be the annual subsistence charge as provided by paragraph 10 of this Scheme, adjusted *pro rata* to the period beginning with the day after the date of the registration or authorisation coming into operation and ending with the last day of March following.
8. In the case of a registration or authorisation in operation at 1st April 1993 and granted pursuant to an application submitted between 1st April 1991 and 31st March 1992, the charge shall be the annual subsistence charge as provided by paragraph 10 of this Scheme, together with the supplementary charge as provided by paragraph 11 of this Scheme.
9. In the case of a registration or authorisation granted on or after 1st April 1993 pursuant to an application submitted on or between 1st April 1991 and 31st March 1992, the charge shall be the annual subsistence charge as provided by paragraph 10 of this Scheme adjusted *pro rata* to the period beginning with the day after the date of the registration or authorisation coming into operation and ending with the last day of March following, together with the supplementary charge as provided by paragraph 11 of this Scheme.
10. (1) The annual subsistence charge shall be as follows:

(a) Registration under section 1 or section 3 of the Act:	
(i) for one or more closed source(s) none of which exceeds 4 terabecquerels in activity content:	**Nil**
(ii) for one or more closed source(s), any one of which exceeds 4 terabecquerels in activity content:	**£80** per registration

(iii) for a source which is not a closed source, and which is the subject of an authorisation under section 6 or section 7 of the Act, or an application for such an authorisation:	**Nil**	
(iv) for a source which is not a closed source and which is not the subject of an authorisation, or application for an authorisation, under section 6 or section 7 of the Act.	**£80**	
(v) for radioactive material stored in transit	**Nil**	
(b) Registration under section 3 of the Act for the use of mobile radioactive apparatus for testing, measuring or otherwise investigating any of the characteristics of substances or articles:	**£80** per registration	
(c) Registration under section 3 of the Act for the use of mobile radioactive apparatus for releasing quantities of radioactive material into the environment or introducing such material into organisms:	**Nil**	
(d) Authorisation under section 6 or section 7 of the Act, except as described in (e) and (f) below:	**£820** per authorisation	
(e) Authorisation under section 6 or section 7 of the Act in respect of a registration under section 1 of the Act where the registration is solely for the use of Technetium 99M, and the registered holding is less than 10 gigabecquerels.	**£80** per authorisation	
(f) Authorisation under section 6 or section 7 of the Act in respect of registrations under section 1 or section 3 of the Act where the sum of the registered holdings does not exceed 20 megabecquerels.	**£80** per authorisation	

(2) In this paragraph:

"closed source" means an object free from patent defect which consists of or includes one or more radionuclides firmly incorporated on or in or sealed within solid inert non-radioactive material so as to prevent the dispersion of any radioactive material in normal use.

"mobile radioactive apparatus" has the same meaning as in section 18 of the Act.

"stored in transit" means kept securely while in transit from one location to another.

"registered holding" means the upper limit of activity content imposed by the registration.

11. The supplementary charge payable in respect of a registration or authorisation granted pursuant to an application submitted between 1st April 1991 and 31st March 1992 shall be as follows:

(a) Registration under section 1 or section 3 of the Act:	**£80** per registration
(b) Authorisation under section 6 or section 7 of the Act:	**£210** per authorisation

VARIATION FEE

12. (1) Except in those cases described in paragraphs 12(2) and 14 below, a variation fee shall be payable on demand to the Chief Inspector by the holder of a registration or authorisation when the Chief Inspector gives notice on or after 1st April 1993 of the making of a variation of a registration or authorisation under section 5(2) or section 8(8) of the Act.

(2) No variation fee is payable when the variation is, in the opinion of the Chief Inspector, trivial.

13. The variation fee shall be as follows:

Variation of a registration under section 5 of the Act	**£500** per variation
Variation of an authorisation under section 8 of the Act	**£1,385** per variation

SITES SUBJECT TO LICENSING UNDER THE NUCLEAR INSTALLATIONS ACT 1965

14. In the case of a site subject to licensing under section 1 of the Nuclear Installations Act

1965, the fees and charges payable in respect of applications for registration under section 3 of the Act, applications for authorisations under section 6 of the Act, the subsistence of any registrations or authorisations, and variation of any registrations or authorisations, shall consist of the expenditure incurred as from 1st April 1993 by the Chief Inspector (or the Chief Inspector and the Minister) in exercising his (or their) functions under the Act in respect of those applications, registrations, authorisations and variations, as notified from time to time by the Chief Inspector or the Minister.

METHOD OF PAYMENT

15. Payment of fees and charges shall be by cheque, made payable to Her Majesty's Inspectorate of Pollution or to the Ministry of Agriculture, Fisheries and Food as notified, and endorsed "Not Negotiable: A/C Payee only".

Signed by authority of the Secretary of State for the Environment.

I C McBrayne
An Assistant Secretary in the Department of the Environment.

Signed by authority of the Secretary of State for Wales.

A H H Jones
An Assistant Secretary in the Welsh Office.

March 1993

INDEX

References are to section and Schedule numbers

CARRYING OF KNIVES ETC. (SCOTLAND) ACT 1993*

(1993 c. 13)

An Act to provide, as respects Scotland, for it to be an offence to have in a public place an article with a blade or point; and for connected purposes.

[27th May 1993]

PARLIAMENTARY DEBATES

Hansard, H.C. Vol. 220, col. 1283; Vol. 221, col. 1378; H.L. Vol. 544, col. 1213; Vol. 545, cols. 443, 701, 866.

The Bill was discussed in Second Scottish Standing Committee on March 23, 1993.

INTRODUCTION AND GENERAL NOTE

The Criminal Justice Act 1988 (c.33) created certain offences relating to offensive weapons. In particular, by s.139 of that Act, it became an offence to have an article with a blade or point in a public place.

That section creating the new offence applied (a) by s.172(1) of the 1988 Act to England and Wales; and (b) by s.172(3) of the 1988 Act to Northern Ireland. Section 139 did not apply to Scotland.

Public disquiet at the increased prevalence of knives in Scotland led to political pressure for a change in the law: the 1993 Act in effect extends s.139 of the 1988 Act to Scotland with minor modifications.

Offence of having in public place article with blade or point

1.—(1) Subject to subsections (4) and (5) below, any person who has an article to which this section applies with him in a public place shall be guilty of an offence and liable—

    (a) on summary conviction, to imprisonment for a term not exceeding six months or a fine not exceeding the statutory maximum or both; and

    (b) on conviction on indictment, to imprisonment for a term not exceeding two years or a fine or both.

(2) Subject to subsection (3) below, this section applies to any article which has a blade or is sharply pointed.

(3) This section does not apply to a folding pocketknife if the cutting edge of its blade does not exceed three inches.

(4) It shall be a defence for a person charged with an offence under subsection (1) above to prove that he had good reason or lawful authority for having the article with him in the public place.

(5) Without prejudice to the generality of subsection (4) above, it shall be a defence for a person charged with an offence under subsection (1) above to prove that he had the article with him—

    (a) for use at work;

    (b) for religious reasons; or

    (c) as part of any national costume.

(6) Where a person is convicted of an offence under subsection (1) above the court may make an order for the forfeiture of any article to which the offence relates, and any article forfeited under this subsection shall (subject to section 443A of the Criminal Procedure (Scotland) Act 1975 (suspension of forfeiture etc, pending appeal)) be disposed of as the court may direct.

(7) In this section "public place" includes any place to which at the material time the public have or are permitted access, whether on payment or otherwise.

DEFINITIONS

"public place": subs. (7).

"the statutory maximum": see s.289B(6) of the Criminal Procedure (Scotland) Act 1975 and s.17(1) of the Criminal Justice Act 1991; the sum is £5,000.

---

* Annotations by Robert S. Shiels, solicitor in the Supreme Courts of Scotland.

GENERAL NOTE

This Act considerably extends liability for carrying knives and sharp articles. Under s.1 a new general offence of having such an item in a public place (as defined in s.1(7)) is created. The Crown may prosecute summarily or on indictment with an appropriate maximum penalty: see s.1(1)(a) and (b) respectively.

Subs. (1)

Has ... with him in a public place. Identical words appearing in the Prevention of Crime Act 1953, s.1, were interpreted in *R.* v. *Cugullere* [1961] 1 W.L.R. 858 to mean "knowingly has with him in any public place", with the onus on the prosecution to establish knowledge. For an example of a case in which the inference of "having a knife with him" was properly drawn from the facts see *Murdoch* v. *Carmichael* 1993 S.C.C.R. 444.

Subss. (2) and (3)

These subsections define the articles which are prohibited under subs. (1). The effect is that all knives, except small pen-knives, and a wide range of other articles are within the section. Examples, given during the passage of clause 139 of the Criminal Justice Bill in 1988, which could be included were chisels (unless exempted under subs. (5)(a)), knitting needles, brooches, manicure sets, darts, garden shears and drawing pins. In many such cases the accused would be able to establish "good reason or lawful authority" within subs. (4) or a specific defence under subs. (5). The onus will be on him to do so. Unlike the requirement in s.1 of the Prevention of Crime Act 1953, the Crown in Scotland do not need to show that an item within the terms of the 1993 Act is offensive *per se* or intended to cause injury.

Subss. (4) and (5)

These subsections provide possible defences to subs. (1).

Good reason or lawful authority. There is a considerable body of case law under s.1 of the Prevention of Crime Act 1953 as to what constitutes "lawful authority or reasonable excuse" which is the term used in that provision. For a detailed collection of the case law see R. S. Shiels *Offensive Weapons* (Edinburgh, 1992). The principles in the case law flowing from the 1953 Act probably apply to the 1993 Act where appropriate.

For use at work. This defence will allow joiners, plumbers, mechanics and other tradesmen who necessarily carry sharp or bladed items to continue to do so.

For religious reasons. This will include, for example, the carrying of kirpan by a Sikh.

As part of any national costume. This will include, for example, the wearing of a skean-dhu with a kilt; see 1954 S.L.T. (News) 67.

Subs. (6)

This subsection provides a power of forfeiture in addition to the general provisions in ss.223 and 436 of the Criminal Procedure (Scotland) Act 1975.

Subs. (7)

It has been held in relation to other statutes that whether a place is a "public place" is a question of degree and fact: *R.* v. *Waters* (1963) 47 Cr.App.R. 149. Car parks attached to public houses or shops have been held to be public places: *Elkins* v. *Cartlidge* [1947] 1 All E.R. 829. If the public are not invited there after closing they cease to be public "at the material time": *Sandy* v. *Martin* [1974] Crim.L.R. 258. Communal areas in a block of flats are a public place if there is nothing to prevent access: *Knox* v. *Anderton* (1983) 76 Cr.App.R. 156. See also *Williams* v. *D.P.P.* [1992] Crim.L.R. 502.

Extension of constable's power to stop, search and arrest without warrant

2.—(1) Where a constable has reasonable grounds for suspecting that a person has with him an article to which section 1 of this Act applies and has committed or is committing an offence under subsection (1) of that section, the constable may search that person without warrant and detain him for such time as is reasonably required to permit the search to be carried out.

(2) A constable who detains a person under subsection (1) above shall inform him of the reason for his detention.

(3) Where a constable has reasonable cause to believe that a person has committed or is committing an offence under section 1(1) of this Act and the constable—

    (a) having requested that person to give his name or address or both—
        (i) is not given the information requested; or
        (ii) is not satisfied that such information as is given is correct; or
    (b) has reasonable cause to believe that it is necessary to arrest him in order to prevent the commission by him of any other offence in the course of committing which an article to which that section applies might be used.
he may arrest that person without warrant.

    (4) Any person who—
    (a) intentionally obstructs a constable in the exercise of the constable's powers under subsection (1) above; or
    (b) conceals from a constable acting in the exercise of those powers an article to which section 1 of this Act applies,
shall be guilty of an offence and liable on summary conviction to a fine not exceeding level 3 on the standard scale.

    (5) Where a constable has reasonable cause to believe that a person has committed or is committing an offence under subsection (4) above he may arrest that person without warrant.

DEFINITIONS
    "level 3 on the standard scale": see s.289B(6) of the Criminal Procedure (Scotland) Act 1975 and s.17(1) of the Criminal Justice Act 1991; the sum is £1,000.

GENERAL NOTE
    This section extends the power in s.1(3) of the Prevention of Crime Act 1953 and s.4(1) of the Criminal Justice (Scotland) Act 1980 to cover the articles with blades or points provided for in the 1993 Act.
    The new power is not too dissimilar to the terms of s.23 of the Misuse of Drugs Act 1971. For Scots lawyers the case of most interest in that regard is *Wither* v. *Reid* 1979 S.L.T. 192. There, a detective erroneously told a woman that she was under arrest rather than, in terms of s.23, being detained. A search following that error was held to be illegal and on appeal conviction quashed. Lord Robertson said (at p. 197), "There is a vital distinction between 'arrest' and 'detention'. A penal statute must be construed strictly. In my opinion, in deference to the rights of the citizen, it must be made perfectly clear to the person against whom action is being taken under s.23(2)(a) that that is what is being done and that he is not being arrested . . . The police also should know the law and if they were proceeding under s.23 they should have done so explicitly".

Citation, commencement and extent

    3.—(1) This Act may be cited as the Carrying of Knives etc. (Scotland) Act 1993.
    (2) This Act shall not have effect in relation to anything done before it comes into force.
    (3) This Act extends to Scotland only.

GENERAL NOTE
    The 1993 Act came into force on the day on which Royal Assent was granted, thus indicating the urgency with which the problem was dealt with by Parliament.

INDEX

References are to sections

DISABILITY (GRANTS) ACT 1993

(1993 c. 14)

An Act to provide for the making of grants by the Secretary of State and the Department of Health and Social Services for Northern Ireland to the Independent Living (Extension) Fund, the Independent Living (1993) Fund and Motability.   [27th May 1993]

PARLIAMENTARY DEBATES
   Hansard, H.C. Vol. 221, col. 36; Vol. 223, col. 889; H.L. Vol. 545, col. 1536.
   The Bill was discussed in Standing Committee A between March 23 and March 25, 1993.

INTRODUCTION
   This Act makes provisions conferring certain powers on the Secretary of State to make grants to the Independent Living (Extension) Fund, the Independent Living (1993) Fund and Motability. These organisations work to help disabled persons enjoy a more independent life in the community. Similar grants have previously been made under the authority of the Appropriation Acts.

Grants to certain organisations concerned with disabled persons

   1.—(1) The Secretary of State may make grants to—
   (a) the Independent Living (Extension) Fund established by a deed dated 25th February 1993 and made between the Secretary of State for Social Security of the one part and Robin Glover Wendt and John Fletcher Shepherd of the other part,
   (b) the Independent Living (1993) Fund established by a deed of the same date made between the same parties, and
   (c) Motability (a body corporate constituted by Royal Charter),
for such purposes as the Secretary of State may determine.
   (2) Any grant made under this section shall be of such amount, and shall be subject to such conditions, as the Secretary of State may with the consent of the Treasury determine.
   (3) Any grants made under this section shall be payable out of money provided by Parliament.
   (4) This section shall have effect in its application to Northern Ireland with the following modifications—
   (a) for references to the Secretary of State (other than the reference in subsection (1)(a) to the Secretary of State for Social Security) there shall be substituted references to the Department of Health and Social Services for Northern Ireland,
   (b) in subsection (2), for the reference to the Treasury there shall be substituted a reference to the Department of Finance and Personnel in Northern Ireland, and
   (c) in subsection (3), for the reference to money provided by Parliament there shall be substituted a reference to money appropriated by Measure of the Northern Ireland Assembly.

Short title and extent

   2.—(1) This Act may be cited as the Disability (Grants) Act 1993.
   (2) This Act extends to Northern Ireland.

INDEX

References are to sections

PROTECTION OF ANIMALS (SCOTLAND) ACT 1993

(1993 c. 15)

An Act to increase the penalties for certain offences under the Protection of Animals (Scotland) Act 1912. [27th May 1993]

PARLIAMENTARY DEBATES

Hansard, H.C. Vol. 221, col. 1374; H.L. Vol. 544, col. 1435; Vol. 545, cols. 119, 1127, 1732.

INTRODUCTION

This Act amends the Protection of Animals (Scotland) Act 1912 by increasing the penalty for certain acts of cruelty to animals. The 1993 Act substitutes a penalty of imprisonment or a fine or both in place of a fine alone.

Increased penalty for certain acts of cruelty to animals

1. In section 1(1) of the Protection of Animals (Scotland) Act 1912 (actings which as respects animals constitute offence of cruelty), for the words from "a fine" to the end there shall be substituted the words "imprisonment for a term not exceeding six months or to a fine not exceeding level 5 on the standard scale or to both".

Citation, extent and commencement

2.—(1) This Act may be cited as the Protection of Animals (Scotland) Act 1993; and it extends to Scotland only.

(2) This Act shall come into force at the end of the period of two months beginning with the day on which it is passed; and it has no effect in relation to any offence committed before it comes into force.

INDEX

FOREIGN COMPENSATION (AMENDMENT) ACT 1993

(1993 c. 16)

An Act to amend the Foreign Compensation Act 1950 so as to extend the powers to make Orders in Council under section 3 of that Act; and for connected purposes.   [27th May 1993]

PARLIAMENTARY DEBATES
Hansard, H.L. Vol. 539, col. 1545; Vol. 540, cols. 796, 1458; H.C. Vol. 219, col. 492; Vol. 225, col. 205.
The Bill was discussed in Standing Committee D on March 2, 1993.

INTRODUCTION
The Foreign Compensation Commission was established by the Foreign Compensation Act 1950 (later amended by the Foreign Compensation Act 1969). Under those Acts the Commission may be empowered to act by Order in Council. This Act extends the circumstances under which Orders in Council can be made to encompass situations where the Government contemplates receiving or have received compensation paid by another country.

Amendment of the Foreign Compensation Act 1950

1. For section 3 of the Foreign Compensation Act 1950 (compensation payable by governments of other countries under future agreements) there shall be substituted—

"Compensation payable by governments of other countries, international organisations etc.
3.—(1) Her Majesty may by Order in Council provide for any of the matters mentioned in subsection (2) below—
   (a) in contemplation of Her Majesty's Government in the United Kingdom receiving, or
   (b) where Her Majesty's Government in the United Kingdom have received,
compensation paid by another country (or its government), by an international organisation or by an international tribunal.
(2) The matters referred to in subsection (1) above are—
   (a) the prescribing of categories of person who may apply to the Commission for the purpose of establishing claims to participate in the compensation;
   (b) the imposition of conditions that must be fulfilled before such applications can be considered;
   (c) the prescribing of matters that must be established to the satisfaction of the Commission by persons making such applications;
   (d) the registration by the Commission of such claims, and the making of reports by the Commission in respect of such claims;
   (e) the investigation and determination by the Commission of such claims;
   (f) the surrender to the Commission of documents of title relating to property in respect of which claims are established, and the abandonment or extinction of rights in respect of which claims are established;
   (g) the distribution by the Commission of any sums paid to them by Her Majesty's Government in the United Kingdom out of compensation;
   (h) any supplementary or incidental matters for which provision appears to Her Majesty to be necessary or expedient.

(3) In this section—

"international organisation" means an organisation of which two or more countries (or their governments) are members, and includes any committee or other subordinate body of such an organisation, and

"international tribunal" means any tribunal, court or other body or person that in pursuance of—

(a) an agreement between two or more countries (or their governments) or between one or more countries (or their governments) and one or more international organisations, or

(b) a decision or resolution of an international organisation or of a conference attended by representatives of two or more countries (or their governments),

performs, or is appointed (whether permanently or temporarily) to perform, any function of a judicial or quasi-judicial nature."

Financial provision and repeal

2.—(1) There shall be paid out of money provided by Parliament any increase attributable to this Act in the sums so payable under the Foreign Compensation Act 1950.

(2) Section 2(1) and (3) of the Foreign Compensation Act 1969 (which amended and extended section 3 of the Foreign Compensation Act 1950 as originally enacted) shall cease to have effect.

Commencement and short title

3.—(1) This Act shall come into force at the end of the period of two months beginning with the day on which it is passed.

(2) This Act may be cited as the Foreign Compensation (Amendment) Act 1993.

INDEX

References in roman type are to sections of this Act; references in italic are to section 3 of the Foreign Compensation Act 1950

NON-DOMESTIC RATING ACT 1993

(1993 c. 17)

An Act to make further provision with respect to non-domestic rating for the period beginning with 1st April 1993 and ending with 31st March 1995; and for connected purposes.   [27th May 1993]

PARLIAMENTARY DEBATES
Hansard, H.C. Vol. 223, col. 855; Vol. 224, col. 962; H.L. Vol. 546, col. 252.

INTRODUCTION

Two important changes were made to non-domestic rating on April 1, 1990: the introduction of the national non-domestic rate, and the compilation of non-domestic rating lists following a revaluation of non-domestic property. This Act amends the transitional arrangements which phase in the effects of these changes, regulating the amount by which rate increases can grow and ensuring that any shortfall arising as a result of such amendment is made good by the Secretary of State.

Limit on increase in non-domestic rates for 1993 financial year

1.—(1) The provisions of subsections (3) and (4) below have effect for setting at 100, for the financial year beginning in 1993, the value of X in the formula in paragraph 5(2) of Schedule 7A to the Local Government Finance Act 1988, being a formula relevant to the determination of the non-domestic rates for certain hereditaments.

(2) In this Act—

(a) "the 1988 Act" means the Local Government Finance Act 1988;

(b) "the 1992 Act" means the Non-Domestic Rating Act 1992; and

(c) "financial year" has the same meaning as in the 1988 Act.

(3) In paragraph 5 of Schedule 7A to the 1988 Act, at the end of sub-paragraph (2A) (as set out in section 2(1) of the 1992 Act) there shall be added the words "and for that beginning in 1993".

(4) In subsection (2) of section 2 of the 1992 Act (amendment of the Non-Domestic Rating (Transitional Period) (Amendment and Further Provision) Regulations 1990) in paragraph (a) after the words "beginning in 1992" there shall be inserted "or that beginning in 1993".

(5) For the purpose of making similar provision in relation to certain hereditaments shown in a central non-domestic rating list, the formula in each of the following, namely—

(a) article 9 of the British Gas plc (Rateable Values) Order 1989,

(b) article 9(3) of the Electricity Supply Industry (Rateable Values) Order 1989,

(c) article 12(3) of the Railways (Rateable Values) Order 1989, and

(d) article 9(3) of the Water Undertakers (Rateable Values) Order 1989,

shall have effect in relation to the financial year beginning in 1993 as if for the figure "1.2" there were substituted the figure "1".

Non-domestic rating: transitional pooling

2. The modifications of Schedule 8 to the 1988 Act (non-domestic rating: pooling) made by sections 4 and 5 of the 1992 Act shall have effect, in relation to the financial year beginning in 1994, as if in paragraph 9(3A)(a) of that Schedule (as set out in section 4 of the 1992 Act) after the words "the Non-Domestic Rating Act 1992" there were inserted the words "and the Non-Domestic Rating Act 1993".

Financial provisions

3. There shall be paid out of money provided by Parliament any increase attributable to this Act in the sums payable out of money so provided under the 1988 Act.

Subordinate legislation

4. Regulations or orders may be made under any provision of the 1988 Act for the purposes of giving effect to, or in consequence of, any provision of this Act; and any such regulations or orders (including in particular regulations under paragraph 4 of Schedule 8 to that Act) may have retrospective effect.

Effect of certain modifications

5.—(1) Any provision of this Act that an enactment shall have effect with modifications shall be taken, if the context so requires, to include provision that the enactment shall be deemed always to have had effect with those modifications.

(2) Where at any time before the commencement of section 1 above a person's right to pay any non-domestic rates by instalments has been forfeited in pursuance of—

    (a) regulation 8 (failure to pay instalments) of the Non-Domestic Rating (Collection and Enforcement) (Local Lists) Regulations 1989, or

    (b) regulation 8 (failure to pay instalments) of the Non-Domestic Rating (Collection and Enforcement) (Central Lists) Regulations 1989,

nothing in that section as read with subsection (1) above shall be taken as reviving that right.

(3) In this section "enactment" includes any provision made under the 1988 Act.

Short title, commencement and extent

6.—(1) This Act may be cited as the Non-Domestic Rating Act 1993.

(2) This Act shall come into force on such day as the Secretary of State may by order made by statutory instrument appoint; and different days may be appointed for different provisions or for different purposes.

(3) This Act extends to England and Wales only.

INDEX

References are to sections

REINSURANCE (ACTS OF TERRORISM) ACT 1993

(1993 c. 18)

An Act to provide for the payment out of money provided by Parliament or into the Consolidated Fund of sums referable to reinsurance liabilities entered into by the Secretary of State in respect of loss or damage to property resulting from or consequential upon acts of terrorism and losses consequential on such loss or damage.   [27th May 1993]

PARLIAMENTARY DEBATES
Hansard, H.C. Vol. 224, col. 969; H.L. Vol. 546, col. 395.

INTRODUCTION
This Act makes provisions which will allow the Secretary of State to undertake the liability of reinsuring certain risks linked to acts of terrorism. Money will be provided by Parliament to meet any obligations undertaken under this Act.

Financing of reinsurance obligations of the Secretary of State

1.—(1) There shall be paid out of money provided by Parliament such sums as may be necessary to enable the Secretary of State to meet his obligations under—
(a) any agreement of reinsurance which, with the consent of the Treasury, is entered into (whether before or after the passing of this Act) pursuant to arrangements to which this Act applies, or
(b) any guarantee which, with that consent, is entered into (whether before or after that passing) pursuant to any such agreement.

(2) As soon as practicable after the passing of this Act or, if it is later, after he enters into the agreement or guarantee, the Secretary of State shall lay before each House of Parliament a copy of any agreement or guarantee falling within subsection (1) above.

(3) There shall be paid into the Consolidated Fund any sums received by the Secretary of State pursuant to any arrangements to which this Act applies.

Reinsurance arrangements to which this Act applies

2.—(1) This Act applies to arrangements under which the Secretary of State, with the consent of the Treasury, undertakes to any extent the liability of reinsuring risks against—
(a) loss of or damage to property in Great Britain resulting from or consequential upon acts of terrorism; and
(b) any loss which is consequential on loss or damage falling within paragraph (a) above;
and to the extent that the arrangements relate to events occurring before as well as after an agreement of reinsurance comes into being, the reference in section 1(1) above to the obligations of the Secretary of State shall be construed accordingly.

(2) In this section "acts of terrorism" means acts of persons acting on behalf of, or in connection with, any organisation which carries out activities directed towards the overthrowing or influencing, by force or violence, of Her Majesty's government in the United Kingdom or any other government de jure or de facto.

(3) In subjection (2) above "organisation" includes any association or combination of persons.

Citation and extent

3.—(1) This Act may be cited as the Reinsurance (Acts of Terrorism) Act 1993.

(2) This Act does not extend to Northern Ireland.

INDEX

References are to sections

TRADE UNION REFORM AND EMPLOYMENT RIGHTS ACT 1993*

(1993 c. 19)

---

* Annotations by Gareth Thomas, LL.B., B.C.L., Lecturer in Law, University of East Anglia.

An Act to make further reforms of the law relating to trade unions and industrial relations; to make amendments of the law relating to employment
rights and to abolish the right to statutory minimum remuneration; to
amend the law relating to the constitution and jurisdiction of industrial
tribunals and the Employment Appeal Tribunal; to amend section 56A of
the Sex Discrimination Act 1975; to provide for the Secretary of State to
have functions of securing the provision of careers services; to make further provision about employment and training functions of Scottish Enterprise and of Highlands and Islands Enterprise; and for connected
purposes.   [1st July 1993]

PARLIAMENTARY DEBATES
  Hansard, H.C. Vol. 214, cols. 168, 253; Vol. 219, cols. 156, 247, 326; Vol. 226, cols. 738, 868;
H.L. Vol. 534, cols. 422, 1342, 1418, 1557, 1624; Vol. 544, cols. 467, 509, 726, 802, 837, 1718; Vol.
545, cols. 808, 818, 868, 1856; Vol. 546, cols. 12, 81, 117.
  The Bill was discussed in Standing Committee F from November 26, 1992 to February 4, 1993.

INTRODUCTION
  The Trade Union Reform and Employment Rights Act 1993 is the tenth major piece of
employment legislation since 1980, and the largest and most wide-ranging employment statute
(consolidations apart) since the Employment Protection Act 1975. The Act falls into three distinct parts. Part I ("Trade Unions") maintains the relentless pace of the step-by-step legislative
reform of trade unions which began in 1980. Most of the measures in Part I derive from the
Green Paper, *Industrial Relations in the 1990s* (Cm. 1602, 1991), although several were added
during the Act's passage through Parliament. Sections 1 to 6 tighten up the existing requirements on union elections and political fund ballots, particularly in relation to independent scrutiny of the ballot and the accuracy of union membership records, and extend the balloting
requirements to merger ballots, while s.7 repeals the provisions whereby unions may claim reimbursement from the State of the cost of holding a postal ballot. Sections 8 to 12 make significant
changes to the rules on union financial affairs, in line with the recommendations of the Green
Paper, with the aim of improving the flow of information to union members regarding the
finances of their union and strengthening the enforcement procedures. The Certification Officer is given sweeping new powers of investigation into union finances, and imprisonment and
disqualification from union office are added to the penalties for a contravention of the requirements. The provisions in ss.13 to 16 concerning the rights of union members have generated
considerable controversy, with criticism coming from both sides of industry. Employers have
expressed concern over the introduction by s.14 of a right to join a union of one's choice, which
undermines the operation of the Bridlington Principles and which it is feared may have destabilising effect on industrial relations; and the restrictions in s.15 on the operation of check-off
arrangements for the collection of union subscriptions have met with a decidedly lukewarm
response, even after the original proposals were modified so that authorisation is now only
required once every three years instead of annually, as originally proposed in the Green Paper.
The most controversial of the reforms relating to union membership, the provisions in s.13 which
enable an employer to offer sweeteners to employees to persuade them to accept personal contracts instead of collective bargaining, was added so late that the Government were forced to
take the exceptional step of recommitting the Bill to Committee in the Lords in order to introduce it. Finally, ss.17 to 22 of Part I contain several very significant and highly controversial
reforms of the law on industrial action, some of which had been considered during the passage of
earlier legislation and rejected as either unworkable or undesirable. Thus, the requirements of
compulsory postal voting and independent scrutiny are extended to industrial action ballots, as
proposed in the 1991 Green Paper, albeit with a special dispensation in the case of the latter for
small ballots involving not more than 50 members, and a union will in future have to give
employers at least seven days' notice of its intention to hold a ballot and, more controversially, of
the actual timing of the industrial action itself; s.22 introduces a new "citizen's right" (derived
from the Citizen's Charter), whereby an individual who is deprived, or likely to be deprived, of
goods or services as a result of unlawful industrial action may seek an order from the High Court
restraining that unlawful action, with assistance from a new Commissioner for Protection
against Unlawful Industrial Action. The potential impact of this reform cannot be overestimated. It represents a quite breathtaking extension of liability, extending the range of potential
plaintiffs to embrace anyone adversely affected by unlawful industrial action, irrespective of
whether that person has a cause of action in tort or contract or indeed any entitlement to be

supplied with the goods or services in question. It seems certain to have a major impact on the use of the law in industrial disputes.

Part II of the Act ("Employment Rights") has an entirely different tone. It introduces a range of new and improved individual employment protection rights, many of which are designed to bring U.K. law into line with EEC Directives, and it graphically demonstrates the continued importance of EEC law as a source of employment rights, even after the opt-out of the Social Charter negotiated at Maastricht. Sections 23 to 25 overhaul the existing law on maternity rights to implement EEC Directive 92/85 on the Protection of Pregnant Women at Work, adopted in October 1992; s.23 introduces a new right to 14 weeks' maternity leave for all pregnant employees, regardless of length of service or hours of work, which is additional to the existing right to return to work up to 29 weeks after childbirth. Further legislation is expected introducing a right to be paid during the maternity leave period. The protection against dismissal or selection for redundancy on the grounds of pregnancy or childbirth is strengthened by s.24, and will in future apply irrespective of length of service or hours of work, while s.25 introduces a new right for a woman who is pregnant, has recently given birth or is breastfeeding, to be suspended from work on full pay by her employer on maternity grounds. The employee's right to a written statement of employment particulars is heavily amended by s.26, in line with EEC Directive No. 91/533 on information concerning employment conditions, while s.27 removes the five-year service qualification for an itemised pay statement from most employees who work between eight and 16 hours a week.

Part II also contains important new protection against unfair dismissal or victimisation of employees. Thus, there is a new right in s.28 not to be dismissed or subjected to any detriment on specified health and safety grounds, regardless of length of service, hours of work or age. This new right implements part of the EEC Framework Directive 89/391 on the introduction of measures to encourage improvements in the health and safety of workers at work, which requires Member States to legislate for the protection of workers with designated health and safety responsibilities and for workers who leave their workstations in circumstances of serious, imminent and unavoidable danger. The section, therefore, extends to all workers with health and safety responsibilities the protection given to offshore workers by the Offshore Safety (Protection Against Victimisation) Act 1992, and that Act is repealed by s.51, Sched. 10. In addition, s.29 enacts an important new right not to be dismissed or selected for redundancy for asserting a statutory employment right, again regardless of length of service, hours of work or age. The protection applies whether or not the employee was entitled to the right in question, and whether or not that right was in fact infringed; the only requirement is that the employee must have acted in good faith in asserting it. This new right, one of the few in Part II which does not owe its existence to EEC law, represents a significant advance in the rights of employees against heavy-handed action by employers. Section 30 amends the rules governing the award of compensation for unfair dismissal to enable an industrial tribunal to compensate the complainant fully where the employer has failed to comply with a reinstatement or re-engagement order; and Sched. 7, para. 1 removes the usual qualifying period of service where an employee is unfairly selected for redundancy on trade union grounds.

Finally in Part II, there are a series of important amendments concerning sex discrimination, the transfer of undertakings and consultation on redundancies, again to comply with EEC requirements. Thus, s.32 provides a mechanism whereby an employee (or prospective employee) may seek a declaration that a term in a collective agreement discriminates on the grounds of sex and is therefore void, thereby remedying a glaring omission in the Sex Discrimination Act 1986, s.6; s.33 amends the Transfer of Undertakings (Protection of Employment) Regulations 1981 (S.I. 1981 No. 1794) following the instigation of infringement proceedings by the European Commission against the U.K. Government for its alleged failure fully to transpose EEC Directive No. 77/187 (the Acquired Rights Directive) into domestic law; and s.34 amends the statutory redundancy consultation procedures to bring U.K. law more closely into line with EEC Directive No. 75/129 on the Approximation of the Laws of the Member States Relating to Collective Redundancies, recently amended by EEC Directive No. 92/56. In all three cases, however, there remain doubts as to whether the amendments go far enough to meet the U.K.'s obligations under the relevant directives.

Part III ("Other Employment Matters") contains a number of miscellaneous employment measures mainly concerned with institutional matters. By far the most controversial measure in the Act is the abolition of the Wages Councils by s.35, thereby leaving the Agricultural Wages Board as the only remaining vestige of minimum wage machinery in the U.K.; ss.36 to 42 contain a series of important provisions concerning industrial tribunals and the E.A.T. which, *inter alia*, amend the constitution of industrial tribunals and the E.A.T. to permit chairmen and E.A.T. judges to sit alone in certain circumstances; make technical amendments to the power of the Secretary of State to extend the jurisdiction of industrial tribunals to claims for breach of contract; permit binding settlements of employment disputes without the involvement of an

ACAS conciliator where the applicant has received independent legal advice; empower industrial tribunals and the E.A.T. to impose restrictions on the reporting of cases involving allegations of sexual misconduct; and empower the E.A.T. (on the application of the Attorney General or, in Scotland, the Lord Advocate) to make a restriction of proceedings order against a vexatious litigant. There is a small but nevertheless significant change to the terms of reference of ACAS in s.43, which removes its duty to encourage the extension of collective bargaining and the development and reform of collective bargaining machinery, while s.44 allows ACAS to charge for its services, and gives the Secretary of State a controversial new power to direct the Service to impose charges for specified functions. Finally there are important changes in ss.45 and 46 in respect of careers services, transferring the duty to secure the provision of careers services in Great Britain from local education authorities to the Secretary of State; s.47 extends the existing powers of Scottish Enterprise and Highlands and Islands Enterprise to provide work experience schemes for the unemployed.

PART I

TRADE UNIONS ETC.

Union elections and ballots

Election scrutineer to check register

1.—(1) In the Trade Union and Labour Relations (Consolidation) Act 1992 (referred to in this Act as "the 1992 Act"), in section 49 (appointment of independent scrutineer for election)—
(a) after paragraph (a) of subsection (3) (terms of appointment of scrutineer) there shall be inserted—
"(aa) to—
(i) inspect the register of names and addresses of the members of the trade union, or
(ii) examine the copy of the register as at the relevant date which is supplied to him in accordance with subsection (5A)(a), whenever it appears to him appropriate to do so and, in particular, when the conditions specified in subsection (3A) are satisfied;",
(b) in paragraph (d) (scrutineer to retain custody of voting papers) of that subsection, after the words "purposes of the election" there shall be inserted the words "and the copy of the register supplied to him in accordance with subsection (5A)(a)" and after the words "of the papers" there shall be inserted the words "or copy",
(c) after that subsection there shall be inserted—
"(3A) The conditions referred to in subsection (3)(aa) are—
(a) that a request that the scrutineer inspect the register or examine the copy is made to him during the appropriate period by a member of the trade union or candidate who suspects that the register is not, or at the relevant date was not, accurate and up-to-date, and
(b) that the scrutineer does not consider that the suspicion of the member or candidate is ill-founded.
(3B) In subsection (3A) "the appropriate period" means the period—
(a) beginning with the first day on which a person may become a candidate in the election or, if later, the day on which the scrutineer is appointed, and
(b) ending with the day before the day on which the scrutineer makes his report to the trade union.
(3C) The duty of confidentiality as respects the register is incorporated in the scrutineer's appointment.",

(d) after subsection (5) there shall be inserted—
>"(5A) The trade union shall—
>> (a) supply to the scrutineer as soon as is reasonably practicable after the relevant date a copy of the register of names and addresses of its members as at that date, and
>> (b) comply with any request made by the scrutineer to inspect the register.
>
> (5B) Where the register is kept by means of a computer the duty imposed on the trade union by subsection (5A)(a) is either to supply a legible printed copy or (if the scrutineer prefers) to supply a copy of the computer data and allow the scrutineer use of the computer to read it at any time during the period when he is required to retain custody of the copy.", and

(e) after subsection (7) there shall be inserted—
>"(8) In this section "the relevant date" means—
>> (a) where the trade union has rules determining who is entitled to vote in the election by reference to membership on a particular date, that date, and
>> (b) otherwise, the date, or the last date, on which voting papers are distributed for the purposes of the election.".

(2) In section 52 of the 1992 Act (scrutineer's report on election), after subsection (2) there shall be inserted—
>"(2A) The report shall also state—
>> (a) whether the scrutineer—
>>> (i) has inspected the register of names and addresses of the members of the trade union, or
>>> (ii) has examined the copy of the register as at the relevant date which is supplied to him in accordance with section 49(5A)(a),
>> (b) if he has, whether in the case of each inspection or examination he was acting on a request by a member of the trade union or candidate or at his own instance,
>> (c) whether he declined to act on any such request, and
>> (d) whether any inspection of the register, or any examination of the copy of the register, has revealed any matter which he considers should be drawn to the attention of the trade union in order to assist it in securing that the register is accurate and up-to-date,
>
> but shall not state the name of any member or candidate who has requested such an inspection or examination.".

GENERAL NOTE

This section amends the Trade Union and Labour Relations (Consolidation) Act 1992 (hereinafter referred to as the 1992 Act), s.49, which provides for the appointment of an independent scrutineer in trade union executive elections and sets out the statutory functions of the scrutineer, and s.52, which lays down the information which must be contained in the scrutineer's report on the conduct of the election. In addition to the scrutineer's existing duties (which include supervising the production and distribution of ballot papers, compiling a report in accordance with s.52 of the 1992 Act, and retaining custody of the ballot papers for at least a year after the date on which the result of the ballot is announced), subs. (1) adds the additional requirement that the scrutineer must be required by the terms of his appointment to inspect the union's membership register (or a copy thereof) whenever he considers it appropriate to do so, and in particular when requested to do so by a union member or an election candidate who suspects that the register is not accurate and up to date. He need not act on the request if he considers the suspicion ill-founded, or the request is made outside the time period specified in new s.49(3B). Section 1 also imposes a duty on a trade union to supply the scrutineer with a copy of the membership register, which he must keep for the same period as he is required to retain custody of the ballot papers, and to comply with any request from the scrutineer to inspect the register (new s.49(5A)). Unusually, this latter duty does not appear to be qualified by any test of reasonable practicability, so that (in theory at least) the scrutineer could demand to inspect the register in the middle of the night! Where the register is computerised the union may either supply a legible printed copy or, if the scrutineer prefers, provide him with a copy of the computer data and allow him access to a computer to read it.

Subsection (2) adds to the information which must be contained in the scrutineer's report to the union. The report must state whether the scrutineer has inspected the register (or examined a copy thereof), and whether the inspection revealed anything which might indicate that the register is not accurate or up to date. The report must also indicate whether the inspection was on the request of a member or candidate, but may not reveal the identity of anyone who has requested the scrutineer to make such an inspection.

These new requirements originated in the Green Paper, *Industrial Relations in the 1990s* (Cm. 1602, 1991), which reported the Government's concern at a number of alleged cases of ballot-rigging and irregularities in certain union membership registers, and concluded that the existing statutory provisions on trade union executive elections did not go far enough in ensuring compliance by unions with their statutory duties. Union members already have a right to check whether they are entered on their union's membership register, free of charge and at any reasonable time, and to request a copy of their entry (s.24(3) of the 1992 Act), but the Green Paper went further by proposing that union members be given a right to inspect the entire membership register. This proposal was, however, dropped after concerns were expressed that it would invade members' privacy and might infringe the Data Protection Act 1984. The compromise was to give a right of access to the scrutineer instead, but with a duty of confidentiality attached (see the note to s.6, below). The new requirements apply to election ballots held on or after August 30, 1993, unless the scrutineer has begun to carry out his functions in relation to the ballot before that date: Trade Union Reform and Employment Rights Act 1993 (Commencement No. 1 and Transitional Provisions) Order 1993 (S.I. 1993 No. 1908), reg. 3(1). Similar requirements are applied to political fund ballots and merger ballots (but not to industrial action ballots) by ss.3 and 4 respectively.

Subs. (1)

Register of names and addresses of members. The duty to maintain an accurate and up to date register of members' names and addresses is contained in s.24 of the 1992 Act. That section gives a union member the right, on reasonable notice, to check that his or her name is on the register, but does not confer a right of access on anyone else, hence the right conferred on the independent scrutineer by this section. The Green Paper, *Industrial Relations in the 1990s* (Cm. 1602, 1991) proposed that union members should be given a statutory right to inspect the whole membership register, but this does not appear in the Act.

The duty of confidentiality. New s.24A of the 1992 Act, inserted by s.6 below, requires a union to impose a duty of confidentiality on the independent scrutineer in respect of the membership register. See the note to s.6.

Counting of election votes etc. by independent person

2.—(1) After section 51 of the 1992 Act there shall be inserted—

"Counting of votes etc. by independent person

51A.—(1) The trade union shall ensure that—
    (a) the storage and distribution of the voting papers for the purposes of the election, and
    (b) the counting of the votes cast in the election,
are undertaken by one or more independent persons appointed by the union.

    (2) A person is an independent person in relation to an election if—
    (a) he is the scrutineer, or
    (b) he is a person other than the scrutineer and the trade union has no grounds for believing either that he will carry out any functions conferred on him in relation to the election otherwise than competently or that his independence in relation to the union, or in relation to the election, might reasonably be called into question.

    (3) An appointment under this section shall require the person appointed to carry out his functions so as to minimise the risk of any

contravention of requirements imposed by or under any enactment or the occurrence of any unfairness or malpractice.

(4) The duty of confidentiality as respects the register is incorporated in an appointment under this section.

(5) Where the person appointed to undertake the counting of votes is not the scrutineer, his appointment shall require him to send the voting papers back to the scrutineer as soon as reasonably practicable after the counting has been completed.

(6) The trade union—

(a) shall ensure that nothing in the terms of an appointment under this section is such as to make it reasonable for any person to call into question the independence of the person appointed in relation to the union,

(b) shall ensure that a person appointed under this section duly carries out his functions and that there is no interference with his carrying out of those functions which would make it reasonable for any person to call into question the independence of the person appointed in relation to the union, and

(c) shall comply with all reasonable requests made by a person appointed under this section for the purposes of, or in connection with, the carrying out of his functions.".

(2) In section 52 of the 1992 Act (scrutineer's report on election)—

(a) in subsection (1), after paragraph (d) there shall be inserted ", and

(e) the name of the person (or of each of the persons) appointed under section 51A or, if no person was so appointed, that fact.",

(b) in subsection (2)(b), after the word "made" there shall be inserted "(whether by him or any other person)", and

(c) after subsection (2A) (which is inserted by section 1 above) there shall be inserted—

"(2B) Where one or more persons other than the scrutineer are appointed under section 51A, the statement included in the scrutineer's report in accordance with subsection (2)(b) shall also indicate—

(a) whether he is satisfied with the performance of the person, or each of the persons, so appointed, and

(b) if he is not satisfied with the performance of the person, or any of them, particulars of his reasons for not being so satisfied.".

GENERAL NOTE

Under the existing provisions on trade union executive elections, the independent scrutineer is required to supervise the production and distribution of the voting papers, but the scrutineer's duties do not extend to the actual distribution and counting of the voting papers. This section adds a new s.51A to the 1992 Act, which requires the voting papers for union executive elections to be stored and distributed, and the votes to be counted, by one or more "independent persons" appointed by the union. An "independent person" may be the scrutineer, or any other person whom the union believes will carry out his functions competently and whose independence in relation to the union or the election cannot reasonably be called into question. The independent person is required to carry out his functions so as to minimise the risk of any illegality, unfairness or malpractice, and the union must ensure that there is no interference with the independent person which could reasonably call his independence into question. The union must also comply with all reasonable requests made by the independent person in the performance of his duties. These requirements are similar to those which apply to the appointment of an independent scrutineer under s.49 of the 1992 Act. Subsection (2) amends s.52 of the 1992 Act, requiring the scrutineer's report on the conduct of the election to include the name of the independent person or persons, and to state whether or not the scrutineer is satisfied with the way in which the independent person performed his duties, and if not to explain the reasons why. The new requirements apply to election ballots held on or after August 30, 1993, unless the scrutineer has begun to carry out his functions in relation to the ballot before that date: Trade Union Reform and Employment Rights Act 1993 (Commencement No. 1 and Transitional Provisions) Order 1993 (S.I. 1993 No. 1908), reg. 3(1). As in the case of s.1 above, similar requirements are applied to political fund ballots and merger ballots (but not to industrial action ballots) by ss.3 and 4 respectively.

Political fund ballots

3. Schedule 1 to this Act (which makes in relation to political fund ballots provision corresponding to that made in relation to elections by sections 1 and 2 above) shall have effect.

GENERAL NOTE

This section gives effect to Sched. 1, which introduces to political fund ballots the same additional requirements as are applied to union executive elections by ss.1 and 2 (amending ss.74 to 78 of the 1992 Act). The Certification Officer must be satisfied that the political fund ballot rules of the union satisfy these additional requirements before giving those rules his approval. The new requirements apply to political fund ballots in which votes may only be cast on or after August 30, 1993, unless the Certification Officer's approval of the ballot rules was sought after January 1, 1993 and obtained before July 1, 1993, and the voting in the ballot is completed on or before December 31, 1993.

Ballots for union amalgamations and transfers of engagements

4. For section 100 of the 1992 Act (requirement of resolution to approve instrument of amalgamation or transfer) there shall be substituted—

"**Requirement of ballot on resolution**

100.—(1) A resolution approving the instrument of amalgamation or transfer must be passed on a ballot of the members of the trade union held in accordance with sections 100A to 100E.

(2) A simple majority of those voting is sufficient to pass such a resolution unless the rules of the trade union expressly require it to be approved by a greater majority or by a specified proportion of the members of the union.

Appointment of independent scrutineer

100A.—(1) The trade union shall, before the ballot is held, appoint a qualified independent person ("the scrutineer") to carry out—

   (a) the functions in relation to the ballot which are required under this section to be contained in his appointment; and

   (b) such additional functions in relation to the ballot as may be specified in his appointment.

(2) A person is a qualified independent person in relation to a ballot if—

   (a) he satisfies such conditions as may be specified for the purposes of this section by order of the Secretary of State or is himself so specified; and

   (b) the trade union has no grounds for believing either that he will carry out any functions conferred on him in relation to the ballot otherwise than competently or that his independence in relation to the union, or in relation to the ballot, might reasonably be called into question.

An order under paragraph (a) shall be made by statutory instrument which shall be subject to annulment in pursuance of a resolution of either House of Parliament.

(3) The scrutineer's appointment shall require him—

   (a) to be the person who supervises the production of the voting papers and (unless he is appointed under section 100D to undertake the distribution of the voting papers) their distribution and to whom the voting papers are returned by those voting;

   (b) to—

      (i) inspect the register of names and addresses of the members of the trade union, or

(ii) examine the copy of the register as at the relevant date which is supplied to him in accordance with subsection (9)(a),

whenever it appears to him appropriate to do so and, in particular, when the conditions specified in subsection (4) are satisfied;

(c) to take such steps as appear to him to be appropriate for the purpose of enabling him to make his report (see section 100E);

(d) to make his report to the trade union as soon as reasonably practicable after the last date for the return of voting papers; and

(e) to retain custody of all voting papers returned for the purposes of the ballot and the copy of the register supplied to him in accordance with subsection (9)(a)—

(i) until the end of the period of one year beginning with the announcement by the union of the result of the ballot; and

(ii) if within that period a complaint is made under section 103 (complaint as regards passing of resolution), until the Certification Officer or Employment Appeal Tribunal authorises him to dispose of the papers or copy.

(4) The conditions referred to in subsection (3)(b) are—

(a) that a request that the scrutineer inspect the register or examine the copy is made to him during the appropriate period by a member of the trade union who suspects that the register is not, or at the relevant date was not, accurate and up-to-date, and

(b) that the scrutineer does not consider that the member's suspicion is ill-founded.

(5) In subsection (4) "the appropriate period" means the period—

(a) beginning with the day on which the scrutineer is appointed, and

(b) ending with the day before the day on which the scrutineer makes his report to the trade union.

(6) The duty of confidentiality as respects the register is incorporated in the scrutineer's appointment.

(7) The trade union shall ensure that nothing in the terms of the scrutineer's appointment (including any additional functions specified in the appointment) is such as to make it reasonable for any person to call the scrutineer's independence in relation to the union into question.

(8) The trade union shall, before the scrutineer begins to carry out his functions, either—

(a) send a notice stating the name of the scrutineer to every member of the union to whom it is reasonably practicable to send such a notice, or

(b) take all such other steps for notifying members of the name of the scrutineer as it is the practice of the union to take when matters of general interest to all its members need to be brought to their attention.

(9) The trade union shall—

(a) supply to the scrutineer as soon as is reasonably practicable after the relevant date a copy of the register of names and addresses of its members as at that date, and

(b) comply with any request made by the scrutineer to inspect the register.

(10) Where the register is kept by means of a computer the duty imposed on the trade union by subsection (9)(a) is either to supply a legible printed copy or (if the scrutineer prefers) to supply a copy of

the computer data and allow the scrutineer use of the computer to read it at any time during the period when he is required to retain custody of the copy.

(11) The trade union shall ensure that the scrutineer duly carries out his functions and that there is no interference with his carrying out of those functions which would make it reasonable for any person to call the scrutineer's independence in relation to the union into question.

(12) The trade union shall comply with all reasonable requests made by the scrutineer for the purposes of, or in connection with, the carrying out of his functions.

(13) In this section "the relevant date" means—

(a) where the trade union has rules determining who is entitled to vote in the ballot by reference to membership on a particular date, that date, and

(b) otherwise, the date, or the last date, on which voting papers are distributed for the purposes of the ballot.

Entitlement to vote

100B. Entitlement to vote in the ballot shall be accorded equally to all members of the trade union.

Voting

100C.—(1) The method of voting must be by the marking of a voting paper by the person voting.

(2) Each voting paper must—

(a) state the name of the independent scrutineer and clearly specify the address to which, and the date by which, it is to be returned, and

(b) be given one of a series of consecutive whole numbers every one of which is used in giving a different number in that series to each voting paper printed or otherwise produced for the purposes of the ballot, and

(c) be marked with its number.

(3) Every person who is entitled to vote in the ballot must—

(a) be allowed to vote without interference or constraint, and

(b) so far as is reasonably practicable, be enabled to do so without incurring any direct cost to himself.

(4) So far as is reasonably practicable, every person who is entitled to vote in the ballot must—

(a) have a voting paper sent to him by post at his home address or another address which he has requested the trade union in writing to treat as his postal address, and

(b) be given a convenient opportunity to vote by post.

(5) No voting paper which is sent to a person for voting shall have enclosed with it any other document except—

(a) the notice which, under section 99(1), is to accompany the voting paper,

(b) an addressed envelope, and

(c) a document containing instructions for the return of the voting paper,

without any other statement.

(6) The ballot shall be conducted so as to secure that—

(a) so far as is reasonably practicable, those voting do so in secret, and

(b) the votes given in the ballot are fairly and accurately counted.

For the purposes of paragraph (b) an inaccuracy in counting shall be disregarded if it is accidental and on a scale which could not affect the result of the ballot.

Counting of votes etc. by independent person

100D.—(1) The trade union shall ensure that—

(a) the storage and distribution of the voting papers for the purposes of the ballot, and

(b) the counting of the votes cast in the ballot,

are undertaken by one or more independent persons appointed by the trade union.

(2) A person is an independent person in relation to a ballot if—

(a) he is the scrutineer, or

(b) he is a person other than the scrutineer and the trade union has no grounds for believing either that he will carry out any functions conferred on him in relation to the ballot otherwise than competently or that his independence in relation to the union, or in relation to the ballot, might reasonably be called into question.

(3) An appointment under this section shall require the person appointed to carry out his functions so as to minimise the risk of any contravention of requirements imposed by or under any enactment or the occurrence of any unfairness or malpractice.

(4) The duty of confidentiality as respects the register is incorporated in the scrutineer's appointment.

(5) Where the person appointed to undertake the counting of votes is not the scrutineer, his appointment shall require him to send the voting papers back to the scrutineer as soon as reasonably practicable after the counting has been completed.

(6) The trade union—

(a) shall ensure that nothing in the terms of an appointment under this section is such as to make it reasonable for any person to call into question the independence of the person appointed in relation to the union,

(b) shall ensure that a person appointed under this section duly carries out his functions and that there is no interference with his carrying out of those functions which would make it reasonable for any person to call into question the independence of the person appointed in relation to the union, and

(c) shall comply with all reasonable requests made by a person appointed under this section for the purposes of, or in connection with, the carrying out of his functions.

Scrutineer's report

100E.—(1) The scrutineer's report on the ballot shall state—

(a) the number of voting papers distributed for the purposes of the ballot,

(b) the number of voting papers returned to the scrutineer,

(c) the number of valid votes cast in the ballot for and against the resolution,

(d) the number of spoiled or otherwise invalid voting papers returned, and

(e) the name of the person (or of each of the persons) appointed under section 100D or, if no person was so appointed, that fact.

(2) The report shall also state whether the scrutineer is satisfied—

(a) that there are no reasonable grounds for believing that there was any contravention of a requirement imposed by or under any enactment in relation to the ballot,

(b) that the arrangements made (whether by him or any other person) with respect to the production, storage, distribution, return or other handling of the voting papers used in the ballot, and the arrangements for the counting of the votes, included all such security arrangements as were reasonably practicable for the purpose of minimising the risk that any unfairness or mal-practice might occur, and

(c) that he has been able to carry out his functions without any such interference as would make it reasonable for any person to call his independence in relation to the union into question;

and if he is not satisfied as to any of those matters, the report shall give particulars of his reasons for not being satisfied as to that matter.

(3) The report shall also state—

(a) whether the scrutineer—

(i) has inspected the register of names and addresses of the members of the trade union, or

(ii) has examined the copy of the register as at the relevant date which is supplied to him in accordance with section 100A(9)(a),

(b) if he has, whether in the case of each inspection or examination he was acting on a request by a member of the trade union or at his own instance,

(c) whether he declined to act on any such request, and

(d) whether any inspection of the register, or any examination of the copy of the register, has revealed any matter which he con-siders should be drawn to the attention of the trade union in order to assist it in securing that the register is accurate and up-to-date,

but shall not state the name of any member who has requested such an inspection or examination.

(4) Where one or more persons other than the scrutineer are appointed under section 100D, the statement included in the scruti-neer's report in accordance with subsection (2)(b) shall also indicate—

(a) whether he is satisfied with the performance of the person, or each of the persons, so appointed, and

(b) if he is not satisfied with the performance of the person, or any of them, particulars of his reasons for not being so satisfied.

(5) The trade union shall not publish the result of the ballot until it has received the scrutineer's report.

(6) The trade union shall within the period of three months after it receives the report—

(a) send a copy of the report to every member of the union to whom it is reasonably practicable to send such a copy; or

(b) take all such other steps for notifying the contents of the report to the members of the union (whether by publishing the report or otherwise) as it is the practice of the union to take when matters of general interest to all its members need to be brought to their attention.

(7) Any such copy or notification shall be accompanied by a state-ment that the union will, on request, supply any member of the trade union with a copy of the report, either free of charge or on payment of such reasonable fee as may be specified in the notification.

(8) The trade union shall so supply any member of the union who makes such a request and pays the fee (if any) notified to him.".

GENERAL NOTE

This section imposes on merger ballots a set of requirements which are substantially the same as those which apply to union elections and political fund ballots. Thus, the ballot must be fully postal and subject to independent scrutiny, and the additional requirements imposed on union elections and political fund ballots by ss.1 to 3 are also applicable. Hitherto s.100 of the 1992 Act merely set out certain minimum requirements for a valid merger ballot, and subject to those requirements the union's committee of management or other governing body (typically the national executive) was entitled to determine the arrangements for the conduct of the ballot as it thought fit, irrespective of the union's normal balloting procedures, unless the union's rules expressly provided that that power was not to apply. A simple majority of the votes recorded was sufficient to pass a merger resolution, notwithstanding anything in the rules of the union requiring a greater majority or a minimum turn-out, but as before this provision was overridden where the union's rules expressly provided that it was not to apply in relation to the union. The new requirements are set out in ss.100 to 100E, discussed below, and apply to all merger ballots in which votes may only be cast on or after August 30, 1993, unless the instrument of amalgamation or transfer was approved by the Certification Officer before July 1, 1993 and the voting is completed before December 31, 1993.

New s.100 of the 1992 Act
As before, new s.100(2) of the 1992 Act provides that a simple majority of those voting will be sufficient to pass a merger resolution, but in future the union's rules may expressly require it to be approved by a greater majority or by a specified proportion of members; it is no longer necessary for the rules to include an express clause excluding the requirements of the Act if it wishes to impose a requirement other than a simple majority. Previously there was an argument that the union's rules might specify a level of support *lower* than a simple majority, but on the amended wording this is no longer arguable.

New s.100A of the 1992 Act
These provisions mirror those governing the appointment of an independent scrutineer in trade union executive elections and political fund ballots (ss.49 and 75 respectively of the 1992 Act). See the note to s.49 of the 1992 Act, as amended by s.1, above.
Qualified independent person. See the Trade Union Ballots and Elections (Independent Scrutineer Qualifications) Order 1993 (S.I. 1993 No. 1909), which provides that those previously qualified to act as independent scrutineers in union elections or political fund ballots will in future be qualified to act as scrutineers in a merger ballot. See the note to s.49(2) of the 1992 Act.

New s.100B of the 1992 Act
The same form of wording may be found in ss.50(1) and 76 of the 1992 Act (entitlement to vote in union elections and political fund ballots respectively), but note that (unlike union elections) in this context a union cannot restrict entitlement to vote by a rule excluding certain classes of member, for example, apprentices, unemployed members or those in arrears with their subscriptions, even if those members are excluded by the rules from voting in other union ballots. Previously s.100(1)(a) of the 1992 Act provided that "every member of the union must be entitled to vote on the resolution", and the Certification Officer held that "every member" should not be construed literally as including every person identified by the rules as a member, and that in certain exceptional circumstances a member might have such a tenuous connection with the union that the denial of a right to vote on a merger ballot might be justifiable (see, for example, *National Association of Colliery Overmen, Deputies and Shotfirers (Staffordshire Area), Re* (CO/1964/9, 1990), where the denial of a vote to retired members was upheld on the basis that their interest in the union was *de minimis*, and that Parliament could not have intended to insist that they should have a vote on such an important matter as a merger). However, in the context of union elections the Certification Officer has held that the right to complain of an improperly constituted executive or an incomplete register of members extends to every member (see *Society of Graphical and Allied Trades 1982, Re* (D/3/90), where entitlement to vote was accorded to "honorary over-age members").

New s.100C of the 1992 Act
These provisions are similar to those applicable in trade union executive elections and political fund ballots (ss.51 and 77 of the 1992 Act respectively). See the note to s.51 of the 1992 Act. Note, however, that in those contexts only interference or constraint by the union, its members, officials or employees is prohibited, whereas here the prohibition is a general one. One further difference may be found in subs. (5) of s.100C, which provides that the voting paper may not be accompanied by any document other than the notice required under s.99 of the 1992 Act (as amended by s.5, below), an addressed envelope for returning the voting paper and instructions for the return of the voting paper. Under the previous provisions the Certification Officer had held that urging members to vote in favour of a merger did not constitute an interference in the ballot (see *Millar and the National Union of Agricultural and Allied Workers*, Certification Officer's Report for 1982; also *Ammonds and the Society of Lithographic Artists Designers Engravers and Process-Workers*, Certification Officer's Report for 1982); however, the new restrictions on the content of the notice introduced by s.5 mean that a union will no longer be

able to send out material with the voting paper which expresses any opinion about the proposed merger or recommends members to vote in a particular way. See the note to s.5, below.

New s.100D of the 1992 Act
See the note to s.2, above.

New s.100E of the 1992 Act
These provisions are the same as those which apply in trade union executive elections and political fund ballots (ss.52 and 78 of the 1992 Act respectively). See the note to s.52 of the 1992 Act, as amended by s.1, above. An application for the registration of an instrument of transfer or amalgamation may not be sent to the Certification Officer until subs. (6) (which requires the union to notify its members of the contents of the scrutineer's report within three months of receiving it) has been complied with: s.101(3) of the 1992 Act, as inserted by Sched. 8, para. 55.

Ballots for union amalgamations and transfers of engagements: notice not to include influential material

5. In section 99 of the 1992 Act (notice relating to proposed amalgamation or transfer), after subsection (3), there shall be inserted—
    "(3A) The notice shall not contain any statement making a recommendation or expressing an opinion about the proposed amalgamation or transfer.".

GENERAL NOTE
Section 99 of the 1992 Act provides that the notice which is required to be sent to union members in advance of a merger ballot setting out details of the instrument of amalgamation or transfer must be approved by the Certification Officer. This section adds the further requirement that the notice shall not contain any statement "making a recommendation or expressing an opinion about the proposed amalgamation or transfer". Taken together with new s.100C(5) of the 1992 Act (inserted by s.4, above), which provides that no document may be enclosed with the voting paper other than the notice, an addressed envelope and a document containing instructions for the return of the ballot paper, this means that a union may not send out anything with the voting paper which might influence members to vote in a particular way in the merger ballot. There is, however, nothing to prevent a union from communicating its views on a proposed merger to its members by other means, *e.g.* by a separate letter, or through the union's journal. For the commencement provisions, see the note to s.4, above.

Confidentiality of trade union's register of members' names and addresses

6. After section 24 of the 1992 Act there shall be inserted—

"Securing confidentiality of register during ballots
24A.—(1) This section applies in relation to a ballot of the members of a trade union on—
    (a) an election under Chapter IV for a position to which that Chapter applies,
    (b) a political resolution under Chapter VI, and
    (c) a resolution to approve an instrument of amalgamation or transfer under Chapter VII.
    (2) Where this section applies in relation to a ballot the trade union shall impose the duty of confidentiality in relation to the register of members' names and addresses on the scrutineer appointed by the union for the purposes of the ballot and on any person appointed by the union as the independent person for the purposes of the ballot.
    (3) The duty of confidentiality in relation to the register of members' names and addresses is, when imposed on a scrutineer or on an independent person, a duty—
    (a) not to disclose any name or address in the register except in permitted circumstances; and
    (b) to take all reasonable steps to secure that there is no disclosure of any such name or address by any other person except in permitted circumstances;

and any reference in this Act to "the duty of confidentiality" is a reference to the duty prescribed in this subsection.

(4) The circumstances in which disclosure of a member's name and address is permitted are—

(a) where the member consents;

(b) where it is requested by the Certification Officer for the purposes of the discharge of any of his functions or it is required for the purposes of the discharge of any of the functions of an inspector appointed by him;

(c) where it is required for the purposes of the discharge of any of the functions of the scrutineer or independent person, as the case may be, under the terms of his appointment;

(d) where it is required for the purposes of the investigation of crime or of criminal proceedings.

(5) Any provision of this Part which incorporates the duty of confidentiality as respects the register into the appointment of a scrutineer or an independent person has the effect of imposing that duty on the scrutineer or independent person as a duty owed by him to the trade union.

(6) The remedy for failure to comply with the requirements of this section is by way of application under section 25 (to the Certification Officer) or section 26 (to the court).

The making of an application to the Certification Officer does not prevent the applicant, or any other person, from making an application to the court in respect of the same matter.".

GENERAL NOTE

This section requires a trade union to impose a duty of confidentiality on the scrutineer and the independent person in relation to the register of members' names and addresses. The duty is a duty not to disclose, and to take all reasonable steps to ensure that nobody else discloses, any name or address in the register, except in "permitted circumstances" as defined in the new s.24A (4) of the 1992 Act. The permitted circumstances are where the member consents, where disclosure is requested by the Certification Officer or required by an inspector appointed by him (see the note to s.10, below), where it is required to enable the scrutineer or independent person to discharge his functions under the terms of his appointment, or where it is required for the purposes of a criminal investigation or criminal proceedings. A union member who claims that his union has failed to impose the duty of confidentiality may complain to the Certification Officer or to the court under ss.25 and 26 of the 1992 Act respectively (Sched. 8, paras. 40 and 41). Such a complaint must be brought within one year of the last day on which votes may be cast in the ballot. However, while the new s.24A(5) of the 1992 Act provides that the scrutineer's duty of confidentiality is owed to the trade union, there would appear to be no mechanism in the Act whereby an aggrieved union member may complain that the scrutineer or independent person has infringed that duty.

Ballots: repeal of provisions for financial assistance and use of employers' premises

7.—(1) Sections 115 and 116 of the 1992 Act (financial assistance towards expenditure on certain ballots and obligations of employers to make premises available) shall cease to have effect.

(2) No application under regulations under section 115 (whether made before or after its repeal) shall be entertained by the Certification Officer in relation to expenditure in respect of a ballot if the date of the ballot falls after 31 March 1996 or in respect of arrangements to hold a ballot which is not proceeded with if the date of the ballot would have fallen after that date; but, for the purposes of applications made after (as well as before) the repeal in relation to expenditure not excluded by this subsection, the regulations shall continue in force notwithstanding the repeal.

(3) In subsection (2) above, the "date of the ballot" means, in the case of a ballot in which votes may be cast on more than one day, the last of those days.

(4) Subsection (1) above shall come into force on 1 April 1996.

GENERAL NOTE

This section repeals ss.115 and 116 of the 1992 Act, with effect from April 1, 1996. Section 115 empowers the Secretary of State to establish a scheme whereby a trade union may claim reimbursement from public funds of the costs of holding a secret postal ballot for certain purposes. The announcement of the phasing out of the current trade union ballot funding scheme was first made in December 1992, and the Regulations containing the scheme (the Funds for Trade Union Ballots Regulations 1984 (S.I. 1984 No. 1654), as amended) were revoked with effect from April 1, 1996 by the Funds for Trade Union Ballots Regulations (Revocation) Regulations 1993 (S.I. 1993 No. 233). The 1993 Regulations provide that no reimbursement will be made under the scheme for ballots falling on or after April 1, 1996, and that payments for ballots before that date will be progressively reduced, to 75 per cent. where the date of the ballot falls after March 31, 1993 but before April 1, 1994; 50 per cent. where the date of the ballot falls after March 31, 1994 but before April 1, 1995; and 25 per cent. where the date of the ballot falls after March 31, 1995 but before April 1, 1996. Subsection (2) makes it clear that no payment may be made under the scheme in respect of a ballot'where the date of the ballot (defined in subs. (3) as the last day on which votes may be cast) falls after March 31, 1996, even if expenditure in connection with the ballot was incurred *before* that date. By the same token, expenditure incurred *after* that date will be recoverable provided the last day of voting was no later than that date. For an account of the history and details of the current scheme, see the note to s.115 of the 1992 Act.

It is not necessary to look very hard to find the reason for the abolition of the scheme. At a time of intense pressure on the Government to reduce the public sector borrowing requirement, public funding for trade union ballots was a predictable target for savings, especially in view of the dramatic increase in the amount paid over in recent years. During 1992, 80 unions made applications for refunds in respect of 644 ballots, and the Certification Officer made payments under the scheme in excess of £4.25m., as compared with £2.6m. in 1990, £1.1m. in 1987, and only £72,496 in 1984. Not surprisingly, the abolition of the scheme has caused considerable dismay within the trade union movement, which will in future have to look to union members to bear the cost of ballots. It is of course true that trade unions were obliged to meet balloting costs from their own resources before the state funding scheme was introduced in 1980 (indeed many continued to do so for several years thereafter, as a consequence of the TUC's boycott of the scheme) but it is also true that a significant proportion of the cost of holding a trade union ballot is attributable to the requirements imposed on trade unions by law, in particular compulsory postal ballots and independent scrutiny.

This section also repeals s.116 of the 1992 Act, which entitles a recognised trade union to request the use of the employer's premises to hold a workplace ballot in certain circumstances. The increased emphasis on fully postal balloting (a mandatory requirement in union executive elections and political fund ballots since 1988, and extended to strike ballots and merger ballots by this Act) has reduced the significance of the right to hold a workplace ballot on the employer's premises, since that right only arises where the ballot in question is one which is not required to be postal (s.116(3)(a)). However, there are still several types of union ballot falling within the scope of s.116 which are not (yet?) required by law to be fully postal (*e.g.* ballots on the *ending* of industrial action, election to an office not covered by s.46 of the 1992 Act, and ballots on rule changes and on offers of terms and conditions by the employer), so it can hardly be said that the extension of compulsory postal balloting has rendered the section otiose. The explanation given for the repeal of s.116 is that it will be "rendered meaningless" by the repeal of s.115 ([1993] *Employment Gazette* 347), since the right conferred by s.116 only arises in respect of ballots for purposes falling within the Regulations made under s.115, and those Regulations are now to be revoked. Technically it would have been possible to rescue s.116 by amending it to include the list of purposes currently contained in reg. 5 of the 1984 Regulations, but the right contained in it is clearly out of tune with the Government's current preference for postal balloting, hence its repeal. There is of course nothing to prevent an employer from continuing to allow a trade union to use the employer's premises for the purposes of a workplace ballot.

Subs. (2)

Regulations under s.115

See the Funds for Trade Union Ballots Regulations 1984 (S.I. 1984 No. 1654), as amended by S.I. 1988 No. 1123, S.I. 1988 No. 2116 and S.I. 1990 No. 2379. The 1984 Regulations were revoked by the Funds for Trade Union Ballots Regulations (Revocation) Regulations 1993 (S.I. 1993 No. 233), with effect from April 1, 1996.

Financial affairs of unions etc.

Annual return to contain additional information

8. In section 32(3) of the 1992 Act (contents of annual return)—
  (a) after paragraph (a) there shall be inserted—
        "(aa) details of the salary paid to and other benefits provided to or in respect of—
            (i) each member of the executive,
            (ii) the president, and
            (iii) the general secretary,
        by the trade union during the period to which the return relates,", and
  (b) after paragraph (c) there shall be inserted ", and
      (d) in the case of a trade union required to maintain a register by section 24, a statement of the number of names on the register as at the end of the period to which the return relates and the number of those names which were not accompanied by an address which is a member's address for the purposes of that section;".

GENERAL NOTE

This is the first of five sections amending the rules on trade union financial affairs contained in ss.28 to 45 of the 1992 Act. That Act requires a trade union (other than a federated union) to keep proper accounting records with respect to its transactions, assets and liabilities, and to establish and maintain a satisfactory system of control of its accounting records, its cash holdings and all its receipts and remittances; the accounting records must give a true and fair view of the state of the affairs of the union and explain its transactions (s.28 of the 1992 Act). The union must keep its accounting records available for inspection for six years (*ibid.*, s.29), and union members have a right to inspect those records, accompanied by an accountant if so desired (*ibid.*, s.30). In addition, a trade union must appoint auditors to audit its accounts (*ibid.*, s.33), and the audited accounts, together with the auditor's report, must be submitted to the Certification Officer as part of the union's annual return (*ibid.*, s.32). Auditors have a statutory right of access to all documents relating to the union's affairs, and may require information and explanations from union officers; they also have a right to attend and speak at union general meetings (*ibid.*, s.37). A trade union which "refuses or wilfully neglects" to perform any of the above duties commits a criminal offence punishable by a fine, as does any officer of the union responsible under the rules of the union for discharging the duty in question (*ibid.*, s.45).

The new measures on union financial affairs are of two kinds: this section, together with s.9 below, extends the range of information which must be made available to union members about their union's financial affairs, while ss.10 to 12 below introduce significant new powers of investigation into union finances, and increase the penalties for a contravention of the new requirements. The case for further legislation in this area was made in the Green Paper, *Industrial Relations in the 1990s* (Cm. 1602, 1991), which reported the abortive attempt of the Certification Officer to bring proceedings against the National Union of Mineworkers, its President and General Secretary, alleging failure to keep proper accounting records and other offences under the Trade Union and Labour Relations Act 1974, s.12 (now s.45 of the 1992 Act). Those proceedings arose following the publication of the findings of an independent inquiry into the financial affairs of the union by Gavin Lightman Q.C. (*The Lightman Report on the NUM*, 1990), which was commissioned by the National Executive of the NUM following allegations in the media of financial irregularities within the union during the 1984–85 miners' strike. The controversy centred around money alleged to have been received by the NUM during the strike from Libya and the U.S.S.R., and the alleged use of such money by national officials of the union to repay home loans to the union. The charges were dismissed in Sheffield Magistrates' Court in June 1991, the stipendiary magistrate having ruled that much of the prosecution evidence (which was based on the Lightman report) was inadmissible. The Green Paper concluded that the powers of the Certification Officer to investigate union financial irregularity and malpractice were inadequate, and that members should be kept more closely informed about the financial affairs of their union and advised what steps they might take if concerned about any irregularity in the conduct of those affairs.

This section extends the range of information which must be included in a trade union's annual return. Section 32(3) of the 1992 Act already specifies that the annual return must contain the union's revenue accounts, a balance sheet, the auditor's report, a copy of the union's rules, and such other accounts and documents as the Certification Officer may require. To that must now be added details of the salary and other benefits provided to the president, the general secretary and each member of the union's executive, and that information must also be supplied to individual union members under s.9, below. In addition, where a union is required to maintain a membership register, the annual return must include a statement of the number of names on the register, and the number of names which are not accompanied by an address (this latter requirement apparently inspired by allegations that UCATT's membership register included the names of "ghost" members). The new requirements come into force on January 1, 1994.

Member of the executive. This is given the same extended meaning that applies in the context of trade union executive elections (new s.32(7) of the 1992 Act, inserted by Sched. 8, para. 42) and therefore includes those who, under the rules or practice of the union, may attend and speak at some or all of the meetings of the executive, other than those whose function is simply to provide the committee with factual information or with technical or professional advice. See the note to s.46 of the 1992 Act. "Executive" is defined in s.119 of the 1992 Act as "the principal committee of the union exercising executive functions, by whatever name it is called". See the note to s.46 of the 1992 Act.

A trade union required to maintain a register. The duty to compile and maintain an accurate and up to date register of members applies to all trade unions with the exception of those within one year of formation, whether by amalgamation or otherwise (s.43(2) of the 1992 Act), and certain federated trade unions (s.118(6) of the 1992 Act). See the note to s.24 of the 1992 Act.

A member's address. Section 24(5) of the 1992 Act provides that a member's address means either his home address or another address (*e.g.* his work address) which he has requested the union in writing to treat as his postal address. There is no obligation on a union member to inform the union of his home address or to notify the union when he moves, nor is there any obligation on an employer to disclose the addresses of members to unions.

Statement to members following annual return

9. After section 32 of the 1992 Act there shall be inserted—

> **"Statement to members following annual return**
>
> 32A.—(1) A trade union shall take all reasonable steps to secure that, not later than the end of the period of eight weeks beginning with the day on which the annual return of the union is sent to the Certification Officer, all the members of the union are provided with the statement required by this section by any of the methods allowed by subsection (2).
>
> (2) Those methods are—
>
> (a) the sending of individual copies of the statement to members; or
>
> (b) any other means (whether by including the statement in a publication of the union or otherwise) which it is the practice of the union to use when information of general interest to all its members needs to be provided to them.
>
> (3) The statement required by this section shall specify—
>
> (a) the total income and expenditure of the trade union for the period to which the return relates,
>
> (b) how much of the income of the union for that period consisted of payments in respect of membership,
>
> (c) the total income and expenditure for that period of any political fund of the union, and
>
> (d) the salary paid to and other benefits provided to or in respect of—
>
> > (i) each member of the executive,
> >
> > (ii) the president, and
> >
> > (iii) the general secretary,
> >
> > by the trade union during that period.
>
> (4) The requirement imposed by this section is not satisfied if the statement specifies anything inconsistent with the contents of the return.
>
> (5) The statement—

(a) shall also set out in full the report made by the auditor or auditors of the union on the accounts contained in the return and state the name and address of that auditor or of each of those auditors, and

(b) may include any other matter which the union considers may give a member significant assistance in making an informed judgment about the financial activities of the union in the period to which the return relates.

(6) The statement—

(a) shall also include the following statement—

"A member who is concerned that some irregularity may be occurring, or have occurred, in the conduct of the financial affairs of the union may take steps with a view to investigating further, obtaining clarification and, if necessary, securing regularisation of that conduct.

The member may raise any such concern with such one or more of the following as it seems appropriate to raise it with: the officials of the union, the trustees of the property of the union, the auditor or auditors of the union, the Certification Officer (who is an independent officer appointed by the Secretary of State) and the police.

Where a member believes that the financial affairs of the union have been or are being conducted in breach of the law or in breach of rules of the union and contemplates bringing civil proceedings against the union or responsible officials or trustees, he may apply for material assistance from the Commissioner for the Rights of Trade Union Members and should, in any case, consider obtaining independent legal advice."; and

(b) may include such other details of the steps which a member may take for the purpose mentioned in the statement set out above as the trade union considers appropriate.

(7) A trade union shall send to the Certification Officer a copy of the statement which is provided to its members in pursuance of this section as soon as is reasonably practicable after it is so provided.

(8) Where the same form of statement is not provided to all the members of a trade union, the union shall send to the Certification Officer in accordance with subsection (7) a copy of each form of statement provided to any of them.

(9) If at any time during the period of two years beginning with the day referred to in subsection (1) any member of the trade union requests a copy of the statement required by this section, the union shall, as soon as practicable, furnish him with such a copy free of charge.".

GENERAL NOTE

This section, inserting a new s.32A into the 1992 Act, requires a trade union to take all reasonable steps to provide each member with a statement about the union's financial affairs within eight weeks of sending the annual return to the Certification Officer. The statement must include details (for the period covered by the return) of the matters listed in new s.32A(3), *viz.*: the total income and expenditure of the union; how much of that income consisted of membership payments; the total income and expenditure of any political fund; the salary and benefits of the president, general secretary and each member of the executive; the report of the auditors on the accounts contained in the annual return (along with the name and address of the auditors); and any other matter which the union considers may assist members in making an informed judgment about the financial activities of the union. The statement, which must not be inconsistent with the contents of the annual return (new s.32A(4)), must also include the lengthy statement set out in new s.32A(6)(a) specifying the steps which members may take if they are concerned about some irregularity in the conduct of the union's financial affairs and informing them of the availability of financial assistance from the Commissioner for the Rights of Trade

Union Members in bringing civil proceedings against their union, its officials or trustees. Under the original proposals the union would have been required to send an individual copy of the statement to each member, but the Government were persuaded that this was not necessary in order to achieve the desired objective, and new s.32A(2) now allows the union to provide the information to members by using its normal methods of disseminating information amongst the membership (*e.g.* via the union newsletter); a similar formula applies in the context of the publication of the scrutineer's report in executive elections, political fund ballots, etc., (see, *e.g.* s.52(4) of the 1992 Act). Individual members are entitled to request their own copy of the statement within two years of the date mentioned above, and the union must provide it as soon as reasonably practicable and free of charge (new s.32A(9)). A copy of the statement provided to members must also be sent to the Certification Officer (new s.32A(7)). Refusal or wilful neglect to perform the duty imposed by this section constitutes an offence under s.45 of the 1992 Act (as amended by s.11, below).

Investigation of financial affairs

10. After section 37 of the 1992 Act there shall be inserted—

"Investigation of financial affairs

Power of Certification Officer to require production of documents etc.

37A.—(1) The Certification Officer may at any time, if he thinks there is good reason to do so, give directions to a trade union, or a branch or section of a trade union, requiring it to produce such relevant documents as may be specified in the directions; and the documents shall be produced at such time and place as may be so specified.

(2) The Certification Officer may at any time, if he thinks there is good reason to do so, authorise a member of his staff or any other person, on producing (if so required) evidence of his authority, to require a trade union, or a branch or section of a trade union, to produce forthwith to the member of staff or other person such relevant documents as the member of staff or other person may specify.

(3) Where the Certification Officer, or a member of his staff or any other person, has power to require the production of documents by virtue of subsection (1) or (2), the Certification Officer, member of staff or other person has the like power to require production of those documents from any person who appears to the Certification Officer, member of staff or other person to be in possession of them.

(4) Where such a person claims a lien on documents produced by him, the production is without prejudice to the lien.

(5) The power under this section to require the production of documents includes power—

(a) if the documents are produced—

(i) to take copies of them or extracts from them, and
(ii) to require the person by whom they are produced, or any person who is or has been an official or agent of the trade union, to provide an explanation of any of them; and

(b) if the documents are not produced, to require the person who was required to produce them to state, to the best of his knowledge and belief, where they are.

(6) In subsections (1) and (2) "relevant documents", in relation to a trade union or a branch or section of a trade union, means accounting documents, and documents of any other description, which may be relevant in considering the financial affairs of the trade union.

(7) A person shall not be excused from providing an explanation or making a statement in compliance with a requirement imposed under

subsection (5) on the ground that to do so would tend to expose him to proceedings for an offence; but an explanation so provided or statement so made may only be used in evidence against the person by whom it is made or provided—

(a) on a prosecution for an offence under section 45(9) (false explanations and statements), or

(b) on a prosecution for some other offence where in giving evidence the person makes a statement inconsistent with it.

Investigations by inspectors

37B.—(1) The Certification Officer may appoint one or more members of his staff or other persons as an inspector or inspectors to investigate the financial affairs of a trade union and to report on them in such manner as he may direct.

(2) The Certification Officer may only make such an appointment if it appears to him that there are circumstances suggesting—

(a) that the financial affairs of the trade union are being or have been conducted for a fraudulent or unlawful purpose,

(b) that persons concerned with the management of those financial affairs have, in connection with that management, been guilty of fraud, misfeasance or other misconduct,

(c) that the trade union has failed to comply with any duty imposed on it by this Act in relation to its financial affairs, or

(d) that a rule of the union relating to its financial affairs has not been complied with.

(3) Where an inspector is, or inspectors are, appointed under this section it is the duty of all persons who are or have been officials or agents of the trade union—

(a) to produce to the inspector or inspectors all relevant documents which are in their possession,

(b) to attend before the inspector or inspectors when required to do so, and

(c) otherwise to give the inspector or inspectors all assistance in connection with the investigation which they are reasonably able to give.

(4) Where any person (whether or not within subsection (3)) appears to the inspector or inspectors to be in possession of information relating to a matter which he considers, or they consider, to be relevant to the investigation, the inspector or inspectors may require him—

(a) to produce to the inspector or inspectors any relevant documents relating to that matter,

(b) to attend before the inspector or inspectors, and

(c) otherwise to give the inspector or inspectors all assistance in connection with the investigation which he is reasonably able to give;

and it is the duty of the person to comply with the requirement.

(5) In subsections (3) and (4) "relevant documents", in relation to an investigation of the financial affairs of a trade union, means accounting documents, and documents of any other description, which may be relevant to the investigation.

(6) A person shall not be excused from providing an explanation or making a statement in compliance with subsection (3) or a requirement imposed under subsection (4) on the ground that to do so would tend to expose him to proceedings for an offence; but an explanation so provided or statement so made may only be used in evidence against the person by whom it is provided or made—

(a) on a prosecution for an offence under section 45(9) (false explanations and statements), or

(b) on a prosecution for some other offence where in giving evidence the person makes a statement inconsistent with it.

Inspectors' reports etc.

37C.—(1) An inspector or inspectors appointed under section 37B—

(a) may, and if so directed by the Certification Officer shall, make interim reports, and

(b) on the conclusion of their investigation shall make a final report,

to the Certification Officer.

(2) Any report under subsection (1) shall be written or printed, as the Certification Officer directs.

(3) An inspector or inspectors appointed under section 37B may at any time, and if so directed by the Certification Officer shall, inform the Certification Officer of any matters coming to his or their knowledge as a result of the investigation.

(4) The Certification Officer may direct an inspector or inspectors appointed under section 37B to take no further steps in the investigation, or to take only such further steps as are specified in the direction, if—

(a) it appears to the Certification Officer that matters have come to light in the course of the investigation which suggest that a criminal offence has been committed and those matters have been referred to the appropriate prosecuting authority, or

(b) it appears to the Certification Officer appropriate to do so in any other circumstances.

(5) Where an investigation is the subject of a direction under subsection (4), the inspector or inspectors shall make a final report to the Certification Officer only where the Certification Officer directs him or them to do so at the time of the direction under that subsection or subsequently.

(6) The Certification Officer shall publish a final report made to him under this section.

(7) The Certification Officer shall furnish a copy of such a report free of charge—

(a) to the trade union which is the subject of the report,

(b) to any auditor of that trade union or of any branch or section of the union, if he requests a copy before the end of the period of three years beginning with the day on which the report is published, and

(c) to any member of the trade union if—

(i) he has complained to the Certification Officer that there are circumstances suggesting any of the states of affairs specified in section 37B(2)(a) to (d),

(ii) the Certification Officer considers that the report contains findings which are relevant to the complaint, and

(iii) the member requests a copy before the end of the period of three years beginning with the day on which the report is published.

(8) A copy of any report under this section, certified by the Certification Officer to be a true copy, is admissible in any legal proceedings as evidence of the opinion of the inspector or inspectors in relation to any matter contained in the report; and a document purporting to be a certificate of the Certification Officer under this subsection shall be

received in evidence and be deemed to be such a certificate unless the contrary is proved.

Expenses of investigations

37D.—(1) The expenses of an investigation under section 37B shall be defrayed in the first instance by the Certification Officer.

(2) For the purposes of this section there shall be treated as expenses of an investigation, in particular, such reasonable sums as the Certification Officer may determine in respect of general staff costs and overheads.

(3) A person who is convicted on a prosecution instituted as a result of the investigation may in the same proceedings be ordered to pay the expenses of the investigation to such extent as may be specified in the order.

Sections 37A and 37B: supplementary

37E.—(1) Where—

(a) a report of the auditor or auditors of a trade union, or a branch or section of a trade union, on the accounts audited by him or them and contained in the annual return of the union, or branch or section—

    (i) does not state without qualification that the accounts give a true and fair view of the matters to which they relate, or

    (ii) includes a statement in compliance with section 36(4), or

(b) a member of a trade union has complained to the Certification Officer that there are circumstances suggesting any of the states of affairs specified in section 37B(2)(a) to (d),

the Certification Officer shall consider whether it is appropriate for him to exercise any of the powers conferred on him by sections 37A and 37B.

(2) If in a case where a member of a trade union has complained as mentioned in subsection (1)(b) the Certification Officer decides not to exercise any of the powers conferred by those sections he shall, as soon as reasonably practicable after making a decision not to do so, notify the member of his decision and, if he thinks fit, of the reasons for it.

(3) Nothing in section 37A or 37B—

(a) requires or authorises anyone to require the disclosure by a person of information which he would in an action in the High Court or the Court of Session be entitled to refuse to disclose on grounds of legal professional privilege except, if he is a lawyer, the name and address of his client, or

(b) requires or authorises anyone to require the production by a person of a document which he would in such an action be entitled to refuse to produce on such grounds.

(4) Nothing in section 37A or 37B requires or authorises anyone to require the disclosure of information or the production of documents in respect of which the person to whom the requirement would relate owes an obligation of confidence by virtue of carrying on the business of banking unless—

(a) the person to whom the obligation is owed is the trade union, or any branch or section of the union, concerned or a trustee of any fund concerned, or

(b) the person to whom the obligation of confidence is owed consents to the disclosure or production.

(5) In sections 37A and 37B and this section—

(a) references to documents include information recorded in any form, and

(b) in relation to information recorded otherwise than in legible form, references to its production are to the production of a copy of the information in legible form.".

GENERAL NOTE

This section inserts new ss.37A to E into the 1992 Act, giving sweeping new powers to the Certification Officer to investigate union financial affairs. The Certification Officer already has the power under s.32 of the 1992 Act to require the production of union accounts and related documents other than those normally contained in the annual return. However, until now the Certification Officer has had no power of investigation as such, and the collapse of the prosecution case against the NUM and its national officials in 1991 revealed the dangers in seeking to rely on information uncovered by a third party in bringing proceedings for failure to comply with the statutory requirements on union financial affairs. As seen in the note to s.8, above, the Green Paper, *Industrial Relations in the 1990s* (Cm. 1602, 1991) concluded that the existing powers of the Certification Officer were inadequate, and proposed giving him greater powers to examine and investigate trade union financial affairs, including the power to require the production of documents and to appoint inspectors to carry out an investigation and prepare a written report, the findings of which would be admissible as evidence in civil and criminal proceedings. Even before the changes introduced by this section, the role of the Certification Officer involved a somewhat ambiguous mixture of judicial and administrative functions; the addition of a new investigatory role has the potential to transform the nature of the Certification Officer, and concern has been expressed that this new area of activity might undermine the confidence of the trade union movement in his impartiality.

New s.37A of the 1992 Act

This empowers the Certification Officer, or any person authorised by him, to direct a trade union to produce specified "relevant documents" (defined in subs. (6) as accounting and other documents which may be relevant in considering the "financial affairs" of the union), if he thinks there is good reason to do so. Production of relevant documents may also be required of any person who appears to be in possession of them. The power includes a power to take copies of the documents, to require an explanation of those documents from the person by whom they are produced or from any person who is or has been an official or agent of the union and, if they are not produced, to require information as to their whereabouts. The Certification Officer is required by the new s.37E(1) to consider exercising the power conferred by this section in two situations: first, where an auditor's report on the accounts contained in the annual return does not state without qualification that the accounts give a true and fair view of the matters to which they relate, or includes a statement (i) that the union has failed to comply with its duty under s.28 of the 1992 Act to keep proper accounting records and to establish and maintain a satisfactory system of control of its accounting records, etc., or (ii) that the accounts do not agree with the accounting records; and secondly, where a union member complains to the Certification Officer that there are circumstances suggesting financial irregularity in the conduct of the union's financial affairs (see new s.37B(2)). If in such a situation the Certification Officer decides not to act he must notify the member of his decision as soon as reasonably practicable, but need not give his reasons unless he thinks it fit to do so (new s.37E(2)).

A failure to comply with any of these requirements will be an offence under s.45(5) of the 1992 Act (inserted by s.11(1), below), but a person ordered to produce documents has a defence if he is able to prove that the documents were not in his possession and that it was not reasonably practicable for him to comply with the requirement (new s.45(6)). New s.37A(7) provides that a person who is required to explain documents or to state their whereabouts may not refuse to comply on the grounds of self-incrimination, but will be protected from prosecution on the basis of such evidence unless the explanation or statement is false in a material particular and he knows it to be false or makes it recklessly (new s.45(9)), or in the course of a prosecution for some other offence he makes a statement inconsistent with it.

Documents. This includes information recorded in any form (including on computer disk), and where the information required to be produced is not recorded in legible form, a copy in legible form must be provided (s.37E(5)).

Agent of the trade union. This is defined as "a banker or solicitor of, or any person employed as an auditor by, the union or any branch or section of the union" : s.119 of the 1992 Act, inserted by Sched. 8, para. 63. *Cf.* new s.37E(3), which provides that a person may not be required to disclose information (other than the name and address of his client) or to produce documents where he would be entitled to refuse to do so in the High Court or Court of Session on grounds of legal professional privilege; new s.37E(4) extends similar protection to bankers in respect of their obligation of confidence, unless the obligation is owed to the union or its trustees, or the person to whom the obligation is owed consents to the disclosure or production.

Financial affairs. These are defined as "affairs of the union relating to any fund which is applicable for the purposes of the union (including any fund of a branch or section of the union which is so applicable)": s.119 of the 1992 Act, inserted by Sched. 8, para. 63.

New s.37B of the 1992 Act

This empowers the Certification Officer to appoint an inspector or inspectors to investigate and report upon the financial affairs of a trade union. This power may, however, only be exercised where it appears to the Certification Officer that there are circumstances suggesting financial irregularity in the conduct of the union's financial affairs, as specified in subs. (2), *viz.*, where it appears that those affairs are being conducted for a fraudulent or unlawful purpose; that persons concerned with the management of those affairs have (in connection with that management) been guilty of fraud, misfeasance or other misconduct; that the union has infringed the relevant statutory requirements; or that the union has failed to comply with one of its own rules relating to its financial affairs. As with s.37A, the Certification Officer is required to consider the exercise of this power in the circumstances specified in s.37E(1). Subsection (3) imposes a duty on all officials and agents of the union to produce to the inspector all relevant documents in their possession, to attend before the inspector when requested to do so, and otherwise to give the inspector all reasonable assistance; s.37B(4) extends that duty to any other person who appears to the inspector to be in possession of relevant information. A person who contravenes a duty or requirement imposed under this section commits an offence under new s.45(5) of the 1992 Act, but once again has a defence where relevant documents were not in his possession and it was not reasonably practicable for him to comply with the requirement (new s.45(6)). The provisions on self-incrimination in subs. (6) mirror those in s.37A(7), discussed in the note to that section. Note that s.37D provides that where a person is convicted on a prosecution instituted as a result of an investigation by an inspector under this section, that person may be ordered by the court in those proceedings to pay the expenses of the investigation.

Financial affairs. See the note to s.37A, above.

Relevant documents. These are defined in subs. (5) as accounting and other documents which may be relevant to the investigation. For the definition of "documents", see the note to s.37A.

Agent of the trade union. See the note to s.37A. The protection of legal professional privilege and banker's obligation of confidence conferred by s.37E also applies here.

New s.37C of the 1992 Act

Where an inspector is appointed, a final report on the investigation must be made to the Certification Officer, who is required to publish the report (subs. (6)), and to provide a copy, free of charge, to the union, to any auditor of the union who requests a copy within three years of its publication, and to any member of the union who has complained to the Certification Officer of irregularity in the conduct of the union's financial affairs, if the Certification Officer considers that the report contains findings relevant to that complaint and the member requests a copy of the report within three years of its publication (subs. (7)). The Certification Officer may direct that an investigation be discontinued if he considers it appropriate to do so, and in particular if matters have come to light which suggest that a criminal offence has been committed and those matters have been referred to the appropriate prosecuting authority (subs. (4)). Crucially, subs. (8) provides that a certified copy of the report will be admissible in any legal proceedings as evidence of the opinion of the inspector in relation to any matter contained in the report.

Offences

11.—(1) In section 45 of the 1992 Act (offences), for subsection (5) there shall be substituted—

"(5) If a person contravenes any duty, or requirement imposed, under section 37A (power of Certification Officer to require production of documents etc.) or 37B (investigations by inspectors) he commits an offence.

(6) In any proceedings brought against a person in respect of a contravention of a requirement imposed under section 37A(3) or 37B(4) to produce documents it is a defence for him to prove—
   (a) that the documents were not in his possession, and
   (b) that it was not reasonably practicable for him to comply with the requirement.

(7) If an official or agent of a trade union—

(a) destroys, mutilates or falsifies, or is privy to the destruction, mutilation or falsification of, a document relating to the financial affairs of the trade union, or

(b) makes, or is privy to the making of, a false entry in any such document,

he commits an offence unless he proves that he had no intention to conceal the financial affairs of the trade union or to defeat the law.

(8) If such a person fraudulently—

(a) parts with, alters or deletes anything in any such document, or

(b) is privy to the fraudulent parting with, fraudulent alteration of or fraudulent deletion in, any such document,

he commits an offence.

(9) If a person in purported compliance with a duty, or requirement imposed, under section 37A or 37B to provide an explanation or make a statement—

(a) provides or makes an explanation or statement which he knows to be false in a material particular, or

(b) recklessly provides or makes an explanation or statement which is false in a material particular,

he commits an offence.".

(2) After that section there shall be inserted—

"Penalties and prosecution time limits

45A.—(1) A person guilty of an offence under section 45 is liable on summary conviction—

(a) in the case of an offence under subsection (1) or (5), to a fine not exceeding level 5 on the standard scale;

(b) in the case of an offence under subsection (4), (7), (8) or (9), to imprisonment for a term not exceeding six months or to a fine not exceeding level 5 on the standard scale or to both.

(2) Proceedings for an offence under section 45(1) relating to the duty imposed by section 32 (duty to send annual return to Certification Officer) may be commenced at any time before the end of the period of three years beginning with the date when the offence was committed.

(3) Proceedings for any other offence under section 45(1) may be commenced—

(a) at any time before the end of the period of six months beginning with the date when the offence was committed, or

(b) at any time after the end of that period but before the end of the period of twelve months beginning with the date when evidence sufficient in the opinion of the Certification Officer or, in Scotland, the procurator fiscal, to justify the proceedings came to his knowledge;

but no proceedings may be commenced by virtue of paragraph (b) after the end of the period of three years beginning with the date when the offence was committed.

(4) For the purposes of subsection (3)(b), a certificate signed by or on behalf of the Certification Officer or the procurator fiscal which states the date on which evidence sufficient in his opinion to justify the proceedings came to his knowledge shall be conclusive evidence of that fact.

(5) A certificate stating that matter and purporting to be so signed shall be deemed to be so signed unless the contrary is proved.

(6) For the purposes of this section—

(a) in England and Wales, proceedings are commenced when an information is laid, and

(b) in Scotland, subsection (3) of section 331 of the Criminal Procedure (Scotland) Act 1975 (date of commencement of proceedings) applies as it applies for the purposes of that section.".

GENERAL NOTE

This section amends s.45 of the 1992 Act, which provides for offences on infringement of the duties imposed by ss.27 to 42 of the 1992 Act. Subsection (1) creates a series of new offences for breach of the duties or requirements imposed in connection with the exercise of the powers of direction or investigation conferred on the Certification Officer under new ss.37A and 37B, while subs. (2) inserts a new s.45A, which increases the maximum penalties for the existing offences and introduces penalties for the new offences. A conviction under s.45(1) of the 1992 Act (refusal or wilful neglect to perform a statutory duty imposed by ss.27 to 42 of that Act) will in future carry a fine of up to £5,000, as will a conviction under new s.45(5) (contravention of a duty or requirement to produce documents or to co-operate with an inspector appointed by the Certification Officer); the other offences under subs. (4) (wilful alteration of a document with intent to falsify); subs. (7) (destruction, mutilation or falsification of a document, unless done without intent to conceal the financial affairs of the union or to defeat the law); subs. (8) (fraudulently parting with, altering or deleting a document); and subs. (9) (knowingly or recklessly providing a false explanation or statement), will carry a maximum penalty of imprisonment for up to six months or a fine of up to £5,000, or both. New s.45A(2) extends the time-limit for proceedings for an offence relating to the duty to send an annual return to the Certification Officer to three years from the date of the offence; proceedings for any other offence *under s.45(1)* may be commenced within six months of the offence, but if evidence sufficient to justify proceedings comes to the knowledge of the Certification Officer (or the procurator fiscal in Scotland) after that date, proceedings may be commenced within 12 months of it doing so, subject to an overriding limit of three years from the date of the offence (s.45A(3)). There is no express time-limit for the prosecution of offences under s.45(4) to (9), which presumably means that the normal six month limitation period for summary offences applies.

Disqualification of offenders

12. After section 45A of the 1992 Act (which is inserted by section 11 above) there shall be inserted—

"Duty to secure positions not held by certain offenders

45B.—(1) A trade union shall secure that a person does not at any time hold a position in the union to which this section applies if—
    (a) within the period of five years immediately preceding that time he has been convicted of an offence under subsection (1) or (5) of section 45, or
    (b) within the period of ten years immediately preceding that time he has been convicted of an offence under subsection (4), (7), (8) or (9) of that section.

(2) Subject to subsection (4), the positions to which this section applies are—
    (a) member of the executive,
    (b) any position by virtue of which a person is a member of the executive,
    (c) president, and
    (d) general secretary.

(3) For the purposes of subsection (2)(a) "member of the executive" includes any person who, under the rules or practice of the union, may attend and speak at some or all of the meetings of the executive, otherwise than for the purpose of providing the committee with factual information or with technical or professional advice with respect to matters taken into account by the executive in carrying out its functions.

(4) This section does not apply to the position of president or general secretary if the holder of that position—
    (a) is not, in respect of that position, either a voting member of the executive or an employee of the union,

(b) holds that position for a period which under the rules of the union cannot end more than thirteen months after he took it up, and

(c) has not held either position at any time in the period of twelve months ending with the day before he took up that position.

(5) In subsection (4)(a) "a voting member of the executive" means a person entitled in his own right to attend meetings of the executive and to vote on matters on which votes are taken by the executive (whether or not he is entitled to attend all such meetings or to vote on all such matters or in all circumstances).

Remedies and enforcement

45C.—(1) A member of a trade union who claims that the union has failed to comply with the requirement of section 45B may apply to the Certification Officer or to the court for a declaration to that effect.

(2) On an application being made to him, the Certification Officer—

(a) shall, where he considers it appropriate, give the applicant and the trade union an opportunity to be heard,

(b) shall ensure that, so far as is reasonably practicable, the application is determined within six months of being made,

(c) may make or refuse the declaration asked for, and

(d) shall, whether he makes or refuses the declaration, give reasons for his decision in writing.

(3) Where an application is made to the Certification Officer, the person who made that application, or any other person, is not prevented from making an application to the court in respect of the same matter.

(4) If, after an application is made to the Certification Officer, an application in respect of the same matter is made to the court, the court shall have due regard to any declaration which has been made by the Certification Officer.

(5) Where the court makes a declaration it shall also, unless it considers that it would be inappropriate, make an order imposing on the trade union a requirement to take within such period as may be specified in the order such steps to remedy the declared failure as may be so specified.

(6) Where an order has been made, any person who is a member of the trade union and was a member at the time the order was made is entitled to enforce the order as if he had made the application on which the order was made.".

GENERAL NOTE

This section provides for the disqualification of any person convicted of an offence under s.45 of the 1992 Act from serving as a member of the union's executive, or from holding office within the union as its president, general secretary or any other office by virtue of which a person is a member of the executive (new s.45B). The disqualification is for a period of five or 10 years, depending on the gravity of the offence. The only exception is for a person holding office as president or general secretary in an honorary capacity, *i.e.* a person who is not "a voting member of the executive" as defined in new s.45B(5) (the definition includes a person with limited voting rights, *e.g.* a casting vote) or an employee of the union, who cannot hold office for a period of more than 13 months, and who has not held either office in the 12 months before taking up the honorary post. Such persons are also excluded from the requirement to stand for election under the statutory election requirements (see s.46(4) of the 1992 Act). It is for the trade union to secure that a person excluded from holding office under these provisions does not hold such an office during the period of the exclusion, and any union member who claims that the union has failed to comply with the disqualification provisions may apply to the Certification Officer or to the court under new s.45C for a declaration to that effect, and in the case of the court, an order requiring the union to take steps to remedy the declared failure. Such an order may be enforced by any member of the trade union who was a member at the time the order was made. A member wishing to make an application to the court under s.45C may apply for assistance from the Commissioner for the Rights of Trade Union Members (s.109(1) of the 1992 Act, as amended by Sched. 8, para. 58).

The disqualification of offenders from holding union office may be contrasted with the position of company directors under the Company Directors Disqualification Act 1986. In that context the court generally has a discretion whether or not to disqualify company directors (except in the case of unfit directors of insolvent companies, where there is a discretion over the *length* of the disqualification), whereas here the disqualification is automatic. The discrepancy in the treatment of the two groups has been a predictable point of criticism of the new measures.

Rights in relation to union membership

Action short of dismissal: non-infringing actions

13. In section 148 of the 1992 Act (consideration of complaint of action short of dismissal), after subsection (2) there shall be inserted—

"(3) In determining what was the purpose for which action was taken by the employer against the complainant in a case where—

(a) there is evidence that the employer's purpose was to further a change in his relationship with all or any class of his employees, and

(b) there is also evidence that his purpose was one falling within section 146,

the tribunal shall regard the purpose mentioned in paragraph (a) (and not the purpose mentioned in paragraph (b)) as the purpose for which the employer took the action, unless it considers that the action was such as no reasonable employer would take having regard to the purpose mentioned in paragraph (a).

(4) Where the action which the tribunal determines to have been the action taken against the complainant was action taken in consequence of previous action by the employer paragraph (a) of subsection (3) is satisfied if the purpose mentioned in that paragraph was the purpose of the previous action.

(5) In subsection (3) "class", in relation to an employer and his employees, means those employed at a particular place of work, those employees of a particular grade, category or description or those of a particular grade, category or description employed at a particular place of work.".

GENERAL NOTE

The addition of this section to the Bill at a very late stage in its passage through Parliament caused a considerable amount of controversy. It amends s.148 of the 1992 Act, which states that on a complaint by an employee under s.146 of that Act that action short of dismissal has been taken against him by his employer on grounds related to union membership or activities, it shall be for the employer to show the purpose for which that action was taken. This section provides that where there is evidence that the employer's purpose in taking action against an employee was "to further a change in his relationship with all or any class of his employees", and there is also evidence that his purpose was one prohibited by s.146, the tribunal must regard the former purpose as the only purpose for which the action was taken (*i.e.* it must disregard the prohibited purpose), unless it considers that no reasonable employer would have taken that action for that purpose. This amendment is designed to reverse the effect of the rulings in *Associated Newspapers* v. *Wilson*; *Associated British Ports* v. *Palmer* [1993] IRLR 336, where the Court of Appeal held that offering financial incentives (or "sweeteners") to employees in an attempt to persuade them to sign personal contracts and to give up their right to have their terms and conditions negotiated collectively amounted to unlawful action short of dismissal against those who refused to sign such contracts, contrary to s.146. Despite Government claims that the purpose of this amendment to s.148 was merely "to clarify the effect of the law in this area", the effect of the change is likely, in practice, to weaken significantly the protection enjoyed by union members against action by employers which discourages union membership.

Section 146(1)(a) of the 1992 Act provides that an employee has the right not to have action short of dismissal taken against him as an individual by his employer for the purpose of preventing or deterring him from being or seeking to become a member of an independent trade union, or penalising him for doing so; the section also protects union members against victimisation for their union activities, and protects non-union members against discrimination on account of their non-membership of a trade union. In *Associated Newspapers* v. *Wilson*, above, the employer derecognised the NUJ and offered pay increases to those signing individual contracts. The applicant refused to sign, along with a number of fellow employees, and was denied the pay increase. The E.A.T., reversing the industrial tribunal's decision, held (see [1992] I.C.R. 681) that the employer's actions did not constitute action short of dismissal against those refusing to agree to the new arrangements because the purpose of the employer's actions was not to prevent or deter employees from continuing to be union members, or to penalise them for doing so, but rather to end collective bargaining. On appeal the Court of Appeal reversed the E.A.T.'s decision, holding that there had in fact been a breach of the section: the withholding of the pay increase from the applicant amounted to action taken against him as an individual, and the "purpose" of the employer's action was to persuade the employees to give up their right to representation, and ultimately to deter them from being union members; the employer's actions therefore constituted action short of dismissal which both deterred employees from being union members and penalised them for their union membership if they refused to agree to the new arrangements. Dillon L.J. stressed that the decision did not dispute an employer's right to derecognise a union and make consequential changes to terms and conditions of employment: "The employer only enters a potential danger area if he offers a douceur to employees who will support his policy, which is to be withheld from those who are not prepared to support it". (at p. 342). The Court of Appeal overturned the decision of the E.A.T. in *Associated British Ports* v. *Palmer* [1993] IRLR 63 on similar grounds, holding that the employer's purpose in offering extra pay to those signing new personal contracts was to persuade employees to abandon union representation by making the new contracts so attractive that the union would "wither on the vine", thereby deterring those employees from being union members.

These two decisions were considered by the Government to threaten the trend away from collective bargaining and towards individual contracting, hence the introduction of this section as a late amendment to the Bill at Third Reading stage in the Lords. Indeed, the amendment came so late that the Government were forced to take the exceptional step of recommitting the Bill to Committee in the Lords in order to introduce it. The adoption of this unusual procedure allowed little opportunity for mature consideration of the implications of the change, and only served to add to the controversy which it aroused.

Evidence of the employer's purpose. For the section to operate the employer need only provide some evidence that his purpose was to bring about a change in his relationship with his employees; it is not necessary for the employer to show that this was the sole or even the main purpose of his actions.

To further a change in his relationship with all or any class of his employees. This delphic phrase represents the crux of the section, but unfortunately it is unclear exactly what circumstances it is intended to include. The Government's stated objective was to reverse the effect of the decisions in *Wilson* and *Palmer* (see above) by preventing claims under s.146 of the 1992 Act from succeeding where the employer can show that his purpose in taking the action in question was to change his bargaining arrangements with all or part of his workforce, *i.e.* where the employer's purpose was "to bring about *a change in the way he conducts his relationship* with his employees" (*Hansard*, H.L. Vol. 546, col. 24, italics supplied). However, the section as drafted seems to go further than this, in that it applies where the employer's purpose is to further *a change in his relationship* with his employees, not merely a change in the way in which that relationship is conducted, and if broadly construed this could result in complaints under s.146 being ruled out in all cases other than those where discriminatory action is targeted against specific individuals: "so long as the employer is not singling out trade union members, and penalising them for being trade union members, then such action has nothing to do with the law on action short of dismissal" (*ibid.*, col. 39). It would seem to follow that action against a class or group of employees (as opposed to action against individual employees) will in future be outside the scope of s.146: "[the section] was intended to prevent individual discrimination and not class discrimination" (*ibid.*, col. 41). The objection to this approach is that it appears to be based on a misunderstanding of the distinction between individual and collective issues, in that it equates action taken against a group or collection of employees with collective action taken against a trade union (*e.g.* a withdrawal of bargaining rights) which has a consequential effect on union members; it may be correct to say that s.146 was never intended to be used to claim rights which are essentially collective, but it by no means follows that it should only apply where action is taken against individual employees rather than against a group or class of employees.

Class. This is defined for present purposes in new s.148(5) of the 1992 Act as "those employed at a particular place of work, those employees of a particular grade, category or description or those of a particular grade, category or description employed at a particular place of work". Although the section does not make it clear, the intention is to allow an employer to define a class of employees by reference to their membership of a particular trade union or trade unions: "an employer may wish to alter his bargaining arrangements and, to achieve that effect, offer incentives to encourage employees to accept a new arrangement under which a certain trade union does not negotiate terms on their behalf. If he wishes to do that, in some circumstances he may well have to identify the group of employees in making the offer by reference to membership of that trade union. There is no reason why we should seek to prevent that". (*ibid.*, col. 96). This will obviously cover situations where an employer wishes to offer an incentive to employees to accept personal contracts, as in *Wilson* and *Palmer*; but presumably it would also allow an employer to restrict pay rises to those employees who are not members of a union, or of a particular union, on the basis that the purpose of that action was to further a change in his relationship with that class of employees. If this reasoning is correct it would seem to follow that a case like *National Coal Board* v. *Ridgway and Fairbrother* [1987] I.C.R. 641, would be decided differently under the new provisions (see the note to s.146 of the 1992 Act). It would also mean that an employer could offer a financial incentive to employees to *join* a particular union, *e.g.* as part of a move towards single-union bargaining.

Right not to be excluded or expelled

14. For sections 174 to 177 of the 1992 Act (right not to be unreasonably excluded or expelled from union where employment subject to union membership agreement) and the heading immediately preceding them there shall be substituted—

"Right to membership of trade union

Right not to be excluded or expelled from union

174.—(1) An individual shall not be excluded or expelled from a trade union unless the exclusion or expulsion is permitted by this section.

(2) The exclusion or expulsion of an individual from a trade union is permitted by this section if (and only if)—

    (a) he does not satisfy, or no longer satisfies, an enforceable membership requirement contained in the rules of the union,

    (b) he does not qualify, or no longer qualifies, for membership of the union by reason of the union operating only in a particular part or particular parts of Great Britain,

    (c) in the case of a union whose purpose is the regulation of relations between its members and one particular employer or a number of particular employers who are associated, he is not, or is no longer, employed by that employer or one of those employers, or

    (d) the exclusion or expulsion is entirely attributable to his conduct.

(3) A requirement in relation to membership of a union is "enforceable" for the purposes of subsection (2)(a) if it restricts membership solely by reference to one or more of the following criteria—

    (a) employment in a specified trade, industry or profession,

    (b) occupational description (including grade, level or category of appointment), and

    (c) possession of specified trade, industrial or professional qualifications or work experience.

(4) For the purposes of subsection (2)(d) "conduct", in relation to an individual, does not include—

    (a) his being or ceasing to be, or having been or ceased to be—

        (i) a member of another trade union,

        (ii) employed by a particular employer or at a particular place, or

        (iii) a member of a political party, or

    (b) conduct to which section 65 (conduct for which an individual may not be disciplined by a trade union) applies or would apply if the references in that section to the trade union which is relevant for the purposes of that section were references to any trade union.

(5) An individual who claims that he has been excluded or expelled from a trade union in contravention of this section may present a complaint to an industrial tribunal.

Time limit for proceedings
175. An industrial tribunal shall not entertain a complaint under section 174 unless it is presented—
- (a) before the end of the period of six months beginning with the date of the exclusion or expulsion, or
- (b) where the tribunal is satisfied that it was not reasonably practicable for the complaint to be presented before the end of that period, within such further period as the tribunal considers reasonable.

Remedies
176.—(1) Where the industrial tribunal finds a complaint under section 174 is well-founded, it shall make a declaration to that effect.

(2) An individual whose complaint has been declared to be well-founded may make an application for an award of compensation to be paid to him by the union.

The application shall be made to an industrial tribunal if when it is made the applicant has been admitted or readmitted to the union, and otherwise to the Employment Appeal Tribunal.

(3) The application shall not be entertained if made—
- (a) before the end of the period of four weeks beginning with the date of the declaration, or
- (b) after the end of the period of six months beginning with that date.

(4) The amount of compensation awarded shall, subject to the following provisions, be such as the industrial tribunal or the Employment Appeal Tribunal considers just and equitable in all the circumstances.

(5) Where the industrial tribunal or Employment Appeal Tribunal finds that the exclusion or expulsion complained of was to any extent caused or contributed to by the action of the applicant, it shall reduce the amount of the compensation by such proportion as it considers just and equitable having regard to that finding.

(6) The amount of compensation calculated in accordance with subsections (4) and (5) shall not exceed the aggregate of—
- (a) an amount equal to thirty times the limit for the time being imposed by paragraph 8(1)(b) of Schedule 14 to the Employment Protection (Consolidation) Act 1978 (maximum amount of a week's pay for basic award in unfair dismissal cases), and
- (b) an amount equal to the limit for the time being imposed by section 75 of that Act (maximum compensatory award in such cases);

and, in the case of an award by the Employment Appeal Tribunal, shall not be less than £5,000.

(7) The Secretary of State may by order increase the sum specified in subsection (6).

(8) An order under subsection (7)—
- (a) shall be made by statutory instrument which shall be subject to annulment in pursuance of a resolution of either House of Parliament, and

(b) may contain such incidental, supplementary or transitional provisions as appear to the Secretary of State to be necessary or expedient.

Interpretation and other supplementary provisions

177.—(1) For the purposes of section 174—

(a) "trade union" does not include an organisation falling within paragraph (b) of section 1,

(b) "conduct" includes statements, acts and omissions, and

(c) "employment" includes any relationship whereby an individual personally does work or performs services for another person (related expressions being construed accordingly).

(2) For the purposes of sections 174 to 176—

(a) if an individual's application for membership of a trade union is neither granted nor rejected before the end of the period within which it might reasonably have been expected to be granted if it was to be granted, he shall be treated as having been excluded from the union on the last day of that period, and

(b) an individual who under the rules of a trade union ceases to be a member of the union on the happening of an event specified in the rules shall be treated as having been expelled from the union.

(3) The remedy of an individual for infringement of the rights conferred by section 174 is by way of a complaint to an industrial tribunal in accordance with that section, sections 175 and 176 and this section, and not otherwise.

(4) Where a complaint relating to an expulsion which is presented under section 174 is declared to be well-founded, no complaint in respect of the expulsion shall be presented or proceeded with under section 66 (complaint of infringement of right not to be unjustifiably disciplined).

(5) The rights conferred by section 174 are in addition to, and not in substitution for, any right which exists apart from that section; and, subject to subsection (4), nothing in that section, section 175 or 176 or this section affects any remedy for infringement of any such right.".

GENERAL NOTE

This section substitutes ss.174 to 177 of the 1992 Act, which gave a person in (or seeking to be in) employment governed by a closed-shop agreement the right not to be unreasonably expelled or excluded from a trade union, with a new, more general right not to be excluded or expelled from a union. Unlike the former provisions, the new right is not restricted to those in, or seeking to work in, closed-shop employment, and is not subject to a broad test of reasonableness. Instead, the section provides a limited number of reasons for which the exclusion or expulsion of a person from a union will be permitted. The permitted reasons include the fact that a person does not qualify for membership because he does not satisfy an "enforceable membership requirement" contained in the rules of the union, *i.e.* one which restricts membership to those who are employed in a specified trade, industry or profession, are of a particular occupational description, or possess specified trade, industrial or professional qualifications or work experience; a union may also exclude or expel those who do not qualify for membership because the union only accepts members from a particular geographical area (an obvious example would be an area union within the NUM), or because the union is a single employer union; and finally, it is permitted for a union to exclude or expel a person where the exclusion or expulsion is entirely attributable to his conduct, although certain types of conduct must be disregarded. These new provisions impose an extremely tight strait-jacket on union admissions and expulsions, particularly as there is no overall test of reasonableness under which the tribunal may exercise its discretion in deciding whether to uphold the union's actions—an exclusion or expulsion for reasons falling outside the permitted categories will be unlawful.

As before, a person who claims to have been excluded or expelled in contravention of the section may present a complaint to an industrial tribunal within six months of the expulsion or exclusion (unless not reasonably practicable, in which case a further reasonable period will be allowed), and if the tribunal finds the complaint well-founded it must make a declaration to that effect. No award of compensation may be made at this stage, but a person who has been admitted (or readmitted) to the union pursuant to the declaration may subsequently present a claim for an award of compensation to an industrial tribunal, although he must wait at least four weeks (but not more than six months) after the date of the declaration before doing so. If the applicant has not been admitted or readmitted to membership following the declaration, the application for compensation lies directly to the E.A.T. In both cases the amount of compensation will be what the tribunal or the E.A.T. considers just and equitable in all the circumstances, subject to a maximum amount which is tied to the maximum sum of the basic and compensatory awards for unfair dismissal (currently £17,150); in the case of the E.A.T., provision is again made for a minimum award of £5,000. Given the increased protection which now exists under ss.137 to 167 of the 1992 Act for those who are dismissed, victimised or refused employment by employers because of their non-membership of a trade union, the retention of these very high levels of compensation for those denied union membership is surely difficult to justify.

The repeal of the existing provisions came as little surprise in view of the steady decline of the closed-shop as a force in British industrial relations over the last decade or so. In 1984 there were estimated to be some 3.5 to 3.7m. employees covered by closed-shop arrangements (Millward and Stevens, *British Workplace Industrial Relations 1980–1984*, 1986), but by the time of the follow-up survey in 1990 the estimated figure had fallen to between 0.3 and 0.5m. (Millward, Stevens, Smart and Hawes, *Workplace Industrial Relations in Transition*, 1992, Ch. 3). With the inexorable tightening of the statutory controls on the enforcement of a closed-shop by employers in the decade between 1980 and 1990, and the removal of the statutory immunities from industrial action taken to enforce union membership, it could be argued that there was no longer any need for statutory regulation of union exclusions and expulsions, as the connection between union membership and access to employment which was previously used to justify the statutory controls no longer applied. However, the Government's view, as expressed in the Green Paper, *Industrial Relations in the 1990s* (Cm. 1602, 1991), was that individuals should not only have the right to decide whether or not to belong to a trade union but should also have the right to join the union of their choice, even where union membership is not a condition of employment, a view which reflects a strongly individualistic conception of freedom of association with the interests of the individual taking precedence over the interests of the group. Hence the repeal of the existing measures on unreasonable expulsion and exclusion and their replacement with a new, more general right not to be excluded or expelled from a trade union.

The acknowledged target of the new provisions are the procedures developed by the TUC governing disputes over membership between TUC-affiliated unions (the Bridlington Principles), reflecting the Government's view that the freedom of an individual to belong to the union of his or her choice should not be constrained by spheres of influence arrangements between unions. The Green Paper referred to a number of cases in recent years of union members who wished to change unions but were prevented from doing so by the Bridlington Principles. Under the former provisions it was never clearly established whether the expulsion or exclusion of a union member to comply with a decision of the TUC's Disputes Committee under the Bridlington Principles would be held to be unreasonable, although the Code of Practice on Closed Shop Agreements and Arrangements, revoked as from June 1, 1991 (by the Employment Codes of Practice (Revocation) Order 1991 (S.I. 1991 No. 1264)) suggested that in deciding whom to accept into membership a union might properly have regard to matters such as whether admission would involve any infringement of the Bridlington Principles. However, in *Cheall* v. *APEX* [1983] A.C. 180, the House of Lords held that it was not contrary to public policy for a union to expel a member under a rule allowing expulsion in order to comply with a decision of the TUC Disputes Committee, and in that case Lord Diplock reaffirmed the traditional common law stance towards membership of unincorporated associations when he stated: "freedom of association can only be mutual; there can be no right of an individual to associate with other individuals who are not willing to associate with him". As seen above, the Government's conception of freedom of association (as reflected in the new provisions) is a very different one.

Employer reaction to the new right not to be excluded or expelled from a trade union has been guarded. Commenting on the original Green Paper proposals, the IPM warned of the possible destabilising effect on industrial relations, and of the dangers of fragmentation of union representation, while the CBI and the Association of British Chambers of Commerce expressed concern that the new provisions could threaten single union agreements and single table bargaining; the EEF was, however, less pessimistic in its verdict. It is of course true that the Act places no obligation on an employer to recognise a trade union, so that there is no necessary reason why the introduction of a right to join a union of one's choice should have this effect; however, it is not difficult to envisage circumstances where a disaffected group of union members might leave the recognised union to join a non-recognised union, which might itself then press hard for recognition, with potentially harmful consequences for industrial relations.

New s.174 of the 1992 Act

Excluded. Note that a person will be deemed to have been excluded from a union where there has been an unreasonable delay in processing his application for membership (see new s.177(2)(a)).

Expelled. Under the previous provisions the E.A.T. held that there is no concept of "constructive expulsion", so that a union member who resigned his membership in protest at his treatment by the union was unable to claim (*McGhee* v. *Transport and General Workers' Union* [1985] I.C.R. 503 affirmed in (1985) 82 L.S. Gaz. 3701). As before, it is provided that termination of membership through the operation of an automatic expulsion or automatic forfeiture rule (for example, where membership lapses in the event of non-payment of subscriptions) is to be treated as an expulsion (see new s.177(2)(b)). A union will be entitled to point to non-payment of subscriptions as conduct justifying the exclusion of a member (see below), but may find it difficult to satisfy the tribunal that an exclusion is "entirely attributable" to that conduct where for example the member concerned has recently refused to take part in industrial action, particularly if the lapsing rule is not applied automatically in every case.

Enforceable membership requirement. This is defined in subs. (3) as a requirement which restricts membership *solely* by reference to one or more of the following: (a) employment in a specified trade, industry or profession; (b) occupational description (including grade, level or category of appointment); and (c) possession of specified trade, industrial or professional qualifications or work experience. It will still be possible for unions to exercise control over access to membership by means of carefully drafted membership rules, but given the existing high levels of competition for members, particularly among general unions, the loss of flexibility which this is likely to entail may make it too high a price to pay.

Entirely attributable to his conduct. A union may deny access to those who are not eligible for membership under its rules, but it may only exclude or expel a person falling *within* one of those categories where that expulsion or exclusion is entirely attributable to that person's conduct. "Conduct" here includes statements, acts and omissions (see the new s.177(1)(b)), but subs. (4) provides that certain types of conduct cannot be advanced as a reason for an exclusion or expulsion and must therefore be disregarded. So, "conduct" here does not include current or former membership of another trade union, current or former employment by a particular employer or at a particular place, or current or former membership of a political party; moreover, "conduct" is deemed not to include the type of conduct for which an individual has the right not to be disciplined by his trade union under s.65 of the 1992 Act. So for example, a union will be entitled to expel a member who is in arrears with his subscriptions, or refuse membership to an applicant who is under discipline with another union, but it may not refuse membership simply because that person previously belonged to another union, or had refused to take part in industrial action while a member of that union. Note also that the exclusion or expulsion must be *entirely* attributable to conduct, which may be difficult for a union to establish. The Government resisted attempts during the passage of the Bill to substitute a requirement that conduct merely be the *principal* reason for the exclusion or expulsion, on the grounds that this "would be to allow the Bridlington Principles in through the back door" (*Hansard*, H.L. Vol. 543, col. 1577).

New s.175 of the 1992 Act

Not reasonably practicable. For the meaning of this phrase, see Sweet and Maxwell's *Encyclopedia of Employment Law*, para. 1·1633 *et seq.*

New s.176 of the 1992 Act

These remedies are similar to those which previously applied in the case of an unreasonable expulsion or exclusion, save that the upper limit on compensation is now the same in both the E.A.T. and in an industrial tribunal, and in both cases compensation will be such as the tribunal or the E.A.T. considers "just and equitable in all the circumstances". Previously only the E.A.T. was able to award compensation on a just and equitable measure, the industrial tribunal being empowered to award compensation only to the extent necessary to compensate the applicant for the actual loss sustained by him in consequence of the unreasonable expulsion or exclusion. As before, compensation may be reduced on account of the contributory fault of the applicant (subs. (5)), although curiously the applicant is no longer under an express duty to mitigate his loss. On contributory fault under the previous provisions (which were identical on this point) see *Howard* v. *National Graphical Association* [1985] I.C.R. 101, where compensation was reduced because the unsuccessful applicant had taken up closed-shop employment while his application for membership was being considered. The remedy for an infringement of the rights conferred by the new s.174 is by way of a complaint to an industrial tribunal (new s.177(3)), and the existence of those rights is without prejudice to any existing common law rights (new s.177(5)). The potential jurisdictional clash between new s.174 and s.64 (the right not to be unjustifiably disciplined) is resolved by new s.177(4). Previously, the position was that in the event of an overlap the complaint lay under s.176, not under s.66, but if the exclusion or expulsion infringed the right not to be unjustifiably disciplined it was deemed to be unreasonable. The position is now greatly simplified, in that once a complaint relating to an expulsion is declared to be well-founded under new s.174, no complaint in respect of that expulsion may be brought under s.66; there is a parallel provision in s.66(4), as substituted by Sched. 8, para. 50.

Right not to suffer deduction of unauthorised or excessive subscriptions

15. For section 68 of the 1992 Act (right to require employer to stop deduction of union dues on termination of membership) and the heading immediately preceding it there shall be substituted—

"Right not to suffer deduction of unauthorised or excessive union subscriptions

Right not to suffer deduction of unauthorised or excessive subscriptions
68.—(1) Where arrangements ("subscription deduction arrangements") exist between the employer of a worker and a trade union relating to the making from workers' wages of deductions representing payments to the union in respect of the workers' membership of the union ("subscription deductions"), the employer shall ensure—
    (a) that no subscription deduction is made from wages payable to the worker on any day ("the relevant day") unless it is an authorised deduction, and
    (b) that the amount of any subscription deduction which is so made does not exceed the permitted amount.
(2) For the purposes of subsection (1)(a) a subscription deduction is an authorised deduction in relation to the relevant day if—
    (a) a document containing the worker's authorisation of the making from his wages of subscription deductions has been signed and dated by the worker, and
    (b) the authorisation is current on that day.
(3) For the purposes of subsection (2)(b) an authorisation is current on the relevant day if that day falls within the period of three years beginning with the day on which the worker signs and dates the document containing the authorisation and subsection (4) does not apply.
(4) This subsection applies if a document containing the worker's withdrawal of the authorisation has been received by the employer in time for it to be reasonably practicable for him to secure that no subscription deduction is made from wages payable to the worker on the relevant day.
(5) For the purposes of subsection (1)(b) the permitted amount in relation to the relevant day is—
    (a) the amount of the subscription deduction which falls to be made from wages payable to the worker on that day in accordance with the subscription deduction arrangements, or
    (b) if there is a relevant increase in the amount of subscription deductions and appropriate notice has not been given by the employer to the worker at least one month before that day, the amount referred to in paragraph (a) less the amount of the increase.

(6) So much of the increase referred to in subsection (5)(b) is relevant as is not attributable solely to an increase in the wages payable on the relevant day.

(7) In subsection (5)(b) "appropriate notice" means, subject to subsection (8) below, notice in writing stating—

(a) the amount of the increase and the increased amount of the subscription deductions, and

(b) that the worker may at any time withdraw his authorisation of the making of subscription deductions by giving notice in writing to the employer.

(8) Where the relevant increase is attributable to an increase in any percentage by reference to which the worker's subscription deductions are calculated, subsection (7) above shall have effect with the substitution, in paragraph (a), for the reference to the amount of the increase and the increased amount of the deductions of a reference to the percentage before and the percentage after the increase.

(9) A worker's authorisation of the making of subscription deductions from his wages shall not give rise to any obligation on the part of the employer to the worker to maintain or continue to maintain subscription deduction arrangements.

(10) Where arrangements, whether included in subscription deduction arrangements or not, exist between the parties to subscription deduction arrangements for the making from workers' wages of deductions representing payments to the union which are additional to subscription deductions, the amount of the deductions representing such additional payments shall be treated for the purposes of this section (where they would otherwise not be so treated) as part of the subscription deductions.

(11) In this section and section 68A "employer", "wages" and "worker" have the same meanings as in Part I of the Wages Act 1986.

Complaint of infringement of rights

68A.—(1) A worker may present a complaint to an industrial tribunal that his employer has made a deduction from his wages in contravention of section 68—

(a) within the period of three months beginning with the date of the payment of the wages from which the deduction, or (if the complaint relates to more than one deduction) the last of the deductions, was made, or

(b) where the tribunal is satisfied that it was not reasonably practicable for the complaint to be presented within that period, within such further period as the tribunal considers reasonable.

(2) Where a tribunal finds that a complaint under this section is well-founded, it shall make a declaration to that effect and shall order the employer to pay to the worker—

(a) in the case of a contravention of paragraph (a) of subsection (1) of section 68, the whole amount of the deduction, and

(b) in the case of a contravention of paragraph (b) of that subsection, the amount by which the deduction exceeded the amount permitted to be deducted by that paragraph,

less any such part of the amount as has already been paid to the worker by the employer.

(3) Where the making of a deduction from the wages of a worker both contravenes section 68(1) and involves one or more of the contraventions specified in subsection (4) of this section, the aggregate amount which may be ordered by an industrial tribunal or court (whether on the same occasion or on different occasions) to be paid in respect of the contraventions shall not exceed the amount, or (where

different amounts may be ordered to be paid in respect of different contraventions) the greatest amount, which may be ordered to be paid in respect of any one of them.

(4) The contraventions referred to in subsection (3) are—

(a) a contravention of the requirement not to make a deduction without having given the particulars required by section 8 (itemised pay statements) or 9(1) (standing statements of fixed deductions) of the Employment Protection (Consolidation) Act 1978,

(b) a contravention of section 1(1) of the Wages Act 1986 (requirement not to make unauthorised deductions), and

(c) a contravention of section 86(1) or 90(1) of this Act (requirements not to make deductions of political fund contributions in certain circumstances).".

GENERAL NOTE

This section has sent shock waves through the trade union movement. It substitutes s.68 of the 1992 Act, and introduces a new requirement for employers who operate check-off arrangements (*i.e.* where union subscriptions are deducted at source and passed on to the union) to ensure that no subscription deduction is made unless it has been authorised by the worker concerned, in writing, within the last three years and authorisation has not subsequently been withdrawn; it also provides that where there is an increase in the amount of the subscription, the employer may not deduct the increased amount unless the worker has been given at least one month's written notice of that increase *by the employer* (notification of the increase by the union will not suffice), and has been reminded in that notice that he may at any time withdraw his authorisation for the check-off. The new provisions specifically declare that a worker's authorisation of the making of subscription deductions does not give rise to any obligation on the part of the employer to maintain or continue a check-off arrangement, a statement heavy with significance in view of the growing tendency of employers to use the threat to end check-off arrangements as a way of bringing pressure to bear on a union in a trade dispute. As might be expected, these new procedures have generated considerable controversy, particularly the need for periodic renewal of the authorisation (a requirement which does not apply in the case of other deductions from pay) and they have been widely viewed by the trade union movement as a thinly veiled attempt to encourage workers to terminate their union membership.

Union members have had the right since the Employment Act 1988 to require employers to stop deducting union subscriptions from their wages on receiving notice that they have terminated (or are about to terminate) their union membership (see the note to the old s.68 of the 1992 Act). However, until now there has been no requirement for periodic renewal of the check-off authorisation; moreover, in the Green Paper, *Industrial Relations in the 1990s* (Cm. 1602, 1991), concern was expressed that some union members were having their union subscriptions deducted at source in pursuance of collective agreements without having given their consent to that arrangement. Check-off arrangements are of course subject to the restrictions on deductions from pay in the Wages Act 1986, s.1(1), which makes it unlawful for an employer to make a deduction from a worker's wages unless that deduction is authorised by statute or by any "relevant provision" of the worker's contract, or the worker has previously given his written agreement or consent to the making of that deduction; s.1(5) provides that the general restrictions on deductions in s.1 do not apply where deductions are made in pursuance of a check-off arrangement, but this exclusion only applies where that arrangement has been established in accordance with a term which has been included in the contract with the written agreement or consent of the worker, or otherwise with the worker's prior written agreement or consent. In the case of check-off arrangements falling outside s.1(5) it seems that the general rules in s.1(1) apply, so that where a check-off arrangement is incorporated into a worker's contract of employment from a collective agreement the deduction will be lawful under the 1986 Act provided it is authorised by a "relevant provision" of the worker's contract, *i.e.* a written term or terms of which the employer has given the worker a copy prior to making the deduction, or a term or terms (express or implied, oral or written) whose existence and effect has been notified to the worker in writing before the deduction is made (see the Wages Act 1986, s.1(3)). It can therefore be seen that under the existing law there is no blanket requirement for workers to give their written agreement or consent to a check-off arrangement which applies to them, provided they are made aware of those arrangements either by being supplied with a copy of the relevant terms or by being notified of their existence and effect. This section of the 1993 Act extends the statutory protection by requiring written authorisation in all cases, with a right to notice of any increase in the amount to be deducted, and a requirement of periodic renewal of the authorisation. The existing right to terminate the check-off continues to apply (see new s.68(4)), but is no longer restricted to situations where the employee certifies to his employer that his union membership has terminated or is about to terminate.

The remedy for a breach of the new right is by way of complaint to an industrial tribunal. If the tribunal upholds the complaint it will make a declaration to that effect and will order the employer to repay any amount unlawfully deducted. Where a deduction involves a contravention both of new s.68 and of one of the other statutory requirements listed in s.68A(4) (*e.g.* the requirement not to make unauthorised deductions under the Wages Act 1986), the aggregate amount of compensation which may be ordered in respect of that deduction may not exceed the greatest amount which may be ordered in respect of any one of them.

These new requirements came into force on August 30, 1993 in respect of workers entering into check-off arrangements on or after that date. Under the transitional arrangements set out in Sched. 9, para. 2, existing check-off arrangements which pre-date the coming into force of the section remain valid for a period of one year from that date (*i.e.* until August 29, 1994), unless a worker gives written notice to the employer withdrawing from the check-off arrangement before that date. This means that an employer wishing to continue with the check-off after August 29, 1994 must obtain written authorisation from the workers concerned before then.

New s.68 of the 1992 Act

Authorised deduction. For a subscription deduction to be authorised a worker must have signed and dated a document which authorises that deduction, and the authorisation must be current, *i.e.* the deduction must be made within three years of the date of the document (subs. (3)), unless the worker has withdrawn the authorisation in accordance with subs. (4).

Permitted amount. The amount deducted must not exceed the "permitted amount", *i.e.* the amount payable in accordance with the check-off arrangement (subs. (5)). However, where there is an increase in the subscription rate the employer may not lawfully deduct that increased amount unless the worker has been given the "appropriate notice" (see below) at least one month in advance, although this notice requirement does not apply where the increase in the amount to be deducted is attributable solely to an increase in the wages payable to that worker, *e.g.* where the amount of the subscription is expressed as a percentage of pay rather than as a flat rate (subs. (6)).

Appropriate notice. The notice of the increase in subscriptions must be in writing, must state the amount of the increase and the increased amount to be deducted (unless subscriptions are calculated by reference to a percentage, in which case the notice must state the percentage before and after the increase) and must also inform the worker that he may withdraw his authorisation for the check-off on giving written notice to that effect to the employer (subss. (7) and (8)).

Wages. The definition of "wages" contained in the Wages Act 1986, s.7 ("any sums payable to the worker by his employer in connection with his employment") applies here. See Sweet & Maxwell's *Encyclopedia of Employment Law*, para. 1·5306.

Employer/worker. Again, the definitions in the Wages Act 1986 are used here in preference to those in s.296 of the 1992 Act.

New s.68A of the 1992 Act

Not reasonably practicable. For the meaning of this phrase, see Sweet and Maxwell's *Encyclopedia of Employment Law*, para. 1·1633 *et seq.*

Extension of right not to be unjustifiably disciplined

16.—(1) In section 65(2) of the 1992 Act (conduct for which an individual may not be disciplined by a trade union), after paragraph (e) there shall be inserted the following paragraphs—

"(f) failing to agree, or withdrawing agreement, to the making from his wages (in accordance with arrangements between his employer and the union) of deductions representing payments to the union in respect of his membership,

(g) resigning or proposing to resign from the union or from another union, becoming or proposing to become a member of another union, refusing to become a member of another union, or being a member of another union,

(h) working with, or proposing to work with, individuals who are not members of the union or who are or are not members of another union,

    (i) working for, or proposing to work for, an employer who employs or who has employed individuals who are not members of the union or who are or are not members of another union, or

    (j) requiring the union to do an act which the union is, by any provision of this Act, required to do on the requisition of a member.".

(2) In section 65(7) of the 1992 Act (definitions), after the definition of "representative", there shall be inserted the following—

    " "require" (on the part of an individual) includes request or apply for, and "requisition" shall be construed accordingly.".

GENERAL NOTE

Section 64 of the 1992 Act provides that a trade union member may not be "unjustifiably disciplined" by his trade union, and s.65(2) of that Act specifies certain types of conduct for which the imposition of discipline will be deemed to be unjustifiable and therefore unlawful. This section adds to the list of conduct for which individuals have a right not to be disciplined, to take account of the new rights conferred by ss.14 and 15 of this Act. For an account of the existing provisions on unjustifiable discipline, see the notes to ss.64 to 67 of the 1992 Act. Note also Sched. 8, para. 50, substituting a new s.66(4), which provides for the potential overlap between the rights conferred by s.64 (unjustifiable discipline) and s.174 (expulsion or exclusion from a trade union) of the 1992 Act. Previously, where an expulsion infringed the right not to be unjustifiably disciplined, the complaint lay under s.174 rather than under the present section, and the expulsion was deemed to be unlawful; see the note to s.66(4) of the 1992 Act. In future, however, the complainant may choose whether to proceed under s.66 or under s.174, but new s.66(4) provides that where a complaint under s.66 is declared to be well-founded, no complaint in respect of the expulsion may be presented or proceeded with under s.174; similarly, where a complaint under s.174 is declared to be well-founded, no complaint in respect of the expulsion may be presented or proceeded with under s.66 (new s.177(4), inserted by s.14, above).

Industrial action

Requirement of postal ballot

17. In section 230 of the 1992 Act (conduct of ballot), for subsections (2) and (3) (method of voting) there shall be substituted—

    "(2) Except as regards persons falling within subsection (2A), so far as is reasonably practicable, every person who is entitled to vote in the ballot must—

    (a) have a voting paper sent to him by post at his home address or any other address which he has requested the trade union in writing to treat as his postal address; and

    (b) be given a convenient opportunity to vote by post.

    (2A) Where a merchant seaman to whom this subsection applies is entitled to vote in the ballot he must, so far as is reasonably practicable—

    (a) have a voting paper made available to him while he is on board the ship or is at a place where the ship is; and

    (b) be given an opportunity to vote while he is on board the ship or is at a place where the ship is.

    (2B) Subsection (2A) applies to a merchant seaman who the trade union reasonably believes will, throughout the period during which votes may be cast in the ballot, be employed in a ship either at sea or at a place outside Great Britain.

    (2C) In subsections (2A) and (2B) "merchant seaman" means a person whose employment, or the greater part of it, is carried out on board sea-going ships.".

GENERAL NOTE

This section introduces a requirement of "fully postal" voting (where ballot papers are sent out and returned by post) in an industrial action ballot. Failure by a trade union to hold a fully postal ballot before calling for industrial action will lead to a withdrawal of the statutory immunities against liability in tort, conferred by s.219 of the 1992 Act, and will also render the union liable in proceedings brought by a union member under s.62 of the 1992 Act (which gives union members the right to a ballot before industrial action), or by an individual under the new "citizen's right" introduced by s.22, below. The new requirements apply to any ballot in which votes may only be cast on or after August 30, 1993.

Fully postal ballots have been compulsory in union executive elections and political fund ballots since 1988 (see the note to s.51 of the 1992 Act), but until now workplace balloting and "semi-postal" ballots (where ballot papers are made available at the workplace or at some other more convenient location, and returned by post) have been a permitted option in industrial action ballots, provided the other statutory requirements (secret voting, absence of interference or constraint, etc.) were satisfied. The fact that workplace industrial action ballots have survived for as long as they have is a reflection of practical industrial relations: fully postal ballots take time to organise and are expensive, and until recently it had been widely accepted that it would be inappropriate to insist on their use in industrial action ballots, where speed of decision-making is usually of the essence and where relatively few workers may be involved. This is acknowledged by the Code of Practice on Trade Union Ballots on Industrial Action, which gives guidance as to "desirable practices" in relation to the conduct of industrial action ballots, for while the Code (which was revised in 1991) recommends that fully postal balloting should be the "preferred choice", it also states that a semi-postal or workplace ballot might be appropriate where it is impracticable to hold a fully postal ballot in the time available, where only a few members are entitled to vote and/or where voting would only take place at a few locations, or where speed of response is of the essence (para. 20). However, despite some evidence that workplace balloting achieves a higher rate of participation than postal balloting (see Undy and Martin, *Ballots and Trade Union Democracy* (1984); Leopold (1986) Ind Rels J 287), the present Government has increasingly taken the view that fully postal voting should be preferred as it provides the best security against interference, manipulation and malpractice. It was therefore no surprise when the Green Paper, *Industrial Relations in the 1990s* (Cm. 1602, 1991), proposed the imposition of fully postal voting in industrial action ballots. Interestingly, the Green Paper would only have required a postal ballot where more than 50 union members were involved, but the section contains no such provision, although the Government was persuaded to make an exclusion for small ballots in the case of the requirement of independent scrutiny (see s.20(4), inserting the new s.226C into the 1992 Act); here, the only exception relates to merchant seamen who the union reasonably believes will be at sea or outside Great Britain during the ballot, who are allowed to vote on board ship or at the place where the ship is located: new s.230(2A).

There is little doubt that the imposition of compulsory secret ballots before official industrial action has had a significant impact on the organisation of industrial action in the U.K. A major survey conducted in 1990 by Millward, Stevens, Smart and Hawes (*Workplace Industrial Relations in Transition*, 1992) revealed that union members had been consulted before the start of industrial action (whether official or unofficial) in at least 75 per cent. of cases, and in the case of strike action among non-manual workers the figure rose to almost 90 per cent. Significantly, in the case of *strike* action, postal ballots were already being used in nearly 60 per cent. of cases involving non-manual workers, whereas among manual workers postal ballots were only slightly more prevalent than a secret workplace ballot or a show of hands. However, the statutory balloting requirements appear to have had less of an impact on *non-strike* action, as the survey revealed that secret ballots of any kind were relatively rarely used in such cases, the single most common method of consulting with members still being a vote by show of hands (72 per cent. for manual workers, 39 per cent. for non-manual workers). Postal ballots were used before non-strike action in 12 per cent. of cases involving non-manual workers, but in only 2 per cent. of cases involving manual workers (*op. cit.* pp. 297 to 302).

So far as is reasonably practicable. Under the former provisions it was held that an inadvertent failure to supply ballot papers to some members (*e.g.* where ballot papers are accidentally misdirected as a result of changes of address) will not invalidate the ballot if the union has done what is reasonably practicable in the circumstances (*British Railways Board* v. *National Union of Railwaymen* [1989] I.C.R. 678, C.A.).

Post. This is defined in s.298 of the 1992 Act. The definition does not include internal mailing systems.

Notice of ballot and sample voting paper for employers

18.—(1) In subsection (1) of section 226 of the 1992 Act (industrial action not protected unless it has support of a ballot), for the words from "is not protected" to the end there shall be substituted the words "—

(a) is not protected unless the industrial action has the support of a ballot, and

(b) where section 226A falls to be complied with in relation to the person's employer, is not protected as respects the employer unless the trade union has complied with section 226A in relation to him.".

(2) After that section there shall be inserted—

"Notice of ballot and sample voting paper for employers

226A.—(1) The trade union must take such steps as are reasonably necessary to ensure that—

(a) not later than the seventh day before the opening day of the ballot, the notice specified in subsection (2), and

(b) not later than the third day before the opening day of the ballot, the sample voting paper specified in subsection (3),

is received by every person who it is reasonable for the union to believe (at the latest time when steps could be taken to comply with paragraph (a)) will be the employer of persons who will be entitled to vote in the ballot.

(2) The notice referred to in paragraph (a) of subsection (1) is a notice in writing—

(a) stating that the union intends to hold the ballot,

(b) specifying the date which the union reasonably believes will be the opening day of the ballot, and

(c) describing (so that he can readily ascertain them) the employees of the employer who it is reasonable for the union to believe (at the time when the steps to comply with that paragraph are taken) will be entitled to vote in the ballot.

(3) The sample voting paper referred to in paragraph (b) of subsection (1) is—

(a) a sample of the form of voting paper which is to be sent to the employees who it is reasonable for the trade union to believe (at the time when the steps to comply with paragraph (a) of that subsection are taken) will be entitled to vote in the ballot, or

(b) where they are not all to be sent the same form of voting paper, a sample of each form of voting paper which is to be sent to any of them.

(4) In this section references to the opening day of the ballot are references to the first day when a voting paper is sent to any person entitled to vote in the ballot.

(5) This section, in its application to a ballot in which merchant seamen to whom section 230(2A) applies are entitled to vote, shall have effect with the substitution in subsection (3), for references to the voting paper which is to be sent to the employees, of references to the voting paper which is to be sent or otherwise provided to them.".

GENERAL NOTE

This is the first of three sections in the Act imposing notice requirements on a trade union. It requires a union which intends to hold an industrial action ballot to take reasonable steps to ensure that it gives written notice of that intention to an employer of those entitled to vote in the ballot; the notice must be received at least seven days before the opening day of the ballot (see below). The notice must: (i) state that the union intends to hold a ballot; (ii) specify the date which the union believes will be the opening day of the ballot, and (iii) describe "so that he can readily ascertain them" the employees who the union reasonably believes will be entitled to vote in the ballot. The purpose of this new requirement is to give employers an opportunity to put the case against industrial action to their employees in advance of the ballot. However, concern has been expressed that it might facilitate employer interference in the ballot, particularly if the union is required to disclose the identity of individual participants. The union must also provide each employer, no later than three days before the opening day of the ballot, with a sample of the voting paper (or papers) to be used in the ballot. These new requirements only have effect in relation to ballots the opening day of which falls on or after September 6, 1993.

Subs. (1)

Is not protected as respects the employer. Failure to comply with the requirements of new s.226A will result in loss of the protection against proceedings in tort conferred by s.219 of the 1992 Act, but *only* at the suit of an employer who has not been given the appropriate notice; in other words, although a breach of the statutory balloting requirements usually results in the complete withdrawal of the statutory immunities, in this context the loss of immunity is only partial. Failure to comply will not be grounds for a challenge by a union member under s.62 of the 1992 Act. There is, however, a catch, in that such a failure *will* render the industrial action "unlawful" for the purposes of the "citizen's right" conferred by s.22 of this Act, so that any individual deprived of goods or services as a consequence of the industrial action will be able to seek an order restraining that action. See the note to s.22, below.

Subs. (2)

Opening day of the ballot. This is defined in subs. (4) as the first day on which voting papers are sent to members (or, in the case of merchant seamen, otherwise provided to them).

Describing (so that he can readily ascertain them). The union is required to describe to the employer "so that he can readily ascertain them" those of his employees who it is reasonable for the union to believe (at the time the notice is given) will be entitled to vote in the ballot. It is unclear whether a union could be forced to disclose the identity of individual participants in order to comply with this requirement; when pressed on the point during the debates on the Bill, the Minister stated that he could "envisage no circumstances" in which it would be necessary for the union to do so (Standing Committee F, December 15, 1992, col. 247).

Ballot result for employers

19. After section 231 of the 1992 Act there shall be inserted—

"Employers to be informed of ballot result

231A.—(1) As soon as reasonably practicable after the holding of the ballot, the trade union shall take such steps as are reasonably necessary to ensure that every relevant employer is informed of the matters mentioned in section 231.

(2) In subsection (1) "relevant employer" means a person who it is reasonable for the trade union to believe (at the time when the steps are taken) was at the time of the ballot the employer of any persons entitled to vote.".

GENERAL NOTE

This section requires a trade union, as soon as reasonably practicable after holding an industrial action ballot, to take such steps as are reasonably necessary to inform each employer of a person entitled to vote in that ballot of the result of the ballot. Failure to do so will result in loss of the statutory immunities against liability in tort. Note that here, unlike under s.18 above, the withdrawal of the immunity is complete, and *not* restricted to an employer who has not been informed of the result (s.226(2) of the 1992 Act, as amended by Sched. 8, para. 73); as before, such a failure will be "unlawful" for the purposes of the "citizen's right" conferred by s.22 of this Act, but will not be grounds for a challenge by a union member under s.62 of the 1992 Act. The effect of this section is to give the force of law to the recommendation in the Code of Practice on Trade Union Ballots on Industrial Action that unions should "respond positively" to requests from employers for details of the ballot result (para. 53). The union is of course already required to provide this information to those entitled to vote in the ballot, by virtue of s.231 of the 1992 Act. The new requirement applies to all ballots in which votes may only be cast on or after August 30, 1993.

The matters mentioned in s.231. The details which must be provided to employers are the same as those which the union is required to give to those entitled to vote in the ballot, *viz.* the number of votes cast in the ballot, the number of "yes" and "no" votes (for each question, if more than one question was asked), and the number of spoiled voting papers.

Scrutiny of ballots

20.—(1) After section 226A of the 1992 Act (which is inserted by section 18 above) there shall be inserted—

"**Appointment of scrutineer**

226B.—(1) The trade union shall, before the ballot in respect of the industrial action is held, appoint a qualified person ("the scrutineer") whose terms of appointment shall require him to carry out in relation to the ballot the functions of—

(a) taking such steps as appear to him to be appropriate for the purpose of enabling him to make a report to the trade union (see section 231B); and

(b) making the report as soon as reasonably practicable after the date of the ballot and, in any event, not later than the end of the period of four weeks beginning with that date.

(2) A person is a qualified person in relation to a ballot if—

(a) he satisfies such conditions as may be specified for the purposes of this section by order of the Secretary of State or is himself so specified; and

(b) the trade union has no grounds for believing either that he will carry out the functions conferred on him under subsection (1) otherwise than competently or that his independence in relation to the union, or in relation to the ballot, might reasonably be called into question.

An order under paragraph (a) shall be made by statutory instrument which shall be subject to annulment in pursuance of a resolution of either House of Parliament.

(3) The trade union shall ensure that the scrutineer duly carries out the functions conferred on him under subsection (1) and that there is no interference with the carrying out of those functions from the union or any of its members, officials or employees.

(4) The trade union shall comply with all reasonable requests made by the scrutineer for the purposes of, or in connection with, the carrying out of those functions.".

(2) In section 229 of that Act (voting paper), after subsection (1) there shall be inserted—

"(1A) Each voting paper must—

(a) state the name of the independent scrutineer,

(b) clearly specify the address to which, and the date by which, it is to be returned,

(c) be given one of a series of consecutive whole numbers every one of which is used in giving a different number in that series to each voting paper printed or otherwise produced for the purposes of the ballot, and

(d) be marked with its number.

This subsection, in its application to a ballot in which merchant seamen to whom section 230(2A) applies are entitled to vote, shall have effect with the substitution, for the reference to the address to which the voting paper is to be returned, of a reference to the ship to which the seamen belong.".

(3) After section 231A of that Act (which is inserted by section 19 above) there shall be inserted—

"**Scrutineer's report**

231B.—(1) The scrutineer's report on the ballot shall state whether the scrutineer is satisfied—

(a) that there are no reasonable grounds for believing that there was any contravention of a requirement imposed by or under any enactment in relation to the ballot,

(b) that the arrangements made with respect to the production, storage, distribution, return or other handling of the voting papers used in the ballot, and the arrangements for the counting of the votes, included all such security arrangements as were reasonably practicable for the purpose of minimising the risk that any unfairness or malpractice might occur, and

(c) that he has been able to carry out the functions conferred on him under section 226B(1) without any interference from the trade union or any of its members, officials or employees;

and if he is not satisfied as to any of those matters, the report shall give particulars of his reason for not being satisfied as to that matter.

(2) If at any time within six months from the date of the ballot—

(a) any person entitled to vote in the ballot, or

(b) the employer of any such person,

requests a copy of the scrutineer's report, the trade union must, as soon as practicable, provide him with one either free of charge or on payment of such reasonable fee as may be specified by the trade union.".

(4) After section 226B of the 1992 Act there shall be inserted—

"Exclusion for small ballots

226C. Nothing in section 226B, section 229(1A)(a) or section 231B shall impose a requirement on a trade union unless—

(a) the number of members entitled to vote in the ballot, or

(b) where separate workplace ballots are held in accordance with section 228(1), the aggregate of the number of members entitled to vote in each of them,

exceeds 50.".

GENERAL NOTE

This section extends the requirement of independent scrutiny, compulsory in union executive elections and political fund ballots since 1988 and now extended to union merger ballots by s.4 above, to industrial action ballots. As was proposed in the Green Paper, *Industrial Relations in the 1990s* (Cm. 1602, 1991), it gives the force of law to the recommendation in para. 22 of the Code of Practice on Trade Union Ballots on Industrial Action that adequate arrangements be made for independent scrutiny of industrial action ballots. There is however a special dispensation in the case of small ballots in which the total number of members entitled to vote does not exceed 50. As seen in the note to s.17, no such dispensation was made from the requirement to hold a fully postal ballot, despite a proposal to that effect in the Green Paper. Failure to comply with this new requirement will result in loss of the statutory immunities against liability in tort, and will also expose the union to an action brought by a union member under s.62 of the 1992 Act or by an individual deprived of goods or services under the new "citizen's right" conferred by s.22, below. The requirement applies to all ballots in which votes may only be cast on or after August 30, 1993.

The provisions on the appointment of the scrutineer are similar to those which already apply in union election and political fund ballots, and the people currently qualified to act as scrutineers in those contexts are also qualified to act here (see the note to subs. (1), below). However, in this context the requirements in relation to independent scrutiny are less onerous. As usual, the voting paper must state the name of the scrutineer (subs. (2), inserting a new s.229(1A) to the 1992 Act), but there is no requirement that the union notify its members of the name of the scrutineer *before* he begins to perform his duties, nor need the union wait for the scrutineer's report before publishing the result of the ballot; this last point is of course particularly important because the four-week time-limit on industrial action ballots imposed by s.234 of the 1992 Act begins to run from the last day of voting, not from the date on which the ballot result is announced. The scrutineer's report must be made available on request within six months of the ballot to any member entitled to vote in the ballot (and also to the employer of any such person), but the usual requirement to take steps to notify members of the contents of the report (*e.g.* by publication in the union's journal) does not apply here. Note also that the new rules requiring the counting of votes by an independent person, introduced by ss.2 to 4 above, do not apply to industrial action ballots.

Subs. (1)

In a departure from the usual provisions on independent scrutiny, the scrutineer's terms of appointment need not require him to be the person who supervises the production and distribution of the voting papers and to whom they are returned, nor is he expressly required to inspect the membership register or to retain custody of the voting papers for any fixed period after the ballot (compare ss.49(3), 75(3) and 100A(3) of the 1992 Act); the scrutineer is, however, under a duty to make a report on the conduct of the ballot as soon as is reasonably practicable after its completion (and in any event within four weeks of the ballot), and in that report he must state whether he is satisfied that there are no reasonable grounds for believing that the ballot contravened any of the statutory requirements, that the arrangements for producing, storing, distributing, returning and counting the voting papers included all reasonably practicable security arrangements to minimise the risk of unfairness and malpractice, and that he has been able to carry out his functions without interference from the union, its members, officials or employees (see subs. (3), inserting new s.231B to the 1992 Act).

Qualified person. See the Trade Union Ballots and Elections (Independent Scrutineer Qualifications) Order 1993 (S.I. 1993 No. 1909). The order specifies as qualified to act: Electoral Reform Ballot Services, The Industrial Society, Unity Security Balloting Services, solicitors holding a current practising certificate, and those qualified to act as auditors under s.34 of the 1992 Act, unless the individual in question is disqualified by virtue of membership, office or employment within the union in question in the preceding 12 months, or by some previous failure to perform the duties of a scrutineer independently. On the appointment and qualifications of an independent scrutineer generally, see the note to s.49 of the 1992 Act.

Notice of industrial action for employers

21. After section 234 of the 1992 Act there shall be inserted—

"Requirement on trade union to give notice of industrial action

Notice to employers of industrial action

234A.—(1) An act done by a trade union to induce a person to take part, or continue to take part, in industrial action is not protected as respects his employer unless the union has taken or takes such steps as are reasonably necessary to ensure that the employer receives within the appropriate period a relevant notice covering the act.

(2) Subsection (1) imposes a requirement in the case of an employer only if it is reasonable for the union to believe, at the latest time when steps could be taken to ensure that he receives such a notice, that he is the employer of persons who will be or have been induced to take part, or continue to take part, in the industrial action.

(3) For the purposes of this section a relevant notice is a notice in writing which—

    (a) describes (so that he can readily ascertain them) the employees of the employer who the union intends to induce or has induced to take part, or continue to take part, in the industrial action ("the affected employees"),

    (b) states whether industrial action is intended to be continuous or discontinuous and specifies—

        (i) where it is to be continuous, the intended date for any of the affected employees to begin to take part in the action,

        (ii) where it is to be discontinuous, the intended dates for any of the affected employees to take part in the action, and

    (c) states that it is given for the purposes of this section.

(4) For the purposes of subsection (1) the appropriate period is the period—

    (a) beginning with the day when the union satisfies the requirement of section 231A in relation to the ballot in respect of the industrial action, and

    (b) ending with the seventh day before the day, or before the first of the days, specified in the relevant notice.

(5) For the purposes of subsection (1) a relevant notice covers an act done by the union if the person induced is one of the affected employees and—

(a) where he is induced to take part or continue to take part in industrial action which the union intends to be continuous, if—
    (i) the notice states that the union intends the industrial action to be continuous, and
    (ii) there is no participation by him in the industrial action before the date specified in the notice in consequence of any inducement by the union not covered by a relevant notice; and

(b) where he is induced to take part or continue to take part in industrial action which the union intends to be discontinuous, if there is no participation by him in the industrial action on a day not so specified in consequence of any inducement by the union not covered by a relevant notice.

(6) For the purposes of this section—

(a) a union intends industrial action to be discontinuous if it intends it to take place only on some days on which there is an opportunity to take the action, and

(b) a union intends industrial action to be continuous if it intends it to be not so restricted.

(7) Where—

(a) continuous industrial action which has been authorised or endorsed by a union ceases to be so authorised or endorsed otherwise than to enable the union to comply with a court order or an undertaking given to a court, and

(b) the industrial action has at a later date again been authorised or endorsed by the union (whether as continuous or discontinuous action),

no relevant notice covering acts done to induce persons to take part in the earlier action shall operate to cover acts done to induce persons to take part in the action authorised or endorsed at the later date and this section shall apply in relation to an act to induce a person to take part, or continue to take part, in the industrial action after that date as if the references in subsection (3)(b)(i) to the industrial action were to the industrial action taking place after that date.

(8) The requirement imposed on a trade union by subsection (1) shall be treated as having been complied with if the steps were taken by other relevant persons or committees whose acts were authorised or endorsed by the union and references to the belief or intention of the union in subsection (2) or, as the case may be, subsections (3), (5) and (6) shall be construed as references to the belief or the intention of the person or committee taking the steps.

(9) The provisions of section 20(2) to (4) apply for the purpose of determining for the purposes of subsection (1) who are relevant persons or committees and whether the trade union is to be taken to have authorised or endorsed the steps the person or committee took and for the purposes of subsection (7) whether the trade union is to be taken to have authorised or endorsed the industrial action.".

General Note

    This section places a requirement on a trade union to give at least seven days' notice of official industrial action to the employer of those induced to take part in that action. The notice must be in writing, must describe "so that he can readily ascertain them" the employees who the union intends to call upon to take part in the industrial action, and must indicate whether industrial action is intended to be continuous or discontinuous; it must also state that it is given for the purposes of the section. If the action is to be continuous, the notice must state when it is to start; if intended to be discontinuous, *i.e.* if the union does not intend to take action on all the days on which it could do so, the notice must state the particular dates on which it is to take place. Failure to give the requisite strike notice will result in withdrawal of the statutory immunities, but only as respects the employer of a person induced to take part in the action and an individual under the new "citizen's right" introduced by s.22 below. The immunities will not be withdrawn as long as the person induced to take part in the action is one of those described in the notice, and that person participates in the industrial action only on the dates specified in the notice. The new provisions came into force on August 30, 1993, and apply irrespective of whether the ballot in question was subject to any of the other requirements introduced by this Act.

This is one of the more controversial provisions in the Act. The introduction of a compulsory period of notice before industrial action was proposed in the Green Paper, *Industrial Relations in the 1990s* (Cm. 1602, 1991), apparently prompted by the disruption caused by a series of one-day strikes on the London Underground in 1989. The Green Paper noted that strike notice requirements of one form or another exist in a number of other European countries (for details, see *The Regulation of Industrial Conflict in Europe*, EIRR Report No. 2, 1989), and opined that such a requirement would "help to safeguard businesses and jobs, and to protect the community from the effects of precipitate industrial action". The new requirements will obviously deprive unions of the element of surprise in organising industrial action, and the requirement to give advance notice of the precise days on which discontinuous action is to take place means that the threat of a series of random one-day strikes is unlikely to be as coercive in the future as has hitherto been the case. As a consequence of new s.234A(7), where continuous action is called off by the union (*e.g.* to allow negotiations to take place), fresh notice will have to be given before the union is able to call for the action to resume. It remains to be seen whether this will act as a disincentive to breaking off industrial action in an attempt to reach a negotiated settlement of a dispute.

Finally, given that the earliest date on which notice may be given to the employer is the day on which the employer is informed of the result of the ballot, and that an industrial action ballot only remains valid for four weeks from the date of the ballot itself (*i.e.* from the last day of *voting*), it is clear that the imposition of a seven day waiting period after the announcement of the ballot result (which is itself likely to be later in future as a result of the postal ballot requirements introduced by s.17 above) means that the window of opportunity within which the ballot may be implemented is significantly foreshortened by the notice requirement.

An act done by a trade union. The notice requirements only apply to official industrial action, *i.e.* industrial action which is authorised or endorsed by the union according to the statutory test of vicarious liability contained in s.20 of the 1992 Act (subs. (9)). Following the extension of that test by the Employment Act 1990 to include all union officials and committees, most industrial action is likely to be prima facie "official" (in the sense that, unless repudiated, it will be deemed to have been authorised or endorsed by the union) and therefore subject to the notice requirements. Note that subs. (8) provides that notice which is given to the employer by any of the persons or committees for whose actions the union is deemed responsible under s.20 will be treated as notice given by the union for the purposes of this section.

Is not protected as respects his employer. The statutory immunities are only removed as respects the employer of a person induced to take part in the industrial action. *Cf.* s.219(4) of the 1992 Act (as amended by Sched. 8, para. 72) which states that "not protected" means "excluded from the protection afforded by [s.219] or, where the expression is used with reference to a particular person, excluded from that protection as respects that person".

Such steps as are reasonably necessary. Failure to give notice of industrial action to the employer of a member induced to take part in that action will not lead to the withdrawal of the statutory immunities provided the union has taken "such steps as are reasonably necessary" to ensure that the employer receives notice of that action. Moreover, subs. (2) provides that the union need only give notice to an employer whom it is reasonable for the union to believe is the employer of members induced to take part in the action.

Appropriate period. The union must ensure that the notice to employers is received within the "appropriate period" as defined in subs. (4), *i.e.* after the employer has been informed of the result of the ballot (see the note to s.19 above), but at least seven days before the industrial action is due to begin.

A relevant notice covering the act. A "relevant notice" is a notice which satisfies the requirements of subs. (3), as described in the General Note. Such a notice will "cover the act in question provided the person induced to take part in the action is one of the "affected employees" (*i.e.* one of those described in the notice), and that person does not participate in industrial action other than on the dates specified in the notice (subs. (5)).

Describes (so that he can readily ascertain them). The same phrase appears in the provisions which require employers to be notified of the intention to hold a ballot (see the note to s.18). The concerns expressed in that context over potential victimisation of individual union members apply with equal (if not greater) force here.

Continuous or discontinuous. Action will be "discontinuous" where it takes place only on some days on which there is an opportunity to take the action (subs. (6)). Action not so restricted will be "continuous".

industrial action affecting supply of goods or services to an individual

22. After section 235 of the 1992 Act there shall be inserted—

"Industrial action affecting supply of goods or services to an individual

Industrial action affecting supply of goods or services to an individual
235A.—(1) Where an individual claims that—

(a) any trade union or other person has done, or is likely to do, an unlawful act to induce any person to take part, or to continue to take part, in industrial action, and

(b) an effect, or a likely effect, of the industrial action is or will be to—

(i) prevent or delay the supply of goods or services, or
(ii) reduce the quality of goods or services supplied,
to the individual making the claim,

he may apply to the High Court or the Court of Session for an order under this section.

(2) For the purposes of this section an act to induce any person to take part, or to continue to take part, in industrial action is unlawful—

(a) if it is actionable in tort by any one or more persons, or

(b) (where it is or would be the act of a trade union) if it could form the basis of an application by a member under section 62.

(3) In determining whether an individual may make an application under this section it is immaterial whether or not the individual is entitled to be supplied with the goods or services in question.

(4) Where on an application under this section the court is satisfied that the claim is well-founded, it shall make such order as it considers appropriate for requiring the person by whom the act of inducement has been, or is likely to be, done to take steps for ensuring—

(a) that no, or no further, act is done by him to induce any persons to take part or to continue to take part in the industrial action, and

(b) that no person engages in conduct after the making of the order by virtue of having been induced by him before the making of the order to take part or continue to take part in the industrial action.

(5) Without prejudice to any other power of the court, the court may on an application under this section grant such interlocutory relief (in Scotland, such interim order) as it considers appropriate.

(6) For the purposes of this section an act of inducement shall be taken to be done by a trade union if it is authorised or endorsed by the union; and the provisions of section 20(2) to (4) apply for the purposes of determining whether such an act is to be taken to be so authorised or endorsed.

Those provisions also apply in relation to proceedings for failure to comply with an order under this section as they apply in relation to the original proceedings.

Application for assistance for proceedings under section 235A
235B.—(1) An individual who is an actual or prospective party to proceedings to which this section applies may apply to the Commissioner for Protection Against Unlawful Industrial Action (in this section and section 235C referred to as "the Commissioner") for assistance in relation to the proceedings, and the Commissioner shall, as soon as reasonably practicable after receiving the application, consider it and decide whether and to what extent to grant it.

(2) This section applies to proceedings or prospective proceedings to the extent that they consist in, or arise out of, an application to the court under section 235A brought with respect to an act of a trade union; but the Secretary of State may by order provide that this section shall also apply to such proceedings brought with respect to an act of a person other than a trade union.

Any order shall be made by statutory instrument; and no such order shall be made unless a draft of it has been laid before and approved by a resolution of each House of Parliament.

(3) The matters to which the Commissioner may have regard in determining whether, and to what extent, to grant an application under this section include—

  (a) whether it is unreasonable, having regard to the complexity of the case, to expect the applicant to deal with it unaided, and

  (b) whether, in the Commissioner's opinion, the case involves a matter of substantial public interest or concern.

(4) If the Commissioner decides not to provide assistance, he shall, as soon as reasonably practicable after making the decision, notify the applicant of his decision and, if he thinks fit, of the reasons for it.

(5) If the Commissioner decides to provide assistance, he shall, as soon as reasonably practicable after making the decision—

  (a) notify the applicant, stating the extent of the assistance to be provided, and

  (b) give him a choice, subject to any restrictions specified in the notification, as to the financial arrangements to be made in connection with the provision of the assistance.

(6) The assistance provided may include the making of arrangements for, or for the Commissioner to bear the costs of—

  (a) the giving of advice or assistance by a solicitor or counsel, and

  (b) the representation of the applicant, or the provision to him of such assistance as is usually given by a solicitor or counsel—

    (i) in steps preliminary or incidental to the proceedings, or

    (ii) in arriving at or giving effect to a compromise to avoid or bring an end to the proceedings.

Provisions supplementary to section 235B

235C.—(1) Where assistance is provided under section 235B with respect to the conduct of proceedings—

  (a) it shall include an agreement by the Commissioner to indemnify the applicant (subject only to any exceptions specified in the notification) in respect of any liability to pay costs or expenses arising by virtue of any judgment or order of the court in the proceedings,

  (b) it may include an agreement by the Commissioner to indemnify the applicant in respect of any liability to pay costs or expenses arising by virtue of any compromise or settlement arrived at in respect of the matter in connection with which the assistance is provided in order to avoid or bring proceedings to an end, and

  (c) it may include an agreement by the Commissioner to indemnify the applicant in respect of any liability to pay damages pursuant to an undertaking given on the grant of interlocutory relief (in Scotland, an interim order) to the applicant.

(2) Where the Commissioner provides assistance in relation to any proceedings, he shall do so on such terms, or make such other

arrangements, as will secure that a person against whom the proceedings have been or are commenced is informed that assistance has been or is being provided by the Commissioner in relation to them.

(3) In England and Wales, the recovery of expenses incurred by the Commissioner in providing an applicant with assistance (as taxed or assessed in such manner as may be prescribed by rules of court) shall constitute a first charge for the benefit of the Commissioner—

(a) on any costs which, by virtue of any judgment or order of the court, are payable to the applicant by any other person in respect of the matter in connection with which the assistance is provided, and

(b) on any sum payable to the applicant under a compromise or settlement arrived at in connection with that matter to avoid or bring proceedings to an end.

(4) In Scotland, the recovery of such expenses (as taxed or assessed in such manner as may be prescribed by rules of court) shall be paid to the Commissioner, in priority to other debts—

(a) out of any expenses which, by virtue of any judgment or order of the court, are payable to the applicant by any other person in respect of the matter in connection with which the assistance is provided, and

(b) out of any sum payable to the applicant under a compromise or settlement arrived at in connection with that matter to avoid or bring proceedings to an end.

(5) Where a person is receiving assistance in relation to proceedings, there shall, if he so wishes, be added after his name in the title of the proceedings the words "(assisted by the Commissioner for Protection Against Unlawful Industrial Action)".

(6) The addition of those words shall not be construed as making the Commissioner a party to the proceedings or as liable to be treated as a party for any purpose; and the omission of those words shall be treated as an irregularity only and shall not nullify the proceedings, any step taken in the proceedings or any document, judgment or order therein.

(7) Where the Commissioner grants an application to a person who for the purposes of the application—

(a) has made a statement which he knew to be false in a material particular, or

(b) has recklessly made a statement which was false in a material particular,

he is entitled to recover from that person any sum paid by him to that person, or to any other person, by way of assistance; but nothing in this subsection affects the power of the Commissioner to enter into any agreement he thinks fit as to the terms on which assistance is provided.

(8) Nothing in section 235B or this section affects the law and practice regulating the description of persons who may appear in, conduct, defend and address the court in any proceedings.

(9) In section 235B and this section "applicant", in relation to assistance, means the individual on whose application the assistance is provided.".

GENERAL NOTE

This section establishes a new "citizen's right" for an individual to seek an order restraining unlawful industrial action where an effect, or likely effect, of the industrial action is to prevent or delay the supply of goods or services to that person, or to reduce the quality of the goods or services which are supplied. This right derives from proposals in the White Paper on the Citizen's Charter (Cm. 1599, 1991) and the Green Paper, *Industrial Relations in the 1990s* (Cm. 1602, 1991), in which the view was expressed that members of the public affected by unlawful industrial action should be able to seek the protection of the law where an employer is unwilling to act or does not act quickly enough. Those proposals were however restricted to industrial action affecting the public services within the scope of the Citizen's Charter; the right as enacted in this section goes considerably further, in that it applies to all industrial action, not just to action affecting the public services. Its potential impact cannot be overestimated, for it extends the range of potential plaintiffs to embrace anyone adversely affected by unlawful industrial action, irrespective of whether that person himself has a cause of action in tort or contract, or indeed any entitlement to be supplied with the goods or services in question (the aim apparently being to ensure that frustrated commuters stranded on station platforms are not denied the right to restrain unlawful industrial action by technical arguments over whether they have a cause of action in tort or a contractual entitlement to travel on any particular train). The only requirements are that the organisation of industrial action must be "unlawful", in the sense that it must be actionable in tort by at least one person (*e.g.* by the employer in dispute), or capable of forming the basis of an application by a member under s.62 of the 1992 Act (which gives union members the right to be balloted before industrial action); and the industrial action must affect the supply of goods or services to the complainant (although it seems that the complainant need not have suffered any quantifiable financial loss or damage). The result is that any technical failure to comply with the detailed statutory requirements on the organisation of industrial action (*e.g.* on balloting) will render the industrial action restrainable by anyone adversely affected by it. It should be noted however that the section does not provide any right to damages.

The citizen's right represents a quite breath-taking extension of liability, overturning at a stroke of the legislative pen the common law principles which limit the range of potential plaintiffs in such cases, in particular the (probable) requirement that the defendant must have intended to harm the plaintiff (in the sense that the unlawful act must have been directed at the plaintiff) in order for an action for inducing breach of contract or interference with contract to lie. Admittedly in *Falconer* v. *A.S.L.E.F. and N.U.R.* [1986] IRLR 331, the plaintiff, a frustrated customer of British Rail unable to travel by train because of industrial action by the rail unions, successfully sued the defendant unions in tort and was awarded damages of £153, the county court rejecting as "naïve and divorced from reality" the unions' argument that their intent was to harm British Rail, not the plaintiff. However, the decision in that case has been widely criticised, and appears to extend liability for the tort of inducement well beyond the existing authorities (see, *e.g. Thomson (D.C.) & Co.* v. *Deakin* [1952] Ch. 646 and *Barretts & Baird (Wholesale)* v. *Institution of Professional Civil Servants* [1987] 1 FTLR 121, where Henry J. considered that intent to injure the plaintiff must be the "predominant purpose" of the action; but *cf. Hill (Edwin) & Partners* v. *First National Finance Corp.* [1988] 3 All E.R. 801). Fears have also been expressed that the citizen's right may have a destabilising effect on industrial relations by hindering attempts to reach a negotiated settlement of a dispute, *e.g.* where the employer has deliberately chosen not to pursue legal remedies for fear of inflaming the situation. The new right has generally met with a cool response from employers, largely as a result of fears of this kind. However, the Government remained unmoved by such concerns, the Minister of State in Committee putting the case for the new right in blunt terms: "Why should citizens be inconvenienced because a gutless and spineless employer fails to seek a remedy for unlawful action which results in loss?": (Standing Committee F, December 15, 1992, col. 270).

Finally, the section provides for a new Commissioner for Protection Against Unlawful Industrial Action (CPAUIA) to assist individuals in bringing proceedings against a trade union under the new citizen's right. In determining whether and to what extent to grant assistance, the Commissioner may, *inter alia*, have regard to whether it is unreasonable in view of the complexity of the case to expect the applicant to deal with it unaided; and whether the case involves a matter of substantial public interest or concern. If granted, the assistance may include making arrangements for, or meeting the cost of, legal advice and representation, and indemnifying the applicant in respect of any costs and expenses arising out of the proceedings or from any settlement of the matter. The detailed provisions governing the powers of the new Commissioner are virtually identical to those which apply to the Commissioner for the Rights of Trade Union Members (CROTUM) under ss.109 to 114 of the 1992 Act, and the present CROTUM has been appointed by the Secretary of State as the new Commissioner with effect from August 30, 1993 (the date on which the new citizen's right came into force). Predictably, the establishment of yet another specialist Commissioner (at an anticipated cost of £300,000 per annum) at a time of cut backs in legal aid has been heavily criticised. The proposal for a new Commissioner did not appear in the 1991 Green Paper.

PART II

EMPLOYMENT RIGHTS

Maternity

Right to maternity leave and right to return to work

23.—(1) In the Employment Protection (Consolidation) Act 1978 (referred to in this Act as "the 1978 Act"), for Part III (maternity: right to return to work) there shall be substituted—
  (a) the sections 33 to 38A set out in subsection (2) below (which provide for a new right to maternity leave), and
  (b) the sections 39 to 44, together with the heading, set out in Schedule 2 to this Act (which continue in effect the right to return to work with amendments to take account of the new right).
(2) The provisions referred to in subsection (1)(a) above are—

"PART III

MATERNITY

General right to maternity leave

General right to maternity leave

33.—(1) An employee who is absent from work at any time during her maternity leave period shall, subject to sections 36 and 37, be entitled to the benefit of the terms and conditions of employment which would have been applicable to her if she had not been absent (and had not been pregnant or given birth to a child).

(2) Subsection (1) does not confer any entitlement to remuneration.

Commencement of maternity leave period

34.—(1) Subject to subsection (2), an employee's maternity leave period commences with—
  (a) the date which, in accordance with section 36, she notifies to her employer as the date on which she intends her period of absence from work in exercise of her right to maternity leave to commence, or
  (b) if earlier, the first day on which she is absent from work wholly or partly because of pregnancy or childbirth after the beginning of the sixth week before the expected week of childbirth.

(2) Where childbirth occurs before the day with which the employee's maternity leave period would otherwise commence, her maternity leave period shall commence with the day on which childbirth occurs.

(3) The Secretary of State may by order vary either of the provisions of subsections (1) and (2).

(4) No order shall be made under subsection (3) unless a draft of the order has been laid before Parliament and approved by a resolution of each House of Parliament.

Duration of maternity leave period

35.—(1) Subject to subsections (2) and (3), an employee's maternity leave period shall continue for the period of fourteen weeks from its commencement or until the birth of the child, if later.

(2) Subject to subsection (3), where any requirement imposed by or under any provision of any enactment or of any instrument made

under any enactment, other than a provision for the time being specified in an order made under section 45(3), prohibits her working for any period after the end of the period mentioned in subsection (1) by reason of her having recently given birth, her maternity leave period shall continue until the expiry of that later period.

(3) Where an employee is dismissed after the commencement of her maternity leave period but before the time when (apart from this subsection) that period would end, the period ends at the time of the dismissal.

(4) The Secretary of State may by order vary any of the provisions of this section.

(5) No order shall be made under subsection (4) unless a draft of the order has been laid before Parliament and approved by a resolution of each House of Parliament.

Notice of commencement of leave

36.—(1) An employee shall not have the right conferred by section 33 unless—

   (a) she notifies her employer of the date (within the restriction imposed by subsection (2)) ("the notified leave date") on which she intends her period of absence from work in exercise of her right to maternity leave to commence—
      (i) not less than twenty-one days before that date, or
      (ii) if that is not reasonably practicable, as soon as is reasonably practicable,
   (b) where she is first absent from work wholly or partly because of pregnancy or childbirth before the notified leave date or before she has notified such a date and after the beginning of the sixth week before the expected week of childbirth, she notifies her employer as soon as is reasonably practicable that she is absent for that reason, or
   (c) where childbirth occurs before the notified leave date or before she has notified such a date, she notifies her employer that she has given birth as soon as is reasonably practicable after the birth,

and any notice she is required to give under paragraphs (a) to (c) shall, if her employer so requests, be given in writing.

(2) No date may be notified under subsection (1)(a) which occurs before the beginning of the eleventh week before the expected week of childbirth.

(3) Where, in the case of an employee, either paragraph (b) or (c) of subsection (1) has fallen to be satisfied, and has been so satisfied, nothing in paragraph (a) of that subsection shall impose any requirement on the employee.

Requirement to inform employer of pregnancy etc.

37.—(1) An employee shall not have the right conferred by section 33 unless she informs her employer in writing at least twenty-one days before her maternity leave period commences or, if that is not reasonably practicable, as soon as is reasonably practicable—

   (a) that she is pregnant, and
   (b) of the expected week of childbirth or, if the childbirth has occurred, the date on which it occurred.

(2) An employee shall not have the right conferred by section 33 unless, if requested to do so by her employer, she produces for his inspection a certificate from a registered medical practitioner or a registered midwife stating the expected week of childbirth.

Requirement to inform employer of return during maternity leave period

37A.—(1) An employee who intends to return to work earlier than the end of her maternity leave period shall give to her employer not less than seven days notice of the date on which she intends to return.

(2) If an employee returns to work as mentioned in subsection (1) without notifying her employer of her intention to do so or without giving him the notice required by that subsection her employer shall be entitled to postpone her return to a date such as will secure, subject to subsection (3), that he has seven days notice of her return.

(3) An employer is not entitled under subsection (2) to postpone an employee's return to work to a date after the end of her maternity leave period.

(4) If an employee who has been notified under subsection (2) that she is not to return to work before the date specified by her employer does return to work before that date the employer shall be under no contractual obligation to pay her remuneration until the date specified by him as the date on which she may return.

Special provision where redundancy during maternity leave period

38.—(1) Where during an employee's maternity leave period it is not practicable by reason of redundancy for the employer to continue to employ her under her existing contract of employment, she shall be entitled, where there is a suitable available vacancy, to be offered (before the ending of her employment under that contract) alternative employment with her employer or his successor, or an associated employer, under a new contract of employment which complies with subsection (2) (and takes effect immediately on the ending of her employment under the previous contract).

(2) The new contract of employment must be such that—

(a) the work to be done under the contract is of a kind which is both suitable in relation to the employee and appropriate for her to do in the circumstances; and

(b) the provisions of the new contract as to the capacity and place in which she is to be employed and as to the other terms and conditions of her employment are not substantially less favourable to her than if she had continued to be employed under the previous contract.

Contractual right to maternity leave

38A.—(1) An employee who has the right to maternity leave under section 33 and a right to maternity leave under a contract of employment or otherwise may not exercise the two rights separately but may, in taking maternity leave, take advantage of whichever right is, in any particular respect, the more favourable.

(2) The provisions of sections 34 to 38 shall apply, subject to any modifications necessary to give effect to any more favourable contractual terms, to the exercise of the composite right described in subsection (1) as they apply to the exercise of the right under section 33.".

GENERAL NOTE

This is the first of three sections making radical changes to the law on maternity rights, implementing the requirements of EEC Directive 92/85 on the Protection of Pregnant Women at Work, adopted on October 19, 1992. It substitutes Pt. III of the Employment Protection (Consolidation) Act 1978 (the 1978 Act), and introduces a new right to 14 weeks' maternity leave for all pregnant employees, irrespective of length of service, hours of work or size of firm, during which all normal contractual rights will be maintained (except for remuneration, which is specifically excluded). This new statutory right to maternity leave is additional to the existing right of employees with at least two years' continuous employment (or five years, if they work between eight and 16 hours a week) to return to work up to 29 weeks after childbirth, and, like the right to return, it is subject to detailed notice requirements. The existing provisions on the right to return are preserved by Sched. 2, with modifications to take account of the new right to maternity leave. The Government has made clear its intention to bring the new provisions into force by October 19, 1994, the deadline set by the Directive.

In its final form, the Pregnancy Directive represents a considerable watering-down of the European Commission's initial proposals, which were for a minimum entitlement of 18 weeks leave at 80 per cent. of full pay for all pregnant employees. This was unacceptable to the U.K. Government, and in a display of brinkmanship in which the draft directive nearly lapsed through passage of time (it was finally adopted at a meeting of E.C. Fisheries Ministers only hours within the deadline, after the meeting of Employment Ministers had failed to reach agreement), a compromise was reached involving a minimum entitlement of 14 weeks' maternity leave, during which a woman is entitled to be paid an amount equivalent to the amount of state benefit she would receive if she were absent due to sickness. The Italian Government objected to the equation of maternity with sickness, but were placated by the inclusion of a statement in the directive which declares that the reference to sickness benefit "is not intended in any way to imply that pregnancy and childbirth be equated with sickness". The Directive also provides that entitlement to pay during maternity leave may not be made conditional on periods of previous employment in excess of 12 months before the expected date of childbirth. As the Directive was brought forward as a health and safety measure under Art. 118A of the Treaty of Rome, it required only qualified majority approval; in the event both the Italian and the U.K. Governments abstained in the vote on its adoption.

The Act itself makes no provision for pay during the maternity leave period, the intention being to introduce the right to paid maternity leave via amendments to the relevant social security legislation. At the time of writing the Department of Social Security had issued a Consultation Document outlining the options for implementing the requirements of the Directive (*Changes in Maternity Pay*, DSS, August 1993). That document sets out two broad choices for bringing Statutory Maternity Pay (SMP) into line with the Directive. The cheapest option involves increasing the lower rate of SMP to the higher rate of Statutory Sick Pay (SSP) for 14 weeks (necessary because lower rate SSP is currently *below* lower rate SMP), followed by payment at the current rate for the remaining four weeks; higher rate SMP would be payable for the first six weeks to women who have worked for at least 37 weeks for their current employer at the qualifying week (*i.e.* the fifteenth week before the expected week of confinement), the reduction in the qualifying period for higher rate SMP (currently two years at the qualifying week) being necessary to comply with the new 12-month limit mentioned above. The problem with this solution is that it would introduce further complication into an already difficult area of the law; for example a woman employed for more than 37 weeks would receive no fewer than three different rates of payment over the 18 week SMP period. The second, simpler, option would be to increase the lower rate of SMP to the higher rate of SSP for the entire 18 week maternity pay period, with higher rate SMP payable for the first six weeks to women who had worked for at least 26 weeks with their current employer, and lower rate SMP payable to any woman employed in the qualifying week (*i.e.* dropping the current 26-week qualifying period for lower rate SMP). This would also have the advantage of bringing the maternity pay provisions into line with the provisions in this section concerning maternity leave, which apply irrespective of length of service. The drawback is of course the additional cost involved (at £50m., the second option is reckoned to be some £15m. more expensive than the first one); at the present time, employers are entitled to 100 per cent. reimbursement of the amount paid out by way of SMP, plus an extra 4.5 per cent. to cover the additional N.I.C.'s payable on SMP. To meet the cost of implementing the maternity pay aspects of the Directive, the consultation document proposes a reduction in the reimbursement rate of SMP (as occurred in the case of Statutory Sick Pay in 1989), with special help for small employers.

New s.33 of the 1978 Act

The Pregnancy Directive requires that all contractual rights (other than pay) must be maintained during the maternity leave period. This implies that the contract of employment will continue to subsist during the maternity leave period, although the section does not expressly state that this will be the case; instead, it states that the employee will be "entitled to the benefit of the terms and conditions of employment which would have been applicable to her if she had not been absent", which probably amounts to the same thing. Under the previous provisions on the right to return, s.33(3) of the 1978 Act stated that the right applied whether or not the employee's contract of employment subsisted throughout her period of maternity absence, and whether the contract did in fact subsist was a question of fact in every case. The E.A.T. has recently held in *Institute of the Motor Industry* v. *Harvey* [1992] I.C.R. 470, that a woman's contract of employment is likely to continue during her maternity absence unless terminated by agreement, resignation or dismissal, which suggests that unless some such positive step is taken the contract will continue; premature resignation is obviously a danger here, but in the past the tribunals have been reluctant to interpret a statement by an employee that she does not intend to return to work as a resignation (*Hughes* v. *Gwynedd Area Health Authority* [1978] I.C.R. 161). This issue of contractual status will still be important where a woman is entitled to a further period of maternity absence after the expiration of her 14 week maternity leave, and it is unfortunate that the opportunity has not been taken to clarify that issue. In the absence of any specific provision in the Act concerning the remedies available to a woman denied the benefits of her contract of employment during the maternity leave period, it seems that the remedy will be an action for breach of contract in the ordinary courts (unless of course the opportunity is taken to confer jurisdiction on industrial tribunals in such cases under the extended powers in s.38 of this Act: see below).

Remuneration. As originally drafted, this section excluded all entitlement to "pay", which would have included the totality of the consideration which an employee receives from her employer, whether in the form of wages, salary or non-wage benefits such as private medical insurance, company car, accommodation allowance, etc., however, the Bill was amended in Committee and the reference to "pay" was replaced by "remuneration". This is not defined in the Act, but the Government's intention is that it should include wages and salary but not other, non-wage, benefits. The term "remuneration" also appears in the calculation of a "week's pay" under Sched. 14 to the 1978 Act, where it is similarly undefined; in that context it has been held to include, in addition to wages or salary, any regular bonuses, commission or supplements to which the employee is entitled (*Weevsmay* v. *Kings* [1977] I.C.R. 244; *Marcusfield (A. & B.)* v. *Melhuish* [1977] IRLR 484), but not payments in kind, payments from a third party (*e.g.* tips: *Palmanor* v. *Cedron* [1978] I.C.R. 1008), unless distributed by the employer (*Keywest Club* (*t/a Veeraswamys Restaurant*) v. *Choudhury* [1988] IRLR 51), or expenses, unless there is an element of profit or surplus (*S. & U. Stores* v. *Wilkes* [1974] I.C.R. 645). The same interpretation is likely to apply in this context. It follows that a pregnant employee will be entitled to the benefit of the non-wage elements of her remuneration package throughout her statutory maternity leave period. Whether she continues to be entitled to those benefits after the end of the maternity leave period will be a matter of her contract of employment.

New s.34 of the 1978 Act

Within certain limits it is for the employee to decide when her maternity leave period commences. She must normally give notice to her employer of her pregnancy and of the date on which she intends her maternity leave to begin (the "notified leave date") at least 21 days before that date, which may not be earlier than the beginning of the eleventh week before the expected date of childbirth (see the note to new s.36), and her maternity leave period will then normally begin on the date notified to her employer. There are however two exceptions to the above. First, if before the notified leave date and after the beginning of the sixth week before the expected week of childbirth (EWC) she is absent from work wholly or partly because of pregnancy or childbirth, the maternity leave period will be automatically triggered on the first day of that absence; and secondly, if childbirth occurs before the maternity leave period would otherwise have commenced, the maternity leave period will begin to run on the date of the birth. Under the original proposals the maternity leave period would in all cases have commenced automatically with the first day of pregnancy absence after the beginning of the eleventh week before the EWC, but this was amended in Committee following objections that it removed the woman's right to choose when to start her maternity leave, and in cases where childbirth was late could even lead to the absurdity of the 14 week maternity leave period expiring before the date of childbirth (although see new s.35(2), below). Postponement of the automatic triggering provisions until the sixth week before the EWC means that a woman suffering from an antenatal illness who does not qualify for the right to return under new s.39 will still have the possibility of up to eight weeks' leave post-childbirth. However, in such cases the temptation will always be to delay the start of the maternity leave period for as long as possible so as to guarantee the maximum period of leave after the birth, and there must be a danger that some women will try to continue working through antenatal illness in an attempt to avoid the automatic triggering provisions. Such a consequence would be particularly unfortunate given the fact that these new measures derive from an EEC Directive designed to improve the health and safety protection of pregnant women at work. The Government considered that the automatic triggering provisions were necessary in order to avoid the possibility of a woman suffering from antenatal illness delaying the start of her maternity leave by relying on her entitlement to sick leave. However, it is only absence "wholly or partly because of pregnancy or childbirth" which sets the clock running, and given the widespread propensity to assume that *any* illness during pregnancy is pregnancy related, we can no doubt expect some difficult conflicts of evidence where the reason for the absence is disputed. One assumes that a woman who is permitted by her employer to take time off work for antenatal care under s.31A of the 1978 Act will not be "absent from work wholly or partly because of pregnancy or childbirth" within these provisions, although this is not made explicit. It would be most unfortunate if this were not the case.

Expected week of childbirth. This is defined in s.153(1) of the 1978 Act (as amended by Sched. 8, para. 25) as "the week, beginning with midnight between Saturday and Sunday, in which it is expected that childbirth will occur". Note that the correct definition of week in this context is the one in Sched. 13, para. 24 to the 1978 Act ("week means a week ending with Saturday"), and not the more complex definition in s.153(1): *Secretary of State for Employment* v. *Ford (A.) & Son (Sacks)* [1986] I.C.R. 882. "Childbirth" is defined in s.153(1) as "the birth of a living child or the birth of a child whether living or dead after twenty-four weeks of pregnancy". The previous provisions used the concept of the "expected week of *confinement*", which referred to the birth of a child after *28* weeks of pregnancy.

New s.35 of the 1978 Act

The maternity leave period will normally continue for 14 weeks from the commencement date. However, there are three exceptions: first, subs. (1) provides that if childbirth is late, the maternity leave period continues until the birth of the child, even if this extends it beyond the normal 14-week limit; secondly, subs. (2) provides that where the employee is prohibited by law from working within a certain period after childbirth, her maternity leave period will continue until the expiry of that period; this anticipates the introduction of new regulations by the Health and Safety Executive providing for two weeks' compulsory maternity leave after childbirth, as required by the Pregnancy Directive (although under the Directive the two-week period may be before or after birth); and thirdly, subs. (3) provides that where the employee is dismissed during the maternity leave period, the period will end at the time of the dismissal. Such a dismissal will however be automatically unfair under the new s.60 (see the note to s.24, below). Note the special provisions which apply where the employee is made redundant during the maternity leave period (see new s.38, below).

New ss.36 and 37 of the 1978 Act

The entitlement to maternity leave is subject to detailed notice requirements similar to those which formerly applied to the right to return to work; these notice requirements also apply to the right to return to work: see the note to new s.39. New s.36(1) requires the employee to give her employer at least 21 days' notice (in writing, if the employer so requests) of the date on which she intends her maternity leave to commence, or if that is not reasonably practicable she must give notice as soon as is reasonably practicable; new s.37 provides that at that same time she must also give written notice of the fact that she is pregnant, and of the expected week of childbirth (or, if childbirth has already occurred, the date of the birth). The employer may also ask for a certificate from a registered medical practitioner or registered midwife confirming the expected week of childbirth. These requirements are similar to those which previously applied to the right to return to work. Where the maternity leave period is automatically triggered by a day of absence after the sixth week before the EWC (see new s.34, above), s.36(3) provides that the notice requirement in s.36(1)(a) does not apply, but the employee must notify her employer as soon as is reasonably practicable that she is absent for that reason; similarly, where childbirth occurs before the start of the maternity leave period, she must give notice to her employer, as soon as is reasonably practicable, that she has given birth. As mentioned above, these notice requirements also apply to the right to return to work under new s.39, but an employee who wishes to exercise her right to return under that section must include with the initial written notice to the employer the information that she intends to return to work (see new s.40(1)). As before, the employer may subsequently ask her to confirm her intention to return to work, but whereas under the old provisions that request could be made no earlier than 49 days after the beginning of the EWC, in future the request may be made no earlier than 21 days before the end of the 14-week maternity leave period; this means that an employee who started her maternity leave period at the beginning of the eleventh week before the EWC (*i.e.* at the earliest opportunity) may be required to give confirmation of her intention to return to work in the very week that she is due to give birth, and if childbirth is late she may have to do so even *before* giving birth! See the note to s.40(2).

Not reasonably practicable. In cases under the former provisions on the right to return to work, the E.A.T. indicated that in determining whether it was "not reasonably practicable" to give the required 21 days' notice, the tribunal should adopt the interpretation of those words as used in the context of the time limit for claiming unfair dismissal (see *Nu-Swift International* v. *Mallinson* [1979] I.C.R. 157 (employee's delay in deciding whether or not to return to work did not make it "not reasonably practicable" for her to inform the employer at the appropriate time)).

New s.37A of the 1978 Act

A woman who is absent from work on maternity leave is not required to give notice to her employer of her intention to return to work at the end of the 14-week maternity leave period, either before, during or towards the end of that period. This contrasts with the right to return after maternity absence, where notice of the intention to return must still be given at the beginning and at the end of the period of absence, and where written confirmation of that intention may be requested by the employer during the period of maternity leave (see the note to Sched. 2). However, this section provides that a woman who wishes to return to work *before* the end of her maternity leave period must give her employer seven days' notice (not necessarily in writing) of the date of her intended return; if she fails to do so, the employer may postpone her return to the extent necessary to give the required seven days' notice (although not beyond the end of the maternity leave period), and is under no obligation to pay her if she does insist on returning to work before that notice period expires.

New s.38 of the 1978 Act

A woman who is made redundant during her maternity leave period is entitled to be offered alternative employment with her employer (or his successor, or an associated employer) where there is a suitable available vacancy, defined in subs. (2) as a contract involving work which is suitable in relation to the employee, appropriate for her to do in the circumstances, and on terms and conditions which are not substantially less favourable than those which she enjoyed under her previous contract. The offer must be made before her original contract ends, and must take effect immediately on the ending of that contract. Failure to make such an offer will render the dismissal automatically unfair (s.60(f) of the 1978 Act, as substituted by s.24 of this Act, below), but where an offer of suitable alternative employment is made, an employee who unreasonably refuses that offer will lose her right to a redundancy payment (s.82(5) of the 1978 Act), and her dismissal is likely to be held to be fair. The right conferred by this section mirrors the long-standing right (now contained in new s.41) of a woman who is made redundant during maternity absence to be offered suitable alternative employment (see the note to Sched. 2), and the cases decided under those provisions will be relevant here. Note that in that context the E.A.T. has held in *Community Task Force* v. *Rimmer* [1986] I.C.R. 491, that the employer's failure to offer the employee an alternative job because of undesirable financial implications (loss of funding from the Manpower Services Commission) rendered her dismissal automatically unfair; the consequences for the employer of offering her the job were not relevant: "The test of availability … is not expressed to be qualified by considerations of what is economic or reasonable. The tribunal must simply ask themselves whether a suitable vacancy is available".

Redundancy. The usual definition of redundancy contained in the 1978 Act, s.81(2) applies. See Sweet & Maxwell's *Encyclopedia of Employment Law*, para. 1·6502.

Suitable available vacancy. The alternative work must be "suitable" in relation to the employee and "appropriate" for her to do in the circumstances. Neither requirement is defined. In the context of entitlement to redundancy payments it has been held that the suitability of an offer of alternative employment is a question of fact and degree for the tribunal (see *Taylor* v. *Kent County Council* [1969] 2 Q.B. 560). The issue of suitability is likely to turn on matters such as the nature and status of the job, pay, hours of work, place of work and working conditions in general. The alternative employment must also be "appropriate for her to do in the circumstances"; the tribunal must therefore take into account the particular personal circumstances of the employee, including the fact that she has a new baby, in considering the suitability of the offer of alternative employment. Factors likely to be relevant include the location of the work, hours of work, domestic considerations, etc. The requirement of appropriateness does not appear in the redundancy payments provisions, although in that context the tribunal must consider whether the employee's refusal of an offer of alternative employment was unreasonable, a test which probably performs a similar function. Note that unlike the position where the employee exercises her right to return to work after maternity absence, where the terms and conditions must be no less favourable than those which would have been applicable to her had she not been absent (see new s.39(2)), here the terms and conditions of the new job *may* be less favourable than those of her original job, provided they are not *substantially* so. Once again this will be a question of fact for the tribunal. On the availability of alternative employment, see *Community Task Force* v. *Rimmer* [1986] I.C.R. 491, discussed above.

Associated employer. The usual definition in the 1978 Act, s.153(4) applies. See Sweet & Maxwell's *Encyclopedia of Employment Law*, para. 1·2014.

New s.38A of the 1978 Act

A woman who also has a contractual right to maternity leave may not exercise her contractual and statutory rights separately, but may take advantage of whichever is, in any particular respect, the more favourable. In exercising this composite right the normal statutory requirements will still apply, suitably modified to give effect to any more favourable terms in the contract. This mirrors the existing provision for a composite right to return to work after maternity absence previously contained in s.48 of the 1978 Act, and now to be found in new s.44. In that context, the Court of Appeal has held that the statutory requirements will apply unless there is evidence that the parties have expressly or impliedly agreed to some modification of them: see *Lavery* v. *Plessey Telecommunications* [1983] I.C.R. 534.

In any particular respect. In *Bovey* v. *Board of Governors of the Hospital for Sick Children* [1978] I.C.R. 934, a case under the predecessor of s.44, the E.A.T. interpreted these words restrictively, refusing to allow a woman with a statutory right to return to work full-time on her original grade and a contractual right to return part-time on a lower grade to construct a composite right to return part-time on her original grade: "There must be a limit to the extent to which the right in question, to return to work, can be sub-divided, so as to identify the particular respects in which it is more favourable".

Sched. 2

This Schedule, substituting new ss.39 to 44 of the 1978 Act, preserves (with the necessary amendments to take account of the right to maternity leave) the existing right of a woman who has at least two years' continuous service at the beginning of the eleventh week before the expected week of childbirth (or five years' service for those who work between eight and 16 hours per week) to return to work at any time up to 29 weeks after the week of childbirth. To qualify for the right to return, the employee must have complied with the notice requirements for the right to maternity leave as set out in new ss.36 and 37, and must also have notified her employer at that time of her intention to exercise her right to return to work after maternity absence. As before, while she is on leave her employer may request that she confirm in writing her intention to return to work, and she must comply with that request within 14 days or, if not reasonably practicable, within a further reasonable period. However, in a significant departure from the previous provisions, which stated that such a request could not be made earlier than 49 days after the beginning of the EWC, the request for confirmation may now be made no earlier than 21 days before the end of the 14 week maternity leave period (which may of course have started anything up to 11 weeks before the EWC). In many cases the result of this change will be that a woman will have very little (if any) time after giving birth to decide whether or not she still wishes to return to work, and where childbirth is delayed by more than two weeks (which is by no means uncommon) she could even be required to give confirmation before she has given birth. It is submitted that this is a most unfortunate development, as the period immediately around the time of childbirth is not the most appropriate time for a woman to be expected to make important decisions about her future employment. The latitude with which the tribunals are prepared to interpret the test of reasonable practicability is likely to be crucial here. It should also be remembered that under the 1978 Act there is nothing to prevent a woman who has confirmed her intention to return to work from subsequently changing her mind (*quaere* whether in such a case she might be held disqualified from receiving unemployment benefit on the grounds that she has "without good cause neglected to avail [herself] of a reasonable opportunity of employment" within the Social Security Contributions and Benefits Act 1992, s.28(1)(c)).

In other respects the new provisions on the right to return are as before: she is entitled to return to her previous job on terms and conditions no less favourable than those which would have applied had she not been absent from work after the end of the maternity leave period (new s.39(2)); where it is impracticable because of redundancy for the employer to permit her to return, she is entitled to be offered alternative employment where there is a suitable available vacancy (new s.41); she must give at least 21 days' notice in writing of her proposed date of return (new s.42); and where she has both a statutory and a contractual right to return, she may take advantage of whichever is in any particular respect the more favourable (new s.44). The exemption for small employers (*i.e.* those employing five or fewer employees) from the obligation to permit a woman to return to work after maternity absence where not reasonably practicable to do so still applies (s.56A of the 1978 Act), although it should be noted that there is no such exemption from the newly introduced right to maternity leave. For further details of the right to return to work, see Sweet & Maxwell's *Encyclopedia of Employment Law*, para. 1·5511 *et seq.*

Dismissal rights

24.—(1) For section 60 of the 1978 Act (dismissal on ground of pregnancy) there shall be substituted—

"Dismissal on ground of pregnancy or childbirth

60. An employee shall be treated for the purposes of this Part as unfairly dismissed if—

   (a) the reason (or, if there is more than one, the principal reason)
       for her dismissal is that she is pregnant or any other reason con-
       nected with her pregnancy,
   (b) her maternity leave period is ended by the dismissal and the
       reason (or, if there is more than one, the principal reason) for
       her dismissal is that she has given birth to a child or any other
       reason connected with her having given birth to a child,
   (c) the reason (or, if there is more than one, the principal reason)
       for her dismissal, where her contract of employment was ter-
       minated after the end of her maternity leave period, is that she
       took, or availed herself of the benefits of, maternity leave,
   (d) the reason (or, if there is more than one, the principal reason)
       for her dismissal, where—
           (i) before the end of her maternity leave period, she gave
       to her employer a certificate from a registered medical prac-
       titioner stating that by reason of disease or bodily or mental
       disablement she would be incapable of work after the end of
       that period, and
           (ii) her contract of employment was terminated within the
       four week period following the end of her maternity leave
       period in circumstances where she continued to be
       incapable of work and the certificate relating to her inca-
       pacity remained current,
       is that she has given birth to a child or any other reason connec-
       ted with her having given birth to a child,
   (e) the reason (or, if there is more than one, the principal reason)
       for her dismissal is a requirement or recommendation such as is
       referred to in section 45(1), or
   (f) her maternity leave period is ended by the dismissal, and the
       reason (or, if there is more than one, the principal reason) for
       her dismissal is that she is redundant and section 38 has not
       been complied with.
   For the purposes of paragraph (c) above a woman "takes maternity
leave" if she is absent from work during her maternity leave period
and a woman "avails herself of the benefits of maternity leave" if,
during her maternity leave period, she avails herself of the benefit of
any of the terms and conditions of her employment preserved by section 33 during that period.".
   (2) In section 59 of the 1978 Act (dismissal on ground of redundancy),—
   (a) for the words "employer, and" there shall be substituted the words
       "employer, and either—
           (a) that the reason (or, if more than one, the principal reason) for
       which the employee was selected for dismissal was an inadmissible
       reason; or"; and
   (b) there shall be inserted at the end, as subsection (2), the following—
           "(2) For the purposes of this section "inadmissible", in relation to
       a reason, means that it is one of those specified in section 60(a) to
       (e)";
       and the words preceding that subsection (2) shall become subsection
       (1).
   (3) In section 64 of the 1978 Act (qualifying period for right not to be
unfairly dismissed), after subsection (2) there shall be inserted—
       "(3) Subsection (1) shall not apply to the dismissal of an employee if it
   is shown that the reason (or, if more than one, the principal reason) for
   the dismissal or, in a redundancy case, for selecting the employee for
   dismissal, was an inadmissible reason.
       (4) For the purposes of subsection (3) "inadmissible", in relation to
   a reason, means that it is one of those specified in section 60(a) to (e).

(5) Subsection (1) shall not apply to a case falling within section 60(f).".

(4) In section 53 of that Act (written statement of reasons for dismissal), after subsection (2) there shall be inserted—

"(2A) An employee shall be entitled (without making any request and irrespective of whether or not she has been continuously employed for any period) to be provided by her employer with a written statement giving particulars of the reasons for her dismissal if she is dismissed—

    (a) at any time while she is pregnant, or

    (b) after childbirth in circumstances in which her maternity leave period ends by reason of the dismissal.".

GENERAL NOTE

This section significantly improves the protection enjoyed by pregnant women and those who have recently given birth against dismissal or redundancy selection on the grounds of pregnancy or childbirth, in line with EEC Directive 92/85 on the Protection of Pregnant Women at Work. Such a dismissal will in future be automatically unfair, irrespective of the length of service or hours of work of the dismissed employee. Hitherto the protection conferred by s.60 of the 1978 Act against dismissal on the ground of pregnancy only applied to those able to satisfy the usual service qualification for unfair dismissal of two years' continuous employment (or five years for those working between eight and 16 hours a week). However, the Directive requires Member States to implement measures prohibiting the dismissal of any worker from the beginning of her pregnancy to the end of her maternity leave period, irrespective of her length of service or hours of work, unless the dismissal is for a reason unconnected with pregnancy or childbirth. The section also provides that an employee who is dismissed while pregnant or during her maternity leave period shall be entitled to a written statement giving the reasons for her dismissal, irrespective of her length of service and without having to make any request for those reasons. In normal circumstances the right to a written statement is subject to the usual service qualification, and need only be provided on request. Presumably an employer who does not know of the employee's pregnancy at the time of dismissal will not be held to have infringed this requirement provided the written reasons are given as soon as he learns of the pregnancy.

The two-year service requirement significantly weakened the scope of the protection afforded by s.60 of the 1978 Act, particularly as regards women working part-time. At the time of the 1989 Labour Force Survey, more than 40 per cent. of working women had been in their present job for less than two years, and 42 per cent. of women in employment were in part-time work. The failure of the employment protection legislation to afford a remedy in such cases led those affected to seek redress under the Sex Discrimination Act 1975 (which is not subject to any service qualification), on the grounds that as only women can become pregnant, a dismissal for pregnancy or a reason connected with pregnancy must inevitably constitute unlawful discrimination on the grounds of sex. While this line of argument has an obvious logical attractiveness, it runs up against the problem that under the 1975 Act the tribunal, in determining whether the applicant has been treated less favourably than a man on the grounds of her sex, is required to make a comparison between her treatment and that of a man in circumstances which are "not materially different" (1975 Act, s.5(3)), a comparison which strictly speaking cannot be made (*Turley* v. *Allders Department Stores* [1980] I.C.R. 66). However, in *Hayes* v. *Malleable Working Men's Club and Institute* [1985] I.C.R. 703, the E.A.T. held that this requirement could be satisfied by comparing the treatment of a pregnant woman with that of a man in comparable circumstances, *e.g.* a man suffering from some temporary disability such as a hernia. It is, however, a moot point whether this comparative approach satisfies the requirements of E.C. law, since the European Court of Justice (E.C.J.) has held that less favourable treatment of a woman because of her pregnancy constitutes direct discrimination on the grounds of sex in contravention of the Equal Treatment Directive (Directive 76/207), without the need for any comparison to be made of the treatment of a hypothetical male in similar circumstances (see *Dekker* v. *Stichting Vormingscentrum voor Jonge Volwassenen Plus* [1991] IRLR 27; *Handels-og Kontorfunktionaerernes Forbund i Danmark* (*Union of Clerical and Commercial Employees*) (*For Hertz*) v. *Dansk Arbejdsgiverforening* (*Danish Employers' Association*) (*For Aldi Marked K/S*) [1992] I.C.R. 332). The matter was referred back to the E.C.J. by the House of Lords in *Webb* v. *Emo Air Cargo (U.K.)* [1992] 4 All E.R. 929, but the outcome of that reference was still outstanding at the time of writing. For a fuller account of these developments see Sweet and Maxwell's *Encyclopedia of Employment Law*, para. 1·5507.

The removal of the two-year qualifying period for unfair dismissal by this section means that the practical importance of this issue in pregnancy dismissal cases will be considerably reduced once the new provisions come into force; it will, however, still be of great significance where the complaint is one of discriminatory action short of dismissal on grounds of pregnancy.

Subs. (1)

This substitutes s.60 of the 1978 Act, and sets out a new, improved regime of protection whereby it is automatically unfair to dismiss an employee, regardless of her hours of work or length of service, if the reason (or principal reason) for the dismissal is: (a) that she is pregnant, or any other reason connected with her pregnancy (*e.g.* a miscarriage); (b) that she has given birth to a child or any other reason connected with her having given birth to a child, and the dismissal occurred during her maternity leave period; (c) that she took, or availed herself of the benefits of, maternity leave, and the dismissal occurred after the end of her maternity leave period; (d) that she has given birth to a child or any other reason connected with her having given birth to a child, and her contract was terminated within four weeks of the end of the maternity leave period, where before the end of her maternity leave period she gave the employer a medical certificate stating that she would be incapable of work after the end of that period; (e) that she is suspended from work on maternity grounds under new s.45(1) of the 1978 Act (*i.e.* because of a statutory requirement or a recommendation in a code of practice) or (f) that she is made redundant during her maternity leave period and has not been offered suitable alternative employment.

Subs. (2)

This amends s.59 of the 1978 Act, so that a redundancy dismissal will be automatically unfair where the reason (or principal reason) for which the employee was selected for redundancy was one of the "inadmissible reasons" set out in (a) to (e) above.

Subs. (3)

This disapplies the usual qualifying period for unfair dismissal complaints in cases falling within new s.60. Note also that the usual exclusion from the unfair dismissal protection of those taking part in industrial action at the date of the dismissal does not apply where the reason (or principal reason) for the dismissal (or, in a redundancy case, for selecting the employee for dismissal) was one of those specified in s.60 (Sched. 8, paras. 76 and 77, amending ss.237 and 238 of the 1992 Act).

Rights on suspension on maternity grounds

25. After section 44 of the 1978 Act (set out in Schedule 2 to this Act) there shall be inserted as provisions of Part III the sections 45 to 47, together with the heading, set out in Schedule 3 to this Act (which makes provision conferring rights on employees suspended from work on grounds of maternity).

GENERAL NOTE

This section gives effect to Sched. 3 (substituting new ss.45 to 47 of the 1978 Act) and confers important new rights on employees who are suspended from work on "maternity grounds" in consequence of a relevant statutory requirement or a recommendation in a code of practice issued or approved under s.16 of the Health and Safety at Work, etc., Act 1974. An employee will be regarded as suspended from work on "maternity grounds" if she is suspended from work by her employer on the ground that she is pregnant, has recently given birth or is breast-feeding a child. The Schedule confers two main rights on a woman suspended on maternity grounds: first, new s.46 confers a right to be offered any "suitable alternative work" before being suspended on maternity grounds, with a right of complaint to an industrial tribunal if the employer fails to make an offer of alternative work; the right of complaint is subject to the usual three month time-limit calculated from the first day of suspension, unless not reasonably practicable to do so (s.46(4)), and where the tribunal upholds the complaint it may award such compensation as it considers just and equitable in all the circumstances (s.46(5)); and secondly, new s.47 confers a right to be paid by her employer during the period of the suspension, unless she has unreasonably refused an offer of suitable alternative work for the period in question (s.47(2)). Once again there is a right of complaint to an industrial tribunal that the employer has failed to pay the amount due. Here, the complaint must be brought within three months from the day in respect of which the remuneration was not paid, unless not reasonably practicable to do so (s.47(7)), and where the tribunal upholds the complaint it will order the employer to pay to the employee the remuneration which it finds due to her. The amount of remuneration payable under these provisions is a week's pay (calculated in accordance with Sched. 14 of the 1978 Act) for each full week of suspension, with payment on a pro rata basis for part-weeks for which remuneration is payable. Any remuneration paid under the contract goes towards discharging the employer's liability under these provisions, and vice versa.

Relevant provision. i.e. a provision specified in an order made by the Secretary of State under new s.45(3). No such order had been made at the time of writing.

Suspended from work. This refers to a situation where an employee continues to be employed by her employer, but is not provided with work or does not perform the work she normally performed before the suspension (new s.45(2)).

Suitable alternative work. The definition of "suitable alternative work" in new s.46(2) (*i.e.* work which is suitable in relation to her, appropriate for her to do in the circumstances, and on terms and conditions not substantially less favourable than those under which she normally works) echoes the familiar concept of "suitable available vacancy" discussed in the note to new s.38, above.

Employment particulars

Right to employment particulars

26. For sections 1 to 6 of the 1978 Act (particulars relating to employment) there shall be substituted the sections set out in Schedule 4 to this Act.

GENERAL NOTE

This section gives effect to Sched. 4, which substitutes ss.1 to 6 of the 1978 Act. It makes important changes to an employee's right to be given a written statement of employment particulars, implementing EEC Directive No. 91/533 (adopted on October 14, 1991) on information concerning employment conditions, which requires employers to notify their employees of "the essential aspects of the contract or employment relationship". The right of an employee to be provided with written particulars of the terms of employment was introduced by the Contracts of Employment Act 1963, subsequently re-enacted in the Contracts of Employment Act 1972 and later consolidated in the 1978 Act. In some respects, in particular the scope of the information to be disclosed, the existing law already exceeded the requirements of the Directive. The main changes required to implement the Directive concern the time within which the written statement must be provided to the employee, the range of employees entitled to receive a written statement, and matters in respect of which particulars must be given, and the extent to which the statement may refer to some other document rather than itself giving the necessary details. Taking these points in turn, under the previous provisions the written statement had to be given to the employee within 13 weeks of starting work, whereas new s.1(1) now provides that the information must be provided within two months of the start of employment; previously, only employees who worked for more than 16 hours a week (or who had worked for between eight and 16 hours a week for at least five years) were entitled to receive a written statement, whereas under the new provisions an employee need only work for eight hours a week to qualify, an exemption permitted by the Directive (employees whose employment continues for less than one month are also excluded); certain additional information must be included, *e.g.* on how long a job which is not permanent is expected to continue, the employee's place of work, the existence of any relevant collective agreements, and arrangements where the employee is required to work outside the U.K. for more than one month; and finally, while under the previous provisions it was permissible for the written statement to refer the employee to some other reasonably accessible document (*e.g.* a company handbook or a collective agreement) for all or any of the relevant particulars, in future only particulars relating to sickness entitlement, pensions and disciplinary rules and procedures may be provided in this way, although for details of notice periods the employee may be referred to the provisions of the general law or to a relevant collective agreement. However, as a result of a late amendment in the Lords, the written statement may be provided in instalments, as long as the main particulars (the "principal statement") are included in a single document. The rules on notification of changes in relevant terms and conditions are also tightened up, with employees now being entitled to receive individual written notification of any changes at the earliest opportunity, and in any event within one month of the change; this contrasts with the previous provisions, under which the employer was only required to inform employees of the changes, with no requirement to provide employees with an individual written statement detailing those changes.

The new requirements do not apply to existing employees, *i.e.* those whose employment began before the coming into force of the new provisions (November 30, 1993), but an existing employee is entitled to request a new style statement (albeit on one occasion only) and must also be notified of any changes in the particulars in accordance with the new requirements, even if the employee's full statement was given under the old provisions (Sched. 9, para. 3).

New s.1 of the 1978 Act

As seen in the General Note, above, the written statement must now be given within two months of the beginning of employment, rather than 13 weeks as before, although subs. (1)

allows it to be given in instalments provided that all the particulars are given within the two month deadline. The main particulars, listed in new s.2(4), must however be included in a single document (the "principal statement"). To the existing list of particulars are added paras. (g) to (k) concerning, respectively, the period for which the employment is expected to continue (where it is not intended to be permanent), or the date when it is to end (where it is for a fixed term); the place of work (or if work may be at various places, an indication of that fact and of the employer's address); any collective agreements directly affecting the terms and conditions of employment, including (where the employer is not a party) the persons by whom they were made; and, where the employee is required to work outside the U.K. for more than a month, details of the period for which he is to work outside the U.K., the currency in which he is to be paid, any additional pay and benefits by reason of working outside the U.K., and any terms and conditions relating to his return to the U.K. The position of those working outside the U.K. is further strengthened by the new requirement in new s.2(5) that where an employee is to begin work outside the U.K. within two months of starting employment, the written statement must be given before the employee departs.

A written statement is not a contract of employment *per se*, nor does it become one simply because the employee signs a receipt for it without objecting to the terms set out therein, unless the evidence is that the employee in fact signed the written statement as a contract: see *Gascol Conversions* v. *Mercer* [1974] I.C.R. 420. In normal circumstances the written statement simply provides evidence of what the main terms of employment are: see *Turriff Construction* v. *Bryant* [1967] I.T.R. 292 and *Parkes Classic Confectionery* v. *Ashcroft* [1973] I.T.R. 43. In *System Floors (U.K.)* v. *Daniel* [1982] I.C.R. 54 (a case where the employer was arguing that the written statement was not accurate), Browne-Wilkinson J. put it thus: "It seems to us, therefore, that in general the status of the statutory statement is this. It provides very strong prima facie evidence of what were the terms of the contract between the parties, but does not constitute a written contract between the parties. Nor are the statements of the terms finally conclusive: at most, they place a heavy burden on the employer to show that the actual terms of the contract are different from those which he has set out in the statutory statement".

Browne-Wilkinson J. added that as against an *employee* the written statement will be "no more than persuasive" evidence, which might be rebutted, *e.g.* by evidence of statements made at a job interview or in letters of appointment. These dicta were subsequently approved by the Court of Appeal in *Robertson* v. *British Gas Corp.* [1983] I.C.R.351.

There is one further aspect of the relationship between the s.1 statement and the contract of employment which should be noted. The old s.5 expressly provided that the right to a written statement did not apply where the employee had a written contract of employment containing express terms covering all those matters required to be included in the written statement, provided the employee had been given a copy of that contract or a copy was made reasonably accessible to him. There is no such provision in the substituted provisions, and on the face of it this seems to suggest that a written statement must be provided even where the employee has been provided with a full written contract. If correct, this must be considered as an unfortunate development, particularly in view of the fact (as seen in the General Note above) that the circumstances where a written statement may refer the employee to some other document are now greatly constrained (see the note to new s.2). Presumably it would be open to a tribunal in such a case to hold that the written contract constitutes a "written statement" within the meaning of this section; such an interpretation would at least have the merit of avoiding what might be considered needless duplication.

Employee, employer, employment. The usual definitions in s.153 of the 1978 Act apply.

Period of continuous employment. This is to be calculated in accordance with the 1978 Act, Sched. 13. Employment with a previous employer must be included if it counts towards the employee's period of continuous employment, although whether in fact continuity is preserved for the purposes of the employee's statutory rights must be determined in accordance with the provisions of Sched. 13: see *Secretary of State for Employment* v. *Globe Elastic Thread Co.* [1980] A.C. 506, overruling *Evenden* v. *Guildford City Association Football Club* [1975] Q.B. 917.

Place of work. This is not defined. *Cf.* the definition in s.228 of the 1978 Act, where an employee's "place of work" is defined (for the purposes of the law on separate workplace ballots) as "the premises occupied by his employer at or from which that person works or, where he does not work at or from any such premises or works at or from more than one set of premises, the premises occupied by his employer with which his employment has the closest connection".

New s.2 of the 1978 Act
Subsection (1) of the new section repeats the wording of the previous provisions in stating that where there are no particulars to be given for any of the items covered in the statement, that fact must be indicated. On the face of it this seems to suggest that no particulars need be given under any of the headings where none have been agreed, but in *Eagland* v. *British Telecommunications*

19–66

[1992] IRLR 323, the Court of Appeal held that it is necessary to distinguish between "mandatory terms", *i.e.* essential terms which the written statement must contain, and "non-mandatory terms", where no particulars need be given if there is no evidence that the parties have reached an agreement on that matter. The particulars in s.1(2)(a) to (c) (the parties, the commencement of employment and continuity of employment) and s.1(3)(a), (b), (e) and (f) (rate of pay, interval of payment, notice requirements and job title) were said to be mandatory terms, while the particulars in s.1(3)(c) and (3) (hours of work, holidays, sickness and pensions) were non-mandatory, since the wording of the section ("any terms and conditions relating to...") clearly envisaged that there might not be any agreed terms on those matters. The Court of Appeal disapproved of the suggestion in *Mears* v. *Safecar Security* [1982] 3 W.L.R. 366, that the duty of the tribunal under s.11(1) of the 1978 Act "to determine what particulars ought to have been included" means that the tribunal may ultimately have to "invent" a term in circumstances where no express term has been agreed and where there is no evidence upon which a term can be implied. In the case of non-mandatory terms such as pensions, holidays and sick pay, Parker L.J. (giving the leading judgment of the court) stated that the tribunal has no power to impose on the employer any such terms if either the parties had agreed that there should be no such terms, or no agreement at all had been reached on those matters (there being no entitlement to such terms as a necessary legal incident of the employment relationship). In the case of mandatory terms, Parker L.J. considered that it was difficult to imagine how such a case could arise; one possibility might be where there is no evidence of any agreement on the length of notice, but in such a case the tribunal would be able to imply a term that there must be reasonable notice, as that is a term which would normally be implied in the absence of an express agreement as one of the ordinary requirements of the employment relationship. That is not to say, however, that the tribunal has the power to invent a term simply to fill the gap in the written statement: "I do not consider that even in mandatory cases the Tribunal have power to impose on parties terms which have not been agreed". Taking this to its logical conclusion, Leggatt L.J. suggested that a failure to reach agreement on one of the mandatory terms might well lead to a finding that the contract fails for uncertainty: "If an essential term, such as a written statement must contain, has not been agreed, there will be no agreement".

Of the new particulars added by this Act, those in s.1(2)(g) and (h) (non-permanent employment and place of work) would appear to be mandatory, while those in s.1(2)(j) (any collective agreements) are presumably non-mandatory; the particulars in s.1(2)(k) relating to employment abroad are a mixture of the two.

Subsection (2) mirrors the provision formerly contained in s.2(3), but with the important difference that whereas previously the employer was entitled to refer the employee to some other reasonably accessible document for all or any of the particulars required to be included in the written statement, the employer may now only refer the employee to another document for particulars relating to sickness entitlement, pensions and, under new s.3(1), any relevant disciplinary rules and procedures; subs. (3) allows the employer to refer the employee to the provisions of the general law or to a reasonably accessible collective agreement, but only for details of notice periods. In the past widespread use has been made of this power of incorporation by reference, particularly through the provision of company handbooks, and the restriction of this practice has been criticised as adding significantly to the administrative costs of employers. In a modest concession new s.1(1) allows the written statement to be given in instalments, provided all the particulars are given within the two month deadline, but the particulars set out in subs. (4) must be included in a single document (the "principal statement"). Where within two months of starting employment an employee is to begin work outside the U.K. for a period of more than one month, the written statement must be given before the employee departs (subs. (5)), and certain additional information relating to the employment overseas must be included in the written statement; see the note to new s.1. Finally, while an employee cannot insist on being given a written statement within two months of the start of employment, the right to receive the statement is not lost if the employment ends before that period expires (subs. (6)), although new s.5(1)(a) provides that the right will only arise where the employment has continued for at least one month.

New s.3 of the 1978 Act

This section, which re-enacts the provisions previously contained in ss.1(4) and 2A of the 1978 Act, sets out the information relating to disciplinary rules and procedures which must be included in the written statement. In brief, the statement must contain a note specifying any disciplinary rules applicable to the employee, or referring him to a reasonably accessible document which specifies those rules; it must specify a person to whom the employee may apply if dissatisfied with a disciplinary decision relating to him or if seeking redress of a grievance relating to his employment, and the manner in which such an application should be made; it must explain any further steps in the employer's disciplinary or grievance procedures consequent on such an application, or refer the employee to a reasonably accessible document which explains those steps; and it must state whether a contracting out certificate issued by the Occupational Pensions Board under Pt. III of the Social Security Pensions Act 1975 is in force for the employment in question. Subsection (2) provides that the first three of the above requirements do not apply to rules and procedures relating to health and safety, and subs. (3) exempts small firms (*i.e.* firms employing less than 20 employees) from all those requirements other than the requirement to specify how and to whom the employee may apply if seeking redress of a grievance relating to his employment. In determining the "relevant number of employees", the tribunal must take account of all the employees of the employer, irrespective of status, and must also include in the headcount those employed by any associated employer (subs. (4)). For the definition of "associated employer", see the 1978 Act, s.153(4); the concept is discussed further in Sweet & Maxwell's *Encyclopedia of Employment Law*, para. 1·2014.

New s.4 of the 1978 Act

This section tightens up considerably the procedures which employers must follow in notifying employees of changes in any of the matters covered by the written statement. Previously the employer was not required to give notice of changes to each employee individually, but could inform an employee of any changes by means of a written statement which the employee had a reasonable opportunity of reading at work or which was reasonably accessible to him in some other way; alternatively, the employer could simply refer the employee to some other document, provided once again that the employee had a reasonable opportunity of reading that document at work or it was otherwise reasonably accessible to him. Furthermore, the employer was entitled to indicate in the original written statement that any future changes in the particulars would be recorded in that document, and if the changes were duly noted up within one month of the change this relieved the employer of the need to take other steps to inform employees of the change. In future, the employer will generally have to give the employee an individual written statement giving details of the changes, whether or not the original statement was given in instalments; this will have to be provided at the earliest opportunity, and at the latest within one month of the change (or even earlier if the change results from the employee being sent to work outside the U.K. for more than one month). There are two relatively minor concessions: first, the statement of changes may refer the employee to some other reasonably accessible document, to the general law or to a relevant collective agreement for the actual details of those changes, where such a reference across would have been allowed in the original statement (subs. (3)); and secondly, where the name or the identity of the employer changes, the employer will not have to issue a new s.1 statement unless the employee's continuity of employment is broken by the change of identity or there are changes in any of the matters (other than the names of the parties) required to be included in the written statement (subs. (4)).

It is important to realise that observance of this requirement to notify employees of changes in their terms and conditions of employment does not of itself give the employer the right to vary the terms of the contract of employment unilaterally. Any such variation is subject to the ordinary common law rules on the variation of contracts, and it has long been established under the previous provisions that the mere fact that an employee does not object to a unilateral alteration of the written particulars does not imply assent to a variation of the contract, particularly where the change in question has no immediate practical effect (*Jones* v. *Associated Tunnelling Co.* [1981] IRLR 477; *Robertson* v. *British Gas Corp.* [1983] I.C.R. 351). Conversely, a failure by the employer to comply with the statutory requirements will not nullify a variation which is in fact contractually valid (*e.g.* where there has been an agreed oral variation of the contract).

New s.5 of the 1978 Act

Certain types of employees are excluded from the right to a written statement. The main exclusions, contained in subs. (1), affect those who have been employed for less than one month and part-time workers. Both exclusions are permitted by Directive No. 91/533, although note that to meet the requirements of the directive the usual 1978 Act definition of a part-time worker (*i.e.* an employee whose contract normally involves employment for less than 16 hours weekly) has had to be modified; under the new provisions, an employee need only be employed under a contract normally involving employment for at least eight hours a week to qualify for a written statement. The existing exclusions in respect of those working wholly or mainly outside Great Britain (s.141 of the 1978 Act) and mariners (s.144) continue to apply, although Crown servants, House of Commons and House of Lords staff are no longer excluded.

Subsection (2) provides that an employee who ceases to be excluded from the right to a written statement is to be treated as if his employment started at that time, save that by virtue of subs. (3) the written statement must specify the actual date on which his employment began. Under the old provisions the employer was required in such a case to provide a written statement within one month of the employee ceasing to come within the exclusion, rather than within the usual time-limit of 13 weeks, but there is no such measure in the new provisions and so the normal two-month period applies.

Entitlement to itemised pay statement

27. After section 146(4) of the 1978 Act (provisions disapplied in relation to employment below minimum number of hours weekly) there shall be inserted—

"(4A) Subject to subsection (4B), subsection (4) shall have effect as respects section 8 subject to the following modifications, namely—

(a) the substitution of a reference to eight hours weekly for the reference to sixteen hours weekly, and

(b) the omission of the words "Subject to subsections (5), (6) and (7)".

(4B) Subsection (4A) shall not apply in relation to employment if, at the relevant date, the number of employees employed by the employer, added to the number employed by any associated employer, is less than twenty.

(4C) For the purposes of subsection (4B) "relevant date" means the date on which any payment of wages or salary is made to an employee in respect of which he would, apart from subsection (4B), have the right to an itemised pay statement.".

GENERAL NOTE

This section extends the right to an itemised pay statement to an employee working under a contract of employment which normally involves employment for between eight and 16 hours a week. Previously such an employee was only entitled to an itemised pay statement after five years' service; in future, qualification for the right will be automatic. There is however an exception for small employers, in that the existing service qualification (five years' continuous employment at between eight and 16 hours a week) will still apply where the employer (together with any associated employer) employs fewer than 20 employees on the date on which payment is due.

Employment protection in health and safety cases

Rights to claim unfair dismissal and not to suffer detriment

28. Schedule 5 to this Act (which makes amendments of the 1978 Act for protecting employees against dismissal, and being subjected to other detriment, in health and safety cases) shall have effect.

GENERAL NOTE

This section implements part of the EEC Framework Directive (Directive 89/391/EEC) on the introduction of measures to encourage improvements in the health and safety of workers at work. Most of the Directive's requirements were implemented by the Management of Health and Safety at Work Regulations 1992 (S.I. 1992 No. 2051, in force from January 1, 1993), but the Government considered that primary legislation was necessary in order to implement those parts of the Directive requiring protection for workers with designated health and safety responsibilities (Art. 7(2)) and for workers who leave their workstations in circumstances of serious, imminent and unavoidable danger (Art. 8(4)) against being placed at a disadvantage because of their actions; hence this section, which gives effect to Sched. 5 to the Act.

The new provisions give employees the right not to suffer any detriment or to be dismissed for taking certain types of health and safety-related action. The new s.22A of the 1978 Act gives an employee the right not to be subjected to any detriment (whether by an act or a deliberate failure to act) on any of the specified grounds, while new s.57A makes a dismissal automatically unfair if the reason (or principal reason) is one of those specified; it is also automatically unfair to select an employee for redundancy on those grounds. The new protection is not subject to any qualifying period of continuous employment, and applies irrespective of the number of hours worked or the employee's age; in certain circumstances it also carries enhanced compensation, in the form of a special award for unfair dismissal (on top of the usual basic and compensatory awards) and a minimum basic award, and there is also the possibility of claiming interim relief pending the hearing. In many respects it therefore mirrors the protection against victimisation on trade union grounds conferred by ss.146 to 167 of the 1992 Act.

The five circumstances where the new protection applies are set out in the new ss.22A(1) and 57A(1) of the 1978 Act, and can be divided into two broad categories: the first two grounds concern employees with some specific health and safety responsibility at the workplace, *viz.*, (a) where an employee is dismissed or suffers detriment for carrying out or proposing to carry out health and safety activities at work, having been designated by the employer to do so; (b) where a health and safety representative or member of a safety committee (whether in accordance with arrangements made under statute or by the employer's acknowledgement) is dismissed or suffers detriment for performing or proposing to perform any of his functions as such. The other three grounds concern employees who have no specific health and safety responsibility, but who take action (which might include "whistle-blowing" or walking off the job) in response to a perceived health and safety risk: (c) where an employee is dismissed or suffers a detriment for bringing to his employer's attention, by reasonable means, circumstances which he reasonably believes to be harmful or potentially harmful to health or safety (in circumstances where there is no safety representative or safety committee, or it was not reasonably practicable to raise the matter with them); (d) where an employee is dismissed or suffers a detriment for leaving or proposing to leave his place of work, or for refusing to return to it, "in circumstances of danger which he reasonably believed to be serious and imminent" and which he could not reasonably be expected to avert; and finally (e) where an employee is dismissed or suffers a detriment in such circumstances for taking or proposing to take "appropriate steps" (see below) to protect himself or others from the danger.

New s.22A of the 1978 Act

This section gives an employee the right not to be subjected to any detriment by an employer on one of five grounds specified above. In the last of those specified grounds (*i.e.* taking or proposing to take appropriate steps to protect himself or other persons from danger), subs. (2) provides that whether steps were "appropriate" must be judged by reference to all the circumstances, including the employee's state of knowledge and the facilities and advice available to him at the time. However, there will be a defence under subs. (3) if in such a case the employer is able to show that it was (or would have been) so negligent for the employee to take those steps that a reasonable employer might have treated him as the employer did.

Employee. The right conferred by the new s.22A only extends to employees, although s.149 of the 1978 Act (as amended by Sched. 7, para. 13) gives the Secretary of State the power to amend the 1978 Act and thereby to extend that right to cover persons other than employees. It is unclear whether the confinement of the new rights to employees is in conformity with the directive, which requires measures protecting the health and safety of "workers", a wider concept in U.K. law.

Subjected to any detriment. "Detriment" is not defined for these purposes. That concept also appears in the Sex Discrimination Act 1975, where it forms part of the definition of indirect discrimination in s.1(1)(b)(iii); it is also used in s.6(2)(b) of that Act to define the scope of unlawful discrimination in the employment field (see also the Race Relations Act 1976, ss.1(1)(b)(iii) and 4(2)(c)). In that context it has been held that "detriment" is to be given its ordinary, common sense meaning of being put under a disadvantage (*Ministry of Defence* v. *Jeremiah* [1980] Q.B. 87). In the parallel protection against victimisation for trade union reasons in s.146 of the 1992 Act, somewhat different terminology is used; that section gives an employee the right not to have "action short of dismissal" taken against him, and it has been established in that context that an employer takes action against an employee if he subjects the employee to any positive detriment, for example, suspension, demotion, transfer to less desirable work, withholding of bonuses or other financial penalty. It seems likely that a similar interpretation will be applied here. Under s.146, "action" includes omission (by virtue of s.298), so that the protection still applies where the employer subjects the employee to some disadvantage by denying him a benefit, for example, by refusing promotion or a parking permit, or by denying the employee the right to be represented by an official from his union (*Carlson* v. *Post Office* [1981] I.C.R. 343; *Cheall* v. *Vauxhall Motors* [1979] IRLR 253). The protection under this section appears to be narrower, as it only applies where there is a *deliberate* failure to act, whereas under s.146 a simple omission to act will suffice. It is unclear whether an employee is "subjected to any detriment" for present purposes where the employer *threatens* to subject the employee to some disadvantage. Under s.146 it has been held that "action short of dismissal" includes a threat to report employees to a disciplinary tribunal for holding a union meeting on the employer's premises without permission (*Carter* v. *Wiltshire County Council* [1979] IRLR 331), but there are dicta to the contrary in *Brassington* v. *Cauldon Wholesale* [1978] I.C.R. 405.

New s.22B of the 1978 Act

It will be for the employee to show at the outset that the employer has subjected him to a detriment, but s.22B(2) places the burden of proof on the employer to show the ground on which the act (or failure to act) was done. This echoes the position under s.146 of the 1992 Act, where the employer has to show the purpose for which action was taken against the complainant. Subsection (3) contains the usual three-month time-limit, extendable where it was not reasonably practicable for the complaint to be presented within that period.

Where an act extends over a period. Where an act extends over a period the time-limit will not begin to run until the act ceases. This provision also appears in the Sex Discrimination Act 1975, s.76(6)(c), where it has been held to apply only to a *continuing* act of discrimination, and not to a situation where a *single* act or event of discrimination has continuing *consequences*. So, for example, in *Amies* v. *Inner London Education Authority* [1977] I.C.R. 308, the E.A.T. rejected the complainant's argument that the employer's failure to appoint her to a particular post was a continuing act of discrimination; in contrast, in *Calder* v. *James Finlay Corporation (Note)* [1989] I.C.R. 157, the employer's refusal to allow the complainant access to a mortgage subsidy scheme was held by the E.A.T. to be a continuing discrimination against her, so that she was entitled to bring her complaint more than three months after the refusal. These cases were approved by the House of Lords in *Barclays Bank* v. *Kapur* [1991] 2 A.C. 355 under the analogous provisions in the Race Relations Act 1976, s.68(7)(c). In that case, the employer's refusal to recognise the complainant's previous service for pensions purposes was held to be a continuing act of discrimination; the case was distinguished by the E.A.T. in *Sougrin* v. *Haringey Health Authority* [1991] I.C.R. 791 (affirmed in [1992] I.C.R. 650), where the employer's decision on grading was held not to be a continuing act of discrimination.

New s.22C of the 1978 Act

The remedies for a breach of the new right conferred by s.22A mirror those available in cases of action short of dismissal for trade union reasons. See the note to s.149 of the 1992 Act. Note in particular that compensation under this section is not restricted to pecuniary loss, and that there is no upper limit on the amount which may be awarded.

New s.57A of the 1978 Act

This section gives an employee the right not to be dismissed for one of the five specified reasons set out in the General Note, and parallels the right not to suffer detriment on those grounds conferred by new s.22A. A dismissal for one of the specified reasons will be automatically unfair, save that subs. (3) provides that a dismissal for the last of the five reasons (*i.e.* taking or proposing to take appropriate steps to protect himself or other persons from danger) will not be unfair if the employer is able to show that it was (or would have been) so negligent for the employee to take those steps that a reasonable employer might have dismissed him for taking (or proposing to take) them. Paragraph 4 of Sched. 5, amending s.59 of the 1978 Act, renders it automatically unfair to select an employee for redundancy for any of the specified reasons. In both cases, the right is not conditional on the employee's length of service, age or hours of work (para. 5). Where the dismissal is for one of the "inadmissible reasons" specified in s.57A(1)(a) or (b) (*i.e.* carrying out designated health and safety activities, or performing functions as a health and safety representative or member of a safety committee), the employee is entitled to the enhanced remedies which apply in the case of a dismissal for trade union reasons. Thus, provision is made for a minimum basic award of not less than £2,700, and a special award (on top of the basic and compensatory awards) where the complainant has requested the tribunal to make an order of reinstatement or re-engagement; interim relief is also available. In other cases the remedies are those which apply in an ordinary unfair dismissal complaint. Finally, following concern that employees dismissed for refusing to work in circumstances of danger might be held to be taking part in industrial action, and therefore be excluded by ss.237 and 238 of the 1992 Act from the unfair dismissal protection, Sched. 8, paras. 76 and 77 provide that the usual exclusion of those taking part in industrial action at the date of the dismissal does not apply where the reason (or principal reason) for the dismissal (or, in a redundancy case, for selecting the employee for dismissal) was one of those specified in the new s.57A.

If the reason ... or ... the principal reason. As in all unfair dismissal cases, the burden of proof will initially be on the employee to show that he was dismissed within the meaning of the definition contained in s.55(2) of the 1978 Act. Once the employee has discharged that burden, then with one exception (discussed below) it will fall to the employer to show the reason for the dismissal in the usual way. The employee does not have to prove that the dismissal was for one of the specified reasons. Where the reason for dismissal is disputed, the employee will be required to produce some evidence that casts doubt upon the reason given by the employer (*i.e.* evidence sufficient to raise the issue), but the onus remains upon the employer to establish the true reason for the dismissal to the satisfaction of the tribunal (*Maund* v. *Penwith District Council* [1984] I.C.R. 143). If the employer is not able to satisfy the tribunal as to the reason for the dismissal, he will fail to discharge the burden of proof placed upon him and the dismissal will be unfair. The one exception as regards the burden of proof arises where the complainant lacks the qualifying period of continuous employment normally required to bring an unfair dismissal complaint, or is over retirement age. In such a case the tribunal will only have jurisdiction to hear the complaint if the reason for the dismissal is one of those specified in subs. (1) (unless of course the reason falls into one of the other categories where no qualifying period is necessary, *viz*, dismissal for trade union reasons, pregnancy or childbirth, or assertion of a statutory right), and so the burden of proof will be on the complainant to show that the dismissal was for such a reason (see *Smith* v. *Hayle Town Council* [1978] I.C.R. 996).

New s.75A of the 1978 Act
   See the note to s.158 of the 1992 Act.

New ss.77 to 79 of the 1978 Act
   See the notes to ss.161 to 166 of the 1992 Act.

Unfair dismissal: assertion of statutory right

Dismissal on ground of assertion of statutory right

   29.—(1) After section 60 of the 1978 Act (as substituted by section 24 of this Act), there shall be inserted—

   "Dismissal on grounds of assertion of statutory right
      60A.—(1) The dismissal of an employee by an employer shall be regarded for the purposes of this Part as having been unfair if the reason for it (or, if more than one, the principal reason) was that the employee—
         (a) brought proceedings against the employer to enforce a right of his which is a relevant statutory right; or
         (b) alleged that the employer had infringed a right of his which is a relevant statutory right.
      (2) It is immaterial for the purposes of subsection (1) whether the employee has the right or not and whether it has been infringed or not, but, for that subsection to apply, the claim to the right and that it has been infringed must be made in good faith.
      (3) It shall be sufficient for subsection (1) to apply that the employee, without specifying the right, made it reasonably clear to the employer what the right claimed to have been infringed was.
      (4) The following statutory rights are relevant for the purposes of this section, namely—
         (a) any right conferred by—
            (i) this Act, or
            (ii) the Wages Act 1986,
            for which the remedy for its infringement is by way of a complaint or reference to an industrial tribunal;
         (b) the right conferred by section 49 (minimum notice);
         (c) the rights conferred by the following provisions of the Trade Union and Labour Relations (Consolidation) Act 1992, namely, sections 68, 86, 146, 168, 169 and 170 (deductions from pay, union activities and time off).".

   (2) In section 59 of the 1978 Act (dismissal on ground of redundancy), in subsection (2) (inserted by section 24(2) of this Act), after the word "(e)" there shall be inserted the words "or 60A(1) (read with (2) and (3))".

   (3) In section 64 of the 1978 Act (qualifying period for right not to be unfairly dismissed), in subsection (4) (inserted by section 24(3) of this Act), after the word "(e)" there shall be inserted the words "or 60A(1) (read with (2) and (3))".

GENERAL NOTE

This section introduces important new protection against being dismissed for asserting a statutory right. Subsection (1) inserts a new s.60A into the 1978 Act, which makes it automatically unfair to dismiss an employee (regardless of length of service, hours of work or age) if the reason or principal reason for the dismissal was that the employee had either brought proceedings against the employer to enforce a "relevant statutory right", or had alleged that the employer had infringed such a right. Subsection (2) amends s.59 of the 1978 Act to make it automatically unfair to select an employee for redundancy for such a reason. The new protection applies whether or not the employee was entitled to the right in question, and whether or not it was in fact infringed, provided that the employee acted in good faith in asserting it; nor is it necessary for the employee to have specified the right in question to the employer, provided that he made it reasonably clear which right it was that he was claiming had been infringed. The "relevant statutory rights" to which the section applies are those specified in s.60A(4), which lists all those rights conferred by the 1978 Act or the Wages Act 1986 for which the remedy is by way of complaint to an industrial tribunal; the right to a minimum period of notice laid down in s.49 of the 1978 Act; and the rights relating to deductions from pay, discrimination for trade union reasons and time off for trade union duties and activities which an employee may exercise against an employer under the 1992 Act.

This new protection will be especially valuable to those employees who do not have sufficient continuity of employment to bring an ordinary unfair dismissal complaint, and who might therefore be reluctant to assert their statutory rights for fear of being dismissed. Obvious examples would be employees making complaints within the first two years of employment (or the first five years in the case of part-timers working between eight and 16 hours per week) over matters such as incorrect written particulars of employment or unauthorised deductions from pay. The protection is greatly strengthened by s.60A(2), which makes it unnecessary for the employee to show that he actually qualified for the right in question or that the right had in fact been infringed: the only requirement is that he must have made his claim in good faith. When taken together with the improved protection against dismissal on grounds of pregnancy or childbirth introduced by s.24, and the protection against dismissal in health and safety cases introduced by s.28 (both of which are similarly exempt from the normal qualifying period), this represents a significant advance in the rights of employees against heavy-handed action by employers.

Subs. (1)
  If the reason ... or ... the principal reason. See the note to new s.57A.

Reinstatement orders: compensation

Compensation for unfair dismissal when reinstatement or re-engagement ordered

30.—(1) Sections 71, 74 and 75 of the 1978 Act (awards of compensation for unfair dismissal) shall be amended in accordance with subsections (2), (3) and (4).

(2) In section 71—

(a) in subsection (1), for the words "section 75" there shall be substituted the words "subsection (1A)"; and

(b) after subsection (1) there shall be inserted—

"(1A) Subsection (1) is subject to section 75 except that the limit imposed by that section may be exceeded to the extent necessary to enable the award fully to reflect the amount specified as payable under section 69(2)(a) or (4)(d), as the case may be.".

(3) In section 74—

(a) in subsection (1), for the words "sections 75 and 76" there shall be substituted the words "subsection (8) and section 76"; and

(b) after subsection (7) there shall be inserted—

"(8) Subsection (1) is subject also to section 75 except that, in the case of an award of compensation under section 71(2)(a) where an additional award falls to be made, the limit imposed by section 75 may be exceeded to the extent necessary to enable the award fully to reflect the amount specified as payable under section 69(2)(a) or (4)(d), as the case may be, if that limit would otherwise reduce the amount of the compensatory award when added to the additional award.".

(4) In section 75(1), after the word "shall" there shall be inserted the words "(save where the exception in section 71(1A) or 74(8) applies)".

GENERAL NOTE

This section makes a small but nevertheless important reform to the rules which govern the award of compensation for unfair dismissal in cases where the employer has failed to comply with a reinstatement or re-engagement order. It allows an industrial tribunal to disregard the normal statutory limit on compensation where this is necessary in order to compensate the complainant fully for the employer's failure to comply with such an order, and so removes any incentive which the employer might otherwise have to disregard the order.

The problem arose in the following way: where a reinstatement or re-engagement order is made under s.69 of the 1978 Act, the tribunal is required to make an order for monetary compensation "in respect of any benefit which the complainant might reasonably be expected to have had but for the dismissal, including arrears of pay, for the period between the date of termination of employment and the date of [reinstatement or re-engagement]" (s.69(2)(a) and (4)(d) respectively). If the complainant is subsequently reinstated or re-engaged but the terms of the order are not fully complied with, the tribunal will make an award of compensation under s.71(1) of the 1978 Act "of such amount as the tribunal thinks fit, having regard to the loss sustained by the complainant in consequence of the failure to comply fully with the terms of the order"; if the order is not complied with *at all*, the tribunal will make a basic and compensatory award of compensation, and will also make an additional award unless the employer is able to satisfy the tribunal that it was not practicable to comply with the order (s.71(2)). However, in either case the award of compensation was subject to the statutory maximum laid down in s.75(1), which applies to a compensatory award under s.71(2) and to a compensation award under s.71(1). The unfortunate consequence was that in cases where the monetary element of the reinstatement or re-engagement order was greater than the statutory maximum (which might well be the case where the complainant was a high earner), the tribunal was unable to compensate the complainant fully, and the employer might well be better off financially by disregarding an order for reinstatement or re-engagement. In *Conoco (U.K.)* v. *Neal* [1989] I.C.R. 114, the E.A.T. sought to avoid such a conclusion by holding that the complainant could elect to enforce the order for compensation made by the tribunal under s.69(2)(a), instead of proceeding under s.71(2); however, that decision was subsequently overruled by the Court of Appeal in *O'Laoire* v. *Jackel International* [1990] IRLR 70, the court holding that where an order for reinstatement or re-engagement is not complied with, the employee's only remedy is under s.71. In that case Lord Donaldson M.R. expressed concern at the practical implications of this ruling, commenting that the statutory maximum level of award fixed by s.75 "can positively discourage employers from complying with an order for reinstatement, contrary to the interests [*sic*] of Parliament, and in addition causes injustice to higher paid employees. In these circumstances, there may be a case for a much more fundamental review of the s.75 limits than is called for simply by inflation".

In this section the Government have responded to such criticisms by allowing a tribunal, in awarding compensation under s.71, to exceed the limit set by s.75 "to the extent necessary to enable the award fully to reflect the amount specified as payable" under s.69. Note, however, that in cases falling under s.71(2) (*i.e.* where the order is not complied with at all) it seems that the s.75 limits may only be exceeded in calculating a compensatory award where an additional award is also made.

The limit imposed by s.75. At the time of writing the limit was £11,000, with effect from June 1, 1993, (S.I. 1993 No. 1348).

Service in armed forces

Application of 1978 Act to service in armed forces

31.—(1) In section 138 of the 1978 Act (application of Act to Crown employment) for subsection (3) (service in the armed forces excepted) there shall be substituted—

"(3) This section applies to service as a member of the naval, military or air forces of the Crown but only in accordance with section 138A and it applies also to employment by any association established for the purposes of Part VI of the Reserve Forces Act 1980.".

(2) After section 138, there shall be inserted—

"Application of Act to armed forces
138A.—(1) The provisions of this Act which apply, by virtue of section 138, to service as a member of the naval, military or air forces of the Crown are—
Part I;
in Part II, sections 19 to 22 and 31A;
Part III;
in Part IV, section 53;
Part V, except sections 57A and 80;
Part VIII; and
this Part.
(2) Her Majesty may, by Order in Council,—
(a) amend subsection (1) above by making additions to, or omissions from, the provisions for the time being specified in that subsection by an Order under this subsection; and
(b) make any provision apply to service as a member of the naval, military or air forces of the Crown subject to such exceptions and modifications as may be specified in the Order.
(3) Subject to subsection (5) below, modifications made under subsection (2) above may include provision precluding the making of a complaint or reference to any industrial tribunal unless the person aggrieved has availed himself of the service procedures for the redress of complaints applicable to him.
(4) Where modifications include the provision authorised by subsection (3) above the Order in Council shall also include provision designed to secure that the service procedures for the redress of complaints result in a determination, or what is to be treated under the Order as a determination, in sufficient time to enable a complaint or reference to be made to an industrial tribunal.
(5) No provision shall be made by virtue of subsection (3) above which has the effect of substituting, for any period specified as the normal period for a complaint or reference on any matter to an industrial tribunal, a period longer than six months.
(6) No recommendation shall be made to Her Majesty to make an Order in Council under subsection (2) above unless a draft of the Order has been laid before Parliament and approved by a resolution of each House of Parliament.
(7) In this section—
"the normal period for a complaint or reference", in relation to any matter within the jurisdiction of an industrial tribunal, means the period specified in the relevant enactment as the period within which the complaint or reference must be made, disregarding any provision permitting an extension of that period at the discretion of the tribunal; and
"the service procedures for the redress of complaints" means the procedures, excluding those which relate to the making of a report on a complaint to Her Majesty, referred to in sections 180 and 181 of the Army Act 1955, sections 180 and 181 of the Air Force Act 1955 and section 130 of the Naval Discipline Act 1957.".

GENERAL NOTE
This section extends most of the provisions of the 1978 Act to members of the armed forces. The provisions which are to apply are listed in new subs. 138A(1) of the 1978 Act, and include provisions on the right to written particulars of employment and to itemised pay statements, the right to suspension from work on medical grounds and to time off for ante-natal care, maternity rights, written statement of reasons for dismissal, unfair dismissal, and the resolution of employment disputes. The following rights are not on the list: guarantee payments; time off for public duties and to look for work during notice of redundancy; minimum periods of notice; protection

against dismissal or other detriment for taking action on health and safety grounds (see s.28, above); redundancy payments and insolvency payments.

The application of the 1978 Act to the armed forces is subject to new s.138A(2) of that Act, which permits the usual provisions to be modified by an Order in Council. Subsection (3) provides that such an Order may preclude the making of a complaint or reference to an industrial tribunal unless the complainant "has availed himself of the service procedures for the redress of complaints applicable to him", provided those procedures result in a determination in sufficient time to enable a complaint or reference to be made to a tribunal; subs. (5) provides that the normal limitation period for a complaint or reference to a tribunal may not be replaced under these powers by a period longer than six months.

Sex discrimination

Right to declaration of invalidity of discriminatory terms and rules

32. In section 6 of the Sex Discrimination Act 1986 (application of section 77 of the Sex Discrimination Act 1975, which provides for discriminatory terms of contracts to be void, to terms of collective agreements, employers' rules and rules of certain organisations), after subsection (4) there shall be inserted—

"(4A) A person to whom this subsection applies may present a complaint to an industrial tribunal that a term or rule is void by virtue of subsection (1) of the said section 77 if he has reason to believe—

(a) that the term or rule may at some future time have effect in relation to him, and

(b) where he alleges that it is void by virtue of paragraph (c) of that subsection, that—

(i) an act for the doing of which it provides may at some such time be done in relation to him, and

(ii) the act would be, or be deemed by virtue of subsection (3) above to be, rendered unlawful by the 1975 Act if done in relation to him in present circumstances.

(4B) In the case of a complaint about—

(a) a term of a collective agreement made by or on behalf of—

(i) an employer,

(ii) an organisation of employers of which an employer is a member, or

(iii) an association of such organisations of one of which an employer is a member, or

(b) a rule made by an employer,

subsection (4A) applies to any person who is, or is genuinely and actively seeking to become, one of his employees.

(4C) In the case of a complaint about a rule made by an organisation, authority or body to which subsection (2) above applies, subsection (4A) applies to any person—

(a) who is, or is genuinely and actively seeking to become, a member of the organisation, authority or body,

(b) on whom the organisation, authority or body has conferred an authorisation or qualification, or

(c) who is genuinely and actively seeking an authorisation or qualification which the organisation, authority or body has power to confer.

(4D) When an industrial tribunal finds that a complaint presented to it under subsection (4A) above is well-founded the tribunal shall make an order declaring that the term or rule is void.".

GENERAL NOTE

This section provides a mechanism whereby an employee (whether actual or prospective) may bring proceedings in an industrial tribunal requesting a declaration that a term in a collective agreement discriminates on grounds of sex and is therefore void. It has a complicated history. The Sex Discrimination Act 1975, s.77(1), provides that a term of a contract is void where its inclusion would render the making of the contract unlawful under the 1975 Act, or it is included in furtherance of an unlawful act of discrimination, or it provides for the doing of such an unlawful act. However, s.77(2) provides that where the victim of the unlawful discrimination is a party to the contract, the term is not void but is unenforceable against that party, and subs. (5) provides that any person "interested in a contract to which subs. (2) applies" may apply to the county court (or sheriff court) for an order to have the term modified or removed. In *E.C. Commission* v. *United Kingdom* (No. 165/82) [1984] 1 All E.R. 353, the E.C.J. held that U.K. law failed to comply with the requirements of Directive 76/207/EEC (the "equal treatment" Directive) because s.77 only applied to discrimination in contracts, and did not extend to collective agreements, works rules and the rules of professional bodies, whereas Art. 3 of the Directive states that: "Any provisions contrary to the principle of equal treatment which are included in collective agreements, individual contracts of employment, internal rules of undertakings and rules governing independent occupations and professions shall be, or may be declared, null and void or may be amended". This ruling necessitated a change in domestic law, and the Sex Discrimination Act 1986, s.6, duly extended s.77 of the 1975 Act to cover the terms of collective agreements, works rules and the rules of professional bodies, whether or not intended to be legally binding, in order to comply with the requirements of the Directive. Section 6(3) of the 1986 Act specifically provides that any term in a collective agreement will be void in so far as it provides for the inclusion in a contract of employment of a term which would be caught by an equality clause under the Equal Pay Act 1970. However, one glaring deficiency in the Sex Discrimination Act 1986 was that it failed to provide any new mechanism whereby an employee or prospective employee could seek to have a discriminatory term in a collective agreement removed or modified; it merely declared that any such term or rule was void, and left those adversely affected with their existing remedies under the Equal Pay Act 1970 and the Sex Discrimination Act 1975, s.6. Crucially, the right to apply for an order removing or modifying a discriminatory term or rule under s.77(5) of the 1975 Act only applies to the *parties* to a collective agreement, and does not therefore extend to employees. The Government was urged during the passage of the Sex Discrimination Act 1986 to provide a mechanism whereby a discriminatory collective agreement could itself be challenged, but argued that the existing remedies under the Equal Pay Act 1970 and the Sex Discrimination Act 1975 were adequate, and that the main objective of s.6 of the 1986 Act was to provide an incentive for employers and trade unions to renegotiate collective agreements. However, while an employee may be able to challenge a discriminatory contract term under the 1970 Act, or a discriminatory offer of terms under s.6 of the 1975 Act, those remedies only apply where the discriminatory terms in question are already in force or have been offered by the employer, and do not therefore assist a prospective employee.

This section seeks to remedy that deficiency by amending the Sex Discrimination Act 1986 s.6, so as to allow an employee or prospective employee to obtain a declaration from an industrial tribunal that a term or rule in a collective agreement or works rule is void under s.77 of the 1975 Act, if that person believes that the term or rule may be applied to him in future or that it provides for the doing of an unlawful act which may be done to him in future (new subs. (4A)). In the case of a prospective employee, this right applies to a person who is genuinely and actively seeking to become an employee of the employer by or on whose behalf the collective agreement or works rule was made (new subs. (4B)). The right applies, mutatis mutandis, to a member or prospective member of a trade or professional organisation, and also to complaints in relation to bodies with power to confer a trade or professional authorisation or qualification (new subs. (4C)). If the tribunal upholds the complaint it must make an order declaring that the term or rule is void (new subs. (4D)). However, in contrast with the powers conferred on the county court under s.77(5) of the 1975 Act, the tribunal has no power to *modify* a discriminatory term so as to render it non-discriminatory, an omission which must be considered a major point of weakness in the new provisions. As was pointed out by the Equal Opportunities Commission for Northern Ireland in its comments on the clause, as quoted in Committee, this means that "where the term in question confers a benefit on members of one sex only, rather than modifying the term to ensure that both sexes benefit, the term would be declared void, thus denying both sexes the benefit". (Standing Committee F, January 19, 1993, col. 474). In cases under Art. 119 involving indirectly discriminatory collective agreements the E.C.J. has held that the national court should remove the discrimination by extending to members of the disadvantaged group the benefits applied to other employees, *i.e.* a levelling up rather than a levelling down (see *Kowalska* v. *Freie und Hansestadt Hamburg* [1990] IRLR 447; *Nimz* v. *Freie und Hansestadt Hamburg* [1991] IRLR 222), but the Government's view is that levelling up is not required under the directive. Where possible, there may therefore be some advantage in arguing a case under Art. 119 rather than under this section.

Transfer and redundancy rights

Amendments of transfer of undertakings regulations

33.—(1) The Transfer of Undertakings (Protection of Employment) Regulations 1981 shall be amended as follows.

(2) In Regulation 2(1), in the definition of "undertaking" (which excludes from the Regulations undertakings, and parts of undertakings, not in the nature of a commercial venture), the words from "but does not" to the end shall cease to have effect.

(3) In Regulation 3(4) (transfers to which the Regulations apply), for the words from "one" to the end there shall be substituted the words "one—

(a) may be effected by a series of two or more transactions; and

(b) may take place whether or not any property is transferred to the transferee by the transferor.".

(4) In Regulation 5 (effect of relevant transfer on contracts of employment, etc.)—

(a) in paragraph (1), at the beginning, there shall be inserted the words "Except where objection is made under paragraph (4A) below,";

(b) in paragraph (2) after the words "paragraph (1) above" there shall be inserted the words "but subject to paragraph (4A) below,";

(c) after paragraph (4), there shall be inserted—

"(4A) Paragraphs (1) and (2) above shall not operate to transfer his contract of employment and the rights, powers, duties and liabilities under or in connection with it if the employee informs the transferor or the transferee that he objects to becoming employed by the transferee.

(4B) Where an employee so objects the transfer of the undertaking or part in which he is employed shall operate so as to terminate his contract of employment with the transferor but he shall not be treated, for any purpose, as having been dismissed by the transferor."; and

(d) in paragraph (5), for the words "Paragraph (1) above is" there shall be substituted the words "Paragraphs (1) and (4A) above are".

(5) Regulation 7 (exclusion of occupational pension schemes) shall be re-numbered as paragraph (1) of that Regulation and after that provision as so re-numbered there shall be inserted—

"(2) For the purposes of paragraph (1) above any provisions of an occupational pension scheme which do not relate to benefits for old age, invalidity or survivors shall be treated as not being part of the scheme.".

(6) At the end of Regulation 10(5) (duty to consult) there shall be added the words "with a view to seeking their agreement to measures to be taken.".

(7) In Regulation 11 (remedies for failure to inform or consult)—

(a) paragraph (7) (deduction from compensation of any payments relating to failure to consult on redundancy) shall cease to have effect, and

(b) in paragraph (11) (compensation subject to maximum of two weeks' pay for employee in question), for the words "two weeks' pay" there shall be substituted the words "four weeks' pay".

GENERAL NOTE

This section makes a number of important amendments to the Transfer of Undertakings (Protection of Employment) Regulations 1981 (S.I. 1981 No. 1794) (the TUPE regulations), following the instigation of infringement proceedings by the European Commission against the U.K. Government in October 1992 for its alleged failure fully to transpose EEC Directive No. 77/187 (the Acquired Rights Directive) into domestic law. The most important of the amendments is the extension of the definition of "undertaking" to include undertakings not in the nature of a commercial venture, previously excluded by reg. 2(1) (see the note to subs. (2)). The significance of this development for the contracting-out of public services is considered below. The section also: extends the regulations to cover transfers effected by two or more transactions, and transfers which do not involve the transfer of property (subs. (3)); gives an employee the right to object to the transfer of his contract of employment to the transferee, as required by the decision of the E.C.J. in *Katsikas* v. *Konstantinidis* [1993] IRLR 179 (subs. (4)); provides for the automatic transfer of any provisions of a pension scheme which do not relate to benefits for old-age, invalidity or survivors (subs. (5)); modifies the duty of consultation with union representatives over measures to be taken in connection with the transfer so that the consultation must be undertaken "with a view to seeking their agreement to measures to be taken" (subs. (6)); and amends the remedies for a failure to comply with the duty to consult over the transfer (subs. (7)). The amendments came into force on August 30, 1993, and the transitional provisions provide that the amendments to the regulations will not have effect in relation to any transfer taking place before that date (Sched. 9, para. 4).

These amendments address most of the concerns raised by the European Commission in its complaint, but signally fail to deal with the objection that the TUPE regulations do not comply with the Acquired Rights Directive because the employer's duty to inform and consult under reg. 10 only arises in relation to the representatives of recognised trade unions, whereas the directive requires there to be "consultations with workers' representatives" and does not restrict the duty to the representatives of recognised trade unions. The Commission has asked the European Court to declare that the U.K. has infringed its obligations under the directive by failing "to provide for the designation of employee representatives where this does not occur voluntarily in practice" (*i.e.* where there is no recognised trade union). The Commission has requested a similar declaration in relation to the redundancy consultation provisions: see the note to s.34.

It is a matter of regret that the Act does not clarify the position regarding the application of the TUPE regulations to the practice of contracting out and compulsory competitive tendering. The Attorney-General, invited to attend the Standing Committee on the Bill to explain the position, stressed that the extension of the regulations to non-commercial undertakings was simply intended to ensure that they applied to transfers which involved undertakings not run on commercial lines (*e.g.* charities), which had previously been held to be outside the scope of the regulations, and that it did not follow that the contracting-out of services in the public sector would now automatically fall within the regulations (Standing Committee F, January 21, 1993, col. 504). However, the argument that the contracting-out of a service does not constitute a transfer of an undertaking within the meaning of the regulations is increasingly difficult to sustain in the light of decisions like that in *Stichting (Sophie Redmond)* v. *Bartol* (C-29/91) [1992] IRLR 366 (see the note to subs. (2)) and *Rask and Christensen* v. *ISS Kantineservice A/S* (C-209/91) [1993] IRLR 133, where the E.C.J. held that the directive did apply where the running of a canteen was contracted out to a service company. In *Kenny* v. *South Manchester College* [1993] IRLR 265, the High Court held that a similarly wide approach should be taken in domestic law (see also *Wren* v. *Eastbourne Borough Council and U.K. Waste Control* [1993] IRLR 425 and *Porter and Nanayakkara* v. *Queen's Medical Centre (Nottingham University Hospital)* [1993] IRLR 486). A narrower view was, however, taken by the E.A.T. in *Dines* v. *Initial Health Care Services and Pall Mall Services Group* [1993] IRLR 521, where it was stressed that whether or not there is a transfer within the meaning of the regulations in any particular case is a question of fact for the tribunal to decide, having considered all the relevant factors. Regrettably, the application of the regulations in such cases remains a matter of acute uncertainty even after the amendments made by this section; any further guidance will have to come from the courts.

Subs. (2)

As explained in the General Note, this subsection extends the definition of an "undertaking" in reg. 2(1) to include undertakings not in the nature of a commercial venture, which were previously excluded from the scope of the regulations (see, *e.g. Expro Services* v. *Smith* [1991] I.C.R. 577). It is designed to bring U.K. law into line with the Acquired Rights Directive following the decision of the E.C.J. in *Stichting (Sophie Redmond)* v. *Bartol* (C-29/91) [1992] IRLR 366, which established that the exclusion of non-commercial undertakings was inconsistent with the directive. The amendments do not have effect in relation to transfers which took place before the coming into force of the section on August 30, 1993, but in *Wren* v. *Eastbourne Borough Council and U.K. Waste Control* [1993] IRLR 425 (a case which pre-dated the new provisions), the E.A.T. suggested that the limitation of the regulations to commercial undertakings should be "interpreted" so as to conform with EEC law.

Subs. (3)

This subsection amends the definition of a "relevant transfer" in reg. 3(4) to make it clear that it includes a transfer effected by two or more transactions, and may take place whether or not property is transferred to the transferee by the transferor. This confirms the trend of the decisions of the E.C.J. in recent cases such as *Bork (P.) International A/S* v. *Foreningen af Arbejdsledere i Danmark* [1989] IRLR 41 and *Stichting (Sophie Redmond)* v. *Bartol* (above), and casts doubt on the correctness of the decisions of the domestic courts in cases such as *Seligman (Robert) Corp.* v. *Baker* [1983] I.C.R. 770 and *Stirling* v. *Dietsmann Management Systems* [1991] IRLR 368.

Subs. (4)

This subsection amends reg. 5, which provides for the automatic transfer of an employee's contract of employment from the transferor to the transferee where there is a relevant transfer within the scope of the regulations, to take account of the recent decision of the E.C.J. in *Katsikas* v. *Konstantinidis* [1993] IRLR 179. Previously reg. 5 provided that on a relevant transfer the contracts of employment of the transferor's employees were transferred automatically to the transferee in every case, irrespective of the wishes of the parties (*Premier Motors (Medway)* v. *Total Oil Great Britain* [1984] 1 W.L.R. 377; *Newns* v. *British Airways* [1992] IRLR 575), in effect overriding the fundamental common law principle that an employee cannot be transferred from one employer to another without his consent (*Nokes* v. *Doncaster Amalgamated Collieries* [1940] A.C. 1014). Until recently this was thought to be in line with the Acquired Rights Directive (*Berg (Harry) and Busschers (Theodorus Maria)* v. *Besselsen (Ivo Marten)* (C-144-5/87) [1988] ECR 2559). However, in *Katsikas* the E.C.J. held that under the directive an employee is not precluded from objecting to the transfer of his contract of employment to the transferee, although the E.C.J. also held that it was up to each Member State to determine the fate of the contract of employment or of the employment relationship in such cases, and that the directive does not oblige Member States to provide that the contract of employment or the employment relationship continues with the transferor. This provision, a late amendment at Report stage in the House of Lords, therefore states that an employee's contract of employment will not in future be automatically transferred by a relevant transfer if the employee informs the transferor or the transferee that he objects to becoming employed by the transfer (new reg. 5(4A)); instead, the transfer will operate in such a case so as to terminate his contract of employment with the transferor, but with the catch that the employee will not be treated "for any purpose" as having been dismissed by the transferor (new reg. 5(4B)), effectively excluding any possibility of a claim by the employee against the transferor for unfair dismissal or a redundancy payment, or indeed any contractual claim arising on a dismissal. In effect, the employee will be deemed to have resigned. This is likely to make the option of objecting to the transfer so unattractive in practice as to rule it out in most cases. Surprisingly, there is no requirement for the employee's notice of objection to the transfer to be in writing, and the section gives no clear indication of when the notice of objection must be given, although the fact that the employee may inform the transferor or the transferee of his objection suggests that notice need not be given in advance of the transfer. Given the drastic consequences for the employee of objecting to the transfer, it is to be hoped that the tribunals will require clear evidence before holding that an employee's contract has not been transferred.

Subs. (5)

This subsection amends reg. 7 (which provides that rights, duties and liabilities under an occupational pension scheme are not transferred to the transferee employer) to ensure that any provisions of such a scheme which do not relate to benefits for old-age, invalidity or survivors *are* automatically transferred along with the rest of the employee's contract. It is designed to ensure that where redundancy provisions and other termination benefits are contained in an employee's pension scheme, those provisions are transferred on a relevant transfer.

Subs. (6)

This subsection modifies the duty to consult with union representatives before the transfer to require that the consultation be undertaken "with a view to seeking their agreement to measures to be taken"; for the similar amendment to the duty to consult over redundancies, see the note to s.34. As seen in the General Note, above, it is arguable that the consultation provisions still fail to comply fully with the requirements of the directive in this area because under the TUPE regulations consultation need only take place where there is a recognised trade union.

Subs. (7)

This subsection makes two modest amendments to the remedies for a failure to comply with the duty to inform and consult with union representatives in relation to a proposed transfer. The maximum award of compensation is increased from two weeks' pay to four weeks' pay, and the former restriction on double payments is removed, so that any compensation which an industrial tribunal may award for the employer's failure to inform or consult under the TUPE regulations need not in future be offset against any protective award (*i.e.* an award under s.190 of the 1992

Act for failing to consult over redundancy) or payment of wages or pay in lieu of notice payable by the employer in respect of the protected period, and vice versa. *Cf.* the removal of the parallel provision on double payments in s.190(3) of the 1992 Act by s.34(3), below.

Redundancy consultation procedures

34.—(1) Chapter II of Part IV of the 1992 Act (procedure for handling redundancies) shall be amended in accordance with subsections (2) to (5) below.

(2) In section 188 (duty of employer to consult trade union representatives)—

(a) in subsection (4) (information to be disclosed to representatives), after paragraph (e) there shall be inserted "and

(f) the proposed method of calculating the amount of any redundancy payments to be made (otherwise than in compliance with an obligation imposed by or by virtue of any enactment) to employees who may be dismissed.",

(b) for subsection (6) there shall be substituted—

"(6) The consultation required by this section shall include consultation about ways of—

(a) avoiding the dismissals,

(b) reducing the numbers of employees to be dismissed, and

(c) mitigating the consequences of the dismissals,

and shall be undertaken by the employer with a view to reaching agreement with the trade union representatives.", and

(c) at the end of subsection (7) (exception from requirements in special circumstances) there shall be inserted—

"Where the decision leading to the proposed dismissals is that of a person controlling the employer (directly or indirectly), a failure on the part of that person to provide information to the employer shall not constitute special circumstances rendering it not reasonably practicable for the employer to comply with such a requirement.".

(3) In section 190 (entitlement under protective award), subsection (3) (avoidance of double payments) shall cease to have effect.

(4) In section 193 (duty of employer to notify Secretary of State of certain redundancies), at the end of subsection (7) (exception from requirements in special circumstances) there shall be inserted—

"Where the decision leading to the proposed dismissals is that of a person controlling the employer (directly or indirectly), a failure on the part of that person to provide information to the employer shall not constitute special circumstances rendering it not reasonably practicable for the employer to comply with any of those requirements.".

(5) For section 195 there shall be substituted—

"Construction of references to dismissal as redundant etc.

195.—(1) In this Chapter references to dismissal as redundant are references to dismissal for a reason not related to the individual concerned or for a number of reasons all of which are not so related.

(2) For the purposes of any proceedings under this Chapter, where an employee is or is proposed to be dismissed it shall be presumed, unless the contrary is proved, that he is or is proposed to be dismissed as redundant.".

(6) Section 283 of the 1992 Act (which excepts employment as a merchant seaman from the provisions of Chapter II of Part IV) shall cease to have effect.

GENERAL NOTE

This section amends the redundancy consultation procedures contained in ss.188 to 198 of the 1992 Act, whereby an employer is placed under a duty to consult with representatives of a recognised, independent trade union if he proposes to make redundant any employees in respect of whom the union is recognised by him, subject to a defence where there are special circumstances which make it not reasonably practicable for him to comply. The redundancy consultation provisions were first introduced in the Employment Protection Act 1975, to give effect to EEC Directive No. 75/129 on the Approximation of the Laws of the Member States Relating to Collective Redundancies. The original directive was amended in June 1992 by Directive No. 92/56, which aims, *inter alia*, to remove from an employer who fails to comply with the duty to consult any defence that he did not do so because the decision to make the redundancies was made by a controlling interest which did not provide him with the necessary information.

The amending directive is required to be implemented by June 1994, and it was therefore necessary for the Government to introduce legislation to comply with its provisions. However, even before the adoption of the amending directive by the Social Affairs Council in 1992 it had become increasingly clear that the provisions on redundancy consultation in the 1975 Act fell some way short of the requirements of Directive 75/129. The main grounds of objection were as follows: first, the 1975 Act only required consultation in workplaces where there is a recognised trade union, whereas the directive requires there to be "consultation with workers' representatives" and does not restrict the right to be consulted to the representatives of recognised trade unions; secondly, under the 1975 Act the obligation to consult arose where the employer was "proposing to dismiss" an employee as redundant, whereas the directive requires consultations to begin "where an employer is contemplating collective redundancies", which seems to refer to an earlier point in time; thirdly, the directive requires the employer to consult workers' representatives "with a view to reaching an agreement", a requirement which did not appear in the 1975 Act; fourthly, under the 1975 Act consultation was only required where the employee was dismissed for redundancy, as defined for the purposes of the unfair dismissal and redundancy payment provisions of the 1978 Act, whereas the directive defines redundancy for these purposes more widely, as a dismissal "for one or more reasons not related to the individual workers concerned"; fifthly, the sanctions under the 1975 Act were inadequate, particularly in view of the rule which required the tribunal to offset compensation awarded for a failure to consult against any payment of wages or pay in lieu of notice in respect of that period, which could wipe out the protective award altogether; and finally, the directive does not appear to make provision for a "special circumstances" defence.

In October 1992 the European Commission initiated infringement proceedings against the U.K. Government for its alleged failure fully to transpose the 1975 directive into domestic law. This section is intended to meet those objections, and also to implement the amendments to the 1975 directive adopted in June 1992. The detailed changes are explained below, but surprisingly the Government has not taken the opportunity provided by this Act to address all the criticisms of the European Commission, in particular the complaint that the domestic consultation provisions fail to provide for the situation where there is no recognised trade union at the workplace. Moreover, there is still great uncertainty over whether the domestic provisions require consultation to begin at a sufficiently early stage to satisfy the requirements of the directive (as explained above). That uncertainty was fuelled by the decision of the Divisional Court in *R.* v. *British Coal Corporation and Secretary of State for Trade and Industry, ex p. Vardy* [1993] IRLR 104, where Glidewell L.J. stated that "the difference between the wording of the Directive and the wording of s.188 of the 1992 Act is such that the section cannot be interpreted as having the same meaning as the Directive ... The verb 'proposes' in its ordinary usage relates to a state of mind which is much more certain and further along the decision-making process than the verb 'contemplate';" (p. 116). It is not yet established whether the collective redundancies directive has direct effect in the domestic courts (Glidewell L.J. expressed no final view on the matter), but in any event it could only have "vertical" direct effect against the state or an emanation thereof (*Foster* v. *British Gas* (No. C-188/89) [1991] 1 Q.B. 405, and Art. 1(1) provides that the directive shall not apply "to workers employed by public administrative bodies or by establishments governed by public law", which makes the question of direct effect of little practical relevance. However, in view of the fact that the domestic provisions were enacted to implement the directive, it is clearly arguable that they should be construed purposively so as to accord with the directive (*e.g.* by reading "proposing" as "contemplating") even if to do so would involve a strained interpretation of the ordinary literal meaning of the Act (see *Litster* v. *Forth Dry Dock and Engineering Co.* [1990] 1 A.C. 546, H.L.; *Marleasing S.A.* v. *La Comercial Internacional de Alimentacion S.A.* (C-106/89) [1992] 1 C.M.L.R. 305). The Government's failure to take the opportunity presented by this Act to address these issues means that the infringement proceedings initiated by the Commission seem likely to continue. Moreover, the possibility of a claim for compensation *against the State* by individual workers who suffer loss as a result of its failure properly to implement the directive cannot be ruled out (see *Francovich* v. *Italy* (Joined cases C-6/90 and C-9/90) [1992] IRLR 84).

The new provisions came into force on August 30, 1993, but do not have effect in relation to any dismissal which takes place within 90 days after that date (S.I. 1993 No. 1908, para. 3(12)).

Subs. (2)

This subsection makes three important changes to the provisions in s.188 of the 1992 Act. Paragraph (a) extends the information which must be provided by the employer to the trade union representatives to include details of the proposed method of calculating the amount of any extra-statutory redundancy payments to the affected employees. Paragraph (b) replaces the existing s.188(6), which required the employer in the course of consultations to consider and reply to any representations made by the trade union representatives, with a more specific provision (modelled on Arts. 2(1) and 2(2) of the directive) which imposes an obligation to consult, *inter alia*, about ways of avoiding, or at least reducing, the redundancies, and mitigating their consequences, and stipulates that the consultation must be undertaken "with a view to reaching agreement with the trade union representatives". This should not be taken to mean that the employer will be under a duty to reach a compromise agreement with union representatives in every case—the duty is one of consultation, not negotiation, and the E.C.J. has clearly held in *Dansk Metalarbejderforbund* v. *Neilsen (H.) & Son, Maskinfabrik A/S* (C-284/83) [1985] ECR 554 that the directive does not restrict the employer's right to decide when redundancies are necessary; however, it does seem to imply a duty on the part of the employer to act in good faith in seeking to reach an agreed solution. Finally, para. (c) amends the "special circumstances" defence in s.188(7), in line with Directive 92/56 (see the General Note), by providing that the defence will not apply where the employer's failure to consult arose because a person controlling the employer (whether directly or indirectly) did not provide the employer with information. Subsection (4) places the same limitation on the special circumstances defence in relation to the duty to notify the Secretary of State of collective redundancies under s.193 of the 1992 Act.

Subs. (3)

This subsection removes s.190(3) of the 1992 Act, which provided for the avoidance of double payments. In future the compensation which an industrial tribunal may award for the employer's failure to consult (referred to as the "protective award") may not be offset against any payment of wages or pay in lieu of notice by the employer in respect of the protected period, and vice versa. This simple amendment addresses the criticisms referred to in the General Note concerning the adequacy of the sanctions for a failure to consult, but only in a modest way. An opposition amendment which would have enabled a union to apply for an order from the High Court restraining a redundancy dismissal until the consultation procedures were properly carried out was rejected as unnecessary and disproportionate (Standing Committee F, January 26, 1993, col. 569). The parallel provision in the TUPE regulations is removed by s.33(7), above.

Subs. (4)

See the note to subs. (2), above.

Subs. (5)

As seen in the General Note, one of the criticisms levelled by the European Commission at the redundancy consultation provisions was that they were too limited in their scope, in that they adopted the 1978 Act definition of redundancy (which focuses on the availability of work) whereas Art. 1 of the directive defines redundancy for these purposes more widely, as a dismissal "for one or more reasons not related to the individual workers concerned". This subsection duly widens the definition of redundancy in s.195 of the 1992 Act to include any dismissal for one or more reasons not related to the individual concerned; as before, it will be presumed that the dismissal is for redundancy unless the contrary is proved. It is crucial to note that this wider definition applies *only* for the purposes of the statutory redundancy consultation provisions: the narrower definition still applies for the purposes of individual employment rights.

The precise scope of the new definition will need to be worked out by the courts, but it is likely that under the amended provisions the duty to consult will be held to arise where an employer, having failed to secure the agreement of employees to a change in their terms and conditions (*e.g.* as part of a reorganisation), proposes to dismiss the existing workforce and to re-engage them on the amended terms, as it could be argued in such a case that the reason for the dismissals was not related to the individuals concerned, so giving rise to a duty to consult before imposing the new contracts; against that, however, the employer might seek to argue that the reason for the dismissals was the failure of each individual employee to agree to the new terms, and that the dismissls *were* therefore for a reason related to the individuals concerned, an argument which, if accepted by the court, would prevent the duty to consult from arising.

Subs. (6)

This subsection extends the scope of the redundancy consultation provisions to merchant seamen.

PART III

OTHER EMPLOYMENT MATTERS

Abolition of right to statutory minimum remuneration

Repeal of Part II of Wages Act 1986

35. Part II of the Wages Act 1986 (which provides for statutory minimum remuneration for certain workers in accordance with wages orders made by wages councils) shall cease to have effect.

GENERAL NOTE

This section, the shortest in the Act, undoubtedly generated the greatest amount of political controversy during its passage through Parliament. It repeals Pt. II of the Wages Act 1986, thereby abolishing the remaining 26 Wages Councils and with them the system for the fixing of statutory minimum rates of pay for certain groups of workers. The only remaining vestige of the machinery for the fixing of minimum wages is the Agricultural Wages Board. The repeal took effect from August 30, 1993, and all wages orders ceased to have effect at that date. This means that employers in industries formerly covered by Wages Councils will no longer be obliged to pay the statutory minimum rates to new employees. However, the repeal does not affect the contractual entitlements of existing employees, who will continue to be entitled to be paid in accordance with their existing contracts of employment until those contracts are varied by agreement with the employer; any attempt by the employer to impose a unilateral reduction in pay on existing employees is likely to constitute a breach of contract in accordance with ordinary contractual principles. There are transitional provisions in Sched. 9, para. 5 which provide that the enforcement procedures in s.16 of the 1986 Act continue to have effect after August 30, 1993, in respect of underpayments occurring before that date, and so the failure by an employer to pay the statutory minimum rate before abolition could still be the subject of a claim and/or prosecution by the wages inspectorate. The provisions in ss.19 and 20 of the 1986 Act relating to the keeping of records by employers and enforcement by the wages inspectorate remain in force for six months after abolition.

The decision finally to abolish the Wages Council came as little surprise. The idea of attempting to impose minimum wage levels is at odds with the present Government's commitment to deregulation of the labour market and its preference for individual bargaining, added to which the Government has consistently maintained that Wages Councils maintained pay rates at unrealistically high levels thereby acting as a disincentive to job creation (see for example the 1988 Consultation Document, which leaned heavily towards abolition). Such claims are of course acutely controversial, but in view of the hostile political environment it is perhaps surprising that the Wages Councils survived for as long as they did.

Constitution and jurisdiction of tribunals

Constitution of industrial tribunals

36.—(1) Section 128 of the 1978 Act (industrial tribunals) shall be amended as follows.

(2) After subsection (2) there shall be inserted—

"(2A) Subject to the following provisions of this section, proceedings before an industrial tribunal shall be heard by—

    (a) the person who, in accordance with regulations made under subsection (1), is the chairman, and

    (b) two other members, or (with the consent of the parties) one other member, selected as the other members (or member) in accordance with regulations so made.

(2B) Subject to subsection (2F), the proceedings to which subsection (2C) applies shall be heard by the person specified in subsection (2A)(a) alone.

(2C) This subsection applies to—

19–84

(a) proceedings on an application under section 77, 78A or 79 of this Act or under section 161, 165 or 166 of the Trade Union and Labour Relations (Consolidation) Act 1992,

(b) proceedings on a complaint under section 124 of this Act or under section 5 of the Wages Act 1986,

(c) proceedings in respect of which an industrial tribunal has jurisdiction by virtue of an order under section 131,

(d) proceedings in which the parties have given their written consent to the proceedings being heard in accordance with subsection (2B) (whether or not they have subsequently withdrawn it),

(e) proceedings in which the person bringing the proceedings has given written notice withdrawing the case, and

(f) proceedings in which the person (or, where more than one, each of the persons) against whom the proceedings are brought does not, or has ceased to, contest the case.

(2D) The Secretary of State may by order amend the provisions of subsection (2C).

(2E) No order shall be made under subsection (2D) unless a draft of the order has been laid before Parliament and approved by a resolution of each House of Parliament.

(2F) Proceedings to which subsection (2C) applies shall be heard in accordance with subsection (2A) if a person who, in accordance with regulations made under subsection (1), may be the chairman of an industrial tribunal, having regard to—

(a) whether there is a likelihood of a dispute arising on the facts which makes it desirable for the proceedings to be heard in accordance with subsection (2A),

(b) whether there is a likelihood of an issue of law arising which would make it desirable for the proceedings to be heard in accordance with subsection (2B),

(c) any views of any of the parties as to whether or not the proceedings ought to be heard in accordance with either of those subsections, and

(d) whether there are other proceedings which might be heard concurrently but which are not proceedings to which subsection (2C) applies,

decides (at any stage of the proceedings) that the proceedings are to be heard in accordance with subsection (2A).".

(3) After subsection (4) there shall be inserted—

"(5) Regulations made under Schedule 9 may provide that in such circumstances as the regulations may specify any act required or authorised by the regulations to be done by an industrial tribunal may be done by the person specified in subsection (2A)(a) alone.

(6) Where a Minister of the Crown so directs in relation to any proceedings on grounds of national security, the proceedings shall be heard and determined, and any act required or authorised by regulations made under Schedule 9 to be done by an industrial tribunal in relation to the proceedings shall be done, by the President of Industrial Tribunals (England and Wales) appointed in accordance with regulations made under subsection (1), or the President of Industrial Tribunals (Scotland) so appointed, alone.".

GENERAL NOTE

Industrial tribunals normally consist of a legally qualified chairman and two lay members, one drawn from a panel of employers' representatives and the other from a panel of employees' representatives. As full members of the tribunal the side members are entitled to participate fully in the hearing of a case, using their knowledge or experience of industrial relations to help the tribunal in reaching a sensible and practicable decision (which may be by a majority). This section, which amends s.128 of the 1978 Act, provides for the chairman of an industrial tribunal to sit alone (*i.e.* without any side members) in any of the following cases (as set out in new subs. (2C)), *viz.:*

(a) applications for interim relief in health and safety cases (see the note to s.28, above) and dismissals for trade union reasons;

(b) claims against the Secretary of State for payments on insolvency, and claims under the Wages Act 1986;

(c) claims of breach of contract brought by virtue of a s.131 order (see the note to s.38, below);

(d) where the parties have given their written consent to the chairman sitting alone;

(e) where the applicant has given written notice withdrawing the complaint;

(f) where the respondent is not contesting the case.

Any such proceedings are to be heard by the chairman alone, unless the chairman decides (at any stage of the proceedings) to hear the case in accordance with the normal procedures (see new subs. (2F)); in so deciding, the chairman must have regard to: the likelihood of a dispute arising on the facts (which might make it desirable for the proceedings to be heard by a full tribunal); the likelihood of an issue of law arising (which might make it desirable for the proceedings to be heard by the chairman alone); the views of the parties; and whether there are other proceedings which might be heard concurrently but which would have to be heard by a full tribunal. Section 37 similarly amends the constitution of the E.A.T. to allow a judge to sit alone on any appeal from a decision of an industrial tribunal reached by the chairman sitting alone.

One does not have to look very far to find an explanation for the introduction of these new procedures. The number of applications to industrial tribunals has risen significantly in recent years, fuelled in part by a sharp increase in the number of complaints under the Wages Act 1986. In 1990–91 there were a total of 35,826 tribunal applications, as against 31,913 in 1989–90, an increase of some 12.3 per cent. ([1991] Employment Gazette 681; the figures for 1991–92 were not available at the time of writing). Of these, 6,238 (or 17.4 per cent.) were applications under the Wages Act, compared with only 522 such complaints in 1987–88. There was also a significant rise in the number of complaints concerning redundancy payments (to 5,022, an increase of 31 per cent. over 1989–90), as might be expected during a recession. One predictable consequence of this increased work-load has been a substantial increase in waiting times for tribunal hearings. In 1990–91, only 39 per cent. of industrial tribunal applications in England and Wales reached a first hearing within 12 weeks of the original application, some 20 per cent. short of the target figure set by the Department of Employment; the provisional figure for the first half of 1991–92 was under 24 per cent. and in five of the 11 tribunal regions in England and Wales it fell below 15 per cent. (House of Commons debate, October 17, 1991, col. 222). It seems inevitable that the extension of tribunal jurisdiction to hear breach of contract claims (see the note to s.38, below) will lead to a further increase in the work-load of tribunals. In the past the Government has addressed the problem of delay in the industrial tribunal system by allocating extra funding, thereby enabling greater use to be made of part-time chairmen. On this occasion the Government has taken a different approach, altering the constitution of industrial tribunals by removing the side members from certain types of case. However, most cases will still be heard by a full tribunal, and the Government has emphasised that even in those cases where the tribunal chair may sit alone, he or she retains the discretion to decide that in the circumstances the case should be heard by a full tribunal. The Secretary of State may add to (or reduce, although this seems unlikely) the list of cases by regulations, using the affirmative resolution procedure (new subss. (2D) and (2E)).

Whether the desire to reduce delay is a sufficient reason for doing away with the "industrial jury", even in a limited range of cases, is of course a matter of acute controversy. It should be noted, however, that there is a long standing (albeit very narrow) precedent for dispensing with the side members of a tribunal, in that under the existing law (as set out in the Industrial Tribunals (England and Wales) Regulations 1965 (S.I. 1975 No. 1101), reg. 5(1A), as amended by S.I. 1967 No. 301 and S.I. 1977 No. 1473), a chairman may sit alone to make an order:

(a) dismissing the proceedings where the applicant has given written notice of the abandonment of his application;

(b) allowing an appeal against an assessment to industrial training levy under the Industrial Training Act 1982 where the Industrial Training Board has given written notice that the appeal is not contested;

(c) deciding an application in accordance with the written agreement of the parties;

(d) dealing with any interlocutory matter or application;

(e) making a costs order in connection with any of the above.

An industrial tribunal may also dispense with *one* of the side members with the consent of the parties (reg. 5(1); this is now stated expressly in new subs. (2A)).

Constitution of Employment Appeal Tribunal

37. In Schedule 11 to the 1978 Act (Employment Appeal Tribunal), for paragraph 16 (Appeal Tribunal to consist of judge and two or four other members or, if parties consent, judge and one other member) there shall be substituted—
"16.—(1) Subject to sub-paragraphs (2) to (4), proceedings before the Appeal Tribunal shall be heard by a judge and either two or four appointed members, so that in either case there is an equal number of persons whose knowledge or experience of industrial relations is as representatives of employers and whose knowledge or experience of industrial relations is as representatives of workers.
(2) With the consent of the parties proceedings before the Appeal Tribunal may be heard by a judge and one appointed member or by a judge and three appointed members.
(3) Proceedings on an appeal on a question arising from any decision of, or arising in any proceedings before, an industrial tribunal consisting of the person specified in section 128(2A)(a) alone shall be heard by a judge alone unless a judge directs that the proceedings shall be heard in accordance with sub-paragraphs (1) and (2).
(4) Where a Minister of the Crown so directs in relation to any proceedings on grounds of national security, the proceedings shall be heard by the President of the Appeal Tribunal alone.".

GENERAL NOTE

This section amends the constitution of the E.A.T. to allow a judge to sit alone on any appeal from a decision of an industrial tribunal (or on a question arising in proceedings before an industrial tribunal) where the tribunal chairman heard the case alone in accordance with the measures introduced by s.36 above. Hitherto the only circumstances where a case could be dealt with otherwise than by a full division of the E.A.T. (consisting of a judge and either two or four appointed members) was where the parties consented to it being heard by a judge and one side member, or in the case of interlocutory applications, which may be disposed of by the Registrar or referred by him to the President or a judge, who may dispose of it himself, refer it to a full division of the E.A.T., or refer it back to the Registrar with directions (Employment Appeal Tribunal Rules 1980 (S.I. 1980 No. 2035), r.16(2)); where an interlocutory application is disposed of by the Registrar there is a right of appeal to a judge, who may determine the appeal himself or refer it to a full division of the E.A.T. (*ibid.*, r.17(1)).

The reasons for this change are the same as those noted above in the context of industrial tribunals (see the note to s.36). In June 1992, the Employment Minister reported that the average time taken for a case to reach a hearing by the E.A.T. was two years in England and Wales and four months in Scotland (House of Commons debate, June 18, 1992, col. 137). Additional judge time has frequently been allocated in the past to address the problem of delays before the E.A.T., but the Government has now turned to other solutions to that problem. As with industrial tribunals, the side members of the E.A.T. are appointed on the basis of their special knowledge or experience of industrial relations, either as representatives of employers or as representatives of workers, and the decision may be by a majority. While the rationale for having side members in industrial tribunals is self-evident, their rôle in the E.A.T. has occasioned greater debate, especially in view of the fact that appeals lie to the E.A.T. only on points of law (the only exception being an appeal from a decision of the Certification Officer on the independence of a trade union under the 1992 Act, s.9, which may be on law or fact). The scope of the right of appeal has been further circumscribed by a number of factors; first, the tendency of the Court of Appeal to classify many issues as pure questions of fact for the industrial tribunal to decide (one blatant example is the characterisation of the question of what constitutes "other industrial action" under the 1992 Act, ss.237 and 238 as a question of fact: see *Coates* v. *Modern Methods and Materials* [1983] Q.B. 192, C.A., and the comments of Browne-Wilkinson J. in *Naylor* v. *Orton & Smith* [1983] I.C.R. 665); secondly, the confinement of the scope of errors of law to *ex facie* errors of law, cases where there is no evidence to support a finding of fact, and decisions which are perverse (*British Telecommunications* v. *Sheridan* [1990] IRLR 27 C.A., disapproving a third category, *i.e.* where the tribunal misunderstood or misapplied the facts); and thirdly, the narrow approach to perversity taken by the Court of Appeal in *Neale* v. *Hereford and Worcester County Council* [1986] I.C.R. 471 and *Piggott Brothers* v. *Jackson* [1992] I.C.R. 85. The narrowness of the right of appeal inevitably raises questions as to the appropriateness of involving non-lawyers in the appellate process at all. However, Wood P. has recently reaffirmed the important contribution made by the lay members of the E.A.T., in particular their ability to bring their industrial experience and practice to bear in applying the perversity test (*East Berkshire Health Authority* v. *Matadeen* [1992] I.C.R. 723). On the rôle of the side members generally, see also Browne-Wilkinson [1982] *The rôle of the E.A.T. in the 1980s* 11 I.L.J. 69; Waite [1986] *Lawyers and laymen as judges in industry* 15 I.L.J. 32.

Extension of power to confer on industrial tribunals jurisdiction in respect of contracts of employment etc.

38. In section 131 of the 1978 Act (power to confer on industrial tribunals jurisdiction in respect of claims for damages for breach of contract of employment and similar claims)—

    (a) for subsection (1) (appropriate Minister to have power to make order in respect of claims satisfying certain conditions) there shall be substituted—

        "(1) The appropriate Minister may by order provide that proceedings in respect of—

        (a) any claim to which this section applies, or

        (b) any such claim of a description specified in the order,

        may, subject to such exceptions (if any) as may be specified in the order, be brought before an industrial tribunal.",

    (b) for subsection (3) there shall be substituted—

        "(3) This section does not apply to a claim for damages, or for a sum due, in respect of personal injuries.",

    (c) after subsection (4) (tribunal to order payment of amount which it finds due) there shall be inserted—

        "(4A) An order under this section may provide that an industrial tribunal shall not in proceedings in respect of a claim, or a number of claims relating to the same contract, order the payment of an amount exceeding such sum as may be specified in the order as the maximum amount which a tribunal may order to be paid in relation to a claim or in relation to a contract.",

    (d) after subsection (5) there shall be inserted—

        "(5A) An order under this section may make different provision in relation to proceedings in respect of different descriptions of claims.", and

    (e) in subsection (7), in the definition of "appropriate Minister", for the words "Secretary of State" there shall be substituted the words "Lord Advocate".

GENERAL NOTE

    This section amends s.131 of the 1978 Act, which empowers the Lord Chancellor (or the Lord Advocate in Scotland) to make an order extending the jurisdiction of the industrial tribunals to cover claims for damages or any other sums due in respect of breach of a contract of employment. The Government first announced its intention of issuing a s.131 order in 1991, but subsequently decided that the existing powers were inadequate because they were restricted to contractual claims which arose or were outstanding on the termination of employment or where there was some other related tribunal complaint. Changes to the primary legislation were therefore needed in order to achieve the desired objective. This section makes the necessary changes, amending s.131 so as to enable an order to be made allowing contractual claims to be brought before an industrial tribunal in a much wider range of matters. Indeed, under the amended provisions the only type of claim over which a s.131 order may not confer jurisdiction is a claim for damages or for a sum due in respect of personal injuries. The order may however be subject to exceptions, and may make different provision in respect of different types of claim; it may also set an upper limit on the amount which a tribunal may order in respect of a claim or a number of claims relating to the same contract. The Government has indicated its intention to set the limit at the current maximum compensatory award for unfair dismissal (£11,000 at the time of writing).

The new provisions came into force on August 30, 1993, and a draft s.131 order was widely anticipated at the time of writing.

Agreements not to take proceedings before industrial tribunal

39.—(1) In section 140 of the 1978 Act (restrictions on contracting out)—
   (a) in subsection (2) (exceptions), after the paragraph (fa) inserted by paragraph 21 of Schedule 8 to this Act, there shall be inserted—
      "(fb) to any agreement to refrain from instituting or continuing any proceedings specified in section 133(1) (except (c)) or 134(1) before an industrial tribunal if the conditions regulating compromise agreements under this Act are satisfied in relation to the agreement."; .
   (b) after subsection (2), there shall be inserted—
      "(3) The conditions regulating compromise agreements under this Act are that—
      (a) the agreement must be in writing;
      (b) the agreement must relate to the particular complaint;
      (c) the employee must have received independent legal advice from a qualified lawyer as to the terms and effect of the proposed agreement and in particular its effect on his ability to pursue his rights before an industrial tribunal;
      (d) there must be in force, when the adviser gives the advice, a policy of insurance covering the risk of a claim by the employee in respect of loss arising in consequence of the advice;
      (e) the agreement must identify the adviser; and
      (f) the agreement must state that the conditions regulating compromise agreements under this Act are satisfied.
      (4) In subsection (3)—
         "independent", in relation to legal advice to the employee, means that it is given by a lawyer who is not acting in the matter for the employer or an associated employer; and
         "qualified lawyer" means—
      (a) as respects proceedings in England and Wales—
            (i) a barrister, whether in practice as such or employed to give legal advice, or
            (ii) a solicitor of the Supreme Court who holds a practising certificate;
      (b) as respects proceedings in Scotland—
            (i) an advocate, whether in practice as such or employed to give legal advice, or
            (ii) a solicitor who holds a practising certificate.".

(2) Schedule 6 to this Act shall have effect for making corresponding amendments in the Sex Discrimination Act 1975, the Race Relations Act 1976, the Wages Act 1986 and the Trade Union and Labour Relations (Consolidation) Act 1992.

GENERAL NOTE

This section makes an important change to the provisions restricting contracting out of the employment protection legislation by providing that an agreement to settle proceedings will be binding if it constitutes a valid "compromise agreement" (or "compromise contract" in the case of the anti-discrimination legislation), the principal requirements of which are that it must be in writing, and the employee must have received independent legal advice from a qualified lawyer as to the terms and effect of the proposed agreement and its effect on his ability to pursue his statutory rights before a tribunal. Hitherto an agreement to settle proceedings was only valid if reached with the involvement of an ACAS conciliation officer, an important safeguard designed to ensure "that both sides are adequately informed, and fully understand the range of options open to them and the consequences of the different decisions they may take". (*Individual Employment Rights—ACAS Conciliation between Individuals and Employers*, ACAS, p.7). The courts have tended to give ACAS a wide discretion in such cases. In *Duport Furniture Products* v. *Moore* [1982] I.C.R. 84, the House of Lords held that it was not necessary for a conciliation officer to investigate the fairness of a settlement already worked out between the parties or to give the applicant further advice in order for the agreement to be binding. However, as seen above, ACAS' stated policy has been to seek to ensure that the parties make decisions on a properly informed basis, and this caused serious problems for ACAS during the 1980s as there was a sharp rise in the number of cases being referred to them where no formal complaint had been made to an industrial tribunal (non-IT1 cases), and where ACAS was in effect being asked to rubber stamp an agreement which had already been reached. The relevant statutory provisions state that a settlement will only be binding where a conciliation officer has "taken action" under his statutory duties (see, *e.g.* the 1978 Act, s.140(2)(d) and (e)), and following legal advice ACAS adopted a new policy in July 1990 of only exceptionally dealing with non-IT1 cases and refusing to rubber stamp agreements reached independently unless the terms of the agreement were capable of being changed as a result of the intervention of the conciliation officer (ACAS Annual Report 1991, p.45). As a result, the number of non-IT1 cases received by ACAS fell from 17,724 (or 36 per cent. of the total caseload) in 1989, to only 2,431 (three per cent. of the total) in 1992. One important consequence of the adoption of this more restrictive policy was that there was no longer any mechanism whereby a settlement freely reached between the parties but without the assistance of an ACAS conciliator could be given legal force, and this led to the risk of IT1 applications being made simply in order to ensure that such a settlement might become binding. The procedure introduced by this section (which came into force on August 30, 1993) allows the parties to reach a binding "compromise agreement" without ACAS involvement, and is intended to reduce the pressure on the tribunal system by avoiding unnecessary applications. However, to be effective a compromise agreement must satisfy a number of detailed requirements as set out in new s.140(3), and the possibility of an agreement being ruled invalid for some technical defect must be a very real one. Two issues in particular are worthy of note: first, it is unclear whether a compromise agreement may cover more than one complaint, as subs. (3)(b) states that "the agreement must relate to the particular complaint"; and secondly, the requirement that there must be in force a "policy of insurance" covering the risk of a claim by the employee against the legal adviser may be a potential stumbling-block, particularly as it is unclear whether the Solicitors' Indemnity Fund constitutes a "policy of insurance".

Subs. (1)

This amends s.140(2) of the 1978 Act so that an agreement to refrain from instituting or continuing certain specified tribunal proceedings under that Act will be enforceable provided it fulfils all the requirements of a valid compromise agreement as set out in new s.140(3). Those requirements are as follows:

(i) the agreement must be in writing;

(ii) the agreement must relate to the particular complaint, so that a blanket agreement which purports to cover any statutory complaint which the individual might bring will not be valid; if an agreement is intended to cover more than one type of complaint, it must spell out each complaint to which it is intended to apply (see also (vi) below);

(iii) the individual must have received independent legal advice from a qualified lawyer, *i.e.* a barrister (or, in Scotland, an advocate) who is in practice as such or is employed to give legal advice, or a solicitor holding a practising certificate. Advice will be "independent" for these purposes if it is given by a lawyer "who is not acting *in the matter* for the employer or an associated employer" (new s.140(4), italics supplied), which seems to imply that the lawyer may be acting or have acted for the employer in some *other* capacity; curiously, while the amendment in Sched. 6 to the Wages Act 1986 follows the wording of the 1978 Act, the amendments to the parallel provisions in the Sex Discrimination Act 1975, Race Relations Act 1976 and the 1992 Act simply require that the lawyer "is not acting for the other party or for a person who is connected with that other party", which seems to rule out the possibility of the lawyer acting for the other party in any capacity; *quaere* whether the different wording is intended to imply that a greater degree of independence is required in such cases;

(iv) the legal advice must cover the terms and effect of the proposed agreement and in particular its effect on the individual's ability to pursue his rights before an industrial tribunal;

(v) there must be a policy of insurance in force at the time when the advice is given covering the risk of a claim (*e.g.* of professional negligence) by the individual in respect of loss arising in consequence of the advice (on the significance of this requirement for a solicitor covered by the Solicitors' Indemnity Fund, see above);

(vi) the agreement must identify the adviser, and must state that the conditions regulating compromise agreements under the Act are satisfied; where a single compromise agreement is intended to cover claims under more than one statute, it seems that the agreement must expressly state that the requirements of each of those Acts are satisfied; this is because the relevant provisions all require a compromise agreement to state that "the conditions regulating compromise agreements *under this Act* are satisfied" [italics supplied]. This is presumably designed to avoid the type of confusion which arose in *Livingstone* v. *Hepworth Refractories* [1992] I.C.R. 287, where the E.A.T. held that a conciliated settlement "in full and final settlement of all claims" reached under the 1978 Act was not binding in respect of a subsequent claim of unlawful sex discrimination.

Where these requirements are satisfied, new s.140(2)(fb) of the 1978 Act provides that a compromise agreement may preclude an individual from instituting or continuing proceedings in relation to any of the following matters: itemised pay statements, guarantee payments, medical suspension pay, the new right not to suffer a detriment in health and safety cases (see s.28, above), time off for public duties, time off to look for work or training while under notice of redundancy, time off for antenatal care, written statement of reasons for dismissal, the new right to alternative work and to pay on maternity suspension (see s.25, above), complaints of unlawful deductions from pay under the Wages Act 1986, and unfair dismissal.

Subs. (2)

This gives effect to Sched. 6, which makes corresponding provision in respect of tribunal complaints relating to sex discrimination and equal pay, race discrimination, deductions from pay and the rights of trade union members.

Restriction of publicity in cases involving sexual misconduct: industrial tribunals

40.—(1) Schedule 9 to the 1978 Act (regulations for industrial tribunals) shall be amended by the insertion in paragraph 1 of the following.

(2) After sub-paragraph (5) there shall be inserted—

"(5A) The regulations may include provision—

(a) for cases involving allegations of the commission of sexual offences, for securing that the registration or other making available of documents or decisions shall be so effected as to prevent the identification of any person affected by or making the allegation;

(b) for cases involving allegations of sexual misconduct, enabling an industrial tribunal, on the application of any party to proceedings before it or of its own motion, to make a restricted reporting order having effect (if not revoked earlier) until the promulgation of the decision of the tribunal.

In this sub-paragraph—

"identifying matter", in relation to a person, means any matter likely to lead members of the public to identify him as a person affected by, or as the person making, the allegation;

"restricted reporting order" means an order prohibiting the publication in Great Britain of identifying matter in a written publication available to the public or its inclusion in a relevant programme for reception in Great Britain;

"sexual misconduct" means the commission of a sexual offence, sexual harassment or other adverse conduct (of whatever nature) related to sex, and conduct is related to sex whether the relationship with sex lies in the character of the conduct or in its having reference to the sex or sexual orientation of the person at whom the conduct is directed;

"sexual offence" means any offence to which section 141A(2) of the Criminal Procedure (Scotland) Act 1975, section 4 of the Sexual Offences (Amendment) Act 1976 or the Sexual Offences (Amendment) Act 1992 applies (offences under

the Sexual Offences Act 1956, the Sexual Offences (Scotland) Act 1976 and certain other enactments);
and "written publication" and "relevant programme" have the same meaning as in that Act of 1992.".

(3) In sub-paragraph (6), after the word "send" there shall be inserted the words "(subject to any regulations under sub-paragraph (5A)(a))".

(4) After sub-paragraph (7) there shall be inserted—

"(8) If any identifying matter is published or included in a relevant programme in contravention of a restricted reporting order the following persons shall be guilty of an offence and liable on summary conviction to a fine not exceeding level 5 on the standard scale—

(a) in the case of publication in a newspaper or periodical, any proprietor, any editor and any publisher of the newspaper or periodical;

(b) in the case of publication in any other form, the person publishing the matter; and

(c) in the case of matter included in a relevant programme—

(i) any body corporate engaged in providing the service in which the programme is included; and

(ii) any person having functions in relation to the programme corresponding to those of an editor of a newspaper.

Expressions used in this sub-paragraph and in sub-paragraph (5A) have the same meaning in this sub-paragraph as in that sub-paragraph.

(9) Where a person is charged with an offence under sub-paragraph (8) it shall be a defence to prove that at the time of the alleged offence he was not aware, and neither suspected nor had reason to suspect, that the publication or programme in question was of, or (as the case may be) included, the matter in question.

(10) Where an offence under sub-paragraph (8) committed by a body corporate is proved to have been committed with the consent or connivance of, or to be attributable to any neglect on the part of—

(a) a director, manager, secretary or other similar officer of the body corporate, or

(b) a person purporting to act in any such capacity,

he as well as the body corporate shall be guilty of the offence and liable to be proceeded against and punished accordingly.

(11) In relation to a body corporate whose affairs are managed by its members "director", in sub-paragraph (10), means a member of the body corporate.".

GENERAL NOTE

This section introduces important new restrictions on the reporting of cases involving sexual misconduct in industrial tribunals, following concerns that people wishing to bring complaints of such conduct might be deterred from doing so by the prospect of being subjected to high profile, intrusive media coverage like that seen in certain recent cases involving allegations of sexual harassment. The section amends Sched. 9 to the 1978 Act (regulations for industrial tribunals) thereby allowing for the amendment of the Industrial Tribunals (Rules of Procedure) Regulations to give the tribunal a discretion to make a "restricted reporting order" prohibiting the publication in cases involving allegations of "sexual misconduct" of anything which would be likely to identify the person making the allegation or a person affected by the allegation. However, such an order will only remain in force until the tribunal has issued its decision, so that once a case has finished there will be no restriction on the disclosure of those involved (although there are special rules preserving anonymity in cases involving allegations of the commission of a sexual offence; see below). The assumption appears to be that the media will have lost interest in reporting a case involving sexual misconduct once it has finished, but this may be overly optimistic. Contravention of the order will be a criminal offence triable summarily and punishable by a fine of up to £5,000 (at current rates). The offence may be committed, in the case of publication in a newspaper or periodical, by the proprietor, editor and publisher of that newspaper or periodical; in the case of publication in any other form, by the person publishing the material;

and in the case of material broadcast in a relevant programme, by the broadcasting company, the editor of the programme and, where an offence by the broadcasting company is committed with the consent or connivance of or through the neglect of a director, manager, secretary or other similar officer of that company, by that person. It will be a defence for a person charged with the offence to show that he was not aware, and neither suspected nor had reason to suspect, that the publication or programme in question included the restricted material, but it seems that ignorance of the restricted reporting order will not be a defence.

The section also provides for the amendment of the industrial tribunal rules to prevent the identification of any person who alleges the commission of a sexual offence or is affected by such an allegation in any document or decision made available to the public by the tribunal. This is necessary to enable tribunals to avoid infringing the provisions of the Sexual Offences (Amendment) Act 1992, which makes it a criminal offence to disclose the identity of the victim of a sexual offence during that person's lifetime without written consent; however, the section appears to go further than is strictly necessary in order to comply with that legislation, in that it allows for the protection of the identity of any person "affected by" such an allegation, which presumably would include the alleged perpetrator.

There are parallel provisions in s.41 concerning the E.A.T., but the powers of the E.A.T. to make a restricted reporting order are very limited.

Sexual misconduct. This is defined as the commission of a sexual offence, sexual harassment or other adverse conduct related to sex, including conduct which relates to the sex or sexual orientation of the person at whom it is directed; it would therefore cover a case where an employee claims to have been dismissed because of his or her sexual orientation.

Restricted reporting order. This is an order prohibiting the publication in Great Britain, in a "written publication" or a "relevant programme", of anything likely to lead to the identification of the person making the allegation or a person affected by the allegation. The making of such an order is entirely at the discretion of the tribunal, and it only remains in force until the tribunal promulgates its decision, unless it is revoked earlier. It should be noted that the order does not prohibit all reporting of the case—it merely prevents the publication in the media of anything which might identify anyone involved in the allegations.

Written publication. This is defined for present purposes in the Sexual Offences (Amendment) Act 1992, s.6, as including "a film, a sound-track and any other record in permanent form", but excluding any document prepared for use in particular legal proceedings.

Relevant programme. This means a programme included in a programme service, within the meaning of the Broadcasting Act 1990: Sexual Offences (Amendment) Act 1992, s.6.

Restriction of publicity in cases involving sexual misconduct: Employment Appeal Tribunal

41.—(1) Schedule 11 to the 1978 Act (Employment Appeal Tribunal) shall be amended by the insertion after paragraph 18 (rules) of the following—
  "**18A.**—(1) Without prejudice to the generality of paragraph 17 the rules may, as respects proceedings to which this paragraph applies, include provision—
  (a) for cases involving allegations of the commission of sexual offences, for securing that the registration or other making available of documents or decisions shall be so effected as to prevent the identification of any person affected by or making the allegation; and
  (b) for cases involving allegations of sexual misconduct, enabling the Appeal Tribunal, on the application of any party to the proceedings before it or of its own motion, to make a restricted reporting order having effect (if not revoked earlier) until the promulgation of the decision of the Appeal Tribunal.
  (2) This paragraph applies to—
  (a) proceedings on an appeal against a decision of an industrial tribunal to make, or not to make, a restricted reporting order; and
  (b) proceedings on an appeal against any interlocutory decision of an industrial tribunal in proceedings in which the industrial tribunal has made a restricted reporting order which it has not revoked.
  (3) If any identifying matter is published or included in a relevant programme in contravention of a restricted reporting order the fol-

lowing persons shall be guilty of an offence and liable on summary conviction to a fine not exceeding level 5 on the standard scale—

    (a) in the case of publication in a newspaper or periodical, any proprietor, any editor and any publisher of the newspaper or periodical;

    (b) in the case of publication in any other form, the person publishing the matter; and

    (c) in the case of matter included in a relevant programme—

        (i) any body corporate engaged in providing the service in which the programme is included; and

        (ii) any person having functions in relation to the programme corresponding to those of an editor of a newspaper.

(4) Where a person is charged with an offence under sub-paragraph (3) it shall be a defence to prove that at the time of the alleged offence he was not aware, and neither suspected nor had reason to suspect, that the publication or programme in question was of, or (as the case may be) included, the matter in question.

(5) Where an offence under sub-paragraph (3) committed by a body corporate is proved to have been committed with the consent or connivance of, or to be attributable to any neglect on the part of—

    (a) a director, manager, secretary or other similar officer of the body corporate, or

    (b) a person purporting to act in any such capacity,

he as well as the body corporate shall be guilty of the offence and liable to be proceeded against and punished accordingly.

(6) In relation to a body corporate whose affairs are managed by its members "director", in sub-paragraph (5), means a member of the body corporate.

(7) In this paragraph—

    "identifying matter", in relation to a person, means any matter likely to lead members of the public to identify him as a person affected by, or as the person making, the allegation;

    "restricted reporting order" means an order prohibiting the publication in Great Britain of identifying matter in a written publication available to the public or its inclusion in a relevant programme for reception in Great Britain;

    "sexual misconduct" means the commission of a sexual offence, sexual harassment or other adverse conduct (of whatever nature) related to sex, and conduct is related to sex whether the relationship with sex lies in the character of the conduct or in its having reference to the sex or sexual orientation of the person at whom the conduct is directed;

    "sexual offence" means any offence to which section 141A(2) of the Criminal Procedure (Scotland) Act 1975, section 4 of the Sexual Offences (Amendment) Act 1976 or the Sexual Offences (Amendment) Act 1992 applies (offences under the Sexual Offences Act 1956, the Sexual Offences (Scotland) Act 1976 and certain other enactments);

and "written publication" and "relevant programme" have the same meaning as in that Act of 1992.".

<small>GENERAL NOTE</small>

This section allows for the amendment of the E.A.T. Rules to enable it to make a restricted reporting order in the same way and to the same effect as an industrial tribunal, but only in very limited circumstances. Such an order may only be made in proceedings on an appeal against a decision of an industrial tribunal to make or not to make a restricted reporting order, or on an appeal against an interlocutory decision of an industrial tribunal in a case in which the tribunal made a restricted reporting order which has not yet been revoked. Other than in these two situations, the E.A.T. will not be able to make a restricted reporting order on an ordinary appeal from an industrial tribunal, even where the tribunal proceedings were subject to such an order. The thinking behind this is presumably that since the order made by the industrial tribunal would have lapsed once the tribunal issued its decision, the imposition of a further order on appeal would serve no purpose, as the identities of those involved might already have been disclosed; furthermore, it could be argued that those involved in appeals on a point of law to the E.A.T. are less likely to be subjected to sensational media coverage than are those appearing before an industrial tribunal. Whether or not the new powers of the E.A.T. are adequate to achieve the desired objective remains to be seen. As in the case of the industrial tribunal, a restricted reporting order made by the E.A.T. will lapse once the Appeal Tribunal promulgates its decision, unless revoked earlier. Penalties for non-compliance are as in s.40 (see the note to that section). The section also allows the E.A.T. Rules (Sched. 11 to the 1978 Act) to be amended to prevent the identification of anyone making or affected by allegations of a sexual offence in any document or decision made available to the public by the E.A.T. This echoes the similar provision in s.40.

Restriction of vexatious proceedings

42. After section 136 of the 1978 Act there shall be inserted—

> ## "Restriction of vexatious proceedings
>
> 136A.—(1) If, on an application made by the Attorney General or the Lord Advocate under this section, the Appeal Tribunal is satisfied that any person has habitually and persistently and without any reasonable ground—
>
> (a) instituted vexatious proceedings, whether in an industrial tribunal or before the Appeal Tribunal, and whether against the same person or against different persons; or
>
> (b) made vexatious applications in any proceedings, whether in an industrial tribunal or before the Appeal Tribunal,
>
> the Appeal Tribunal may, after hearing that person or giving him an opportunity of being heard, make a restriction of proceedings order.
>
> (2) A "restriction of proceedings order" is an order that—
>
> (a) no proceedings shall without the leave of the Appeal Tribunal be instituted in any industrial tribunal or before the Appeal Tribunal by the person against whom the order is made;
>
> (b) any proceedings instituted by him in any industrial tribunal or before the Appeal Tribunal before the making of the order shall not be continued by him without the leave of the Appeal Tribunal; and
>
> (c) no application (other than one for leave under this section) shall be made by him in any proceedings in any industrial tribunal or in the Appeal Tribunal without the leave of the Appeal Tribunal.
>
> (3) A restriction of proceedings order may provide that it is to cease to have effect at the end of a specified period, but shall otherwise remain in force indefinitely.
>
> (4) Leave for the institution or continuance of, or for the making of an application in, any proceedings in an industrial tribunal or before the Appeal Tribunal by a person who is the subject of a restricted proceedings order shall not be given unless the Appeal Tribunal is satisfied that the proceedings or application are not an abuse of the process of the tribunal in question and that there are reasonable grounds for the proceedings or application.
>
> (5) No appeal shall lie from a decision of the Appeal Tribunal refusing leave for the institution or continuance of, or for the making of an application in, proceedings by a person who is the subject of a restriction of proceedings order.
>
> (6) A copy of a restriction of proceedings order shall be published in the London Gazette and in the Edinburgh Gazette.".

GENERAL NOTE

This section, added at Report stage in the House of Lords, empowers the E.A.T. (on the application of the Attorney General or, in Scotland, the Lord Advocate) to make a "restriction of proceedings order" against a vexatious litigant, *i.e.* a person who has habitually and persistently and without any reasonable ground instituted vexatious proceedings or made vexatious applications to an industrial tribunal or to the E.A.T. The provisions follow closely the measures in the Supreme Court Act 1981, s.42, which empower the High Court to make a civil proceedings order restricting vexatious legal proceedings in the High Court or in any inferior court. The effect of a restriction of proceedings order (which remains in force indefinitely unless subject to an express time limitation) is that the person against whom it is made may not institute or continue proceedings or make any application in an industrial tribunal or before the E.A.T. without first seeking the leave of the E.A.T., which will only be given if the E.A.T. is satisfied that the proceedings or application are not an abuse of the process of the tribunal in question and that there are reasonable grounds for them. Before making such an order the E.A.T. must give the individual concerned an opportunity to be heard, and that person may appeal against the making of the order in the usual way under s.136(4) of the 1978 Act. There is however no appeal from a decision of the E.A.T. to refuse leave under a restriction of proceedings order. A copy of the restriction of proceedings order will be published in the London Gazette and the Edinburgh Gazette.

This is the latest in a series of measures designed to discourage unmeritorious and ill-founded applications to industrial tribunals. A tribunal has the power to strike out or amend any originating application or notice of proceedings on the grounds that it is "scandalous, frivolous or vexatious" (Industrial Tribunals (Rules of Procedure) Regulations 1985 (S.I. 1985 No. 16), r. 12(2)(e)), and tribunals have had the power since 1974 to make a costs order where a party in bringing or conducting proceedings has "acted frivolously or vexatiously"; that rule was widened in 1980 to cover cases where a party has acted "otherwise unreasonably" (*ibid.*, r. 11), and at the same time the pre-hearing assessment (PHA) was introduced (*ibid.*, r. 6). The PHA is a preliminary review of the case by a full tribunal, on the application of either of the parties or of its own accord. If, on a PHA, the tribunal considers that one of the parties has no reasonable prospect of success it may warn that party that costs may be awarded against him under r. 11 if he continues with the case (a "costs warning"). Awards of costs following a PHA are rare; in 1990–91, 381 PHAs were ordered (slightly more than 1 per cent. of the total number of cases disposed of), and 167 costs warnings were made. Over 83 per cent. of those who received a costs warning settled or withdrew their applications, and of the 21 who proceeded to a full hearing, 18 lost their cases, of whom seven subsequently had costs orders made against them. In all, costs were awarded in 175 cases, or less than 0.5 per cent. of all the cases disposed of ([1991] Employment Gazette 681; the figures for 1991–92 were not available at the time of writing). The Government considered the PHA procedure to have been of only limited success as a device for weeding out ill-founded claims to industrial tribunals, and accordingly the Employment Act 1989, s.20, empowered the Secretary of State to introduce regulations providing for "pre-hearing reviews", at which a party might be required to pay a deposit of up to £150 in order to continue with the proceedings. At the time of writing no such regulations had been made, although the Government had indicated its intention of amending the Rules of Procedure (S.I. 1985 No. 16) to implement pre-hearing reviews and deposits as part of a wider review of tribunal procedures following the coming into force of the Act (House of Commons debate, March 23, 1993, col. 565).

The introduction of yet another device to discourage ill-founded claims while the pre-hearing review procedure has still to be implemented has occasioned some surprise, but the Government believes that the new restrictions of proceedings orders are necessary in order to deal with persistent vexatious applicants who are not discouraged by the threat of having costs orders made against them or the possibility of having to pay a deposit (one example given in debate in the Lords was of an individual who is reported to have made over 100 tribunal applications). The number of applicants affected by this new procedure is likely to be small.

Habitually and persistently and without any reasonable ground. This phrase also appears in the analogous provisions in the Supreme Court Act 1981, s.42(1).

Vexatious. There is no definition of "vexatious", but in the context of the power of an industrial tribunal to award costs the expression has been construed narrowly. In *Marler (E.T.)* v. *Robertson* [1974] I.C.R. 72, Sir Hugh Griffiths considered that conduct would be regarded as vexatious "if an employee brings a hopeless claim not with any expectation of recovering compensation but out of spite to harass his employers or for some other improper motive". However, in the context of striking out, the expression has been interpreted more widely in the sense of an abuse of process. In *Acrow (Engineers)* v. *Hathaway* [1981] 2 All E.R. 161, the E.A.T. struck out a second complaint of unfair dismissal on the grounds that it was vexatious, the applicant having withdrawn his first complaint shortly before it was due to be heard on account of illness. In cases under the analogous provisions in the Supreme Court Act 1981, s.42, it has been held that in considering whether proceedings are vexatious the court must examine the whole history of the matter, and that proceedings may be found to be vexatious even where there may have been reasonable grounds for the proceedings in each individual case (see *Att.-Gen.* v. *Vernazza* [1960] A.C. 965).

ACAS

Functions of ACAS

43.—(1) In section 209 of the 1992 Act (general duty of ACAS to promote improvement of industrial relations), for the words following "industrial relations" there shall be substituted ", in particular, by exercising its functions in relation to the settlement of trade disputes under sections 210 and 212.".

(2) For section 213 of the 1992 Act (powers of ACAS to give advice) there shall be substituted—

> "**Advice**
> 213.—(1) ACAS may, on request or otherwise, give employers, employers' associations, workers and trade unions such advice as it thinks appropriate on matters concerned with or affecting or likely to affect industrial relations.
>
> (2) ACAS may also publish general advice on matters concerned with or affecting or likely to affect industrial relations.".

(3) In section 249(2) of the 1992 Act (chairman to be full time, but other members full or part time), the first sentence shall be omitted, and, in the second sentence, after the word "as", in the first place where it occurs, there shall be inserted the words "chairman, or as".

GENERAL NOTE

This is the first of two sections amending the provisions of the 1992 Act concerning the duties and activities of ACAS, in the wake of the five-yearly review of ACAS conducted by the Department of Employment in 1992 (see *ACAS Annual Report 1992*, Ch. 2). Subsection (1) amends the terms of reference of ACAS in s.209 of the 1992 Act to remove its duty "to encourage the extension of collective bargaining and the development and, where necessary, reform of collective bargaining machinery". ACAS remains under a general duty to promote the improvement of industrial relations, but the statute now directs its attention towards its function of providing conciliation and arbitration in trade disputes (*i.e.* its "fire-fighting" activities) and away from those activities which are more akin to "fire prevention". The expunging of the duty to encourage the extension of collective bargaining, which dates from the Employment Protection Act 1975, was perhaps predictable in view of the present Government's attitude towards collectivism and its widely-expressed preference for individual bargaining between employers and employees as the means of determining terms and conditions of employment, but its removal, while clearly of symbolic importance, is unlikely to have any practical impact on ACAS' activities.

Subsection (2) removes the prohibition on ACAS charging for advice (see the note to s.44, below), and restricts the matters on which ACAS may give advice to those concerned with or affecting industrial relations; previously ACAS was also empowered to give advice on matters concerned with employment policies. The detailed list of matters on which advice may be given has also been removed. For an evaluation of the advisory work of ACAS, see Armstrong [1985] Employment Gazette 143.

Subsection (3) enables the ACAS Chairman to be appointed on a part-time basis.

Fees for exercise of functions by ACAS

44. After section 251 of the 1992 Act there shall be inserted the following section—

"Fees for exercise of functions by ACAS

251A.—(1) ACAS may, in any case in which it thinks it appropriate to do so, but subject to any directions under subsection (2) below, charge a fee for exercising a function in relation to any person.

(2) The Secretary of State may direct ACAS to charge fees, in accordance with the direction, for exercising any function specified in the direction, but the Secretary of State shall not give a direction under this subsection without consulting ACAS.

(3) A direction under subsection (2) above may require ACAS to charge fees in respect of the exercise of a function only in specified descriptions of case.

(4) A direction under subsection (2) above shall specify whether fees are to be charged in respect of the exercise of any specified function—

(a) at the full economic cost level, or

(b) at a level less than the full economic cost but not less than a specified proportion or percentage of the full economic cost.

(5) Where a direction requires fees to be charged at the full economic cost level ACAS shall fix the fee for the case at an amount estimated to be sufficient to cover the administrative costs of ACAS of exercising the function including an appropriate sum in respect of general staff costs and overheads.

(6) Where a direction requires fees to be charged at a level less than the full economic cost ACAS shall fix the fee for the case at such amount, not being less than the proportion or percentage of the full economic cost specified under subsection (4)(b) above, as it thinks appropriate (computing that cost in the same way as under subsection (5) above).

(7) No liability to pay a fee charged under this section shall arise on the part of any person unless ACAS has notified that person that a fee may or will be charged.

(8) For the purposes of this section—

(a) a function is exercised "in relation to" a person who avails himself of the benefit of its exercise, whether or not he requested its exercise and whether the function is such as to be exercisable in relation to particular persons only or in relation to persons generally; and

(b) where a function is exercised in relation to two or more persons the fee chargeable for its exercise shall be apportioned among them as ACAS thinks appropriate.".

GENERAL NOTE

This section inserts a new s.251A into the 1992 Act which empowers ACAS to charge for its services where it considers it appropriate to do so; more controversially, it also gives the Secretary of State, after consultation with ACAS, the power to direct the Service to charge fees for specified functions. These changes follow the five-yearly review of ACAS in 1992, which recommended that the Service might consider charging for certain of its publications, and perhaps for arranging arbitrations. While the ACAS Council was ready to accept the first recommendation, it was "wholly resistant" to the idea of applying charges for other activities, and in particular to any proposal to charge for arbitration (*ACAS Annual Report 1992*, p.28). However, the Secretary of State subsequently decided to take a reserve power to direct ACAS to charge for its services, a move greeted with considerable dismay by the ACAS Council, which wrote to the Secretary of State unanimously opposing that decision. The reasons for the Council's opposition are spelt out in the 1992 Annual Report, at p.29: "The Council is clear that the freedom from Ministerial direction which was given to the Service on its creation in 1975 has been the essential foundation of its independence and proven impartiality between employers and employees. A reserve power could well be regarded as a continuing threat to seek to influence or govern the ways in which, under the Council's direction, the Service exercises any, or all, of its statutory duties". It would indeed be unfortunate if the Service's carefully guarded reputation for impartiality were to be undermined in the pursuit of short-term financial advantage.

Careers services

Careers services

45. For sections 8 to 10 of the Employment and Training Act 1973 (careers services of education authorities) and the heading immediately preceding them there shall be substituted—

"Careers services

Duty of Secretary of State to ensure provision of careers services for school and college students

8.—(1) It shall be the duty of the Secretary of State to secure the provision of relevant services for assisting persons undergoing relevant education to decide—

(a) what employments, having regard to their capabilities, will be suitable for and available to them when they cease undergoing such education, and

(b) what training or education is or will be required by and available to them in order to fit them for those employments,

and for assisting persons ceasing to undergo relevant education to obtain such employments, training and education.

(2) In subsection (1) of this section and section 9 of this Act "relevant services" means—

(a) giving of assistance by collecting, or disseminating or otherwise providing, information about persons seeking, obtaining or offering employment, training and education,

(b) offering advice and guidance, and

(c) other services calculated to facilitate the provision of any services specified in paragraphs (a) and (b) of this subsection.

(3) In this section and section 9 of this Act "relevant education" means—

(a) education involving full-time attendance at any educational institution in Great Britain, other than an educational institution within the higher education sector, and

(b) education involving part-time attendance at any educational institution in Great Britain, other than an educational institution within the higher education sector, which is education of a description commonly undergone by persons in order to fit them for employment.

(4) The references in subsection (3) of this section to an educational institution within the higher education sector shall be construed—

(a) as respects England and Wales, in accordance with section 91(5) of the Further and Higher Education Act 1992 or, if this section is in force at any time before section 65 of that Act comes into force, in accordance with section 61(3)(a) of that Act until that section comes into force, and

(b) as respects Scotland, in accordance with section 56(2) of the Further and Higher Education (Scotland) Act 1992.

Power of Secretary of State to arrange for provision of careers services for others

9. The Secretary of State shall have power to secure the provision of relevant services, or any description of relevant services, for assisting persons other than those undergoing relevant education, or any description of such persons, to decide—

    (a) what employments, having regard to their capabilities, are or will be suitable for and available to them, and

    (b) what training or education is or will be required by and available to them in order to fit them for those employments,

and for assisting those persons to obtain such employments, training and education.

Provision of services

10.—(1) The Secretary of State may perform the duty imposed on him by section 8 of this Act, and exercise the power conferred on him by section 9 of this Act, by making arrangements with—

    (a) local education authorities or (in Scotland) education authorities,

    (b) persons of any other description, or

    (c) local education authorities or education authorities and persons of any other description acting jointly,

under which they undertake to provide, or arrange for the provision of, services in accordance with the arrangements; and in doing so the Secretary of State shall have regard to the requirements of disabled persons.

(2) The Secretary of State may also perform the duty imposed on him by section 8 of this Act, and exercise the power conferred on him by section 9 of this Act, by giving directions to local education authorities or education authorities requiring them to provide, or arrange for the provision of, services in accordance with the directions; and in doing so the Secretary of State shall have regard to the requirements of disabled persons.

(3) Directions given under this section may require local education authorities and education authorities—

    (a) to provide services themselves or jointly with other authorities or persons,

    (b) to arrange for the provision of services by other authorities or persons, or

    (c) to consult and co-ordinate in the provision, or in arranging for the provision, of services with other authorities or persons.

(4) Arrangements made, and directions given, under this section may include provision for the making of payments by the Secretary of State, whether by way of grant or loan or otherwise, to the persons with whom they are made or to whom they are given.

(5) Arrangements made, and directions given, under this section in exercise of the power conferred by section 9 of this Act may include provision permitting the making of charges for the provision of the services to which they relate.

(6) Arrangements made, and directions given, under this section shall require the person with whom they are made or to whom they are given—

    (a) to provide, or arrange for the provision, of services in accordance with such guidance of a general character as the Secretary of State may give, and

    (b) to furnish the Secretary of State, in such manner and at such times as he may specify in the arrangements or directions or in guidance given under paragraph (a) of this subsection, with such information and facilities for obtaining information as he may so specify.

(7) The Secretary of State may give directions to local education authorities and education authorities requiring them to transfer (on

such terms as may be specified in the directions) to any persons who are providing, or are to provide, services in accordance with arrangements made, or directions given, under this section any records of the authorities which may be relevant in the provision of the services.

(8) Local education authorities and education authorities shall have power—

(a) to provide services or arrange for the provision of services in accordance with arrangements made, or directions given, under this section (including services provided outside their areas) by any such means (including by the formation of companies for the purpose) as they consider appropriate, and

(b) to employ officers and provide facilities for and in connection with the provision of the services or arranging for the provision of the services;

but, where directions are given to local education authorities and education authorities, the power conferred on them by this subsection shall be exercised in accordance with the directions.

(9) Where services are being provided in pursuance of arrangements made, or directions given, under this section, the authority with whom the arrangements are made or to whom the directions have been given shall have power, with the consent of the Secretary of State, to provide, or arrange for the provision of, more extensive (relevant) services than the arrangements authorise or the directions require and to employ more officers and provide more facilities accordingly.

(10) Nothing in sections 8 and 9 and this section shall make it unlawful for a local education authority or education authority to defray the cost of exercising their powers under this section from resources other than payments of the Secretary of State.

(11) A direction given under this section may be revoked or varied by another direction so given.

(12) Nothing in this section shall be taken to limit the arrangements which may be made under section 2 of this Act.".

Careers services: ancillary services

46. After section 10 of the Employment and Training Act 1973 (which is inserted by section 45 above) there shall be inserted—

"Provision of ancillary goods and services

10A.—(1) The functions of a local education authority or education authority shall include power to enter into agreements for the supply of goods or services authorised by this section with any person (other than an authority) who provides, or arranges for the provision of, relevant services and is a person with whom this section authorises such arrangements to be made.

(2) This section authorises the making of such arrangements with any person—

(a) who, under arrangements (or joint arrangements) made with that person under section 10(1) or (3) of this Act provides, or arranges for the provision of, the services;

(b) who provides the services jointly with an authority under section 10(3) of this Act;

(c) who is the means by which, under section 10(8), an authority provides, or arranges for the provision of, the services.

(3) Subject to subsections (4), (5) and (6) below, this section authorises—

(a) the supply by the authority to the person of any goods;
(b) the provision by the authority for the person of any administrative, professional or technical services;
(c) the use by the person of any vehicle, plant or apparatus belonging to the authority and, without prejudice to paragraph (b)
above, the placing at the disposal of the person of the services
of any person employed in connection with the vehicle or other
property in question;
(d) the carrying out by the authority of works of maintenance in
connection with land or buildings for the maintenance of which
the person is responsible;

and the authority may purchase and store any goods which in their
opinion they may require for the purposes of paragraph (a) above.

(4) The supply by an authority of goods or services to any person is
authorised by this section only for the purpose of the provision by that
person of relevant services.

(5) The supply by an authority of goods or services to any person is
authorised by this section only during the period of two years beginning with the day on which that person first provides relevant services
in the area of that authority.

(6) Goods and services shall be supplied on such terms as can
reasonably be expected to secure that the full cost of making the
supply is recovered by the authority.

(7) The supply by an authority of goods or services to any person is
authorised outside as well as within the area of that authority.

(8) This section is without prejudice to the generality of any other
enactment conferring functions on local education authorities or education authorities.

(9) In this section—
      "goods" includes materials; and
      "relevant services" has the meaning given in section 8(2) of
         this Act.".

Training etc. in Scotland

**Employment and training functions of Scottish Enterprise and Highlands
and Islands Enterprise**

47.—(1) In section 2 of the Employment and Training Act 1973 (functions
of the Secretary of State), after subsection (3) there shall be inserted—
      "(3A) Without prejudice to subsection (2)(f) of this section, the
Secretary of State may wholly or partly perform his duty under subsection (1) of this section in relation to Scotland by authorising or
directing Scottish Enterprise or Highlands and Islands Enterprise to
act on his behalf—
      (a) in the making of arrangements under this section in such cases
         or for such purposes as may be specified in or determined
         under the authorisation or direction;
      (b) in the taking of such steps for the purposes of, or in connection
         with, the carrying out of any arrangements under this section
         (including any made otherwise than by Scottish Enterprise or
         Highlands and Islands Enterprise) as may be so specified or
         determined,
and the power under this subsection to give authorisations or directions shall include power to revoke or vary any authorisation or
direction so given.

      (3B) Where Scottish Enterprise or Highlands and Islands Enter-
prise make arrangements under this section in pursuance of an authorisation or direction made by the Secretary of State under subsection

(3A)(a) above, they shall, at such times as the Secretary of State may require, report to him what provision, if any, they have included in those arrangements in relation to disabled persons.".

(2) The Enterprise and New Towns (Scotland) Act 1990 shall be amended in accordance with the following provisions of this section.

(3) In paragraphs (a)(ii) and (b)(ii) of section 1 (Scottish Enterprise and Highlands and Islands Enterprise), after the word "Act," there shall be inserted the words "maintaining and".

(4) In section 2 (functions in relation to training for employment etc.)—

(a) in subsection (3), after paragraph (c) there shall be inserted "; and

> (d) providing temporary employment for persons who are without employment.", and

(b) in subsection (4), for the word "training", in both places where it occurs, there shall be substituted the words "employment and training".

(5) After section 14 there shall be inserted—

"Power of Ministers to confer or impose functions

14A.—(1) Without prejudice to the foregoing provisions of this Act, the functions of each of Scottish Enterprise and Highlands and Islands Enterprise shall include—

(a) a power to do anything in connection with unemployment, training for employment or employment which it is authorised to do by a Minister of the Crown; and

(b) a duty to do anything in connection with unemployment, training for employment or employment which it is required to do by or under a direction given to it by a Minister of the Crown.

(2) Scottish Enterprise and Highlands and Islands Enterprise shall each—

(a) from time to time submit to the Secretary of State particulars of what it proposes to do for the purpose of carrying out the functions conferred or imposed upon it by or under subsection (1) above; and

(b) ensure that all its activities in relation to those functions are in accordance with such proposals submitted by it to the Secretary of State as have been approved by him and with such modifications (if any) of those proposals as are notified to the body in question by him.

(3) The power of a Minister of the Crown by virtue of subsection (1) above to authorise or direct Scottish Enterprise or Highlands and Islands Enterprise to do anything shall include the power to delegate powers conferred on him by any enactment; but nothing in this section shall authorise any Minister of the Crown to delegate a power to make subordinate legislation (within the meaning of the Interpretation Act 1978).".

PART IV

SUPPLEMENTARY

Interpretation

48. In this Act—

> "the 1978 Act" means the Employment Protection (Consolidation) Act 1978, and

> "the 1992 Act" means the Trade Union and Labour Relations (Consolidation) Act 1992.

Miscellaneous and consequential amendments

49.—(1) The enactments specified in Schedule 7 to this Act shall have effect subject to the amendments there specified (which are miscellaneous amendments).

(2) The enactments specified in Schedule 8 to this Act shall have effect subject to the amendments there specified (which are consequential amendments).

Transitional provisions and savings

50. The transitional provisions and savings set out in Schedule 9 to this Act shall have effect.

Repeals and revocations

51. The enactments mentioned in Schedule 10 to this Act (which include enactments which are unnecessary) are repealed, and the instruments mentioned in that Schedule are revoked, to the extent specified in the third column of that Schedule.

Commencement

52. Subject to any other commencement provision, the preceding sections of, and the Schedules to, this Act shall not come into force until such day as the Secretary of State may appoint by order made by statutory instrument; and different days may be appointed for different provisions and different purposes.

Financial provision

53. There shall be paid out of money provided by Parliament—
(a) any expenditure of the Secretary of State under this Act, and
(b) any increase attributable to this Act in the sums payable out of money so provided under any other Act.

Northern Ireland

54.—(1) An Order in Council under paragraph 1(1)(b) of Schedule 1 to the Northern Ireland Act 1974 (legislation for Northern Ireland in the interim period) which states that it is made only for purposes to which this subsection applies—
(a) shall not be subject to paragraph 1(4) and (5) of that Schedule (affirmative resolution of both Houses of Parliament), but
(b) shall be subject to annulment in pursuance of a resolution of either House of Parliament.

(2) The purposes to which subsection (1) above applies are purposes corresponding to those of—
(a) sections 23 to 25 and Schedules 2 and 3,
(b) section 26 and Schedule 4,
(c) section 27,
(d) section 28 and Schedule 5,
(e) sections 29, 30 and 31,
(f) section 32,
(g) section 34,
(h) section 35,
(i) sections 36, 38 and 39 and Schedule 6,
(j) section 40, and

(k) this Part (including Schedules 7, 8, 9 and 10).

(3) The following provisions of this Act (and no others) extend to Northern Ireland—

(a) section 3 and Schedule 1 (but only for the purposes of their application
to trade unions and unincorporated employers' associations having
their head or main office outside Northern Ireland),

(b) sections 33, 48, 49, 50, 51, 52 and 55 and this section,

(c) paragraphs 2, 6 and 7 of Schedule 8,

(d) paragraphs 1 and 4 of Schedule 9, and

(e) Schedule 10 so far as it relates to enactments or instruments which
extend there.

Short title

55. This Act may be cited as the Trade Union Reform and Employment
Rights Act 1993.

SCHEDULES

Section 3   SCHEDULE 1

POLITICAL FUND BALLOTS

1. In section 74(3) of the 1992 Act (requirements which Certification Officer must be satisfied
would be met in relation to political fund ballot held by trade union in accordance with its rules),
after the entry relating to section 77 there shall be inserted—

"section 77A (counting of votes etc. by independent person), and".

2. In section 75 of that Act (appointment of independent scrutineer for political fund ballot)—

(a) in paragraph (a) (scrutineer to supervise certain matters) of subsection (3) (terms of
appointment of scrutineer), for the words "and distribution of the voting papers" there
shall be substituted the words "of the voting papers and (unless he is appointed under
section 77A to undertake the distribution of the voting papers) their distribution",

(b) after that paragraph there shall be inserted—

"(aa) to—

(i) inspect the register of names and addresses of the members of the trade
union, or

(ii) examine the copy of the register as at the relevant date which is supplied to
him in accordance with subsection (5A)(a),

whenever it appears to him appropriate to do so and, in particular, when the conditions specified in subsection (3A) are satisfied;",

(c) in paragraph (d) (scrutineer to retain custody of voting papers) of that subsection—

(i) after the words "purposes of the ballot" there shall be inserted the words "and the
copy of the register supplied to him in accordance with subsection (5A)(a)", and

(ii) after the words "of the papers" there shall be inserted the words "or copy",

(d) after that subsection there shall be inserted—

"(3A) The conditions referred to in subsection (3)(aa) are—

(a) that a request that the scrutineer inspect the register or examine the copy is made to
him during the appropriate period by a member of the trade union who suspects that
the register is not, or at the relevant date was not, accurate and up-to-date, and

(b) that the scrutineer does not consider that the member's suspicion is ill-founded.

(3B) In subsection (3A) "the appropriate period" means the period—

(a) beginning with the day on which the scrutineer is appointed, and

(b) ending with the day before the day on which the scrutineer makes his report to the
trade union.

(3C) The duty of confidentiality as respects the register is incorporated in the scrutineer's
appointment.",

(e) after subsection (5) there shall be inserted—

"(5A) The trade union shall—

(a) supply to the scrutineer as soon as is reasonably practicable after the relevant date a
copy of the register of names and addresses of its members as at that date, and

(b) comply with any request made by the scrutineer to inspect the register.

(5B) Where the register is kept by means of a computer the duty imposed on the trade
union by subsection (5A)(a) is either to supply a legible printed copy or (if the scrutineer

prefers) to supply a copy of the computer data and allow the scrutineer use of the computer to read it at any time during the period when he is required to retain custody of the copy.",
and
(f) after subsection (7) there shall be inserted—
"(8) In this section "the relevant date" means—
(a) where the trade union has rules determining who is entitled to vote in the ballot by reference to membership on a particular date, that date, and
(b) otherwise, the date, or the last date, on which voting papers are distributed for the purposes of the ballot.".
3. After section 77 of that Act there shall be inserted—

"Counting of votes etc. by independent person
77A.—(1) The trade union shall ensure that—
(a) the storage and distribution of the voting papers for the purposes of the ballot, and
(b) the counting of the votes cast in the ballot,
are undertaken by one or more independent persons appointed by the union.
(2) A person is an independent person in relation to a ballot if—
(a) he is the scrutineer, or
(b) he is a person other than the scrutineer and the trade union has no grounds for believing either that he will carry out any functions conferred on him in relation to the ballot otherwise than competently or that his independence in relation to the ballot, might reasonably be called into question.
(3) An appointment under this section shall require the person appointed to carry out his functions so as to minimise the risk of any contravention of requirements imposed by or under any enactment or the occurrence of any unfairness or malpractice.
(4) The duty of confidentiality as respects the register is incorporated in an appointment under this section.
(5) Where the person appointed to undertake the counting of votes is not the scrutineer, his appointment shall require him to send the voting papers back to the scrutineer as soon as reasonably practicable after the counting has been completed.
(6) The trade union—
(a) shall ensure that nothing in the terms of an appointment under this section is such as to make it reasonable for any person to call into question the independence of the person appointed in relation to the union,
(b) shall ensure that a person appointed under this section duly carries out his functions and that there is no interference with his carrying out of those functions which would make it reasonable for any person to call into question the independence of the person appointed in relation to the union, and
(c) shall comply with all reasonable requests made by a person appointed under this section for the purposes of, or in connection with, the carrying out of his functions.".
4. In section 78 of that Act (scrutineer's report on ballot)—
(a) in subsection (1), after paragraph (d) there shall be inserted "and
(e) the name of the person (or of each of the persons) appointed under section 77A or, if no person was so appointed, that fact.",
(b) in subsection (2)(b), after the word "made" there shall be inserted "(whether by him or any other person)", and
(c) after that subsection there shall be inserted—
"(2A) The report shall also state—
(a) whether the scrutineer—
(i) has inspected the register of names and addresses of the members of the trade union, or
(ii) has examined the copy of the register as at the relevant date which is supplied to him in accordance with section 75(5A)(a),
(b) if he has, whether in the case of each inspection or examination he was acting on a request by a member of the trade union or at his own instance,
(c) whether he declined to act on any such request, and
(d) whether any inspection of the register, or any examination of the copy of the register, has revealed any matter which he considers should be drawn to the attention of the trade union in order to assist it in securing that the register is accurate and up-to-date,
but shall not state the name of any member who has requested such an inspection or examination.
(2B) Where one or more persons other than the scrutineer are appointed under section 77A, the statement included in the scrutineer's report in accordance with subsection (2)(b) shall also indicate—

(a) whether he is satisfied with the performance of the person, or each of the persons, so appointed, and

(b) if he is not satisfied with the performance of the person, or any of them, particulars of his reasons for not being so satisfied.".

Section 23   SCHEDULE 2

MATERNITY: THE RIGHT TO RETURN TO WORK

Right to return to work

Right to return to work

39.—(1) An employee who—

(a) has the right conferred by section 33, and

(b) has, at the beginning of the eleventh week before the expected week of childbirth, been continuously employed for a period of not less than two years,

shall also have the right to return to work at any time during the period beginning at the end of her maternity leave period and ending twenty-nine weeks after the beginning of the week in which childbirth occurs.

(2) An employee's right to return to work under this section is the right to return to work with the person who was her employer before the end of her maternity leave period, or (where appropriate) his successor, in the job in which she was then employed—

(a) on terms and conditions as to remuneration not less favourable than those which would have been applicable to her had she not been absent from work at any time since the commencement of her maternity leave period,

(b) with her seniority, pension rights and similar rights as they would have been if the period or periods of her employment prior to the end of her maternity leave period were continuous with her employment following her return to work (but subject to the requirements of paragraph 5 of Schedule 5 to the Social Security Act 1989 (credit for the period of absence in certain cases)), and

(c) otherwise on terms and conditions no less favourable than those which would have been applicable to her had she not been absent from work after the end of her maternity leave period.

(3) The Secretary of State may by order vary the period of two years specified in sub-section (1) or that period as so varied.

(4) No order shall be made under subsection (3) unless a draft of the order has been laid before Parliament and approved by a resolution of each House of Parliament.

Requirement to give notice of return to employer

40.—(1) An employee shall not have the right to return to work under section 39 unless she includes with the information required by section 37(1) the information that she intends to exercise the right.

(2) Where, not earlier than twenty-one days before the end of her maternity leave period, an employee is requested in accordance with subsection (3) by her employer, or a successor of his, to give him written confirmation that she intends to exercise the right to return to work under section 39, the employee shall not be entitled to that right unless she gives the requested confirmation within fourteen days of receiving the request or, if that is not reasonably practicable, as soon as is reasonably practicable.

(3) A request under subsection (2) shall be—

(a) made in writing, and

(b) accompanied by a written statement of the effect of that subsection.

Special provision where redundancies occur before return to work

41.—(1) Where an employee has the right to return to work under section 39, but it is not practicable by reason of redundancy for the employer to permit her to return in accordance with that right, she shall be entitled, where there is a suitable available vacancy, to be offered alternative employment with her employer (or his successor), or an associated employer, under a new contract of employment complying with subsection (2).

(2) The new contract of employment must be such that—

(a) the work to be done under the contract is of a kind which is both suitable in relation to the employee and appropriate for her to do in the circumstances; and

(b) the provisions of the new contract as to the capacity and place in which she is to be employed and as to the other terms and conditions of her employment are not substantially less favourable to her than if she had returned to work pursuant to her right to return.

Exercise of right to return to work

42.—(1) An employee shall exercise the right to return to work under section 39 by giving written notice to the employer (who may be her employer before the end of her maternity leave period or a successor of his) at least twenty-one days before the day on which she proposes to return of her proposal to return on that day (the "notified day of return").

(2) An employer may postpone an employee's return to work until a date not more than four weeks after the notified day of return if he notifies her before that day that for specified reasons he is postponing her return until that date, and accordingly she will be entitled to return to work with him on that date.

(3) Subject to subsection (4), an employee may—

(a) postpone her return to work until a date not exceeding four weeks from the notified day of return, notwithstanding that that date falls after the end of the period of twenty-nine weeks beginning with the week in which childbirth occurred; and

(b) where no day of return has been notified to the employer, extend the time during which she may exercise her right to return in accordance with subsection (1), so that she returns to work not later than four weeks from the end of that period of twenty-nine weeks;

if, before the notified day of return (or the end of the period of twenty-nine weeks), she gives the employer a certificate from a registered medical practitioner stating that by reason of disease or bodily or mental disablement she will be incapable of work on the notified day of return (or the end of that period).

(4) Where an employee has once exercised a right of postponement or extension under subsection (3)(a) or (b), she shall not again be entitled to exercise a right of postponement or extension under that subsection in connection with the same return to work.

(5) If an employee has notified a day of return but there is an interruption of work (whether due to industrial action or some other reason) which renders it unreasonable to expect the employee to return to work on the notified day of return, she may instead return to work when work resumes after the interruption or as soon as reasonably practicable afterwards.

(6) If—

(a) no day of return has been notified,

(b) there is an interruption of work (whether due to industrial action or some other reason) which renders it unreasonable to expect the employee to return to work before the end of the period of twenty-nine weeks beginning with the week in which childbirth occurred, or which appears likely to have that effect, and

(c) in consequence, the employee does not notify a day of return,

the employee may exercise her right to return in accordance with subsection (1) so that she returns to work at any time before the end of the period of twenty-eight days from the end of the interruption notwithstanding that she returns to work outside the period of twenty-nine weeks.

(7) Where the employee has either—

(a) exercised the right under subsection (3)(b) to extend the period during which she may exercise her right to return, or

(b) refrained from notifying the day of return in the circumstances described in subsection (6),

the other of those subsections shall apply as if for the reference to the end of the period of twenty-nine weeks there were substituted a reference to the end of the further period of four weeks or, as the case may be, of the period of twenty-eight days from the end of the interruption of work.

Supplementary

43.—(1) Schedule 2 shall have effect for the purpose of supplementing the preceding sections in relation to an employee's right to return to work under section 39.

(2) Sections 56 and 86 also have effect for that purpose.

(3) Subject to subsection (4), in sections 56 and 86 and Schedule 2 "notified day of return" has the same meaning as in section 42.

(4) Where—

(a) an employee's return is postponed under subsection (2) or (3)(a) of section 42, or

(b) the employee returns to work on a day later than the notified day of return in the circumstances described in subsection (5) of that section,

then, subject to subsection (4) of that section, references in those subsections and in sections 56 and 86 and Schedule 2 to the notified day of return shall be construed as references to the day to which the return is postponed or that later day.

Contractual rights

44.—(1) An employee who has the right to return to work under section 39 and a right to return to work after absence because of pregnancy or childbirth under a contract of employment or otherwise may not exercise the two rights separately but may, in returning to work, take advantage of whichever right is, in any particular respect, the more favourable.

(2) The provisions of sections 39, 41 to 43, 56 and 86 and paragraphs 1 to 4 and 6 of Schedule 2 shall apply, subject to any modifications necessary to give effect to any more favourable contractual terms, to the exercise of the composite right described in subsection (1) as they apply to the exercise of the right to return to work under section 39.

Section 25   SCHEDULE 3

SUSPENSION FROM WORK ON MATERNITY GROUNDS

Suspension from work on maternity grounds

Suspension from work on maternity grounds

45.—(1) For the purposes of sections 46 and 47 an employee is suspended on maternity grounds where, in consequence of—

(a) any requirement imposed by or under any relevant provision of any enactment or of any instrument made under any enactment, or

(b) any recommendation in any relevant provision of a code of practice issued or approved under section 16 of the Health and Safety at Work etc. Act 1974,

she is suspended from work by her employer on the ground that she is pregnant, has recently given birth or is breastfeeding a child.

(2) For the purposes of this section, sections 46 and 47 and section 61 an employee shall be regarded as suspended from work only if, and so long as, she continues to be employed by her employer, but is not provided with work or (disregarding alternative work for the purposes of section 46) does not perform the work she normally performed before the suspension.

(3) For the purposes of subsection (1) a provision is a "relevant provision" if it is for the time being specified as a relevant provision in an order made by the Secretary of State under this subsection.

Right to offer of alternative work

46.—(1) Where an employer has available suitable alternative work for an employee the employee has a right to be offered to be provided with it before being suspended on maternity grounds.

(2) For alternative work to be suitable for an employee for the purposes of this section—

(a) the work must be of a kind which is both suitable in relation to her and appropriate for her to do in the circumstances; and

(b) the terms and conditions applicable to her for performing the work, if they differ from the corresponding terms and conditions applicable to her for performing the work she normally performs under her contract of employment, must not be substantially less favourable to her than those corresponding terms and conditions.

(3) An employee may present a complaint to an industrial tribunal that her employer has failed to offer to provide her with work in contravention of subsection (1).

(4) An industrial tribunal shall not entertain a complaint under subsection (3) unless it is presented to the tribunal before the end of the period of three months beginning with the first day of the suspension, or within such further period as the tribunal considers reasonable in a case where it is satisfied that it was not reasonably practicable for the complaint to be presented within the period of three months.

(5) Where the tribunal finds the complaint well-founded it may make an award of compensation to be paid by the employer to the employee.

(6) The amount of the compensation shall be such as the tribunal considers just and equitable in all the circumstances having regard to the infringement of the complainant's right under subsection (1) by the employer's failure complained of and to any loss sustained by the complainant which is attributable to that failure.

Right to remuneration on suspension

47.—(1) An employee who is suspended on maternity grounds shall be entitled to be paid remuneration by her employer while she is so suspended.

(2) An employee shall not be entitled to remuneration under this section in respect of any period during which her employer has offered to provide her with work which is suitable alternative work for the purposes of section 46 and the employee has unreasonably refused to perform that work.

(3) The amount of remuneration payable by an employer to an employee under this section shall be a week's pay in respect of each week of the period of suspension; and if in any week remuneration is payable in respect only of part of that week the amount of a week's pay shall be reduced proportionately.

(4) Subject to subsection (5), a right to remuneration under this section shall not affect any right of an employee in relation to remuneration under her contract of employment (in subsection (5) referred to as "contractual remuneration").

(5) Any contractual remuneration paid by an employer to an employee in respect of any period shall go towards discharging the employer's liability under this section in respect of that period; and, conversely, any payment of remuneration in discharge of an employer's liability under this section in respect of any period shall go towards discharging any obligation of the employer to pay contractual remuneration in respect of that period.

(6) An employee may present a complaint to any industrial tribunal that her employer has failed to pay the whole or any part of remuneration to which she is entitled under this section.

(7) An industrial tribunal shall not entertain a complaint relating to remuneration under this section in respect of any day unless the complaint is presented to the tribunal before the end of the period of three months beginning with that day, or within such further period as the tribunal considers reasonable in a case where it is satisfied that it was not reasonably practicable for the complaint to be presented within the period of three months.

(8) Where an industrial tribunal finds a complaint under subsection (6) well-founded the tribunal shall order the employer to pay the complainant the amount of remuneration which it finds is due to her.

Section 26   SCHEDULE 4

PROVISIONS SUBSTITUTED FOR SECTIONS 1 TO 6 OF 1978 ACT

PART I

EMPLOYMENT PARTICULARS

Written particulars of employment

Employer's duty to give statement of employment particulars

1.—(1) Not later than two months after the beginning of an employee's employment with an employer, the employer shall give to the employee a written statement which may, subject to subsection (3) of section 2, be given in instalments before the end of that period.

(2) The statement shall contain particulars of—
   (a) the names of the employer and employee,
   (b) the date when the employment began, and
   (c) the date on which the employee's period of continuous employment began (taking into account any employment with a previous employer which counts towards that period).

(3) The statement shall also contain particulars, as at a specified date not more than seven days before the statement or instalment of the statement containing them is given, of—
   (a) the scale or rate of remuneration or the method of calculating remuneration,

(b) the intervals at which remuneration is paid (that is, weekly, monthly or other specified intervals),

(c) any terms and conditions relating to hours of work (including any terms and conditions relating to normal working hours),

(d) any terms and conditions relating to any of the following—

(i) entitlement to holidays, including public holidays, and holiday pay (the particulars given being sufficient to enable the employee's entitlement, including any entitlement to accrued holiday pay on the termination of employment, to be precisely calculated),

(ii) incapacity for work due to sickness or injury, including any provision for sick pay, and

(iii) pensions and pension schemes,

(e) the length of notice which the employee is obliged to give and entitled to receive to terminate his contract of employment,

(f) the title of the job which the employee is employed to do or a brief description of the work for which the employee is employed,

(g) where the employment is not intended to be permanent, the period for which it is expected to continue or, if it is for a fixed term, the date when it is to end,

(h) either the place of work or, where the employee is required or permitted to work at various places, an indication of that and of the address of the employer,

(j) any collective agreements which directly affect the terms and conditions of the employment including, where the employer is not a party, the persons by whom they were made, and

(k) where the employee is required to work outside the United Kingdom for a period of more than one month—

(i) the period for which he is to work outside the United Kingdom,

(ii) the currency in which remuneration is to be paid while he is working outside the United Kingdom,

(iii) any additional remuneration payable to him, and any benefits to be provided to or in respect of him, by reason of his being required to work outside the United Kingdom, and

(iv) any terms and conditions relating to his return to the United Kingdom.

(4) Subsection (3)(d)(iii) shall not apply to the employees of any body or authority if—

(a) the employees' pension rights depend on the terms of a pension scheme established under any provision contained in or having effect under any Act of Parliament, and

(b) the body or authority are required by any such provision to give to new employees information concerning their pension rights or the determination of questions affecting their pension rights.

Section 1: supplementary

2.—(1) If, in the case of a statement under section 1, there are no particulars to be entered under any of the heads of paragraph (d) or (k) of subsection (3) of that section, or under any of the other paragraphs of subsection (2) or (3) of that section, that fact shall be stated.

(2) A statement under section 1—

(a) may refer the employee to the provisions of some other document which—

(i) the employee has reasonable opportunities of reading in the course of his employment, or

(ii) is made reasonably accessible to him in some other way,

for particulars of any of the matters specified in heads (ii) and (iii) of paragraph (d) of subsection (3) of section 1, and

(b) may refer the employee to the law, or, subject to subsection (3), to the provisions of any collective agreement which directly affects the terms and conditions of the employment, for particulars of either of the matters specified in paragraph (e) of that subsection.

(3) A statement under section 1 may refer the employee to the provisions of a collective agreement under subsection (2)(b) if, and only if, it is an agreement which—

(a) the employee has reasonable opportunities of reading in the course of his employment, or

(b) is made reasonably accessible to him in some other way.

(4) The particulars required by section 1(2) and the following provisions of subsection (3)—

(a) paragraphs (a) to (c),

(b) head (i) of paragraph (d),

(c) paragraph (f), and

(d) paragraph (h),

shall be included in a single document (in this Part referred to as the "principal statement").

(5) Where before the end of the period of two months after the beginning of his employment an employee is to begin to work outside the United Kingdom for a period of more than one

month, the statement under section 1 shall be given to him not later than the time when he leaves the United Kingdom in order to begin so to work.

(6) A statement shall be given to a person under section 1 notwithstanding that his employment ends before the end of the period within which the statement is required to be given.

Statement to include note about disciplinary procedures

3.—(1) A statement under section 1 shall include a note—

(a) specifying any disciplinary rules applicable to the employee or referring the employee to the provisions of a document which—

(i) the employee has reasonable opportunities of reading in the course of his employment, or

(ii) is made reasonably accessible to him in some other way,

and which specifies such rules,

(b) specifying, by description or otherwise—

(i) a person to whom the employee can apply if he is dissatisfied with any disciplinary decision relating to him, and

(ii) a person to whom the employee can apply for the purpose of seeking redress of any grievance relating to his employment,

and the manner in which any such application should be made,

(c) where there are further steps consequent on any such application, explaining those steps or referring to the provisions of a document which—

(i) the employee has reasonable opportunities of reading in the course of his employment, or

(ii) is made reasonably accessible to him in some other way,

and which explains them, and

(d) stating whether a contracting-out certificate is in force for the employment.

(2) Subsection (1)(a) to (c) shall not apply to rules, disciplinary decisions, grievances or procedures relating to health or safety at work.

(3) The note need not comply with the following provisions of subsection (1)—

(a) paragraph (a),

(b) in paragraph (b), sub-paragraph (i) and the words following sub-paragraph (ii) so far as relating to sub-paragraph (i), and

(c) paragraph (c),

if on the date when the employee's employment began the relevant number of employees was less than twenty.

(4) In subsection (3) "the relevant number of employees", in relation to an employee, means the number of employees employed by his employer added to the number of employees employed by any associated employer.

Employer's duty to give statement of changes

4.—(1) If, after the date to which a statement given under section 1 relates, or, where no such statement is given, after the end of the period within which a statement under section 1 is required to be given, there is a change in any of the matters particulars of which are required by sections 1 to 3 to be included or referred to in a statement under section 1, the employer shall at the earliest opportunity and, in any event, not later than—

(a) one month after the change, or

(b) where the change results from the employee being required to work outside the United Kingdom for a period of more than one month, the time when he leaves the United Kingdom in order to begin so to work, if that is earlier,

give to the employee a written statement containing particulars of the change.

(2) In a case where the statement under section 1 is given in instalments, subsection (1) applies—

(a) in relation to—

(i) matters particulars of which are required to be (whether they are or not) included in the instalment comprising the principal statement, and

(ii) other matters particulars of which are included or referred to in that instalment;

(b) in relation to matters particulars of which are included or referred to in any other instalment; and

(c) in relation to any change occurring after the end of the two-month period within which a statement under section 1 is required to be given in matters particulars of which were required to be included in the statement given under section 1 but which were not included in any instalment;

as it applies in relation to matters particulars of which are required to be included or referred to in a statement under section 1 not given in instalments.

(3) A statement under subsection (1)—
(a) may refer the employee to the provisions of some other document which—
    (i) the employee has reasonable opportunities of reading in the course of his employment, or
    (ii) is made reasonably accessible to him in some other way,
for a change in any of the matters specified in sections 1(3)(d)(ii) and (iii) and 3(1)(a) and (c), and
(b) may refer the employee to the law, or, subject to subsection (4), to the provisions of any collective agreement which directly affects the terms and conditions of the employment, for a change in either of the matters specified in section 1(3)(e).

(4) A statement under subsection (1) may refer the employee to the provisions of a collective agreement under subsection (3)(b) if, and only if, it is an agreement which—
(a) the employee has reasonable opportunities of reading in the course of his employment, or
(b) is made reasonably accessible to him in some other way.

(5) Where after an employer has given to an employee a statement under section 1—
(a) either—
    (i) the name of the employer (whether an individual or a body corporate or partnership) is changed without any change in the identity of the employer, or
    (ii) the identity of the employer is changed in circumstances in which the continuity of the employee's period of employment is not broken, and
(b) the change does not involve any change in any of the matters (other than the names of the parties) particulars of which are required by sections 1 to 3 to be included in the statement,
the person who immediately after the change is the employer shall not be required to give to the employee a statement under section 1 but the change shall be treated as a change falling within subsection (1) of this section.

(6) A statement under subsection (1) which informs an employee of a change such as is referred to in subsection (5)(a)(ii) shall specify the date on which the employee's period of continuous employment began.

Exclusion of sections 1 to 4 in case of certain employees

5.—(1) Sections 1 to 4 shall not apply to an employee if—
(a) his employment continues for less than one month, or
(b) he is employed under a contract which normally involves employment for less than eight hours weekly.

(2) Sections 1 to 4 shall apply to an employee who at any time comes or ceases to come within the exceptions from those sections provided for by subsection (1)(b) and sections 141 and 144, and under section 149, as if his employment with his employer terminated or began at that time.

(3) The fact that section 1 is directed by subsection (2) to apply to an employee as if his employment began on his ceasing to come within the exceptions referred to in that subsection shall not affect the obligation under section 1(2)(b) to specify the date on which his employment actually began.

Power of Secretary of State to require particulars of further matters

6. The Secretary of State may by order provide that section 1 shall have effect as if particulars of such further matters as may be specified in the order were included in the particulars required by that section; and, for that purpose, the order may include such provisions amending that section as appear to the Secretary of State to be expedient.

Section 28   SCHEDULE 5

EMPLOYMENT PROTECTION IN HEALTH AND SAFETY CASES

1. After section 22 of the 1978 Act there shall be inserted—

"Right not to suffer detriment in health and safety cases

Right not to suffer detriment in health and safety cases

22A.—(1) An employee has the right not to be subjected to any detriment by any act, or any deliberate failure to act, by his employer done on the ground that—
(a) having been designated by the employer to carry out activities in connection with preventing or reducing risks to health and safety at work, he carried out, or proposed to carry out, any such activities,
(b) being a representative of workers on matters of health and safety at work, or a member of a safety committee—
    (i) in accordance with arrangements established under or by virtue of any enactment, or

(ii) by reason of being acknowledged as such by the employer,

he performed, or proposed to perform, any functions as such a representative or a member of such a committee,

(c) being an employee at a place where—

    (i) there was no such representative or safety committee, or

    (ii) there was such a representative or safety committee but it was not reasonably practicable for the employee to raise the matter by those means,

he brought to his employer's attention, by reasonable means, circumstances connected with his work which he reasonably believed were harmful or potentially harmful to health or safety,

(d) in circumstances of danger which he reasonably believed to be serious and imminent and which he could not reasonably have been expected to avert, he left, or proposed to leave, or (while the danger persisted) refused to return to, his place of work or any dangerous part of his place of work, or

(e) in circumstances of danger which he reasonably believed to be serious and imminent, he took, or proposed to take, appropriate steps to protect himself or other persons from the danger.

(2) For the purposes of subsection (1)(e) whether steps which an employee took, or proposed to take, were appropriate shall be judged by reference to all the circumstances including, in particular, his knowledge and the facilities and advice available to him at the time.

(3) An employee shall not be regarded as having been subjected to any detriment on the ground specified in subsection (1)(e) if the employer shows that it was, or would have been, so negligent for the employee to take the steps which he took, or proposed to take, that a reasonable employer might have treated him as the employer did.

(4) Except where an employee is dismissed in circumstances in which, by virtue of section 142, section 54 does not apply to the dismissal, this section shall not apply where the detriment in question amounts to dismissal.

Proceedings for contravention of section 22A

22B.—(1) An employee may present a complaint to an industrial tribunal on the ground that he has been subjected to a detriment in contravention of section 22A.

(2) On such a complaint it shall be for the employer to show the ground on which any act, or deliberate failure to act, was done.

(3) An industrial tribunal shall not consider a complaint under this section unless it is presented—

(a) before the end of the period of three months beginning with the date of the act or failure to act to which the complaint relates or, where that act or failure is part of a series of similar acts or failures, the last of them, or

(b) where the tribunal is satisfied that it was not reasonably practicable for the complaint to be presented before the end of that period, within such further period as it considers reasonable.

(4) For the purposes of subsection (3)—

(a) where an act extends over a period, the "date of the act" means the last day of that period, and

(b) a deliberate failure to act shall be treated as done when it was decided on;

and, in the absence of evidence establishing the contrary, an employer shall be taken to decide on a failure to act when he does an act inconsistent with doing the failed act or, if he has done no such inconsistent act, when the period expires within which he might reasonably have been expected to do the failed act if it was to be done.

Remedies

22C.—(1) Where the industrial tribunal finds that a complaint under section 22B is well-founded, it shall make a declaration to that effect and may make an award of compensation to be paid to the complainant in respect of the act or failure to act complained of.

(2) The amount of the compensation awarded shall be such as the tribunal considers just and equitable in all the circumstances having regard to the infringement complained of and to any loss which is attributable to the act or failure which infringed his right.

(3) The loss shall be taken to include—

(a) any expenses reasonably incurred by the complainant in consequence of the act or failure complained of, and

(b) loss of any benefit which he might reasonably be expected to have had but for that act or failure.

(4) In ascertaining the loss, the tribunal shall apply the same rule concerning the duty of a person to mitigate his loss as applies to damages recoverable under the common law of England and Wales or Scotland.

(5) Where the tribunal finds that the act or failure complained of was to any extent caused or contributed to by action of the complainant, it shall reduce the amount of the compensation by such proportion as it considers just and equitable having regard to that finding.".

2. In subsection (3) of section 57 of that Act (general provisions as to fairness of dismissal), for the words "sections 59 to 61" there shall be substituted the words "sections 57A to 61".

3. After that section there shall be inserted—

"Dismissal in health and safety cases

57A.—(1) The dismissal of an employee by an employer shall be regarded for the purposes of this Part as having been unfair if the reason for it (or, if more than one, the principal reason) was that the employee—

(a) having been designated by the employer to carry out activities in connection with preventing or reducing risks to health and safety at work, carried out, or proposed to carry out, any such activities,

(b) being a representative of workers on matters of health and safety at work, or a member of a safety committee—

    (i) in accordance with arrangements established under or by virtue of any enactment, or

    (ii) by reason of being acknowledged as such by the employer,

performed, or proposed to perform, any functions as such a representative or a member of such a committee,

(c) being an employee at a place where—

    (i) there was no such representative or safety committee, or

    (ii) there was such a representative or safety committee but it was not reasonably practicable for the employee to raise the matter by those means,

brought to his employer's attention, by reasonable means, circumstances connected with his work which he reasonably believed were harmful or potentially harmful to health or safety,

(d) in circumstances of danger which he reasonably believed to be serious and imminent and which he could not reasonably have been expected to avert, left, or proposed to leave, or (while the danger persisted) refused to return to, his place of work or any dangerous part of his place of work, or

(e) in circumstances of danger which he reasonably believed to be serious and imminent, took, or proposed to take, appropriate steps to protect himself or other persons from the danger.

(2) For the purposes of subsection (1)(e) whether steps which an employee took, or proposed to take, were appropriate shall be judged by reference to all the circumstances including, in particular, his knowledge and the facilities and advice available to him at the time.

(3) Where the reason (or, if more than one, the principal reason) for the dismissal of an employee was that specified in subsection (1)(e), the dismissal shall not be regarded as having been unfair if the employer shows that it was, or would have been, so negligent for the employee to take the steps which he took, or proposed to take, that a reasonable employer might have dismissed him for taking, or proposing to take, them.".

4. In section 59 of the 1978 Act (dismissal on ground of redundancy), in subsection (2) (inserted by section 24(2) of this Act), between the words "section" and "60" there shall be inserted the words "57A(1) (read with (2) and (3))".

5. In section 64 of the 1978 Act (qualifying period etc for right not to be unfairly dismissed), in subsection (4) (inserted by section 24(3) of this Act), between the words "section" and "60" there shall be inserted the words "57A(1) (read with (2) and (3))".

6. In section 71 of the 1978 Act (compensation for failure to comply with section 69)—

(a) in subsection (2)(b) (additional award), after the word "unless" there shall be inserted the words "the case is one where this paragraph is excluded or"; and

(b) after that subsection there shall be inserted—

"(2A) Subsection (2)(b) is excluded where the reason (or, if more than one, the principal reason) for the dismissal or, in a redundancy case, for selecting the employee for dismissal, was an inadmissible reason.

(2B) For the purposes of subsection (2A) a reason is "inadmissible" if it is one of those specified in section 57A(1)(a) and (b).".

7. In section 72 of the 1978 Act (compensation for unfair dismissal) there shall be inserted at the end the following—

"(2) Where the reason (or, if more than one, the principal reason) for the dismissal or, in a redundancy case, for selecting the employee for dismissal, was an inadmissible reason, then, unless—

(a) the complainant does not request the tribunal to make an order under section 69, or
(b) the case falls within section 73(2),

the award shall include a special award calculated in accordance with section 75A.

(3) For the purposes of subsection (2) a reason is "inadmissible" if it is one of those specified in section 57A(1)(a) and (b)."

and the preceding words shall become subsection (1) of section 72.

8. In section 73 of the 1978 Act (calculation of basic award)—

(a) in subsection (1), for "(6)" there shall be substituted "(6A)";
(b) after subsection (6) there shall be inserted—

"(6A) Where the reason (or, if more than one, the principal reason) for the dismissal or, in a redundancy case, for selecting the employee for dismissal, was an inadmissible reason the amount of the basic award (before any reduction under the following provisions of this section) shall not be less than £2,700.

(6B) For the purposes of this section a reason is "inadmissible" if it is one of those specified in section 57A(1)(a) and (b).

(6C) The Secretary of State may by order increase the sum specified in subsection (6A).

(6D) No order shall be made under subsection (6C) unless a draft of the order has been laid before Parliament and approved by a resolution of each House of Parliament."; and

(c) in subsection (7C), for the words following "apply" there shall be substituted the words "in a redundancy case unless the reason for selecting the employee for dismissal was an inadmissible reason; and, in that event, subsection (7B) shall apply only to so much of the basic award as is payable because of subsection (6A)".

9. After section 75 of that Act there shall be inserted—

"Calculation of special award

75A.—(1) Subject to the following provisions of this section, the amount of the special award shall be—

(a) one week's pay multiplied by 104, or
(b) £13,400,

whichever is the greater, but shall not exceed £26,800.

(2) Where the award of compensation is made under section 71(2)(a) then, unless the employer satisfies the tribunal that it was not practicable to comply with the preceding order under section 69, the amount of the special award shall be increased to—

(a) one week's pay multiplied by 156, or
(b) £20,100,

whichever is the greater, but subject to the following provisions of this section.

(3) In the case where the amount of the basic award is reduced under section 73(5), the amount of the special award shall be reduced by the same fraction.

(4) Where the tribunal considers that any conduct of the complainant before the dismissal (or, where the dismissal was with notice, before the notice was given) was such that it would be just and equitable to reduce or further reduce the amount of the special award to any extent, the tribunal shall reduce or further reduce that amount accordingly.

(5) Where the tribunal finds that the complainant has unreasonably—

(a) prevented an order under section 69 from being complied with, or
(b) refused an offer by the employer (made otherwise than in compliance with such an order) which if accepted would have the effect of reinstating the complainant in his employment in all respects as if he had not been dismissed,

the tribunal shall reduce or further reduce the amount of the special award to such extent as it considers just and equitable having regard to that finding.

(6) Where the employer has engaged a permanent replacement for the complainant, the tribunal shall not take that fact into account in determining for the purposes of subsection (2) whether it was practicable to comply with an order under section 69 unless the employer shows that it was not practicable for him to arrange for the complainant's work to be done without engaging a permanent replacement.

(7) The Secretary of State may by order increase any of the sums specified in subsections (1) and (2).

(8) No order shall be made under subsection (7) unless a draft of the order has been laid before Parliament and approved by a resolution of each House of Parliament.".

10. After section 76 of that Act there shall be inserted—

Interim relief pending determination of complaint of unfair dismissal

77.—(1) An employee who presents a complaint to an industrial tribunal that he has been unfairly dismissed by his employer and that the reason (or, if more than one, the principal reason) for the dismissal was one of those specified in section 57A(1)(a) and (b) may apply to the tribunal for interim relief.

(2) The tribunal shall not entertain an application for interim relief unless it is presented to the tribunal before the end of the period of seven days immediately following the effective date of termination (whether before, on or after that date).

(3) The tribunal shall determine the application for interim relief as soon as practicable after receiving the application.

(4) The tribunal shall give to the employer (not later than seven days before the date of the hearing) a copy of the application together with notice of the date, time and place of the hearing.

(5) The tribunal shall not exercise any power it has of postponing the hearing of an application for interim relief except where it is satisfied that special circumstances exist which justify it in doing so.

Procedure on hearing of application and making of order

77A.—(1) If on hearing an employee's application for interim relief it appears to the tribunal that it is likely that on determining the complaint to which the application relates the tribunal will find that the reason (or, if more than one, the principal reason) for his dismissal was one of those specified in section 57A(1)(a) and (b) the following provisions shall apply.

(2) The tribunal shall announce its findings and explain to both parties (if present) what powers the tribunal may exercise on the application and in what circumstances it will exercise them, and shall ask the employer (if present) whether he is willing, pending the determination or settlement of the complaint—

    (a) to reinstate the employee, that is to say, to treat him in all respects as if he had not been dismissed, or

    (b) if not, to re-engage him in another job on terms and conditions not less favourable than those which would have been applicable to him if he had not been dismissed.

(3) For this purpose "terms and conditions not less favourable than those which would have been applicable to him if he had not been dismissed" means, as regards seniority, pension rights and other similar rights, that the period prior to the dismissal should be regarded as continuous with his employment following the dismissal.

(4) If the employer states that he is willing to reinstate the employee, the tribunal shall make an order to that effect.

(5) If the employer states that he is willing to re-engage the employee in another job and specifies the terms and conditions on which he is willing to do so, the tribunal shall ask the employee whether he is willing to accept the job on those terms and conditions; and—

    (a) if the employee is willing to accept the job on those terms and conditions, the tribunal shall make an order to that effect, and

    (b) if he is not, then, if the tribunal is of the opinion that the refusal is reasonable, the tribunal shall make an order for the continuation of his contract of employment, but otherwise the tribunal shall make no order.

(6) If on the hearing of an application for interim relief the employer fails to attend before the tribunal, or states that he is unwilling either to reinstate the employee or re-engage him as mentioned in subsection (2), the tribunal shall make an order for the continuation of the employee's contract of employment.

Orders for continuation of contract of employment

78.—(1) An order under section 77A for the continuation of a contract of employment is an order that the contract of employment continue in force—

    (a) for the purposes of pay or of any other benefit derived from the employment, seniority, pension rights and other similar matters, and

    (b) for the purposes of determining for any purpose the period for which the employee has been continuously employed, from the date of its termination (whether before or after the making of the order) until the determination or settlement of the complaint.

(2) Where the tribunal makes such an order it shall specify in the order the amount which is to be paid by the employer to the employee by way of pay in respect of each normal pay period, or part of any such period, falling between the date of dismissal and the determination or settlement of the complaint.

(3) Subject as follows, the amount so specified shall be that which the employee could reasonably have been expected to earn during that period, or part, and shall be paid—
- (a) in the case of payment for any such period falling wholly or partly after the making of the order, on the normal pay day for that period, and
- (b) in the case of a payment for any past period, within such time as may be specified in the order.

(4) If an amount is payable in respect only of part of a normal pay period, the amount shall be calculated by reference to the whole period and reduced proportionately.

(5) Any payment made to an employee by an employer under his contract of employment, or by way of damages for breach of that contract, in respect of a normal pay period, or part of any such period, shall go towards discharging the employer's liability in respect of that period under subsection (2); and, conversely, any payment under that subsection in respect of a period shall go towards discharging any liability of the employer under, or in respect of breach of, the contract of employment in respect of that period.

(6) If an employee, on or after being dismissed by his employer, receives a lump sum which, or part of which, is in lieu of wages but is not referable to any normal pay period, the tribunal shall take the payment into account in determining the amount of pay to be payable in pursuance of any such order.

(7) For the purposes of this section, the amount which an employee could reasonably have been expected to earn, his normal pay period and the normal pay day for each such period shall be determined as if he had not been dismissed.

Application for variation or revocation of order

78A.—(1) At any time between the making of an order under section 77A and the determination or settlement of the complaint, the employer or the employee may apply to an industrial tribunal for the revocation or variation of the order on the ground of a relevant change of circumstances since the making of the order.

(2) Sections 77 and 77A apply in relation to such an application as in relation to an original application for interim relief except that, in the case of an application by the employer, section 77(4) has effect with the substitution of a reference to the employee for the reference to the employer.

Consequence of failure to comply with order

79.—(1) If on the application of an employee an industrial tribunal is satisfied that the employer has not complied with the terms of an order for the reinstatement or re-engagement of the employee under section 77A(4) or (5), the tribunal shall—
- (a) make an order for the continuation of the employee's contract of employment, and
- (b) order the employer to pay the employee such compensation as the tribunal considers just and equitable in all the circumstances having regard—
  - (i) to the infringement of the employee's right to be reinstated or re-engaged in pursuance of the order, and
  - (ii) to any loss suffered by the employee in consequence of the non-compliance.

(2) Section 78 applies to an order under subsection (1)(a) as in relation to an order under section 77A.

(3) If on the application of an employee an industrial tribunal is satisfied that the employer has not complied with the terms of an order for the continuation of a contract of employment, the following provisions apply.

(4) If the non-compliance consists of a failure to pay an amount by way of pay specified in the order, the tribunal shall determine the amount owed by the employer on the date of the determination.

(5) If on that date the tribunal also determines the employee's complaint that he has been unfairly dismissed, it shall specify that amount separately from any other sum awarded to the employee.

(6) In any other case, the tribunal shall order the employer to pay the employee such compensation as the tribunal considers just and equitable in all the circumstances having regard to any loss suffered by the employee in consequence of the non-compliance.".

SCHEDULE 6

COMPROMISE CONTRACTS

Sex Discrimination Act 1975 (c. 65)

1. In section 77 of the Sex Discrimination Act 1975 (validity, etc. of contracts)—
(a) in subsection (4), after paragraph (a), there shall be inserted—
    "(aa) to a contract settling a complaint to which section 63(1) of this Act or section 2 of
        the Equal Pay Act 1970 applies if the conditions regulating compromise contracts
        under this Act are satisfied in relation to the contract;"; and
(b) after subsection (4) there shall be inserted—
    "(4A) The conditions regulating compromise contracts under this Act are that—
        (a) the contract must be in writing;
        (b) the contract must relate to the particular complaint;
        (c) the complainant must have received independent legal advice from a qualified
            lawyer as to the terms and effect of the proposed contract and in particular its
            effect on his ability to pursue his complaint before an industrial tribunal;
        (d) there must be in force, when the adviser gives the advice, a policy of insurance
            covering the risk of a claim by the complainant in respect of loss arising in conse-
            quence of the advice;
        (e) the contract must identify the adviser; and
        (f) the contract must state that the conditions regulating compromise contracts under
            this Act are satisfied.
    (4B) In subsection (4A)—
        "independent", in relation to legal advice to the complainant, means that it is given by a
            lawyer who is not acting for the other party or for a person who is connected with
            that other party; and
        "qualified lawyer" means—
            (a) as respects proceedings in England and Wales—
                (i) a barrister, whether in practice as such or employed to give legal
                    advice, or
                (ii) a solicitor of the Supreme Court who holds a practising certificate;
            (b) as respects proceedings in Scotland—
                (i) an advocate, whether in practice as such or employed to give legal
                    advice, or
                (ii) a solicitor who holds a practising certificate.
    (4C) For the purposes of subsection (4B) any two persons are to be treated as "connec-
ted" if one is a company of which the other (directly or indirectly) has control, or if both are
companies of which a third person (directly or indirectly) has control.".

Race Relations Act 1976 (c. 74)

2. In section 72 of the Race Relations Act 1976 (validity, etc. of contracts)—
(a) in subsection (4), after paragraph (a) there shall be inserted—
    "(aa) to a contract settling a complaint to which section 54(1) applies if the conditions
        regulating compromise contracts under this Act are satisfied in relation to the con-
        tract;"; and
(b) after subsection (4) there shall be inserted—
    "(4A) The conditions regulating compromise contracts under this Act are that—
        (a) the contract must be in writing;
        (b) the contract must relate to the particular complaint;
        (c) the complainant must have received independent legal advice from a qualified
            lawyer as to the terms and effect of the proposed contract and in particular its
            effect on his ability to pursue his complaint before an industrial tribunal;
        (d) there must be in force, when the adviser gives the advice, a policy of insurance
            covering the risk of a claim by the complainant in respect of loss arising in conse-
            quence of the advice;
        (e) the contract must identify the adviser; and
        (f) the contract must state that the conditions regulating compromise contracts under
            this Act are satisfied.
    (4B) In subsection (4A)—
        "independent", in relation to legal advice to the complainant, means that it is given by a
            lawyer who is not acting for the other party or for a person who is connected with
            that other party; and

"qualified lawyer" means—
> (a) as respects proceedings in England and Wales—
>> (i) a barrister, whether in practice as such or employed to give legal advice, or
>> (ii) a solicitor of the Supreme Court who holds a practising certificate.
> (b) as respects proceedings in Scotland—
>> (i) an advocate, whether in practice as such or employed to give legal advice, or
>> (ii) a solicitor who holds a practising certificate.

(4C) For the purposes of subsection (4B) any two persons are to be treated as "connected" if one is a company of which the other (directly or indirectly) has control, or if both are companies of which a third person (directly or indirectly) has control.".

Wages Act 1986 (c. 48)

3. In section 6 of the Wages Act 1986 (remedies for Part I contraventions and restriction on contracting out)—
> (a) in subsection (3) after the words "apply to" there shall be inserted "(a)" and at the end of the words so constituted paragraph (a) there shall be inserted the words "; or
>> (b) an agreement to refrain from presenting or continuing with a complaint if the conditions regulating compromise agreements under this Part of this Act are satisfied in relation to the agreement"; and
> (b) after subsection (3) there shall be inserted—

"(4) The conditions regulating compromise agreements under this Part of this Act are that—
> (a) the agreement must be in writing;
> (b) the agreement must relate to the particular complaint;
> (c) the worker must have received independent legal advice from a qualified lawyer as to the terms and effect of the proposed agreement and in particular its effect on his ability to pursue his complaint before an industrial tribunal;
> (d) there must be in force, when the adviser gives the advice, a policy of insurance covering the risk of a claim by the worker in respect of loss arising in consequence of the advice;
> (e) the agreement must identify the adviser; and
> (f) the agreement must state that the conditions regulating compromise agreements under this Part of this Act are satisfied.

(5) In subsection (4)—
"independent", in relation to legal advice to the worker, means that it is given by a lawyer who is not acting in the matter for the employer or for a person who is connected with the employer; and
"qualified lawyer" means—
> (a) as respects proceedings in England and Wales—
>> (i) a barrister, whether in practice as such or employed to give legal advice, or
>> (ii) a solicitor of the Supreme Court who holds a practising certificate;
> (b) as respects proceedings in Scotland—
>> (i) an advocate, whether in practice as such or employed to give legal advice, or
>> (ii) a solicitor who holds a practising certificate.

(6) For the purposes of subsection (5) any two persons are to be treated as "connected" if one is a company of which the other (directly or indirectly) has control, or if both are companies of which a third person (directly or indirectly) has control.".

Trade Union and Labour Relations (Consolidation) Act 1992 (c. 52)

4. In section 288 of the 1992 Act (restrictions on contracting out)—
> (a) after subsection (2) there shall be inserted—

"(2A) Subsection (1) does not apply to an agreement to refrain from instituting or continuing any proceedings, other than excepted proceedings, specified in section 290 before an industrial tribunal if the conditions regulating compromise agreements under this Act are satisfied in relation to the agreement.

(2B) The conditions regulating compromise agreements under this Act are that—
> (a) the agreement must be in writing;
> (b) the agreement must relate to the particular complaint;
> (c) the complainant must have received independent legal advice from a qualified lawyer as to the terms and effect of the proposed agreement and in particular its effect on his ability to pursue his rights before an industrial tribunal;

(d) there must be in force, when the adviser gives the advice, a policy of insurance covering the risk of a claim by the complainant in respect of loss arising in consequence of
the advice;

(e) the agreement must identify the adviser; and

(f) the agreement must state that the conditions regulating compromise agreements
under this Act are satisfied.

(2C) The proceedings excepted from subsection (2A) are proceedings on a complaint of
non-compliance with section 188."; and

(b) after subsection (3) there shall be inserted—

"(4) In subsection (2B)—

"independent", in relation to legal advice to the complainant means that it is given by a
lawyer who is not acting for the other party or for a person who is connected with
that other party; and

"qualified lawyer" means—

(a) as respects proceedings in England and Wales—

(i) a barrister, whether in practice as such or employed to give legal
advice, or

(ii) a solicitor of the Supreme Court who holds a practising certificate;

(b) as respects proceedings in Scotland—

(i) an advocate, whether in practice as such or employed to give legal
advice, or

(ii) a solicitor who holds a practising certificate.

(5) For the purposes of subsection (4) any two persons are to be treated as "connected" if
one is a company of which the other (directly or indirectly) has control, or if both are companies of which a third person (directly or indirectly) has control.".

Section 49(1)   SCHEDULE 7

MISCELLANEOUS AMENDMENTS

Unfair selection for dismissal in redundancy cases: exclusion of qualifying conditions

1. In section 154 of the 1992 Act (exclusion of requirement for qualifying period of employment, etc. where reason for dismissal related to trade union membership or activities)—

(a) for the words "was one of those specified in section 152(1)" there shall be substituted the
words "or, in a redundancy case, for selecting the employee for dismissal, was an inadmissible reason.", and

(b) there shall be inserted after those words, as subsection (2), the following—

"(2) For the purposes of this section—

"inadmissible", in relation to a reason, means that it is one of those specified in section
152(1); and

"a redundancy case" means a case where the reason or principal reason for the dismissal was that the employee was redundant but the equal application of the circumstances to non-dismissed employees required by section 153(a) is also
shown.",

and the words preceding that subsection (2) shall become subsection (1).

Qualifying period for unfair dismissal protection: small businesses

2. Section 64A of the 1978 Act (extended qualifying period for right not to be unfairly dismissed where no more than twenty employees) shall be omitted.

Application of 1978 Act to Crown Employment and House of Commons Staff

3. In section 138 of the 1978 Act (application to Crown)—

(a) in subsection (1) (which applies Part I to Crown employees only so far as it relates to
itemised pay statements), the words "(so far as it relates to itemised pay statements)" shall
be omitted, and

(b) in subsection (4) (disapplication of any provision which would otherwise apply to Crown
employment where national security certificate in force), for the words "For the purposes
of this section, Crown employment does not include any employment" there shall be
substituted the words "Part I (so far as it relates to itemised pay statements), Part II
(except sections 22A to 22C and 31A), section 53 (apart from subsection (2A)), Part V
(except so far as relating to a dismissal which is regarded as unfair by reason of section

57A, 59(1)(a) or 60) and Part VIII and this Part (so far as relating to any of those provisions) shall not have effect in relation to any Crown employment".

4. In section 139(1) of the 1978 Act (application of Part I to House of Commons staff only so far as it relates to itemised pay statements), the words "(so far as it relates to itemised pay statements)" shall be omitted.

Restrictions on disclosure of information, etc. on grounds of national security

5. After section 146 of the 1978 Act there shall be inserted—

"National Security

146A.—(1) Where in the opinion of any Minister of the Crown the disclosure of any information would be contrary to the interests of national security—

(a) nothing in any of the provisions to which this section applies shall require any person to disclose the information, and

(b) no person shall disclose the information in any proceedings in any court or tribunal relating to any of those provisions.

(2) This section applies to—

(a) Part I so far as it relates to employment particulars,

(b) sections 22A to 22C and section 31A,

(c) Part III,

(d) section 53(2A),

(e) Part V so far as relating to a dismissal which is regarded as unfair by reason of section 57A, 59(1)(a) or 60, and

(f) Part VIII and this Part so far as relating to any of the provisions in paragraphs (a) to (e).".

6. In Schedule 9 of the 1978 Act (industrial tribunals)—

(a) in paragraph 1 (regulations as to procedure), after sub-paragraph (4), there shall be inserted—

"(4A) Without prejudice to sub-paragraph (5) or paragraph 2, a Minister of the Crown may on grounds of national security direct an industrial tribunal to sit in private when hearing or determining any proceedings specified in the direction.", and

(b) in paragraph 2 (national security), in sub-paragraph (2), for the words "A certificate" there shall be substituted the words "Except where the complaint is that a dismissal is unfair by reason of section 57A, 59(1)(a) or 60, a certificate".

7. In paragraph 18 of Schedule 11 to the 1978 Act (Employment Appeal Tribunal Rules), for sub-paragraph (c) (power for rules to enable private hearings) there shall be substituted—

"(c) for requiring or enabling the Appeal Tribunal to sit in private in circumstances in which an industrial tribunal is required or empowered to sit in private by virtue of paragraph 1 of Schedule 9;".

Extension of employment protection provisions and related legislation to House of Lords Staff

8. In section 1 of the Equal Pay Act 1970 (requirement of equal treatment for men and women), after subsection (10A) there shall be inserted—

"(10B) This section applies in relation to employment as a relevant member of the House of Lords staff as in relation to other employment.

In this subsection "relevant member of the House of Lords staff" has the same meaning as in section 139A of the Employment Protection (Consolidation) Act 1978; and subsection (6) of that section applies for the purposes of this section.".

9. After section 85A of the Sex Discrimination Act 1975 (application to House of Commons staff) there shall be inserted—

"Application to House of Lords staff

85B.—(1) Parts II and IV apply in relation to employment as a relevant member of the House of Lords staff as they apply in relation to other employment.

(2) In this section "relevant member of the House of Lords staff" has the same meaning as in section 139A of the Employment Protection (Consolidation) Act 1978; and subsection (6) of that section applies for the purposes of this section.".

10. After section 75A of the Race Relations Act 1976 (application to House of Commons staff) there shall be inserted—

"Application to House of Lords staff

75B.—(1) Parts II and IV apply in relation to employment as a relevant member of the House of Lords staff as they apply in relation to other employment.

(2) In this section "relevant member of the House of Lords staff" has the same meaning as in section 139A of the Employment Protection (Consolidation) Act 1978; and subsection (6) of that section applies for the purposes of this section.".

11. After section 139 of the 1978 Act there shall be inserted—

"House of Lords staff

Provisions as to House of Lords staff
139A.—(1) The provisions of Parts I, II, III, V and VIII, and this Part and section 53 shall apply in relation to employment as a relevant member of the House of Lords staff as they apply to other employment.

(2) Nothing in any rule of law or the law or practice of Parliament shall prevent a relevant member of the House of Lords staff from bringing a civil employment claim before the court or from bringing before an industrial tribunal proceedings of any description which could be brought before such a tribunal by a person who is not such a member.

(3) For the purposes of the application of the enactments applied by subsection (1) in relation to a relevant member of the House of Lords staff—
  (a) the reference in paragraph 1(5)(c) of Schedule 9 to a person's undertaking or any undertaking in which he works shall be construed as a reference to the national interest or, if the case so requires, the interests of the House of Lords; and
  (b) any other reference to an undertaking shall be construed as a reference to the House of Lords.

(4) Where the terms of his contract of employment restrict the right of a relevant member of the House of Lords staff to take part in—
  (a) certain political activities, or
  (b) activities which may conflict with his official functions,
nothing in section 29 shall require him to be allowed time off work for public duties connected with any such activities.

(5) In this section—
  "relevant member of the House of Lords staff" means any person who is employed under a contract of employment with the Corporate Officer of the House of Lords;
  "civil employment claim" means a claim arising out of or relating to a contract of employment or any other contract connected with employment, or a claim in tort arising in connection with a person's employment; and
  "the court" means the High Court or the county court.

(6) For the purposes of the application of the enactments applied by subsection (1) and of any civil employment claim in relation to a person continuously employed in or for the purposes of the House of Lords up to the time when he became so employed under a contract of employment with the Corporate Officer of the House of Lords, his employment shall not be treated as having been terminated by reason only of a change in his employer before or at that time.".

12. In section 277 of the 1992 Act (House of Lords staff)—
(a) in subsection (1), for the words "Sections 137 to 143 (rights in relation to trade union membership: access to employment)" there shall be substituted the words "The provisions of this Act (except those specified below)",
(b) after that subsection there shall be inserted—
"(1A) The following provisions are excepted from subsection (1)—
  sections 184 and 185 (remedy for failure to comply with declaration as to disclosure of information),
  Chapter II of Part IV (procedure for handling redundancies).",
(c) in subsection (2), after the word "bringing" there shall be inserted the words "a civil employment claim before the court or from bringing",
(d) after that subsection there shall be inserted—
"(2A) For the purposes of the application of the other provisions of this Act as they apply by virtue of this section—
  (a) the reference in section 182(1)(e) (disclosure of information for collective bargaining: restrictions) to a person's undertaking shall be construed as a reference to the national interest or, if the case so requires, the interests of the House of Lords; and
  (b) any other reference to an undertaking shall be construed as a reference to the House of Lords.", and
(e) for subsections (3) to (6) there shall be substituted—

"(3) In this section—
"relevant member of the House of Lords staff" means any person who is employed under a contract of employment with the Corporate Officer of the House of Lords;
"civil employment claim" means a claim arising out of or relating to a contract of employment or any other contract connected with employment, or a claim in tort arising in connection with a person's employment; and
"the court" means the High Court or a county court.".

Power to extend 1978 Act in certain health and safety cases

13. In section 149 of the 1978 Act (general power to amend Act), after subsection (2) there shall be inserted—
"(2A) The Secretary of State may by order provide that, subject to any such modifications and exceptions as may be prescribed in the order, sections 22A to 22C (and any other provisions of this Act so far as relating to those sections) shall apply to such descriptions of persons other than employees as may be prescribed in the order as they apply to employees (but as if references to their employer were references to such person as may be so prescribed).".

Power to provide for continuity of employment following reinstatement or re-engagement

14. In Schedule 13 to the 1978 Act (computation of period of employment), in paragraph 20 (re-instatement or re-engagement of dismissed employee)—
   (a) in sub-paragraph (2)(a), for the words "complaint under section 67" there shall be substituted the words "relevant complaint of dismissal";
   (b) in sub-paragraph (2)(c), for the words "section 134(3)" there shall be substituted the words "his relevant conciliation powers or";
   (c) after sub-paragraph (2)(c), there shall be inserted—
   "(d) of the making of a relevant compromise contract.";
   and
   (d) after sub-paragraph (2) there shall be inserted—
   "(3) In sub-paragraph (2)—
   "relevant complaint of dismissal" means a complaint under section 67 of this Act, a complaint under section 63 of the Sex Discrimination Act 1975 arising out of a dismissal or a complaint under section 54 of the Race Relations Act 1976 arising out of a dismissal;
   "relevant conciliation powers" means section 134(3) of this Act, section 64(2) of the Sex Discrimination Act 1975 or section 55(2) of the Race Relations Act 1976; and
   "relevant compromise contract" means an agreement or contract authorised by section 140(2)(fa) or (fb) of this Act, section 77(4)(aa) of the Sex Discrimination Act 1975 or section 72(4)(aa) of the Race Relations Act 1976.".

Codes of practice on employment: use in proceedings

15. In section 56A of the Sex Discrimination Act 1975 (codes of practice in the field of employment), in subsection (10) (relevance of codes in proceedings under that Act before industrial tribunals), after the words "under this Act" there shall be inserted the words "or the Equal Pay Act 1970".

Parliamentary procedure: orders modifying application of redundancy provisions

16. In section 149 of the 1978 Act (general power to amend Act)—
   (a) in subsection (4) (orders to be subject to affirmative procedure), for the words "subsection (1)" there shall be inserted the words "this section, other than one to which subsection (5) applies,", and
   (b) after subsection (4) there shall be inserted—
   "(5) This subsection applies to an order under subsection (1)(b) which specifies only provisions contained in Part VI.".

Miscellaneous minor corrections and amendments

17. In section 21(6) of the 1992 Act (repudiation by trade union of certain acts) for the words "six months" there shall be substituted the words "three months".
18. In section 34(5) of the 1992 Act (eligibility for appointment as auditor), the second sentence shall be omitted.
19. In section 35(5) of the 1992 Act (appointment and removal of auditors)—
   (a) for the words "subsections (1) to (6)" there shall be substituted the words "subsections (1) to (4)", and

(b) for the words "subsection (7)" there shall be substituted the words "subsection (5)".

20. In section 110(3) of the 1992 Act (consideration by Commissioner of application for assistance for certain legal proceedings) for the word "(f)" there shall be substituted the word "(e)" and for the words "or ballot" there shall be substituted the words "or political ballot".

21. In section 158 of the 1992 Act (special award in cases of dismissal on grounds related to union membership or activities) after subsection (6) there shall be inserted—

"(7) Schedule 14 to the Employment Protection (Consolidation) Act 1978 (calculation of a week's pay) shall apply for the purposes of this section with the substitution, for paragraph 7, of the following:—

For the purposes of this Part in its application to section 158 of the Trade Union and Labour Relations (Consolidation) Act 1992, the calculation date is—

(a) where the dismissal was with notice, the date on which the employer's notice was given;

(b) where paragraph (a) does not apply, the effective date of termination.".

22. In section 166(1) of the 1992 Act (consequences of failure to comply with order of reinstatement or re-engagement, for "(5)(a)" there shall be substituted "(5)".

23. In section 187(2) of the 1992 Act (meaning of refusal to deal where refusal on grounds of union exclusion), paragraph (c) shall become subparagraph (iii) of paragraph (b) and there shall be inserted as paragraph (c) the following, preceded by "or", namely—

"(c) he terminates a contract with that person for the supply of goods or services.".

24. In section 228 of the 1992 Act (separate workplace ballots before action by trade union) after subsection (3) there shall be inserted—

"(4) In this section "place of work", in relation to any person who is employed, means the premises occupied by his employer at or from which that person works or, where he does not work at or from any such premises or works at or from more than one set of premises, the premises occupied by his employer with which his employment has the closest connection.".

25. In section 229(3) of the 1992 Act (voting paper for industrial action ballot) for the word "20(3)" there shall be substituted the word "20(2)".

26. In section 246 of the 1992 Act (minor definitions relating to industrial action provisions) the definition of "place of work" shall be omitted.

27. In section 278(4)(c) of the 1992 Act (House of Commons staff), after the word "in" there shall be inserted the word "section".

Section 49(2)   SCHEDULE 8

CONSEQUENTIAL AMENDMENTS

The Factories Act 1961 (c. 34)

1. In section 119A of the Factories Act 1961 (notice of employment of a young person to be sent to local careers office), in subsection (2)(a) (definition of "local careers office"), for the words from ", under" to "the arrangements)" there shall be substituted the words "services are provided in pursuance of arrangements made, or a direction given, under section 10 of the Employment and Training Act 1973 in the area".

The Parliamentary Commissioner Act 1967 (c. 13)

2. In Schedule 2 to the Parliamentary Commissioner Act 1967 (departments and authorities subject to investigation) there shall be inserted at the appropriate place—

"Office of the Commissioner for Protection Against Unlawful Industrial Action.".

The Chronically Sick and Disabled Persons Act 1970 (c. 44)

3. In section 13(2) of the Chronically Sick and Disabled Persons Act 1970 (youth employment service), for the words "section 10(1)" there shall be substituted the words "section 10(6)".

The Employment Agencies Act 1973 (c. 35)

4. In section 13(7) of the Employment Agencies Act 1973 (exclusions from provisions of that Act), after paragraph (g) there shall be inserted—

"(ga) services provided in pursuance of arrangements made, or a direction given, under section 10 of the Employment and Training Act 1973;".

The Employment and Training Act 1973 (c. 50)

5. In section 5(2)(a) of the Employment and Training Act 1973 (power to appoint advisers with respect to performance of certain functions), for the words from "on him" to the end there shall be substituted the words "or imposed on him by sections 2, 8 to 10 and 12 of this Act; and".

The House of Commons Disqualification Act 1975 (c. 24)

6. In Part III of Schedule 1 to the House of Commons Disqualification Act 1975 (other disqualifying offices) there shall be inserted at the appropriate place—
"Commissioner for Protection Against Unlawful Industrial Action.".

The Northern Ireland Assembly Disqualification Act 1975 (c. 25)

7. In Part III of Schedule 1 to the Northern Ireland Assembly Disqualification Act 1975 (other disqualifying offices) there shall be inserted at the appropriate place—
"Commissioner for Protection Against Unlawful Industrial Action.".

The Sex Discrimination Act 1975 (c. 65)

8. In section 15 of the Sex Discrimination Act 1975 (employment agencies etc.)—
(a) for subsection (2) there shall be substituted—
"(2) It is unlawful for a local education authority or education authority or any other person to do any act in providing services in pursuance of arrangements made, or a direction given, under section 10 of the Employment and Training Act 1973 which constitutes discrimination.", and
(b) in subsection (5), for the words "or an education authority" there shall be substituted the words ", education authority or other person".

The Race Relations Act 1976 (c. 74)

9. In section 14 of the Race Relations Act 1976 (employment agencies etc.)—
(a) for subsection (2) there shall be substituted—
"(2) It is unlawful for a local education authority or education authority or any other person to do any act in providing services in pursuance of arrangements made, or a direction given, under section 10 of the Employment and Training Act 1973 which constitutes discrimination.", and
(b) in subsection (5), for the words "or an education authority" there shall be substituted the words ", education authority or other person".

The Employment Protection (Consolidation) Act 1978 (c. 44)

10. In section 11 of the 1978 Act (enforcement of right to employment particulars)—
(a) in subsection (1) (references to determine what statement an employer ought to have given the employee), after the words "as required by section 1 or 4(1) or 8" there shall be inserted the words "(that is to say, either because he gives him no statement or because the statement he gives does not comply with those requirements)";
(b) in subsection (4)(b) (questions as to particulars which ought to have been included in a note about disciplinary procedures), for the words "a note under section 1(4)" there shall be substituted the words "the note required by section 3 to be included in the statement under section 1"; and
(c) in subsection (9) (time limit of three months for applications to industrial tribunals), at the end, there shall be inserted the words—
"or—
(b) within such further period as the tribunal considers reasonable in a case where it is satisfied that it was not reasonably practicable for the application to be made before the end of that period of three months";
and after the word "made" (in the second place where it occurs) there shall be inserted "(a)".

11. In section 53 of the 1978 Act (written statement of reasons for dismissal), in subsection (4) (complaint on ground of unreasonable refusal to provide written statement under subsection (1))—
(a) for the words "refused to provide a written statement under subsection (1)" there shall be substituted the words "failed to provide a written statement under this section", and
(b) for the words "that subsection" there shall be substituted the words "this section".

12. In section 56 of the 1978 Act (failure to permit woman to return to work under section 47 treated as dismissal for purposes of unfair dismissal provisions), for the words "is entitled to return to work and has exercised her right to return in accordance with section 47" there shall be substituted the words "has the right to return to work under section 39 and has exercised it in accordance with section 42".

13. In section 56A of the 1978 Act (exclusion of section 56)—
(a) in subsection (1)(a), for the words "her absence began" there shall be substituted the words "the end of her maternity leave period (or, if it ends by reason of dismissal, immediately before the dismissal)", and

(b) in subsections (1)(b), (2)(a) and (3)(b), for the words "section 45(1)" there shall be substituted the words "section 39".

14. In section 59 of the 1978 Act (dismissal on ground of redundancy)—

(a) for the word "he", in both places where it occurs, and the word "him" there shall be substituted the words "the employee",

(b) for the words "in his case" there shall be substituted the words "in the case of the employee", and

(c) at the end, there shall be inserted as subsection (3)—

"(3) For the purposes of this Part "a redundancy case" means a case where the reason or principal reason for the dismissal was that the employee was redundant but the equal application of the circumstances to non-dismissed employees is also shown.".

15. In section 61 of the 1978 Act (dismissal of replacement)—

(a) in subsection (1)(a) (dismissal of employee on return to work of employee absent because of pregnancy or confinement)—

(i) for the words "return to work of" there shall be substituted the words "resumption of work by", and

(ii) for the word "confinement" there shall be substituted the word "childbirth", and

(b) in subsection (2) (dismissal of employee on resumption of work by employee suspended as mentioned in section 19)—

(i) after the word "19" there shall be inserted the words "or 45", and

(ii) for the words "other employee to resume his original work" there shall be substituted the words "resumption of work by the other employee".

16. In section 65 of the 1978 Act (exclusion in respect of dismissal procedures agreement), in subsection (4) (disapplication of subsection (3) in case of right not to be dismissed for any reason mentioned in section 60(1) or (2)), for the words from "right" to the end there shall be substituted the words "right conferred by section 60 or 60A(1).".

17. In section 86 of the 1978 Act (failure to permit woman to return to work under section 47 treated as dismissal for purposes of redundancy provisions), for the words "is entitled to return to work and has exercised her right to return in accordance with section 47" there shall be substituted the words "has the right to return to work under section 39 and has exercised it in accordance with section 42".

18. In section 122 of the 1978 Act (employee's rights on insolvency of employer), in subsection (4) (amounts treated as arrears of pay), after paragraph (c) there shall be inserted—

"(ca) remuneration on suspension on maternity grounds under section 47;".

19. In section 132 of the 1978 Act (recoupment of benefits), in subsection (1)(b) (payments from which provision for recoupment may be made), after the words "or section" there shall be inserted the words "47 or".

20. In section 133(1)(a) of the 1978 Act (conciliation)—

(a) after the word "19", there shall be inserted the word "22A,", and

(b) after the word "31A", there shall be inserted the words "46, 47,".

21. In section 140 of the 1978 Act (restrictions on contracting-out), in subsection (2) (exceptions), after paragraph (f) there shall be inserted—

"(fa) to any agreement to refrain from instituting or continuing any proceedings before an industrial tribunal where the tribunal has jurisdiction in respect of the proceedings by virtue of an order under section 131;".

22. In section 141(1) of the 1978 Act (disapplication of sections 1 to 4 in case of employees engaged in work wholly or mainly outside Great Britain), for the words "unless the employee ordinarily works in Great Britain and the work outside Great Britain is for the same employer" there shall be substituted the words "unless—

(a) the employee ordinarily works in Great Britain and the work outside Great Britain is for the same employer, or

(b) the law which governs his contract of employment is the law of England and Wales or of Scotland".

23. In section 144 of the 1978 Act (mariners), for subsection (1) there shall be substituted—

"(1) Sections 1 to 4 and 49 to 51 do not apply to a person employed as a seaman in a ship registered in the United Kingdom under a crew agreement the provisions and form of which are of a kind approved by the Secretary of State.".

24. In section 149(2) of the 1978 Act (provisions to which power to make orders amending that Act does not apply)—

(a) after the word "57," there shall be inserted the word "57A,",

(b) after the word "67," there shall be inserted the words "73(6C) and (6D),", and

(c) after the word "75," there shall be inserted the words "75A(7) and (8),".

25. In section 153 of the 1978 Act (interpretation)—

(a) in subsection (1) (definitions)—
>>(i) after the definition of "business" there shall be inserted—
" "childbirth" means the birth of a living child or the birth of a child whether living or dead after twenty-four weeks of pregnancy;",
>>(ii) for the definition of "expected week of confinement" there shall be substituted—
" "expected week of childbirth" means the week, beginning with midnight between Saturday and Sunday, in which it is expected that childbirth will occur;",
>>(iii) after the definition of "job" there shall be inserted—
" "maternity leave period" shall be construed in accordance with sections 34 and 35;",
>>(iv) in the definition of "notified day of return", for the words "has the meaning given by section 47(1) and (8)" there shall be substituted the words "shall be construed in accordance with section 43(3) and (4)", and
>>(v) after that definition there shall be inserted—
" "notified leave date" shall be construed in accordance with section 36;", and
(b) in subsection (5) (irrelevance of what law governs a person's employment), for the word "For" there shall be substituted the words "Subject to section 141(1)(b), for".
26. In Schedule 2 to the 1978 Act (maternity)—
(a) in paragraph 2—
>>(i) in sub-paragraph (1), in the substituted sub-section (3), for the words "sections 59 to 61" there shall be substituted the words "sections 57A to 61",
>>(ii) in sub-paragraph (2), for the words "section 45(3)" there shall be substituted the words "section 41(1)", and
>>(iii) in sub-paragraph (5), for the words "the original contract of employment" there shall be substituted the words "her contract of employment immediately before the beginning of her maternity leave period",
(b) in paragraph 4—
>>(i) in sub-paragraph (1), for paragraph (c) there shall be substituted—
"(c) the reference in section 84(3) to the provisions of the previous contract shall be construed as a reference to the provisions of the contract under which the employee worked immediately before the beginning of her maternity leave period.", and
>>(ii) in sub-paragraph (4), for the words "the original contract of employment" there shall be substituted the words "her contract of employment immediately before the beginning of her maternity leave period",
(c) in paragraph 5—
>>(i) after the words "return to work" there shall be inserted the words "in accordance with section 42", and
>>(ii) for the words from "during her absence" to "confinement" there shall be substituted the words "on a day falling after the commencement of her maternity leave period and before the notified day of return",
(d) in paragraph 6—
>>(i) for sub-paragraph (1) there shall be substituted—
"(1) This paragraph applies where an employee has the right to return to work under section 39 and either her maternity leave period ends by reason of dismissal or she is dismissed after her maternity leave period.", and
>>(ii) in sub-paragraph (2), for the words "during the period of her absence" there shall be substituted the words "after her maternity leave period" and for the words "section 48" there shall be substituted the words "section 44", and
(e) in paragraph 7(1), for the words "section 48" there shall be substituted the words "section 44".
27. In Schedule 3 to the 1978 Act (rights of employees in period of notice)—
(a) in paragraph 2—
>>(i) in sub-paragraph (1), after paragraph (b) there shall be inserted—
"(ba) the employee is absent from work wholly or partly because of pregnancy or childbirth; or",
>>(ii) in sub-paragraph (1), after the words "paragraphs (a), (b)" there shall be inserted ", (ba)", and
>>(iii) in sub-paragraph (2), after the words "statutory sick pay," there shall be inserted the words "maternity pay, statutory maternity pay,", and
(b) in paragraph 3(3)—
>>(i) after paragraph (a) there shall be inserted—
"(aa) in respect of any period during which the employee is absent from work wholly or partly because of pregnancy or childbirth, or", and

(ii) after the words "statutory sick pay," there shall be inserted the words "maternity pay, statutory maternity pay,".

28. In Schedule 9 to the 1978 Act (industrial tribunals)—

(a) in paragraph 1(4)(b) (regulations as to procedure), for the word "confinement" there shall be substituted the word "childbirth",

(b) in sub-paragraph (1) of paragraph 1A (power to authorise pre-hearing reviews), for paragraph (a) there shall be substituted—

"(a) for authorising the carrying out by an industrial tribunal of a preliminary consideration of any proceedings before it ("a pre-hearing review"); and", and

(c) after that paragraph there shall be inserted—

"1B. The regulations may also include provision for authorising an industrial tribunal to hear and determine any issue relating to the entitlement of any party to proceedings to bring or contest the proceedings in advance of the hearing and determination of the proceedings by that or any other industrial tribunal.".

29. In paragraph 18(aa) of Schedule 11 to the 1978 Act (power for Employment Appeal Tribunal rules to regulate certain applications), for the words from "an application" to the end there shall be substituted the words "any application to the Appeal Tribunal may be made;".

30. In paragraph 18(e) of Schedule 11 to the 1978 Act (power for Employment Appeal Tribunal rules to provide for interlocutory proceedings to be dealt with otherwise than in accordance with paragraph 16), for the word "proceedings" there shall be substituted the words "matters arising on any appeal or application to the Appeal Tribunal".

31. In Schedule 13 to the 1978 Act (computation of period of employment)—

(a) in paragraph 9(1)(d), for the word "confinement" there shall be substituted the word "childbirth", and

(b) in paragraph 10—

(i) for the words "section 45(1)" there shall be substituted the words "section 39", and

(ii) for the word "confinement" there shall be substituted the word "childbirth".

32. In Schedule 14 to the 1978 Act (calculation of week's pay), in paragraph 7(1) (the calculation date)—

(a) after paragraph (e) there shall be inserted—

"(ea) where the calculation is for the purposes of section 47, the day before the suspension referred to in section 45(1) begins or where that day falls within an employee's maternity leave period or within the further period up to the day on which an employee exercises her right to return to work under section 39, the day before the beginning of the maternity leave period;", and

(b) after paragraph (i) there shall be inserted—

"(ia) where the calculation is for the purposes of section 75A and the dismissal was with notice, the date on which the employer's notice was given;

(ib) where the calculation is for the purposes of section 75A but sub-paragraph (ia) does not apply, the effective date of termination;".

The Agricultural Training Board Act 1982 (c. 9)

33. In section 4(1)(f) of the Agricultural Training Board Act 1982 (functions of the Agricultural Training Board), at the end there shall be inserted the words "and may provide services or arrange for the provision of services in pursuance of arrangements made, or a direction given, under section 10 of the Employment and Training Act 1973 (careers services)".

The Industrial Training Act 1982 (c. 10)

34. In section 5(3)(e) of the Industrial Training Act 1982 (functions of industrial training boards), at the end there shall be inserted the words "and may provide services or arrange for the provision of services in pursuance of arrangements made, or a direction given, under section 10 of the Employment and Training Act 1973 (careers services)".

The Insolvency Act 1986 (c. 45)

35. In paragraph 13(2) of Schedule 6 to the Insolvency Act 1986 (amounts treated as remuneration), in paragraph (b), after the word "Act" there shall be inserted the words "or remuneration on suspension on maternity grounds under section 47 of that Act".

The Wages Act 1986 (c. 48)

36. In section 30(1) and (3) of the Wages Act 1986 (excluded employments), for the words "Parts I and II do" there shall be substituted the words "Part I does".

37. In section 33(4) of that Act (commencement), for the words "paragraphs 4 to 7" there shall be substituted the words "paragraph 4".

The Employment Act 1988 (c. 19)

38. In subsection (1) of section 26 (status of trainees etc.) of the Employment Act 1988—
(a) after the words "under section 2(3)" there shall be inserted the words "or section 14A"; and
(b) for the words "the said section 2, or as the case may be the said section 2(3)" there shall be substituted the words "any of those three sections".

The Legal Aid Act 1988 (c. 34)

39. In Part II of Schedule 2 to the Legal Aid Act 1988 (excepted proceedings), after paragraph 5A there shall be inserted—
"5B. Proceedings to the extent that they consist in, or arise out of, an application to the court under section 235A of the Trade Union and Labour Relations (Consolidation) Act 1992,".

The Trade Union and Labour Relations (Consolidation) Act 1992 (c. 52)

40. In section 25 of the 1992 Act (application to Certification Officer as respects failures in relation to the register of members)—
(a) in subsection (1), after the words "section 24" there shall be inserted the words "or 24A"; and
(b) after subsection (7), there shall be inserted—
"(8) The Certification Officer shall not entertain an application for a declaration as respects an alleged failure to comply with the requirements of section 24A in relation to a ballot to which that section applies unless the application is made before the end of the period of one year beginning with the last day on which votes could be cast in the ballot.".
41. In section 26 of the 1992 Act (application to court as respects failures in relation to the register of members)—
(a) in subsection (1), after the words "section 24" there shall be inserted the words "or 24A"; and
(b) after subsection (6) there shall be inserted—
"(7) The court shall not entertain an application for a declaration as respects an alleged failure to comply with the requirements of section 24A in relation to a ballot to which that section applies unless the application is made before the end of the period of one year beginning with the last day on which votes could be cast in the ballot.".
42. In section 32 of the 1992 Act (annual return), after subsection (6) there shall be inserted—
"(7) For the purposes of this section and section 32A "member of the executive" includes any person who, under the rules or practice of the union, may attend and speak at some or all of the meetings of the executive, otherwise than for the purpose of providing the committee with factual information or with technical or professional advice with respect to matters taken into account by the executive in carrying out its functions.".
43. In section 43(1) (provisions not to apply in case of newly-formed trade unions)—
(a) in paragraph (b) (disapplication of sections 32 to 37), after the words "annual return," there shall be inserted the words "statement for members,", and
(b) after that paragraph there shall be inserted—
"(ba) sections 37A to 37E (investigation of financial affairs), and".
44. In section 44 of the 1992 Act (discharge of duties in case of union having branches or sections)—
(a) in subsections (2) and (4), for the words "sections 32 to 37" there shall be substituted the words "sections 32 and 33 to 37", and
(b) after subsection (4) there shall be inserted—
"(5) Where the duty falling on a trade union under section 32 to send to the Certification Officer a return relating to its affairs is treated as discharged by the union by virtue of subsection (2) or (4) of this section, the duties imposed by section 32A in relation to the return shall be treated as duties of the branch or section of the union, or the trade union of which it is a branch or section, by which that duty is in fact discharged.".
45. In section 45(1) of the 1992 Act (offences for breach of duty under sections 32 to 37 etc.), after the words "annual return," there shall be inserted the words "statement for members,".
46. In section 49(3)(a) of the 1992 Act (election scrutineer to supervise certain matters) for the words "and distribution of the voting papers" there shall be substituted the words "of the voting papers and (unless he is appointed under section 51A to undertake the distribution of the voting papers) their distribution".

47. In section 62 of the 1992 Act (right of trade union members to obtain order to prevent inducement to take part in industrial action not having support of a ballot)—

(a) at the end of subsection (1) (stating the right) there shall be inserted the following paragraph—

"In this section "the relevant time" means the time when the application is made."; and

(b) in subsection (2) (circumstances in which action has such support), for paragraphs (a) to (c) there shall be substituted—

"(a) the union has held a ballot in respect of the action—

(i) in relation to which the requirements of section 226B so far as applicable before and during the holding of the ballot were satisfied,

(ii) in relation to which the requirements of sections 227 to 231 were satisfied, and

(iii) in which the majority voting in the ballot answered "Yes" to the question applicable in accordance with section 229(2) to industrial action of the kind which the applicant has been or is likely to be induced to take part in;

(b) such of the requirements of the following sections as have fallen to be satisfied at the relevant time have been satisfied, namely—

(i) section 226B so far as applicable after the holding of the ballot, and

(ii) section 231B; and

(c) the requirements of section 233 (calling of industrial action with support of ballot) are satisfied.

Any reference in this subsection to a requirement of a provision which is disapplied or modified by section 232 has effect subject to that section.".

48. In section 64 of the 1992 Act (right not to be unjustifiably disciplined), in subsection (5) (enforcement provisions not to affect remedy for infringement of other rights), for the words "and nothing" there shall be substituted the words "and, subject to section 66(4), nothing".

49. In section 65(7) of the 1992 Act (definitions related to unjustifiable discipline)—

(a) in the definition of "contract of employment", at the end, there shall be inserted the words ", "employer" includes such a person and related expressions shall be construed accordingly;"; and

(b) at the end, there shall be inserted the following definition, preceded by the word "and"— " "wages" shall be construed in accordance with the definitions of "contract of employment", "employer" and related expressions.".

50. In section 66 of the 1992 Act (complaint of infringement of right not to be unjustifiably disciplined), for subsection (4) there shall be substituted—

"(4) Where a complaint relating to an expulsion which is presented under this section is declared to be well-founded, no complaint in respect of the expulsion shall be presented or proceeded with under section 174 (right not to be excluded or expelled from trade union).".

51. In section 67 of the 1992 Act (compensation for right not to be unjustifiably disciplined)—

(a) in subsection (8) (application of maximum and minimum limits of compensation)—

(i) for the words "awarded against a trade union on an application under this section" there shall be substituted the words "calculated in accordance with subsections (5) to (7)", and

(ii) for the words "156(1) of this Act (minimum basic award in certain cases of unfair dismissal)" there shall be substituted the words "176(6) of this Act (minimum award by Employment Appeal Tribunal in cases of exclusion or expulsion from union)", and

(b) subsection (9) (limits to be applied before reduction for failure to mitigate etc.) shall cease to have effect.

52. In section 97(1)(b) and (2)(b) of the 1992 Act (amalgamation or transfer of engagements), for the words "sections 99 and 100 (notice to members and passing of resolution)" there shall be substituted the words "section 99 (notice to members) and section 100 (resolution to be passed by required majority on ballot held in accordance with sections 100A to 100E)".

53. In section 98(1) of the 1992 Act (instrument of amalgamation or transfer to be submitted for approval of Certification Officer before resolution to approve it is voted on by members), for the words from "the resolution" to the end there shall be substituted the words "a ballot of the members of any amalgamating union, or (as the case may be) of the transferor union, is held on the resolution to approve the instrument.".

54. In section 99(1) of the 1992 Act (notice of instrument to be supplied to members), for the words from "that, not less" to "supplied with" there shall be substituted the words "that every voting paper which is supplied for voting in the ballot on the resolution to approve the instrument of amalgamation or transfer is accompanied by".

55. In section 101 of the 1992 Act (registration of instrument of amalgamation or transfer), after subsection (2) there shall be inserted—

"(3) An application for registration of an instrument of amalgamation or transfer shall not be sent to the Certification Officer until section 100E(6) has been complied with in relation to the scrutineer's report on the ballot held on the resolution to approve the instrument.".

56. In section 103 of the 1992 Act (complaints about passing of resolution approving instrument of amalgamation or transfer), for subsection (1) there shall be substituted—

"(1) A member of a trade union who claims that the union—
(a) has failed to comply with any of the requirements of sections 99 to 100E, or
(b) has, in connection with a resolution approving an instrument of amalgamation or transfer, failed to comply with any rule of the union relating to the passing of the resolution,
may complain to the Certification Officer.".

57. In section 106 of the 1992 Act (amalgamation or transfer involving Northern Ireland union)—
(a) in subsection (2), for the words "98 to 100 (approval of instrument; notice to members; passing of resolution)" there shall be substituted the words "98 to 100E and 101(3) (approval of instrument, notice to members and ballot on resolution)", and
(b) in subsection (4), for the words "section 103" there shall be substituted the words "sections 103 and 104".

58. In section 109 of the 1992 Act (proceedings in relation to which assistance may be provided by Commissioner)—
(a) in subsection (1)—
(i) in paragraph (c) after the word "members" there shall be inserted the words "or secure confidentiality"; and
(ii) after paragraph (d) there shall be inserted—
"(da) an application to the court under section 45C (remedy for failure to comply with duty to secure positions not held by certain offenders);", and
(b) in subsection (2), for the words from "in the High Court" to "arise out of" there shall be substituted the words "to the extent that they consist in, or arise out of, proceedings in the High Court or the Court of Session with respect to".

59. In section 110(1) of the 1992 Act (application for assistance from Commissioner for the Rights of Trade Union Members for certain legal proceedings), for the words "to the Commissioner" there shall be substituted the words "to the Commissioner for the Rights of Trade Union Members (in this Chapter referred to as "the Commissioner")".

60. In section 111 of the 1992 Act (provision of assistance by that Commissioner), for subsection (3) there shall be substituted—
"(3) Where assistance is provided with respect to the conduct of proceedings—
(a) it shall include an agreement by the Commissioner to indemnify the applicant (subject only to any exceptions specified in the notification) in respect of any liability to pay costs or expenses arising by virtue of any judgment or order of the court in the proceedings,
(b) it may include an agreement by the Commissioner to indemnify the applicant in respect of any liability to pay costs or expenses arising by virtue of any compromise or settlement arrived at in order to avoid the proceedings or bring the proceedings to an end, and
(c) it may include an agreement by the Commissioner to indemnify the applicant in respect of any liability to pay damages pursuant to an undertaking given on the grant of interlocutory relief (in Scotland, an interim order) to the applicant.".

61. In section 117(5) of the 1992 Act (provisions operating only in relation to certain positions in case of special register bodies), for the words "Chapter IV (elections for certain union positions) only applies" there shall be substituted the words "Sections 45B and 45C (disqualification) and Chapter IV (elections) apply only".

62. In section 118(4) of the 1992 Act (provisions not to apply in case of federated trade unions consisting wholly or mainly of representatives of constituent or affiliated organisations)—
(a) in paragraph (c) (disapplication of sections 32 to 37), after the words "annual return," there shall be inserted the words "statement for members,", and
(b) after that paragraph there shall be inserted—
"(ca) sections 37A to 37E (investigation of financial affairs), and".

63. In section 119 of the 1992 Act (expressions relating to trade unions)—
(a) before the definition of "branch or section" there shall be inserted—
" "agent" means a banker or solicitor of, or any person employed as an auditor by, the union or any branch or section of the union;", and
(b) after the definition of "executive" there shall be inserted—

" "financial affairs" means affairs of the union relating to any fund which is applicable for the purposes of the union (including any fund of a branch or section of the union which is so applicable);".

64. In section 131(1) of the 1992 Act (administrative provisions applying to employers' associations)—

(a) for the words "sections 32 to 37" there shall be substituted the words "section 32(1), (2), (3)(a), (b) and (c) and (4) to (6) and sections 33 to 37",

(b) after the word "audit)," there shall be inserted—

"sections 37A to 37E (investigation of financial affairs),", and

(c) for the words "section 45" there shall be substituted the words "sections 45 and 45A".

65. For section 133 of the 1992 Act (employers' associations: amalgamations etc.) there shall be substituted—

"Amalgamations and transfers of engagements

133.—(1) Subject to subsection (2), the provisions of Chapter VII of Part I of this Act (amalgamations and similar matters) apply to unincorporated employers' associations as in relation to trade unions.

(2) In its application to such associations that Chapter shall have effect—

(a) as if in section 99(1) for the words from "that every" to "accompanied by" there were substituted the words "that, not less than seven days before the ballot on the resolution to approve the instrument of amalgamation or transfer is held, every member is supplied with";

(b) as if the requirements imposed by sections 100A to 100E consisted only of those specified in sections 100B and 100C(1) and (3)(a) together with the requirement that every member must, so far as is reasonably possible, be given a fair opportunity of voting, and

(c) with the omission of sections 101(3) and 107.".

66. In section 135(3) of the 1992 Act (provisions not to apply in case of federated employers' associations consisting wholly or mainly of representatives of constituent or affiliated organisations)—

(a) in paragraph (c) (disapplication of sections 32 to 37), for the words "sections 32 to 37" there shall be substituted the words "section 32(1), (2), (3)(a), (b) and (c) and (4) to (6) and sections 33 to 37", and

(b) after that paragraph there shall be inserted—

"(ca) sections 37A to 37E (investigation of financial affairs), and".

67. In section 154 of the 1992 Act (exclusion of requirement of qualifying period), the words "and 64A" shall be omitted and for the words "Sections" and "do" there shall be substituted the words "Section" and "does".

68. In section 158(2) of the 1992 Act (minimum amount of special award in certain cases), the words ", but subject to the following provisions of this section," shall be inserted at the end.

69. In section 164(1)(a) of the 1992 Act (order in such a case for continuation of contract for purposes of pay or any benefit derived from the employment), for the words "any benefit" there shall be substituted the words "any other benefit".

70. In section 191(1)(a) of the 1992 Act (no remuneration under protective award for period after fair dismissal for a reason other than redundancy), for the words "for a reason other than redundancy" there shall be substituted the words "otherwise than as redundant".

71. In section 198(1)(b) of the 1992 Act (power to adapt provisions in case of collective agreement establishing arrangements for the handling of redundancies), for the words "the handling of redundancies" there shall be substituted the words "handling the dismissal of employees as redundant".

72. In section 219 of the 1992 Act (protection of acts in contemplation or furtherance of trade dispute from certain tort liabilities), in subsection (4) for the words from "to section 226" to the end there shall be substituted the words "to sections 226 (requirement of ballot before action by trade union) and 234A (requirement of notice to employer of industrial action); and in those sections "not protected" means excluded from the protection afforded by this section or, where the expression is used with reference to a particular person, excluded from that protection as respects that person.".

73. In section 226 of the 1992 Act (act of trade union not protected unless industrial action has support of a ballot)—

(a) at the end of subsection (1) (requiring the ballot) there shall be inserted the following paragraph—

"In this section "the relevant time", in relation to an act by a trade union to induce a person to take part, or continue to take part, in industrial action, means the time at which proceedings are commenced in respect of the act.";

(b) in subsection (2) (circumstances in which action has such support) for paragraphs (a) to (c) there shall be substituted—

"(a) the union has held a ballot in respect of the action—
(i) in relation to which the requirements of section 226B so far as applicable before and during the holding of the ballot were satisfied,
(ii) in relation to which the requirements of section 227 to 231A were satisfied, and
(iii) in which the majority voting in the ballot answered "Yes" to the question applicable in accordance with section 229(2) to industrial action of the kind to which the act of inducement relates;
(b) such of the requirements of the following sections as have fallen to be satisfied at the relevant time have been satisfied, namely—
(i) section 226B so far as applicable after the holding of the ballot, and
(ii) section 231B; and
(c) the requirements of section 233 (calling of industrial action with support of ballot) are satisfied.

Any reference in this subsection to a requirement of a provision which is disapplied or modified by section 232 has effect subject to that section."; and

(c) in subsection (3) (separate workplace ballots), for the words from "section 228(1)," to "in relation" there shall be substituted the words "section 228(1)—
(a) industrial action shall be regarded as having the support of a ballot if the conditions specified in subsection (2) are satisfied, and
(b) the trade union shall be taken to have complied with the requirements relating to a ballot imposed by section 226A if those requirements are complied with,
in relation".

74. In section 232 of the 1992 Act (balloting of overseas members)—

(a) in subsection (1) (sections 227 to 230 not to apply), for the words "227 to 230" there shall be substituted the words "226B to 230 and 231B", and

(b) for subsection (2) (operation of section 231) there shall be substituted—

"(2) Where overseas members have voted in the ballot—
(a) the references in sections 231 and 231A to persons entitled to vote in the ballot do not include overseas members, and
(b) those sections shall be read as requiring the information mentioned in section 231 to distinguish between overseas members and other members.".

75. In section 235 of the 1992 Act (meaning of "contract of employment" and related expressions)—

(a) for "234" there shall be substituted "234A"; and

(b) for the words "and related expressions" there shall be substituted the words "and "employer" and other related expressions".

76. In section 237 of the 1992 Act (no right to complain of unfair dismissal in case of employee taking part in unofficial industrial action), after subsection (1) there shall be inserted—

"(1A) Subsection (1) does not apply to the dismissal of the employee if it is shown that the reason (or, if more than one, the principal reason) for the dismissal or, in a redundancy case, for selecting the employee for dismissal was one of those specified in section 57A or 60 of the Employment Protection (Consolidation) Act 1978 (dismissal in health and safety cases and maternity cases).

In this subsection "redundancy case" has the meaning given in section 59 of that Act.".

77. In section 238 of the 1992 Act (tribunal not to determine whether or not dismissal is fair where there is a lock-out or industrial action), after subsection (2) there shall be inserted—

"(2A) Subsection (2) does not apply to the dismissal of the employee if it is shown that the reason (or, if more than one, the principal reason) for the dismissal or, in a redundancy case, for selecting the employee for dismissal was one of those specified in section 57A or 60 of the Employment Protection (Consolidation) Act 1978 (dismissal in health and safety cases and maternity cases).

In this subsection "redundancy case" has the meaning given in section 59 of that Act.".

78. In section 254 of the 1992 Act (Certification Officer), after subsection (5) there shall be inserted—

"(5A) Subject to subsection (6), ACAS shall pay to the Certification Officer such sums as he may require for the performance of any of his functions.".

79. For section 266 of the 1992 Act (Commissioner for the Rights of Trade Union Members) and the heading immediately preceding it there shall be substituted—

"The Commissioner for the Rights of Trade Union Members and the Commissioner for Protection Against Unlawful Industrial Action

The Commissioners

266.—(1) There—

(a) shall continue to be an officer called the Commissioner for the Rights of Trade Union Members whose function is to provide assistance in accordance with Chapter VIII of Part I of this Act in connection with certain legal proceedings, and

(b) shall be an officer called the Commissioner for Protection Against Unlawful Industrial Action whose function is to provide assistance in accordance with sections 235B and 235C of this Act in connection with proceedings brought by virtue of section 235A.

(2) Each of the Commissioners shall be appointed by the Secretary of State.

(3) Each of the Commissioners shall have an official seal for the authentication of documents required for the purposes of his functions.

(4) Anything authorised or required by or under this Act to be done by either of the Commissioners may be done by a member of his staff authorised by him for that purpose, whether generally or specifically.

An authorisation given for the purposes of this subsection continues to have effect during a vacancy in the office of the Commissioner concerned.

(5) Neither of the Commissioners nor any member of the staff of either of the Commissioners shall, in that capacity, be regarded as a servant or agent of the Crown or as enjoying any status, immunity or privilege of the Crown.".

80. In section 267 of the 1992 Act (terms of appointment of Commissioner for the Rights of Trade Union Members)—

(a) in subsection (1), for the words "The Commissioner" there shall be substituted the words "Each of the Commissioners",

(b) in subsection (2), for the words "the Commissioner" there shall be substituted the words "one of the Commissioners", and

(c) in subsection (3)—

    (i) for the words "that office" there shall be substituted the words "office as one of the Commissioners", and

    (ii) for the words "his functions as the Commissioner" there shall be substituted the words "the functions of the office".

81. In section 268 of the 1992 Act (remuneration, pension etc. of Commissioner)—

(a) in subsection (1), for the words "the Commissioner" there shall be substituted the words "each of the Commissioners",

(b) in subsection (2), for the words "any holder of the office of Commissioner" there shall be substituted the words "any person who holds office as one of the Commissioners", and

(c) in subsection (3), for the words "the Commissioner" there shall be substituted the words "one of the Commissioners".

82. In section 269 of the 1992 Act (staff of Commissioner)—

(a) in subsection (1), for the words "The Commissioner" there shall be substituted the words "Each of the Commissioners",

(b) in subsection (2), for the words "the Commissioner" there shall be substituted the words "one of the Commissioners",

(c) in subsection (3)—

    (i) for the words "the Commissioner becomes the Commissioner" there shall be substituted the words "one of the Commissioners becomes one of the Commissioners", and

    (ii) for the words "the Commissioner shall be treated for the purposes of the scheme as service as an employee of the Commissioner" there shall be substituted the words "Commissioner shall be treated for the purposes of the scheme as service as an employee", and

(d) in subsection (4), for the words "The Commissioner is not" there shall be substituted the words "Neither of the Commissioners is".

83. In section 270 of the 1992 Act (financial provisions relating to Commissioner)—

(a) in subsection (1), for the words "The Commissioner" there shall be substituted the words "Each of the Commissioners", and

(b) in subsection (2)—

    (i) for the words "to the Commissioner" there shall be substituted the words "to each of the Commissioners", and

    (ii) for the words "by the Commissioner" there shall be substituted the words "by him".

84. In section 271 of the 1992 Act (annual report and accounts of Commissioner)—
(a) in subsection (1), for the words "the Commissioner" there shall be substituted the words "each of the Commissioners", and
(b) in subsections (2) and (3), for the words "The Commissioner" there shall be substituted the words "Each of the Commissioners".

85. In section 278 of the 1992 Act (House of Commons staff)—
(a) after subsection (2) there shall be inserted—
"(2A) Nothing in any rule of law or the law or practice of Parliament prevents a relevant member of the House of Commons staff from bringing a civil employment claim before the court or from bringing before an industrial tribunal proceedings of any description which could be brought before such a tribunal by any person who is not such a member.", and
(b) in subsection (3) at the end there shall be inserted—
" "civil employment claim" means a claim arising out of or relating to a contract of employment or any other contract connected with employment, or a claim in tort arising in connection with a person's employment; and
"the court" means the High Court or the county court.".

86. In section 290 of the 1992 Act (functions of conciliation officers in relation to certain proceedings), after paragraph (a) there shall be inserted—
"(aa) section 68 (right not to suffer deduction or unauthorised or excessive union subscriptions);".

87. In section 291 of the 1992 Act (right of appeal from industrial tribunal)—
(a) subsection (1) (appeal on question of law or fact in the case of section 174), and
(b) in subsection (2) (appeal on question of law in the case of any other provision of 1992 Act) the words "any other provision of",
shall cease to have effect.

88. In section 296 of the 1992 Act (meaning of "worker" and "employer"), after subsection (2) there shall be inserted—
"(3) This section has effect subject to section 68(11).".

89. In section 299 of the 1992 Act (index of defined expressions)—
(a) after the entry relating to "advertisement" there shall be inserted—
"agent (of trade union)   section 19",
(b) after the entry relating to "dismiss and dismissal" there shall be inserted—
"the duty of confidentiality"   section 24A(3)", and
(c) after the entry relating to "executive" there shall be inserted—
"financial affairs (of trade union)   section 119".

Section 50   SCHEDULE 9

TRANSITIONAL PROVISIONS AND SAVINGS

General

1.—(1) An order under section 52 of this Act may contain such transitional provisions and savings as appear to the Secretary of State to be appropriate.
(2) Nothing in the following provisions of this Schedule prejudices the generality of sub-paragraph (1) above.
(3) Nothing in this Schedule prejudices the operation of sections 16 and 17 of the Interpretation Act 1978 (effect of repeals).

Deduction of trade union subscriptions

2. For the purposes of section 68 of the 1992 Act (as substituted by section 15 of this Act) a deduction representing a payment to a trade union in respect of a worker's membership which is made in accordance with arrangements existing between his employer and the union immediately before the day on which section 15 comes into force under which deductions were made in his case before that day shall be treated as an authorised deduction where—
(a) the day on which the deduction is made falls before the end of the period of one year beginning with the day on which section 15 comes into force, and
(b) written notice from the worker stating that he does not wish such deductions to be made has not been received by the employer in time for it to be reasonably practicable for him to secure that the deduction is not made.

Employment particulars

3.—(1) In this paragraph "existing employee" means an employee whose employment with his employer has begun before the day on which section 26 of this Act comes into force (whether or not the provisions of sections 1 to 6 of the 1978 Act applied to him before that day).

(2) Subject to the following provisions of this paragraph, the provisions substituted for sections 1 to 4 and 6 of the 1978 Act by section 26 of this Act shall not apply to any existing employee.

(3) Where an existing employee, at any time—

(a) on or after the day on which section 26 of this Act comes into force, and

(b) either before the end of his employment or within the period of three months beginning with the day on which his employment ends,

requests from his employer a statement under section 1 of the 1978 Act (as substituted by section 26), the employer shall (subject to section 5 and any other provision disapplying or having the effect of disapplying section 1) be treated as being required by section 1 to give him a written statement under that section, in accordance with the provisions of the 1978 Act as so substituted, not later than two months after the request is made; and section 4 of that Act (as so substituted) shall, subject as aforesaid, apply in relation to the existing employee after he makes the request.

(4) An employer shall not be required to give a statement under section 1 by virtue of sub-paragraph (3) above to an existing employee on more than one occasion by virtue of that sub-paragraph.

(5) Where—

(a) on or after the day on which section 26 of this Act comes into force there is in the case of any existing employee a change in any of the matters particulars of which would, had he been given a statement of particulars as at that day under section 1 of the 1978 Act (as substituted by that section), have been included or referred to in the statement, and

(b) he has not previously requested a statement under sub-paragraph (3) above,

subsections (1) and (5) of section 4 of the 1978 Act (as substituted by section 26 of this Act) shall be treated (subject to section 5 and any other provision disapplying or having the effect of disapplying section 4) as requiring his employer to give him a written statement containing particulars of the change at the time specified in subsection (1) of section 4; and subsections (3) and (6) of that section shall apply accordingly.

(6) Nothing in any enactment providing for the application of sections 1 to 4 of the 1978 Act to a person who comes or ceases to come within any of the exceptions from those sections specified in that Act shall have effect in relation to an existing employee by reason of his coming or ceasing to come within that exception by virtue of any of the amendments of the 1978 Act made by this Act.

Transfers of undertakings

4. The amendments of the Transfer of Undertakings (Protection of Employment) Regulations 1981 made by section 33 of this Act shall not have effect in relation to any transfer of an undertaking taking place before the date on which that section comes into force; and, accordingly, the repeal by this Act of—

(a) section 94 of the 1978 Act, and

(b) section 23 of the Contracts of Employment and Redundancy Payments Act (Northern Ireland) 1965,

shall have effect only in relation to any change in the ownership of a business occurring on or after that date.

Wages Councils

5.—(1) Notwithstanding the repeal of Part II of the Wages Act 1986 by section 35 of this Act, the provisions of that Part specified or referred to below shall continue to have effect, on and after the day appointed for the repeal ("the appointed day"), in accordance with the following provisions.

(2) Section 16 (effect and enforcement of wages orders under section 14) shall have effect in relation to a failure occurring or continuing on or after the appointed day to pay, with respect to any period ending before that day, an amount equal to or exceeding the statutory minimum remuneration as it has effect in relation to such a failure before the appointed day; and, subject to the following provisions, the other sections of Part II which relate to section 16 shall continue to have effect accordingly.

(3) Section 19(1) and (4) (obligation to keep records etc.) shall have effect on and after the appointed day as if—

    (a) the reference to the provisions of Part II being complied with in relation to the payment of remuneration were a reference to their having been complied with in relation to payments of remuneration made—

        (i) before the appointed day, or

        (ii) on or after the appointed day with respect to any period ending before that day;

    (b) the reference to deductions or payments made were references to deductions or payments so made; and

    (c) in a case where the three-year retention period for records would end after the expiry of the period of six months beginning with the appointed day, the retention period were—

        (i) that period of six months, or

        (ii) if within that period of six months a court so orders, such longer period as is specified by the court;

and, subject to the following provisions, the other sections of Part II which relate to section 19 shall continue to have effect accordingly.

(4) Section 20 (wages inspectors) shall continue to have effect on and after the appointed day for the purposes of this paragraph; but—

    (a) the powers conferred by subsections (3) and (4) shall not be exercisable after the end of the period of six months beginning with the appointed day, and

    (b) subsection (6) shall not authorise the institution of proceedings by a wages inspector after the end of the period of six months beginning with the appointed day.

(5) Paragraph 4 of Schedule 3 shall continue to have effect on and after the appointed day in relation to orders under section 14 made before that day.

(6) In the operation of any provision of Part II by virtue of this paragraph, references to a wages order applying shall have effect as references to an order under section 14 having applied at any time before the appointed day.

Section 51   SCHEDULE 10

REPEALS AND REVOCATIONS

Chapter or Number	Title	Extent of repeal or revocation
9 & 10 Eliz. 2 c. 34.	Factories Act 1961.	Section 117(5)(b).
1965 c. 19 (N.I.).	Contracts of Employment and Redundancy Payments Act (Northern Ireland) 1965.	Sections 23 and 23A. In section 29(1), the words "(except section 23)". Section 32(4). Section 54(2). In Schedule 5, paragraph 2.
1968 c. 73.	Transport Act 1968.	Section 94(10).
1969 c. 32.	Finance Act 1969.	In section 58(4), in the Table, the entries relating to a local education authority in England and Wales and an education authority in Scotland.
1970 c. 44.	Chronically Sick and Disabled Persons Act 1970.	Section 13(1).
1973 c. 50.	Employment and Training Act 1973.	In section 4(3)(e)(ii), the words "a local education authority,". In section 4(5)(d), the words "a local education authority or" and "by section 8 of this Act or, as the case may be,".
1975 c. 24.	House of Commons Disqualification Act 1975.	In Part III of Schedule 1, the first entry beginning "Member of a Wages Council".
1975 c. 25.	Northern Ireland Assembly Disqualification Act 1975.	In Part III of Schedule 1, the first entry beginning "Member of a Wages Council".

Chapter or Number	Title	Extent of repeal or revocation
S.I. 1976/1043 (N.I. 16).	Industrial Relations (Northern Ireland) Order 1976.	In Schedule 5, in Part II, paragraphs 19, 20 and 23(3).
1978 c. 44.	Employment Protection (Consolidation) Act 1978.	Section 11(3) and (7). In section 18, in subsection (1), the words "council or", subsection (2)(a), in subsection (3)(a), the words "(a) or", and in subsection (5), the words "council or". In section 53(4), the words "against his employer". In section 55(5) and (6), ", 64A". Section 64A. Section 93(4). Sections 94 and 95. In section 100(1), the words "(except section 94)". In section 123(4), the words ", maternity pay under Part III of this Act". In section 128(4), the words "paragraph 1 of". In section 133(1)(c), the words "or claims". In section 138, in subsection (1) the words "(so far as it relates to itemised pay statements)" and in subsection (2) the words ", subject to subsections (3) to (5),". In section 139(1), the words "(so far as it relates to itemised pay statements)". In section 146(4), the words "1, 4,". In section 149(1)(c), "64A(1),". In section 153, in subsection (1), the definitions of "confinement", "expected week of confinement" and "original contract of employment" and subsection (3). In Schedule 9, in paragraph 1A(2)(a) the words "person or" and paragraph 8. In Schedule 12, paragraph 13. In Schedule 13, in paragraph 11(1), ", 64A(1)". In Schedule 15, paragraph 10(2).
1979 c. 36.	Nurses, Midwives and Health Visitors Act 1979.	In Schedule 7, paragraph 31.
1980 c. 42.	Employment Act 1980.	Section 8(1). Section 11. In Schedule 1, paragraphs 10, 21(a) and 32.
1980 c. 44.	Education (Scotland) Act 1980.	Sections 126 to 128.
S.I. 1981/1794.	Transfer of Undertakings (Protection of Employment) Regulations 1981.	In Regulation 2(1), in the definition of "undertaking", the words from "but does not" to the end. Regulation 11(7).
1982 c. 9.	Agricultural Training Board Act 1982.	In section 4(1)(f), the words "or 8".
1982 c. 10.	Industrial Training Act 1982.	In section 5(3)(e), the words "or 8".
1982 c. 46.	Employment Act 1982.	In Schedule 2, paragraphs 8(1) to (4) and (5)(a).
1986 c. 48.	Wages Act 1986.	Section 9(3). Part II. Section 31(a) and (b).

Chapter or Number	Title	Extent of repeal or revocation
		In section 33, in subsection (2) the entries relating to sections 24 and 25(1) to (3), in subsection (4) the words from "Part II (excluding" to "relating to Part II;" and in subsection (7) the words from "paragraphs 5" to "thereto,".
		Schedules 2 and 3.
		In Schedule 4, paragraphs 5 to 7.
		In Schedule 6, paragraphs 1 to 8.
1986 c. 50.	Social Security Act 1986.	In Schedule 10, paragraph 75.
1988 c. 1.	Income and Corporation Taxes Act 1988.	In section 175(4), the words "Part II of the Wages Act 1986,".
1989 c. 13.	Dock Work Act 1989.	Section 6(2).
1989 c. 24.	Social Security Act 1989.	In Schedule 5, paragraph 15.
1989 c. 38.	Employment Act 1989.	Section 13.
		In Schedule 6, paragraph 18.
1990 c. 35.	Enterprise and New Towns (Scotland) Act 1990.	In section 2(3), the word "and" at the end of paragraph (b).
1992 c. 24.	Offshore Safety (Protection Against Victimisation) Act 1992.	The whole Act.
1992 c. 52.	Trade Union and Labour Relations (Consolidation) Act 1992.	Section 24(4).
		In section 32(3), the word "and" at the end of paragraph (b).
		In section 34(5), the second sentence.
		In section 43(1), the word "and" at the end of paragraph (b).
		In section 52(1), the word "and" at the end of paragraph (c).
		In section 65(2), the word "or" at the end of paragraph (d).
		In section 65(7), the word "and" following the definition of "contract of employment".
		Section 67(9).
		In section 74(3), the word "and" at the end of the entry relating to section 77.
		In section 78(1), the word "and" at the end of paragraph (c).
		Sections 115 and 116.
		In section 118(4), the word "and" at the end of paragraph (c).
		In section 135(3), the word "and" at the end of paragraph (c).
		In section 154, the words "and 64A".
		In section 188(4), the word "and" at the end of paragraph (d).
		Section 190(3).
		In section 209, the words from "and in particular" to the end.
		In section 246, the definition of "place of work".
		In section 249(2), the first sentence.
		Section 256(4).
		Section 273(4)(c).
		In section 277(2), the words "under those sections".
		Section 283.

Chapter or Number	Title	Extent of repeal or revocation
		In section 288(1)(b), the word "unreasonable".
		In section 290(e), the word "unreasonable" and the words "where employment subject to union membership agreement".
		In section 291, subsection (1) and, in subsection (2), the words "any other provision of".
		In section 299, the entries relating to "the Commissioner" and "redundancy".
		In Schedule 2, paragraphs 15, 24(3) and 34(3).

INDEX

References in roman type are to sections of this Act whilst references in italic are to sections of other Acts amended thereby

ACAS,
advice by, 43(2)
fees for exercise of functions, 44
functions, 43(1)
AMENDMENTS,
consequential, 49(2), Sched. 8
miscellaneous, 49(1), Sched. 7
ARMED FORCES,
service in, 31
ASSERTION OF STATUTORY RIGHT,
unfair dismissal for, 29

CAREERS SERVICES,
ancillary services, 46
provision of, 45
COMMENCEMENT, 52

ELECTIONS AND BALLOTS,
amalgamations and transfers of engagements, 4, *100*
notices not to include influential material, 5, *99*
confidentiality of register, 6, *24*
counting of votes, 2, *51*
counting of votes by independent person, 2, *51*
financial assistance and use of premises discontinued, 7, *113, 116*
independent persons, 2, *51*
political fund ballots, 3, Sched. 1
postal ballot, requirement of. *See* INDUSTRIAL ACTION
scrutineers,
to check register, 1, *49*
independence, 2(1), 4, *51, 100*
reports, *100E*, 1, 4, *52*
EMPLOYMENT APPEAL TRIBUNAL,
constitution of, 37
sexual misconduct cases, restriction of publicity, 41
vexatious proceedings, 42
EMPLOYMENT PARTICULARS,
disciplinary procedures, Sched. 3, para. 3
employer's duty to give statement, Sched. 3, paras. 1–2
excluded employees, Sched. 3, para. 5
further matters, Sched. 3, para. 6
itemised pay statement, 27
right to, 26, Sched. 4
statement of changes, Sched. 3, para. 4
EMPLOYMENT RIGHTS,
armed forces, 31

EMPLOYMENT RIGHTS—*cont.*
assertion of statutory right: compensation, 29
reinstatement orders: compensation, 30
sex discrimination, 32
transfer and redundancy, 33–34
See also EMPLOYMENT PARTICULARS; HEALTH AND SAFETY; MATERNITY

FINANCIAL AFFAIRS OF UNIONS,
annual return, contents of, 8, *32(3)*
investigation of, 10
auditor's report, arising from, 10, *37E*
complaints by members, 10, *37E*
disclosure of information, 10, *37E*
disqualification of offenders, 12, *45B*
remedies and enforcement, 12, *45C*
expenses of, 10, *37D*
inspectors appointed for, 10, *37B*
offences, 11, *45*
penalties, 11, *45A*
production of documents, 10, *37A*
prosecution time limits, 11, *45A*
report of inspectors, 10, *37C*
statement to members following annual return, 9, *32*
FINANCIAL PROVISION, 53

HEALTH AND SAFETY, EMPLOYMENT PROTECTION,
right not to suffer detriment, Sched. 5, para. 1
rights to claim, 28, Sched. 5
unfair dismissal, Sched. 5, para. 3
continuation of employment, Sched. 5, para. 10
failure to comply with order, Sched. 5, para. 10
interim relief, Sched. 5, para. 10
procedure on hearing, Sched. 5, para. 10
special award, calculation of, Sched. 5, para. 9
variation of order, Sched. 5, para. 10

INDUSTRIAL ACTION,
affecting supply of goods or services to an individual, 22, *235A*
application for assistance for proceedings, 22, *235B–C*
Commissioner for Protection Against Unlawful Industrial Action, 22, *235B–C*
notice of, for employers, 21, *234A*

19–143

LICENSING (AMENDMENT) (SCOTLAND) ACT 1993*

(1993 c. 20)

An Act to amend section 23(2) of the Licensing (Scotland) Act 1976 in relation to certain planning certificates.   [1st July 1993]

PARLIAMENTARY DEBATES
Hansard, H.C. Vol. 219, col. 1195; Vol. 221, col. 1334; H.L. Vol. 545, col. 775.

GENERAL NOTE

This Act corrects a defect in Scottish licensing law following the amendment of the Town and Country Planning (Scotland) Act 1972 by the Planning and Compensation Act 1991.

By s.23(1) of the Licensing (Scotland) Act 1976, a licensing board may not entertain an application for the grant or provisional grant of a new licence (other than an off-sale licence) unless the applicant produces, *inter alia*, a certificate of suitability in relation to planning. By s.23(2), as previously enacted, that certificate was required to state that the applicant had obtained in respect of the premises planning permission (or outline planning permission in the case of an application for a provisional grant) under the 1972 Act, or a determination under s.51 of that Act that planning permission was not required.

Section 42 of the 1991 Act substituted new ss.90–90C for the original s.90 (certification of established use) of the 1972 Act, the purpose of which was to provide a single procedure in place of the former ss.51 and 90 whereby a planning authority can issue a certificate that any specified use or operation (whether or not instituted before the application) can be carried on without planning permission. The Act repealed s.51 of the 1972 Act (Scheds. 13 and 19) but unfortunately did not make the necessary consequential amendment to s.23(2) of the 1976 Act, with the result that applicants for new licences might be required to obtain a certificate which planning authorities were no longer able to grant.

Section 1(2) of the 1993 Act accordingly amends s.23(2) by adding the alternative of a certificate under the new s.90A of the 1972 Act (certificate of lawfulness of proposed use or development) to a determination under s.51. Section 90A, and the repeal of s.51, were brought into effect from September 25, 1992 by S.I. 1992 No. 1937, which also contains a saving for s.51 determinations made before that date or following on an application made before that date, including a determination made on appeal.

The Bill was introduced as a Private Member's Bill by Phil Gallie M.P. but was drafted by the Scottish Office and received all-party support in its parliamentary passage, which it survived unamended. It also had the support of the Law Society of Scotland, the Scottish licensed trade and the Convention of Scottish Local Authorities.

Amendment of section 23(2) of the Licensing (Scotland) Act 1976

1.—(1) Section 23 of the Licensing (Scotland) Act 1976 (production of certificates on application for new licence) shall be amended as mentioned in subsection (2) below.

(2) In subsection (2) (certificate in relation to planning) at the end there shall be added "or a certificate under section 90A of that Act that the proposed use or operations would be lawful as mentioned in the said section 90A."

Short title and extent

2.—(1) This Act may be cited as the Licensing (Amendment) (Scotland) Act 1993.

(2) This Act extends to Scotland only.

---

* Annotations by Peter Nicholson, LL.B., Solicitor.

INDEX

References are to sections

CERTIFICATES, PRODUCTION OF,
application for new licence, 1(1)
planning, 1(2)

EXTENT, 2(2)

SHORT TITLE, 2(1)

OSTEOPATHS ACT 1993*

(1993 c. 21)

---

* Annotations by Professor Paul Jackson, LL.D., Head of Department of Law, University of Reading.

An Act to establish a body to be known as the General Osteopathic Council; to provide for the regulation of the profession of osteopathy, including making provision as to the registration of osteopaths and as to their professional education and conduct; to make provision in connection with the development and promotion of the profession; and for connected purposes. [1st July 1993]

PARLIAMENTARY DEBATES

Hansard, H.C. Vol. 216, col. 1170; Vol. 224, col. 391; H.L. Vol. 546, col. 488; Vol. 547, col. 657.

The Bill was discussed in Standing Committee C between February 3 and 10, 1993.

INTRODUCTION AND GENERAL NOTE

As a theory of the causes of illness and disease, osteopathy can date its origin to the writings of Andrew Taylor Still who published his theory of osteopathy in Missouri in 1894. The members of both Houses of Parliament concerned with the passage of the Bill which became the Osteopaths Act 1993 clearly, however, saw themselves as concerned with regulating the practice of non-contentious methods of controlling back pain. Osteopathy has become in the words of Earl Baldwin of Bewdley: "this most orthodox of the unorthodox professions" (*Hansard*, H.L. Vol. 546, col. 494).

Efforts to secure statutory recognition and regulation began sixty years ago. The impetus for the most recent and successful campaign was identified by the Under-Secretary of State for Health (Mr. Tom Sackville) as coming from a luncheon hosted at Kensington Palace by the Prince of Wales in 1988. Subsequently the King's Fund established a working party on osteopathy, chaired by Bingham L.J., (as he then was). A draft Bill which was appended to the working party's report and introduced in the House of Lords by Lord Walton of Detchant in 1991 failed to complete all its stages before the dissolution of Parliament in March 1992. Mr. Malcolm Moss, who introduced a re-drafted Bill, was more fortunate in ensuring the enactment of what was described as "the largest Private Member's Bill ever in Parliament's history" (Mr. Tom Sackville, *Hansard*, H.C. Vol. 224, col. 443).

The importance of the new Act is seen by its proponents as going beyond providing regulation for a profession estimated to number around 2000 persons in the U.K.: it is a milestone on the road to recognition for complementary medicine as a whole and provides a model for the future for statutory regulation of other—including older—medical professions. (References were made during the debates in particular to the outmoded terms of the Professions Supplementary to Medicine Act 1960 which regulates Chiropodists, Dietitians, Medical Laboratory Technicians, Occupational Therapists, Orthoptists, Physiotherapists, Radiographers and Remedial Gymnasts). The hope was expressed of similar legislation in perhaps the next session of Parliament to extend recognition to Chiropractic, on which form of treatment a King's Fund report appeared in May 1993. The more optimistic (or less realistic) looked forward to statutory recognition of iridology and phrenology.

References to complementary and alternative forms of medicine in the discussion of the draft Bill revealed the difficulty of giving a precise meaning to these terms. Modern statutory regulation of "practitioners in medicine and surgery" began with the Medical Act 1858, which recognised in a preamble that it was "expedient that persons requiring medical aid should be enabled to distinguish qualified from unqualified practitioners". In one sense any form of treatment not used or approved by such recognised practitioners is complementary or alternative. It can be argued that such forms of treatment require regulation to protect the public from "unqualified cowboys and unscrupulous quacks" (Mr. David Atkinson, *Hansard*, H.C. Vol. 216, col. 1187). But yesterday's unqualified cowboys may be today's alternative therapists and, as was pointed out, there are dangers in respectability; "In welcoming osteopathy to its place in the sun . . . we should do nothing that could lead it to lose its soul or . . . to abandon its unique therapeutic flavour" (*Hansard*, H.L. Vol. 546, col. 494).

A remarkable feature of the Act, to which only one reference was made in the course of the debates on the Bill (*Hansard*, H.C. Vol. 216, col. 1183), is that it offers no definition of osteopathy. In moving the Bill in the House of Commons Mr. Malcolm Moss defined it as "a system of diagnosis and treatment that lays its main influence on the structural and mechanical problems of the body ... Osteopathic treatment predominantly comprises gentle manual methods. It utilises a diagnostic procedure similar to conventional medical examination, but it pays especial attention to the patient's musculo-skeletal system" (*Hansard*, H.C. Vol. 216, col. 1170). Similar words were used by Lord Walton (*Hansard*, H.L. Vol. 546, col. 489). The only response to criticism of a lack of statutory definition was made at the Committee stage when it was said, rather unhelpfully:

"[The Hon. Member for Rochdale] asked for a definition of "osteopathy" in the Bill. It was felt almost impossible to separate what osteopaths, chiropractors and some of the manipulators do. There is almost cross-referencing, and cross-referral techniques are used. We should concentrate in the Bill on regulating a group who are prepared to call themselves osteopaths and keep to a certain level of professional expertise and training." (Standing Committee C, col. 22).

Such a response offers no help in the case of the registered practitioners who claim that they are remaining true to the principles of osteopathy and the General Council which is trying to remove their name from the register has abandoned those principles; nor in the case of applicants for registration who argue that non-registration of their qualifications arises from abandonment by the General Council of the principles of osteopathy. It could be argued that osteopathy means, in crude terms, whatever the General Council says it means. The prospect of judicial intervention in any dispute about the meaning of osteopathy would depend on whether the courts could be persuaded that the term had such a generally agreed meaning that it was possible to hold that no reasonable Council could interpret the term as the General Council had done: *Associated Provincial Picture Houses* v. *Wednesbury Corporation* [1948] 1 K.B. 223; *Brutus* v. *Cozens* [1973] A.C. 854. Secondly, it might be possible to argue that a clear meaning for "osteopathy" as used in the Act could be discerned from the frequent descriptions of this branch of medicine in both Houses by reference to the "musculo-skeletal system" and "gentle manual methods": *Pepper (Inspector of Taxes)* v. *Hart* [1992] 3 W.L.R. 1032.

The main object of the Act is to establish a General Osteopathic Council to be responsible for making provision for a system of statutory registration of osteopaths. The Act also establishes four statutory committees of the General Council; an Education Committee, an Investigating Committee, a Professional Conduct Committee and a Health Committee. The statutory system of registration will replace a voluntary system which has existed for almost sixty years. The Act makes it a criminal offence to use the title "osteopath" without being registered under the Act (s.32) but it does not attempt to regulate the use of osteopathic techniques: a distinction referred to as "closure of title, not closure of function". (See further under s.32). The General Council has wide powers to make rules to give effect to the provisions of the Act. Ultimate responsibility for supervising the exercise of these powers and for exercising a final appellate jurisdiction is conferred on the Privy Council.

The General Council and its committees

The General Osteopathic Council and its committees

1.—(1) There shall be a body corporate to be known as the General Osteopathic Council (referred to in this Act as "the General Council").

(2) It shall be the duty of the General Council to develop, promote and regulate the profession of osteopathy.

(3) The General Council shall have such other functions as are conferred on it by this Act.

(4) Part I of the Schedule shall have effect with respect to the constitution of the General Council.

(5) There shall be four committees of the General Council, to be known as—

(a) the Education Committee;
(b) the Investigating Committee;
(c) the Professional Conduct Committee; and
(d) the Health Committee.

(6) The four committees are referred to in this Act as "the statutory committees".

(7) Each of the statutory committees shall have the functions conferred on it by or under this Act.

(8) The General Council may establish such other committees as it considers appropriate in connection with the discharge of its functions.

(9) Part II of the Schedule shall have effect with respect to the statutory committees.

(10) At the request of the General Council, Her Majesty may by Order in Council make such provision with respect to the matters dealt with by the Schedule as Her Majesty considers appropriate in consultation with the General Council.

(11) Any such Order in Council shall be subject to annulment in pursuance of a resolution of either House of Parliament.

(12) Any provision under subsection (10) may be made either in substitution for, or as an addition to, that made by any provision of the Schedule.

GENERAL NOTE

Subs. (2)

According to the Parliamentary Under-Secretary of State, Department of Health (Baroness Cumberlege) the General Council, in being encouraged to develop and promote the profession, is given a much broader remit than the statutory bodies of other comparable schemes which signals a new and exciting model for self-regulation for the future (*Hansard*, H.L. Vol. 546, col. 499).

The wording of the subsection, however, is too general to offer a real prospect of judicial review of these responsibilities of the Council.

Subs. (3)

Other functions include the appointment of the Registrar of Osteopaths (s.2); the making of rules under various sections (*e.g.*, ss.4, 5, 6, and 17); publishing the register of osteopaths (s.9); determining the standard of proficiency required for the safe practice of osteopathy (s.13); recognition of qualifications (s.14); publishing a Code of Practice (s.19); the making of interim orders for suspension of registration (s.21); and the removal of names from the register (s.22).

Subs. (4)

Until the statutory system of registration has come into effect it will not be possible for the General Council to be constituted according to Pt. I of the Schedule and the transitional provisions of Pt. III of the Schedule will have effect: see s.42(6).

Subs. (10)

This subsection allows for the constitution of the General Council and of its statutory committees to be varied by Order in Council, thus affording the flexibility of responding to changing circumstances without the need for primary legislation.

Registration of osteopaths

GENERAL NOTE

The Act provides for three types of registration; full, conditional and provisional.

Full registration will, once the Act is fully operative, be granted to applicants holding a recognised qualification in osteopathy and satisfying other statutory requirements (s.3(2)). For a transitional period, however, full registration will be granted to osteopaths in practice before the opening of the statutory register who satisfy the statutory requirements (s.3(3)).

Conditional registration is provided for by s.4 as a qualified, transitional form of registration for applicants who rely on practical experience before the Act but are unable to satisfy the terms of s.3(3).

Under s.5 the General Council may by rules introduce a system of provisional registration to provide for registration for a limited period for applicants entitled to full registration by virtue of obtaining a recognised qualification within the terms of s.3(2). It is envisaged that such a scheme will operate on the lines of the pre-registration year for doctors.

The Registrar of Osteopaths

2.—(1) The General Council shall appoint a person to be the registrar for the purposes of this Act.

(2) The person appointed shall be known as the Registrar of Osteopaths (referred to in this Act as "the Registrar") and shall hold office for such period and on such terms as the General Council may determine.

(3) It shall be the duty of the Registrar to establish and maintain a register of osteopaths in accordance with the provisions of this Act.

(4) The Registrar shall have such other functions as the General Council may direct.

(5) Where the terms on which the Registrar holds office include provision for the payment to him of any allowances or expenses, the rate at which those allowances or expenses are paid shall be determined by the General Council.

(6) The terms on which the Registrar holds office may, in addition to providing for his remuneration, include provision for the payment of such pensions, allowances or gratuities to or in respect of him, or such contributions or payments towards provision for such pensions, allowances or gratuities, as may be determined by the General Council.

DEFINITIONS
"the General Council": s.41.
"transitional period": s.3(7).

Full registration

3.—(1) Subject to the provisions of this Act, any person who satisfies the conditions mentioned in subsection (2) shall be entitled to be registered as a fully registered osteopath.

(2) The conditions are that the application is made in the prescribed form and manner and that the applicant—

(a) has paid the prescribed fee;

(b) satisfies the Registrar that he is of good character;

(c) satisfies the Registrar that he is in good health, both physically and mentally; and

(d) has a recognised qualification.

(3) Where an application for registration is made during the transitional period by a person who was in practice as an osteopath at any time before the opening of the register, he shall be treated as having a recognised qualification if he satisfies the Registrar that for a period of at least five years (which need not be continuous) he has spent a substantial part of his working time in the lawful, safe and competent practice of osteopathy.

(4) For the purposes of subsection (3), no account shall be taken of any work done by the applicant before the beginning of the period of seven years ending with the opening of the register.

(5) For the purposes of subsection (3), the question whether the applicant has spent any part of his working time in the lawful, safe and competent practice of osteopathy shall be determined in accordance with such rules (if any) as may be made by the General Council.

(6) The General Council may by rules provide for treating a person who—

(a) has obtained a qualification in osteopathy outside the United Kingdom,

(b) does not hold a recognised qualification, but

(c) satisfies the Registrar that he has reached the required standard of proficiency,

as holding a recognised qualification for the purposes of this Act.

(7) In this section "transitional period" means the period of two years beginning with the opening of the register.

DEFINITIONS
"the Registrar": s.41.
"recognised qualification": s.14.

GENERAL NOTE

Subs. (1)

Full registration is to be contrasted with conditional (s.4) and provisional (s.5).

All three types of registration entitle an osteopath to describe himself as a "registered osteopath" (s.41).

Subs. (2)

Paragraphs (b) and (c) follow the similar provision in s.15 of the Dentists Act 1984.

Paragraph (b) offers no guidance as to what is meant by good character. It is difficult to believe that *any* moral fault, civil finding of fault or criminal conviction is sufficient to deprive an applicant of a good character for the purpose of being a suitable person to practise as an osteopath.

The scope of the requirement can be tested if the registrar refuses registration by resort to the appeal procedures contained in ss.29 and 31 which are considered below.

Paragraph (c) is designed to ensure that the Registrar is not required to register an applicant whose health would then constitute a ground for removal from the register under s.20(1)(d). (The Medical Act 1983 does not contain a similar provision, perhaps because medical qualifications cannot be obtained by persons who are not in good health, both physical and mental).

Paragraph (d) is in many ways the heart of s.3. It recognises for the future the existence of statutorily regulated qualifications, the possession of which *prima facie* entitles the holder to registration.

Subs. (3)

This is a temporary provision which provides for the full registration of persons in practice before the opening of the statutory register. Applications must be made within two years of the opening of the register (subs. (7) defining transitional period) on the basis of five years', not necessarily continuous, practice in the seven years before the opening of the register (subs. (4)).

A period of four years' work within the six years before the opening of the register may entitle an applicant to conditional registration under s.4.

Considerable discussion took place at the Committee stage on the meaning of the requirement that the qualifying practice must have been "safe, lawful and competent". There was concern at the phrase's vagueness and uncertainty whether the burden of proof was on the applicant or the Registrar. The requirement, however, that the applicant must satisfy the Registrar seems to place the burden clearly on the applicant.

Subs. (5)

This subsection provides that the question whether an applicant has spent time in "lawful safe and competent practice" shall be determined by reference to such rules, if any, as may be made by the General Council.

Sections 6(2) and (3) provide for the making of rules relating to the form and manner in which applications for registration are to be made, the documentary and other evidence which must accompany applications and the manner in which the Registrar is to satisfy himself as to the competence of any person applying for registration.

Such rules when made may solve the concerns expressed during the passage of the Bill. Whether they are within the powers of the Council will be open to judicial review.

Subs. (6)

This subsection allows the General Council to treat a person who has obtained a qualification which is not a "recognised qualification" within s.14 as holding a recognised qualification.

Subs. (7)

Transitional periods, here and elsewhere, are defined by reference to periods measured from "the opening of the register", a phrase which is itself defined by s.41 as meaning the date on which s.3 comes into force.

Conditional registration

4.—(1) Subject to the provisions of this Act, any person who satisfies the conditions mentioned in subsection (2) shall be entitled to be registered as a conditionally registered osteopath.

(2) The conditions are that the application is made in the prescribed form and manner during the transitional period and that the applicant—

(a) has paid the prescribed fee;

(b) satisfies the Registrar that he is of good character;
(c) satisfies the Registrar that he is in good health, both physically and mentally;
(d) satisfies the Registrar that for a period of at least four years (which need not be continuous) he has spent a substantial part of his working time in the lawful, safe and competent practice of osteopathy;
(e) if required to do so by the Registrar in accordance with rules made by the General Council, passes—
  (i) the prescribed test of competence; or
  (ii) such part of that test as the Registrar may specify; and
(f) gives the required undertaking.

(3) In the application of subsection (2)(d), in relation to any person, no account shall be taken of any work done by him before the beginning of the period of six years ending with the opening of the register.

(4) The General Council may by rules provide for the conversion, in prescribed circumstances and subject to the osteopath concerned complying with such conditions (if any) as may be prescribed, of conditional registration into full registration.

(5) Unless it is converted into full registration in accordance with the rules, any conditional registration shall cease to have effect—
(a) at the end of the period of five years beginning with the opening of the register; or
(b) where a shorter period has been specified by the Registrar in accordance with subsection (10) in relation to the osteopath in question, at the end of that shorter period.

(6) In dealing with an application for registration made during the transitional period by a person who—
(a) cannot meet the requirement of subsection (2)(d), but
(b) has a qualification in osteopathy which, while not being a recognised qualification, has not been refused recognition by the General Council,
the Registrar shall refer the matter to the Education Committee.

(7) Where a reference is made to the Education Committee under subsection (6), it shall be the duty of the Committee to advise the General Council.

(8) If, after considering the advice of the Education Committee, the General Council is satisfied that it is appropriate to do so, it shall direct the Registrar to disregard subsection (2)(d) in relation to the application in question.

(9) For the purposes of subsection (2)(d), the question whether the applicant has spent any part of his working time in the lawful, safe and competent practice of osteopathy shall be determined in accordance with such rules (if any) as may be made by the General Council.

(10) In this section—
  "required undertaking" means an undertaking that the person giving it will, before the end of the period of five years beginning with the opening of the register or such shorter period as the Registrar may specify in relation to the applicant—
    (a) complete such additional training and acquire such experience as may be specified by the Registrar in accordance with rules made by the General Council; and
    (b) comply with such other conditions (if any) as may be imposed on him by the Registrar in accordance with such rules; and
  "transitional period" means the period of two years beginning with the opening of the register.

(11) Rules made by virtue of paragraph (b) in the definition of "required undertaking" in subsection (10) may, in particular, provide for the Registrar

to be able to impose, as a condition, the passing of a test of competence specified by the Registrar.

GENERAL NOTE

Conditional registration, as explained above, is a transitional, restricted form of registration for applicants who rely on a period of practice before the opening of the statutory register.

It lasts for a limited time except in cases where rules made by the General Council provide for conversion into full registration.

Subs. (2)

This subsection follows the form of s.3, except that four years' practice is substituted for five and the period preceding the opening of the register is six years, not seven. Provision is also made to allow the Registrar to require an applicant to pass a test of competence and give such undertaking as he may require under subs. (10).

Subs. (5)

This subsection provides for a normal maximum period of five years for any conditional registration from the opening of the register. The Registrar is, however, empowered to specify a shorter period and to impose a requirement of additional training and compliance with any other conditions imposed under rules made by the General Council, in particular the passing of a test of competence (subss. (10) and (11)).

Subss. (6)–(8)

These subsections entitle the General Council to direct the Registrar, in dealing with an application for conditional registration, to ignore the requirement of sufficient, satisfactory practice within s.4(2)(d), on the advice of the Education Committee where the applicant has a qualification in osteopathy which has not been recognised by the Council but has not been refused recognition.

Subs. (9)

See the General Note to s.3(3).

Subss. (10) and (11)

These regulate the power of the Registrar to impose conditions on applications for conditional registration, whether under subs. (2)(f), (5) or (6).

Provisional registration

5.—(1) The General Council may make rules providing for all applicants for registration who are entitled to be registered with full registration, or all such applicants falling within a prescribed class, to be registered initially with provisional registration.

(2) No such rules shall be made before the end of the period of two years beginning with the opening of the register.

(3) Before making any rules under subsection (1), the General Council shall take such steps as are reasonably practicable to consult those who are registered osteopaths.

(4) The General Council may by rules provide for the conversion, in prescribed circumstances and subject to the osteopath concerned complying with such conditions (if any) as may be prescribed, of provisional registration into full registration.

(5) Unless it is converted into full registration in accordance with the rules, any provisional registration shall cease to have effect at the end of the period of one year beginning with the date on which it is entered in the register.

(6) A provisionally registered osteopath shall not practise osteopathy except under the supervision of a fully registered osteopath who is approved by the General Council for the purposes of this subsection.

(7) The General Council shall maintain a list of those fully registered osteopaths who are for the time being approved by the Council for the purposes of subsection (6).

GENERAL NOTE
This section authorises the General Council to make rules to provide for provisional registration of applicants for a period of one year during which time the registered persons shall practise under the supervision of approved fully registered osteopaths. Although these will normally be newly qualified osteopaths the provisions of the section are sufficiently broad to include practitioners returning to the profession after an absence of some time.

Subs. (2)
The delay of two years from the opening of the register is designed to allow the General Council to deal with the work likely to arise from dealing with conditional registrations under s.4.

Subs. (3)
The requirement that before the Council introduces provisional registration it must take reasonably practicable steps to consult registered osteopaths reflects the need to have the general approval of the profession to a system which requires its willingness to devote time to supervising the work of newly qualified osteopaths.
The meaning of a requirement to consult has been considered in a number of cases. There must be a real opportunity for the body or persons consulted to make their views known: *Port Louis Corporation* v. *Att.-Gen. of Mauritius* [1965] A.C. 1111; *R.* v. *Secretary of State for the Environment,* ex p. *Association of Metropolitan Authorities* [1986] 1 W.L.R. 1; *R.* v. *Secretary of State for Health,* ex p. *United States Tobacco International Inc.* [1992] 1 Q.B. 353. The process of consultation must not be a cosmetic exercise. Failure to consult at all is likely to be regarded as breach of a mandatory requirement, so rendering the decision in question invalid: *Agricultural, Horticultural and Forestry Industry Training Board* v. *Aylesbury Mushrooms* [1972] 1 W.L.R. 190. In the case of a provision such as that contained in subs. (3) the question, where there has been some consultation, is likely to be whether the steps taken were reasonably practicable. A circular addressed to all registered osteopaths at their last known addresses would presumably constitute reasonably practicable steps even if it were not received by one or two practitioners; an advertisement in a journal which there was no reason to believe was widely read within the profession would probably not: see further *Grunwick Processing Laboratories* v. *Advisory, Conciliation and Arbitration Service* [1978] A.C. 655.

Subs. (6)
"Supervision" will clearly cover the giving of treatment by a provisionally registered osteopath in the presence of and under the direction of an approved fully trained osteopath. The Act, however, gives no guidance on what degree of control is required.

Registration: supplemental provision

6.—(1) The register shall show, in relation to each registered osteopath—
(a) whether he is registered with full, conditional or provisional registration; and
(b) the address at which he has his practice or principal practice or, if he is not practising, such address as may be prescribed.
(2) The General Council may make rules in connection with registration and the register and as to the payment of fees.
(3) The rules may, in particular, make provision as to—
(a) the form and keeping of the register;
(b) the form and manner in which applications for registration are to be made;
(c) the documentary and other evidence which is to accompany applications for registration;
(d) the manner in which the Registrar is to satisfy himself as to the good character and competence of any person applying for registration and the procedure for so doing;
(e) the manner in which the Registrar is to satisfy himself as to the physical and mental health of any person applying for registration and the procedure for so doing;
(f) the description of persons from whom references are to be provided for persons applying for registration;

(g) in the case of an application for conditional registration, the conditions or kinds of condition which may be imposed on the osteopath concerned;
(h) the making, periodic renewal and removal of entries in the register;
(i) the giving of reasons for any removal of, or refusal to renew, an entry in the register;
(j) any failure on the part of a registered osteopath to comply with any conditions subject to which his registration has effect, including provision for the Registrar to refuse to renew his registration or for the removal of his name from the register;
(k) the issue and form of certificates;
(l) the content, assessment and conduct of any test of competence imposed under section 4;
(m) the meaning of "principal practice" for the purposes of subsection (1).
(4) The rules may, in particular, also make provision—
(a) prescribing the fee to be charged for making an entry in the register or restoring such an entry;
(b) prescribing the fee to be charged in respect of the retention in the register of any entry in any year following the year in which the entry was first made;
(c) providing for the entry in the register of qualifications (whether or not they are recognised qualifications) possessed by registered osteopaths and the removal of such an entry;
(d) prescribing the fee to be charged in respect of the making or removal of any entry of a kind mentioned in paragraph (c);
(e) authorising the Registrar—
    (i) to refuse to make an entry in the register, or restore such an entry, until the prescribed fee has been paid;
    (ii) to remove from the register any entry relating to a person who, after the prescribed notice has been given, fails to pay the fee prescribed in respect of the retention of the entry.
(5) A person who has failed to renew his registration as an osteopath shall be entitled to have his entry restored to the register on payment of the prescribed fee.

GENERAL NOTE
   Section 6 consists, as the head note succinctly states, of provisions supplemental to the organising and keeping of a register of names.

Suspension of registration

   7.—(1) Where the Registrar suspends the registration of an osteopath in accordance with any provision of this Act, the Registrar shall enter in the register a note of—
(a) the suspension;
(b) the period of the suspension; and
(c) the provision under which the suspension was made.
   (2) Where the period of the suspension is extended, the Registrar shall note the extension in the register.
   (3) Any osteopath whose registration has been suspended shall, for the period of his suspension, cease to be a registered osteopath for the purposes of section 32(1).

GENERAL NOTE

Subss. (1) and (2)
   These subsections provide for the formal consequences of suspension of the registration of an osteopath.
   The power to suspend is found in ss.10(3), 21(2), 22(4)(c), 23(2)(b) and (5), and 24(2).

Restoration to the register of osteopaths who have been struck off

8.—(1) Where a person who has had his entry as a fully registered osteopath removed from the register as the result of an order under section 22(4)(d) wishes to have his entry restored to the register he shall make an application for registration to the Registrar.

(2) No such application may be made before the end of the period of ten months beginning with the date on which the order under section 22(4)(d) was made.

(3) Any application for registration in the circumstances mentioned in subsection (1) (an "application for restoration") shall be referred by the Registrar to the Professional Conduct Committee for determination by that Committee.

(4) For the purposes of determining an application for restoration—
(a) the Committee shall exercise the Registrar's functions under section 3; and
(b) subsection (2) of that section shall have effect as if paragraph (d) were omitted.

(5) The Committee shall not grant an application for restoration unless it is satisfied that the applicant not only satisfies the requirements of section 3 (as modified) but, having regard in particular to the circumstances which led to the making of the order under section 22(4)(d), is also a fit and proper person to practise the profession of osteopathy.

(6) On granting an application for restoration, the Committee—
(a) shall direct the Registrar to register the applicant as a fully registered osteopath; and
(b) may make a conditions of practice order with respect to him.

(7) The provisions of section 22 shall have effect in relation to a conditions of practice order made by virtue of subsection (6) as they have effect in relation to one made by virtue of subsection (4)(b) of that section.

(8) The General Council may by rules make provision in relation to the restoration to the register of conditionally registered osteopaths or provisionally registered osteopaths, and any such rules may provide for restoration, in prescribed circumstances, as a fully registered osteopath.

GENERAL NOTE

Subsections (1) to (7) of this section deal with the formal requirements relating to an application to be restored to the register by an applicant whose entry as a fully registered osteopath has been removed by the General Council under s.22(4)(d), that is following consideration of an allegation referred to it by the Professional Conduct Committee (either as a result of allegations of conduct in breach of s.20 or under s.26(2)(a) which provides for the making of rules to allow for the referral to the Professional Conduct Committee by the Health Committee of matters which it considers would be better dealt with by the former committee).

Subsection (8) allows the General Council to make rules for the restoration of the names of conditionally or provisionally registered osteopaths and provides that restoration may be as fully registered osteopaths.

Access to the register etc.

9.—(1) The General Council shall—
(a) make the register available for inspection by members of the public at all reasonable times; and
(b) publish the register before the end of the period of twelve months beginning with the opening of the register and at least once in every succeeding period of twelve months.

(2) Any person who asks the General Council for a copy of the most recently published register shall be entitled to have one on payment of such reasonable fee as the Council may determine.

(3) Subsection (2) shall not be taken as preventing the General Council from providing copies of the register free of charge whenever it considers it appropriate.

(4) Any copy of, or extract from, the published register shall be evidence (and in Scotland sufficient evidence) of the matters mentioned in it.

(5) A certificate purporting to be signed by the Registrar, certifying that a person—

(a) is registered in a specified category,

(b) is not registered,

(c) was registered in a specified category at a specified date or during a specified period,

(d) was not registered in a specified category, or in any category, at a specified date or during a specified period, or

(e) has never been registered,

shall be evidence (and in Scotland sufficient evidence) of the matters certified.

<small>GENERAL NOTE</small>

Subss. (1)–(3)

These subsections ensure public access to the register and, having provided for the right to charge a fee (by subs. (2)), expressly provides, to avoid any doubt, that the Council may, where it considers it appropriate, provide copies of the register free of charge.

Fraud or error in relation to registration

10.—(1) The Registrar shall investigate any allegation that an entry in the register has been fraudulently procured or incorrectly made and report on the result of his investigation to the General Council.

(2) An entry which has been restored to the register under section 6(5) or section 8, or under rules made by virtue of section 8(8), may be treated for the purposes of this section as having been fraudulently procured or incorrectly made if any previous entry from which the restored entry is derived was fraudulently procured or incorrectly made.

(3) The Registrar may, at any time during his investigation, suspend the registration in question if he is satisfied that it is necessary to do so in order to protect members of the public.

(4) The General Council shall by rules make provision, in relation to any case where the Registrar proposes to suspend an osteopath's registration under subsection (3)—

(a) giving the osteopath concerned an opportunity to appear before the Investigating Committee and argue his case against suspension;

· (b) allowing him to be legally represented; and

(c) for the Registrar to be made a party to the proceedings.

(5) If, having considered any report of the Registrar, the General Council is satisfied that the entry in question has been fraudulently procured or incorrectly made it may order the Registrar to remove the entry.

(6) Where such an order is made, the Registrar shall without delay notify the person whose entry is to be removed—

(a) of the order; and

(b) of the right of appeal given by subsection (7).

(7) Where such an order is made, the person whose entry is to be removed may appeal to Her Majesty in Council.

(8) Any such appeal—

(a) must be brought before the end of the period of 28 days beginning with the date on which the order is made; and

(b) shall be dealt with in accordance with rules made by Her Majesty by Order in Council for the purposes of this section.

(9) On an appeal under this section, the General Council shall be the respondent.

(10) The Judicial Committee Act 1833 shall apply in relation to the General Council as it applies in relation to any court from which an appeal lies to Her Majesty in Council.

(11) Without prejudice to the application of that Act, on an appeal under this section to Her Majesty in Council the Judicial Committee may, in their report, recommend to Her Majesty in Council—

(a) that the appeal be dismissed; or

(b) that it be allowed and the order appealed against quashed.

(12) The General Council may by rules make such further provision as it considers appropriate with respect to suspensions under subsection (3), including in particular provision as to their duration.

GENERAL NOTE

This section is modelled on s.39(1) of the Medical Act 1983, but with the additional provision of a possibility of suspension pending investigation (subs. (3)).

A right to appear before the Investigating Committee to argue against suspension is given by subs. (3). The procedure for hearing such an application is set out in s.20.

A right of appeal lies to Her Majesty in Council (subs. (7)). This right of appeal is not limited to a question of law, as for example, under s.31. The position of the Privy Council under comparable legislative provisions was considered in *Felix* v. *General Dental Council* [1960] A.C. 704 and *Fox* v. *General Medical Council* [1960] 1 W.L.R. 1017.

Professional education

GENERAL NOTE

This part of the Act deals with the powers and duties of the Education Committee and of the General Council with regard to training, educating and maintaining standards in the profession of osteopathy.

The Education Committee

11.—(1) The Education Committee shall have the general duty of promoting high standards of education and training in osteopathy and keeping the provision made for that education and training under review.

(2) Where it considers it to be necessary in connection with the discharge of its general duty, the Education Committee may itself provide, or arrange for the provision of, education or training.

(3) The General Council shall consult the Education Committee on matters relating to education, training, examinations or tests of competence.

(4) It shall be the duty of the Education Committee to give advice to the General Council on the matters mentioned in subsection (3), either on being consulted by the Council or where it considers it appropriate to do so.

DEFINITIONS

"Education Committee": s.1(5)(a); Sched., Part II.

GENERAL NOTE

The Education Committee is not merely charged with the duty of promoting high standards of education and training (subs. (1)) but is authorised, if necessary, to provide, or arrange for the provision of education or training. At the Committee stage this section was described as "the cornerstone of the statutory scheme" (Standing Committee C, col. 42).

Visitors

12.—(1) The Education Committee may appoint persons to visit any place at which or institution by which or under whose direction—

(a) any relevant course of study is, or is proposed to be, given;

(b) any examination is, or is proposed to be, held in connection with any such course;

(c) any test of competence is, or is proposed to be, conducted in connection with any such course or for any other purpose connected with this Act.

(2) In subsection (1) "relevant course of study" means any course of study which forms, or is intended to form, part of—

(a) the complete course of study required in order to obtain a recognised qualification or a qualification for which recognition is being sought; or

(b) any training which a registered osteopath may be required to undergo after registration.

(3) No person appointed as a visitor may exercise his functions under this section in relation to—

(a) any place at which he regularly gives instruction in any subject; or

(b) any institution with which he has a significant connection.

(4) A person shall not be prevented from being appointed as a visitor merely because he is a member of—

(a) the General Council; or

(b) any of its committees.

(5) Where a visitor visits any place or institution, in the exercise of his functions under this section, he shall report to the Education Committee—

(a) on the nature and quality of the instruction given, or to be given, and the facilities provided or to be provided, at that place or by that institution; and

(b) on such other matters (if any) as he was required to report on by the Committee.

(6) Requirements of the kind mentioned in subsection (5)(b) may be imposed by the Education Committee—

(a) generally in relation to all visits;

(b) generally in relation to all visits made to a specified kind of place or institution; or

(c) specifically in relation to a particular visit.

(7) Where a visitor reports to the Education Committee under subsection (5), the Committee shall on receipt of the report—

(a) send a copy of it to the institution concerned; and

(b) notify that institution of the period within which it may make observations on, or raise objections to, the report.

(8) The period specified by the Committee in a notice given under subsection (7)(b) shall not be less than one month beginning with the date on which a copy of the report is sent to the institution under subsection (7)(a).

(9) The Education Committee shall not take any steps in the light of any report made under subsection (5) before the end of the specified period.

(10) The General Council may—

(a) pay fees, allowances and expenses to persons appointed as visitors; or

(b) treat any such person, for the purposes of paragraph 15(2)(c) to (e) of the Schedule, as a member of its staff.

(11) In the case of a visitor who is also such a member as is mentioned in subsection (4), any payment made to him in his capacity as a visitor shall be in addition to any to which he is entitled as such a member.

GENERAL NOTE

In order to obtain information about the nature and quality of institutions offering training in osteopathy the Education Committee is authorised to appoint visitors. In the Bill as originally drafted, this power was explicitly limited to institutions within the U.K. That restriction was deleted at the Committee stage where it was recognised that the Education Committee might have to advise the General Council on the recognition of qualifications awarded by overseas institutions.

The standard of proficiency

13.—(1) The General Council shall from time to time determine the standard of proficiency which, in its opinion, is required for the competent and safe practice of osteopathy.

(2) The Council shall publish a statement of the standard of proficiency determined by it under this section.

(3) If the Council at any time varies the standard so determined it shall publish—

(a) a statement of the revised standard; and

(b) a statement of the differences between that standard and the standard as it was immediately before the revision.

(4) No variation of the standard shall have effect before the end of the period of one year beginning with the date on which the Council publishes the statement required by subsection (3) in connection with that variation.

GENERAL NOTE

The Act does not explain the purpose or function of the publication by the General Council of a standard of proficiency. Nor is there any indication of the link between the standard of proficiency promulgated under s.13 and the Code of Practice which the General Council is required to publish by s.19. The section is the descendant of a clause in the original Bill which did not, in addition, provide for a Code of Practice.

In the Standing Committee Mr. Malcolm Moss expressed the view that the standard would "provide the bench mark for determining whether a qualification should be recognised for the purpose of registration . . . It will also be used as the plumbline when allegations of unacceptable professional conduct are being considered by the Professional Conduct Committee" (Standing Committee C, col. 43).

Recognition of qualifications

14.—(1) For the purposes of this Act, a qualification is a "recognised qualification" if it is recognised by the General Council under this section.

(2) Where the General Council is satisfied that—

(a) a qualification granted by an institution in the United Kingdom is evidence of having reached the required standard of proficiency, or

(b) a qualification which such an institution proposes to grant will be evidence of having reached that standard,

it may, with the approval of the Privy Council, recognise that qualification for the purposes of this Act.

(3) Where the General Council is satisfied that a qualification granted by an institution outside the United Kingdom is evidence of having reached the required standard of proficiency, or of reaching a comparable standard, it may, with the approval of the Privy Council, recognise that qualification for the purposes of this Act.

(4) The General Council may by rules—

(a) impose additional conditions for registration, or

(b) provide for any provision made by this Act in relation to conditions for registration to have effect subject to prescribed modifications,

in the case of any application for registration based on a person's holding a qualification which is recognised under subsection (3).

(5) The General Council shall maintain and publish a list of the qualifications which are for the time being recognised under this section.

(6) Before deciding whether or not to recognise a qualification under this section, the General Council shall consult the Education Committee.

(7) When requesting the approval of the Privy Council for the purposes of subsection (2) or (3), the General Council shall make available to the Privy Council—

(a) the information provided to it by the Education Committee; or

(b) where the Privy Council considers it appropriate, the summary of that information.

(8) The Privy Council shall have regard to the information made available to it under subsection (7) before deciding whether or not to give its approval.

(9) The General Council may by rules make provision requiring the Education Committee to publish a statement indicating—

(a) matters on which the Committee will wish to be satisfied before advising the General Council to recognise a qualification under subsection (2); and

(b) matters which may cause the Committee to advise the General Council not to recognise a qualification under subsection (2).

(10) Where, by virtue of Community law a person ("the osteopath") is to be authorised to practise the profession of osteopathy on the same conditions as a person who holds a recognised qualification—

(a) the osteopath shall be treated for the purposes of this Act as having a recognised qualification; but

(b) the General Council may, subject to Community law, require him to satisfy specified additional conditions before being registered.

(11) In subsection (10) "Community law" means any enforceable Community right or any enactment giving effect to a Community obligation.

GENERAL NOTE

This section and s.15 set out the rules relating to the recognition of qualifications by the General Council. Possession of a recognised qualification will be, once two years have elapsed since the opening of the register, the only way of securing registration as an osteopath (see s.3(2), *supra*).

The General Council may only recognise a qualification after it has consulted the Education Committee (subs. (6)) and secured the approval of the Privy Council. Recognition may be given to qualifications granted by institutions whether situated inside or outside the U.K. (subss. (2) and (3)).

The obligation to recognise qualifications by virtue of Community Law is explicitly referred to in subs. (10).

Recognition of qualifications: supplemental

15.—(1) A qualification may be recognised by the General Council under section 14—

(a) only in respect of awards of that qualification made after a specified date;

(b) only in respect of awards made before a specified date; or

(c) only in respect of awards made after a specified date but before a specified date.

(2) Any date specified under subsection (1) may be earlier than the date on which this Act is passed.

(3) Where the General Council recognises a qualification in one or other of the limited ways allowed for by subsection (1), the limitation shall be specified in the list issued by the Council under section 14(5).

(4) The General Council may, in recognising a qualification under section 14, direct that the qualification is to remain a recognised qualification only so long as such conditions as the General Council sees fit to impose are complied with in relation to the qualification.

(5) Any such condition may at any time be removed by the General Council.

(6) The General Council shall not exercise any of its functions under subsection (4) or (5) without the approval of the Privy Council.

(7) Any institution which is, or is likely to be, affected by a direction given by the General Council under subsection (4) shall be notified by the Council of the direction as soon as is reasonably practicable.

(8) Where an application is made by any institution for the recognition of a qualification under section 14, the General Council shall notify the institution of the result of its application as soon as is reasonably practicable after the Council determines the application.

(9) Where the General Council refuses such an application it shall, when notifying the institution concerned, give reasons for its refusal.

Withdrawal of recognition

16.—(1) Where, as a result of any visitor's report or other information acquired by the Education Committee, the Committee is of the opinion—
  (a) that a recognised qualification is no longer, or will no longer be, evidence of having reached the required standard of proficiency,
  (b) that a proposed qualification which has yet to be granted, but which was recognised by virtue of section 14(2)(b), will not be evidence of having reached that standard, or
  (c) that a condition for the continued recognition of a qualification (imposed under section 15(4)) has not been complied with,
it shall refer the matter to the General Council.

(2) If the General Council is satisfied that the circumstances of the case are as mentioned in subsection (1)(a), (b) or (c) it may, with the approval of the Privy Council, direct that the qualification is no longer to be a recognised qualification for the purposes of this Act.

(3) A direction under subsection (2) shall have effect from the date of the direction or from such later date as may be specified in the direction.

(4) In considering any matter referred to it under subsection (1), the General Council shall have regard to the information on which the Education Committee formed its opinion together with any other relevant information which the Council may have.

(5) When requesting the approval of the Privy Council for the purposes of subsection (2), the General Council shall make available to the Privy Council the information to which it had regard under subsection (4).

(6) The Privy Council shall have regard to the information made available to it under subsection (5) before deciding whether or not to give its approval.

(7) Where the recognition of any qualification is withdrawn under this section, the General Council shall use its best endeavours to secure that any person who is studying for that qualification at any place, at the time when recognition is withdrawn, is given the opportunity to study at that or any other place for a qualification which is recognised.

(8) The withdrawal under this section of recognition from any qualification shall not affect the entitlement of any person to be registered by reference to an award of that qualification made to him before the date on which the direction withdrawing recognition had effect.

GENERAL NOTE
  This section deals with the withdrawal of recognition of a formerly recognised qualification by the General Council on the advice of the Education Committee and with the approval of the Privy Council.

Post registration training

17.—(1) The General Council may make rules requiring registered osteopaths to undertake further courses of training.

(2) The rules may, in particular, make provision with respect to registered osteopaths who fail to comply with any requirements of the rules, including provision for their registration to cease to have effect.

(3) Before making, or varying, any rules under this section the General Council shall take such steps as are reasonably practicable to consult those who are registered osteopaths and such other persons as the Council considers appropriate.

GENERAL NOTE
  The General Council is empowered to make rules requiring registered osteopaths to undertake post-registration training. It was frankly admitted at the Committee stage that in its early years the Council would have other more pressing concerns.
  Subsection (3) requires that before making or varying rules under the section the General Council must take "such steps as are reasonably practicable" to consult registered osteopaths

and "such other persons as the Council considers appropriate". On the necessity to consult generally, see General Note to s.5(3), *supra*.

The obligation to consult "such other persons as the Council considers appropriate" is subject to judicial review: despite the subjectivity of the word "considers" there can be little doubt that the provision would be judicially interpreted as meaning such persons as a reasonable Council, in the *Wednesbury* sense of reasonable, considers appropriate: *Secretary of State for Education and Science* v. *Tameside Metropolitan Borough Council* [1977] A.C. 1014.

Information to be given by institutions

18.—(1) This section applies to any institution by which, or under whose direction—

(a) any relevant course of study is, or is proposed to be, given;

(b) any examination is, or is proposed to be, held in connection with any such course; or

(c) any test of competence is, or is proposed to be, conducted in connection with any such course or for any other purpose connected with this Act.

(2) In subsection (1) "relevant course of study" has the same meaning as in section 12.

(3) Whenever required to do so by the General Council, any such institution shall give to the Council such information as the Council may reasonably require in connection with the exercise of its functions under this Act.

(4) The matters with respect to which the General Council may require information under subsection (3) include—

(a) the requirements which must be met by any person pursuing the course of study, undergoing the course of training or taking the examination or test in question;

(b) the financial position of the institution;

(c) the efficiency of the institution's management.

(5) Where an institution refuses any reasonable request for information made by the General Council under this section, the Council may on that ground alone—

(a) give a direction under section 16(2) (with the required approval of the Privy Council) in respect of the qualification in question; or

(b) refuse to recognise that qualification under section 14.

Professional conduct and fitness to practise

GENERAL NOTE

The first section in this Part of the Act (s.19) deals with the publication of a Code of Practice by the General Council. Its connection to the other sections (ss.20–31) arises from the evidential significance in disciplinary proceedings of a failure by a registered osteopath to observe the terms of the Code.

Section 19 is obviously relevant to claims that the Act incorporates "the most up to date thinking on professional self regulation" (*Hansard*, H.C. Vol. 216, col. 1197) and "that it will serve as a model for statutory regulation for other professions" (Standing Committee C, col. 18). Codes of Practice are noticeably absent from the Medical Act 1983 and the Dentists Act 1984. The nearest approach to such a provision is to be found in s.35 of the Medical Act 1983 which provides that the powers of the General Council shall include the power to provide, in such manner as the Council thinks fit, advice for members of the medical profession on standards of professional conduct or on medical ethics.

The Code of Practice

19.—(1) The General Council shall prepare and from time to time publish a Code of Practice—

(a) laying down standards of conduct and practice expected of registered osteopaths; and

(b) giving advice in relation to the practice of osteopathy.

(2) It shall be the duty of the General Council to keep the Code under review and to vary its provisions whenever the Council considers it appropriate to do so.

(3) Before issuing the Code or varying it, the General Council shall consult such representatives of practising osteopaths as it considers appropriate.

(4) Where any person is alleged to have failed to comply with any provision of the Code, that failure—

    (a) shall not be taken, of itself, to constitute unacceptable professional conduct on his part; but

    (b) shall be taken into account in any proceedings against him under this Act.

(5) Any person who asks the General Council for a copy of the Code shall be entitled to have one on payment of such reasonable fee as the Council may determine.

(6) Subsection (5) is not to be taken as preventing the General Council from providing copies of the Code free of charge whenever it considers it appropriate.

GENERAL NOTE

"Codes of practice . . . offer 'practical guidance', are of evidential value and may, reverse the onus of proof" (R. Baldwin and J. Houghton, "Circular Arguments: The Status and Legitimacy of Administrative Rules" [1986] P.L. 239, 243).

A provision for the publication of such a Code Practice is increasingly common in modern legislation and s.19 follows the normal pattern in requiring the promulgating body to enter into consultations before issuing the Code (subs. (3)) and in providing that a breach of the Code does not in itself constitute a wrong or offence—or, in the instant case, "unacceptable professional conduct" (subs. (4)(a))—but such breach may be taken into account in legal proceedings (subs. (4)(b)).

Subs. (3)

The discretion to determine which representatives the General Council thinks fit is not untrammelled: see notes to ss.5(3) and 17(3).

Professional conduct and fitness to practise

20.—(1) This section applies where any allegation is made against a registered osteopath to the effect that—

    (a) he has been guilty of conduct which falls short of the standard required of a registered osteopath;

    (b) he has been guilty of professional incompetence;

    (c) he has been convicted (at any time) in the United Kingdom of a criminal offence; or

    (d) his ability to practise as an osteopath is seriously impaired because of his physical or mental condition.

(2) In this Act conduct which falls short of the standard required of a registered osteopath is referred to as "unacceptable professional conduct".

(3) Where an allegation is made to the General Council, or to any of its committees (other than the Investigating Committee), it shall be the duty of the Council or committee to refer the allegation to the Investigating Committee.

(4) The General Council may make rules requiring any allegation which is made or referred to the Investigating Committee to be referred for preliminary consideration to a person appointed by the Council in accordance with the rules.

(5) Any rules made under subsection (4)—

    (a) may allow for the appointment of persons who are members of the General Council; but

    (b) may not allow for the appointment of the Registrar.

(6) Any person to whom an allegation is referred by the Investigating Committee in accordance with rules made under subsection (4) shall—

    (a) consider the allegation with a view to establishing whether, in his opinion, power is given by this Act to deal with it if it proves to be well founded; and

    (b) if he considers that such power is given, give the Investigating Committee a report of the result of his consideration.

(7) Where there are rules in force under subsection (4), the Investigating Committee shall investigate any allegation with respect to which it is given a report by a person appointed under the rules.

(8) Where there are no such rules in force, the Investigating Committee shall investigate any allegation which is made or referred to it.

(9) Where the Investigating Committee is required to investigate any allegation, it shall—

    (a) notify the registered osteopath concerned of the allegation and invite him to give it his observations before the end of the period of 28 days beginning with the day on which notice of the allegation is sent to him;

    (b) take such steps as are reasonably practicable to obtain as much information as possible about the case; and

    (c) consider, in the light of the information which it has been able to obtain and any observations duly made to it by the registered osteopath concerned, whether in its opinion there is a case to answer.

(10) The General Council may by rules make provision as to the procedure to be followed by the Investigating Committee in any investigation carried out by it under this section.

(11) In the case of an allegation of a kind mentioned in subsection (1)(c), the Investigating Committee may conclude that there is no case to answer if it considers that the criminal offence in question has no material relevance to the fitness of the osteopath concerned to practise osteopathy.

(12) Where the Investigating Committee concludes that there is a case to answer, it shall—

    (a) notify both the osteopath concerned and the person making the allegation of its conclusion; and

    (b) refer the allegation, as formulated by the Investigating Committee—

        (i) to the Health Committee, in the case of an allegation of a kind mentioned in subsection (1)(d); or

        (ii) to the Professional Conduct Committee, in the case of an allegation of any other kind.

(13) Where the Investigating Committee concludes that there is no case to answer, it shall notify both the osteopath concerned and the person making the allegation.

(14) In this section "allegation" means an allegation of a kind mentioned in subsection (1).

DEFINITIONS

    "allegation": s.20(14).

    "Investigating Committee": s.1(5)(6); Sched., Pt. II, paras. 30–33.

GENERAL NOTE

    This section sets out the procedure to be followed where an allegation is made against a registered osteopath which falls within one of the four categories defined in subs. (1). Any such allegation will be referred to the Investigating Committee although provision is made by subs. (4) for the preliminary consideration of a complaint by a person under rules made by the General Council. Where the Investigating Committee concludes that an allegation falls within subs. (1) and is well founded it will refer the case, as appropriate, to the Professional Conduct Committee or the Health Committee (ss.22 and 23).

    The provisions of this Part of the Act and the sections dealing with rights of appeal have been designed "to safeguard the human rights of osteopaths . . . great care has been taken to ensure the panoply of appeal provisions . . . are founded firmly on the principles of natural justice and reflect European law on human rights" (*Hansard*, H.C. Vol. 216, col. 1180).

Subs. (1)

Para. (a)
This type of conduct is defined in subs. (2) as "unacceptable professional conduct". It is a comparable provision to that in the Medical Act 1983, s.36(1)(b): "serious professional misconduct".

Para. (b)
The recognition of professional incompetence, without more, as a ground for disciplinary proceedings was singled out at the Committee Stage as one of the features of the statutory scheme not yet to be found in legislation governing other health care professions. Such a provision may enable appropriate steps to be taken, for example, an admonition or a conditions of practice order under s.22(4), which ensure that it does not become necessary to attempt to prove later more serious shortcomings which fall within para. (a).

Para. (c)
Although this provision makes no attempt to limit the range of criminal convictions which may be made the subject of allegations (provided that they were within the U.K.) two later provisions make it clear that proceedings may be dismissed if the offence in question has no "material relevance" to the fitness of the osteopath to practise osteopathy (subs. (11) and s.22(3)). Thus a conviction for driving under the influence of alcohol might be held to have no material relevance to fitness to practise. But such a conviction might be relevant where it discloses an addiction to alcohol of a kind which may interfere with the osteopath's ability to carry out his professional duties.
In the case of a conviction outside the U.K. it would be open to a complainant to proceed under para. (a) or (b).

Para. (d)
Allegations of serious impairment arising from physical or mental condition if found by the Investigating Committee to be well-founded are referred to the Health Committee.

Subs. (9)
This subsection ensures that an osteopath against whom an allegation has been made knows the charge which he has to meet and is given an adequate opportunity to prepare a response—both aspects of natural justice.
In contrast to hearings before the Professional Conduct Committee and the Health Committee (ss.22(11) and 23(10)) there is, however, no explicit right to be legally represented. This might be said to be an example of implied exclusion of such a right by reference to the principle *expressio unius* but this principle should, at least in the realm of natural justice, only be applied with great caution: *R* v. *Huntingdon District Council*, ex p. *Cowan* [1984] 1 W.L.R. 501; noted (1984) 100 L.Q.R. 367. Perhaps a stronger argument, here, is that hearings by the Investigating Committee are a prelude to the taking of a decision at a later stage, akin to investigations by the police or a prosecutor where fairness is required but not necessarily the full panoply of natural justice. Even in such a case, however, it can be argued that a tribunal must, if asked, consider in its discretion whether the relevant circumstances require the granting of a request for legal representation.

Interim suspension powers of the Investigating Committee

21.—(1) This section applies where, under section 20, the Investigating Committee is investigating an allegation against a registered osteopath.

(2) If the Committee is satisfied that it is necessary to do so in order to protect members of the public, it may order the Registrar to suspend the osteopath's registration.

(3) The order shall specify the period of the suspension, which shall not exceed two months beginning with the date on which the order is made.

(4) The Committee shall not—

(a) make an order in any case after it has referred the allegation in question to the Professional Conduct Committee or the Health Committee; or

(b) make more than one order in respect of the same allegation.

(5) Before making an order, the Investigating Committee shall give the osteopath concerned an opportunity to appear before it and to argue his case against the making of the proposed order.

(6) At any such hearing the osteopath shall be entitled to be legally represented.

GENERAL NOTE
A power of temporary suspension, exercisable before the Investigating Committee has decided that there is evidence to justify referring an allegation to the Professional Conduct Committee or the Health Committee, is justifiable only by reference to the need to protect the public.

An order of temporary suspension cannot be made before the osteopath concerned has been given an opportunity to argue his case against the making of the order (subs. (5)). Such an order cannot last for longer than two months (subs. (3)).

As in s.20 there is no explicit right to legal representation although there is such a right under s.24 when the Professional Conduct Committee or the Health Committee is exercising a similar power.

Consideration of allegations by the Professional Conduct Committee

22.—(1) Where an allegation has been referred to the Professional Conduct Committee under section 20 or by virtue of any rule made under section 26(2)(a), it shall be the duty of the Committee to consider the allegation.

(2) If, having considered it, the Committee is satisfied that the allegation is well founded it shall proceed as follows.

(3) If the allegation is of a kind mentioned in section 20(1)(c), the Committee may take no further action if it considers that the criminal offence in question has no material relevance to the fitness of the osteopath concerned to practise osteopathy.

(4) Otherwise, the Committee shall take one of the following steps—
(a) admonish the osteopath;
(b) make an order imposing conditions with which he must comply while practising as an osteopath (a "conditions of practice order");
(c) order the Registrar to suspend the osteopath's registration for such period as may be specified in the order (a "suspension order"); or
(d) order the Registrar to remove the osteopath's name from the register.

(5) A conditions of practice order shall cease to have effect—
(a) if a period is specified in the order for the purposes of this subsection, when that period ends;
(b) if no such period is specified but a test of competence is so specified, when the osteopath concerned passes the test; or
(c) if both a period and a test are so specified, when the period ends or when the osteopath concerned passes the test, whichever is the later to occur.

(6) At any time while a conditions of practice order is in force under this section or by virtue of a recommendation under section 31(8)(c), the Committee may (whether or not of its own motion)—
(a) extend, or further extend, the period for which the order has effect;
(b) revoke or vary any of the conditions;
(c) require the osteopath concerned to pass a test of competence specified by the Committee;
(d) reduce the period for which the order has effect; or
(e) revoke the order.

(7) Where the period for which a conditions of practice order has effect is extended or reduced under subsection (6), or a test of competence is specified under that subsection, subsection (5) shall have effect as if—
(a) the period specified in the conditions of practice order was the extended or reduced period; and
(b) the test of competence was specified in that order.

(8) At any time while a suspension order is in force with respect to an osteopath under this section or by virtue of a recommendation under section 31(8)(c), the Committee may (whether or not of its own motion)—
(a) extend, or further extend, the period of suspension; and

(b) make a conditions of practice order with which the osteopath must comply if he resumes the practice of osteopathy after the end of his period of suspension.

(9) The period specified in a conditions of practice order or in a suspension order under this section, and any extension of a specified period under subsection (6) or (8), shall not in each case exceed three years.

(10) Before exercising its powers under subsection (4), (6) or (8), the Committee shall give the osteopath concerned an opportunity to appear before it and to argue his case.

(11) At any such hearing the osteopath shall be entitled to be legally represented.

(12) In exercising its powers under subsection (6) or (8), the Committee shall ensure that the conditions imposed on the osteopath concerned are, or the period of suspension imposed on him is, the minimum which it considers necessary for the protection of members of the public.

(13) The Committee shall, before the end of the period of twelve months beginning with the commencement of this section, and at least once in every succeeding period of twelve months, publish a report setting out—
  (a) the names of those osteopaths in respect of whom it has investigated allegations under this section and found the allegations to be well founded;
  (b) the nature of those allegations; and
  (c) the steps (if any) taken by the Committee in respect of the osteopaths so named.

(14) Where the Committee has investigated any allegation against an osteopath under this section and has not been satisfied that the allegation was well founded, it shall include in its report for the year in question a statement of that fact if the osteopath so requests.

DEFINITIONS
"Professional Conduct Committee": s.1(5)(c); Sched., Pt. II, paras. 34–37.

GENERAL NOTE
Allegations may be referred to the Professional Conduct Committee by the Investigating Committee under s.20 or by the Health Committee under s.26(2)(a) where it thinks that an allegation referred to it would be better dealt with by the Professional Conduct Committee.

Subs. (2)
The Committee is directed to consider for itself whether an allegation is well founded, although a complaint cannot come before it until the Investigating Committee has similarly satisfied itself that it is well founded.

Subs. (3)
See the note to s.20(1)(c).

Subss. (4)–(8)
These subsections set out the sanctions open to the Committee, ranging from admonition (subs. (4)(a)), to removal from the register (subs. (4)(d)).

Subss. (10) and (11)
The Committee, before exercising its powers under subss. (4)–(8), must give the osteopath an opportunity to appear before it and argue his case.

In contrast to s.20, the minimum period of notice of a hearing is not laid down in this section but the matter is dealt with later in s.26 which provides for the making of rules to regulate the procedure for the consideration of allegations under ss.22 and 23. Again, in contrast to s.20, the right to legal representation is explicitly recognised: see the note to s.20(9) above.

Consideration of allegations by the Health Committee

23.—(1) Where an allegation has been referred to the Health Committee under section 20 or by virtue of any rule made under section 26(2)(a), it shall be the duty of the Committee to consider the allegation.

(2) If, having considered it, the Committee is satisfied that the allegation is well founded, it shall—

   (a) make an order imposing conditions with which the osteopath concerned must comply while practising as an osteopath (a "conditions of practice order"); or

   (b) order the Registrar to suspend the osteopath's registration for such period as may be specified in the order (a "suspension order").

(3) Any condition in a conditions of practice order under this section shall be imposed so as to have effect for a period specified in the order.

(4) At any time while a conditions of practice order is in force under this section or under section 30 or by virtue of a recommendation under section 31(8)(c), the Committee may (whether or not of its own motion)—

   (a) extend, or further extend, the period for which the order has effect; or

   (b) make a suspension order with respect to the osteopath concerned.

(5) At any time while a suspension order is in force with respect to an osteopath under this section or under section 30 or by virtue of a recommendation under section 31(8)(c), the Committee may (whether or not of its own motion)—

   (a) extend, or further extend, the period of suspension;

   (b) replace the order with a conditions of practice order having effect for the remainder of the period of suspension; or

   (c) make a conditions of practice order with which the osteopath must comply if he resumes the practice of osteopathy after the end of his period of suspension.

(6) On the application of the osteopath with respect to whom a conditions of practice order or a suspension order is in force under this section or under section 30 or by virtue of a recommendation under section 31(8)(c), the Committee may—

   (a) revoke the order;

   (b) vary the order by reducing the period for which it has effect; or

   (c) in the case of a conditions of practice order, vary the order by removing or altering any of the conditions.

(7) Where an osteopath has made an application under subsection (6) which has been refused ("the previous application"), the Committee shall not entertain a further such application unless it is made after the end of the period of twelve months beginning with the date on which the previous application was received by the Committee.

(8) The period specified in a conditions of practice order or in a suspension order under this section, and any extension of a specified period under subsection (4) or (5), shall not in each case exceed three years.

(9) Before exercising its powers under subsection (2), (4), (5) or (6), the Committee shall give the osteopath concerned an opportunity to appear before it and to argue his case.

(10) At any such hearing the osteopath shall be entitled to be legally represented.

(11) In exercising any of its powers under this section, the Committee shall ensure that any conditions imposed on the osteopath concerned are, or any period of suspension imposed on him is, the minimum which it considers necessary for the protection of members of the public.

DEFINITIONS
"Health Committee": s.1(5)(d) and Sched., Pt. II, paras. 38–41.

GENERAL NOTE
This section follows the form of s.22. Allegations that an osteopath's ability to practise is seriously impaired by reason of his physical or mental condition may be referred to the Committee directly by the Investigating Committee under s.20 or by the Professional Conduct

Committee under s.26(2)(a) where it thinks an allegation referred to it could be better dealt with by the Health Committee.

Interim suspension powers of the Professional Conduct Committee and the Health Committee

24.—(1) This section applies where—

(a) an allegation against a registered osteopath has been referred under section 20, or by virtue of any rule made under section 26(2)(a), to the Professional Conduct Committee or the Health Committee and the Committee has not reached a decision on the matter; or

(b) the Professional Conduct Committee or the Health Committee reaches a relevant decision on any such allegation.

(2) The Committee concerned may, if it is satisfied that it is necessary to do so in order to protect members of the public, order the Registrar to suspend the registration of the osteopath concerned.

(3) An order under subsection (2) (an "interim suspension order") shall cease to have effect—

(a) in a case falling within subsection (1)(a), when the Committee reaches a decision in respect of the allegation in question; and

(b) in a case falling within subsection (1)(b)—

(i) if there is no appeal against the decision, when the period for appealing expires; or

(ii) if there is an appeal against the decision, when the appeal is withdrawn or otherwise disposed of.

(4) Before making an interim suspension order, the Committee shall give the osteopath in question an opportunity to appear before it and to argue his case against the making of the proposed order.

(5) At any such hearing the osteopath shall be entitled to be legally represented.

(6) Where an interim suspension order has been made, the osteopath concerned may appeal against it to the appropriate court.

(7) Any such appeal must be brought before the end of the period of 28 days beginning with the date on which the order appealed against is made.

(8) On an appeal under subsection (6) the court may terminate the suspension.

(9) On such an appeal the decision of the court shall be final.

(10) In this section—

"the appropriate court" means—

(a) in the case of an osteopath whose registered address is in Scotland, the Court of Session;

(b) in the case of an osteopath whose registered address is in Northern Ireland, the High Court of Justice in Northern Ireland; and

(c) in any other case, the High Court of Justice in England and Wales;

"relevant decision" means an order under section 22(4)(c) or (d), or an order under section 23(2)(b).

GENERAL NOTE

The Professional Conduct Committee and the Health Committee possess similar powers to the Investigating Committee to order interim suspension from the register before reaching a conclusion on a reported allegation. They also have a power to order a temporary suspension after reaching a decision to cover the interval between making the decision and the lapse of time within which an appeal may be brought: subss. (1)(b) and (3)(b). In the case of the Committees acting under this section they must allow legal representation although the order is an interim order (subs. (5)) and an appeal against the making of an order lies to the appropriate court (subss. (6) and (10)). These provisions no doubt reflect the view that, although interim, orders made by these bodies are likely to have more serious consequences and be regarded more seriously than those made initially at an early stage in an investigation.

Revocation of interim suspension orders

25.—(1) On an application made by the osteopath concerned, in a case falling within section 24(1)(a), an interim suspension order may be revoked by the Committee which made it on the ground that a change in the circumstances of the case has made the order unnecessary.

(2) Where an osteopath has made an application under subsection (1) which has been refused, he may appeal to the appropriate court against the refusal.

(3) Where, in relation to an interim suspension order—

(a) an appeal has been made under section 24(6) against the making of the order, or

(b) a further application for the order to be revoked has been made after an unsuccessful appeal under this section against the refusal of an earlier application,

leave of the appropriate court shall be required for any appeal under subsection (2) in relation to that order.

(4) Except in a case falling within subsection (5), no application under subsection (1) shall be entertained by the Committee concerned if it is made before the end of the period of six months beginning—

(a) with the date on which the order was imposed; or

(b) where an unsuccessful appeal against the order has been made under section 24(6), the date on which the appeal was dismissed.

(5) Where a previous application has been made under subsection (1) in relation to an interim suspension order, no further such application shall be entertained by the Committee concerned if it is made before the end of the period of six months beginning with the date on which the previous application was finally disposed of.

(6) Any appeal under subsection (2) must be brought before the end of the period of 28 days beginning with the date on which notice of the refusal is sent to the osteopath.

(7) On an appeal under subsection (2) the court may terminate the suspension.

(8) On such an appeal the decision of the court shall be final.

(9) In this section "the appropriate court" has the same meaning as in section 24.

GENERAL NOTE

This section provides for applications for revocations of orders of suspension made under s.24 on the grounds of a change in circumstances and for appeals to the courts against a refusal of such an application.

Investigation of allegations: procedural rules

26.—(1) The General Council shall make rules as to the procedure to be followed by the Professional Conduct Committee or the Health Committee in considering any allegation under section 22 or 23.

(2) The rules shall, in particular, include provision—

(a) empowering each Committee to refer to the other any allegation which it considers would be better dealt with by that other Committee;

(b) requiring the osteopath to whom the allegation relates to be given notice of the allegation;

(c) giving the osteopath an opportunity to put his case at a hearing if—

(i) before the end of the period of 28 days beginning with the date on which notice of the allegation is sent to him, he asks for a hearing; or

(ii) the Committee considers that a hearing is desirable;

(d) entitling the osteopath to be legally represented at any hearing in respect of the allegation;

(e) securing that—
    (i) any hearing before the Professional Conduct Committee is held in public unless the Committee decides that it is in the interests of the person making the allegation, or of any person giving evidence or of any patient, to hold the hearing or any part of it in private; and
    (ii) any hearing before the Health Committee is held in private unless the Committee considers that it is appropriate to hold the hearing or any part of it in public;
(f) requiring the osteopath to be notified by the Committee of its decision, its reasons for reaching that decision and of his right of appeal;
(g) requiring the person by whom the allegation was made to be notified by the Committee of its decision and of its reasons for reaching that decision;
(h) empowering the Committee to require persons to attend and give evidence or to produce documents;
(i) about the admissibility of evidence;
(j) enabling the Committee to administer oaths.
(3) No person shall be required by any rules made under this section to give any evidence or produce any document or other material at a hearing held by either Committee which he could not be compelled to give or produce in civil proceedings in any court in that part of the United Kingdom in which the hearing takes place.

GENERAL NOTE
This section provides for the making of rules regulating the conduct of hearings by the Professional Conduct Committee and the Health Committee.

Subs. (2)

Para. (a)
This provision, for the referring by one Committee to the other of any allegation, ensures that an allegation cannot be defeated by attempting to show that it falls outside the jurisdiction of the Committee to which it was initially sent by the Investigating Committee.

Paras. (b), (c) and (d)
These provisions ensure that natural justice is complied with by giving osteopaths against whom allegations have been made (and found to be well founded) notice of the hearings and time to prepare their cases.

Para. (e)
The presumption in the case of hearings before the Professional Conduct Committee is that proceedings will be held in public. Conversely, the presumption in the case of hearings before the Health Committee is that proceedings will take place in private.

Legal assessors

27.—(1) The General Council shall appoint persons to be legal assessors.
(2) They shall have the general function of giving advice to—
(a) any person appointed in accordance with rules made under section 20(4),
(b) the Investigating Committee,
(c) the Professional Conduct Committee, or
(d) the Health Committee,
on questions of law arising in connection with any matter which he or (as the case may be) the committee is considering.
(3) They shall also have such other functions as may be conferred on them by rules made by the General Council.
(4) To be qualified for appointment as a legal assessor under this section, a person must—

(a) have a 10 year general qualification (within the meaning of section 71 of the Courts and Legal Services Act 1990);

(b) be an advocate or solicitor in Scotland of at least 10 years' standing; or

(c) be a member of the Bar of Northern Ireland or solicitor of the Supreme Court of Northern Ireland of at least 10 years' standing.

(5) The General Council may pay such fees, allowances and expenses to persons appointed as legal assessors as it may determine.

(6) In the case of a legal assessor who is also a member of the General Council or of any of its committees, any such payment made to him in his capacity as a legal assessor shall be in addition to any to which he is entitled as such a member.

Medical assessors

28.—(1) The General Council may appoint registered medical practitioners to be medical assessors.

(2) They shall have the general function of giving advice to—

(a) any person appointed in accordance with rules made under section 20(4),

(b) the Investigating Committee,

(c) the Professional Conduct Committee, or

(d) the Health Committee,

on matters within their professional competence arising in connection with any matter which he or (as the case may be) the committee is considering.

(3) They shall also have such other functions as may be conferred on them by rules made by the General Council.

(4) The General Council may pay such fees, allowances and expenses to persons appointed as medical assessors as it may determine.

(5) In the case of a medical assessor who is also a member of the General Council or of any of its committees, any such payment made to him in his capacity as a medical assessor shall be in addition to any to which he is entitled as such a member.

Appeals

GENERAL NOTE

Sections 29–31 deal specifically with appeals, although provisions for appeals in relation to interim suspension orders are to be found in ss.24 and 25.

Appeals against decisions of the Registrar

29.—(1) Where the Registrar—

(a) refuses to register an applicant for registration under this Act,

(b) registers such an applicant with provisional or conditional registration,

(c) refuses to renew any registration,

(d) removes the name of a registered osteopath from the register on the ground that he has breached one or more of the conditions subject to which his registration had effect (otherwise than under an order of the Professional Conduct Committee), or

(e) refuses to grant an application for the conversion of a conditional, or provisional, registration into full registration,

the person aggrieved may appeal to the General Council.

(2) Any such appeal shall be subject to such rules as the General Council may make for the purpose of regulating appeals under this section.

(3) An appeal to the General Council must be made before the end of the period of 28 days beginning with the date on which notice of the Registrar's decision is sent to the person concerned.

(4) Any person aggrieved by the decision of the General Council on an appeal under this section may appeal, on a point of law, to the appropriate court.

(5) Any right of appeal given by this section shall be in addition to any right which the person concerned may otherwise have to appeal to a county court or, in Scotland, to the sheriff; but only one such right of appeal may be exercised in relation to the same decision.

(6) In this section "the appropriate court" means—

(a) in the case of a person whose registered address is (or if he were registered would be) in Scotland, the Court of Session;

(b) in the case of a person whose registered address is (or if he were registered would be) in Northern Ireland, the High Court of Justice in Northern Ireland; and

(c) in any other case, the High Court of Justice in England and Wales.

DEFINITIONS
"appropriate court": s.29(6).

GENERAL NOTE
This section applies to appeals against decisions of the Registrar in regard to registration under the Act. Appeal lies to the General Council and then, on a point of law, to the appropriate court.

Subs. (4)
It should be noted that the right of appeal under s.10(7) is, unlike the right granted by this subsection, not limited to a point of law.

Appeals against decisions of the Health Committee

30.—(1) Any person with respect to whom a decision of the Health Committee is made under section 23 may, before the end of the period of 28 days beginning with the date on which notification of the decision is sent to him, appeal against it in accordance with the provisions of this section.

(2) An appeal under subsection (1) shall lie to an appeal tribunal, consisting of a chairman and two other members, established for the purposes of the appeal in accordance with rules made by the General Council for the purposes of this section.

(3) The General Council shall make rules as to the procedure to be followed by an appeal tribunal hearing an appeal under this section.

(4) The rules may, in particular, make similar provision to that made by virtue of section 26(2)(d), (f), (g), (h), (i) or (j).

(5) No decision against which an appeal may be made under this section shall have effect before—

(a) the expiry of the period within which such an appeal may be made; or

(b) the appeal is withdrawn or otherwise disposed of.

(6) The chairman of an appeal tribunal—

(a) shall be selected in accordance with rules made by the General Council; and

(b) shall be qualified as mentioned in section 27(4).

(7) Each of the other two members of an appeal tribunal shall be selected in accordance with rules made by the General Council—

(a) one of them being a fully registered osteopath, and

(b) the other being a registered medical practitioner.

(8) The rules may not provide for the selection of any member of an appeal tribunal to be by the General Council.

(9) The chairman of an appeal tribunal shall appoint a person approved by the members of the tribunal to act as clerk of the tribunal.

(10) Subject to any provision made by the rules, an appeal tribunal shall sit in public and shall sit—

(a) in Northern Ireland, in the case of an osteopath whose registered address is in Northern Ireland;

(b) in Scotland, in the case of an osteopath whose registered address is in Scotland; and

(c) in England and Wales, in any other case.

(11) On any appeal under this section—

(a) the appeal shall be by way of a rehearing of the case;

(b) the General Council shall be the respondent; and

(c) the tribunal hearing the appeal shall have power to make any decision which the Health Committee had power to make under section 23.

(12) An appeal tribunal shall have the same powers of interim suspension as the Health Committee has under section 24(1)(b) and that section shall have effect in relation to suspension orders made by appeal tribunals with the necessary modifications.

(13) No person shall be required by any rules made under this section to give any evidence or produce any document or other material at a hearing held by an appeal tribunal which he could not be compelled to give or produce in civil proceedings in any court in that part of the United Kingdom in which the hearing takes place.

(14) An appeal tribunal shall have power to award costs.

(15) Any expenses reasonably incurred by a tribunal, including any incurred in connection with the appointment of a clerk, shall be met by the General Council.

GENERAL NOTE

In the case of the Health Committee alone, a right of appeal by way of re-hearing is provided to a specially constituted appeal tribunal the members of which are qualified to consider questions of evidence relating to the appellant's physical or mental health. This is another novel feature of the legislation in comparison with that regulating other professions in the field of medicine.

Subs. (2)

Members of the tribunal are selected for each appeal according to rules made by the General Council. (See subs. (8), below).

Subs. (6)

The Chairman of the tribunal must be legally qualified, as defined in s.27(4), *i.e.* a legal practitioner of ten years' experience.

Subs. (7)

The professional qualifications required of the other two members emphasise that the tribunal is to come to its own conclusion on questions of fact relating to medical matters.

Subs. (8)

This subsection guarantees the independence of the tribunal. The General Council makes the rules for selecting the members of a tribunal but their rules cannot give the power of selection to the General Council.

Subs. (10)

Appeals, in contrast to proceedings before the Health Committee which are normally heard in private (s.26(2)(e)) will normally be heard in public. Two justifications have been offered for the distinction. First, that the appeal is initiated by the osteopath himself. Secondly, the provision accords with Article 6.1 of the European Convention on Human Rights which states:
"In the determination of his civil rights and obligations or of any criminal charge against him, everyone is entitled to a fair and public hearing within a reasonable time by an independent and impartial tribunal established by law" (*Hansard*, H.C. Vol. 224, col. 397).

Subs. (11)

This provision makes clear that an appeal under the section is by way of re-hearing.

Subs. (14)

The tribunal has power to award costs. The absence of a similar provision in the case of the

Professional Conduct Committee and the Health Committee was referred to as a possible source of injustice in the course of debate in the House of Lords (*Hansard*, H.L. Vol. 546, col. 498).

Appeals against decisions of the Professional Conduct Committee and appeal tribunals

31.—(1) Any person with respect to whom—

(a) a decision of the Professional Conduct Committee is made under section 22, or

(b) a decision is made by an appeal tribunal hearing an appeal under section 30,

may, before the end of the period of 28 days beginning with the date on which notification of the decision is sent to him, appeal against it in accordance with the provisions of this section.

(2) No such decision shall have effect—

(a) before the expiry of the period within which an appeal against the decision may be made; or

(b) where an appeal against the decision has been duly made, before the appeal is withdrawn or otherwise disposed of.

(3) An appeal under this section shall lie to Her Majesty in Council.

(4) An appeal under subsection (1)(b) may only be on a point of law.

(5) Any such appeal shall be dealt with in accordance with rules made by Her Majesty by Order in Council for the purposes of this section.

(6) On an appeal under this section, the General Council shall be the respondent.

(7) The Judicial Committee Act 1833 shall apply in relation to the Professional Conduct Committee, the Health Committee and the General Council as it applies in relation to any court from which an appeal lies to Her Majesty in Council.

(8) Without prejudice to the application of that Act, on an appeal under this section to Her Majesty in Council, the Judicial Committee may in their report recommend to Her Majesty in Council—

(a) that the appeal be dismissed;

(b) that the appeal be allowed and the decision questioned by the appeal quashed;

(c) that such other decision as the Professional Conduct Committee or (as the case may be) Health Committee could have made be substituted for the decision questioned by the appeal; or

(d) that the case be remitted to the Committee or appeal tribunal concerned to be disposed of in accordance with the directions of the Judicial Committee.

GENERAL NOTE

Appeals from decisions of the Professional Conduct Committee and the Appeal Tribunal lie to Her Majesty in Council on a point of law only. This section follows the pattern set by earlier legislation relating to the medical professions, currently to be found in the Medical Act 1983, s.40 and the Dentists Act 1984, s.29.

Offences

Offences

32.—(1) A person who (whether expressly or by implication) describes himself as an osteopath, osteopathic practitioner, osteopathic physician, osteopathist, osteotherapist, or any other kind of osteopath, is guilty of an offence unless he is a registered osteopath.

(2) A person who, without reasonable excuse, fails to comply with any requirement imposed by—

(a) the Professional Conduct Committee,

(b) the Health Committee, or
(c) an appeal tribunal hearing an appeal under section 30,
under rules made by virtue of section 26(2)(h) or under any corresponding rules made by virtue of section 30(4) is guilty of an offence.

(3) A person guilty of an offence under this section shall be liable on summary conviction to a fine not exceeding level five on the standard scale.

GENERAL NOTE

Subs. (1)
   The use of the terms listed in this subsection is made an offence in itself. Earlier legislation relating to medical and allied professions had prohibited not the use of professional titles, but false claims to be registered members of the relevant professions, *e.g.*, Professions Supplementary to Medicine Act 1960, s.6; Medical Act 1983, s.49.
   The Opticians Act 1989, s.28, both prohibits the use of certain titles by persons who are not registered and the use of any title or description falsely implying that they are registered in any relevant register. In the latter case it is a defence to prove that the title or description was used in circumstances where it would have been unreasonable for people to believe that the person using the title or description was in fact registered in one of the registers.

Monopolies and competition

Competition and anti-competitive practices

33.—(1) In this section "regulatory provision" means—
(a) any rule made by the General Council;
(b) any provision of the Code of Practice issued by the Council under section 19; and
(c) any other advice or guidance given by the Council, any of its committees or any sub-committee of such a committee.

(2) Schedule 8 to the Fair Trading Act 1973 (powers exercisable when making certain orders) shall, for the purposes of a competition order, have effect in relation to a regulatory provision as it has effect in relation to an agreement, but with the necessary modifications.

(3) A competition order may be made so as to have effect in relation to a regulatory provision even though that provision was properly made in exercise of functions conferred by this Act.

(4) In this section "a competition order" means—
(a) an order under section 56 of the Act of 1973 (orders following reports on monopoly references); or
(b) an order under section 10 of the Competition Act 1980 (orders following reports on competition references).

(5) For the purposes of any order under section 56 of the Act of 1973 or section 10 of the Act of 1980, section 90(4) of the Act of 1973 (power to apply orders to existing agreements) shall have effect in relation to a regulatory provision as it has effect in relation to an agreement.

GENERAL NOTE
   The rules of the non-statutory associations of osteopaths fell within the monopoly provisions of the Fair Trading Act 1973 and anti-competitive practices provisions of the Competition Act 1980. The effect of this section is to ensure that the rules of the new statutorily regulated profession will continue to fall within these Acts.

Miscellaneous

Default powers of the Privy Council

34.—(1) If it appears to the Privy Council that the General Council has failed to perform any functions which, in the opinion of the Privy Council, should have been performed, the Privy Council may give the General Council such direction as the Privy Council considers appropriate.

(2) If the General Council fails to comply with any direction given under this section, the Privy Council may itself give effect to the direction.

(3) For the purpose of enabling it to give effect to a direction under subsection (1), the Privy Council may—

(a) exercise any power of the General Council or do any act or other thing authorised to be done by the General Council; and

(b) do, of its own motion, any act or other thing which it is otherwise authorised to do under this Act on the instigation of the General Council.

GENERAL NOTE

   This section confers default powers on the Privy Council, again following provisions to be found, for example, in the Medical Act 1983, s.50.

Rules

35.—(1) The approval of the Privy Council shall be required for any exercise by the General Council of a power to make rules under this Act.

(2) Any rules made by the General Council or by Order in Council under this Act may make different provision with respect to different cases, or classes of case and, in particular, different provision with respect to different categories of osteopath or registered osteopath.

(3) Any Order in Council made under section 10(8)(b) or 31(5) shall be subject to annulment in pursuance of a resolution of either House of Parliament.

(4) Nothing in any rules made under this Act shall be taken to oblige or entitle any person to act in breach of the law relating to confidentiality.

Exercise of powers of Privy Council

36.—(1) Where the approval of the Privy Council is required by this Act in respect of the making of any rules by the General Council, it shall be given by an order made by the Privy Council.

(2) Any power of the Privy Council under this Act to make an order shall be exercisable by statutory instrument.

(3) Any order approving rules made under section 5, 8(8), 17 or 30 shall be subject to annulment in pursuance of a resolution of either House of Parliament.

(4) For the purposes of exercising any powers conferred by this Act (other than the power of hearing appeals) the quorum of the Privy Council shall be two.

(5) Any act of the Privy Council under this Act shall be sufficiently signified by an instrument signed by the Clerk of the Council.

(6) Any document purporting to be—

(a) an instrument made by the Privy Council under this Act, and

(b) signed by the Clerk of the Privy Council,

shall be evidence (and in Scotland sufficient evidence) of the fact that the instrument was so made and of its terms.

Professional indemnity insurance

37.—(1) The General Council may by rules make provision requiring—

(a) registered osteopaths who are practising as osteopaths, or

(b) prescribed categories of registered osteopaths who are practising as osteopaths,

to secure that they are properly insured against liability to, or in relation to, their patients.

(2) The rules may, in particular—

(a) prescribe risks, or descriptions of risk, with respect to which insurance is required;

    (b) prescribe the amount of insurance that is required either generally or with respect to prescribed risks;

    (c) make such provision as the General Council considers appropriate for the purpose of securing, so far as is reasonably practicable, that the requirements of the rules are complied with;

    (d) make provision with respect to failure to comply with their requirements (including provision for treating any failure as constituting unacceptable professional conduct).

GENERAL NOTE

Concern was expressed during the Third Reading of the Bill in the House of Commons that this section authorises but does not require the General Council to establish a scheme of professional indemnity insurance. The House, however, accepted that responsibility for making the appropriate decision relating to insurance should be left to the General Council.

Data protection and access to personal health information

38.—(1) In section 2(1) of the Access to Health Records Act 1990 (definition of health professionals), after paragraph (f) there shall be inserted—
        "(ff) a registered osteopath;".

(2) The following instruments shall be amended as mentioned in subsection (3)—

    (a) the Data Protection (Subject Access Modification) (Health) Order 1987;

    (b) the Access to Personal Files (Social Services) Regulations 1989;

    (c) the Access to Personal Files (Social Work) (Scotland) Regulations 1989;

    (d) the Access to Personal Files (Housing) Regulations 1989; and

    (e) the Access to Personal Files (Housing) (Scotland) Regulations 1992.

(3) In each case, at the end of the Table in the Schedule there shall be inserted—

"Registered osteopath	Osteopaths Act 1993, section 41."

(4) The reference in section 2(1) of the Access to Medical Reports Act 1988 to the order mentioned in subsection (2)(a) shall be read as a reference to that order as amended by this section.

(5) The amendments made by this section shall not be taken to prejudice the power to make further orders or (as the case may be) regulations varying or revoking the amended provisions.

GENERAL NOTE

The amendments effected by this section give individuals who have received treatment from osteopaths the same right of access to the records of that treatment as in the case of other medical professions.

Exemption from provisions about rehabilitation of offenders

39.—(1) In this section—
    "the 1975 Order" means the Rehabilitation of Offenders Act 1974 (Exceptions) Order 1975 (professions etc. with respect to which provisions of the Act of 1974 are excluded); and
    "the 1979 Order" means the Rehabilitation of Offenders (Exceptions) Order (Northern Ireland) 1979 (professions etc. with respect to which provisions of the Rehabilitation of Offenders (Northern Ireland) Order 1978 are excluded).

(2) In Part I of Schedule 1 to the 1975 Order, there shall be inserted at the end—
        "11. Registered osteopath."

(3) In Part I of Schedule 1 to the 1979 Order, there shall be inserted at the end—

"10. Registered osteopath."

(4) In both the 1975 Order and the 1979 Order, in each case in Part IV of Schedule 1, there shall be inserted in the appropriate place—

" "registered osteopath" has the meaning given by section 41 of the Osteopaths Act 1993."

(5) The amendment of the 1975 Order and the 1979 Order by this section shall not be taken to prejudice the power to make further orders varying or revoking the amended provisions.

Financial provisions

40.—(1) The General Council shall keep proper accounts of all sums received or paid by it and proper records in relation to those accounts.

(2) The accounts for each financial year of the General Council shall be audited by persons appointed by the Council.

(3) No person may be appointed as an auditor under subsection (2) unless he is eligible for appointment as a company auditor under section 25 of the Companies Act 1989 or Article 28 of the Companies (Northern Ireland) Order 1990.

(4) As soon as is reasonably practicable after the accounts of the General Council have been audited, the Council shall—

(a) cause them to be published, together with any report on them made by the auditors; and

(b) send a copy of the accounts and of any such report to the Privy Council.

(5) The Privy Council shall lay any copy sent to them under subsection (4) before each House of Parliament.

Supplemental

Interpretation

41. In this Act—

"conditionally registered osteopath" means a person who is registered with conditional registration;

"fully registered osteopath" means a person who is registered with full registration;

"the General Council" means the General Osteopathic Council;

"interim suspension order" has the meaning given in section 24(3);

"opening of the register" means the date on which section 3 comes into force;

"prescribed" means prescribed by rules made by the General Council;

"provisionally registered osteopath" means a person who is registered with provisional registration;

"recognised qualification" has the meaning given by section 14(1);

"the register" means the register of osteopaths maintained by the Registrar under section 2;

"registered" means registered in the register;

"registered address", in relation to a registered osteopath, means the address which is entered in the register;

"registered osteopath" means a person who is registered as a fully registered osteopath, as a conditionally registered osteopath or as a provisionally registered osteopath;

"the Registrar" has the meaning given in section 2(2);

"the required standard of proficiency" means the standard determined by the General Council under section 13;

"the statutory committees" has the meaning given by section 1(6);

"unacceptable professional conduct" has the meaning given by section 20(2);

"visitor" means a person appointed under section 12.

Short title, commencement, transitional provisions and extent

42.—(1) This Act may be cited as the Osteopaths Act 1993.

(2) This Act shall come into force on such day as the Secretary of State may by order appoint.

(3) The power conferred by subsection (2) shall be exercisable by statutory instrument.

(4) Different days may be appointed by an order under subsection (2) for different purposes and different provisions.

(5) Any order under subsection (2) may make such transitional provision as the Secretary of State considers appropriate.

(6) The transitional provisions of Part III of the Schedule shall have effect.

(7) This Act extends to the United Kingdom except that—
(a) section 38(1) and section 39(2) extend only to Great Britain;
(b) section 38(2)(c) and (e) extends only to Scotland;
(c) section 39(3) extends only to Northern Ireland; and
(d) section 38(2)(b) and (d) extends only to England and Wales.

GENERAL NOTE

Subss. (2) and (4)

The Act is to come into force on such day as the Secretary of State may by order appoint. Different days may be appointed for different purposes and different provisions.

These two provisions, commonly found in legislation, have particular importance because of the number of sections in the Act that measure periods of time from the "opening of the register" which is defined by s.41 as the date on which s.3 comes into force. (See, for example, ss.3(4) and 4(3)). Other sections (for example, s.3(3) and (7)) and the Schedule, Pt. III, refer to transitional provisions which are defined as periods of time running from the opening of the register.

SCHEDULE

GENERAL NOTE

Part I deals with the composition of the General Council and Part II with the composition of the Statutory Committees. Part III consists of transitional provisions which bring into existence the first General Council. Only then can a register of osteopaths be created and members of a General Council be elected by registered osteopaths as required in Pt. I.

Sections 1 and 42(3) THE GENERAL COUNCIL AND COMMITTEES

PART I

GENERAL NOTE

The General Council when established under this Part of the Schedule will consist of 12 members elected by fully registered osteopaths and an equal number consisting of eight members appointed by the Privy Council, three appointed by the Education Committee and one appointed by the Secretary of State.

A close link between osteopaths and the medical profession is ensured by the requirement that one of the twelve elected osteopaths must also be a registered medical practitioner (para. 9(3) and (4)) and that one of the eight members appointed by the Privy Council must be a registered medical practitioner.

THE GENERAL COUNCIL

Membership

1. The General Council shall consist of—
(a) 12 members elected by fully registered osteopaths;
(b) 8 members appointed by the Privy Council;
(c) 3 members appointed by the Education Committee; and
(d) 1 member appointed by the Secretary of State.

2. The quorum of the General Council shall be 12.

3. Subject to paragraphs 4 to 7, each member's term of office shall be for a period of 5 years.

4.—(1) This paragraph applies where a member fails to complete his full term of office.

(2) In such circumstances as may be prescribed, if the unexpired term is less than the prescribed period the vacancy need not be filled before the end of that term.

(3) If the member's successor is elected or (as the case may be) appointed during the unexpired term, the successor's term of office shall, subject to paragraphs 5 to 7, be for the residue of the unexpired term.

(4) Rules made by the General Council under sub-paragraph (2) shall not prescribe a period of more than twelve months.

(5) In this paragraph "the unexpired term" means the period beginning with the date on which the member ceased to be a member and ending with the date on which his full term of office would have expired.

5. Any member may at any time resign by notice in writing addressed to the Registrar.

6. Every member shall retire on reaching the age of 70.

7. The General Council shall by rules make provision as to the grounds (such as repeated absence from meetings or unacceptable professional conduct) on which any member may be removed from office and the procedure involved.

8. No person shall be prevented from being elected or from being appointed merely because he has previously been a member of the General Council.

Members elected by fully registered osteopaths

9.—(1) This paragraph and paragraph 10 apply in relation to the 12 members elected by fully registered osteopaths.

(2) Each member—

(a) shall be a fully registered osteopath at the time of his election, and

(b) may be a registered medical practitioner.

(3) One member shall be expressly elected as a member who is both a fully registered osteopath and a registered medical practitioner at the time of his election.

(4) The member mentioned in sub-paragraph (3) shall be elected by fully registered osteopaths whose registered addresses are in the United Kingdom.

(5) Of the other 11 members—

(a) 8 shall be elected by fully registered osteopaths whose registered addresses are in England;

(b) 1 shall be elected by fully registered osteopaths whose registered addresses are in Wales;

(c) 1 shall be elected by fully registered osteopaths whose registered addresses are in Scotland; and

(d) 1 shall be elected by fully registered osteopaths whose registered addresses are in Northern Ireland.

10. The General Council shall make further provision by rules in relation to the election of the 12 members and as to by-elections.

Members appointed by the Privy Council

11.—(1) Of the 8 members appointed by the Privy Council—

(a) 1 shall be a registered medical practitioner at the time of his appointment and shall be appointed after consultation with the Conference of Medical Royal Colleges and their Faculties in the United Kingdom; and

(b) the other 7 shall be persons who are not registered osteopaths at the time of their appointment.

(2) If the body mentioned in sub-paragraph (1)(a) ceases to exist, the Privy Council shall appoint the member in question after consultation with such other representative body or bodies as they think fit.

(3) The member appointed in accordance with sub-paragraph (1)(a) shall not be a registered osteopath.

(4) Any of the other members may be a registered medical practitioner.

Members appointed by the Education Committee

12.—(1) The 3 members appointed by the Education Committee shall be persons appearing to the Committee to be qualified to advise the General Council on matters relating to education and training in osteopathy.

(2) Before making any such appointment, the Committee shall consult—

(a) those institutions in the United Kingdom by which or under whose direction any relevant course of study is given; and

(b) such other bodies (if any) as the Education Committee considers appropriate.

(3) In this paragraph "relevant course of study" has the same meaning as in section 12(2).

The member appointed by the Secretary of State

13. The member appointed by the Secretary of State shall be a person appearing to him to be qualified to advise the General Council on matters relating to professional education.

The Chairman

14.—(1) The members of the General Council shall elect a Chairman from among themselves.

(2) The Chairman may resign the office of Chairman at any time by notice in writing addressed to the Registrar.

(3) The Chairman shall hold office until—

(a) he resigns as Chairman;

(b) he ceases to be a member of the General Council;

(c) he is removed by a majority vote of the other members of the Council; or

(d) a period of 7 years, beginning with his assuming office as Chairman, has elapsed and no other person has been elected (and served) as Chairman during that time.

(4) A person shall not be prevented from being elected as Chairman merely because he has previously been Chairman, but if he has ceased to hold office by virtue of sub-paragraph (3)(d) he may not be elected as Chairman until some other person has served as the elected Chairman.

(5) The General Council shall by rules—

(a) make further provision in relation to the election of a Chairman; and

(b) make provision for the appointment of an acting Chairman in the event of a vacancy in the office of Chairman or in such other circumstances as may be prescribed.

Powers of the General Council

15.—(1) Subject to any provision made by or under this Act, the General Council shall have power to do anything which is calculated to facilitate the discharge of its functions or which is incidental or conducive to the discharge of its functions.

(2) The General Council shall, in particular, have power—

(a) to borrow;

(b) to appoint such staff as it may determine;

(c) to pay its staff such salaries as it may determine;

(d) to pay its staff, and the members of its committees and any of their sub-committees, such allowances and expenses as it may determine;

(e) to make such provision for the payment of such pensions, allowances or gratuities, or such contributions or payments towards provision for such pensions, allowances or gratuities, to or in respect of its staff as it may determine;

(f) to establish such sub-committees of any of its committees as it may determine;

(g) subject to any provision made by or under this Act, to regulate the procedure of any of its committees or their sub-committees;

(h) to abolish any of its committees, other than a statutory committee, or any sub-committee of any of its committees;

(i) to delegate to any of its committees any functions of the General Council other than any power to make rules.

(3) The powers of the General Council may be exercised even though there is a vacancy among its members.

(4) No proceedings of the General Council shall be invalidated by any defect in the election or appointment of a member.

(5) Subject to any provision made by or under this Act, the General Council may regulate its own procedure.

PART II

THE STATUTORY COMMITTEES

General

16.—(1) The members of the statutory committees, other than co-opted members, shall be appointed by the General Council from among the members of the Council.

(2) The General Council shall make provision by rules as to the procedure for such appointments.

17.—(1) The co-option of any person to any of the statutory committees shall be subject to the approval of the General Council.

(2) A co-opted member of any of the statutory committees may also be a member of the General Council.

(3) The term of office of a co-opted member shall not exceed the period of 3 years beginning with the date of his co-option.

(4) The General Council shall make further provision by rules in relation to co-option, including provision as to the procedure involved.

18. A person shall not be prevented from being a member of a statutory committee merely because he has previously been a member of that committee.

19. Any member of a statutory committee (other than a co-opted member) shall hold office until he ceases to be a member of the General Council or, where he is a member of the committee by virtue of being Chairman of the General Council, until he ceases to be Chairman of the General Council.

20. The General Council may by rules make provision with respect to any sub-committee of a statutory committee including, in particular, provision as to the functions and powers to be conferred on the sub-committee, its composition and its relationship with the statutory committee.

21.—(1) The General Council shall make rules regulating the procedure of the statutory committees and their sub-committees (if any) including, in particular, provision as to rules of evidence to be observed in proceedings before any such committee or sub-committee.

(2) Subject to any rules made under sub-paragraph (1), and to any provision made by the General Council under paragraph 15(2)(g), each statutory committee and any sub-committee of such a committee may regulate its own procedure.

22.—(1) If it appears to the General Council that any statutory committee is failing to perform its functions adequately, the General Council may give a direction as to the proper performance of those functions.

(2) Where the General Council, having given a direction under sub-paragraph (1), is satisfied that the committee has failed to comply with the direction, it may exercise any power of that committee or do any act or other thing authorised to be done by that committee.

23.—(1) The powers of any statutory committee may be exercised even though there is a vacancy among its members.

(2) No proceedings of a statutory committee shall be invalidated by any defect in the appointment of a member.

24.—(1) A person may be a member of more than one statutory committee.

(2) No member of the Professional Conduct Committee or the Health Committee shall take part in dealing with an allegation referred to either committee by another committee if he is also a member of the committee which referred the allegation.

The Education Committee

25.—(1) The Education Committee shall consist of—

(a) 6 of the members of the General Council elected by fully registered osteopaths;

(b) 3 of the members of the General Council appointed by the Privy Council;

(c) the 3 members of the General Council appointed by the Education Committee;

(d) the member of the General Council appointed by the Secretary of State.

(2) In appointing the members of the Committee, the General Council shall secure, so far as is compatible with the provisions of sub-paragraph (1), that its Chairman is a member of the Committee.

26. The Committee may co-opt up to 8 further members.

27.—(1) Subject to sub-paragraph (2), the members of the Committee shall elect a Chairman from among themselves.

(2) The Chairman shall not be the Chairman of the General Council or a co-opted member of the Committee.

(3) In the event of a tie in any voting, the Chairman of the Committee shall have an additional casting vote.

28. The quorum of the Committee shall be 7, of whom at least 4 shall be members of the General Council.

29.—(1) The 3 members appointed to the General Council by the Committee shall not be entitled to take part in the appointment of any of their successors.

(2) The member appointed to the General Council by the Secretary of State shall also not be entitled to take part in the appointment of any of the successors to the 3 members mentioned in sub-paragraph (1).

(3) Where the Chairman of the Committee is prevented by sub-paragraph (1) or (2) from taking part in an appointment the appointment shall be made in accordance with rules made by the General Council.

The Investigating Committee

30. The Investigating Committee shall consist of at least 8 members of the General Council, of whom at least 2 shall be members of the General Council appointed by the Privy Council.

31. The Committee may co-opt up to 8 further members.

32.—(1) Subject to sub-paragraph (2), the members of the Committee shall elect a Chairman from among themselves.

(2) The Chairman shall not be the Chairman of the General Council or a co-opted member of the Committee.

(3) In the event of a tie in any voting, the Chairman of the Committee shall have an additional casting vote.

(4) In the event of a tie in voting in respect of a decision under section 20(9)(c) or section 21(2), the Chairman shall cast his additional vote in favour of the osteopath concerned.

33. The quorum of the Committee shall be 7, of whom at least 4 shall be members of the General Council.

The Professional Conduct Committee

34. The Professional Conduct Committee shall consist of at least 6 members of the General Council, of whom at least 2 shall be members of the General Council appointed by the Privy Council.

35. The Committee may co-opt up to 4 further members.

36.—(1) If the Chairman of the General Council is a member of the Committee he shall be Chairman of the Committee.

(2) If he is not a member of the Committee, the members shall elect a Chairman from among those members who are not co-opted members.

(3) In the event of a tie in any voting, the Chairman of the Committee shall have an additional casting vote.

(4) In the event of a tie in voting in respect of a decision under section 22 or section 24, the Chairman shall cast his additional vote in favour of the osteopath concerned.

37. The quorum of the Committee shall be 5, of whom at least 3 shall be members of the General Council.

The Health Committee

38. The Health Committee shall consist of at least 6 members of the General Council, of whom—

(a) at least 2 shall be members of the General Council appointed by the Privy Council; and

(b) at least one shall be a registered medical practitioner at the time of his appointment.

39. The Committee may co-opt up to 4 further members.

40.—(1) If the Chairman of the General Council is a member of the Committee he shall be Chairman of the Committee.

(2) If he is not a member of the Committee, the members shall elect a Chairman from among those members who are not co-opted members.

(3) In the event of a tie in any voting, the Chairman of the Committee shall have an additional casting vote.

(4) In the event of a tie in voting in respect of a decision under section 23 or section 24, the Chairman shall cast his additional vote in favour of the osteopath concerned.

41. The quorum of the Committee shall be 5, none of whom need be registered medical practitioners but at least 3 of whom shall be members of the General Council.

Part III

DEFINITIONS
"the five year transitional period": para. 43.
"the four year transitional period": para. 43.
"the three year transitional period": para. 43.

GENERAL NOTE
The initial membership of the General Council "will" as to 23 members, depend on nomination by the Privy Council, one member being appointed by the Secretary of State. The Chairman of the Council will be appointed by the Privy Council from among the eight lay members.

The transitional provisions require that in appointing 12 members—equivalent to those later to be elected by registered osteopaths—the Privy Council will appoint persons appearing to be practising osteopaths, after consultation with bodies in the U.K. appearing to the Privy Council to represent practising osteopaths.

Appointment of the 12 osteopathic members will be for a three year transitional period which is defined as beginning with the passing of the Act and ending with the third anniversary of the opening of the register (para. 43).

The lay members, who correspond to those to be appointed under Pt. I, para. 1(b), are to be appointed for a five year transitional period.

The three members corresponding to the members appointed by the Education Committee under Pt. I, para. 1(c) are to be appointed by the Privy Council for a four year transitional period and the Secretary of State's initial appointment will similarly be until the expiration of the four year transitional period.

The appointed Chairman will serve until the end of the first meeting of the Council to be held after the first election by registered osteopaths.

TRANSITIONAL PROVISIONS

The initial membership of the General Council

42. When first constituted, the membership of the General Council shall be determined in accordance with the provisions of this Schedule as modified by this Part.

The transitional periods

43. In this Part—
   "the three year transitional period" means the period beginning with the passing of this Act and ending with the third anniversary of the opening of the register;
   "the four year transitional period" means the period beginning with the passing of this Act and ending with the fourth anniversary of the opening of the register; and
   "the five year transitional period" means the period beginning with the passing of this Act and ending with the fifth anniversary of the opening of the register.

The osteopathic members

44.—(1) During the three year transitional period, paragraph 1(a) shall have effect as if it provided for the appointment of 12 members by the Privy Council.

(2) Each of those members shall be appointed by the Privy Council after consultation with bodies in the United Kingdom appearing to the Privy Council to represent practising osteopaths.

(3) When appointing any such member the Privy Council shall designate him as a person appointed as one of the 12 members provided for by paragraph 1(a) (as modified by this paragraph).

(4) In this paragraph "osteopathic member" means a member designated under this paragraph.

(5) Each of the osteopathic members shall, at the time of his appointment, be a person appearing to the Privy Council to be a practising osteopath.

(6) One of the osteopathic members shall be expressly appointed as a member who is also a registered medical practitioner at the time of his appointment.

(7) Paragraph 6 shall not apply to any of the osteopathic members.

(8) Subject to paragraphs 4, 5 and 7, the term of office of each of the osteopathic members shall end at the end of the three year transitional period.

The lay members

45.—(1) The members appointed by the Privy Council under paragraph 1(b) during the five year transitional period shall each be designated by the Privy Council as a person appointed under paragraph 1(b).

(2) In this Part "lay member" means a member designated under this paragraph.

(3) Paragraph 11 shall have effect during the five year transitional period as if "registered osteopaths" and "registered osteopath" read, respectively, "persons appearing to the Privy Council to be practising osteopaths" and "a person appearing to the Privy Council to be a practising osteopath".

(4) Subject to paragraphs 4 to 7, the term of office of each of the lay members shall end at the end of the five year transitional period.

The education members

46.—(1) During the four year transitional period, paragraph 1(c) shall have effect as if it provided for the appointment of 3 members by the Privy Council.

(2) Each of those members shall be appointed by the Privy Council after consultation with the Secretary of State.

(3) When appointing any such member the Privy Council shall designate him as a person appointed as one of the 3 members provided for by paragraph 1(c) (as modified by this paragraph).

(4) The 3 education members shall be persons appearing to the Privy Council to be qualified to advise the General Council on matters relating to education and training in osteopathy.

(5) In this paragraph "education member" means a member designated under this paragraph.

(6) Paragraph 6 shall not apply to any of the education members.

(7) Subject to paragraphs 4 to 7, the term of office of each of the education members shall end at the end of the four year transitional period.

The Secretary of State's nominee

47. Subject to paragraphs 4, 5 and 7, the term of office of any person appointed by the Secretary of State under paragraph 1(d) during the four year transitional period shall come to an end at the end of that period.

Appointment of first Chairman

48.—(1) The first Chairman of the General Council shall be appointed by the Privy Council from among the lay members to serve as such until the end of the first meeting of the Council to be held after the first election of members under paragraph 1(a).

(2) If a person appointed as Chairman of the Council during the three year transitional period fails to serve his full term of office as Chairman, his successor as Chairman shall be appointed by the Privy Council from among the lay members for the residue of the unexpired term.

(3) Paragraph 14(3) shall have effect in relation to any Chairman appointed by the Privy Council under this paragraph as if for paragraph (c) there were substituted—

"(c) his removal by the Privy Council, where the Privy Council agrees to a request for his removal made by a majority of the other members of the General Council;".

(4) Paragraph 14(3)(d) shall not apply in relation to any person serving as the Chairman appointed by the Privy Council under this paragraph.

INDEX

MERCHANT SHIPPING (REGISTRATION, ETC.) ACT 1993*

(1993 c. 22)

An Act to amend and restate the law relating to the registration of ships and related matters, to make provision in relation to ships on bareboat charter and to make amendments designed to facilitate, or otherwise desirable in connection with, the consolidation of the enactments relating to shipping and seamen.   [1st July 1993]

PARLIAMENTARY DEBATES
Hansard, H.C. Vol. 223, col. 695; H.L. Vol. 545, col. 1916; Vol. 547, col. 96.
The Bill was discussed in Standing Committee D between March 17 and 31, 1993.

INTRODUCTION AND GENERAL NOTE

Purpose of Act
The 1993 Act has two broad purposes; the first is to amend the law relating to the registration of ships, the second is to introduce amendments necessary before the consolidation of the Merchant Shipping Acts 1894–1988. Sections 1–6 and Sched. 1 deal with ship registration generally, while s.7 introduces the possibility of a bareboat charterer registering a foreign vessel under the British flag. Section 8 and Scheds. 2–5 deal with various amendments consequential on the new provisions, while Sched. 4 deals particularly with pre-consolidation amendments.

The 1993 Act began life as a Private Member's Bill introduced by Richard Page, Conservative member for Hertfordshire South West. At the Committee Stage in the Commons, the Labour spokesperson, Joan Walley, congratulated the Government for having "successfully bareboat-chartered a Private Member's Bill". This was a particularly apt description, in view of the Bill's new provision on bareboat charterering-in to the British register. The Bill was really a vehicle for normal Department of Transport (DOT) merchant shipping legislation which would otherwise have been squeezed out of the parliamentary timetable by the pressures of the European Communities (Amendment) Bill, amongst others. Indeed, such were the pressures from Maastricht that there was not time for a Second Reading debate in the Commons—a fact which drew some criticism from the Opposition.

---

* Annotations by Nicholas Gaskell, Reader in Maritime Law, Institute of Maritime Law, Faculty of Law, University of Southampton.

Drafting of merchant shipping legislation

The modern legislative approach, preferred by Government departments such as the DOT, is to leave an increasing amount of detail to be dealt with by statutory instrument. This tendency is particularly marked in respect of the new ship registration provisions, where much material, previously appearing in legislation such as the Merchant Shipping Acts 1894 and 1988, will now be covered by regulations issued under s.3 of the 1993 Act.

In the annotation to the Merchant Shipping Act 1988 in *Current Law Statutes Annotated*, the writer indicated the hope that by 1994 it would be possible to see a thorough consolidation of the Merchant Shipping Acts in time for the centenary of the principal Act, the Merchant Shipping Act 1894. Section 8 of the 1993 Act, and Scheds. 4 and 5, herald the possibility that 1994 will see the long-awaited consolidation. These provisions of the 1993 Act pave the way for consolidation by tidying up the Statute Book. As a consolidating Bill cannot usually introduce changes in the law it is usual to have a pre-consolidation Act which contains any necessary substantive changes. Some venerable provisions dating back to the last century will be repealed, the most remarkable perhaps being s.514 of the Merchant Shipping Act 1894 (re-enacting an 1854 provision) which gave the receiver of a wreck power to "suppress plunder"!

Other states which inherited the imperial Merchant Shipping Act 1894 have already undertaken the process of restructuring it. New Zealand, for example, introduced a 547-section long Transport Law Reform Bill earlier in 1993.

Scope of the Act

Although essentially a non-political and uncontroversial measure which had the broad support of all sides in Parliament, the precise scope of the Bill was a matter of some debate. The Opposition would have preferred more financial support for the British fleet, but this was clearly not a matter for a Private Member's Bill. The proposer of the Bill (Mr Page, *i.e.* the DOT) conceded a number of points on safety when he withdrew what was cl.8 (see the General Note to s.7, on bareboat charterering-out) and agreed to what is now s.7(9). However, it is worth commenting on two areas which were dealt with (or not) by the 1993 Act, namely international maritime conventions and mortgages.

First, the Opposition pressed for the Bill to be amended to allow ratification of the 1989 Salvage Convention. An Opposition Private Member's Bill had been introduced on February 2, 1993, but failed for lack of time. At Committee stage in the Commons the Minister for Transport in London, Mr Norris, gave an undertaking that the Government would take an early legislative opportunity to incorporate the Convention. The Government's view was that it was only lack of parliamentary time that prevented ratification, but that the present Bill's title (referring to pre-consolidation measures) precluded it from being used as a ratification vehicle. It may be a matter of regret that the title was drafted so as to exclude this possibility, although it may be that there was not sufficient time to produce the necessary drafts. It is also the normal practice for ratification of conventions to be undertaken in a government Bill, although the 1993 Act was a government Act in all but name. It is likely that the DOT will have to introduce primary legislation in order to ratify the 1992 Protocols to the Civil Liability Convention 1969 and the Fund Convention 1971, dealing with liability for oil pollution (see the notes to Sched. 4, para. 17, below), and the International Convention on Pollution Preparedness and Response 1992. There is also a possibility of ratifying the 1990 Protocol to the Athens Convention 1974 on the carriage of passengers by sea, which would increase the damages payable after disasters such as that at Zeebrugge in 1987. There are consultations taking place which might, however, see more radical changes to this Convention. Although the latter might not need a new statute it would be convenient to have all three sets of international materials introduced by a single Act. It would seem to make little sense to have a major consolidation which would then be subject to almost immediate and predictable amendment. There have, however, been unfortunate precedents for this. It was hoped that there would be room for a Bill on the oil and salvage Conventions in the Government's programme for 1993–4, but the Queen's speech of November 1993 contained no proposals. However, it is understood that another Private Member's Bill, the Merchant Shipping (Salvage and Pollution) Bill, may be introduced.

Secondly, there are two matters of some significance relating to ship mortgages that may be noted. The Act contains no attempt to reverse the decision in *Shizelle, The* [1992] 2 Lloyd's Rep. 444, which leaves the buyers of unregistered ships such as yachts at risk of having unregistered and undiscoverable mortgages enforced against them. Although the drafting of the Act would in all probability have been done before the decision, it must have been available before consideration began in the Commons on March 17, 1993. It should also be noted that, although the 1993 Act does not make dramatic changes to private law, *e.g.* in Sched. 1, it does appear that a restriction has been placed upon what was thought to be an absolute power of sale granted to a mortgagee by s.35 of the Merchant Shipping Act 1894. This matter is discussed in the notes to Sched. 1, para. 9, below.

Commencement

The Act received Royal Assent on July 1, 1993, but under s.10(2) will come into force on days to be appointed by the Secretary of State.

ABBREVIATIONS

CMI	: Comite Maritime International
DOT	: Department of Transport
DOT/GCBS 1990 Report	: *British Shipping: Challenges and Opportunities* (HMSO, 1990)
GCBS	: General Council Of British Shipping
IMO	: International Maritime Organisation
RYA	: Royal Yachting Association
SSR	: Small Ships Register

Registration of British ships

GENERAL NOTE

A major theme in debates on the transport industry has been the dramatic decline in the British merchant fleet. The Opposition has accused the Government of failing to provide enough support to the industry, particularly in the form of financial incentives to encourage shipowners to operate under the British flag with British seafarers. Consistent with its non-interventionist approach, the Government has been more concerned to remove obstacles facing British shipowners. A number of minor measures were introduced in the Merchant Shipping Act 1988, ss.38–40 to counter unfair competition. However, during the Gulf crisis, concerns were again voiced about the declining level of investment in the British fleet. In 1990, a joint working party set up to investigate the future of British shipping was chaired by the then Secretary of State for Transport, Cecil Parkinson, and the President of the General Council of British Shipping, Sir Jeffrey Sterling. The trade unions were deliberately excluded from the discussions. Later that year, the DOT and the GCBS produced a joint report, *British Shipping: Challenges and Opportunities*, HMSO, 1990. The report was concerned only with economic, and not defence, considerations and focused largely on a number of regulatory policy options that could assist investment. In particular it recommended change or action to: (1) press ahead with moves in the E.C. to secure the liberalisation of cabotage; (2) speed up and simplify technical procedures and regulations governing the DOT's registration requirements; (3) allow demise-chartered vessels to be registered in the U.K. and vice versa; (4) introduce more flexibility into the rules governing the nationality of officers on British ships; and (5) raise the profile of marine training.

The first recommendation was given effect on December 7, 1992 when the E.C. Council agreed Regulation (EEC) No. 3577/92 (O.J. L364/7) applying the principle of freedom to provide services to maritime transport within Member States (maritime cabotage). This agreement on cabotage (coastal trade between the ports of individual Member States) may open up some markets in the Mediterranean to British shipowners. Recommendations 4 and 5, above, have not been the subject of any legislative changes, in this Act or elsewhere.

The second recommendation is reflected in the changes that have now been introduced by ss.1–6 of and Sched. 1 to the 1993 Act. The third recommendation is given partial effect in s.7.

A number of other states offer inducements to foreign shipowners to register under their flags, *e.g.* by creating parallel international registers in addition to financial incentives, such as exemption from seafarers' income tax (DOT/GCBS 1990 Report, para. 3.7). In fact, British shipowners have access to offshore registries in the overseas possessions, such as the Isle of Man, Bermuda, and the Cayman Islands (and see the General Note to s.11 of the Merchant Shipping Act 1988, in *Current Law Statutes Annotated* 1988). The Baltic Exchange has argued for the creation of a new "British Open Register", available to overseas owners which would have, *inter alia*, freedom from U.K. taxation on international earnings of owners registered under the new flag and a relaxation of requirements concerning the nationality of officers (see *The Baltic*, April 1993, p. 12). A formal proposal was presented to the Secretary of State for Transport on December 3, 1993, but did not suggest changes to the existing tax régime. The proposals in s.7 do not create such a new register and it is doubtful whether one could be introduced by regulations under s.3, without the need for the full political scrutiny that primary legislation would entail. Certainly, the DOT could offer tax incentives to ships bareboat chartered-in under s.7 (see ss.2(8) and 7(9), below). The European Court has recently ruled that the German International Ship Register is compatible with the Treaty of Rome (*Firma Sloman Neptun Schiffahrts A.G.*, March 17, 1993 (unreported), noted by Greaves, [1993] L.M.C.L.Q. 471, 473).

Central register of British ships

1.—(1) There shall be established, for all registrations of ships in the United Kingdom under this Act, a register of British ships which shall be available for public inspection.

(2) The register shall be maintained by the Registrar General of Shipping and Seamen as registrar.

(3) The Secretary of State may designate any person to discharge, on behalf of the registrar, all his functions or such of them as the Secretary of State may direct.

(4) The Secretary of State may give to the registrar directions of a general nature as to the discharge of any of his functions.

(5) The register shall be so constituted as to distinguish, in a separate part, registrations of fishing vessels and may be otherwise divided into parts so as to distinguish between classes or descriptions of ships.

(6) The register shall be maintained in accordance with registration regulations and the private law provisions for registered ships and any directions given by the Secretary of State under subsection (4) above.

(7) On the appointed day for the opening of the new register established under subsection (1) above the following existing registers shall close, that is to say—

(a) the register of British ships maintained under Part I of the Merchant Shipping Act 1894;

(b) the register of small British ships maintained under section 5 of the Merchant Shipping Act 1983; and

(c) the register of British fishing vessels maintained under section 13 of the Merchant Shipping Act 1988;

and all registrations in those registers in force on that day shall become registrations in the new register.

DEFINITIONS

"British ship": s.8(2) and Sched. 3.
"directions": subs. (4).
"private law provisions for registered ships": ss.6 and 9(2).
"register": s.9(2).
"registrar": s.9(2).
"registration regulations": ss.3 and 9(2).
"Secretary of State": Sched. 1 to the Interpretation Act 1978.
"United Kingdom": Sched. 1 to the Interpretation Act 1978.

GENERAL NOTE

As a result of a century of developments, there existed by 1993 the three shipping registers referred to in subs. (7). The old register under Pt. I of the 1894 Act was administered by H.M. Customs and Excise at individual ports all around the country. Most ordinary British merchant ships have been registered under Pt. I. The register of small ships under the Merchant Shipping Act 1983 was set up in order to remove many pleasure craft from the full register which, at one time, was comprised of 80 per cent. of such craft. The full Pt. I registry functions were only needed for title purposes, for example in respect of craft for which it was necessary to register a mortgage. The Small Ships Register (SSR) was administered by the RYA under regulations (Merchant Shipping (Small Ships Register) Regulations 1983 (S.I. 1983 No. 1470)). Following the amendments introduced by the Merchant Shipping Act 1988, Pt. II, there was a new centralised register of British fishing vessels which replaced the old fishing boat register under Pt. IV of the 1894 Act.

In 1988, the Government clearly wished to centralise the Pt. I registry functions in Cardiff but, probably to avoid political opposition, postponed the decision (see the General Note to the Merchant Shipping Act 1988, Pt. I in *Current Law Statutes Annotated*). There continued to be 112 traditional ports of registry, but the number of ports at which business was transacted was reduced from 86 to the present total of 14. The new 1988 fishing boat register was, however, centralised (*ibid.*, General Note to Pt. II).

Section 1 of the 1993 Act finally establishes a single central register of British ships (and see s.8(2) and Sched. 3), maintained (probably) in Cardiff by a Registrar General of Shipping and Seamen. The register will probably be computerised. The Registrar, and any lawfully designated delegate, is effectively under the administrative control of the Secretary of State who may give "directions" under s.1(3). Presumably the powers under s.1(3) have been drafted sufficiently widely so as to allow privatisation of the service, a possibility that gave rise to some Opposition fears during debates (see also s.3(6)(b), below). Once the new register is opened (see s.10, below), s.1(7) provides that all existing registrations under the 1894, 1983 and 1988 Acts will be automatically transferred to the new register. Registration regulations under s.3 will allow applicants to choose a port to which the ship belongs. Accordingly, the traditional ports of registry will only survive in the sense that a ship may be marked with the port of choice (see ss.3(2)(f) and 9(5)). Under s.9(4), references in any other Act to ship registration will have to be construed as referring to the system established under the 1993 Act.

Subs. (1)
   The original Bill did not have the requirement that the register "shall be available for public inspection". Some concern was expressed that there would be difficulties for members of the public in checking on the ownership and histories of ships (such as the ill-fated bulk carrier *Derbyshire*). The Opposition tabled an amendment that would have enabled "public inspection" and for it to be "free of charge". The proposer of the Bill (in effect the DOT) was not prepared to accept any reduction in income. At present, personal inspections of ships under Pt. I of the 1894 Act cost £10 per entry and £25 per transcript (£5 and £10, respectively, for fishing vessels), although exceptions are sometimes made for genuine scholars. In Committee it was agreed that the first part of the amendment should be accepted and the second part withdrawn.

Subs. (5)
   This subsection provides that there will continue to be a separately recorded list for fishing vessels. There is also provision to allow for sub-dividing the register into other parts, *e.g.* so as to maintain a separate register for small ships, or possibly for ships bareboat chartered-in (see s.7). There must be a separate fishing part, but other parts are optional.

Subs. (6)
   The key change, apart from centralisation, is brought about by subs. (6). This follows the practice adopted in the 1983 and 1988 legislation by transferring all the detailed provisions relating to merchant ship registration from the primary statute to regulations (governed by s.3, below). Naturally, this will give the DOT greater flexibility to introduce technical changes to a register which had hitherto been enshrined in the 1894 Act.
   The register will have to be operated to take account, not only of the registration regulations and any directions given by the Secretary of State, but also the "private law provisions for registered ships". Essentially, these are the provisions dealing with matters such as title and mortgages (see ss.6(1), 9(2) and Sched. 1).

Registration of ships: basic provisions

   2.—(1) A ship is entitled to be registered if—
   (a) it is owned, to the prescribed extent, by persons qualified to own British ships; and
   (b) such other conditions are satisfied as are prescribed under subsection (2)(b) below;
(and any application for registration is duly made).
   (2) It shall be for registration regulations—
   (a) to determine the persons who are qualified to be owners of British ships, or British ships of any class or description, and to prescribe the extent of the ownership required for compliance with subsection (1)(a) above;
   (b) to prescribe other requirements designed to secure that, taken in conjunction with the requisite ownership, only ships having a British connection are registered.
   (3) The registrar may, if registration regulations so provide, refuse to register a ship or terminate the registration of a ship if, having regard to any relevant requirements of the Merchant Shipping Acts he considers it would be inappropriate for the ship to be or, as the case may be, to remain registered.
   (4) The registrar may, if registration regulations so provide, register a fishing vessel notwithstanding that the requirement of subsection (1)(a) above is not satisfied in relation to a particular owner of a share in the vessel if the vessel otherwise has a British connection.
   (5) Where a ship becomes registered at a time when it is already registered under the law of a country other than the United Kingdom, the owner of the

ship shall take all reasonable steps to secure the termination of the ship's registration under the law of that country.

(6) Subsection (5) above does not apply to a ship which becomes registered on a transfer of registration to the register from a relevant British possession.

(7) Any person who contravenes subsection (5) above shall be guilty of an offence and liable on summary conviction to a fine not exceeding level 3 on the standard scale.

(8) In subsection (3) above "the relevant requirements of the Merchant Shipping Acts" means the requirements of those Acts (including requirements falling to be complied with after registration) relating to—

(a) the condition of ships or their equipment so far as relevant to their safety or any risk of pollution; and

(b) the safety, health and welfare of persons employed or engaged in them.

(9) In this Act references to a ship's having a British connection are references to compliance with the conditions of entitlement imposed by subsection (1)(a) and (b) above and "declaration of British connection" is to be construed accordingly.

DEFINITIONS
"British connection": subs. (2) and s.9(2).
"British ship": s.8(2) and Sched. 3.
"Merchant Shipping Acts": s.9(2).
"qualified to own British ships": subs. (2)(a) and s.9(3).
"register": s.9(2).
"registered": s.9(2).
"registrar": s.9(2).
"registration regulations": ss.3 and 9(2).
"relevant British possession": s.9(2).
"relevant requirements of the Merchant Shipping Acts": subs. (8).
"standard scale": s.37 of the Criminal Justice Act 1982.
"United Kingdom": Sched. 1 to the Interpretation Act 1978.

GENERAL NOTE

Entitlement to register
As the marginal heading indicates, this section sets out the basic criteria for entitlement to be registered on the new British register. In fact, the section says very little about the substance of those criteria. This contrasts with, for example, s.3 of the Merchant Shipping Act 1988, which laid down extensive and detailed rules about those persons entitled to be owners of British ships. The reason for the generality of s.2 is that the detailed criteria will be prescribed by the regulations issued under s.3. However, it appears that by continuing to refer to "entitlement" to register, the 1993 Act preserves the voluntary registration régime introduced by the Merchant Shipping Act 1988, s.4. It has already been suggested that the concept of voluntary registration is not particularly welcome, except perhaps in the case of special categories of small ships (see the General Note to s.4(2) of the Merchant Shipping Act 1988 in *Current Law Statutes Annotated* 1988). It is submitted that maritime safety, the preservation of the environment and the prevention of drug and arms trafficking all demand an accurate and up to date record of all ships having the nationality of a particular state such as the U.K.

It is generally accepted in international law that there should be a "genuine link" between the ship and the state of registry (*e.g.* Art. 5 of the 1958 Geneva Convention on the High Seas and Art. 92 of the 1982 U.N. Convention on the Law of the Sea). Sections 3–5 and 14 of the Merchant Shipping Act 1988 set out requirements which related to the identity of the shipowner (*e.g.* whether it was a British or Hong Kong company) and the nature of its presence in the U.K. (if a U.K. citizen was qualified, but non-resident, there would be the necessity to appoint a representative person in the U.K.). It is generally accepted that such provisions satisfy the international requirement of the "genuine link" and it is the intention of the DOT that the registration regulations issued under s.3 of the 1993 Act will reaffirm the 1988 provisions. A "British ship" is defined in Sched. 3, below.

British Connection
Subsections (1) and (2) focus on two requirements before a ship can be registered; both are

designed to ensure that a ship has a British connection. First, ships must be owned only by persons qualified to own British ships and, secondly, other conditions may be included in regulations to ensure that qualified owners have a sufficient connection with Britain. In particular, the regulations may deal with issues such as whether a ship may be registered if a minority of shares in it are held by non-qualified persons.

The exact nature of the connection that ought to exist between shipowners and Britain is one of some political and commercial sensitivity. The Merchant Shipping Act 1988 restricted somewhat the category of persons who were qualified to own British ships, mainly by removing or redefining the rights of persons who formerly had rights from the days of the empire. A state which enquires too much into the beneficial ownership of corporations themselves registered in that state will not succeed in encouraging such companies to register ships under its flag.

Part II of the 1988 Act was particularly restrictive in respect of fishing vessels. It attempted in s.14 to impose British nationality requirements in order to deter the perceived practice of "quota-hopping", allegedly committed by many Spanish fishing vessels which were re-registered under the British flag in order to take advantage of British fishing quotas allocated under the Common Fishing Policy of the E.C. (and see the General Note to the Merchant Shipping Act 1988, Pt. II, in *Current Law Statutes Annotated* 1988). In the *Factortame* litigation, the European Court ruled that the relevant parts of the 1988 Act could contravene E.C. law on discrimination against the nationals of other Member States and the House of Lords was eventually obliged to declare that E.C. law could give interim relief to override the 1988 Act (see *R.* v. *Secretary of State for Transport*, ex p. *Factortame (No. 2)* (C–213/89) [1991] A.C. 603; see also *R.* v. *Secretary of State for Transport*, ex p. *Factortame* [1990] 2 A.C. 85). A regulation had to be passed, in the meantime, to give effect to the order of the European Court (see the Merchant Shipping Act 1988 (Amendment) Order 1989 (S.I. 1989 No. 2006)). The result of the litigation was to leave the nationality provisions of the Merchant Shipping Act 1988, Pt. II in some disarray, although the Minister for Transport in London, Mr Steven Norris, indicated at the Committee stage of the 1993 Bill that the judgment of the Court was "currently being administratively implemented in respect of all three registers" (Standing Committee D, col. 28, March 17, 1993). At that stage, the Opposition were concerned to learn the exact approach that the DOT would take in dealing with *Factortame* and the extent to which fishermen would be protected. The promoter of the 1993 Bill played down the quota-hopping problem by stating that there were 64 Spanish vessels registered under Pt. II of the 1988 Act, a total of 0.6 per cent. of the fishing fleet, and 28 vessels of other E.C. States, with a total of about 0.3 per cent. of the fleet. The decision of the European Court had not specifically outlawed other provisions in s.14(1) of the Merchant Shipping Act 1988 requiring, *e.g.* the fishing vessel to be managed, and its operations directed and controlled, from within the U.K. It may still be possible for the DOT to insist on these and other genuine links with the U.K. It is for that reason that the requirement as to "British connection" have been framed widely in the section, so that it may be applied to vessels of all types, whether they are fishing vessels, tankers, or pleasure craft, and to British citizens who may be resident abroad. For that reason, an Opposition amendment requiring an "economic connection" was recognised as being too narrow and was withdrawn.

Subsection (4) repeats a discretion granted by s.14(4) of the Merchant Shipping Act 1988 whereby the Secretary of State was entitled to allow a fishing vessel to be registered even where its owners did not pass the relevant eligibility tests. An example of a case where such discretion might be exercised would be where a non-E.C. citizen had been resident and fishing in the U.K. for some time and it would cause hardship to refuse registration. Apparently, only 13 such dispensations have been given since 1988.

Refusal and termination of registration

Under ss.6, 7, 15 and 16 of the Merchant Shipping Act 1988 the Secretary of State was given the power to refuse to register a ship, or to direct its removal from the register. Subsection (3) reproduces similar powers, which will now be filled out by regulations made under s.3. The registrar is given a discretion to refuse to register a ship or terminate the registration of a ship, but the cases in which it will be exercised are fairly well known and are indicated by the reference to the "relevant requirements of the Merchant Shipping Acts", as defined in subs. (8). These relate to safety and pollution requirements, *e.g.* that the ship has the relevant certification under international Conventions such as MARPOL 1973/78 (as amended) or SOLAS 1974 (as amended) which indicate that it has been regularly surveyed and poses no hazard to human safety or to the environment. However, the DOT (through the promoter) resisted any attempt to add "passengers" to the list of persons mentioned in subs. (8)(b), apparently because the provision was merely meant to replicate s.6(3) of the Merchant Shipping Act 1988 (with which it is broadly comparable): see also the General Note to s.7(9), below. Further powers to allow deregistration are provided for in s.3(2)(j), but presumably these are subject to an implied limitation in s.2(4) (arising from the matters specifically listed in subs. (8)). It does seem curious that a registrar could refuse to register a ship that had unsafe working conditions for the crew, but not a ship which was unsafe for passengers (such as the ferry *Celtic Pride*, the defective sewerage system of which caused the death of two children in August 1992). Subsection (8) is specific in its reference to the Merchant Shipping Act requirements and other legislation applying to ships (*e.g.* relating to taxation of seafarers) need not be complied with before an application can be made to register (*cf.* s.7(6)(b) and (c), below).

Registration may also be terminated under subs. (4) where a ship ceases to be owned by a qualified person, *e.g.* where it is sold to a company seated abroad.

Subsection (5) deals with a related matter, namely that of the practical problems occurring when a ship transfers from a foreign registry to the British register. In practice, it may not always be technically possible to make deregistration abroad a pre-condition of entry onto the U.K. register, as there may be delays in communications with foreign administrations. The Merchant Shipping Act 1988, s.9 accordingly introduced a duty on the shipowner to take all reasonable measures to secure deregistration abroad and subs. (5) is to similar effect. Section 7(5) now makes specific provision, in one particular instance, for the possibility of simultaneous registration in the registries of two states, namely where a ship is allowed to be entered in the U.K. register by a bareboat charterer. The requirement of subs. (5) does not apply where the ship is transferred from one of the Crown Dependencies or Dependent Territories, such as Jersey or Hong Kong (see subs. (6) and s.9(2)).

Subsection (7) sets out the appropriate fine for failing to comply with subs. (5) according to the standard scale set out in s.37 of the Criminal Justice Act 1982 (as amended), currently £500.

Registration regulations

3.—(1) The Secretary of State shall by regulations (to be known as "registration regulations") make provision for and in connection with the registration of ships as British ships.

(2) Without prejudice to the generality of subsection (1) above, registration regulations may, in particular, make provision with respect to any of the following matters—

(a) the persons by whom and the manner in which applications in connection with registration are to be made;

(b) the information and evidence (including declarations of British connection) to be provided in connection with such applications and such supplementary information or evidence as may be required by any specified authority;

(c) the shares in the property in, and the number of owners (including joint owners) of, a ship permitted for the purposes of registration and the persons required or permitted to be registered in respect of a ship or to be so registered in specified circumstances;

(d) the issue of certificates (including provisional certificates) of registration, their production and surrender;

(e) restricting and regulating the names of ships registered or to be registered;

(f) the marking of ships registered or to be registered, including marks for identifying the port to which a ship is to be treated as belonging;

(g) the period for which registration is to remain effective without renewal;

(h) the production to the registrar of declarations of British connection or other information relating thereto, as respects registered ships, at specified intervals or at his request;

(i) the survey and inspection of ships registered or to be registered and the recording of their tonnage as ascertained (or reascertained) under the tonnage regulations;

(j) the refusal, suspension and termination of registration in specified circumstances;

(k) matters arising out of the expiration, suspension or termination of registration (including the removal of marks and the cancellation of certificates);

(l) the charging of fees in connection with registration or registered ships;

(m) the transfer of the registration of ships to and from the register from and to registers or corresponding records in countries other than the United Kingdom;

(n) inspection of the register;

(o) any other matter which is authorised or required by this Act to be prescribed in registration regulations;

but no provision determining, or providing for determining, the fees to be charged or prescribing any arrangements for their determination by other persons shall be made without the approval of the Treasury.

(3) Registration regulations may—

(a) make different provision for different classes or descriptions of ships and for different circumstances;

(b) without prejudice to paragraph (a) above, make provision for the granting of exemptions or dispensations by the Secretary of State from specified requirements of the regulations, subject to such conditions (if any) as he thinks fit to impose; and

(c) make such transitional, incidental or supplementary provision as appears to the Secretary of State to be necessary or expedient, including provision authorising investigations and conferring powers of inspection for verifying the British connection of a ship.

(4) Registration regulations—

(a) may make provision for the registration of any class or description of ships to be such as to exclude the application of the private law provisions for registered ships and, if they do, may regulate the transfer, transmission or mortgaging of ships of the class or description so excluded;

(b) may make provision for any matter which is authorised or required by those provisions to be prescribed by registration regulations; and

(c) shall make provision precluding notice of any trust being entered in the register or being receivable by the registrar except as respects specified classes or descriptions of ships or in specified circumstances.

(5) Registration regulations may create offences subject to the limitation that no offence shall be punishable with imprisonment or punishable on summary conviction with a fine exceeding level 5 on the standard scale.

(6) Registration regulations may provide for—

(a) the approval of forms by the Secretary of State; and

(b) the discharge of specified functions by specified authorities or persons.

(7) Registration regulations may provide for any of their provisions to extend to places outside the United Kingdom.

(8) The power to make registration regulations shall be exercisable by statutory instrument which shall be subject to annulment in pursuance of a resolution of either House of Parliament.

(9) Any document purporting to be a copy of any information contained in an entry in the register and to be certified as a true copy by the registrar shall be evidence (and, in Scotland, sufficient evidence) of the matters stated in the document.

(10) Any fees received by the Secretary of State in pursuance of registration regulations shall be paid into the Consolidated Fund.

DEFINITIONS

"British connection": s.9(2).
"British ship": s.8(2) and Sched. 3.
"person": Sched. 1 to the Interpretation Act 1978.
"private law provisions for registered ships": ss.6 and 9(2).
"register": s.9(2).
"registered": s.9(2).
"registrar": s.9(2).
"registration regulations": ss.3 and 9(2).

"Secretary of State": Sched. 1 to the Interpretation Act 1978.
"standard scale": s.35 of the Criminal Justice Act 1982.
"tonnage regulations": s.9(2); s.1 of the Merchant Shipping Act 1965.
"United Kingdom": Sched. 1 to the Interpretation Act 1978.

GENERAL NOTE

The DOT/GCBS 1990 Report, para. 3.12, noted that changes to registration requirements always required amendment to the Merchant Shipping Acts. By contrast, aircraft registration requirements have been promulgated through delegated legislation, namely Air Navigation Orders made under the Civil Aviation Act 1982. It was said that "this is a more flexible arrangement which allows technical changes to be made quickly in response to modern developments and practice" (*ibid.*). Admittedly, it is inconvenient to the DOT to have to fight for parliamentary time for technical changes. However, some changes to registration law have been politically sensitive, *e.g.* where centralisation has been seen to affect local fishing interests, and registration rules are often related to issues such as manning and labour costs. It might be thought that a movement towards the use of delegated legislation also removes possibilities for political opposition to market oriented policies favoured by shipowners. On balance, though, the lack of parliamentary time for merchant shipping matters and the relatively technical nature of the subject matter of registration probably justify the approach taken by s.3, which gives effect to the DOT/GCBS recommendations.

Part II of the Merchant Shipping Act 1988 had already removed most of the detailed requirements for fishing vessels from the body of the Act to Sched. 2. The process has simply moved a stage further and, as outlined in the General Note to the 1993 Act, above, s.3 removes from the Merchant Shipping Acts altogether the detailed registration requirements for all ships and puts them into delegated legislation. This purpose is achieved by s.3(1). It is anticipated that regulations will be published in January 1994 to come into effect on March 21, 1994.

Subss. (2), (6) and (7)

Subsection (2) outlines the general scope of the registration regulations, without in any way limiting the general rule making power (subject, perhaps to the comments made in relation to s.2(4), above). Most of the matters listed are already established features of the ship registration system (*cf.* Sched. 2, para. 2 to the Merchant Shipping Act 1988) and do not call for separate comment. The DOT has indicated, however, that innovations are contemplated in connection with the computerisation of the register (which is not specifically mentioned) and by the introduction of a finite five-year registration period for all vessels (falling within s.3(2)(g)). Existing practice allows for there to be a large number of "ports of registry", *e.g.* Southampton, London, etc., in which all the records for a ship are kept. Ships have traditionally borne the name of this port on their sterns and there is a certain sentimental attachment to the practice. The centralisation of the registry, and its probable computerisation, means that there will not be separate registries, as such. However, it is envisaged that registration regulations will allow applicants to choose a port to which the ship belongs (see subs. (2)(f)). The "belonging" would seem to have no other legal significance for registration purposes than the fact that the ship must be marked according to the choice. According to s.9(5) registration regulations may provide that references in other legislation to the traditional port of registry, or the port to which a ship belongs, are to be construed as referring to the port indicated by the marking on the ship. Subsection (6)(a) allows for the approval by the Secretary of State of standard forms, *e.g.* mortgages and bills of sale (see Sched. 1, paras. 2 and 7). Subsection (6)(b) seems to overlap with s.1(3), above, in that it allows for the delegation of functions. Regulations may provide for the privatisation of certain parts of the registrar's work, such as inspections or the maintenance of computerised records. Subsection (7) allows regulations to extend to places outside the U.K. to deal with circumstances where, for example, provisional certificates are granted at ports outside the U.K.

Subs. (3)

This subsection contains ancillary provisions which preserve the general flexibility of the powers granted by subs. (1). If, for example, there are separate parts of the register for pleasure craft (in addition to one for fishing vessels) the regulations may set out different requirements for each part. Exemptions may also be granted, *e.g.* under s.2(4), above. Powers of inspection are granted by para. (c) in order to check whether a shipowner has the necessary British connection required by s.2. Presumably, an inspector may be empowered to check whether a fishing vessel is effectively controlled and managed from the U.K. It is clear that the work of surveying and inspecting under subs. (2)(i) may be sub-contracted to the private sector and much work is already delegated to classification societies such as Lloyd's Register of Shipping. In November 1992, the Government had announced that the work of the Surveyor-General's Department would be a candidate for "agency" status and would be known from April 1, 1994 as the Maritime Safety Agency.

Subs. (4)

This subsection is an important provision for those interested in the private law aspects of shipping registration. At present, the small ships register under the Merchant Shipping Act 1983 is not a title register, that is, it does not contain any proof of title and does not allow for mortgages to be registered. Owners of pleasure craft, and lenders to such owners, must presently seek an entry on the full register if they want recognition of such private law rights. Full registration may impose too many burdens for the comparatively small sums involved and the subsection allows for a part of the new register to exclude the "private law provisions for registered ships", as defined in ss.6 and 9(2), below. This would preserve the current position, but para. (a) also allows regulations specifically to deal with the transfer or transmission of such ships (*e.g.* by sale or inheritance) or for their mortgaging (*cf.* ss.31–38 of the Merchant Shipping Act 1894). Paragraph (c) will enable a provision to substantially re-enact s.56 of the Merchant Shipping Act 1894, although that section contains an absolute prohibition on trusts being entered in the register while the new provision retains the flexibility of allowing such entries in circumstances to be defined.

Subs. (5)

This subsection allows for the creation of offences and the current level of fine under the Criminal Justice Act 1982 is £5000.

Offences relating to a ship's British connection

4.—(1) Any person who, in relation to any matter relevant to the British connection of a ship—

    (a) makes to the registrar a statement which he knows to be false or recklessly makes a statement which is false; or

    (b) furnishes to the registrar information which is false,

shall be guilty of an offence.

(2) If at any time there occurs, in relation to a registered ship, any change affecting the British connection of the ship the owner of the ship shall, as soon as practicable after the change occurs, notify the registrar of that change; and if he fails to do so he shall be guilty of an offence.

(3) Any person who intentionally alters, suppresses, conceals or destroys a document which contains information relating to the British connection of a ship and which he has been required to produce to the registrar in pursuance of registration regulations shall be guilty of an offence.

(4) A person guilty of an offence under this section shall be liable—

    (a) on summary conviction, to a fine not exceeding the statutory maximum;

    (b) on conviction on indictment, to imprisonment for a term not exceeding two years or a fine, or both.

(5) This section applies to things done outside, as well as to things done within, the United Kingdom.

DEFINITIONS

    "British connection": s.9(2).

    "person": Sched. 1 to the Interpretation Act 1978.

    "registered": s.9(2).

    "registrar": s.9(2).

    "United Kingdom": Sched. 1 to the Interpretation Act 1978.

GENERAL NOTE

This section effectively reproduces s.8 of the Merchant Shipping Act 1988 (and the equivalent in respect of fishing vessels—the Merchant Shipping Act 1988, Sched. 2, para. 5). Thus, under subs. (1), offences are created if any person knowingly or recklessly makes a false statement to the registrar or provides false information. An example might be where an agent handling the registration declares that a ship has already been deregistered elsewhere when he knows that an application to deregister is still pending. In a number of respects the new provision goes beyond its forbear. Under subs. (1), para. (b) there appears to be no requirement that the information should be knowingly or recklessly furnished, in contrast with para. (a) and the 1988 provision. Mr Page, the Bill's promoter, sought to justify the distinction on the basis that para. (b) was designed to deal with the person who arranges for an agent to provide false information, *e.g.* forgeries, to the registrar. The explanation was not entirely convincing and there does appear to be the possibility of a strict liability offence, as Terry Davis M.P. warned at Committee Stage (Standing Committee D, col. 74, March 31, 1993). Subsection (2) creates an offence if the ship-owner fails to notify the registrar of a change that affects the British character of the ship, *e.g.* where after a reasonable period of time the shipowner deliberately fails to tell the registrar that the ship has been sold to a foreign citizen or company. A further offence is created by subs. (3) and is designed to prevent the deliberate concealment, suppression, alteration or destruction of a document that might affect the British connection of a ship, *e.g.* where an executive destroys a document which indicates that a fishing vessel is being controlled from abroad. The penalties created by subs. (4) have been increased (on indictment) from those in the Merchant Shipping Act 1988, from an unlimited fine to imprisonment for two years. Subsection (5) purports to extend offences to that which is done outside, as well as within, the U.K.

Supplementary provisions as respects fishing vessels

5.—(1) Subject to subsection (2) below, if a fishing vessel which—
  (a) is either—
        (i) entitled to be registered, or
        (ii) wholly owned by persons qualified to be owners of British
     ships, but
  (b) is registered neither under this Act in the part of the register relating to
     fishing vessels nor under the law of any country outside the United
     Kingdom,
fishes for profit the vessel shall be liable to forfeiture and the skipper, the owner and the charterer of the vessel shall each be guilty of an offence.

(2) Subsection (1) above does not apply to fishing vessels of such classes or descriptions or in such circumstances as may be specified in regulations made by the Secretary of State by statutory instrument subject to annulment in pursuance of a resolution of either House of Parliament.

(3) If the skipper or owner of a fishing vessel which is not registered in the United Kingdom does anything, or permits anything to be done, for the purpose of causing the vessel to appear to be a vessel registered in the United Kingdom, then, subject to subsection (4) below, the vessel shall be liable to forfeiture and the skipper, the owner and any charterer of the vessel shall each be guilty of an offence.

(4) Where the registration of a fishing vessel has terminated by virtue of any provision of registration regulations, any marks prescribed by registration regulations displayed on the fishing vessel within the period of 14 days beginning with the date of termination of that registration shall be disregarded for the purposes of subsection (3) above.

(5) Any person guilty of an offence under this section shall be liable—
  (a) on summary conviction, to a fine not exceeding £50,000;
  (b) on conviction on indictment, to imprisonment for a term not exceeding two years or a fine, or both.

(6) Proceedings for an offence under this section shall not be instituted—
  (a) in England and Wales, except by or with the consent of the Attorney
     General, the Secretary of State or the Minister; or
  (b) in Northern Ireland, except by or with the consent of the Attorney
     General for Northern Ireland, the Secretary of State or the Minister.

(7) In subsection (6) above "the Minister"—
  (a) in relation to England and Wales, means the Minister of Agriculture,
     Fisheries and Food; and
  (b) in relation to Northern Ireland, means the Secretary of State con-
     cerned with sea fishing in Northern Ireland.

(8) This section applies to things done outside, as well as to things done within, the United Kingdom.

(9) Sections 8 and 9 of the Sea Fisheries Act 1968 (general powers of British sea-fishery officers and powers of sea-fishery officers to enforce conventions) shall apply in relation to any provision of this section or of registration regulations in their application to fishing vessels or fishing vessels of any class or description as they apply in relation to any order mentioned in section 8 of that Act and in relation to any convention mentioned in section 9 of that Act respectively; and sections 10 to 12 and 14 of that Act (offences and supplemental proceedings as to legal proceedings) shall apply accordingly.

DEFINITIONS
"British ship": s.8(2) and Sched. 3.
"person": Sched. 1 to the Interpretation Act 1978.
"register": s.9(2).
"registered": s.9(2).
"registration regulations": ss.3 and 9(2).
"Secretary of State": Sched. 1 to the Interpretation Act 1978.
"United Kingdom": Sched. 1 to the Interpretation Act 1978.

GENERAL NOTE
This section reiterates s.22 of the Merchant Shipping Act 1988 (and see the General Note to that section in *Current Law Statutes Annotated* 1988). Although the Merchant Shipping Act 1988 introduced a system of voluntary registration for non-fishing vessels, s.22 of that Act, and s.5 of the 1993 Act, impose drastic penalties in respect of vessels fishing for profit which are not registered in the U.K. or overseas. Not only may the skipper, owner and charterer be guilty but the fishing vessel is liable to forfeiture. Subsection (2) repeats the possibility, raised by the Merchant Shipping Act 1988, s.22(2), of exemption for certain types of unregistered fishing vessels. Currently, only salmon cobles are exempted.

Subsection (3) effectively repeats s.22(5) of the Merchant Shipping Act 1988 and imposes sanctions on those who cheat by trying to make it appear that the fishing vessel is registered in the U.K., *e.g.* by painting on a false name and port of registry. Again, in addition to the personal penalties set out in subs. (5), the vessel may be forfeited. Subsection (4) has a similar effect as s.22(8) of the 1988 Act and allows a 14-day period of grace after the termination of registration (*e.g.* where the vessel has been sold to a foreign corporation for registration abroad) within which there is no offence committed under subs. (3). The period may be necessary where the registrar orders deregistration while the vessel is at sea.

Subsections (5)–(7) replace s.24 of the 1988 Act with identical penalties. Like s.4(5) of the 1993 Act, offences under s.5 can be committed outside the U.K., *e.g.* on the high seas.

Subsection (9) re-enacts s.24(3) of the 1988 Act and continues the extension of the powers of sea fishery officers under the Sea Fisheries Act 1968.

Private law provisions for registered ships and liability as owner

6.—(1) Schedule 1 (which makes provision relating to the title to, and the registration of mortgages over, ships) shall have effect.

(2) Schedule 1 does not apply in relation to ships which are excluded from its application by registration regulations under section 3(4)(a).

(3) Where any person is beneficially interested, otherwise than as mortgagee, in any ship or share in a ship registered in the name of some other person as owner, the person so interested shall, as well as the registered owner, be liable to any pecuniary penalties imposed by or under the Merchant Shipping Acts or any other Act on the owners of registered ships.

(4) Where the registration of any ship terminates by virtue of any provision of registration regulations, the termination of that registration shall not affect any entry made in the register so far as relating to any undischarged registered mortgage of that ship or of any share in it.

(5) In subsection (4) above "registered mortgage" has the same meaning as in that Schedule.

(6) In this Act "the private law provisions for registered ships" means the provisions of Schedule 1 and registration regulations made for the purposes of that Schedule or the provisions of registration regulations made under section 3(4)(a).

DEFINITIONS
"private law provisions for registered ships": subs. (6) and s.9(2).
"registered": s.9(2).
"registered mortgage": subs. (5) and Sched. 1.
"registration regulations": ss.3 and 9(2).

GENERAL NOTE
This section is important providing for particular private law provisions to apply to registered ships. At present, ss.24–30 of the Merchant Shipping Act 1894 lay down the procedures for the transfer of, and transmission of property in, a ship; ss.31–38 set out the rather antiquated provisions relating to ship mortgages; ss.56–60 set out some equally venerable provisions relating to title, beneficial interests and liabilities of owners. Sections 19–21 of and Sched. 3 to the Merchant Shipping Act 1988 contain the equivalent transfer, transmission and mortgage provisions for fishing vessels (and see also the Merchant Shipping (Registration of Fishing Vessels) Regulations 1988 (S.I. 1988 No. 1926)). Schedule 5 to the 1993 Act will repeal all these provisions and s.6 of and Sched. 1 to the 1993 Act contain the necessary replacements and re-enactments. The private law provisions of Sched. 1 are not, however, designed to be applied to ships which are included on a part of the register from which, under s.3(4)(a), the Secretary of State has decided to exclude them (see subs. (2)). One such category may consist of pleasure craft which, under the present provisions of the small ship register established by the Merchant Shipping Act 1983, are not presently registered for title.
The general intention of the new provisions is, for the most part, to re-enact the earlier provisions, although note the changes introduced to the mortgagee's power of sale in Sched. 1, para. 9, below. The opportunity has been taken to remove some of the more archaic language from the 1894 Act. Thus, subs. (3) re-enacts s.58 of the 1894 Act, dealing with the liability of beneficial owners. It provides that a person with beneficial interests in a registered ship can be jointly liable with the registered shipowner for any pecuniary penalties imposed under the Merchant Shipping Acts (or other legislation) on a registered shipowner. The new subsection omits the final phrase of the original s.58 of the Merchant Shipping Act 1894 which spelt out, rather unnecessarily, that joint proceedings could be taken. Those familiar with the 1894 provisions will have to learn to navigate around the new Act to find equivalent provisions (see, *e.g.* the old s.56 of the 1894 Act and Sched. 1, para. 1(1) and (3) to the 1993 Act, below, and the old s.57 and Sched. 1, para. 1(2), below).
Similarly, subs. (4) is a modernised version of s.21(1) of the 1894 Act (as amended by the Merchant Shipping Act 1906, s.52(1)). The general effect of the new provision is to preserve the rights of the registered mortgagee when the registration is terminated, *e.g.* when the ship is sold abroad and re-registered. A registered mortgage is one entered on the register in accordance with Sched. 1, para. 7 (see subs. (5)). On ship mortgages generally, see A. Clarke, "Ship Mortgages"; Chap. 3 of N. Palmer, E. McKendrick (eds.), *Interests in Goods* (1993); N. Gaskell, C. Debattista, R. Swatton, *Chorley and Giles Shipping Law* (8th ed., 1987), Chap. 6; M. Thomas, D. Steel, *Temperley: Merchant Shipping Acts* (7th ed., 1976), pp. 24–40, 45–47.

Special provisions for ships on bareboat charter

Ships bareboat chartered-in by British charterers

7.—(1) This section applies to any ship which—
(a) is registered under the law of a country other than the United Kingdom ("the country of original registration"),
(b) is chartered on bareboat charter terms to a charterer who is a person qualified to own British ships, and
(c) is so chartered in circumstances where the conditions of entitlement to registration prescribed under section 2(2)(b), read with the requisite modifications, are satisfied as respects the charterer and the ship.
(2) The "requisite modifications" of those conditions are the substitution for any requirement to be satisfied by or as respects the owner of a ship of a corresponding requirement to be satisfied by or as respects the charterer of the ship.
(3) A ship to which this section applies is entitled to be registered if an application for registration is duly made, but section 2(3) applies also in relation to registration by virtue of this section.
(4) The registration of a ship registered by virtue of this section shall remain in force (unless terminated earlier by virtue of registration regu-

22–14

lations and subject to any suspension thereunder) until the end of the charter period and shall then terminate by virtue of this subsection.

(5) Section 2(5) does not apply to a ship registered by virtue of this section but registration regulations shall include provision for securing that the authority responsible for the registration of ships in the country of original registration is notified of the registration of the ship and of the termination of its registration whether by virtue of subsection (4) above or registration regulations.

(6) Accordingly, throughout the period for which a ship is registered by virtue of this section—

(a) the ship shall, as a British ship, be entitled to fly the British flag;

(b) the Merchant Shipping Acts shall, subject to subsections (7) and (8) below, apply to the ship as a British ship or as a registered ship as those Acts apply to other British ships and to registered ships; and

(c) any other enactment applicable to British ships or ships registered under those Acts shall, subject to subsection (8) below, apply to the ship as a British ship or as a registered ship.

(7) The private law provisions for registered ships shall not apply to a ship registered by virtue of this section and any matters or questions corresponding to those for which the private law provisions for registered ships make provision shall be determined by reference to the law of the country of original registration.

(8) Her Majesty may, subject to subsection (9) below, by Order in Council, provide that any enactment falling within subsection (6)(b) or (c) above—

(a) shall not have effect in accordance with that subsection in relation to a ship registered by virtue of this section, or

(b) shall so have effect subject to such modifications (if any) as may be specified in the Order.

(9) No provision shall be made by an Order in Council under subsection (8) above which would have the effect of relaxing the relevant requirements of the Merchant Shipping Acts (within the meaning of section 2(3)) in their application to a ship to which this section applies.

(10) An Order in Council under subsection (8) above—

(a) may make such transitional, incidental or supplementary provision as appears to Her Majesty to be necessary or expedient (including provision divesting or providing for the divestment of ownership in the ship); and

(b) shall be subject to annulment in pursuance of a resolution of either House of Parliament.

(11) In this section—

"bareboat charter terms", in relation to a ship, means the hiring of the ship for a stipulated period on terms which give the charterer possession and control of the ship, including the right to appoint the master and crew; and

"the charter period" means the period during which the ship is chartered on bareboat charter terms.

DEFINITIONS
"bareboat charter terms": subs. (11).
"British ship": s.8(2) and Sched. 3.
"charter period": subs. (11).
"country of original registration": subs. (1).
"Merchant Shipping Acts": s.9(2).
"private law provisions for registered ships": ss.6 and 9(2).
"qualified to own British ships": s.9(3).
"registered": s.9(2).
"registration regulations": ss.3 and 9(2).
"requisite modifications": subs. (2).
"United Kingdom": Sched. 1 to the Interpretation Act 1978.

The general aim of this section is to allow a ship registered abroad, but, for example, bareboat chartered to a British company, to be registered in the U.K. The legal effect of such registration will be that British public law regulatory rules will apply to the ship, whereas certain private law rules of the state of original registry will continue to be applied. For example, U.K. law will govern matters such as the safe maintenance and operation of the vessel (*cf.* ss.30–32 of the Merchant Shipping Act 1979) and the foreign law will govern issues such as the title to the ship and the existence and priority of mortgages made in respect of it. Thus, the new section makes a distinction between the law of the state of registration and the law of the flag.

Bareboat chartering
A bareboat or demise charter is a contract of hire, similar to a lease, which differs from a time charter in that the bareboat charterer is given the right of possession and control of the ship, appointing its master and crew (and see s.7(11)). Thus, in the Barecon A Standard Bareboat Charter, cl. 8, the vessel is stated to be "in the full possession and at the absolute disposal for all purposes of the charterers and under their complete control in every respect". It follows that, in law, it is the bareboat charterer who is treated as the owner of the ship *pro hac vice* and is, for example, vicariously responsible for the faults of the master and crew in navigating and operating the vessel. By contrast, a time charterer merely has the right to give orders to the master (employed by the shipowner) in respect of the employment of the vessel (see, *e.g.* cl. 8 of the Asbatime charter-party).

The DOT/GCBS 1990 Report, para. 6.4, recognised that "demise chartering (with temporary re-registration) has been allowed both 'in' and 'out' for aircraft by U.K. law for a number of years". The report also noted that:

"U.K. law does not allow a vessel owned in a foreign country but chartered to a U.K. company who acts as the owner (bareboat or demise chartering), to be registered in the U.K. This means that when ownership of the ship must remain in a foreign country to secure or retain the most advantageous fiscal benefits, U.K. companies cannot take advantage of the flexibility provided by demise chartering-in to obtain the right to fly the British flag. Nor does U.K. law allow for demise chartering outwards on a similar basis. This would enable a ship owned in the U.K. to be registered temporarily in a foreign country in order to secure cost savings, as an alternative to leaving the U.K. register altogether. The Working Party was of the view that registration law should be amended to allow demise chartering-in or out with temporary change of flag, so long as there were adequate safeguards regarding safety and availability in time of war for ships demise chartered-out" (*ibid.*, para. 3.11).

It was partly as a result of this recommendation that the original Bill, as introduced in the Commons, contained two provisions, cls. 7 and 8, which dealt with chartering-in and out. The final version of the Bill contained only what is now s.7.

Legal problems with bareboat charter registers
There are theoretical legal problems with the whole question of temporary bareboat charter registers, concerning both public and private law (see N. Ready, *Ship Registration* (1991), Chap. 3). One public law issue concerns the precise responsibilities of the original state of registry and that of the temporary registry. In general terms, it is the flag state which has traditionally exercised control over its ships wherever they are in the world and over ships of all nations when they are in its territorial waters. The existence of dual registration raises the possibility of confusion over which state has the obligation to see that international safety standards are maintained and to ensure that correct operational procedures are followed in order to reduce accidents and pollution. Moreover, one of the criticisms of the practice of flagging-out is that it is merely a device for shipowners to cut costs by avoiding the more stringent safety requirements of states such as the U.K. by obtaining registration in a "flag of convenience" state which has little or no control over the ships which fly its flag.

The U.N. Convention on Conditions for Registration of Ships 1986
The U.N. Convention on Conditions for Registration of Ships 1986 (to which the U.K. is not a party) requires in Art. 11.5, that in the case of a ship bareboat chartered-in, a State should assure itself that the right to fly the flag of the former flag state is suspended. It does not say in terms that the former flag state must be notified of the bareboat registration, but this must surely be implied. Under Art. 12.5, the former flag state also has to be notified of any termination of registration: see subs. (5), below. Article 12.4 provides that the state should ensure that a ship bareboat chartered-in and flying its flag will be subject to its full jurisdiction and control (see subs. (6), below).

There are also theoretical problems of private law where bareboat registries are used. The owner of the ship will still usually be a national of the original state of registry and there will normally be loans secured by way of mortgage and registered in the port of registry. Articles 12.3 and 12.6 of the U.N. Convention on Conditions for Registration of Ships 1986 make it clear that the bareboat registration does not affect the existing ownership and other rights set out in the charter contract (see subs. (7), below, on the private law issue).

Bareboat Chartering-out
Where there is an application for the registration of a ship, on the register of one state, to be suspended for a period of time, while it is bareboat chartered-out and registered elsewhere, there must be a provision in the law of the original state allowing the suspension. Otherwise there is a real potential for conflict between the respective national administrations as to which is to exercise supervisory control. Clause 8 of the Bill, as originally introduced into the Commons, provided for ships registered in the U.K. to be bareboat chartered outwards, as recommended in the DOT/GCBS 1990 Report. The commercial attraction of chartering-out was that a ship owned in the U.K. might be temporarily registered overseas, in circumstances where cost savings were required, as an alternative to leaving the register altogether (*ibid.*, para. 3.11, above). The provision would have allowed for such vessels to remain on the U.K. register for the purposes of private law (*e.g.* mortgages), but for the state of temporary bareboat registry to apply its public law provisions. However, this provision, the reverse of the present s.7, was withdrawn by the promoter at Committee stage in the Commons, following strong representations from the Opposition. The concern was that ships bareboat chartered-out could then be subject to lower safety and other standards. Many so-called "flag of convenience" states allow for bareboat chartering-in and out, as well as more traditional shipowning states such as Italy and Australia. It is from the registers of such states that ships may come to be bareboat chartered-in to the U.K. under s.7. The original draft of the Bill worked on the supposition that a state could hardly provide for chartering-in without allowing a mirror facility for chartering-out. However, it was pointed out by the Opposition that there were even flag of convenience states, such as Cyprus, which allowed for chartering-in, but not chartering-out. On that basis, the promoter was able to withdraw cl. 8, without affecting cl. 7, as he conceded that the shipping companies had not claimed that the clause was vital.
It follows that there are no provisions which would allow the registration of a British registered ship to be suspended so that it could temporarily be flagged out to another register. The DOT would thus continue to exercise full regulatory control over the vessel.

Subss. (1)–(5)
Entitlement to registration
Subsection (1) defines the ships which may be included on the register under s.7 by reference to three criteria. First, they must already be registered in another country (*e.g.* Greece). Normally, ships cannot be registered in the U.K. if they are already registered elsewhere (see, *e.g.* the offence in, and General Note to, s.2(5), above). Section 7 creates a special exemption to this general principle (see subs. (5)).
Secondly, the ship has to be "chartered on bareboat terms" to a person qualified to own British ships. Bareboat charter terms are defined in subs. (11) in a way which would include the standard bareboat charters in use worldwide (such as Barecon A, described above). The definition in subs. (11) does not depend for its application on how the contract in question is described, but on what is its effect. Some arrangements may well be described as a lease, or long-term charter agreement, but the crucial issue concerns possession and control of the ship. In modern shipping practice, great use is made of firms of professional ship managers, whose functions may or may not include the hiring of a crew (or the use of a crewing agency to do this). Shipowners and operators are not always keen to make it clear to the outside world where the exact control of a ship lies, partly in order to avoid private law litigation. Although a ship management agreement (such as Bimco's Shipman Contract) between owner and manager would usually be considered as an agency agreement, some care may be needed to ensure that this is the true legal effect of the contract and that the "ship manager" has not, in effect, employed the crew in its own name and taken possession and control of the ship. The qualification to own a British ship, referred to in the subsection, will be determined by registration regulations made under s.2(2), above (see s.9(3)). The regulations are expected to adopt the same broad approach as the Merchant Shipping Act 1988, s.3, as modified by the *Factortame* litigation (see the General Note to s.2, above). For "British ships", see s.8(2) of and Sched. 3 to the 1993 Act.
Thirdly, in addition to being chartered to a qualified person, the ship will have had to be chartered in circumstances where it has a prescribed British connection (see s.2(2)(b) and (9), above). The type of circumstances envisaged might be those where regulations (made under s.2(2)(b)), require a degree of management and control to be exercised from within the U.K. (as with s.14(1)(b) of the Merchant Shipping Act 1988). A further example might be where British citizens, resident abroad, are required to appoint "representative persons" in the U.K.

on whom legal documents could be served (*cf.* s.5 of the Merchant Shipping Act 1988). Section 7(1)(c) refers to the requirements being subject to "requisite modifications". This technical reservation means no more than that the requirements would have to be read as referring, in the case of a s.7 application, to the bareboat charterer, as opposed to the shipowner (see subs. (2)). The Opposition failed in an attempted amendment, involving a more substantial "modification", to insert in subs. (2) a requirement for the use of U.K.-domiciled seafarers. The prevailing view (in effect of the Government) was that this would be a disincentive to shipowners to bareboat charter-in.

Assuming that the ship falls within subs. (1) it may be registered, as of right, on an application being made, subject only to the overriding discretion of the registrar under s.2(3), above (see subs. (3)). There is no requirement to register the fact that a ship has been bareboat chartered to a British company, although a failure to do so would mean that the ship was not entitled to fly the British flag (and see s.8(2) and Sched. 3).

The registration of a ship will normally continue indefinitely unless, for example, regulations specify a time-limit (see s.3(2)(g)), or there is any suspension (see s.3(2)(j)). However, under subs. (4) a bareboat charter will terminate automatically at the end of the "charter period". Subsection (11) defines the period simply as one during which the ship is actually chartered on bareboat terms. There could be any length of time laid down in the original agreement, although it would usually be a period of years. The section does not concentrate on this figure as, presumably, the period could include any expressly agreed extension, or any implied extension, *e.g.* where the ship continues after the prescribed period in the actual control and possession of a charterer continuing to pay hire on the basis of the agreement. The definition is sufficiently wide to cover the case where the parties agree to terminate the charter before the full agreed period. The registration will terminate in such a case at the earlier time. More difficult is the case where the contract is frustrated, or where one of the parties elects to treat it as having been repudiated. Where the termination of a charter is disputed, *e.g.* where the charterer denies it has been in fundamental breach or declines to accept a repudiation by the shipowner (*cf. Attica Sea Carriers Corporation* v. *Ferrostaal Poseidon Bulk Reederei G.m.b.H.*; *Puerto Buitrago, The* [1976] 1 Lloyd's Rep. 250), it may be uncertain for some time whether the ship is still chartered on bareboat terms. Ultimately, an arbitration award or court decision may resolve the rights of the parties, but there may be a period during which it is not clear whether the bareboat charter has terminated—and registration along with it. It seems that the vessel will remain on the register until a court decides otherwise, or the charterer requests closure. The matter is not without significance, as it ought not to be left undecided whether the U.K. or the state of original registration should be exercising regulatory control.

Registration regulations may have to deal with the point, but the question may arise as to whether the bareboat charterer who fails to inform the registrar of any such dispute can be guilty of any offence. Section 2(5), above, does not really address this issue and in any event is expressly disapplied by subs. (5), but there may be an offence under s.4(2), above if the charterer does not give notification of a change to the British connection of a ship. The problem is that a charterer might argue that there *had* been no change (on its interpretation of the contractual dispute). The "change" would be the alleged termination and it could be argued that it *might* affect the British connection, but may not definitely do so. Section 3(2)(h) does require the production to the registrar of certain information "at specified intervals or at his request" and the furnishing of positively wrong information is an offence under s.4(1). Section 3(2)(h) does not seem to have in mind the voluntary provision of information by a charterer arising out of changes between any "specified intervals". It would be best if the registration regulations clarified the matter and, although no doubt an *ultra vires* argument might be raised over the creation of any offence on the part of the charterer, it would be sensible to adopt a wide interpretation of s.4(2) so as to put a continuing obligation on a bareboat charterer to keep the registrar informed of disputes which might reasonably be considered to have terminated the charter-party.

Subsection (5) is in accordance with Arts. 11.5 and 12.5 of the U.N. Convention on Conditions for Registration of Ships 1986, which require that in the case of a ship bareboat chartered-in, a State should ensure that the former flag state is notified of the bareboat registration and its eventual termination. The subsection will achieve this through registration regulations issued under s.3, above.

Subss. (6), (8) and (10)
Extent of British control
   Subsection (6) sets out the consequences, in public law, of bareboat registration under the section. First, the ship will be considered as a British ship and be entitled to fly the British flag (for detailed provisions on that right, see s.8(2) and Sched. 3, below). Also, presumably, the bareboat charterer will be able to call on the protection of the Royal Navy, in time of conflict, in the same way as with other British ships. Secondly, the whole regulatory force of the Merchant Shipping Acts, applying to British ships or British registered ships, will be applied in the same

manner to the bareboat chartered ship. The Merchant Shipping Acts and, more importantly, the delegated legislation issued under them, cover safety issues (such as crewing, health and safety, ship operation and maintenance), pollution prevention (*e.g.* through restrictions on operational discharges of oil and on dumping) and security (*e.g.* in relation to terrorism), as well as matters such as casualty prevention and investigation. Thirdly, there is a host of general enactments and delegated legislation which have been extended to ships. These include general social security, taxation and employment law. Such enactments shall also apply to the bareboat chartered ship.

It is apparent that not all the various enactments included in subs. (6)(b) and (c) may be appropriate to the situation of a bareboat chartered ship. In their application to such ships subs. (8) allows an Order in Council to be made which will either (a) exclude totally the effect of a particular enactment, or (b) make modifications to the enactment. There may be rare occasions where the enactment is totally excluded. The example was given of the Merchant Shipping (Oil Pollution) Act 1971, s.1 which imposes strict liability for oil pollution damage on a shipowner. The Act was designed to give effect to the International Convention on Civil Liability for Oil Pollution Damage 1969 which deliberately chose to channel liability to the registered shipowner only, requiring the shipowner to obtain liability insurance, and in exchange it was provided that any pollution claimant would not be able to sue third parties under the Convention or at common law (see Art. III(4) of the Convention and s.3 of the Act and the annotations made by the writer to Sched. 4 to the Merchant Shipping Act 1988 in *Current Law Statutes Annotated* 1988). It may be necessary to exclude the application of that legislation to make it clear that "registered owner" does not include a bareboat charterer, although it is submitted that this is probably clear from the context. An obvious example of a modification under subs. (8)(b) would be the substitution of the word "bareboat charterer" for "shipowner" in any regulations made under s.117 of the Social Security Contributions and Benefits Act 1992.

One of the key questions in debates was whether subs. (8) might be used by the DOT to provide lower standards for ships which were chartered-in than for ships which were on the register in the ordinary way. The promoter of the Bill accepted that exactly the same requirements would be imposed on a ship bareboat chartered-in as to any other ship which it is sought to register in the U.K. A certificate of survey must be produced and the ship will be inspected. However, to meet legitimate concerns about lowering of standards, the promoter (in effect, the DOT) introduced what is now subs. (9) at Committee stage in the Commons. Subsection (9) imposes a specific limitation on the Order making power in subs. (8) by forbidding any relaxation of the "requirements of the Merchant Shipping Acts" within s.2(3), above. It is clear that this is meant to stop the bareboat chartered ships having lower standards than other British ships of condition or equipment, pollution control, or health and safety of those employed or engaged in them (see the definition in s.2(8)). However, the specific reference to "Merchant Shipping Acts" makes it clear that there can be discrimination in favour of the bareboat chartered-in ships in respect of other legislation normally applicable to British ships, *e.g.* relating to the taxation of seafarers (see the comments on s.7(6)(c), above). It has already been noted in relation to s.2(8)(b), above, that an attempt to add "passengers" to the list of persons mentioned in s.2(8)(b) was successfully resisted. It seems highly unlikely that the DOT intended that lower safety standards were envisaged for passengers, although the restrictive reference in para. (b) is still slightly puzzling. The better view might be that passenger safety is covered generally in para. (a).

Subsection (10), although phrased as an ancillary provision to subs. (8), contains what appears to be a very wide rule-making power in para. (a), namely that the Order can include provision for the divestment of ownership in the ship. The apparent width of the provision might seem to suggest that the DOT could be given unlimited powers of confiscation. However, it is clear that the power must be read in the context of the section as a whole and subs. (8) in particular, which is aimed at modifying existing provisions applying to ships (ordinarily owned and registered) to those now to be bareboat chartered-in. An example given by the DOT was where existing legislation allowed for forfeiture, or for a power of sale to be exercised. The latter can be demonstrated by s.20 of the Prevention of Oil Pollution Act 1971 which allows a vessel to be sold where there is non-payment of a fine for illegal oil pollution. The divestment reference was included out of an abundance of caution, so as to allow such a sale even where the offence is committed by the bareboat charterer who, by definition, is not the owner. In theory, the rights of the owner are protected by an indemnity under the charter-party and, presumably, by its claim to any monies left in court after the order for sale is exercised. The British owner of a British registered ship, subject to a bareboat charter, would already be faced by this risk. Any Order is subject to the negative resolution procedure.

Subs. (7)
Application of U.K. private law
    This subsection is particularly important to the question of the application of U.K. private

law to a bareboat chartered ship registered in the U.K. It must be directly contrasted with the previous subsection, as it provides that U.K. "private law provisions for registered ships" are not to be extended to a ship bareboat chartered-in. At first sight this would appear to suggest that, although public law matters are to be dealt with by U.K. public law (see subs. (6)), all private law question will fall to be dealt with according to the law of the country of original registration. It is not as simple as that for, as is shown by the reference, above, to the application of the Merchant Shipping (Oil Pollution) Act 1971, U.K. law on private liabilities may continue to be applied to the bareboat chartered ship. The "private law provisions" referred to in the subsection are those defined in ss.6(6) and 9(2) of and Sched. 1 to the Act. As can be seen from Sched. 1, the term deals with issues concerning title, *e.g.* the rights of the registered owner, the existence of beneficial interests, the creation and priority of mortgages and the transfer of rights of ownership and mortgages. All these issues, which in most legal systems relate directly to the process of registration, will be dealt with by the law of the country of original registration. Matters not strictly falling within the definition of "private law provisions" could be covered by U.K. private law rules. However, there is nothing surprising in this as, under the usual principles of the conflict of laws, the U.K. courts may already have to apply the law of the appropriate part of the U.K. to the ship, *e.g.* where the Commercial Court decides on substantive disputes arising out of the bareboat charter as a result of an English choice of law clause, or where the Admiralty Court applies English salvage or collision law following a casualty on the high seas. United Kingdom courts are not forbidden from deciding questions of title to a foreign registered ship to which the foreign law applies provided, of course, that there is jurisdiction to do so—again according to ordinary conflicts principles. It appears to be intended that, for a ship bareboat chartered-in, the existence of the foreign mortgage may be recorded on the U.K. register, albeit that this will be for information only. It must be emphasised that all questions relating to such registered mortgages, *e.g.* as to their priority, will be governed by the foreign law.

Supplementary and pre-consolidation provisions

Amendments and repeals including those for purposes of consolidation

8.—(1) Schedule 2 to this Act shall have effect for making amendments consequential on the provisions of this Act.

(2) Schedule 3 to this Act (which substantially re-enacts certain provisions of the Merchant Shipping Acts relating to British ships and the British flag) shall have effect.

(3) Schedule 4 to this Act shall have effect for making amendments designed to facilitate, or otherwise desirable in connection with, the consolidation of the enactments relating to merchant shipping.

(4) The enactments mentioned in Schedule 5 to this Act (which include enactments which are spent or are of no practical utility) are hereby repealed to the extent specified in the third column of that Schedule, subject, however, to the saving at the end of the Schedule.

GENERAL NOTE

Schedule 2 contains various consequential amendments to existing legislation to take account of the new provisions in ss.1–7 concerning registration.

Schedule 3 contains provisions which are a re-enactment of legislation relating to British ships and the British flag, *e.g.* the Merchant Shipping Act 1988, s.2.

Schedule 4 deals with the second main object of the 1993 Act, namely the preparation of the Statute Book for the consolidation of all the Merchant Shipping Acts dating back to 1894. As mentioned in the General and Introductory Note, above, the merchant shipping legislation on the Statute Book is unwieldy. The Schedule should allow for the Acts to be consolidated in 1994, taking into account the fact that one more piece of merchant shipping legislation will be required in the meantime to allow for the ratification of a number of important IMO (International Maritime Organisation) Conventions on marine salvage and pollution.

The Schedule amends the language used throughout the Merchant Shipping Acts, particularly in the 1894 Act, both (i) updating it and (ii) making sure that concepts are applied uniformly across the Acts to be consolidated. For example, (i) it removes references to carts and (ii) ensures that there are uniform provisions on jurisdiction, *mens rea*, documentation, evidence, powers of officers and fees. Amongst the important and diverse matters covered are: the definition of "ship"; powers of detention; the revision of wreck law; lighthouses and light dues; the application of rules to overseas possessions. It is ironic that, in sweeping away provisions that the Merchant Shipping Act 1894 applied across the world, it has been necessary to correct defects that were contained in the Act itself in relation to its application to Scotland.

Detailed annotations follow the various Schedules. Acknowledgement is made of the DOT Notes on Clauses.

Interpretation, etc.

9.—(1) This Act shall be construed as one with the Merchant Shipping Acts 1894 to 1988.

(2) In this Act—

"British connection" and "declaration of British connection" have the meaning given in section 2(9);

"the Merchant Shipping Acts" means the Merchant Shipping Acts 1894 to 1988 and this Act;

"the private law provisions for registered ships" has the meaning given in section 6;

"the register" means the register maintained for the United Kingdom under section 1 and "registered" (except with reference to the law of another country) is to be construed accordingly;

"the registrar" means the Registrar General of Shipping and Seamen in his capacity as registrar or, as respects functions of his being discharged by another authority or person, that authority or person;

"registration regulations" means regulations under section 3;

"relevant British possession" means—

    (a) the Isle of Man,

    (b) the Channel Islands, or

    (c) any colony; and

"the tonnage regulations" means regulations under section 1 of the Merchant Shipping Act 1965.

(3) Where, for the purposes of any enactment, the question arises whether a ship is owned by persons qualified to own British ships, the question shall be determined by reference to registration regulations made under section 2(2)(a).

(4) Any reference in any other Act or in any instrument made under any other Act to the registration of a ship (or fishing vessel) under any of the enactments mentioned in section 1(7) shall be construed, unless the context otherwise requires, as, or as including, a reference to registration under this Act; and connected phrases shall be construed accordingly.

(5) Registration regulations may provide that any reference in any other Act or in any instrument made under any other Act to the port of registry of a ship or the port to which a ship belongs shall be construed as a reference to the port identified by the marks required for the purpose by registration regulations.

(6) The Secretary of State may, by order made by statutory instrument subject to annulment in pursuance of a resolution of either House of Parliament, make such amendments of any local Act or instrument so far as it provides for the registration of ships in local registers as appear to him to be appropriate in view of the provision made by section 1.

GENERAL NOTE

This section contains the usual set of definitions. It also contains provisions designed to ensure that references in other legislation are consistent with the new principles introduced by the Act. Thus, subs. (3) subjects other enactments to the test of qualification to own British ships laid down in the 1993 Act; subs. (4) provides that references in other enactments to registration have to be construed according to the 1993 Act; and subs. (5) deals with the abolition of individual ports of registry (see the General Notes to ss.1 and 3(2), above). Subsection (6) deals with the possibility that there may be local legislation dealing with the registration of ships. There are probably hundreds of local Acts that may apply and the Secretary of State is given the power to amend them by statutory instrument where necessary.

Short title, commencement and extent

10.—(1) This Act may be cited as the Merchant Shipping (Registration, etc.) Act 1993; and this Act and the Merchant Shipping Acts 1894 to 1988 may be cited together as the Merchant Shipping Acts 1894 to 1993.

(2) This Act shall come into force on such day as the Secretary of State may appoint by order made by statutory instrument, and different days may be appointed for different provisions or different purposes.

(3) An order under subsection (2) above may include such transitional, saving and supplementary provision (including modifications of any enactment) as appear to the Secretary of State to be appropriate in connection with the transition to the new register or the partial operation of section 1 or in connection with the amendments made by Schedule 4 to this Act.

(4) This Act extends to England and Wales, Scotland and Northern Ireland.

SCHEDULES

Section 6   SCHEDULE 1

PRIVATE LAW PROVISIONS FOR REGISTERED SHIPS

General

1.—(1) Subject to any rights and powers appearing from the register to be vested in any other person, the registered owner of a ship or of a share in a ship shall have power absolutely to dispose of it provided the disposal is made in accordance with this Schedule and registration regulations.

(2) Sub-paragraph (1) above does not imply that interests arising under contract or other equitable interests cannot subsist in relation to a ship or a share in a ship; and such interests may be enforced by or against owners and mortgagees of ships in respect of their interest in the ship or share in the same manner as in respect of any other personal property.

(3) The registered owner of a ship or of a share in a ship shall have power to give effectual receipts for any money paid or advanced by way of consideration on any disposal of the ship or share.

Transfers etc. of registered ships

2.—(1) Any transfer of a registered ship, or a share in such a ship, shall be effected by a bill of sale satisfying the prescribed requirements, unless the transfer will result in the ship ceasing to have a British connection.

(2) Where any such ship or share has been transferred in accordance with sub-paragraph (1) above, the transferee shall not be registered as owner of the ship or share unless—

    (a) he has made the prescribed application to the registrar; and

    (b) the registrar is satisfied that the ship retains a British connection and that he would not refuse to register the ship.

(3) If an application under sub-paragraph (2) above is granted by the registrar, the registrar shall register the bill of sale in the prescribed manner.

(4) Bills of sale shall be registered in the order in which they are produced to the registrar for the purposes of registration.

3.—(1) Where a registered ship, or a share in a registered ship, is transmitted to any person by any lawful means other than a transfer under paragraph 2 above and the ship continues to have a British connection, that person shall not be registered as owner of the ship or share unless—

    (a) he has made the prescribed application to the registrar; and

    (b) the registrar is satisfied that the ship retains a British connection and that he would not refuse to register the ship.

(2) If an application under sub-paragraph (1) is granted by the registrar, the registrar shall cause the applicant's name to be registered as owner of the ship or share.

4.—(1) Where the property in a registered ship or share in a registered ship is transmitted to any person by any lawful means other than a transfer under paragraph 2 above, but as a result the ship no longer has a British connection, the High Court or the Court of Session may, on application by or on behalf of that person, order a sale of the property so transmitted and direct that the proceeds of sale, after deducting the expenses of the sale, shall be paid to that person or otherwise as the court direct.

(2) The court may require any evidence in support of the application they think requisite, and may make the order on any terms and conditions they think just, or may refuse to make the order, and generally may act in the case as the justice of the case requires.

(3) Every such application must be made within the period of 28 days beginning with the date of the occurrence of the event on which the transmission has taken place, or within such further time (not exceeding one year) as the court may allow.

(4) If—

(a) such an application is not made within the time allowed by or under sub-paragraph (3) above; or

(b) the court refuse an order for sale,

the ship or share transmitted shall be liable to forfeiture.

5.—(1) Where any court (whether under paragraph 4 above or otherwise) order the sale of any registered ship or share in a registered ship, the order of the court shall contain a declaration vesting in some named person the right to transfer the ship or share.

(2) The person so named shall be entitled to transfer the ship or share in the same manner and to the same extent as if he were the registered owner of the ship or share.

(3) The registrar shall deal with any application relating to the transfer of the ship or share made by the person so named as if that person were the registered owner.

6.—(1) The High Court or Court of Session may, if they think fit (without prejudice to the exercise of any other power), on the application of any interested person, make an order prohibiting for a specified time any dealing with a registered ship or share in a registered ship.

(2) The court may make the order on any terms or conditions they think just, or may refuse to make the order, or may discharge the order when made (with or without costs or, in Scotland, expenses) and generally may act in the case as the justice of the case requires.

(3) The order, when a copy is served on the registrar, shall be binding on him whether or not he was made a party to the proceedings.

Mortgages of registered ships

7.—(1) A registered ship, or share in a registered ship, may be made a security for the repayment of a loan or the discharge of any other obligation.

(2) The instrument creating any such security (referred to in the following provisions of this Schedule as a "mortgage") shall be in the form prescribed by or approved under registration regulations.

(3) Where a mortgage executed in accordance with sub-paragraph (2) above is produced to the registrar, he shall register the mortgage in the prescribed manner.

(4) Mortgages shall be registered in the order in which they are produced to the registrar for the purposes of registration.

Priority of registered mortgages

8.—(1) Where two or more mortgages are registered in respect of the same ship or share, the priority of the mortgagees between themselves shall, subject to sub-paragraph (2) below, be determined by the order in which the mortgages were registered (and not by reference to any other matter).

(2) Registration regulations may provide for the giving to the registrar by intending mortgagees of "priority notices" in a form prescribed by or approved under the regulations which, when recorded in the register, determine the priority of the interest to which the notice relates.

Registered mortgagee's power of sale

9.—(1) Subject to sub-paragraph (2) below, every registered mortgagee shall have power, if the mortgage money or any part of it is due, to sell the ship or share in respect of which he is registered, and to give effectual receipts for the purchase money.

(2) Where two or more mortgagees are registered in respect of the same ship or share, a subsequent mortgagee shall not, except under an order of a court of competent jurisdiction, sell the ship or share without the concurrence of every prior mortgagee.

Protection of registered mortgagees

10. Where a ship or share is subject to a registered mortgage—

(a) except so far as may be necessary for making the ship or share available as a security for the mortgage debt, the mortgagee shall not by reason of the mortgage be treated as owner of the ship or share; and

(b) the mortgagor shall be treated as not having ceased to be owner of the ship or share.

Transfer of registered mortgage

11.—(1) A registered mortgage may be transferred by an instrument made in the form prescribed by or approved under registration regulations.

(2) Where any such instrument is produced to the registrar, the registrar shall register the transferee in the prescribed manner.

Transmission of registered mortgage by operation of law

12. Where the interest of a mortgagee in a registered mortgage is transmitted to any person by any lawful means other than by a transfer under paragraph 11 above, the registrar shall, on production of the prescribed evidence, cause the name of that person to be entered in the register as mortgagee of the ship or share in question.

Discharge of registered mortgage

13. Where a registered mortgage has been discharged, the registrar shall, on production of the mortgage deed and such evidence of the discharge of the mortgage as may be prescribed, cause an entry to be made in the register to the effect that the mortgage has been discharged.

Definitions

14. In this Schedule—
   "mortgage" shall be construed in accordance with paragraph 7(2) above;
   "prescribed" means prescribed in registration regulations; and
   "registered mortgage" means a mortgage registered under paragraph 7(3) above.

DEFINITIONS
   "British connection": s.9(2).
   "mortgage": para. 14.
   "person": Sched. 1 to the Interpretation Act 1978.
   "prescribed": para. 14.
   "registered": s.9(2).
   "registered mortgage": para. 14.
   "registrar": s.9(2).

GENERAL NOTE
   This Schedule sets out certain private law provisions which (i) are to apply to British registered ships according to s.1(6), or (ii) may be excluded in their application to certain kinds of registered ships under s.3(4), or (iii) shall not be applied to ships bareboat chartered-in to the British register under s.7. As mentioned in the General Note to s.6(3), above, the provisions are essentially those from the Merchant Shipping Act 1894 in a more updated form. They deal with matters such as rights of ownership, transfer and mortgages. In general, the existing provisions have been modernised by the removal of arcane or unnecessary language and the breaking up of large complex sections into more manageable subparagraphs. Where appropriate the origin of the provision will be given.

Para. 1
   Subparagraph (1) is derived from the Merchant Shipping Act 1894, s.56. It gives the registered shipowner the absolute right to sell the ship in accordance with the new Schedule and any regulations made under s.3. References here and elsewhere to "shares" in a ship refer to the traditional division of the ship into 64 shares effected by s.5 of the Merchant Shipping Act 1894. Section 5 will be repealed by Sched. 5 to the 1993 Act, but registration regulations under s.3(2) (c) can be expected to preserve the existing position. The shares referred to must not be confused with the shares which might exist in a company which itself had an interest in the ship (*e.g.* by holding all 64 shares under s.5 of the 1894 Act).
   Examples of rights and powers which might exist in another person would be the priority accorded by para. 8 to a mortgagee whose mortgage was registered under para. 7 and the power of sale given to a mortgagee under para. 9. The final part of the old s.56 is now in subpara. (3) (see *Barclay* v. *Poole* [1907] 2 Ch. 284, *Temperley*, p. 46).
   The original s.57 of the Merchant Shipping Act 1894 contained a definition of "beneficial interests" for the purpose, *inter alia*, of s.58 (itself now re-enacted in s.6(3)). It will now be found, in a slightly different form, in subpara. (2), but with the omission of three rather distracting "without prejudice to" references which appeared in the middle of the old s.57 (relating to ss.35, 56 and 1 of the 1894 Act). The effect of the subparagraph is to make it clear that there may be contractual or other equitable rights (*e.g.* an equitable mortgage) in a ship which are not

recorded on the register. These may be enforced against the shipowner or mortgagee, but in the event of insolvency they may not enjoy the same priority as that accorded to a registered mortgage. The section was originally passed to reverse the effect of *Liverpool Borough Bank* v. *Turner* (1860) 30 L.J. Ch. 379 (see *Temperley*, p. 46 and Clarke, *op. cit.*, p. 79). The provision would not seem to cover the position of a *legal* mortgage of an unregistered ship and it could not be implied from the 1894 Act that an unregistered mortgage of an unregistered ship had to be treated as an equitable mortgage (see *Shizelle, The* [1992] 2 Lloyd's Rep. 445, but *cf.* Clarke, *op. cit.*, pp. 85, 88). The effect of *The Shizelle* was that bona fide purchasers for value without notice of an unregistered yacht were held bound by an unregistered and undiscoverable mortgage. Unfortunately, the opportunity has not been taken to fill in what the judge in that case described as a statutory lacuna, although it is conceivable that the matter might be dealt with by registration regulations under s.3 (but note s.3(4)(a)). It is submitted that it should still be considered open for the higher courts to overrule the decision and hold that the implication of the old s.31 (now para. 7, below) was that all unregistered mortgages must be equitable.

Transfers of ships
    Paragraphs 2–6 deal with the transfer of registered ships and restate ss.24–30 of the Merchant Shipping Act 1894 (dealing with ships generally) and ss.19 and 20 of the Merchant Shipping Act 1988 (dealing with fishing vessels).

Para. 2
    Under subpara. (1) transfers of ships, or any of the 64 shares in them, have to be made by a bill of sale (see s.24 of the 1894 Act). At one time the format of the bill of sale was set out in s.24(2) of the 1894 Act. The 1993 Act now allows the whole question of approved forms to be dealt with by registration regulations (see s.2(6), above). Under s.24(1) as substituted by the Merchant Shipping Act 1988, Sched. 1, para. 15, there was a reference to the bill of sale requirement not applying where a majority interest in the ship is sold to a non-qualified person (*cf.* s.19(1) of the 1988 Act). The new version is an example of the greater flexibility brought about by the 1993 Act, as it leaves the precise British connection requirements to registration regulations. The bill of sale requirement will not apply, for example, if the ship is sold to a foreign company not entitled to own a British ship under s.2.
    Subparagraph (2) deals with the circumstances when the transferee can be registered as owner (*cf.* s.25 of the 1894 Act, as amended by Sched. 1, para. 16 of the 1988 Act, and s.19(3) of the 1988 Act).
    Under subpara. (3), once the application is granted the registrar will register the bill of sale (*cf.* s.26 of the 1894 Act and s.19(4) of the 1988 Act).
    Under subpara. (4), the bills of sale are registered in the order of their production (*cf.* s.26(2) of the 1894 Act and s.19(5) of the 1988 Act).

Para. 3
    This paragraph replaces s.27 of the Merchant Shipping Act 1894 and s.20(1) of the Merchant Shipping Act 1988. The old s.27 dealt with the transfer of a ship by means such as death, bankruptcy, marriage, etc., but was amended by Sched. 1, para. 16 to the 1988 Act to refer, like s.20(1), to transfers generally other than by way of bill of sale (see now para. 2 of this Schedule, above). Paragraph 3 is to the same effect, but has the added flexibility given by the ability to produce registration regulations (as explained in relation to para. 2(1), above). The paragraph is designed for those examples of transfers which operate automatically as a matter of law. Thus on the death of a registered owner, an heir would be entitled to be registered as owner, provided he could satisfy the registrar as to his British connection as required in s.2, *e.g.* that he was a British citizen and, if resident abroad, that he had appointed a representative person in the U.K.

Para. 4
    If property is automatically transmitted by operation of law (*e.g.* on bankruptcy) to a transmittee who could not demonstrate the necessary British connection required by s.2, the court may order a sale of the ship, as previously provided for by s.28 of the Merchant Shipping Act 1894, as amended by Sched. 1, para. 16 of the Merchant Shipping Act 1988 (*cf.* s.20(4) of the 1988 Act). The penalty for failing to apply for any order within the strict time-limits is severe, namely the potential forfeiture of the vessel. Although subpara. (4) uses the word "shall", the words "be liable to", which follow, indicates that there is a court discretion. It would seem unlikely that the court would order forfeiture in the type of case where administrative delays and communication difficulties arose as a result of death or insolvency (see s.76 of the 1894 Act on forfeiture). The attitude might differ where there was some evidence of the unqualified transmittee

deliberately trying to run the ship under the British flag, knowing that there was not the necessary British connection. Presumably, the transmittee might wish to continue its ownership of the ship. To maintain the U.K. registration it would be necessary for the ship to be transferred to some associated person, *e.g.* a U.K. company, which could satisfy the criteria in s.2(2).

Para. 5
    Where a court does order the sale of a ship, *e.g.* under para. 4, the buyer will want to deal with someone who has the same status as the registered owner and who can give effective receipts under para. 1(3), above. Paragraph 5 re-enacts s.29 of the Merchant Shipping Act 1894 by allowing the court to declare that a particular person has the right to transfer the ship. There appears to be no legal reason why that person cannot be the transmittee. The power of a court to order a sale of a ship might arise in circumstances other than para. 4, *e.g.* where mortgagees have arrested the ship for non-payment and have obtained a judgment *in rem* which they seek to enforce by an order of sale. It is a general principle that sale by court order gives the purchaser a title free of all liens and encumbrances (*Cerro Colorado, The* [1993] 1 Lloyd's Rep. 58, *Acrux, The* [1962] 1 Lloyd's Rep. 405 and *cf. Blitz, The* [1992] 2 Lloyd's Rep. 441).

Para. 6
    This paragraph re-enacts s.30 of the Merchant Shipping Act 1894 and allows an interested person to apply for an order delaying dealing in a ship. In effect, there is a form of interim injunction and the order might be used where a mortgagee suspected fraudulent dealings, or where it appeared that a purchaser would not pay the purchase money.

Mortgages
    Paragraphs 7–13 deal with mortgages and restate ss.31–43 of the Merchant Shipping Act 1894 (ships generally) and s.21 of and Sched. 3 to the Merchant Shipping Act 1988 (fishing vessels).

Para. 7
    The wording used in this paragraph is taken from s.31 of the Merchant Shipping Act, as it was amended by the Merchant Shipping Act 1988, Sched. 1, para. 21, and is substantially similar to that introduced in Sched. 3 to the Merchant Shipping Act 1988 for fishing vessels. The mortgage is simply the instrument containing the security and its precise form will be set out in the registration regulations. Mortgages are registered in the order in which they are produced to the registrar, although there is no longer the requirement in s.31(2) of the Merchant Shipping Act 1894 that the registrar include a handwritten memorandum of the date and hour.
    The statute does not deal with mortgage obligations, which are generally dealt with by contract (see Clarke, *op. cit.*, p. 75). There is still some dispute about whether the registered ship mortgage is a *sui generis* "statutory security perfectable by registration" or whether it is a "chattel mortgage whose attributes have been modified by statute" (*ibid.*, p. 74). Neither the original s.31 *et seq.*, nor the present provisions, give any clear answer to this rather fundamental point. The traditional view (and the recent rather unsatisfactory decision in *Shizelle, The* [1992] 2 Lloyd's Rep. 445) support the latter view, although there are persuasive arguments to the contrary in favour of the former (see Clarke, *op. cit.*, generally). The provisions unfortunately do not make clear what is the nature of unregistered mortgages, particularly in respect of unregistered ships (see *Shizelle, The*, above).

Para. 8
    The priority of registered mortgages between themselves is determined by the order in which they are *registered* under para. 7 and not the date of their *creation* (restating s.33 of the Merchant Shipping Act 1894 and Sched. 3, para. 3 to the Merchant Shipping Act 1988). The priority of registered mortgages against other forms of security, such as unregistered mortgages, or maritime liens, will be determined by general maritime law principles. Thus, for instance, a registered mortgage will take priority over a subsequent statutory lien for repairs, but not over a maritime lien (*cf. Bankers Trust International* v. *Todd Shipyard Corp.; Halcyon Isle, The* [1981] A.C. 221 and see further, *Chorley and Giles Shipping Law* 8th ed. 1987, pp. 78–81).
    Schedule 3, para. 3 to the Merchant Shipping Act 1988 introduced a new and useful provision whereby the interests of intending mortgagees could be recorded on the register. The facility was only available under that Act for fishing vessels, but para. 8(2) of Sched. 1 to the 1993 Act, allows the registration regulations to produce a similar system for all ships. The subparagraph allows intending mortgagees to give notices, in prescribed form, which "determine" priority when recorded on the register. The provision does not fully define priority notices, or state

exactly how they will determine priority, but it seems to be envisaged that a system will be used similar to that in Sched. 3, para. 4(3) to the Merchant Shipping Act 1988. Under that provision, once notice of an intended mortgage is given and recorded the mortgage will, if later executed and registered, take priority over another registered mortgage—even where the latter was the first to be actually registered in the ordinary way. To this extent, subpara. (2) derogates from the general priority principle under subpara. (1). The provision is sensible and helpful, because there may be a gap in time between the execution of the mortgage and its registration, during which the owner might persuade others to execute a mortgage. Clearly, an intending mortgagee cannot be expected to have a provisional priority recorded for an indefinite period of time. The 1988 Act allowed an initial, renewable, period of 30 days (Sched. 3, para. 4(4) and (5)), but the 1993 Act leaves this issue to regulations.

Para. 9(1)
Mortgagees have a variety of remedies available to them in the event that they are not happy about the security provided by the mortgage. Many of these remedies arise expressly from the mortgage contract, or derive from the common law (see *Temperley*, pp. 28–34, Clarke, *op. cit.*, pp. 91–99, *Chorley and Giles Shipping Law*, pp. 63–65). Section 35 of the Merchant Shipping Act 1894 gave a statutory power of sale to the mortgagee which could be exercised without leave of the court. There were doubts as to whether any implied limitation could have been placed on the apparently wide power of the mortgagee under s.35, *e.g.* so as to require that the security of the mortgage be threatened in some way (see Clarke, *op. cit.*, p. 93). Section 34 of the 1894 Act (now para. 10, below) contained a limitation on the extent to which the mortgagee can be treated as owner (*e.g.* where it can take over control), namely where it may be necessary to make the ship "available" as security for the mortgage debt. It might be strange to have this limitation, yet grant an unfettered right of sale.

Paragraph 9 restates the mortgagee's statutory power of sale given by s.35 of the 1894 Act, but reproduces it in the modernised version first introduced in respect of fishing vessels by the Merchant Shipping Act 1988, Sched. 3, para. 5. Section 35 of the 1894 Act is thereby replaced (being repealed by Sched. 5), but there are two differences in wording between s.35 and the new provision which may be of some significance. First, s.35 referred to the registered mortgagee having the power "absolutely" to dispose of the ship and there were no express limitations on the right (for the doubts about implied limitations, see above). Secondly, subpara. (1) now makes the power exercisable "if the mortgage money or any part of it is due" (the wording used for fishing vessels in Sched. 3, para. 5 to the 1988 Act).

Has the removal of the word "absolutely", either alone or together with the newly added words, imposed restrictions on the power of sale? The answer must be in the affirmative. It is not entirely clear if the changes have been made by inadvertence. Clearly, the mortgagee can now only exercise the power of sale under the Act in the circumstance specified, namely "if the mortgage money or any part of it is due". "Mortgage money" is not defined (although para. 7(1) refers to a loan) and could refer to the capital sum, or repayments, and interest due under it (or possibly both). It is submitted that any change in the law has been made partly as a result of a reliance on the law relating to land mortgages set out in s.101(1) of the Law of Property Act 1925 (see generally J. Farrand, *Wolstenholme and Cherry's Conveyancing Statutes* (13th ed., 1972), p. 206 *et seq.*). Section 101(1)(i) sets out the mortgagee's power "when the mortgage money has become due, to sell…". Section 205(xvi) defines "mortgage money" to be "money or money's worth secured by a mortgage". On this basis the money would be "due" once the legal date for redemption of the loan had passed. If it was repayable by instalments of capital, the power could apparently be exercised not only when the whole sum was in arrears, but when any instalment was in arrears (*Payne* v. *Cardiff Rural District Council* [1932] 1 K.B. 241). In the *Payne* case, instalments of capital and interest upon them were due and the mortgagee was held entitled to exercise its rights under the Act to sell, but *only* in respect of that instalment that had fallen due and not future instalments. In fact the only claim in that case was for the instalments in arrears (and the case did not concern a normal loan, but a statutory charge under public works legislation).

The 1993 Act appears to reflect the *Payne* decision, as subpara. (1) expressly refers to "part" of the money becoming due. The 1925 Act refers to money which "has become due", while the 1993 Act talks of money which "is due", although it is submitted that there is no material difference. However, the 1925 Act contains, in s.103, express limitations on the power of the mortgagee to *exercise* the power of sale, *e.g.* (i) that a notice to pay has been served and thereafter there has been a default for three months, or (ii) that interest is two months overdue, or (iii) that there has been a breach of some other provision in the mortgage deed. No equivalent provisions exist in the 1993 Act and it is extremely unlikely that they can now be implied. If this view is right, the extreme view that s.35 of the 1894 Act imposed no restrictions whatsoever has been narrowed, so that some money must at least be due. If the correct view of the 1894 Act was that it was subject to an implied limitation by virtue of s.34, or one requiring the type of defaults listed in s.103 of the 1894 Act, then the scope of the power of sale has been widened. Either way, it is arguable that the result is not particularly coherent in the context of ship mortgages.

Whether any new limitation will have a great effect in practice may, perhaps, be doubted. As noted by Clarke (*op. cit.*, p. 76) sale by court order following a mortgagee's action *in rem* may be preferable in many circumstances to the extra-judicial power of sale under s.35 (now para. 9(1)), in that the former will involve a sale free of encumbrances (*cf. Cerro Colorado, The* [1993] 1 Lloyd's Rep. 58 and para. 5, above). Moreover, there is no reason why the mortgage contract could not also provide for a power of sale, which may not require any notice to be given (see *e.g.* N. Meeson, *Ship and Aircraft Mortgages* (1989), p. 73). In practice, the mortgage covenant will also provide a large number of circumstances of default when the outstanding indebtedness will become due, including failure to pay any sum, failure to observe specific covenants (*e.g.* illegal trading), or conduct which imperils the security (*ibid.*, p. 72).

Para. 9(2)

This paragraph re-enacts the second part of s.35 of the 1894 Act and Sched. 3, para. 5(2) to the 1988 Act and provides that a registered mortgagee cannot sell the ship without the agreement of prior (registered) mortgagees. It follows that the mortgagee can sell without the agreement of subsequent registered mortgagees and mortgagees whose mortgages are unregistered.

Para. 10

The paragraph re-enacts s.34 of the Merchant Shipping Act 1894, referred to in para. 9(1), above. The mortgagee has a number of remedies at common law, including the right to take possession of the ship in certain circumstances. Rights may be, and in practice are, granted by the mortgage covenant (and see Meeson, *op. cit.*). The extent of the general rights and the effect that this has on the status of the mortgagee has been the subject of much litigation and discussion (see *Temperley*, pp. 28–44; Clarke, *op. cit.*, pp. 91–99). It might have been helpful if the Merchant Shipping Acts could have codified and clarified some of the issues under discussion. However, the general effect of the paragraph is simply stated, namely that the mortgagor does not cease to be treated as a shipowner where there is a registered mortgage and the mortgagee is not treated as the shipowner, except where it has taken possession and control in order to protect its security (*cf.* s.6(3)).

Para. 11

This paragraph repeats in substance s.37 of the 1894 Act (as amended by Sched. 1, para. 23 to the 1988 Act) and its more modern counterpart for fishing vessels, Sched. 3, para. 6 to the 1988 Act. A mortgagee is allowed to transfer a mortgage in accordance with registration regulations under s.3 and the registrar will register the name of the transferee accordingly.

Para. 12

This paragraph repeats in substance s.38 of the 1894 Act and its more modern counterpart for fishing vessels, Sched. 3, para. 7 to the 1988 Act. It allows transmission of a mortgage, *e.g.* by inheritance or insolvency, and the name of the transferee is recorded accordingly. *Cf.* para. 3, above.

Para. 13

This paragraph repeats in substance s.38 of the 1894 Act and its more modern counterpart for fishing vessels, Sched. 3, para. 8 to the 1988 Act. It allows for the discharge of the mortgage on production to the registrar of such information as is required by the registration regulations under s.3. Note also s.6(3), above.

Section 8(1)   SCHEDULE 2

CONSEQUENTIAL AMENDMENTS

1.—(1) Section 26 of the Sea Fisheries Act 1868 (see fishing boats within British waters to have official papers) shall be amended as follows.

(2) In subsection (1)—

(a) for the words "Part II of the Merchant Shipping Act 1988" there shall be substituted the words "the Merchant Shipping (Registration, etc.) Act 1993"; and

(b) for the words "that Part of that Act" there shall be substituted the words "registration regulations under section 3 of that Act".

(3) In subsection (5), in the definition of "foreign sea-fishing boat", for paragraphs (a), (b) and (c) there shall be substituted the following—

"(a) is not registered in the United Kingdom, the Channel Islands or the Isle of Man, and

(b) is not wholly owned by persons qualified to own British ships for the purposes of the Merchant Shipping (Registration, etc.) Act 1993.".

2. In the Merchant Shipping Act 1894—

(a) in section 82 (tonnage on registration to be registered tonnage of ship), for the words from "the same" to the end there shall be substituted the words "that tonnage shall be treated as the tonnage of the ship except so far as registration regulations provide, in specified circumstances, for the ship to be re-measured and the register amended accordingly."; and

(b) in section 742 (definitions), there shall be inserted as the first two definitions the following—

" "the register" means the register of British ships kept under section 1 of the Merchant Shipping (Registration, etc.) Act 1993;

"registration regulations" means regulations under section 3 of that Act;" ".

3. In section 80(1) of the Merchant Shipping Act 1906 (power to register Government ships)—

(a) for the words from "for the purpose" to "those Acts" there shall be substituted the words "in the United Kingdom under the Merchant Shipping (Registration, etc.) Act 1993, and the Merchant Shipping Acts,"; and

(b) for the words "in manner provided by those Acts" there shall be substituted the words "in accordance with that Act".

4. In section 6(1)(c) of the Contracts of Employment and Redundancy Payments Act (Northern Ireland) 1965 (excluded categories of employees), from the word "registered" to the end there shall be substituted the words "registered under the Merchant Shipping (Registration, etc.) Act 1993".

5.—(1) In section 163(3) of the Fisheries Act (Northern Ireland) 1966 (names of owners to be painted on fishing boats registered under Part IV of the 1894 Act) for the words "Part IV of the Merchant Shipping Act 1894" there shall be substituted the words "the Merchant Shipping (Registration, etc.) Act 1993".

(2) In section 174(4) of that Act (examination of certificates for fishing boats) for the words from "Part IV" to the end there shall be substituted the words "the Merchant Shipping (Registration, etc.) Act 1993".

6. In section 1 of the Sea Fish (Conservation) Act 1967 (size, limits, etc. for fish) for subsection (9) (definitions) there shall be substituted the following subsection—

"(9) In this section—

"British fishing boat" means a fishing boat which either is registered in the United Kingdom under the Merchant Shipping (Registration, etc.) Act 1993 or is owned wholly by persons qualified to own British ships for the purposes of that Act; and

"foreign fishing boat" means any fishing boat other than a British fishing boat.".

7. In section 5(8) of the Sea Fish (Conservation) Act 1967 (restriction on scope of certain orders), in paragraph (b), for the words "Merchant Shipping Act 1894" there shall be substituted the words "Merchant Shipping (Registration, etc.) Act 1993".

8. In section 22(1) of the Sea Fish (Conservation) Act 1967 (definitions), in the definition of "British-owned", for the words "(within the meaning of the Merchant Shipping Act 1894)" and "(within the meaning of that Act)" there shall be substituted the words "for the purposes of the Merchant Shipping (Registration, etc.) Act 1993" and "for those purposes" respectively.

9. In section 19(1) of the Sea Fisheries Act 1968 (definitions)—

(a) for the definitions of "British fishing boat" and "foreign fishing boat" there shall be substituted the following definition—

" "British fishing boat" means a fishing boat which either is registered in the United Kingdom under the Merchant Shipping (Registration, etc.) Act 1993 or is wholly British-owned"; and

(b) in the appropriate places there shall be inserted the following definitions—

" "foreign fishing boat" means any fishing boat other than a British fishing boat;"

" "wholly British-owned" means wholly owned by persons qualified to own British ships for the purposes of the Merchant Shipping (Registration, etc.) Act 1993;" ".

10. In section 8 of the Fishery Limits Act 1976 (definitions)—

(a) for the definition of "foreign fishing boat" there shall be substituted the following definition—

" "foreign fishing boat" means a fishing boat which is not—

(a) registered in the United Kingdom, the Channel Islands or the Isle of Man; or

(b) wholly British-owned;" and

(b) in the appropriate place there shall be inserted the following definition—
" "wholly British-owned" means wholly owned by persons qualified to own British fishing boats for the purposes of the Merchant Shipping (Registration, etc.) Act 1993;".

11. In section 144(1)(b) of the Employment Protection (Consolidation) Act 1978 (mariners), for the words following "registered", there shall be substituted the words "under the Merchant Shipping (Registration, etc.) Act 1993".

12. In section 81(7) of the Customs and Excise Management Act 1979 (power to regulate small craft), for the words from "fishing vessel" to "1988", there shall be substituted the words "fishing vessel registered under the Merchant Shipping (Registration, etc.) Act 1993".

13. In section 9 of the British Fishing Boats Act 1983 (definitions)—
(a) for the definition of "British fishing boat" there shall be substituted the following definition—
" "British fishing boat" means a fishing boat which either is registered in the United Kingdom under the Merchant Shipping (Registration, etc.) Act 1993 or is wholly British-owned"; and
(b) in the appropriate place there shall be inserted the following definition—
" "wholly British-owned" means wholly owned by persons qualified to own British ships for the purposes of the Merchant Shipping (Registration, etc.) Act 1993;".

14. In section 9(1) of the Inshore Fishing (Scotland) Act 1984 (definitions)—
(a) for the definition of "British fishing boat" there shall be substituted the following definition—
" "British fishing boat" means a fishing boat which either is registered in the United Kingdom under the Merchant Shipping (Registration, etc.) Act 1993 or is wholly British-owned;" and
(b) in the appropriate place there shall be inserted the following definition—
" "wholly British-owned" means wholly owned by persons qualified to own British ships for the purposes of the Merchant Shipping (Registration, etc.) Act 1993;".

15.—(1) The Merchant Shipping Act 1988 shall be amended as follows.
(2) In section 11 (regulation of registration in British territories overseas)—
(a) in subsection (1), for the words from "of ships" to "territories" there shall be substituted the words "in relevant British possessions of ships other than small ships and fishing vessels";
(b) in subsection (2)—
(i) in paragraph (a) for the words "under Part I of the 1894 Act" there shall be substituted the words "in such possessions";
(ii) in paragraphs (b) and (c), for the words "overseas territory" there shall be substituted the words "British possession"; and
(iii) in paragraph (c), for the words from "Part I" to the end there shall be substituted the words "the law of that possession";
(c) in subsection (3)—
(i) for the word "territory" there shall be substituted the word "possession"; and
(ii) the words "under Part I of the 1894 Act" shall be omitted; and
(d) at the end insert—
"(5) In this section—
"relevant British possession" has the meaning given in paragraph 4 of Schedule 4 to the Merchant Shipping (Registration, etc.) Act 1993; and
"small ship" has the meaning given in paragraph 1(2) of Schedule 3 to that Act".
(3) In section 47 (application of Merchant Shipping Acts to ships chartered by demise to the Crown)—
(a) in subsections (3) and (5), for the words "registration enactments" there shall be substituted the words "Merchant Shipping (Registration, etc.) Act 1993";
(b) in subsection (7)—
(i) after the definition of "Government ship" there shall be inserted the following definition—
" "the Merchant Shipping Acts" means the Merchant Shipping Acts 1894 to 1986, this Act and the Merchant Shipping (Registration, etc.) Act 1993;"; and
(ii) the definition of "the registration enactments" shall be omitted.
(4) In section 52 (disclosure of information to the Secretary of State by other government departments)—
(a) in subsection (1), after paragraph (a), there shall be inserted—
"(aa) to the registrar of British ships (within the meaning of the Merchant Shipping (Registration, etc.) Act 1993), or"; and
(b) in subsections (1) and (3), for the words "Part I or Part II" there shall be substituted the words "the Merchant Shipping (Registration, etc.) Act 1993".

General Note
This Schedule amends existing legislation to take account of amendments brought about by the Act itself. In general, the changes reflect the replacement of the existing system of registration and the future importance of registration regulations made by s.3. The opportunity has also been taken to correct one omission in the Merchant Shipping Act 1988, namely the failure to remove the reference in the Fisheries Act (Northern Ireland) 1966, s.163 to Pt. IV of the Merchant Shipping Act 1894 (which was replaced by Pt. II of the 1988 Act and is, in turn, now replaced by the 1993 Act).

Paragraph 15 relates to the Merchant Shipping Act 1988 powers to regulate the shipping registers in certain colonies, described there (and in s.57(2)) as "relevant overseas territories". The new terminology is "relevant British possession" as now defined in Sched. 4, para. 4 to the 1993 Act, below.

Section 8(2)   SCHEDULE 3

British Ships

British ships

1.—(1) A ship is a British ship if—
(a) the ship is registered in the United Kingdom under this Act; or
(b) the ship is registered in the United Kingdom in pursuance of an Order in Council under section 80 of the Merchant Shipping Act 1906 (Government ships); or
(c) the ship is registered under the law of a relevant British possession; or
(d) the ship is a small ship other than a fishing vessel and—
  (i) is not registered under this Act, but
  (ii) is wholly owned by qualified owners, and
  (iii) is not registered under the law of a country outside the United Kingdom.
(2) For the purposes of sub-paragraph (1)(d) above—
  "qualified owners" means persons of such description qualified to own British ships as is prescribed by regulations made by the Secretary of State for the purposes of that sub-paragraph; and
  "small ship" means a ship less than 24 metres in length ("length" having the same meaning as in the tonnage regulations).
(3) The power to make regulations for the purposes of sub-paragraph (1)(d) above shall be exercisable by statutory instrument which shall be subject to annulment in pursuance of a resolution of either House of Parliament.

The British flag

2.—(1) The flag which every British ship is entitled to fly is the red ensign (without any defacement or modification) and, subject to sub-paragraphs (2) and (3) below, no other colours.
(2) Sub-paragraph (1) above does not apply to Government ships within the meaning of section 80 of the Merchant Shipping Act 1906.
(3) The following are also proper national colours, that is to say—
(a) any colours allowed to be worn in pursuance of a warrant from Her Majesty or from the Secretary of State;
(b) in the case of British ships registered in a relevant British possession, any colours consisting of the red ensign defaced or modified whose adoption for ships registered in that possession is authorised or confirmed by Her Majesty by Order in Council.

Penalty for carrying improper colours

3.—(1) If any of the following colours, namely—
(a) any distinctive national colours except—
  (i) the red ensign,
  (ii) the Union flag (commonly known as the Union Jack) with a white border, or
  (iii) any colours authorised or confirmed under paragraph 2(3)(b) above; or
(b) any colours usually worn by Her Majesty's ships or resembling those of Her Majesty, or
(c) the pendant usually carried by Her Majesty's ships or any pendant resembling that pendant,
are hoisted on board any British ship without warrant from Her Majesty or from the Secretary of State, the master of the ship, or the owner of the ship (if on board) and every other person hoisting them shall be guilty of an offence.
(2) A person guilty of an offence under sub-paragraph (1) above shall be liable—

(a) on conviction on indictment, to a fine;

(b) on summary conviction, to a fine not exceeding the statutory maximum.

(3) If any colours are hoisted on board a ship in contravention of sub-paragraph (1) above, any of the following, namely—

(a) any commissioned naval or military officer,

(b) any officer of customs and excise, and

(c) any British consular officer,

may board the ship and seize and take away the colours.

(4) Any colours seized under sub-paragraph (3) above shall be forfeited to Her Majesty.

(5) In this paragraph—

"colours" includes any pendant;

"commissioned naval officer" means a commissioned officer in Her Majesty's navy on full pay and "commissioned military officer" has a corresponding meaning.

Duty to show British flag

4.—(1) Subject to sub-paragraph (2) below, a British ship, other than a fishing vessel, shall hoist the red ensign or other proper national colours—

(a) on a signal being made to the ship by one of Her Majesty's ships (including any ship under the command of a commissioned naval officer); and

(b) on entering or leaving any foreign port; and

(c) in the case of ships of 50 or more tons gross tonnage, on entering or leaving any British port.

(2) Sub-paragraph (1)(c) above does not apply to a small ship (as defined in paragraph 1(2) above) registered under this Act.

(3) In this paragraph "commissioned naval officer" has the same meaning as in paragraph 3 above.

Offences relating to British character of ship

5.—(1) If the master or owner of a ship which is not a British ship does anything, or permits anything to be done, for the purpose of causing the ship to appear to be a British ship then, except as provided by sub-paragraphs (2) and (3) below, the ship shall be liable to forfeiture and the master, the owner and any charterer shall each be guilty of an offence.

(2) No liability arises under sub-paragraph (1) above where the assumption of British nationality has been made for the purpose of escaping capture by an enemy or by a foreign ship of war in the exercise of some belligerent right.

(3) Where the registration of any ship has terminated by virtue of any provision of registration regulations, any marks prescribed by registration regulations displayed on the ship within the period of 14 days beginning with the date of termination of that registration shall be disregarded for the purposes of sub-paragraph (1) above.

(4) If the master or owner of a British ship does anything, or permits anything to be done, for the purpose of concealing the nationality of the ship, the ship shall be liable to forfeiture and the master, the owner and any charterer of the ship shall each be guilty of an offence.

(5) Without prejudice to the generality of sub-paragraphs (1) and (4) above, those sub-paragraphs apply in particular to acts or deliberate omissions as respects—

(a) the flying of a national flag;

(b) the carrying or production of certificates of registration or other documents relating to the nationality of the ship; and

(c) the display of marks required by the law of any country.

(6) Any person guilty of an offence under this paragraph shall be liable—

(a) on summary conviction, to a fine not exceeding £50,000;

(b) on conviction on indictment, to imprisonment for a term not exceeding two years or a fine, or both.

(7) This paragraph applies to things done outside, as well as to things done within, the United Kingdom.

Duty to declare national character of ship

6.—(1) An officer of customs and excise shall not grant a clearance or transire for any ship until the master of such ship has declared to that officer the name of the nation to which he claims that the ship belongs, and that officer shall thereupon enter that name on the clearance or transire.

(2) If a ship attempts to proceed to sea without such clearance or transire, the ship may be detained until the declaration is made.

Status of certificate of registration

7. The certificate of registration of a British ship shall be used only for the lawful navigation of the ship, and shall not be subject to detention to secure any private right or claim.

GENERAL NOTE

This Schedule brings together from the Merchant Shipping Acts 1894 and 1988 a number of provisions relating to the national character and flag of ships. The provisions are to have effect generally, and not simply in relation to the 1993 Act.

Para. 1

This paragraph declares which ships are British and substantially re-enacts s.2 of the Merchant Shipping Act 1988 (see the annotations in *Current Law Statutes Annotated* 1988). In all cases except subpara. (1)(d) a British ship will be registered in the U.K. (or a U.K. colony). Small ships whose owners may wish to exercise the entitlement not to register can still be considered British if they satisfy the three criteria mentioned. Clearly, there may be ships which are unregistered, but owned by persons who would be entitled to register them as British ships. An example would be ships over 24 metres in length. For the treatment of unregistered ships, see the General Note to Sched. 4, para. 5, below.

Para. 2

This paragraph describes the red ensign which British ships are entitled to fly and substantially re-enacts s.73(1) of the Merchant Shipping Act 1894.

Para. 3

This paragraph sets out the offence of flying the wrong colours and specifies the appropriate penalty and restates s.73(2) of the Merchant Shipping Act 1894. Powers given by s.73(3) of the Merchant Shipping Act 1894 to remove colours are restated.

Para. 4

This paragraph restates s.74 of the Merchant Shipping Act 1894 and sets out duties to display the ensign at stated times.

Para. 5

This paragraph restates parts of various enactments (see ss.69(1) and 70 of the Merchant Shipping Act 1894, as amended). It creates offences where non-British ships are made to appear as British and the penalty can include forfeiture. British masters who conceal the nationality of their ships can also commit offences. On the termination of registration, 14 days is allowed in which to remove British markings. *Cf.* s.4 of the 1993 Act, above. See also s.5 in respect of fishing vessels (restating s.22(8) of the Merchant Shipping Act 1988).

Para. 6

This paragraph restates s.68 of the Merchant Shipping Act 1894 imposing duties to declare the nationality of a ship.

Para. 7

This paragraph restates s.15(1) of the Merchant Shipping Act 1894.

Section 8(3)   SCHEDULE 4

PRE-CONSOLIDATION AMENDMENTS

Preliminary

1.—(1) In this Schedule—
    "the 1894 Act" means the Merchant Shipping Act 1894, and so for any other Merchant Shipping Act of a specified year;
    "the Merchant Shipping Acts" means the Merchant Shipping Acts 1894 to 1988 and this Act and also the Maritime Conventions Act 1911 and the Prevention of Oil Pollution Act 1971 except sections 2(1) and 3 (and so much of it as relates to them);
    "the Oil Pollution Act" means the Prevention of Oil Pollution Act 1971; and
    "United Kingdom ship" means a ship registered in the United Kingdom under this Act.
    (2) Any power under any provision in this Schedule to make regulations or orders shall be exercisable by statutory instrument subject to annulment in pursuance of a resolution of either House of Parliament.

Terminology and construction

2.—(1) Except as mentioned in sub-paragraph (2) below, in the Merchant Shipping Acts—

(a) "ship" includes every description of vessel used in navigation;

(b) any reference to a vessel, except in the expression "fishing vessel", shall be construed as a reference to a ship (as so defined);

(c) "fishing vessel" means a vessel for the time being used (or, in the context of an application for registration, intended to be used) for or in connection with fishing for sea fish, other than a vessel used (or intended to be used) for fishing otherwise than for profit; and for the purposes of this definition "sea fish" includes shellfish, salmon and migratory trout (as defined by section 44 of the Fisheries Act 1981);

(d) a vessel for the time being used (or intended to be used) wholly for the purpose of conveying persons wishing to fish for pleasure is not a fishing vessel;

(e) "foreign", in relation to a ship, means that it is neither a United Kingdom ship nor a small ship (as defined in paragraph 1(2) of Schedule 3 to this Act) which is a British ship;

(f) "master", in relation to a fishing vessel, means the skipper; and

(g) any reference to "home trade ships" shall be construed as a reference to ships employed in trading or going between places in the limited trading area, as defined for the time being in regulations; and similarly as respects any reference to a "home trade passenger ship";

and any enactment in which "ship" or "vessel" has the same meaning as in the Merchant Shipping Acts shall be construed in accordance with (a) and (b) above.

(2) Sub-paragraph (1)(a) and (b) above do not apply in relation to Part IX of the 1894 Act and sections 16 and 17 of the 1974 Act.

(3) In the Merchant Shipping Acts—

(a) "United Kingdom waters" means the sea or other waters within the seaward limits of the territorial sea of the United Kingdom;

(b) "national waters", in relation to the United Kingdom, means United Kingdom waters landward of the baselines for measuring the breadth of its territorial sea;

and in section 544 of the 1894 Act the reference to British waters shall be construed as a reference to United Kingdom waters.

(4) In the Merchant Shipping Acts any reference to, or to any of, the tackle, equipments, furniture or apparel of a ship shall be construed as a reference to the equipment of a ship.

(5) In the Merchant Shipping Acts any reference to carriages, wagons or carts shall be construed as a reference to vehicles.

3. Without prejudice to the effect of any provision for the construction of any Act ("the Act in question") included in the Merchant Shipping Acts 1894 to 1988 as one with the previous Acts so included, references in the Acts so previously included to the Merchant Shipping Acts shall be construed as including references to the Act in question.

Extent and application: generalised provisions

4.—(1) Her Majesty may by Order in Council direct that any provision of the Merchant Shipping Acts and instruments made under them shall, with such exceptions, adaptations and modifications (if any) as may be specified in the Order, extend to any relevant British possession.

(2) Her Majesty may, in relation to any relevant British possession, by Order in Council direct that, with such exceptions, adaptations and modifications (if any) as may be specified in the Order, any of the provisions of those Acts shall have effect as if references in them to the United Kingdom included a reference to that possession.

(3) An Order in Council under this paragraph may make such transitional, incidental or supplementary provision as appears to Her Majesty to be necessary or expedient.

(4) Without prejudice to the generality of sub-paragraph (3) above, an Order in Council under this paragraph may, in its application to any relevant British possession, provide for such authority in that possession as is specified in the Order to furnish the Secretary of State or the registrar with such information with respect to the registration of ships in that territory under its law as is specified in the Order or as the Secretary of State may from time to time require, and for any such information to be so furnished at such time or times and in such manner as is or are so specified or (as the case may be) as the Secretary of State may so require.

(5) In this paragraph "relevant British possession" means—

(a) the Isle of Man;

(b) any of the Channel Islands; and

(c) any colony.

5.—(1) The Secretary of State may make regulations specifying any description of non-United Kingdom ships and directing that such of the provisions of the Merchant Shipping Acts and of instruments under those Acts as may be specified in the regulations—

    (a) shall extend to non-United Kingdom ships of that description and to masters and seamen employed in them, or

    (b) shall so extend in such circumstances as may be so specified, with such modifications (if any) as may be so specified.

(2) Regulations under this paragraph may contain such transitional, supplementary and consequential provisions as appear to the Secretary of State to be necessary or expedient.

(3) In this paragraph "non-United Kingdom ships" means ships which are not registered in the United Kingdom.

Extent of application of Acts

6.—(1) The following provisions of the Merchant Shipping Acts (which expressly or by implication apply to or in relation to British ships), namely—

    (a) in the 1894 Act—

        section 458 (shipowner's obligation as to seaworthiness);

        section 544 (saving life outside United Kingdom waters);

        section 689 (returns in cases of offences abroad);

        section 723 (powers to require production of ship's documents, etc.); and

    (b) section 18 of the 1979 Act (exclusion of liability),

shall apply only to United Kingdom ships.

(2) The following provisions of those Acts (duties of masters of ships to give assistance at sea), namely—

    (a) section 422 of the 1894 Act;

    (b) section 6 of the Maritime Conventions Act 1911; and

    (c) section 22 of the 1949 Act,

shall apply in relation to United Kingdom ships and to foreign ships when in United Kingdom waters.

(3) Sections 16 and 17 of the 1974 Act (regulations for submersible and supporting apparatus) shall have effect with the omission, in section 16(1)(b), of the words following "United Kingdom".

(4) Sections 21 and 22 of the 1979 Act (safety regulations) shall have effect with the substitution in section 21(1)(c), for the reference to a port in the United Kingdom, of a reference to United Kingdom national waters.

Masters and seamen

7. In section 458 of the 1894 Act (obligation of shipowner to crew with respect to seaworthiness)—

    (a) in subsection (1), for the words "contract of service, express or implied" substitute "contract of employment"; and

    (b) in subsection (2), omit paragraph (b).

8. In the 1970 Act omit the following provisions (for which corresponding provision is made by other enactments), namely, sections 6 (control of employment agencies), 19 (safety regulations) and 87 (uniform).

9. In section 11(1) of the 1970 Act (restriction on assignment of and charges upon wages), after paragraph (a) insert—

    "(aa) the wages shall not, in Scotland, be subject to any diligence other than those provided for in section 46(1) of the Debtors (Scotland) Act 1987;"

10. In section 17 of the 1970 Act (claims against seamen's wages for maintenance, etc.), in subsection (10), omit "Ministry of Home Affairs for Northern Ireland" and substitute "that Department" for "either of those Ministries" and, in subsection (11), omit "the Ministry of Home Affairs for Northern Ireland or".

Safety

11.—(1) Omit sections 446 to 448 of the 1894 Act (provisions about dangerous goods substantially superseded by safety regulations).

(2) Section 449 shall be amended as follows—

    (a) in subsection (1), for the words "as aforesaid" (in both places) substitute "as required by safety regulations";

    (b) in subsection (2), for the words "this Act" substitute "safety regulations"; and

    (c) after subsection (2) insert—

      "(3) In this section—

"dangerous goods" means goods that are designated as dangerous goods by safety regulations; and

"safety regulations" means regulations under section 21 of the Merchant Shipping Act 1979.".

12.—(1) Omit sections 459 to 461 of the 1894 Act (provisions for the detention of unsafe ships no longer reflected in modern practice).

(2) After section 30 of the 1988 Act (offences where ship is unsafe), there shall be inserted the following section—

"Power to detain unsafe ship

30A.—(1) Where a ship in a port in the United Kingdom appears to a relevant inspector to be an unsafe ship the ship may be detained.

(2) The power of detention conferred by subsection (1) above is exercisable in relation to foreign ships as well as United Kingdom ships.

(3) The officer detaining the ship shall serve on the master of the ship a detention notice which shall—

(a) state that the relevant inspector is of the opinion that the ship is an unsafe ship;
(b) specify the matters which, in the relevant inspector's opinion, make the ship an unsafe ship; and
(c) prohibit the ship from going to sea until it is released by competent authority.

(4) In the case of a ship which is not a British ship the officer detaining the ship shall cause a copy of the detention notice to be sent as soon as practicable to the nearest consular officer for the country to which the ship belongs.

(5) In this section—

"competent authority" means any officer mentioned in section 692(1) of the 1894 Act;
"relevant inspector" means any person mentioned in paragraph (a), (b) or (c) of section 76(1) of the Merchant Shipping Act 1970; and
"unsafe ship" means a ship which is not fit to go to sea as mentioned in section 30(1) of this Act;

and the reference to going to sea shall be construed in accordance with subsection (9) of section 30.".

(3) Sections 4 and 5 of the 1984 Act (arbitration and compensation) shall apply in relation to a detention notice under section 30A of the 1988 Act and the matters specified in the notice as those sections apply in relation to a prohibition notice under section 2 of that Act and the matters specified in a prohibition notice, subject, however, to the following modifications.

(4) The modifications referred to above are as follows:

(a) the substitution of references to the relevant inspector (within the meaning of section 30A) for references to the inspector referred to in those sections;
(b) the right to refer a question to the arbitrator shall be available to the owner of the ship whether or not the master of the ship also exercises that right;
(c) the giving of the notice referring the question to the arbitrator shall not suspend the operation of the detention notice unless, on the application of the person referring the question, the arbitrator so directs;
(d) the arbitrator shall have regard, in coming to his decision, to any other matters not specified in the detention notice which appear to him to be relevant to whether the ship was or was not an unsafe ship;
(e) the arbitrator shall include in his decision a finding whether there was or was not a valid basis for the detention of the ship as an unsafe ship.

(5) In the application of sub-paragraphs (3) and (4) above to Scotland any reference to an arbitrator shall be construed as a reference to an arbiter.

(6) Any provision of the Merchant Shipping Acts which deems a ship to be an unsafe ship for the purposes of section 459 or 462 of the 1894 Act shall be construed as deeming the ship to be an unsafe ship for the purposes of section 30A of the 1988 Act.

13.—(1) In section 21 of the 1979 Act (regulations to secure health and safety on ships) insert the following subsection—

"(3A) The power to make regulations conferred by subsection (1)(a) above shall extend also to the making of regulations for the prevention of collisions between seaplanes on the surface of water and between ships and seaplanes and subsection (3)(k) above and subsections (4) to (6) below and section 22(l) shall have effect accordingly.".

(2) In consequence of that extension of powers, omit sections 418 and 419 (collision regulations for seaplanes) and 421 (power to make local regulations) of the 1894 Act.

(3) In section 22(l) of the 1979 Act (provisions supplementary to s.21), at the end insert—

"(e) make provision for compensation to be paid, where a signal is used or displayed otherwise than in accordance with the regulations, for any expense or loss caused in consequence of the signal's being taken for a signal of distress;

and any compensation falling to be paid by virtue of regulations under paragraph (e) above may, without prejudice to any other remedy, be recovered in the same manner as salvage.".

Offences by and in relation to passengers

14. In section 287 of the 1894 Act (offences by passengers)—
(a) in subsection (1), omit paragraphs (f) and (g);
(b) in subsection (2), for "injure" substitute "damage"; and
(c) in subsection (3), for the words from "convey" to the end substitute "deliver that person to a constable".
15. In section 76(3) of the 1906 Act (false statements for returns of passengers), for "gives any false information for the purpose" substitute ", for that purpose, gives to the master information which he knows to be false or recklessly gives to him information which is false".

Fishing vessel certificates: incidental offences

16. Sections 280 to 282(a) of the 1894 Act (delivery up and posting of certificates and penalty for falsity) as applied by section 3(4) of the Fishing Vessels (Safety Provisions) Act 1970 shall have effect—
(a) with the substitution in section 281 of a reference to a copy of the certificate for the reference to a duplicate; and
(b) with the omission in section 282(a) of the words "knowingly and".

Pollution prevention: assimilation of inspection powers

17. For the purposes of the Oil Pollution Act other than sections 2(1) and 3—
(a) the functions of inspectors under section 728 of the 1894 Act to report to the Secretary of State on the matters specified in that section shall include the function of reporting to him on the matters specified in section 18(1)(a) and (b) of the Oil Pollution Act, and the functions of inspectors under the said section 18 shall not include that function; and sections 18(2) and 30(3) shall have effect accordingly;
(b) the powers conferred by section 18(6) of the Oil Pollution Act (which are conferred on harbour masters as respects vessels in their harbours) shall not be available, but the corresponding powers conferred by section 27 of the 1979 Act shall be available to harbour masters in relation to ships in their harbours;
(c) the extension of the power to test equipment effected, in relation to section 18 of the Oil Pollution Act, by section 29(5) of that Act shall be treated as an extension of the corresponding power in section 27 of the 1979 Act; and
(d) for references in section 30 to the Department of Commerce for Northern Ireland substitute references to the Department of the Environment for Northern Ireland;
and, in section 18(1)(a), the reference to obligations shall be read as a reference to requirements and the reference to compliance as a reference to contravention.
18. The amendments made in the 1971 and 1974 Acts (liability and compensation for oil pollution damage) by section 34 of and Schedule 4 to the 1988 Act (in consequence of certain Conventions of 1984 which cannot now come into force) shall not have effect.

Wreck and salvage

19. Omit section 514 of the 1894 Act (receiver's power to suppress plunder and disorder by force).
20. In section 515 of the 1894 Act (liability for plundering vessel)—
(a) omit the words "and tumultuously"; and
(b) for the words from "council" to "permit" substitute "regional or islands council within whose area, or nearest to whose area, the plundering, damage or destruction took place and as if entitlement to such compensation arose under section 10 of the Riotous Assemblies (Scotland) Act 1822.".
21. In section 516 of the 1894 Act (exercise of powers of receiver in his absence)—
(a) for subsection (1) substitute—
    "(1) Where any function is conferred on the receiver by any of the preceding sections of this Act that function may be discharged by any officer of customs and excise or any principal officer of the coastguard."; and
(b) in subsection (2) omit "and shall place the same in the custody of the receiver".
22. In section 518 of the 1894 Act (duties of finder of wreck, etc.)—
(a) in paragraph (a), omit the words "of the district";
(b) in paragraph (b), for the words following "thereof" substitute "give notice to the receiver that he has found or taken possession of it and, as directed by the receiver, either hold it to the receiver's order or deliver it to the receiver;";

    (c) after "recovered" insert ", except in Scotland,";

    (d) the existing words so amended shall be subsection (1) of the section; and

    (e) after that subsection add—

        "(2) In Scotland, any sum payable under subsection (1) above to the owner of the wreck or to the persons entitled to the wreck shall, for the purposes of the sum's recovery, be regarded as a debt due to the owner or as the case may be to those persons.".

    23. In section 520 of the 1894 Act (notice of wreck), for paragraphs (a) and (b), substitute—

    "(a) make a record describing the wreck and any marks by which it is distinguished;

       (b) if, in his opinion, the value of the wreck exceeds £5,000 also transmit a similar description to the chief executive officer of Lloyds in London; and that officer shall cause it to be posted in some conspicuous place for inspection.

    The record made by the receiver under paragraph (a) above shall be kept by him available for inspection by any person during reasonable hours without charge.".

    24. In section 522 of the 1894 Act (immediate sale in certain cases)—

    (a) for "five pounds" substitute "£5,000"; and

    (b) for "warehousing" substitute "storage".

    25. In section 524 of the 1894 Act (notice of unclaimed wreck to person entitled), for the words from the beginning to "he" substitute "Any person who is entitled to unclaimed wreck found on any place in the United Kingdom or in United Kingdom waters".

    26. Omit section 528 of the 1894 Act (power of Secretary of State to purchase rights to wreck).

    27. Omit section 529 of the 1894 Act (restriction on interfering with wreck by persons exercising Admiralty jurisdiction).

    28. In section 537(2) of the 1894 Act (reward for information), for "five pounds" substitute "£100".

    29. Omit section 543 of the 1894 Act (marking of anchors).

    30. In sections 552(3), 555(1) and 556 of the 1894 Act (detention where claim exceeds £200 and apportionment of salvage up to, or exceeding, £200) for "two hundred pounds" substitute "£5,000".

    31.—(1) In section 566 of the 1894 Act (appointment of receivers of wreck for districts) for the words following "appoint" substitute "one or more persons to be receiver of wreck for the purposes of this Part of this Act and a receiver so appointed shall discharge such functions as are assigned to him by the Secretary of State.

    (2) Such public notice of appointments to the office of receiver shall be given as appears to the Secretary of State to be appropriate.".

    32. In section 567(1) of the 1894 Act (receivers' fees) for the words from "the several matters" to "as may be directed" substitute "such matters as may be prescribed by regulations made by the Secretary of State by statutory instrument such fees as may be so prescribed".

    33. In section 551(1) of the 1894 Act (valuation of property by receiver) omit the words from "of the district" to "made".

    34. Omit sections 558 to 564 of the 1894 Act (salvage by naval ships).

Lighthouses, etc.

    35. Omit sections 47 and 48 of the Malicious Damage Act 1861 (offences relating to false signals and damage, removal or concealment of buoys and other sea marks).

    36. In section 634(1) of the 1894 Act (areas for which general lighthouse authorities exercise functions) omit "and the Channel Islands", "and at Gibraltar" and "and the Isle of Man".

    37. In section 638 of the 1894 Act (general powers of lighthouse authorities), at the end, insert—

        "Any reference in this Part of this Act to a lighthouse, buoy or beacon includes its appurtenances.".

    38. In section 639(1) of the 1894 Act (land acquisition powers), for the words from "and for that purpose" to the end, substitute—

        "(1A) For the purpose of the acquisition of land by a general lighthouse authority under subsection (1) above the following provisions shall apply—

       (a) if the land is in England and Wales, the provisions of Part I of the Compulsory Purchase Act 1965 (so far as applicable) except sections 4 to 8, 27 and 31;

       (b) if the land is in Scotland, the provisions of the Lands Clauses Acts (so far as applicable) except sections 120 to 125, 127, 142 and 143 of the Lands Clauses Consolidation (Scotland) Act 1845;

       (c) if the land is in Northern Ireland, the provisions of the Land Clauses Acts (so far as applicable) except sections 16 to 18, 19, 20, 92 to 94, 123, 127 to 132, 150 and 151 of the Lands Clauses Consolidation Act 1845.".

39. In section 642 of the 1894 Act (additions to lighthouses), insert "or beacon" after "light" in both places where it occurs.

40. In section 643 of the 1894 Act (general light dues), at the beginning, insert—

"A general lighthouse authority may demand, take and recover dues in respect of light-houses, buoys and beacons under their management (in this Part of this Act called light dues) in accordance with the following provisions of this Part of this Act and for that purpose appoint persons to collect them.".

41. After section 643 of the 1894 Act insert—

"Information to determine light dues

643A.—(1) A general lighthouse authority may, for the purpose of determining whether any and, if so, what light dues are payable in respect of any ship, require any relevant authority or any person who is liable to pay light dues in respect of the ship, to furnish to the general lighthouse authority such information in that authoritys' or person's possession or control relating to the arrival or departure of the ship at or from any port within their area as they may reasonably require for that purpose.

(2) A general lighthouse authority may require any relevant authority to furnish to them such information in the relevant authoritys' possession or control relating to the movements within the relevant authoritys' area of ships or ships of any class or description for the purpose of determining whether any and, if so, what light dues are payable in respect of the ships.

(3) The powers conferred on a general lighthouse authority by subsections (1) and (2) above shall also be available to the person appointed by them to collect dues at a port.

(4) It shall be the duty of a relevant authority or person of whom a requirement for information is made under subsection (1), (2) or (3) above to furnish information as soon as is reasonably practicable.

(5) In this section "relevant authority" means—

(a) a harbour authority;

(b) the Commissioners of Customs and Excise; and

(c) a conservancy authority.".

42. For section 647 of the 1894 Act (light dues tables and regulations to be posted up in customs houses) substitute—

"Availability of light dues regulations for inspection

647. A copy of the regulations in force under section 5(2) of the Merchant Shipping (Mercantile Marine Fund) Act 1898 (as substituted by section 36(2) of the Merchant Shipping Act 1979) in respect of light dues shall be kept at—

(a) the principal office of the general lighthouse authority, and

(b) the office of the appointed collector at every port where such dues are collected;

and shall be open for inspection there during reasonable hours by any person without charge.".

43. In section 648(3) of the 1894 Act (accounts of light dues), for "and the authority receiving the dues" substitute "(4) A general lighthouse authority receiving dues (whether themselves or from a collector)".

44. In section 649 of the 1894 Act (recovery of light dues)—

(a) in subsection (1), after "dues may" insert ", except in Scotland,"; and

(b) after subsection (1) insert—

"(1A) In Scotland light dues shall, for the purposes of their recovery, be regarded as a debt due to the general lighthouse authority.".

45. In section 650 of the 1894 Act (distress on ship for light dues)—

(a) in subsection (1), omit "guns";

(b) in subsection (2)—

(i) for "three" substitute "five"; and

(ii) for "appraised by two sufficient persons or sworn appraisers, and thereupon sell the same" substitute "independently appraised and thereupon sold by public auction"; and

(c) at end add—

"(3) This section does not apply to Scotland.".

46. In section 651 of the 1894 Act (detention of ship pending production of receipt for light dues)—

(a) for the words from "by the person" to "paying the same" substitute "to the person paying them by the authority or person receiving them from him"; and

(b) for the words from "where" to "for the light dues" substitute "until the receipt for any dues in respect of the ship" and at the end insert "or the person appointed to collect light dues at the port".

47. Section 655 of the 1894 Act (local light dues) shall, so far as it extends to Northern Ireland, cease to have effect.

48. In section 656(2) of the 1894 Act (account of local light dues), omit the words from "and shall" (where first occurring) to the end.

49. In section 664 of the 1894 Act (accounts of general lighthouse authorities)—

(a) for "their receipts from light dues" substitute "the light dues and other sums received by or accruing to them by virtue of, or in connection with, the discharge of their functions under this Part of this Act or Part IX of this Act"; and

(b) for "books of account" substitute "accounting records".

50. For section 666(1) of the 1894 Act (offence of damaging, etc. lighthouses, etc.) substitute—

"(1) A person who, without lawful authority—

(a) intentionally or recklessly damages—

(i) any lighthouse or the lights exhibited in it, or

(ii) any lightship, buoy or beacon;

(b) removes, casts adrift or sinks any lightship, buoy or beacon; or

(c) conceals or obscures any lighthouse, buoy or beacon;

commits an offence.

(1A) A person who, without reasonable excuse,—

(a) rides by,

(b) makes fast to, or

(c) runs foul of,

any lightship, buoy or beacon commits an offence.".

51. In section 667 of the 1894 Act (prevention of false lights)—

(a) omit "fire" and "burnt" wherever occurring together with the word "or" in conjunction with those words;

(b) in subsection (4), after "damage; and" insert ", except in Scotland,"; and

(c) after subsection (4) add—

"(4A) In Scotland any such expenses as are mentioned in subsection (4) above shall, for the purposes of their recovery, be regarded as a debt due by the owner or person on whom the notice has been served to the general lighthouse authority.".

52. Omit section 669 of the 1894 Act (restriction on exercise of powers in Channel Islands).

53. For section 679 of the 1894 Act (auditing and laying before Parliament of accounts of General Lighthouse Fund) substitute—

"**Auditing and laying before Parliament of accounts of General Lighthouse Fund**

679.—(1) The accounts of the General Lighthouse Fund for each year shall be examined by the Comptroller and Auditor General who shall send a copy of the accounts certified by him to the Secretary of State.

(2) The Secretary of State shall lay copies of the accounts before each House of Parliament.".

54. In the Merchant Shipping (Mercantile Marine Fund) Act 1898 omit the following provisions (relating to colonial lights)—

(a) in section 2, subsections (3), (4) and (5);

(b) section 7; and

(c) in Schedule 3, the entry for the lighthouse on Cape Pembroke, Falkland Islands.

55. In section 30(2) of the Harbours Act 1964 (list of charges to be available to the public at price not exceeding 5p) for "a price not exceeding 5p. for each copy" substitute "such reasonable price (if any) as the authority determine".

Enforcement powers: generalisation

56. In section 728 of the 1894 Act (Departmental inspectors to report on certain matters)—

(a) the repeal of paragraph (a) by the 1988 Act shall not have effect;

(b) for paragraph (b) substitute—

"(b) whether any requirements, restrictions or prohibitions imposed by or under the Merchant Shipping Acts have been complied with or (as the case may be) contravened;" and

(c) at the end (instead of the amendment made in paragraph (b) by section 26 of the 1979 Act) insert "and the reference to requirements, restrictions or prohibitions under the Merchant Shipping Acts includes any such requirements, restrictions or prohibitions constituting the terms of any approval, licence, consent or exemption given in any document issued under those Acts".

57. In section 27(1)(h)(iii) of the 1979 Act (powers of Departmental inspectors) for "regulations" substitute "instruments".

Legal proceedings and offences: assimilation and modernisation

58. In section 681(2) of the 1894 Act (mode of enforcing recovery of certain sums), after "England" insert "or Northern Ireland".

59. Section 683 of the 1894 Act (time limit for summary proceedings) shall apply in relation to offences under the Oil Pollution Act instead of section 19(4) of that Act (corresponding provision); and for the word "after" in section 683(1) substitute "beginning with" where that word first appears and, where that word secondly appears, substitute "beginning with the date on which".

60. Section 684 of the 1894 Act (jurisdiction in relation to offences) shall apply in relation to offences under the Oil Pollution Act instead of section 19(5) of that Act (corresponding provision).

61. Section 686(1) (jurisdiction over offences on board ship) shall—

(a) so far as it applies to British subjects, apply only to British citizens (within the meaning of the British Nationality Act 1981); and

(b) so far as it applies to British ships, apply only to United Kingdom ships.

62. For section 687 of the 1894 Act (offences by British seamen overseas) substitute—

"Offences committed by British seamen

687.—(1) Any act in relation to property or person done in or at any place (ashore or afloat) outside the United Kingdom by any master or seaman who at the time is employed in a United Kingdom ship, which, if done in any part of the United Kingdom, would be an offence under the law of any part of the United Kingdom, shall—

(a) be an offence under that law, and

(b) be treated for the purposes of jurisdiction and trial as if it had been done within the jurisdiction of the Admiralty of England.

(2) Subsection (1) above also applies in relation to a person who had been so employed within the period of three months expiring with the time when the act was done.

(3) Subsections (1) and (2) above apply to omissions as they apply to acts.".

63. After section 687 of the 1894 Act insert the following—

"Offences by officers of bodies corporate

687A.—(1) Where a body corporate is guilty of an offence under the Merchant Shipping Acts or any instrument made under those Acts, and that offence is proved to have been committed with the consent or connivance of, or to be attributable to any neglect on the part of, a director, manager, secretary or other similar officer of the body corporate or any person who was purporting to act in such a capacity, he as well as the body corporate shall be guilty of that offence and shall be liable to be proceeded against and punished accordingly.

(2) Where the affairs of a body corporate are managed by its members, subsection (1) above shall apply in relation to the acts and defaults of a member in connection with his functions of management as if he were a director of the body corporate.

Offences by partners, etc. in Scotland

687B. Where, in Scotland, a partnership or unincorporated association (other than a partnership) is guilty of an offence under the Merchant Shipping Acts or any instrument made under those Acts, and that offence is proved to have been committed with the consent or connivance of, or to be attributable to any neglect on the part of, a partner in the partnership or, as the case may be, a person concerned in the management or control of the association, he as well as the partnership or association shall be guilty of that offence and shall be liable to be proceeded against and punished accordingly.".

64. In section 689 of the 1894 Act (return of offenders to the United Kingdom)—

(a) in subsection (2), after "may" insert ", where no more convenient means of transport is available (or is available only at disproportionate expense),"; and

(b) in subsection (3), omit the words from "and that officer" to the end.

65. In section 693 of the 1894 Act (how sums ordered to be paid are leviable), for the words from "direct" to the end substitute—

"—

    (a) except in Scotland, direct the amount remaining unpaid to be levied by distress,

    (b) in Scotland, grant warrant authorising the arrestment and sale,

of the ship and its equipment.".

66. In section 20 of the Oil Pollution Act (enforcement and application of fines), for the words from "to direct" to the end substitute—

"—

    (a) except in Scotland, to direct the amount remaining unpaid to be levied by distress,

    (b) in Scotland, to grant warrant authorising the arrestment and sale,

of the ship and its equipment.".

67. In section 695 of the 1894 Act (certification of copies for evidence)—

  (a) in subsection (2) (provision of copies), for the reference to payment of a reasonable sum not exceeding an amount prescribed by regulations substitute a reference to payment of a reasonable price determined by the Secretary of State;

  (b) in subsection (3) (offence) for "eighteen months" substitute "two years"; and

  (c) after subsection (3) insert—

"(3A) Without prejudice to section 6(1) of the Civil Evidence (Scotland) Act 1988 (production of copy documents), subsection (2) above shall not apply, for the purposes of civil proceedings in Scotland, as respects the admissibility of a copy document; but subsection (3) above shall apply to a person purporting to authenticate any such document and to authentication as it applies to an officer purporting to certify any such document and to certification.".

68. For section 696 of the 1894 Act (service of documents) substitute the following—

"Service of documents

    696.—(1) Any document authorised or required to be served on any person may be served on that person—

    (a) by delivering it to him;

    (b) by leaving it at his proper address; or

    (c) by sending it by post to him at his proper address.

    (2) Any such document authorised or required to be served on the master of a ship may be served—

    (a) where there is a master, by leaving it for him on board the ship with the person appearing to be in command or charge of the ship;

    (b) where there is no master—

      (i) on the managing owner of the ship; or

      (ii) if there is no managing owner, on any agent of the owner; or

      (iii) where no such agent is known or can be found, by leaving a copy of the document fixed to the mast of the ship.

    (3) Any document authorised or required to be served on any person may—

    (a) in the case of a body corporate, be served on the secretary or clerk of that body;

    (b) in the case of a partnership, be served on a partner or a person having the control or management of the partnership business or, in Scotland, on the firm.

    (4) Any notice authorised or required by, or by regulations under, the Merchant Shipping (Registration, etc.) Act 1993 to be served on the Secretary of State may be served by post.

    (5) Any notice authorised by Part I of the Merchant Shipping Act 1984 to be given to an inspector may be given by delivering it to him or by leaving it at, or sending it by post to, his office.

    (6) Any document authorised or required by or under any enactment to be served on the registered owner of a registered ship shall be treated as duly served on him if served on such person, in such circumstances and by such method, as may be specified in registration regulations.

    (7) For the purposes of this section and of section 7 of the Interpretation Act 1978 (service of documents by post) in its application to this section, the proper address of any person on whom any document is to be served shall be his last known address, except that—

    (a) in the case of a body corporate or their secretary or clerk it shall be the address of the registered or principal office of that body;

    (b) in the case of a partnership or a person having the control or management of the partnership business, it shall be the principal office of the partnership;

and for the purposes of this subsection the principal office of a company registered outside the United Kingdom or of a partnership carrying on business outside the United Kingdom shall be their principal office in the United Kingdom.

(8) If the person to be served with any notice has (whether in pursuance of registration regulations or otherwise) specified an address in the United Kingdom other than his proper address within the meaning of subsection (7) above as the one at which he or someone on his behalf will accept notices of the same description as that notice, that address shall also be treated for the purposes of this section and section 7 of the Interpretation Act 1978 as his proper address.

(9) For the purposes of the said section 7 a letter containing—

(a) a notice to be served on any person in pursuance of subsection (6) above, or

(b) a notice authorised or required to be served under registration regulations on a representative person (within the meaning of those regulations),

shall be deemed to be properly addressed if it is addressed to that person at the address for the time being recorded in relation to him in the register; and a letter containing any other notice under registration regulations shall be deemed to be properly addressed if it is addressed to the last known address of the person to be served (whether of his residence or of a place where he carries on business).".

69. In section 697 of the 1894 Act (proof etc. of exemption), the existing words shall be subsection (1), and after that subsection add—

"(2) This section does not apply to Scotland.".

70. In section 76 of the 1894 Act (proceedings on forfeiture of ship) omit—

(a) in subsection (1), the words from "and may award" to the end; and

(b) in subsection (2), the words "either" and "or criminally".

71. For section 66 of the 1894 Act (forgery of documents: Scotland) substitute—

"Forgery of documents: Scotland

66.—(1) In Scotland if any person forges or fraudulently alters—

(a) any entry or endorsement in the register kept under section 1 of the Merchant Shipping (Registration, etc.) Act 1993; or

(b) subject to subsection (2) below, any other document as respects which provision is made by, under or by virtue of that Act or this Part of this Act (or any entry or endorsement, in or on such other document and as respects which provision is so made),

he shall be liable—

(i) on summary conviction, to a fine not exceeding the statutory maximum or to imprisonment for a term not exceeding six months or to both; or

(ii) on conviction on indictment, to a fine or to imprisonment or to both.

(2) Subsection (1)(b) above does not apply in respect of actings which constitute an offence under section 695(4) or 722(1) of this Act.".

72. For section 695(4) of the 1894 Act (offences as respects documents admissible in evidence) substitute—

"(4) Subject to subsection (5) below, in Scotland if any person forges the seal, stamp or signature of any document (or copy document) declared by this Act to be admissible in evidence or tenders in evidence any such document (or copy document) with, and knowing it to have, a false or counterfeit seal, stamp or signature he shall be liable—

(a) on summary conviction, to a fine not exceeding the statutory maximum or to imprisonment for a term not exceeding six months or to both; or

(b) on conviction on indictment, to a fine or to imprisonment for a term not exceeding seven years or to both.

(5) Subsection (4) above does not apply in respect of actings which constitute an offence under section 722(1) of this Act.".

73. For section 722(1) of the 1894 Act (offences as to use of forms) substitute—

"(1) In Scotland, if any person forges any seal or distinguishing mark on any form issued under this Act or fraudulently alters any such form he shall be liable—

(a) on summary conviction, to a fine not exceeding the statutory maximum or to imprisonment for a term not exceeding six months or to both; or

(b) on conviction on indictment, to a fine or to imprisonment or to both.".

74. In any offence-creating provision of the Merchant Shipping Acts—

(a) any reference to doing a thing "wilfully" shall be construed as a reference to doing it "intentionally";

(b) any reference to "suffering" or "allowing" a thing to be done shall be construed as a reference to "permitting" it to be done; and

(c) any reference to the absence of a reasonable "cause" shall be construed as a reference to the absence of a reasonable "excuse".

Procedure in Scotland

75. Omit sections 704 to 709 of the 1894 Act.

76. In section 710 (savings for Scots law), for the words "or punishment of offences at the instance or by the direction of the Lord Advocate" substitute "of offences at the instance or on the authority or with the concurrence of the Lord Advocate or on the authority of the High Court or to any punishment consequent on such prosecution".

77. In paragraph 5 of Schedule 5 to the 1974 Act (provision as to regulations relating to submersible and supporting apparatus)—
   (a) in sub-paragraph (b), after "regulations" insert "(other than proceedings to which paragraph (bb) below applies)"; and
   (b) after sub-paragraph (b) insert—
      "(bb) may provide that in any proceedings in Scotland for an offence under the regulations a statement in any complaint or indictment of any such fact as is mentioned in sub-paragraph (b) above shall, until the contrary is proved, be sufficient evidence of the fact as so stated,".

Supplemental: surveyors

78. In section 724 of the 1894 Act (surveyors of ships) subsections (3) and (5) shall be omitted save, in (3), for the power of the Secretary of State to remove surveyors.

Generalised power to charge fees

79.—(1) The Secretary of State may, with the consent of the Treasury, make regulations prescribing fees to be charged in respect of—
   (a) the issue or recording in pursuance of the Merchant Shipping Acts of any certificate, licence or other document; or
   (b) the doing of any other thing in pursuance of those Acts.
   (2) All fees received by the Secretary of State under those Acts shall be paid into the Consolidated Fund.

GENERAL NOTE
   See the Introduction and General Note to the Act, and the General Note to s.8, above. Although the 1993 Act is in part a pre-consolidation measure, it was not suitable for large scale amendments of the previous law, but was designed to effect a modernisation of the somewhat archaic language of the Statute Book.

Para. 1
   This paragraph provides for definitions in this Schedule only and provides a shorthand method of reference to amendments. It is noticeable from the Acts mentioned that a number of Acts have to be treated as part of the merchant shipping legislation although not termed Merchant Shipping Acts. This indicates some of the incoherence of the present state of the Statute Book. The task of reconciling expressions across some 30 Acts which used different drafting techniques is a formidable one and it would not be surprising if further inconsistencies were to be found in the ultimate consolidation.

Para. 2

Terminology and construction
   This paragraph will be of central importance in the consolidated Act as it contains definitions which must be consistent between all the legislation consolidated. It is not possible here to give an exhaustive interpretation of the expressions, which will replace some of those in s.742 of the Merchant Shipping Act 1894 (but see *Temperley*, pp. 274–282). Section 742 will presumably be repealed by the consolidating measure.

Para. 2(1) and (2)
   Ship. It might be thought that defining "ship" was the simplest of tasks. Unfortunately, there has been a mass of litigation on whether a particular structure is a ship for a variety of purposes, from marine salvage to the application of safety regulations and time bars (see *Temperley*, pp. 276 and 277). Suffice it to say that the courts have generally taken a rather restrictive view of what is a ship and have laid particular emphasis on the expression "used in navigation" (see, *e.g. Gas Float Whitton, The (No. 2)* [1897] A.C. 337). Sometimes that emphasis has been artificial and seemingly only designed to protect personal injury claimants where the operation of a maritime rule would disadvantage them. Thus, in an unconvincing judgment, Sheen J. declared that a jet ski was not a ship, partly because it was not used in "navigation" in a traditional sense (see *Steedman* v. *Scofield* [1992] 2 Lloyd's Rep. 163). Similarly, Henry J. held that a sailing dinghy used on a reservoir was not used in navigation, as the users were merely "messing about in

boats" (*Curtis* v. *Wild* [1991] 4 All E.R. 172). Whatever the merits of the individual cases, the reasoning is not always consistent. The real question is not so much whether particular craft fall within a simple definition of ship, but the more complex one of whether substantive maritime rules of many different types and on many different subjects (*e.g.* regulations on safety, limits of liability, time bars, registration) can and should be applied to craft of vastly differing size and construction and designed for a multiplicity of purposes. Thus, one may quite rationally want to apply strict regulatory safety requirements on pleasure craft operating on a reservoir, but might think it quite inappropriate or unfair to apply limits of liability or time bars, designed for merchant ships, which will provide radically different remedies to those injured in a bus crash. Similarly, at sea, there is great uncertainty how the definition of ship is to be applied to whole categories of modern offshore craft, such as semi-submersible platforms and jack-up oil rigs (see M. Summerskill, *Oil Rigs: Law and Insurance* (1979), where the author wrestles for the best part of Chap. 2 in an attempt to define oil rigs). The definition of "ship" does use the word "includes", so that there is the possibility of recognising new craft as ships. Note that s.41 of the Merchant Shipping Act 1979 gave the Secretary of State power to declare that certain structures such as oil rigs were or were not ships, but this useful power has not been exercised. The CMI (Comite Maritime International) produced in 1977 a draft Convention on Offshore Mobile Craft. In 1991 the 64th Session of the IMO Legal Committee recorded sufficient interest in an updated study of the earlier draft that the subject was placed on the work programme of the Legal Committee. An International Sub-committee of the CMI has since discussed the subject at meetings in 1992 and 1993.

The 1993 Act does not solve any of the modern problems, although it does remove one anachronism in s.742 of the 1894 Act definition of ship. That section stated that "ship" included every description of vessel used in navigation "not propelled by oars". The new definition has removed the quoted phrase, so that a rowing boat can be a "ship". This seemed to be the only distinction between ship and "vessel" in s.742. "Vessel" can thus be absorbed into "ship" except in relation to wreck and submarines, as provided by subpara. (2), and fishing vessels, which are separately defined in subpara. (1)(c). However, if judges wish to exclude the application of rules such as those relating to limitation of liability (which under the Merchant Shipping Act 1979 Sched. 4, Pt. II, para. 2 do not depend on a vessel being seagoing) to rowing boats they will have to continue a strained interpretation of "used in navigation". It would be better if, after consolidation, a detailed look was taken at each part of the consolidated Act and a principled decision was taken on how far the relevant provisions should extend to particular maritime craft. To some extent, this is the approach that has always been taken for fishing vessels, below, for wrecks (in Pt. IX of the 1894 Act) and for midget submarines and submersibles (in ss.16 and 17 of the Merchant Shipping Act 1974).

Fishing vessel. The definition of fishing vessel in subpara. (1)(c) is that used in the Merchant Shipping Act 1988, s.12(1). It is intended to apply to commercial fishing operations (*cf.* the definition in the Merchant Shipping Act 1894, s.370, as amended by the Merchant Shipping Act 1970, s.100(3) and Sched. V). It would not include the fishing boat operated by an individual for the sport of fishing or, apparently, the fishing boat used by a company as a courtesy leisure craft for clients. Nor would it extend to the type of fishing boat found in holiday resorts which, for payment, offer to take private fishermen for a day's recreational fishing (see subpara. (1)(d), taken from s.12(2) of the Merchant Shipping Act 1988). But in this latter case the fishing boat must be used *wholly* for that purpose: if its owner was a part-time commercial fisherman, who took pleasure fishers along on his trips, it would fall within the definition of a fishing vessel. The definition of fishing vessel relates to its usage for the time being (as did s.370 of the 1894 Act), a recognition of the fact that boats are used for a variety of purposes.

Para. 2(3)

Subparagraph (3) provides consistent expressions for use when it is necessary to refer to territorial or national waters, for example, s.27 of the Merchant Shipping Act 1894 (as amended by s.32 of the Merchant Shipping Act 1988) which creates an offence where seafarers endanger ships in waters now within the definition in subpara. (3)(a). Section 544 of the Merchant Shipping Act 1894 sets out the circumstances when life salvage is payable for services performed in "British waters", an expression that is now to be read as the territorial sea.

Para. 2(4) and (5)

There are many references to particular pieces of ship's equipment in the Merchant Shipping Act 1894 which date from the days of sail. Section 544 of the 1894 Act (para. 2(3) above) refers to the apparel of a ship. The use of the word "equipment" can now cover all such references. References to means of conveyance are also updated (*cf.* s.512(1)(c) of the 1894 Act).

Para. 3
The drafting technique that has generally been used with the Merchant Shipping Acts is to have a provision stating that a particular Act is "to be construed as one" with the 1894 and other Merchant Shipping Acts (see, *e.g.* s.12(2) of the Merchant Shipping (Liability of Shipowners and Others) Act 1958, or s.57(1) of the Merchant Shipping Act 1988). It has also been the practice to provide that the Acts may be cited together as the Merchant Shipping Acts (as was also done in s.12(3) of the 1958 Act and s.58(1) of the 1988 Act). When the construing provision was first introduced in this context, in the Merchant Shipping (Mercantile Marine Fund) Act 1898, s.9(2), it may have been anticipated that the Acts could easily be read together. Now there are some 30 Merchant Shipping Acts and it is not always easy or possible to see how they are to be construed together. The difficulty of the consolidator's task is shown by the handful of provisions which make it clear that such references in the previous Acts include the last one of the accumulating series (see, *e.g.* the Merchant Shipping (Load Lines) Act 1967, s.34(2), the Merchant Shipping Act 1974, s.23(1), the Merchant Shipping Act 1979, s.37(5) and the Safety at Sea Act 1986, s.5(3)). Paragraph 3 now generalises this drafting proposition in order to avoid any implication that the same does not hold true for other Acts which have not used the formula.

Para. 4
There are 15 Merchant Shipping Acts which allow their provisions to be extended overseas by Order in Council. The existence of the empire and an empire register meant that many merchant shipping provisions were applied to the colonies. Early references were to dominions and territories (*e.g.* the Maritime Conventions Act 1911, s.9(1)), but later references had to take account of mandates and trust territories and all the other confusing array of countries over which the U.K. has exercised some form of control. The Merchant Shipping Act 1988, s.57(2) used the expression "relevant overseas territory" to refer to Crown Dependencies and Dependent Territories. Paragraph 4 now sets out a set of uniform provisions for applying merchant shipping legislation to the possessions now listed in subpara. (5). This will entail the repeal of a number of provisions of the 1894 Act which applied to the colonies, so that regulations can be made (see, *e.g.* paras. 36 and 52, below).

Para. 5
Much merchant shipping legislation applies to U.K. ships, *i.e.* ships registered in the U.K. It might be questioned whether an unscrupulous shipowner could avoid responsibilities by failing to register a ship. A number of Acts dealt with particular problems by extending their operation to unregistered ships. Thus, the Merchant Shipping Act 1894, s.72 (as amended by the Merchant Shipping Act 1988, Sched. 1, para. 44) provided for the liabilities of unregistered ships. In particular, ships which were not registered elsewhere but could have been registered in the U.K. were treated as British ships in respect of dues, fines, forfeiture and "the punishment of offences committed on board the ship, or by any persons belonging to the ship" (*cf.* the Merchant Shipping Act 1894, s.734, the Merchant Shipping (Load Lines) Act 1967, s.29, the Merchant Shipping Act 1970, s.92, the Prevention of Oil Pollution Act 1971, s.22 and the Merchant Shipping Act 1988, s.50). Section 72 (and the other provisions listed) will be repealed by Sched. 5 to the 1993 Act. It appears that para. 5 of Sched. 4 to the 1993 Act will enable them to be replaced by regulations. There will thus be little point in failing to register in order to avoid the regulatory effects of the Merchant Shipping Acts. Note that the paragraph does extend to foreign ships and ships which would otherwise be British ships within Sched. 3 if they had been registered. The expression "non-United Kingdom ships" in subpara. (1)(a) must be read in accordance with para. 1(1) and does not exclude from the powers in para. 5 ships, for example, which were based in the U.K. but unregistered. *Cf.* para. 61, below.

Para. 6
The definition of British ships in Sched. 3, para. 1 is wider than that of U.K. ships within Sched. 4, para. 1, as it could include ships registered in colonies (see Sched. 3, para. 1(1)(c)). There are many examples of provisions scattered around the Merchant Shipping Acts which include references (expressly or by implication) to British ships (*cf.* s.458(2)(b) of the 1894 Act and para. 7, below). The general international principle of law is that a state can regulate its own (*e.g.* registered) ships wherever they are and foreign ships when they are in national waters. Paragraph 6 has the effect of bringing the various provisions listed into line with these principles. Subparagraph (4) actually extends the power to make health and safety regulations under ss.21 and 22 of the Merchant Shipping Act 1979 from port limits to U.K. national waters.

Paras. 7–10

Masters and seamen

Section 458(2)(b) of the 1894 Act sets out the obligation of a shipowner to use reasonable methods to ensure the seaworthiness of the ship, but used the dated terminology "contract of service". This usage was superseded by that of "contract of employment" by the Merchant Shipping Act 1970, which introduced the concept of written crew agreements. Paragraph 7 acknowledges this change (which was presumably missed in 1970) and also removes subpara. (2)(b) which extended the section to all British possessions.

Paragraph 8 repeals provisions where there is an overlap with existing legislation.

Paragraph 9 corrects an error in the Debtors (Scotland) Act 1987 where the diligence of arrestment and furthcoming remained available against seamen, but not fishers, because of the way "earning" was defined.

Paragraph 10 reflects administrative changes in respect of Northern Ireland. Paragraph 54, below, also brings the law of Northern Ireland into line with that of England and Wales.

Para. 11

Dangerous goods are now regulated by the Merchant Shipping (Dangerous Goods) Regulations 1981 (S.I. 1981 No. 1747), as amended, issued under s.21 of the Merchant Shipping Act 1979. In effect these have made ss.446–448 redundant and the provisions will be repealed. Section 449 of the 1894 Act allowed for forfeiture of dangerous goods carried without being marked or under a false description. Subparagraph (2) adapts this provision to reflect that the obligations will be set out in the regulations and not in s.446.

Para. 12

Sections 459–461 established a rigorous system (for its day) for the detention of British and foreign ships which were found to be unsafe in a British port. Gradually, these powers have been superseded by more specific provisions laid down in later Acts and in individual regulations. Some procedural provisions, such as provisional and final detention (s.459(4)) and courts of survey (s.459(7)), do not reflect modern practice and it is entirely appropriate to effect a repeal. Subparagraph (2) is a modern replacement which enables an inspector to serve a detention notice on a master. The structure of the new provision is based upon the equivalent concept of a prohibition notice, set out in the Merchant Shipping Act 1984, s.2. The new section is inserted in the Merchant Shipping Act 1988, because that Act established (in ss.30–33) a number of new provisions dealing with maritime safety as a result of the Zeebrugge disaster. The new s.30A of the 1988 Act will follow s.30, dealing with the criminal liability of shipowners and masters in respect of dangerously unsafe ships, and the definitions of "unsafe ship" and "going to sea" are made common. There is also harmonisation of references in the Merchant Shipping Act 1984 to the arbitration and compensation system established there to deal with disputes about the validity of improvement and prohibition notices (see subparas. (3)–(5)).

Para. 13

As has already been noted, most safety matters are now dealt with in detail by regulations issued under the Merchant Shipping Act 1979, s.21. Sections 22(3) of the 1979 Act gave wide powers to the Secretary of State to repeal or modify the Merchant Shipping Acts by regulations. This was done, for instance, in respect of the redundant powers to make collision regulations given by ss.418 and 419 of the Merchant Shipping Act 1894, which were repealed by the Merchant Shipping (Distress Signals and Prevention of Collision) Regulations 1983 (S.I. 1983 No. 708). The 1993 Act continues the policy of repealing redundant rules contained in the primary Acts, especially the Merchant Shipping Act 1894, by repealing the remaining parts of ss.418 and 419, dealing with the minor topic of collision regulations for seaplanes. Specific action was needed by the 1993 Act because of the extension to the rule-making power which needed to be made by subpara. (1). An extension was similarly necessary in subpara. (3), in order to allow regulations to provide for compensation for reliance by a master on misleading distress signals given by another ship. Those powers are currently contained in the Merchant Shipping (Safety Convention) Act 1949, which will eventually be repealed by Sched. 5 (and see *Temperley*, p. 484, note 7).

The repeal of s.421, a saving power for local navigation rules, is presumably justified because the international collision regulations, applied by the latest statutory instruments (S.I. 1989 Nos. 1798 and 2400 and S.I. 1991 No. 638), themselves contain in reg. 1(b) a saving for local rules.

Para. 14

Section 287 of the Merchant Shipping Act 1894 has the title "offences in connection with passenger steamers", which betrays its ancestry dating from the time of emigrant ships. Paragraph 14 modernises it by: removing fare-dodging provisions (now covered by the Theft Act 1968); using the word "damage" instead of "injury" in relation to the ship and its equipment; and removing a requirement that offenders be delivered to a justice of the peace. The original Bill included provisions to update other references in s.287 of the 1894 Act so that there would be an offence not only for being "drunk", but also "under the influence of drink or drugs", and so that "molests" would include annoyance of other passengers. The drink and drugs provision seemed unremarkable (*cf.* s.27(3)(b) of the Merchant Shipping Act 1970, as amended by the Merchant Shipping Act 1988, s.32), but one MP objected at Committee stage that the suggested provisions were too vague. Perhaps in order to speed the passage of the Bill without opposition, the promoter, Mr Page, agreed to the deletion of what were subparas. (4)(a) and (b). It is submitted that the objection was unfounded and unfortunate.

Para. 15
Section 76(3) of the Merchant Shipping Act 1906 creates an offence where a master provides a false return as to the number of passengers carried. The amendment imposes a more modern mental element for the offence.

Para. 16
The Fishing Vessels (Safety Provisions) Act 1970, s.3(4) applies certain enforcement provisions of the 1894 Act, relating to passenger steamer certificates, which are no longer appropriate.

Para. 17
The Prevention of Oil Pollution Act 1971 is an example of a piece of legislation relating to merchant shipping that was not integrated with the Merchant Shipping Acts. The consolidation cannot really leave out the oil pollution provisions and it is therefore necessary to achieve harmonisation of the various inspection powers. In effect, this means that the general merchant shipping powers in s.27 of the Merchant Shipping Act 1979 are to prevail. See also paras. 59 and 60, below.

Para. 18
The whole system of compensation for oil pollution damage was reformed by two Protocols in 1984. These have not entered into force, mainly as a result of the failure of the USA to ratify them and by the enactment of its own Oil Pollution Act 1990. The Protocols were given effect by s.34 of and Sched. 4 to the Merchant Shipping Act 1988 (which were never brought into force). The background and effect of those provisions was explained in some detail by the writer in the General Note to Sched. 4 in *Current Law Statutes Annotated* 1988 and will not be repeated here. Paragraph 18 recognises the effective end to the 1984 Protocols. However, it should be noted that an international compromise has produced two more Protocols in 1992 (see N. Gaskell, "Compensation for Oil Pollution: 1992 Protocols to the Civil Liability Convention and the Fund Convention" (1993) 8 International Journal of Marine and Coastal Law, pp. 286–290). The U.K. will almost certainly ratify these Protocols and new legislation will be needed (see the Introduction and General Note, above), hopefully to be passed before the 1994 consolidation.

Paras. 19–34
Wreck
Many of the provisions of Pt. IX of the 1894 Act dealing with wreck and salvage are totally inappropriate to deal with modern conditions (see generally, S. Dromgoole, N. Gaskell, "Interests in Wreck", in N. Palmer, E. McKendrick, *Interests in Goods* (1993), Chap. 13). Paragraphs 19–34 attempt to remove some absurdities in the old law and to modernise it where appropriate. It must be emphasised that the amendments are largely cosmetic and the thorough reform of wreck law that is required must await another day. "Wreck" is still defined in s.510 of the 1894 Act.

In practice, the receiver of wreck service has declined in importance (*op. cit.*, pp. 352–354). The powers of a receiver have been exercised by H.M. Customs and the hierarchy of officials mentioned, *e.g.* in s.516, does not operate. Paragraph 31 amends s.566 of the 1894 Act on the appointment of receivers so as to allow for there to be a single central receiver, if desired (see also para. 21). Receivers' fees will be set out in statutory instruments (see para. 32, amending s.567).

Section 518 of the 1894 Act imposes an obligation on a finder of wreck brought within the U.K. (see the Merchant Shipping Act 1906, s.72 and *Pierce* v. *Bernis*; *Lusitania, The* [1986] Q.B. 384) to report the find and to "deliver the same to the receiver". In practice there are very few reports made (some 25 in 1990 (Gaskell and Dromgoole, *op. cit.*, p. 353)) and the Customs service has no real mechanism for the receiving and conservation of finds which may have some historical importance. Still less does it desire to receive artefacts. The assumption of the 1894 Act was that it was in the public good for a wreck to be brought ashore, but the Act was designed to deal with commercial property issues, where removal, sale and disposal was the sensible alternative. These days there may well be heritage considerations in relation to an ancient wreck. Archaeologists may prefer for the wreck *not* to be moved from its situation, *e.g.* on the seabed, where it may constitute a time capsule with each artefact having a significance in relation to the others. More destruction to the archaeological integrity of the site may occur by attempts to remove the wreck and, ironically, to comply with s.518. Paragraph 22 therefore constitutes a welcome and significant change in the law, by removing the obligation of a finder always to *deliver* a wreck to the receiver. Instead, a person who finds or takes possession of the wreck must still report that fact (under s.518(a)), but must obey any instruction then given by the receiver. That instruction might be to hold the wreck (or artefacts), or actually to deliver it as before.

   The amended provision still leaves many problems of interpretation. First, what are the relative meanings of the expressions "finding" and "taking possession" as utilised in the section? In particular, does a person "find" a wreck by discovering it, or is finding in this context a synonym for taking possession? The distinction is of some significance, because a failure to report or deliver is a criminal offence. If a diver spots a hulk on the seabed, must this be reported? If a stroller on a beach comes across some flotsam, must that be reported? Reporting is an important feature for the establishing of any archaeological record, but that is not what Pt. IX was originally designed to achieve (although see now para. 23, below). It is difficult to see how s.72 of the Merchant Shipping Act 1906 can refer to a wreck found outside the U.K. and brought within it unless the finding is the equivalent of taking possession. It is submitted that the context shows that there must be more than mere discovery for s.518 to operate and that in most contexts "finding" must involve the taking into possession of the wreck (and see *Tubantia, The* [1924] P. 78 and Dromgoole and Gaskell, "Interests in Wreck", *op. cit.*, pp. 386–398), or the exercising of some control over it. In the nineteenth century there must have been little prospect of deep sea recovery and most finding will have occurred on the sea-shore. If the shore was privately owned, the landowner who discovered it might also be said to have found it, in that he may have been able to exercise control over it without physically reducing it into possession. It may well be that this was the type of finding that the section had in mind. More likely is that the provision was either loosely drafted or used a general colloquial expression followed by a more specific legal concept (justifying a kind of *ejuisdem generis* approach).

   Secondly, what powers does the receiver have under the amended s.518(b)? The finder may be obliged to hold the wreck to the "receiver's order". Can any conditions be attached to this direction? Does the direction relate merely to the exercise of the two options given, or can the receiver require the finder to hold the wreck and conserve it, or keep it in a particular place, or make it available to members of the public or researchers? Who is to bear any costs involved? Presumably, if the finder is directed to hold the wreck to the receiver's order the latter ought to bear any costs involved, *e.g.* in storage or conservation. It may be unlikely that this was what the Government intended, yet it would be unjust if a specific request as to storage made by the receiver was complied with but no remuneration was provided. It would seem that there is little sanction in the section for precise onerous conditions to be attached to any direction without there being a concomitant obligation for the receiver to pay for them. These conclusions would also follow from s.522, which allows the receiver to sell a wreck if its value would not justify the costs of "storage" (and see para. 24(b)). In practice, it seems unlikely that the receiver would give such directions, except where it is generally convenient for remains to be left where they are. Although it may not be possible for a receiver to impose onerous conditions, other than that the finder shall retain possession to the order of the receiver, it may well be in the interests of the finder voluntarily to incur expenditure to preserve the wreck in order to be able to maintain or reinforce a salvage claim under ss.521 or 525.

   Paragraph 22(e) contains a specific provision to deal with the recovery of sums under s.518 in Scottish law. Section 518 makes the amount recoverable summarily in a magistrates' court in England and Wales as a civil debt. For Scotland it is apparently unnecessary for any special procedure to be mentioned and it is sufficient for s.518 and diligence that the sum be treated as a debt (see also paras. 44, 45, 51, 65, 66 below). Note also paras. 75–77 on Scottish procedure.

   Paragraph 23 updates s.520 of the 1894 Act in relation to the action which has to be taken by receivers to publicise the taking possession of a wreck by them. Section 520(1) originally required the receiver to post a description of the wreck and any marks in the nearest customs house to where the wreck was found or seized. This was designed to allow the owners to find out about their lost property, but probably has little significance today. The new subpara. (a) merely requires the receiver to make a "record" and this may well be kept centrally (*cf.* para. 33, amending s.551(1)). It will probably be as useful to archaeologists as owners, particularly as inspection is to be free of charge. Subparagraph (b) reflects the fact that the person with most interest in a wreck is likely to be the insurer of it (see Dromgoole and Gaskell, "Interests in Wreck", *op. cit.*, pp. 366–375). The 1894 provision required notice to be given to Lloyd's when the value of the wreck exceeded £20: that figure has now been increased to £5000. Of course, there may be plenty of underwriters who are not based at Lloyd's, although it would be quite common for insurance companies to have a line on a Lloyd's slip.

A number of wreck provisions are removed altogether by the 1993 Act. Section 528 (omitted by para. 26) allowed the Secretary of State to purchase rights to a wreck. It is not clear if this was ever used as a compulsory purchase provision, but the state no longer exercises the power. It is not clear, either, exactly why the provision was repealed. If there is no restriction on the extent to which the state could contract to buy wrecks in the ordinary way, the provision was surplussage. If specific power was needed, there may well be occasions in the future when it is in the national interest to purchase historic wrecks but where no power will exist. Section 529 (omitted by para. 27), dealing with powers of those exercising Admiralty jurisdiction, has no significance today. Section 543 (omitted by para. 29), dealt with the marking of anchors, a subject now dealt with by the Anchors and Chain Cables Act 1967 and which in future will be dealt with by regulation (on the repeal of the 1967 Act by Sched. 5). Sections 558–564 (omitted by para. 34), dealt with salvage by naval vessels, particularly overseas. The decline in size of the navy and the existence of specialist salvors means that there is little call for such work, at least for that which would involve special procedures. The Crown Proceedings Act 1947, s.8 now regulates salvage claims by or against Crown vessels and there is nothing to prevent the Crown making use of standard contracts such as the Lloyd's Open Form Salvage Agreement 1990.

There are a number of specific amendments designed to remove anachronistic references in the 1894 Act. Paragraph 19 repeals a delightful provision from another era (s.514 of the Merchant Shipping Act 1894), which gave the receiver of a wreck the right to suppress plunder! Wreck law is more concerned today with the environment and underwater archaeology than it is with deliberate plunder. Paragraph 20 removes a similarly anachronistic reference to persons riotously and tumultuously assembled to plunder. For riots, see now the Public Order Act 1986. Section 524(1) deals with claims and notices by purported owners of wreck. The wording is changed by para. 25 to remove specific references to Lords of the Manor and the like, but does not effect a change of substance. A number of other paragraphs increase figures in the 1894 Act which have become hopelessly outdated (see, *e.g.* s.522(a) (para. 24); s.537(2) (para. 28); and ss.552(3), 555(1) and 556 (para. 30)).

Paras. 35–55
Lighthouses, etc.

Paragraphs 35–55 deal with the general issue of lighthouse authorities. There are a large number of general amendments and many dealing with light dues. The miscellaneous provisions will be mentioned first.

Paragraphs 36, 52 and 54 repeal provisions which applied to colonies. Those matters will be dealt with in the consolidation by the powers given in para. 4, above. See also para. 47, necessary because the Harbours Act 1964, s.29 (which abolished the fixing of light dues by Order) did not extend to Northern Ireland. Paragraph 50 modernises the offence in s.666 of the Merchant Shipping Act 1894, of damaging lighthouses, lightships, buoys or the automatic beacons that are widely used at sea. As a consequence, para. 35 repeals superfluous provisions in the Malicious Damage Act 1861. There are many modern appliances, often unstaffed, that now do the work of lighthouses and lightships. Paragraph 39 makes it clear that additions to lighthouses under s.642 include radio beacons and racons. Section 638(1) of the 1894 Act gave a lighthouse authority power to construct a lighthouse, etc., with all requisite roads and appurtenances. Under s.654(3) the appurtenances would pass on sale to the acquirer (and see s.33 of the Ports Act 1991). Paragraph 37 makes general, throughout Pt. IX, references to appurtenances, as opposed to it referring only to s.638. Paragraph 38 modernises the land acquisition references to take account of the current practices under the Compulsory Purchase Act 1965. Section 667 deals with the powers of a General Lighthouse Authority (GLA) to prevent misleading lights being used in the vicinity of a lighthouse. Paragraph 51 removes the mischief of burning fires from the section.

The Harbours Act 1964, s.29(2) gives local lighthouse authorities the power to levy light dues on ships to help defray the costs of running the service, but the power of a GLA under the 1894 Act arises only by implication. For the consolidation it was thought that it was necessary to include express powers and this is done by para. 40 (see also ss.41–45 of and Sched. 5 to the Merchant Shipping Act 1988 on the financing and administration of the lighthouse service). Paragraph 41 allows the GLA to require the provision of information to it so that it can calculate the dues payable. These powers did not exist before under the 1894 Act. Effectively, it is the harbour authority which will be the likely source of the information, but the shipowner may also be required to give it. As noted above, in relation to a wreck, the practice of posting information at customs houses no longer operates as a reliable source of shipping knowledge. Paragraph 42 now requires the display of light dues tables at the GLA's central office and at the offices of the local collector of dues. Paragraph 55 amends the charging procedure under the Harbours Act 1964, s.30(2) for local lighthouse authorities which are not harbour authorities.

The payment of light dues has always been enforced through customs officers requiring the production of a receipt before giving clearance to the ship and allowing it to sail. The assumption in s.651 of the 1894 Act (and s.648) has been that the receipt will be given by the local collector, who in turn pays the GLA. It appears that, in practice, payment is often made directly to the GLA and paras. 43 and 46 recognise this fact by obliging the GLA to give a receipt. Paragraph 44 deals with the mode of recovering light dues throughout the U.K. under s.649(1) (and see the note to para. 22, above). Section 650 gives the collector of dues the power to levy distress in respect of moveables on the ship. A number of changes are made by para. 45 to the procedures envisaged. Guns cannot be distrained. The period of non-payment after which distraint can be exercised is increased from three to five days. Valuation is no longer to be by a process of "appraisal", but by independent valuation and sale at auction. The local lighthouse authorities need no longer send accounts to the DOT as required by s.656(2) (see para. 48). However, under para. 49, GLA's are to be obliged to account to the DOT for other sources of income, *e.g.* property. Paragraph 53 reforms the auditing requirements of s.679 to accord with contemporary practice.

Paras. 56 and 57
Enforcement powers
Inspectors are appointed to report on various matters under s.728 of the 1894 Act, although the powers once contained in s.729 have been replaced by those in the Merchant Shipping Act 1979, s.27. It appears that some problems were anticipated on consolidation and so paras. 56 and 57 achieve some harmonisation. The Merchant Shipping Act 1988, Sched. 7 repealed the power of inspectors to make reports on accidents at sea under s.728(a). That repeal is prevented from coming into force. Subparagraph (b) rewords the power to inquire into compliance with the Merchant Shipping Acts generally to take into account the wider requirements of modern merchant shipping legislation, often made by statutory instrument.

Paras. 58–77
Legal proceedings
Paragraphs 58–77 deal with a variety of matters relating to legal proceedings, *e.g.* criminal jurisdiction.

Section 686 of the 1894 Act allowed British subjects to be prosecuted for offences on ships almost anywhere in the world, *e.g.* on British ships on the high seas, in foreign ports, or on foreign ships to which they did not "belong" (*cf. R.* v. *Keyn; Franconia, The* (1876) 46 LJMC 17). Foreigners could be prosecuted for offences on board British ships on the high seas. Paragraph 61 is designed to reduce what has been described as an extraordinary jurisdiction in two ways. First, it restricts the criminal jurisdiction to British citizens as defined in the British Nationality Act 1981, Pt. I. This means that the personal jurisdiction is founded on having a link with the U.K. closer than that envisaged in the days of empire when British subjects included a variety of persons with allegiance to the Crown, *e.g.* commonwealth citizens (see *Temperley*, p. 4, note 1 and the General Note to s.3(1) of the Merchant Shipping Act 1988, in *Current Law Statutes Annotated* 1988). Secondly, the criminal jurisdiction will extend only to offences on U.K. ships (*i.e.* U.K. registered ships, see para. 1, above). Presumably, this amendment may be read subject to the power granted by para. 5, above, *e.g.* in respect of unregistered ships.

It seems that nineteenth century legislation did not draw the same distinctions that modern legislation does between conferring (i) local criminal jurisdiction over offences committed outside the U.K. and (ii) making acts done outside the U.K. offences against U.K. law. The assumption seems to have been that doing the former implied the latter. Thus, s.687 makes seamen employed on British ships liable for offences committed afloat or ashore outside the U.K. Apparently, the section is treated in practice as an offence-making provision. Paragraph 62 restates the section in the modern form used in, *e.g.* the Civil Aviation Act 1982, s.92 and the Oil and Gas Enterprise Act 1982, s.22.

Merchant shipping legislation normally makes express provision for offences which may be committed by companies, *e.g.* where the shipowner is liable for having a dangerously unsafe ship under the Merchant Shipping Act 1988, s.30. There is not much point in fining a company if the senior management cannot also be convicted for their connivance in the companies breaches. Accordingly, it is now usual to have a provision creating offences by the officers of bodies corporate (see, *e.g.* s.51 of the Merchant Shipping Act 1988, and the comments on it in *Current Law Statutes Annotated* 1988). The 1988 Act, Sched. 5 extended the provision to regulations made under the Merchant Shipping Act 1979. Paragraph 63 of Sched. 4 to the 1993 Act now unifies the provisions for all the Merchant Shipping Acts and delegated legislation both for England and Wales and Scotland.

Section 689 of the 1894 Act gives power, which is occasionally used, to British consular officers to order a master to allow an offender to be transported back to the U.K. for trial. Paragraph 64 amends the requirement so that a discretion is given where there are more convenient or less expensive means of transport (*e.g.* air).

Section 693 of the 1894 Act and s.20 of the Prevention of Oil Pollution Act 1971 allow for certain sums to be levied against a ship by distress but, as this system is not known in Scottish law, separate provision is made by paras. 65 and 66 (and see the note to para. 22, above).

Paragraph 67 makes three small changes to the evidentiary requirements set out in s.695 of the 1894 Act.

A number of provisions in the 1894 Act deal with the service of documents. Paragraph 68 provides a modern uniform version to replace s.696. Separate provision is already made for Scotland in ss.66 and 312(v) of the Criminal Procedure (Scotland) Act 1975 and so para. 69 disapplies s.697 to Scotland.

Section 76 of the 1894 Act deals with the appropriate procedure for forfeiture of a ship under the Merchant Shipping Acts. Paragraph 70 amends it by removing the power to award detaining officers' expenses out of the proceeds of sale and by making it clear that officers can be criminally (though not civilly) liable for their actions.

The Forgery and Counterfeiting Act 1981 repealed ss.66, 695 and 722(1) of the 1894 Act, as respects England and Wales. Paragraphs 71–73 replace the provisions with more appropriate language for Scotland.

The necessary *mens rea* for offences has been expressed differently over the years and para. 74 effects a general change from the use of the word "wilfully" to "intentionally" and from "suffering" or "allowing" a thing to be done to "permitting" it to be done.

Paras. 75–77
Scottish procedure

A number of procedural rules, *e.g.* relating to warrants, the utility of which has always been open to doubt, are repealed by para. 75. It also appears that offences were never punishable at the instance or direction of the Lord Advocate, as suggested in s.710. The provision is amended by para. 76 to reflect Scottish law more accurately. Paragraph 77 amends the Merchant Shipping Act 1974, Sched. 5, para. 5 to use appropriate Scottish terms.

Para. 78

It is no longer desired to regulate the activities of surveyors by regulation, as set out in s.724, and para. 78 amends the section accordingly.

Para. 79

It is common for merchant shipping legislation to provide for the payment of fees (see, *e.g.* the Merchant Shipping Act 1979, s.51(2)) and fees regulations are issued regularly. Paragraph 79 provides for a uniform general fee prescribing power which will apply in all cases, except for ship registration (see s.3(2)(l), above). Existing provisions will ultimately be repealed.

Section 8(4)   SCHEDULE 5

Repeals

Part I

Repeals consequential on this Act

Chapter	Short title	Extent of repeal
1894 c. 60.	Merchant Shipping Act 1894.	Section 4(1) and (3). Sections 5 to 18. Sections 20 to 38.

Chapter	Short title	Extent of repeal
		Sections 47 to 53B.
		Sections 56 to 60.
		Section 61(2).
		Sections 62 to 65.
		Sections 67 to 70.
		Sections 72 to 74.
		In section 422(1)(b), the words "of the port to which she belongs, and also".
		Section 694.
		Section 698.
		Schedule 1 Part II.
1898 c. 44.	Merchant Shipping (Mercantile Marine Fund) Act 1898.	Section 3.
1906 c. 48.	Merchant Shipping Act 1906.	Sections 50 and 53.
1921 c. 8.	Merchant Shipping Act 1921.	Section 1(1)(3).
1983 c. 13.	Merchant Shipping Act 1983.	Section 5.
		Sections 7 and 8.
		Section 9(1).
		Sections 10 and 11.
		The Schedule.
1988 c. 12.	Merchant Shipping Act 1988.	Sections 1 to 10.
		In section 11(3), the words "under Part I of the 1894 Act".
		Sections 12 to 25.
		In section 47(7), the definition of "the registration enactments".
		Schedule 1 except paragraph 48.
		Schedules 2 and 3.
		In Schedule 6, the entries relating to the—
		Contracts of Employment and Redundancy Payments Act (Northern Ireland) 1965;
		Sea Fish (Conservation) Act 1967;
		Sea Fisheries Act 1968;
		Fishing Vessels (Safety Provisions) Act 1970;
		Fishery Limits Act 1976;
		Employment Protection (Consolidation) Act 1978;
		Customs and Excise Management Act 1979;
		British Fishing Boats Act 1983;
		Merchant Shipping Act 1983;
		Inshore Fishing (Scotland) Act 1984; and Safety at Sea Act 1986.

PART II

PRE-CONSOLIDATION REPEALS

Chapter	Short title	Extent of repeal
1854 c. 120.	Merchant Shipping Repeal Act 1854.	Section 7.
1861 c. 97.	Malicious Damage Act 1861.	Sections 47 and 48.

Chapter	Short title	Extent of repeal
1894 c. 60.	Merchant Shipping Act 1894.	Section 75.
		In section 76, in subsection (1), the words from "and may award" to the end and, in subsection (2), the words "either" and "or criminally".
		Sections 83, 86 and 87.
		Section 126.
		In section 282(a) the words "knowingly and".
		Sections 284 to 286.
		In section 287(1), paragraphs (f) and (g).
		Section 356.
		Section 359.
		Sections 366 and 367.
		Sections 418 and 419.
		Section 421.
		Sections 427 to 433.
		Section 436.
		Sections 446 to 448 and 450.
		Section 458(2)(b).
		Sections 459 to 462.
		Section 478.
		Sections 480 to 490.
		Section 514.
		In section 515, the words "and tumultuously".
		In section 516(2), the words "and shall place the same in the custody of the receiver".
		Section 517.
		In section 518(a), the words "of the district".
		Section 526.
		Sections 528 and 529.
		Section 543.
		Sections 547 to 549.
		Section 550.
		In section 551(1), the words from "of the district" to "made".
		Section 554.
		Sections 558 to 565.
		In section 634(1), the words "and the Channel Islands", "and at Gibraltar" and "and the Isle of Man".
		In section 650(1), the word "guns".
		Section 655 (so far as in force in Northern Ireland).
		In section 656(2), the words from "and shall" (where first occurring) to the end.
		In section 667, the words "fire" and "burnt" wherever occurring together with the word "or" in conjunction with either of those words.
		Section 669.
		Section 676(1)(c).
		In section 677(1)(f), the words "on account of the property of deceased seamen or".
		Section 686(2).
		In section 689(3), the words from "and that officer" to the end.
		Section 694.
		Sections 698 to 700.

Chapter	Short title	Extent of repeal
		In section 702, the words "Subject to section 703 of this Act", the words from "or criminal" to "sheriff court", and "and with imprisonment in default of payment" and the words from "or in the case" to the end.
		Sections 704 to 709.
		Section 716.
		Section 719.
		Section 724(3) and (5) except, in subsection (3), the words "may remove any surveyors of ships".
		Sections 733 and 734.
		Section 737.
		Schedule 20 so far as unrepealed.
1898 c. 44.	Merchant Shipping (Mercantile Marine Fund) Act 1898.	Section 2(3), (4) and (5).
		Section 7.
		In Schedule 3, the entry for the lighthouse on Cape Pembroke, Falkland Islands.
1906 c. 48.	Merchant Shipping Act 1906.	Sections 2 and 6.
		Sections 15 and 16.
		Section 27.
		Section 44.
		Section 49.
		Section 58.
		Section 77
1923 c. 4.	Fees (Increase) Act 1923.	The whole Act.
1925 c. 37.	Merchant Shipping (Equivalent Provisions) Act 1925.	The whole Act.
1932 c. 9.	Merchant Shipping (Safety and Load Line Conventions) Act 1932.	Section 12.
		Section 27.
		Sections 29 to 31.
		Section 36.
1934 c. 18.	Illegal Trawling (Scotland) Act 1934.	Section 2.
		In section 6, the definitions of "fishing boat" and "voyage".
1949 c. 43.	Merchant Shipping (Safety Convention) Act 1949.	Sections 1 to 6.
		Section 19.
		Section 21.
		Section 23.
		Sections 27 to 30.
		Section 33.
		Section 35(4) and (6).
		In section 36(1), the definitions of "collision regulations", "construction rules", "principal Act", "radio navigational aid", "radio rules", "rules for direction finders", "rules for life-saving equipment", and "United Kingdom ship".
		Schedule 2.
1958 c. 62.	Merchant Shipping (Liability of Shipowners and Others) Act 1958.	Section 11 so far as applying to the Merchant Shipping (Liability of Shipowners and Others) Act 1900 (c. 32).
1964 c. 47.	Merchant Shipping Act 1964.	Section 2.
		Section 8.
		Section 10.
		Section 15.
1965 c. 47.	Merchant Shipping Act 1965.	Section 6.

Chapter	Short title	Extent of repeal
1967 c. 27.	Merchant Shipping (Load Lines) Act 1967.	Sections 26, 27(2), 28 and 29.
1967 c. 64.	Anchors and Chain Cables Act 1967.	The whole Act.
1970 c. 27.	Fishing Vessels (Safety Provisions) Act 1970.	Section 4(4). Section 6. Section 8. In section 9(1), the definitions of "collision regulations", "fishing vessel", "radio rules", "rules for direction finders", "rules for life-saving appliances" and "rules for radio navigational aids".
1970 c. 36.	Merchant Shipping Act 1970.	Section 6. In section 17, in subsection (10), the words "Ministry of Home Affairs for Northern Ireland" and, in subsection (11), the words "the Ministry of Home Affairs for Northern Ireland or". Section 19. Section 84. Section 87. Section 90. Sections 92 to 94. Section 95(6).
1971 c. 59.	Merchant Shipping (Oil Pollution) Act 1971.	Section 11(3)(a). Section 18.
1971 c. 60.	Prevention of Oil Pollution Act 1971.	Section 18 except in its application to sections 2(1) and 3. Section 22. Section 25(1).
1974 c. 43.	Merchant Shipping Act 1974.	Section 20. Section 22. In Schedule 5, in paragraph 5(g), the words from "including" to the end.
1977 c. 24.	Merchant Shipping (Safety Convention) Act 1977.	The whole Act.
1979 c. 39.	Merchant Shipping Act 1979.	Section 19(2) and (3). In section 20(3)(b), the words from "and the payment" to the end. Section 21(3)(r). Sections 46 and 47.
1981 c. 10.	Merchant Shipping Act 1981.	In section 4(2) the words from the beginning to "that section; and".
1984 c. 5.	Merchant Shipping Act 1984.	Section 13.
1986 c. 23.	Safety at Sea Act 1986.	Sections 1 to 6. Section 9(4). In section 13(1), the definition of "fishing vessel". Section 14.
1988 c. 12.	Merchant Shipping Act 1988.	Section 34. Sections 50 and 51. Section 54. Section 56. Schedule 4. In Schedule 5, paragraph 4 of the amendments of the 1894 Act.

Saving

Notwithstanding the repeal by this Act of the following provisions, instruments in force immediately before the repeal under the provisions specified in the left-hand column shall continue in force until superseded by regulations under section 21 of the 1979 Act (safety regulations) and the related provisions specified in the right-hand column shall continue in force for the purposes of those instruments:

Empowering provision		*Related provisions*
1894 Act: section 427	—	Section 430.
1949 Act: section 3	—	Sections 3(5) and (6) and 28.
section 21	—	Section 21(3).
1964 Act: section 2	—	—
1967 Act (c. 64): section 1	—	Section 1(2) and (3).
1977 Act: section 2	—	—

INDEX

References are to sections and Schedule numbers

ASYLUM AND IMMIGRATION APPEALS ACT 1993*

(1993 c. 23)

ARRANGEMENT OF SECTIONS

An Act to make provision about persons who claim asylum in the United Kingdom and their dependants; to amend the law with respect to certain rights of appeal under the Immigration Act 1971; and to extend the provisions of the Immigration (Carriers' Liability) Act 1987 to transit passengers. [1st July 1993]

PARLIAMENTARY DEBATES
Hansard, H.C. Vol. 213, col. 21; Vol. 216, cols. 637, 727; Vol. 226, col. 26; H.L. Vol. 541, col. 1147; Vol. 542, cols. 533, 536, 619, 767, 769, 788, 839, 1024, 1087; Vol. 543, cols. 343, 540, 617, 643, 1151; Vol. 547, col. 935.
The Bill was discussed in Standing Committee A between November 10 and December 15, 1992.

INTRODUCTION AND GENERAL NOTE
This Act originated in the Asylum Bill, which was presented to the House of Commons by the then Home Secretary, Kenneth Baker, on November 13, 1991. It was introduced to achieve three main purposes. The first was to accelerate the process of immigration control to cope with the growth in the number of asylum-seekers, the second to deal with what the Home Secretary described as: "... blatant misuse of the asylum procedures" (*Hansard*, H.C. Vol. 198, col. 1094), and the third was to extend rights of appeal for asylum–seekers. There was, at that time, a widely shared perception of the inadequacy of the appeal process for asylum-seekers under the Immigration Act 1971. The Bill included provisions for the fingerprinting of asylum-seekers

*Annotations by Dr Christopher Vincenzi, University of Huddersfield. The writer acknowledges with thanks the valuable assistance of David Marrington, LL.B., Immigration Consultant of Oldham.

to avoid multiple applications and limited the obligations of local housing authorities in relation to the provision of emergency housing to asylum-seekers and their dependants. It met considerable opposition, especially in the House of Lords, largely because it was thought that the new appeal procedures gave insufficient opportunity for those refused asylum to challenge decisions effectively. The Bill was lost when Parliament was dissolved, prior to the general election, in March 1992.

When the Bill was re-presented to the new Parliament in November 1992, significant additions had been made affecting the appeal rights of visitors, short-term and prospective students and their dependants and its title had been changed to reflect its broader character. Concern was expressed in both Houses about the loss of appeal rights under s.10 and an amendment introduced in the House of Lords to monitor the effect of abolition was accepted in a modified form by the Government (see s.13(3AA) of the 1971 Act as inserted by s.10 of this Act). The focus had moved to a more general one of improving: "the efficiency and the speed of the operation of the immigration system. [The Bill] seeks to ensure that resources are used more effectively in deciding questions which really matter" (Lord Ferrars, *Hansard*, H.L. Vol. 541, col. 1147). One of the most important, and least discussed, changes in the Bill was the abolition of appeal rights in "mandatory" refusal cases under s.11. Although these were presented by the Government as "hopeless" appeals which, in certain circumstances such as the absence of relevant documents, or the age or nationality of the appellant, required a refusal by an immigration officer, such facts, or their interpretation, may not be beyond dispute. Lord Donaldson of Lymington, the former Master of the Rolls, expressed his surprise at what he described as "either a naïvety or an arrogance in the attitude of the Home Office that its immigration officers must inevitably be right" (*Hansard*, H.L. Vol. 541, col. 1170).

The main thrust of the original Bill as a measure designed to prevent abuses of the system and to improve the way in which asylum applications are dealt with remains. The principal change from the 1991 Bill in relation to asylum applications is the abolition of the requirement for leave to appeal before the appeal to a special adjudicator can be commenced. However, an element of the "fast track" process that characterised the 1991 Bill remains in relation to those claims which are certified by the Secretary of State as being "without foundation" on the grounds that the application does not raise issues relating to the Geneva Convention or is otherwise "frivolous or vexatious" (Sched. 2, para. 5). In such cases there will only be an appeal to a special adjudicator appointed under the Act, and no further appeal. In all other cases (except non-asylum-seekers without a right of appeal under s.5(1) of the Immigration Act 1988), it will be possible to appeal, with leave, on a point of law, to the Immigration Appeal Tribunal and the Court of Appeal (or, in Scotland, the Court of Session). This is a significant innovation for both asylum and non-asylum appeals and should reduce the number of applications for judicial review of immigration cases, were it not for the fact that abolition of appeal rights for visitors, short-term students, their dependants and for "mandatory refusal" cases by ss.10 and 11 is likely to lead to a whole new category of such applications.

Concern about time-limits for appeals appears at least partly to have been met by amendments to the Appeals Procedure Rules, so that the time-limit for giving notice of appeal is now ten days instead of the two days allowed in the draft Appeals Procedure Rules 1991 (see now, para. 5(1) of the Asylum Appeals (Procedure) Rules 1993 (S.I. 1993 No. 1661) (reproduced as Appendix 2 to these annotations), except where the Secretary of State certifies that the claim is "frivolous or vexatious" or "without foundation". Here the time-limit for serving notice of appeal remains at two days (*ibid.*, para. 5(2)).

Attempts to provide special protection for young, unaccompanied asylum-seekers, although successful in the House of Lords, were subsequently frustrated when the Bill returned to the Commons (*Hansard*, H.C. Vol. 226, col. 52). As a concession, however, the Government agreed to fund a non-statutory panel established and administered by the Refugee Council. This panel will provide support and assistance to child asylum-seekers and will liaise with the relevant local authority social services department. Although there is now no provision for this in the Act, the new Immigration Rules (H.C. 725) (see Appendix 1), which came into effect on July 26, 1993, contain, in paras. 180P, 180Q, and 180R rules as to the way in which unaccompanied children are to be treated, with a general direction that "close attention should be given to the welfare of the child at all times".

Under the Immigration Act 1971 ("the 1971 Act") the primary difficulty for asylum-seekers has been that, under s.13(3), if they are refused asylum at the port of entry, they can only appeal against refusal of leave from abroad if they have no entry clearance. An entitlement to be considered under the Convention does not confer on an applicant a right to remain until a decision is given (*Bugdaycay* v. *Secretary of State for the Home Department*; *Nelidow Santis* v. *Same*; *Norman* v. *Same*; *Musisi, Re* [1987] 1 A.C. 514). An appeal from abroad in such circumstances is clearly of limited value. Although judicial review is available, despite the failure of the applicant to exhaust the appeals process (*R.* v. *Chief Immigration Officer, Gatwick Airport*, ex p. *Kharrazi* [1980] 1 W.L.R. 1396) it can only examine *the way* in which the decision has been reached and not the *merits* of the case (see *Bugdaycay* above). The Act addresses this problem by prohibiting the removal of asylum claimants while their claims are being considered and during the appeal process (s.6 and paras. 8 and 9 of Sched. 2) and by conferring upon them a specific right of appeal through a new, and separate, appeal system, to a special adjudicator and from thence, with leave, to the Immigration Appeal Tribunal and to the Court of Appeal or, in Scotland, to the Court of Session (ss.8, 9 and Sched. 2). The new process is intended to create a system under which, with the exception of those claimants whose claims are certified by the Home Secretary as either "unfounded" or "frivolous or vexatious" under para. 5(3) of Sched. 2, the merits of each applicant's claim under the Geneva Convention can be fully examined.

A further difficulty for asylum applicants has been that under the unamended Immigration Rules (H.C. 251, March 1990), although requiring that "where a person is a refugee full account is to be taken of the Geneva Convention and Protocol relating to the Status of Refugees (Cmnd. 9171 and Cmnd. 3096)", such consideration did not have to be given until the applicant had reached the U.K. This accords with the obligation of the U.K. to refrain from *refoulement*, the return of a refugee to "the frontiers of territories where his life or freedom would be threatened on account of his race, religion, nationality, membership of a particular social group or political opinion" (Art. 33 of the Geneva Convention; see the General Note to s.2). The new Rules (paras. 75, 75A, 75B and 75C) (H.C. 725) (see Appendix 1) also appear to be predicated on a port application. Only port applications have to be referred to the Home Secretary and a condition for the grant of asylum under para. 180B(a) of the new Immigration Rules is that the applicant "is in the United Kingdom or has arrived at a port of entry in the United Kingdom". There will therefore continue to be no obligation to consider applications made to British posts abroad, although, the Home Secretary may, as he has recently done in relation to Bosnia, consider applications from abroad as an extra-statutory concession.

For individuals without prior entry clearance, the prospect of reaching this country to make a claim for asylum has been diminished by the Immigration (Carriers Liability) Act 1987 which can result in the imposition of severe penalties on airlines and shipping companies bringing passengers to the U.K. without clearance or an entitlement to enter. As a consequence, many applicants arrive with forged or stolen documents. Critics of the Bill, who objected that the 1987 Act effectively relegated the exclusion or admission of asylum claimants to carriers, were told that it was not an obligation of the Geneva Convention "to encourage or facilitate the ability of would-be applicants to travel to a particular country to claim asylum" (Parliamentary Under Secretary of State for the Home Department, Standing Committee A, col. 481, December 1, 1992). The new Immigration Rules (see Appendix 1, below) are, however, intended to ensure that the need to use some form of deception to secure entry should not work to the disadvantage of the genuine asylum-seeker, provided that "a reasonable explanation" is offered and "a prompt and full disclosure made" where false representations, either orally or in writing have been used (paras. 180F and 180G(b)).

For individuals who have obtained prior entry clearance for some other purpose, to come, for example as a visitor or student, the application for asylum can be made on or after entry and the appeal can be heard in the usual way if refugee status is refused. Applicants are expected to apply for asylum "forthwith" upon arrival (*ibid.*, para. 180G(a)). In the case of those who become *refugees sur place*, that is, their return has become dangerous after having been given leave and after having entered the country, the applicant should apply as soon as he becomes aware of the circumstances that put him at risk. In such cases the application will be to vary the existing leave to enable the applicant to remain as a refugee. Under the new provisions, an appeal against a refusal to vary leave on asylum grounds will go to a special adjudicator under the Act (s.8(2)). Unsuccessful in-state applications could now result in revocation or curtailment of any existing leave (s.7). The Minister, however, made it clear that such a course would not be automatic and would usually only be followed if the asylum application raised doubts about the genuineness of the circumstances surrounding the grant of the original leave (Standing Committee A, col. 415, December 1, 1992, Mr Charles Wardle).

The decision on whether or not a person seeking asylum is to be granted refugee status will remain with the Home Secretary, who has regard to the views of the United Nations High Commissioner for refugees, "reports of the refugee unit of his own Department compiled from sources such as press articles, journals and Amnesty International publications, and also information supplied to him by the Foreign Office" (see *R.* v. *Home Secretary*, ex p. *Sivakumaran*; *Same* v. *Same*, ex p. *Vaithialingam*; *Same* v. *Same*, ex p. *Vilvarajah*; *Same* v. *Same*, ex p. *Vathanan*; *Same* v. *Same*, ex p. *Rasalingam*; *Same* v. *Same*, ex p. *Navaratnaam* (*United Nations High Commissioner for Refugees intervening*) [1988] 1 A.C. 958 at 995 (Lord Keith)). The High Commissioner is closely involved in monitoring the treatment of refugees and the U.K. Representative of the United Nations Commissioner has the right to be treated as a party to an appeal under para. 8(2) of the Asylum Appeals Procedure Rules (see Appendix 2, below). The procedure for dealing with asylum-seekers and the criteria for dealing with them are contained in the new Immigration Rules (H.C. 725) (see Appendix 1). A failure to adhere to the Rules will ground an appeal under s.19 of the 1971 Act, but any inconsistency between the Rules and the Geneva Convention should, under s.1 of the Act, be resolved in favour of the Convention.

Advice to asylum-seekers, assistance with interviews and with the completion of the asylum questionnaire form (PAQ) will still be available on legal aid, although there had been some indication during the debates on the 1991 Asylum Bill that this would be withdrawn (*Hansard*, H.L. Vol. 535, col. 459). Help that was previously available from the U.K. Immigrants' Advisory Service, which closed in 1992, is now available from the Home Office funded Refugee Legal Centre.

Main provisions of the Act

Section 1 defines a claim for asylum by reference to the U.N. Convention relating to the Status of Refugees.

Section 2 provides that the provisions of the Geneva Convention prevail over any inconsistent provisions of the Immigration Rules.

Section 3 provides for a person who has made a claim for asylum to be required to have his fingerprints taken, or to attend for fingerprinting, and empowers an immigration officer or constable to arrest without warrant a person who fails to comply with a requirement to attend.

Sections 4 and 5 modify the duties of housing authorities under the homelessness legislation in relation to asylum-seekers and their dependants while a decision on the asylum claim is pending.

Section 6 protects a person from removal, or being required to leave, while his claim to asylum is under consideration.

Section 7 enables the Secretary of State to curtail the leave of a person with limited leave to enter or remain whose application for asylum has been refused, and to order the detention of such a person pending his deportation.

Section 8 provides a right of appeal in cases where a claim for asylum is refused.

Section 9 provides for a right of appeal on a point of law to the Court of Appeal or the Court of Sessions from a final determination of the Immigration Appeal Tribunal in an asylum case.

Section 10 abolishes the right of appeal of visitors, short-term and prospective students and their dependants against refusal of leave to enter or of an entry clearance.

Section 11 removes the right of appeal against a refusal of leave to enter or of an entry clearance, and the right of appeal against the refusal to vary leave to enter or remain where the refusal is mandatory under the Immigration Rules.

Section 12 amends the 1987 Act to enable the Secretary of State to require by order that certain transit passengers are to hold entry clearance and to impose penalties on carriers for failure to comply.

Commencement and Transitional Provisions

Section 1 (except in so far as it related to ss.4–11), 2, 3, 12, 13, 14 and 15 became effective on July 1, 1993. The remainder of the Act came into effect on July 26, 1993 by virtue of the Asylum and Immigration Appeals Act 1993 (Commencement and Transitional Provisions) Order 1993 (S.I. 1993 No. 1655 (C.31)).

However, the new appeal rights created by s.8 of the Act do not apply to decisions refusing leave to enter the U.K., decisions to vary or to refuse to vary leave, to make or refuse to revoke a deportation order, or to remove a person from the U.K., made before July 26, 1993. Appeals against final determinations of the Immigration Appeal Tribunal to the Court of Appeal or Court of Session (s.9) will not be available in relation to determinations given by the Tribunal before July 26, 1993. The loss of appeal rights resulting from ss.10 and 11 will apply to refusals of leave to enter, refusal of entry clearance or refusal to vary leave made on or after the same date.

Extent

The Act extends to Northern Ireland (s.15(2)) and may, by Order in Council under s.15(1), be extended to any of the Channel Islands and the Isle of Man.

Immigration Rules

Amendments to give effect to the Act

These amendments to the Rules are contained in H.C. 725 and came into effect on July 26, 1993. A copy is contained in Appendix 1 at the end of these annotations. They are referred to throughout the annotations as "the new Immigration Rules".

Appeals Procedure Rules

The new immigration appeals procedures under the Act are contained in the Asylum Appeals (Procedure) Rules 1993 (S.I. 1993 No. 1661) and the Immigration Appeals (Procedure) Amendment Rules 1993 (S.I. 1993 No. 1662). Copies of both sets of Rules are attached as Appendix 2 to these annotations. These Rules came into effect on July 26, 1993. Statutory Instrument 1993 No. 1661 is referred to hereafter as "the new Appeals Procedure Rules".

ABBREVIATIONS

The Act	: the Asylum and Immigration Appeals Act 1993.
The 1971 Act	: the Immigration Act 1971.
The 1985 Act	: the Housing Act 1985.
The 1987 Act	: the Immigration (Carriers Liability) Act 1987.
The 1988 Act	: the Immigration Act 1988.
the Geneva Convention	: the Geneva Convention relating to the Status of Refugees (Geneva, July 28, 1951) and Protocol
the new Immigration Rules	: H.C. 725.

Introductory

Interpretation

1. In this Act—

"the 1971 Act" means the Immigration Act 1971;

"claim for asylum" means a claim made by a person (whether before or after the coming into force of this section) that it would be contrary to the United Kingdom's obligations under the Convention for him to be removed from, or required to leave, the United Kingdom; and

"the Convention" means the Convention relating to the Status of Refugees done at Geneva on 28th July 1951 and the Protocol to that Convention.

GENERAL NOTE

The Act amends the 1971 Act, which provides the legal basis for all decisions relating to entry, residence, deportation and appeals made by immigration officers, the Secretary of State and all officers acting under his authority (*R.* v. *Secretary of State for the Home Department*, ex p. *Oladehinde*; *R.* v. *Same*, ex p. *Alexander* [1991] 1 A.C. 254). "A claim for asylum" can, under the Rules, cover a situation in which a formal application is made and also one in which a "person subject to immigration control . . . may otherwise indicate a fear of being required to return to his country of origin or habitual residence", (para. 75 of the new Immigration Rules; see Appendix 1). Such cases should be referred to the Home Secretary together with formal requests for asylum. The actual process of granting or refusing leave under the 1971 Act remains with the immigration officer, except in those cases where "exceptional leave" is granted by the Secretary of State outside the framework of the 1971 Act and the Rules. This process remains untouched by the Act and it is envisaged that many cases which are regarded as meritorious but which fall outside the terms of the Geneva Convention will continue to be dealt with in this way.

In the case of port and "in-state" applications, a full interview with the applicant should be conducted to establish the relevant facts. Such interviews should be conducted fairly, preferably with the assistance of an adviser; "Asylum decisions are of such moment that only the highest standards of fairness will suffice" (*R.* v. *Secretary of State for the Home Department*, ex p. *Thirukumar* [1989] Imm AR 402, 414, C.A., Bingham L.J.). A record of the interview and a completed questionnaire (PAQ) will be sent to the Home Office, which will then consider the application in relation to the information available to it concerning the country from which the applicant has fled and on the basis of the U.N. High Commission for Refugees *Handbook on Procedures and Criteria for Determining Refugee Status*. Paragraph 180F of the new Immigration Rules directs that "a failure, without reasonable explanation, to make a prompt and full disclosure of material factors, either orally or in writing, or otherwise to assist the Secretary of State to the full in establishing the facts of the case may lead to the refusal of an asylum application. This includes . . . failure to complete an asylum questionnaire, or failure to comply with a request to attend an interview concerning the application".

During the period in which the claim is under consideration an applicant will normally be allowed "temporary admission" under para. 21(1) of Sched. 2 to the 1971 Act. In the case of applications which are perceived, *ab initio*, under para. 5 of Sched. 2 (below) to be "manifestly unfounded", it is likely that the applicant will be detained in custody throughout consideration of the application and exhaustion of the more limited appeal process. Once the decision has been made, it must be conveyed to the applicant. In cases of refusal there should be a further interview, at which the applicant should be reminded of what he had previously said and of those statements which formed the basis of the decision. This may involve referring a claim back to the Secretary of State where further facts come to the attention of the immigration officer at this second interview (*R*. v. *Secretary of State for the Home Department*, ex p. *Thirukumar*, (above)). Under para. 75B of the new Immigration Rules, after a final refusal of asylum is communicated to the applicant, the officer must then resume examination of the passenger to determine whether or not to grant him leave to enter under any other provision of the Rules. An applicant who is refused must be informed in writing of the decision, the reasons, his rights of appeal and how they may be exercised (para. 180N).

The new Immigration Rules contain provisions relating to "group" applications under which "if an individual is part of a group whose claims are clearly not related to the criteria for refugee status ... he may be refused without examination of his individual claim" (para. 180K). Although the rule also requires the Home Secretary to "have regard to any evidence produced by an individual to show that his claim should be distinguished from the rest of the group", there is clearly a risk that a person with different circumstances from those with whom he travelled to this country and no knowledge of English, may find that a decision is made against him without proper consideration of his individual circumstances. Article 5(1)(f) of the European Convention on Human Rights authorises detention of individuals to prevent unlawful entry and detention and examination of asylum applicants clearly falls within this provision. However, the protection is given on an *individual* basis and it is hard to see how such collective decisions would be compatible with the European Convention on Human Rights. The Act does not, of course, incorporate the European Convention but it may be used as an aid to the interpretation of, *inter alia*, immigration law (*Waddington* v. *Miah* [1974] 1 W.L.R. 693 H.L.). See also the General Note to s.2).

The scope and application of the Geneva Convention is considered in the General Note to s.2.

Primacy of Convention

2. Nothing in the immigration rules (within the meaning of the 1971 Act) shall lay down any practice which would be contrary to the Convention.

GENERAL NOTE

The object of the provisions of ss.1 and 2 is to ensure the U.K.'s compliance with the 1951 Geneva Convention relating to the Status of Refugees and the Protocol. The Geneva Convention has been held by the Court of Appeal in *R*. v. *Secretary of State for the Home Department*, ex p. *Singh (Parminder)*, *The Times*, June 8, 1987 to have been "incorporated into English law" by the Immigration Rules, although, since the Rules are not law but merely directions to immigration officers, this is probably incorrect (*R*. v. *Secretary of State for Home Affairs*, ex p. *Hosenball* [1977] 1 W.L.R. 766, C.A.). The effect of s.1(2) will not be directly to incorporate the Geneva Convention, but it will ensure that the Secretary of State is bound to observe it. Under Sched. 2, para. 1(3) of the 1971 Act, immigration officers are bound to act only in accordance with instructions given to them by the Secretary of State in a manner "consistent with the Immigration Rules". The new Immigration Rules incorporate the Geneva Convention by virtue of para. 180A which requires that: "All asylum applications will be determined by the Secretary of State in accordance with the U.K.'s obligations under the U.N.'s Convention and Protocol relating to the Status of Refugees". Decisions made by either immigration officers or the Home Secretary which are not in accordance with this country's obligations should result in a successful appeal under s.19(1)(a) of the 1971 Act (see *R*. v. *Secretary of State for the Home Department*, ex p. *Chahal*, *The Times*, October 27, 1993). The criteria for granting an application and the procedure for dealing with applications are set out in paras. 180B to 180R of the new Immigration Rules.

Attempts in Committee Stage in both the Commons (Standing Committee A, cols. 35–60, November 12, 1992) and the Lords (*Hansard*, H.L. Vol. 542, cols. 536–552) to broaden the scope of the Government's obligations to take formal account of other international conventions and agreements affecting human rights, such as the European Convention on Human Rights, the United Nations Convention against Torture and the International Covenant on Civil and Political Rights were unsuccessful. The Court in *Chahal* (above), while confirming that the 1984 United Nations Convention against Torture, and the European Convention on Human Rights were not part of national law, said that the provisions of these Conventions would ordinarily have to be taken into account. However, where there was an issue of torture, it could be assumed that that had already been considered by the Secretary of State, since, under the 1951 Geneva Convention, torture was "implicitly an aspect of persecution". (See *R*. v. *Secretary of State for the Home Department*, ex p. *Chahal*, *The Times*, October 27, 1993).

The Parliamentary Under Secretary of State for the Home Department (Mr Charles Wardle) explained the Government's reasons for excluding reference in the Act to other internation conventions by which the U.K. was bound (Standing Committee A, col. 52, November 12, 1992):

"Our asylum system is designed primarily to ensure the protection of refugees as defined in the 1951 Geneva Convention. In operating that system, we ensure that we do not breach any of the U.K.'s obligations under the other conventions, and that we respond to other compelling humanitarian factors in every case where such exist. ... The rare cases which raise issues under any of those conventions but do not fall within the 1951 Geneva Convention, are appropriately dealt with by the grant of exceptional leave to remain. That will continue to be the case".

During the period 1990 to 1991 only a small proportion of applicants were actually accepted as refugees under the Geneva Convention. "The majority–over 60 per cent. in 1991–received exceptional leave to remain. That is not the same as asylum. In some cases it may be given for genuine humanitarian reasons. Often, it is simply as a result of the delays in determining the claims that it becomes impossible to enforce a person's removal" (*per* Lord Ferrars, *Hansard*, H.L. Vol. 542, col. 546).

Individuals who are given exceptional leave are in a somewhat anomalous position. Such leave, where it is granted, is given both outside the 1971 Act and the Immigration Rules. There is no provision in the Act under which the Secretary of State may grant leave, and there would appear to be no prerogative power enabling him to do so, or to direct immigration officers to grant leave to enter in circumstances not falling within the Rules (para. 1(3) of Sched. 2 to the 1971 Act, and see C.L. Vincenzi, *Extra-Statutory Ministerial Discretion in Immigration Law* [1992] P.L. 300). Such decisions and any conditions which may be attached to them, although judicially reviewable, are not appealable to an adjudicator (*Somasundaram* v. *Entry Clearance Officer, Colombo* [1990] Imm AR 16, 19). However, a decision to refuse asylum under the Geneva Convention will itself be appealable under s.8 below. Those who are given exceptional leave do not enjoy refugee status, with the considerable benefits attached to it under both domestic and international law (see *The Law of Refugee Status*, J.C. Hathaway (1992)).

Although the European Convention on Human Rights, which is particularly relevant to the position of refugees in relation to expulsion (Arts. 5(1) and (3)), is not part of U.K. law as such, it has a growing European Community law dimension. It should also inform decisions and act as an aid to interpretation in cases of ambiguity (*R.* v. *Secretary of State for the Home Department, ex p. Brind* [1991] 1 A.C. 696). Within the formal legal decision-making process of the E.C., immigration from states outside the Community has remained firmly within the province of the national law of the Member States. Attempts by the Commission to develop a common Community immigration policy has been held to fall beyond Community competence (*Immigration of Non-Community Workers: Germany* v. *E.C. Commission* (*Nos. 281/85, 283–285/85, 287/85*) [1988] 1 C.M.L.R. 11). However, since the Single European Act 1986 and the creation of the Single European Market from January 1, 1993 which "shall comprise an area without internal frontiers in which the free movement of goods, persons, services and capital is ensured ... " (Art. 7A of the E.C. Treaty as amended by the Treaty on European Union) [emphasis added], it is arguably within the competence of the Community to regulate the movement of nationals of third states, at least once they are within the external borders of the Community.

This is the view of the Commission, although it is one that is not accepted by the British Government and is yet to be tested before the European Court of Justice. If the Court upholds the view of the Commission, then the way is open to the application of the European Convention on Human Rights to any measures taken by the Community on refugee and asylum policy, since the Court has held on several occasions that the Convention is to be regarded as legally binding in relation to powers exercised under Community law (*Nold (J.)* v. *E.C. Commission* (*No. 4/73*) [1975] E.C.R. 985). In the meantime, Community interior ministers have continued to address problems of immigration from third states outside the formal Community decision-making process, through the ad hoc group of immigration ministers or the Trevi Group of home affairs ministers. This process has been modified under the European Treaty on European Union (Maastricht Treaty), which inserted a new Art. 100C into the Treaty of Rome, under which the Council of Ministers of the European Community will be able to determine for the Community as a whole which third state nationals will require visas to enter any Member State. Such decisions will require unanimity, so that U.K. immigration and asylum policy will not be modified without the concurrence of the Government. However, under new Art. 100C(2), under a majority vote, a Community visa policy may be introduced in "an emergency situation in a third country posing a threat of a sudden inflow of nationals from that country into the Community".

The inter-governmental process has already produced the Dublin Convention Determining the State Responsible for Examining Applications for Asylum lodged in one of the Member States of June 15, 1990 (reproduced in [1990] Imm AR 604). To date, only five states have ratified the Convention, but it is, nonetheless, being applied by the British Government. A number of asylum-seekers have unsuccessfully challenged decisions to return them to other Member States of the Community which would have no obligation to deal with their applications under the criteria laid down in Arts. 4 to 8 of the Convention. These decisions have been partly based on a perceived "connection" with the Member State, even where the asylum-seeker has only passed through that State as a transit passenger (*R.* v. *Secretary of State for the Home Department*, ex p. *Karali* [1991] Imm AR 199) and partly on a Home Office policy statement by the then Home Secretary, David Waddington, on July 25, 1990 (reproduced in full in [1990] Imm AR 573 (note) and see E. Guild, *Towards an European Asylum Law*, Imm. and Nat. L. & P. 1993, Vol. 7, No. 3, p.88).

In his statement the Minister said that the Refugee Convention:

"is an investment of last resort–not a licence for refugees to travel the world in search of an ideal place of residence. . . . Accordingly, an application for asylum from a country other than the country in which he fears persecution will not normally be considered substantively. The passenger will be returned to the country from which he embarked, or to another country in which he has been since he left the country of feared persecution. . . . However, in consider-ing any individual case I shall take into account any evidence of substantial links with the U.K. which in my view would make it reasonable for the claim for asylum exceptionally to be considered here".

Paragraph 180K of the new Immigration Rules largely reproduces the substance of this statement, except that the reference is not to a country where the asylum applicant is safe from "persecution" but in which "his life or freedom would not be threatened". This accords with Art. 33 of the Geneva Convention, but is less generous than Art. 1A, which defines "refugee" with regard to "persecution", an expression that includes threats to life and liberty, but also includes forms of harassment that fall short of them (see below). Applicants who have travelled from third states ("safe" countries through which the applicant has passed : see *Karali* (above), including, but not confined to Dublin Convention countries) will continue not to receive substantive consideration and it may well be that they will be certified as "without foundation" under para. 5(1) of Sched. 2 (below), and attract only limited rights of appeal. However, it will remain the case that the Home Office will have to investigate whether or not the third state from which the asylum-seeker has come is indeed "safe", and will not, despite assurances to the contrary, return the asylum-seeker to the country of alleged persecution (*Bugdaycay* v. *Secretary of State for the Home Department*; *Nelidow Santis* v. *Same*; *Norman* v. *Same*; *Musisi, Re* [1987] A.C. 514). The new Rule also reflects the decision of the Court in *R.* v. *Secretary of State for the Home Department*, ex p. *Yassine* (*Khalil*) [1990] Imm AR 354, that there must be clear evidence that the "safe" third country will, in fact, admit the applicant (*ibid.*, para. 180K(b)).

There is also a more general agreement on an external border control policy, which has not yet been signed because of differences between Spain and the U.K. on the status of Gibraltar. The process of inter-governmental co-operation will undoubtedly lead to an increasing harmonisation of the asylum and immigration policy of the Member States, but the Parlia-mentary Under-Secretary of State for the Home Department has emphasised that ". . . there is no question of handing over responsibility for controlling access to each Member State's territory" (Standing Committee A, cols. 477 and 478, December 2, 1992).

The important provisions of the Geneva Convention which must be observed when applica-tions for asylum are dealt with by the Home Office are Arts. 1A(2), 32 and 33 (see I.A. Macdonald and N.J. Blake, *Macdonald's Immigration Law and Practice*, (1991) pp. 289–314, G. Goodwin-Gill, *The Refugee in International Law*, (1983) and F. Lindsley, *Best Practice Guide to the Preparation of Asylum Applications*, (1992)).

Article 1A(2) provides that the term "refugee" applies to any person who "(2) . . . owing to a well-founded fear of being persecuted for reasons of race, religion, membership of a particular social group or political opinion, is outside the country of his nationality and is unable, or, owing to such fear, is unwilling to avail himself of the protection of that country; or who, not having a nationality and being outside the country of his former habitual residence . . . is unable or, owing to such fear, is unwilling to return to it . . .".

Well-founded fear

The applicant must be genuinely afraid of persecution in his country of residence or national-ity, but that fear must be based on objective evidence, and was not merely to be accepted on the basis of the state of mind of the applicant (*R.* v. *Secretary of State for the Home Department*, ex p. *Sivakumaran*; *Same* v. *Same*, ex p. *Vaithialingam*; *Same* v. *Same*, ex p. *Vilvarajah*; *Same* v. *Same*, ex p. *Vathanan*; *Same* v. *Same*, ex p. *Rasalingam*; *Same* v. *Same*, ex p. *Navaratnaam* (*United Nations High Commissioner for Refugees intervening*) [1988] A.C. 958).

"In general, the applicant's fear should be considered well-founded if he can establish, to a reasonable degree, that his continued stay in his country of origin has become intolerable to him for the reasons stated in the definition, or would for the same reasons be intolerable if he returned there". (See para. 42 of the *Handbook on Procedures and Criteria for Determining Refugee Status*, issued by the United Nations High Commissioner for Refugees, September 1979).

The standard of proof to be demanded in these cases is less than the balance of probabilities, and could be "a reasonable chance" or "a serious possibility" of persecution (see *Fernandez* v. *Government of Singapore* [1971] 1 W.L.R. 987, followed in *Sivakumaran*, above).

Persecution

This expression has been held to embrace not only torture and ill-treatment but conduct which amounted to pursuit "with malignancy and injurious action, especially to oppress for holding a heretical opinion or belief" (Nolan J. in *R.* v. *Immigration Appeal Tribunal*, ex p. *Jonah* [1985] Imm AR 7). However, in *R.* v. *Secretary of State for the Home Department*, ex p. *Ahmad (Gulzar)* [1990] Imm AR 61, the Court of Appeal held that a Pakistan Government Ordinance which prohibits Ahmadis from practising their religion or seeking converts did not, in fact, amount to persecution because Ahmadis who did not attempt to evangelise were left untroubled.

In *Asante* v. *Secretary of State for the Home Department* [1991] Imm AR 78 the Immigration Appeal Tribunal held that persecution could consist of the likelihood of "persistent hounding" of the applicant because of the suspicion as to his involvement in an embezzlement, his detention and the lack of a fair trial. It went on to hold that it was not necessary for the applicant to manifest any political opinion for that to form the reason for his persecution, if those in power believed that "the individual held certain political opinions or was thought likely to commit acts in support of a political cause". A number of cases have supported the Government position that a state may still be safe for an individual if he can avoid persecution by moving elsewhere within it. In *R.* v. *Secretary of State for the Home Department*, ex p. *Gunes (Hidir)* [1991] Imm AR 278, for example, the Divisional Court held that a decision by the Home Secretary that an applicant who had been driven by beatings from his home village was not in fear of persecution because he could leave peaceably was not perverse. These decisions are now reflected in para. 180I of the new Immigration Rules which provides that "if there is part of the country from which the applicant claims to be a refugee in which he would not have a well-founded fear of persecution, and to which it would be reasonable to expect him to go, the application may be refused". Whether or not part of a country is indeed safe for the applicant, or whether it would be reasonable to expect him to go there is, of course, a matter of fact which can be explored on appeal before a special adjudicator.

Membership of a particular social group

The fact that a group is subjected to military action in a civil war does not, *per se*, amount to persecution. If, however, that action far exceeds the bounds of military necessity and amounts to a breach of the laws of war, then the victims of a civil war may also be the victims of persecution (see N. Blake, *Life after the Lords*, Imm. and Nat. L. & P. 1989, Vol. 4, No. 1, p.7 (an account of the subsequent successful appeal, after removal, of the Tamil appellants in *R.* v. *Secretary of State for the Home Department*, ex p. *Sivakumaran*, supra)). A person may be one of a group which is persecuted, and it is not therefore necessary for him to show that he would be "singled out" for persecution (*R.* v. *Secretary of State for the Home Department*, ex p. *R.*, *The Times*, June 8, 1987). Whether or not a person is a member of such a group is a matter of fact to be determined, in the first instance, by the Home Secretary.

In a number of recent cases, it has been held that it was not unreasonable for the Home Secretary to hold that homosexuals were not, *per se*, members of such a group. Following *R.* v. *Secretary of State for the Home Department*, ex p. *Mendis* [1989] Imm AR 6, where it had been decided that a person could not claim asylum on the basis of fear of persecution arising from some future activity in which he could refrain from taking part, it was held in *R.* v. *Secretary of State for the Home Department*, ex p. *Binbasi* [1989] Imm AR 595, that, although in that case homosexuality was punished by the criminal law, homosexuals were not a social group suffering persecution under the Geneva Convention.

Under Art. 32 of the Geneva Convention a refugee "lawfully in [the] territory" should not be expelled save on the grounds of public order and national security. However, this provision only applies to those who have been given leave to enter, and not merely where a person has been given temporary admission. In such cases, Art. 33 will apply and should prevent a person from being returned to the country of persecution (*R.* v. *Secretary of State for the Home Department*, ex p. *Singh (Parminder)*, *The Times*, June 8, 1987). In cases where national security was involved and the individual was in the country with leave, the Secretary of State was not required to place all details of the relevant evidence before the court. It was enough if he sufficiently identified the grounds on which he had, in the context of Art. 32(2), regarded the applicant as a danger to the country (*R.* v. *Secretary of State for the Home Department*, ex p. *Chahal*, *The Times*, March 12, 1993). Except in such security cases, "the refugee shall be allowed to submit evidence to clear himself, and to appeal to, and be represented for the purpose before the competent authority".

By Art. 33 of the Geneva Convention, the U.K. has undertaken not to return "a refugee in any manner whatsoever to the frontiers of territories where his life or freedom would be threatened on account of his race, religion, nationality, membership of a particular social group or political opinion".

Essentially, the test here is the same as that for a refugee, although there, the criterion is whether the applicant has a well-founded fear of persecution and here it is concerned with a threat to the refugee's life or freedom (*R*. v. *Secretary of State for the Home Department*, ex p. *Sivakumaran*; *Same* v. *Same*, ex p. *Vaithialingam*; *Same* v. *Same*, ex p. *Vilvarajah*; *Same* v. *Same*, ex p. *Vathanan*; *Same* v. *Same*, ex p. *Rasalingan*; *Same* v. *Same*, ex p. *Navaratnaam* (*United Nations High Commissioner for Refugees intervening*) [1988] A.C. 958). Paragraph 180K of the new Immigration Rules, which deals with third country cases, adopts the less liberal test of Art. 33 of the Geneva Convention, which could mean that an asylum-seeker is returned to a state where he is likely to be subjected to harassment amounting to persecution but falling short of a threat to his life and liberty.

Treatment of persons who claim asylum

Fingerprinting

    3.—(1) Where a person ("the claimant") has made a claim for asylum, an immigration officer, constable, prison officer or officer of the Secretary of State authorised for the purposes of this section may—

    (a) take such steps as may be reasonably necessary for taking the claimant's fingerprints; or

    (b) by notice in writing require the claimant to attend at a place specified in the notice in order that such steps may be taken.

    (2) The powers conferred by subsection (1) above may be exercised not only in relation to the claimant but also in relation to any dependant of his; but in the exercise of the power conferred by paragraph (a) of that subsection, fingerprints shall not be taken from a person under the age of sixteen ("the child") except in the presence of a person of full age who is—

    (a) the child's parent or guardian; or

    (b) a person who for the time being takes responsibility for the child and is not an immigration officer, constable, prison officer or officer of the Secretary of State.

    (3) Where the claimant's claim for asylum has been finally determined or abandoned—

    (a) the powers conferred by subsection (1) above shall not be exercisable in relation to him or any dependant of his; and

    (b) any requirement imposed on him or any dependant of his by a notice under subsection (1)(b) above shall no longer have effect.

    (4) A notice given to any person under paragraph (b) of subsection (1) above—

    (a) shall give him a period of at least seven days within which he is to attend as mentioned in that paragraph; and

    (b) may require him so to attend at a specified time of day or between specified times of day.

    (5) Any immigration officer or constable may arrest without warrant a person who has failed to comply with a requirement imposed on him by a notice under subsection (1)(b) above (unless the requirement no longer has effect) and, where a person is arrested under this subsection,—

    (a) he may be removed to a place where his fingerprints may conveniently be taken, and

    (b) (whether or not he is so removed) there may be taken such steps as may be reasonably necessary for taking his fingerprints,

before he is released.

    (6) Fingerprints of a person which are taken by virtue of this section must be destroyed not later than the earlier of—

    (a) the end of the period of one month beginning with any day on which he is given indefinite leave under the 1971 Act to enter or remain in the United Kingdom; and

(b) the end of the period of ten years beginning with the day on which the fingerprints are taken.

(7) Where fingerprints taken by virtue of this section are destroyed—

(a) any copies of the fingerprints shall also be destroyed; and

(b) if there are any computer data relating to the fingerprints, the Secretary of State shall, as soon as it is practicable to do so, make it impossible for access to be gained to the data.

(8) If—

(a) subsection (7)(b) above falls to be complied with, and

(b) the person to whose fingerprints the data relate asks for a certificate that it has been complied with,

such a certificate shall be issued to him by the Secretary of State not later than the end of the period of three months beginning with the day on which he asks for it.

(9) In this section—

(a) "immigration officer" means an immigration officer appointed for the purposes of the 1971 Act; and

(b) "dependant", in relation to the claimant, means a person—

 (i) who is his spouse or a child of his under the age of eighteen; and

 (ii) who has neither a right of abode in the United Kingdom nor indefinite leave under the 1971 Act to enter or remain in the United Kingdom.

(10) Nothing in this section shall be taken to limit the power conferred by paragraph 18(2) of Schedule 2 to the 1971 Act.

DEFINITIONS

"finally determined": s.33(4) of the 1971 Act.

"immigration officer": Sched. 2, para. 1(1) to the 1971 Act.

"indefinite leave": s.33(1) of the 1971 Act.

"prison officer": s.8 of the Prison Act 1952.

"right of abode": s.2(1) of the 1971 Act.

GENERAL NOTE

This section makes specific the powers of fingerprinting already implied in the general powers conferred on immigration officers and other authorised officers under para. 18(2) of Sched. 2 to the 1971 Act to take steps to identify a person detained for examination and extends this to all asylum-seekers who will not, generally, be detained while their claims are determined.

The primary reason given for the need for greater fingerprinting powers was the increasing incidence of multiple asylum applications and associated attempted benefit fraud, together with problems arising from the fact that so many applicants were obliged to travel on admittedly false documentation or without travel documents at all (Standing Committee A, col. 191, November 19, 1992). Concern was expressed at Committee stage of the Bill, about the security of such fingerprint records, and the Minister (Mr Charles Wardle) assured the Committee that all such records would be kept fully secure, and when placed on computer, would be protected by the provisions of the Data Protection Act 1984 (Standing Committee A, col. 263, November 24, 1992). The security of those records is, however, subject to the purposes for which they have been made.

"The only inquiries to the Home Office about an asylum-seeker's status are likely to come from the Department of Social Security, from local authorities in connection with the Bill's housing provisions and, occasionally, from the police. There will be no routine trawling of Home Office records during criminal inquiries. There may legitimately be matters that need to be raised with the Home Office, for example, the identification of bodies, but control will remain with the Home Office. That is fundamental" (Standing Committee A, col. 262, November 24, 1992).

Fingerprints will only be destroyed when a person is given indefinite leave to remain, so that those who are given exceptional leave (normally renewed on an annual basis) as well as those whose applications for asylum have been refused, will have to wait ten years before their prints are destroyed under s.3(6)(b).

Protection under the Data Protection Act 1984 must be subject to the primacy of E.C. law. Currently there is no Community legislation on data of this kind. However, following the ratification of the Treaty on European Union, under which limited competence is conferred on the Community in relation to immigration from third states under Art. 100C, the fingerprint information which is likely to be passed to the new European Automated Fingerprinting Recognition System (EURODAC) might be lost to Home Office control under s.3(7)(b). (On EURODAC, see E. Guild, *Lawyers' Europe*, Spring, 1993, p. 4). This system, which seems to have been put in hand to contain fingerprints of all persons who apply for asylum in the E.C., would be an important concomitant to implementation of the Dublin Convention (see the General Note to s.2). To date, EURODAC is described by the junior Minister at the Home Office as no more than a "limited feasibility study" (Standing Committee A, col. 431).

Subs. (1)

It would seem that the power to fingerprint, will arise not only in relation to formal asylum claims but also in relation to the "deemed claim" situations, where no formal claim has been made but the applicant's case has been referred to the Home Secretary as an asylum applicant in cases where the passenger has clearly demonstrated a fear of return to his country of origin or residence (para. 75 of the new Immigration Rules).

There is no statutory definition of a constable, but the term should be confined to those who have been appointed and attested as such (the Police Act 1984, s.19(1)). A police cadet would, therefore, have no power to fingerprint under this section (s.17(1)).

"Such steps as may be reasonably necessary" will include the application of reasonable force, but only after the claimant has been given a proper opportunity to comply voluntarily, either by a direct request or by a notice properly served under subs. (4). During the Commons Committee Stage of the Bill, the Parliamentary Under-Secretary of State at the Home Department indicated that notices are only likely to be sent out where facilities for fingerprinting at the port were not available. Such a notice would state to an asylum-seeker who is being required to report for fingerprinting "the power under which he is being required to do so, as well as pointing out the consequences of his failing to comply with the notice" (Standing Committee A, col. 210, November 19, 1992). Until such a notice is served and the time for compliance has expired, application of force would not be "necessary" (*Swales* v. *Cox* [1981] Q.B. 849). Under para. 180F of the new Immigration Rules, failure to comply with a notice issued by the Secretary of State under this subsection, "without reasonable explanation . . . may lead to refusal of an asylum application".

Subs. (2)

These powers compare to those conferred by s.65 of the Police and Criminal Evidence Act 1984, although the Government rejected any suggestion that routine compulsory fingerprinting would criminalise asylum-seekers (Standing Committee A, col. 190, November 19, 1992). Mr Charles Wardle, the Parliamentary Under-Secretary at the Home Department, stated during the Committee Stage of the Bill, that "it is not anticipated that it will be necessary to fingerprint every child, and we do not intend to fingerprint routinely very young children" (*ibid.*, col. 222). There are general provisions in paras. 180P, Q and R of the new Immigration Rules relating to applications for asylum by unaccompanied child asylum-seekers. It is emphasised that "in view of their potential vulnerability, particular priority and care is to be given to the handling of their cases" (para. 180B).

In relation to fingerprinting procedures under the Police and Criminal Evidence Act 1984, Code C, para. 1.7 the "responsible adult" means, in relation to the fingerprinting of a juvenile, a parent, guardian or "another responsible adult of 18 or over who is not a police officer or employed by the police" (and see s.57 of the Police and Criminal Evidence Act 1984).

Under this subsection, "a person who for the time being takes responsibility for the child" is likely to be a specialist adviser from a non–statutory panel established and administered by the Refugee Council or a social worker. During the final stages of the Bill, when the House of Commons was considering the amendments made to the Bill in the House of Lords, the Secretary of State for the Home Department, Mr Charles Wardle, described the process which the Government intended for assisting child asylum-seekers: "The function of the adviser would principally be to ensure that the social services department was aware of the child's wishes and of relevant cultural considerations and that the child understands as far as possible what is happening and what choices he or she has" (*Hansard*, H.C. Vol. 226, col. 29).

Subs. (3)

Under s.33(4) of the 1971 Act an appeal is not "finally determined", in the case of an appeal to an adjudicator, "so long as a further appeal can be brought by virtue of s.20 nor, if such an appeal is duly brought, until it is determined or withdrawn". In the case of asylum appeals, this is to be read as an appeal to a special adjudicator, with an additional appeal, with leave, on a question of law, to the Immigration Appeal Tribunal and from thence, on the same basis, to the Court of Appeal (see s.9 and para. 4 of Sched. 2, below). Essentially, a final determination can be identified when the appeal time-limits under the Asylum Appeals (Procedure) Rules 1993 (S.I. 1993 No. 1661) (see Appendix 2) have expired or the appeal process under ss.8 and 9 has been exhausted. The grant of exceptional leave to remain will not entitle the claimant to destruction of the fingerprint records, because such leave is normally limited and renewed annually.

"Abandoned" could cover either a failure to pursue the claim or a more formal revocation. It is likely that a finding of an abandonment of an appeal by a special adjudicator under r. 9(4)(a) of the Appeals Procedure Rules will be regarded as an abandonment of a claim.

The effect of this provision is that once a person has been granted refugee status neither he nor his dependants (see subs. (3)(b)) can be fingerprinted.

Subs. (5)

A power to arrest without warrant for the purposes of examination, ". . . if need be by force" already exists by virtue of para. 17(2) of Sched. 2 and the effect of this provision is to extend that power to those no longer liable to detention for examination because they have been granted leave to enter under the 1971 Act as, say, a student or visitor, and have subsequently made an application for asylum.

Subss. (7) and (8)

Fingerprint records are to be held securely at the Lunar House offices of the Immigration and Nationality Department. Fingerprints are to be destroyed "in batches" after the conclusion of the ten year period, and destruction will not depend on an application made by the person whose prints are held. The Government rejected proposals that the individuals affected should be able to witness the destruction of their fingerprints on the grounds that this would only delay that destruction and would pose problems of confidentiality (Standing Committee A, col. 230, November 19, 1992). This contrasts with the position of those who have had fingerprints taken under suspicion of an involvement in a criminal offence, where there is a right to witness destruction (see s.64(6) of the Police and Criminal Evidence Act 1984 and Code D, paras. 3.1 and 5.7 and see, also, H. Levenson and F. Fairweather, *Police Powers* (1992)). There is a very similar entitlement to a certificate of compliance under s.64(6A)(b) of the Police and Criminal Evidence Act 1984.

Subs. (10)

The broad powers of taking steps, including fingerprinting, for the purpose of identifying anyone liable to be detained for examination under para. 18(2) of Sched. 2 to the 1971 Act remain unaffected by this section. Most importantly, perhaps, the section does not confer on individuals whose fingerprints have been taken under those powers the right to have them destroyed (and see s.64(7)(a) of the Police and Criminal Evidence Act 1984).

Housing of asylum-seekers and their dependants

4.—(1) If a person ("the applicant") makes an application under the homelessness legislation for accommodation or assistance in obtaining accommodation and the housing authority who are dealing with his case are satisfied—

(a) that he is an asylum-seeker or the dependant of an asylum-seeker, and

(b) that he has or has available for his occupation any accommodation, however temporary, which it would be reasonable for him to occupy,

nothing in the homelessness legislation shall require the housing authority to secure that accommodation is made available for his occupation.

(2) In determining for the purposes of subsection (1)(b) above whether it would be reasonable for the applicant to occupy accommodation, regard may be had to the general circumstances prevailing in relation to housing in the district of the housing authority who are dealing with the applicant's case.

(3) Where, on an application made as mentioned in subsection (1) above, the housing authority are satisfied that the applicant is an asylum-seeker or the dependant of an asylum-seeker, but are not satisfied as mentioned in paragraph (b) of that subsection, then, subject to subsection (4) below,—

(a) any duty under the homelessness legislation to secure that accommodation is made available for the applicant's occupation shall not continue after he ceases to be an asylum-seeker or a dependant of an asylum-seeker; and

(b) accordingly, so long as the applicant remains an asylum-seeker or the dependant of an asylum-seeker, any need of his for accommodation shall be regarded as temporary only.

(4) If, immediately before he ceases to be an asylum-seeker or the dependant of an asylum-seeker, the applicant is occupying accommodation (whether temporary or not) made available in pursuance of the homelessness legislation, that legislation shall apply as if, at that time—

(a) he were not occupying that accommodation; and

(b) he had made an application under that legislation for accommodation or assistance in obtaining accommodation to the housing authority who secured that accommodation was made available.

(5) Schedule 1 to this Act (which makes supplementary provision with respect to housing of asylum-seekers and their dependants) shall have effect.

DEFINITIONS

"accommodation": s.58(2) of the Housing Act 1985.
"asylum-seeker": ss.1 and 5(2).
"available for occupation": s.5(8); s.75 of the Housing Act 1985.
"dependants": s.5(3)(a) and (5).
"housing authority": s.5(6)(b).

GENERAL NOTE

The object of ss.4 and 5 and the more detailed provisions of Sched. 1 is to ensure that only temporary accommodation is to be made available to asylum-seekers and their dependants by local housing authorities under the emergency housing powers conferred on them by Pt. III of the Housing Act 1985 ("the 1985 Act"), and that local housing authorities need not recognise a need for accommodation where an asylum-seeker applicant or a dependant of such a person has "temporary" accommodation, which must, nonetheless be "reasonable". This restricted obligation continues until the asylum claim has been determined. The problem which these sections seek to address is largely London related, where, in a few boroughs, it was stated in Committee on the Bill, as many as ten per cent. of those accepted as homeless under the 1985 Act were refugees, applicants for asylum or their dependants (Standing Committee A, col. 292, November 24, 1992, Mr Robin Squire, Parliamentary Under-Secretary of State for the Department of the Environment). Failure to disclose asylum-seeker status in the course of the inquiries which a housing authority is obliged to make before making a decision under the 1985 Act will be an offence under s.74 of that Act. Amendments are to be made to the Code of Guidance on the operation of Pt. III of the 1985 Act to make local housing authorities aware of their new obligations under the Act (*Hansard*, H.L. Vol. 543, col. 588). The Code is not law, but authorities must "have regard" to it while carrying out their duties (s.71 of the 1985 Act; and see *De Falco* v. *Crawley Borough Council*; *Silvestri* v. *Crawley Borough Council* [1980] Q.B. 460).

Once a local housing authority is made aware of an applicant's status, further inquiries will have to be made about the applicant, his dependants and progress of the application. This check, and the inevitable delay that it will cause, should not absolve local housing authorities from their obligation to provide at least temporary accommodation to those asylum-seekers and their dependants who are in priority need under s.59(1) of the 1985 Act, if they have no other accommodation (*Hansard*, H.L. Vol. 543, col. 294).

Subs. (1)(b)

"'However temporary' does not mean 'however unsatisfactory'. Although the floor of a church hall or a couch in a friend's flat might meet the criteria of 'however temporary', such accommodation would probably not be reasonable for an asylum-seeker and his family. The test of reasonableness would embrace both levels of overcrowding, hygiene and safety as well as cost and the willingness of friends and relatives to continue to provide accommodation" (*Hansard*, H.L. Vol. 543, col. 587). Accommodation would have to be reasonable, albeit temporary. These observations would appear to be an attempt to dispel fears that asylum-seekers would be placed in a post-*Puhlhofer* situation (*R.* v. *Hillingdon London Borough Council*, ex p. *Puhlhofer* [1986] A.C. 484, H.L.) before s.14(2) of the Housing and Planning Act 1986 imposed a requirement that accommodation had not only to be available but that it had to be "reasonable" to continue occupying it, but having regard to the general housing circumstances of the area (see subs. (2), below, and see C. Hunter and S. McGrath, *Homeless Persons: Arden's Guide to the Housing Act 1985, Pt. III*, p. 43 (note)).

During the Report Stage in the House of Lords, Lord Strathclyde described the purpose of this subsection, which is central to the housing provisions of the Act:

"The term 'however temporary' is used in subsection (1)(b), in distinction to the requirements that flow from Pt. III of the Housing Act 1985, under which someone is defined as homeless if he has no interest in a property or licence to occupy it—in broad terms, if he has no degree of security in his existing accommodation. The provisions of the 1985 Act are a direct route into settled accommodation for homeless households that meet the criteria set out in that Act. Although most homeless families these days do have a spell in temporary accommodation, that is not a necessary part of the Act. In the [1985] Act the yardstick for homelessness is set by reference to the security of tenure that flows from the duty of authorities to secure that accommodation is available for homeless families by reference to the security of such accommodation.

The housing provisions of the [Act] are directed towards a different concern. They will ensure that an asylum-seeker has adequate temporary accommodation, but they relieve authorities of the duty to provide permanent accommodation until he has been given leave to remain in this country. It is therefore appropriate that the need for an authority to intervene in providing accommodation should be set by reference to criteria based on the type of accommodation that the authority has a duty to provide in such instances at that time; namely temporary accommodation. Once a local authority has accepted responsibility to provide temporary accommodation for an asylum-seeker and his dependants, there is no reason that this should be any different in quality from the accommodation provided for other homeless families" (*Hansard*, H.L. Vol. 543, col. 587).

Subs. (3)
This provision, together with para. 6 of Sched. 1, ensures that asylum applicants will not acquire security of tenure in any accommodation which they are provided either by or under arrangements made by the local housing authority. Essentially, once an asylum-seeker's claim has been determined, he will be treated, if he has been given leave to remain, as a person who has just made an application for emergency housing provision and who is in temporary accommodation. If his application for asylum is refused it may be followed by removal and the relevance of the permanence of the accommodation will not arise. Paragraph 6(1) of Sched. 1 retains an option for the landlord, whether public or private, to grant a secure or an assured tenancy, if he so chooses.

Housing: interpretative provisions

5.—(1) The provisions of this section have effect for the purposes of section 4 above and Schedule 1 to this Act; and that section and Schedule are in the following provisions of this section referred to as "the housing provisions".

(2) For the purposes of the housing provisions a person who makes a claim for asylum—
  (a) becomes an asylum-seeker at the time when his claim is recorded by the Secretary of State as having been made; and
  (b) ceases to be an asylum-seeker at the time when his claim is recorded by the Secretary of State as having been finally determined or abandoned.

(3) For the purposes of the housing provisions, a person—
  (a) becomes a dependant of an asylum-seeker at the time when he is recorded by the Secretary of State as being a dependant of the asylum-seeker; and
  (b) ceases to be a dependant of an asylum-seeker at the time when the person whose dependant he is ceases to be an asylum-seeker or, if it is earlier, at the time when he is recorded by the Secretary of State as ceasing to be a dependant of the asylum-seeker.

(4) References in subsections (2) and (3) above to a time when an event occurs include references to a time before as well as after the passing of this Act.

(5) In relation to an asylum-seeker, "dependant" means a person—
  (a) who is his spouse or a child of his under the age of eighteen; and
  (b) who has neither a right of abode in the United Kingdom nor indefinite leave under the 1971 Act to enter or remain in the United Kingdom.

(6) Except in their application to Northern Ireland, in the housing provisions—

(a) "the homelessness legislation" means, in relation to England and Wales, Part III of the Housing Act 1985 and, in relation to Scotland, Part II of the Housing (Scotland) Act 1987;

(b) "housing authority" means—

(i) in relation to England and Wales, any authority which is a local housing authority for the purposes of Part III of the Housing Act 1985; and

(ii) in relation to Scotland, any authority which is a local authority for the purposes of Part II of the Housing (Scotland) Act 1987;

and references to a housing authority who are dealing with an applicant's case shall be construed as references to the authority to whom the application is made or (as the case may be) the authority who under the homelessness legislation are the notified authority in relation to the applicant.

(7) In the application of the housing provisions to Northern Ireland—

(a) "the homelessness legislation" means Part II of the Housing (Northern Ireland) Order 1988;

(b) "housing authority" means the Northern Ireland Housing Executive and references to a housing authority who are dealing with an applicant's case shall be construed as references to that Executive; and

(c) references to the district of a housing authority shall be construed as references to Northern Ireland.

(8) For the purposes of the housing provisions accommodation shall be regarded as available for the applicant's occupation only if it is available for occupation both by him and by any other person who might reasonably be expected to reside with him and references to securing accommodation for his occupation shall be construed accordingly.

GENERAL NOTE

These interpretative provisions and those in Sched. 1 are primarily intended to give operational effect to the substantive provisions of s.4 in England, Wales, Scotland and Northern Ireland (see the General Note to s.4 above). It should be noted that the effect of subs. (4) of the section is to make the Act retrospective in relation to housing applications, in that individuals who had made asylum claims before the Act came into effect may now be treated as asylum-seekers for the purpose of emergency housing provision under the Act. It does not, however, mean that asylum applicants who are currently in local authority or other accommodation will lose any security of tenure which they currently possess (see para. 8(1)(a) of Sched. 1). Nor do the new provisions affect applications for emergency housing which were pending when the Act came into effect. "Pending" in this context means that the housing authority has commenced the inquiries about the applicant which it is obliged to make under s.62 of the 1985 Act.

Subs. (8)

This provision, which mirrors s.75 of the 1985 Act, has the important effect of broadening the category of persons whose housing position must be considered under the Act when determining whether or not an applicant is homeless or threatened with homelessness under the 1985 Act. Section 58(2) refers to "no accommodation which he [the applicant], together with any other person who normally resides with him as a member of his family or in circumstances in which it is reasonable for that person to reside with him"; that "other person" may well be a cohabitee, or another family member having indefinite leave. Neither of the latter would be "dependants" for the purposes of subs. (5), although there would be an obligation to consider their housing needs in conjunction with those of the asylum-seeker. It is clear that local housing authorities may have difficulties in reconciling their obligation to provide only temporary accommodation to the asylum-seeker and his or her dependants and their duty to provide permanent accommodation to other members of the family unit who are in priority need under s.59 of the 1985 Act but are not dependants as defined in subs. (5).

Protection of claimants from deportation etc.

6. During the period beginning when a person makes a claim for asylum and ending when the Secretary of State gives him notice of the decision on the claim, he may not be removed from, or required to leave, the United Kingdom.

DEFINITIONS
  "claim for asylum": s.1.
  "removed": para. 8(1) of Sched. 2 to the 1971 Act.
  "required to leave": s.5(1) of the 1971 Act.

GENERAL NOTE
  Asylum applicants who have arrived at ports of entry have, in the past, generally been admitted to the U.K. on a temporary basis under the 1971 Act without being given leave. While here awaiting a decision they are not lawfully "in" the U.K. under the 1971 Act (ss.3 and 11(1)). See *R.* v. *Secretary of State for the Home Department*, ex p. *Parminder Singh, The Times*, June 8, 1987. In some cases this has meant that they have been held in custody under Sched. 2 to the 1971, or have been allowed bail. They have not been, in such cases, secure from removal, especially after an asylum application has been refused. Even an application made for judicial review of any decision affecting them, including a decision on their refugee status (*R.* v. *Secretary of State for the Home Department*, ex p. *Muboyayi* [1991] 3 W.L.R. 442) has not sufficed to protect them from removal. However, following the decision of the House of Lords in *M.* v. *Home Office* [1993] 3 W.L.R. 433, breach of an undertaking not to remove the applicant would be a contempt, and it is now clear that the court may grant an injunction to prevent removal of the applicant pending the outcome of the hearing. An injunction would also be available against the Home Secretary, if removal of an asylum applicant in breach of this section seemed imminent.
  This new provision was added by the Government after the Committee Stage of the Bill in the House of Commons (*Hansard*, H.C. Vol. 216, col. 637). It protects asylum applicants from removal from the moment a claim for asylum is made to an immigration officer until they have been accepted as refugees or been given notice of refusal. Removal is also prohibited by para. 9 of Sched. 2, below, once notice of appeal has been given. There is, however, a gap in the period of immunity from removal. After an application for asylum is refused, under the Immigration Appeals (Procedure) Rules 1993, an applicant has up to ten days in which to serve notice of appeal (r. 5(1)), or two days if the Secretary of State has certified the claim to be without foundation and where the notice of refusal has been served personally on the applicant (r. 5(2) and para. 5 of Sched. 2 (below)). During this period, in which an appellant is considering, or being advised on, an appeal, he is at risk. The Home Secretary did, however, give this assurance during the debate on this clause in the House of Commons: ". . . if someone reaches these shores and applies for asylum the application will be properly considered. No one will be removed without his case having been properly determined in the light of the rules" (*Hansard*, H.C. Vol. 216, col. 639). He added that the combined effect of protection against removal while the application is under consideration and the protection against removal during the appeal process "will be to cover the period between a decision being taken and a possible appeal being filed" (*Hansard*, H.C. Vol. 216, col. 642).
  It is not, however, clear that the period between the Home Secretary's decision on the application and the service of notice of appeal is, in fact, covered and applicants will remain at risk of removal during this period. The Government resisted an attempt to provide the necessary protection from removal in the House of Lords on the ground that someone who did not wish to appeal would have to remain here for another ten days, "probably in detention and at considerable public expense" (*Hansard*, H.L. Vol. 542, col. 840).
  Paragraph 75C of the new Immigration Rules prohibits removal of an applicant for asylum who has applied for leave to enter "so long as *any appeal which he may bring is pending*" [emphasis added]. Prima facie, this would appear to cover appeals which are contemplated in the permitted period of notice, as well as those of which notice has already been given. However, para. 28(1) of Sched. 2 to the 1971 Act speaks in terms of a situation in which an appeal is pending in relation to circumstances "where a person in the U.K. *appeals*" [emphasis added]. It would seem, therefore, that the Rules, like the Act, only provide protection while an application is being considered and *after* a notice of appeal against a refusal to grant asylum has been lodged.

Curtailment of leave to enter or remain

7.—(1) Where—
  (a) a person who has limited leave under the 1971 Act to enter or remain in the United Kingdom claims that it would be contrary to the United

Kingdom's obligations under the Convention for him to be required to leave the United Kingdom after the time limited by the leave, and

(b) the Secretary of State has considered the claim and given to the person notice in writing of his rejection of it,

the Secretary of State may by notice in writing, given to the person concurrently with the notice under paragraph (b) above, curtail the duration of the leave.

(2) No appeal may be brought under section 14 of the 1971 Act or section 8(2) below against the curtailment of leave under subsection (1) above.

(3) The power conferred by subsection (1) above is without prejudice to sections 3(3) and 4 of the 1971 Act and the immigration rules (within the meaning of that Act).

(4) Where—

(a) the duration of a person's leave under the 1971 Act to enter or remain in the United Kingdom has been curtailed under subsection (1) above, and

(b) the Secretary of State has decided to make a deportation order against him by virtue of section 3(5) of that Act,

he may be detained under the authority of the Secretary of State pending the making of the deportation order; and the references to sub-paragraph (2) of paragraph 2 of Schedule 3 to that Act in sub-paragraphs (3), (4) and (6) of that paragraph (provisions about detention under sub-paragraph (2)) shall include references to this subsection.

DEFINITIONS
"claim for asylum": s.1.
"Convention": s.1.
"immigration rules": ss.3(2) and 33(1) of the 1971 Act.
"limited leave": s.33(1) of the 1971 Act.

GENERAL NOTE

All foreign and commonwealth nationals, except those who are exempt from immigration control by virtue of having a right of abode under s.1(1) of the 1971 Act, or as seamen, diplomats or in some other exempt category under s.8 of the 1971 Act, or s.7 of the 1988 Act, or have been granted indefinite leave under s.3(3)(a) of the 1971 Act, will be in the U.K. with some kind of limited leave. Within the limits imposed by the rules (or, in some circumstances, outside the rules : *R.* v. *Immigration Appeal Tribunal* ex p. *Singh (Bakhtaur)* [1986] 1 W.L.R. 910) such leave may, from time to time be varied, curtailed or revoked by the Secretary of State (s.3(3)(a) of the 1971 Act).

The object of this section is to make it a specific ground for curtailment of leave that a person has made an application for asylum that raises doubts about the circumstances of the original grant of leave and to provide an accelerated and more limited appeal right in such cases. It still leaves the Secretary of State free to curtail a person's leave on any other ground (subs. (3) below). Under para. 100 of the Immigration Rules (H.C. 251), a person's leave may, for example, be curtailed because false representations have been made to secure the initial leave or a previous variation. Such conduct should not, however, prejudice the claim of a genuine asylum-seeker. Article 31.1 of the Geneva Convention prohibits the imposition of penalties for illegal entry on asylum-seekers, "provided they present themselves without delay and show good cause for their illegal entry or presence". The new Immigration Rules provide that the Home Secretary will "have regard to matters which may damage an asylum-seeker's credibility if no reasonable explanation is given". Among these are failing to apply forthwith for asylum on arrival in the U.K. (unless the application is based on events which have happened since arrival) and the making of false representations, orally or in writing, on arrival or the damage or destruction of travel documents (para. 180G).

Under this section, where a decision has been taken to curtail a person's leave, following an unsuccessful asylum application, there will only be a combined right of appeal against both the decision to curtail and the linked decision to deport. "We intend that the appellant should be able to argue on his appeal against the deportation decision not only that the deportation would contravene obligations under the Convention, but that the Secretary of State has exercised wrongly his discretion in deciding to deport" (Standing Committee A, col. 415, December 1, 1992, Mr Charles Wardle).

Concurrently. The word "concurrently" is important. The notice of curtailment must be served at the same time as the notice of refusal of asylum. It will not be possible for the Home Secretary to serve notice of curtailment, as an afterthought, at a later date:

"When it is decided at the time the asylum claim is determined, that a person no longer qualifies to remain here, the intention has always been that the notices should be served simultaneously: the person would be notified of the refusal of his claim, the curtailment of his leave and the decision to make a deportation order against him" (*Hansard*, H.C. Vol. 216, col. 697).

The effect of the section is that a person cannot circumvent the new provisions by appealing under s.14(1) of the 1971 Act on non-asylum grounds, and then raising the issue of asylum at a subsequent deportation appeal. Where an application to vary has been refused on non-asylum grounds and an appeal is pending to an "ordinary" adjudicator, the Asylum Appeals (Procedure) Rules (see Appendix 2, below) provide that the "ordinary" appeal and the "special appeal" will be dealt with together (r. 29(1)).

Since s.5(1) of the 1988 Act offers limited powers of appeal in the case of those who have been in the U.K. for less than seven years and are to be deported for breach of conditions of leave or being family members of those ordered to be deported, the Under-Secretary of State has promised to bring forward an Order in Council under s.5(2) of the 1988 Act to enable those claiming asylum to be exempted from those appeal restrictions (*Hansard*, H.C. Vol. 216, col. 415).

The Government emphasised in Committee in the House of Commons that curtailment of leave would remain discretionary and would be decided upon the facts of each case:

"Curtailment of leave to enter or remain will not be automatic . . . the key criteria will be whether the claim for asylum has raised questions about the continuing legitimacy of a person's stay under the ordinary immigration rules, the majority of which impose an obligation to leave the country in due course, after expiry of limited leave" (*Hansard*, H.C. Vol. 216, col. 415).

Subs. (2)

The effect of this provision is to confine appeals against curtailment of leave, where asylum has been claimed and rejected, to the new appeal route in relation to appeals against deportation orders under s.8(3), below. Where an appeal raises, or has raised, non-asylum issues, then the rules as to "mixed appeals" will mean that such appeals are dealt with by the special adjudicator (r. 29). The transfer of the appeal to the special adjudicator should not be to the prejudice of any steps taken by the parties under the 1984 Rules (Immigration Appeals (Procedure) Rules 1984 (S.I. 1984 No. 2041)). However, the restriction on appeal rights only applies to a situation where the leave is revoked on these grounds. If a person applies near the end of his leave for a variation, it will then be too late to revoke the leave, even if the Home Secretary were minded to do so. In such a case an appeal may be lodged, provided that the application to vary was made during the currency of the leave (see the Immigration (Variation of Leave) Order 1976 (S.I. 1976 No. 1572)).

Subs. (3)

This preserves the broad powers of the Secretary of State to vary leave and to impose conditions on the basis of criteria, some of which are currently contained in para. 100 of the 1990 Immigration Rules (H.C. 251). A person's leave may, for example, be curtailed "if false representations have been made . . . in order to obtain leave to enter" or if a person "ceases to meet the requirements of the rules under which he was granted leave".

Subs. (4)

Curtailment of leave does not, *per se*, give rise to a power to detain. A person will normally only be liable to detention after his curtailed leave has expired and he is then liable to deportation under s.5 of and para. 2(2) of Sched. 3 to the 1971 Act. This subsection does not mean that it will be possible for a person to be detained *before* the expiry of a curtailed leave if, in addition to curtailment, the Secretary of State has decided to make a deportation order under s.3(5) of the 1971 Act, because the power to deport only arises where he has breached a condition of that leave or remained beyond the time limited by the leave. Detention will not be routine in such cases. "We will exercise the power to detain only if we do not think that the person would keep in touch; and that a failure to detain would frustrate our intention to enforce departure" (*Hansard*, H.C. Vol. 216, col. 698).

Rights of appeal

Appeals to special adjudicator

8.—(1) A person who is refused leave to enter the United Kingdom under the 1971 Act may appeal against the refusal to a special adjudicator on the ground that his removal in consequence of the refusal would be contrary to the United Kingdom's obligations under the Convention.

(2) A person who has limited leave under the 1971 Act to enter or remain in the United Kingdom may appeal to a special adjudicator against any variation of, or refusal to vary, the leave on the ground that it would be contrary to the United Kingdom's obligations under the Convention for him to be required to leave the United Kingdom after the time limited by the leave.

(3) Where the Secretary of State—
(a) has decided to make a deportation order against a person by virtue of section 3(5) of the 1971 Act, or
(b) has refused to revoke a deportation order made against a person by virtue of section 3(5) or (6) of that Act,
the person may appeal to a special adjudicator against the decision or refusal on the ground that his removal in pursuance of the order would be contrary to the United Kingdom's obligations under the Convention; but a person may not bring an appeal under both paragraph (a) and paragraph (b) above.

(4) Where directions are given as mentioned in section 16(1)(a) or (b) of the 1971 Act for a person's removal from the United Kingdom, the person may appeal to a special adjudicator against the directions on the ground that his removal in pursuance of the directions would be contrary to the United Kingdom's obligations under the Convention.

(5) The Lord Chancellor shall designate such number of the adjudicators appointed for the purposes of Part II of the 1971 Act as he thinks necessary to act as special adjudicators for the purposes of this section and may from time to time vary that number and the persons who are so designated.

(6) Schedule 2 to this Act (which makes supplementary provision about appeals under this section) shall have effect; and the preceding provisions of this section shall have effect subject to that Schedule.

DEFINITIONS
"Convention": s.1.
"deportation order": s.5(1) of the 1971 Act.
"directions": para. 8(1)(a) of Sched. 2 to the 1971 Act.
"leave": s.3 of the 1971 Act.
"removal": para. 8(1) of Sched. 2 to the 1971 Act.
"variation of . . . leave": s.3(3)(a) of the 1971 Act.

GENERAL NOTE
This section confers, for the first time, an "in-state" right of appeal on asylum-seekers refused at the port of entry, and is central to the legislation. Unlike the earlier provision in the 1991 Asylum Bill, such right is not now dependent upon first obtaining leave to appeal. The requirement to obtain prior leave before an asylum refusal could be appealed had met sustained opposition, especially in the House of Lords among cross–bench peers. The process of obtaining leave had been described by Lord Ackner as an application to "a faceless adjudicator relying on documents, some of which the applicant may well believe he has never seen, [who] makes a final and vital decision without hearing the applicant" (*Hansard*, H.L. Vol. 535, col. 507). This has now been replaced by a prima facie entitlement to a full right of appeal to a special adjudicator, with a reserve power to the Secretary of State to designate certain applications as "without foundation" where the application does not relate to Convention issues or is "frivolous or vexatious" under para. 5(1) of Sched. 2.

The section also transfers the existing function of an ordinary adjudicator to a special adjudicator in relation to existing appeal rights under the 1971 Act, where an application to vary an existing leave has been refused, and it is alleged that removal would be contrary to the Geneva Convention, and, similarly, in relation to appeals against refusal to revoke a deportation order and against the terms of a direction for removal. Special adjudicators are to be appointed from those already holding office as ordinary adjudicators under s.12 of and Sched. 5 to the 1971 Act.

Paragraph 180B of the new Immigration Rules provides that a person will be granted asylum if he is a refugee as defined by the Convention *and* refusal of his application would result in his being required to go to a country in which his life or freedom would be threatened. The second of these criteria is that contained in Art. 33 of the Geneva Convention. The case law of British courts and the decisions of the Immigration Appeal Tribunal have produced a much broader definition of "persecution" than one confined to threats to life and liberty (see the General Note to s.2). If refusal of an application will result in the applicant being returned to his country of origin or country of habitual residence if he has no nationality, then the question of the possibility of persecution will be paramount. However, a threatened removal to a "safe" third country may attract only the lesser protection afforded by Art. 33. These will be material issues on an appeal which will turn, ultimately, on interpretation of the Convention, not the Rules (s.1).

Under r. 5(1) of the Immigration Appeal Rules appeals must be lodged within ten days of the service of the notice of refusal of an asylum application. In the case of an applicant whose application has been certified under Sched. 2 as being "manifestly ill-founded", the period will be two days in relation to port refusals where the person has been detained (Standing Committee A, col. 511, December 3, 1992). Where notice of appeal is served out of time the recipient (normally the Secretary of State, except where the appellant is in custody (r. 5(4)), may decide to accept it where he is of the opinion that it would be "just and right" to do so. In addition, a special adjudicator may extend any time-limit "provided he considers it necessary in the interests of justice" (r. 5(7)). In such cases, if the appellate authority exercises its discretion to allow such an appeal to proceed, it is not entitled to deal with the substantial merits of the case without first giving the parties adequate time to prepare.

The section also creates a new right of appeal on asylum grounds for individuals who have been recommended for deportation by a court. In such cases, where the rights of appeal against a recommendation had been exhausted through the criminal appeal process, there was no further right of appeal against the decision of the Secretary of State to implement the recommendation (s.6(5) of the 1971 Act). Under subs. (3)(b) of this section, such an individual will have a right of appeal where he has applied to have such a deportation order revoked on asylum grounds. This change meets criticisms from both domestic courts and the European Commission of Human Rights and gives effect to an undertaking by the then Secretary of State (*R.* v. *Immigration Appeal Tribunal*, ex p. *Murugunandarajah*; *R.* v. *Immigration Appeal Tribunal*, ex p. *Sureshkuman* [1986] Imm AR 382 (and see *Macdonald's Immigration Law and Practice* (1991), p.391)).

Subs. (1)

Note that a removal will normally follow a refusal of leave under the 1971 Act, Sched. 2, para. 8(1). An immigration officer will refuse leave under s.4(1) of the 1971 Act after an adverse decision of the Secretary of State. Applicants will need to be told by the officer why the Home Secretary is minded to refuse and give an opportunity to the applicant to clarify any relevant facts and provide any new information (*R.* v. *Secretary of State for the Home Department*, ex p. *Thirukumar* [1989] Imm AR 402). Under the Asylum Appeals (Procedure) Rules 1993 (S.I. 1993 No. 1661), r.5, applicants will have ten days in which to serve notice of appeal, or two days in the case of applications which the Secretary of State has certified, in his decision, as "without foundation" under para. 5 of Sched. 2 (r. 5(2)(b)) and notice of the refusal has been served in person on the applicant. The restriction on removal which applies *after* notice of appeal has been lodged under s.6 does not apply while those who are refused are making up their minds whether or not to appeal, and they are, in theory at least, liable to removal during that period (see the General Note to s.6 and Sched. 2).

Subs. (2)

"Limited leave" can include any kind of leave limited in duration, including "extra-statutory" leave and exceptional leave, granted by the Secretary of State (*R.* v. *Secretary of State for the Home Department*, ex p. *Kaur (Rajinder)* [1987] Imm AR 278). All can be varied by the Secretary of State under s.4(1) of the 1971 Act. However, it does not apply to temporary admission granted under para. 8(2) of Sched. 2 to those whose applications for asylum and leave to enter are under consideration (see *Kaur*, above). There is no "leave" in such cases to vary.

A "variation" could include a curtailment of leave, either under s.7(1) above following an unsuccessful asylum application, or under the more general powers of the Home Secretary under ss.3 and 4 of the 1971 Act and under, for example, para. 100 of the current Immigration Rules (H.C. 251) as amended by the new Immigration Rules.

Subs. (3)

This provision transfers to the jurisdiction of the special adjudicator appeals which would hitherto have gone to an ordinary adjudicator under s.15(1) of the 1971 Act. However, there was no right to appeal to an adjudicator against a decision to implement a recommendation by a court following a criminal conviction under s.3(6). That right now exists by virtue of subs. (3)(b) in relation to a refusal to revoke such an order. Appellants only have one opportunity to appeal, either against the decision to make the order or the refusal to revoke it on the grounds that to implement the order would constitute an infringement of the Geneva Convention.

Appeals from Immigration Appeal Tribunal

9.—(1) Where the Immigration Appeal Tribunal has made a final determination of an appeal brought under Part II of the 1971 Act (including that Part as it applies by virtue of Schedule 2 to this Act) any party to the appeal may bring a further appeal to the appropriate appeal court on any question of law material to that determination.

(2) An appeal under this section may be brought only with the leave of the Immigration Appeal Tribunal or, if such leave is refused, with the leave of the appropriate appeal court.

(3) In this section "the appropriate appeal court" means—

(a) if the appeal is from the determination of an adjudicator or special adjudicator and that determination was made in Scotland, the Court of Session; and

(b) in any other case, the Court of Appeal.

(4) Rules of procedure under section 22 of the 1971 Act may include provision regulating, and prescribing the procedure to be followed on, applications to the Immigration Appeal Tribunal for leave to appeal under this section.

(5) In section 33(4) of the 1971 Act—

(a) for the words "in the case of an appeal to an adjudicator, the" there shall be substituted "an"; and

(b) after the words "section 20" there shall be inserted "or section 9 of the Asylum and Immigration Appeals Act 1993".

DEFINITIONS
"Immigration Appeal Tribunal": s.12 of and Sched. 5, Pt. II to the 1971 Act.
"final determination": s.33(4) of the 1971 Act.
"party": r.8 of the Asylum Appeals (Procedure) Rules 1993 (S.I. 1993 No. 1661).

GENERAL NOTE
Under this section an opportunity is created for an appeal on a point of law, with leave, to the Court of Appeal for cases determined by the Immigration Appeal Tribunal in England, Wales and Northern Ireland, and to the Court of Session for determinations in Scotland. The possibility of an appeal in such cases was originally confined in the Bill as introduced at First Reading on October 22, 1992 to cases which had originally been heard before a special adjudicator under ss.7 and 8. As a result of the Government accepting an amendment at Committee Stage in the House of Lords the scope of appeals has been widened to include *all* determinations made by the Immigration Appeal Tribunal, including asylum appeals. This is a substantial innovation and one which, it was hoped, would significantly reduce the number of immigration cases dealt with in judicial review applications to the Divisional Court.

Speaking for the Home Office on the amendment, Earl Ferrers said, "The creation of an avenue of appeal from the Immigration Appeal Tribunal to the courts on a point of law is a change which has been advocated for many years by the Council on Tribunals and by many of those who represent appellants. Judicial review will still be available in some cases where it is an appropriate remedy" (*Hansard*, H.L. Vol. 543, col. 654). A "question of law" is not confined to the "immigration laws" (see s.33(1) of the 1971 Act), but would include any rule of statute or common law that is relevant, the Geneva Convention, European Community law and any provision of international law that is appropriate to the interpretation of English law, for example, the European Convention on Human Rights. There does not appear to be any significance in the fact that the term used here and in r. 20 of the Asylum Appeals (Procedure) Rules 1993 (S.I. 1993 No. 1661) (Appendix 2, below) is "question of law" rather than the "point of law" referred to in r.14(2)(a) of the Immigration Appeals (Procedure) Rules 1984 (S.I. 1984 No. 2041).

Appellants will have 10 days from the final determination to make an application for leave to appeal in connection with an asylum appeal (r. 21(1) of the Asylum Appeals (Procedure) Rules 1993 (S.I. 1993 No. 1661) (see Appendix 2)). The application may be determined without a hearing by the President of the Tribunal or the chairman sitting alone, unless they consider that "there are special circumstances making a hearing necessary or desirable" (*ibid.*, r. 21(4)). The procedure is similar in non–asylum appeals but in those cases the time-limit is 14 days (see new para. 21B of the 1984 Rules as added by para. 2 of the Immigration Appeals (Procedure) Rules 1993 (S.I. 1993 No. 1662), set out in Appendix 3, below).

Subss. (2) and (4)
    The Immigration Appeals (Procedure) Rules (S.I. 1993 No. 1662) (see Appendix 3, below) which came into effect on July 26, 1993, contain provisions on the making of applications for leave to appeal from the Immigration Appeal Tribunal to the Court of Appeal or the Court of Session. They amend the Immigration Appeals (Procedure) Rules 1984 (S.I. 1984 No. 2041, amended by S.I. 1991 No. 1545) to provide non-asylum appellants with an opportunity for a further appeal on a point of law, and allow a time-limit of 14 days after the intended appellant has received written notice of the determination from the Tribunal within which the application for leave to appeal must be made. The Tribunal can, as with the asylum cases, determine the application without a hearing unless it considers that there are special circumstances making a hearing necessary or desirable (r. 21B(4)). Applicants should be given written notice of the determination with reasons (r., 21B(5)).

Visitors, short-term and prospective students and their dependants

10. In section 13 of the 1971 Act (appeals against exclusion from United Kingdom), after subsection (3) there shall be inserted—
    "(3A) A person who seeks to enter the United Kingdom—
        (a) as a visitor, or
        (b) in order to follow a course of study of not more than six months duration for which he has been accepted, or
        (c) with the intention of studying but without having been accepted for any course of study, or
        (d) as a dependant of a person within paragraph (a), (b) or (c) above,
    shall not be entitled to appeal against a refusal of an entry clearance and shall not be entitled to appeal against a refusal of leave to enter unless he held a current entry clearance at the time of the refusal.
    (3AA) The Secretary of State shall appoint a person, not being an officer of his, to monitor, in such manner as the Secretary of State may determine, refusals of entry clearance in cases where there is, by virtue of subsection (3A) above, no right of appeal; and the person so appointed shall make an annual report on the discharge of his functions to the Secretary of State who shall lay a copy of it before each House of Parliament.
    (3AB) The Secretary of State may pay to a person appointed under subsection (3AA) above such fees and allowances as he may with the approval of the Treasury determine."

DEFINITIONS
    "entry clearance": s.33(1) of the 1971 Act.
    "leave to enter": s.3(1) of the 1971 Act.

GENERAL NOTE
    This provision abolishes the right of appeal for visitors, short-term students and those who wish to enter to study but have not yet been accepted for a place on a course, and their dependants. The reason given by the Government for abolition of this right was that it was "intended to streamline the present system of immigration appeals, in order to enable it to deal more quickly with appeals against decisions which have a fundamental impact on the lives of the persons concerned ... there is a backlog of some 23,000 appeals awaiting hearing by adjudicators and the system is not delivering a fair, effective and timely remedy either to would-be visitors or to those seeking to settle here. It is necessary to recognise that the available remedy needs to be proportional to the potential grievance, and to concentrate resources on the cases that vitally affect a person's future" (Standing Committee A, cols. 641–642, December 8, 1992).
    A right of appeal has existed in such cases since the present system of appeals was introduced by the Immigration Appeals Act 1969, and there was considerable opposition to its abolition

both at Committee Stage in the House of Commons and in the House of Lords. Lord Ackner, a Lord of Appeal, observed that it was "wholly unjust to take away an entrenched right of appeal without compelling reasons". He could see no such reason except the "convenience" of saving money on such appeals to fund the new asylum appeals system (*Hansard*, H.L. Vol. 543, cols. 770–771). Section 13(3AA) of the 1971 Act is the result of an amendment successfully moved by Lady Flather in the House of Lords, and reflects the fear expressed in both Houses that the quality of decision-making in such cases by immigration officers will deteriorate in the absence of any effective system of appeal or review. It was also anticipated in the House of Lords that the effect of abolition will be to increase the number of applications for judicial review (*ibid.* col. 771). The Minister seems to have accepted that this would be the case and announced the introduction of the practice of sending a letter "setting out the full background to the case to solicitors who have notified the Home Office that they are applying for judicial review" (Standing Committee A, cols. 672–673, December 8, 1992).

It must be emphasised that this section can have no application to those exercising free movement rights conferred by E.C. law. Despite the failure to bring s.7 of the 1988 Act into force, Community nationals, their families, European Free Trade Area nationals (except the Swiss) when the European Economic Area Treaty is ratified and incorporated, and other nationals coming to the U.K. as business visitors on behalf of E.C. based companies (see *Rush Portuguesa* v. *Office National d'Immigration* (No. 113/89) [1990] 2 C.M.L.R. 818), have a *right* of entry under E.C. law.

Such passengers do not require leave under the 1971 Act, and if refused admission, are entitled to remain in the U.K. to challenge the decision through any available appeal process (Dir. 64/221, Arts. 5 to 9, and see *R.* v. *Pieck* (No. 157/79) [1981] 1 Q.B. 571; *Van Duyn* v. *Home Office* (No. 41/74) [1975] Ch. 358). Vocational students have rights of entry under Dir. 90/366, and any students who are paying course fees are entitled to enter as recipients of services (*Luisi and Carbone* v. *Ministero del Tesoro* (Nos. 286/82 and 26/83) [1984] E.C.R. 377). Although such individuals may be allowed, as a concession, to remain to appeal against a refusal of entry, the failure to make a specific exception in their case in this section is in itself a breach of E.C. law (*French Merchant Seamen, Re; E.C. Commission* v. *France* (No. 167/73) [1974] E.C.R. 359; *E.C. Commission* v. *Germany* (No. 29/84) [1986] 3 C.M.L.R. 579).

S.13(3A)(a), (b) and (c) of the 1971 Act

Section 1(4) of the 1971 Act requires that the Immigration Rules "shall include provision for admitting . . . persons coming for the purpose of taking employment, or for purposes of study, or as visitors, or as dependants of persons lawfully in or entering the U.K.".

In relation to visitors, the current Rules (H.C. 251), paras. 22 to 25, provide that a person seeking entry as a visitor is only to be admitted, "if he satisfies the immigration officer that he is genuinely seeking entry for the period of the visit". Much of the case law is concerned with questions of the "genuineness" of the visit and whether the proposed visitor will return home at the end of it (*R.* v. *Secretary of State for the Home Department*, ex p. *Swati*; *Same* v. *Same*, ex p. *Butt* [1986] 1 W.L.R. 472). In some cases this may involve attempting to distinguish between the wishes and the intentions of the appellant (*Karachiwalla, Re* (1986), unreported, No. 8218 (IAT) and see C. Vincenzi and D. Marrington, *Immigration Law: The Rules Explained* (1992)). Visitors are normally given leave to enter for a maximum of six months, "unless the immigration officer is satisfied that there are particular circumstances which justify the giving of a shorter period of leave" (H.C. 251, para. 25). Visitors given leave for three months may apply to the Home Office to have their leave varied, and, provided they can support themselves without working or becoming a charge on public funds (H.C. 251, para. 1), they may obtain an extension to six months. The only exception to the six months maximium leave for visitors is in relation to people coming for medical treatment (para. 106). It must be emphasised that the abolition of appeal rights in relation to visitors only applies to refusal of *entry* and not in relation to appeals against variation of leave under s.14 of the 1971 Act. Thus, a visitor admitted for three months, or a person admitted for six months for medical treatment, will still have a right of appeal against a refusal to extend that period (see para. 105 as amended by the new Immigration Rules). However, a person who was not admitted for medical treatment and wants an extension beyond six months must be refused, and will now lose his right of appeal by virtue of the "mandatory refusal" provisions of s.11 (see the General Note to s.11, below).

In relation to students, the current rules distinguish between prospective students who have "genuine and realistic intentions of studying in the U.K." but do not yet have a place on a course (H.C. 251, para. 28), and those who have been accepted on a course at a university, polytechnic or further education establishment, independent school or any bona fide private educational institution, provided that not less than 15 hours a week is spent in "organised daytime study" (H.C. 251, para. 27). No distinction has hitherto been made about the duration of such courses. However, a decision will now have to be made about the duration of the course of study. This máy involve difficult practical problems about whether or not periods allowed for dissertations, periods in industrial training and so forth are to be computed as part of a "course of study" under new subs. (3A)(b) and (c) of s.13 of the 1971 Act.

Entry clearance has to be obtained in the country of origin. Any challenge to a refusal will now have to be based on judicial review of the entry clearance officer's decision and the conduct of the interview. The scope for judicial review is, however, limited. It is only available to correct an error of law made by the immigration authorities. In an extreme case, an unreasonable finding of fact may amount to an error of law but, generally, the High Court will not interfere with the factual basis of an immigration decision (*R.* v. *Secretary of State for the Home Department*, ex p. *Jaifrey (Mohammed Nurul Wahab)* [1990] Imm AR 6). Provided that the decision is within the band of reasonable options, the court is not concerned with the merits (*Ayo (Bashir Adebula)* v. *Immigration Appeal Tribunal* [1990] Imm AR 461).

S.13(3AA) of the 1971 Act

The role of the monitor is not yet clear. He will not be an officer of the Secretary of State and will be free to make an independent judgment of the operation of the entry clearance application process (for the position of officers of the Home Office see *R.* v. *Secretary of State for the Home Department*, ex p. *Oladehinde* [1991] A.C. 254). But he will have to liaise closely with both the Home and Foreign Offices. During the final stages of the Bill, in the discussions on the House of Lords' amendments, the junior Minister at the Home Office, Mr Charles Wardle, said:

"We are not contemplating some alternative appeal system by which applicants or sponsors could seek to have the decision in an individual case overturned, but rather, a periodic review or audit of a random sample of entry clearance refusals by an independent person, to ensure that fair and consistent standards of decision-making were maintained ... the person appointed will have a wide degree of independence in the way in which he conducts the exercise. The choice of which cases will be reviewed will be entirely his. However, the exercise must in practice be conducted within agreed guide-lines on such matters as how long the exercise should last, how many posts should be visited and when the report is produced. Those matters must ultimately be the responsibility of the Secretary of State ... the Foreign Secretary because this matter concerns the Foreign and Commonwealth Office" (*Hansard*, H.C. Vol. 226, cols. 80–81).

Refusals which are mandatory under immigration rules

11.—(1) In section 13 of the 1971 Act, after subsection (3AB) (which is inserted by section 10 above) there shall be inserted—

"(3B) A person shall not be entitled to appeal against a refusal of an entry clearance if the refusal is on the ground that—

(a) he or any person whose dependant he is does not hold a relevant document which is required by the immigration rules; or

(b) he or any person whose dependant he is does not satisfy a requirement of the immigration rules as to age or nationality or citizenship; or

(c) he or any person whose dependant he is seeks entry for a period exceeding that permitted by the immigration rules;

and a person shall not be entitled to appeal against a refusal of leave to enter if the refusal is on any of those grounds.

(3C) For the purposes of subsection (3B)(a) above, the following are "relevant documents"—

(a) entry clearances;

(b) passports or other identity documents; and

(c) work permits."

(2) In section 14 of the 1971 Act (appeals against refusals to vary leave to enter or remain), after subsection (2) there shall be inserted—

"(2A) A person shall not be entitled to appeal under subsection (1) above against any refusal to vary his leave if the refusal is on the ground that—

(a) a relevant document which is required by the immigration rules has not been issued; or

(b) the person or a person whose dependant he is does not satisfy a

requirement of the immigration rules as to age or nationality
or citizenship; or

(c) the variation would result in the duration of the person's leave
exceeding what is permitted by the immigration rules; or

(d) any fee required by or under any enactment has not been paid.

(2B) For the purposes of subsection (2A)(a) above, the following are
relevant documents—

(a) entry clearances;
(b) passports or other identity documents; and
(c) work permits."

DEFINITIONS

"dependant": para. 46 of the Immigration Rules (H.C. 251).
"entry clearance": s.33(1) of the 1971 Act.
"fee": para. 15A of the Immigration Rules 1993.
"immigration rules": s.3(1) and (2) of the 1971 Act.
"passports or . . . identity documents": para. 7 of the Immigration Rules (H.C. 251).
"vary . . . leave": s.3(3)(a) of the 1971 Act.
"work permit": para. 34 of the Immigration Rules (H.C. 251).

GENERAL NOTE

The object of this section is to remove a right of appeal from those who are bound, under the
immigration rules, to be refused entry clearance, leave or a variation of leave on the grounds
specified and whose appeals cannot therefore succeed under s.19 of the 1971 Act. Under para.
34 of the current Immigration Rules (H.C. 251), for example, if a person comes to the U.K. to
seek employment and he has no work permit issued by the Department of Employment, he is to
be refused leave to enter. There are a number of other situations under the Rules where refusal
is mandatory. However, the list in this section is exhaustive and the fact that a person does not
satisfy some other provision in the rules does not preclude an appeal, even though immigration
officers are obliged to refuse leave to enter in such cases (para. 78 of the current Immigration
Rules (H.C. 251)). The situations designated in the section, however, involve matters of fact
about which there may be genuine differences of opinion and even the exercise of an element of
discretion by the entry certificate or immigration officer. The Minister explained the scope and
reasons for this provision at Committee Stage:

"Some rules contain requirements which must be met if the application is to succeed, where
the question of whether the requirement is met can be easily determined on the basis of
documentary evidence. When an application is refused because such a requirement is not
met, the adjudicator has no option but to dismiss the appeal when it comes before him. The
existence of a right of appeal in such cases does nothing to redress genuine grievances. It
serves only to enable those appellants who have no claim under the immigration rules to spin
out their stay in this country pursuing hopeless appeals, while delaying the hearing of other
appeals which involve issues of substance" (Mr Charles Wardle, Standing Committee A, col.
703, December 10, 1993).

Lord Donaldson, the former Master of the Rolls, was not reassured during the Second
Reading of the Bill in the House of Lords that such decisions would always be so clear-cut or
that the reasons given (refusal on the grounds of age, lack of appropriate documents) would in
fact be the true basis for that decision.

"Clause 11 is the really vicious clause. I use the word advisedly . . . Subsection (3B) says 'if the
refusal is on the ground that:—'. Those of us who have dealt with immigration cases know that
the proposed immigrant is given a piece of paper on which there is a blank to be filled in by the
immigration officer. I imagine there is an equivalent one for entry clearance certificates. It says
'I have refused leave to enter on the grounds that:—'. He then inserts in manuscript whatever is
the reason . . . Is the Minister seriously saying that if the immigration officer fills in that blank
saying that the applicant does not hold a relevant document required by the immigration rules
. . . or that he has not satisfied me . . . as to his age, nationality or citizenship, then that is an end
of the matter? There is either a naïvety or an arrogance in the attitude of the Home Office that
its immigration officers must inevitably be right" (*Hansard*, H.L. Vol. 541, col. 1170).

He predicted a major increase in applications for judicial review as a result of this provision
and indicated that the courts might well be prepared to treat the grounds tendered by the Home
Office for refusal as "precedent facts". In such a case the courts will entertain a challenge to the
existence or non-existence of that precedent fact "and the burden of proof will be on the Home

Office to prove or disprove it" (*ibid.* col. 1170). (See also *R.* v. *Secretary of State for the Home Department*, ex p. *Khera*; *R.* v. *Secretary of State for the Home Department*, ex p. *Khawaja* [1984] A.C. 74).

Immigration officers are bound, under the Rules, to refuse leave if a person does not have the relevant entry clearance for the purpose for which he comes to this country (paras. 14 and 78 of H.C. 251). The fact that such a mandatory rule effectively deprives immigration officers of the discretion which they are required to exercise in giving leave under s.4 of the 1971 Act was held in *R.* v. *Secretary of State for the Home Department*, ex p. *Kaur* [1987] Imm AR 278 not to invalidate the rule (and see *R.* v. *Secretary of State for the Home Department*, ex p. *Ounejma* [1989] Imm AR 75). Whether a person has or has not a requisite document is a relatively simple question of fact. A question of age may present more difficulties, especially since many countries, including those in the Indian sub-continent, have no compulsory system of registration of births, deaths and marriages. Under para. 7 of the current Rules (H.C. 251) passengers must "furnish the immigration officers with such information as may be required". This may, for example, involve satisfying an entry clearance officer that a child is under the age of 18 for admission as a dependant under para. 53 of the Rules (H.C. 251). Real differences may arise in such cases. In the absence of an appeal right, judicial review will be the only means of challenge. In relation to the assessment of age, for example, issues of fairness about the process could form the basis for an application (*H.K. (An Infant), Re* [1967] 2 Q.B. 617.

S.13(3B)(b) of the 1971 Act

A "dependant" in this context is not the same as a "dependant" under s.3(9)(b) of the 1993 Act, namely a spouse or child under the age of 18. It might, for example, also include an unmarried, but still dependent daughter who still forms part of the family unit and is still under 21 (para. 55 of H.C. 251). The list of "relevant documents" is exhaustive. However, the subsection is much more wide-ranging then it would appear. Under the "no switching" rules (para. 102 of the current Rules (H.C. 251)), a person must be refused if he wants to switch after entry from one category to another; from, say, that of visitor to student, where the new category also requires a specific prior entry clearance for the purpose. Until now, it has been possible to appeal that refusal on, say, *Wednesbury* grounds. That will no longer be possible as the appellant will be lacking the requisite entry clearance.

S.14(2) and (2A) of the 1971 Act

Exceeding what is permitted by the immigration rules. Under para. 105 of H.C. 251, a passenger admitted for six months "shall not be permitted to extend the duration of his visit". Clearly, in such a case, a refusal is mandatory because any kind of extension (except for medical treatment: para. 106) is prohibited. But if the initial leave was for three months and the applicant seeks "an extension" without specifying a period, it is not clear whether this is to be treated as an application to vary for a period exceeding that permitted by the rules. In *Singh*, unreported, the Immigration Appeal Tribunal ruled that an application for an extension must be considered on its merits, even though the application would take the total past the maximum; the Secretary of State has a discretion to grant a lesser period ensuring that the total does not exceed the maximum period laid down by the rules.

Visas for transit passengers

Carriers' liability for transit passengers

12.—(1) The Immigration (Carriers' Liability) Act 1987 shall be amended as follows.

(2) In subsection (1)(b) of section 1 (liability of carrier of person who requires a visa for entry but fails to produce one) for the words ", a visa valid for that purpose," there shall be substituted the words "or by virtue of section 1A below requires a visa for passing through the United Kingdom, a visa valid for the purpose of entering or (as the case may be) passing through the United Kingdom,".

(3) After that section there shall be inserted—

"Visas for transit passengers

1A.—(1) The Secretary of State may by order require persons of any description specified in the order who on arrival in the United Kingdom pass through to another country or territory without entering the United Kingdom to hold a visa for that purpose.

(2) An order under this section—

(a) may specify a description of persons by reference to nationality, citizenship, origin or other connection with any particular
country or territory, but not by reference to race, colour or
religion;

(b) shall not provide for the requirement imposed by the order to
apply to any person who under the Immigration Act 1971 has
the right of abode in the United Kingdom and may provide for
any category of persons of a description specified in the order
to be exempted from the requirement imposed by the order;
and

(c) may make provision about the method of application for visas
required by the order.

(3) An order under this section shall be made by statutory instrument which shall be subject to annulment in pursuance of a resolution
of either House of Parliament."

DEFINITION
"right of abode": s.2(1) of the 1971 Act.

GENERAL NOTE
A large number of foreign and Commonwealth nationals listed in the Appendix to the new
Immigration Rules are required to have a visa endorsed on their passport or identity document,
to secure entry to the U.K. and must be refused admission if they have no such visa or prior
entry clearance (para. 14 of the new Immigration Rules). Hitherto, although transit passengers
may be examined and even refused entry (even if they have no wish to enter) (*R.* v. *Home
Secretary,* ex p. *Caunhye* [1987] Imm AR 478) they have not previously required a visa to pass,
in transit, through the U.K. Under s.11(1) of the 1971 Act, a person is not deemed to enter the
U.K. so long as he remains in the area of the port of entry (often called a "transit lounge")
approved by an immigration officer. Transit passengers may be granted leave to enter the
country for up to 48 hours, but they will require a visa for *entry* for this purpose (para. 25 of H.C.
251 as amended by the new Immigration Rules). The nationals designated as requiring transit
visas may comprise, some, or all, of those who require visas to enter the U.K. No order has yet
been made designating the categories of foreign nationals requiring a visa under this section.

The section extends the liability of carriers to the new visa requirement. Under s.1(1) and (2)
of the 1987 Act, liability is incurred by the carrier if the passenger fails to produce a passport or
identity document and a valid visa for entry to the U.K. (if necessary) when embarking on the
ship or aircraft for the voyage or flight to the U.K. It is likely to make it more difficult for
prospective asylum-seekers to reach the U.K. Some have, hitherto, obtained access to this
country by buying a ticket to another country and using the stop-off in a British airport to make
an asylum application (see, for example, *R.* v. *Secretary of State for the Home Department,* ex p.
Yassine (Khalil) [1990] Imm AR 354).

Supplementary

Financial provision

13.—(1) There shall be paid out of money provided by Parliament—

(a) any expenditure incurred by the Secretary of State under this Act;
and

(b) any increase attributable to this Act in the sums payable out of such
money under any other enactment.

(2) Any sums received by the Secretary of State by virtue of this Act shall
be paid into the Consolidated Fund.

Commencement

14.—(1) Sections 4 to 11 above (and section 1 above so far as it relates to
those sections) shall not come into force until such day as the Secretary of
State may by order appoint, and different days may be appointed for
different provisions or for different purposes.

(2) An order under subsection (1) above—

(a) shall be made by statutory instrument; and

(b) may contain such transitional and supplemental provisions as the Secretary of State thinks necessary or expedient.

(3) Without prejudice to the generality of subsections (1) and (2) above, with respect to any provision of section 4 above an order under subsection (1) above may appoint different days in relation to different descriptions of asylum-seekers and dependants of asylum-seekers; and any such descriptions may be framed by reference to nationality, citizenship, origin or other connection with any particular country or territory, but not by reference to race, colour or religion.

GENERAL NOTE
Details about commencement and the transitional provisions of the Act are contained in the introductory notes, above.

Extent

15.—(1) Her Majesty may by Order in Council direct that any of the provisions of this Act shall extend, with such modifications as appear to Her Majesty to be appropriate, to any of the Channel Islands or the Isle of Man.

(2) This Act extends to Northern Ireland.

GENERAL NOTE
No order to this effect has yet been made (November 1993).

Short title

16. This Act may be cited as the Asylum and Immigration Appeals Act 1993.

SCHEDULES

Section 4(5)   SCHEDULE 1

HOUSING OF ASYLUM-SEEKERS AND THEIR DEPENDANTS: SUPPLEMENTARY

Qualifying persons

1. In this Schedule the expression "qualifying person" means an asylum-seeker or a dependant of an asylum-seeker.

Inquiries about applicants

2. If a housing authority to whom an application is made have reason to believe that the applicant is a qualifying person, they shall include in the inquiries that they are required to make under section 62 of the Housing Act 1985, section 28 of the Housing (Scotland) Act 1987 or, as the case may be, Article 7 of the Housing (Northern Ireland) Order 1988 such inquiries as are necessary to satisfy them as to whether—
   (a) he is a qualifying person; and
   (b) if so, whether any duty is owed to him to secure that accommodation is made available for his occupation.

Notification of decision and reasons

3.—(1) Subject to sub-paragraph (2) below, if a housing authority who are dealing with an applicant's case are satisfied that he is a qualifying person they shall notify him—
   (a) that they are so satisfied;
   (b) that they are or, as the case may be, are not satisfied that a duty is owed to him to secure that accommodation is made available for his occupation;
   (c) if they are the authority to whom the application is made, whether they have notified or propose to notify another housing authority under section 67 of the Act of 1985 or, as the case may be, section 33 of the Act of 1987 (referral of application on grounds of local connection) as modified by paragraph 4 below;
and they shall at the same time notify him of their reasons.

(2) In its application to Northern Ireland, sub-paragraph (1) above shall have effect as if paragraph (c) were omitted.

(3) The notice required to be given to the applicant under sub-paragraph (1) above shall be given in writing and shall, if not received by him, be treated as having been given to him only if it is made available at the authority's office for a reasonable period for collection by him or on his behalf.

(4) Where notice is given under sub-paragraph (1) above, no notice need be given under section 64 of the Act of 1985, section 30 of the Act of 1987 or, as the case may be, Article 9 of the Order of 1988 (notification of decision and reasons).

Referral of application to another housing authority

4.—(1) If a housing authority to whom an application is made are satisfied that the applicant is a qualifying person and that a duty to secure that accommodation is made available for his occupation is owed to him, the homelessness legislation shall have effect as if in section 67 of the Act of 1985 or, as the case may be, section 33 of the Act of 1987 for paragraph (a) of subsection (1) there were substituted—

"(a) are satisfied that an applicant is a qualifying person and that a duty to secure that accommodation is made available for his occupation is owed to him."

(2) Sub-paragraph (1) above does not apply in relation to Northern Ireland.

Offences

5. Section 74 of the Act of 1985, section 40 of the Act of 1987 or, as the case may be, Article 17 of the Order of 1988 applies to statements made or information withheld with intent to induce an authority to believe that a person is or is not an asylum-seeker or a dependant of an asylum-seeker as it applies to statements made or information withheld with the intent mentioned in subsection (1) of section 74, section 40 or, as the case may be, Article 17.

Security of tenure

6.—(1) A tenancy granted in pursuance of any duty under Part III of the Act of 1985 to a person who is a qualifying person cannot be—

(a) a tenancy which is a secure tenancy for the purposes of that Act, or

(b) a tenancy which is an assured tenancy for the purposes of the Housing Act 1988,

before the expiry of the period of twelve months beginning with the date on which the landlord is supplied with written information given by the Secretary of State under paragraph 7 below that the person has ceased to be a qualifying person, unless before the expiry of that period the landlord notifies that person that the tenancy is to be regarded as a secure tenancy or, as the case may be, an assured tenancy.

(2) A tenancy granted in pursuance of any duty under Part II of the Order of 1988 to a person who is a qualifying person cannot be a tenancy which is a secure tenancy for the purposes of Part II of the Housing (Northern Ireland) Order 1983 before the expiry of the period of twelve months beginning with the date on which the landlord is supplied with written information given by the Secretary of State under paragraph 7 below that the person has ceased to be a qualifying person, unless before the expiry of that period the landlord notifies that person that the tenancy is to be regarded as a secure tenancy.

Information

7.—(1) The Secretary of State shall, if requested to do so by a housing authority who are dealing with an applicant's case, inform the authority whether the applicant has become a qualifying person.

(2) Where information which the Secretary of State is required to give to a housing authority under sub-paragraph (1) above is given otherwise than in writing, he shall confirm it in writing if a written request is made to him by the authority.

(3) If the Secretary of State informs an authority that an applicant has become a qualifying person, he shall, when the applicant ceases to be a qualifying person, inform the authority and the applicant in writing of that event and of the date on which it occurred.

Existing applicants

8.—(1) Nothing in section 4 or section 5 of this Act or this Schedule shall affect—

(a) the right of any person to occupy (or to have made available for his occupation) accommodation which, immediately before the day on which section 4 comes into force, is required to be made available for his occupation in pursuance of the homelessness legislation; or

(b) any application made to a housing authority which immediately before that day is a pending application.

(2) For the purposes of sub-paragraph (1) above an application shall be regarded as pending if it is an application in respect of which the authority have not completed the inquiries that they are required to make under section 62 of the Housing Act 1985, section 28 of the Housing (Scotland) Act 1987 or, as the case may be, Article 7 of the Housing (Northern Ireland) Order 1988.

Isles of Scilly

9.—(1) The provisions of sections 4 and 5 of this Act and this Schedule shall apply to the Isles of Scilly subject to such exceptions, adaptations and modifications as the Secretary of State may by order direct.

(2) An order under sub-paragraph (1) above shall be made by statutory instrument which shall be subject to annulment in pursuance of a resolution of either House of Parliament.

GENERAL NOTE

This Schedule, together with ss.4 and 5, modifies the obligations of local housing authorities under the housing legislation relating to emergency housing provisions (principally the Housing Act 1985, Pt. III) and details the procedure to be adopted by local housing authorities in relation to asylum-seekers and their dependants, and the obligations of the Home Office to supply information concerning the status of applicants (see the General Note to s.4). It also prevents asylum-seekers and their dependants from acquiring security of tenure in local authority or other housing while asylum applications are under consideration, but does not affect the security of any tenancy granted to asylum-seekers, or likely to be granted as a result of inquiries which were being made when the Act came into effect. Paragraph 5 extends the scope of offences under s.74 of the 1985 Act, and under Art. 17 of the Housing (Northern Ireland) Order 1988 (S.I. 1988 No. 1990) in relation to Northern Ireland, to include the withholding of information relating to asylum-seeker status.

Section 8(6)   SCHEDULE 2

APPEALS TO SPECIAL ADJUDICATOR: SUPPLEMENTARY

New appeal rights to replace rights under the 1971 Act

1. No appeal may be brought under Part II of the 1971 Act on any of the grounds mentioned in subsections (1) to (4) of section 8 of this Act.

Scope of new rights of appeal

2. A person may not bring an appeal on any of the grounds mentioned in subsections (1) to (4) of section 8 of this Act unless, before the time of the refusal, variation, decision or directions (as the case may be), he has made a claim for asylum.

Other grounds of appeal

3. Where an appeal is brought by a person on any of the grounds mentioned in subsections (1) to (4) of section 8 of this Act, the special adjudicator shall in the same proceedings deal with—
   (a) any appeal against the refusal, variation, decision or directions (as the case may be) which the person is entitled to bring under Part II of the 1971 Act on any other ground on which he seeks to rely; and
   (b) any appeal brought by the person under that Part of that Act against any other decision or action.

Application of procedures in the 1971 Act

4.—(1) Subject to sub-paragraphs (3) and (4) of this paragraph and to paragraph 5 below, the provisions of the 1971 Act specified in sub-paragraph (2) below shall have effect as if section 8 of this Act were contained in Part II of that Act.

(2) The provisions referred to in sub-paragraph (1) above are—
   (a) section 18 (notice of decisions appealable under that Part and statement of appeal rights etc.);
   (b) section 19 (determination of appeals under that Part by adjudicators);
   (c) section 20 (appeal for adjudicator to Immigration Appeal Tribunal);
   (d) section 21 (references of cases by Secretary of State for further consideration);
   (e) section 22(1) to (4), (6) and (7) (rules of procedure for appeals);
   (f) section 23 (grants to voluntary organisations helping persons with rights of appeal); and
   (g) Schedule 5 (provisions about adjudicators and Immigration Appeal Tribunal).

(3) Rules of procedure under section 22 may make special provision in relation to—

(a) proceedings on appeals on any of the grounds mentioned in subsections (1) to (4) of section 8 of this Act; and

(b) proceedings in which, by virtue of paragraph 3 above, a special adjudicator is required to deal both with an appeal on any of those grounds and another appeal.

(4) So much of paragraph 5 of Schedule 5 as relates to the allocation of duties among the adjudicators shall have effect subject to subsection (5) of section 8 of this Act.

Special appeal procedures for claims without foundation

5.—(1) Subject to sub-paragraph (2) below, this paragraph applies to an appeal by a person under subsection (1), (3)(b) or (4) of section 8 of this Act if the Secretary of State has certified that, in his opinion, the person's claim on the ground that it would be contrary to the United Kingdom's obligations under the Convention for him to be removed from the United Kingdom is without foundation.

(2) This paragraph does not apply to an appeal on the ground mentioned in subsection (1) of section 8 of this Act if, by virtue of section 13(3) of the 1971 Act (right of appeal for person with current entry clearance or work permit), the appellant seeks to rely on another ground.

(3) For the purposes of this paragraph a claim is without foundation if (and only if)—

(a) it does not raise any issue as to the United Kingdom's obligations under the Convention; or

(b) it is otherwise frivolous or vexatious.

(4) Rules of procedure under section 22 of the 1971 Act may make special provision in relation to appeals to which this paragraph applies.

(5) If on an appeal to which this paragraph applies the special adjudicator agrees that the claim is without foundation, section 20(1) of that Act shall not confer on the appellant any right to appeal to the Immigration Appeal Tribunal.

(6) If the special adjudicator does not agree that the claim is without foundation, he may (as an alternative to allowing or dismissing the appeal) refer the case to the Secretary of State for reconsideration; and the making of such a reference shall, accordingly, be regarded as disposing of the appeal.

Exception for national security

6. Subsection (5) of section 13, subsection (3) of section 14 and subsections (3) and (4) of section 15 of the 1971 Act shall have effect in relation to the rights of appeal conferred by section 8(1), (2) and (3)(a) and (b) of this Act respectively as they have effect in relation to the rights of appeal conferred by subsection (1) of those sections of that Act but as if references to a person's exclusion, departure or deportation being conducive to the public good were references to its being in the interests of national security.

Suspension of variation of limited leave pending appeal

7. The limitation on the taking effect of a variation and on a requirement to leave the United Kingdom contained in subsection (1) of section 14 of the 1971 Act shall have effect as if appeals under section 8(2) of this Act were appeals under that subsection.

Deportation order not to be made while appeal pending

8. In section 15(2) of the 1971 Act references to an appeal against a decision to make a deportation order shall include references to an appeal against such a decision under section 8(3)(a) of this Act.

Stay of removal directions pending appeal and bail

9. Part II of Schedule 2, and paragraph 3 of Schedule 3, to the 1971 Act shall have effect as if the references to appeals under section 13(1), 15(1)(a) and 16 of that Act included (respectively) appeals under section 8(1), (3) and (4) of this Act and as if sub-paragraph (5) of paragraph 28 of Schedule 2 were omitted.

GENERAL NOTE

Paragraphs 4, 7, 8 and 9 of this Schedule are required to ensure that appeal procedures and the protection of appellants from deportation and removal while an appeal is pending under Pt. II of the 1971 Act in relation to "ordinary" appeals are extended to asylum appeals (see the General Note to s.8). Except in the case of the more limited appeal rights conferred on applicants whose claims have been certified to be without foundation under s.8(1), (3)(b) or (4), which are dealt with in para. 5 of the Schedule, the procedure and the powers of the special adjudicator, are the same as that in Pt. II appeals except that the time-limits for the lodging of appeals are shorter in the case of asylum appeals. (See r. 5 of the Asylum Appeals (Procedure) Rules 1993 (S.I. 1993 No. 1661) reproduced in Appendix 2 to these annotations). The most important paragraphs of this Schedule are para. 5, which defines the circumstances for the certification of "without foundation" claims by the Home Secretary and the more limited appeal rights which result from such certification, para. 6, which enlarges the appeal rights of asylum-seekers threatened with exclusion or deportation on political grounds, and para. 9 which extends protection against removal to asylum appellants.

The effect of s.8 and Sched. 2, paras. 1 and 2 is to create a separate avenue for asylum appeals in relation to applications made for leave to enter, variations or refusals to vary leave already given, decisions to deport and refusals to revoke existing deportation orders and directions for removal from the U.K. Paragraph 2 was added after the Bill returned to the Commons. It would seem, on the face of it, to be otiose, because an appeal against refusal of asylum is only likely to be lodged if an application is refused. However, s.8 confers a right of appeal where the consequences of a refusal of leave, refusal to vary, deportation or removal may result in action contrary to the Convention. Those steps may well result from non-asylum causes, such as a breach of conditions attached to a leave, or the recommendation of a court following a conviction. A failure to make a claim for asylum before the decision may mean, in those cases where there is an existing appeal, that the individual has only the "ordinary" appeal under Pt. II of the 1971 Act. If he makes the claim before the decision, and there are non-asylum issues as well as Convention matters, then the case will go to the special adjudicator as a "mixed" appeal under para. 3 (see r. 29 of the Asylum Appeals (Procedure) Rules 1993 (S.I. 1993 No. 1661)). If the applicant fails to make the claim in time, para. 2 would seem to preclude him from raising asylum issues on the appeal. He may, however, raise the issue before a decision to deport is made, and it will then be heard on appeal before a special adjudicator on the deportation appeal.

Para. 5
This provision creates the "fast-track" system for those described by Government ministers as "bogus" asylum-seekers and whose claims to asylum will be certified by the Home Secretary as being "without foundation". It will apply to port, deportation and illegal entry cases where the notice of refusal has been personally served on the applicant. Under the Asylum Appeals (Procedure) Rules 1993 (S.I. 1993 No. 1661), only two days is given within which to lodge an appeal (r. 5(2)), and special adjudicators are required to determine such appeals within seven days of receiving notice of appeal (r. 9(2)). During the Committee Stage of the Bill in the House of Commons the Parliamentary Under-Secretary of State at the Home Office, Mr Charles Wardle explained the basis on which such certificates will be issued:

"Manifestly unfounded cases fall into three categories. The first is the safe third country cases, where the applicant has previously been in a safe third country . . . . The second category is when the grounds do not bear in any sense on the U.K.'s obligations under the Convention; when, for example, there is no expressed fear of persecution, and, therefore, asylum claims do not apply. The third category is when the application is frivolous or vexatious or when no proper details are provided on request" (Standing Committee A, col. 566, December 3, 1992).

The new Immigration Rules (para. 180K) provide that if the Home Secretary is satisfied that "the asylum applicant has not arrived in the U.K. directly from the country in which he claims to fear persecution and has had an opportunity, at the border or within the territory of a third country, to make contact with that country's authorities in order to seek their protection, or there is clear evidence of his admissibility to a third country" then his claim will not receive "substantive consideration". This will also be the case if a "safe" third country has considered and rejected a claim for asylum (para. 180M). Such cases may raise the issue of whether or not a third country is indeed "safe", and this is a matter which a special adjudicator will have to consider, together with the broader merits of an applicant's appeal, in the more truncated appeal provided for under subpara. (5) of this paragraph (*Bugdaycay* v. *Secretary of State for the Home Department; Nelidow Santis* v. *Same; Norman* v. *Same; Musisi, Re* [1987] A.C. 514 (and see the General Note to s.2)).

There is no definition in the Act of "frivolous or vexatious" claims, but the same words are included in R.S.C., Ord. 18, r. 19 in relation to the striking out of actions. Since the outcome of an unsuccessful asylum application may be so much more serious to an applicant than failure in civil litigation, the expression does not seem altogether well chosen in relation to claims which appear to the Home Secretary to be wholly without merit, or where the applicant is simply using the asylum appeal process to delay his departure.

Para. 6
Article 32(1) of the Geneva Convention prohibits the expulsion of a refugee lawfully in

the territory "save on grounds of national security or public order", and Art. 33(2) restricts the protection of refugees against return or "*refoulement*" in cases where "there are reasonable grounds for regarding [a refugee] as a danger to the security of the country in which he is, or who having been convicted by a final judgment of a particularly serious crime, constitutes a danger to the community of that country".

Article 32 is applicable to refugees who are *lawfully* in the country, that is with leave (*R.* v. *Secretary of State for the Home Department*, ex p. *Singh (Gurmeet)*, *The Times*, March 28, 1988). The more limited protection of Art. 33, in which there are no procedural safeguards, is available to those who are simply "in" the country in the physical sense, having been granted temporary admission under para. 21(1) of Sched. 2 to the 1971 Act (see *Singh*, above).

Those who have refugee status and are liable to expulsion on national security or public order grounds are, by virtue of Art. 32(3), only to be expelled "in pursuance of a decision reached in accordance with due process of law. Except where compelling reasons of national security otherwise require, the refugee shall be allowed to submit evidence to clear himself, and to appeal and be represented for the purpose before competent authority or persons specifically designated by the competent authority".

Under ss.13(5), 14(3) and 15(4) of the 1971 Act a person does not have a right of appeal if the decision to exclude him, refuse to vary his leave or to deport him is taken personally by the Home Secretary and is taken (in the case of an exclusion) on the ground that his exclusion is "conducive to the public good", or (in the case of refusal to vary leave) on the ground that the appellant's departure "would be conducive to the public good, as being in the interests of national security or of the relations between the U.K. and any other country or for other reasons of a political nature", or (in the case of refusal to revoke a deportation order) where the Home Secretary personally refuses to revoke such a decision on the basis that the individual's exclusion would be "conducive to the public good".

The effect of subpara. 6 is to confine those restrictions on appeal rights to national security cases, so that, for example, a decision to revoke an asylum-seeker's leave to be here as a visitor on the grounds that his political activities were damaging to Britain's relations with a friendly state, would be subject to an appeal under s.8 of the Act. In national security cases there will still remain the right to make representations to the "three advisers", although the appellant may be given little or no information as to why a decision has been taken and will have little chance to put up an effective defence to the allegations on which the Home Secretary has based his decision (*R.* v. *Secretary of State for Home Affairs*, ex p. *Hosenball* [1977] 1 W.L.R. 766, C.A.). To satisfy the requirements of Art. 33 of the Geneva Convention, the Court held in *R.* v. *Secretary of State for the Home Department*, ex p. *Chahal*, *The Times*, March 12, 1993 that it was "enough if [the Secretary of State] sufficiently identified the grounds on which he had ... regarded the applicant as a danger to the security of the country" (*per* Potts J.). (See also the decision of the Court of Appeal at, *The Times*, October 27, 1993).

Para. 9

This paragraph extends the protection against removal which is provided by Pt. II of the 1971 Act in relation to appeals against refusal of leave to enter or directions for removal to appeals lodged in asylum cases. Schedule 2, para. 28(5) to the 1971 Act limits the meaning of a "pending" appeal (giving protection against removal following an adverse determination by an adjudicator), to one in which the individual gives notice of appeal, or applies for leave to appeal, against the determination "forthwith". In asylum cases, under this paragraph, as long as notice of appeal is given within the time-limits specified in r. 5 of the Asylum Appeals (Procedure) Rules 1993 (S.I. 1993 No. 1661), an appeal against the determination of a special adjudicator can still be "pending" during the period allowed. A direction to remove a person who *may* appeal to the Immigration Appeal Tribunal during the period allowed may not, therefore, be given. However, the position with regard to appeals against the decision of the Home Secretary that leave to enter should be refused in an asylum case is unaffected. In those cases, protection against removal only becomes operative *after* the notice of appeal has been lodged (and see the General Note to s.6).

APPENDICES

APPENDIX 1

STATEMENT OF CHANGES IN IMMIGRATION RULES

[July 5, 1993; laid before Parliament under s.3(2) of the Immigration Act 1971.]

STATEMENT OF CHANGES IN IMMIGRATION RULES

The Home Secretary has made the changes hereinafter stated in the rules laid down by him as to the practice to be followed in the administration of the Immigration Act 1971 for regulating entry into and the stay of persons in the U.K. and contained in the statement laid before Parliament on March 23, 1990 (HC 251), as amended. [The amending statements were laid before or presented to Parliament on March 26, 1991 (HC 320), April 17, 1991 (HC 356), September 30, 1991 (Cm 1672), October 18, 1991 (HC 670), January 21, 1992 (HC 175), June 10, 1992 (HC 49) and November 5, 1992 (HC 251)].

With the exception of changes in respect of "au pairs", namely paras. 33, 121, 121A and 187 and the Appendix, these changes shall take effect from July 26, 1993. The changes in "au pairs" shall take effect from September 1, 1993. The changes in the Appendix shall take effect from July 6, 1993.

In paragraph 1 after the word 'hydrofoil' there shall be inserted the following words: "or train"

In paragraph 7 after the words 'United Kingdom' (each time that it appears) there shall be inserted the following words:
", or when seeking entry through the Channel Tunnel."

In paragraph 12 after the words 'A passenger arriving in the United Kingdom' there shall be inserted the following words:
", or seeking entry through the Channel Tunnel."

For paragraph 14 there shall be substituted:
"14. The persons specified in the Appendix who need a visa for the United Kingdom (and who are collectively described in these Rules as "visa nationals") and any other person who is seeking entry for a purpose for which prior entry clearance is required under these Rules must produce to the immigration officer a passport or other identity document endorsed with a United Kingdom entry clearance issued for the purpose for which they seek entry. They must be refused leave to enter if they have no such current entry clearance. Any other person who wishes to ascertain in advance whether he is eligible for admission to the United Kingdom must apply for the issue of an entry clearance."

For paragraph 15 there shall be substituted:
"15. An applicant for an entry clearance must be outside the United Kingdom and Islands at the time of the application. An applicant for an entry clearance who is seeking entry as a visitor must apply to a post designated by the Secretary of State to accept applications for entry clearance for that purpose and from that category of applicant. Any other application must be made to the post in the country or territory where the applicant is living which has been designated by the Secretary of State to accept applications for entry clearance for that purpose and from that category of applicant. Where there is no such post the applicant must apply to the appropriate designated post outside the country or territory where he is living".

(For the purposes of this Rule "Post" means a British diplomatic mission, British Consular Post or the office of any person outside the United Kingdom and Islands who has been authorised by the Secretary of State to accept applications for entry clearance. A list of designated posts is published by the Foreign and Commonwealth Office.)

After paragraph 15 there shall be inserted:
"15A. An application for an entry clearance is not made until any fee required to be paid under the Consular Fees Act 1980 (including any Regulations or Orders made under that Act) has been paid."

For paragraph 16 there shall be substituted:
"16. Entry clearance takes the form of a visa or an entry certificate and these are to be taken as evidence of the holder's eligibility for entry to the United Kingdom, and accordingly accepted as "entry clearances" within the meaning of the Act. Applications for entry clearance are to be considered in accordance with the provisions in this statement governing the grant or refusal of leave to enter by an immigration officer and, where appropriate, the term "entry

clearance officer" may be substituted for "immigration officer" accordingly. Applications are to be decided in the light of the circumstances existing at the time of the decision except that an applicant will not be refused an entry clearance under paragraphs 53 to 55 solely on account of his becoming over age between the receipt of his application and the date of the decision on it."

For paragraph 25 there shall be substituted:

"25. A person who satisfies the requirements of paragraph 13 for admission as a passenger in transit will be admitted as a visitor for a period not exceeding 48 hours and be expected to leave the United Kingdom within that period. Any other passenger admitted to the United Kingdom as a visitor, and any dependants accompanying him should be given leave to enter for a period of 6 months unless the immigration officer is satisfied that there are particular circumstances which justify the giving of a shorter period of leave. Visitors should normally be prohibited from taking employment."

For paragraph 33 there shall be substituted:

"33. "Au pair" is an arrangement under which an unmarried person aged 17 to 27 inclusive and without dependants who is a national of Andorra, Austria, Bosnia-Herzegovina, Croatia, Cyprus, Czech Republic, The Faeroes, Finland, Greenland, Hungary, Iceland, Liechtenstein, Macedonia, Malta, Monaco, Norway, San Marino, Slovak Republic, Slovenia, Sweden, Switzerland, or Turkey may come to the United Kingdom to learn the English language and to live for a time as a member of an English speaking family. A person coming for full-time domestic employment requires a work permit; and a person admitted under an "au pair" arrangement has no claim to stay in the United Kingdom in some other capacity. When the immigration officer is satisfied that an "au pair" arrangement has been made he may admit the passenger for a period of up to 2 years with a prohibition on him taking employment. If a passenger has previously spent time in the United Kingdom as an "au pair" he may be admitted for a further period as an "au pair" but the total aggregate period should not exceed 2 years."

For paragraph 75, there shall be substituted:

"75. A person subject to immigration control may seek to enter the United Kingdom by applying for asylum as a refugee or may otherwise indicate a fear of being required to return to his country of origin or habitual residence. All such cases are referred to in these rules as "asylum applications". Every asylum application made by a person at a port or airport in the United Kingdom will be referred by the Immigration Officer to the Home Office for determination by the Secretary of State in accordance with the provisions of Part XIII of these Rules. Until such a case has been determined by the Secretary of State no action will be taken to require the person's departure from the United Kingdom.

75A. If the Secretary of State decides to grant asylum and the person has not yet been given leave to enter the Immigration Officer will grant limited leave to enter.

75B. If a person seeking leave to enter is refused asylum the Immigration Officer will then resume his examination to determine whether or not to grant him leave to enter under any other provision of the Rules. If a person who has been refused leave to enter applies for asylum and that application is refused, leave to enter will again be refused, unless the applicant qualifies for admission under any other provisions of these rules.

75C. A person who is refused leave to enter following the refusal of an asylum application will be provided with a notice informing him of the decision and of the reasons for refusal. The notice of refusal will also explain any rights of appeal available to the applicant and will inform him of the means by which he may exercise those rights. The applicant will not be removed from the United Kingdom so long as any appeal which he may bring is pending".

In paragraph 87 after the word 'ship' there shall be inserted the following words:
", 'aircraft, hydrofoil or train' "

In paragraph 88 after the word 'removal' there shall be inserted the following words:
"from the United Kingdom."

For paragraph 90 there shall be substituted:

"90. Where refusal of leave to enter is confirmed, the passenger should be handed a notice informing him of the decision and the reasons for the refusal. This notice will also inform the passenger whether he has a right of appeal under section 13 of the Act, and, if so, how that right of appeal might be exercised. If he has difficulty in understanding the notice its meaning should be explained to him."

After paragraph 91 there shall be inserted the following paragraph:

"91A. A passenger in possession of a current entry clearance or named in a current work permit who is refused leave to enter when seeking entry to the United Kingdom through the Channel Tunnel may, upon giving notice of appeal, be brought through the tunnel to enable him to pursue his appeal."

For paragraph 92 there shall be substituted:

"92. In other cases where the passenger is entitled to appeal against refusal of leave to enter, except cases involving an asylum application, to which paragraph 75C applies, irrespective of the passenger's national status it should be explained to him that his right of appeal is exercisable only after he has left the United Kingdom."

For paragraph 97 there shall be substituted:

"97. A person may appeal under section 14 of the Act against any variation of his leave to enter or any refusal to vary it, except when a refusal is on one of the grounds specified in section 14(2A). Furthermore there is no such appeal against a variation of leave which reduces its duration, or against a refusal to extend or remove a time limit, if the Secretary of State personally decides that the departure of the person concerned from the United Kingdom would be conducive to the public good as being in the interest of national security or of the relations between the United Kingdom and any other country or for reasons of a political nature. There is no right of appeal either in respect of a variation made by statutory instrument. Where:

(i) an application for variation of leave to enter is refused; or

(ii) a variation is made otherwise than on the application of a person concerned, or is less favourable than that for which he applied,

notice of the decision and, if an appeal lies, of his right of appeal will normally be handed to the person concerned or sent to his last known address. Alternatively it may be so given or sent to a person who has either made the application on behalf of another, or has subsequently been appointed to act on another's behalf in connection with an application. If notice of appeal is given within the period allowed, an explanatory statement summarising the facts of the case on the basis of which the decision was taken will be sent to the independent appellant authorities, who will notify the appellant of the arrangements for any appeal to be heard."

For paragraph 103 there shall be substituted:

"103. A person who has been given leave to enter to join a ship, aircraft, hovercraft, hydrofoil or international train service as a member of its crew, or a crew member who has been given leave to enter for hospital treatment, repatriation or transfer to another ship, aircraft, hovercraft, hydrofoil or international train service in the United Kingdom, should be granted an extension of stay only when this is necessary to fulfil the purpose for which he was given leave to enter, unless he qualifies for an extension of stay in accordance with paragraph 131."

For paragraph 105 there shall be substituted:

"105. A visitor admitted for up to 48 hours for the sole purpose of transit who applies for an extension of stay beyond this period must be refused. Subject to paragraph 106, a visitor who has been admitted for a stay of six months shall not be permitted to extend the duration of his visit. Where any other visitor who has been admitted for a stay of less than 6 months wishes to extend his visit, and provided that he has sufficient means to maintain himself and any dependants without work and without becoming a charge on public funds for the remainder of his proposed stay and intends to leave at the end of it, an extension may be granted provided that the duration of the visit would not as a result exceed 6 months."

For paragraph 121 there shall be substituted:

"121. Where the immigration officer was satisfied that an "au pair" arrangement had been made, the passenger will have been admitted for up to 2 years, with a condition prohibiting his employment. Where he subsequently applies for an extension of stay in the "au pair" capacity, an extension to bring the aggregate of his periods of stay up to 2 years in an "au pair" capacity may be granted if the "au pair" arrangement is satisfactory. Where an extension is granted the applicant should be informed that 2 years is the maximum period permitted."

After paragraph 121 there shall be inserted paragraph 121A:

"121A. A person who was not given leave to enter the United Kingdom as an "au pair" must be refused an extension if he applies to remain as an "au pair"."

In paragraph 139 after the words 'in that capacity for' there shall be inserted the following words,

'a continuous period of'.

For paragraph 140, there shall be substituted:

"140. A person subject to immigration control may seek to prolong his stay in the United Kingdom by applying for asylum as a refugee or may otherwise indicate a fear of being required to return to his country of origin or habitual residence. All such cases are referred to in these rules as "asylum applications". All asylum applications will be determined by the Secretary of State in accordance with the provisions of Part XIII of these Rules."

After paragraph 160 there shall be inserted paragraph 160A:

"160A. In addition to the rights of appeal mentioned above then, except where the ground of the decision to make a deportation order is conducive to the public good and is certified by the Secretary of State as being in the interests of national security, a person who has claimed asylum may also appeal against (a) a decision to make a deportation order against him by virtue of section 3(5), (b) a refusal to revoke a deportation order made against him by virtue of section 3(5) or (6), or (c) directions for their removal from the United Kingdom given under section 16(1)(a) or (b) of the Act, under section [10] of the Asylum and Immigration Appeals Act 1993. In such circumstances the appeal will be before a special adjudicator who will also consider any appeal under Part II of the Act."

For paragraph 173 there shall be substituted:

"173. A deportation order will not be made against any person if his removal in pursuance of the order would be contrary to the United Kingdom's obligations under the Convention and Protocol relating to the Status of Refugees."

After paragraph 180, there shall be inserted:

"PART XIII: ASYLUM

180A. All asylum applications will be determined by the Secretary of State in accordance with the United Kingdom's obligations under the United Nations Convention and Protocol relating to the Status of Refugees. Until an asylum application has been determined by the Secretary of State, no action will be taken to require the departure of the applicant or his dependants from the United Kingdom.

Grant of Asylum

180B. A person will be granted asylum in the United Kingdom if the Secretary of State is satisfied that:
- (a) he is in the United Kingdom or has arrived at a port of entry in the United Kingdom; and
- (b) he is a refugee, as defined by the Convention and Protocol; and
- (c) refusing his application would result in his being required to go, (whether immediately or after the time limited by an existing leave to enter or remain) in breach of the Convention and Protocol, to a country in which his life or freedom would be threatened on account of his race, religion, nationality, membership of a particular social group or political opinion.

180C. If the Secretary of State decides to grant asylum to a person who has been given leave to enter (whether or not the leave has expired) or to a person who has entered without leave, the Secretary of State will vary the existing leave or grant limited leave to remain.

Refusal of asylum

180D. An application which does not meet the criteria in paragraph 180B will be refused. The Secretary of State may decide not to consider the substance of a person's claim to refugee status if he is satisfied that the person's removal to a third country does not raise any issue as to the United Kingdom's obligations under the Convention and Protocol. More details are given in paragraphs 180K and 180M.

180E. When a person in the United Kingdom is notified that asylum has been refused he may, if he is liable to removal as an illegal entrant or to deportation, at the same time be notified of removal directions, served with a notice of intention to make a deportation order, or served with a deportation order, as appropriate. When a person with limited leave is refused asylum the leave may be curtailed if he does not meet the requirements of the rules under which leave was granted; when a person's leave is curtailed under section 7 of the Asylum and Immigration Appeals Act 1993, he may at the same time be served with a notice of intention to make a deportation order. Full account will be taken of all the relevant circumstances known to the Secretary of State, including those listed in paragraph 164.

Consideration of cases

180F. A failure, without reasonable explanation, to make a prompt and full disclosure of material factors, either orally or in writing, or otherwise to assist the Secretary of State to the full in establishing the facts of the case may lead to refusal of an asylum application. This includes failure to comply with a notice issued by the Secretary of State requiring the applicant to report to a designated place to be fingerprinted, or failure to complete an asylum questionnaire, or failure to comply with a request to attend an interview concerning the application.

180G. In determining an asylum application the Secretary of State will have regard to matters which may damage an asylum applicant's credibility if no reasonable explanation is given. Among such matters are:
- (a) that the applicant has failed to apply forthwith upon arrival in the United Kingdom, unless the application is founded on events which have taken place since his arrival in the United Kingdom;

(b) that the applicant has made false representations, either orally or in writing;

(c) that the applicant has destroyed, damaged or disposed of any passport, other document or ticket relevant to his claim;

(d) that the applicant has undertaken any activities in the United Kingdom before or after lodging his application which are inconsistent with his previous beliefs and behaviour and calculated to create or substantially enhance his claim to refugee status;

(e) that the applicant has lodged concurrent applications for asylum in the United Kingdom or in another country.

If the Secretary of State concludes for these or any other reasons that an asylum applicant's account is not credible, the application will be refused.

180H. The actions of anyone acting as an agent of the asylum applicant may also be taken into account in regard to the matters set out in paragraphs 180F and 180G.

180I. If there is a part of the country from which the applicant claims to be a refugee in which he would not have a well-founded fear of persecution, and to which it would be reasonable to expect him to go, the application may be refused.

180J. Cases will normally be considered on an individual basis but if an applicant is part of a group whose claims are clearly not related to the criteria for refugee status in the Convention and Protocol he may be refused without examination of his individual claim. However, the Secretary of State will have regard to any evidence produced by an individual to show that his claim should be distinguished from those of the rest of the group.

Third country cases

180K. If the Secretary of State is satisfied that there is a safe country to which an asylum applicant can be sent his application will normally be refused without substantive consideration of his claim to refugee status. A safe country is one in which the life or freedom of the asylum applicant would not be threatened (within the meaning of Article 33 of the Convention) and the government of which would not send the applicant elsewhere in a manner contrary to the principles of the Convention and Protocol. The Secretary of State shall not remove an asylum applicant without substantive consideration of his claim unless:

(a) the asylum applicant has not arrived in the United Kingdom directly from the country in which he claims to fear persecution and has had an opportunity, at the border or within the territory of a third country, to make contact with that country's authorities in order to seek their protection; or

(b) there is other clear evidence of his admissibility to a third country.

Provided that he is satisfied that a case meets these criteria, the Secretary of State is under no obligation to consult the authorities of the third country before the removal of an asylum applicant.

Previously rejected applications

180L. When an asylum applicant has previously been refused asylum in the United Kingdom and can demonstrate no relevant and substantial change in his circumstances since that date his application will be refused.

180M. When an asylum applicant has come to the United Kingdom from another country which is a party to the United Nations Convention relating to the Status of Refugees or its Protocol and which has considered and rejected an application for asylum from him, his application for asylum in the United Kingdom may be refused without substantive consideration of his claim to refugee status. He may be removed to that country, or another country meeting the criteria of paragraph 180K, and invited to raise any new circumstances with the authorities of the country which originally considered his application.

Rights of appeal

180N. Where asylum is refused the applicant will be provided with a notice informing him of the decision and of the reasons for refusal. At the same time that asylum is refused the applicant may be notified of removal directions or served with a notice of intention to deport, as appropriate. The notice of refusal of asylum will also explain any rights of appeal available to the applicant and will inform him of the means by which he may exercise those rights.

Dependants

180O. A husband or wife or minor children accompanying a principal applicant may be included in an application for asylum. If the principal applicant is granted asylum any such dependants will be granted leave to enter or remain of the same duration. The case of any dependant who claims asylum in his own right and who would otherwise be refused leave to enter or remain will be considered individually in accordance with paragraph 180B. It will not normally be necessary separately to interview or otherwise investigate the status of children accompanying a parent who is an asylum applicant except in so far as this is necessary to establish the child's identity. (In this paragraph, and paragraphs 180P–180R, a child means a person who is under 18 years of age, or who, in the absence of documentary evidence, appears to be under that age.)

Unaccompanied Children

180P. Unaccompanied children may also apply for asylum and, in view of their potential vulnerability, particular priority and care is to be given to the handling of their cases.

180Q. A person of any age may qualify for refugee status under the Convention and the criteria in paragraph 180B apply to all cases. However, account should be taken of the applicant's maturity and in assessing the claim of a child more weight should be given to objective indications of risk than to the child's state of mind and understanding of his or her situation. An asylum application made on behalf of a child should not be refused solely because the child is too young to understand his situation or to have formed a well-founded fear of persecution. Close attention should be given to the welfare of the child at all times.

180R. A child will not be interviewed about the substance of his claim to refugee status if it is possible to obtain by written enquiries or from other sources sufficient information properly to determine the claim. When an interview is necessary it should be conducted in the presence of a parent, guardian, representative or another adult who for the time being takes responsibility for the child and is not an immigration officer, an officer of the Secretary of State or a police officer. The interviewer should have particular regard to the possibility that a child will feel inhibited or alarmed. The child should be allowed to express himself in his own way and at his own speed. If he appears tired or distressed, the interview should be stopped".

After paragraph 186 there shall be inserted paragraph 187:

"187. Paragraph 121A shall not apply to any application for an extension of stay as an "au pair" made by a girl whose current leave to enter or remain was granted before July 5, 1993."

STATEMENT OF CHANGES IN IMMIGRATION RULES

1. The following shall be substituted for the Appendix of the said statement:

"APPENDIX

VISA REQUIREMENTS FOR THE UNITED KINGDOM

1. Subject to paragraph 2 below the following persons need a visa for the United Kingdom:
(*a*) Nationals or citizens of the following countries or territorial entities:

Afghanistan	Gabon	Philippines
Albania	Georgia	Romania
Algeria	Ghana	Russia
Angola	Guinea	Rwanda
Armenia	Guinea-Bissau	Sao Tome e Principe
Azerbaijan	Haiti	Saudi Arabia
Bangladesh	India	Senegal
Belarus	Indonesia	Somalia
Benin	Iran	Sri Lanka
Bhutan	Iraq	Sudan
Bosnia-Herzegovina	Jordan	Syria
Bulgaria	Kazakhstan	Taiwan
Burkina	Kirgizstan	Tajikistan
Burma	Korea (North)	Thailand
Burundi	Laos	Togo
Cambodia	Lebanon	Tunisia
Cameroon	Liberia	Turkey
Cape Verde	Libya	Turkmenistan
Central African	Macedonia	Uganda
Republic	Madagascar	Ukraine
Chad	Mali	Uzbekistan
China	Mauritania	Vietnam
Comoros	Moldova	Yemen
Congo	Mongolia	Zaire
Cuba	Morocco	The territories formerly
Djibouti	Mozambique	comprising the
Egypt	Nepal	Socialist Federal
Equatorial Guinea	Nigeria	Republic of
Eritrea	Oman	Yugoslavia excluding
Ethiopia	Pakistan	Croatia and Slovenia

(*b*) Persons who hold passports or travel documents issued by the former Soviet Union or by the former Socialist Federal Republic of Yugoslavia.

(*c*) Stateless persons.

(*d*) Persons who hold non-national documents.

2. The following persons do not need a visa for the United Kingdom:

(*a*) those who qualify for admission to the United Kingdom as returning residents in accordance with paragraph 58;

(*b*) those who seek leave to enter the United Kingdom within the period of their earlier leave unless that leave:

    (i) was for a period of six months or less; or

    (ii) was extended by statutory instrument".

(*c*) those holding refugee travel documents issued under the 1951 Convention relating to the Status of Refugees by countries which are signatories of the Council of Europe Agreement of 1959 on the Abolition of Visas for Refugees if coming on visits of 3 months or less.

APPENDIX 2

IMMIGRATION

THE ASYLUM APPEALS (PROCEDURE) RULES 1993

(S.I. 1993 No. 1661)

Made - - - - - - -	*5th July 1993*
Laid before Parliament - - - -	*5th July 1993*
Coming into force - - - - -	*26th July 1993*

ARRANGEMENT OF RULES

SCHEDULE

The Lord Chancellor, in exercise of the powers conferred by section 22 of, and paragraph 25 of Schedule 2 to, the Immigration Act 1971 (c. 77; s.22 was extended by the Asylum and Immigration Appeals Act 1993 (c. 23), s.8(6) and Sched. 2, paras. 4(3) and 5(4) and s.9(4)) and now vested in him (the Transfer of Functions (Immigration Appeals) Order 1987 (S.I. 1987 No. 465)), after consultation with the Council on Tribunals in accordance with section 8 of the Tribunals and Inquiries Act 1992 (c. 53), hereby makes the following Rules:

PART I

INTRODUCTION

Citation, commencement and revocation
   1.—(1) These Rules may be cited as the Asylum Appeals (Procedure) Rules 1993 and shall come into force on 26th July 1993.
   (2) In the 1984 Rules—
   (a) rule 14(2)(b) is hearby revoked; and
   (b) in rule 28, for the words "Rule 8(5)" there shall be substituted the words "Rule 8(4)".

Interpretation
   2.—(1) In these Rules—
"the 1984 Rules" means the Immigration Appeals (Procedure) Rules 1984 (S.I. 1984 No. 2041);
"the 1971 Act" means the Immigration Act 1971;
"the 1993 Act" means the Asylum and Immigration Appeals Act 1993 (c. 23);
"asylum appeal" means any appeal made under any of the subsections (1) to (4) of section 8 of the 1993 Act (including any further appeal that is made in relation to such an appeal) and shall include any appeal which, by virtue of paragraph 3 of Schedule 2 to that Act, shall be dealt with in the same proceedings as the appeal brought under any of those subsections;
"special adjudicator" means an adjudicator designated under section 8(5) of the 1993 Act; and
"the Tribunal" means the Immigration Appeal Tribunal.
   (2) In these Rules—
   (a) the time by which any act must be done shall be calculated in the manner provided in rule 32; and
   (b) an application or an appeal is determined when a decision is made as to whether the application should be granted or the appeal allowed.

Application
   3.—(1) These Rules shall apply to all asylum appeals.
   (2) Subject as provided by these Rules, the 1984 Rules shall not apply to asylum appeals.
   (3) These Rules shall apply only to asylum appeals brought in respect of decisions made after these Rules have come into force.

PART II

APPEALS TO SPECIAL ADJUDICATORS

Application of Part II
   4. This Part applies to asylum appeals to a special adjudicator.

Notice of appeal

5.—(1) Subject to paragraph (2), a person making an asylum appeal ("the appellant") shall give notice of appeal not later than 10 days after receiving notice of the decision against which he is appealing.

(2) The time limit for giving notice of appeal shall be 2 days in a case where—

(a) the appeal is made under section 8(1) of the 1993 Act;

(b) the appeal is one to which paragraph 5 of Schedule 2 to the 1993 Act applies (Secretary of State certifies claim to be without foundation); and

(c) there has been personal service on the appellant of the notice of the decision against which he is appealing.

(3) Subject to paragraph (4), notice of appeal shall be given—

(a) by serving on an immigration officer, in the case of appeal under section 8(1) or (4) of the 1993 Act; and

(b) by serving upon the Secretary of State, in the case of appeal under section 8(2) or (3) of the 1993 Act,

the Form prescribed in the Schedule to these Rules (Form A1) which shall be accompanied by the notice (or a copy of the notice) informing the appellant of the decision against which he is appealing and the reasons for the decision.

(4) In any case where an appellant is in custody, service under paragraph (3) may be upon the person having custody of him.

(5) Where any notice of appeal is not given within the appropriate time limit, it shall nevertheless be treated for all purposes as having been given within that time limit if the person to whom it was given under paragraph (3) is of the opinion that, by reason of special circumstances, it is just and right for the notice to be so treated.

(6) Upon receipt of notice of appeal (whether or not the notice was given within the time limit), the immigration officer or (as the case may be) the Secretary of State shall send to the appellant, to a special adjudicator and to the United Kingdom Representative of the United Nations High Commissioner for Refugees the documents specified in paragraph (3) together with (in the case of the appellant and the special adjudicator only) the original or copies of any notes of interview and of any other document referred to in the decision which is being appealed.

(7) A special adjudicator may extend any time limit for giving notice of appeal provided he considers it necessary in the interests of justice.

(8) An extension may be made under paragraph (7) notwithstanding that the period prescribed by the time limit has already expired.

Notification of hearing

6.—(1) The special adjudicator shall not later than 5 days after receiving a notice of appeal serve on—

(a) the appellant;

(b) the immigration officer or (as the case may be) the Secretary of State; and

(c) (if he has given notice in accordance with rule 8(2)) the United Kingdom Representative of the United Nations High Commissioner for Refugees

a notice of the date, time and place fixed for the hearing of the appeal.

(2) The period specified in paragraph (1) shall be 3 days in a case where the appeal is one to which paragraph 5 of Schedule 2 to the 1993 Act applies (Secretary of State certifies claim to be without foundation).

Variation of notice of appeal

7. The notice of appeal may, with the leave of the special adjudicator, be varied by the appellant.

Parties

8.—(1) The parties to an appeal shall be the appellant and the Secretary of State.

(2) The United Kingdom Representative of the United Nations High Commissioner for Refugees shall be treated as a party to an appeal upon giving written notice to the special adjudicator at any time during the course of the appeal that he desires to be so treated.

Determination of appeal

9.—(1) Subject to rule 31, a special adjudicator shall determine an appeal not later than 42 days after receiving notice of the appeal.

(2) The period specified in paragraph (1) shall be 7 days in a case where the appeal is one to which paragraph 5 of Schedule 2 to the 1993 Act applies (Secretary of State certifies claim to be without foundation).

(3) Where an appeal is remitted to a special adjudicator by the Tribunal pursuant to rule 17(3), the special adjudicator shall determine the appeal within 42 days of the appeal being so remitted.

(4) Subject to rule 35 of the 1984 Rules (as applied by these Rules) an appeal shall be determined by hearing unless—

    (a) the special adjudicator is satisfied, having regard to the material before him or to the conduct of the appellant, that the appeal has been abandoned by the appellant; or

    (b) the decision being appealed against has been withdrawn or reversed, and the special adjudicator is satisfied that written notice of the withdrawal or reversal has been given to the appellant.

(5) The special adjudicator shall determine the appeal without a hearing upon being satisfied in accordance with paragraph (4)(a) or (b).

Adjournment of hearings

10.—(1) Subject to rule 9(1) and (2), a special adjudicator may grant an application for an adjournment of a hearing upon being satisfied that there is a good cause for the adjournment.

(2) Where a hearing is adjourned, the special adjudicator shall give notice either orally or in writing to every party to the proceedings of the time and place of the adjourned hearing.

Promulgation of determination and reasons therefor

11.—(1) Subject to paragraph (4), the special adjudicator shall, wherever practicable, pronounce the determination and the reasons therefor at the conclusion of the hearing.

(2) Subject to paragraph (4), the special adjudicator shall send to every party to the appeal, not later than 10 days after the conclusion of the hearing, written notice of the determination and reasons.

(3) A notice sent under paragraph (2) shall not be invalid by virtue of any failure to comply with the time limit prescribed in that paragraph.

(4) In an appeal to which paragraph 5 of Schedule 2 to the 1993 Act applies (Secretary of State certifies claim to be without foundation), if the special adjudicator agrees that the claim is without foundation, he shall at the conclusion of the hearing pronounce the determination and the reasons therefor and furnish every party to the appeal with written notice of that determination and reasons.

PART III

APPEALS TO TRIBUNAL FROM SPECIAL ADJUDICATOR

Application of Part III

12. This Part applies to appeals to the Tribunal from the determination of a special adjudicator.

Leave to appeal

13.—(1) An appeal shall be brought only with the leave of the Tribunal.

(2) An application for leave to the Tribunal shall be made not later than 5 days after the person making it ("the appellant") has received notice of the determination against which he wishes to appeal.

(3) An application for leave shall be made by serving upon the Tribunal the Form prescribed in the Schedule to these Rules (Form A2) which shall be accompanied by the document (or copy of the document) recording the special adjudicator's determination.

(4) An application for leave shall be determined not later than 5 days after its receipt by the Tribunal.

(5) An application for leave shall be determined without a hearing unless the Tribunal considers that there are special circumstances making a hearing necessary or desirable.

(6) When an application for leave has been determined, the Tribunal shall forthwith send to the parties to the appeal a notice recording the determination of the application for leave and, where leave to appeal is refused, the reasons for the refusal.

Notice of appeal

14.—(1) The application for leave to appeal shall be deemed to be the appellant's notice of appeal and may (as such a notice of appeal) be varied by the appellant with the leave of the Tribunal.

(2) The Tribunal shall not later than 5 days after leave to appeal has been granted serve on the parties to the appeal a notice of the date, time and place fixed for the hearing.

Parties
   15.—(1) The parties to an appeal shall be the persons who were the parties to the appeal before the special adjudicator.
   (2) Where he would not otherwise be a party by virtue of paragraph (1), the United Kingdom Representative of the United Nations High Commissioner for Refugees shall be treated as a party to an appeal upon giving written notice to the Tribunal at any time during the course of the appeal that he desires to be so treated.

Time within which appeal is to be determined
   16. Subject to rule 31, every appeal under this Part shall be determined not later than 42 days after the date of service on the Tribunal of the appellant's notice of appeal.

Determination of appeal
   17.—(1) Subject to rule 35 of the 1984 Rules (as applied by these Rules) an appeal shall be disposed of by hearing unless—
   (a) the Tribunal is satisfied, having regard to the material before it or to the conduct of the appellant, that the appeal has been abandoned by the appellant; or
   (b) the decision which was the subject of the asylum appeal has been withdrawn or reversed, and the Tribunal is satisfied that written notice of the withdrawal or reversal has been given to the appellant.
   (2) The Tribunal shall determine the appeal without a hearing upon being satisfied in accordance with paragraph (1)(a) or (b).
   (3) Where the Tribunal considers it appropriate to do so, it may instead of determining the appeal, remit the case to a special adjudicator for determination by him in accordance with any directions given to him by the Tribunal.

Adjournment of hearings
   18.—(1) Subject to rule 16, the Tribunal may grant an application for an adjournment of a hearing upon being satisfied that there is good cause for the adjournment.
   (2) Where a hearing is adjourned, the Tribunal shall give notice either orally or in writing to every party to the proceedings of the time and place of the adjourned hearing.

Promulgation of determination and reasons therefor
   19. The Tribunal shall record the determination on any appeal, and the reasons therefor, and shall send to every party to the appeal, not later than 10 days after the conclusion of the hearing, written notice of the determination and reasons.

PART IV

APPEALS FROM TRIBUNAL

Application of Part IV
   20. This Part applies to applications for leave to appeal, on a question of law, from a final determination of an asylum appeal by the Tribunal.

Leave to appeal
   21.—(1) An application to the Tribunal for leave to appeal shall be made not later than 10 days after the party seeking to appeal has received written notice of the determination.
   (2) An application for leave shall be made by serving upon the Tribunal a notice of application for leave to appeal in the Form prescribed in the Schedule to these Rules (Form A3).
   (3) An application may be determined by the President or a chairman of the Tribunal acting alone.
   (4) The Tribunal shall determine the application without a hearing unless it considers that there are special circumstances making a hearing necessary or desirable.
   (5) The Tribunal shall determine the application, and shall give the parties to the proceedings written notice of the determination and the reasons therefor, not later than 10 days after the Tribunal has received the application.

PART V

GENERAL PROCEDURE

Application of Part V
   22.—(1) This Part applies to—

(a) proceedings to which Part II applies (appeals to special adjudicator);
(b) proceedings to which Part III applies (appeals to the Tribunal from special adjudicator);
(c) proceedings to which Part IV applies (applications for leave to appeal from the Tribunal); and
(d) applications for bail.

(2) Rule 18 of the 1984 Rules shall apply to this Part as it applies to Part III of the 1984 Rules.

(3) Rules 23, 25 to 36, 37 (except paragraph (a)), 38, 40 to 42, 44 and 45 of the 1984 Rules (as applied by this Part) shall apply to this Part as they apply to Part IV of the 1984 Rules.

(4) In the 1984 Rules applied by paragraphs (2) and (3)—
(a) references to "adjudicator" (other than the reference in rule 33(1) to the chief adjudicator) shall be taken to be references to a special adjudicator; and
(b) references to "appellate authority" shall be taken to be references to a special adjudicator or the Tribunal.

(5) Rules 23 to 28 amend the application of the 1984 Rules for the purposes of this Part.

Conduct of proceedings at hearings

23.—In rule 28 of the 1984 rules, the words "and after complying where appropriate with the provisions of Rule 8(4) or 11(3)" shall be omitted.

Burden of proof

24.—In rule 31 of the 1984 Rules, the reference in paragraphs (1) and (2) to "the Act" shall be taken to include a reference to the 1993 Act.

Hearing of appeal in absence of appellant or other party

25.—In rule 34 of the 1984 Rules—
(a) the reference in paragraph (2) to rule 24 (of the 1984 Rules) shall be taken to be a reference to rules 6 and 10(2) of these Rules (in the case of a hearing before a special adjudicator) and to rules 14(2) and 18(2) of these Rules (in the case of a hearing before the Tribunal); and
(b) paragraph (5)(a) shall be omitted.

Summary determination of appeals

26.—In rule 35 of the 1984 Rules, the reference in paragraph (1) to "previous proceedings" shall be treated as including proceedings under the 1993 Act.

Performance of functions of Tribunal

27.—In rule 42 of the 1984 Rules—
(a) sub-paragraph (c)(i) shall be omitted;
(b) the reference in sub-paragraph (c)(ii) to rule 21(1) shall be taken to be a reference to rule 17(3) of these Rules; and
(c) paragraph (c) shall be construed as if it included a reference to rule 31 of these Rules (Tribunal's power to extend time limit).

Notices etc.

28.—In rule 44(1) of the 1984 Rules—
(a) in paragraph (c) for the words "to the Immigration and Nationality Department (Appeals Section)" there shall be substituted the words "to the Appeals Support Section of the Asylum Division"; and
(b) paragraph (d) shall be omitted.

Mixed appeals

29.—(1) This rule applies in any case where a person ("the appellant") is appealing to a special adjudicator or to the Tribunal in relation to any of the grounds mentioned in subsections (1) to (4) of section 8 of the 1993 Act ("the section 8 appeal") and is also appealing to an adjudicator or to the Tribunal in relation to other grounds under Part II of the 1971 Act ("the Part II appeal").

(2) Where the appellant lodges his Part II appeal before his section 8 appeal has been determined by a special adjudicator or (as the case may be) the Tribunal, the special adjudicator or the Tribunal shall deal with both appeals in the same proceedings.

(3) Where the appellant lodges his section 8 appeal before his Part II appeal has been determined by an adjudicator or (as the case may be) the Tribunal, the special adjudicator or (as the case may be) the Tribunal dealing with his section 8 appeal shall deal with both appeals in the same proceedings.

(4) These Rules (so far as they relate to appeals to special adjudicators and to the Tribunal) shall apply to the Part II appeal as if that appeal had been a section 8 appeal and shall continue so to apply even if the section 8 appeal is determined before the Part II appeal.

(5) Nothing in paragraph (4) shall—

(a) prejudice any steps taken under the 1984 Rules before the appellant lodged the section 8 appeal; or

(b) require any step to be taken under these Rules which is analogous to a step already taken under the 1984 Rules.

(6) An adjudicator, a special adjudicator or the Tribunal may adjourn a section 8 appeal or a Part II appeal so far as is necessary or expedient for complying with a requirement in this rule to deal with both appeals in the same proceedings.

(7) For the purposes of this rule, a person shall be taken to be appealing if he has given a notice of appeal in accordance with these Rules (in the case of a section 8 appeal) or in accordance with the 1984 Rules (in the case of a Part II appeal) and, in either case, the appeal has not yet been determined.

Deemed grant of application

30. Where the Tribunal fails to determine any application for leave under rule 13 within the time prescribed, the application shall be deemed to have been granted.

Extension of time limit

31.—(1) Where under these Rules—

(a) a special adjudicator or the Tribunal is required to determine an appeal; or

(b) the Tribunal is required to provide written notification of the determination (and the reasons therefor)

at or within a time prescribed, the special adjudicator or (as the case may be) the Tribunal may if necessary extend the time so prescribed either to enable it fairly to determine the appeal or (as the case may be) to provide the notification.

(2) An extension may be made notwithstanding that the time prescribed by the time limit in any case has already expired.

Time

32.—(1) Subject to paragraph (2), any notice or other document that is sent or served under these Rules shall be deemed to have been received—

(a) where the notice or other document is sent by post, on the second day after which it was sent; and

(b) in any other case, on the day on which the notice or other document was served.

(2) Where under these Rules a notice or other document is sent by post to a special adjudicator or to the Tribunal, it shall be deemed to have been received on the day on which it was in fact received by the special adjudicator or, as the case may be, by the Tribunal.

(3) For the purpose of these Rules, a notice or other document is received by a special adjudicator or by the Tribunal when it is received by any person employed as a clerk to the special adjudicator or Tribunal.

(4) Where under these Rules, an act is to be done not later than a specified period after any event, the period shall be calculated from the expiry of the day on which the event occurred.

(5) Where the time provided by these Rules by which any act must be done expires on a Saturday, Sunday or a bank holiday, Christmas Day or Good Friday, the act shall be done in time if done on the next working day.

(6) Where, apart from this paragraph, the period in question being a period of 10 days or less would include a Saturday, Sunday or bank holiday, Christmas Day or Good Friday, that day shall be excluded.

(7) In this rule, "bank holiday" means a day that is specified in, or appointed under, the Banking and Financial Dealings Act 1971 (1971 c.80) as a bank holiday.

5th July 1993   Mackay of Clashfern, C.

SCHEDULE

Rule 5(3)

FORM A1

Notice of an appeal to
a Special Adjudicator
against a refusal of asylum

Asylum Appeal (Form A1)

> Immigration Appellate Authority
> Case Number:

*   See Notes 1 and 5

| Part 1   **About you**

Your surname or family name:

Your other names:

Your address: *Say where you are living now.*
If you are in a detention centre put its address.

Telephone   *Please give a number where you can be contacted during the day.*
number:

Your date of birth:

Your nationality or citizenship:

Have you ever made **any other appeal** which was about **Immigration**?

Put **No** *or* **Yes**:

If you have put **Yes** say
● when you made the appeal: *Please give the case number, if you can.*

● what was the appeal about:

| Part 2   **Help with your appeal**   (See Note 2)

Will anyone help you prepare or present your appeal?   *Put* **No** *or* **Yes**:

If you have put **Yes** give
The person's name:

Address:

Telephone number: FAX number:

Form A1   Rule 5(3) Asylum Appeals (Procedure) rules 1993.

Part 3   The grounds of your appeal

Please give the **Reference Number** of this Notice of Refusal (Notice of Decision):

This number is on the cover of the Notice.

Please say why you think the decision to refuse you asylum was wrong:

---

*Part 4   **Declaration**   (See Note 6)*

You, not the person helping you, should sign this form.

I declare that the information I have given is true and complete to the best of my knowledge and belief.

I appeal to the Special Adjudicator against the decision to refuse me asylum.

Your signature: Date:

---

*Part 5   **Documents which you are sending**   (See Note 4)*

- **You must send the Notice of Refusal (Notice of Decision), or a copy of it, with this form.**

- Are you sending **any other** documents with this form?   *Put* **No** *or* **Yes:**

If you have put **Yes**, say what papers or photographs you are sending:

You do not have to fill in any more parts of this form.

For the use of the Home Office, the Immigration Officer or Custody Officer

The appeal was received at

on

at   am/pm

Who received the appeal?

The application was received by hand □ by post □ The envelope is attached to this form.

Signed   Date

What to do next

To the Custody Officer   You must give, or send, the form to
                                    the Home Office **or** an Immigration Officer.

To the Home Office
or Immigration Officer   You must send to the Immigration Appellate Authority **at**
                                    once:
                                    ● this form
                                    ● the Notice of Decision
                                    ● Interview notes and other documents referred to in the
                                       decision.

For the use of the Immigration Appellate Authority

The appeal was received at

on

at   am/pm

Who received the appeal?

The application was received by hand □ by post □ The envelope is attached to this form.

Signed   Date

Notice of an appeal
to a Special Adjudicator
against a refusal of asylum

Notes

Use this form if you have been given a Notice of Refusal (Notice of Decision) and you want to appeal against the decision to refuse you asylum.

1   When to appeal

You must appeal within the time which the law allows (see Rule 5 of the Asylum Appeals (Procedure) Rules 1993).

Warning: the time may be as little as 2 working days.

2   Help with your appeal

Someone may help you prepare your appeal. They may fill in this form for you but **you** should sign Part 4.

3   Presenting your appeal

You may present your appeal (put your case) to the Special Adjudicator or someone may do it for you. This person is called your representative and may be anyone who can be a representative **by law** (see Rule 26 of the Immigration Appeals (Procedure) Rules 1984).

4   Sending other documents

You must send the Notice of Refusal (Notice of Decision), or a copy of it, with this form.

If you want the Special Adjudicator to see other papers or photographs please send them with this form, if you can.

5   What to do

Fill in parts 1, 2, 3, 4 and 5 of the form. If you need more space use another sheet of paper and put your name on it.

6   When you have filled in the form

The Notice of Refusal (Notice of Decision) will tell you the **Section** of the Asylum and Immigration Appeals Act 1993 under which you may appeal.

- If you appeal under **Section 8(1) or 8(4):**
  serve this form on **or** send it to
  an Immigration Officer.
  The address is on the Notice of Refusal (Notice of Decision).
- If you appeal under **Section 8(2) or 8(3):**
  serve this form on **or** send it to
  The Secretary of State for the Home Department.
  The address is on the Notice of Refusal (Notice of Decision).

If you are in custody

you may serve this form on the person who has custody of you.

Form A1 Rule 5(3) Asylum Appeals (Procedure) Rules 1993.

FORM A2   Rule 13(3)

Application for leave to appeal to the
Immigration Appeal Tribunal against   **Asylum Appeal (Form A2)**
a decision of a Special Adjudicator

- Please put the case number in the box: | Immigration Appellate Authority
  (*this number is on the Special Adjudicator's* | Case Number:
  decision)

- See Notes 1 and 5

| Part 1   **About you**

Your surname or family name:

Your other names:

Your address: *Say where you are living now.*
                   If you are in a detention centre put its address.

Telephone   *Please give a number where you can be contacted during the day.*
number:

Your date of birth:

Your nationality or citizenship:

Have you ever applied for leave to appeal, **or** appealed, to the Tribunal?

                                               Put **No** *or* **Yes**:

If you have put **Yes** say
   • when you applied for leave to appeal, or appealed: *Please give the case number,*
   if you can.

   • what the application, or the appeal, was about:

| Part 2   **Help with your appeal**   (See Note 2)

Will anyone help you prepare or present your appeal?   *Put* **No** *or* **Yes**:

If you have put **Yes** give
The person's name:

Address:

Telephone number: FAX number:

Form A2   Rule 13(3) Asylum Appeals (Procedure) Rules 1993.

Part 3 **The grounds of your appeal**

Please say why you think the Special Adjudicator's decision was wrong:

Part 4 **Declaration** (See Note 6)

You, not the person helping you, should sign this form.

I declare that the information I have given is true and complete to the best of my knowledge and belief.

I appeal for leave to appeal to the Immigration Appeal Tribunal against the Special Adjudicator's decision

Your signature: Date:

Part 5 **Documents which you are sending** (See Note 4)

• **You must send the Special Adjudicator's decision, or a copy of it, with this form.**

• Are you sending **any other** documents with this form?   *Put* **No** *or* **Yes:**

If you have put **Yes**, say what papers or photographs you are sending:

You do not have to fill in any more parts of this form.

For the use of the Immigration Appeal Tribunal

The application was received on

_____ at _____ am/pm

Who received the application?

_____

The application was received by hand ☐ by post ☐ The envelope is attached to this form.

_____

Signed   Date

_____

Asylum Appeal (Form A2)

Application for leave to appeal to the
Immigration Appeal Tribunal against
a decision of a Special Adjudicator

Notes

If you want to appeal to the Immigration Appeal Tribunal against a decision of a Special Adjudicator, you must first get permission to appeal. This is called leave to appeal.
But you have no right to apply for leave to appeal if the Special Adjudicator has agreed with the Secretary of State that your claim to asylum is without foundation.

1 *When to apply for leave to appeal*

You must apply for leave to appeal **within 5 days** of getting the Special Adjudicator's decision (see Rule 13(2) of the Asylum Appeals (Procedure) Rules 1993).

2 *Help with your application*

Someone may help you prepare your application. They may fill in this form for you but **you** should sign Part 4.

3 *Presenting your application*

You may present your application (put your case) to the tribunal or someone may do it for you. This person is called your representative and may be anyone who can be a representative by law (see Rule 26 of the Immigration Appeals (Procedure) Rules 1984).

4 *Sending other documents*

You must send the Special Adjudicator's decision, or a copy of it, with this form.
If you want the Tribunal to see other papers, or photographs please send them with this form, if you can.

5 *What to do*

• Use this form to apply for leave to appeal
• Fill in Parts 1, 2, 3, 4 and 5 of the form.
   If you need more space use another sheet of paper and put your name on it.

6 *When you have filled in the form*

Serve it on **or** send it to
   The Chief Clerk
   Immigration Appeal Tribunal
   231 Strand
   LONDON WC2R 1DA
If you are in custody
you may serve this form on the person who has custody of you.

Form A2 Rule 13(3) Asylum Appeals (Procedure) Rules 1993.

FORM A3   Rule 21(2)

Application to the
Immigration Appeal Tribunal
for leave to appeal against its decision

Asylum Appeal (Form A3)

Immigration Appellate Authority Case Number:

- Please put the case number in the box:
  (*this number is on the tribunal's decision*)

- See Notes 1 and 4

⌐ *Part 1* **About you**

Your surname or family name:

Your other names:

Your address: *Say where you are living now.*
                     If you are in a detention centre put its address.

Telephone   *Please give a number where you can be contacted during the day.*
number:

Your date of birth:

Your nationality or citizenship:

Have you ever applied for leave to appeal,
or appealed to the Court of Appeal or Court of Session (in Scotland),
against a decision of the Immigration Appeal Tribunal?

                                        Put **No** *or* **Yes**:

If you have put **Yes** say
- when you applied for leave to appeal, or appealed: *Please give the case number,*
  if you can.

- what the application, or the appeal, was about:

⌐ *Part 2* **Help with your appeal**   (See Note 2)

Will anyone help you prepare or present your appeal?   *Put* **No** *or* **Yes**:

If you have put **Yes** give
The person's name:

Address:

Telephone number: FAX number:

Form A3   Rule 21(2) Asylum Appeals (Procedure) Rules 1993.

Part 3   The grounds of your appeal

Please say why you think the Tribunal's decision was wrong:
(Remember that   you can appeal against
                          only **the final decision** of the Tribunal
                  and   only because you think the decision
                          was wrong **on a question of law)**

Part 4   Declaration   (See Note 5)

You, not the person helping you, should sign this form.

I declare that the information I have given is true and complete to the best of my knowledge and belief.

I apply to the Immigration Appeal Tribunal for leave to appeal to the Court of Appeal or Court of Session (if the decision was made in Scotland) against the decision of the Immigration Appeal Tribunal.

Your signature:

Date:

You do not have to fill in any more parts of this form.

For the use of the Immigration Appeal Tribunal

The application was received on

                                        at   am/pm

Who received the application?

The application was received by hand □ by post □ The envelope is attached to this form.

Signed   Date

Application to the
Immigration Appeal Tribunal
for leave to appeal against its decision

Notes

If you want to appeal to the Court of Appeal (or Court of Session in Scotland), against a decision of the Immigration Appeal Tribunal, you must first get permission to appeal. This is called leave to appeal. You apply to the Immigration Appeal Tribunal for leave to appeal.

You may appeal against
      only **the final decision** of the Tribunal
and only because you think the decision was
      wrong **on a question of law.**

1   *When to apply for leave to appeal*

You must apply **within 10 days** of getting the Tribunal's decision (see Rule 21(1) of the Asylum Appeals (Procedure) Rules 1993).

2   *Help with your application*

Someone may help you prepare your application. They may fill in this form for you but **you** should sign Part 4.

3   *Presenting your application*

You may present your application (put your case) to the tribunal or someone may do it for you. This person is called your representative and may be anyone who can be a representative **by law** (see Rule 26 of the Immigration Appeals (Procedure) Rules 1984). .

4   *What to do*

- Use this form to apply for leave to appeal in **an asylum case.**
- Fill in parts 1, 2, 3, 4 and 5 of the form.
  If you need more space use another sheet of paper and put your name on it.

5   *When you have filled in the form*

Serve it on **or** send it to
    The Chief Clerk
    Immigration Appeal Tribunal
    231 Strand
    LONDON WC2R 1DA

Form A3 Rule 21(2) Asylum Appeals (Procedure) Rules 1993.

APPENDIX 3

IMMIGRATION

THE IMMIGRATION APPEALS (PROCEDURE) (AMENDMENT) RULES 1993

(S.I. 1993 No. 1662)

Made - - - - - - -	*5th July 1993*
Laid before Parliament - - - -	*5th July 1993*
Coming into force - - - - -	*26th July 1993*

The Lord Chancellor, in exercise of the powers conferred by section 22 of, and paragraph 25 of Schedule 2 to, the Immigration Act 1971 (c. 77; s.22 was extended by the Asylum and Immigration Appeals Act 1993 (c. 23), s.9(4) and now vested in him (The Transfer of Functions (Immigration Appeals) Order 1987 (S.I. 1987 No. 465)), after consultation with the Council on Tribunals in accordance with section 8 of the Tribunals and Inquiries Act 1992 (c. 53), hereby makes the following rules:

Citation, commencement and interpretation

1.—(1) These Rules may be cited as the Immigration Appeals (Procedure) (Amendment) Rules 1993 and shall come into force on 26th July 1993.

(2) In these Rules, "the 1984 Rules" means the Immigration Appeals (Procedure) Rules 1984 (S.I. 1984 No. 2041, amended by S.I. 1991 No. 1545).

Appeals from Immigration Appeal Tribunal

2. After Part III of the 1984 Rules there shall be inserted the following—

"PART IIIA

APPEALS FROM TRIBUNAL

Application of Part IIIA

21A. This Part applies to applications for leave to appeal on any question of law from a final determination of the Tribunal made under section 20 of the Act.

Leave to appeal

21B.—(1) An application to the Tribunal for leave to appeal shall be made not later than 14 days after the party seeking to appeal has received written notice of the determination.

(2) An application for leave shall be made by serving upon the Tribunal a notice of application for leave to appeal in Form 4.

(3) An application may be determined by the president or a chairman of the Tribunal acting alone.

(4) The Tribunal shall determine the application without a hearing unless it considers that there are special circumstances making a hearing necessary or desirable.

(5) The Tribunal shall give the parties to the proceedings written notice of the determination and of the reasons therefor."

Application of Part IV of the 1984 Rules

3. In Rule 22 (application of Part IV) after paragraph (1) there shall be inserted the following—

"(1A) Rules 23 and 26 shall apply in relation to an application for leave under Part IIIA."

Form of notice of application for leave to appeal

4. The form set out in the Schedule to these Rules shall be added as Form 4 to the forms in the Schedule to the 1984 Rules.

5th July 1993

Mackay of Clashfern, C.

SCHEDULE   Rule 4

FORM 4

Application to the   **Immigration Appeal (Form 4)**
Immigration Appeal Tribunal
for leave to appeal against its decision | Immigration Appellate Authority
                                             | Case Number:

- Please put the case number in the box:
  (*this number is on the tribunal's decision*)

- See Notes 1 and 4

| Part 1   **About you**

Your surname or family name:

Your other names:

Your address: *Say where you are living now.*
                  If you are in a detention centre put its address.

Telephone   *Please give a number where you can be contacted during the day.*
number:

Your date of birth:

Your nationality or citizenship:

Have you ever applied for leave to appeal,
or appealed to the Court of Appeal or Court of Session (in Scotland),
against a decision of the Immigration Appeal Tribunal?
                                             Put **No** *or* **Yes**:

If you have put **Yes** say
- when you applied for leave to appeal, or appealed: *Please give the case number,*
  if you can.

- what the application, or the appeal, was about:

| Part 2   **Help with your appeal**   (See Note 2)

Will anyone help you prepare or present your appeal?   *Put* **No** *or* **Yes**:

If you have put **Yes** give
The person's name:

Address:

Telephone number: FAX number:

Form 4   Rule 21B Immigration Appeals (Procedure) Rules 1984
as amended by the Immigration Appeals (Procedure) (Amendment) Rules 1993.

Part 3   *The grounds of your appeal*

Please say why you think the Tribunal's decision was wrong:
(**Remember** that   you can appeal against
                        only **the final decision** of the Tribunal
            and   only because you think the decision
                        was wrong **on a question of law)**

Part 4   *Declaration*   (See Note 5)

You, not the person helping you, should sign this form.

I declare that the information I have
given is true and complete to the best of
my knowledge and belief.

I apply to the Immigration Appeal
Tribunal for leave to appeal to the Court
of Appeal or Court of Session (if the
decision was made in Scotland) against
the decision of the Immigration Appeal
Tribunal.

Your signature: Date:

You do not have to fill in any more parts of this form.

For the use of the Immigration Appeal Tribunal

The application was received on

                    at   am/pm

Who received the application?

The application was received by hand □ by post □ The envelope is attached to this form.

Signed   Date

Application to the
Immigration Appeal Tribunal
for leave to appeal against its decision

Notes

If you want to appeal to the Court of Appeal (or Court of Session in Scotland), against a decision of the Immigration Appeal Tribunal, you must first get permission to appeal. This is called leave to appeal. You apply to the Immigration Appeal Tribunal for leave to appeal.

You may appeal against

only **the final decision** of the Tribunal

and only because you think the decision was

wrong **on a question of law.**

1 When to apply for leave to appeal

You must apply **within 14 days** of getting the Tribunal's decision (see the Immigration Appeals (Procedure) (Amendment) Rules 1993).

2 Help with your application

Someone may help you prepare your application. They may fill in this form for you but **you** should sign Part 4.

3 Presenting your application

You may present your application (put your case) to the tribunal or someone may do it for you. This person is called your representative and may be anyone who can be a representative **by law** (see Rule 26 of the Immigration Appeals (Procedure) Rules 1984).

4 What to do

- Use this form to apply for leave to appeal in any immigration case.
  Do not use it if the appeal is about asylum.
  In an asylum appeal use Form A3.
- Fill in parts 1, 2, 3, 4 and 5 of the form.
  If you need more space use another sheet of paper and put your name on it.

5 When you have filled in the form

Serve it on **or** send it to
The Chief Clerk
Immigration Appeal Tribunal
231 Strand
London WC2R 1DA

INDEX

References are to sections and Schedule numbers

VIDEO RECORDINGS ACT 1993

(1993 c. 24)

An Act to amend the Video Recordings Act 1984 and, so far as it relates to evidence by certificate in respect of offences under the 1984 Act, the Criminal Justice (Scotland) Act 1980. [20th July 1993]

Parliamentary Debates
Hansard, H.L. Vol. 541, col. 1013; Vol. 542, col. 902; Vol. 543, col. 1286; Vol. 544, col. 790.

Introduction
This Act provides for a number of amendments to the Video Recordings Act 1984.

Section 4 is amended to allow the Secretary of State power to designate the relevant person or authority responsible for assigning a unique title to a video work in respect of which a classification certificate is to be issued. Section 14, which covers the supply of video recordings containing false indications as to classification, is amended to incorporate a general defence to the offences under the Act. Section 15 of the 1984 Act provides for the various penalties which can be incurred under the Act; a new subs. (3) is inserted to instigate time limits for prosecutions. Section 19, which provides for evidence by certificate, is extended; Sched. 1 to the Criminal Justice (Scotland) Act 1980 is also amended to allow for evidence by certificate for that jurisdiction.

Titles to be assigned to video works for identification purposes

1.—(1) In subsection (1) of section 4 of the Video Recordings Act 1984 (arrangements for classification of video works), in paragraph (b) before sub-paragraph (i) there shall be inserted the following sub-paragraph—
"(ia) for assigning a unique title to each video work in respect of which a classification certificate is to be issued".

(2) In paragraph (c) of that subsection the words from "including" to the end shall be omitted and after that subsection there shall be inserted the following subsections—
"(1A) A title assigned to a video work under subsection (1)(b)(ia) above shall consist of—
(a) the title under which the video work was determined to be suitable for the issue of a classification certificate; and
(b) a registration number (which may contain letters and other symbols as well as figures).
(1B) The record maintained under subsection (1)(c) above shall include, in relation to each video work in respect of which a classification certificate has been issued, a video recording which—
(a) contains the video work; and
(b) shows, or shows on its spool, case or other thing on or in which the recording is kept—
(i) the title assigned to the video work under subsection (1)(b)(ia) above; and
(ii) the determination or determinations made in respect of the video work."
(3) In subsection (2) of section 7 of that Act (contents of classification certificate), after the words "must contain" there shall be inserted "the title assigned to the video work in accordance with section 4(1)(b)(ia) of this Act and."

General defence to offences under the 1984 Act

2. After section 14 of the Video Recordings Act 1984 there shall be inserted the following section—

"General defence to offences under this Act

14A. Without prejudice to any defence specified in the preceding provisions of this Act in relation to a particular offence, it is a defence to a charge of committing any offence under this Act to prove—

    (a) that the commission of the offence was due to the act or default of a person other than the accused, and

    (b) that the accused took all reasonable precautions and exercised all due diligence to avoid the commission of the offence by any person under his control."

Time limit for prosecutions

3. In section 15 of the Video Recordings Act 1984 (penalties) after subsection (3) there shall be inserted the following subsections—

"(3A) No prosecution for an offence under this Act shall be brought after the expiry of the period of three years beginning with the date of the commission of the offence or one year beginning with the date of its discovery by the prosecutor, whichever is earlier.

(3B) In Scotland the reference in subsection (3A) above to the date of discovery by the prosecutor shall be construed as a reference to the date on which evidence sufficient in the opinion of the Lord Advocate to warrant proceedings came to his knowledge; and for the purposes of that subsection—

    (a) a certificate signed by him or on his behalf and stating the date on which such evidence came to his knowledge shall be conclusive evidence of that fact (a certificate purporting to be so signed being presumed to be so signed unless the contrary is proved); and

    (b) a prosecution shall be deemed to be brought on the date on which a warrant to apprehend or to cite the accused is granted provided that the warrant is executed without undue delay."

Extension of procedure for evidence by certificate

4. In section 19 of the Video Recordings Act 1984 (evidence by certificate) after subsection (3) there shall be inserted the following subsections—

"(3A) In any proceedings in England and Wales or Northern Ireland for an offence under this Act, a certificate purporting to be signed by a person authorised in that behalf by the Secretary of State and stating—

    (a) that he has examined the record maintained in pursuance of arrangements made by the designated authority, and

    (b) that the record shows that, on the date specified in the certificate, no classification certificate had been issued in respect of a video work having a particular title,

shall be admissible as evidence of the fact that, on that date, no classification certificate had been issued in respect of a work of that title.

(3B) In any proceedings in England and Wales or Northern Ireland for an offence under this Act, a certificate purporting to be signed by a person authorised in that behalf by the Secretary of State and stating—

    (a) that he has examined the record maintained in pursuance of arrangements made by the designated authority, and

    (b) that the record shows that, on the date specified in the certificate under this subsection, a classification certificate was issued in respect of a video work having a particular title and that a document identified by the certificate under this subsection is a copy of the classification certificate so issued,

shall be admissible as evidence of the fact that, on that date, a classification certificate in terms of the document so identified was issued in respect of a work of that title."

Evidence by certificate: amendment of Scottish provisions

5. In Schedule 1 to the Criminal Justice (Scotland) Act 1980 (certain certificates to be sufficient evidence in relation to statutory offences), for the words in the second and third columns of the entry relating to the Video Recordings Act 1984, there shall be substituted the words in, respectively, the left and right hand columns below—

"A person authorised to do so by the Secretary of State, being a person who has examined the record maintained in pursuance of arrangements made by the designated authority and in the case of a certificate in terms of—

(a) sub-paragraph (a) in column 3, the video work mentioned in that sub-paragraph;

(b) sub-paragraph (b) in that column, both video works mentioned in that sub-paragraph.

That the record shows any of the following—

(a) in respect of a video work (or part of a video work) contained in a video recording identified by the certificate, that by a date specified no classification certificate had been issued;

(b) in respect of a video work which is the subject of a certificate under sub-paragraph (a) above, that the video work differs in a specified way from another video work contained in a video recording identified in the certificate under this sub-paragraph and that, on a date specified, a classification certificate was issued in respect of that other video work;

(c) that, by a date specified, no classification certificate had been issued in respect of a video work having a particular title;

(d) that, on a date specified, a classification certificate was issued in respect of a video work having a particular title and that a document which is identified in the certificate under this sub-paragraph is a copy of the classification certificate so issued;

expressions used in column 2, or in this column, of this entry being construed in accordance with that Act; and in each of sub-paragraphs (a) to (d) above "specified" means specified in the certificate under that sub-paragraph."

Short title, commencement and extent

6.—(1) This Act may be cited as the Video Recordings Act 1993.

(2) This Act shall come into force at the end of the period of two months beginning with the day on which it is passed.

(3) Section 5 above extends to Scotland only.

(4) This Act (apart from section 5) extends to Northern Ireland.

INDEX

References are to sections

LOCAL GOVERNMENT (OVERSEAS ASSISTANCE) ACT 1993

(1993 c. 25)

An Act to enable local authorities in Great Britain to provide advice and assistance as respects matters in which they have skill and experience to bodies engaged outside the United Kingdom in the carrying on of any of the activities of local government. [20th July 1993]

PARLIAMENTARY DEBATES
   Hansard, H.C. Vol. 215, cols. 1105, 1134; Vol. 221, col. 340; Vol. 227, col. 1213; H.L. Vol. 545, col. 72; Vol. 546, col. 1283; Vol. 547, col. 527.

INTRODUCTION
   This Act gives local authorities power to provide advice and assistance to bodies outside the U.K. if engaged in activities of local government. Activities of local government mean activities which are the equivalent of, or are comparable to, any activities which in Great Britain are carried on by local authorities. The Secretary of State is responsible for authorising such cooperation.

Power to provide advice and assistance

1.—(1) Subject to subsections (3) to (6) below, a local authority may provide advice and assistance as respects any matter in which they have skill and experience to a body engaged outside the United Kingdom in the carrying on of any of the activities of local government.

(2) In relation to any place outside the United Kingdom, activities shall be taken for the purposes of this Act to be activities of local government wherever they are the equivalent of, or are comparable to, any activities which in any part of Great Britain are carried on, by virtue of the functions vested in them, by local authorities.

(3) The power conferred by subsection (1) above shall not be exercised except with the consent of the Secretary of State or in accordance with a general authorisation given by him.

(4) Before giving any general authorisation under subsection (3) above, the Secretary of State shall consult with such persons appearing to him to represent local authorities as he thinks appropriate.

(5) A consent or authorisation under subsection (3) above may be given subject to such conditions as the Secretary of State thinks fit.

(6) Nothing in this section authorises a local authority to provide any financial assistance by—

(a) making a grant or loan,
(b) giving a guarantee or indemnity, or
(c) investing by acquiring share or loan capital.

(7) The Secretary of State shall provide local authorities with such guidance about the exercise of their powers under this section as he thinks appropriate.

(8) There shall be paid out of money provided by Parliament any increase attributable to this section in the sums payable out of money so provided under any other enactment.

(9) In this section, "local authority" means—

(a) a county or district council in England and Wales, a London borough council, the Common Council of the City of London, the Council of the Isles of Scilly or a body mentioned in subsection (10) below; or
(b) a regional, islands or district council in Scotland or a joint board within the meaning of section 235(1) of the Local Government (Scotland) Act 1973.

(10) The bodies referred to in subsection (9) above are—

(a) a fire authority constituted in England and Wales by a combination scheme under the Fire Services Act 1947;
(b) a combined police authority established by an amalgamation scheme under the Police Act 1964;
(c) an authority established under section 10 of the Local Government Act 1985 (waste disposal authorities);
(d) a joint authority established by Part IV of that Act (police, fire services, civil defence and transport);
(e) a joint authority established by an order under section 21 of the Local Government Act 1992 (joint authorities established in connection with structural or boundary changes);
(f) the Broads Authority;
(g) a joint or special planning board constituted for a National Park by an order under paragraph 1 or 3 of Schedule 17 to the Local Government Act 1972.

(11) The Secretary of State may by order made by statutory instrument amend subsection (9) or (10) above so as to add any body or description of body to the bodies which are local authorities for the purposes of this section; and any statutory instrument containing an order under this subsection shall be subject to annulment in pursuance of a resolution of either House of Parliament.

Short title, commencement and extent

2.—(1) This Act may be cited as the Local Government (Overseas Assistance) Act 1993.

(2) This Act shall come into force at the end of the period of two months beginning with the day on which it is passed.

(3) This Act does not extend to Northern Ireland.

INDEX

References are to sections

BAIL (AMENDMENT) ACT 1993*

(1993 c. 26)

An Act to confer upon the prosecution a right of appeal against decisions to grant bail.   [20th July 1993]

PARLIAMENTARY DEBATES

Hansard, H.C. Vol. 227, col. 1235; H.L. Vol. 546, col. 1004; Vol. 547, cols. 660, 990.
The Bill was discussed in Standing Committee E on April 21, 1993.

INTRODUCTION

This Act was introduced to the House of Commons as a Private Members Bill by the Honourable Member for Shoreham. The Bill reflected, and was a response to the serious concern of the public in respect of offences committed by persons who, at the time they commit such offences, are on bail. The majority of those offences relate to burglary and vehicular crime.

Records of the number of persons who commit offences while on bail have been gathered since 1989 by Northumbria Police under the supervision of Professor Openshaw of Newcastle University. Those statistics suggested that in the case of offences of theft or the taking of motor vehicles 44.6 per cent. of such detected crimes were committed by a person on bail. In the case of house burglaries 53.5 per cent. of all detected crimes were committed by a person on bail.

The above must be seen in the context, between the years 1989 and 1992, of an increase in the theft of cars of some 45 per cent., together with an associated increase in offences of theft from cars of 48 per cent. In the year ending June 1992, 28 per cent. of all recorded crimes were vehicle-related offences.

Prosecution right of appeal

1.—(1) Where a magistrates' court grants bail to a person who is charged with or convicted of—

    (a) an offence punishable by a term of imprisonment of 5 years or more, or

    (b) an offence under section 12 (taking a conveyance without authority) or 12A (aggravated vehicle taking) of the Theft Act 1968,

the prosecution may appeal to a judge of the Crown Court against the granting of bail.

    (2) Subsection (1) above applies only where the prosecution is conducted—

    (a) by or on behalf of the Director of Public Prosecutions; or

    (b) by a person who falls within such class or description of person as may be prescribed for the purposes of this section by order made by the Secretary of State.

    (3) Such an appeal may be made only if—

    (a) the prosecution made representations that bail should not be granted; and

    (b) the representations were made before it was granted.

    (4) In the event of the prosecution wishing to exercise the right of appeal set out in subsection (1) above, oral notice of appeal shall be given to the magistrates' court at the conclusion of the proceedings in which such bail has been granted and before the release from custody of the person concerned.

    (5) Written notice of appeal shall thereafter be served on the magistrates' court and the person concerned within two hours of the conclusion of such proceedings.

    (6) Upon receipt from the prosecution of oral notice of appeal from its decision to grant bail the magistrates' court shall remand in custody the person concerned, until the appeal is determined or otherwise disposed of.

---

* Annotations by G. P. Scanlan, LL.B, Solicitor, Lecturer in Law, University of Liverpool.

(7) Where the prosecution fails, within the period of two hours mentioned in subsection (5) above, to serve one or both of the notices required by that subsection, the appeal shall be deemed to have been disposed of.

(8) The hearing of an appeal under subsection (1) above against a decision of the magistrates' court to grant bail shall be commenced within forty-eight hours, excluding weekends and any public holiday (that is to say, Christmas Day, Good Friday or a bank holiday), from the date on which oral notice of appeal is given.

(9) At the hearing of any appeal by the prosecution under this section, such appeal shall be by way of re-hearing, and the judge hearing any such appeal may remand the person concerned in custody or may grant bail subject to such conditions (if any) as he thinks fit.

(10) In relation to a child or young person (within the meaning of the Children and Young Persons Act 1969)—

    (a) the reference in subsection (1) above to an offence punishable by a term of imprisonment is to be read as a reference to an offence which would be so punishable in the case of an adult; and

    (b) the reference in subsection (5) above to remand in custody is to be read subject to the provisions of section 23 of the Act of 1969 (remands to local authority accommodation).

(11) The power to make an order under subsection (2) above shall be exercisable by statutory instrument and any instrument shall be subject to annulment in pursuance of a resolution of either House of Parliament.

GENERAL NOTE

This section provides for the first time in English law for the prosecution to appeal against a magistrates' court's decision to grant bail. Such a right already exists in Scotland. This right of appeal is subject to safeguards set out in subs. (2) onwards.

Subs. (1)

The right of the prosecution to appeal against a magistrates' court's decision to grant bail to a party is restricted to such persons who have been charged with or convicted of an offence or offences specified in the subsection. The offences specified include offences which are punishable by a term of imprisonment of five years or more. This would include, *e.g.* all offences of theft. The offences of taking a conveyance without authority under s.12 of the Theft Act 1968 and aggravated vehicle taking under s.12A of that Act were also specified in the subsection, principally because these offences are regarded as dangerous to the public, and are commonly committed by individuals who at the time they commit such offences are on bail. Neither of the above offences carry a penalty of five years imprisonment, and therefore were not included within the ambit of subs. (1)(a).

An appeal by the prosecution against the granting of bail is to a judge of the Crown Court. The subsection as originally drafted also permitted such an appeal to be made to a High Court judge. This route of appeal was, however, removed since such an appeal would have required in many instances the granting to the defendant or convicted person of civil legal aid. The granting of such aid could not be guaranteed swiftly enough to permit the commencing of the appeal within the time specified within the section (see s.1(7) below).

The prosecution now have an express right to appeal against the granting of bail following conviction of a defendant and pending sentence.

Subs. (2)

The Bill as originally drafted would have permitted private prosecutors to bring appeals against the granting of bail. It was considered that the existence of such a right might conceivably cause miscarriages of justice, especially if such appeals were brought in a capricious manner. Subsection (2) therefore limits the bodies which are able to bring prosecution, and which may subsequently make an appeal against the granting of bail.

The prosecutors who may make an appeal against the granting of bail under the section are prosecutors acting on behalf of the Director of Public Prosecutors (see s.1(2)(a)). This provision would appear to cover Crown Prosecutors. Section 1(2)(b) permits other types of prosecutors (for example Inland Revenue and Customs & Excise officers) to be given by the order of the Secretary of State the power to appeal against the granting of bail.

Subs. (3)

This subsection provides that an appeal against the granting of bail can only be made if representation against the granting of bail is made before it is granted. Rules of court provide that the court clerk must record any representations made against the granting of bail during the proceedings, so as to remove any doubt that such representations (within the terms of the subsection) were made.

Assurances were made by the Government during the passage of the Bill (see *Hansard*, H.L. Vol. 547, col. 993) that guidance will be issued to Crown Prosecutors making it clear that appeals against the granting of bail should not be made by junior prosecutors without seeking approval from more senior Crown Prosecutors. It is thought that senior Crown Prosecutors mean prosecutors of at least four years' experience within the Crown Prosecution Service. It is also intended that Crown Prosecutors should, wherever possible, seek prior authority to exercise the right of appeal. Crown Prosecutors should also subsequently review their decision to appeal against the granting of bail with Senior Crown Prosecutors, within the time limit for giving written notice of appeal (see s.1(5) below). There will be a power to discontinue appeals.

The Crown Prosecution Service is to draft guidelines for its prosecutors, setting out the circumstances in which the prosecution's right of appeal against bail should be exercised.

The guidance will emphasise that an appeal should not be lodged as a matter of routine, solely on the basis that the granting of bail has been opposed. The right of appeal will only be used in cases of grave concern, *e.g.* where the safety of the public is paramount. The appeal will be exercisable by any Crown Prosecutor (subject to consultation and review by senior Crown Prosecutors) but not by agents without specific authority.

The factors which will be relevant to the decision to exercise the right of appeal will include the following:

    (a) The gravity of the offence.

    (b) The risk of harm to the public should bail be granted to the individual, *e.g.* that the person concerned may interfere with witnesses or commit further serious offences.

    (c) The risk that a defendant or convicted person will fail to appear for trial or sentence.

In assessing the cogency of the above factors, reference will be made to the previous conduct of the person concerned.

Subss. (4) and (5)

The procedure for initiating an appeal under the section is fully set out in subss. (4) and (5). The procedure requires first oral notice of an appeal to be given to the court, followed by written notice. It is proposed that the written notice shall be in a prescribed standard form. It is intended that a standard form of written notice of appeal will lessen the burden of preparing such forms and thus enable the prosecutor to satisfy the requirement that written notice of appeal be served on the Magistrates' Court within two hours of the conclusion of the original proceedings. The consequences of failure to serve such a written notice are set out in s.1(7) (see below).

Subs. (7)

The effect of this provision is that if the prosecution fails to lodge either oral or written notice of appeal within the one or two hour periods prescribed under subss. (4) and (5), then the appeal is deemed to have failed and the defendant or person convicted must be released on bail. The same consequence ensues where an appeal is otherwise "disposed of" within the terms of subs. (6) (set out above).

Subs. (8)

It is to be noted that the appeal against the granting of bail shall by virtue of this subsection be *commenced* within 48 hours. The provision of course does not require that the appeal be *disposed* of within that period. In calculating the 48 hour period weekends and public holidays shall be disregarded. Disquiet was expressed during the passage of the Bill that the effect of this subsection would be that the defendant or person convicted could be detained in custody for inordinate lengths of time. Accordingly, the Minister of State, Home Affairs, Mr David Maclean gave the following assurance to the House of Commons. *Hansard*, H.C. Vol. 227, col. 1242:

> "In this context, it may be right to refer to the views expressed by the Lord Chief Justice—I assure the House that he has been consulted, although with less time for deliberation than we would have wished—on the introduction of a prosecution right of appeal via the Bill. He came back to the Government on one point in particular: to ask that everything possible is done to ensure that defendants spend as little time as possible in prison, pending the hearing of the appeal.

To that end, the Lord Chancellor's Department proposes to consult the judiciary with a view to providing guidance to the effect that, in cases where the time limit would, but for the formula provided in the Bill as it now stands, expire on a Saturday or a public holiday, everything possible should be done to expedite the hearing. If that proves impossible, consideration will be given to the possibility of making special local arrangements to bring on the appeal on a Saturday or public holiday. That encompasses the desire expressed by the Lord Chief Justice, on being consulted about the prosecution right of appeal, that everything should be done to avoid the necessity of defendants being held in custody for long periods. Lord Taylor said that if the appeal is launched just before a weekend or bank holiday he would expect it to be heard wherever possible on the same day".

Subs. (10)
This subsection provides that subject to modifications the provisions of the section shall apply to children and young persons.

Subs. (11)
The power of the Secretary of State to make an order under subs. (2) noted above is subject by virtue of this subsection to full Parliamentary control.

Citation, commencement and extent

2.—(1) This Act may be cited as the Bail (Amendment) Act 1993.
(2) This Act (except this section) shall come into force on such day as the Secretary of State may by order made by statutory instrument appoint.
(3) This Act extends to England and Wales only.

INDEX

References are to sections

LOCAL GOVERNMENT (AMENDMENT) ACT 1993

(1993 c. 27)

An Act to amend section 11 of the Local Government Act 1966 to permit grants to be made to local authorities making special provisions in exercising their functions, in consequence of the presence within their areas of persons belonging to ethnic minorities; and for connected purposes.

[20th July 1993]

PARLIAMENTARY DEBATES
Hansard, H.L. Vol. 546, col. 1293.
The Bill was discussed in Standing Committee C on May 12, 1993.

INTRODUCTION
This Act provides for the amendment of the Local Government Act 1966. Section 11 of that Act provides for the making of grants for certain expenditure due to immigrant population. This Act substitutes a new s.11 in the 1966 Act to encompass an ethnic minority population. The new s.11 extends the application of the provision to any joint authority established by Pt. IV of the Local Government Act 1985. Financial provisions are made in s.2 to ensure that Parliament will provide funding for expenses and sums payable under this Act.

Amendment of section 11 of Local Government Act 1966

1.—(1) For section 11 of the Local Government Act 1966 there shall be substituted the following—

"Grants for certain expenditure due to ethnic minority population

11.—(1) Subject to the provisions of this section the Secretary of State may pay, to local authorities who in his opinion are required to make special provision in the exercise of any of their functions in consequence of the presence within their areas of persons belonging to ethnic minorities whose language or customs differ from those of the rest of the community, grants of such amounts as he may with the consent of the Treasury determine on account of expenditure of such description (being expenditure in respect of the employment of staff) as he may so determine.

(2) This section shall apply to a joint authority established by Part IV of the Local Government Act 1985 as it applies to a local authority."

(2) Subsection (1) above does not apply in any case where the expenditure was incurred before 1st April 1993.

Financial provisions

2. There shall be paid out of moneys provided by Parliament—
(a) any expenses of the Secretary of State incurred in consequence of this Act; and
(b) any increase attributable to this Act in the sums payable out of money so provided under any other enactment.

Citation, commencement and extent

3.—(1) This Act may be cited as the Local Government (Amendment) Act 1993.

(2) This Act shall come into force at the end of the period of two months beginning with the day on which it is passed.

(3) This Act does not extend to Northern Ireland or to Scotland.

INDEX

References are to sections